THE ILLUSTRATED ENCYCLOPEDIA OF
AMERICAN TRUCKS
AND COMMERCIAL VEHICLES

Albert Mroz

Published by

700 E. State Street • Iola, WI 54990-0001
Telephone: 715/445-2214

Please call or write for our free catalog of automotive publications. Our toll-free number to place an
order or obtain a free catalog is 800-258-0929 or please use our regular business telephone 715-445-
2214 for editorial comment
and further information.

Library of Congress Catalog Number: 95-82431
ISBN: 0-87341-368-7

Printed in the United States of America

CONTENTS

Abbreviations

BBC - bumper to back of cab

COE - cab over engine

GCW - gross combination weight

GPM - gallons per minute

GVW - gross vehicle weight

HP - horsepower

MPG - miles per gallon

MPH - miles per hour

PSI - pounds per square inch

Acknowledgements

The author would like to thank the following individuals and organizations for help in obtaining information and inspiration to complete the writing of this book:

Museum of Alaska Transportation, American Truck Historical Society, James Anderson, Antique Truck Club of America, Jim Beach, Behring Museum at Blackhawk, Car and Carriage Caravan, Cole Land Transportation Museum, Harold Day, Doug Delano, Ralph Dunwoodie, Chad Elmore, Deborah Faupel, Eric Foley, Forney Museum, FWD/Seagrave Museum, David Gallagher, Al and Margaret Garcia, Evelyn Garcia, Cindy Gates, G.N. Georgano, Steve Greenberg, John Gunnell, Hartford Heritage Auto Museum, Hartung's Automotive Museum, Hasting's Museum, Elwood Haynes Museum, A.W. Hays, Don and Naomi Hays, Hays Antique Truck Museum, Dennis Hurry, Paul Hyland, Pat Klug, Ron Kowalke, Chet Krause, James V. Lee, C.B. Lewis Museum, Marcy Lucas, Joseph and Grace Mazzarella, Military Vehicle Preservation Association, Dale Miller, S. Ray Miller Foundation, Walter Miller, Ed and Teresa Mroz, Daphne Mroz, New Brunswick Museum, Old Rhinebeck Aerodrome, Owls Head Transportation Museum, Pacific Northwest Truck Museum, Petit Jean Mountain Museum, Pioneer Auto & Antique Town, Bill Powk, Reilly Classic Motorcars, Dirk Roberts, Ed Roberts, Randy Shapiro, William Smith, Society of Automotive Engineers, Society of Automotive Historians, Van Horn Truck Museum, Venerable Fire Collection, Virginia Museum of Transportation, Whoop-N-Holler Museum, Wilson Historical Society, and Zunker Museum.

A

A & B 1914-1922 — The American and British Manufacturing Company of Providence, Rhode Island, built two-wheel assemblies for tractors in order to convert horsedrawn steam pumpers into self-propelled vehicles. These conversions were hybrid-powered in that a four-cylinder gasoline engine turned a generator that powered electric motors in both front wheels. Some standard 3-ton and 5-ton trucks were also assembled during and just after World War I before the company closed down permanently.

1913 A & R   **RD**

A & R 1912-1915 — The Abendroth and Root Manufacturing Company built A & R marque trucks in Newburgh, New York, for just under four years. Offices were in New York City. These vehicles were forward control design using four-cylinder engines and three-speed transmissions. Power to the rear wheels was achieved with double-chain drive on the three models that were built: 3-ton, 4-ton and 5-ton, with the latter having a governor that limited its top speed to 8.5 mph. Solid rubber tires were used on all models. The company slogan in 1913 was "Study the lines." The Abendroth and Root company was formerly known as Frontenac, which was the name of the passenger car manufacturer that was in existence only briefly. Frontenac trucks were built from 1906 to 1912.

A.B.C. See WAVERLY ELECTRIC

A.B.C. 1908-1910 — A.B.C. Motor Vehicle Manufacturing of St. Louis, Missouri, built highwheelers. Amedee B. Cole was the founder and president who used his own initials to their best advantage. Amid a plethora of passenger cars, A.B.C. also built a 1/2-ton delivery van using an 18 hp two-cylinder engine that could be ordered as air-cooled or water-cooled. The van had a wheelbase of 90 inches and was priced at $700 in 1908. In 1909 as the Model F it was priced at $650 or $700, depending on the cooling system.

ABENDROTH & ROOT see FRONTENAC

ABRESCH-CRAMER; ABRESCH-KREMERS 1910-1912 — Charles Abresch, proprietor of the Abresch Carriage Company since 1871, announced the incorporation of the Abresch-Cramer Truck Company of Milwaukee, Wisconsin, which began building high wheel commercial vehicles about 10 years after *Automobile Review* announced his entry into the truck building business. For a time the company specialized in automobile body manufacturing. The Abresch-Kremers were assembled trucks, and like the first similar Internationals, used two-cylinder engines which were either water or air cooled. The water-cooled model was $50 more than the air-

cooled model which sold for $600 in 1911. By 1910 Abresch-Cramer offered a 4-ton capacity truck with a 40 hp four-cylinder motor. Sub-frames were provided for the engines and transmission. Front springs were full-elliptic and platform springs were used in the rear. Artillery wheels carried 36x4 front and 42x3 rear dual solid rubber tires.

1910 ABRESCH-CRAMER   **RD**

Reference to the company as the "Abresch-Cramer" company is not an error. It appears Abresch's partner Kremers changed his last name for euphony or in order to be listed earlier alphabetically at a time when there were dozens of similar builders in the region. The Charles Abresch Company survived until 1965 in the machine business, but it was unrelated to truck manufacturing after 1912 when Abresch passed away.

1915 ACASON TRUCK CHASSIS   **LIAM**

ACASON 1915-1925 — Though relatively small, the Acason Motor Truck Company was started in Detroit, Michigan, at a time when numerous such companies were springing up in the Midwest. The first model was a 1/2-ton, which was quickly followed by 2-ton and 3-1/2-ton models. Each of the conventional assembled trucks used four-cylinder Waukesha engines with four-speed transmissions. Timken worm drive rear axles were standard. A 1-1/2 ton model was added in 1917, and a year later a 5-ton model was added to the line. The company also began manufacturing both light and heavy tractors. By 1921 all but the 2-1/2-ton and 3-1/2 ton models were discontinued, and by 1925 the company shut down altogether.

ACE 1918-1927 — After the Blair Manufacturing Company was reorganized it became the American Motor Truck Company of Newark, Ohio, which produced the Ace line of trucks and buses. The first model of 1918 was a 2-1/2 ton and featured a Buda WU four-cylinder engine with electric starting, which had been introduced by Cadillac when Charles Kettering developed the design six years earlier. The truck featured left-hand drive.

The following year 2-ton and 3-ton models were introduced which used Buda engines as well. These trucks featured headlights that moved as the steering wheel was turned, an unusual design that was later adapted in some luxury passenger cars. Prices ranged from $3,100 up to $5,050 for the most expensive long wheelbase model.

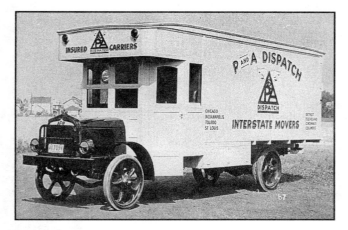

1922 ACE   OCW

In the last three years the company produced a 2-1/2-ton model truck. This was called the Model 56 by 1924, which used a 28.9 hp Buda EBU engine, and chassis price was $3,350. It had a wheelbase of 156 inches using 36x4 front and 36x8 rear pneumatic tires as standard. This model also used a Zenith carburetor and Eisemann ignition, Brown-Lipe clutch and transmission, Timken front and rear axles, steering by Ross Gear, and the wheels were made by Dayton Steel Foundry. The bare chassis weighed 5,650 pounds.

From the beginning of the new decade bus manufacturing met with some success when the company offered the Model A 20/22 passenger and Model B 26/28 passenger bus. In 1923 the Model C was introduced, which was a 30/32 passenger bus that for the first two years used a Midwest engine. For the last years of production the Model C had a Continental six-cylinder 6B or six-cylinder 7T engine. The company was liquidated in 1927.

1930 ACF P-45 COACH   MBS

ACF/ACF-BRILL/BRILL 1926-1953 — The American Car and Foundry Company of Detroit, Michigan, was already a successful railway car manufacturer when it acquired the J.G. Brill Company of Philadelphia, Pennsylvania, in 1925. The goal was to expand the model line to include buses, and the Fageol Motors Company of Ohio was also bought. Brill had been building streetcars for 30 years, but the business was declining as buses became more affordable and reliable while proving their worth through versatility. In addition, the Brill Company was composed of the C.C. Kuhlman Company of Cleveland, Ohio, and the American Car Company of St. Louis, Missouri, which the company had acquired prior to being absorbed by ACF.

The Fageol buses were being manufactured in Kent, Ohio, and in 1926 American Car and Foundry moved the operation to their facilities in Detroit, Michigan. The Fageol brothers accepted positions as vice-presidents of ACF while continuing their manufacturing operations of Fageol trucks in Oakland, California, still under the Fageol name.

When a Twin Coach two-engine 40-passenger bus design was rejected by ACF management, the Fageol brothers resigned in 1927. However, ACF continued to use the Fageol name on its buses until 1929 after the chassis were redesigned and strengthened in 1927 with influence from the Twin Coach design. The Lang Body Company of Cleveland, Ohio, built most of the city bus and parlor coach bodies at that time.

Minor improvements in the chassis and body of the conventional buses met with new model designations, although the changes were not significant, and all conventional models of this vintage used six-cylinder Hall-Scott engines. In contrast, a new design called the "Metropolitan" was simultaneously produced from 1928. Its primary feature was its under-floor engine design that could be ordered in either "gas-mechanical" or "gas-electric" configuration, but this family of designs met only with limited success particularly due to its introduction at the outset of the Depression. In order to make its buses more attractive from a cost point of view at this time, a small front-engine bus design was introduced in 1930 using a Hercules engine. The following year ACF also built trucks that used Hall-Scott 160 or 175 motors, but only 25 were assembled through 1932. These included the ACF TT175 articulated trucks.

1931 ACF TT 175 ARTICULATED TRUCK   NAHC

1931 ACF MODEL M URBAN COACH   OCW

By the end of 1932 bus manufacturing was moved to Philadelphia, Pennsylvania. The front-engine transit buses were discontinued while a new under-floor engine design was introduced in 1933 at a time when business was at a near standstill, and only a few units actually sold. Business continued to be poor, but in 1937 a new streamline design was introduced. That year several size buses were offered including the 26-, 31-, 36-, 41- and 45-passenger models. With some success, parlor coaches were also offered in 25-, 29- and 35-passenger versions. All of these models used 175 and later 180 Hall-Scott engines, and a few were offered with hydraulic transmissions. Manufacturing continued until 1942 when factories were converted to military production.

After World War II the first model numbers were C-36 and C-44 for city buses and IC-41 for inter-city buses, designations that marked the number of passengers. These were under-floor engine designs using six-cylinder Hall-Scott engines. In 1947 Spicer hydraulic transmissions were offered and these buses were known as ACF-Brill.

The following year the model line also included the C-27 and C-31 models. These were new designs with International gasoline engines mounted in back. In order to distinguish these models from the ones using Hall-Scott engines, the new models were called

Brill. Hence, vehicles built by American Car and Foundry Company were known under three marques. During the Korean "conflict" ACF Brill built "Ambulbus" for the U.S. Air Force, which could carry 18 litter patients or 50 ambulatory persons. This bus ambulance was powered by a 361-cubic inch 126 hp GMC six-cylinder engine.

1938 ACF UNDERFLOOR ENGINE BUS MBS

It should be noted that Brill also built trolley coaches from 1921 at its streetcar facilities. They called these "railless" coaches and, once they became accepted, Brill built many of them during the 1930s. However, once the bus and trolley bus market fell in the early 1950s, ACF-Brill reduced production and by 1953 ceased manufacturing altogether, unable to compete with GMC. As late as 1954 plans to liquidate ACF-Brill by selling all interests to Twin Coach did not materialize. The following year records show stockholders voting for spin-off of Hall-Scott Division and finally merging with Big Bear Markets of Michigan.

ACME 1904-1906 — The Acme Motor Car Company, which was started in Reading, Pennsylvania, first began building passenger cars before introducing a truck in 1905 when Frank A. Devlin took over the small company. The model offered was a 1/2-ton delivery with a two-cylinder 16 hp engine that incorporated chain drive, cone clutch and a three-speed progressive transmission. The truck was listed until 1906 when the company went into temporary receivership in July of that year. However, passenger car production continued until 1910 before the company stopped manufacturing. It is uncertain what number of trucks, if any, were actually produced, and this company should not be confused with Acme of Cadillac, Michigan, and Acme Wagon Company of Emigsville, Pennsylvania.

1925 ACME LIAM

ACME 1915-1931 — Acme trucks were first built by the Cadillac Auto Truck Company of Cadillac, Michigan. Its first model line included standard assembled trucks in the 1-ton, 2-ton and 3-1/2-ton range using four-cylinder Continental motors. By 1917 the 2-

ton Acme featured a 40 hp Continental motor, 148-inch wheelbase and full-floating Timken rear axle. This was the year that the Cadillac Motor Company of Detroit successfully sued the Cadillac Auto Truck Company to prevent the newer company from using the name Cadillac. The company changed its name to Acme.

By 1924 Acme had several models to offer. The Acme Flyer was the lightest rated at 1-ton. It had a 130-inch wheelbase and was powered by a Continental S4 engine using a Zenith carburetor and Auto-Lite ignition. The clutch and transmission were by Brown-Lipe, while the front and rear axles were made by Columbia axle of Cleveland, Ohio. This model used 30x5 front and rear tires on Smith Wheels.

The 20L Model 1-1/2-ton differed from the Flyer in that it had a 136-inch wheelbase and was powered by a Continental 8R engine. Rear axle was a Timken 1452. Tires were 34x5 both front and rear on Bimel wheels. Next up was the Model 40 with 141-inch wheelbase using a Continental J4 engine, while the Model 40L with 147-inch wheelbase used a Continental K-4 motor. Both of these models were rated at 2-ton capacity. Acme offered the 3-ton Model K, Model 60 and Model 60L. These used Continental motors 6B, K-4 and L-4, respectively, the latter which was also used in the 4-ton Model 90. However, the two largest Model 90L and Model 125 in the mid 1920s used a Continental B-5 engine with Beneke and Kropf carburetor. All but the Flyer, which used Auto-Lite, and the 20L Model, which used Bosch, had Eisemann ignition, as well as Borg and Beck clutches and Cotta transmissions with Timken rear axles. The 3-ton Model K was listed as the longest wheelbase at 200 inches.

A line of truck tractors was also offered that included Models 40, 40L, 60, 60L, 90, 90L and 125. In 1927 Acme acquired United Truck Company of Grand Rapids, Michigan, and soon thereafter built its largest truck tractor which was rated at 7-1/2-ton using a Continental six-cylinder engine. Also, 16- and 21-passenger buses were built during the mid to late 1920s before the company closed down in 1931.

1918 ACME SUBURBAN OCW

1918 ACME AMBULANCE OCW

ACME 1916-1919 — The Acme Wagon Company of Emigsville, Pennsylvania, was incorporated in 1888. Edward K. Emig became president of the company in 1905 with J. Albert Emig as vice-president and J.S. Miller as secretary.

The company briefly built 1-ton conventional assembled trucks that used 17 hp four-cylinder engines. This model line was only a small portion of overall production which concentrated on farm wagons and truck bodies usually mounted on Ford chassis. The truck model used a four-cylinder engine stamped "Acme," (most likely purchased elsewhere and only tagged with the company's name) and a dry plate clutch and three-speed transmission with bevel drive at the rear axle. The company discontinued its truck manufacturing in 1919, although wagon and body production continued into the mid 1920s.

1910 ACORN   **KP**

ACORN 1910-1912 — A light motorized delivery wagon was built by Acorn Motor Car Company in Cincinnati, Ohio. The vehicle had a 1/2-ton capacity and was powered by an 18 hp two-cylinder horizontally-opposed engine with an unusual (for that time) transverse mounting in the front. A three-speed roller friction transmission was used with power transmitted by double chain drive. This company was not affiliated with the later Acorn Motor Truck Company of Chicago, Illinois.

ACORN 1925-1931 — The Acorn Motor Truck Company of Chicago, Illinois, built conventional assembled trucks for a little over six years. Records show models ranging from 1 to 5 tons. The first year of manufacture Acorn offered the 2-1/2-ton Model 50 and 4-ton Model 70. The lighter truck had a standard wheelbase of 156 inches, although other sizes were available on order. It used a Buda EBU engine with Zenith carburetor and Eisemann ignition, Brown-Lipe clutch and transmission, Timken front and rear axles, Ross steering and wheels were by Prudden Wheel Company with 36x4 front and 36x8 rear tires. Pneumatics were available at extra cost. The Model 70 differed in that it had a set 166-inch wheelbase, was powered by a Buda YBUI engine with Bosch ignition, and wheels were from Interstate Foundry carrying 36x5 front and 40x10 rear tires. For that year chassis price for the Model 50 was $3,250, and for the Model 70 it was $4,250. Soon after the Depression began, the company ceased manufacturing.

1912 ADAMS   **RD**

ADAMS 1910-1916 — The Adams Brothers of Findlay, Ohio, began building 3/4-ton delivery trucks in 1910. The light delivery van used a two-cylinder engine with a three-speed transmission.

Power to the rear wheels was achieved with shaft drive, and the vehicles used pneumatic tires as standard equipment. All of the delivery vans had the radiator behind the motor with sloping hoods that resembled the early Macks and Internationals. The cooling fan was on the flywheel and a filling cap was located on each side of the radiator.

In the second year of manufacture a 1-ton van was offered with a wheelbase of 120 inches. It was powered by a four-cylinder engine. In 1913 1-1/2-ton and 2-ton vans were added. Maximum wheelbase on the 2-ton truck was 152 inches. In 1915 the company changed names to the Adams Truck, Foundry and Machine Company but was still at the same location. That year the company developed a dump bed, and in the final year of production 1-, 2- and 2-1/2-ton trucks were offered before the company ceased to exist.

ADMIRAL 1913-1915 — The Admiral Motor Car Company was located in St. Louis, Missouri. The company offered a Model C truck powered by a four-cylinder motor using a three-speed transmission. Power to the rear wheels was transmitted by double chain. The Model C was available as an express or stake body. Either one had a 125-inch wheelbase and was priced at $1,475.

AEROCOACH 1940-1952 — The General American Aerocoach of Chicago, Illinois, became a subsidiary of the General American Transportation Corporation in 1939. The former company was in business as a builder and lessor of railroad cars when it bought out Gar Wood Industries and set up a new manufacturing facility in Chicago at the beginning of 1940.

Once new production facilities were set up, the smaller buses, which had been designed at Gar Wood, were phased out from the model line and larger 29- and 33-passenger buses were built using the relatively new method of welded tube framework. The last Gar Wood buses of 1939-1940 had the Aerocoach emblem and so were nearly identical in outer appearance to the first units built by General American Aerocoach.

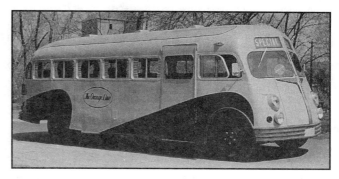

1940 AEROCOACH   **MBS**

The new, larger buses were manufactured without any substantial changes up to the time the company stopped production. These had International engines and used Clark five-speed transmissions as standard equipment. During World War II manufacturing was halted in 1943 due specifically to material shortages as the war effort went into full production. Sales records show that by this time the company had sold 250 Aerocoaches of the Gar Wood design, as compared with 300 of the new welded tube framework design. Material shortages notwithstanding, production started up again in April of 1944. Postwar manufacturing records show that a total of 2,350 buses were built up to 1952.

By 1947 a Continental engine was also offered in addition to the standard International engine and some changes, mostly in the front sheet metal, were made in 1949 and 1951. However, the basic design having become somewhat antiquated, Aerocoaches were sold more often to customers in other countries than in the United States where competition was much more keen. In 1948 Aerocoach attempted to enter the inter-city bus market with 36- and 45-passenger models, which had such amenities as automatic heating and ventilating systems. However, the competition was too tough, and this model line soon met its demise. Aerocoach tried to supplement its business by rebuilding prewar Greyhound

Yellow Coach buses with diesel engines and refurbished interiors under contract with Greyhound, but by 1952 the company ceased operation.

1916 AETNA 2-1/2-TON   **HAYS**

AETNA 1915-1916 — The Aetna Motor Truck Company of Detroit, Michigan, built conventional assembled trucks after starting in 1910 with a prototype of a five-passenger torpedo touring car that never went into production. The two Aetna trucks were offered as 1-1/2-ton and 2-1/2-ton capacity and featured underslung 3/4 elliptical springs and worm-drive rear axles. The small company only lasted for two years in the truck building business. Another Aetna Motor enterprise, which has been listed as a manufacturer of trucks and of which little is known, appears to have existed briefly in New York City in 1920.

1919 AHRENS-FOX PUMPER   **KP**

AHRENS-FOX 1911-1957, (1961-1977) — The Ahrens-Fox Fire Engine Company of Cincinnati, Ohio, was started by John P. Ahrens and Charles H. Fox. Ahrens' family had built horsedrawn steam pumpers starting in 1868. Fox was assistant chief of the Cincinnati Fire Department.

The Rockford, Illinois, Fire Department was its first customer in 1911 and the first motor fire engine called the Model A was built for them early the following year. The fire engine had a Herschell-Spillman six-cylinder 80 hp engine with a two-cylinder pumper that was capable of 750 gallons per minute. Ahrens-Fox received orders from other fire departments and a total of 12 were built in 1912. The production number for 1913 was 13 and for the following year it was 11. All of these were basically the same design except for a steamer that was powered by an electric motor front-wheel drive and sold in 1912. In 1913 the company also offered a Model E-C Battalion Roadster, equipped with some fire fighting equipment, intended for fire chiefs to be able to get to a fire at 50 mph. Also for that year, Charles H. Fox developed a triple combination fire engine with a gasoline-powered centrifugal pump mounted in front of the radiator fed by an auxiliary water tank that became known as the booster tank.

By 1914 Ahrens-Fox produced its own six-cylinder engine that was larger than the Herschell-Spillman. It was a monobloc casting and was used on all production fire engines until 1927. The well-known spherical air chamber and front-mounted pump appeared in 1915. The company introduced the Model M in 1915, which used a double-acting four-cylinder pump mounted in front of the engine. The spherical brass chamber on top of the pump was an easily identifiable component associated with Ahrens-Fox fire engines up to 1952. According to records, apparently only one man knew how to fabricate the hand-tooled brass sphere, and when he died the company was forced to switch to a more conventional and less remarkable two-piece steel ball that was forged.

Several other vehicle models were offered besides the well-known fire engines. Ahrens-Fox built tractors to pull horsedrawn ladder wagons as modernizing retrofits. The company also produced hose trucks, chemical engines and articulated aerial ladder trucks with rear wheel tiller steering. Peter Pirsch in Kenosha, Wisconsin, built most of the specialized equipment under contract with Ahrens-Fox. All of the models up to 1920 used chain drive to the rear wheels except the Model J introduced in 1919 with shaft drive.

1931 AHRENS-FOX QUAD 1000 GPM PUMPER   **BS**

Over the years the company was known for its innovations. The problem of frozen hydrants in the winter was overcome with a boiler that was attached to the exhaust manifold. Ladders were double banked for additional stability as well as firemen's mobility, and the tall ladders were extended using a motorized hoist powered by a compressor that was driven by the engine. As a crowning achievement in 1917 Ahrens-Fox was first to spray water over the Woolworth Building in New York City. At 60 stories high it was the world's tallest building at that time.

In 1915 the Model L offered a six-cylinder pump as did the Model P of 1921, which had a maximum capacity of 1,300 gallon per minute (gpm). Shaft drive to the rear differential was still an option in 1920. It became standard equipment four years later. By 1927 the chemical trucks featured Continental engines, and Hercules and Waukesha engines were optional by 1935 when customers opted not to rely on the Ahrens-Fox engine. By 1936 the company merged with the LeBlond-Schacht Truck Company of Cincinnati, Ohio. Because of the Depression few trucks were sold and Ahrens-Fox was forced to build small rotary pumpers on Dodge, Ford, Republic and Studebaker chassis as well as its own. But the HT series of 1937 with 1,000 gpm capacity were well-known over their 15 years of production.

The LeBlond-Schacht merger remained intact until 1951 when Walter Walkenhorst, also of Cincinnati, bought Ahrens-Fox. He held onto it for less than a year before selling to C.D. Beck Company in 1953, which manufactured buses. It was he, however, who discontinued the piston pumpers with the steel ball, believing them to be too antiquated. Although sales and service remained in Cincinnati, fire engine production was transferred to the Sidney, Ohio, Beck operations.

Beck continued to build the Ahrens-Fox in its previous versions, but also introduced a cab-forward design with Continental or Waukesha engines in 1956. Later the same year Mack bought out Ahrens-Fox, although according to some records the last Ahrens-

Fox was a 1957 model. The new parent company eliminated the Ahrens-Fox name from its model lineup but did adopt the cab-forward design for its own fire trucks. Mack built some of its trucks at the Sidney, Ohio, factory before consolidating its manufacturing at Allentown, Pennsylvania. Over the years overall production of units on Ahrens-Fox chassis was 900. Only a few were built on other makes' chassis in the 1930s.

Richard C. Nepper, a former employee of Ahrens-Fox, acquired all assets, patterns, parts and factory equipment in 1961 and continued to build one truck every five years through the 1970s while servicing and repairing about 200 Ahrens-Fox trucks that were still on the road.

A.I.C. 1912-1914 — A.I.C. was the abbreviation of American Ice Manufacturing Company of New York, New York. It was not in the business of truck manufacturing but because specialized trucks of adequate capacity were difficult to find during that time, A.I.C. built a few of its own vehicles. The truck had a 5-ton capacity, which was considered large at that time, and used a big 40 hp four-cylinder engine with a 6-3/4-inch stroke. It was mounted under the cab. A cone clutch was used with the three-speed selective sliding gear transmission. The wheelbase was 136 inches and the chassis weighed nearly four tons. Springs were semi-elliptic front and rear. The dual rear wheels used 40x5 solid rubber tires to accommodate such a load. The truck used dual chain drive and three lamps and a horn were standard equipment. This was a right-hand drive vehicle with controls on the right as well. Chassis price in 1913 was $3,500.

AIR-O-FLEX 1918-1920 — The Air-O-Flex Auto Corporation of Detroit, Michigan, built several fire engine pumpers. In the first two years a 2-ton model was offered and in 1920, the last year of production, a 1-1/2-ton model powered by a four-cylinder Buda engine with piston driven pump was produced. The truck had a wheelbase of 180 inches and used a four-speed transmission with shaft drive to the rear differential.

AJAX ELECTRIC 1901-1903 — Walter Simpson, along with some family members, incorporated the Ajax Motor Vehicle Company in New York City during 1901. A.L. Simpson was president. The company built electric runabouts using the slogan "An Honest Automobile at an Honest Price." For 1903 a Light Delivery Wagon powered by a 6 hp motor was offered for $1,500. Its capacity was 500 pounds. Advertising showed only a simple drawing of this commercial vehicle, and manufacture of the Ajax Light Delivery Wagon has not been substantiated. It is known that the company did build electric passenger cars.

AKRON 1912-1914 — The Akron Motor Car and Truck Company was founded in Akron, Ohio. The company produced very few vehicles in all, but offered numerous models. The Model A truck was rated at 3/4-ton in either delivery or open bed variations. Special order vehicles included ambulance, bus, hearse and police wagon. Prices varied starting at $1,460 for the lightest truck without accessories. This company should not be confused with Akron Multi-Truck of Kent, Ohio, or the Akron Company that briefly existed from 1899 to 1901 in Akron, building a few stanhopes.

AKRON MULTI-TRUCK 1920-1921 — The marque name not withstanding, the Thomart Motor Company of Kent, Ohio, briefly built only a single model truck rated at 1-ton. The Model 20 had a wheelbase of 133 inches and used a Hinkley four-cylinder Model 400 engine. The truck used a three-speed transmission and featured pneumatic tires. Whether or not it was later actually built under the Thomart name is uncertain, although literature of that period suggests it.

ALCO 1909-1913 — The American Locomotive Company of Providence, Rhode Island, got into the business of building heavy-duty trucks in 1909. The 2-, 3-1/2-, 5- and 6-1/2-ton models were known for their ruggedness, and in fact the company built the gasoline-powered trucks with the same durability in mind as with its steam locomotives. It had built some 51,000 of them starting in 1835. As might be appropriate, one customer used an Alco truck to pull a road train of four trailers loaded with 36,000 pounds of coal. Alco also produced a luxury line of passenger cars, as well as taxis, at about the same time as its trucks. By 1912 the company had sold a total of about 1,000 trucks.

1912 ALCO 5-TON   RD

The cab-over design was universal on Alco trucks. By 1912 the sturdy vehicles used 453-cubic inch four-cylinder or 579-cubic inch six-cylinder engines with artillery wheels and solid tires. The chassis had semi-elliptic springs and power to the rear wheels was accomplished with dual chain drive. The 2-ton model with 112-inch wheelbase used a four-cylinder 32.4 hp engine, while the larger models starting with the 3-1/2-ton on a 126-inch wheelbase used a four-cylinder 40 hp engine, one of the largest at that time with 471-cubic inch displacement. The 5-ton and 6-1/2-ton trucks both had a 144-inch wheelbase. The standard solid rubber tire sizes ranged from single front 36x4 and 36x3 rear dual wheels to 36x5, 36x6 and 36x7 front and 36x4, 42x5 and 42x6 rear, respectively. All engines used dual ignition and Newcombe carburetors. Maximum speed ranged from 17 mph for the lightest truck to 8 mph for the heaviest. Tractors for articulated fire trucks were built with the same mechanical configurations utilizing the fifth wheel concept and shorter wheelbase. These were advertised as retrofits for horsedrawn ladder trucks. The Schenectady Fire Department in New York used Alco trucks in this application. Advertising claimed that a 3-1/2-ton model Alco could supplant five horses and carry three tons daily on a 40 mile route. One customer claimed disposing of 20 horses after buying a 5-ton Alco. All models used a 27-1/2 gallon gasoline tank.

The Alco engines used a water pump for cooling. The clutch was a steel and bronze multiple disc design, and each truck had a three-speed transmission mounted centrally. The lightest model started at $2,950 going up to $5,500 for the 6-1/2-ton truck. Passenger cars had been produced since 1905. However, automotive and truck manufacturing was not profitable and ended suddenly in 1913 after about 5,000 Alcos had been built in 54 models of cars and trucks. The company built steam and later diesel-electric locomotives up to 1969, after which it continued to build Alco Power diesel engines from 700 hp to 4000 hp for various applications.

Alco made history in 1912 when a crew of four men, including photographer John Cambon, set out on a first-ever attempt at transcontinental delivery of merchandise by motor truck. On board was E.L. Ferguson and drivers Frank Morin and Walter Dick. On June 20 they set out in a 3-1/2-ton model with three tons of Parrott Brand Olive Silk Soap consigned to Carlson Currier Company in Petaluma, California. The projected route took them first to New York, then Albany, Buffalo, Chicago, Omaha, Salt Lake City, Reno, Sacramento, San Francisco and finally 40 miles further north to Petaluma, California. A third driver, Frank Colburn, relieved Walter Dick in Denver.

In each city the company made much fanfare of the truck's rail-road pedigree, and enthusiastic crowds showed up to cheer on the truck and its crew. However, roads were nearly nonexistent in those days, and the crew fought one obstacle after another to get across country. They dug out of the mud after torrential rains bogged them down near Point of Rocks, Wyoming. They reinforced bridges along the way, which were never built to handle the many tons the truck and its cargo weighed. A few bridges were damaged and had to be rebuilt. In the Sierra Nevada the crew blazed its own trail. Finally, after 4,145 miles which took a total 776 hours with 412 hours actually on the road, the truck and its cargo arrived in good condition in Petaluma, setting a precedent with a remarkable achievement. Average speed during the entire trip was a fraction over 10 mph.

1913 ALCO MOBILE CHURCH MROZ

The United States Postal Transfer Service ordered 80 Alco trucks in 1913. The order represented $225,000, but it was one of the last ones that Alco would fulfill in truck production. One of the company's last efforts in motor vehicle production was a motor chapel complete with cathedral glass. The company exhibited this vehicle stating, "The equipment of the motor chapel is complete in every respect, including all the paraphernalia prescribed by the rubric of the Catholic Church." After 1913 the company went back to locomotive manufacturing.

ALDEN-SAMPSON See SAMPSON

ALENA STEAM 1922 — The Alena Steam Products Company was a short-lived enterprise in Indianapolis, Indiana. The company built a few trucks, tractors and a passenger car using a two-cylinder 115-cubic inch displacement engine.

1921 ALL-AMERICAN KP

ALL-AMERICAN 1918-1925 — The All-American Super Truck of Chicago, Illinois, was produced in the former Ogren car factory and was also known under the name of A.A., especially in the overseas

market to Great Britain. The standard and only 1-ton Model A had a 130-inch wheelbase. It was powered by a four-cylinder Herschel-Spillman engine and used a three-speed transmission. Front and rear wheels carried 20x7.5 pneumatic tires. The basic truck cost $1,595 in 1919. An all-wood enclosed cab was available from the factory, as was the eight-in-one body for agricultural uses. Manufacturing was transferred to Fremont, Ohio, in 1922 before the company closed in 1925.

1916 ALLIS-CHALMERS B-6 HALF-TRACK A-C

ALLIS-CHALMERS 1915-1918 — Better known for its heavy machinery, electrical equipment and components, as well as for its tractors, the Allis-Chalmers Manufacturing Company of Milwaukee, Wisconsin, made a brief foray into truck production under the leadership of president General Otto H. Falk. The Allis-Chalmers Tractor Truck's design was in the form of a half-track that used artillery-type steel wheels in front for steering. It was powered by a 68 hp T-head four-cylinder motor, and its rated capacity as a truck was five tons. Top speed was 10 mph in fourth gear. Suggested price was $5,000. Ten of these vehicles were sold to Russia during World War I, but other countries did not put in orders. Only a few of these vehicles were built up to 1918, the last one serving as a snowplow and tow vehicle around the Allis-Chalmers factory. The concept was later revived and both a Chase and Dodge truck were fitted with similar half-track axles at the Aberdeen Proving Grounds in 1924 and 1925. The results met with only limited success.

ALLIANCE 1916 — The Alliance Manufacturing Company was briefly in the business of building hearses in Streator, Illinois. The single model of vehicle used a six-cylinder Lycoming 40 hp engine.

ALL-POWER 1918-1920 — The All-Power Truck Company of Detroit, Michigan, briefly built a single model 3-1/2-ton known as the SV 4. The truck had a 150-inch or 168-inch wheelbase and used a 32.4 hp four-cylinder Continental engine with a three-speed transmission and shaft drive to the Timken rear axle. Available in bare chassis only, the vehicle sold for $4,800. The company did not build a four-wheel-drive truck, much as the name might imply. For 1921 the company offered a truck called Mor-Power.

ALMA 1913-1914 — The Alma Motor Truck Company was listed as a commercial vehicle builder in Alma, Michigan. The Alma Model B was a 1-ton truck powered by a Continental motor with Schebler carburetor and Eisemann ignition and used a Covert transmission with double chain drive. This company became the Republic Motor Truck Company in 1914, and subsequent listings were under the name Republic.

ALTER 1914-1916 — Alter trucks were built in Cincinnati, Ohio, by Cincinnati Motors Manufacturing Company. It appears the company was reorganized in Plymouth, Michigan, in 1915. Three model were offered from 1/2 ton to 1,800-pound capacity. All models used a four-cylinder engine, although six-cylinder engines were available in the Model F touring car. The company name changed three times after it moved to Grand Haven, Michigan, under the control of various investors. C.A. Alter was the vice-president. All models totaled a production figure of 1,000. Guy Hamilton, president of Alter, founded Hamilton Motors Company after Alter went bankrupt, and built Apex trucks.

1911 AMERICAN 5-TON   NAHC

AMERICAN 1906-1912 — The American Motor Truck Company, of Lockport, New York, began in 1906 before moving to Findlay, Ohio, in 1911 under the name of Findlay Motor Car Company. In Lockport, forward-control American trucks were available in 3-ton and 5-ton capacity. The company built heavy trucks using four-cylinder motors from 20 hp to 60 hp with power to the rear wheels with double chain drive.

By 1911 both conventional and forward control models were built. The 60 hp model used an epicyclic transmission usually found on lighter trucks. In 1912 the company merged with Ewing-American Motor Car Company, also in Findlay, Ohio. Builder of taxicabs and light commercial vehicles, Ewing-American built the American truck for its last year of production.

1911 AMERICAN 5-TON   NAHC

AMERICAN 1906-1912 — The American Motor Truck Company of Detroit, Michigan, though overlapping in time of manufacture with the earlier truck builder of Lockport, New York, by the same name, built one of the first four-wheel-drive, four-wheel-steering trucks. It used a four-cylinder engine that was centrally mounted and drove both front and rear axles by chain. The front and rear axles were identical, simplifying manufacturing and maintenance.

The company advertised "patent double drive and double steer" that used chain drive to the front and rear axle. By 1911 the 1-ton was priced at $1,400, the 2-ton was $1,900 and the 3-ton was $2,700. However, four-wheel-steering was highly impractical to use for delivery in the city where it was difficult to pull away from a curb and impossible to turn away when stopped next to a wall or other large obstacle.

AMERICAN 1913-1918 — A second American Motor Truck Company was formed in Detroit, Michigan, but it was not related to the prior company started in 1910. The first model offered had a 108-inch wheelbase. It was rated as a 1-ton and used a four-cylinder Continental motor with a three-speed Brown-Lipe transmission. A

3-1/2-ton model appeared in 1917, which was also powered with a Continental engine but used a Covert four-speed transmission with Sheldon worm drive.

AMERICAN 1916-1917 — Another truck overlapping in time of manufacture with a truck builder of the same name was the American Motor Truck Company of Hartford, Connecticut. At the time small truck builders sold only locally, but some confusion probably existed among buyers. This American was a 2-ton truck with a stake body that used a four-cylinder engine with a three-speed transmission and worm-drive. It was one of the earliest trucks to offer an electric starter and lighting as standard equipment.

AMERICAN 1918 — The American Motor Vehicle built a 1/2-ton truck in LaFayette, Indiana, but it was actually known for its pedal vehicles built for children.

AMERICAN 1920-1924 — Yet another truck by the same name, The American Truck and Tractor Company of Portland, Connecticut, began building 159-inch wheelbase trucks that were either 2-1/2-ton or 4-ton models for 1920 and 1921. The trucks used four-cylinder Wisconsin engines with four-speed transmissions and worm-drive. In 1923 the 4-ton model was rated as a 5-ton without any known mechanical upgrades. For the last year of production only the Model 25 2-1/2-ton was manufactured.

AMERICAN-ARGO see ARGO

1938 AMERICAN BANTAM PICKUP   KP

AMERICAN AUSTiN / BANTAM 1929-1941 — The American Austin Car Company was incorporated in 1929 in Delaware with manufacturing facilities in Butler, Pennsylvania. The first cars rolled off the assembly line in 1930. The American version was a mirror image of the British Austin 7 in that the steering was on the left side. Hayes Body Company of Detroit, Michigan, supplied most of the coachwork, which at first included a roadster, coupe and 1/4-ton sedan delivery, hence the company can be considered a commercial vehicle manufacturer.

The first year was also the best year for American Austin with 8,558 total vehicles sold. At the time, even the sedan delivery was 16 inches narrower and 28 inches shorter than any car in the United States. It has been claimed it was the first car to carry its battery under the hood. All models were powered by a four-cylinder 15 hp engine. The sedan delivery cost $550 for 1930 and 1931 with the price going down to $495 for 1932 and eventually hitting a low of $365 for 1934.

The company went into receivership in 1932, but thanks to businessman Roy Evans it stayed afloat through 1934 before bankruptcy was filed. Production stopped for 1936 and 1937, but Evans brought the company back into operation as American Bantam Car Company with a restyled look for 1938 with the Model 60. Designer Alexis de Sakhnoffsky reportedly charged only $300 for the new aerodynamic design, and sufficient changes were made to the engine in order to avoid paying patent royalties to British Austin. A synchromesh transmission was introduced and several different delivery body styles were added to the lineup, including the stylish Boulevard Delivery of 1939. For 1940 a three-bearing 49-cubic inch engine was incorporated, but the company continued to lose money.

That same year Karl Probst was hired to design a 1/4-ton four-wheel-drive vehicle for the U.S. Army. The new vehicle used a four-cylinder Continental 45 hp engine, and this design beat Ford and Willys to become the prototype for the military jeep of which Bantam built 2,500 in 1941, the last year of its Model 65 production. During the war Bantam continued to produce two-wheel trailers, which it had done since 1939, but manufacturing did not resume after World War II.

1939 AMERICAN BANTAM 60 BOULEVARD DELIVERY   JAW

1941 AMERICAN BANTAM LIGHT RECONNAISANCE TRUCK   RD

AMERICAN CARRIER EQUIPMENT 1971 to date — American Carrier Equipment started its manufacturing facilities in Fresno, California. The company began producing complete buses in 1971, having already been in the business of fabricating truck bodies and trailers. That year the company supplied Yosemite National Park in California with three 100-passenger open-top double-decker buses powered with a six-cylinder Ford motor converted to propane. The trucks used Allison fully automatic transmissions. Previously, the company built open sided sightseeing trailers for parks and tourism under the "Shuttlecraft" nameplate. The company has manufactured several more similar buses for other parks and recreational areas in the United States. During the 1980s the company built 15 more buses on Ford chassis for the San Diego Zoo. American Carrier Equipment has continued to build buses on a custom basis only.

AMERICAN COULTHARD 1905-1906 — The American Coulthard Company of Boston, Massachusetts, contracted with the Corwin Manufacturing Company of Peabody, Massachusetts, to build a large steam-powered truck based on the British Coulthard design. It used a two-cylinder cross compound steam engine rated at 30 hp, which was fed by a boiler standing upright between the seats of the fireman and driver. The chassis was a 130-inch wheelbase with steel-clad wheels. The company could not compete with electric and gasoline powered trucks, which rapidly became the preferred means of propulsion after the turn of the century.

1905 AMERICAN COULTHARD   RD

AMERICAN EAGLE 1911-1912 — The American Eagle Motor Car Company of New York, New York, built a single model 1-1/2-ton truck with a 103-inch wheelbase and used a four-cylinder 25 hp engine.

AMERICAN ELECTRIC 1900-1902 — Numerous models of electric vehicles were built by American Electric starting in 1896. The early models were essentially motorized carriages with tiller steering and a range of 60 miles at 12 mph. Between 1900 and 1902 the company expanded its model line to 21 different variations including an omnibus, emergency vehicle and light delivery truck. The latter sold for $1,650. Argo also used the American Electric name a decade later.

1912 AMERICAN LAFRANCE TYPE 12   A-L

1920 AMERICAN LAFRANCE TYPE 40   A-L

AMERICAN LAFRANCE 1910-1985, (1986-1994) — The American LaFrance Fire Engine Company started in Elmira, New York, and was actually formed in 1903 from several small outfits, one of which dated back to 1832. The two largest of these companies lent their names to form American LaFrance -- the American Fire Engine Company of Seneca Fall, New York, and LaFrance Fire Engine Company of Elmira.

Prior to building a motorized fire engine, prototypes of steam-powered fire engines were built starting in 1905. For 1907 the company built a chemical car on a 30 hp Packard chassis. It was delivered to the city of Boston but returned months later when the fire department neglected to pay for the vehicle. In 1909 the company produced a chemical and hose truck powered by a four-cylinder Simplex engine. That same year the company also began manufacturing its own four-cylinder and six-cylinder engines, so that after 1910 American LaFrance did not use purchased engines.

The year 1910 marked the delivery of Register No. 1, a Type 5 combination chemical and hose truck. The following year American LaFrance began offering the Type 10 (500 gallons per minute) and Type 12 (750 gpm) rotary-gear pumping engines.

1924 AMERICAN LAFRANCE   **CHRIS STUDIO**

1929 AMERICAN LAFRANCE TYPE 270   **A-L**

By 1913 the company began producing Type 16 and Type 30, two gasoline-electric-hybrid vehicles, as well as the Type 31, which was a front-drive retrofit unit used to convert horsedrawn wagons. It was similar to that built by A & B Manufacturing of Providence, Rhode Island. The Type 31 was built until 1929, including complete factory-built front-drive vehicles with wagons. The Type 17 was the largest at the beginning of manufacturing with a six-cylinder 105 hp engine. The last American LaFrance steam pumper was built in 1914 using a Type 31 tractor. The company also built long ladder trucks with wheelbases from 239 to 383 inches, which had tiller-steer rear axles operated at the back by a steersman.

The popular Type 14 was introduced for 1916, and by 1921 this vehicle was offered in a quadruple combination with a full set of ladders, hose, a volume pump, and either a booster pump or chemical equipment. American LaFrance built commercial trucks from 1913 until 1929 from 2-ton to 7-1/2-ton. All of these trucks used American LaFrance engines, and in 1923 a new factory was started in Bloomfield, New Jersey, especially for this production. For example, in the mid 1920s the company built the 2-1/2-ton Model 2R with optional wheelbase and 36x4 front and 36x7 rear

tires on Dayton wheels. The engine was also designated as 2R using a Zenith carburetor and Splitdorf ignition. The company built its own clutch and transmission as well as front and rear axles. The Model 2R price was $3,950. The 3-1/2-ton Model 3R was $4,950, 5-ton Model 5R $5,500, 5-ton Model 5R $5,750, 6-ton Model 5R $6,000. At this time American LaFrance also built truck tractors including a 5-ton for $3,950, 7-ton for $4,950, 10-ton for $5,500, 13-ton for $5,750 and 15-ton for $6,000. All of these trucks used the company's own engines, clutches, transmissions and axles, and all used Dayton wheels, Zenith carburetor and Splitdorf ignition.

The smallest rotary gear pumper was the Type 40 with a capacity of 350 gpm introduced in 1915, built in the mid 1920s when American LaFrance equipment was also available on special Brockway chassis. A major design change was initiated in 1926, and the new models were designated Series 100. The Foamite-Childs Corporation was acquired in 1927 creating the American LaFrance Foamite Corporation. This company had built fire engines under the name Childs Thoroughbred using Kearns-Dughie chassis.

In 1928 American LaFrance cooperated with General Motors to build the American LaFrance-GMC Type 199 powered by a Buick engine to be used as a mid-size chemical, hose or pumper truck.

One of the most important developments for American LaFrance was its 240 hp 30 degree V-12 engine that came out in 1929. Also that year American LaFrance merged with the Republic truck company to form the commercial truck manufacturing division of LaFrance-Republic, which was acquired by Sterling in 1931.

The V-12 engine was used not only by American LaFrance in its fire trucks but also in Brockway trucks, army tanks and the Budd Streamliner railroad locomotive. This was the same year that four-wheel brakes were also introduced in production. A smaller 170 hp V-12 was developed in 1935, which was based on the Auburn V-12 engine. That year chain drive was discontinued, which had still been used on the 400 series models. The smaller 500 gpm pumpers had straight-eight engines made by Lycoming, and van pumpers were introduced in 1936.

1939 AMERICAN LAFRANCE 500 SERIES   **RD**

1940 AMERICAN LAFRANCE 575 CC   **A-L**

The following year American LaFrance built four Metropolitan Duplex Pumpers for the Los Angeles Fire Department. Each of these trucks utilized two of the large V-12 engines. One propelled the truck and drove the pump mounted on the front cowl, the second drove the rear main pump. The hose was carried in a separate manifold wagon.

In 1938 the company introduced the streamlined Series 500 models that looked far different from their predecessors, and the following year a new cab-forward design aerial ladder truck was added to the model line. By the end of World War II the Series 700, based on the earlier cab-forward, began production and was available in 1947. The conventional truck design was discontinued as American LaFrance concentrated strictly on the cab-forward 700 series, which was built until 1956.

1950 AMERICAN LAFRANCE PUMPER　　　　　OCW

At the same time the company was awarded a large contract from the Air Force in 1950 to build the Model 0-10 and 0-11 six-wheel airfield fire trucks that used remote-controlled foam turrets. Marmon-Herrington was also given a contract for these vehicles and between the two companies 1,100 were built up until 1953.

For the first time since its infancy the company adapted purchased engines in 1955. The lighter Ranger, Protector and Crusader trucks began using a Continental six-cylinder engine. The following year the Series 700 was discontinued to make way for the Series 800. This series was similar in design and appearance to the 700 with open and closed cab options, as well as rigid or articulated versions. Along with the Continental engine the American LaFrance V-12 motor continued to be offered until 1958 when a new V-8 was also added. Only a few trucks were fitted with the V-12 after 1958.

In 1960 American LaFrance built several fire trucks using Boeing gas turbine engines. The first was ordered by the City of San Francisco Fire Department, and the pumper was fitted with a 330 hp Boeing 502-10MA gas turbine that weighed 450 pounds, compared to a 335 hp Continental gasoline engine that weighed 2,100 pounds. The two engines were compared after Seattle, Washington, evaluated another Boeing turbine fire truck, which was a tractor-trailer ladder rig.

San Francisco was the optimum hill climbing and acceleration test ground, but the turbine engine was geared too low for optimum results, despite having better performance. Shortcomings in acceleration, efficiency and reliability put the turbine engine project to rest. By 1965 the turbine-powered fire trucks (including one in Mt. Vernon, Virginia) were taken out of operation, and Boeing sold the gas turbine designs to Caterpillar for industrial applications. In 1961 the V-12 was phased out entirely. The company did not give up on gas-turbine power until 1972 when another experimental truck was built with this design.

A new series of airfield fire engines was started in 1962. These were based on the 900 series but had four-wheel-drive and were called Airport Chief. Two years later lower cost trucks were introduced as the Pioneer Series. In appearance they had square cabs compared with the round 900 series. In 1965 diesel engines were introduced, and beginning with the 1000 series of 1970, diesel engines became standard equipment although the trucks remained the same in appearance as those since 1958.

1952 AMERICAN LAFRANCE 700 SERIES　　　　　OCW

The following year 285 hp International gasoline engines were utilized as standard equipment in the Pioneer Series, while 216 or 265 hp Detroit Diesel engines became optional. In 1972 a new model with Cincinnati cab and Detroit Diesel called Pacemaker was introduced, priced between the Pioneer and the Model 1000. In 1974 the Century Series with wider cab was produced as the top of the line American LaFrance. It could be ordered as a two-wheel-drive or four-wheel-drive three-axle in both rigid and articulated tractor versions. At this time both 216 to 380 hp Detroit Diesel or 225 to 350 hp Cummins diesel engines were available.

These models continued through the 1970s, until the company additionally offered commercial trucks in 1981. The 4x2 and 6x4 chassis was incorporated primarily for use in refuse collection or general hauling. These trucks, with a total of 14 different wheelbases on the two chassis, used the Caterpillar 3208 as a standard engine, but a total of five Cummins and Detroit Diesel engines were also available. The Allison MT653 automatic transmission was standard with optional Fuller or Spicer manual transmissions. The trucks also offered right-hand drive, AM/FM radio and air-conditioning as options.

The last complete American LaFrance fire engine was delivered to Monroeville, Pennsylvania, in June of 1985. It had a Detroit 8V-92TA diesel engine, 300-gallon tank and 2,000 gpm pump. American LaFrance then continued under Figgie International as a marketing group selling complete pumps and aerial ladders manufactured by Kersey Manufacturing Company of Bluefield, Virginia. Some small component manufacturing continued by the company, but it met its final demise in 1994.

AMERICAN MOTOR BUS See CHICAGO MOTOR BUS

AMERICAN SAURER See HEWITT and/or SAURER

1921 AMERICAN STEAMER 4-TON CHASSIS　　　　　MROZ

AMERICAN STEAM 1912-1913; 1918-1922 — The American Steam Truck Company of Lansing, Michigan, built a large vehicle with a steam engine of its own design that had eight cylinders using a quadruple expansion system. The low pressure cylinders started with 7 inch bores and progressively increased in pressure from 5, 3.25

with 2.5 diameter being the highest pressure cylinders. With 300 psi of steam the engine produced 53 hp. Although the steam vehicle was a road truck, the model was called the Locomotive. Weighing 3-1/2 tons with a 144-inch wheelbase, it was priced at $4,500 in 1912 when there were 471 truck builders in the United States. It appears the company stopped production for several years before briefly resuming business in Elgin, Illinois, from 1918 to 1922.

AMERICAN STEAMER 1922-1924 — Not affiliated with the earlier American Steam Truck Company of Lansing, Michigan, this later American Steam Truck Company was founded by R.R. Howard in Chicago, Illinois, during 1922. A brochure printed late in 1921 proclaimed "First Truck in America to be Successfully Operated by Steam." The 4-ton truck was offered with "100 horsepower as compared with gas engines." A number of advantages were touted, some of them quite compelling, but it would appear few trucks were built.

Instead, Howard began building passenger cars by May of 1922. The $1,650 touring cars, likened in appearance to Lincolns, were considerably more affordable than the $4,800 truck chassis, but success did not arrive. By April of 1924 bankruptcy was filed with assets of $75,000 and liabilities nearly double that. At that time the company's offices were listed in Elgin, Illinois.

1973 AM GENERAL METROBUS   OCW

AM GENERAL 1974 to date — AM General is a descendant of the Kaiser Jeep Corporation (via American Motors purchase in 1970), which built approximately 350,000 jeeps during World War II. The factory has been located in former Studebaker headquarters in South Bend, Indiana, and with facilities in Wayne, Michigan; Mishawaka, Indiana; and Marshall, Texas. AM General has been a subsidiary of LTV Aerospace and Defense Company and its primary role has been building military and post office vehicles, as well as transit buses.

The company was founded in 1972 when arrangements were made with Flyer Industries in Winnipeg to supply finished bodies for buses that were similar to those of General Motors and Flxible. Final assembly included adding windows and air conditioning, along with a transverse Detroit Diesel 6V-71 or 8V-71 engine with an Allison transmission as on the GM and Flxible iterations, which used inline engines with Spicer transmissions. The Washington transit system initially placed an order for 620 buses.

By 1975 2,250 buses had been sold. These were either of two designs: 35 feet or 40 feet long and 96 or 102 inches wide. Subsequently, a new order called for 398 articulated buses for 11 different customers. Bodies and engines were supplied by M.A.N. and finished in Marshall, Texas, by AM General. These 55- or 60-foot long buses have been considered the first true articulated buses in the United States. AM General also built 219 trolley coaches for Seattle and Philadelphia.

AM General began building the Jeep Dispatcher 100 by 1977. These were 4x2 "jeeps" with sliding side doors used for multi-stop delivery and were widely used by the Postal Service. The vehicles were powered by a 121-cubic inch 80 hp four-cylinder engine permitting an average of 25 mpg.

The company has built 5-ton trucks and 15-ton 6x6 tank and heavy equipment carriers, although some have been actually manufactured by Crane Carrier Corporation. When the Mishawaka factory was closed in 1978, production was transferred to Marshall,

Texas. AM General built the M915 6x4 truck tractor that was rated at 15-ton throughout the 1980s. AM General withdrew from the controversial "Transbus" project in 1978. Other bus manufacturers joined AM General in refusing to bid on bus contracts calling for "Transbus" specifications.

1977 AM GENERAL 5-TON CARGO TRUCK   AM-GENERAL

Eighty percent of AM General's business has been through government contracts. This has included 100,000 High Mobility Multipurpose Wheeled Vehicles (HMMWV) otherwise known as Humvees or Hummers, which were built for the U.S. Army according to new military specifications beginning in 1978, although procurement did not start until 1981. The four-wheel-drive vehicle had to operate in the desert as well as the arctic, with or without armor, and had to be easily adapted to various applications as troop carrier, tow missile carrier, armament carrier, ambulance and other variations. During the Desert Storm operations in Kuwait, Saudi Arabia and Iraq, the Marine Corps, Army, Navy and Air Force used a total of 20,000 Hummers.

1993 AM GENERAL HUMVEE (HUMMER)   AM-GENERAL

The 130-inch wheelbase Hummer, either two- or four-passenger, has used a 6.2-liter diesel V-8 with 150 hp and 250 pounds of torque with a maximum towing capacity of 5,000 pounds and a cruising range of 275 miles. The vehicle has had a central pneumatic regulator allowing the driver to control pressure of the 36-inch diameter tires on 16.5 wide rims for on/off road driving. On or off road driving can be accomplished with one or more tires deflated. The Hummer has a 72-inch track allowing it to handle 40 percent side slopes. Also, the vehicle could climb 60 percent slopes and ford 30-inch deep water. AM General began to sell the Hummer to the civilian market in 1992. Actor Arnold Schwarzenegger was one of the first civilians to buy the vehicle. The basic model started at $40,000 that year.

AMTRAN 1981 to date — The AmTran Corporation evolved out of Ward Transportation, and the company became known as AmTran in 1981. School bus manufacturing has been the specialty of the company, and the conventional Volunteer model with 236-inch wheelbase has been produced for over a decade. Since 1991 the

Genesis bus has been a successful model line incorporating a special forward-control front-engine chassis. It has used the International DT 466 diesel engine and Allison AT or MT transmission.

1993 AMTRAN VOLUNTEER SCHOOL BUS　　　　　　**AMTRAN**

AmTran has also built the rear-engine Model RE school bus. It has also been powered by the International DT 466 diesel engine, and with a 234-inch wheelbase has been listed with a capacity of up to 90 passengers. The smallest has been listed as a 48-passenger version. The Genensis 72-seat school bus has also been converted to electric power by APS Systems of Oxnard, California.

1909 ANDERSON MODEL B　　　　　　　　　　　**WLB**

ANDERSON 1909-1910 — The Anderson Carriage Manufacturing Company of Anderson, Indiana, briefly built a highwheeler commercial vehicle. It used a two-cylinder engine with a planetary transmission that powered the rear wheels with chain drive. The wheelbase of the light truck was 70 inches and it weighed 1,300 pounds. Its crude frame was considered obsolete even at the time of its manufacture. It cost $700, but only a few were actually sold.

ANDOVER 1915-1917 — The Andover Motor Vehicle Company located in Andover, Massachusetts, built an electric truck rated at 1-1/2-ton capacity. Power was supplied by batteries. It is uncertain whether the Andover truck was actually built by Joly and Lambert Electric Auto Company of Andover. Only a few of the trucks were produced and plans for a passenger car never materialized.

ANHEUSER-BUSCH 1903/1917 — The Anheuser-Busch Company of St. Louis, Missouri, decided to use trucks to deliver beer throughout the city. These were the largest trucks ever built at that time -- 24 feet long and 10 feet wide able to carry 15 tons of beer. They were electrically powered but not successful due to their unwieldy size. Subsequently, Anheuser-Busch opened a vehicle department in its offices and designed truck and bus bodies during Prohibition when beer was illegal and to survive the company made Ginger-Ale, Carcho, Grape Bouquet, Buschtee and Bevo. The latter inspired an unusual promotional vehicle called the Bevo-Boat. It was built on a Pierce-Arrow chassis and in fact resembled a boat.

During World War I it was used to promote war bonds and two more were built in the 1920s. Once Prohibition was repealed the Bevo-Boats became the Budweiser Cars.

ANN ARBOR 1911-1912 — One of many upstart truck builders at that time, the Huron River Manufacturing Company of Ann Arbor, Michigan, built a single model of an open delivery truck with 3/4-ton capacity. The vehicle, called the Ann Arbor, had a 100-inch wheelbase and used a two-cylinder engine with a planetary transmission powering the rear wheels by double chain drive. Tires were pneumatic on all four wheels.

APEX 1918-1921 — Originating as Cincinnati Motors before moving to Grand Haven, Michigan, the Apex was built by the Hamilton Motors Company whose name was linked with Alter trucks built by Cincinnati Motors and then Alter Motor Car Company. For the three years that Apex was in production, a 1-ton, 1-1/2-ton and 2-1/2-ton model was offered. The first two models had a 130-inch wheelbase and the 2-1/2-ton had a 150-inch wheelbase. Each used a three-speed Fuller transmission and Torbensen internal-gear rear axle. See also ALTER.

APPLETON 1922-1927 — The Appleton Motor Truck Company of Appleton, Wisconsin, was organized as an outgrowth of the Reliance Motor Truck Company of that city. Reliance trucks were first built in Appleton in 1917 and were not affiliated with Reliance of Owosso, Michigan, and later Detroit, which was absorbed by GMC. A.G. Brusewitz, M. Rossmeissl and W.G. Jamisen were the incorporators who were working with $25,000 in capitalization. A.G. Brusewitz was one of the principals of the earlier Reliance company, which was forced into bankruptcy.

The Appleton Motor Truck Company appears to have completed the assembly of a few earlier Reliance trucks, which were 1-1/2-ton and 2-1/2-ton capacity with four-cylinder Buda engines and three-speed or four-speed transmissions and Badger internal gear drive. The company was listed as late as 1927, although complete truck manufacturing faded out in the early 1920s. Appleton probably continued as a parts and repair facility for the maintenance of the trucks built between 1917 and 1922.

1995 APS ELECTRIC SHUTTLE　　　　　　　　　**APS**

APS 1994 to date — APS Systems was incorporated in 1983 and has been located in Oxnard, California. The initial business concentration was in the area of aviation test and ground support equipment. In 1991 the company initiated research and development of battery-powered transit vehicles and their components. APS began retrofitting diesel- and gasoline-powered buses, and one of the first vehicles to go into service was the MTD Villager shuttle bus. This vehicle used two 50-kilowatt electric motors with 260-pound-feet of torque, and with 78-kilowatt-hours of battery power that permitted a 45-mile range at an average 20 mph with a top speed of 40 mph.

The APS 22-foot 19-passenger electric shuttle bus with 144-inch wheelbase has been available with a 95-mile range and a top speed of 40 mph. GVW has been listed at 16,800 pounds and battery weight was listed at 3,800 pounds for the Nickel-Cadmium pack and 5,600 pounds for the lead acid pack. APS Systems converted a school bus to electric power using 100-kilowatt electric motor power with 107-kilowatt-hour battery capacity permitting a maximum speed of 55 mph and a 70-mile range at an average 20 mph average speed.

A 35-foot electric bus has been developed by APS Systems that has been listed with a 70-mile range and a top speed of 60 mph. The company has built several 22-foot 20-passenger battery-powered shuttle buses for the city of Santa Barbara. For 1996 APS Systems has announced 22-, 25-, 29-, 35- and 40-foot electric and hybrid electric transit buses and chassis.

1912 ARGO   LIAM

ARGO 1911-1915 — The Argo Electric Vehicle Company of Saginaw, Michigan, built 1/2-ton and 1-ton model trucks, along with a line of passenger car models. The standard electric truck design of the period provided a top speed of 16 mph using a 40-cell battery and shaft drive. A 100-inch wheelbase was standard and the longest on the market for an electric vehicle. Gemmer wheel steering was state-of-the-art at that time. Argo got a late start in the electric vehicle business, and further delays at the former Sommer Brothers Match Company in Saginaw postponed the production of cars until 1912, and trucks were not built until 1913.

In 1914 Argo merged with Broc and Borland electric companies to form the new American Electric Car Company. Plans to build all three makes in three factories continued for only one year before all manufacturing was consolidated in the Saginaw plant, although all three trucks were produced under their individual names until 1916 when operations were shut down. Columbia Motors Company of Detroit bought Argo to get the National Automobile Chamber of Commerce license for national car shows. The Argo factory was acquired by the Saginaw Motor Car Company, which built the Yale 8, and subsequently Jumbo trucks were built by the Nelson Motor Truck Company at the same plant.

1976 ARGOSY MINIATURE BUS   ARGOSY

ARGOSY 1976-1984 — The Argosy Company of Versailles, Ohio, was a relative newcomer to the business of building commercial vehicles, which have been in the form of small buses. They were often used where local government provides low-density area transportation without having to rely on larger less efficient designs. The Argosy Company has been offering Airstream aluminum travel trailers, A-Van truck bodies and 25-foot buses for 25 to 29 passengers, depending on the accommodations and wheelchair lift. Shuttle bus production faded out in the early 1980s.

ARKLA 1965 — In 1965 the Arkansas-Louisiana Gas Company of Little Rock, Arkansas, built 100 1/4-ton trucks for its own use. These were powered by 45.5 hp air-cooled "flat" two-cylinder engines and were coupled by an automatic centrifugal clutch. The small utility trucks had a capacity of 840 pounds. The cab, hood and fenders were made of fiberglass. The Arkla light trucks were produced for only one year.

ARMLEDER 1910-1936 — Otto Armleder was known in Ohio's Cincinnati brewing industry during the 1890s as an experienced wagon builder. The O. Armleder Company began producing trucks in 1910 in a large six-story factory. The first model line was a series of conventional assembled trucks ranging from 3/4-ton to 3-ton capacity. By 1917 another model was added that was 3-1/2 ton. The same year the chain drive design was supplanted with worm-drive. During World War I the company successfully extended its dealer network throughout the United States.

1920 ARMLEDER 6-TON ARTICULATED TRUCK   FLP

1924 ARMLEDER 1-1/2-TON MODEL 21   HAYS

Armleder trucks during the 1920s were offered from 1-ton to 3-1/2 ton with Buda, Continental or Hercules engines. An articulated 2-1/2 ton model was offered in 1920. The 1-1/2-ton Model 30 of 1925 had a wheelbase of 148 inches with 34x5 front and rear wheels and used a 25.6 hp four-cylinder Hercules OX engine with Zenith carburetor and Bosch ignition. The Model 50, offered with a 152-inch or optional wheelbase and 36x4 front and 36x8 rear wheels, used a Buda EBU1 28.9 hp engine and was rated at 2-1/2-ton. The Models KWB and KWC, both with 156-inch (or optional) wheelbase rated at 3-1/2 ton, used a Buda YTU 32.4 hp engine while the KWC truck used a Continental E-4 engine rated at the same hp. On each of these models the transmission and clutch were Brown-Lipe with front and rear axles by Timken, as well as Bosch ignition and Zenith carburetor.

In 1927 a six-cylinder engine was available in addition to the four-cylinder. The 3-1/2 ton used structural I beams and during the 1920s various models used wheels made by St. Marys Wheel Co. of St. Marys, Ohio, as well as steering gear made by Ross Gear and Tool Co. of Lafayette, Indiana. Variable rate rear suspension was available on most models over these years when production averaged eight units per month.

Armleder was absorbed by Cincinnati's LeBlond-Schacht Truck Company in 1928, becoming a division of the parent company and was gradually merged with the Schacht badge of trucks. Buda, Continental and Hercules engines continued to be used, and the articulated model was continued. The last year Armleder trucks were made was 1936. Schacht listed 19 models in 1937 but the following year LeBlond-Schacht was out of business.

ARROW 1973-1974 — The Arrow Manufacturing Company of Denver, Colorado, built a terminal truck tractor used as a yard jockey. The six-wheel truck featured a half-cab, 152-inch wheelbase and full engine cowling. It was powered by a 210 hp 361-cubic inch Ford V-8 engine. Manufacture after 1974 has not been substantiated.

ARROWHEAD 1936 — At a cost of $8,000 the Arrowhead Spring Water Company of Los Angeles contracted Everett Miller to design a promotional vehicle for the company that could serve as a jitney. The Arrowhead was a three-wheel vehicle in the shape of a water droplet. It was powered by a V-8 engine mounted at the rear but driving the two front wheels. The single vehicle, steered with the rear wheel and similar to Buckminster Fuller's Dymaxion, remains extant.

ASPROOTH-LEONI ELECTRIC 1924-1927 — A.M. Leoni started in 1924 by building a prototype truck chassis in Philadelphia. This was followed by a taxicab chassis that had the engine incorporated with the rear axle using planetary gearing. The chassis used Hofmann air springs front and rear to compensate for the solid tires that Leoni considered optimal considering the great frictional power loss with pneumatic tires, which affected the performance of his electric vehicle.

Leoni devised a method of using quick-exchange batteries so that fresh power was available at all times for the taxicabs, but these only went as far as the prototype stage before the venture closed.

ASTOR 1925 — The M.P. Moller Motor Car Company was located in Hagerstown, Maryland, and manufactured Astor Cabs, as well as Luxor Cabs and Dagmar passenger cars. The Astor Cabs were built under contract from Astor Cab Sales of New York City. The vehicle used a four-cylinder Buda engine and featured disc wheels. Its V-shaped radiator was distinctive from other makes. There were also body styles incorporating the limousine and landaulet taking the price up to $2,695 from a base cab that sold for $2,295.

ATCO 1919-1921 — The American Truck and Trailer Corporation of Kankakee, Illinois, started in business by building a 2-ton truck powered by a four-cylinder Buda engine using a three-speed transmission and worm-drive rear axle. The eight-spoke cast steel wheels had solid rubber tires. In 1920 pneumatic tires were available and the following year the trucks were rated at 1-1/2-ton and 2-1/2-ton capacity. The latter model used a Fuller four-speed transmission.

ATLANTIC 1912-1921 — The Atlantic Vehicle Company of Newark, New Jersey, started building electric trucks rated at 1-, 2-, 3-1/2- and 5-ton capacity. These were designed by Arthur J. Slade, chief engineer, formerly of Commercial Motor Car Company of New York City. A year-and-a-half of design and experimentation went into the truck before it was offered for sale. The factory was located at the former Royal Machine Company.

The smaller truck was capable of 15 mph with an average range of 50 miles using standard lead-acid batteries. The trucks were of conventional design using chain drive. The 1-ton Model 1-C cost

$2,665 while the 2-ton Model 2-C cost $3,215. The 5-ton model with 115-inch wheelbase was built with a fitted body for hauling beer kegs and was priced at $4,400. A similar 5-ton stake body truck was $4,575. It used large 44-cell Exide batteries mounted under the midsection of the chassis. In 1912 the Royal Machine Company factory was acquired and Atlantic bid on postal vehicles.

1914 ATLANTIC MODEL 1-C   **KP**

By 1914 the model line consisted of 1/2-, 1-, 1-1/2-, 3-1/2-, and 5-ton capacity electric trucks. Only the 1/2-ton used shaft drive, and this model was dropped in 1920. But by 1914 the company was in receivership under the control of A.P. Osborn and H.L. Davisson, who blamed financial trouble on the extravagance of the sales department.

In 1915 the company was reorganized as the Atlantic Electric Vehicle Company in Newark, New Jersey. In 1916 six new models were offered using General Electric motors and controllers, although overall design remained unchanged to the end. In 1917 four model sizes were available, and by 1920 five were offered. For the last year of production the company switched to Hycap batteries. The company also built a taxicab, which never went beyond the prototype stage.

1906 ATLAS 2-TON   **NAHC**

ATLAS 1907-1912 — Sometimes listed as two separate Atlas trucks, the first series was built by the Knox Motor Truck Company of Springfield, Massachusetts, which had been started by Harry A. Knox, who had left the Knox Automobile Company that built air-cooled cars since 1900. Knox Automobile Company sued Harry Knox for the use of the Knox name, and he started the Atlas Motor Car Company late in 1906. One of the first Atlas trucks had a water-cooled engine and transmission mounted just ahead of the rear axle on a coil-spring-suspended channel frame. At this time Knox persuaded the Sunset Automobile Company of San Francisco, which had just lost its factory to the 1906 earthquake, to allow him to build under license Sunset's two-stroke engines, which were used in the later series of trucks built by Atlas.

The earlier series included the Type A model, which had a 96-inch wheelbase and was rated at 2-ton. It used a 25 hp two-cylinder motor and shaft drive. The Type B was rated as a 3-ton with a wheelbase of 113 inches and used the same engine. The 1-1/2-ton Model C appeared in 1907 as did the Type D, which was a bus. In the final years the company built only 2-ton and 3-ton models. The Knox Motor Truck Company was also known for its three-wheel Martin tractor called the Knox-Martin.

1907 ATLAS SPRINKLER TRUCK   RD

Atlas also built a taxicab called the Model T, which was powered by the same two-stroke engine that was advertised as "The Perfected Two-Cycle Engine." The Delivery Car of 1909 used this engine and sold for $1,800. By 1910, the taxicab was priced at $2,400. The two-cylinder engine developed 20 hp and was used in the 1,250-pound capacity delivery vans. The taxi first appeared in 1908 as did the Atlas delivery vans.

Harry Knox continued to develop the two-stroke engine, and a three-cylinder version was built, touted as having the "continuous power of the ordinary six-cylinder engine...with only seven moving parts." A 60 hp four-cylinder engine was developed by 1909, the year Knox entered the Vanderbilt Cup race. He was the first to enter the well-known long distance competition with a two-stroke engine and finished fifth overall. In 1911, a 3/4-ton truck was developed using a three-speed transmission, shaft drive and pneumatic tires. The four-cylinder engine was used in the 2-ton Atlas express model of 1912, which had a 144-inch wheelbase.

The two-stroke engine did not prove to be successful and by 1912, Knox adapted the Knight sleeve-valve engine, which was used in Atlas touring cars. By this time truck production was ended and in 1913, the company went into bankruptcy. Harry Knox left for Indianapolis where he went in business with the Lyons brothers producing the Lyons-Knight automobile. The later Atlas trucks from York, Pennsylvania, were built by another business entity related only indirectly through Milton Martin who was the entrepreneur behind the Martin-Parry Corporation.

ATLAS 1916-1923 — The more recent trucks by this name built in the United States, as a business entity Atlas went through many incarnations. In its inception the Martin-Parry Corporation built Atlas trucks, having taken over from the Martin Carriage Works when Milton Martin passed away in 1916. The following year the Martin Truck and Body Company and Atlas trucks were names used by the Martin-Parry Corporation of York, Pennsylvania.

1916 ATLAS 3/4-TON   OCW

Atlas was a direct successor to Martin trucks. Over almost eight years of production some 3,500 Atlas trucks rolled off the line. The first model offered was a 3/4-ton model that used a 19.6 hp four-cylinder Lycoming engine. Some 550 of these were built in 1917 and another 550 for 1918, while for 1919 sales increased to 740 for the year.

1916 ATLAS GLASS SIDE BUS   WM

In 1920 a 1-ton model was introduced. According to some records a Buda engine was used, although the company used Lycoming engines throughout most of its production. For 1920 the company sold 365 of the heavier truck model. Sales dropped to 217 trucks in the recessionary year of 1921, but the following year a 2-ton model was added as the 3/4-ton was discontinued. In 1916 the 3/4-ton cost $690, but within three years the price had nearly doubled. In the early 1920s Martin-Parry claimed to have half of the truck body building in the United States. The company also built bodies for the Ford Model T at 500 units per day.

The company merged with Selden in 1922, and as the new parent company took over dealerships, Selden trucks succeeded Atlas. But it appears that Atlas trucks were manufactured until 1923 in Rochester, New York. That year sales for Martin-Parry reached $5,951,000, but when the Ford Model T was abandoned, the company was stuck with a huge inventory, which ended up getting bought out by Chevrolet. The Atlas Truck Company was listed in New York directories as late as 1925, but by that time it was a dealership. The Martin-Parry business continued building third axles for heavy field artillery as well as steel wallboard, which was a type of wood grain painted metal paneling for buildings. The company's final demise came in 1948.

1930 ATTERBURY   HAYS

ATTERBURY 1910-1935 — Starting out as the Buffalo truck, the Atterbury Motor Car Company of Buffalo, New York, built conventional assembled trucks. George W. Atterbury began as an electrical engineer for Westinghouse, which he left in 1902. He teamed up with Henry Brunn, a Buffalo carriage builder. In 1903 he joined the Conrad Motor Carriage Company as general manager and started the Auto-Car Equipment Company, which changed names to Atterbury in 1909. As early as 1903 he received an order for 50 electric buses for the St. Louis Exposition, as well as for some two-cylinder gasoline-powered trucks. The Atterbury company built vehicles under the name Buffalo until 1910. See BUFFALO.

Starting with the Model 100 in 1910 the company offered 1-, 2-, 3-, and 5-ton models still using chain drive for its heaviest truck until 1917 when worm-drive was utilized for all models. A large ten-passenger touring car was produced for the jitney market in 1911. In 1925 Atterbury offered the 1-1/2-ton Model 24R, 2-1/2-ton Model 22C and 22CLWB, the 3-1/2-ton Model 22D and the 5-ton Model 24E and 24E-LWB. The LWB suffixes only referred to the long-wheelbase (and slightly higher price). The Model 22R had a 150-inch wheelbase and used a 25.6 hp Buda KTU engine with Zenith carburetor and Bosch ignition coupled to a Brown-Lipe clutch and transmission. Axles were Timken front and rear and solid tires as standard 34x4 front and 34x6 rear duals on Archibald wheels. The price was $2,450.

The 22C model with 156-inch wheelbase costing $3,375 (180-inch LWB $3,475) used a 27.2 hp Continental K-4 engine with Zenith carb and Eisemann ignition. The 22D Model costing $4,275 had a 174-inch wheelbase and used a 32.4 hp Continental L-4 engine. Wheel size on this model was 36x5 front and rear duals 40x6. The largest model used a 40.1 hp Continental B-7 engine with Zenith carb and Bosch ignition. Price for the heaviest truck was $5,350 and up to $5,500 for the LWB.

Atterbury was unable to compete with Pierce-Arrow and other upscale manufacturers, although the Canadian market just across the border provided some business in Ontario. Just before the stock market fell in 1929 the yearly production figure for the year at Atterbury was only 141 trucks. The company offered nine models by that time from 1-1/4-ton to 7-ton capacity with various engines available from Buda, Continental and Lycoming. At a cost of $1,595 the 1930 1-1/2-ton Model K with 145-inch wheelbase used a six-cylinder Lycoming engine with Brown-Lipe four-speed transmission and Timken bevel rear axle. By 1931 the company narrowed its model line ranging from 2-ton to 5-ton, and these remained unchanged until the very end in 1935. In terms of identifying some of the last models it should be noted that in order to save money Atterbury used radiator sheet metal from Larrabee-Deyo trucks. These were no longer in production, but suppliers still had stock and tooling, although such cost-saving measures did not save the Atterbury Motor Car Company.

AUBURN See HANDY WAGON

AUBURN 1936; 1938; 1941 — Auburn, Indiana, was the location of the Auburn Automobile Company. At the end of its financial slide during the Depression management at Auburn, where high-quality expensive cars had been built, decided to go into the ambulance and hearse-building business. This was a last gasp effort utilizing the 852-series cars, which had Lycoming straight-eight engines. The production figure for these vehicles was about 5,000 in 1936, the last year of manufacturing. How many of these were actually commercial vehicles has not been determined.

In 1938 when the Auburn-Central Manufacturing Corporation was formed after Auburn-Cord-Duesenberg went bankrupt, the Pak-Age-Car truck line was bought from Stutz and moved to the new factory in Connersville, Indiana. In 1941 Willys-Overland awarded Auburn Central a contract for 492,000 jeep bodies for World War II military production, which continued from 1945 to 1948 with the CJ2 Jeep bodies.

AUGLAIZE 1911-1916 — The Auglaize Motor Car Company was located in New Bremen, Ohio. The conventional highwheeler was rated as a 1/2-ton truck using a two-cylinder water-cooled engine with a planetary transmission driving the solid rubber wheels with two chains. The Model B was built as an express van. The Model C, which was rated as a 3/4-ton, used a four-cylinder engine with three-speed transmission and the same double chain drive. It was also built as an express van.

1914 AUGLAIZE MODEL H   OCW

A year after it was introduced, the lightest model was discontinued and the 3/4-ton built exclusively from there on until 1916. The model designations changed chronologically from Model D to Model H, but aside from the adaptation of shaft drive, the one 3/4-ton truck that was offered kept the same basic design until the company closed.

AULTMAN 1901-1902 — Henry Aultman built his first experimental steam vehicle in 1898. By 1901 he had built 10 auto-buggy steam carriages. Aultman and Company of Canton, Ohio, built a steam road engine that used a friction transmission. This would be considered unconventional if not unnecessary with a steam engine. The four-wheel-drive steam wagon, which was rated as a 5-ton truck, had the rear wheels driven with double chain drive while the front, which had narrower tread, were driven with a bevel gear shaft. The two-cylinder steam engine was rated at 16 hp. A prototype was the only example of this vehicle. Aultman also experimented with a gasoline engine, briefly, and the one model of the steam auto-buggy was continued until 1905.

AURORA 1908 — Aurora, Illinois, was the home of the Aurora Motor Works for the one year of its short existence. The one model offered, which had a wheelbase of only 80 inches, was rated as a 3/4-ton and used a two-cylinder two-stroke water-cooled engine coupled to a planetary transmission with shaft drive to the rear wheels. It is believed only one such truck was built. The company also briefly produced the Aurora Emancipator, but the factory was suddenly sold in 1909.

1933 AUSTIN UTILITY COACH   MBS

AUSTIN UTILITY COACH 1933-1934 — The Austin Utility Coach got its start when the Pickwick Corporation, a large holding company, went into receivership in 1932. The general manager of Pickwick, Dwight Austin, acquired the factory and built his own version of a 21-passenger transit bus. He had patented a right angle drive for rear transverse engines and this was the heralded feature of the Austin Utility Coach. However, Dwight Austin was hired by Yellow Coach in 1934 and his patent was used by Yellow and General Motors for the following three decades, the Austin System manufacturing having been closed down late that same year.

AUTO-CAR 1904-1908 — Preceding the more famous Autocar Company of Pennsylvania, the Auto-Car was built in Buffalo by Auto-Car Equipment Company. The company offered 2-ton electric-powered models at first, which were built in three different versions: closed delivery van, 24-passenger bus or trackless trolley. Also gasoline-powered trucks with delivery van bodies were produced using two-cylinder motors.

By 1906 the company expanded its model line with a 3-ton model that was powered by a 35 hp four-cylinder engine. This used the cab-over design and the following year a similar 5-ton model was available, both as a truck or 20-passenger jitney. Light electric buses for 10 passengers continued to be produced, and in the last year of business, this Auto-Car Company built an electric 24-passenger bus and a 6-ton platform body truck, as well as an electric ambulance. The company simultaneously built gasoline-powered vehicles in the form of 3-ton and 5-ton trucks, as well as a 20-passenger bus. The Auto-Car Company became the Buffalo Truck manufacturer in 1908 before changing names again to Atterbury in 1910.

1907 AUTOCAR COMMERCIAL   HE

1910 AUTOCAR TRACTOR-TRAILER   DH

AUTOCAR 1907-1995 — The Autocar Company got its original start as the Pittsburgh Motor Car Company founded in 1897 by Louis S. Clark and his brother John S. Clark. The Pittsburgh, Pennsylvania, company began with a motorized tricycle and a small automobile called the Pittsburger. The name was changed to the Autocar Company in 1899. At the turn of the century the company was moved to Ardmore, Pennsylvania, and from 1908 produced many thousands of trucks there until 1953 when White Motor Car Company of Exton, Pennsylvania, bought controlling interest, continuing to build Autocar Trucks. The Autocar emblem appeared as recently as 1995 on heavy trucks sold by White-GMC-Volvo.

Autocar started building passenger cars in 1900. The first experimental commercial vehicle was tested in 1907 and by 1908 the Type XVIII was offered as part of the model line. The truck had a wheelbase of only 85 inches, was rated as a 1-ton and used a horizontally-opposed 18.1 hp two-cylinder motor with a three-speed transmission and shaft drive. The Type XXI was almost identical except it had a 97-inch wheelbase and was rated as a 2-ton. By the time these were discontinued in 1926, 30,000 of them had been produced, many of them as buses.

Autocar trucks met with such success that passenger cars were discontinued in 1911. The two models of commercial vehicles continued through World War I as common all-purpose trucks for the United States, Canada and Great Britain until 1919 when four-cylinder "engine-under-seat" models from 2-ton to 5-ton began production. That year a pair of the new model trucks made a successful promotional, coast-to-coast round trip fully loaded, including side trips to the top of Pike's Peak and bottom of Yosemite Valley. The 2-ton used on the trip (and 3-ton) were powered by a 25.6 hp engine while the 4-ton and 5-ton had 28.9 hp engines. In addition to these gasoline-powered trucks, three electric trucks of 1-, 2- and 3-ton capacity were built.

1920 AUTOCAR HOTEL BUS   LIAM

1926 AUTOCAR 2-TON   HAYS

Prior to 1926 when a new series of commercial vehicles was introduced, Autocar offered 20 models in all variations. The lightest Model F with 97-inch wheelbase sold for $2,200. Model G with 120-inch wheelbase sold for $2,300. This series was available as 1-, 1-1/4-, 1-1/2- and 2-ton using the Autocar two-cylinder engine, but the 2-ton Model H and Model K used the 25.6 hp four-cylinder. All Autocars of this period used Stromberg carburetors and Bosch ignition. The 5-ton Model L and Model M, which differed only in wheelbase from 156-inch to 120-inch, respectively, were priced at $4,800 and $4,650. The heavier trucks used a 28.9 hp motor and 34x6 front and 36x12 rear solid rubber tires, as well as Autocar's own clutches, transmissions and axles. Wheels on all models of this period were by Hoopes Brothers and Darlington.

A new series was produced starting in 1926, which ranged from 1-1/2-ton to 7-1/2-ton capacity. The two-cylinder was no longer used as four-cylinder and six-cylinder motors were utilized. The stone grille guard in front and use of high grade bolts instead of rivets became standard features. The four-cylinder and six-cylinder models continued into the early 1930s. When Robert P. Page was elected president in 1927, Autocar began building some special application trucks under his new direction.

Off highway work provided Autocar with the opportunity to develop a heavy 4x4. Setting example for Mack, GMC and White, Autocar reintroduced the cab-over design, which continued on the 1933 U series. Autocar broke with the tradition of using its own engines when a Waukesha diesel was utilized in 1935, and trucks with Cummins diesels soon followed, such as the Model DC 4x4 dump truck. The cab-over, becoming increasingly popular, was available along with conventional models. These included 4x2 and 6x2 tractors for articulated haulers and 4x2 and 6x2 rigid chassis, with the larger trucks using five-speed transmissions. In 1936 the company introduced the UD series, which could be identified by their more streamlined cabs. This design continued until after World War II. Autocars were assembled in Amsterdam in 1938 and 1939, and these were called Autocar-Kromhouts, used primarily as refuse and fire trucks.

1936 AUTOCAR COE VAN   **KP**

1938 AUTOCAR STAKE BODY   **KP**

Between 1936 and 1946 Autocar used nine different engines from 33.7 hp (90 brake hp) to 48.6 hp (130 brake hp) including its own motors, as well as Cummins and Hercules powerplants. Transmissions were made by Autocar, Brown-Lipe, Clark or Fuller, and driving axles were by Autocar, Eaton or Timken. Brakes were made by Bendix, Lockheed, Timken or Westinghouse. For 1937 alone Autocar offered 14 different six-wheel trucks priced from $2,715 to $9,500, and four 4x4 models were built starting at $5,000 up to $7,250. The same year Autocar offered 35 lighter

trucks starting at $1,980 up to $6,650 including 14 cab-over models. Most of the 1937 models used Autocar engines and transmissions.

1941 AUTOCAR LINE TRUCK   **MC**

Starting in 1940 Autocar began large scale production of military trucks. The company received a contract for thousands of halftracks, as well as 4x4 and 4x6 prime movers. Halftrack production ended quickly in 1940 and the company built 3,000 trucks for civilian use before going back into dedicated military production.

1944 AUTOCAR ARTICULATED TANKER   **OCW**

After World War II production was quickly shifted back to civilian use with 5,320 Autocar trucks built in 1946 alone. In the early 1950s a new deluxe cab was offered, later to be used on some White and Diamond Reo trucks.

With financial trouble brewing, Autocar was acquired by White Motor Company in 1953 and manufacturing was transferred to nearby Exton, Pennsylvania. The Autocar became the top of the line marque for White. Marketing focused primarily on specialized applications, such as construction, logging, mining, quarrying and oil industries. The largest of these trucks from the mid 1950s was the 40-ton Model AP40 that used a 600 hp V-12 diesel.

The A series using lightweight aluminum chassis was started in 1958 reducing the truck's weight by one-fourth so that payload could be increased by 2-1/4 tons. At the same time some Model C65 and Model C90 with stainless steel cab were custom built using the 490 White gasoline and C180 and C220 Cummins diesel engines. In the 1960s diesel engines made by Cummins and Caterpillar became the mainstay of the production line. Trucks and truck tractors were built in 4x2, 4x4, 6x4 and 8x4 configurations. After 1965 all Autocars were powered by diesel engines with trucks ranging from 23-ton GVW to 100-ton GCW. Also, special chassis for cement mixers, including the cab-over design, were built in 6x4, 8x4 and 6x6 configurations. In the 1970s Cummins diesel engines from 230 hp to 350 hp and Caterpillar engines from 220 hp to 375 hp were available.

For 1975 Autocar introduced the Contractor with offset cab, and the Constructor 2 series came in 1978 with both fiberglass and steel hoods, axles forward or set back and engines from 210 hp to 430 hp. A "B" suffix indicated a set back front axle while an "F" suffix indicated the axle set forward. Detroit Diesel engines were also made available.

1993 WHITEGMC AUTOCAR   **GMC**

In 1980 Autocars stopped production in Exton, and all manufacturing was transferred to Ogden, Utah. A new High Hat Cab with extra headroom was introduced in 1984. By this time the DC series was available with a Caterpillar 3406 325 hp six-cylinder turbocharged diesel with a displacement of 16.6 liters, or a Caterpillar 3408 450 hp V-8 turbocharged diesel with a displacement of 18 liters. Transmission was a Fuller 6F 1R with a three-speed auxiliary unit. Rear axle was a Rockwell SSHP single reduction hypoid, and the frame design was a channel section double plate ladder type. Top speed was 45 mph.

As part of White-GMC-Volvo, Autocar was badge-engineered as a symbol of one of the earliest marques to have begun its successful life in America. White-GMC-Volvo dropped the Autocar name as of July 1995.

AUTOHORSE 1917-1922 — The One Wheel Truck Company of St. Louis, Missouri, built a motorized unit that attached as a retrofit to a horsedrawn wagon for converting it into a primitive truck at a time when the motor industry was proving that the internal combustion engine was more reliable, durable and efficient than the horse. Many fire departments and some businesses opted to use motor power but did not want to pay for an entire new truck and all of its equipment. The aptly-named Autohorse used a 22.5 hp Continental engine that was offset-mounted but counterbalanced by a 56-gallon water tank for the radiator. The unit had a Borg and Beck clutch and Warner three-speed transmission, and final drive was by internal gearing. The Autohorse had no turntable, unlike some similar contraptions of the time, but was bolted to the steerable front axle of the wagon.

The St. Louis Fire Department ordered 40 such units in 1918, but they turned out to be too much of a compromise for both horse and machine. Only five were produced and sold. Steam wagon builder Taskers of Andover, Great Britain, planned to continue building the Autohorse, but none were manufactured there, although some U.S.-built units were used in England.

AUTOMATIC ELECTRIC 1922 — A small electric truck was briefly built by the Automatic Transportation Company of Buffalo, New York, which made the unsubstantiated claim to be the largest electric truck and tractor manufacturer at that time. The company also built passenger cars. The 1/4-ton truck had a wheelbase of only 65 inches and overall length of 102 inches, and was essentially a modified runabout. It used a 24-volt system to drive one rear wheel by chain and had tiller steering. The company was acquired by Walker Electric by 1922.

AUTOMOBILE FORE CARRIAGE 1900 — The Automobile Fore Carriage Company of New York was not so much a builder of commercial vehicles as it was a manufacturer of an engine attachment for wagons used in commerce or privately. The two-wheel-drive

system, which could be retrofitted to replace a horse, had been developed by Kullstein-Vollmer in Germany, but only two prototypes were known to have been built and used in the United States.

1928 AUTOMOTIVE SYNDICATE STEAM BUS   **MBS**

AUTOMOTIVE SYNDICATE 1928 — Organized in 1927 by William Parrish who was the former vice-president of the Wills-St. Claire Motor Company, the Automotive Syndicate was a rather late and brief endeavor to develop a steam-powered bus, although investment in the enterprise was substantial. Part of the design was copied from the British Clarkson steam buses that had been built 15 years earlier. The steam bus design was under license from the Electrol Corporation, which held a patent on the flash boiler and control system that had been originally, though unsuccessfully, tested on the Standard Steam Truck.

The large six-wheel bus prototype was built entirely of steel and was to hold 40 passengers. A V-8 steam engine under the floor drove both rear axles directly. A second smaller steam engine ran the air compressor, condenser cooling fan, electric generator and water pumps. Testing of the bus continued until the stock market crash of 1929, and no further progress was ever made on this vehicle.

AUTO TRACTOR see AUTO MOWER

AUTO-TRICAR 1914 — The Auto-Tricar was a three-wheel vehicle built by A.E. Osborn in New York City. Several models including a light delivery model was available. The single wheel was in front and the vehicle was powered either by a single or double cylinder water-cooled Prugh side-valve motor. Wheelbase was 96 inches for the one-cylinder model and 108 inches for the two-cylinder model, and prices ranged from $250 to $400. The company only lasted approximately one year.

AUTO-TRUCK 1916 — The Auto-Truck Company of Bangor, Pennsylvania, built a single model 1-ton truck that sold for $1,250. It used a 20 hp four-cylinder Buda engine and was produced only as a stake body truck.

1935 AVAILABLE 6-TON TANKER   **RJ**

AVAILABLE 1910-1957 — Available trucks were built by the Available Truck Company of Chicago, Illinois, for their entire duration of manufacture except for the last year when the company became a division of Crane Carrier Corporation of Tulsa, Oklahoma. In 1910 the first model was a 3/4-ton "engine-under-driver-seat" forward control type that used a 22 hp flat two-cylinder engine, two-speed planetary transmission and chain drive to the rear wheels. In design and appearance, with its radiator guard, it was similar to the Autocar Type XXI.

1912 AVAILABLE OPEN GRILL EXPRESS   MROZ

Responding to the needs of the rapidly growing trucking industry in 1914, Available brought out a 1-ton 32 hp four-cylinder model again using the "engine-under-driver-seat" design, which over the years, as cabs became standard equipment, became known as the cab-over-engine (COE) design. The following year, however, the company returned to conventional truck design with 1-ton and 2-ton models using three-speed transmissions and shaft worm-drive.

The model line was expanded in 1917 when Available trucks were offered up to 5-ton capacity with four-cylinder Continental engines, four-speed transmissions and either Timken or Wisconsin rear axles. The 7-ton Invincible model was introduced in 1920 using a 50 hp Waukesha engine, but few sold and the line of heavy trucks was discontinued. For 1925 when pneumatic tires were available, the 1-1/2-ton JH model with 145-inch wheelbase used a 25.6 hp Hercules engine with Zenith carburetor and Bosch ignition coupled to a Brown-Lipe transmission and clutch.

The 2-ton JH-2 and 2-1/2-ton JH-2-1/2 models both used the same engine and transmission as the smaller truck. The JH-3-1/2 used a 32.4 hp Hercules MU-3 engine. The H5 Model with 190-inch wheelbase used a 40 hp Hercules T-3 engine. By 1928 six-cylinder engines were offered.

The 1930s were not lucrative years for the truck industry and Available was no exception. Many models were advertised but only some were actually built. Cab-over designs including six-wheel chassis continued to be produced up to 6-ton capacity, which were notably used as tankers. The wide range of trucks included a 3/4-ton pickup by 1937 as well as heavier trucks in both conventional and forward-control versions.

Available built a variety of vehicles for the military during World War II. Those included 6x4 trucks, buses, tow trucks and mobile cranes. After the war Buda and Cummins diesels and Waukesha gasoline engines continued to be the choice as were Fuller, Spicer or Warner transmission. The model line included a fire truck and all together 10 different capacities from 15,000 to 32,000 pounds GVW were produced. Buses were built by 1952 using Ford V-8 engines, which were either front cab-over or rear mounted. That year Available bought a series of crane carriers called Model OW63M for the U.S. Army. They were powered by a 450-cubic inch overhead-valve six-cylinder engine and used a five-speed transmission with a two-speed transfer case. The mounted Quick-Way crane had a 13,000-pound maximum capacity.

Because of Available's 6x4 chassis, which had been used for cranes and cement mixers, the Crane Carrier Corporation bought the Available Company in 1957. After a 47-year production of 2,500 trucks, Available trucks were briefly built under Crane Carrier Corporation ownership before wearing the C.C.C. emblem.

1916 AVERY 2-TON   RD

AVERY 1910-1923 — Builders of tractors and farm equipment, the Avery Company of Peoria, Illinois, began building trucks primarily for the agricultural market. The design included wide steel-clad tires and wheels for soft ground, as well as a crankshaft extension for power take-off to run pumps, saws and other machinery.

The company introduced the truck line with a 1-ton model using a four-cylinder engine, open cab and chain drive. Heavier trucks with solid rubber tires rated at 2-ton and 3-ton were produced starting in 1912. C-cabs were available the following year, and by 1917 the cab-over-engine design was utilized with enclosed chain drive. However, by 1921 Averys were conventional trucks with electric starter and lights, as well as enclosed cabs. A six-cylinder engine the company developed and introduced in 1921 was short-lived when the company closed less than two years later.

1911 AVERY 3-TON   RD

1921 AVERY 1-TON GRAIN BODY   RD

AVS see SPECIALTY VEHICLE

AYERS 1913 — The Ayers Steam Truck Company was organized in New York City by R.B. Ayers, president and John T. Bell, secretary. That year the California National Bank sued the Ayers company for $2,769, and no further activity has been substantiated regarding this ephemeral truck company.

B

BABCOCK 1911-1918 — The H.H. Babcock Company of Watertown, New York, briefly built a 3/4-ton van that used a two-cylinder engine mounted under the driver's seat and a three-speed transmission with double chain drive. The Model G, the only model available which also remained unchanged during its short production life, cost $1,650 in 1911. H.H. Babcock also built passenger cars, Models A through K, which ranged from $1,050 to $3,000 in 1909. By 1913 passenger car production was discontinued and Babcock, employing some 800 people, built truck and ambulance components during World War I.

BACKUS 1925-1937 — Production was limited to 150 vehicles during the dozen-plus years of the Backus Motor Truck Company of East Rutherford, New Jersey. These were assembled trucks from 1-1/2-ton to 6-ton capacity. Remarkably, the lightest model was powered by a six-cylinder engine while the heavier models were powered with four-cylinder engines. All engines were made by Waukesha with Brown-Lipe clutches and transmissions and Timken rear axles. Buses were put into production in 1927 and were built in small numbers for the next 10 years. Backus buses were used locally. In appearance the Backus radiators resembled those of Packards from that era.

1937 BACKUS BUS   FTS

1914 BAILEY MODEL E   KP

BAILEY ELECTRIC 1912-1914 — S.R. Bailey and Company built a light electric van using a passenger car chassis. As a builder of passenger electric cars the company existed from 1907 to 1916. The two commercial versions had a 106-inch wheelbase and a capacity of only 300 pounds. Two General Electric motors were powered by 60-cell Edison alkaline batteries. The Model E had a sloping hood and looked quite aerodynamic for a vehicle of this period. Pneumatic tires were also standard at that time, which was unusual then for electric commercial vehicles. Top speed was 16 mph and range was 80 miles on a single charge. The light van was almost identical to the light service car but for the box body. The Bailey Electric Roadsters, which sold from $2,000 to $3,300 between 1908 and 1916, were quite popular before the company declared bankruptcy.

BAKER 1908-1930 — The earlier Baker vehicle company should not be confused with the later one, both being located in Cleveland, Ohio. The Baker Electrics were the first by that name in the United States and primarily built electric passenger cars, but numerous electric battery-powered trucks ranging from 1/2-ton to 5-ton were also produced.

1913 BAKER DELIVERY TRUCK IN TOKYO   RD

The Baker Electric Company, started in 1899 by Walter C. Baker, did not begin building trucks until 1908. Baker had been involved in building the Electrobat taxis of 1893 for the Columbia World Exposition. He pioneered ball bearings for automotive use and engineered lightweight alloy axles for the Ford Model T. He was known for his record-setting 1902 Torpedo Baker Electric.

Baker's company sold truck fleets to customers such as American Express, which had over 30 Baker electric trucks by 1912. A Depot Wagon, the lightest truck, sold for $2,200 in 1911. Baker Electric 2-ton trucks were used as far away as Tokyo (Tokio), Japan, by the Mitsui Company in 1913. Other users at that time could be found in Sao Paulo, Brazil; Bangkok, Siam and Melbourne, Australia.

When the Baker company merged with Rauch-Lang in 1916, becoming the Baker-Rauch-Lang, commercial cars were no longer made. However, Baker's name continued on with the Baker Industrial Truck Division, forklift builders, a part of Otis Elevator Corporation in Cleveland, Ohio.

1921 BAKER RAM 1-TON TRUCK   MROZ

BAKER 1926-1928 — A second venture by the same name in Cleveland built a steam-powered bus chassis. The engine was an unusual five-cylinder rotary, reciprocating design, and auxiliary pumps and pulleys were driven with electric motors. "The Rotobaker Engine" was advertised widely, and a single example was displayed in 1928, but no further production was evident. The Steam Appliance Corporation of America, also located in Cleveland, used the Rotobaker engine again in a second chassis in 1928.

BAKER-BELL 1913-1914 — The Baker-Bell Motor Company of Philadelphia, Pennsylvania, briefly built light delivery vans alongside a passenger car model called the Hummingbird, which lasted only the first year. The lightest truck had a capacity of 1/4 ton and had a wheelbase of 90 inches. It cost $600 in 1913. Two other delivery vehicles, a 1/2-ton and 3/4-ton, were also produced. When Baker-Bell stopped production, the company became an agent for Commerce Trucks until 1916.

BALDWIN STEAM 1896-1901 — Baldwin Steam of Providence, Rhode Island, first built a steam van in 1896 for a local department store named Shepard and Company. L.F.N. Baldwin designed the vehicle, and it was built by Cruickshank Steam Engine Works where Baldwin was superintendent. Another vehicle was built there for Cross Steam Cars, but it is believed only one commercial type was ever produced by Baldwin before he sold his patents to a group of entrepreneurs from Connellsville, Pennsylvania, who built a few Baldwin steam cars at a separate company in the first few years of the century.

BANTA 1911 — The Banta Motor Truck Company was capitalized in 1911 at $100,000 in Detroit, Michigan. The stockholders were Jacob H. Stoerkel, George H. Banta, Hiram P. Stalker and Daniel P. Cassidy. Plans were made to build a delivery wagon priced at $700, but after announcements in the press no manufacture has been substantiated.

BANTAM See AMERICAN AUSTIN

BANKS 1923 — The Banks Motor Corporation built ornate carved hearses for one year in Louisville, Kentucky. The vehicle had a chassis built by Banks but used a Model T engine and transmission made by Ford. This company should not be confused with the Robert Banks Company of Stanton, Delaware, which built a steam car for Banks' own use 23 years earlier.

BARBER 1917-1918 — The Barber Motors Corporation built a special design truck tractor with narrow gauge 24-inch track for the rear wheels. This was accomplished by using a worm-drive rear axle with no differential and its associated large housing. A forward control design was utilized in this short production truck, which was claimed to be able to pull 12 tons and was priced at only $2,500.

1914 BARKER MODEL U KP

BARKER 1911-1913 — Two Barker truck builders with the same nameplate overlapped in time of manufacturing, but the one that got its earlier start was located in North Los Angeles, California. It was not affiliated with its contemporary in Norwalk, Connecticut. The company built 3-ton and 5-ton trucks that shared a chassis with 150-inch wheelbase, and both used 40 hp four-cylinder motors. The company provided several different commercial bodies including closed van, open express and stake bed.

BARKER 1912-1917 — The C.L. Barker Company of Norwalk, Connecticut, built several truck models ranging from 1/2-ton to 5-ton capacity. The wide model line did not prove lucrative and by 1914, at a time when heavy trucks did not sell in large numbers, only the lightest model was made available with a new worm-drive design. In 1915 a 2-ton truck with 137-inch wheelbase was also produced before the company's ultimate demise.

BARROWS 1927-1928 — The brief venture of Barrows Motor Truck Company of Indianapolis, Indiana, built trucks of three capacities: 1-1/2-, 2-1/2- and 3-1/2-ton. Each truck was powered by a four-cylinder engine using a four-speed transmission and shaft drive. This company should not be confused with the Barrows Vehicle Company of New York City, which lasted from 1895-1899.

1975 BATTRONIC ELECTRIC VAN BATTRONIC

BATTRONIC 1964-1980 — Boyertown, Pennsylvania, has been the location of the Battronic Truck Corporation since 1964. Battronic has been financed by Boyertown Auto Body Works in Pennsylvania with Smith Delivery Vehicles, Gateshead-on-Tyne, England, and the Exide Division of the Electric Storage Battery Company. Originally, Exide provided the batteries and motors for the production of an electric minivan, and Smith provided the chassis, while Boyertown built steel forward-control bodies and the assembly facilities.

The minivan was built in conjunction with the Electric Vehicle Council, a non-profit organization dedicated to the proliferation of electric-powered transportation. Its members included electric utilities, manufacturers of related products, research organizations, university members and individuals in government encompassing 19 countries throughout the world.

Smith withdrew from the manufacturing in 1966 and Exide followed in 1969. The first Battronic truck was built in 1964. It had a 1-1/4-ton capacity, top speed of 25 mph and 62-mile range. Chassis were built in Boyertown starting in 1966. An improved version of the truck followed using an SCR controller, series-wound 112-volt motor and patented quick-change batteries that provided a top speed of 60 mph with a 75-mile range.

The Battronic Minivan was distributed to 64 U.S. utility companies in 32 states. The Electric Vehicle Council tabulated data for research purposes. By 1971 the company offered four models including the minivan, 11-passenger bus, and 15-passenger and 25-passenger transit buses. In 1978 22-passenger buses began serving a 42-mile route in Montevideo, Minnesota, for a 6-1/2 hour work day. Both the vans and buses used the quick-change battery design. Paul Hafer, president of Boyertown, left the company in 1980 when the Battronic also ceased being built, and Boyertown closed down in 1993.

BAUER 1914-1917 — Bauer Machine Works Company, located in Kansas City, Missouri, built Bauer trucks from leftover parts for Gleason Trucks that the company had acquired. Two models were produced with a 1/2-ton and 3/4-ton capacity. Both used a four-cylinder engine and three-speed transmission with a wet clutch.

The drivetrain was advertised as a double-reduction drive. All components, including engine, transmission, chassis and axles were built by Bauer.

BEAN 1973-1993 — The John Bean Corporation, a Division of Food Machinery Corporation in Tipton, Indiana, built a high-pressure steam system during World War II. Originally, this equipment was mounted on various commercial chassis before Bean began building its own cab-forward custom chassis starting in 1973. Manufacturing continued sporadically in Hogansville, Georgia, until 1993.

BEARDSLEY 1914-1915 — Volney Beardsley started in Ohio as a partner in the Beardsley and Hobbs company, which built the Darling automobile. After going west and joining the Auto Vehicle Company, later the California Automobile Company, in 1913 Beardsley formed his own company with Watt Moreland, who built the Moreland trucks, and the Beardsley Electric Company built a few electric trucks in Los Angeles, California. However, the truck manufacturing operation was soon absorbed by Moreland. A few of the little-known 1/2-ton and 1-ton trucks were sold in Southern California prior to World War I.

1915 BEARDSLEY ELECTRIC   **JO VALENTINE**

BEAVER 1914-1915 — The Beaver State Motor Company of Portland, Oregon, built two passenger car prototypes. As was common during this period, manufacturers first dabbled in passenger car production, then moved to heavier vehicles as orders trickled in. No data is available on the Beaver electric vehicles, if in fact they were produced. At a cost of $2,650, a gasoline-powered truck was offered with 112-inch wheelbase using a 28 hp four-cylinder engine, but there is no substantiation that manufacturing of this vehicle ever took place.

This company should not be confused with the Beaver Truck company of Hamilton, Ontario, Canada, where production of various models from 1-1/2-ton to 3-ton lasted from 1918 to 1923.

The two known Beaver passenger car prototypes from Portland both disappeared, one mysteriously during bankruptcy, the other in a bonfire in 1929. See also BEAVER of Beaver Falls, Ohio.

1950 BEAVER MODEL B-35-PT   **MBS**

BEAVER 1934-1956 — Beaver buses were named after Beaver Falls, Ohio, where the Beaver Transit Equipment Company began in 1934 when G.M. Davis, who was a sales manager for ACF, decided to go out on his own to build buses. In the Depression year of 1934 there was some demand for new buses, but most orders were for light and economical models. Under contract, the Traver Engineering Company built a prototype bus using a Ford front-engine commercial chassis. The bus was shown to local and nearby transit companies, and with enough orders, the Beaver Company was formed. In 1935 the enterprise was incorporated as the Beaver Metropolitan Coaches.

The original 83-inch wide body was enlarged to accommodate double seats on each side, but the chassis remained the same with Chevrolet and International engines also being offered. In 1938 a rear-engine design was introduced and buses from 20-passenger to 35-passenger were available. The company advertised its flat sheet metal body for its economical repair and replacement. Only the four roof corners had compound curves. After World War II this design was replaced by a more aerodynamic design with opening slide windows.

After Davis left the company, a flood shut down factory operations in 1953. Davis and investors reacquired the factory in 1955, naming it the National Coach and Manufacturing Company, but the effort to restart the operation did not meet with success. By this time small transit companies that had bought light buses had either consolidated or closed, and those still in business were much more likely to buy used buses or diesel-powered vehicles of more modern design. During its years of production almost 1,000 buses were manufactured by Beaver.

BECK / BECK-HAWKEYE 1911-1921 — Several incarnations of the manufacturer built the early Beck trucks and buses in Cedar Rapids, Iowa, which should not be confused with the later Beck Company of Sidney, Ohio. The first two models consisted of a 120-inch truck chassis and an 18-passenger bus with 130-inch wheelbase. Both used a 40 hp four-cylinder engine. In 1914, when the Cedar Rapids Auto Works became Beck and Sons, the model line was expanded to include a 2-ton and 3-ton commercial chassis. A 1/2-ton truck was introduced for the 1915 model year. Later that year a 1-1/2-ton truck was offered using a 134-inch wheelbase. It had a three-speed transmission and used solid rubber tires. The rear axle used a double reduction drive.

In 1917 the company changed names to Beck Motor Truck Works before merging with Hawkeye and becoming Beck-Hawkeye, continuing to build trucks from 1-1/2-ton to 3-ton capacity using Continental, Herschell-Spillman or Buda engines with a price of $3,700 for the heaviest truck. To the end of production in 1921 a 1-ton and 2-1/2-ton model were available.

BECK 1934-1957 — C.D. Beck and Company began in Sidney, Ohio, when the founder, a salesman for Fremont Metal Body Company (C.D. Beck) bought the Anderson Body Company with the help of several investors and dealers. Briefly still under the name of Anderson, the company first built buses called Model 10 in five different sizes from 12 seats to 28 seats. There was also a Model 15 and a Model 20 with seating capacity up to 33 passengers. Chevrolet and Ford extended chassis with up to a 188-inch wheelbase were used with Airstream bodies. Buses were built for schools in New York, which had instituted a set of specifications, providing Beck with the opportunity to fill orders given the new regulations.

The first Airstream-bodied Beck buses were delivered to the Kerrville Bus Company in Texas. Kerrville was a silent partner in the Beck manufacturing venture. Other buses were delivered to Consolidated Bus Lines, Bowen Motor Coaches, Southwest Coaches and Parrish Stage Lines. Since the vogue at the time was for streamlining, the squarish Model 10 did not sell nearly as well. Eighteen carriers bought Beck Airstream buses in 1934 alone. By June of 1934 the name Anderson was entirely gone from all company advertising.

About 100 buses were built for each of the first and second years of production by Beck, not including the first few vehicles sold under the Anderson name. The Airstream buses were built on Chevrolet and Reo chassis, and transit buses were also built on International D-35 chassis as well as Dodge and Reo chassis.

Late in 1936 Beck introduced the Fleetway, which was an 11-passenger "airport" sedan built to compete with similar models produced by Crown, FitzJohn Body and Pierce-Arrow. The second new model for that year was called the Cosmopolitan, a COE-type bus with seating capacity for 15 passengers built on 166-inch Reo and 170-inch White chassis.

1935 BECK AIRSTREAM   MCA

1938 BECK STEELINER SUPER 19   MBS

For 1937 Beck began building the Metropolitan, which was similar to the Cosmopolitan except that it had transit seats and folding doors. It was built on several forward-control chassis such as the Mack Jr. 90-MJA, Reo 2LM, Studebaker Metropolitan ZMB and White 706-M. Wood over aluminum with steel angle construction continued to be used along with canvas tops. The Metropolitan Intercity bus was listed with a weight of 9,350 pounds and a price tag of $4,795 before Interstate Commerce Commission specifications were enacted.

Saddled with new all-metal construction requirements, Beck answered with the Steeliner, which looked much like the previous design but incorporated the necessary material changes. The original chassis had a 190-inch wheelbase, and the essential design was built until 1950. The Airstream design was also updated per ICC specifications, but the Model 10 and Fleetway series were discontinued. The Airstream series was built until 1939. Beck built special-order buses such as the 213-inch-chassis-based Diamond T transit bus for Willet Motor Coach Company of Chicago in 1937.

Integral construction was the next advance in design, and Beck joined the competitors of FitzJohn and Flxible in 1938. Airstreams and Steeliners were both introduced with integral construction, although in appearance they were nearly indistinguishable from the "body-on-chassis" design. In 1939 Beck also introduced its 29-passenger parlor bus with a Chevrolet engine at the rear and new front sheet metal styling, and these were called the Super Steeliner. The Scout was a stripped-down model of this bus.

After only 85 Super Steeliners were built and 7 Scouts, Beck discontinued the model lines in 1940 and introduced the rear-engined 33-passenger Mainliners and more expensive Luxury Liners. The first Mainliners were large enough to hold 29 reclining or 33 stationary seats, and from the 185-inch wheelbase Beck lengthened the next version to 220 inches, which was 33 feet long in overall length. This model had 37 seats, and International Red Diamond engines that superseded the earlier Chevrolet engines that Beck discontinued after 1939.

During World War II bus production was stopped by the War Production Board in 1942. By that time Beck had built 1,714 buses out of which 420 were integral design units. Because the War Production Board found the Beck factory unsuitable for war production, a few months later in 1943 Beck was back into bus

manufacturing. The buses Beck built were on 220-inch wheelbases without luggage racks, decorative trim or any special accoutrements. These were called the Commuter Express and were built of materials approved by the ODT. One hundred of the 41-passenger buses were built between April 1943 and February 1944, possibly the only production buses built in the United States at that time.

After the war a new factory was built, which opened in July of 1946. Beck built only the Steeliner and the Mainliner using virtually unchanged designs from 1942. Almost all used the RED-450 engine, except for Hercules diesel engines that were fitted in buses exported to Cuba and Mexico. Domestic buses used 269-cubic inch Blue Diamond and 361-cubic inch Red Diamond International engines.

1940 BECK LUXURY LINER COACH   MBS

The Mainliner II 3000 series arrived in 1948 and had a completely new appearance. The windshield was entirely symmetrical and so interchangeable left to right. Silver-sided versions were called Silverliners and air-conditioned buses were dubbed Luxury Liners. Welded tubing construction was reinforced with X-shaped side pieces. Glass-roof versions were called Skyliners, but only seven were built in the 3500 and 4000 series, which were built until 1951.

In February of 1951 Beck introduced a revised Mainliner known as the 5000 series, which used the RD-450 or Cummins diesel engine. Beck acquired Ahrens-Fox in 1953 and moved the fire engine manufacturing to the plant in Sidney, Ohio. The Highway Post Office was called the 6000 series and the 8000 series C-33 arrived in 1954. There was also the 9200 series Airglide Cruiser of 1954, the 9600 series Semi-deck-and-a-half of 1956 and the DH1040 series 40-foot deck-and-a-half of 1955. That year C.D. Beck bought out his original partners. The largest buses Beck built were the 40-foot deck-and-a-half, but only 12 were built. Seven were sold to Cuba but were repossessed and returned to the United States where they were rebuilt with Mack engines.

1957 BECK DECK-AND-A-HALF COACH   MBS

Mack bought out Beck in 1956 in order to expand fire engine and bus production (in effect acquiring Ahrens-Fox), but after getting out of bus manufacturing and reducing fire engine building the plant was sold to Westinghouse Air Brake. Twenty-five Mack Cruiser buses were built in Sidney in 1958. Records show that Beck built a total of 3,150 buses, not including the Mack Cruisers.

BEECH CREEK 1915-1917 — The Beech Creek Truck and Auto Company of the town by the same name in Pennsylvania was a short-lived manufacturer of four-wheel-drive four-wheel-steering 3-ton trucks. The truck's design was based on two patents obtained in 1914 and 1915 by Paul J. Smith, a machinist in Galeton, Pennsylvania. The patents covered a simple mechanism that included a pair of driveshafts from a transmission located amidship and full-floating front and rear axles that were pivoted from their centers. The first prototype based on an existing chassis was finished in 1914 with the financial help of William H. Ward, a wealthy lumberman who later became a major stockholder in the company. A second truck chassis, which was fabricated by the company, used a 40 hp four-cylinder Pittsburgh Model Engine with governor and Remy magneto.

The first prototype was demonstrated in Beech Creek, a small mining town of 800 people at that time. The company was soon incorporated with authorized capital of $100,000, with half of the stock issued for sale. Henry H. Salisbury was elected president but almost immediately moved out of town. George F. Hess took his place, and David M. Packer was secretary while I.J. Rohrbaugh was treasurer.

The first truck was rated at 3-ton capacity. Its steering gear was built by the DuBois Iron Works and transmission was supplied by the Philadelphia gear works. Wheelbase was 132 inches. The truck was priced at $3,850, roughly twice what it cost to build. Two trucks were sold in 1916, but there is no evidence that any more were built after that. The company continued as an automobile dealership and repair shop until 1920. A 1918 listing offered the Beech Creek truck with a 29 hp Waukesha engine, but it is doubtful that any were built.

1915 BEECH CREEK 4X4   SAH

BELL 1913-1915 — Bell steam trucks were built for only three years but under four names. All in Yonkers, New York, the company names were listed as Bell and Waring or Bell Locomotive Company and American Motor Freight Company in 1913, and Bell and Waring Steam Vehicle in 1914. The large truck had a capacity of six tons using a dump bed. The steam engine used double acting cylinders of 4.5-inch bore and 6.5-inch stroke with power supplied directly to the rear wheels.

BELL 1916-1921 — Not affiliated with Bell of Yonkers, the Bell Motor Car Company of York, Pennsylvania, built passenger cars in the former Baily Manufacturing Company located in York. Ernest T. Gilliard, already associated in York with Pullman and Sphinx automobiles, invested in the enterprise in 1915 and production started the next year. Henry M. Stauffer was president and Dr. Harry W. Posey was vice-president.

The company built one model of truck on a touring car chassis. It had a capacity of 1,200 pounds and used a 19 hp four-cylinder Lycoming engine. The truck was priced the same as a Model 16 touring or roadster at $775. In 1918 a 1-1/2-ton truck was offered, but that year the company was moved to the closed Pullman factory and it is not certain if truck production continued. By 1919 Herschell-Spillman engines were available. In 1921 the company was taken over by Charles E. Riess who changed the name to Riess Royal, but no manufacturing ensued.

BELL 1919-1923 — A number of sound business ideas went into forming the Iowa Motor Truck Company in Ottumwa, Iowa. H.L. Bell chose the location due to its proximity to the Des Moines hydro-electric plant where power was more affordable, and four available railroad companies would give Bell the flexibility of long-distance transportation. Labor was cheaper and conditions were better than in the East. A large farm market for trucks waited in Iowa, Nebraska, Colorado and the Dakotas, and Bell intended to fill its needs.

Once manufacturing began in 1919 the Iowa Motor Truck Company built 15 trucks per month. The vehicles were conventional assembled 1-1/2-ton and 2-1/2-ton trucks that used four-cylinder Buda engines and Russel internal-gear rear axle. In the final two years of production a 1-ton model was also offered. The chassis design for the two larger trucks was described as having been made from six-inch channel with five-inch crossmembers, the truck being well proportioned. The radiator was well inside the front of the frame, creating a form of bumper. Along with the extended frame, the radiator was protected with six vertical polished bars. Artillery wheels and solid rubber tires were standard for agricultural work during that time, but pneumatic tires became optional. Prices started at $2,000 for the "short-haul" local market and $2,650 for the 2-1/2-ton aimed at the Colorado "long-haul" market. Standard equipment was described as C-cab, cushions, driver's seat, klaxon, sidelamps, storm curtains, taillamps, and windshield.

BELLABEY See DUFOUR

BELLSTROM 1916-1921 — The Bellstrom Company was located in Battle Creek, Michigan, then moved to Detroit, Michigan, in 1916. The company first built 3/4-ton trucks and later went into limited production of larger trucks. Other details have not been available.

BELMONT 1919-1923 — In 1918 Belmont Motors Corporation bought the defunct Dile Motor Car Company of Reading, Pennsylvania. After assembling a few leftover Dile cars, the small business of Belmont Motors Corporation, located in Lewistown, Pennsylvania, began building trucks. The two models offered were conventional assembled trucks rated at 3/4-ton and 1-1/2-ton and carried price tags of $1,150 and $1,950, respectively. The two models, of which few were built, both used a 26 hp four-cylinder Continental engine. In 1920 the factory burned to the ground but was reopened in 1922. The Kearns truck company took over Belmont Motors and it became a dealership solely for the parent company.

BENDIX 1908-1909 — Chicago, Illinois, was the location of the Bendix Company during its brief entry into the truck manufacturing business. The company was started by Vincent Bendix who left his home of Moline, Illinois, at age 16 in 1899 and became an elevator operator in New York City. He teamed up with aircraft pioneer Glenn Curtiss to build motorcycles in 1901 and later returned to Chicago as a sales manager for the Holmsman Automobile Company. In 1907 he started the Bendix Company after purchasing the Triumph Motor Car Company of Chicago. The first prototype car was called the Duplex, the second was called a Bendix. In 1908 the Bendix factory was moved to Logansport, Indiana. About 7,000 cars were built under the name Bendix.

Bendix also built a light commercial vehicle. The 110-inch wheelbase highwheeler was powered by a four-cylinder engine with a friction transmission using double chain drive to the rear wheels. It looked somewhat like the light International highwheeler truck of that era yet the Bendix was advertised as a 1-1/4-ton vehicle during its short life as a model line for the company with its famous name. Except for a streamline showcase car of 1934, Bendix vehicles were no longer built after 1909 when Vincent Bendix joined

F.A. Ames in component manufacturing at Owensboro, Kentucky. There he went on to fame and fortune building magnetos, generators and brakes, each carrying the Bendix name.

BERGDOLL 1910-1913 — The three wealthy Bergdoll brothers of Philadelphia, Pennsylvania, were known for their European car tastes and penchant for racing. The Louis J. Bergdoll Motor Company was started by the middle brother as what has been termed a pet project. With a tidy investment Bergdoll opened his seven-story 100,000-square-foot factory in downtown Philadelphia. He spared no expense at building excellent cars and some light trucks. Both Model 30 and 40 used an inlet-over-exhaust-valve four-cylinder engine. Standard were annular ball bearings throughout, full-floating rear axle and oversize brakes. An electric starter was available the first year it appeared on Cadillac -- 1912. The two models were advertised as capable of 35 mph -- racing cars for that time. Prices started at $1,600 for the light van, which was built on an unmodified passenger car chassis, up to $2,600 for special taxi or limousine.

Concentrating on high quality and performance did not preclude the eventual financial disintegration of the company. It was sold in 1913 for $45,000 to an undisclosed party.

BERKSHIRE 1905-1912 — Berkshire cars and trucks were built in Pittsfield, Massachusetts, while the company struggled to exist, changing names to Berkshire Motor Company, Berkshire Automobile Company, Berkshire Motor Car Company, and finally Berkshire Auto-Car Company, when it was bought and moved to Cambridge in 1912. The Berkshire vehicles were advertised as having been made and tested in the Berkshire hills where negotiating the grades was advanced as the proof of quality. The company built several delivery vans on standard Model A, B, C or D chassis with engines from 18 hp to 50 hp. Wheelbases ranged from 86-inch to 122-inch and prices ranged from $1,750 for the lightest vehicle to $4,500 for a seven-passenger limousine. In 1907 a few 3-ton trucks with forward control were built using a three-speed transmission and double chain drive. Total production of all vehicles was approximately 150.

1912 BESSEMER 1-TON DELIVERY WAGON   MROZ

1912 BESSEMER 1-TON DELIVERY WAGON   **MROZ**

BESSEMER 1911-1926 — The Bessemer Motor Truck Company of Grove City, Pennsylvania, started building 1-ton and 2-ton trucks in 1911, and both models were powered by four-cylinder Continental engines. A cone clutch and progressive three-speed transmission design was incorporated along with chain drive. For 1913 Bessemer offered trucks of three capacities: 3/4-, 2- and 2-1/2-ton priced at $1,250, $1,800 and $2,100, with wheelbases of 108, 120 and 136 inches, respectively. Advertised features included a long-stroke Continental engine, Timken axles and bearings, left-side drive and center control.

A selective three-speed transmission was offered by 1916 when a 1-ton model with internal gear drive was produced. A 1-1/2-ton model used chain drive, after which the heavier models, including 2-, 3-1/2-, and 5-ton trucks used worm-drive. The lightest truck was priced at $975 and the 5-ton was priced at $3,400.

The vehicles were modernized when chain drive was discontinued and a standard dry plate clutch was utilized by 1918. By 1920 the cost of a Bessemer truck varied from $1,835 to $4,295, depending on the model.

A new factory was built in Philadelphia, yet instead of moving there the Bessemer company merged with American Motors Corporation of Plainfield, New Jersey, in 1923. Another merger with Northway and Winther never took place despite the press releases in 1924. Production of Bessemer trucks began in Plainfield, New Jersey, along with a light 16-passenger bus. The same year a new 3-ton model was introduced.

In 1925 the Bessemer 1-ton Model G with 124-inch wheelbase used a 19.6 hp Continental N engine with Stromberg carburetor and Bosch ignition and a Fuller clutch and transmission. The truck rode on Ross wheels with 35x5 front and rear tires with pneumatics at extra cost. The 1-1/2-ton Model H2 with 144-inch wheelbase also used a Continental N engine, but it was rated at 22.5 hp and used a Borg and Beck clutch and Brown-Lipe transmission. It rode on 36-inch solid rubber tires. The 4-ton Model K2 with 175-inch wheelbase used a 32.4 hp Continental E-7 engine with Shuler rear axle and 36x5 front and 36x10 rear solid rubber tires. In the final year of production a speed truck was offered with pneumatic tires and high ratio rear axle. It was rated as a 1-ton using a six-cylinder Continental engine with a price tag of $1,250.

1912 BEST PANEL DELIVERY   **LIAM**

BEST 1898-1899, 1913-1914 — Located in the San Francisco Bay Area, Best Manufacturing Company of San Leandro, California, was known for its traction engines. It was operated by three brothers: Otto, Leo and Daniel Best. The first vehicle was a huge gasoline-powered surrey powered by a 7 hp two-cylinder engine that had gasoline sprayed into it for combustion. It was capable of carrying eight passengers at a speed of 18 mph. In 1908 the Holt Manufacturing Company took over Best. Four years later 1-ton and 1-1/2-ton trucks were built, with the smaller using a two-cylinder engine, a friction transmission and double chain drive. The heavier truck used a four-cylinder engine and selective transmission with shaft drive. The 1-ton cost $1,370 in 1914, the year Sequoia Motor Car Company absorbed Best and Holt and began building the Sequoia passenger cars.

BEST 1912-1915 — Overlapping in time with the San Leandro Best company, the Durant-Dort Carriage Company in Flint, Michigan, built a light van also called Best. The light commercial vehicle had a wheelbase of 76 inches and was available both as an open or closed delivery truck. These were powered by a two-cylinder engine and used a friction transmission with double chain drive. Early on in production the closed delivery van cost $875. This company should not be confused with Best of Indianapolis, Indiana, which was incorporated in 1908 with plans to manufacture vehicles in 1910, but it appears no production followed for the earlier Indiana company.

1919 BETHLEHEM 3-1/2-TON   RD

BETHLEHEM 1917-1926 — The Bethlehem Automobile Company of Bethlehem, Pennsylvania, did not build trucks. The Bethlehem Motors Corporation of Allentown, Pennsylvania, did. The early models were rated at 1-1/4-ton and used 23 hp Golden, Belknap and Swartz motors. The 2-1/4-ton had a 26 hp North American engine. Both models used internal gear drive. Prices were $1,245 and $1,775, respectively. The first few years were lucrative for Bethlehem and in 1919 it built 3,500 trucks.

In 1920 Bethlehem absorbed North American Motors in Pottstown, Pennsylvania, thereby acquiring facilities for engine manufacturing. That year four models from 1-ton to 4-ton were offered with Bethlehem engines for the first time. This was the year that Bethlehem announced the production of an export passenger car that was named Ideal. This refers back to the Bethlehem Company of Bethlehem, Pennsylvania, which built a single car named Ideal in 1907-1908. The new Ideal auto, one of a dozen by that name over the years, was a four-passenger sport touring car powered by a 40 hp Bethlehem engine using Timken axles and was priced at $3,000. For 1923 Bethlehem unveiled its 1-ton Airline truck with four-wheel-brakes and pneumatic tires. Optimism abounded when Bethlehem also announced it would begin building buses. Total yearly production of vehicles was planned to be 20,000. But instead Bethlehem went into receivership the next year, and the Ideal car was immediately discontinued.

The new management focused on truck production, but it had fallen to 42 trucks by 1924. This was the year Bethlehem offered the seven-speed "California Special," which was developed for road building with a Brown-Lipe clutch and transmission mounted amidships with gear ratios from 8:1 up to 98:1. The following year Bethlehem still offered its 1-ton Model KN with 125-inch wheelbase priced at $1,595. The 19.6 hp Bethlehem KN engine used a Zenith carburetor and Bosch ignition. The transmission was made by Detroit Gear and was used with a Borg and Beck clutch. Both front and rear axles were made by Eaton and pneumatic tires 33x5 front and rear were standard. The 2-ton Model GN with 137-1/2-inch wheelbase sold for $2,495. It used the 25.6 hp Bethlehem GN engine. The rear axle was made by Wisconsin while the front axle was from Sheldon, and Smith wheels used 36x4 front and 33x7 rear tires. The 2-1/2-ton Model L with 145-inch wheelbase

sold for $3,195. It was similar to the Model GN using the same engine but had a Fuller clutch and transmission. The 3-1/2-ton Model M was also similar but had a 168-inch wheelbase, dual 36x5 wheels in the rear and sold for $3,795. In the last few years of production few of these trucks were built. First Lehigh Company merged with Bethlehem in 1925, then Hahn and Company bought the factory in early 1927.

1923 BETHLEHEM 2-TON   HAYS

BETZ 1919-1929 — An earlier Betz company that built a few automobiles in Chicago, Illinois, was not affiliated with the Betz Motor Truck Company of Hammond, Indiana. The first model was rated at 2-1/2 tons and used a four-cylinder Buda engine. By 1924 the 1-ton Model J-3 with 140-inch wheelbase sold for $1,850. It used a 22.3 hp Betz J-3 engine and well-known components such as Zenith carburetor and Bosch ignition, Brown-Lipe clutch and transmission and Timken front and rear axles. Pneumatic tires 34x5 front and rear were standard. The 2-1/2-ton Model D-3 with 160-inch wheelbase sold for $2,985. It was powered by the 28.9 hp Betz D-3 engine. Buda four- and six-cylinder engines were also available.

1911 BEYSTER-DETROIT DELIVERY VAN   NAHC

BEYSTER-DETROIT 1910-1911 — At the factory of Beyster in Detroit, Michigan, the Beyster-Detroit Motor Car Company focused on building light delivery vehicles. The passenger cars used Hupmobile 20 engines, and the 1,200-pound capacity delivery vehicles used the 25 hp four-cylinder engine. The light truck with 105-inch wheelbase also used a cone clutch in oil, a selective slide transmission and double brakes and double enclosed chain drive at the rear wheels, which were 34x2. Before closing in 1911 the company announced that in truck manufacturing "the field was too crowded and the competition too strenuous."

BIDDLE-MURRAY 1905-1907 — Organized in Chicago, the Biddle-Murray Motor Truck Company of Oak Park, Illinois, was incorporated in Maine for the sake of legal expediency. The Oak Park factory did build a forward control 3-ton model truck with a 24 hp four-cylinder engine and four-speed transmission using chain drive to the rear wheels. The price tag was $3,500.

1926 BIEDERMAN 4-TON TANKER NAHC

BIEDERMAN 1920-1955 — The Biederman Motors Corporation of Cincinnati, Ohio, produced special application trucks in small numbers, as well as trucks for the military. As early as 1921 the company offered a six-cylinder Continental engine that was built along Charles Biederman's specifications. A 1-ton and 1-1/2-ton model were powered by a four-cylinder engine, while 2- and 3-ton capacity trucks had a six-cylinder engine. By 1923 four-cylinder engines were discontinued.

Biederman was known for its variable-rate suspension design. In 1932 5-ton and 7-ton trucks were offered. An unusual Biederman truck was the 3-ton Model A of 1934 with non-driving front axle, which was built for the U.S. military. It was powered by a 76 hp 318-cubic inch Continental E600 engine and used a Fuller 5A-290 transmission permitting a top speed of 50 mph. By 1936 Biederman also built a 7-1/2-ton model. These were available with both Continental and Lycoming engines.

In 1937 Biederman offered eight models listed consecutively from Model 10 to Model 80, the latter being rated at 7-1/2-ton capacity with wheelbases from 145-inch to 187-inch. Each model, with the exception of the Model 30, was powered by a different six-cylinder engine as follows in chronological order: 70 hp Continental 25A, 75 hp Waukesha 6BL, 75 hp Waukesha 6BL, 84 hp Waukesha 6BK, 88 hp Continental E601, 92 hp Continental E602, 98 hp Hercules WXC3 and 110 hp Hercules RX8. The lightest two models used Warner T-9 transmissions with Clark front and rear axles, while the heaviest two models used Fuller transmissions with Timken front axles and Wisconsin rear axles. The rest used Fuller transmissions and Clark front and rear axles. Chassis prices were $1,095, $1,295, $1,560, $1,750, $2,205, $2,750, $3,600 and $4,200, respectively.

Also for 1937 the first military contracts arrived, and Biederman built a 3-ton truck tractor as well as a 4-ton and 5-ton 6x6 trucks. The company offered a multitude of truck models by 1938 from 1-ton to 7-1/2-ton with a cab-over-engine design available and encompassing numerous applications such as buses, refuse and snow removal trucks, as well as fire engines. However, many of the illustrated models never made it to the production line despite a wide range of engine choices including Continental, Hercules and Lycoming gasoline engines, Cummins and Detroit diesel engines and even a Waukesha-Hesselman oil-burning engine. Chevrolet cabs were used at times before World War II.

Because of previous experience with the U.S. Army, war production boosted the company's output with demand for the Biederman 6x6 trucks powered by Hercules engines. Similar trucks were built by Federal and Reo under military specifications, and for Biederman the enlarging war production effort also meant entering the civilian market after the war in strong financial condition.

The new postwar model was named National Standard (NS) and was similar to the army truck being available in four-wheel and six-wheel design. It also used a Hercules gasoline engine and Timken axles, among other standard purchased components. The early 1950s brought a setback to the truck manufacturing industry and Biederman was badly affected. A total of only a few dozen trucks were built in the 1950s including large cab-over-engine tow trucks for use in New York's Lincoln tunnel. By 1956 the relatively small Biederman factory became Cincinnati's largest Chevrolet dealership.

BIG FOUR See GOLDEN WEST

BILLINGS see TOLEDO

BIMEL 1916 — The Bimel Buggy Company of Sidney, Ohio, built a 1/2-ton light truck chassis and offered it for $485 in 1916. The company also built the Elco passenger automobile between 1915 and 1917.

BINGHAM 1914-1915 — Herbert Bingham organized the Bingham Manufacturing Company in Cleveland, Ohio, and with new investors the following year, he reorganized as the Bingham Motor Car Company. Plans were to build both cars and trucks but only a truck model was offered by 1914. This vehicle was a conventional delivery van with a 115-inch wheelbase with a capacity of 1,250 pounds. It used a four-cylinder Continental engine, an early L-head cast enbloc design, and friction drive, which was advertised as good for 10,000 miles. Final drive was with Coventry dual chains. Steering was left-hand drive, unlike many of its contemporaries. The body could be ordered as an open express, panel or stake bed with a semi-enclosed cab. Passenger car production never materialized and the delivery truck was the only model built before the company ceased operations.

BINGHAMTON 1912-1913 — The Binghamton Motor Car Company of Binghamton, New York, announced production of light trucks in December of 1912. W.G. Fatz was the owner of the company who told the press that 35 men would be employed at his company on Water Street. No production has been substantiated.

BIRCH 1918-1923 — The Birch truck was assembled by students of the Birch Motor College of Chicago, Illinois. It was put on the market in 1918 at $735 for chassis or $795 with box body. It was rated at 1/2-ton capacity and was powered by a four-cylinder engine. The Birch Motor College continued its existence until at least 1923.

All Steel Dump Body

1920 BIRCH DUMP TRUCK MROZ

The company began in 1916 as an adjunct to the Birch Motor College of Chicago where students assembled vehicles in addition to the units produced for the company by various factories such as Crow-Elkhart in Indiana and Seneca in Ohio.

All vehicles were sold by mail order, and it appears that by 1919 Birch offered a 1-ton chassis. Distributors, such as Pittevil & Company, were agents for Birch as far away as London, England. Specifications included a 36 hp overhead valve engine cast enbloc with Connecticut ignition and Stromberg carburetor. A three-speed transmission and clutch was from Fuller and rear axle was Clark internal gear type. Wheelbase was 132 inches. Tires were 32x3-1/2 front and 32x4 rear solid or 35x5 pneumatic. An all steel dump body with 32 cubic feet capacity was offered at extra cost. The Birch warranty included a disclaimer for any of its trucks "which have been operated at a speed exceeding 15 miles per hour."

By 1923 production of both passenger cars and trucks ceased. It is not known how many Birch trucks were produced, but the number was far smaller than that of passenger car production.

BLACK / BLACK CROW 1908-1912 — Black Crow derived its name from two companies: the Black Manufacturing Company of Chicago, Illinois, and the Crow Motor Car Company of nearby Elkhart, Indiana. The former company showed its highwheeler at the Iowa State Fair in 1908, which resulted in $50,000 worth of orders. The Black used a two-cylinder air-cooled engine, planetary transmission and double chain drive. Another vehicle was marketed as the Chicago Motor Buggy. The Type 30 closed delivery van that sold for $900 was one of two commercial vehicles the company built. The other later van with 112-inch wheelbase was powered by a four-cylinder engine with a three-speed transmission and shaft drive. By 1911 Crow canceled the contract with Black and this meant the demise of the company. A few 1/2-ton highwheeler delivery trucks were reportedly built in 1912.

1911 BLACKER 3-TON   RD

BLACKER 1910-1912 — John H. Blacker & Company was located in Chillicothe, Ohio, and built three models of commercial vehicles rated at 1/2-, 1- and 3-ton capacity. The 1/2-ton Model N with 78-inch wheelbase used a 13 hp two-cylinder engine and was priced at $670. The 3-ton Model S with 120-inch wheelbase used a 40 hp four-cylinder engine and sold for $3,300. Only a handful of these vehicles were built.

1912 BLAIR 1-1/2-TON   RD

BLAIR 1911-1918 — Although several companies by the name of Blair entered the motorcar manufacturing business, only the Blair Manufacturing Company (by 1914 the Blair Motor Truck Company) of Newark, Ohio, actually built trucks. The company was organized by Frank M. Blair and investors in late 1911. The design was an unusual one for the time using a three-point suspended frame on which the engine, transmission, driveshaft and rear axle were held, while the main frame held the body, front axle, steering and controls. The patented drive system allowed the engine and driveline to move with the rear wheels. This direct connection between engine and rear axle eliminated the need for universal joints, which were the weak link in the drivetrain during the early days of motor truck manufacturing.

All three Blair model trucks used a four-cylinder Continental engine. The models were rated at 1-1/2-, 2-1/2- and 3-1/2-ton capacity. They were priced at $3,000, $3,250 and $3,750, respectively. A standard stake body cost $150. The design was a

forward-control type, but with seats significantly lower on both sides of the engine. In 1918 the company reemerged as the American Motor Truck Company, manufacturers of Ace commercial vehicles. Total production of Blair Trucks over the years amounted to two dozen.

1952 BLUE BIRD TRAVELER BUS   MBS

BLUE BIRD 1927 to date — The Blue Bird Body Company of Fort Valley, Georgia, was the development of A.L. Luce, who was a Ford dealer in nearby Perry, Georgia. There were two previous ventures by the name of Bluebird in New York and Connecticut, which were unrelated. Luce designed a bus body that was produced on a Ford commercial chassis at a time when customers were difficult to find. The first Blue Bird school bus was built in 1927. A few such buses were sold to schools. The design utilized angle iron roof bows instead of wooden construction, which was being phased out by safety regulations. However, the new all-metal bus body with canvas roof had no window sashes; therefore, none of the windows opened. The economical aspect of a less-expensive bus appealed to enough customers that Luce's dealership survived through the Depression years. In 1932, based on the color of one of the demonstrator buses, the Blue Bird name became a model line advertised as the economical choice for custom-built buses.

In 1937 window sashes and all-steel roof design were adopted, although some wood in the cross sills was used during World War II when steel shortages became a factor. Luce traveled to France in 1948 where at the Paris Salon he viewed a forward-control GMC chassis. GMC refused to sell him such a chassis, and Luce ended up importing an entire GMC bus from Belgium to get his hands on the new bus design. Once back in Georgia, Luce copied the forward-control bus and after modifying a few conventional chassis, his company began offering the All American Blue Bird in 1952 with its own forward-control chassis, which the company began to build that year. In order to customize its model line, the company offered several engines and transmissions in both conventional and forward-control versions per customer specs.

Ten years later the All American Wanderlodge motor home was introduced. Blue Bird also sold 50 tandem axle beverage delivery trucks that used GMC V-6 engines. A rear engine chassis was introduced in 1976, and the company's market was expanded to Canada and South and Central America. About the time Luce's three sons took over the company, assembly plants in Canada and Guatemala were opened, as well as factories in Mount Pleasant, Iowa, and Buena Vista, Virginia.

In 1992 Blue Bird built its first natural gas-powered buses. The Mount Pleasant, Iowa, plant has continued to operate along with two new factories in LaFayette and Fort Valley. The Buena Vista, Virginia, plant has not been used since. Blue Bird has offered several school bus models, which include the Mini-Bird for up to 36 students, MB-20 for up to 35 students, Micro-Bird for up to 21 students, MB-II for up to 20 students, a Special Needs transit-style bus, the CV2000, which is a conventional bus on a GM chassis, the TC/2000 medium-duty transit-style bus for 48 to 84 students and the All American bus, a premium transit-style vehicle with a capacity of up to 90 passengers.

1969 BLUE BIRD   BB

1994 BLUE BIRD MOBILE WORK STATION   BB

The latest school bus design from Blue Bird is the Electric Bus Model TCEV with a seating capacity of up to 72 passengers with a wheelbase of 193 inches. GVW rating has been listed at 33,000 pounds and the bus has used a 230 hp AC induction three-phase electric motor with 112 batteries in four packs of 28 for a total of 336 volts DC. Top speed has been given as 55 mph with a range of 80 miles between charges.

Blue Bird has also offered the CS series buses in 10 sizes from 24-foot to 39-foot length with passenger capacity from 29 to 49 and GVW ratings from 26,300 pounds to 33,000 pounds. Also offered to date has been the Q-Bus Series in 29-foot and 37-foot lengths. Both versions have been available in tour, charter and commuter layouts as well as in the form of the Work Station Q mobile offices. All of these have been offered with Cummins diesel engines from 190 hp to 300 hp and gasoline engines up to 235 hp, which could be converted to natural gas power. Power systems for CNG, LNG and bi-fuel have also been available. Transmission choices have been the Allison AT545 as standard with optional Allison MT643, MTB643 as well as B300 and B300R World Transmissions. These buses have used all-steel floor and body construction.

1995 BLUE BIRD CS SERIES   BB

In addition Blue Bird has offered the 29-foot Q-Bus, 37-foot Q-Bus and CS series with natural gas power using any of five engines: 195 hp Cummins 5.9 Liter, 225 hp John Deere 6.8 Liter, 250 hp John Deere 8.1 Liter, 235 hp GM 427 Bi-Fuel Engine and 190 hp Hercules 5.6 Liter, all of them rear-mounted and available by 1995. The John Deere 6.8 Liter has been offered for 1996.

BOARD 1911-1913 — The B.F. Board Motor Truck Company was located in Alexandria, Virginia. The company built open panel trucks in 1/2-, 1-, 2- and 3-ton capacities. Each of these trucks used forward-control design and four-cylinder engines. The 1/2-ton model had shaft drive while the heavier trucks used double chain drive. Little else is known about this early and brief enterprise.

B.O.E. 1911-1913 — The Motor Conveyance Company of Milwaukee, Wisconsin, built a few trucks that were quite large for that period. Few were actually sold. The B.O.E. nameplate was an abbreviation for Best On Earth. The company built 2-, 3- and 6-ton flatbed trucks each powered by a four-cylinder engine. The largest was a 6-ton model, which itself weighed 4 tons, using a structural steel frame. It was powered by an enormous 11.3-liter four-cylinder engine.

1911 B.O.E. 6-TON   MROZ

BOLLSTROM 1915-1921 — Maurice Ballstrom was an engineer who started the Bollstrom Sales Company in Battle Creek, Michigan, in 1915. His first design was a 1/2-ton capacity four-wheel-drive chassis that he planned to use in a variety of vehicles including roadster, touring car and delivery van. This chassis was the basis for a few prototypes, but it is uncertain how many Bollstrom built before announcing full production that never materialized. In 1920 he announced a Model A truck with 144-inch wheelbase, which used his own four-cylinder engine with Bosch ignition and a four-speed transmission. Bollstrom Motors was incorporated in Detroit, Michigan, in 1916, but few trucks and cars were ever produced.

BOLTON See BRADSHAW

BORLAND 1910-1916 — Electric car and truck production was the business that the Borland-Grannis Company was involved with in Chicago, Illinois. The company started in 1910 as the Ideal Electric Car Company, changing names in 1912 when the car builder Bruce Borland became partners with U.B. Grannis and first displayed a vehicle at the Chicago Automobile Show. A Borland car made a test run from Chicago to Milwaukee on a single battery charge, a distance of 104 miles, which was considered quite a technical breakthrough at that time (and is to date). Borland merged with Argo Electric and Broc Electric to form the American Electric Car Company. Vehicles under all three names continued until 1916.

Borland built two model trucks: the Model 10 and Model 15. Both models used an 81-inch wheelbase and carried 1,200 pounds of Exide batteries. The Model 10 was an open express while the Model 15 was a closed body van. Final drive to the rear wheels was with chain, and top speed was 15 mph. Fifty miles was the advertised range for the trucks, although some Borland cars it was claimed would go 100 miles on a single charge.

BOSS STEAM 1897-1909 — In 1892 James Eck started the Boss Knitting Machine Works in Reading, Pennsylvania. By 1897 he had built his first steam car. The design involved an unsprung subframe that held the running gear, which could be bought as a unit separately for $140. Eck advertised the benefits of steam power by pointing out the danger of fires in barns during refueling of gasoline, yet at the same time he promoted kerosene to heat the boiler because it was cheaper and much easier to find than gasoline at that time.

Eck built 22 steam cars, among them a 1/2-ton delivery van Model D with 72-inch wheelbase. This light truck, which sold at a base price of $800, used a Mason double-acting steam engine with tiller steering and the engine-under-driver-seat design.

1903 BOSWORTH STEAM WLB

BOSWORTH 1903-1904 — The Bosworth was built by Frank C. Bosworth. It was a 7-1/2 hp steam delivery vehicle. It was registered in the Massachusetts Automobile Register as No. 8634 in 1904. Frank Bosworth used the vehicle in his hometown of Saugus, Massachusetts, but it does not appear that he built any more vehicles.

BOULDING STEAM 1905 — George Boulding of Salt Lake City, Utah, built a giant steam surrey to transport passengers across the desert. Assessed as "a freak of a looker..." by *Motor Field* in 1905, it was a goliath vehicle with giant wheels to run over sagebrush and ruts, along with front-wheel-drive to pull out of chuck holes. Boulding's vehicle never went further than its first test drive.

BOUR-DAVIS 1916-1922 — Robert Davis, a steam ship engineer in Chicago, and advertising man Charles Bour gave their names to the popular cars and about 100 trucks, which were built in three different states during various incarnations of the company as it moved from Detroit, Michigan, in 1918 to Frankfort, Indiana, then to Cedar Grove, Louisiana, in 1919 when the company was reorganized as the Louisiana Motor Car Company of Shreveport. Only scant records show that Bour-Davis built a model of 2-1/2-ton trucks around 1919 at the factory in Cedar Grove.

BOURNE 1915-1919 — The Bourne Magnetic Truck Company of Philadelphia, Pennsylvania (which was also occupied by the Biddle Motor Car Company), offered an unique magnetic transmission designed by Justus B. Entz and used in Owen-Magnetic and Deering-Magnetic passenger cars. The Owen-Magnetic cars were some of the most luxurious of that day, but the magnetic transmission proved to be too expensive and complicated.

1918 BOURNE MODEL V-M 2-TON RD

In the meantime, Stephen Bourne built several experimental trucks for the Atlantic Refining Company. The first was a 2-ton model powered by a four-cylinder Hercules engine and was priced at $3,150 and later $3,500. A 3-1/2-ton model, which had the same motor was priced at $3,850 and later $4,200. Both had worm-drive at the rear axle, left-hand steering, semi-enclosed cab and artillery wheels with solid rubber tires. The 2-ton Bourne was dubbed the Model VM and the 3-1/2-ton became the Model XM, both of which were still advertised as late as October 1919. "The Most Advanced Truck in America" and "The Aladdin of Motor Power Transmissions" were the company's two slogans. In its last year of production the company moved to New York City.

1914 BOWLING GREEN MODEL F KP

BOWLING GREEN See MODERN

1916 BOYD 3-TON 4X4 RD

BOYD 1908-1916 — The James Boyd & Brother Incorporated motor vehicle company resided in Philadelphia, Pennsylvania. The company built fire engines, including hose and chemical wagons, which had a 144-inch wheelbase and used a four-cylinder engine. Top speed was advertised at 50 mph with the vehicle weighing over 4,600 pounds. In the last year of production Boyd built a four-wheel-drive 3-ton truck that was advertised for its patented steerable front axle. It does not appear that manufacturing continued past the year 1916.

BRADFIELD See KISSEL

BRADFORD See JOWETT

1904 BRAMWELL OCW

BRAMWELL 1904-1905 — W.C. Bramwell and son C.C. Bramwell invested in the Springfield Automobile Company, in Springfield, Ohio, in order to build their own vehicles in a factory that had some experience in the business, although the Springfield factory had already tried and failed to build a car in 1899. The car was listed as a 72-inch wheelbase chassis, but a small delivery van has also been listed with a 76-inch wheelbase. The light runabout used an 8 hp one-cylinder two-stroke engine and was priced at $800, whereas the van used a 20 hp two-cylinder engine, weighed 1,700 pounds and was priced at $1,250.

BRANDENBURGH 1902 — The Brandenburgh Wagon Company was incorporated in New Jersey in 1902 for the purpose of building motor vehicles. The incorporators were William L. Glorieaux, George E. Brandenburgh, C. William Pfiel, Henry Berefeld and Benjamin F. Jones. Manufacture has not been substantiated.

BRANDON see TWYFORD

1916 BRASIE PACKET   HAYS

BRASIE 1913-1917 — Frank Brasie had a new vehicle in mind after building Twin City trucks at his Brasie Motor Truck Company in 1913. Twin City trucks were 2-ton forward-control design and used chain drive. At the Brasie Motor Car Company a cyclecar was designed and called the Messenger Roadster, while the delivery was called the Packet. Both were on 100-inch wheelbases and the Packet Delivery cost $450. The Packet used a 12 hp four-cylinder engine with friction transmission and belt drive. See also PACKET.

BRAZIL 1917 — The Brazil Motors Company was incorporated in 1917 with a capitalization of $150,000 in Brazil, Indiana. It moved into the Brazil Fence Company with the intention to build a front-drive truck, according to the press. Motor vehicle production has not been substantiated.

BRECHT 1901-1904 — Brecht vehicles were built by the Brecht Automobile Company, a subsidiary of Brecht Butcher Supply Company in St. Louis, Missouri, which was run by the Brecht Brothers: Gus, Frank and Charles. Numerous vehicles were listed but it is not certain which of these were actually built. Some of the Brecht vehicles were sold without engines "ready for power." Electric passenger cars were offered as well as the steam Rushmobile. One version was the Fancy Steam Delivery Wagon that used a 12 hp two-cylinder steam engine that was double-acting and reversible. It was rated at 1,800-pound capacity with a top speed of 15 mph.

H.R. Borbein, manager of the automobile division from the start of the company, bought out Brecht by 1904, and the Brecht brothers went back to their butcher supply business.

BREEDING 1916 — William Breeding built one steam truck in Cincinnati, Ohio. The 5-ton truck, which has survived to date, was built with a 177-inch wheelbase and used a Stanley Steamer two-cylinder engine and internal gear rear axle. Tires used were 36x6

front and 42x6 rear, both solid rubber. It is uncertain whether Breeding built other gasoline-powered trucks during his brief engagement in the business of building commercial vehicles.

BRENNAN 1908; 1913 — The Brennan Manufacturing Company of Syracuse, New York, built engines, supplying them to various vehicle makers including George Selden. Brennan built a runabout in 1904, which was discontinued after 1908. In November of 1908 Brennan displayed a 1,200-pound capacity commercial car that had been built for the Harrall Buggy Company of South Boston, Virginia. It was called the Model 7 and was powered by an 18 hp two-cylinder water-cooled engine. A planetary transmission was used with side chain drive.

Subsequently, the company offered commercial vehicles in 1913. These consisted of 2-, 3- and 5-ton trucks with either stake beds or flatbeds. The 5-ton truck was a forward-control design and cost $4,600. It is uncertain how many of these trucks were built, but they were offered for only one year.

BRIDGEPORT 1920-1927 — The Bridgeport Motor Truck Company was not affiliated with the earlier Bridgeport steam auto of 1901, both located in Bridgeport, Connecticut. Although the Morrissey Motor Car Company was listed as the parent company, only trucks and buses under the Bridgeport insignia were produced.

In 1920 the Bridgeport trucks included a 4-1/2-ton and 6-ton model, both powered by Hercules engines. In 1923 Bridgeport switched to lighter truck production. The 1-1/2-ton Model A with 144-inch wheelbase sold for $2,350. It was powered by a 22.5 hp Buda WTU engine. The 2-1/2-ton Model B with 155-inch wheelbase sold for $299. It used a 28.9 hp Buda ETU engine. The 4-ton Model C with 175-inch wheelbase used a 32.4 hp Buda YTU engine and cost $3,990. All three models used a Zenith carburetor and Bosch ignition, Brown-Lipe clutch and transmission, Timken rear axle, Ross steering and wheels by Jones, Phineas and Company. Pneumatic tires were available at extra cost on all three models with 34-inch wheels on the smaller truck and 36-inch on the two larger models. After 1925 only a 30-seat bus called the Bridgeport 45 was available.

BRILL see A.C.F.

BRINTON 1913-1926 — Brinton trucks were built in Coatesville, Pennsylvania, for the first three years where 76 were built before the company moved to Philadelphia for the duration of its existence. The first truck had a tapered hood like an early International, used chain drive and was rated at 3/4-ton. However, the first production model was a conventional 2-ton model that used a four-cylinder Rutenber engine. By the last year of production the 1-1/2-ton Model C with 138-inch wheelbase sold for $2,500. It was powered by a 22.5 hp engine with Stromberg carburetor and used a Brown-Lipe clutch and transmission. Timken front and rear axles were used with Ross steering. The 2-1/2-ton Model D with 150-inch wheelbase sold for $2,975. It was powered by a 27.2 hp Continental C-4 engine. The Model C used 34x4 front and 34x5 rear solid tires while the Model D used 36x4 front and 36x8 rear solid tires. Listings for both models stated that the ignition system was not supplied, an arrangement apparently allowing the buyer more flexibility. Total production for Brinton was 287 trucks over 12 years.

BRISCOE 1915-1921 — Benjamin Briscoe was an innovator in the motor car business. At first he was a partner in the Maxwell automobile, but his United States Motor Car Company could not compete with General Motors. Briscoe left for France where he developed a cyclecar that he brought back to the United States and marketed as the Argo. Another car developed by Briscoe was the Cloverleaf. It used a cyclops headlight, which turned out to be illegal in many states, and a papier-mache body. A Ferro V-8 engine was offered along with the four-cylinder and was available as a retrofit for the customer who changed his mind after purchase and wanted more power.

The first Briscoe trucks were built on the passenger car chassis and were rated at 1/2-ton. These had a three-speed transmission on the rear axle and were available with a canopy top or panel body. In 1918 a 1-ton model was available with double chain drive. Internal gear shaft drive was introduced for 1920 on the one model offered until the company shut down before Benjamin Briscoe went on to oil drilling in California and gold mining in Colorado.

BRISTOL 1909-1911 — The Bristol Engineering Company designed a five-passenger landaulet taxicab that was built by the New Departure Manufacturing Company of Bristol, Connecticut. The chassis employed half-elliptical springs in front, three-quarter elliptical in the rear. Although referred to as the Bristol, the taxi, which used a four-cylinder engine and three-speed transmission, was marketed under the trade name of Rockwell. It appears this is the only commercial vehicle built by New Departure. This company was not affiliated with the earlier Bristol company of Chicago, nor Bristol of Bristol, Connecticut, and it was not connected with Bristol of England.

BROBECK 1971 — William M. Brobeck had been an employee of Abner Doble who built steam-powered vehicles in Emeryville, California. William M. Brobeck and Associates were located in Berkeley, California, and were best known for high-energy particle accelerators such as cyclotrons. The company built a steam-powered bus in 1969 when the Department of Transportation awarded $450,000 to the state of California to develop and test steam-powered buses.

After hearing testimony from Norman Lear, the California Assembly held a series of hearings that seemed to show the feasibility of steam power. Eleven bids were received in May of 1969 and the scope of the project was expanded when federal funding was increased to $1,121,000. Four manufacturers were chosen: Steam Power Systems of San Diego, General Steam Corporation of Newport Beach, William M. Brobeck & Associates and Lear Motors Corporation of Reno, Nevada.

The Brobeck bus, using the body and chassis of a 1969 GM T6H-5305-231, was the first to be finished. It used a three-cylinder compound engine with one high-pressure cylinder and two low-pressure cylinders. The design incorporated the three-throw crankshaft used in the 6V-71 diesel engine. The bus was displayed in Washington D.C. in November of 1971. The Secretary of Transportation and his staff, as well as members of the legislature and guests, rode the bus. When the burner was running, a sound much like a jet engine was found distracting, and plumbing leaks elevated the temperature in the bus considerably. Idling at the curb large amounts of soot emanated from the bus, but in testing it turned out to be cleaner running than the equivalent AC Transit diesel bus.

General Steam bowed out of the project leaving Steam Power Systems and Lear as the other vendors. Under the direction of general manager Richard D. Burtz the Steam Power System engine was a two-cylinder compound type installed in a 1968 Flxible 111CC-D51-53447 bus. Lear developed a rotary-type steam turbine and installed it in a 1969 GM T8H-5305A-026 bus. Its geared steam turbine produced 240 hp yet the wheels were only 5.5 inches in diameter and weighed only 22 pounds. Another similar project was also developed in Dallas, Texas, under the name LTV-Sundstrand, which used tulol as the working fluid in a turbine delivered by Highway Products. The DOT steam bus project faded out as political interests lost enthusiasm and cut off further funding.

BROC ELECTRIC 1909-1914 — Broc got its start as a builder of auto bodies in 1904 in Cleveland, Ohio, but did not build a car of its own until 1909. Advertising for this vehicle included mention of theft-proof safety appliances, continuous torque control, efficiency and durability and interchangeable bodies and parts, among other claims. The company built mostly passenger cars, but also built 1/2-ton and 1-ton trucks. The larger truck used a 100-inch wheelbase and had a gross vehicle weight (GVW) of 3,400 pounds with a 15 mph top speed. Although production of the Broc continued, in 1914 the company merged with Argo and Borland-Grannis forming the American Electric Car Company, which moved to Saginaw, Michigan, before these three were absorbed by the Columbian Motor Company of Detroit, Michigan, in 1916.

1912 BROCKWAY   NAHC

BROCKWAY 1912-1977 — William Brockway was a carriage builder, having started his company in 1851 in Homer, New York. His son George Brockway started the Brockway Motor Truck Company in Cortland, New York, with $100,000 and built his first truck in 1912.

The first Brockway, a highwheeler similar to the 1912 Chase in appearance and design, was powered by a three-cylinder two-stroke air-cooled engine and used a two-speed planetary transmission. For 1913 the 3/4-ton Model B sold for $1,450, Model C van was priced at $1,400, and the 2-ton Model D stake body was offered at $1,925. For 1915 two trucks up to 2-ton capacity were added using a four-cylinder Continental engine and a selective sliding gear transmission.

1920 BROCKWAY TANKER   KP

With this basic design, Brockway built 587 Class B Liberty trucks for the military during World War I, as well as numerous fire engines for the protection of camps, ports and explosives factories. After World War I, Brockway went back into civilian production with conventional models by 1919, starting with the 2-ton Model K-3. The next year the company listed a 1-1/2-ton Model S2 for $2,100, 2-1/2-ton Model K-4 for $3,000, 3-1/2-ton Model R2 for $3,900 and a 5-ton Model T for $5,000. Designations continued to change, but the basic design remained the same through the early 1920s.

By 1925 Brockway offered four models: 1-1/2-, 2-1/2-, 3-1/2- and 5-ton capacities. The 1-1/2-ton Model S12 with 140-inch wheelbase used a 25.6 hp Wisconsin SU engine. The 2-1/2-ton Model K with 153-inch wheelbase used a 27.2 hp Continental K-4 engine. The 3-1/2-ton Model R12 used a 32.4 hp Continental L-4 engine, while the 5-ton Model T with 174-inch wheelbase used a 40 hp Continental B-7 engine. Each engine used a Stromberg carburetor with Eisemann ignition except for the Model S12, which used a Zenith carb. All models used Brown-Lipe clutch and transmission, Timken front and rear axles and steering by Gemmer Manufacturing. The two lighter models had pneumatic tires available at extra cost. All used 36-inch wheels except the 5-ton which had 40-inch duals on the rear.

1930 BROCKWAY MODEL 220 TANKERS   TEX

By 1927 the model line had changed somewhat, a 3-ton Model K with 148-inch wheelbase was available at $3,300. In 1928 Brockway bought the Indiana Truck Corporation and the two companies' combined assets amounted to $9 million that year, although a month later the company was recapitalized at $3 million. A substantial part of Brockway's business was supplying chassis for buses and fire trucks during this period.

From 1928 on, six-cylinder engines were used. That year Brockway reached production of 5,500, one of the largest in the United States and net profit was over $1 million. New numerical model designations began in 1930. The purchase of Indiana opened the market westward and into some foreign countries; however, in 1932 the Depression forced Brockway to sell Indiana truck manufacturing to White trucks. Brockway was reorganized in 1932 as the Brockway Motor Company, Incorporated, and operations continued without any major interruptions.

For five years starting with 1933, Brockway built electric trucks ranging from 1/4-ton to 7-ton capacity. The electric trucks and gasoline-powered trucks were advertised as "The Brockway Idea - The Same Truck With Different Motive-Power Units." The Series 50 E (electric) was a drop-frame side-entrance delivery van. One of its salient features was that it could be left safely unattended while the delivery driver was busy, whereas with a gasoline-powered vehicle the motor would be running and potential for vehicle theft was obvious. Brockway sold electric trucks mainly in large cities such as New York.

In 1934 the company introduced the Model V1200, one of the largest trucks in the United States at the time, which used a 240 hp American LaFrance V-12 engine. The truck was rated at 30 ton with a top speed of 45 mph and the chassis cost $10,500. Since a number of states had weight limits per axle, sales of the V1200 were limited and the model was listed only until 1937. Built as a truck tractor, one of the versions had a sleeper cab for 1934. At this time Brockway offered 15 gasoline-powered model trucks and a "full line of electrics." Front end styling was updated in 1935 and standardization was incorporated in all non-load carrying parts such as fenders, runningboards, gas tanks, hood, radiator shell, headlights, bumper and cab. The model line ranged from 1-1/2-ton to 15-ton including tandem and third axle versions for the heaviest trucks.

For 1937, besides the V1200, Brockway offered 26 models ranging in capacity from 1-1/2-ton to 10-ton and in price from $895 to $6,380. The models listed were as follows: 78, 87, 88, 90X, 92, 94, 96, 110, 125X, 130, 145, 150X-4, 150X-5, 120, 140, 141, 130-PS, 160X, 170X, 165X, 175X, 195X, 220X, 240X, 260X and 260S. All except the V1200 used Continental six-cylinder engines from 71 hp to 135 hp. By 1940 the Brockway Metropolitan was offered as a cab forward van that was modified as a crew cab for utility and power companies. Prices ranged from $895 for the Model 78 to $6,380 for the Model 260-S that year.

During World War II Brockway was again under contract with the military. The Army Corps of Engineers cooperated with Brockway to build a 6x6 6-ton truck for hauling pontoons and treadways to build combat bridges. Production began in early 1942, and the truck was equipped with inflation equipment for the rubber pontoons, as well as a hydraulic loading device for the steel treadways. This truck was also built as a general load carrier, crane and airfield fire truck. All the production focused on military equipment and also included a smaller 4x2 truck used by both the United States and Britain. The War Production Board allowed Brockway to build 1,237 trucks for civilian use in 1944.

Directly after the war, production began with the 260 series using the new overhead valve Continental BD engine, and a sleeper cab truck tractor was available in 1946 when Brockway built 4,212 trucks. Production dropped to 2,919 by 1948 as the market began to become saturated. The two-speed Eaton axle was available on most models through the 1940s and 1950s.

In the early 1950s 20 Brockway models were available, all using Continental gasoline engines, Fuller transmissions and Timken axles. The company focused on sales through company branches instead of dealerships. The model line continued in a range from the 88 series to the 260 series. Sales and share of the market continued to slip. By 1952 total sales for the year was 1,752 trucks, which amounted to 0.2 percent of the overall truck market. By 1954 sales had slipped to 611 and 0.1 percent of the market.

In 1956 Mack acquired Brockway, although the company had some autonomy and continued to build trucks under the Brockway emblem, which was modernized for 1957. That year Brockway introduced off highway oil field rigs and heavy-duty short tractors, and Brockway designers introduced a new series called the Huskie in 1958, which was distinguished by a chrome huskie emblem on the radiator grille. The Model 258 Huskie truck tractor measured 87 inches from bumper to back of cab, and in 1960 a sleeper cab was offered. Brockway continued to produce chassis for custom body builders that mainly built fire trucks.

In 1961 Brockway advertised 14 models in the medium and medium-heavy truck line with engines from 125 hp to 200 hp. These truck tractors measured 90 inches BBC and were rated from 45,000 to 60,000 pounds gross combination weight (GCW). Gross vehicle weight (GVW) ratings were from 23,000 to 36,000 pounds for cargo units, while the tandem versions were rated from 40,000 to 60,000 GVW. Cabs were similar to previous design but called "new all-steel." The frontal area was enlarged for larger radiators and "set-aside" fenders were used for easier access to the engine area. The 200 hp overhead valve engine with 478-cubic inch displacement was built by Brockway in conjunction with Continental and introduced in the 158 series in 1961.

For the Brockway company the 50-year golden anniversary took place in 1962, and a golden emblem superseded the chrome one used to that point. That year Brockway offered seven Continental six-cylinder engines from 330 to 602 cubic inch displacement, as well as four Cummins diesel six-cylinder engines from 464 to 743 cubic inch displacement.

In 1963 Brockway began offering a cab-over-engine design that used a modified Mack F series cab. These became increasingly popular, but conventional design trucks were also offered with Continental gasoline engines, as well as Cummins and Detroit diesel engines. Two years later gasoline engines were discontinued, and in addition Caterpillar diesel engines became available. The 300 series was introduced in 1965, and a diesel V-8 engine was available that year, as well as the NH-250 Cummins six-cylinder diesel engine with 855 cubic inch displacement.

1938 BROCKWAY TANKER   TEX

In 1968 the company offered the Huskiedrive, which consisted of a five-speed transmission and two-speed rear axle. This was increased to an eight-speed transmission with a total of 16 forward speeds.

For the 1970s Brockway introduced the Huskiteer beginning in 1971, which was a low-profile cab-over-engine design with two axles, which was immediately expanded to three axles. For 1971 the Brockway slogan was "The Most Rugged Truck in the World." By the following year, along with Cummins diesel engines, the Caterpillar 1673 six-cylinder engine was available, as were three Detroit Diesel engines: the six-cylinder 6-71N, the V-8 8V-71N and the V-12 12V-71N.

1973 BROCKWAY REFUSE TRUCK   OCW

In 1973 and 1974, due to an economic downturn based on fuel costs, Brockway interrupted its production, which was resumed when Iran ordered 575 trucks the following year. By 1977 Brockway built 4x2 and 6x4 rigid as well as tractor trucks with engines up to 500 hp and load capacity up to 53,000 pounds GVW. But the company was in trouble.

Beset by the full gamut of financial problems and difficulties with the new anti-skid brake-implement legislation, Mack decided to divest in 1977 just when many new sales outlets had been formed out of former Diamond Reo dealers when that company went bankrupt and was sold. Local community effort could not save the last major truck manufacturer in New York that year, and Mack, the parent company, decided to shut it down permanently.

BRODESSER 1910-1911 — The Brodesser Motor Truck Company got its start in Milwaukee, Wisconsin, when Peter Brodesser, who arrived from Cologne, Germany, formed the enterprise as a sideline to his elevator company. The 1,200-pound capacity Model A used a 20 hp two-cylinder engine that was a horizontally-opposed design with pressurized oil lubrication. The Model B used a 26 hp four-cylinder engine of the same configuration. The large 1-ton truck chassis was also used for 25-passenger buses.

1910 BRODESSER   RD

The trucks were of a square cab-over design and used a friction transmission and chain drive. Solid rubber tires were mounted on artillery wheels. For 1911 the company offered the 1-ton C1, the 2-ton C2 and the 3-ton F3. The latter was powered by a 45 hp four-cylinder water-cooled engine and had a wheelbase of 140 inches.

The Juno Motor Truck Company of Juneau, Wisconsin, bought out Brodesser in 1912. However, that year it appears the Brodesser trucks were renamed Juno in anticipation of the takeover. Juno trucks were built until 1914.

BROGAN 1946-1948 — Built initially as a tiny three-wheel runabout, the vehicle resembled a bumper car. The B & B Specialty Company of Rossmoyne, Ohio, also built a Brogan Package Car on a 60-inch wheelbase chassis using a one-cylinder or two-cylinder Onan engine. Factory price was $600 and shipping weight was 450 pounds. Production totaled 30 including both models. For 1949 a roadster was introduced.

1912 BRONX 2-TON ELECTRIC   NAHC

BRONX 1912-1913 — Despite its obscurity, records show that Bronx electric trucks were in fact built in Bronx, New York. One was a small van with an 800-pound capacity and wheelbase of 76 inches. Top speed was 14 mph with a range of 50 miles before battery recharging. The second Bronx truck was also electric powered. It was rated at 2-ton capacity and had a 108-inch wheelbase. Its top speed was 9 mph with a range of 40 miles between charges. It is not certain if there were two companies existing simultaneously by this name in Bronx, but that is doubtful.

BROOKS 1911-1913 — The Brooks Manufacturing Company of Saginaw, Michigan, built a lightweight highwheeler that was powered by a two-cylinder air-cooled engine mounted under the body using a friction transmission and double chain drive. It was advertised as cheaper than a horse and wagon with three times the mileage at one-third the upkeep. Both open and closed delivery bodies were available at a price of $625 and $675, respectively. The business changed names to the Brooks Motor Wagon Company in 1912, and the following year it was purchased by Charles Duryea becoming part of the Duryea Auto Company. The factory itself was bought by A.R. Thomas to build a cyclecar that started out as the Detroit Speedster.

BROOKS 1927-1928 — The Brooks Steam Motors Company actually got its start in Stratford, Ontario, Canada, when American insurance broker Oland Brooks decided in 1923 to build steam vehicles patterned after the Stanley cars. His factory built about 180 steam passenger cars, and some records show a few cars being assembled in Buffalo, New York. In 1927 a steam-powered bus with an aluminum body was built and shown to the public. Its main feature was that the flash boiler could build up 750 psi within 40 seconds. The vehicle was capable of 60 mph and used four-wheel air brakes. The company also converted an ACF bus to steam power in 1928, but nobody was willing to place orders and the business failed. Ironically, the original steam bus was converted to gasoline power and used in that configuration until 1937.

BROUGH 1904 — George Brough was a mailman in Randall, Kansas, who built his own motorized buggy, which can be considered a commercial vehicle considering Brough's profession. The local blacksmith in Randall helped Brough build the simple vehicle, which used a one-cylinder engine mounted up front and chain drive. Despite being quite primitive, Brough used the vehicle to deliver mail for several years. The motor buggy remains extant to date at Stone Mountain, Georgia.

BROWN 1912-1914 — One of many early and little-known vehicle manufacturers by this name, the Brown Commercial Car Company of Peru, Indiana, built a 3/4-ton and a 1-ton delivery van. The van used a four-cylinder engine with a three-speed transmission and shaft drive. Pneumatic tires were standard and top speed was 16 mph, which was controlled by a governor on the engine.

BROWN 1916 — The Brown Carriage Company of Cincinnati, Ohio, was a well-known carriage builder before going briefly into motor vehicle manufacturing. The first development project was a five-passenger touring car with a 105-inch wheelbase. The second, presumably on the same chassis, was a light delivery vehicle similar to the successful Dodge "business car." It was powered by an L-head four-cylinder LeRoi engine and used a Walker-Weiss rear axle and Allis-Chalmers electrical system. The passenger car was priced at $735 and the delivery at $675. Neither vehicle progressed past the prototype stage.

BROWN 1922-1924 — The Saint Cloud Truck Company of Duluth, Minnesota, began building a 2-1/2-ton commercial vehicle that could be ordered as a stake or dump truck. It was powered by a 28.9 hp Buda ETU engine and was priced from $3,650 to $4,400, depending on equipment, with pneumatic tires and electric lights at extra cost. The company name changed to the Brown Truck Company of Duluth before finally closing its doors.

1914 BROWN MODEL F   **OCW**

BROWN 1936-1938 — Spokane, Washington, was the location of Brown Industries which displayed a bus called the Sunset Coach in 1936. The design used airplane-type frameless construction for weight savings. The bus was powered by a rear-mounted Ford V-8, but the company changed to Hercules engines the same year. The first design was a 24-passenger model with reclining seats, and a 28-passenger bus was also introduced. Less than a total of 50 Brown buses were built prior to 1939.

BROWN 1939-1953 — Under the direction of H.D. "Buddy" Horton, owner of Horton Motor Lines of Charlotte, North Carolina, the company's chief engineer, J.L. Brown, designed a truck tractor to be used exclusively by the parent transport business. The Brown truck was similar to the Corbitt truck built in Henderson, North Carolina, and Horton had several in his fleet. The Brown Equipment and Manufacturing Company of Charlotte was listed as a builder of truck trailers, and in 1940 it was reorganized as a builder of trucks, trailers, trailer bodies and equipment accessories. One such accessory was the patented Marko-Lite trailer clearance light that became an industry standard in the eastern United States.

First, the oldest Corbitt trucks in the Horton fleet were retrofitted with new 12-volt electrical systems and the badges were changed over to Brown. In 1942 Horton merged with six other truck transport firms, forming Associated Transport after a lengthy battle with the Anti-Trust Division of the Justice Department due to fears of freight monopoly on the eastern seaboard. Corbitt trucks were rebuilt and updated using new Corbitt cabs with custom trim including Brown badges.

1949 BROWN TRACTOR-TRAILER   **RD**

Brown trucks, specifically the Model 513, were made available on the public market for the first time after World War II. These used Parish frames, Continental or Buda engines and Fuller transmissions. Brown plants were located in Charlotte, as well as in Taunton and Westfield, Massachusetts. The Corbitt integral sleeper was used before Alcoa Aluminum built a new cab called the L-5 in regular and sleeper form. The quality was considered high, but by 1948 Brown trucks were selling for $4,450, at the time when Cummins diesel engines were first offered.

Due to length and weight regulations the industry demand was for lighter and shorter trucks. A new COE design was introduced in 1952 (dubbed the "flying saucer" by drivers), but it was too late for the company to continue the extravagance of building its own rugged trucks when customers were few and far between. Associated Transport decided to buy less expensive mass-produced trucks, such as International and White, and stopped manufacturing the Brown after 1953.

Associated Transport survived as an entity until 1976 when, ironically after concern over monopoly, it went bankrupt even after merging with Eastern Freightways the previous year. The trailer plant was sold to Fruehauf Trailer Company and the truck tractor plant was sold to International Harvester. About 1,000 Brown trucks were built during all the postwar years of production.

1986 BROYHILL UTILITY PARK SERVICE TRUCK   **EK**

BROYHILL 1986 — The Broyhill Manufacturing Company, located in Wayne, Nebraska, built an articulated COE utility truck for the Park Maintenance Department of Clearwater, Florida. Further specifications are lacking.

1910 BRUNNER RD

BRUNNER 1910 — The Brunner Motor Car Company built a touring car that was made in Buffalo, New York, and also offered a commercial vehicle on the same 90-inch wheelbase chassis, although a 1-ton and 2-ton truck were advertised, but in all probability it was never actually produced. The 1/2-ton used a 16 hp two-cylinder engine that had separate exhaust and muffler systems. The vehicles used a planetary transmission, shaft drive, full-elliptic springs and solid rubber tires on 36-inch front and 38-inch rear wheels.

BRUSH 1908-1913 — The Brush Motor Car Company built a popular runabout that was powered by a 6 hp one-cylinder engine and used axles and frame made of oak, hickory and maple. Designer Alanson Brush, who had helped in the development of the first one-cylinder Cadillac, stated that he believed he had reached perfection of an original idea in motor car construction. The Brush runabout had successfully finished the 2,636-mile Glidden Tour of 1909, crossed the continent and had climbed Pike's Peak in eight hours. In order to promote the light cars, early advertising advocated the idea that prospective buyers reflect upon the reason a squirrel can climb a tree better than an elephant.

The first light 1/4-ton van based on the passenger car was a semi-forward-control configuration and was discontinued after 1909 before being reintroduced in 1912 with pneumatic tires and conventional driver position. A light taxi called the Titan was also produced on this chassis. For 1912 Brush sold its 1911 production, and in 1913 Brush was absorbed by the United States Motor Corporation. This company was not affiliated with the British Brush Electric.

1911 BRUSH PANEL DELIVERY VAN NAHC

BRYAN 1918-1923 — As chief inspector for the Santa Fe Railroad, George Bryan adapted the super-heat system in locomotives for light powerplant application in road vehicles. After building an experimental steam car, which he thoroughly tested in the deserts

and mountains of New Mexico, Bryan and his father, Oscar Bryan built a factory in Peru, Indiana, to manufacture vehicles. The boiler of the Bryan featured 44 seven-foot tubes with a Bunsen-type burner giving a maximum steam pressure of 600 psi. Bryan built a prototype steam truck, but it may be the only one the company produced. While also developing a tractor, Bryan designed a home heating plant, and by 1925 the company name had changed to Bryan Steam Corporation, marketing steam boilers, as well as gas and oil heating burners that were sold for building application in 43 states and overseas.

BUCK 1925-1927 — Nine conventional models were offered by the Buck Motor Truck Company of Bellevue, Ohio. These ranged from 1-1/2-ton to 7-1/2-ton capacity. Two of these trucks were "speed" models powered by a four-cylinder engine, and two were powered by a six-cylinder engine. The rest were heavy trucks that used transmissions with seven forward speeds and two speeds in reverse.

All the truck models used steel-spoke wheels and solid rubber tires with duals on the rear. The rectangular C-cabs' doors slid to the back for better access to the cargo area. The radiator shell and hood were inspired by the Rolls-Royce of that era. All trucks had Moto-meters, electric lights, front tow hooks and four vertical grille bars as standard equipment. A tenth heavy-duty model was added in 1926 also using a six-cylinder engine, unlike the five lightest models that used four-cylinder engines.

BUCKEYE 1911 — The Buckeye Wagon Company of Dayton, Ohio, built horsedrawn delivery wagons when a company decision was made in 1910 to enter the motor truck market. In 1911 the company added "& Motor Car" to its name and began producing a highwheeler motor buggy using 100-inch wheelbase and a 25 hp four-cylinder motor. The 1-1/2-ton truck featured all four fenders as standard equipment, chain drive and a vertical steering column. The company advertised its selective transmission as being immune to having gears stripped, a common and severe problem during this era of motor car development. Other advertising beckoned prospective buyers to compare, but they had less than half a year to do so before Buckeye went entirely back to horsedrawn carriage production.

BUCKLEN 1912-1916 — The H.E. Bucklen, Jr. Motor Truck Company had a brief endeavor in Elkhart, Indiana. The Model A light truck was rated at 3/4-ton, Model B was 1-1/2-ton and Model C was rated as 3-ton capacity. Several body designs were advertised including express, stake bed and delivery van. For some reason the derated 3-ton capacity van was offered as a 2-1/2-ton in 1914, but the Bucklen truck's design remained the same until the company's demise in 1916.

1905 BUCKMOBILE BUSINESS WAGON RD

BUCKMOBILE 1903-1905 — By the time a commercial vehicle was built by the name of Buckmobile, the company had merged with the Black Diamond Automobile Company of Utica, New York, which never marketed a car under its own name. As with so many other companies during this time, the Buckmobile started out as a runabout before a delivery van called the Business Wagon was added to the model line in 1905. Despite the name, Buckmobile's advertising department adopted the slogan "Ease of Riding Without a Peer." The 1-ton delivery van with 83-inch wheelbase priced at $1,100 (compared to $900 for the 1905 runabout) used a 15 hp two-cylinder water-cooled engine with a planetary transmission and unusually long double chain drive. After Diamond Autombile took over, few Buckmobiles were produced before the company was sold in a Utica sheriff's bankruptcy sale. Total production of Buckmobiles has been estimated at 40 vehicles.

1910 BUFFALO 1-TON   NAHC

BUFFALO 1908-1910 — The Atterbury Manufacturing Company of Buffalo, New York, built the early Buffalo trucks as a continuation of the Auto-Car trucks. Auto-Car was abandoned as a name and emblem to avoid confusion with the Autocar trucks of Ardmore, Pennsylvania, which were to survive all other "Buffalo" commercial vehicle endeavors numbering at least a baker's dozen over the years. This Buffalo used a single chassis but offered several models. A 10-passenger and 20-passenger bus were also available. Later a 1/2-ton model was built, as well as a 2-ton, which was offered with either a four- or six-cylinder engine. Several electric trucks were also available. There was also the Model F bus and a stake body 5-ton model.

In 1910 the company produced the 1/2-ton Model K and the Model O, which was a 1-ton delivery van. There was also the 2-ton Model N with a 40 hp engine, 5-ton Model S electric truck, 3-ton Model M with a 50 hp engine and a Model H, which was a 20-passenger Sight-Seeing Car. All of these vehicles used solid rubber tires and chain drive. The name was changed back to Atterbury at the end of 1910.

1914 BUFFALO 1-TON ELECTRIC   KP

BUFFALO ELECTRIC 1912-1916 — Confusing as it might be, a similar electric Buffalo truck was built in Buffalo, New York, by the Buffalo Electric Vehicle Company only two years after Atterbury built its line of Buffalos. This company also built electric passenger

cars from 1901 to 1906 and later from 1912 to 1915. The original company, called the Buffalo Electric Carriage Company, was taken over by Babcock in 1906.

All of these Buffalo vehicles used General Electric motors and shaft drive. Battery recharging was claimed to take only 45 minutes. The 1-ton truck with 102-inch wheelbase weighed 3,700 pounds with batteries and was available with an enclosed express body. For 1914 only, a 3/4-ton was offered on the same chassis. All models used solid rubber tires and remained unchanged until the company stopped production in 1916.

BUFFALO 1920-1925 — Another Buffalo truck was built by the Buffalo Truck and Tractor Company of Buffalo, New York. The company offered several models that were powered by Hercules engines. The first was a 2-ton truck that used a four-cylinder Hercules CU-3 engine, Detroit transmission and Wisconsin or Sheldon rear axle. In 1921 the company built a 2-1/2-ton truck that featured two three-speed transmissions mounted in tandem to provide a gear with a countershaft in between for power takeoff with a ratio of 130:1 and permitted hauling heavy loads as well as using the engine as a brake down steep hills.

For regular production a 1-1/2-ton model was added for 1921, which became the 2-ton model for 1922, while the 2-ton was upgraded to a 3-ton capacity. For 1923 an unusual feature was added to the radiator in the form of three copper balls mounted in front. The radiator water could be directed through these balls for extra cooling when the engine was being taxed extra hard. The slogan for the company was "The truck that sells," yet the company sold only 45 trucks in 1921 and 25 in 1922.

For 1924 and selling at $2,750, the 2-ton Model 9 and Model 10 on 140-inch wheelbase were powered by a 22.6 hp Hercules O engine that used a Stromberg carburetor and Bosch ignition. The 3-ton Model 6 and Model 12 with 155-inch wheelbase sold for $4,850. All four models used Covert clutch and transmission with Sheldon front and rear axles. Front tires on both models were on 34-inch wheels, pneumatics were at extra cost and the 3-ton models had dual wheels on the rear. That year the company went through bankruptcy and was reorganized, but it appears no more vehicles were built. Between 1920 and 1925 approximately 130 trucks were produced with this Buffalo badge.

1930 BUFFALO FIRE ENGINE   KP

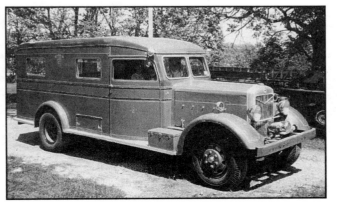

1937 BUFFALO   KP

BUFFALO 1927-1948 — The Buffalo Fire Appliance Corporation was located in Buffalo, New York, starting in 1920, perhaps adding more confusion to the Buffalo name. Until 1927 Buffalo built fire trucks on Larrabee and Reo chassis, but from that year forward the company produced its own chassis. Some of the smaller fire trucks were built on Ford Model A chassis, and starting in 1937 "limousine pumpers" were also built. A new streamlined series was introduced in 1939, and directly after World War II the trucks had a new front grille but were otherwise unchanged until 1948 when production stopped.

BUICK 1910-1918, 1922-1923, 1928 Buick entered the commercial vehicle market after starting in the passenger car business during 1903 in Flint, Michigan. The first commercial chassis was the Model 2, which was powered by a 22 hp two-cylinder horizontally-opposed engine also used in the Buick Model F passenger car. The 3/4-ton truck utilized an engine-under-driver-seat design with a planetary transmission and double chain drive. Choice of 92-inch and 110-inch wheelbase was offered. Stake bed and delivery van bodies were available, as was a light hotel bus.

In 1912 the two-cylinder was superseded by a Buick four-cylinder engine for the 1/2-ton Model 3 and 3/4-ton Model 4. These models were continued until 1918 when truck manufacturing was stopped. The four-cylinder model was also called the D-4 and was advertised as capable of doing four times the work of a couple of mules. It was priced at $1,250 in 1916 with express body, $1,150 for chassis only. Wheelbase was 122 inches and 35x5 pneumatic tires front and rear were standard. The engine and three-speed transmission were mounted on a subframe using three-point suspension, and the clutch was a leather-faced cone type. External contracting brakes were on rear wheels only. Standard equipment was electric headlights with dimmer, electric taillights, trouble lamp with extension, electric horn, extra demountable rim, tire pump and complete set of tools. The Buick engine was called "Valve-in-Head" and was rated at 37 hp.

1910 BUICK MOTOR BUS MROZ

1910 BUICK LONG BODY COMMERCIAL CAR MROZ

1916 BUICK 1-TON D-4 KP

Buick introduced an inexpensive new car in 1922, which also served as the basis for the SD4 light truck of which 2,740 were built up to 1923 when management at General Motors decided to concentrate truck production under the Chevrolet and GMC badges. In 1928 an experimental Buick van was built on an extended Buick chassis. It was used for several years by the Flxible Company as a long-distance bus. Ambulances and hearses were built on Buick chassis by the Knightstown company and Sayers & Scovill at various times since the company's inception.

BULKLEY-RIDER 1914-1917 — Marcus Bulkley was a distributor for Autocar and Knox, but also went into the business of manufacturing. The Bulkley-Rider Tractor Company of Los Angeles, California, built mostly tractors for farm work, but the company also produced a large tractor for road use. It was designed by James Fouch and William Rider and was powered by a 90 hp engine, which was mounted under a hood for the first two years, and then in 1916 it was located under the floorboards of the cab. A three-speed transmission with double reduction gearing was used, giving a total of six speeds with double chain drive at the rear. Top speed was 25 mph, but the lowest gear had a 96:1 ratio, which was the highest reduction for any road vehicle at the time. The vehicle used a double frame design where the engine was mounted on an inner sub-frame on separate springs from the ones that supported the main frame. Steel "tires" were used for most applications; however, rubber tires could be mounted on the rear for road use.

BULL DOG 1924-1925 — The Bull Dog Motor Truck Company of Galena, Illinois, assembled conventional trucks for a brief time. The single model truck offered was rated at two tons and was powered by a 30 hp four-cylinder Continental N engine. It sold for $1,800, but few were produced.

BULLEY see MERCURY

1922 BURFORD 1-1/2-TON BR

BURFORD 1914-1938 — The H.G. Burford Company built and sold trucks in both North Kennsington, England, as well as in Fremont, Ohio. H.G. Burford, being manager of G.F. Milnes & Company and having founded Milnes-Daimler Limited where he became managing director in 1905, introduced a new truck on the British market using his own name as the emblem in 1914. The truck was actually a Fremont-Mais made in Fremont, Ohio, and at first sold under that name. The 2-ton truck with solid rubber tires was powered by a 28.9 hp four-cylinder Buda engine with a three-speed transmission and internal gear drive. Within one year of introduction the name was changed to Burford by the man importing the trucks. At that time the trucks began to be sold in both countries. However, in 1917 the Taylor Truck Company bought out the Burford company of Fremont, and as production continued, the name was immediately changed to Taylor. Taylor trucks were built with the Burford name only for the British market. The trucks sold in the United States were called Taylor.

After World War I Burford trucks were either 1-ton powered by a 19.6 hp four-cylinder engine, or 2-ton and powered by a 27.3 hp four-cylinder engine. The same internal gear drive design was continued, and the chassis was also used to build passenger cars. By 1921 four-wheel-brakes were added to the passenger cars, but this was not standardized until 1927.

Forward control was first introduced in 1923. The next year Burford/Taylor built a 3/4-ton van that could be used as a light bus. It was a forward-control-type with a two-cylinder horizontally-opposed engine built by Anzani in England, which was mounted ahead of the driver's seat as he straddled the engine between his legs. It used a three-speed transmission and chain drive, selling for 150 British pounds. These light buses were specifically aimed at railroad companies for shuttle use, and Great Western Railway bought several but not with the two-cylinder Anzani engines.

A Burford/Kegresse halftrack vehicle was introduced in 1924 as the company tried to expand its market. Burford's entry into halftrack manufacturing stemmed from the previous import of the Cletrac crawler, which was sold in Britain under the name Burford-Cleveland. The Burford-Kegresse was powered by a 5.1-liter four-cylinder engine, considerably larger than the other four-cylinder engines previously employed. The halftrack used the larger forward-control chassis with an additional two-speed reduction unit giving the vehicle eight speeds forward and two speeds in reverse. These were sold to the War Office including an armored version in 1928.

The original Burford company in England was liquidated in 1926 and D.C.H. Gray, a former manager, bought the remaining assets. Limited production of 1-1/2-ton and 2-1/2-ton trucks continued using forward-control and four-cylinder engines. The production facilities in North Kensington were sold, and by 1931 a new factory was leased in Teddington. These were conventional trucks except for the Kegresse halftrack. In 1934 the company was once again taken over, this time by Lacre, which built a few Burfords with the Lacre emblem on them. Few of these trucks were built after 1936 although the company was listed as a manufacturer until 1938.

BUS MFR USA see CLEAN AIR TRANSIT

BUTLER 1913-1914 — Starting in 1901 the Butler Company of Butler, Pennsylvania, began experimenting with motorized vehicles. Engines were supplied by the Motor Vehicle Power Company of Philadelphia, but the vehicles never made it past the prototype stage. Finally, in 1913 the Huselton Automobile Company, possibly an outgrowth of the Butler company, marketed a 3/4-ton truck that cost $1,650 and was powered by a 30 hp four-cylinder engine.

BYRON 1912 — All that is known about the fleeting Byron Motor Car Company of Denver, Colorado, was that it built 1-, 2- and 3-ton gasoline-powered trucks for less than one year.

C

C

CADILLAC 1904 to date — The well-known marque of Cadillac, located in Detroit, Michigan, started in 1903 and the following year began building small delivery vans mounted on Model B passenger car chassis. In 1905 they were mounted on the Model F, and for 1906 through 1908 the Model M was used, which had a wheelbase of 76 inches. In 1908 the Model M was offered only as a delivery van. Each of these used an 8.2 hp one-cylinder Leland and Faulconer engine, which was upgraded to 9 hp in 1905. It was water-cooled and used a two-speed planetary transmission with single chain drive to the rear axle spur gear differential. A steering wheel was utilized, as were pneumatic tires, both considered innovations at that time.

1906 CADILLAC LIGHT DELIVERY   RD

The small vans had approximately 45 cubic feet of cargo space and were rated between 600 and 900 pounds. The C-cab design was used on all vans, and no windshield was provided, which was a standard design shortcoming for that period. Headlights were not standard equipment until 1910. In 1904 the price started at $900 and four years later had risen by $50. Coincidentally, these were about the same prices for the touring models.

1913 CADILLAC POLICE WAGON   KP

Although Cadillac did not build vans or trucks after 1909, over the years the company has built commercial vehicles in the form of hearses, ambulances, police patrol wagons and limousines. A seven-passenger limousine priced at $3,000 was listed as early as 1910. In 1916 an ambulance, police patrol car and hearse were listed at prices of $3,455, $2,955 and $3,880, respectively. These were built on three different chassis of 122-inch, 135-inch or 145-inch. A 90 degree L-head V-8 was used, which had been introduced the previous year. Slightly over 18,000 Cadillacs of all models and

body styles were sold for that model year with Henry Leland as president and general manager. The year 1916 was also when the Cadillac Motor Car Company successfully sued the Cadillac Auto Truck Company to prevent the latter from using the name Cadillac. The Cadillac Auto Truck Company built the Acme truck for a brief period in Cadillac, Michigan.

By 1926 Cadillac listed commercial vehicles for its specialty coach builders. These models included two hearses, an ambulance and an armored car, each powered by an 80 hp V-8 engine with a three-speed selective sliding gear transmission that was cast in unit with the engine block. In 1927 General Motors launched the LaSalle, which was essentially a Cadillac with a new price and badge named after the French explorer who ventured into the Mississippi Valley in 1682. LaSalle professional chassis were used for ambulances and hearses until the make was discontinued in 1940.

1954 CADILLAC MILLER FLOWER CAR   RD

In 1930 a new Cadillac V-16 engine with 185 hp was introduced. The following year a V-12 engine was also added. By 1933 a 140-inch wheelbase was used for the commercial versions, and the next year that was increased to 149 inches.

Since World War II approximately 2,000 commercial vehicles per year have been built by specialty coach builders using Cadillac chassis, not including limousines. By 1975 the three major coach builders of hearses and ambulances were Miller-Meteor, S & S, and Superior. These have been built to date on Series 75 chassis lengthened by over six inches.

CAFFREY ELECTRIC 1897 — W.G. Caffrey of Reno, Nevada, built a four-wheel electric carriage that did not use batteries but got its electrical power from overhead wires much as a trolley would. One such prototype was built and Caffrey set up a series of poles with electrical wire and a dynamo outside his Reno foundry. The trial run was successful, according to the reports of that day, and Caffrey planned on building a system in outlying districts of Reno where hydrodymanic electric power was available. However, the trolley-type vehicle, although envisioned for possible commercial use, never made it past the experimental stage.

1924 CALECTRIC DELIVERY   RD

CALECTRIC 1924 — The Calectric Vehicle Company was formed in Oakland, California, during 1924. The electric delivery truck was built primarily for milk delivery, and had a load capacity of 45 cases of quart bottles. The vehicle used a 44-cell Exide Iron Clad battery mounted under the hood, which powered a General Electric Motor. Cruising speed was 15 mph over a 25-mile route that required up to 400 stops. It is uncertain how many of these vehicles were actually produced.

CALIMOBILE 1902 — The California Automobile Company first built a model California car in 1900 and 1901 powered by electricity, gasoline or steam. New managers William Corbin, Dr. J.G. Crawford and E.R. Harper decided to concentrate on steam powered vehicles in 1902. Little is known about the technical aspects of these vehicles, but it is known that three nine-passenger stagecoaches were built that year along with other smaller vehicles, some of these sold to the well-known and extravagant Palace Hotel in San Francisco. The company did not survive into the following year.

CAMERON 1912 — Everett and Forrest Cameron began by building steam-powered vehicles called Eclipse and Taunton at the turn of the century in Easton and Taunton, Massachusetts. Believing steam power would not be the optimum method of propelling vehicles, the two brothers switched to gasoline power with a one-cylinder air-cooled engine, and by 1903 hired the James Brown Company, a textile machinery builder, to produce their first Cameron auto. The air-cooled design was successful, but the company was reorganized in 1906 in Brockton, Massachusetts, where a rear-mounted transmission was developed and used on all subsequent models. Four and six-cylinder air-cooled engines were also developed, and in 1912, Alma, Michigan, was the location of the plant where Cameron trucks were briefly built. Little is known about the trucks, but most likely they were built on the 120-inch wheelbase touring chassis also using the 36 hp six-cylinder air-cooled Cameron engine. Despite numerous moves to various factory locations and bankruptcy, the Cameron name would not easily die as a manufacturer. A new water-cooled engine was developed in 1919 and used in a front-wheel-drive tractor called the Cameron. Everett Cameron continued to build aviation and marine engines after 1920.

CANTONO ELECTRIC 1904-1907 — Eugene Cantono, a Captain in the Italian Army, arrived in Marion, New Jersey, with an idea to motorize horsedrawn surreys with an electric fore-carriage. Batteries were mounted on the front axle and electric motors were geared to both front wheels of the vehicle. These sold for $1,750 in 1904 and 1905, and Cantono also built complete broughams using this design for $3,500. *Motor World* magazine commented at that time that the captain's design was a ponderous creation that failed to cut a figure in the electric field. The company was bankrupt by 1907.

1910 CAPITOL ELECTRIC VAN   WJP

CAPITOL 1909-1912 — The Washington Motor Vehicle Company began by building 1/2-ton electric trucks called Washington. The name was changed to Capitol (and Capitol Car) in 1911. The District of Columbia business produced trucks but also built a few passenger cars. A 1-1/4-ton truck was also available in 1910, and prices were $1,600 and $2,300, respectively. An unusual move for the company in 1911 was reducing the two trucks' capacities

to 800-pounds and 1,500-pounds, respectively. They were cab-over design and could be furnished with panel bodies. Centrally located below the floorboards were either Edison nickel-iron batteries or more conventional lead acid batteries that weighed over 270 pounds each. It was claimed the Edison batteries provided a 70 mile range, while the lead acid only allowed 40 miles. The 1/2-ton truck weighed 2,400 pounds with Edison batteries, even more with lead acid. Voltages for the motors were either 40 or 80. Chain drive was standard with full-elliptical springs in front. However, the rear employed platform springs usually associated with expensive automobiles of that era.

1914 CAPITOL   JAW

CAPITOL 1914 — Soon after the demise of the Capitol electric trucks in Washington D.C., the unaffiliated Capitol Truck Manufacturing Company began business in Denver, Colorado, albeit briefly. The company built a light electric delivery van powered by a General Electric series-wound motor with a continuous torque drum providing four forward speeds and one reverse. Shaft drive was provided with a floating-type rear axle. Tiller or wheel steering were both available.

The suspension was of a semi-elliptic design on the conventional chassis, which had an open cargo body as standard equipment. A braced windshield was also provided as well as a folding buggy-style canvas top. Headlights were also standard. Batteries containing 30 cells were scattered throughout the truck -- some in front under the hood, some on the sides. The full-length runningboards ended as curved rear fenders while the front were of an unusual shape rising vertically about 12 inches, then protruding forward at a 50 degree angle over the axle and then curving again forward for another 12 inches. The truck weighed 1,800 pounds with batteries that gave a range of about 50 to 60 miles per charge. The company lasted for exactly one year.

CAPITOL 1920-1921 — The Capitol trucks built by Capitol Motors Corporation were built in Fall River, Massachusetts. Three models were offered, each powered by four-cylinder Wisconsin engines. The capacities were 1-1/2-, 2-1/2- and 3-1/2-ton. The lightest truck had a wheelbase of 144 inches, the heaviest 168 inches. All of the trucks used four-speed Cotta transmissions as well as Wisconsin worm-drive, and all had solid rubber tires, although for an extra $550 the 2-1/2-ton was available with pneumatic tires.

CARHARTT 1911-1912 — Hamilton Carhartt advertised in 1911 that his automobile venture was an outcome of 28 years of progressive manufacturing success. Those 28 years, however, had been spent making overalls, but like many entrepreneurs of that era, Carhartt could not resist trying his hand at a motor car venture. He first built eight models of passenger cars on a 118-inch wheelbase with either a 25 hp or 35 hp engine. In 1912 he built fewer models but with horsepower increased to 30 and 50, respectively. Subsequently, he built a 3-ton Model T truck with a 38 hp engine and three-speed transmission using double chain drive. The price for the truck was $3,000 compared to the Carhartt Model B 50 hp limousine that sold for $3,500.

CARL 1913 — Arnold Goss, A.O. Garford, H. Sulzberger and C.A. Neracher organized the Carl Electric Vehicle Company in Toledo, Ohio. Most of the equipment to manufacture was bought from the Chicago Electric Motor Car Company in 1913, and a commercial vehicle was planned, but records do not show whether production actually took place.

CARLSON 1904-1910 — Having been repair manager for the Winton Motor Carriage Company in Cleveland, Ohio, Charles A. Carlson started his own company in 1903 in Brooklyn, New York. Some confusion exists between this company and another named Carlson-Wenstrom of Philadelphia, which did not build commercial vehicles. At first a 20 hp runabout using a 90-inch wheelbase was built in 1904. The following year Carlson focused on building forward-control trucks using the same 20 hp horizontally-opposed engine that was cooled using a water pump, an innovation at the time. The trucks had right-hand steering and the engine was mounted in a cradle under the driver's seat. The chassis used an unusual bent-channel design instead of the customary riveted type of the time, although the crossbars were hot riveted. Chain drive was standard, as were coil springs. The first models had a capacity of one ton and also weighed one ton.

In the last year of production Carlson built 3-ton models, still powered by the same engine and using solid rubber tires. These used semi-elliptic springs and utilized some innovative features for that time. The crankcase cover was removable, as was the entire engine, with ease for fleet maintenance and interchangeability. Pressurized lubrication was provided and advertised as allowing 3,000 miles of operation with five gallons of oil. The Carlson Sliding Case Transmission had been given the first patents on the sliding case principle. Steering was shock-proofed. The 3-ton model used a 108-inch wheelbase and weighed 4,300 pounds. Standard body was a screen-side. Despite such recognized innovations, the company stopped production after 1910.

CARLTON HILL 1915 — The Carlton Hill Motor Car Company had a brief existence building 1-1/2-ton trucks that were used locally in East Rutherford, New Jersey, by the Bobkins and Atkins gardens. The trucks' specifications are not known, but several fire engines were also built. Total production for the one year of operation was 25 vehicles.

1936 CARPENTER SCHOOL BUS   **CARPENTER**

CARPENTER 1923 to date — Ralph H. Carpenter started his body works company in Mitchell, Indiana, during 1919 after having learned the blacksmith trade from his father. He began building horsedrawn wagons for transporting school children in 1919 when he set up his own business. His entry into the motor car business started in 1923 when he produced his first wood-frame bus body built for a truck chassis. The body was entirely of wood including the roof, which was covered with a coated canvas material. He continued building coach bodies, gradually utilizing more sheet

metal until all-steel construction was adopted by 1935. The company incorporated under the same name in the same location in 1941.

The limited production coach builder built conventional school bus bodies, which had been standardized although not built on an assembly line until a new 165,000-square foot plant was built in Mt. Vernon, Indiana. Design variations and custom accessories have been available on the serial bodies, which range from 29-passenger to 72-passenger. Several truck manufacturers including General Motors have manufactured chassis specifically for Carpenter school bus bodies.

By 1970 Carpenter began building three new buses. The Cadet CV design seated 26 passengers (or 32 children for school bus application). Chevrolet and GMC Step-Van chassis for this model have been built by A.O. Smith of Milwaukee, Wisconsin. This type of bus has also been available in a forward-control variation mounted on an Oshkosh V-series chassis using the Carpenter curved windshield. Two wheelbases have been available: 139-inch and 246-inch. Several engines were fitted with this design including Ford and International gasoline engines, as well as Caterpillar, Cummins and Detroit diesel engines. The third bus design has been the Carpenter Corsair series, which had the engine mounted in the rear and has been built by Hendrickson of Chicago.

1968 CARPENTER SCHOOL BUS   **EK**

Carpenter's model line to date has included the Classmate S.W. built on a Ford E-350 Cutaway chassis with single rear wheels. Capacity has been listed at 22 children or 10 adults. Lift gate and door have been available in front or behind the rear wheelhouse. Carpenter has also offered the Classmate D.W.C., Classmate D.W., Classmate II, Cadet, Classic, Counselor and Coach school buses.

The Counselor and Coach chassis have been designated as SB1912-2B, CMI 4027 and CC2322-2CRB. The first two are forward-control front engine chassis that have been available with Cummins diesel or Hercules CNG engine choices. The second chassis is a rear-engine type. AT545 and MT643 transmissions have been listed with these chassis. The rear-engine Coach bus has been listed with an 84-passenger capacity, which has been the largest school bus available from Carpenter to date.

1996 CARPENTER REAR-ENGINE COACH   **CARPENTER**

Carpenter acquired Crown Commercial Buses in 1991, and for 1996 these have been designated as "Crown by Carpenter." Also, APS Systems has converted Carpenter buses to electric power using two 50-kilowatt motors and 7,960 pounds of batteries giving a maximum speed of 35 mph and a 70-mile range at an average 20 mph.

In 1994 Carpenter acquired the tooling, engineering and rights to Wayne. Plans to use both the 167,000-square foot Mitchell, Indiana, plant and the Wayne plant in Richmond, Indiana, shifted, and all Carpenter operations were to be moved for 1996 to the more modern 533,000-square foot plant that Wayne had built during the 1960s. However, the Wayne name was dropped by Carpenter.

1908 CARTERCAR MODEL C   **JAW**

CARTERCAR 1906-1912 — Some of the complexity of early motor car manufacturers' history is exemplified by a company such as Cartercar. Byron J. Carter organized the Cartercar company in Detroit, Michigan, after leaving the Jackson Automobile Company in 1905 and starting the Motorcar Company in Jackson, Michigan. He had built an experimental steam vehicle at the turn of the century, but it did not progress beyond the prototype stage. In 1907 the company was again moved to the Pontiac Spring and Wagon Works in Pontiac, Michigan, where production of passenger cars began. The cars were powered by two-cylinder engines and used a friction transmission that allowed "a thousand speeds...no clutch to slip...no gears to strip...no universal joints to break...no shaft drive to twist...no bevel gears to wear and howl...no noise to annoy." The paper fiber rims of the transmission could be replaced every 4,000 miles for three to five dollars.

Besides a model line of passenger cars, light delivery vans and taxis were built on chassis using wheelbases from 96 to 110 inches. The Cartercar was quite popular, rising to a production number of 325 in 1908. However, that year Carter died suddenly of pneumonia at age 44.

1910 CARTERCAR LIGHT TRUCK   **WJP**

The company was bought by William Crapo Durant in 1909 and became one of 30 firms incorporated under General Motors. A four-cylinder engine was introduced, but otherwise the vehicles remained unchanged, including its double chain drive. When Durant was removed from General Motors by the board of directors, they also decided to drop the Cartercar and to use the factory to build the Oakland, another company Durant had acquired.

1905 CASADAY 3-TON   **RD**

CASADAY 1905-1906 — The W.L. Casaday Manufacturing Company of South Bend, Indiana, built 3-ton and 5-ton trucks powered by a 40 hp four-cylinder engine. A three-speed sliding gear transmission was available, but friction drive was also offered. The lighter chassis had a 108-inch wheelbase and was priced at $3,000. The heavier chassis was $3,500. A variety of bodies was available including police patrol, depot bus, fire hose cart, 18-passenger brake, postal delivery wagons and brewery trucks at prices from $400 to $600. It is not clear how long the Casaday company lasted.

CASCO 1922-1930 — Casco Motors first built Casco trucks in Sanford, Maine, when the company was incorporated in 1922. Until 1924 production was concentrated on a 1-ton speed truck that had a 130-inch wheelbase. The Model A Casco was powered by a four-cylinder Buda MU motor and featured pneumatic tires and electric lighting and starting. Axles were provided by Columbia. At that time the chassis price was $1,784. It was available with different bodies as well as power hoists. The factory was located in the basement of a huge dance hall called the "Palace of Joy."

By 1927 the company had been reorganized and was called the Sanford Automotive Corporation still located in Sanford, Maine. Models from 1-ton to 4-ton were available at a chassis price of $1,700 to $4,150. In 1928 a six-cylinder Buda engine was introduced and the 3-ton and 4-ton models had a 170-inch wheelbase.

In January of 1929 Perley R. Ford, the general manager, died suddenly just prior to signing a contract with the Maine Highway Commission for an order for 27 trucks. Casco introduced its Highway Monarch model, which was rated at 4-ton capacity in the last years of production. It featured a four-speed Fuller transmission, a Wisconsin double reduction axle, and like other Casco trucks, it had no radius rods. There was also a 3/4-cab "Contractor's Special" and the Model A was rated at 1-1/2-ton by then, but when the Depression began the company lasted only through 1930 still offering trucks of 1-1/2-, 2-, 2-1/2-, 3- and 4-ton capacity, though few if any were built by that time. Total production over the years was about 300 Casco trucks.

CASE 1910-1913 — Apparently, there is no connection between this Case company and the one located in Racine, Wisconsin, and in operation concurrently. The Case Motor Car Company of New Bremen, Ohio, built two models of commercial vehicles. The Model B was a 1,200-pound capacity delivery van on a 100-inch wheelbase. The Model C was a 96-inch wheelbase 1-ton with an open express body. Both were powered by two-cylinder two-stroke engines. For the Model B the engine was rated at 20 hp and for the Model C the engine was rated at 24 hp.

1910 CASS   **NAHC**

CASS 1910-1915 — Port Huron, Michigan, was the location of the Cass Motor Truck Company for the first few years when the company produced several models of light trucks of 1-ton capacity. The conventional trucks were powered by a 30 hp four-cylinder engine using three-speed sliding gear transmissions and double chain drive. There was a choice of platform stake, panel or covered express bodies, and the base price was $1,950 in 1910.

Starting in 1912 3/4-, 1- and 1-1/2-ton capacity models were added to the existing 2-ton series. Once Independent Motors Company of Port Huron bought Cass Motors the name also changed in 1915.

1974 CATERPILLAR COAL HAULER MODEL 772   **KP**

CATERPILLAR 1962 to date — The Caterpillar Tractor Company has a long tradition even if it can be considered a relatively new entry into the truck manufacturing business. The origins of the company go back to the steam tractors that Daniel Best and Benjamin Holt built in the 1890s, as well as the crawler tractor introduced by Holt in 1925. The Caterpillar Tractor Company was formed by Best and Holt that year and has become one of the world's largest industrial manufacturers. Caterpillar introduced proprietary engines to their line of products in 1932.

In 1962 the company introduced a range of off highway dump trucks for large road and construction applications. The rigid four-wheel trucks were listed as the 35-ton Model 769B (later the 769C), the 50-ton Model 773 (later the 773B), and the 85-ton Model 777. There were also three truck tractors: Model 768B, Model 772 and Model 776. In addition Caterpillar built two bottom dump coal haulers. These were the 100-ton Model 772 and 150-ton Model 776. All engines were made by Caterpillar and included the 415 hp six-cylinder and the 600 hp and 870 hp V-8 turbocharged diesels. The largest V-8 had a displacement of 29.3 liters. The trucks had nine-speed planetary transmissions, full-floating rear axles, oil-cooled disc brakes and fully hydraulic steering. Each wheel was suspended by independent oil-nitrogen cylinders.

In the early 1980s Caterpillar also used the 650 hp 3412 V-12 turbocharged diesel with a 27-liter displacement for trucks such as the Model 773B. This engine was coupled to a Caterpillar 7F 1R automatic transmission with torque converter drive on reverse and first gear and double reduction rear axle. The frame design consisted of a full box section with torque tube crossmember and box section rear crossmember. Top speed was 40 mph. Brakes were dual system air/hydraulic.

By the mid-1990s Caterpillar's model line consisted of models 769C, 771C, 773B, 775B, 777C, 789B and 793B. The two lightest models have been powered by the 450 hp Cat 3408 diesel engine driving though a lock-up torque converter, planetary power shift transmission and differential. The next two models, 773B and 775B, have been powered by the 650 hp CAT 3412 diesel engine through a lock-up torque converter and planetary power shift transmission that is located at the rear on the differential, which eliminates the drive shaft used on the 769C and 771C. SAE 2:1 capacity has been rated at 44.6 cubic yards and 51.4 cubic yards for the 773B and 775B trucks, respectively.

The three largest Caterpillar trucks have been rated at 150-, 195- and 240-ton capacity. The 785B model has used the 1,380 hp CAT 3516 engine, the 789B has had the same engine rated at 1,800 hp and the 793B has used a 2,057 hp Caterpillar diesel engine. Top speed for the 785B and 789B trucks has been listed at 35 mph while the heaviest has been listed at 33 mph. Maximum gross machine weight for the heaviest 793B truck has been listed at a hefty 830,000 pounds. All of the Caterpillar trucks have been designed with mechanical drive. What appears as headlights at the front of the trucks are actually giant air cleaners for the huge diesel engine.

1975 CATERPILLAR 85-TON MODEL 777   **TWC**

1994 CATERPILLAR MODEL 789B   **CAT**

Although Caterpillar has operated 11 factories throughout the United States with headquarters in Peoria, Illinois, the Decatur, Illinois, plant that was opened in 1955 has produced all the dump trucks. For 1996 Caterpillar announced an increase up to 550 hp for its 3406E engine. The new "King of the Hill" rating has also been listed at 1,850 pound-feet of torque at 1200 rpm. Top engine speed could be set from 1600 to 2100 rpm. Caterpillar reported that the new engine achieved over eight miles per gallon in a fuel economy field test.

1995 CATERPILLAR MODEL 775B QUARRY TRUCK　　CAT

CAVAC 1910-1911 — The Small Motor Car Company of Plymouth, Michigan, built a roadster using a 24 hp L-head four-cylinder engine on a 100-inch wheelbase. When this venture did not produce lucrative results, the company also built a light three-wheel delivery vehicle. All of the prototypes were manufactured at a local machine shop, and after the company incorporated as the Cavac Motor Car Company of Philadelphia, Pennsylvania, it soon ceased to exist.

1974 C.C.C. CENTURY SERIES 6X6　　CCC

C.C.C. 1953 to date — The Crane Carrier Corporation got its start in Tulsa, Oklahoma, when the Zeligson Truck and Equipment Company was formed in 1946 to convert and rebuild surplus military vehicles and equipment. Crane Carrier Corporation was formed in 1953 to build custom-engineered vehicles for the construction industry.

The first truck was built for the city of Brunswick, Georgia. It was a 6-ton carrier chassis. In 1954 a second factory was established in Toronto, Canada, and the following year a larger factory was acquired from Hinderlitor Tool Company in Tulsa. More important acquisitions followed. In 1957 Crane Carrier Corporation purchased the well-known Available Truck Company of Chicago. This allowed the company to re-establish its manufacturing facilities in Tulsa. Another important takeover took place in 1959 when C.C.C. bought its rival, the Maxi Corporation of Los Angeles, California, and moved its manufacturing facilities to Tulsa as well.

By the 1960s the primary application for C.C.C. trucks was for transporting cranes, 9-ton to 60-ton capacity. Chassis were built in 6x4, 8x4 and 6x6 configurations, but 2x4 chassis were also built for quarry load carriers, as well as for several integral-construction buses. At this time Chrysler, Cummins, General Motors, International and Waukesha engines were available in any number of custom C.C.C. heavy-duty vehicles. C.C.C. design included H-

beam frames entirely welded and lightweight cabs with greater visibility and other features that set precedence in the no-nonsense specialty truck manufacturing field.

1977 C.C.C. CENTURY 6X4 TIPPER　　CCC

To date C.C.C. has built 6x4, 8x4 and 6x6 chassis for numerous applications. These include crane carriers, cement mixers, roll-off container transporters, waste disposal trucks with low profile full-cab as opposed to standard half-cabs, and conventional 6x4 Centaur models, which by the mid 1980s were often powered by a 240 hp six-cylinder Cummins PT-240 14-liter displacement engine with Allison MT-654CR automatic transmission and Rockwell SSHD single reduction hypoid rear axle. Besides Cummins, other engine choices have been Caterpillar, Detroit Diesel and Waukesha. Into the 1990s Fuller transmissions were also an option, and suspensions were built by Hendrickson.

C. de L. 1913 — The C. de L. Engineering Works of Nutley, New Jersey, built four-cylinder passenger cars and offered two truck models in bare chassis form only. The two chassis were either 118-inch wheelbase or 140-inch wheelbase. Engines were available from 20 hp to 60 hp. Prices were from $1,500 to $2,800. Pistons of the engines were advertised as "single- or double-acting at the pleasure of the operator."

CECO 1914-1915 — The cyclecar that John Pfeffer designed started out as the Continental in Minneapolis, Minnesota. Investors allowed Pfeffer to build a larger car when the Continental Engineering Company (hence CECO) was formed and the operation was moved to Chicago. Besides a roadster, Ceco also built light delivery and parcel post delivery van models on the standard 103-inch wheelbase chassis. All of the models were powered by a 12 hp four-cylinder engine using a friction transmission. Prices started at $350 and went up to $395 for the parcel post delivery, which weighed 630 pounds and had a 36-inch track.

CHADWICK 1915-1916 — Having learned about motor cars at Searchmont and being familiar with the record-setting Mors racer, Lee Sherman Chadwick began building the Chadwick automobile at the Fairmount Engineering Works in Philadelphia, Pennsylvania. The company became the Chadwick Engineering Works of Pottstown, Pennsylvania, in 1907 when the Chadwick Six was put on the market. The 706-cubic inch displacement engine produced 75 hp at 1100 rpm and propelled the touring car up to 80 mph as early as 1908. The transmission was a double bevel gear direct-drive with final double chain drive using a cone clutch, which Chadwick patented along with the carburetor, cylindrical copper water jackets and aluminum dust-proof covers.

Chadwick never intended to get into the commercial vehicle market. In fact his goal was racing, and the Chadwick Six won at the inaugural Indianapolis Motor Speedway contest in 1909, besting Barney Oldfield, as well as in numerous other major events up to 1911 when Chadwick himself quit racing. He also quit working at the Chadwick company, having moved on to other pursuits. But without new engineering ambitions to further drain the company by the perfectionist founder, Chadwick vehicles continued to be built a few at a time, and it was at this point the limping enterprise tried its luck with a little-known 1/2-ton delivery truck priced at $620 and powered by a 16 hp four-cylinder LeRoi engine. After the company went bankrupt in 1915 the factory was used by an armaments manufacturer during World War I.

CHALLENGE-COOK See COOK

CHALLENGER See M.C.I.

1905 CHAMPION 1-TON ELECTRIC   **JAW**

CHAMPION 1904-1905 — The Champion Wagon Works of Oswego, New York, offered a 1-ton battery-powered truck using a forward-control design and double chain drive. The only versions were either a closed van or open-sided van with a roof. The McCrea Motor Truck Company of Chicago, Illinois, marketed such a truck in 1906, and the two are believed to be one and the same, although neither this nor actual manufacture has been substantiated.

CHAMPION 1907 — The McCrea Motor Truck Company of Cleveland, Ohio, built a 1/2-ton and 2-ton electric truck under the name Champion. The Model L with a delivery body sold for $1,850. It is not clear if this company later moved to Chicago.

CHAMPION 1913-1913 — The Champion was a name used by the Milwaukee Auto Truck Manufacturing Company that built a 1-ton Model A priced at $2,000 and a 2-ton Model B and 3-ton Model C. The company was located in Milwaukee, Wisconsin, and produced vehicles for just over one year.

CHAMPION ELECTRIC 1912-1913 — Although there existed 10 different companies by this name that built motor vehicles, the Champion Electric Vehicle Company of New York, New York, is only one of five listed to have built trucks, and briefly at that. The company offered a light delivery wagon and a 1-ton truck that were shown at the New York Automobile Show in 1912. The prototypes were as far as the venture progressed. Champion Wagon Works of Oswego, New York, was listed as a builder of trucks, and the two are sometimes confused.

CHAMPION 1917 — Little is known about this ephemeral Champion built in Fulton, Illinois, except that a 1/2-ton and 3/4-ton delivery chassis was offered powered by a four-cylinder L-head engine and three-speed transmission with shaft drive.

CHANCE 1976 to date — Chance Corporation started out building amusement rides in the early 1960s. By 1976 bus manufacturing had been organized in Wichita, Kansas, and the company has built three model lines of people movers: the RT-52 Transit Coach, the American Heritage Streetcar built on the same chassis, and the Ford-based Tramstar Low Floor open tram with up to three trailers.

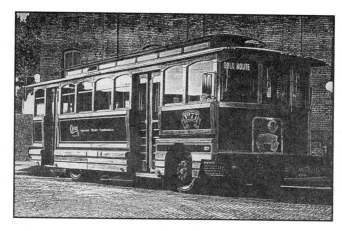

1996 CHANCE AMERICAN HERITAGE STREETCAR BUS   **CHA**

The RT-52 Transit Coach, with up to 23-passenger capacity, has been listed with a 160 hp (190 hp optional) Cummins 6B 5.9 turbocharged diesel engine and an Allison AT-545 (AT-643 optional) automatic transmission.

Actually a bus, the Chance Streetcar was developed originally for the City of San Antonio, Texas. The first Chance Streetcars were built in 1980. That design had an open platform at the front and rear of bus, which was styled after streetcars built at the turn of the century. The AH28 model, which has a maximum capacity of 28 passengers, has been redesigned to include a fully-enclosed forward-control body and has been available with wheelchair lift and air conditioning. The retro-styled bus was listed with the more powerful 190 hp Cummins 6B 5.9 turbocharged, air to air, after-cooled diesel engine at a base price for 1996 of $199,500.

1912 CHASE OPEN EXPRESS   **RM**

1912 CHASE SCREENSIDE DELIVERY   **OCW**

CHASE 1907-1917 — Aurin Chase, former vice-president of the Syracuse Chilled Plow Company, started the Chase Motor Truck Company in Syracuse, New York. The large highwheeler that Chase built could be easily transformed between passenger and light truck iterations. From a business runabout or a five-passenger surrey it could easily be converted into a 700-pound capacity truck with 100-inch wheelbase. Engines were two-, three- and four-cylinder two-cycle, and later Continental engines were used. By 1908 a 3-ton forward-control truck was also offered. Many of the early vehicles were powered by a Chase 160-cubic inch 20 hp three-cylinder two-stroke air-cooled engine with Bosch ignition. The suspension was full-elliptic leaf springs front and rear, with rear transverse semi-elliptic auxiliary leaf spring. Priced at $1,250, the 1912 1-ton Model H with 106-inch wheelbase used 34x2 front and 34x2-1/2 rear solid rubber tires on wagon-type wood spoke wheels. Top speed was 12 mph. The year 1912 was when Chase stopped building passenger cars.

The 3-ton truck used a 30 hp engine of the same design. Only the trucks had three-speed sliding gear transmissions while the runabouts were fitted with two-speed planetary units, although a few light trucks were also fitted with the simpler transmission. Prices for the runabout and light truck started at $750, and went up to $3,500 for the 3-ton model. Chase trucks were sold on the British market by Henry Spurrier of Leylands. The Chase became conventional by 1914 and was powered by a four-cylinder Continental engine with four-speed sliding transmission and worm-drive. Models were offered as 1-, 2- and 3-ton capacity, but by 1917 the range was expanded from 3/4-ton to 3-1/2-ton.

CHAUTAUQUA 1914 — Not to be confused with the Chappaqua Garage of East Orange, New Jersey, the Chautauqua Cyclecar Company of Jamestown, New York, had a brief encounter with reality when designer and president H.J. Newman, veteran of Stoddard-Dayton, built an unremarkable cyclecar, which was sometimes fitted with a van body. The only unusual aspect of the Chautauqua van, besides its name, was that the gearshift was mounted on the steering column. The vehicle was powered by a 12 hp two-cylinder Spacke engine using a friction transmission and belt drive to the rear wire-spoke wheels. While the roadster sold for $400, the van was $415. Newman announced plans to upgrade the vehicles with four-cylinder engines and shaft drive, but time ran out quickly for this venture.

1923 CHECKER TAXI   HAC

CHECKER 1920-1982 — The original Checkers were actually cars made by Commonwealth Motors with bodies made by the Markin Auto Body Corporation, the two of which merged. The cars were specially built for the Checker Taxicab Company of Chicago, Illinois, hence the origin of the name. Commonwealth Motors Company was located in Joliet, Illinois, and remained there when it became the Checker Cab Manufacturing Company in 1922 before moving to Kalamazoo, Michigan, in 1923.

The first few Checker cabs used Lycoming engines but switched to Herschell-Spillman engines when Commonwealth Motors made the change. After the merger in 1921 Commonwealth passenger cars were discontinued as the company focused solely on Checker cabs. The Checker operation moved to Kalamazoo at the former Handley-Knight factory. Herschell-Spillman engines were no longer

used as the company again switched to a 22.5 hp Buda engine, which was standardized for five years when Checker production reached 900 cabs per year, the best selling cab in America at that time.

Checker built cabs in sedan and landaulet bodies, some of the latter of which were exported to Britain. For 1924 a five-passenger taxi cost $2,440. By 1927 a six-cylinder Buda engine was offered, and late the following year four-wheel hydraulic brakes were introduced with the Model K. A number of these were bought for private use by those who trusted Checker's reliability and appreciated the design and price. A few custom-built cars were also produced in the early 1930s, notably a bulletproof sedan for Sam Insull. Prices for the standard cabs remained stable up to the Great Depression.

For 1931 Checker expanded its model line to include the Suburban. This was a versatile design with folding seats and tailgate that could be used as a station wagon, ambulance or hearse. Checker also built a light delivery truck. At a price of $1,795, and using either 122-inch or 127-inch wheelbase, the Suburban Utility was dubbed the MU6 and was powered by a 61.5 bhp Buda J-214 engine. The standard Model K at this time used a 27.3 hp Buda CS6 engine. For 1933 Checker introduced the Model T with a 98 hp Lycoming straight-eight engine. After 500 light trucks were built by 1933, the model was discontinued, but the Suburban was produced until the following year when the total production reached 1,000.

E.L. Cord gained control of Checker in 1933 through a purchase of Morris Markin's stock. At that time Checker began making a car called the Saf-T-Cab for Cord's Auburn Automobile Company of Indiana. The Model T for this version had a different grille and trim, and the cabs were used primarily in Cleveland, Ohio. Markin regained control in 1936 and held it until he died in 1970 at the age of 77 when his family took over.

In the meantime Checker produced a less-expensive Model Y that had an 80 hp six-cylinder Continental engine and was used on the long wheelbase six-door Suburban of 1935, a predecessor of the Aerobus, also known as the airport limousine. The Model Y was also available with the 148 hp straight-eight Lycoming engine for that year. For 1937 through 1939 only the powerful 148 hp (30.01 hp S.A.E.) eight-cylinder Lycoming GFD engine was available.

1941 CHECKER RECONNAISANCE   KP

During World War II Checker was utilized to make trailers and for some experimental work with a four-wheel-drive four-wheel-steering jeep. Also, rear engine and front-wheel-drive with transverse engine designs were built as prototypes, but when Checker went back into production in 1947, a standard Model A of 1940 to 1941 was the basis for the body design without the unusual front fender cuts and open rear body removable section.

The Series E bus was an entirely new field for Checker in 1948 when the chassis were built for Transit Buses, Incorporated. However, after two years of production, Checker bought Transit Buses in 1950, and with a slight redesign and change in appearance they were sold under the Checker emblem. These were powered with Continental engines, and the first series of 450 buses was sold to the Detroit Transit System. In the following two years 40 more of the same buses that seated 31 passengers were sold to various companies in the northwestern United States.

1956 CHECKER TAXI   **OCW**

In 1952 the prototype of a new bus design was built. The proposed new line was powered by a LeRoi engine rear-mounted inline, but not enough interest was generated regarding these city and suburban coaches with seating from 28 to 42 passengers. The Transit-design buses continued to be built through 1953 before bus production ceased. However, a gradual evolution of the cabs took place throughout the early 1950s until the Model A8 was built in 1956. The overall appearance of the cabs changed little from that time on. By 1958 independent front suspension was used with coil springs on the A8 model. The following year Checker introduced the heavy four-headlight body design, which was to stay with the company until the end. During this period the 226-cubic inch Continental engine was available in either side-valve or overhead-valve configurations with 80 hp and 122 hp, respectively.

The Marathon name of the 1950s was added to the Suburban name in 1961. The 120-inch wheelbase sedan cost $3,320, while the Marathon was $3,345. A Marathon station wagon cost $3,615. That year Checker switched from 15-inch wheels to 14-inch. In 1962 an eight-passenger limousine, which cost $7,500, was offered using a 129-inch wheelbase. Production would never again beat the year's 8,173 vehicles built, most of them taxis. It was not until 1965 that Chevrolet 195 hp 283-cubic inch and 250 hp 327-cubic inch V-8 engines were available.

Upon his father's death in 1970, David Markin took over the helm of the Checker company. It went into a steady decline, but not as much due to the new leadership as it had to do with the economics of the marketplace. Competition for fleet sales, especially after the OPEC oil crisis, greatly increased at the same time as Edward N. Cole, retired General Motors Corporation president, joined Checker to begin a new model program. Cole was killed in an airplane crash before he could see to the plans. The company's fixed volume production capabilities and high overhead brought costs up and production down to 500 vehicles per year after 1975. Many Checkers stayed on the road before the six-cylinder was dropped in 1979 to be replaced for the last three years with a 115 hp 229-cubic inch V-6 engine. The Chevrolet 350-cubic inch V-8, which continued down in horsepower from 300 in 1969 to 145 in 1975, was available until 1982 with 105 hp.

Prices continued to rise relentlessly during the 1970s from $4,000 for a standard sedan in 1973 to $5,400 in 1975 and $8,000 by 1980. The year 1974 also brought federally-mandated crash bumpers, which did not accentuate the Checker's well-tested appearance. A Ghia coachworks design was commissioned but rejected also. Autodynamics' 1975 proposal, "Galva II" was also dismissed, primarily for lack of capital for even a simple retooling. Another prototype, inspired by Ed Cole's earlier influence, was built using front-wheel-drive GM X-car components as a basis for a

square-lined four-door hatchback. The project went only as far as a full scale mockup, and Checker closed its doors for the last time in 1982.

1982 CHECKER TAXI   **OCW**

CHELSEA 1914-1915 — One source indicates that Chelsea built a panel van with a 1/4-ton capacity using an 18 hp four-cylinder engine. What is certain is that the Chelsea Manufacturing Company of Newark, New Jersey, actually built about 500 roadsters powered by 12 hp four-cylinder engines by 1915. With shaft drive and 102-inch wheelbase, the company tried a commercial vehicle application towards its final struggle as a viable business, but was not successful.

CHEVALIER 1974-1979 — Monarch Manufacturing Corporation of Nappanee, Indiana, and Chatsworth, California, marketed a cabover truck named the Chevalier CC, which was based on the Monarch motorhome chassis available as 125-inch, 137-inch or 158-1/2-inch wheelbase. Also, 350-cubic inch and 454-cubic inch Chevrolet engines were available. Dual rear wheels, automatic transmission and power steering and brakes were standard equipment. Cabs were built in Indiana and Monarch assembled the vehicles, while the Chevalier was sold at Chevrolet dealerships. It appears the company faded out by the end of the decade.

1922 CHEVROLET 1/2-TON MODEL 490   **KUNTZ**

CHEVROLET 1918 to date — The primary division of General Motors of Detroit, Michigan, and beginning as an independent company founded in 1912 by William Crapo Durant, Chevrolet started in the truck building business with 1/2-ton and 1-ton trucks in 1918. The first 1-ton trucks were not unusual, with solid rubber tires and worm-drive using a 225-cubic inch four-cylinder splash-lubricated overhead-valve Chevrolet engine. Features of the new-comer truck included coil ignition, complete electrical and three-speed transmission. Total truck production for the first year was 879. By the end of 1919 another 7,300 had been built.

1948 CHEVROLET 2-TON COE   HE

1932 CHEVROLET TRACTOR-TRAILER   A&A

1939 CHEVROLET 1-TON TOW TRUCK   GROSS

1941 CHEVROLET COE   HE

1927 CHEVROLET 1-TON CAPITOL AA UTILITY DUMP OCW

1986 CHEVROLET BLAZER BUSHWACKER   CHEV

1976 CHEVROLET TITAN 90 TANDEM DIESEL TRACTOR CHEV

At this time Chevrolet built the "490" series passenger car, which had been introduced in 1914 with a price tag of $490 (what the Ford Model T cost). Using the "490" chassis, a light van was also built. By 1919 Samson had become a subsidiary of General Motors, and many Samson trucks were powered by Chevrolet engines until the Samson division was liquidated in 1923.

As head of Chevrolet, Durant had reacquired General Motors in 1915, seven years after having founded the expanding conglomerate. Race driver Louis Chevrolet, for which the make was named, had previously severed ties with the company. The Chevrolet emblem was conceived by Durant, who said it was to resemble a bow tie that he claimed he had seen in a wallpaper pattern at a hotel in Paris.

1951 CHEVROLET SERIES 6400 DUMP   **GMC**

1951 CHEVROLET SERIES 1500 SEDAN DELIVERY   **MROZ**

Having over-extended the enterprise once again, when a postwar recession hit in 1920, Durant lost control of General Motors, and Pierre du Pont became president. Du Pont favored scuttling the Chevrolet line, but Alfred Sloan Jr., who had been brought in by du Pont to clean up after Durant and who was to become president in 1923, talked him into keeping it. It was at this time that Charles Kettering, who had invented the electric starter motor in 1912, tried to develop four- and six-cylinder air-cooled engines for Chevrolet and Oakland. These were called "copper-cooled" engines, and the 500 cars and light trucks that were produced with these engines turned out to be defective due to then-insurmountable metallurgical, ignition and fuel problems. The light van continued to be built parallel to the passenger car line, both with water-cooled engines, but when the F-series cars were discontinued in 1923, the 1-ton trucks got a 170-cubic inch four-cylinder water-cooled Chevrolet engine and bevel drive.

The H-series was introduced in 1924, and the following year a six-wheel trailing axle version was also offered. An enclosed cab R-series and a panel truck were also introduced in 1925. For that year the Chevrolet Superior commercial chassis cost $410. It had a 103-inch wheelbase and was rated as a 1/2-ton. The 21.7 hp Chevrolet engine used a Zenith carburetor and Remy ignition. Pneumatic 30x3-1/2 front and rear tires were standard. The 1-ton Superior chassis was listed at $550. It used a 120-inch wheelbase and had the same engine as the 1/2-ton. Hayes wheels were pro-

vided on both size trucks with the larger using 31x4 front and 34x4-1/2 rear pneumatic tires. A commercial roadster and roadster pickup were developed in 1926, and the coupe edition from 1928 was offered until 1942. A delivery van on the 1-ton chassis called the "Step-N-Drive" was introduced in 1928.

A new 26.3 hp 194-cubic inch six-cylinder engine with Carter carburetor was introduced in 1929, the year total production of Chevrolet trucks reached one-half million. Wheelbase was 107-inch for the 1/2-ton AC series, which used a three-speed transmission, and 124-inch for the 1-1/2-ton LQ series, which had a four-speed transmission. The new six-cylinder, advertised as "six for the price of four" and sometimes called the "stovebolt six," was also cast iron and retained splash lubrication. Hydraulic shock absorbers, vacuum windshield wipers and exterior mirrors also became standard equipment.

For the year 1930, when Chevrolet sold over 188,000 trucks, improvements included dual rear wheel option, stronger rear axles and all-expanding brakes with the rear fully enclosed. Like the passenger cars, the trucks were fitted with new instrument panels that included an electric gasoline gauge. Chevrolet factory-assembled the Commercial Chassis, Chassis and Cab including Roadster Delivery, and the Sedan Delivery. Other commercial bodies were purchased from outside sources such as Hercules until the Martin Parry Body Company was acquired in 1930. The Chevrolet commercial engine developed 46 hp by this time. The dual-wheel 1-ton became popular as a fire engine, such as the Chevrolet/Howe combination.

For 1931 Chevrolet introduced a Deluxe Sedan Delivery with plated headlights, radiator shell and wire wheels, as well as whitewall tires. A Panel truck was offered with insulated box sides and disc wheels. A 1/2-ton Canopy Express was produced with open body sides optional with curtains or screens. For 1932 the Sedan Delivery had the passenger car front end look, including a new hood with louvers. The Light Delivery series was equipped with the new Silent Synchromesh transmission. Trucks did not get the engine improvements that passenger cars got and used a less powerful 53 hp six-cylinder engine, but a downdraft carburetor was standardized that year. Styling tended to lag behind passenger cars by one year.

In truck sales Chevrolet outproduced Ford in 1933 for the first time ever. The first factory-built station wagon, called the eight-passenger Suburban, was offered in 1935. Midway through 1936 a streamlined low-roof cab and hydraulic brakes were standardized.

By 1936 the 1-1/2-ton truck was available with either 131-inch or 159-inch wheelbase. Short wheelbase truck tractors were produced and sold well. One truck hauling a trailer with five tons of cargo up Pikes Peak was the year's promotional stunt. At this time some of Chevrolet's mechanical components began to be used by other General Motors vehicles, such as the Yellow Coach PSV between 1937 and 1942. The General Motors Cab from 1936 to 1938 was an extended-chassis version of the Chevrolet Master Six sedan.

"Steel Stream Styling" was a dramatic new look for 1937 when the Model GE 1-ton truck with 122-1/4-inch wheelbase was added to the line. That year a new 216.5-cubic inch four-main-bearing engine was offered in both trucks and passenger cars. The cab-over-engine (COE) design was also introduced by Chevrolet for that year but for export only, as was the 77 hp diesel engine option. By this time Chevrolet had assembly plants in Flint, Michigan; Tarrytown, New York; St. Louis, Missouri; Kansas City, Kansas; Oakland and Los Angeles, California; Atlanta, Georgia; Norwood, Ohio; Baltimore, Maryland; Janesville, Wisconsin; as well as Canada and Great Britain. For 1937 chassis prices varied from the Model GC 112-inch wheelbase 1/2-ton at $360 up to the Model SD 157-inch wheelbase 1-1/2-ton at $640. All trucks used the 216-cubic inch six-cylinder rated at 78 hp. The 1-1/2-ton models used 6.00x20 tires front and rear.

For 1939, intermediate 3/4-ton Model JD and JE, as well as the Model VA 1-ton were offered. The one-piece windshields were replaced with a new two-piece V design, and a new heavier grille was used. Hypoid rear axles, used since 1937, were standardized in 1940. A new model for that year was the KP Dubl-Duti walk-through van with forward control (COE) used for urban delivery work.

During this time automatic transmissions of the closed-circuit torque converter fluid-turbine type were being developed by the GMC Truck and Coach engineering staff. The first such transmission was tested in 1937 on a bus, and by the end of 1941 the Engineering Staff Transmission Development Group was working on adaptation for passenger and light truck applications. The beginning of World War II halted this project, but the automatic transmissions, called Hydra-Matic, were utilized for M-3 and M-4 tanks, and large numbers of these were built during the war by General Motors.

From 1940 to 1945 General Motors produced about $12 billion worth of military equipment. Passenger car production was halted entirely between the beginning of 1942 to the end of 1945. One of the numerous yet most unusual vehicles Chevrolet built at the beginning of World War II on an experimental basis was an extra-lightweight jeep-type vehicle powered by a 90-degree V-type air-cooled 20.5 hp 45.44-cubic inch Indian motor. This 64-inch wheelbase vehicle had a tubular frame, independent suspension all around with transverse leaf springs, inboard rear brakes and integral transmission and transfer case for its four-wheel-drive. After completing only 3,223 miles of a 10,650-mile test it was dropped as a viable vehicle.

At the beginning of the war, the Transmission Development Group designed a specialized tank transmission and steering system known at the "cross drive" for large vehicles over 50 tons. Chevrolet built 60,257 trucks in 1943 and 71,631 in 1944, almost all of them for the war effort. The War Production Board concluded there were five classes of haulers who could buy new civilian trucks, and 640 were approved out of 33,000 applications.

A new heavy-duty 231-cubic inch six-cylinder engine became optional in 1941, and was standardized for 1942 in all 1-1/2-ton models. For the first full year of war, Chevrolet built 15 models ranging from 1/2-ton to 2-ton capacity, including two bus chassis. The company also built the short-lived M38 Armored Car in 1945. General Motors of Oshawa, Ontario, Canada, built the first Chevrolet four-wheel-drive called the GS series. It was the Canadian Army's standard load carrier. Its reverse angle two-piece windshield was designed to reduce the possibility of reflection to aerial reconnaissance.

For the immediate postwar years Chevrolet used 1942 designs, and during 1946 and 1947 all trucks had painted grilles, bumpers, hubcaps and hood trim. The first face lift came midyear in 1947 with the all-new Advanced Design truck series, although the model line remained the same as before with sedan delivery, vans and trucks from 1/2-ton to 2-ton capacity including a 1-1/2-ton COE design, as well as a school bus with 54 seats. Engines also remained unchanged with the 216-cubic inch six-cylinder producing 90 hp and the 235-cubic inch producing 105 hp. Cab styling was called "Unisteel" and frames and interiors were improved. Five broad horizontal bars constituted the new grille, a complete departure from the earlier vertical bars. Forester green was the standard color, and chrome grilles were optional. For 1949 the sedan delivery was changed with a new 115-inch wheelbase and new body based on a combination of sedan and station wagon sheet metal.

1954 CHEVROLET SERIES 3600 STAKE　　　　　　　**KP**

For the new decade Chevrolet again offered Step-N-Drive vans in 1951. Introduced were the Powerglide automatic transmission and full-pressure engine lubrication, while horsepower was increased to 92 in the 216-cubic inch engine. By this time Chevrolet was restricted by the Korean War to 35 percent of the light-duty truck market. For 1952 a 90 hp four-cylinder two-stroke Detroit Diesel was optional but rarely utilized. In 1954 restyling of the conventional trucks included a new one-piece windshield and a massive cross-bar front grille, as well as several other details. Two forward-control Dubl-Duti chassis were reintroduced using the Loadmaster 235-cubic inch six-cylinder with updraft carburetor, which was rated at 110 hp. A 16-passenger school bus on a 1-ton chassis Model 3802 was also available.

1963 CHEVROLET SERIES 10 SUBURBAN EMERGENCY　　**KP**

1978 CHEVROLET BRUIN (LEFT) AND 70 SERIES　　　　**CHEV**

Another complete midyear restyling took place in 1955 when the 145 hp Taskmaster short-stroke overhead-valve V-8 was introduced in the 2-ton trucks, and the new 265-cubic inch V-8 with up to 180 hp became optional with all light trucks. This was the year that the wrap-around windshields were adopted, as was a 12-volt electrical system and four-speed Hydramatic transmission on all models except the sedan delivery.

A record 393,315 commercial vehicles were sold by Chevrolet in 1955 when the stylish Cameo Carrier pickup debuted. Chevrolet was the largest truckmaker in the United States at this time with 31.55 percent of the market share, having attained top sales from 1951 until Ford took over in 1970. Tubeless tires became standard in 1956, and the V-8 engine was available in most trucks. The 2-ton was uprated to 2-1/2-ton and power steering and six-speed automatic transmission were optional. The first factory-built four-wheel-drive pickup trucks arrived in 1957. On heavier trucks the five-speed transmission was all-synchromesh for that year, and air/hydraulic brakes were optional, as was a more powerful 205 hp V-8.

1978 CHEVROLET BISON　　　　　　　　　**CHEV**

Dual-headlight restyling arrived in 1958, as did full air brakes. The 283-cubic inch V-8 was optional with up to 250 hp. Along with a 348-cubic inch V-8 with up to 335 hp, for 1959 Chevrolet introduced its El Camino sedan pickup to compete with Ford's Ranchero. For 1960 torsion-bar independent front suspension was adopted on all trucks, but this was used only for three years. A new range of COE models with GVW weight up to 40,000 pounds was also offered. Detroit Diesel four-cylinder engines reappeared as an option. The 1960 Corvair-based Corvan with a six-cylinder air-cooled horizontally-opposed engine was all new for 1961 when the sedan delivery was discontinued. The forward-control Corvan, which was also available in pickup form, featured a uni-body construction and all-independent suspension, which became quite controversial after the book *Unsafe At Any Speed* was published.

The El Camino pickup was continued in 1961, but it was based on the midsize Chevelle. Diesel engines were available for all large Chevrolet trucks. Although most light trucks had a V-8 option, 82 percent were still powered by six-cylinder engines. The eight millionth Chevrolet truck was sold in 1962. The following year a new four-cylinder five-main-bearing engine, primarily developed for the new compact Chevy II, was available in some light trucks but for a brief time only. This was the year that new ladder-type frames in place of the X-brace type were adopted. For heavy trucks diesel engines were optional, as were Fuller Roadranger transmissions. The largest Chevrolet trucks were 6x4 and used 195 hp V-6 Detroit Diesel engines.

The Corvan was discontinued after 1964, although the Corvair was still produced. A standard forward-control van with four- or six-cylinder inline engines superseded the relatively unsuccessful Corvan. Vans could be ordered with a three-cylinder Detroit Diesel engine. The 327-cubic inch V-8 appeared midway in 1965 for trucks, the year factory air-conditioning was available. This was also the year Chevrolet showcased its new Turbo Titan III, which was gas-turbine powered. It featured automatic transmission, power tilt cab, power windows, retractable headlamps, stereo and CB. Large trucks were available up to 48,000 pounds GVW.

Chevrolet trucks remained relatively unchanged through the generally successful 1960s. For its 50-year anniversary in 1968 Chevrolet offered a special gold and white paint option. Front and rear safety sidemarker lights were introduced. For 1969 Chevrolet introduced the 4x4 Blazer, at first based on the K10 4x4 pickup. Also new was the forward-control step-van model with independent front suspension, coil springs, power steering and V-8.

By 1969 Chevrolet entered the heavy truck market with the 65,000-pound GCW Titan truck tractor. This was a tilt cab design available in 4x2 and 6x4 versions. Detroit Diesel V-6, V-8 and V-12 engines were available up to 390 hp and Cummins diesel engines with up to 319 hp were offered. The Titan also featured twin-disc clutches, air brakes and suspension, power steering, and 10-speed or 13-speed transmissions. In 1970 the Titan's GCW was increased to 76,800 pounds. This was also the year of some disruptive labor strikes for Chevrolet.

As popular and successful as the Blazer was, the new Vega Panel Express of 1971 was plagued with design problems. This was also the year truck engines were modified to run on unleaded gasoline. All con-

ventional light-duty trucks and vans had front disc brakes, and independent front suspension was adopted on vans. Also for this year, the fuel evaporative smog-control system, which had been first mandated in California, became standard on all 1/2-ton trucks. A total of 345 V-6 engines were used on light trucks up to 1-ton capacity. Exhaust valve rotators were added to the 307-, 350- and 400-cubic inch displacement engines.

With A.T. Olson as the top man of the truck division in 1972, Chevrolet imported the light LUV pickup (Light Utility Vehicle), which was built by Isuzu of Japan. By 1975 85 percent of Chevrolet trucks used V-8 engines. The Chevy Blazer was appointed with a roll bar in 1976, and the Vega was discontinued at the end of 1977, the year a 1-ton 4x4 model was first offered. Also, along with the Titan, Chevrolet introduced a conventional 6x4 heavy truck called the Bison, whose GMC counterpart was the General. It was rated at 50,500 pounds gross vehicle weight (GVW) and 80,000 pounds gross combination weight (GCW). Diesel engines up to 490 hp were by Cummins or Detroit Diesel, and a five-speed automatic transmission was standard.

For 1978 Chevrolet offered the most complete commercial vehicle model line ever. Starting with the light LUV pickup, the lineup included the El Camino, Suburban, various vans and pickups up to the Series 70 and Series 90 Bruin, Bison and COE Titan heavy trucks. Medium conventional trucks were offered upward from 13,000 GVW. A relatively unsuccessful 5.7-liter diesel engine for the light trucks was supplied by Oldsmobile. Also new was a turbocharged four-cylinder Detroit Diesel engine. There was a choice of 18 transmissions from four-speed up to 13-speed. Air brakes were standard on heavy trucks, some of which had fiberglass tilt hoods. Caterpillar engines also became available.

Chevrolet continued to produce its Step Van model line and bus chassis up to 72-passenger on a 274-inch wheelbase. Also offered were front-wheel-drive mobile home chassis with gasoline engines, front disc brakes and independent front suspension. The mobile home market peaked in 1976 with 18 major specialty body manufacturers, but by the end of the 1970s this production was nearly phased out by Chevrolet. The 4x4 LUV was introduced in 1979.

For 1980 Chevrolet offered the 199 hp Caterpillar 3208 and the 212 hp Cummins VT-225 along with Detroit Diesel and Allison "Fuel Pincher" engines in its large trucks. The fiberglass tilt hood was called the Kodiak. Although a new Chevrolet 6.2-liter diesel was introduced, the company discontinued its heavy-duty trucks after 1980. This was also the year that the four-cylinder two-cycle Detroit Diesel engine was replaced with the four-cycle Detroit V-8.

The Chevrolet compact S-10 pickup was introduced midyear in 1981 as a 1982 model line. The S-10 Blazer followed in 1983. Medium-duty trucks for 1984, when Isuzu started making new tilt cabs for Chevrolet medium-duty trucks, included the COE Tiltmaster with a new 165 hp turbocharged diesel engine. This truck was available on 142-, 165-, 181- and 197-inch wheelbases. Also that year, the U.S. Army purchased 30,000 full-size 4x4 pickups and 23,000 full-size Blazers with 6.2-liter diesel engines.

With new front grilles for 1985 full-size Chevrolet trucks, the cab-over-engine Tiltmaster was available in wheelbases from 137-inch to 209-inch. The medium-duty trucks were still called the C-50, C-60 and C-70, the latter with a Kodiak cab option and 13-speed Fuller transmission. Standard transmission for the medium-duty trucks was the GM 4F 1R all-synchromesh with Rockwell single reduction rear axle. Also for that year, the new Astro van with 111-inch wheelbase and V-6 engine was offered.

1986 CHEVROLET W4 DIESEL (LEFT) AND W7　　　　　　**CHEV**

1989 CHEVROLET 3/4-TON CHEYENNE EXTENDED CAB **MROZ**

1992 CHEVROLET K3500 CREW CAB **CHEV**

By 1990 the Caterpillar 3116 engine was offered by Chevrolet. The Kodiak model line has continued to use this engine, as well as the 6.0L (366-cubic inch) and 7.0L (427-cubic inch) gasoline V-8s. Specifications for the Kodiak have been identical to those of the GMC Topkick and model numbers have been identical through 1996. The only difference was in the badge and warranty between Chevrolet and GMC.

For the mid-1990s Chevrolet has continued to offer a full line of light- and medium-duty trucks and vans. The All-Wheel-Drive Astro van debuted in 1990. Other models have included the Lumina Cargo Minivan with 3.1L standard engine and three-speed automatic transmission on a 109.8-inch wheelbase with GVW rating of 5,126 pounds. The Astro Cargo Van has used a 4.3L engine with a four-speed base automatic overdrive transmission and a 111-inch wheelbase. The extended body version of the Astro Cargo Van has had the same wheelbase but nearly 20 more cubic feet of cargo room and a GVW rating of up to 5,700 pounds.

The Full Size Chevy Van has been available as the G10, G20, G30, G30 Extended Body and G Cutaway Van. All of these have had the 4.3L engine as standard except the Cutaway, which has been powered by the 5.7L engine. Transmissions have been the four-speed automatic overdrive on all five of these vans. The G30 Extended Body has had a GVW rating of up to 9,200 pounds with a payload capacity of 3,796 pounds. The G Cutaway Van has had a GVW rating of up to 10,500 pounds with a load capacity of up to 6,121 pounds.

1994 CHEVROLET S-10 SS PICKUP **CHEV**

The S series pickup has used the 2.2L engine with a five-speed manual base transmission on wheelbases of 108.3, 117.9 and 122.9 inches. These have included the Regular Cab Short Box, Regular Cab Long Box and Extended Cab Short Box. The C series full-size pickup has been available in seven basic versions that included: Regular Cab Sportside, Extended Cab Sportside, Regular Cab Short Box, Regular Cab Long Box, Extended Cab Short Box, Extended Cab Long Box and Crew Cab Long Box. Standard engine on the first five versions has been the 4.3L and base transmission has been the five-speed manual. The Extended Cab Long Box and Crew Cab Long Box has used the 5.7L heavy-duty V-8 engine and the five-speed manual overdrive transmission. The heaviest GVW rating of 10,000 pounds for these pickups has applied to the Regular Cab Long Box, Extended Cab Long Box and Crew Cab Long Box.

1995 CHEVROLET C1500 EXTENDED CAB SPORTSIDE **CHEV**

The C Full-Size Chassis Cab has been offered as the C2500 and C3500 with regular frame, C3500 straight frame and C3500 Crew Cab regular frame. All four of these have been powered by the 5.7L heavy-duty V-8 engine and have used the five-speed manual overdrive base transmission. The Forward Control P Chassis has had the 4.3L base engine and four-speed overdrive base transmission on wheelbases of 125, 133, 157 and 178 inches. The P Chassis has been GVW rated up to 14,000 pounds. For the complete history of Chevrolet light trucks see Krause Publications' *Standard Catalog of American Light-Duty Trucks*.

CHICAGO 1910-1911 — Two truck versions were built by the Chicago Commercial Car Company for a brief time. One was a 3/4-ton and the other a 1-ton, both with open van bodies. The Model P16 3/4-ton had a 16 hp two-cylinder engine. This was an "engine-under-driver-seat" design with planetary transmission, double chain drive and solid rubber tires. The Model S-25 1-ton used a 20 hp engine and selective slide gear transmission, also with double chain drive and solid rubber tires. The price of the Model P-16 was $1,500 and for the Model S-25 it was $1,700.

1919 CHICAGO 2-1/2-TON **MROZ**

CHICAGO 1919-1932 — Although the Chicago Motor Truck Company of Chicago, Illinois, was in business some 13 years, only limited information exists regarding its product line of trucks. It was not affiliated with the earlier Chicago commercial vehicle producers. What is known is the company built trucks from 1-ton to 5-ton capacity throughout the 1920s. Its first offering was a 2-1/2-ton with 168-inch wheelbase powered by a 27.2 hp four-cylinder Continental engine using a four-speed transmission (mounted amidships) and a Huck rear bevel drive. All of the later trucks were powered by Hercules engines until 1927 when the company switched to Waukesha engines. In 1930 a six-wheel truck was added to the model line in two versions: 8-ton and 12-ton capacity. By 1930 all engines were Waukesha six-cylinder, but the Depression took its final toll on Chicago Motor Trucks in 1932.

1927 CHICAGO 12-TON FURNITURE TRUCK   KP

CHICAGO BUSINESS 1912 — This brief venture known as the Chicago Business Car Company built one truck model in 1912. Its wheelbase was 87 inches and capacity was 800 pounds for this light commercial vehicle. It was powered by a 14 hp two-cylinder engine. Only a few of these were built before the company folded.

CHICAGO ELECTRIC 1913-1916 — The Chicago Electric Motor Car Company existed for a few months building a handful of battery-powered passenger cars before the Carl Electric Vehicle Company of Toledo, Ohio, bought the manufacturing equipment with the intention to build commercial vehicles. At the same time the Walker Vehicle Company of Chicago bought the design for the passenger car, which continued to be built until 1916. Walker electric trucks were made until 1942.

CHICAGO MOTOR BUGGY See BLACK / BLACK CROW

1917 CHICAGO FRONT-DRIVE DOUBLE DECK   MBS

CHICAGO MOTOR BUS 1916-1923 — Yet another Chicago enterprise that built vehicles, out of some two dozen that existed over the years, the Chicago Motor Bus Company specialized in bus manufacturing including an unusually-designed front-wheel-drive model. Beginning in 1916, the company assembled 50 open-top double-decker buses. The St. Louis Car Company built the bodies. The detachable front-wheel-drive unit was assembled in Chicago using a Moline-Knight sleeve-valve engine. The entire powerplant assembly was similar to the one produced by MacDonald in San

Francisco around the same time, and it allowed a completely flat, low bed -- in the case of the Chicago buses for easy passenger entry and clearance purposes of the upper deck.

In 1919 two experimental buses were constructed. One was a conventional rear-wheel-drive design that proved to be too high for upper deck clearances. The second was a front-wheel-drive with enclosed upper deck, which was the first of such a bus design in the United States. In the economic slump of 1920 the company reorganized, splitting into two organizations. The Chicago Motor Bus Company continued in the business of operating buses, while the new American Motor Bus Company became the manufacturer of buses. Subsequently, the latter outfit built 23 double-decker enclosed top buses with front-wheel-drive. The company also designed and built a new rear-wheel-drive open-top bus, known as the Type K, which seated 67 passengers. A total of 71 such buses were built within two years starting in 1922.

Chicago Motor Bus, the parent company, was bought by John D. Hertz late in 1923. This led to the American Bus Company being succeeded by the Yellow Coach Manufacturing Company. At the same time the bus operating business became the Chicago Motor Coach Company, which in 1928 built one experimental six-wheel bus that was a single-deck design.

CHICAGO MOTOR WAGON 1910-1912 — One model of commercial vehicle was built by the Chicago Motor Wagon Company of Chicago, Illinois. It was a 1-ton capacity truck powered by a 20 hp two-cylinder engine using a friction transmission and standard double chain drive to the rear wheels. The 90-inch wheelbase chassis weighed 2,300 pounds. This vehicle was priced at $1,000 with open express body.

CHICAGO RUNABOUT   See DUER

CHIEF 1910 — The Michigan Steam Motor Company of Pontiac, Michigan, evolved from the Belknap Motor Company of Detroit in 1907. It should not be confused with the Michigan Steam car built by Byron Carter in 1901 in Grand Rapids. It is not certain whether two other steam vehicle builders by the name of Belknap, one of Portland, Maine, the other of Newark, New Jersey, were related. The Michigan Steam Motor Company built one steam-powered truck in 1910, but specifications are not available.

CHILDS See AMERICAN LAFRANCE or KEARNS

1914 CHRISTIE 2-WHEEL TRACTOR W/STEAM PUMPER   KP

CHRISTIE 1909-1930 — The Front Drive Motor Company of Hoboken, New Jersey, was founded by John Walter Christie who was a pioneer of front-wheel-drive starting in 1904. Originally, the Christie Iron Works of New York became the Christie Direct Action Motor Car Company in 1906, which evolved into the Christie Automobile Company in 1908. Christie built front-wheel-drive racing cars to prove his ideas, which were patented in the United States, Russia, Europe and Australia.

The first car Christie took to Ormond-Daytona Beach in 1904 was powered by a 30 hp four-cylinder engine mounted transversely, the crankshaft acting as the front axle with front wheels driven directly by flywheels coupled with leather-faced clutches and telescoping universal joints, packed with grease, carrying the wheels. One of the half-dozen racers Christie built had two 60 hp engines both fore and aft. This was the first American entry in the French Grand Prix in 1907, and it was powered by the largest ever engine to start in the famous competition. The V-4 engines had a displacement of 19.88 liters each, but Christie did not win the race.

Once the Direct Action company went into receivership, Christie formed a new business and built a $2,300 taxicab model for the City of New York. Only three of these were built before Christie resumed racing circa 1909. However, partly as a result of continuous financial problems, Christie decided to focus his front-wheel-drive design on utilitarian applications, and he formed the Front Drive Motor Company in 1912.

First he built two-wheel tractors that were intended as substitutes for horses used for steam pumper fire engines. Fire departments could not afford to buy an entire new fleet of such expensive equipment, and so in some cases opted to use devices such as Christie's. The first such tractor was built for the New York Fire Department in 1911 using a 90 hp four-cylinder engine mounted longitudinally ahead of the front axle. A two-speed transmission used chain to rotate a countershaft at the ends of which four spur gears meshed with the internal gears of the road wheels. A power-operated turntable was utilized that could pivot 60 degrees, which, along with the 30 degree steering capability, allowed for a 90 degree angle so that the vehicle could turn in its own length. This was especially effective when some ladder trucks were up to 80 feet long.

1915 CHRISTIE FRONT DRIVE WATER TOWER   LIAM

Although the first such tractor had a longitudinally mounted engine, all subsequent units had the engine transversely mounted under the seat or beneath a short hood. Compressed-air engine starters were incorporated into the design after the early hand-cranked engines turned out to be difficult to handle. The New York Fire Department bought 186 Christie tractors over the years of production. In addition Boston, Chicago, Philadelphia, Pittsburgh and Manila, Philippines, bought Christie tractors, with total production going just over 600.

Christie built a front-drive four-wheel articulated prime mover for pulling artillery in 1916. This pilot model was steered by braking one drive wheel and used a transversely-mounted 60 hp engine. It does not appear to have been tested or purchased by any of the military branches.

Once horsedrawn fire engines stopped being produced circa 1912, the attachable tractor design (also made by Autohorse, Cross, LaFrance, Martin and Seagrave) had a finite lifespan, and motorized vehicles gradually came into use by fire departments and businesses. Christie's tractors served as long as 1945 in Toledo, Ohio.

Although Christie's Front Drive Motor Company ceased production of the tractors, Christie continued to build vehicles for specialized applications. In 1928 Christie built a 6x4 10-ton truck. Each of the two rear axles had four wheels, hence Christie called it "Eight Wheel Drive." The wheels were essentially drums with solid rubber

tires. A chain drive assembly operated between each set of drums. A steel traction device could be fitted over the two sets of wheels creating a "poor man's halftrack," which did not attract buyers.

1930 CHRISTIE TRUCKTOR   RD

A Christie Crawler under the name Trucktor, built by the Trucktor Corporation of New Jersey, appeared in January of 1930. The six-wheel truck had detachable 24-inch tracks so that the vehicle could be quickly converted to a standard truck. It does not appear that this vehicle went beyond the pilot model either. Christie experimented with various crawler devices into the 1930s but these could not be considered trucks or commercial vehicles. Born in 1864, Walter John Christie passed away in 1944 after being involved in tank development during World War II.

1928 CHRYSLER SERIES 62 1/2-TON   CP

CHRYSLER 1925-1928, 1938, 1958-1965, 1978, 1990 to date — In 1924 Walter Chrysler became president of Maxwell, and the last Maxwell was built the following year. Aside from many passenger car models, Chrysler offered 1/2-ton and 3/4-ton commercial vehicles for export in 1925. The Chrysler name was used on light Plymouth trucks sold in Great Britain in 1938.

In 1958 Chrysler built a 2-1/2-ton aluminum-body 8x8 for the U.S. Army. This truck was called the XM410 and was built of riveted panels so as to be floatable. The engine was a Continental LD-465-2 and the vehicle was fitted with low pressure 14x18 tires. Only a half dozen were delivered to the Army for testing. Further development resulted in the XM410E1, which was fitted with a closed cab. It used the same 150 hp engine and had a semi-automatic transmission. The 22-foot long trucks were floatable with the spinning tires used as propulsion.

1996 CHRYSLER TOWN AND COUNTRY VAN   CHRYS

1978 CHRYSLER EXPANDED MOBILITY VEHICLE   MROZ

In 1980 Chrysler submitted its Expanded Mobility Vehicle to the military for evaluation in the High Mobility Multi-Purpose Wheeled Vehicle (HMMWV) or "Hummer" project. Its "Hummer" prototype was powered by a Deutz air-cooled V-8 and used a Chrysler A727 three-speed automatic transmission.

In 1983 Lee Iacocca was named an honorary member of the Antique Automobile Club of America. Part of the reason for getting such an award was Iacocca's ability to turn Chrysler around from a loss of more than $1 billion in 1979 to a profit figure of $1.84 per share by 1982. Iacocca spent many years at Ford Motor Company. Having had differences with Henry Ford II, which resulted in Iacocca being fired as president and being relegated to a distant warehouse office, apparently did not dampen his enthusiasm for the industry.

More recently, Chrysler Corporation brought out a series of minivans that have sometimes been used commercially for light-duty use. The Chrysler Town & Country minivan was introduced in 1990 equipped with a V-6 motor. The larger Chrysler minivan was added to the lineup after the introduction of the Plymouth in 1984. The V-6 engine has been available in 3.3- and 3.8-liter displacements through 1996. The Town & Country LX, Town & Country AWD and Town & Country LXi and LXi AWD have used four-speed automatic transmissions. With seats easily removable, cargo space has been listed at 146.2 cubic feet and 172.3 cubic feet, respectively. However, as the most luxurious of the Mopar vans, it would be used as a light delivery commercial vehicle less often than the similar Dodge Caravan and Plymouth Voyager.

CHUTING STAR 1976-1985 — Forward, Incorporated, of Huron, South Dakota, specialized in 6x6 cement mixers, hence the pun in its name. These were front discharge design with a rear mounted Cummins VT 555 turbocharged engine and Sundstrand DMT 250 transmission. The cement mixer version had a low cab; however, the chassis was designed for other applications such as crane carrying, highway maintenance and public utility trucks. How many complete trucks were built is uncertain, and the company faded out by mid-decade.

CINO 1910-1913 — Haberer and Company of Cincinnati, Ohio, built two models of truck, along with a well-crafted touring car, during its brief existence. For 1910, when there were an even half-dozen automobile manufacturers in Cincinnati, the company built a conventional 1/2-ton truck with a wheelbase of 113 inches. This truck was powered by a 40 hp engine. For 1913 a 1/4-ton chassis was built with a price of $1,300. Both trucks were similar except for their capacity rating.

Al Haberer entered his touring car in dirt track racing around Cincinnati, and the Cino car did quite well, winning 32 prizes in 44 starts. The decision to close the factory came as a surprise.

Haberer explained to the press that the Ohio River had flooded the plant in the spring of 1913, inundating the equipment, most of which was ruined.

CLARK 1900-1909 — Edward S. Clark began by building steam boilers in Boston in 1895. This led to experimentation with steam engines, and by the turn of the century, he built a steam car powered by a 20 hp horizontally-opposed steam engine with flash boiler under the hood. This might have been the first car to feature a tilt steering wheel, which also locked the throttle valve "removing the danger of starting the car by unauthorized persons."

Although Clark never bothered to incorporate his business, he went on for several years experimenting with and repairing various vehicles. He built a few 1/2-ton steam-powered vans. Later he built a 3-ton and 5-ton truck, both powered by four-cylinder two-stroke gasoline engines that were mounted under the body. The 5-ton capacity truck weighed 7,200 pounds, had a wheelbase of 144 inches and a price tag of $4,400.

CLARK 1910-1912 — Clark and Company started out in the buggy business in 1865. Albert Clark's son, Frank G. Clark, was an early automobile enthusiast who built the first car body for Ransom Olds in nearby Detroit, Michigan. His father resisted going into the nascent motor car business, so it was not until he died in 1901 that Frank Clark got into the automobile manufacturing field wholeheartedly. This company would eventually be known as the Clark Power Wagon Company.

The first vehicle was a 7 hp one-cylinder runabout, and the Clarkmobile company slogan was "They Go and Go Right." However, by 1905 Clark was the one to go when he sold his business to the New Way Motor Company and teamed up with Claude Furgason who ran a machine shop in Lansing, Michigan. They established the Furgason Motor Company and called the new car the Clark. It was powered by a 20 hp two-cylinder engine, and a 1/2-ton and 3/4-ton express van was offered on a 92-inch wheelbase. Some records also show a 1-ton model. All used planetary transmissions and shaft drive. The Clark vehicles were marketed for two years before Frank Clark moved into the Furgason shop and started the Clark Power Wagon Company in 1911. This venture lasted just over a year before Clark moved to Pontiac, Michigan, where he started the Columbia Motor Truck and Trailer Company, which he headed until his retirement in 1929.

1911 CLARK POWER WAGON   WOM

1914 CLARK 3/4-TON FLARE BOARD WITH STAKES   KP

CLARK 1910-1914 — The A.C. Clark & Company began in Chicago, Illinois, at Grand Crossing. The company was started by another commercial vehicle builder named Albert Clark, this one the founder of the A.C. Clark Carriage Company, which had for years built horsedrawn wagons. In 1910 Clark reincorporated as the Clark Delivery Car Company and built a 3/4-ton delivery van with a 24 hp four-cylinder engine. It had a three-speed transmission, shaft drive and used pneumatic tires. The following year a forward-control design was used to build a 1-ton truck with stake body. By 1914 only the 3/4-ton was produced with 144-inch wheelbase. It was powered by a four-cylinder Continental engine with a three-speed Brown-Lipe transmission and shaft drive.

1925 CLARK 1/2-TON DUMP 3-WHEELER   **HAYS**

CLARK 1919-1929 — This three-wheel gasoline-powered vehicle was built in Chicago, Illinois, for about one decade. This Clark company was not related to the earlier A.C. Clark & Company. *Motor Truck Magazine* announced Clark's "Tructractor" in 1919 and stated that the manufacturer claimed it was the "first specially designed gasoline industrial truck and tractor on the market...replacing hand trucks, wheelbarrows and horsedrawn equipment in factories, foundries, warehouses, construction and contracting industries..."

The rear-mounted four-cylinder engine drove the two front wheels through a dry disc clutch and three-speed selective transmission. A cargo body, dump bed or flat platform were available, and the single rear wheel steered the vehicle whose top speed was 15 mph. Wheelbase was 72 inches and load capacity was 1-1/2 tons. The vehicle weighed 2,050 pounds and was priced at $1,135. Clark faded out in the late 1920s and the stock market crash appears to have led to its final demise.

1992 CLEAN AIR TRANSIT ELECTRIC BUS   **TM**

CLEAN AIR TRANSIT 1991-1994 — Clean Air Transit was located in Santa Barbara, California. In 1991 the company acquired the rights to the Electric Shuttle Vehicle from Bus Manufacturing USA Incorporated and placed the prototypes into service around Santa Barbara. Plans were made to build and sell 100 18-seat shuttles for 1992, but these plans did not materialize.

The shuttle bus was powered by a Nelco DC 216-volt 30-kilowatt front axle drive motor and used a Chloride transistorized armature/field chopper 400-amp controller. Both body and chassis were built from steel and GVW was 14,480 pounds. Battery weight was 4,104 pounds.

Top speed was listed at 40 mph and a maximum range between charges was given as 60 miles. The Clean Air Transit shuttle had both heating and ventilation. Several of these vehicles have been used to date in and around the Santa Barbara downtown waterfront, but manufacturing was suspended in 1994.

1906 CLEMICK-HIRSCH 2-TON OPEN DELIVERY   **RD**

CLEMICK-HIRSCH 1905-1906 — The Clemick-Hirsch Company of Milwaukee, Wisconsin, briefly built 2-ton delivery trucks. They were powered by a 24 hp "double-opposed" cylinder engine and used solid rubber tires. Wheelbase was 102 inches and the vehicle weight was 3,000 pounds. It is unclear how long this company lasted after 1907.

1913 CLEVELAND OPEN EXPRESS   **KP**

CLEVELAND 1913-1914 — This obscure make of 3/4-ton trucks was manufactured by the E.C. Clark Motor Company of Jackson, Michigan. The actual name was derived from the location of the C.D. Paxon Company, the truck builder's marketing agent located in Cleveland, Ohio. The most remarkable feature of the Cleveland truck was its four-cylinder engine with overhead valves that were at a 45 degree angle to the cylinder head, which also carried an overhead camshaft -- notably the first such truck engine design in the United States. The few trucks that were produced used shaft drive and pneumatic tires and were also known as the New Cleveland.

1905 CLIMAX LIGHT COMMERCIAL   **RD**

CLIMAX 1906-1907 — The Hinde & Dauch Paper Company of Sandusky, Ohio, had an idea to create a "convertible" vehicle before the word was associated with "cabriolet." In the case of the Climax it meant using an 80-inch car that could be switched from roadster to touring to delivery body in a matter of minutes. As a delivery vehicle it weighed 1,400 pounds with a 1/2-ton capacity. The vehicle was powered by an 8 hp one-cylinder horizontal engine that was water cooled with the aid of a water pump. The transmission was a two-speed sliding gear type with final drive by single chain to the rear axle. The angle steel frame had semi-elliptic springs. Top speed was 15 mph with either pneumatic tires or artillery wheels and solid rubber tires. Another Climax car was built at about the same time in New Salem, Massachusetts, but it was not a commercial vehicle in any sense. It appears Hinde & Dauch hired the Dunbar Manufacturing Company to build these vehicles.

CLIMBER 1920-1923 — The Climber Motor Corporation started in 1919 by building touring, roadster or sedan passenger cars in Little Rock, Arkansas. These were assembled cars using four- or six-cylinder Herschell-Spillman engines. In 1920 the company also offered a 1-1/2-ton truck using the four-cylinder engine with a three-speed Muncie transmission and Torbensen rear axle. The truck had a wheelbase of 146 inches and was priced at $2,450, about the same price for a five-passenger sedan with the same engine.

It is uncertain about how many trucks were actually built, but it is known that about 100 four-cylinder and 100 six-cylinder cars were built over a period of five years. This was far short of the 3,000 cars planned to be built per year. It would appear that parts shortages were one of the main problems plaguing the company before it went into receivership in 1923. As the New Climber Company, a few more vehicles were assembled from remaining parts on hand before the doors were permanently closed.

1967 CLINE 6X4 OMM

CLINE 1952 to date — The Cline Truck Manufacturing Company was founded in Kansas City, Missouri, by ex-Dart Truck salesman Max W. Cline, who also brought over some expatriates from Dart in 1952. The company started out small and had only one order at first; an assembled truck for a local construction company that already had parts on hand including a new Waukesha diesel engine. Nine crane carriers was the second order, and for 1953 Cline built eight more trucks. The company began expanding rapidly, building 24 trucks in 1954.

The St. Joseph Lead Company ordered two 10-ton underground trucks for mining in 1956. This was to be one of Cline's biggest customers during that period purchasing over $1 million worth of Cline trucks. Although Max Cline died in 1957, his business continued to grow and by 1968 the tally for total production was 501 tandem axle trucks, 91 tandem axle trucks with four-wheel trailers, and 169 two-axle truck tractors. Cline's 6x4 35-ton coal hauler became a stalwart in that industry, and along with drilling rigs, accounted for more than half of the company's truck manufacturing. Other fields in which Cline marketed its products were logging, railroad, slag haulers and miscellaneous trailers.

The Cline 12-ton and 20-ton trucks were powered by four-cylinder and six-cylinder Detroit diesel engines, while the 35-ton 4x2 and 6x4 trucks used Cummins NT-380 diesel engines. The largest 6x6 truck, which was introduced in 1970, had a capacity of 72 tons and was powered by 635 hp Cummins turbocharged diesel V-12 engine. Transmissions were Allison, Clark or Fuller, available from five-speed to nine-speed. Timken-Cline made the hypoid rear axles that used planetary gears at the wheels. Offset cabs, half-cabs and conventional cab designs were all offered. Rear rubber suspension was Cline's own design and manufacture.

The IC-A20R was introduced in 1973. This was a one-man cab, front-drive, articulated, low-bed dump truck with a capacity of 20 tons, which was used in the quarry and road building industry. This truck was powered by a six-cylinder Cummins engine with Clark single-stage torque converter and Rockwell differential with planetary drive.

Cline also built some trucks using Hendrickson cabs, which obviously resembled the former company's highway trucks. Specialty trucks for railroad wheel changing and locomotive and rail car re-railing were built with auxiliary railroad conversion wheels. By 1972 Cline was bought by Isco, but the Cline badge was still used. According to George Thomson, Cline has made no significant changes nor introduced any new trucks models during the 1990s, but it appears the company has stayed in production.

CLINTON 1920-1934 — Clinton Motors Corporation was located in New York City and assembled a few conventional trucks until 1923 when the company bought a factory that had belonged to Schwartz Motors. After the move, eight models were offered in 1925. The 1-1/4-ton Clinton Model 20 with 150-inch wheelbase was priced at $2,070. It was powered by a 22.5 hp Buda WTU engine with Zenith carburetor and Bosch ignition, as was standard on all models with larger engines. Pneumatic tires on 30x5 wheels front and rear were standard on this model only. The 2-ton Model 45 with 163-inch wheelbase cost $2,840. It was powered by a 25.6 hp Buda KTU engine, while the Model 65 with 184-inch wheelbase costing $3,550 was powered by a 28.9 hp Buda ETU engine. These used solid rubber tires on 34x4 wheels front and rear and 34x5 wheels front and rear, respectively, with the larger model using duals in back. Two 4-ton models were offered: the Model 90 and Model 90M which cost $4,260 and $4,400, respectively, both using the 32.4 hp Buda YTU engine. Also, two 5-ton models were available: the Model 120L and Model 120LM, both with 204-inch wheelbase, cost $5,140 and $5,150, respectively. These were powered by a 40 hp Buda BTU engine. The heftiest was the 7-ton Model 120SM with 180-inch wheelbase with a price of $5,250. This truck also used the 40 hp Buda engine but had 36x6 front and 40x7 rear solid tires, as opposed to 36x6 front and 33x7 rear solid rubber tires on the two 5-ton models. All models used Brown-Lipe clutches and transmissions with Timken axles front and rear, and all wheels were by St. Mary's Wheel Company.

From 1925 until 1928 30-passenger and 35-passenger bus chassis were produced. For 1927 a six-cylinder Lycoming engine was first offered, and production hit its peak with 135 trucks for that year. However, once the Depression began truck production was on a special-order basis only before the company closed in 1934.

CLINTON E. WOODS 1901 — The son of a carriagemaker, Clinton E. Woods was an early proponent of electric cars. After working in 1896 for the American Electric Vehicle Company in Chicago, Woods designed his own carriage-based car, which was marketed by the Aluminum Motor Vehicle Company in 1897. The Woods Motor Vehicle Company was organized in 1899 when wealthy capitalists invested in a reorganized manufacturing enterprise. However, by 1901 Woods went on his own again, and the Clinton E. Woods was available in four different models including a Light Stanhope, Brougham Cab, Victoria Stanhope and Delivery. The lightest model sold for $850 while the Delivery was priced at $3,100. In 1902 Woods jumped ship once again in order to become a tire salesman for Penn Rubber Company. Meanwhile, the

Woods Motor Vehicle Company was reorganized in Chicago without its founder, and the company went on to success building electric cars for many years.

CLOUGHLEY 1896-1903 — Robert H. Cloughley was honored automobile patents in 1891 and built his first steam surrey five years later. He was the first to offer a taxi service in Cherryvale, Kansas, and it appears he was the first to build a steam car and to offer motorized taxi service west of the Mississippi. With its stove-pipe stack in the back for smoke exhaust, the Cloughley steamer reflected the inventor's earlier involvement in the railroad industry. Even at 25 cents a head to go anywhere in town there were few customers, perhaps due to the fact that the boiler was directly under the rear seat where it affected the comfort of the passengers.

The Cloughley Automobile Manufacturing Company was organized in 1901. The first customer bought a Cloughley Surrey under the condition the car would climb Serber Hill just outside Cherryvale. It did. The 8 hp two-cylinder steam engine was mounted on Cloughley's own chassis, which featured a ball-bearing compensating gear, solid axles with hollow axles turning on the outside and spring blocks forming a case for driving boxes on roller bearings. Cloughley also built his surrey using a gasoline engine that sold for $1,500 in 1903, the last year of production.

CLUB 1911-19123 — The Club Car Company of America was a unique organization started by bankers in New York City. Membership meant ownership of a car, taxi or 3-ton truck, thus avoiding the costs associated with marketing, sales, advertising, racing, et cetera. Merchant and Evans of Philadelphia, Pennsylvania, were the actual manufacturers with engines supplied by American and British Manufacturing of Bridgeport, Connecticut, and coachwork by Biddle and Smart of Amesbury, Massachusetts.

The luxurious passenger cars ranged from the $2,800 runabout to the $3,750 limousine. The taxi was powered by a 16 hp American and British Motor, while all the rest, including the forward-control truck, were powered by a 40 hp four-cylinder engine with a three-speed transmission. Few if any memberships were sold, and Merchant and Evans sold off the remaining vehicles as Devons.

CLUB CAR 1985 to date — Located in Augusta, Georgia, Club Car, Incorporated has been a manufacturer of light commercial and industrial vehicles, having developed a model line in 1985 after many years of building golf carts. According to a company representative Club Car was a spin-off from E-Z-Go, which has also been located in Augusta. The Club Car lineup has consisted of the Carryall I Flatbed/Pickup, Carryall II Flatbed/Pickup, Carryall II Plus, Carryall VI, Carryall VI XL, Trans-Porter, Trans-Sender, Tourall and Resort Villager XL.

1996 CLUB CAR CARRYALL   **CLUB CAR**

The Carryall I and Carryall II Flatbed and Pickup have been powered by a 9 hp four-cycle 286-cubic centimeter air-cooled engine or by a 48-volt DC series-wound electric motor. Suspension has been accomplished with front and rear leaf springs and dual shock absorbers. The Carryall II has been fitted with an anti-sway bar. The Carryall II Plus has had only the gasoline engine option using an 11 hp four-cycle

351-cubic centimeter air-cooled engine, and this powerplant has also been available with the Carryall VI and Carryall VI XL along with the 3.1 hp 48-volt series-wound DC electric motor.

Van box, enclosed cab, hydraulic dump mechanism, tailgate ramp, stake-side kit, canopy and tool boxes have been some of the options available with most of the models listed. Commercial applications for the Club Car vehicles have included personnel carriers at resorts, stadiums, hotels, airports and amusement parks, security patrol, laundry vans, parking lot courtesy vehicles, groundskeeping, warehouse and construction site transporter and food vending. Trailers and a portable refreshment center have also been listed as optional equipment.

1920 CLYDESDALE HIGHWAY EXPRESS   **GOODYEAR**

CLYDESDALE 1916-1938 — Clyde, Ohio, was the location of the Clyde Cars Company (later the Clyde Motor Truck Company), which assembled conventional trucks in a range from 3/4-ton to 6-ton. They were advertised as having been "Tested in the Crucible of War -- and Found Fit." The heavier trucks featured deep, tapered, pressed-frame siderails. Early Clydesdale trucks used a governor called the Krebs Patented Automatic Controller, and the radiator was patterned after the London Omnibus. Suspension was with chrome vanadium springs with pins operating in bronze bushings. In 1920 Clydesdale offered pyramidal headlights with an octagonal front mounted at the sides of the radiator.

By the mid 1920s the Model 10 and Model 10A, both rated at 1-1/4-ton with 138-inch wheelbase, were powered by a 22.5 hp Continental N motor. The 2-1/2-ton Model 8 with 156-inch wheelbase was powered by a 27.2 hp Continental K-4 engine, while the 3-1/2-ton Model 6 with 163-inch wheelbase was powered by 32.4 hp Continental L-4 engine. The 5-ton Model 4 with 177-inch wheelbase was powered by a 36.1 hp Continental B-5 engine, which was also used in the 6-ton Model 2 with 176-inch wheelbase. Every model used the Zenith carburetor and Bosch ignition combination, as well as four-speed Brown-Lipe transmission and Timken front and rear axles. The lightest model used 34x5 front and rear pneumatic tires as standard equipment. Only 36-inch solid rubber tires were standard on all the other models with duals on the Model 6 and Model 4. The Model 2 had 40-inch duals.

Between 1925 and 1930 six-cylinder engines were available. During the Depression, manufacturing came to a near-standstill with only one or two trucks possibly going for export. In 1936 production commenced again with a new line of trucks powered by Buda and early Hercules diesel engines with vehicle capacities from 1-ton to 7-ton. All types were available including 15-ton truck tractors, conventional, short conventional, cab-over-engine with 4x4 and 6x6 trucks for off road work. The 6x6 was powered by a 779-cubic inch Hercules diesel engine, and some were purchased by the U.S. Army.

Despite a production number of less than 200 per year of all the various models available combined, Clydesdale offered a line of light trucks in 1937 that were powered by Waukesha-Hesselman diesel engines. For that year Clydesdale listed eight models, six with optional diesel-powered engines. The 1-1/2-ton Model 34-D with 140-inch to 180-inch wheelbase was powered by a 55 hp Buda 4LD196 engine, used Clark front and rear axles and was priced at $2,795. The 2-ton Model 40-D, with the same wheelbase as the Model 34-D, was powered by a 77 hp Hercules engine, used a Brown-Lipe 2341 transmission, Timken front and rear axles and was priced at $2,945. The 2-1/2-ton Model 70D had essentially the same specs, but Models 75D, 80D and 90D, which ranged in capacity from 3-ton to 6-ton, were each powered by a Buda 6LD engine of increasing size and used Clark transmissions and Timken front and rear axles. Prices were $4,265,

$5,560 and $5,885, respectively. The two heaviest models were the 7-ton Model 105D and the 10-ton Model 125D both with 145-inch to 220-inch wheelbase options and using a Fuller 5A620 transmission, Timken front axle and Wisconsin rear axle. Chassis prices were $6,850 and $8,925, respectively.

1954 COACHETTE   MBS

COACHETTE 1954-1968 — The Coachette Company of Dallas, Texas, was founded by Carl Graham who was a former salesman for Ford and later Marmon-Herrington buses. Graham decided to build his own buses, and the first design was a 21-passenger city transit bus on a 172-inch wheelbase Ford truck chassis. The Ward Body Company was the firm responsible for sheet metal on nearly all the Coachettes. A square design of the front was adopted in 1958. Also, GMC and Chevrolet chassis were available. By the mid 1960s the largest Coachette was a 37-passenger bus with optional air conditioning and sliding windows. Total production number was 330 including all models.

COAST 1958-1974 — Before being acquired by Howe in 1974 this company primarily built fire equipment on commercial chassis as Coast Apparatus Incorporated in Martinez, California. A few standard-design and forward-control-type custom chassis were built with Hall-Scott engines and International cabs.

COATES-GOSHEN see TRI-CAR

COEY 1902; 1916 — Charles A. Coey had a few unusual ideas for his motor car business located in Chicago, Illinois. First was his design of a one-cylinder two-cycle engine that had a water jacket that weighed 225 pounds. His cars carried a five-year guarantee "against imperfect workmanship and poor material." In terms of commercial applications Coey was probably the first "rental car" business in the United States at that time, which he called an "automobile livery and repository." He was also one of the first to organize a driving school, charging $10 to teach someone the nuances of negotiating the road. Eventually, his cars were powered by 24 hp four-cylinder or 48 hp six-cylinder engines, and Coey enjoyed some success in racing before his company was acquired by the Wonder Motor Truck Company in 1916.

1914 COLEMAN MODEL B   KP

COLEMAN 1910-1915 — Coleman trucks and vans were built by the F. Coleman Carriage and Harness Company of Ilion, New York. The first two models were the A-1 and A-2, both powered by 20 hp two-cylinder air-cooled engines and were identical except for the open body of the former and closed van body of the latter. Planetary transmissions were used with double chain drive to the rear wheels. In 1912 the company changed names to the Coleman Motor Truck Company of Ilion. The 1,200-pound capacity trucks were superseded by the 1-ton Model B and the 2-ton Model C, with 107-inch and 117-inch wheelbase, respectively, both of which were powered by four-cylinder water-cooled engines.

COLEMAN 1925-1986 — Coleman Motors Corporation was started by G.L. Coleman in 1923 in Omaha, Nebraska, but production did not begin until two years later when the company moved to Littleton, Colorado, where it became the American Coleman Company. Harley Holmes was the company's design engineer who had invented a durable gear-type steerable axle for four-wheel-drive application.

1948 COLEMAN 4X4   LA

Load carriers and truck tractors in the 4x4 and 6x6 configuration, powered by four-cylinder Buda engines, comprised the first model line from Coleman. These were primarily bought by State Highway Departments for off road highway construction and maintenance, but some were used as fire trucks, log haulers and snow plows -- virtually all of them in Colorado.

The U.S. Army tested a Coleman truck tractor and placed orders for both 4x4 and 6x6 units. Also, fire engines were offered, which could use water both from pressurized hydrants as well as reservoirs, capable of pumping 80 feet into the air.

A 7-1/2-ton 6x6 truck was offered in 1928 for the logging and oil industries. It was powered by a six-cylinder Buda GL engine and a four-speed Fuller with a two-speed Coleman auxiliary transmission giving eight forward speeds. This type of truck was also used in early applications for aircraft refueling. In 1930 and 1931 Coleman entered front-wheel-drive Miller-powered race cars in the Indianapolis 500. These cars were driven by Joe, Louis and Jerry Unser.

In 1936 the company had eight models from 2-ton to 10-ton capacity, all powered by Buda engines. The only exception was the Model E-57 7-3/4-ton, which used a Sterling engine. Buda and Cummins diesel engines were offered in 1938. By 1941 only one 6-ton model was available. Coleman produced crane carriers for the Army Corps of Engineers during World War II, although some of the 4x4 Coleman trucks were fitted with Quick-Way shovels for construction.

After the war Coleman resumed building 4x4 trucks; however, a fractious labor dispute and strike kept the Coleman factory closed for most of 1949 and 1950. During this time the company lost its dealer network, 350 skilled employees as well as numerous customers. This downfall was overcome in 1952 when Coleman obtained a $9-1/2 million contract from the U.S. Air Force to build Mule towing tractors. These trucks featured six-cylinder Buda engines, four-wheel-drive, four-wheel-steering and twin Ford cabs, one at each end of the vehicle.

After 1954 Coleman concentrated on building all-wheel-drive conversion units for standard trucks. Large steerable axles were built for O.E.M. customers starting in 1961. The Space Star, a forward-control truck tractor with four-wheel-drive and four-wheel-steering, was introduced in 1968. In this design a semi-trailer was rigidly attached to the highway tractor allowing a second trailer to be pulled. The Space Star was powered by a 318 hp Detroit Diesel 8V-71N engine and was tested at speeds up to 80 mph. Other features included roll-bar construction in the cab, as well as adjustable air suspension allowing eight inches of vertical travel to match different loading dock heights. Nevertheless, the Space Star did not make it past the prototype stage. Coleman faded out during the early 1980s.

1918 COLLIER 1-TON MODEL 18　　　　　　　**OCW**

COLLIER 1917-1922 — A standard passenger car design was the basis for the Collier trucks even though the company did not actually produce any passenger cars. The Collier Company was located in Cleveland, Ohio, before moving to Bellevue, Ohio, and becoming the Collier Motor Truck Company. Only 1/2-ton trucks and vans were built at first before the company offered heavier constructed 1-ton and 1-1/2-ton trucks powered by four-cylinder Continental engines and worm-drive. In 1920 the model range also included a 2-ton truck with 152-inch wheelbase, which was also powered by a four-cylinder Continental engine using a four-speed Fuller transmission with Selden worm-drive. This truck sold for $3,200.

In 1922 a 2-1/2-ton truck model line was offered using essentially the same drivetrain as the 1-ton versions. During the postwar economic downturn the company ceased operations.

COLLINS 1900 — As manager of the Scranton Electric Works in Scranton, Pennsylvania, Patrick J. Collins had an inspiration to build electric vehicles. He embarked on such a project in 1900 and built a 1-ton delivery wagon that was both powered as well as steered by electric motors. He formed the Collins Electric Vehicle Company and announced to the press that he intended to start production. This did not happen and the 1-ton delivery was the only vehicle Collins built, choosing to remain instead with the Scranton Electric Works which specialized in armature windings and x-ray supplies.

1899 COLUMBIA MARK XVII ELECTRIC CAB　　　　　**CP**

COLUMBIA 1899-1907 — The history of the Columbia Automobile Company is as convoluted as it is relevant to the whole automobile industry that existed in the first decade of the century. The enterprise was started by Colonel Albert Pope who was building "Columbia" bicycles in the 1890s. Intrigued by developments in motorized vehicles, Pope decided to expand his business into that field, and with the managerial help of Hiram Percy Maxim, the company built 500 electric- and 40 gasoline-powered carriages between 1897 and 1899.

At the same time William Collins Whitney bought Isaac Rice's Electric Vehicle Company and negotiated with Pope to form a merger called the Columbia Automobile Company of Hartford, Connecticut, also forming the Electric Vehicle firm as a holding company for the taxicab fleet subsidiaries to be established in numerous cities. In 1900 the entire enterprise was named the Columbia and Electric Vehicle Company of Hartford. By this time the company had acquired the Selden patent on all gasoline-powered vehicles in the United States and decided that enforcing the patent would be a lucrative undertaking in the automotive business. It was, but only briefly. Most auto manufacturers agreed to pay the royalty to Columbia rather than engage in costly and time-consuming litigation. Henry Ford refused to pay the royalty and the lawsuit that took years to resolve in Ford's favor merely accelerated Columbia's ultimate demise in 1913, after having been absorbed by United States Motors in 1910.

1904 COLUMBIA MARK LIII 5-TON　　　　　　　**CP**

1906 COLUMBIA 6-TON 4X4　　　　　　　**NAHC**

During the years of production about 2,000 Columbia electric cabs were built. The first models were based on the earlier Morris and Salom Electrobat cabs, which were quite successful in New York City. The driver of the early Columbia cab was still in the hansom position, but the pneumatic tires were equal size with front-wheel-steering and rear-wheel-drive. These and modernized versions were successfully used in New York and Boston until 1908.

At the same time Columbia was also building heavy electric vans and trucks up to 5-ton capacity. Lighter trucks used a single electric motor while the heavier trucks used two motors connected to the rear wheels with double reduction gears and double chain drive. Batteries were 44-cell Exides giving an approximate range of 25 miles at 6 mph. Power-assisted steering was used on the largest models. Along with 10,000 other make electric trucks by 1907, Columbia trucks totaled 8,000 at a time when gasoline-powered vehicles were outnumbered, especially in the heavier commercial vehicle industry.

In 1903 Columbia offered many models of passenger cars as well as a Surrey for $1,500, Special Service Wagon for $2,000, Hansom Cab for $3,500, Opera Bus for $2,000, Ambulance for $3,500, Police Patrol for $3,500 and two delivery wagons for $1,800 and $2,250, respectively. The company also made 6-passenger and 15-passenger hotel buses, an 11-passenger depot wagon, as well as observation buses for sightseeing, and at least one of the latter was brought over to London, England. After 1907 Columbia discontinued heavy electric vehicle manufacturing and focused on both gasoline and electric passenger car production until 1913 when the Columbia Knight was its last effort in the automotive business.

COLUMBIA 1916-1926 — This company located in Pontiac, Michigan, was not affiliated with the former Columbia vehicle company, nor was it affiliated with any of the other 10 companies that used the same name up to 1926. This Columbia, formerly the Kalamazoo, started out as a 2-ton model in 1917 and a 1-ton model was added by the following year. Both were powered by four-cylinder Buda engines with three-speed Covert transmissions and Russell internal-gear rear axles. Continental engines were adopted for 1918, and a 6-ton truck tractor was offered. The following year three models were offered: 1-1/2-, 2-1/2- and 3-ton. In the last few years Hinkley engines were used.

For 1924 and 1925 the 1-1/2-ton Model H with 140-inch wheelbase sold for $2,175. It was powered by a 22.5 hp Hinkley 300 engine with Stromberg carburetor and Bosch ignition coupled through a Detlaff clutch to a Detroit Gear transmission. Solid rubber tires 34x4 front and 34x6 rear rode on St. Mary's wheels. The 2-1/2-ton Model G with 148-inch wheelbase priced at $2,850 used a 25.6 hp Hinkley 400 engine. The 3-ton Model K with 150-inch wheelbase was priced at $4,850 and used a 28.9 hp Hinkley 500 engine. The heaviest truck used 36x5 front and 36x12 rear solid rubber tires on Van wheels. Production stopped with the 1925 model year, although a few vehicles were sold in 1926.

COLUMBIA CARRIAGE 1915 — The Columbia Carriage & Auto Company was located in Portland, Oregon. The company offered a 1-ton truck that could also be used as a station bus to carry 11 passengers. The vehicle had pneumatic tires and was priced at $1,400.

1903 COLUMBUS   RD

COLUMBUS 1902-1903 — The Columbus Motor Truck and Vehicle Company located in Columbus, Ohio, built a stake bed truck powered by a 12 hp one-cylinder engine late in 1902. Wheelbase was 90-inch and with the stake bed the entire vehicle weighed 3,800 pounds. Tires were solid rubber 33x3-1/2 front and 37x3-1/2 rear. The vehicle used an "expansible pulley" transmission allowing for speeds from 1-1/2 to 15 mph. Final drive was by the usual chain on each side. Both a water pump and gasoline pump were incorporated in this early design. It is not clear how long this company stayed in business.

1914 COMET   KP

COMET 1914 — The Comet Cyclecar Company built a pilot run of 25 Comets. Each had a 100-inch wheelbase and 36-inch track and used a 10 hp two-cylinder air-cooled engine, planetary transmission with final drive by belts to the rear wheels. A few of the 25 units were offered with an attached delivery box constituting the Comet as a commercial vehicle, albeit a very light one. It sold for $450 as the Delivery and $500 as the Tandem Roadster. Advertising asked, "Have you seen the Comet? Not a luminous celestial body..."

The front fenders were attached to the axles turning with the wheels as on a motorcycle. The Comet was designed by Fred B. Mertz and financed by the Parry brothers, one of whom designed the Parry automobile, which lasted a year longer than the Comet. The firm had begun as the Economy Cyclecar Company in Indianapolis, Indiana, but it was quickly changed to Comet when it was discovered another company already existed on the East Coast with that name. It appears that production never went beyond the first set of test vehicles.

COMET 1920-1921 — Comet cars, trucks and tractors built in Decatur, Illinois, came into existence in a rather roundabout way. George W. Jagers was a costing clerk for the J.I. Case Threshing Machine Company when he gained control of the Racine Manufacturing Company, which was located in Racine, Wisconsin, where he had been born. Racine Manufacturing was a maker of toys and novelty items, but Jagers intended to launch his business into the automotive field. He opened offices in Rockford and Chicago and had a dozen prototype Comet cars assembled. After a favorable response at the Chicago Automobile Show in 1917, production began in Decatur. Besides the Comet 6, which had a 125-inch wheelbase and was powered by a 50 hp six-cylinder engine, the company also assembled a conventional 1-1/2-ton truck that used a four-cylinder Lycoming engine and a Wisconsin worm-drive rear axle.

Once the company received an order for 40 cars from Antwerp, Belgium, in 1920, Jagers fell victim to his own excessive enthusiasm when he immediately started the construction of a large, expensive factory capable of 200-car-per-day production capacity. Following the failure of its bond issue in the economically dim year of 1920, the company went into receivership. A smaller four-cylinder car was offered and attempts were made to relocate to Racine. In 1922 there were no bidders when the company was offered on the block, and after Comet was liquidated in 1923, eight former officers were indicted for mail fraud in regard to earlier stock selling operations. Not all of them were cleared of the charges.

COMMERCE 1907-1908 — The American Machine Manufacturing Company of Detroit began in the motor vehicle business in 1906 as a fabricator of parts as well as engines. With David Blumenthal as president and Charles C. Simons as vice-president, the company hired Paul Arthur to design vehicles primarily for commercial use. One model was a passenger car that could be converted into a delivery truck or hotel jitney. The first Commerce truck was a forward control 2-1/2-ton model with 109-inch wheelbase powered by a 30 hp four-cylinder engine. Final drive was with double chain, and this design was used on 1908 3-ton and 5-ton models. The final product line included the Model A with 111-inch wheelbase and a 35 hp four-cylinder engine. The 5-ton Model C had a wheelbase of 130 inches and weighed 8,400 pounds.

1911 COMMERCE NAHC

COMMERCE 1911-1932 — The Commerce Motor Car Company began building trucks in Detroit, Michigan, in 1911. A 1/2-ton panel delivery was the first model offered. It was powered by a 16.9 hp four-cylinder L-head engine with single final chain drive, and it featured right-hand steering. For 1913 the steering was placed on the left side and the following year the Commerce truck was powered by a Northway engine. Between 1911 and 1913 800 Commerce trucks were produced. Also in 1914, capacity was increased to 3/4-ton, with a 1-ton model appearing in 1917. The 3/4-ton and 1-ton were powered by the same engine, but were differentiated in that the heavier truck used internal gear drive as opposed to the lighter truck having bevel drive.

In 1922 Continental engines were introduced in models from 3/4-ton to 2-1/2-ton. The $2,350 10-passenger "charabanc," later perhaps known better as the airport limousine, was built by Commerce at this time. It was advertised as "the wonder of motordom" and "could travel at 40 mph easily."

1919 COMMERCE 1-1/4-TON MODEL T HAYS

By 1924 pressurized lubrication and worm-drive was standard equipment on all models. The following year the company expanded the model line with a choice of four bus chassis from 18-passenger to 28-passenger, a funeral coach, special "powermatic" lumber truck, dump truck and oil truck. The 1-ton Model 11 with 127-inch wheelbase was powered by a 22.5 hp four-cylinder Continental N engine with Zenith carburetor and Bosch ignition. Clutch and transmission were made by Fuller while front and rear axles were made by Salisbury. Smith wheels carried 34x5 front and rear solid rubber tires. The 1-1/4-ton Commerce Super 11 had a 142-inch wheelbase but used a 28.9 hp Continental S4 engine. The 1-1/2-ton Model 14B with 146-inch wheelbase used a 22.5 hp Continental J4 engine, and on this and two heavier models the clutch and transmission were made by Brown-Lipe while the axles front and rear were built by Timken.

Commerce also offered two 2-1/2-ton models in 1925, which were known as the Model 25B and Model 25D with 156-inch wheelbase and 198-inch wheelbase, respectively. The Model 25B was powered by a 27.2 hp Continental K-4 engine while the Model 25D was powered by a 33.7 hp Continental 6B engine. Also, the Model 25B was optional with 36x6 front and 40x8 rear pneumatic tires while the Model 25D was fitted with solid tires of the same size.

In 1926 Commerce changed model specifications and general styling using six-cylinder Continental engines and three-speed transmissions instead of the previous four-speed. A semi-floating spiral bevel rear axle design was also adopted. In 1927 Relay Motors of Wabash, Indiana, bought Commerce and moved the plant into the Service Motors factory that it had also purchased. Later manufacturing was again transferred to the Garford Truck Company plant in Lima, Ohio.

Under Relay control, Commerce Trucks were redesigned once again, this time by Relay engineers who preferred worm-drive. This was basically the same design as the Relay trucks of that year. Relay trucks were available in eight models from 1-ton to 4-ton capacity, all powered by six-cylinder Buda engines and using four-wheel hydraulic brakes. At this time Relay was what would later be called "badge engineered," identical to Commerce, Garford and Service trucks, which had their own emblems. Of these nameplates Commerce sold the fewest in 1928 with a total of 65 trucks produced. The following year that number fell to 16. When the Depression hit, both Commerce and Service truck production was suspended while Garford and Relay continued, but not for much longer.

COMMERCIAL 1903 — A brief venture into the commercial vehicle manufacturing business resulted in the Commercial Motor Company of Jersey City, New Jersey. Once this company absorbed the Pan-American Company, there is indication that Commercial built a few kerosene-burning steam delivery wagons.

COMMERCIAL 1906-1912 — The Commercial Motor Car Company of New York City produced 1-, 2-, 3- and 5-ton capacity trucks during a seven year production run. All models used four-cylinder engines with gear reduction and final chain drive as well as solid rubber tires. The later 3-ton and 4-ton models were forward-control design and were powered by 40 hp engines. This company should not be confused with the Commercial Motor Car Company of Jersey City, New Jersey, which built a single prototype truck in 1903 before going out of business.

COMMERCIAL 1911-1912 — In 1911 Newark, New Jersey, became the home of the new Commercial Truck Companies of America, which built a 1-1/2-ton forward-control model in 1911 powered by a four-cylinder four-stroke engine with a three-speed transmission and shaft drive. Pneumatic or solid tires were available and the closed delivery van version was priced at $2,450 in 1912, the last year of production. Late in 1911 the company's name changed to Commercial Motor Truck Construction Company, still located in Newark.

COMMERCIAL MOTOR VEHICLE see QUADRAY

COMPOUND 1906 — After designing an experimental automobile in San Francisco in 1896, John W. Eisenhuth moved to Newark, New Jersey, to manufacture the car. During the time he experimented in a Newark machine shop he met D.F. Graham, who had developed the Graham-Fox compound engine. Some of its design principles came from steam engines in that it had two ignited cylinders whose exhaust gases operated the large unignited center cylinder that was seven inches in diameter. This saved some power and reduced muffler noise. The prototype was shown at Madison Square Garden in 1903 as the Graham-Fox, but it went into production as the Compound built by the Eisenhuth Horseless Vehicle Company of Middleton, Connecticut, where Eisenhuth had taken over the Keating Automobile Company in 1901. Because of charges of grand larceny and blackmail, Eisenhuth was arrested on two occasions before matters were settled.

The Model Nine Delivery Van with 98-1/2-inch wheelbase powered by the Compound engine and a three-speed transmission was the only commercial vehicle Eisenhuth offered, which was priced at $1,400. The company's name was changed to the Eagle Motor Car Company somewhere along the line, as Eisenhuth's name was perhaps a detraction after his legal problems. Compound cars were built from 1904 to 1908 while it appears the delivery van was built only in 1906. Later Eisenhuth went on to develop another car called the Poppy.

1924 CONCORD 3-TON MODEL B   **HAYS**

CONCORD 1916-1933 — These 1-ton and 2-ton trucks were at first known as Abbot-Downing, which was the name of the manufacturer located in Concord, New Hampshire. After the first year of production the trucks were renamed Concord. They used Buda engines and Timken-David Brown rear axles. A 3-ton model was also added to the line. By 1924 the 1-ton Model E with 135-inch wheelbase was powered by a 25.6 hp Buda GBU engine with Zenith carburetor and Eisemann ignition coupled through a Brown-Lipe clutch to a Brown-Lipe transmission. Timken front and rear axles were used with Ross steering and Archibald wheels carrying 34x5 front and 36x6 rear pneumatic tires as standard. Its price tag was $2,500.

In the 2-ton range Concord offered the Model G with 140-inch wheelbase and the Model H with 150-inch wheelbase. The former was powered by a 25.6 hp Buda GBU engine while the latter used a 28.9 hp Buda EBU engine. The Model G cost $3,250 while the Model H was $3,700. These trucks used 36x4 front and rear tires with pneumatics at extra cost. The 3-ton Model JL with 170-inch wheelbase also used the Buda EBU engine and was listed at $3,600. All other component manufacturers were the same as the 1-ton Model E truck.

CONDOR 1932-1941 — Condor Motors Incorporated of Chicago, Illinois, originally built Gramm trucks, which were renamed Condor in 1933, and these were marketed for export by a subsidiary in Chicago. However, from 1934 the specifications for the Condor and the Gramm diverged considerably when Waukesha-Hesselman engines were adopted for the Condor in place of the Hercules and Cummins engines used in the Gramm trucks. The Waukesha-Hesselman engine was designed to burn light oil and was fitted with spark plugs and an ignition system for use in export areas where fuel was low grade. Most Condor trucks had these special application engines, which were designed to be more tolerant of poor grade fuel than standard diesel engines, although gasoline engines were also offered.

Condor trucks sold in 30 different countries including China where they were sold by Mark L. Moody Inc. of Shanghai. In Belgium and Holland they were fitted with custom European cabs built locally in those countries. They were also sold in Greece, Portugal, Spain and Turkey.

For 1937 Condor listed seven models. The 1-1/2- to 2-1/2-ton Model ACW, the 2- to 3-1/2-ton Model BCW and the 2-1/2- to 4-ton Model CCW were each powered by a 41 hp four-cylinder Waukesha-Hesselman engine and used the Warner T9 transmission. Either Clark or Timken axles were incorporated in the design. The 2- to 3-1/2-ton Model FCW, the 3- to 4-1/2-ton Model GCW,

the 3-1/2- to 5-ton Model CDW and 4- to 5-1/2-ton Model CEW were each powered by a 75 hp six-cylinder Waukesha-Hesselman engine and used Clark transmissions, as well as Timken axles front and rear, with the exception of Model FCW that had a Clark front axle. Chassis prices were $1,565, $1,635, $1,850, $2,160, $2,525, $2,955 and $3,175, respectively. Wheelbases were listed as 136-inch to 220-inch for all models.

The last model year was 1939/1940 when Condor trucks, like the Gramms, used Willys half-ton pickup cabs with long factory-made hoods to house the Buda Lanova diesel engines. Export markets dried up during World War II, which contributed to the company's demise.

CONESTOGA 1917-1920 — The Conestoga Motor Truck was located in Lancaster, Pennsylvania, long enough to produce 700 trucks over almost four years. For 1918 the company offered 1,200-pound capacity and 1-1/2-ton capacity models, both powered by the four-cylinder Light engine. The following year 1-ton and 2-ton models were offered with four-cylinder Continental engines. The "Victory" emblem belonged to Conestoga on 3/4-ton trucks in 1919 when World War I ended. All models used worm gear drive at the rear axle. The Connersville Buggy Company has also been listed as having built a truck by the name of Conestoga. It was a 1,250-pound capacity electric truck.

CONNERSVILLE 1914 — In the era of the cyclecar's popularity, the Connersville Buggy Company built a 1,250-pound prototype electric delivery vehicle in 1914. Howard Van Auken organized the plant to build the electric van model for less than one year. This company should not be confused with the Connersville Motor Company, which was a developmental company for John McFarlan and Sons who went into business in 1909 building McFarlan automobiles.

CONSOLIDATED see MOYEA

CONTINENTAL 1912-1918 — The first commercial vehicle built by the Continental Truck Manufacturing Company was the forward-control 1-1/2-ton Model AE, which was powered by a four-cylinder engine and used a three-speed transmission with double chain final drive. The company was located in Superior, Wisconsin. In 1914 the design was changed to a conventional type with the engine under the hood. It was also the year the company produced a 1-ton model. The following year a 1-1/2-ton and 3-ton were built with a choice of worm- or chain-drive. By the last year of production Continental trucks were available as 1-, 1-1/2-, 2- and 3-1/2-ton, each with worm-drive to the rear axle.

CONTINENTAL 1915-1917 — The Continental Motor Truck Company got its start in Chicago, Illinois, as the Continental Motor Car Company, which produced a single model roadster with a distinctive circular "barrel" hood and a guarantee of 26 mpg using a two-cylinder optional air-cooled or water-cooled engine. However, this venture did not last beyond 1908, and it appears the company was reorganized as a commercial vehicle manufacturer that built 1-, 1-1/2-, 2- and 3-1/2-ton trucks each powered by a four-cylinder engine with a three-speed transmission and worm gear final drive. It went out of business in 1917.

COOK 1905-1906 — The story of the Cook Auto-Sled (also Auto-Sledge) is fascinating even if marginally related to the commercial vehicle industry. It is probably the first "snow-mobile" ever built before such a term was adopted for motorized vehicles designed for traveling entirely on snow and ice.

In many books and encyclopedias Admiral Robert E. Perry is cited as the first man to reach the North Pole in 1909. However, many scholars, including a society named after the explorer, believed that it was Dr. Frederick A. Cook who got there first in 1908. His brother Theodore Cook built an auto-sled called the Calicoon in 1906/1907, which Frederick Cook considered taking on his polar expedition. It was powered by an air-cooled engine and tested in the Catskill Mountains in 1906. Frederick Cook considered it too heavy for the icy arctic crust and set out on a dog-drawn sled instead. Following his return in 1908 and after the controversy erupted, Frederick Cook retired from polar exploration. An unconfirmed report stated Theodore Cook built three 24 hp auto-sleds for F.R. Burch in 1906. It is known that he built dog-drawn sleds for other polar explorers such as Roald Amundsen, who first discovered the South Pole in 1911 and whose claim has not been challenged.

COOK 1905-1906 — The Cook Locomotive Works of Paterson, New Jersey, built a steam truck powered by a 24 (boiler) hp engine. The underslung chassis featured an enclosed cab, and the steel tires rode on wooden spoke wheels. Rear brakes made contact directly to the steel shod wheel rims, as on railway trains. Five of these enormous trucks were built; however, according to records, due to severe reliability problems all of the vehicles went out of service within a year after manufacture.

1920 COOK 1-TON   RD

COOK 1920-1923 — The Cook Motors Corporation was organized in 1920 in Kankakee, Illinois. The Cook truck featured a telescoping frame that could be extended incrementally from 96 inches to 184 inches. It was powered by a 25.6 four-cylinder Hercules CU-3 engine with Stromberg carburetor. Provisions were made to extend the driveshaft and brake linkage, and a tracking trailer was also built using the telescoping design. The truck used a Borg & Beck clutch, Cotta transmission, Lavine steering gear, Shuler I-beam front axle and Kennedy internal gear rear axle. Front and rear springs were semi-elliptic and wood spoke wheels carried 36x6 front and 38x7 rear Firestone Giant Cord pneumatic tires. Standard equipment included side and taillights, jack, tool kit and "explosion whistle." A 20-gallon gasoline tank was mounted under the driver's seat. Price was $3,000. Apparently the telescoping idea was not well accepted (even though it might have some structural integrity) and Cook did not stay in business long.

1942 COOK   BILL POWK

COOK 1942-1964 — The Cook Brothers Equipment Company was located in Los Angeles, California, and was founded some time during World War II. Much of the information about the company's work during that time was classified. However, it is known that the company built experimental trucks during the war, such as the double-bogie vehicle for the Army Desert Training Center in Indio. The truck featured steel pipe roof framework and a flat narrow body with cutouts for the pivoting chain-driven front bogie. The engine was mounted in the rear.

At the end of World War II the Cook brothers built experimental 8x8 army trucks and tractors. Subsequently, six-wheel attachments and chain drive tandems were also produced. Once the company was established as a business entity, the Cook Brothers company began building trucks for the construction industry. A combination of Reo parts and modified sheet metal along with Cummins diesel or Ford V-8 engines were employed in the manufacture under California maximum payload restrictions.

Throughout the 1950s the company focused on special chassis for crane carriers, cement mixers along with bulk-haul beds for brick, gravel and sand transport. A limited number of articulated bottom-dump earth haulers with offset cabs for road construction were also produced during this time. Crane carriers and cement mixers also used offset cabs, and these trucks were available with Reo and Cummins engines that ran on diesel, gasoline or propane. Single reduction, double reduction and chain drive tandem rear axles were available.

In 1958 the company was acquired by Challenge Manufacturing, which built cement mixers. Cook chassis continued to be offered with Challenge equipment, but these gradually became phased out as other chassis were utilized for that purpose. Cook was the last truck manufacturer to use chain drive, which was employed as late as the early 1960s. Challenge stopped building trucks under the Cook name in 1964 with a possible exception of a few custom trucks that have not been documented.

COOLEY STEAM   See GROUT or MOBILE

1908 COPPOCK 1-TON   RD

COPPOCK 1906-1909 — The Coppock Motor Car Company was a predecessor of the Decatur Motor Car Company. In 1907 the Coppock company was located in Marion, Indiana, and produced its 87-inch wheelbase Model A 1-ton truck with forward-control and stake bed. The truck had solid rubber tires and a vertical steering column in an open cab. It was powered by a two-cylinder two-cycle engine that utilized the three-port design and used copper water jackets. A three-speed progressive transmission was employed, which was coupled through a bronze internal-expanding clutch. The bronze friction shoes were 10 inches in diameter with a 2-1/2-inch face, eight percent of which comprised cork inserts. At the end of 1907 the enterprise moved to Decatur, Indiana, before it was reorganized in 1909 when the city's name was adopted for its cars and light commercial vehicles.

CORBIN 1902-1905 — Philip Corbin was a horseless carriage enthusiast with one major advantage over many others -- his family had established the Corbin Screw Company and the Corbin Cabinet Lock Company, divisions of American Hardware. This allowed Corbin and his Corbin Motor Vehicle Company, which was also a wholly owned subsidiary of American Hardware, to experiment with motorized vehicles and set up production without too much concern about the balance sheets.

The first vehicle was built for the Russel & Erwin Company, another hardware firm in New Britain, Connecticut. It had a 96-inch wheelbase and was rated at 3/4-ton capacity. This first commercial vehicle Corbin built was a 3/4-ton truck powered by an 8 hp one-cylinder air-cooled horizontal engine positioned under the floorboards. It had a two-speed transmission, single chain drive and was advertised as capable of either 3 or 10 mph.

Corbin's early models featured metal brake shoes, first in an American production car, though later discontinued. Corbin produced both air-cooled and water-cooled engines for his cars, which included limousines used commercially. These used 32 hp four-cylinder engines and had a wheelbase of up to 120 inches in the last two years of production. When the company announced its cessation of motor vehicle production in 1912, it was not due to lack of funds, but because of Philip Corbin's retirement. American Hardware has continued to do business since that time.

CORBITT 1910-1952, 1957-1958 — Richard J. Corbitt started out in the tobacco business in the 1890s in Henderson, North Carolina, but soon became interested in building wagons and formed the Corbitt Company in 1899. He formed the Corbitt Automobile Company in Henderson in 1907 and began producing highwheelers, which gradually gained some sophistication. In 1910 be built his first truck, which was considerably more successful than his passenger cars and led to his decision to stay with commercial vehicle manufacturing.

1922 CORBITT 1-1/2-TON   NAHC

Corbitt's first production truck was a conventional 1-1/2-ton model powered by a four-cylinder engine with chain drive. By 1915 Corbitt sold school buses and urban transit buses throughout North Carolina. Corbitt also established an export market, and by 1916 Corbitt trucks were sold in 23 countries prompting the press to call his company "the South's largest truck builder."

In the mid 1920s Corbitt trucks ranged in capacity from 1-ton to 5-ton. The 1-ton Model E chassis with 130-inch wheelbase sold for $1,600. It was powered by a 22.5 hp Continental N engine with Stromberg carburetor and Bijur ignition. Electric generator and starter were at extra cost. Clutch and transmission were Brown-Lipe while the axles were made by Sheldon with Ross steering and Bimel wheels, which carried 34x3-1/2 front and 34x4 rear solid rubber tires with pneumatics at extra cost. The 1-1/2-ton Model D-22 chassis with 140-inch wheelbase sold for $2,150 and was powered by a Continental J-4 engine. The 2-ton Model C chassis with 148-inch wheelbase sold for $2,750 and used a 27.2 hp Continental K-4 engine. The 2-1/2-ton Model B chassis with 152-inch wheelbase sold for $3,000 and used the same engine as the previous model. The 3-ton Model R chassis with 158-inch wheelbase had a price tag of $3,250 and was powered by a 32.4 hp Continental L-4 engine. The 4-ton Model A with 178-inch wheelbase cost $3,800, also powered by the L-4 engine, while the 5-ton Model AA with 178-inch wheelbase sold for $4,750 and was powered by a 40 hp Continental B7 engine. All except the lightest model used Bosch ignition, and pneumatic tires were available at extra cost up to the 3-ton model. Otherwise, component manufacturers were the same as on the Model E.

By the early 1930s Corbitt trucks were offered in a variety of sizes and configurations with six-wheel truck tractors rated up to 15-ton. Some of the lighter Corbitt trucks at that time had Auburn passenger car front grilles, body panels and fenders. From 1933 on, Corbitt became a well-established contractor for the U.S. Army, building several models

of heavy trucks. These included a 2-1/2-ton 6x6 cargo carrier powered by a Lycoming straight-eight engine, 8-ton 6x4 and 6x6 artillery prime movers with Hercules six-cylinder engines, and Lycoming-powered armored scout cars.

1934 CORBITT BUS   LIAM

For 1937 Corbitt listed seven models all powered by six-cylinder Waukesha engines. The 1-1/2- to 2-ton Series 12B with 158- to 183-inch wheelbase was powered by a 72 hp 6BL engine, used a Warner T-9 transmission and was priced at $1,095. The Series 14B had a 159- to 208-inch wheelbase and had an 85 hp 6BK engine, used a Clark B-116 transmission and was priced at $1,665. The 2- to 3-ton Series 18 with 163- to 220-inch wheelbase had a 73 hp 6MS engine; the Series 22 with 174-inch wheelbase had an 85 hp 6MK engine; the Series 27 with 178-inch wheelbase had a 90 hp 6MZ engine; the Series 35 and Series 40 rated up to 7-1/2-ton capacity, both with 195-inch wheelbase, both also used a 110 hp 6SRK engine. Series 18 through 40 all used Fuller transmissions and Timken front and rear axles, and were priced $3,050, $3,740, $4,400, $5,115 and $6,160, respectively.

An unusual Corbitt truck of 1938 was the 3-ton Model 18BT powered by a 383-cubic inch six-cylinder Continental E603 engine. The sheet metal was stamped from obsolete Auburn dies giving the truck a swept-back appearance unlike other Corbitt trucks.

In 1940 Corbitt received a contract from the U.S. Coastal Artillery to design and build a 6-ton 6x6 prime mover and cargo carrier. The Corbitt 50 SD6 was later a familiar and reliable hauler for the United States and some of its allies. The truck was particularly known for its 855-cubic inch displacement six-cylinder Hercules engine. Many of these trucks survived to continue work in Austria, Denmark, France, Greece, the Netherlands and Sweden. During World War II Corbitt also manufactured 6x4 truck tractors using six-cylinder Continental engines. Corbitt was involved in building a rear-engine 2-1/2-ton truck and an 8x8 prime mover on an experimental basis, but these did not go into production.

1945 CORBITT 12-TON 8X8   RD

Corbitt sold many truck tractors directly after the war consisting of large 6x2 and 6x4 units powered by Continental gasoline or Cummins diesel engines. In 1946 production totaled over 600 for the year. One of the last Corbitt trucks sold to the military was the Model D800 T35 of 1950. It was powered by a 150 hp six-cylinder Cummins HB600 diesel engine. In the early 1950s sales of independent motor vehicle manufacturers leveled off as an overall industry phenomenon and Corbitt trucks were no exception. Corbitt himself retired and the company was essentially closed in 1952.

In 1957 there was an attempt at reopening the Corbitt production line and custom-built trucks were available. Some Mack 6x6 artillery tractors were rebuilt at the factory during this time. A new emblem with "Henderson, N.C." under "Corbitt" set off the later trucks from the ones produced earlier. Nevertheless, the enterprise permanently closed its doors in 1958 after "Uncle Dick" Corbitt had decided it was time to retire.

1911 CORTLAND 3/4-TON DELIVERY   GMN

CORTLAND 1911-1912 — Located in Cortland, New York, the Cortland Motor Wagon Company built two forward-control "engine-under-driver-seat" trucks. The lighter 3/4-ton model was powered by a 15 hp two-cylinder engine and was priced at $1,100 while the 1-1/2-ton model was powered by a 20 hp two-cylinder engine and was priced at $1,750. The trucks used standard-for-that-day two-speed planetary transmissions and double chain drive to the rear wheels. The Cortland Motor Wagon Company moved to Pittsfield, Massachusetts, before vanishing as a business.

1907 COUPLE-GEAR 2-TON   RD

1908 COUPLE-GEAR 5-TON BEER TRUCK   MROZ

COUPLE-GEAR 1904-1922 — The Couple-Gear Freight Wheel Company was located in Grand Rapids, Michigan. The model line featured 1-, 2- and 5-ton electric battery powered trucks that had a top speed of 6 mph. By 1906 the Couple Gear four-wheel-drive and four-wheel-steer truck was capable of moving directly sideways without first rolling forward or backward. In 1908 a gasoline-electric hybrid was also produced with up to 5-ton capacity and often used as a tanker. The previous year the company had introduced the two lighter models that had front-wheel-drive. All models featured electric motors geared directly to the disc-type wheels with hard rubber including the 5-ton models that had four-wheel-steering. The lighter trucks had a top speed of 9 mph.

In 1910 a test run was made with the heavy hybrid gasoline-electric from Buffalo to Tonawanda. The truck was owned by the Dold Company and carried a load of 7 tons. Total miles covered was 38 with 28 stops. Average speed was 8.14 mph with a consumption of 11 gallons of gasoline and one quart of oil. Total running time was 7 hours and 32 minutes and average fuel consumption was 3.45 mpg. Further tests resulted in similar performance. The city of Boston permitted the operation of a Couple Gear 5-ton truck and 5-ton trailer that year, but the permit was only for 30 days. This was also the year that Couple Gear converted a horsedrawn ambulance into a gas-electric vehicle for the American Society for the Prevention of Cruelty to Animals.

1912 COUPLE-GEAR 5-TON HC GAS ELECTRIC   NAHC

Both battery electric- and gasoline-powered fire engines were also built by Couple-Gear for several fire equipment manufacturers including Ahrens-Fox, Boyd, Peter Pirsch, Seagrave and Webb. One exemplary truck of this series, which was a Couple-Gear/Seagrave combination, was sold in 1914 to the Springfield, Massachusetts, Fire Department. It was 52 feet long, weighed over 20,000 pounds and carried 10 different size ladders. The city of New Bedford, Massachusetts, used a number of Couple-Gear fire engines for over 30 years.

In 1914 a new range of gasoline trucks and tractors was offered with four-wheel-drive, tram-car controls and five forward and reverse speeds. Despite ruggedness and reliability the slow Couple-Gear electric trucks, as with all electric trucks of this period, did not have sufficient energy density available from the batteries to compete with fossil fuel vehicles, whose volatile liquid petroleum-based fuel was available cheaply and conveniently via the simple gas tank, compared to lead-acid chemical power in heavy, bulky casings. Couple-Gear stopped manufacturing after producing two fire engines in 1920 and by 1922 the enterprise was entirely defunct.

1914 COUPLE-GEAR 3-WHEEL CONTRACTOR'S WAGON   KP

COVERT 1906-1907 — In 1902 Byron V. Covert & Company was founded in Lockport, New York. Although it was announced that Covert was going to build a steam car that he had designed, he built a gasoline-powered runabout that year. In 1903 at the New York Automobile Show he exhibited his Covert Chainless with sliding gear transmission, running gear of the "reachless pattern" with a rear transaxle. The car was proved out in the World's Fair Buffalo to St. Louis endurance race in 1904 when it was the only car in its class to reach Missouri. Accolades from the press did not expand Covert's limited marketing much farther than New York.

In 1906 Covert offered a 1/2-ton truck with screenside body. It was a forward-control-type with a two-cylinder engine and two-speed transmission. The chassis wheelbase was 84 inches and worm-drive was used. The truck was offered at $1,000 for the brief time it was available.

C.P.T. See LITTLE GIANT and DUNTLEY C.P.T.

CRANE & BREED 1909-1924 — The Crane and Breed Manufacturing Company specialized in ambulance and hearse chassis. The company was started in 1850 to build these types of carriages, and by 1909 offered professional cars powered by a four-cylinder engine with magneto ignition and a three-speed transmission with side chain-drive. The first Crane & Breed hearse hauled a large reproduction of the tomb of Scipio on its roof. By 1912, concentrating on body manufacturing, the company ceased production of chassis, preferring to use those purchased from Winton, which were powered by six-cylinder engines and available through 1924.

1912 CRAWFORD   RD

CRAWFORD 1911-1917 — Mathias Peter Moller, who was an organ pipe manufacturer, and Robert S. Crawford, a bicycle builder who built a two-cylinder car in 1902, collaborated by forming the Crawford Automobile Company in 1904 in Hagerstown, Maryland. At first two models of runabout were built featuring wheel steering, and both were powered by a 10 hp water-cooled engine coupled to a planetary transmission with final chain drive. A commercial vehicle emerged from the passenger car chassis design with a capacity of 1,200 pounds and wheelbase of 112 inches. The light truck was powered by a 30 hp four-cylinder engine with three-speed transmission, shaft drive and pneumatic tires. It was built as a closed van and sold for $1,300, or open body the price was $1,250 in 1912.

At the same time as the truck production stopped and started between 1911 and 1917 Crawford built several passenger cars with Rutenber engines and later Continental engines. Beginning in 1911 the transmissions were fitted with the rear axles. From 1916 all Crawfords were six-cylinder; however, by 1917 material shortages had reduced the annual output to 38 cars and this was the last year for truck production. Moller proceeded to buy out the company in 1921 and began producing the Dagmar automobile, which was named after his daughter.

CRESCENT 1912-1913 — There were 10 various Crescent motor vehicle manufacturers listed between 1900 and 1914 in the United States, including one obscure company named Crescent Motor Truck of Middletown, Ohio, which apparently moved to Hamilton, Ohio, where production of the little-known 1-, 2- and 3-ton trucks continued briefly until the end of 1913.

1914 CRETORS POPCORN WAGON   PJMMOA

CRETORS 1914-1915 — C. Cretors and Company was a business enterprise that built popcorn machines in Chicago, Illinois. For 1915 the company built nine special popcorn wagons propelled by 22.5 hp Buda QU engines. A Brown-Lipe transmission was used with chain drive. Chain drive was used and service brakes were leather to metal internal expanding on rear wheels. Wheelbase was 132 inches and 34x5 front with 36x5 rear solid rubber tires were used. Each wagon included a complete steam plant using a gas-fired boiler and a mill-type steam engine that powered the popcorn popper as well as the peanut roaster. Price in 1915 was $4,600.

CRICKET 1915 — The Cyclecar Company of Detroit, Michigan, built a package delivery model by the name of Cricket. It was priced at $345 and production lasted for only one year. The vehicle was powered by a 9 hp V-2 engine and had a wheelbase of 84 inches. Tracy Lyon and O.C. Hutchinson sold their Motor Products Company late in 1914. They were the owners of the company that built the engine for the Cricket, thus ending its short production run as well.

1914 CROCE 3/4-TON DELIVERY PANEL BODY   KP

CROCE 1914-1918 — The Croce Automobile Company built passenger cars in Asbury Park, New Jersey, and also marketed a line of delivery trucks. The Model A was priced at $1,700 at the beginning of production. The following year the Model A was up to $1,800 as an open or closed cab van. In 1915 there was also a 1-ton Model C that was priced at $1,850 for the chassis and a Model A-1 also rated at 1 ton capacity and priced at $1,800.

Production was interrupted for 1916, but in 1917 Croce trucks returned to the market. These were designated as the Model 18, 19 and 20. The first was an open cab style truck, the second a closed cab and the Model 20 was either closed or open cab priced at $1,250. Production of Croce ceased in 1918.

CROFTON 1959-1961 — In San Diego, California, the Crofton Marine Engine Company built a lightweight utility vehicle called the Crofton Bug, which resembled a jeep. It was powered by a 44-cubic inch four-cylinder overhead-cam engine, which was similar to the postwar Crosley engine but had 35 hp. In 1961 a Brawny Bug was introduced with a six-speed transmission and optional dual wheels in the rear. The Brawny kit cost $450 and included a PowerLok differential, a crash pan, deluxe seats and 9.00x10 tires. Accessories included a snowplow and an electric winch. The Crofton truck model was called the Tug. Base price was $1,350 and production was 200 over the three years of manufacturing.

1940 CROSLEY PICKUP KP

CROSLEY 1940-1952 — Powel Crosley Jr. built two earlier prototype cars before going into production with the Crosley "miniature" car in 1939. Crosley had become a multi-millionaire with his radio and refrigerator manufacturing. His name was well-known for the "Shelvadoor" refrigerator design, which pioneered shelves mounted in the door, a standard in the industry to date. By 1934 he owned the Cincinnati Redlegs baseball team.

The new Crosley car was called a "wish-fulfillment" by his associates, and its brief successful emergence on the market after World War II during a period of surging sales in the car industry propelled Powel Crosley in his crusade to market the small-car idea in the United States. Crosley's peak sales year was 1948 when a total of 32,000 Crosleys were sold. An indication that he was ahead of his time was one of Crosley's favorite slogans -- "Why Build a Battleship to Cross a River?"

The Crosley car was introduced to the press at the Indianapolis Motor Speedway in April 1939 and to the public at the New York World's Fair in June of that year. At the Fair the Crosley was called "The Car of Tomorrow" and subsequently "The Forgotten Man's Car." Macy's and Bamberger's, for example, became dealers for Crosleys because they already carried other well-known Crosley products. The first Macy's customer in 1939 to buy a Crosley was a Mrs. Averell Harriman.

In 1940 Crosley introduced the Parkway delivery van, thereby entering the commercial vehicle market. It was powered by a 40-cubic inch displacement horizontally-opposed two-cylinder Waukesha engine with 13 hp. In 1940, when sales were only 422 for the whole year, the van sold for $450, compared to the convertible that sold for $299. The following year a more extensive range of commercial bodies was available and a total of 2,289 were built for the year. The vehicles were spartan with a graduated tank dipstick rather than a fuel gauge, as well as a pull-up chain handbrake.

1946 CROSLEY FARM-O-ROAD LA

Once World War II started, production was interrupted at 1,029 Crosleys for 1942. The Army tested an ultra-light 4x4 based on the two-cylinder Crosley, but it proved inadequate, especially in the suspension and steering mechanism. It was called the Crosley Pup and was powered by a 13.5 hp 38.35-cubic inch horizontally-opposed two-cylinder Waukesha engine. It had constant four-wheel-drive and a 65-inch wheelbase. Several experimental versions were built, and a production Crosley Scout Car was accepted by the U.S. Army, but only 36 units were bought.

Crosley experimented with single-fork motorcycles for the military, and the company also built 3x2 three-wheel vehicles that had a seat with side handles at the rear on which two passengers could sit either forward or backward. These were only experimental, but the Crosley company did get a lucrative contract to build the Cobra industrial engine and other machines for military use.

1947 CROSLEY SEDAN DELIVERY JAMES KILLION

After the war, the Crosley company resumed production when it received government approval to build 16,000 cars from July 1945 to March 1946. By mid-1947, when the station wagon was introduced, the company had sold 16,437 cars, of which 4,999 were considered 1946 models. These, like the prewar models, were built on an 80-inch wheelbase chassis, but used the Cobra engine whose block was made out of sheet metal. The pickup cost $839 while the chassis and cab were $819 in 1946. For 1947 the panel truck was $899. The Crosley cars were still quite austere without synchromesh, and even the bumper guard was optional, but the Cobra engine produced 26.5 hp using five copper-brazed main bearings and provided at least 35 mpg. The bodies were now slab-sided with full-length oval fenders, a protruding hood nose and headlamp pods recessed into the front of the body just above the small grille.

The company soon switched to cast-iron engine blocks for 1949, and the body was redesigned for a more modern look. By 1950 aircraft-type disc brakes were used on some models. An all-purpose road vehicle called the Farm-O-Road with six speeds forward and two reverse was introduced in 1951 for the rural market. With sales lagging, Crosley Motors closed in mid-1952 and merged with Aerojet Engineering of Azusa, California, and both companies became part of the General Tire and Rubber Company.

1914 CROSS FRONT DRIVE AERIAL LADDER　　　　　**LA**

CROSS 1914-1916 — Primarily for fire apparatus application, the C.J. Cross Front Drive Tractor Company of Newark, New Jersey, was one of several that built motorized units to take the place of horses. It was similar to the Christie tractor but was positioned longitudinally rather than transversely. The first versions were with the engine ahead of the axle covered with a hood. By 1915 an "engine-under-driver-seat" design was introduced. Cross also offered front-wheel-drive trucks of 3-, 5-, 7- and 10-ton capacity, but few of these were actually sold. The Cross tractors were used by fire departments in New York City and Philadelphia. The company relocated to Rochester, New York, before going out of business as the demand for mechanical horse substitutes was saturated and gradually made obsolete when old fire apparatus was retired.

CROW 1912-1913 — The Crow Motor Company was located in Elkhart, Indiana, and was a result of various automotive experiments as well as the entrepreneurial spirit of Dr. E.C. Crow and his son Martin E. Crow. Dr. Crow became interested in the Menges self-starter design and built a prototype to prove it out, abandoning the starter and keeping the car in the process.

To be exact, the Menges car had been fabricated in the Elkhart shop of the Sterling-Hudson Whip Company. The Crows had been involved with Willard W. Sterling and F.O. Hudson in an automobile development program that resulted in the Sterling car of 1909. However, Albert Menges had already departed for Tennessee and the car was neither a Menges nor a Sterling by the time the Crows took over. The Crow Motor Car Company was incorporated in 1909. Making things even more confusing, during the first two years the Crows did not built their own car but were distributors of the Black Crow, which was manufactured by the Black Manufacturing Company of Chicago.

By 1910 the contract with Black was severed and the Crows went into business building their own car using their own name. In order to differentiate themselves from the Black Crow, the name was soon changed to Crow-Elkhart to draw attention to the Indiana firm that was building the vehicles rather than the former Black company of Chicago.

Crow-Elkharts were conventional cars with many body styles including a Model C.D., which was a 3/4-ton enclosed commercial delivery vehicle with a 114-inch wheelbase. Although Crow used several different engines, including six-cylinder units for their passenger cars, the commercial delivery was powered by a four-cylinder engine with a three-speed transmission and shaft drive. The factory's 30-per-day production capacity was never realized even to half its potential, and the company went into receivership twice before it was liquidated to its own subsidiary, the Century Motors Company, which built the Moriss-London cars for export.

CROWN 1910-1916 — Out of a half-dozen different vehicle manufacturers by the name of Crown, it was the Crown Commercial Car Company of North Milwaukee, Wisconsin, that was one of two to build trucks, albeit briefly. The company's engineering was managed by George Van Rollweiler who arrived after designing for Daimler Motor Gesellschaft in Germany and Milnes-Daimler Ltd. in England, hence the European appearance of the trucks.

The first Crown truck model was a 1/2-ton and powered by a two-cylinder water-cooled engine using a three-speed transmission with double chain drive to the rear wheels. About a year later a 3/4-ton was offered with a four-cylinder T-head engine with cylinders cast separately. A multiple disc clutch was used, and a selective gear three-speed transmission was mounted amidships, with final drive by double chain.

By 1914 the model line had expanded to include 1-1/2-ton and 2-1/2-ton models powered by a four-cylinder Wisconsin T-head engine cast in pairs. While the solid rubber tires were standard and conventional, the frame was not. The channel steel siderails were of adequate size; however, the crossmembers appeared to be pipe stems and a thin X-member was added to the rear axle area for basic alignment and minimum structural integrity. Steel wheels, left-hand steering and worm-drive were used. The company did not survive past 1916.

1995 CROWN CONTINENTAL　　　　　**CARPENTER**

CROWN 1932 to date — The Crown Body and Coach Corporation of Los Angeles, California, started out as the Crown Carriage Company, building carriages and commercial vehicle bodies. It was established by Don M. Brockway in 1904. The first bus body was built in 1915. It was fabricated mostly out of wood and used a Federal chassis. In 1917 the first school bus bodies were built using a similar design. During World War I Crown incorporated and expanded its facilities in downtown Los Angeles.

By the 1920s Crown was building school bus bodies per California specifications, as well as for other Western states. In 1925 Crown began building three biplanes per week called Crown Model B-3, but these were Kinner Airster airplanes built under license. The aircraft division was closed at the beginning of the Depression. The first school bus with dual rear wheels was produced in 1927. A Mack chassis was adopted, and using steel framing, a larger 43-seat bus was built. In 1930 the curtains used until then were superseded by drop-sash metal-frame windows.

The year 1932 marked the first time Crown built a complete school bus. Its design was all-steel, forward-control with a Waukesha engine and featured three independent braking systems. These consisted of standard floor-operated four-wheel hydraulic, hand-controlled vacuum brakes along with an emergency brake acting on the driveline. In order to meet the demand for less expensive vehicles, for 1935 Crown reintroduced buses built on commercial truck chassis, some from Moreland, and these were called Metropolitan or Metro.

By 1937 under-floor Hall-Scott engines were utilized, and although Cummins diesel engines were optional by that time, it appears none were built with such an engine until 1954. The Hall-Scott engine was moved to the rear in 1940. In 1950 a rounder shape was adopted and that design, except for window size, was continued for the next 40 years.

Crown first built a prototype fire truck in 1949. The fire apparatus division was opened in 1951. In 1952 the company became the Crown Coach Corporation. The fire trucks were called Crown Firecoach and were powered by Hall-Scott engines. The company began to build larger fire trucks with telescoping aerials and combination ladder-water towers. The first aerial platform was built in 1961 and was delivered to the city of Downey, California.

Crown fire trucks were built in 4x2 and 6x4 configurations using hydraulically-actuated outriggers. Cummins, Detroit Diesel, Ford and International engines were used after Hall-Scott ceased manufacturing. However good Crown fire engines were, production ended in 1981 after about 880 such trucks were built.

The first tandem-axle bus was built by Crown in 1955, and its seating capacity was for up to 91 students. A bus-truck hybrid was also started that year that had room for 20 passengers and a 20-foot cargo area at the rear. The Crown Cargo Coach was similar, but it used a Crown bus front on a Crown 6x4 chassis with a Trailmobile trailer body. These were used to build mobile offices, libraries, medical trucks and also a heavy-duty wrecker.

Crown Security Coaches were built from the early 1950s, and these were distinguished by bars in the windows for transporting up to 64 prisoners. More contemporary buses built by Crown included 79- or 85-passenger two-axle models and 91- or 97-passenger three-axle models. Each of these have been powered by a Cummins or Detroit Diesel engine.

In 1979 Crown teamed up with Ikarus Coach and Vehicle Works of Budapest, Hungary. Crown built the chassis while Ikarus provided the bodies for these articulated buses. At least 200 such buses were assembled between 1981 and 1989. They were 102 inches wide and 60 feet long and seated up to 76 passengers. The third axle was positioned behind the flexible body joint.

The Brockway family sold its interest in the company in 1980, and the newly formed company was called Crown Coach International, moving to Chino, California, in 1984. The Los Angeles factory was used until it was sold in 1986. In April of 1987 the company went into receivership and the plant, stock and equipment was sold at auction to the GE Railcar Services Company, a subsidiary of the General Electric Company. Manufacturing resumed with a model line including 35-, 38- and 40-foot buses in 4x2, 6x2 and 6x4 configuration. Both mid-engine and rear-engine design was available. These buses were guaranteed for 20 years or 150,000 miles and cost between $90,000 and $135,000. After averaging a production of 100 buses per year through the 1950s and 1960s, and moving up to 500 buses per year for the 1970s and 1980s, the company closed its doors in March of 1991.

In 1991 Carpenter Body Works acquired Crown Commercial Buses, and these have since been listed under Carpenter's headquarters in Mitchell, Indiana. Crown buses have been available to date in five model lines: the Commuter, the Concourse, the Courier, the Continental and the Coastline.

The forward-control front-engine chassis and rear-engine chassis have been available with Cummins diesel or Hercules CNG powerplants. Wheelbases have been offered from 158 inches to 228 inches and a Navistar chassis/engine has also been available. The Continental has been built on the front-engine chassis or the Navistar FC3900 chassis, while the Coastline bus has used the rear-engine chassis with wheelbases from 244 inches to 283 inches for up to 53 passengers. Engine choices have been Caterpillar or Cummins diesel, diesel- or methanol-powered Detroit Diesel Allison engines or a Hercules CNG engine.

For 1996 the company has been listed as "Crown by Carpenter."

CROWTHER-DURYEA 1916 — Henry Crowther founded the Crowther Motor Company in 1915 to market light cars and trucks built by Cresson-Morris of Philadelphia, Pennsylvania. This was the same company that was assembling a cyclecar for Charles E. Duryea, who, with his brother J. Frank Duryea, had built one of America's first gasoline-powered cars back in 1893. Having continued in his bicycle business in Peoria, Illinois, Charles Duryea had designed the transmission for the Crowther car, and he was marketing the Cresson-Morris car under his own name. When Crowther and Duryea got together Cresson-Morris lost two customers.

The Crowther-Duryea was built in Rochester, New York, which was Crowther's hometown. Besides the Crowther-Duryea Model 5-35 passenger car, which was powered by a 23 hp four-cylinder four-cycle engine, a few light, simple 1/2-ton trucks were also built, powered by the same engine with Splitdorf ignition. The design used no clutch but only a "Duryea Roller Drive," which consisted of two small capstans at each end of a jackshaft driving an annular ring by friction, not by gear. The smooth ring was attached to the spokes of the rear wheels. Aside

from this anomalous method of transmitting power to the wheels, the trucks were distinguished by a primitive appearance and did not sell well at all.

1913 CROXTON MODEL A PANEL BODY KP

CROXTON-KEETON 1909-1914 — The story of the Croxton-Keeton is somewhat convoluted. Herbert A. Croxton had previously built the Jewel motor car, and Forrest M. Keeton was from Detroit having been associated with the Pope-Toledo and De Luxe car companies. In 1909 the two of them established the Croxton-Keeton Motor Car Company in Massillon, Ohio, where Croxton was already in the iron and steel business. Their goal was to produce two types of cars. The first was called the "German" car and was based on the Rutenber-engine Jewel car. It was distinguished by a long hood with the radiator in the front of the engine. The second type was the "French," which held its passengers between the axles and positioned the radiator behind the 28 hp engine, along with a Renault-type hood. Both cars used three-speed transmissions. Wheelbase was 115-1/2 inches and the price $3,300. The commercial application was primarily as taxis.

After a year in business with few cars actually manufactured, Croxton announced that the company was in receivership trying to protect the creditors and to keep his reputation. The plan worked, at least temporarily, and Keeton left for Detroit to build a car with his own name on it. Meanwhile, Croxton continued to build the same cars but without the second half of the original name.

By 1913, a Croxton commercial taxi chassis was offered. It was actually the same as the Model A-4 passenger car with a 121-inch wheelbase. The Model B had a 140-inch wheelbase and was powered by 48 hp six-cylinder engine. By 1914, the company had gone through an unsuccessful merger with Royal Tourist to form Consolidated Motor Car Company with Croxton at the top, but Croxton had gone on his own again in 1912 building the final factory in Washington, Pennsylvania. When production was stopped in 1914, the factory was acquired by the Universal Motor Car Company and production of that car began there immediately.

1908 C.T. 30-PASSENGER SIGHTSEEING COACH RD

C.T. 1907-1928 — The Commercial Truck Company of America was founded in 1907 in Philadelphia, Pennsylvania. The vehicles were battery-powered electric, although a few gasoline-electric hybrids were also built by 1915. For 1908 the company advertised itself as the Commercial Truck Company, and showed a 35-passenger omnibus as well as a 30-passenger sight-seeing coach. Already by late 1907 a 3-ton and a 5-ton chassis were available.

Other early models consisted of 1/2-ton to 3-1/2-ton capacity. The 1/2-ton delivery van sold for $2,200. The larger models used General Electric motors geared to each rear dual wheel. The 3-1/2-ton truck had a wheelbase of 114-inches and weighed 10,000 pounds. Top speed was 7 mph.

1911 C.T. 2-TON   NAHC

By 1912 C.T. trucks were available in six different capacities from 1/4-ton to 5-ton. Worm-drive was adopted in 1913. The gasoline-electric hybrid tractor was introduced in 1915 and continued to be built but only for two years. A 6-ton model was added in 1921, and lighter models were improved. Most of the heavier models had four-wheel-drive with an electric motor mounted on each wheel.

1913 C.T. DAIRY DELIVERY   OCW

As an example, C.T. electric trucks were successfully operated in Philadelphia by the Curtis Publishing Company. A fleet of 22 was used by the publisher of *Jack and Jill*, *Holiday*, *Ladies Home Journal* and *Saturday Evening Post*. Two of the trucks were used exclusively to haul coal, while the other 20 delivered the periodicals throughout the city. Loaded with 10 tons of paper and traveling at 10 mph, they silently plied the streets in the early morning hours with nary a puff of exhaust. Curtis used the reliable C.T. fleet as late as 1962. By that time, the trucks were over 40 years old on the average. They still used the original 85 volt 10 amp drive systems that consisted of an electric motor in each wheel.

By 1928, C.T. offered 12 different models to chose from, but the diminishing market for slow electric trucks with limited range forced C.T. to be acquired by the Walker Vehicle Company, an electric truck builder that lasted until 1942.

1916 C.T. 5-TON MODEL 36A   HAYS

1951 CUB 19-PASSENGER BUS   KP

CUB 1950-1951 — Forty Cub buses were built within two years under the leadership of Howard Munshaw, who was once affiliated with Pony Cruiser, Reo, Spartan and Yellow. These were lightweight 19-passenger buses on a 160-inch wheelbase Ford truck chassis.

1901 CUNNINGHAM STEAM WAGON   NMM

CUNNINGHAM 1900-1901 — One of the first four-wheel-drive vehicles to be built in the United States specifically intended as a truck, the Cunningham steam wagon was unconventional in that its centrally-mounted compound engine used chains to drive each wheel. Load capacity on the large flatbed was up to 5 tons. The boiler was a fire-tube fueled by either coal or coke. The Cunningham Engineering Company of Boston, Massachusetts, built the first unit. The company was absorbed by the Massachusetts Steam Wagon Company of Boston in 1901, but further production did not follow.

1926 CUNNINGHAM V-8 FUNERAL COACH　　　　　**LA**

CUNNINGHAM 1909-1934 — Unrelated to the earlier Cunningham steam wagon, James Cunningham, Sons and Company of Rochester, New York, started out as carriagemakers. Upon the death of founder James Cunningham in 1886, Joseph took the reigns and by the turn of the century the company was well known for its top quality berlins, cutters, dogcarts, sleighs, tally-hos, victorias and vis-a-vis. Not unlike many other similar enterprises, Cunningham made the transition to horseless carriages successfully. Just prior to 1900 Cunningham developed an electric vehicle, but it was not until 1907 that the company entered the market with gasoline motor cars. These were powered by Buffalo and Continental engines and used standard components, although the coachwork was on a custom order basis.

The first commercial vehicles were in the form of ambulances and hearses offered in 1909. For the 1911 model year Cunningham began producing cars powered by a 40 hp overhead-valve four-cylinder engine of its own make, and by 1916 the 45 hp Lacey-designed 442-cubic inch V-8 was available. Cunninghams were known for their coachwork with price tags to prove it: $5,000 on the average and going as high as $9,000. Wheelbases up to 142 inches were used, and Cunningham produced many ambulances and hearses besides custom cars for the likes of William Randolph Hearst and Cecil B. De Mille. Aside from totally enclosed six-door ambulances built for the Army and Navy during World War I, Cunningham also became a builder of light tanks, halftracks and wheeled armored cars.

Brakes were on the rear wheels only until 1926, and three-speed and four-speed overdrive transmissions with multi-disc clutches were used until that time. In 1927 Cunningham produced an armored ambulance, and once the Depression hit, concentrated on commercial vehicles. A pickup was built in 1931, but this was the last year of standard production, although some leftover vehicles were sold as new until 1933. Hard times forced the company to revert to using Continental straight-eight engines of which only a dozen were built in this configuration. Commercial bodies began to be mounted on Cadillac, Ford, Lincoln and Packard chassis. Cunningham also built Cadillac-powered halftracks, armored cars and military halftrack conversions of Ford trucks. The last year of any motor car-related manufacturing was 1936, after which Cunningham produced garden tractors in the late 1940s as well as electrical components.

1914 CURTIS 2-TON　　　　　**RJG**

CURTIS 1912-1915 — The Pittsburgh Machine and Tool Company of Braddock, Pennsylvania, first built trucks for inhouse use. The 1-1/2-ton and 2-ton trucks were built entirely within the plant except for wheels and electrical parts. The two sizes of Curtis trucks differed only in terms of tire size. Both were powered by a 27 hp four-cylinder engine with pressurized lubrication and thermo-syphon cooling circulation. The trucks also used a cone-clutch with three-speed transmission and chain drive. In 1913 a 2-ton model cost $3,000 to build. By 1916 essentially the same trucks were offered to the general public as 2-ton and 3-ton capacity trucks.

CURTIS-BILL 1933 — When the Fageol truck company was shut down, Louis H. Bill, who had been associated with the Oakland factory, started his own firm, employing Harry E. Curtis as the designer. The Curtis-Bill vehicles built by the Bill Motors Company of Oakland included a 20-passenger front-drive bus on a 144-inch wheelbase using an eight-cylinder Lycoming engine. The company also built a 10-ton truck of similar configuration.

CURTIS-NATIONAL 1934 — The National Bus Lines of Los Angeles, California, was an unregulated interstate operator that used leased buses. Late in 1934 the company built two custom, low-slung, streamlined 20-passenger buses that were powered by Ford engines. These were known as Curtis-National buses, and only the two were built before the company and the vehicles were sold to All American Bus Lines in 1936.

CURTISS 1917, 1920-1921 — Glenn Curtiss was a well-known aviator, also known for his motorcycle adventures, when he tried to talk Henry Ford into fitting an aviation engine into the Model T. Although Ford showed interest, no such project was ever started by the two men, so Curtiss built his own and very first flying car in 1917. Using standard aircraft wheels, the flying car was powered by a Curtiss OXX engine mounted in front under a hood. Envisioned for possible commercial uses, the flying car was not simple to transform from land to air application with its complicated fasteners and guy wires holding the boom-mounted tail and peculiar wings. It was exhibited at the 1917 New York Pan-American Aeronautic Exposition, and although it was known to have been driven, there is no evidence that it ever flew.

After World War I when Curtiss had a surplus of his Curtiss OX-5 engines he organized the Curtiss Motor Car Company, which was not the only firm at that time to try and adapt the aviation engine for motor vehicle use. Curtiss later had a camp-car designed and built, and this design was expanded to include touring cars and school buses. However, once the stock market crashed, plans for manufacturing were permanently stalled.

1965 CUSHMAN POLICE 3-WHEELER　　　　　**WJP**

CUSHMAN 1936 to date — Cushman Motor Works was founded by brothers Everitt and Clinton in 1901 in Lincoln, Nebraska. Their first product line consisted of two-stroke engines for boats followed by four-stroke water-cooled engines for farm use. In 1903 the company increased its capital stock to $300,000 in order to build automobiles, but this never took place, the Cushman brothers being quite successful with their engine manufacturing. After 1922 their engines were air-cooled.

In 1936, the first Cushman three-wheel vehicles were built based largely on scooter designs. These were first used as golf carts. For commercial purposes Cushman three-wheelers were used as parcel carriers and light delivery vehicles. These were built as sidecars or three-wheelers with two wheels in front. The 4 hp engines were one-cylinder, 15-cubic inch with two speeds and chain drive. They were popular with the U.S. Army and Air Force during World War II, as well as during the Korean War. Load capacities were 350 to 400 pounds. The Model 39 was particularly reliable, and over 600 units were purchased between 1942 and 1944.

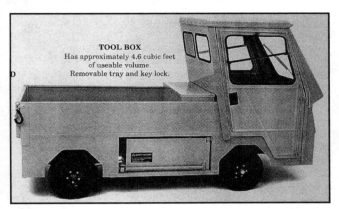

1992 CUSHMAN TITAN   **CUSHMAN**

Cushman Motors became a division of the Outboard Marine Corporation of Lincoln, Nebraska, in 1961. Horizontally-opposed two-cylinder engines with up to 18 hp were introduced. Cushman expanded its product line to include three-wheel as well as four-wheel vehicles with capacities of up to 1-ton. In 1972, the company became OMC-Lincoln, Division of the Outboard Marine Corporation. Both electric motors and gasoline engines have been utilized, and road-going vehicles have been used for police work. About 65 percent were used at golf courses, but Cushman vehicles have also been used at industrial sights and for refuse hauling, airport services, vacation resorts and numerous other such applications. Cabs were available in open, closed and semi-closed configuration using steel construction with fiberglass being utilized more recently. Lighter models used V-belt drive while heavier models used three-speed transmissions with worm-drive.

In the 1980s, Cushman has offered a plethora of electric- and gasoline-powered models. They have included the Minute-Miser three-wheel Model 319 (gasoline-powered) and Model 320 (electric-powered). With 4.80x8 tires the vehicle has been rated at 450-pound capacity. The Model 320 had two speeds allowing 6 mph and 13 mph. The Cushman Electric Executive has been offered as a four-wheel vehicle known as the Model 322 with 900 pound capacity.

The Cushman Electric Titan has been offered in six variations: Models 335, 336, 341, 348, 349 and 351. The Model 348 used a 5.6 hp 48-volt DC series motor (NEMA rating of 22 hp at 1400 rpm) while the Models 335, 336, 348 and 351 used a 3 hp 36-volt DC series motor (NEMA rating of 10.7 hp at 800 rpm). Models 341 and 349 used a 4 hp 48-volt DC series motor (NEMA rating of 19 hp at 900 rpm). Rated capacities were 1,400 pounds for Model 348; 2,400 pounds for Model 335, 336 and 351; 4,000 pounds for Model 341 and 5,000 pounds for Model 349. Each model used 5.70x8 tires except the Model 349, which used 5.00x8 solid rubber tires.

Cushman has also offered the Electric Tug three-wheeler, which used a 3 hp 36-volt DC series motor, with a load capacity of 450 pounds and tow capacity of 3,000 pounds. The company also built an electric Stock Chaser Model 360, as well as the all purpose four-wheel electric (Models 371 and 373) and gasoline (Models 372 and 374) F-2 and F-2J all purpose "flat-bed" vehicles. Electric motors were the same as for previous models while the gasoline engines were 8 hp four-cycle air-cooled with variable V-belt drive.

The Models 371 and 372 were rated at 1,900 pound capacity, while the Models 373 and 373 were rated at 2,400 pound capacity. Factory installed modifications included a fiberglass cab with safety glass windows, vinyl doors and ambulance, fire truck and van bodies with sliding doors.

1993 CUSHMAN ZEV   **CUSHMAN**

Other Cushman models included the Models 369 and 370 Gasoline GT-1 four-wheel hauler with a capacity of 1,200 pounds powered by the 8 hp four-cycle Kohler engine. Other models included the 150 Loadster, 280 B.C.D. Carry-All, 282 B.C.D. Carry-All and Payloader, 282F Thunderbolt, 325 A.B.C. Tote, 535 Errand Master and 539 Chariot.

For the 1990s in order for companies and government agencies to meet the Clean Air Act fleet regulations, Cushman introduced the ZEV (Zero Emission Vehicle) -- a three-wheeler in order to comply with on road Federal Motor Vehicle Safety Administration standards -- as a "motorcycle," even though it weighs 2,300 pounds with a full set of lead acid batteries. It is similar in appearance to the gasoline-powered vehicles but is electric powered using a 10.2 hp (continuous) 72-volt General Electric motor. A wheelbase of 79 inches has been available and load capacity has been specified as 700 pounds including operator. Top speed has been advertised as 39 mph with acceleration 0 to 30 mph in 13 seconds. Many of these with steel doors and cargo box and with fiberglass cabs have been purchased by police departments for parking meter enforcement work.

CUSTER ELECTRIC 1920-1942 — L. Luzern Custer of Dayton, Ohio, started his Custer Specialty Company in 1920, although he claimed to have experimented with electric vehicles as early as 1898. Among the many lightweight electric vehicles he built, which included children's cars, miniature railroads and electric wheelchairs, was a Carrier model, which was a light industrial truck. The vehicle weighed approximately 550 pounds and had a top speed of 8 mph. The Custer Specialty Company was still in business as late as the mid-1960s, but vehicle production stopped at the beginning of World War II.

CYCLOMOBILE 1920 — In January of 1920 the Cyclomobile Manufacturing Company was incorporated with a capital of $600,000. The incorporators were Thomas Davies, John F. Parsons, Charles F.H. Hammel, William E. Jimelhoch and Isaac Mittenthal. The intent was to build cars, motorcycles and trucks. A prototype cyclecar was developed, and after Charles Hammel realized that a one-passenger vehicle would severely limit his market, the vehicle's tread was widened from 36-inches to 44-inches for either two passengers or as a light delivery version. The Cyclomobile did not get past the prototype stage.

D

D

DAGMAR 1922-1935 — Mathias P. Moller owned the Crawford Automobile Company which was located in Hagerstown, Maryland. His company had built the Crawford since 1904, and the Dagmar was intended as a sporty line alongside the Crawford, both powered by 70 hp six-cylinder Continental engines. Named after his daughter, the Crawford was entirely dropped by 1923 as the Dagmar cars began production. Various models were built on the 120-inch wheelbase chassis including taxicabs by the mid 1920s. The company was induced to abandon its Danish coat-of-arms emblem upon protests from the Danish embassy, as it was forced to stop using hexagon hubcaps upon threat of lawsuit from Packard, which had registered the trademark.

A total of 135 Dagmars were built in 1923, the year the flat-fender design was changed to a more standard round fender. In 1924, a Dagmar sport victoria with folding top, considered appropriately ornate for the occasion, was given as one of the prizes to the winner of the Miss America Contest. At this point Moller began building numerous taxis, first under his own name, and subsequently with other names such as Aristocrat, Astor, Blue Light, Five-Boro, Luxor, Paramount, Puritan, Super Paramount and Twentieth Century. Although passenger car production ceased in 1927, the company continued to offer taxis under various names and trucks under the name Elysee until 1934.

DAIN 1912-1917 — Joseph Dain of Ottumwa, Iowa, began building 1-ton trucks in 1912. He subsequently organized the Dain Manufacturing Company later that same year in Ottumwa in order to built 1-, 2- and 3-ton trucks. These were powered by a four-cylinder engine using a friction transmission and speed reduction via internal tooth bull gear inside the rear wheel. It was not until the Style 4 that a worm-drive rear axle was adopted. Most of the models had the driver sitting to the left of the hood, and in the last three years of production only the 1-ton was available. By 1915 the company announced a gross sales revenue of $632,088, but it is not clear how much of this was derived from the sales of trucks.

DAIRY EXPRESS 1926-1930 — The General Ice Cream Corporation of Springfield, Massachusetts, built two models of trucks: a 2-ton powered by a 25.6 hp four-cylinder Hercules OX engine and a 3-ton powered by a six-cylinder Hercules WXB motor. The 2-ton chassis was priced at $1,600 while the 3-ton was priced at $2,000.

DANIELSON 1912-1914 — The Danielson Engine Works of Chicago, Illinois, was capitalized in 1914 with $50,000. The company built a single line of trucks named the Model A. This was a 1-ton truck with a 115-inch wheelbase chassis weighing 3,400 pounds. It was powered by a four-cylinder engine using a three-speed transmission with final chain drive to the rear wheels.

DARBY 1910 — C.T. Darby of St. Louis, Missouri, designed a car in 1908 and was able to obtain the capital for its manufacture with investment by local businessmen Harvey Dunham and Allen Whittemore. The Darby Motor Car Company showed its two prototype models in the 1909 St. Louis Coliseum Exhibition. Production commenced after the show with three-passenger roadsters and four-passenger surreys, but it was not until 1910 that Darby built a small delivery van with a capacity of 800 pounds. It used the same 16 hp two-cylinder two-cycle engine that the passenger cars used, although it was listed with a planetary transmission as opposed to the friction drive used in the former vehicles. All models were built on an even 100-inch wheelbase, and price for the open body commercial was $850 -- $100 more than the roadster.

DART 1903 do date — Dart trucks have been manufactured for over 90 years under nine different company names and three locations. The company started in 1890 as a bicycle manufacturer. From 1903 to 1907 it was the Dart Truck Company of Anderson, Indiana.

Dart first started with 1/2-ton capacity highwheelers that had engines mounted under the floor, and suspension was with full-elliptic springs on all four wheels. These were powered by 20 hp two-cylinder engines with planetary transmissions with a multiple disc clutch. A chain drove a jackshaft from the engine, and power to the rear wheels was with a chain on each side. Wheels were 34 inches in diameter, which had two-inch Diamond tires. The light delivery vehicle weighed 1,800 pounds, and an open body had a loading space of 45 inches by 78 inches. A panel type body was also available, and standard color was Brewster green body with maroon chassis, or an option of a blue body and yellow or maroon chassis. Economy was advertised at 20 mpg with a top speed of 20 mph. Price was $650 for the express model and $690 with a panel body.

1914 DART MODEL B   KP

From 1907 to 1914 the Dart Manufacturing Company moved to Waterloo, Iowa, where the trucks were completely redesigned. A conventional layout using a four-cylinder engine and chain drive was adopted, and shaft drive was introduced in 1912 and three models were available: 1/2-, 1- and 1-1/2-ton. In 1914 the name became the Dart Motor Truck Company, which continued until 1918. During this period Dart also built the 2-ton Model CC, and 325 were sold to the U.S. Army. The Model CC was a conventional truck powered by a four-cylinder Buda engine, as were the lighter models.

The company became the Dart Motor Truck and Tractor Corporation after World War I at the same location. Models up to 3-ton were available. In 1922 a passenger car prototype called the Dart-mobile was fabricated, but it never made it past this initial stage as it was decided not to digress from the commercial vehicle market.

During 1925 the company became the Hawkeye-Dart Truck Company when oil company executive A.H. Howard took control. In 1925 the company was reorganized in Kansas City, Missouri, as the Dart Truck Company when Howard died and Max W. Cline bought the company's assets. Production continued into the 1930s with several models from 1-1/2-ton to 5-ton.

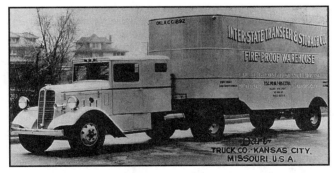

1936 DART 8-TON ARTICULATED VAN   NAHC

In 1938, the company offered newly designed 10-ton rigid or articulated six-wheel trucks, but it was the previous year that Dart began an entirely new model line of heavy-duty trucks for the mining industry. For 1939 Dart built a diesel-electric 6x4 tractor that could tow two 40-ton coal trailers. During World War II Dart built 10-ton 6x4 trucks and 40-ton 6x6 truck tractors as tank transporters that were powered by 250 hp six-cylinder Waukesha engines.

1947 DART MODEL 50 TRUCK TRACTOR   FLP

1948 DART MODEL G TRACTOR-TRAILER   FLP

In 1947, Dart was bought out by the George Ohrstrom Company of New York, and in 1950 it changed ownership to the Carlisle Corporation of Carlisle, Pennsylvania. In the early 1950s heavy-duty tractors up to 20-ton were discontinued. Production was focused on large off-highway dump trucks that reached 70-ton capacity by 1958 when the company was acquired by the Pacific Car and Foundry of Renton, Washington, which was the parent company of Kenworth and Peterbilt. The company changed names in 1961 to KW-Dart Truck Company. By 1962 Dart was building 100-ton capacity dump trucks, and by 1965 the range included trucks from 15-ton rear dump-type to 120-ton bottom-dump tractor/trailer rigs.

By the following year the 110-ton capacity rear-dump KW-Dart D2771 was powered by an 800 hp V-12 diesel engine and used a six-speed powershift torque-converter transmission with automatic lockup and Torqmatic retarding brake. Dual-reduction was through planetary gears in the hub. The truck could turn in a 75-foot radius. Front suspension consisted of free-floating variable rate springs over air springs. Rear suspension used semi-elliptical slip end free-floating variable rate springs with radius rods.

1966 KW-DART 110-TON MODEL D2771   CCJ

In 1970, when the name of the company went back to just Dart, three model lines were available: first, 65-, 75- and 110-ton capacity two-axle diesel mechanical-drive trucks; second, 120- and 150-ton two-axle diesel-electric drive trucks; and third, 100- and 120-ton diesel mechanical-drive articulated three-axle bottom dumpers. Both V-12 and V-16 Caterpillar, Cummins and Detroit diesel engines were available with 635 hp up to 1600 hp.

On the mechanical drive models, Allison and Twin-Disc manual-electric powershift transmissions were offered. The diesel-electric used two General Electric motor units flange-mounted to a tubular wheel housing. Custom orders were available and Dart built two such units in 1969 in the form of a 120-ton tractor pulling three 140-ton capacity trailers, which were used in Baja California for hauling salt from evaporators to the processing plant. Another custom order was from Kuwait to move entire assembled oil well derricks from one site to another. This was dubbed "the world's largest dune buggy," which performed the equivalent work of 14 conventional 25-ton trucks.

Throughout the late 1960s and 1970s Dart also built twin-steer six-wheel fuel tankers for aircraft, as well as front-end loaders, logstackers and snowplows. Production was interrupted in 1973 due to new management policy, but it was resumed with several models of rear-dump and bottom-dump trucks with up to 150-ton capacity. These were powered by Caterpillar, Cummins and Detroit diesel engines as before with up to 1050 hp.

The Dart 4000 series available since the early 1980s included four models: 120-, 130-, 150- and 160-ton articulated bottom-dump coal haulers. The largest Model 4160 was powered by a Cummins KTA2300-C1050 V-12 or Detroit 12V-149T V-12 turbocharged diesel engine, both having a hp rating of 1050. All of these models were fitted with Ingersoll-Rand compressed-air starting motors with tanks of 19-cubic feet capacity. Transmission was an Allison DP8961 6F 1R automatic and rear axle was a Dart DS720 double reduction differential and final planetary reduction in each wheel.

For the 1980s Dart also developed the Model 2085 six-wheel dump truck for off road hauling on steep slopes or soft ground. This truck was designed to carry an 85-ton load up a muddy 16 percent slope, which is in itself 23 percent better than any conventional 85-ton single drive axle dump truck. Engine options were the 800 hp Cummins VTA-1710 or 800 hp Detroit Diesel 16V-92T V-16. Transmission was the same as on the Model 4160 and final drive was a triple reduction type using a Dart DT550 double reduction differential and planetary reduction in each wheel. Top speed was approximately 40 mph.

1994 DART 160-TON MODEL 4160   UNIT RIG

Unit Rig & Equipment Company of Tulsa, Oklahoma, bought the Dart Truck Company from Paccar Incorporated in 1984. Subsequently, Terex Corporation of Green Bay, Wisconsin, acquired Unit Rig and Equipment in 1988.

Up to 1995 Dart has built the 85-ton Model 2085, 100-ton Model 3100 and 130-ton Model 3120, the latter being the largest of four 4x2 rear dump trucks with mechanical drive. The 1200 hp Cummins KTA 2300-C1200 V-12 turbocharged diesel or the 1050 hp Detroit Diesel engines have been available. These were typical specifications with the transmission being the Allison CLBT-9680 6F 1R automatic and rear axle a Dart DS 800 with triple reduction. Dart's two articulated bottom dump trucks have been the Model 4120 and 4160 with 120-ton and 160-ton capacity, respectively. Along with the 600C loader, these trucks have also featured mechanical drive.

1995 DART 85-TON MODEL 2085   **UNIT RIG**

1902 DAVENPORT 12-PASSENGER STAGE   **RD**

DAVENPORT 1902-1903 — The Davenport Manufacturing Company of Minneapolis, Minnesota, built steam stages in 1902. The first was a 12-passenger coach powered by a 15 hp double-cylinder steam engine operating at 250 psi. There were two 16-inch boilers with Kelly generators and burners. Fuel to create steam was provided by two 12-1/2-gallon tanks of gasoline. There was an independent steam air pump, a Moore steam water pump and a power pump attached to the engine. Sarvin wood spoke wheels were used and the vehicle featured Brussels upholstery. Weight of the stage was 3,500 pounds and it was capable of 10 mph. This particular stage was priced at $2,500, but the company also built a 26-passenger bus in 1902, and then in 1903, two 20-passenger buses for Leopold E. Wagner of Binghamton, New York, who operated the buses between downtown and a park several miles outside the city. No other production has been noted after 1903.

DAY-ELDER 1919-1937 — Although Day-Elders were conventional assembled trucks, they were considered good quality. They were first built by the National Motors Manufacturing Company of Irvington, New Jersey. In the early 1920s Day-Elder became nationally distributed with some sales in Canada, also. For 1921 the 2-ton Model D with 170-inch wheelbase was powered by a 27.23 hp Continental four-cylinder engine using a four-speed selective sliding gear transmission and rear axle was Timken worm-drive.

The price of this truck that year was $2,600. Six models from 1-ton to 5-ton were available by 1922, and these were powered by four-cylinder Buda or Continental engines. Transmissions were made by Brown-Lipe, Corvette or Muncie and axles were made by Columbia, Sheldon or Timken.

By 1924 the Day-Elder model line consisted of the 1-1/2-ton Model AN, 2-ton Model BN, 2-1/2-ton Model BN, 3-ton Model CN, 4-ton Model FN and 5-ton Model EN. Model AN with 128-inch wheelbase was powered by a 22.5 hp Buda WTU engine with Zenith carburetor and Bosch ignition, with starter and generator at extra cost. Model BN with 144-inch wheelbase was used a 22.5 hp Continental J-4 engine. Model DN with 144-inch wheelbase used a 27.2 hp Continental K-4 engine. Model CN with 150-inch wheelbase used a 28.9 hp Buda HTU engine. Model FN with 165-inch wheelbase used a 32.4 hp Continental L-4 engine, and Model EN with 170-inch wheelbase was powered by a 36.1 hp Continental B-5 engine. All models used Zenith carbs and Bosch ignition with generator and starter offered at extra cost. The three lightest models used Columbia front axles. Otherwise at this time all axles were Timken, and all clutches and transmissions were made by Brown-Lipe.

In the mid 1920s, on all but the heaviest model, pneumatic tires were available at extra cost. The Model EN had dual wheels on the rear. From 1925 Day-Elder used worm-drive as standard equipment, and by mid-1925 the first six-cylinder engines were offered. A bus chassis was also developed that year and sales peaked about this time. However, by 1928 the market sagged for Day-Elder. A new model line of trucks had been developed, and it was put into production for 1929.

1929 DAY-ELDER 2-TON   **NAHC**

The new 1929 models consisted of the "Super Service Sixes." These were from 1-ton to 6-ton capacity, and all of them were powered by six-cylinder Continental engines. The lighter models had internal hydraulic brakes. The bus chassis was updated and sold as a high-speed van. Day-Elder adopted an unusual, though effective, suspension for the rear axle. A semi-elliptic spring above the axle carried the heavier load and was used in conjunction with a smaller auxiliary leaf below which carried the unladen vehicle. In later years larger International trucks used the same design.

Day-Elder six-wheel trucks also used a Timken bogie. In 1930 the model line was redesigned again in order to compete with Brockway trucks in restricted areas such as New York and New Jersey. The model line ranged from 1-1/2-ton to 8-ton capacity. A bus chassis was offered powered by a Hercules engine. These designs remained unchanged as Day-Elder continued to lose its market share, increasingly becoming a local make until its final demise in 1937.

For the last year of manufacture the company listed seven models: 76, 86, 111, 131, 161, 201 and 241. Wheelbases were 135-, 186-, 186-, 204-, 204-, 204- and 234-inches in chronological order of models. All were powered by six-cylinder Hercules engines with lightest to heaviest models as follows, respectively: 59 hp JXA, 68 hp JXB, 73 hp JXC, 94 hp WXC, 106 hp WXC3, 106 hp WXC3 and 114 hp RXC. The three lightest models up to 2-1/2-ton used Clark T-9 transmissions, while the heaviest four models from 3-ton to 7-ton used Fuller transmissions, and all models used Timken front and rear axles. Chassis prices were $945, $1,245, $1,495, $2,045, $2,495, $2,945 and $4,095, respectively.

DAY STEAM 1901-1902 — The Day Automobile Company of Kansas City, Missouri, started as a dealership for Locomobile steam vehicles and Oldsmobile cars. The company announced upon its commencement as a business enterprise, that there were only two cars in all of Kansas City, both of which were electric. Day built a steam delivery wagon for the George P. Peck Dry Goods Company. The vehicle used a 10 hp steam engine with an 18-inch diameter boiler giving a top speed of up to 18 mph. An anti-freeze device kept the water from freezing in the pipes allowing for operation in cold weather. Although production was intended in St. Louis, this did not materialize, and Day remained an auto dealership.

1914 DAYTON FLAREBOARD EXPRESS   OCW

DAYTON 1914-1915 — The Dayton Electric Car Company of Dayton, Ohio, built a 750-pound capacity electric-powered truck called the Model 15. Chassis price was $1,200 and as a closed panel truck the price was $1,600.

DAY UTILITY 1911-1914 — Former Locomobile dealer Thomas W. Day started the Day Automobile Company in Detroit, Michigan. Hugh Jennings, manager of the Detroit baseball team, became vice-president. The vehicle was designed for use by farmers and its advertising stated "All the room possible is provided for carrying produce." The Day Utility was a combination vehicle, but it was also built as an open express body in the form of the Model D.

The Day Utility started out in 1911 as a 100-inch wheelbase vehicle with a 21 hp four-cylinder engine. In 1912, when a new factory was organized at East Milwaukee Street, the wheelbase grew to 110 inches and hp grew to 26. In the last year of production the Day Utility used a 115-inch wheelbase and a 33 hp motor. All of the models used shaft drive and a three-speed transmission. Prices ranged from $1,150 in 1911 to $1,500 in 1913. Plans were made to move the company to Spokane, Washington, but these never materialized and the Day Utility ceased production.

1920 DEARBORN MODEL F   RD

DEARBORN 1919-1924 — Not to be confused with the obscure Dearborn Automobile Company of Chicago in 1912, the Dearborn Motor Truck Company produced a line of trucks that were 1-1/2-ton and 2-ton capacity starting in 1919. Over the six years of the company's existence, engines were manufactured by Buda, Continental and Hercules. A 1-ton model with pneumatic tires and a 133-inch wheelbase was built for the last two years of production before the enterprise closed in 1924.

1911 DECATUR MOTOR TRUCK   RD

DECATUR 1909-1915 — The somewhat convoluted history of the Decatur Motor Car Company began with Lembert W. Coppock, an engineer who started the Coppock Motor Car Company in Marion, Indiana. After designing and building a light delivery truck, Coppock moved to Decatur, Indiana, when the Decatur Commercial Club came to the rescue of his failing business. The company was reorganized in 1909 as the Decatur Motor Car Company and factory output was increased. Ironically, Coppock left the company about the same time, but the truck he designed remained in production.

1914 DECATUR PARCEL POST KAR   RD

Along with Coppock's Decatur truck, the company offered the "Decatur Utility Car," which sold for $750 and was powered by a two-cylinder air-cooled engine. The rear quarter was easily converted to carry parcels and light cargo. After 200 were built in 1910, the "Utility Car" was discontinued in 1911. It was superseded by the Hoosier Limited truck, which became an instant success. This was a 1-1/2-ton cab-over truck powered by a 30 hp four-cylinder Rutenber engine. It had a three-speed transmission and dual chain drive. With either solid or pneumatic tires, it was offered with 25 different commercial bodies. However, the factory proved to be inadequate to handle the output, and the company accepted a $100,000 offer from Grand Rapids, Michigan, to move its operations there.

Once in Grand Rapids, the company was reorganized in 1912 as the Grand Rapids Motor Truck Company, which became the Parcel Post Equipment Company the following year. A new design, exactly opposite of the previous one, was employed for the new Decatur Parcel Wagon. In this configuration the driver sat at the rear over the axle in back of the cargo area. A V-2 air-cooled engine or four-cylinder water-cooled engine was available with final drive by single chain. The brake was actuated with a single lever pulled towards the seat, which closed an external band inside the differential housing. The same lever when pushed forward and snapped back started the engine. The Parcel Wagons, which had a 600-pound capacity, were sold primarily to the U.S. Post Office. In the final year of production, capacity was increased to 800 pounds, and hp was upped to 14.

Before production stopped at the end of 1915, the company also created the unique Decatur Roadster out of the Parcel Wagon. With the bodies interchangeable, the roadster resembled a large box. The driver still sat over the rear axle, and this created a long hood on the 102-inch wheelbase chassis. The 14 hp engine was the same as on the commercial vehicle, but the unusual roadster used a three-speed selective sliding gear transmission.

1907 DEERE 2-1/2-TON   **RD**

DEERE 1906-1907 — W.E. Clark of Moline, Illinois, began in 1897 when he built an experimental one-cylinder air-cooled car. In 1903 Clark briefly marketed a car called the Blackhawk but without success. By 1905 he persuaded the well-known John Deere to help finance his next motor vehicle venture, and so the Deere-Clark Motor Car Company began in Moline. Coincidentally, John Deere bought out the Clarkmobile Company of Lansing, Michigan, which apparently had no previous connection to W.E. Clark. The machinery and equipment was brought to Moline and manufacture began. Besides a few passenger cars, Deere-Clark also built a 2-1/2-ton truck.

The Deere truck was shown at the end of 1907. It had a horizontally-opposed engine rated at 20 hp mounted in front driving through a clutch that consisted of shoes expanded in a drum. A three-speed progressive sliding gear transmission was used, and final drive was by dual chain. Raymond brakes were used on the rear axle, the other on the countershaft of the transmission. The front axle was a I-beam Elliot-type and the rear axle a square forging. Semi-elliptic springs were used all around. Carnegie channel steel formed the frame, which could be varied to change to the length per customer order. John Deere and his company were not satisfied with the results, neither with the passenger car nor the truck, and proceeded to withdraw their financial stake and name in the Deere-Clark enterprise. Clark reorganized the company and briefly built a car called the Midland, but that venture rapidly faded. Another motor vehicle venture of Moline faired better, the Velie, which was connected to the Deere family through marriage.

1921 DEFIANCE   **HAYS**

DEFIANCE 1917-1930 — Before the Turnbull Motor Truck and Wagon Company began manufacturing the Defiance truck line in Defiance, Ohio, there were two previous ventures called Defiance that did not produce any commercial vehicles. The Turnbull factory was one of the largest operations in Defiance when it was organized in 1916. It later became the Defiance Motor Truck Company in the same location. By 1917, the company began offering conventional trucks from 1-ton to 3-ton. Over the years the company used its own engines, such as in the 1927 1-1/2-ton model, or engines from Continental, Hercules and Wisconsin.

Defiance, which eventually became the Century Motor Truck Company in Defiance, Ohio, in 1925, also built a bus chassis in 1923 powered by a Continental engine. This was a short-lived production run, unlike the company's fire engine chassis that were purchased by Howe to build its Defender series fire trucks. In addition to the factory in Defiance, an assembly plant was built in 1925 in Digby, Nova Scotia, which remained in operation until 1930 when the Depression began.

DEGROOT 1901 — Far ahead of his time, George F. DeGroot was a mailman in Morristown, Pennsylvania, who designed a small parcel wagon in 1900. The wagon was enclosed for the full length of its body to protect both its postal cargo and its mail carrier. A prototype was ready by 1901. It was powered by a 20 hp gasoline engine. Although the vehicle generated much interest in Pennsylvania, and as far away as New York, no further production took place. Ironically, DeGroot continued working for the U.S. Post Office on foot for 25 years, with records estimating that he walked over 146,000 miles during that quarter century of mail service. It appears he did not venture into the commercial vehicle business again after building his unique mail truck.

DEKALB 1914-1918 — Some confusion exists regarding the name DeKalb in connection with commercial vehicles. One company existed in 1915 in St. Louis, Missouri, which built a delivery car using a 130-inch wheelbase and was powered by a 45 hp Beaver engine. This was a brief business venture and appears completely independent of the DeKalb Wagon Works of DeKalb, Illinois, which existed for almost five years.

The latter built trucks that ranged from 1-1/2-ton to 3-1/2-ton capacity. These were powered by four-cylinder Continental engines "under-the-driver-seat." For the first three years chain drive was used exclusively, but by 1916 worm-drive was optional before it became standardized. In 1917 the engines were mounted in front under a hood. The company did not survive past the end of World War I.

DELAHUNTY 1913-1915 — The Delahunty Dyeing Machine Company of Pitton, Pennsylvania, briefly indulged in the motor truck manufacturing business. The early model, priced at $1,800 in 1913, was a 1-ton capacity truck, later upgraded to 1-1/2-ton powered by a 30 hp four-cylinder Continental engine. Later trucks were powered by four-cylinder Buda engines, according to some sources. The engine was coupled to a three-speed transmission via a Hartford cone clutch. Wheelbase was 120 inches and suspension was by semi-elliptic springs. Final drive was through dual chains, and this chassis was priced at $1,800.

1948 DELCAR   **RD**

DELCAR 1947-1949 — The American Motors Incorporated of Troy, New York, built a cab-over delivery van with a short wheelbase of 60 inches. It was powered by a small four-cylinder engine. Its suspension was unusual for the time in that it was independent on all four wheels. The van was priced at $890.

DELLING 1930 — Eric H. Delling was a veteran designer with Stanley Steamer and Mercer car companies. He had also designed and built the Deltal racing car. With his brothers he established Delling Motors Company in West Collingswood, New Jersey. In the early 1920s his company produced small numbers of steam touring cars and sedans priced from $2,500 to $3,200. The steam cars were advertised for their engine power flexibility, which enabled the vehicle to accelerate from 1 mph to 60 mph "without the use of a clutch and without shifting gears."

Another detail worth noting was the claimed kerosene efficiency of 16 mpg. At the time kerosene cost one-third that of gasoline, and it was not taxed by the state. The Delling engine was a three-cylinder double-acting design with poppet valves. A claim in regards to its performance was likened to a 12-cylinder gasoline motor.

The company sought a broad market including taxicabs, buses, tractors, railroad cars, trucks and marine motors. Delling, the chief designer, was capable of building such units, but it is uncertain how many prototypes of these vehicles were built. Delling had also been with the Brooks Steam Motors company, and he eventually formed the Supersteam Service Company to build buses, finding New York investors at the beginning of the Depression.

One bus was built and put into service in 1929 on a route between Philadelphia and Atlantic City logging 40,000 miles. But without orders forthcoming, Delling realized the bus was going to be his only prototype and the company shut down permanently. Some years later, Delling continued with Alma Steam Motors in Newton, Massachusetts.

1918 DEMARTINI BHS

DEMARTINI 1918-1934 — Although some records show that the DeMartini Truck Company was started in 1916, it is believed that production did not begin until 1918 in San Francisco, California. One of the first documented trucks built by DeMartini was a 4-ton self-contained laundry truck built for the U.S. Marine Corps, probably delivered to the Presidio in San Francisco. It was powered by a 28.9 hp 313-cubic inch four-cylinder Buda engine and used a three-speed Brown-Lipe transmission. Its wheelbase was 160 inches and it used 36x4 front and rear solid rubber tires with duals on back.

When most U.S. cities began municipal garbage collection service around the time of World War I, George J. DeMartini saw the potential in building specialized trucks to accomplish this task far better than with horsedrawn wagons. DeMartini had built his own airplane and had worked for the Army-Navy Aircraft Industrial Service.

DeMartini trucks were conventional assembled trucks that usually had dump beds for trash hauling, although a few were built as flatbeds and fire trucks. A small number still in existence that have been converted to flatbeds still have the telltale side steps mounted for refuse collection. Most of the early models had open cabs, although a few C-cabs were built.

The 1925 1-1/2-ton model had a 150-inch wheelbase with 34x4 front and 34x6 rear tires on Smith wheels. It had Buda WTU 22.5 hp engine with Zenith carburetor and Bosch ignition and used a Brown-Lipe clutch and transmission.

1925 DEMARTINI 2-TON HAYS

The same year Model OV 2-ton had a wheelbase of 147 inches and used a Buda HTU 28.9 hp engine also with Zenith carb and Bosch ignition. A Brown-Lipe clutch and four-speed selective slide transmission were standard. Power was transferred to the rear wheels by means of driveshaft to a Sheldon semi-floating worm-drive. The truck used left side Ross steering with the front axle being a standard I-beam design having semi-elliptic leaf springs both front and rear. The wooden spoke wheels had 34x4 front and 36x7 rear solid rubber tires. Price of a new OV model in 1925 was $3,200.

Another 2-ton model of that time offered a 168-inch wheelbase with 36x4 front and 36x7 rear tires. The 3-ton model had a 180-inch wheelbase with a Buda ETU 28.9 hp engine and used 36x5 front and 36x10 rear tires. The 4-ton model, the largest for De-Martini at that time, had a 190-inch wheelbase with a Buda YBU 32.4 hp engine and used 36x6 front and 36x12 rear tires. On each of these last three models the clutch and transmission were Brown-Lipe, the carb Zenith and ignition Bosch, with Ross steering and Smith wheels.

Pneumatic tires were introduced in the late 1920s. By 1933 the Model GW17 used an 85 hp (SAE) engine and had a five-speed transmission. However, after 1931 few DeMartini trucks were built, although the company continued to manufacture dump beds until 1934. George DeMartini had many inventions during the course of his career and business venture, but he stated that he never had a need to patent them.

DE MOTTE 1904 — Like many other early motor vehicle companies, De Motte attempted to build several different models on one chassis. These included "solid and detachable tonneaus, solid and detachable surreys, runabouts, light and heavy deliveries, trucks, passenger coaches." A 10 hp two-cylinder engine was offered with the light delivery wagon, while a 20 hp four-cylinder was offered with the truck.

Chain drive and wheel steering were universal features among all the models. The advertising slogan was "Quaker Staunchness with French Perfection." It has been noted that the truck had the driver's seat located just above the engine in a precarious position.

DENBY 1914-1930 — Of the many conventional assembled trucks, the Denby Motor Truck Company of Detroit, Michigan, entered into the competitive commercial vehicle market in 1914, and its best business years were directly after World War I. However,

Denby never capitalized on its large production potential. In the late 1920s (after Denby incorporated in 1923) most of the oversized plant was sold to a radiator manufacturer.

1915 DENBY 1-1/2-TON   NAHC

During the early years of production Denby offered a model line of trucks ranging from 3/4-ton to 2-ton. The 3/4-ton sold for $890 in 1915. It featured a low express body and solid rubber tires on wooden spoke wheels. For the same year the 1-ton Type B cost $1,475, 1-1/2-ton Type D cost $1,685 and 2-ton Type E cost $1,985. Top, panel body, starting and lighting systems and pneumatic tires were available at extra cost.

1916 DENBY 1-TON   WM

A 3-ton and 7-ton model were available from 1918 to 1922. Subsequently, a 30-passenger bus chassis was built from 1926 to 1930. Disc wheels were a recognizable feature of the Denby trucks, which were mostly powered by Continental engines with the exception of 1-1/2-ton and 2-1/2-ton models from 1924 on, which were powered by Hercules engines. The company did not survive the Great Depression.

DENISON 1898-1902 — Julian F. Denison experimented with gasoline engines before the turn of the century. He developed a two-stroke water-cooled engine in 1898 and established the Denison Motor Carriage Company that year. Named after his partner, the company built a tricycle called Tinkham, as well as four-wheel vehicles under his own name. It appears the only commercial vehicle Denison built was a nine-passenger omnibus for a Torrington company. After 1901 the name of his engines and vehicles was changed to Yale before all production stopped in 1902. However, the Denison Electric Engineering Company did survive as a separate entity.

DENMO 1916-1918 — The Denneen Motor Company of Cleveland, Ohio, was briefly in the business of building a conventional 1-1/4-ton truck model. These were called Denmo and were powered by a four-cylinder Wisconsin engine using a three-speed transmission. Torbensen internal gear drive was used. The front tires were pneumatic while the rear were solid rubber. Few of these trucks were built, and little else is known about the company.

DENNISTON 1911-1912 — As with numerous obscure motor vehicle builders of the early part of the century, conflicting stories abound regarding production and solvency of the E.E. Denniston Company of Buffalo, New York. Early in 1911 the Denniston Company took over the business of E.E. Denniston, recapitalizing with $150,000 for the purpose of building cars and commercial vehicles. Powered by a 15 hp two-cylinder engine, a closed delivery van with 98-inch wheelbase was offered with a capacity of 3/4-ton. A three-speed transmission was utilized with shaft drive to the rear axle. Pneumatic tires were standard and the van was priced at $2,000, but whether such a van was actually produced is in doubt. The company did build some automobile bodies before the Buffalo Electric Vehicle Company moved in to the Denniston factory in 1912.

DEPENDABLE 1914-1925 — The Dependable Truck and Tractor Company of Galesburg, Illinois, made a brief foray into truck manufacturing starting right after World War I when the market was saturated with surplus military trucks. By 1921 the model line included 1-, 1-1/2-, 2-1/2- and 3-1/2-ton trucks powered by Buda engines. By the following year, however, the only models offered were the 1-1/2-ton and the 2-1/2-ton capacity. Fuller three-speed transmissions and Wisconsin worm-drive rear axles were standard throughout.

DESBERON 1901-1904 — The Desberon Motor Car Company had two plants by 1901, one in Manhattan and the other in New Rochelle, New York. Desberon built a few steam-powered as well as gasoline-powered commercial vehicles in the form of delivery vans. Towards the end of their production, the company also produced gasoline-powered trucks with an output of one per month. The engine Desberon used had a patented "cylinder head wherein there are no water joints whatever." Its radiator also used an allegedly optimized design for that era, and bronze bearings were utilized in the same applications where other companies had used ball bearings and roller bearings. The vehicles were not fast as a result, and the company faded away after 1904 for a variety of reasons in a highly competitive market.

DE SCHAUM 1908-1909 — Andrew Schaum moved to Buffalo, New York, and changed his name to William A. de Schaum in 1906. There he designed a highwheeler for the C. Rossler Manufacturing Company. He left the company and established the De Schaum Motor Syndicates Company in Buffalo, where he designed other highwheelers that were known as the "Seven Little Buffaloes." The commercial vehicle was available with a delivery body using an 84-inch wheelbase chassis, and it was powered by a 12 hp two-cylinder engine, with the choice of air or water cooling, and it used a friction transmission with double chain final drive. Capacity was 800 pounds with semi-elliptic front and full-elliptic rear suspension using a 54-inch tread. With some optional equipment prices varied from $750 to $850.

DESERT FLYER 1908 — As a commercial vehicle venture the Desert Flyer was an unusual enterprise. Its origins have been traced to Tonopah, Nevada, where the local newspaper announced in 1907 the formation of the Nevada Motor Car Company, which was to begin manufacturing in Reno by the end of the year. These vehicles were designed as jitneys providing service between various mining districts of Nevada at a time when this mining region was highly active. Only a single prototype was built, but it was not ordinary.

One of the main investors was George Bertzchy of Reno, Nevada, who was a successful silver mine entrepreneur. Other partners included Tex Rickard, George's relative A.J.P. Bretzchy, who had worked for several motor car businesses in Chicago, as well as George W. Tibbetts, a wealthy physician who had invested in the lucrative Nevada mines.

The initial prototype weighed five tons and was powered by an 80 hp four-cylinder engine. It was composed mostly of Pope-Toledo components and used 40-inch solid wooden disc wheels that were iron-bound and had solid rubber tires. It featured a double radiator and enormous fuel and oil capacities for travel through the uninhabited desert. The Desert Flyer was also called the Nevada Flyer and the Reno Flyer. William Clifford of Rawhide, Nevada, became involved briefly in this venture. The original prototype, known as the Nevada Truck, was put into operation in Council Bluffs, Iowa. A.J.P. Bertzchy continued in Council Bluffs with his Bertzchy Motor Company.

1948 DESOTO FUNERAL COACH   OCW

DESOTO 1936-1960 — Not to be confused with de Soto of Auburn, Indiana, DeSoto trucks were badge-engineered for foreign dealers of Chrysler-made commercial vehicles, just as were the related Fargo trucks. DeSoto started out as a record-setting manufacturer for the first year of existence, 1929, when it built 81,065 cars.

It was not until 1937 that DeSoto emblems appeared on trucks, although DeSoto taxis were listed separately in 1936. These were known as seven-passenger jitneys built on extended wheelbase chassis, and production for 1936 was divided between the New York taxi (2,500 total) and California taxi (451 total). These were powered by a 93 hp six-cylinder L-head engine, which was increased to 100 hp in 1940 and 115 hp in 1942. Taxi production fluctuated, but remained low compared to overall output. A few commercial limousines were also built on the long wheelbase chassis, which started out at 130 inches in 1936 and was stretched to 139.5 inches by 1942.

1949 DESOTO S-13-1 DELUXE TAXI   OCW

1958 DESOTO POWER WAGON   CHRYS

The long wheelbase DeSoto jitney and limousine, which usually had two "jump" back seats that folded into the floor, were built through 1954, by that time powered by 170 hp hemi V-8 engines with PowerFlite automatic transmissions.

DeSoto trucks were first exported to Europe as the 1938 model year, and to Australia after World War II. These trucks were identical to Dodge trucks of the same period. In the early 1950s DeSoto trucks were available for export as the J, JA, KA, JM, JMA and KMA series with GVW from 17,250 pounds for the first two series, up to 19,000 pounds for the KMA series. GCW ranged from 32,000 pounds to 36,000 pounds for these series. L-head six-cylinder engines were used throughout with hp at 114 or 120, depending on the series. Transmissions were five-speed with two-speed rear axles as optional equipment. Both COE and conventional cabs were available, and numerous bodies were built for different customers, including tractor and van trailer, beverage trucks, stake body, dump bed, COE tank trucks, refrigerated conventionals and truck tractor tank trailer combinations.

When Chrysler dropped the marque in 1961, truck production using the DeSoto insignia also ceased. A few DeSoto trucks continued to be assembled in India until recently. See Dodge for specifications.

1911 DETROIT ELECTRIC 1/2-TON VAN   NAHC

DETROIT ELECTRIC 1909-1927 — The Anderson Carriage Company, which had been established in Port Huron, Michigan, in 1884, was moved to Detroit, Michigan, in 1895 and began building Detroit Electric vehicles by 1907. Among a dozen manufacturers by the name of Detroit that were organized to build vehicles, the Detroit Electric was the only electric and the only one to build commercial vehicles.

Production increased from 125 in 1907, to 400 in 1908 and 1,500 by 1910. In 1909 Anderson had bought the Elwell-Parker Company of Cleveland, makers of electric motors that had previously been supplied to Baker Electric vehicles. As Anderson was able to build all necessary components besides batteries, tires and wheels, the name of the company was changed to Anderson Electric Car Company in 1911. The year Elwell-Parker was purchased, Anderson offered a 1-ton forward-control truck powered by such an electric motor with side chain drive. By 1912 a 1/2-ton and a 1-1/2-ton model were added to the line, both of which featured wheel steering unlike many of the tiller-steered vehicles of that day.

Anderson undertook a range test to prove that the Detroit Electrics could compete with gasoline-powered vehicles, and in a factory-sponsored run a Detroit Electric ran 211 miles on a single charge, it was claimed. Normal range was actually about 80 miles between charges. In 1912 a taxi was listed. This was the Model 28 with 112-inch wheelbase and a price tag of $3,400. For a brief period around 1913 Detroit Electrics were assembled in Scotland. In 1916 a 2-ton van with a price tag of $2,000 without batteries was offered. This was the year Anderson bought out Chicago Electric, which had been in business since the turn of the century.

By the time World War I had started, production dropped to 3,000 vehicles per year. In 1918 William Anderson retired and M.S. Towsen of Elwell-Parker took over the running of the business. By 1920 the Detroit Electrics were furnished with a hood and false radiator to give them the appearance of gasoline-powered vehicles, which were rapidly gaining favor with the public and the industry. Passenger car production fell drastically, but Detroit Electric light trucks and vans continued to be produced. In 1922 a milk van was built in four iterations: forward control, rear control or from either runningboard.

In 1925, the Detroit Industrial Vehicle Company was formed to develop a gasoline-powered model line of delivery vans, but this did not meet with success. William Anderson died just days before the Great Depression began, and the company's business plummeted after that. The company survived on an individual order basis only, and in some cases coachwork was supplied by Willys-Overland, which resulted in louvered hoods for the electric cars. Shortly after the stock market crash, the company was taken over by A.O. Dunk, known for his business acumen and ability to resurrect dying companies. He kept the company afloat until he himself died in 1936. A few Detroit Electric vehicles were produced until 1938 when the company shut down for good.

DETROIT MOTOR WAGON See Motor Wagon

DETROIT TAXICAB 1914-1915 — The Detroit Taxicab and Transfer Company built its own vehicles on a 121-inch wheelbase when no other company in Detroit was interested in meeting the company's specifications to produce an electric taxi. The prototype was unveiled in mid-1914 at the Hotel Pontchartrain, and after a successful test period 11 more taxis were built. Although detailed specifications are lacking, it is known that the company built a total of 47 electric taxis that remained in service for a number of years before being gradually retired from service around Detroit.

1912 DEVON RD

DEVON 1912-1914 — The Devon began as a vehicle purchased through club membership only, which Merchant & Evans had marketed under the name Club Car. When this failed in New York for lack of memberships, Merchant & Evans moved to Philadelphia, Pennsylvania, and put the Devon emblem on the remaining Club Cars.

Apparently this did not meet with success, and the factory was reorganized as the Devon Engineering Company, which remained in Philadelphia to build some large trucks of 3-1/2-, 5- and 6-ton capacity. The 6-ton Model 6 was an articulated chassis with front-wheel-drive and front-wheel-brakes, while the rear wheels used steel tires to fulfill such a heavy capacity rating for that time. The lighter trucks were powered by a four-cylinder Continental E engine using a Hele Shaw multiple disc clutch and three-speed selective sliding gear transmission with final drive by chain. Front axle was from Sheldon and rear axle was made by Devon. Artillery wheels carried 30x5 front and 40x4 dual rear solid rubber tires. Suspension was semi-elliptic both front and rear. Few of the Devon trucks were built, and by 1914 the company ceased operations altogether.

DE WITT 1984-1986 — The De Witt autobuggy built at this time was a replica of the original De Witt built around 1910. It had a cargo box on the rear deck. The replica was built in North Manchester, Indiana, where the original De Witt vehicles were manufactured.

1909 DEWITT LIGHT DELIVERY KP

1907 DIAMOND MATCH 4-TON RD

DIAMOND MATCH 1907 — The Diamond Match Company of Barberton, Ohio, built its own truck using the "engine-under-driver-seat" design. The 115-inch wheelbase truck was powered by a 45 hp four-cylinder four-cycle water-cooled T-head engine with splash lubrication. A sliding gear transmission was used and final drive was by cardan shaft and pinion-to-internal-gear. Capacity was four tons and top speed was 12 mph. Suspension was by Cleveland-Canton semi-elliptic springs. J.W. Denmead designed and supervised the fabrication of the truck at the Diamond Match machine shop.

1974 DIAMOND REO TRACTOR-TWIN-TRAILER DR

DIAMOND REO 1967 to date — In 1967, Diamond T and Reo trucks were combined to form the Diamond Reo Trucks Division of the White Motor Corporation of Lansing, Michigan. A new emblem was developed and used on all Diamond Reo trucks. Reo dated back to 1904 when Ransom E. Olds, founder of the Oldsmobile, had begun building motor cars, and Diamond T dated back to 1905 when C.A. Tilt began building vehicles.

Diamond Reo continued with essentially the same trucks as Diamond T and Reo in 1966, offering 30 models of the combined marques. Three-axle 6x4 and 8x6 conventional articulated trucks were built along with the more common 4x2 conventional truck tractors. Two models used White cabs, and diesel engines up to 435 hp were available at that time. Seven gasoline engines from 130 hp to 250 hp were available. Both Diamond T and Reo had been manufactured separately by White since the parent company had acquired Diamond T in 1958 and Reo the year before that. Under White, operations had been combined by 1960, although the names had not until that formality took place in 1967.

Loyal Osterlund with his son, Jan Osterlund, were to be major players in Diamond Reo, as well. Loyal Osterlund had become a franchise distributor of Diamond T in 1958, eventually resurrecting the Giant model line in 1977 after Diamond Reo ceased production in 1976. The Giant model line had always been associated with Diamond T and Diamond Reo. By 1977, Osterlund had acquired the rights to the name of Diamond Reo and has continued production to date.

In 1968, the cab-over model line included the CF59 compact, which used a White cab, up to the Trend line, which was available in four models and featured a Royalex cab with steel under-structure. Along with the original 24,000-pound GVW "Trend," Diamond Reo added ratings of 25,500, 26,000 and 27,500 GVW, which were designated as the 255, 260 and 275 series. Cabs were advertised for their luxury and safety. For 1968, the overall model line included the following series: conventional trucks were designated C-90, C-101 and C-114. Cab-over (or cab-forward) were designated as CO-50, CO-78, CF-55, CF-68 and CF-83 series. A maximum 73-seat school bus chassis with 225-inch wheelbase was also available. Each of the above series was designated by the drive axles numbers. Therefore, a CO-50 4x2 was numbered CO-5042. The two largest tractors were the C-9086 and the C-10186 (both 8x6 three axle). Diesel power was available on each model and capacity.

In 1969, the CF-83 series became available with a fiberglass cab, or optional all-steel cab, which weighed 225 pounds more than its predecessor. The Cummins V-6-140 engine was made available with the Trend series, and the Cummins NHCT-270 custom torque engine was available with the C-90, C-114, CO-50 and CO-78. In combination two transmissions were offered: the Spicer 8552A or Fuller T-905J. Gasoline engines from the 6-130 to the V-8-235 were also offered. Diamond Reo also offered the Country Wagon for 1969, which had a removable 20-foot or 22-foot camper body using the Trend chassis/cab configuration.

Known as Cleanaire, in 1970 two LPG engines of either 190 hp or 230 hp were developed for propane fuel. The 8-250 V-8 was added to the gasoline engines available. Diesel engines were made by Caterpillar, Cummins, Detroit Diesel and Perkins. The largest of these produced 475 hp and transmission choices were Allison, Clark, Fuller and Spicer. The Gold Comet gasoline engines continued to be used, with diesel engines gradually becoming more common. Rear axles were made by Rockwell. Tandem trucks were available with a variety of spring and rubber suspensions.

In 1971, Francis L. Cappaert of Birmingham, Alabama, bought Diamond Reo from White for an estimated $16 million. Jack Adams remained as president. At about the same time the Diamond Reo C-116 series was introduced, which featured Cummins NTC-335 engines in combination with Fuller RTO-9513 transmissions. Other engines offered were the Cummins NTC-350, NTA-370 and Detroit Diesel 12V-71N. The CF-65 was also introduced with a full line of diesel and LPG-powered engines.

By 1972, Diamond Reo offered a new sleeper on its C-116 and C92D series. Plant production was increased 10 percent. New design work was instigated resulting in a shortened truck tractor called the C-9264D with the standard engine being the Cummins NTC-335. The cab featured an interior doghouse due to the short-ening of the engine compartment. As before, a fiberglass hood and fender assembly that tilted 90 degrees forward was standard, though steel fenders with a butterfly hood were also available. New highway cab-over trucks called Royale 54 standard and Royale 88 sleeper were also introduced featuring a wide variety of paint schemes, which were popular with independent truckers. The Royale was available with Detroit Diesel six-cylinder, V-8 or a V-12 of 852 cubic inch displacement. Gold Comet gasoline engines from 170 hp to 250 hp and Cleanaire LPG engines from 190 hp to 230 hp continued to be offered.

The new owner, F.L. Cappaert, met with the press in 1972 in order to stymie rumors of his Lansing, Michigan, company's financial woes. This took place after Jack Adams and three vice-presidents resigned in May. Cappaert pointed out the $32.1 million contract with the U.S. military to build 3,868 2-1/2-ton trucks that were slated mostly for South Korea. In late 1973 the company announced the new C-119 series, which were designed to be powered by larger diesel engines including the 425 hp Caterpillar 1693-TA, the 450 hp Cummins KT-450 and the 400 hp Detroit Diesel Allison 8V-92.

The prototype C-119 Raider was shown in 1973 and production was planned for the second quarter of the following year. This truck featured a 13-speed Fuller RTO-12513 transmission, a 15-1/2-inch clutch, Rockwell-Standard SQHD 4.11 rear axle and 10.00x22 tires. GCW was 76,800 pounds on an aluminum frame that had a 236-inch wheelbase. The radiator had a frontal area of 1,600 square inches resulting in a larger grille, which had a column of seven diamonds in the center. A forward axle for Western applications or setback axle for Eastern use were both available. The 152-inch wheelbase truck tractor axle-back prototype used a Caterpillar 1693-TA engine, a 38,000 pound capacity Eaton DS-380 rear axle and an 11-speed Spicer 1211-3A transmission.

For 1974, Diamond Reo also introduced the Rogue CF-60 series. This was a cab-forward design for urban delivery or refuse work. The new cab was 300 pounds lighter than that of the model it replaced by using tubular steel "roll cage" design. It tilted hydraulically 60 degrees forward for repair work, although filter changes, oil checks and routine maintenance could be made without tilting. Engine options included the Gold Comet 6-200 up to the Cummins NTC-290, Caterpillar 3406 and Detroit Diesel 6V-92. Transmission options were Clark, Fuller and Spicer manual and Allison and Cummins-Sundstrand automatic. By this time the company's president was Stan Eaton.

Despite the new model introductions and excellent reputation, Diamond Reo was forced into bankruptcy, filing in court on December 6, 1974. FMC Corporation had demanded $7 million it was due, and Diamond Reo posted $40 million in liabilities with about half that in assets. The president of the company announced a Chapter 11 filing and shut down the production line for a month idling 1,300 employees. A few months later some 300 employees continued finishing trucks still on the assembly line. After much wrangling in court, Diamond Reo was sold to Consolidated International of Columbus, Ohio, which sold off 163 new trucks it had acquired as part of the package deal.

F.L. Cappaert stated he had lost $31 million on Diamond Reo, partly because of the U.S. Army truck deal that, Cappaert stated, short-changed the company by at least $15 million because of a fixed-price contract during times of double digit inflation. The company's assets were sold off for $11 million. A year later Loyal Osterlund and partner Ray Houseal bought the rights to Diamond Reo trucks and made room to continue production in their Harrisburg, Pennsylvania, facility, originally a dealership and maintenance facility. The C-116 was continued in production with the Cummins NTC-290 diesel engine as standard power.

By 1978, Osterlund was building the C-116 Giant in a 4x2 or 6x4 configuration with a Cummins NTC-300 diesel, Fuller RTOF 1160 8LL 1OF 1R transmission and Rockwell-Standard SUHD single reduction hypoid rear axle. A tag axle could be added to the 4x2 and 6x4, but Diamond Reo also built a 6x6 version. Hendrickson RT 440 rear suspension was featured on the Giant, which was the only model Osterlund planned on building. Many of these were used for concrete mixer applications, and some were used for crane carrying and other construction and highway-building related applications. The C-116 remained almost identical as before except the decorative grille was eliminated so that an optional front-mounted power takeoff could be added without obstruction. Production for 1978 was 131 units. Osterlund claimed production capability of 200 trucks per year.

Through the 1980s Diamond Reo trucks continued to be built on a limited production basis. The single model Giant had several applications including dump trucks, concrete mixers and aggregate haulers that were available in 8x4 configuration. In early 1985 Diamond Reo was the first U.S. Class 8 truck company to install an air-cooled, twin-turbocharged Deutz V-8 diesel engine, which produced 315 hp. The new engine application resulted in a modern, aerodynamic, wedge-shaped hood designed by Osterlund because a tall radiator was no longer necessary. This completely changed the appearance of the heretofore square-hooded Diamond Reo trucks.

By 1985, the Harrisburg plant was expanded to be able to produce 10 trucks per day, although output continued at about two per day. The Deutz engine, designated as the model BF8L513, was 10 percent more efficient in terms of mileage and required less maintenance due to lack of liquid cooling components. In 1988, Diamond Reo introduced its new 2WMX 10-cubic yard mixer truck, which had a small cab at the rear for easier, more accurate delivery of wet concrete. At this point the company was headed by chairman Loyal Osterlund, his son Jan as president, and other son, Gary, as factory sales manager. By the late 1980s about 10 percent of sales went overseas. The Giant name was dropped in 1989.

Although the C-116 series continued, in 1991 Diamond Reo announced the new C-120 series with four new models: C12064DBT, C12064DB, C120642DBT and C12042DB. Along with an air-ride cab, the new hood had a 10 degree slope for better aerodynamics and visibility. Engine options were Cummins L10, N14 along with the Caterpillar 3406B engine. Also offered were Rockwell or Eaton axles, Fuller or Allison transmissions, and Hendrickson, Neway or Reyco suspensions.

By the early 1990s Deutz engines were no longer available due to new emission standards. The company continued to build about 150 Class 8 trucks annually through 1995. Glider kits, as well as power glider kits, were also available as recently as 1996. Using a conventional cab with the 4x2, 6x4 and 6x6 models, engine choices were Caterpillar 3406 and Cummins L10 and N14.

1927 DIAMOND T ARTICULATED TANKER   **TEX**

DIAMOND T 1911-1966 — After C.A. Tilt built his first car in 1905, he did not go into production until 1907 with three models of passenger cars. The well-known emblem had been created by Tilt's father, who was a shoe manufacturer. The diamond symbolized quality and the T stood for Tilt.

In 1911, one of Tilt's customers wanted a truck, and this prompted the motor vehicle entrepreneur to focus on truck manufacturing. The first Diamond T truck was the only one to use chain drive. It was powered by a 40 hp 432-cubic inch displacement Continental engine and a three-speed transmission with jackshaft. It had a capacity of 1-1/2 tons. Solid rubber tires were mounted on artillery wheels with duals on back. The truck used Timken axles and the frame was by A.O. Smith. It was still in service in Chicago as late as 1932.

In 1912, the company's largest model was a 5-ton truck with 144-inch wheelbase, and it was powered by a 40 hp four-cylinder engine, used chain drive (contrary to some reports that the first Diamond T truck of 1911 was the only chain driven design built), had a transmission on the jackshaft, right side steering, 36x6 front and rear solid tires with duals in back, and it cost $3,350. The 1-ton Model I with 127-inch wheelbase was powered by a 27.23

hp engine, used shaft drive and a three-speed selective sliding transmission, had 36x3-1/2 front and 36x5 rear solid tires and was priced at $2,250.

1932 DIAMOND T 6X4 1500-GALLON TANKER   **TEX**

In 1914, the 1-1/2-ton Model J had right-hand steering and was powered by a four-cylinder Continental engine, used a three-speed Brown-Lipe transmission with dry disc clutch and had a Timken-David Brown worm-driven axle. The 3-ton and 5-ton models still used chain drive and had disc-in-oil wet clutches. By 1915 Diamond T had developed a network of branches and dealerships that gradually elevated the company to national recognition status.

For 1916, the model line included the 3/4-ton Model JA with a 19.6 hp engine, 1-ton Model JB with the same engine as above, 1-1/2-ton Model J-2 with a 27.23 hp engine, and 2-ton Model J-3 also with the 27.23 hp engine. All of these used worm-drive and were priced at $1,175, $1,485, $2,050 and $2,200, respectively. This was the year the old facilities on the north side of Chicago became inadequate, and a new 250,000-square foot plant was located in Chicago's southwest side.

The following year the model designations changed with J-5 being a 1-ton capacity truck, J-4 1-1/2-ton, J-3 was still a 2-ton and Model L was a 3-1/2-ton. The latter was powered by a 32.4 hp engine and was priced at $3,300. The Model R was a 5-ton truck and was priced at $4,600. A new 1,000-foot progressive assembly line allowed production of 1,500 3-1/2-ton Model B Liberty trucks during 18 months of World War I. With this accomplished, orders for 2,000 more trucks from the military followed after the war. Because of the limitations and shortcomings of rail service during World War I, Diamond T adopted the slogan "The Nation's Freight Car" during this period.

After World War I, the company focused on expanding its dealerships, but by this time the economic picture had changed in the United States. The 1-1/2-ton truck was marketed as the "Farm Special," which had a C-cab and special express body 60-inches long by 30-inches wide and 15-inches deep with a capacity of 62.5 cubic feet. As with other Diamond T trucks of that time it used a Stromberg carburetor and Bosch ignition. Timken axles were utilized with worm-drive at the rear. The "Farm Special" was priced at $2,295.

Having overcome some lean times, Diamond T trucks were built ranging from 1-ton to 5-ton in the early 1920s. "Spring Wheels" were optional by 1920. These expensive wheels with solid outer rubber and inner rubber "spring" inserts were used before pneumatic tires were popular. Hinkley four-cylinder engines were used with three-speed selective sliding transmission and semi-floating worm-drive rear axles. Pneumatic tires were optional, fitted on artillery wheels, and steering was left-hand by 1921. Front bumper and radiator guard were standard, and the price range was from $2,220 to $5,660.

In 1923, Diamond T introduced a closed "coupe" cab, which featured a three-point rubber mounting and new styling. Steel spoke wheels became available on certain models. For that year the company offered eight models that included the 1-ton Model 03, new 1-ton Model 75, 1-1/2-ton Model T, 1-1/2-ton with cab and body Model FS, 2-1/2-ton Model U, 3-1/2-ton Model K, 5-ton Model EL and 5-ton special Model S. The new high-speed Model 75 with 130-inch wheelbase was powered by a Hercules engine with Zenith carb. It used a Covert clutch and transmission and Columbia axles. The truck also used a Hotchkiss drive, 50-inch semi-elliptic springs and 33x5 pneumatic tires.

For 1925, Diamond T offered a variety of models. The 1-ton Model 75 was continued as before powered by a 25.6 hp Hercules OX engine. The 1-1/4-ton Model 03 with 132-inch wheelbase was powered by a 22.5 hp Hinkley 700 engine with Stromberg carburetor and Bosch ignition. Clutch and transmission were made by Covert, but the axles were made by Diamond T. The 1-1/2-ton Model T had a 144-inch wheelbase and used 36x3-1/2 front and 36x5 rear solid tires. Engine, transmission and axles were the same as the Model 03. The 2-1/2-ton Model U2 with 160-inch wheelbase was powered by a 25.6 hp Hinkley 1400 engine with Covert clutch and transmission. Pneumatic 36x4 front tires were optional at extra cost, and rear tires were 36x8 duals. The 3-1/2-ton Model K with 170-inch wheelbase was powered by a 28.9 hp Hinkley 1500 engine. The 5-ton Model S with 180-inch wheelbase was powered by a 36.1 hp Hinkley Class B engine with Brown-Lipe clutch and transmission. All the models from 2-1/2-ton capacity and higher used Timken front and rear axles.

In 1926, Diamond T trucks were redesigned and restyled. Engines were more powerful Hinkley and Hercules four-cylinder units, electric lights took the place of oil lamps, and steel spoke wheels were made standard. However, in 1928 even bigger changes took place in the trucks' engineering and appearance. New six-cylinder seven-bearing engines were utilized. Clutches were multi-disc and transmission was four-speed, driving a spiral-bevel semi-floating rear axle. Brakes were four-wheel internal-expanding hydraulic, and disc wheels were standard. Double-bar bumpers were adopted, and capacities were from 1 ton to 12 ton, including a new six-wheel design.

For 1928, the model line included the 1-1/2 to 2-ton Model T36, 2-1/2-ton Model U46 with solid tires, 1-1/2 to 2-ton Model T46 with pneumatic tires, 2-1/2-ton Model U66 with rear dual pneumatic tires, 1-ton Model 150 and 2-ton Model 302. The new six-wheel four-ton truck with wheelbase from 176-inch to 215-inch had a top speed of 42 mph and was priced at $5,325. Diamond T trucks received chrome plating on many of the exterior components such as headlights, parking lights, radiator shell, cowl molding and even the step plates on the runningboards. The overall effect of re-engineering and new styling was that sales rose by 60 percent over the previous year. Diamond T was setting the pace for other truck manufacturers to follow.

In 1929, Diamond T offered the 1-ton Model 151 with 132-inch wheelbase, the 1-1/2-ton Model 290 with 138-1/2-inch wheelbase, the 2-ton Model 157-3/4-inch wheelbase, the 2-1/2-ton Model 550 with 165-inch wheelbase, the 3-ton Model 600, the 4-ton Model 800, the 8-ton Model 1600, and heavier models including 8-ton and 12-ton six-wheel models. The Model 600 was powered by a new 93.5 hp six-cylinder Hercules engine, while the Model 1600 was powered by a 98 hp Hercules engine. The 3-ton had a seven-speed transmission and had vacuum-operated four-wheel hydraulic brakes. The new Model 1600 used a Timken SW-300 bogie axle configuration. Centrifugal water pumps and pressurized engine lubrication became standard by this time. Also by this time Diamond T had 80 distributors in 60 countries.

In May of 1930, once the stock market had crashed, Diamond T announced the new 1-ton Model 200 four-cylinder truck would be priced at $785, as well as the 1-ton Model 215 six-cylinder version. The four-cylinder engine was a new Buda unit rated at 225 hp (N.A.C.C.), which meant 45 brake hp. With the heavier trucks five different six-cylinder engines were available: 638-cubic inch HXA, 707-cubic inch HXB, 770-cubic inch HXC, 885-cubic inch HXD and 935-cubic inch HXE. These were considered the heavy-duty series ranging from 118 hp to 157.5 hp.

The following year the 4-ton Model 750 with 181-inch wheelbase was added to the line. It was powered by a 125 hp six-cylinder Hercules engine with Zenith carburetor using a Covert clutch and Covert five-speed transmission. Lighting and ignition were by Auto-Lite and final drive was with a Wisconsin double reduction axle. For 1932 the 1-1/2-ton Model 210 was added at a price of $545, which included hood, fenders and all running gear.

In terms of styling, the year 1933 marked another departure from the old. All new cabs with steel roofs had V-type windshields. Also, a V-type grille was utilized and skirted fenders were adopted. Door-type vents were added to the hoods. Chrome hubcaps were standardized over steel spoke wheels. Variable-rate springs were pioneered by Diamond T as well.

By 1934, the company also unveiled its first fully-streamlined tank truck powered by a 110 hp six-cylinder engine mounted longitudinally in the back. This was a 26-foot long forward-control vehicle using a 140-inch wheelbase capable of hauling 1,500 gallons of fuel for the Texaco company. Because of the new design, the front axle to rear axle weight distribution was tremendously improved, intended for states regulating the load limit per axle. Over the following two years, six of these Texaco airport tankers were built. One of the unusual features of this truck was its engine-compartment microphone, which cut out in high gear, so that the driver could hear the engine in order to shift gears at the right rpm.

For 1935, Diamond T announced a new line of trucks from 1-1/2-ton to 12-ton capacity. Super Service engines with electric-furnace alloy blocks were introduced. They also featured a Tocco-hardened counter-balanced crankshaft with precision bearings. The Model 211A powered by an 80 hp engine sold for $555, while the new Model 220 was priced at $666. The 220 was similar to the 211A but had a larger rear axle, a B-K booster, 11-inch clutch and larger engine. Models 243, 244, 311C, 351C and 352 continued as before. The heavy-duty line included models 412B and 512B.

Aside from a new light diesel truck line, for 1936 the same basic mechanical design was continued, but once again the styling was avant-garde. The sales literature compared the new look with the Burlington Zephyr, the most modern and streamlined train of that period. The V-type windshield, which cranked open on most models, now had a 30 degree slant on the all-new aerodynamic cabs. The V-type convex stainless steel grille reflected art deco influence, as did the high-crowned, one-piece pontoon-style front fenders on which teardrop headlights were mounted. C.A. Tilt was personally responsible for all Diamond T design and styling, as has been noted.

At the same time the company also introduced inexpensive pickups and panel trucks called the Model 80 in 1936 and rated at 3/4-ton. Again, eye-catching styling including chrome wheel covers attracted new customers looking for a flashier image for their commercial vehicles. The trucks were powered by Hercules engines, which were moved forward over the front axle. The complete model line ranged from 1-1/2-ton to 6-1/2-ton.

The two high-speed diesel models were introduced as the Model 20 in the 1-1/2-ton to 3-ton capacity and the Model 30 in the 2-1/2-ton to 4-ton capacity. GVW ratings were 13,000 and 17,000 pounds, while prices were $2,150 and $2,750, respectively.

Across the line for heavy trucks, sleeper cabs became available for long haul applications. The new streamlined designs included pontoon fenders over dual rear wheels with detachable fender skirts. The year 1936 was a peak sales record for Diamond T with 8,750 registrations.

Although the cab design was to stay the same until 1951, Diamond T continued to evolve as a truck manufacturer. In 1937, Diamond T listed the following models: 80, 212AS, 212BS, 221S, D20, 2448, 313, 320, 353, 360, D30, 412DR, 512B, 512DR. These ranged from 3/4-ton to 6-1/2-ton. Wheelbase ranged from 119 inches to 225 inches. Prices ranged from $525 to $2,760, and six-cylinder Hercules engines ranged from 61 hp to 118 hp.

Every model in 1937 used 20-inch wheels except for the 3/4-ton pickup, which had 16-inch wheels. The latter, known as the Model 80, was fitted with an all-new welded steel bed made of 13-gauge sheet metal. Mid-year, Diamond T added the Model 301, which was powered by a larger six-cylinder Hercules engine. Fifteen models in total were available in 1937, not including for some Moller taxicabs, which were quite distinctive. Warner and Clark transmissions were used throughout the model line, and axles were supplied by Clark, Eaton, Timken or Wisconsin depending on the model.

Another styling change occurred in 1938, which was called Deluxe Style. It consisted of chrome bumper guards, engine-turned instrument panel with clock and lighter, banjo-style steering wheel, large chrome wheel covers and fine chrome strips in the grille that encircled the hood door-to-door. The design change made an aesthetic impact once again. The 1-ton Model 201 pickup was introduced in 1938, as were two new cab-forward models: Model 306SC and Model 404SC. In 1939, the company became the sales and service agent for the "Pak-Age-Car" delivery van.

1951 DIAMOND T NATIONAL DESIGN AWARD   DT

At the end of 1939 another styling touch took place in the form of adding 10 V-type bars in the front grille, sometimes likened to the 1938 Cadillac. Also, for 1940 Diamond T shocked the industry with a 100,000-mile-or-one-year guarantee on all trucks.

During World War II a few Dart trucks used the same prewar cab as Diamond T. When the United States entered World War II Diamond T was already producing 4-ton 6x6 trucks. In the war years the Diamond T company built 31,245 6x6 4-ton prime movers, 12,424 halftrack scout cars, and 6,554 6x4 12-ton capacity tank-hauler tractors that were diesel-powered using 179 hp 893-cubic inch displacement Hercules DFXE engines with four-speed main and three-speed auxiliary transmissions and 11.56:1 worm-drive axle. A 40,000-pound winch was mounted amidships operated to the front or rear. The truck tractor pulled an M9 trailer at a top speed of 23 mph.

Another common hauler was the 10-ton Model 806. The civilian cab was used on the prime movers and tank truck tractors, but otherwise with substantial military changes to the front sheet metal. One of the unusual versions consisted of a canvas top with folding windshield and track mounting for an anti-aircraft machine gun.

Most of the World War II prime movers were powered by 119 hp Hercules RXC engines using a minimum 70-octane gasoline. These trucks used five-speed transmissions with two-speed transfer cases and a single-disc clutch. Double reduction was used for the front axle. The truck's weight was 18,100 pounds while payload was 8,300 pounds. Several bodies were mounted including cargo, dump and wrecker, as well as a unit for transporting pontoon bridge materiel. By the end of the war production quotas allowed Diamond T to build 2,887 trucks for civilian use in 1944.

The Diamond T models for 1944 through 1946 consisted of the 404H, 404HH, 509, 614H and 806H. For 1947 Models 201, 306, 306H, 703, 809 and 901 were added. C.A. Tilt retired in 1946 to become board chairman for the next 10 years prior to his death in 1956.

After World War II Diamond T continued with the same basic design as from 1942, when only 530 trucks were sold in the first three months of manufacturing before going over to military production. In 1947, there were 14 models ranging from 8,000 pounds to 36,000 pounds GVW. Production figures for 1947 were 10,475, and for 1948, 10,657. Ten of these models used Hercules engines, three Continental, and the heaviest Model 910, which weighed 7 tons, was powered by a Cummins HB600 diesel. By this time the Diamond T factory covered 14 acres with nine buildings.

C.A. Tilt designed a "woodie" station wagon to fill postwar demand, of which two prototypes were built, but this vehicle never went into production. In 1949, Diamond T trucks were no longer produced on a yearly model change basis. This was also the year the Model 201 was discontinued. It was supplanted by the Model 222, but only until 1951 when this series, too, was discontinued.

By 1951, Diamond T dropped the light models altogether and offered trucks from 3-ton capacity or larger. These included Models 660, 720, 722, 920, 921, 921R, 950 and 951. The largest trucks were powered by a 300 hp Cummins NHRBS diesel engine or a 280 hp Buda

6DAS844 diesel engine. As with several other truck manufacturers, Diamond T adopted the new International "comfort cab," which had a curved windshield and concave instrument panel. These cabs were used on and off until 1960.

Diamond T's Tilt-Cab COE of 1953 was given the National Design Award for an industrial product, which had never been bestowed on any truck design ever before. A counterbalance system dispensed with the need for a power unit to tilt the Model 723C cab, which included a dip in the bottom of the side window ventilators that was copied by other truckmakers throughout the world for decades. Hendrickson also used this cab, as did International until 1972.

The 923C cab was used for a full decade. It was centered over the front axle and had an almost vertical, curved, divided windshield. Production continued steadily through the 1950s with approximately 3,000 to 5,000 units per year. In 1954, E.J. Bush, president of Diamond T, and W.C. Schumacher, vice-president of International, announced that the two companies would cooperate in production of additional components. Diamond T would assemble some special models for International, while International would manufacture certain parts for Diamond T. This was the same year that Diamond T also introduced the 723C as a light COE diesel model.

During the 1950s Diamond T built 5-ton 6x6 trucks for the military. These were powered by a 224 hp Continental R6602 engine with synchromesh transmission, automatic six-wheel drive, power steering and special electrical, intake and exhaust system for driving through deep water. Parts were designed to be interchangeable with those from other trucks.

The year before White bought Diamond T, the company introduced the Model 831, which was powered by a 239 hp Hall-Scott 590 engine. With liquid petroleum gas as fuel, it provided 256 hp. Also, the Tilt-Cab Model 911C diesel was offered with the 300 hp Cummins diesel engine.

After much media speculation, White bought Diamond T in 1958. The year before, White had bought Reo, but it was not until 1960 that the Diamond T operations were moved to the Reo factory in Lansing, Michigan. In 1959, Diamond T offered one four-cylinder engine, 14 six-cylinder engines and two eight-cylinder engines. For 1960 two new V-8 models were designated for their horsepower as DT8-207 and DT8-235.

Once the Reo and Diamond T truck production lines were brought to the same location, though still built separately, the two makes used White's wider conventional "D" cab with a wrap-around split windshield, as well as White's other conventional "R" cab with rounded roof line and one-piece curved windshield. Reo also used both cabs. A fiberglass Tilt-Cab was standard on Models 534CG, 634CG and 734CG. There were five six-cylinder gasoline engines available, two V-8 engines, four six-cylinder Cummins diesels and one each of GM's four-cylinder and six-cylinder diesel engines. The Model D-5000 was the largest of the "R" cab series for 1960.

In 1961, the new Model 931C, which was a tall line-haul tilt-cab COE, was shared with Reo (Model DCL) but not with White. It used a grille consisting of two trapezoidal sections, one above the other. A flat V shape was adopted for the windshield. Later, two wrap-around pieces were added to the corners. Engine options consisted of four six-cylinder gasoline units, two V-8s and three Cummins six-cylinder diesel engines. Some of the more unusual "R" cab trucks used a flat grille that was shared with White and Reo at this time. The Diamond T version had a diamond at the intersection of a long T. The same cab was used to build concrete mixers for off-highway use. This was designated as the "P" series, which used some 1940s grille styling.

1951 DIAMOND T MODEL 660 TRACTOR-TRAILER   KP

1960 DIAMOND T COE TANKER OCW

By 1963, Diamond T introduced three new diesel models called the P2000D, P3000D using the "R" cab, as well as the Model 533CG tilt-cab truck tractor that used the fiberglass cab. The Model 990 was the largest Diamond T for 1963. Five six-cylinder gasoline engines were again available, as were five V-8 engines, along with five Cummins Diesel six-cylinder, one Cummins V-6 and one Cummins V-8 diesel. The GM 6-71E six-cylinder diesel was also offered.

By 1965, a Perkins 6-354 six-cylinder diesel was added. This was the year Diamond T announced its 1000 series line of heavy trucks. The first two versions of this series was the 4x2 Model 1044FL and the six-wheel Model 1046FL. Caterpillar, Cummins and Detroit Diesel were available from 218 hp to 335 hp.

By 1966, the 1090 series was offered as a 90-inch BBC conventional. These were built as the 1094 two-axle or 1096 three-axle versions. Light versions with aluminum cabs and Royalex plastic fenders and hood were designated with an "L" after the number. Wheelbases were from 134 inches to 164 inches.

At the same time Diamond T offered the Thousand-line C series, a combination of the long-wheelbase 1044 and 1046 models combined with the 931C COE tilt-cab. Two versions of Caterpillar 1673 engine with up to 245 hp were available, as were five engines from Detroit Diesel with up to 318 hp. This was the last year of a new, light tilt-cab, which was shared with White and, briefly, with Reo in 1967. The new cab was made from Royalex plastic and was called the HF3000, which was also the White 1200. Known as the "Trend," it was Diamond T's only model to use a Chevrolet engine. Also, a Cummins V6-140 was optional.

Although at the same location, Diamond T and Reo had been separate divisions under White's ownership. From a low postwar production number of 1,800 in 1961, Diamond T built 4,000 in 1966. Nevertheless, White merged Diamond T and Reo in May of 1967 to form Diamond Reo. The last Diamond T rolled off the line at the end of the 1966 model year. During its 56 years of manufacturing as the Diamond T, the company had built one-quarter of a million trucks.

1946 DIAMOND T MACDONALD 3-TON LOW-BED MROZ

DIAMOND T MACDONALD See MACDONALD

DIEHL 1918-1927 — The Diehl Motor Truck Works produced a few vehicles in Philadelphia, Pennsylvania. Up to 1923 a 1-ton truck was built along with a 1-1/2-ton version. After 1925 only the heavier truck was listed. The 1-ton Model A with 115-inch wheelbase was powered by a 19.6 hp Continental N engine. From 1921 the 1-1/2-ton Model B with 120-inch wheelbase was powered a Herschell-Spillman 7000 engine. The lighter truck used a Zenith carburetor with a Simms Magneto, while the heavier truck used a Zenith carb with Bosch ignition. Model A used a Borg and Beck clutch with a Durston 02800 transmission, Torrington OX2L front axle and Salisbury 1455 rear axle. Ross steering was utilized, and Schwarz wheels carried 34x4-1/2 front and 35x5 rear pneumatic tires as standard. Model B used a Merchant and Evans clutch with a Durston 02500B transmission and wheels were by Wayne. Axles were the same make as the Model A. There appears to be no connection with G.A. Diehl of Portland, Oregon, who built a streamlined three-wheeled car in 1935.

DIETERICH See KANSAS CITY

1932 DIFFERENTIAL 2-1/2-TON DIFFERENTIAL

DIFFERENTIAL 1931-1936, 1960-1970 — Starting out by building side dumping equipment for railroads as well as for trucks in 1915, the Differential Steel Car Company of Findlay, Ohio, began building three-way dump truck bodies in the 1920s. In 1931 the company built its own chassis, and this truck, which was rated from 2-1/2-ton to 4-ton, was powered by an 85 hp six-cylinder Lycoming engine. It also had a four-speed transmission and Timken spiral bevel rear axle. Wheelbase was 160 inches.

For 1937, only the Model E-131 with 160-inch wheelbase was offered. It was powered by the 85 hp (33.7) Lycoming ASD engine with Tillotson carburetor and Auto-Lite ignition, and used a four-speed Brown-Lipe 314 transmission and Timken axles front and rear. Chassis price for that year was $3,200. Top speed was 44 mph with 34x7 heavy-duty pneumatic tires, which were standard. Also standard were chrome headlights, full instrumentation, front bumper, fender lights and hood and cowl ventilators. Larger trucks were offered having a 6-ton capacity with a four-cubic yard dump body, or 7-1/2-ton capacity with a five-cubic yard dump body.

Differential's specialty was in three-way dump beds, which were called 3-Way Body. Some were mounted on a COE gasoline-electric hybrid chassis. A large part of the production was side-dump bodies for rail cars. Advertising of the 1930s proclaimed "Simple, Powerful, Durable, Profitable, Automatic, Rapid, Safe."

In 1960, another complete truck was built by Differential, which became simply the Differential Company that year. This was a 6x4 off-highway model designed to carry 30 tons of gravel, rock or sand. The truck tractor was also capable of pulling three 30-ton trailers made of welded steel, which gave the overall unit a total 120-ton payload and a gross combined weight of 170 tons. This truck was powered by an 825 hp Continental AVI 1790-8A air-cooled V-12 engine, which was coupled through a torque converter to an Allison transmission with Torqmatic brake. A smaller diesel engine was also available. Final drive was through a Timken-Detroit tandem axle with single reduction differential and final reduction through planetary gears in each wheel. Also standard were power steering and internal-expanding air brakes. The "Wagon Train," as it was referred to, had a total length of 86 feet. In 1970, the company was reorganized as the Difco Company, also of Findlay, Ohio. Difco, Incorporated has stayed in business to date as a specialty railcar builder.

DILVER 1908-1909 — The Dilver Manufacturing Company of Mankato, Minnesota, was listed as a builder of trucks. In 1909, plans to build a new factory in the "Midway district" between St. Paul and Minneapolis was announced, but further details have been unavailable to date.

DISPATCH 1910-1919 — The Dispatch Motor Car Company of Minneapolis, Minnesota, was a builder of both passenger cars and light goods carriers. It appears the first few vehicles were built for stockholders alone, and it is now unknown how many first-year vehicles were built and sold, but different models were available by 1912, including the Model E with a 16 hp two-cylinder air-cooled two-cycle engine, and the Model Four, which was powered by a similar 35 hp four-cylinder engine. The early trucks featured full-elliptic spring suspension and a Renault-type hood. The engines were called Silent Dispatch. The vehicles used a double disc friction transmission and chain drive as late as 1918.

The lighter commercial vehicle had a capacity of 600 pounds, and the heavier one had a 1,100-pound capacity. By 1914 a 23 hp four-cycle Wisconsin engine was used. Material shortages during World War I had a negative impact on manufacturing, and as with other similar companies, the enterprise faded out. It was listed in directories until 1923, but only as a dealership for other vehicles.

DIVCO 1926-1979 — George Bacon, chief engineer for the Detroit Electric Vehicle Car Company, built an electric prototype of a milk delivery truck in 1922 that had four driver positions: from the runningboards on each side, as well as front and rear. In 1925, Bacon, along with H.L. Flinterman, organized the new company, called Detroit Industrial Vehicle Company (DIVCO), which began production the following year. The first Divco trucks were powered by four-cylinder Continental engines using Warner four-speed transmissions. The initial pilot run of 25 vehicles were forward-control vans with a door hinged at the front so that the driver could step out over the front axle, and control from the runningboards was also possible.

In October of 1927, the company was incorporated as the Divco-Detroit Corporation in Detroit. In 1928, the company introduced the Model G, which was a van/open-sided truck with a short hood. Side control was in the normal standing or sitting position. Bacon's design had incorporated a universal control system for the brake, clutch, throttle and transmission. Clutch and parking brake were actuated with the same pedal; half down was the clutch disengagement, all the way down was the brake. A hand throttle was mounted on the transmission lever. A tiller steer was mounted in the center for access from either side of the vehicle.

1927 DIVCO MILK VAN   **A&A**

The Depression took its toll, and by 1931 Divco was in the hands of its creditors. This was the year the company unveiled its Model H, which had a dropped frame creating an aisle from one side of the truck to the other. By the following year Continental bought Divco, and the company's name became Continental-Divco. By then a four-cylinder as well as a six-cylinder engine was offered.

Continental's patent infringement lawsuits from International (regarding the Step Van) resulted in the sale of Divco for $175,000. Divco merged with the Twin Coach Company forming the Divco-Twin Truck Company, known as such until 1944. An all-new design was introduced for 1937 with a welded steel van body and a snub-nose hood, which was used without many changes by Divco since that time. The doors were semi-automatic folding. These vehicles were powered by a four-cylinder Continental engine. Six versions were available from 7,500-pound to 12,000-pound capacity. Production rose to 2,800 units by 1941, up from 1,300 three years before that.

1948 DIVCO BAKERY VAN   **KP**

1948 DIVCO MODEL UM-E MILK DELIVERY   **JM**

In 1940, the first insulated and refrigerated version was produced. After an interruption in manufacturing during World War II, in 1946 the company offered two models: Model UM with 101-inch wheelbase and Model ULM with 127-inch wheelbase. GVW were 9,000 pounds and 12,000 pounds, respectively. The lighter truck used a four-cylinder engine, while the heavier truck used a six-cylinder engine, both built by Continental. Directly after World War II production reached 7,000 trucks per year, which was more than twice the number of any of the prewar years.

By 1954, vans with refrigeration became a regular production option. In 1956 the Dividend series was introduced. That year 80 percent of the Divco trucks built since 1927 were still on the road. During the 1950s L-head four-cylinder and six-cylinder Continental engines as well as six-cylinder Hercules engines were used. By 1956 there were 11 models of the Divco snub-nose truck. A new Model 52-10 was introduced on a 117-inch wheelbase. This body had a 412-cubic foot capacity, which was smaller than the Model 42-12 on a 130-inch wheelbase with a 470-cubic foot van body.

In 1957, Wayne Corporation bought Divco, which remained the Divco-Wayne Corporation through 1967. In 1959, Divco introduced a series of small buses called Plan A, Plan B, Plan C, Plan D, Plan E and Plan F. The first two were 20- and 21-passenger school buses while the rest were small buses with up to 39-passenger capacity. Standard engine was a 102 hp six-cylinder with a four-speed synchromesh transmission. The standard Coachliner bus, as it was called, was priced at $4,609.

In the early 1960s, six-cylinder overhead-valve Nash engines were available, as were three-cylinder two-stroke Detroit Diesel 3-53N engines. Hercules and Ford engines were also offered during the mid-1960s.

The biggest Divco was built in 1961. It was a 6-1/2-ton wholesale delivery model that used the Dividend chassis and cab with a separately-attached van body available in 14-, 16- or 18-foot lengths.

Ford F240 and F300 six-cylinder engines became optional in 1963, but within two years they became standard. Two sizes of the snub-hood model were produced at that time. Also, the forward-control Dividend series was available up to 1966 in three sizes: from 5,300-pound to 9,200-pound payload capacity. In 1968, Divco was bought by Hiway Products of Kent, Ohio, becoming a subsidiary of Transairco Incorporated of Delaware, Ohio. Divco trucks continued to be built as the 300 series with 115-inch wheelbase and the 200 series with 127-1/2-inch wheelbase, which had a payload capacity from 3 ton to 5 ton. Ford F240 and F300 engines were used with an optional three-speed dual-range automatic transmission. Diesel engines made by Caterpillar, Detroit and Deutz were also optional, though apparently rarely ordered.

In 1972, Divco became part of Correct Manufacturing (division of Hughes-Keenan Manufacturing) of Delaware, Ohio, which built sky-worker tree trimmers, often referred to as "cherry-pickers," and "high-risers." Production of the 200 and 300 series Divco trucks continued on a limited, individually-built basis with about 150 trucks per year produced. Also in 1972 a one-man garbage truck with 15-cubic yard packer body was built. Both sitting and standing controls were featured, and the trucks GVW was nine tons. By 1979, truck production ceased, although the parts and repair business continued through the 1980s into the early 1990s.

1928 DIXON SIX-CYLINDER DUMP TRUCK   DJS

DIXON 1921-1928 — The Dixon Motor Truck Company, organized by Frank Dixon in Altoona, Pennsylvania, built commercial vehicles that were well-known for their hill-climbing capability. For the first few years Dixon trucks were powered by four-cylinder Continental engines using worm-drive. Approximately 970 Dixon trucks had been built before the stock market crash of 1929.

By the mid-1920s, Dixon offered five models. The 1-1/2-ton Model D, and similar 2-ton version, with 145-inch wheelbase powered by a 22.5 hp Continental J-4 engine, was priced at $2,650. The 2-1/2-ton Model C with 154-inch wheelbase powered by a 27.2 hp Continental K-4 engine was priced at $3,250. The 3-1/2-ton Model A with 160-inch wheelbase powered by a 32.4 hp Continental L-4 engine was priced at $4,070. A 5-ton model with the same engine and wheelbase was priced at $4,490.

Mobil Oil purchased several tankers but the company also built stake bodies, dump beds, ice-cream vans and dairy delivery trucks. On all of these models a Fuller clutch and transmission were used, and front and rear axles were by Timken. Zenith carburetor and Ross steering were also standard. Dixon trucks used solid rubber tires with 36x3 front and 36x6 rear on the lightest model, while the heaviest used 36x5 front and 36x12 rear single tires.

By 1927, four-cylinder Hercules engines were available, and that year six-cylinder Lycoming engines were offered. The latter featured bevel gear drive and pneumatic tires. The company concentrated its sales in Pennsylvania, where the trucks were popular and gained a good reputation. Of the 970 produced over the years, few have survived to date. The small Dixon Motor Truck Company did not survive the Great Depression as a manufacturer, although offices were listed until 1931.

DMX 1936-1940 — Paul O. Dittmar founded the Dittmar Manufacturing Company in Harvey, Illinois, in 1936 after having established the South Suburban Motor Coach Company in 1927. The motor coach company was organized in order to provide bus service between Chicago rapid transit terminals and nearby communities. Dittmar, along with several investors, created Safeway Lines, Incorporated in 1931. This was a transportation company intended to provide long distance, nonstop coach service between Chicago and New York.

1936 DMX 26-PASSENGER COACH   MBS

Harry A. FitzJohn became Dittmar's partner in the Safeway Lines, and it was he who designed the Autocoach, which was a compact 14-passenger parlor bus. The sedan-style coach, as it has been referred to, was actually built by Reo. However, for his suburban Chicago bus service company, which became the South Suburban Safeway Lines, Dittmar had another bus designed for that purpose. This was the DMX of 1936, which featured an aluminum-alloy body and COE design. It was powered by a Hercules engine, and during five years of production, a total of 150 were built. These varied from 25-passenger to 33-passenger in size, but of the 150 produced, only 33 were used by the South Suburban Safeway Lines, with the rest being sold to other transit companies.

1938 DOANE 7-TON LOW-BED   NAHC

DOANE 1916-1948 — As with MacDonald, another early San Francisco truck builder, Doane began specializing in low-bed vehicles associated with special warehouse applications for longshoremen. These trucks featured low stake-side flatbeds for loading and unloading ships dockside at a time when forklifts were not available.

The first 1916 model was powered by a 16 hp four-cylinder Waukesha engine using double chain drive and low frame design. The first trucks were rated at 6-ton capacity, but cargo weighing four times that was commonly loaded along the piers.

In 1918, a 2-1/2-ton model was added along with the first series. By this time the 6-ton Model HP with 182-inch wheelbase was powered by a 36.2 hp Waukesha engine using a four-speed Brown-Lipe transmission. It used 36x6 front and 40x6 solid tires front and dual at the rear, and it was priced at $3,500. In 1920, a 3-ton model was added to the production line. A rigid six-wheel truck was introduced in 1924 with a capacity of 10-3/4 tons. It used a transmission built by Doane with seven forward speeds and three in reverse allowing a maximum forward speed of 25 mph. Only one heavy chain was used to the leading rear axle. Solid rubber tires were used exclusively throughout the 1920s into the mid-1930s.

One of the six-wheel models was used with a four-wheel trailer to deliver gasoline from refinery to consumer by Mohawk Oil Company of California. This truck had a capacity of 4,900 gallons. Although most Doane trucks were sold on the West Coast, a few sales were recorded in Philadelphia and New York City. In 1928, six-cylinder Waukesha engines were introduced. By 1933, Doane trucks were available as Lo-Bed and Hi-Bed models, as well as six-wheel 10-ton dump trucks.

By 1937, three models were available from Doane. These were rated at 4- to 6-ton, 6- to 9-ton and 10- to 12-ton capacity. This series used six-cylinder Waukesha engines with four-speed Brown-Lipe transmissions, Timken front axles and double reduction rear axles manufactured by Doane. Chevrolet cabs were utilized. Floor to bed height was between 22-1/2 to 24 inches. The company branched out into other applications besides dock work. Doane trucks were used for furniture moving, glass delivery and horse transportation.

In 1946, the company became the Graham-Doane. Production was minimal. The single model was a low-bed truck as before but with forward-control, and it was powered by a six-cylinder Continental engine. It also used a five-speed Clark transmission, and as before the rear axle was built by Doane. It has been noted that at least 10 Doane trucks from 1916 were still operating as late as the early 1950s.

DOBLE 1919-1921 — Abner Doble was born in San Francisco in 1895, the eldest of four brothers. His grandfather, also named Abner, had been successful manufacturing forged mining tools during the California Gold Rush. Abner's father, W.A. Doble along with his brother invented the Doble Water Wheel, and a family fortune was in the making. Abner Doble built his first steam buckboard in 1912 when still in high school. He began attending the Massachusetts Institute of Technology in 1910.

During this time, Doble visited the Stanley brothers' factory in Newton, Massachusetts, and after this experience he planned to better the veterans of steam-powered vehicles. Shortly after the visit, Doble indeed succeeded in improving the steam car design by completely eliminating the exhaust outlet with the use of a Harrison cellular radiator that fully condensed all of the used steam. The Stanley tubular condensers were only partly efficient in this respect, and when Doble visited them at their plant they were truly amazed by Doble's advanced technology. It would be a few years before their steam vehicles were brought up-to-date with efficient condensers. Five such Doble steam cars were built, and these were called the Model A. Four of them were sold, and one was kept for experimentation.

Doble was 19 years old and without business savvy. His under-financed company was not able to produce the scheduled Model B steamer, but after using the prototype to find capital venture backing with C.L. Lewis, who had been head of the Consolidated Car Company, together they started a new company that was called the General Engineering Company. By 1916, the G.E.C. Doble Model C was built, essentially an improved Model B.

The Doble design featured a two-cylinder double-acting single expansion engine with water tube boiler. In the Model C, Doble utilized his uniflow principle, which meant steam flowed in a single direction with lower thermal loss, and along with the elimination of the pilot light, optimized fuel atomization, electric ignition and the use of one fuel for both starting and running, Dobles were the most sophisticated steam vehicles in the world. The Model C made headlines at the New York Automobile Show and by 1917, 11,000 orders were received.

But just as Doble got his running start in the automobile business, material shortages during World War I shut down the General Engineering Company, and Doble reorganized as the Doble-Detroit Steam Motors Company. Nevertheless, in 1919 Doble sold all manufacturing rights to Amalgamated of Chicago and moved to San Francisco with his brothers to continue building a few expensive and exclusive steam cars for the Hollywood set and for such people as Howard Hughes. With coachwork by Murphy, Doble cars sold for as much as $11,000 in 1923.

It was during this short time before moving to Emeryville, California, that the Doble Laboratory in San Francisco built a few steam trucks rated at two tons, although after the first year they were rated at a more realistic one ton. The boiler was paraffin-fired. Wheelbase was 144 inches, and pneumatic tires on wooden spoke wheels were used. The standard express van was priced at $3,300.

1918 DODGE BROS. STAKE BED　　　　　　　　　　　　**KP**

DODGE 1916 to date — After starting a small machine shop in Detroit, John and Horace Dodge supplied 3,000 transmissions to Ransom Eli Olds by 1902 and later axles, engines and transmissions to Henry Ford. As manufacturers and stockholders with Ford, they made a fortune, but the brothers also realized it was time to disengage from Ford, and at the end of 1914, the first of 249 Dodge Brothers cars rolled out of their factory in Detroit, Michigan. The following year the factory produced 45,000 vehicles putting Dodge as third in the industry.

It was not until 1916, however, that the Dodge chassis was fitted with a light truck body. General Pershing used Dodge Brothers touring cars to chase Pancho Villa through Mexican deserts that year, his own car running some 18 hours daily. Dodge advertising mentioned "dependability," a coined term that soon entered into the English language now taken for granted.

In 1916, the Dodge chassis was fitted with a light truck body by numerous Dodge dealers. Dodge began building a truck in 1917, and in form of an ambulance it served in the European war. The civilian version was the Dodge screen-side business truck, which was mounted on the 114-inch passenger chassis and had the same running gear, as well.

By the end of 1918, the U.S. military had bought 2,644 screen side trucks. It would have been difficult to find more trucks overseas during World War I than those made by Dodge, but those screen and express truck bodies were not officially listed until the 1918 model year. By the end of the year a closed panel delivery truck was offered for the civilian market, and any number of commercial applications became available on the Dodge chassis: ambulances, farm wagons, fire engines, funeral cars and special delivery trucks included among them.

In 1919, Dodge continued to build cars and trucks that resembled earlier models and used the same 24 hp four-cylinder engine. That year Dodge Brothers introduced a taxicab, which was only produced for two years, as well as a depot hack with wooden sides and roll-down curtains. A taxi body as well as a fully-enclosed ambulance and hearse were also built by Colt-Stratton Company of New York City. Another quick modification was a box added to the Dodge roadster, and it instantly became a pickup. The Dodge Brothers Business Car, known as a panel delivery, was built without a driver's enclosure, but was quite popular, nevertheless. A tractor-trailer combination featured a Torbensen heavy-duty rear axle, extended frame and custom cab by Colt-Stratton. Some of the modified trucks were rated up to 1-1/2-ton by this time.

101

In 1920, when Dodge became the number two auto producer in the industry, both John and Horace died, having become well-known for their wild bar-wrecking drinking habits. Their widows took over with Frederick Haynes as president of the company. At that time commercial vehicles, called Series One, were identical to those of 1919. After 18,000 of the 22,000-employee workforce were laid off during the recession of 1921, Dodge slipped into third place in vehicle manufacturing but soon rebounded as the nation's economy quickly improved.

1921 DODGE BROS. 1/2-TON SCREENSIDE   **MROZ**

Graham Brothers of Evansville, Indiana, had used Dodge engines in Graham trucks previously, and in 1921 Haynes made arrangements to have Dodge become the exclusive agent for Graham trucks. Dodge's affiliation translated to mean domination, and Graham, de facto, became the Dodge truck division, although not officially until 1924. The Graham/Dodge trucks were first sold in model year 1921 exclusively through Dodge dealers.

The Model A was rated at 1-1/2 tons, and the basic chassis sold for $2,495. Any type of body or bed could be mounted on these trucks, and a 20-seat bus body made mostly of wood was also offered by Graham. Companies such as Anchor Body, Babcock Body, Bridgeton Hearse and Ambulance, E.M. Miller, Eureka, Holcker Manufacturing, Hoover Body, Keystone Vehicle, Stratton-Bliss and Streator Hearse built various bodies for ambulances and hearses.

By 1922, the expanded Dodge factory was producing 600 vehicles per day. This was also the year that a newly-engineered semi-floating rear axle was adopted, as was new front end styling. Also, the new Series Two commercial vehicles were introduced. Mechanically they were essentially the same as previous versions. The 1/2-ton screen side commercial car sold for $880 while the panel delivery was $980. A bare commercial chassis with drivetrain and wheels sold for $730. Numerous commercial bodies were built by Mort, which were called Mort-Dodges.

Graham trucks, which had a complete model line of trucks at that time, complemented the Dodge 1/2-ton, which by 1925 also listed a 3/4-ton model with 116-inch wheelbase powered by the 24 hp four-cylinder engine using a Detroit Lubricator carburetor. Ignition, generator and starter were made by North East Electric Company of Rochester, New York. Kelsey wheels carried 32x4 front and rear pneumatic tires as standard equipment. The chassis price for this truck was $730.

During this period Dodge fell into third place as a manufacturer in 1921, and by 1923 it had fallen to sixth place, the year the company introduced its Series Three commercial vehicles. At this point the Dodge widows decided to sell the company to the New York banking house of Dillon, Read and Company for $146 million, the biggest cash purchase in the history of American industry to date, April 30, 1925.

The new parent company installed E.G. Wilmer as president, a man with no automobile experience, and the company continued to lose its position in the auto industry. At the same time Dodge bought controlling interest in Graham Brothers in 1925.

The Series Four commercial line was introduced in 1926, and Dodge completely took over the Graham operations in Evansville and the assembly plant in Stockton, California. For the first time Dodge built fully enclosed cabs for its trucks, and the standard SAE-blessed shift pattern was adopted for the Dodge transmissions. Dodge began building a new panel truck using a 140-inch wheelbase chassis in 1927.

Late in 1927, a new 60 hp L-head six-cylinder engine with seven main bearings was introduced for the Dodge 2-ton trucks. It had been designed by Dodge, but was actually manufactured by Continental. Most importantly, this was also the year Dillon and Read sold Dodge Brothers to Walter Percy Chrysler for a $170 million stock transaction, and Dodge became a division of the Chrysler Corporation.

At this point, Dodge had slipped into 13th place in the industry, and Wilmer was immediately removed by Chrysler and replaced by K.T. Keller at Dodge's Hamtramck head office.

As Chrysler took over the Graham factories, Graham trucks were completely phased out and superseded by a model line of Dodge trucks and vans up 3-ton capacity. The year 1928 would see the introduction of the first Dodge 3-ton trucks. The new 3/4-ton Dodge Series MD, which sold for $775 in 1928, was a companion to the Standard Six passenger car series.

The light trucks starting with a 1/2-ton model continued to use the four-cylinder engine, but the heavier models used six-cylinder engines with four-speed transmissions, spiral bevel rear axles and hydraulic brakes all around. By 1930, Dodge was in fourth place as far as truck manufacturing was concerned, and this amounted to 15,558 trucks delivered for that year. It was at this time that Brothers began to be gradually dropped from the name Dodge, and by 1935 the word Brothers was entirely dropped. The 4-ton G-80 series was started in 1931.

Although the four-cylinder engines were used up to 1933, six-cylinder engines were also common, but straight-eight engines were utilized as well. For 1931, the 4-ton Dodge truck used a 96 hp 310-cubic inch L-head six-cylinder engine, and from 1933 to just before World War II the G80 series trucks were available with a 385-cubic inch Chrysler Custom Imperial straight-eight engine, which had nine main bearings. It was coupled to a five-speed transmission. These trucks were rated at 4 tons, and the lighter 2-ton and 3-ton trucks used the six-cylinder engines. At this time, the Dodge foreign subsidiary in Great Britain began building Dodge trucks with specifications that were quite different from the American ones.

Just as the Great Depression began, Dodge once again offered a taxi based on the Dodge DC Eight. The standard Dodge panel truck was still rated at 1/2-ton and sold for $545. The new low price reflected the economic hard times of the nation. Dodge began building a new pickup truck, and panel trucks with various lengths and capacities were available. The Series F 30 and VF 30 comprised some of the most common trucks on the road and were rated at 1-1/2-ton.

By 1933, Dodge offered a full model line of commercial vehicles from 1/2-ton to 4-ton capacity. The 1933 Commercial Pickup was the first Dodge truck designed entirely by Chrysler, since the purchase of the Dodge company in 1928. The model line included the Westchester Semi-Sedan Suburban, F10, UF10 and UG21, which carried every conceivable type of body for every conceivable type of business.

Price cuts and many new elegant styling features helped get Dodge out of the Depression sales slump, as did the "show down" ad campaign of 1934. That year Dodge delivered 1,476 chassis units that were built up by so-called "professional" car builders, such as the U.S. Body and Forging Company of Buffalo, New York, which produced the Westchester Semi-Sedan Suburban light trucks, both for civilian and military use. Also, a production ambulance was first offered in 1934, and the first Dodge 4x4 was built for the military. This truck became known as the T214 series, forerunner of the Power Wagon. The commercial sedan cost only $340 that year. The model line still started at 1/2-ton with trucks up to 4-ton capacity, which included the new K-52 Airflow truck built for the Standard Oil Company, among others.

1930 DODGE PANEL DELIVERY   MROZ

1935 DODGE 3-TON PANEL SIDE EXPRESS   TEX

1936 DODGE MODEL LE31 1-1/2-TON   HAYS

1943 DODGE 4X4   MROZ

1938 DODGE COE TANKER   IZZO STUDIOS

1939 DODGE 2-TON SERIES THA 45   A&A

1951 DODGE POWER WAGON   MROZ

1958 DODGE ARMORED CAR   AMT

103

For 1935, the Dodge truck line was headed by the 1/2-ton Series KC vehicles, which were almost identical to the previous year's. "Woodie" station wagons continued to be built by U.S. Body and Forging Company, and the first Dodge promotional trucks in the shape of a milk bottle were built. The light trucks were comprised of Models KC, KCL, KH 15 and KH 17. Dodge built 4x2 trucks for the military, which were designated KC-1 and KCL-1. Three body types were built: the double-level panel, a 1/2-ton pickup and a four-door wood-bodied station wagon. Nearly 4,000 KC-1 and KCL-1 trucks were built in two years for the U.S. military.

In 1935, the 1/2-ton pickup became available in two wheelbases with two respective sizes of beds. The wheelbase option was 111-1/4-inch or 119-inch. Larger models such as the Series K 32, K 38, K 45 and KS 75 continued.

The 1936 model line was not unlike the previous year's in terms of engineering, although the heaviest trucks were usually fitted with hydrovac brakes. However, styling was new and the passenger car grille and fender design were carried over into the heavy trucks as much as possible. The 3-ton K63V truck tractors were commonly used to pull a fleet of trailers, such as for the coast-to-coast operation of the U.S. Truck Company.

By 1937, when truck production neared 65,000, Dodge offered an optional two-speed rear axle, and this was the year of the first forward-control Dodge truck, rated at 1-1/2 tons, which was finished by the Montpelier Company. The Series MC was the light-duty trucks consisting of pickups, sedan delivery and chassis-cowl units, and a few hearses and ambulances continued to be built on Dodges when this type of vehicle was by then more commonly built on larger cars.

By this time, Chrysler was marketing three makes of trucks in Canada: DeSoto, Dodge and Fargo. Fargo trucks were mechanically the same as Dodge in the full model line range, but they did have some trim and styling differences. In the United States, Dodge listed 14 different truck models in 1937: MC, MD15, ME15, MF28, MD20, ME20, MH29, ME30, MF35, MG40, MN45, K50V, K60V and G80. Prices ranged from $410 for the MC chassis to $1,775 for the K60V chassis, which was powered by a 96 hp six-cylinder Dodge engine, with the most powerful 115 hp straight-eight Dodge-built engine in the G80 truck.

For 1938 a new $6 million plant in Warren, Michigan, began producing 98 percent of all Dodge trucks, which were now available with four different six-cylinder engines. The heaviest was the 3-ton RP 66 truck tractor used for pulling heavy trailers. Montpelier continued building COE bodies, both as light vans or heavy haulers. The Airflow trucks continued to be built as the RX-70 and RX-71 for 1938, and about 70 were built this year, mostly as fuel tankers and beer trucks.

Celebrating its 25th anniversary in 1939, Dodge redesigned its entire model line, and the trucks had an all-new look starting with the lightest series TC, which included a pickup for $375. The 3/4-ton Series TD 15 was usually in the guise of a pickup or panel truck, and chassis-cowl units continued to be delivered, as were TL 52 chassis for buses.

Dodge sponsored a Pan American Good Will Tour during which Edison Smith, the world's champion truck driver, toured Peru, Mexico, and the United States before arriving at the New York World's Fair in a Dodge 2-ton Series THA 45 truck. The year 1939 was also the first time Dodge offered a standard diesel engine for two of its trucks including the 3-ton truck tractors. The Airflow trucks were also redesigned in appearance using a 205-inch wheelbase, although the engines remained the same.

For 1940, production of special army vehicles was started with the Lend-Lease and various other defense programs. The Chrysler proving grounds began putting its prototype trucks to extremely heavy testing for military applications. Civilian trucks got a horse-power and torque increase on the 1/2-ton and 2-ton series.

Much of the Canadian operation was turned over to war production of Dodge and Fargo trucks. The Series VLA was the first production Dodge truck with COE design in truck tractor form, which included a sleep cab and optional 95 hp six-cylinder diesel engine with seven main bearings. At this time, the VKD 60 was one of the heaviest of the Dodge trucks.

By 1941, Dodge truck buyers had choices of four clutches, six types of brakes, six engines, 17 axle ratios with eight different axles and 23 chassis. Primarily for Canada and overseas, by this time Chrysler was badge-engineering DeSoto, Fargo and Plymouth trucks along the lines of the Dodge models. All-wheel drive vehicles continued to be produced for the military.

A 1/2-ton Route Van powered by a 95 hp six-cylinder engine was new for 1942. Production was entirely changed over to defense work by February of 1942. The Canadian plant alone built 39,657 military trucks in 1942. Before war production ensued, the Dodge company started using the "job rated" slogan that has continued ever since.

Between 1943 and 1945 Dodge built half a million military trucks of all types, besides a variety of other war materiel for all branches of the military. The most common World War II truck models included the 1/2-ton 4x4 T207-WC3, T207-WC8, T207-WC9, 3/4-ton 4x4 T214-WC52, T214-WC55, T214-WC56, T214-WC57, T214-WC60, 3/4-ton 4x4 WC 52 weapons carrier and the T223-WC62 and T223-WC63.

A few civilian trucks were built in 1944 and 1945, and for 1946 and 1947 Dodge trucks were identical to prewar designs except for the Power Wagon, which was a military design. The year 1947 was the largest single sales year for Dodge trucks to that time. Dodge continued to build many commercial chassis, including the Series WH-49-S with 220-inch wheelbase used for buses, as well as the 1/2-ton Series WC, 1-1/2-ton Series WFA and 2-ton Series WHMA truck tractor. The 3-ton Series WK was the heaviest and was powered by a 128 hp engine with five-speed transmission. Diesel engines were not reintroduced until many years later.

In 1948, Dodge trucks were completely new in terms of styling. The delivery Route Vans were also reintroduced, this time with up to 142-inch wheelbase and 2-ton capacity allowing for a 12-1/2-foot long body and 462 cubic feet of cargo space. The vans were powered by a 102 hp 230-cubic inch displacement six-cylinder engine.

A new assembly plant for both cars and trucks was built in San Leandro, California. A restyled horizontal front grille distinguished all truck models except for the Power Wagon, which continued with its plain military appearance.

For 1949, the styling was kept the same, but model designations changed. The Dodge D-116 was powered by a 95 hp six-cylinder engine, while a 102 hp engine was optional. In the 1-1/2-ton class Dodge offered three models. The largest trucks were powered by a 190 hp 236-cubic inch six-cylinder engine. In 1950, the 331-cubic inch L-head six-cylinder engine was bored out to 377 cubic inches and once again the largest Dodge was rated at 4-ton capacity.

With the Korean War, Dodge began focusing on military vehicle production again, which included the M37 (T245). Based on the 3/4-ton chassis, a 6x4 with optional full air brakes was available. The Model B-108 was still offered as the lightest 1/2-ton pickup, and hundreds were built for the U.S. Navy.

Power Wagons continued to be built both for civilian and military use. These were powered by 94 hp 230-cubic inch six-cylinder engines with eight forward speeds and were often fitted with 7,500-pound capacity winches in front for snow plowing. The military also bought many Series FA trucks that were rated at 7-ton and had wheelbases from 128 inch to 192 inch. The Route Van now featured an electric parking brake and optional fluid-drive semi-automatic, which was also available on some pickups. The semi-automatic was common, if not dependable or efficient, on Chrysler-built passenger cars into the early 1950s.

For 1950, the heavy-duty line received a new five-speed syn-chromesh transmission. An all-new line of trucks was introduced for 1951. The trucks had new styling and there was a broader selection of models. For the 2-1/2-ton the new Dodge Series J and K were powered by 114 hp engines. For the 4-ton and 5-ton trucks the new Series were T, V and Y, and these were powered by twin-carbureted engines with up to 151 hp.

By 1953, the 1/2-ton Series B was powered by a 97 hp six-cylinder engine, which was still an L-head in design, as were all Dodge engines for the last time before hemi V-8 engines were introduced. The 4x4 Power Wagon in various forms saw action in three years of the Korean War. The 2-1/2-ton Series J cab-over-engine truck had either a 112 hp or 118 hp engine and was noted for the shortest turning radius of any COE truck that year -- 37-1/2 feet.

One-piece curved windshields were introduced in the Series B light trucks in 1954. Chrysler's 133 hp 241-cubic inch hemi-head V-8 was now used in the 1-1/2-ton to 2-1/2-ton trucks, and the heaviest models, such as the 3-1/2-ton Model V, with both conventional and COE design, was powered by a 153 hp 331-cubic inch hemi-head V-8.

School bus chassis continued to be offered from 152-inch to 229-inch wheelbase, such as the Model JS-212 built by Superior of Lima, Ohio. The Power Wagon was also occasionally utilized for school bus application for rural areas. The 1/2-ton Series B and 1-1/2-ton Series F were still powered by an L-head six-cylinder engine, 97 hp and 109 hp, respectively.

By 1955, Dodge made V-8 engines available for the entire model line of trucks. The Power-Dome V-8 hemi-head had 145 hp, and could be ordered with a fully automatic transmission on the light-duty models. No styling changes were made in the truck line for that year, but a 12-volt electrical system was introduced, as were tubeless tires for the first time.

1958 DODGE (FOREGROUND) SWEPTSIDE PICKUP   OCW
(AND LEFT TO RIGHT) D100 PICKUP, D100
TOWN-WAGON, D300 STAKE, D100 PANEL AND
D700 6-WHEELER WITH TRAILER

In 1957, the passenger car line was entirely restyled, and a new range of tandem trucks was produced, which were powered by 201 hp or 232 hp V-8 engines. It was not until the following year that trucks were redesigned, having an all-new look with four-headlight configuration. Dodge used hemi-head V-8 engines in its trucks between 1954 and 1959. The 1958 D900, for example, used a 354-cubic inch hemi-head V-8 with dual carbs and dual exhaust.

In 1959, the 383-cubic inch V-8, which could be custom ordered, was offered with electric fuel injection that was rated at 345 hp. The Sweptside 100 pickup was continued from the previous year with either a 120 hp L-head six-cylinder engine, or a 204 hp 314-cubic inch V-8 engine. It was slightly more upscale than the D-100 1/2-ton pickup, but the latter was available in two-tone paint. The D Series styling was extended throughout the line up to the D-400, which was rated at 1-1/2 tons. The 1-ton Series 300 was available with V-8 and a three-speed LoadFlite automatic transmission.

Route Van trucks were either 1-ton P-300 Series or 1-1/2-ton P-400 Series. At this time the heaviest Dodge trucks were the D-800 with a 224 hp V-8 and the D-900 with a 234 hp V-8, which was also used in the T-900 three-axle truck tractor. An eight-wheel amphibious vehicle was developed for the military.

Swing-out front fenders helped with engine access in 1960, which was the year the C models were introduced such as the LCF (Low Cab Forward) series of medium- and heavy-duty gasoline- and diesel-powered Dodges. The C Series began with the designation 600, which had either a 125 hp or 130 hp six-cylinder engine, or a wide range of V-8 power, and five-speed manual or six-speed automatic transmissions. This series included 6x4 trucks and in gross combined

weight (GCW) ratings went up to 53,000 pounds. The heaviest models had full air brakes, and diesel engines were reintroduced for the first time since World War II.

Turbocharged Cummins diesel engines were available typically with 228 hp using twin-plate clutches and 8-speed or 10-speed transmissions. At the other end of the model line, Dodge sedans were becoming quite popular again as taxis and police vehicles. The durable Slant Six (cylinder) engine developed for the Dodge Lancer and Plymouth Valiant was adopted for light trucks from 1/2-ton to 1-ton. Descendent of the Route Van, the P300 Multi Stop vans also used this versatile 225-cubic inch 145 hp Slant Six engine, which was an overhead valve design. The old dependable side-valve L-head continued to be used sparingly in the Power Wagon, a few medium-duty models and some school bus chassis.

For 1961, Dodge restyled the light-duty trucks, which were not recognized for their aesthetic design but were well-engineered. The Series 100 continued to be offered with six-cylinder or eight-cylinder powerplants, as was the Series 300, also considered a Power Wagon, which was available as a 4x4 with a nine-foot bed and a four-speed transmission with two-speed transfer case. The Series 700 was now powered by a 361-cubic inch Power Giant V-8 that produced 194 hp.

The largest Dodge introduced during 1962 was the Series 1000 three-axle truck rated at 5-ton, which was available with gasoline or diesel power. The diesel engine was designated as the Model NH 220 with 743 cubic inch displacement producing 220 hp at a low 2100 rpm.

The first Dodge factory recreational vehicle was marketed by Dodge on a bus chassis in 1962. At this time, the 4x4 Power Wagon was available as the 1/2-ton Series 100, 3/4-ton Series 200 and 1-ton Series 300. Despite the introduction of a modern version, the decades-old military-style Power Wagon continued to be popular. The largest trucks were still the Series 800, 900 and 1000 from 3-ton to 5-ton capacity.

1964 DODGE RESCUE WAGON   AMT

1965 DODGE NL-100 TILT-CAB DIESEL   DODGE
TRACTOR-TRAILER

By 1963, Dodge offered a few innovations. The Ram Charger V-8 now produced 425 hp with a 426-cubic inch displacement. A Perkins diesel engine became an option for the medium-duty model line of

105

trucks. A six-passenger Crew Cab was introduced for the Power Wagon pickups, which were still available as a 4x4. The Series 500 dump truck had a 7-ton capacity and was offered with two V-8 engines, the larger 361-cubic inch at extra cost. Also, Dodge built a Power Wagon Swamp Fox, which had Terra-Tires measuring 46x18x16R front and 46x24x16R rear, making this one of the first all-terrain vehicles that was factory built by one of the Big Three automakers in America.

The largest Series 900 and 1000 were built in standard or COE tilt-cab version with both gasoline and diesel engine options including V-6 and V-8 Cummins. The LN1000 and LNT1000 were first brought out in 1964, and their production continued through 1975.

Dodge observed the burgeoning recreation-vehicle market and filled the growing demand with mobile home chassis and a new camper conversion called Roll-A-Long Sportster Housecar, which eliminated the truck bed entirely and utilized a forward-extending "cab-over" design. This was also the year Dodge unveiled the 90-inch wheelbase Handyvan forward-control van with both rear and side loading. This light truck was designed to compete with Ford's similar Econoline vans. Automatic transmissions were available at first with the Slant Six engine, but a V-8 was offered by 1965.

Dodge built heavy cement mixer chassis and by 1965 an 8x4 with trailing axle truck tractor was built for an 80-ton gross combined weight, as was a 10x4 cement mixer that had a gross vehicle weight of 70,000 pounds and could haul 12-1/2 cubic yards of concrete. The W100 Town Wagon combined the "suburban" style wagon body with the chassis and drivetrain of the Power Wagon. In Canada the Fargo pickups were identical to the Dodges, except for the emblems.

Through 1960, Dodge continued to supply many school bus chassis. The Sweptline received a new and unusual single-headlight treatment. The front grille got a well-deserved makeover in 1968. The A-100 Dodge was offered for numerous applications including law enforcement work. Station wagons were converted into ambulances and hearses by such companies as Automotive Conversions of Troy, Michigan. The squareish styling of the medium- and heavy-duty lines set Dodge apart from other makes.

By 1970, Dodge entered the heavy-duty long distance hauling service with its LM-100 COE tilt-cab. Engine options were up to 318 hp with the Detroit Diesel V-8 and 335 hp with the turbocharged Cummins diesel V-8. Motorhome models gained in popularity and the M-300 and M-375 chassis were supplied to dozens of individual body manufacturers such as the Traveco vehicle, which had an all-fiberglass body. Two similar but heavier chassis were also offered for the school bus market: the S-500 and S-600. Minor frontal restyling took place on the D-100 pickup trucks, and the Polara was commonly used as a police car across the country.

For 1971, the Special Edition Adventurer, as well as the Dude D-100, were some of the more elaborate styling exercises for Dodge pickups in the 1970s. Both Sportsman and Tradesman vans were offered each in two wheelbases. Also by that time the 9-ton 6x4 short-cab was called the Big Horn D-9500 and was available as a three-axle diesel-powered truck tractor.

1975 DODGE CNT900   **RD**

1977 DODGE D600   **DODGE**

At this time, companies such as Wayne Corporation of Richmond, Indiana, produced van-based ambulances, setting the tone in ambulance design for the next two decades. First called Rhino, a name quickly abandoned, the Ramcharger made its debut in 1974. That year Dodge medium-duty trucks received a complete face lift, but at the end of 1975 all heavy-duty Dodge trucks were discontinued. Only 261 Big Horn trucks had been built over three years of their production. A Dodge spokesman stated that the company could not conform to new government regulations, but in reality Dodge was losing money on the heavy-duty truck line.

Concentrating on a more specific part of the market share, including the light- and medium-duty truck lines, resulted in a production increase from 319,694 to 469,197 units by 1977. But in 1977, medium-duty trucks were also discontinued.

By 1978, Dodge expanded its production of the Tradesman and light pickup lines, and both of these featured servo disc front brakes. A new six-cylinder diesel engine became available. Niche marketing included special paint and graphics treatments such as the Warlock and Macho pickup iterations.

The last standard control medium-duty Dodge trucks had a GVW rating of 15,000 to 30,000 pounds. Along with a six-cylinder Perkins diesel, several gasoline V-8 engines were available with four-speed or five-speed synchromesh transmissions, hydrovac air brakes, and optional automatic transmission. The Ramcharger was introduced to compete with the Chevrolet Blazer and Ford Bronco. After a slow start in 1974, Dodge improved its market share of light trucks in the 1980s. The Dodge Mini Pickup built for Dodge by Mitsubishi made its debut in 1979.

The Dodge Power Ram was introduced in 1981, and the Power Wagon name was abandoned. Starting with the 1980s, Dodge, as did other American companies, began importing Japanese-built light trucks, such as the Ram 50 and Raider 4x4 built by Mitsubishi, including a turbo-diesel engine for the Ram 50. The Dakota pickups and Ram pickups continued to be produced with four-cylinder and V-6 engines, but the Dakota Shelby high performance V-8 was an example of the other end of the pickup spectrum.

1988 DODGE GRAND CARAVAN   **DODGE**

The Dodge Caravan made its debut right after the identical Plymouth Voyager began to be produced in 1984. The Dodge Mini-Ram Van for 1985 was nearly identical to the Caravan. The Mitsubishi-built Dodge Colt Vista light van was introduced in 1984 as a front-wheel-drive vehicle, and a year later it was built with four-wheel-drive. Another new 4x4 was the Dodge Dakota of 1987. In 1991 the Dodge Caravan was also offered as a 4x4.

1990 DODGE RAM DIESEL D350   **DODGE**

For 1993, the model line had a new look, and Chrysler Corporation developed a 90-degree V-10 engine, which was intended for its Viper sports car, but by 1995 a high performance V-10-powered pickup was also developed. This truck was built by Dodge as the 300 hp iron block V-10 mounted in a 2500 series 4x4 pickup. An all-aluminum 400 hp 488-cubic inch V-10-powered Ram VTS with a six-speed Borg-Warner T-56 transmission was also factory-built in 1995 as a prototype capable of 0 to 60 mph in 5.9 seconds.

By the mid-1990s, Dodge has offered the Caravan Cargo Van with a 2.5L standard engine and five-speed manual transmission. This minivan, with 2,005-pound payload capacity, has had some light delivery applications and is nearly identical to the Plymouth Voyager. The Dakota Pickup has been the lightest truck from Dodge with a 2.5L standard engine and five-speed manual overdrive transmission, with payload capacity up to 2,600 pounds. The Dakota Club Cab with 131-inch wheelbase has been offered with the same base engine and transmission as the Dakota pickup while 112-inch wheelbase bus has been rated at 2,000-pound capacity. The Dakota Chassis Cab's base engine has been the 3.9L with a 124-inch wheelbase and maximum payload capacity of 2,800 pounds.

The Dodge Ram Full Size Pickup has been available with single rear wheels in the form of the 1500, 2500 and 3500 series with 3.9L, 5.2L and 5.7L engines, respectively. The dual-rear-wheel 3500 series Dodge Ram has used the 5.9L V-8 as the standard engine, and with a five-speed manual overdrive base transmission the GVW rating was 10,500 pounds. The Ram Chassis Cab has been available as a 2500 series heavy-duty or as the 3500 series dual-rear-wheel with GVW rating of 8,800 pounds and 11,000 pounds, respectively.

Full-size vans have included the B150 and B250, both with the 3.9L and three-speed automatic transmission as standard equipment. The B350 has been the heftiest Dodge van with a 5.2L V-8 standard engine and four-speed automatic overdrive transmission and a GVW rating of 8,510 pounds with up to 4,450-pound payload capacity. For complete history of Dodge light-duty commercial vehicle, see Krause Publications' *Standard Catalog of American Light-Duty Trucks.*

1994 DODGE RAM 1500 T-10   **DODGE**

D-OLT 1920-1923 — The D-Olt Motor Truck Company was incorporated in Woodhaven, Long Island, New York, in 1920. Two models were built: a 1-1/2-ton and a 2-1/2-ton, the former being powered by a Herschell-Spillman engine, and the latter by a Midwest 402 engine. Little else is known about the company and its demise in 1923.

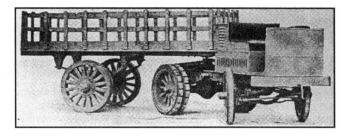

1915 DOMINION ARTICULATED TRACTOR-TRAILER   **HD**

DOMINION 1915-1917 — The Dominion Motor Truck Company built a 90-inch wheelbase truck tractor that was powered by a T-head four-cylinder engine mounted between and under the two front seats. A four-speed transmission was used, and the worm-drive used a design in which torque was dampened through the springs. Having moved from Canada in 1915, the company continued with its original name in Detroit, Michigan.

1914 DORRIS PLATFORM STAKE   **KP**

DORRIS 1911-1928 — George Preston Dorris built a gasoline-powered car prototype between 1891 and 1896 in Nashville, Tennessee. After joining John L. French in organizing the St. Louis Motor Carriage Company in Missouri, he became chief engineer to build "Rigs That Run." When French moved the company to Peoria, Illinois, Dorris remained to start his own company under his own name. The first passenger car, which had a 101-inch wheelbase and was powered by 30 hp four-cylinder Dorris engine, appeared in 1906.

While French's company went under, Dorris was successful, and after testing a truck prototype in 1911, a year later he added light- and medium-duty commercial vehicles to his model line. The 2-ton prototype used a Dorris-made transmission with shaft drive and double reduction rear axle. The Dorris powerplant was located under the seat. Only a few were built.

The 2-ton Model IAW of 1915 was more successful using a 48 hp Dorris engine with three-speed transmission and worm-drive rear axle. Approximately 350 of these were built by 1918. Capital stock of $1 million was raised for expansion, and by World War I both a 2-ton stake bed and 3-ton truck chassis were produced with the Dorris overhead-valve four-cylinder engine. The company president, H.B. Krenning, had stepped aside in 1917 "because of needed rest."

The K-4 model was introduced in 1918 and the K-7 in 1919. The 2-ton K-7 featured a new 312-cubic inch four-cylinder engine with five main bearings and detachable overhead-valve head. Dorris himself held several patents, six of them for improvements in transmission design, although some of his trucks used a four-speed Muncie transmission mounted mid-ship. Warner Gear transmissions were also used. By 1923, the Dorris passenger cars, which had been "practically hand-built," indeed became built only one-by-one by special order. The Dorris company faded out slowly, and commercial vehicles and chassis also continued to be built a few at a time.

By the year 1925, the company had offered seven models of Dorris trucks, but never simultaneously. The 1-ton K-2 of 1925 had an optional wheelbase and was powered by the 25.6 hp Dorris engine with a Warner Gear transmission and Timken front and rear axles on which Muncie wheels carried 33x5 front and rear pneumatic tires as standard equipment. A Stromberg carburetor was used with Bosch ignition along with a Westinghouse starter and generator. Price was $2,490.

The 2-1/2-ton K-4 had the same components except used the larger Dorris engine rated at 28.9 hp coupled to a Brown-Lipe 55 transmission. The price was $3,400 and pneumatic tires were at extra cost. The 3-1/2-ton K-7 used the same engine and transmission as the K-4 with the same components, but the frame and axles were heavier and the wheelbase was set at 174 inches with Smith wheels carrying 36x5 front optional pneumatic and 36x10 rear tires. Price for the K-7 chassis was $4,400.

Starting in 1918, Dorris had also produced a few bus chassis known as the M-4, which was powered by the truck four-cylinder engine, or the L-6, which had either a 38 hp or 80 hp six-cylinder engine also offered in the passenger car line. Over the years, Dorris built limousines with both of these large engines, and some of those could be considered commercial vehicles. A few fire trucks were built on Dorris chassis. It is uncertain if any more than 851 Dorris trucks were built over all years of production, along with 3,100 passenger cars, hence the noted record that total Dorris production over the years was 3,951 units.

1921 DORT 1-TON VAN OMM

DORT 1921-1924 — Josiah Dallas Dort was a close friend with William Crapo Durant. After many years in the carriage-building business, some of them in partnership with Durant, Dort became a motor vehicle manufacturer in 1915 with his own Dort Motor Car Company. His chief engineer was Etienne Planche, the man who had helped Louis Chevrolet build the first car by that name. From the beginning Dort cars were assembled in Canada as well as the main factory in Flint, Michigan. In Canada they were known as the Gray-Dort, after William Gray who owned the plant there. The Dart Motor Truck Company of Waterloo, Iowa, sued Dort for trade name infringement in 1917, but the two names were obviously spelled differently, and the case was thrown out of court that year.

After six years of building Dort passenger cars in considerable numbers (30,000 cars sold in 1920 alone), the first 3/4-ton van was produced in late 1921. All Dorts built after 1919 used a radiator styled after Rolls-Royce, and many of the Dort vehicles were powered by a 19.6 hp four-cylinder Lycoming engine. A 30 hp Lycoming engine was also available by 1920, and a 45 hp six-cylinder Falls engines was introduced in 1923. In a November 1921 advertisement Dort offered its Light Delivery Car with "lamps and brackets, runningboards, windshield and driver's seat" for $685. With driver's cab and duck curtains for the sides and back there was an additional cost of $175. With a steel express body without top the vehicle's price was $780.

Prices ranged from $865 to $1,495 by 1923. All Dort cars and light trucks used a three-speed transmission, and the drivetrain and chassis were shared by passenger and commercial vehicles built by Dort until the last year of production in 1924. A total of 107,000 Dorts were built by that time. In 1925, Dort sold his factory and equipment to A.C. Spark Plug, and during a game of golf in May of that year he died of a heart attack.

DOUBLE DRIVE 1919-1930 — Chicago, Illinois, was hometown to the Double Drive Truck Company before it was moved to Benton Harbour, Michigan, in 1922. The company also made trucks by the name of Front Drive. Double Drive trucks were built up to 3-1/2-ton capacity, while Front Drive was a 1-1/2-ton model.

From 1919 to the time the company moved, Double Drive trucks were powered by a Rutenber engine. After that Buda engines were used on most of the Double Drive and all of the Front Drive trucks. One exception was the 3-1/2-ton Model K that was powered by a Hercules engine.

The Model TT was listed in the mid-1920s for $4,000. It had a 144-inch wheelbase and was powered by a 28.9 hp Buda engine with Zenith carburetor. As with all Double Drive vehicles, the transmission and front and rear axles were made in-house. Standard Company provided the wheels, which had 36x6 front and rear pneumatic tires. Double Drive and Front Drive trucks did not survive the economic downturn of December 1929.

DOUGLAS 1918-1935 — The Drummond Motor Company of Omaha, Nebraska, was succeeded by the Douglas Motor Corporation. The Drummond V-8 engine was revised as the Douglas V-8 with increased power, and the cars had longer wheelbases and higher prices as well. The engines were eventually manufactured by Herschell-Spillman. Douglas built high-powered passenger cars for only two years before turning production entirely over to truck building.

1918 DOUGLAS 2-1/2-TON HAYS

Douglas' marketing strategy focused on the Midwest and Southwest. Regional weight restrictions, which came as an outgrowth of road and bridge building and maintenance costs, resulted in the popularity of rigid six-wheel trucks. Douglas specialized in this type of design before other larger companies entered into the competition.

The initial Douglas trucks were 1-, 1-1/2-, 2-1/2- and 3-ton models powered by either Buda or Weidely engines using Brown-Lipe transmissions and Timken axles. The company withstood a receivership in 1923 but continued production. By 1927, six-cylinder engines were introduced for the 2-ton and 3-ton trucks.

The following year a new 210-inch wheelbase 3-ton truck with Bosch instead of Eisemann ignition was built. Also in 1928 the 6-ton six-wheel F66 was introduced with a Douglas-built bogie suspension that used two Wisconsin worm-drive axles. This truck was marketed for long distance hauling and livestock transport. For the latter, Douglas built a 24-foot two-level rack-type body on a 200-

inch wheelbase. Both four-cylinder and six-cylinder engines were used during the early 1930s, but Douglas was fading out due to the Depression, and all production ceased by 1935.

1929 DOVER PANEL DELIVERY KP

1930 DOVER CANOPY EXPRESS KP

DOVER 1929-1930 — The Essex Motor Company built the Dover 1/2-ton truck, which was a commercial version of the Essex Super Six. Essex cars were built in Detroit, Michigan, and the company was actually part of the Hudson Motor Car Company. The L-head six-cylinder engine, which was used for both the passenger and commercial applications, was rated at 55 hp and was coupled through a single plate oil-immersed clutch to a three-speed sliding gear transmission. Subsequently, vans and pickups were made by Essex and Terraplane under their own names. The name Dover was dropped entirely by 1931, as was Essex by 1933.

1929 DOVER PICKUP KP

DOWAGIAC 1909-1912 — Named after the city of Dowagiac, Michigan, and started by two machinists named Frank Lake and Doras Neff, the Dowagiac Motor Car Company built a light van with 102-inch wheelbase powered by a 24 hp two-cylinder engine. The open van cost $1,400 in 1909.

The Dowagiac Company's history is everything but straightforward. It was bought by J. Victor Lindsley in 1908, but the new owner had no experience in building cars and went into serious debt almost immediately. After his father, a wealthy Dowagiac lumberman, paid off his son's bills, the Dowagiac company was bought in 1909 by a group of local citizens, including Frank Lake who had started the company in the first place.

Unfortunately, Lake was killed in an accident in 1909 along with another Dowagiac official. A few light vans were built, and a larger truck was planned under the phonetic spelling Doe-Wah-Jack. However, in 1912 the company was bought once again and moved to Tulsa, Oklahoma, becoming part of the Tulsa Auto Manufacturing Company, which later built Tulsa trucks.

DOWNING 1913-1915 — The Downing Cyclecar Company of Detroit, Michigan, built what was called a cyclecar with tandem seating. A side-by-side roadster and four-seater were available as well. Utilizing the larger chassis with 105-inch wheelbase and 56-inch track, the Model B was also produced as a light delivery vehicle that weighed 600 pounds. It was powered by an 18 hp four-cylinder engine and had a three-speed transmission with shaft drive. A second plant was opened in Cleveland, Ohio, but that factory did not produce commercial vehicles.

DRAKE 1921-1922 — The Drake Motor and Tire Manufacturing Company was incorporated in 1921 with a capital of $3 million. Its chief organizer and namesake was W.F. Drake, but several wealthy investors were involved who at the time were described as "substantial citizens and men of acknowledged business sagacity." Drake built four-cylinder- and six-cylinder-powered passenger cars, with one notably exceptional custom Six for silent film actor Mildred Reardon.

Drake utilized the Hershell-Spillman six-cylinder 11000 engine for its truck model line at a time when most trucks were powered by smaller four-cylinder engines. The Drake truck's wheelbase was 140 inches and weight was 3,500 pounds for the 2-ton chassis, which cost $2,595. Pneumatic tires were standard.

Despite the substantial investment into the company and advertising proclaiming Drake was "built like the Rock of Gibraltar," the recession of the early 1920s took its toll, and after discounting prices and inviting stock holders to purchase vehicles at a discount with little success, the Drake enterprise ceased production at the end of 1922.

DRESSER see KOMATSU DRESSER

DRIGGS-SEABURY 1912, 1921-1923 — The Driggs Seabury Ordnance Corporation was a U.S. materiel manufacturer that also began building motor vehicles in Sharon, Pennsylvania, and later New Haven, Connecticut. There are references to commercial vehicle production in 1912, and most likely these were built on the 100-inch wheelbase chassis powered by a four-cylinder engine. What is certain is that Driggs also produced taxis from 1921 to 1923.

After discontinuing production of the Driggs-Seabury cyclecar (which was renamed the Sharon cyclecar) in 1915, the Driggs-Seabury reemerged as the Driggs Ordnance and Manufacturing Corporation in 1921, and in 1922 the company switched to building taxis almost exclusively. The company slogan was "Built with the precision of ordnance." Almost all of the Driggs sedans, which sold for $1,975 in 1923, were equipped with taxi meters. These vehicles had a 104-inch wheelbase and were powered by a 22 hp four-cylinder Driggs engine. Reorganization followed receivership in November of 1923, and the company was closed in 1925.

DUDLY 1914-1915 — Classified as a cyclecar, the Dudly Bug was offered as a light closed delivery van for $375. H.F. Tideman along with younger brother, William J. Tideman were the designers of the Dudly Bug. The former was also president of the well-established Dudly Tool Company, located in Menominee, Michigan, where the Dudly Bug was built.

"Everybody is 'Bugs' about the Dudly," was the company slogan. The first version of the vehicle featured a 10 hp two-cylinder engine and two-speed planetary transmission with double belt drive. The front fenders turned with the wheels, and the headlights were mounted in such a way that the Bug's appearance lived up to its name. In 1914, the wheelbase was lengthened from 96 inches to 100 inches, and the vehicle was now powered by a 12 hp four-cylinder engine using chain drive selling, albeit rarely, for $385. Few of these vehicles found new owners, and Tideman went on to build the Menominee Electric, not affiliated with the Menominee trucks later produced in Wisconsin.

DUER 1908-1910 — The Chicago Coach and Carriage Company began building horsedrawn vehicles in 1898. Superintendent Charles Duer persuaded company officials to design a motor vehicle in 1905. Two years later the first Duer Model A highwheeler was built, but it was not until 1910 that the Model C was produced as a light delivery van of 1/2-ton capacity weighing 1,400 pounds. The 90-inch wheelbase vehicle was powered by a 16 hp air-cooled two-cylinder engine with double chain drive, although earlier models used rope drive. A mock radiator was installed in 1908 to modernize the appearance of the Duer, but sales were dismal nevertheless, and the Duer was allowed to fade away. This vehicle was also briefly called the Chicago Runabout.

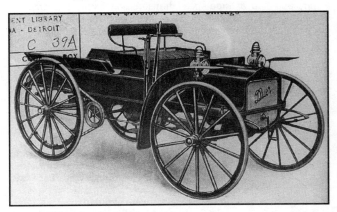

1908 DUER LIGHT DELIVERY   **JAW**

DUESENBERG 1920-1937 — Fred Duesenberg began his career by building bicycles, although not successfully when he filed for bankruptcy in 1903. He went on to build some of the most extravagant cars in the world, and a few of them were used commercially as limousines. "A real Duesy" became an American expression meaning that something was superior in excellence.

With his brother Augie, the Duesenberg company was formed in 1913 in St. Paul, Minnesota, where auto and marine engines were manufactured. With success on the racing circuit, the Duesenberg name became famous, although the Duesenberg brothers were always employees in their business ventures, never owners.

With an infusion of $1.5 million in venture capital by 1916, the Duesenberg company built airplane engines and artillery tractor units at the new Elizabeth, New Jersey, factory under contract with the U.S. military during World War I. After the factory was sold to Willys, and the rights to the Duesenberg four-cylinder engine were acquired by Rochester, the brothers continued in developing their overhead-cam straight-eight engine, which would later power all the Duesenberg cars. Their first car shown in 1920 had hydraulic brakes, which was a first in the industry.

The company was reorganized in Indianapolis, Indiana, and called the Duesenberg Automobile and Motors Corporation. The first production car did not become available until the 1922 model year due to manufacturing problems with the straight-eight engine. In 1925, the company was again reorganized as the Duesenberg Motors Company. After 600 Model A cars were built without profit to the Duesenberg business enterprise, in 1926 Errett Lobban Cord, president of the Auburn auto company, acquired the Duesenberg firm, and the name changed to Duesenberg, Incorporated.

From then on the reputation of Duesenberg entered the top echelon of automobile manufacturing. The straight-eight engine used twin overhead cams and produced 265 hp on the dynamometer. Although the company built its own bodies, numerous coachbuilders were employed to build custom Duesenbergs, with some limousines having up to 153-1/2-inch wheelbases. "He drives a Duesenberg" sufficed as the slogan for those who could afford a car that was priced at $8,500 for chassis alone in the mid-1920s.

In July of 1932 Fred Duesenberg died following a car accident. By that time he had designed the centrifugal supercharger that boosted the Model J's hp to 320, and later to 400 with Augie

Duesenberg's ram's horn. However, the rolling status symbol became affordable to fewer and fewer wealthy customers during the Depression, and E.L. Cord sold his three auto companies in 1937.

DUNLAP 1914 — The Dunlap Electric Truck Company was established in Columbus, Ohio, at the Dunlap Engineering Company facilities. The company was capitalized with $20,000 in order to build a 750-pound capacity electric delivery wagon. T.C. Dunlap was the principal behind the venture along with George R. Hedges, Stewart A. Hoover, Herman R. Tingley and M.E. Heasely. Output was planned at 100 vehicles per month.

A prototype was built and tested in September/October of 1914. The vehicle's weight with batteries was given as 3,553 pounds. It was tested with a payload of 1,100 pounds. The total energy consumption was calculated at 78 watt hours per ton mile. This also translated into the total expense of the vehicle, including upkeep, cost of operation, replacement of batteries and depreciation being an estimated five cents per mile. However, as with many such entrepreneurial adventures, only the names of the organizers, their capital sum and their intent has been documented, whereas no further production has been substantiated.

1910 DUNTLEY 1-TON DELIVERY   **RD**

1911 DUNTLEY C.P.T. COMMERCIAL CAR   **RD**

DUNTLEY 1910-1912 — The Chicago Pneumatic Tool Company was a well-established manufacturer of air compressors, as well as pneumatic and electric tools, when a decision was made to enter the business of building a delivery truck in 1910. The engine developed for the truck was a 20 hp horizontally-opposed two-cylinder-type that was used in conjunction with a two-speed planetary transmission and shaft drive. The company advertised "Strong, Simple, Reliable, Efficient." The 1-ton capacity vehicle was sold in England as the C.P.T. In the United States, the name Little Giant was adopted in 1912, and the make continued to be built until 1918, sometimes also known as Chicago.

1909 DUPLEX 4X4   LA

DUPLEX 1907-1985 — The Duplex Power Car Company was founded in 1907 in Charlotte, Michigan, taking over the factory of the J.L. Dolson company, which had built passenger cars between 1904 and 1907. Contrary to some belief, Dolson and Duplex were completely separate business entities, aside from the fact they both were located in the same plant in the early part of the century. Their management did not share any personnel, and the mechanical design for the trucks was not directly extrapolated from the Dolson car design.

The first Duplex truck was 3/4-ton capacity four-wheel-drive-type and was powered by a 14 hp two-cylinder engine mounted under the driver's seat. After the prototype was built, the first model for production, ostensibly called the Model B, sold well and was the only model built until 1915 when Duplex introduced the 2-ton Model C and the 3-ton Model D.

Due to the loss of all early company records in the Lansing, Michigan, flood of 1975, another controversy exists regarding the two later models. According to some claims, all three early models were four-wheel-drive, but one source states that the Model C was a rear-wheel-drive truck. Possibly, they existed side-by-side in two iterations. What is certain is that they were both powered by 20 hp engines mounted ahead of the driver.

In 1915, a 3-1/2-ton model truck was offered before the company moved to Lansing, Michigan, and changed its name to the Duplex Truck Company in 1916. The new model was powered by a four-cylinder Buda with a three-speed transmission and featured a C-cab. Power was transmitted to a chain-drive case where direct drive or 2:1 ratio was possible, giving the truck full dual range, and in the lowest gear this translated to a 64:1 ratio. Final drive used spur and ring gears inside each wheel carried by dead axles both front and rear relieving the power axles from also carrying the payload and weight of the truck. Also, both differentials had power locks allowing the truck to move if only one of the wheels had traction.

By 1917, Duplex was building four-wheel-drive trucks exclusively. The brake pedal operated a band on the driving side of the chain case while the handbrake was attached to a drum on the driven side giving four-wheel-brakes either way. During World War I, Duplex built trucks for the military. With a $400 price increase to "take care of the war tax," in 1918 the company announced its commitment to re-enter the private commercial market with its new two-wheel-drive truck called the "Limited."

The new "Limited" model truck had a 2-ton capacity. It had pneumatic tires and was designed for higher speeds. As a publicity stunt in 1920, a standard "Limited" production model was fitted with four 55-gallon drums of fuel and sent on a 24-hour endurance run at Indianapolis Motor Speedway. The 935 miles that the truck covered was a record for non-stop running, and the press covered the event closely. The truck started out with a payload of 3,300

pounds of gasoline and averaged 38.96 miles per hour. A pace car was used to pass coffee over to the driver, but apparently he was not allowed to stop even after many cups.

At the beginning of the 1920s, the smaller rear-drive Duplex trucks used Hinckley engines, while the largest 3-1/2-ton trucks were powered by Buda engines. The 2-ton "Limited" with 145-inch wheelbase was priced at $2,575, but this included pneumatic cord tires, windshield, electric lighting and starting, ammeter, Boyce Moto-meter, speedometer, electric horn, tools, jack, rim wrench, alemite grease gun and front fenders. All models had internal gear drive with vertical steering columns and solid rubber tires. Many of the Duplex trucks did not have standard features such as front fenders and some of the accouterments as listed above.

In 1923, Reo Motor Car Company bought the Duplex factory, and this allowed enough cash for a new Duplex plant to be built in Lansing without refinancing. The 1923 Duplex 3-1/2-ton Model E was powered by a 28.9 hp four-cylinder Buda engine with Schebler carburetor and Eisemann ignition and had a four-speed Brown-Lipe selective sliding gear transmission. This four-wheel-drive truck had shaft drive to both front and rear axles that were built by Duplex. Two years later Duplex offered five models ranging from 1-ton to 3-1/2-ton. The 1-ton Model G with 132-inch wheelbase was powered by a 22.5 hp Buda WTU engine with Zenith carburetor and Westinghouse ignition. This model also used a Brown-Lipe transmission and clutch with Timken front and rear axles carrying Motor Wheels that had 33x5 pneumatic tires.

At the same time the 1-1/2-ton Model GH with 138-inch wheelbase had the same engine and engine components but used a Covert clutch and transmission. Front and rear axles were from Sheldon and tires were 35x5 pneumatic front and rear. The next heavier truck was the 2-ton called Model A with 145-inch wheelbase. It was powered by a 25.6 hp Hinckley HAA engine with a Stromberg carb. The other components were the same make as the previous model except pneumatic tires were at extra cost. The 2-1/2-ton Model AC with 160-inch wheelbase was powered by a Hinckley 400 engine with Stromberg carb and Eisemann ignition. The Model AC had a Brown-Lipe clutch and transmission, but front and rear axles were built by Vulcan. Pneumatic tires were at extra cost up front, while the rear 36x8 used solid rubber tires. The heaviest model of this period, which was the 3-1/2-ton Model E, had a 130-inch wheelbase and was powered by a 28.9 hp Buda ETU engine with a Wheeler Schebler carburetor. Brown-Lipe clutch and transmission were used, but on this model the front and rear axles were made by Duplex.

The heavier Duplex trucks sometimes pulled road trains with up to five trailers before this practice was outlawed by state legislatures. Many Duplex trucks saw work as fire engines and were used in logging and construction. By 1929, there were seven models offered, but only one was four-wheel-drive -- the Model EF. The others ranged from 1-1/2-ton to 7-ton in capacity and used both four-cylinder and six-cylinder engines. The 3-ton Model SAC used a seven-speed transmission.

In the 1930s, the capacity of Duplex trucks ranged from 2-ton to 7-ton, and a 10-ton truck was available from 1938 to 1940. Most Duplex trucks were powered by Buda or Hercules engines by that time. During World War II, Duplex built a few 6x4 trucks for the military to carry searchlights, but production was concentrated on large electrical generating equipment.

After World War II, Duplex reintroduced its line of conventional trucks, which were powered by six-cylinder Hercules engines with up to 140 hp using five-speed Fuller transmissions and full-floating Timken rear axles with bevel gears or double-reduction. Duplex also built the LC600-4 using a six-cylinder Cummins diesel engine. With enormous competition from high-volume truck manufacturers, the company began to evolve as a builder of chassis for special applications mostly in the construction, crane carrying and fire apparatus market. For crane carrying Duplex produced 6x4 "half-cab" trucks with Continental engines. One of its largest customers, Gradall Division of Warner and Swasey, also of Lansing, bought Duplex in 1955.

At this point, the name Duplex represented five model lines. First, as off-highway chassis for Gradall; second as 4x4 and 4x6 heavy trucks for highway construction and maintenance; third as special chassis for airport snow removal; fourth as military and civilian airport vehicles; and fifth as generator sets up to 500 kilowatts output. Models T, H and L received the reputable Chicago cabs that were also used by Cline, Coleman, Diamond T, F.W.D., Hendrickson, International and Oshkosh.

1963 DUPLEX 4X4 DUMP   **W&S**

In the early 1960s, Duplex increasingly became an internal subsidiary of Gradall and many of the trucks carried the Gradall emblem. In the late 1960s, Duplex built a 25-ton 8x4 model, with a GVW of 77,000 pounds, powered by International gasoline or Detroit Diesel engines. But the 1960s and 1970s were not a placid time for Duplex, and two labor strikes nearly crippled the company. Duplex was forced to find its own market share as the parent company decided to build its own Gradall trucks.

Although Duplex continued to build some Gradall trucks, emphasis was placed once again on specialized equipment, and Duplex produced four-wheel road-and-rail maintenance vehicles, tunnel maintenance trucks and 4x4 rear-wheel-steering snowplow. Fire engine chassis continued to be built with three cab-forward models in 4x2 and 6x4 configurations.

1975 DUPLEX FIRE ENGINE CHASSIS   **W&S**

In the 1970s, Duplex produced still more fire engine chassis, as well as an off-road terrain forklift. But the second of the two labor strikes closed the factory, and Warner and Swasey decided to shut down truck manufacturing. The forklift line was sold, and in actuality the fire engine chassis line was spared.

Conventional Duplex trucks were 4x4 design with forward-slanting cabs shared by Oshkosh. Caterpillar and Detroit Diesel engines from 225 hp to 318 hp were used. Transmissions were by Fuller or Allison, and front and rear axles were made by Rockwell-Standard. However, customers of Duplex trucks had become wary of production uncertainties, and in 1977 the remaining assets were bought by the Nolan Company of Bowerston, Ohio. A new 10,000-

square foot plant was established in Midvale, Ohio. Under the new ownership of the Nolan Company, Duplex fire trucks were continued in production on a limited scale.

As the plant was expanded to 50,000-square feet, Duplex production rose from an average 50 per year to about 300 per year. During the mid-1980s, Duplex introduced the Model D-350 chassis and cab for fire engine application. One of its latest efforts has been the airport crash and rescue vehicle, which was over nine feet wide and was powered by a rear mounted 492 hp engine. By mid-decade the marque's production was discontinued.

1912 DURABLE DAYTON MODEL K 3-TON   **NAHC**

DURABLE DAYTON 1912-1917 — This make began as the Dayton, which was first manufactured in Dayton, Ohio, by the Dayton Auto Truck Company. The company built three models of forward-control trucks: Model H, Model K and Model M with capacities of 2, 3 and 5 tons, respectively. Most were built with stake or express bodies at prices ranging from $2,500 to $4,500. The trucks' T-head four-cylinder engines were rated at 35, 45 and 60 hp, respectively, for each model. Blocks were cast with cylinders paired and the engines used force-fed cooling. Transmissions were three-speed selective gear-type with final chain drive.

By 1914, the company was renamed as the Durable Dayton Truck Company during reorganization. The same models continued to be offered. The lightest model had a transmission brake, while the 3-ton Model K had external expanding brakes on the rear wheels. The heaviest Durable Dayton had a service brake on the jackshaft. Emergency brakes were internal expanding type on the rear wheels for all models. In the final years of production, models were designated as U, A and E, with 2-, 3-1/2- and 7-1/2-ton capacities and prices ranging from $2,700 to $4,950. The company went out of business during World War I partly as a result of general material shortages.

1928 DURANT 1/2-TON FLARE-SIDE   **JG**

DURANT see STAR

DUROCAR/DURO 1910-1916 — Watt Moreland, a mechanic for Winton, and William M. Varney, a car dealer in Long Beach, California, joined forces to form the Durocar Manufacturing Company of Los Angeles in 1906. Moreland designed the car with a 26 hp two-cylinder water-cooled engine and two-speed planetary transmission with shaft drive. It was shown at the Los Angeles Automobile Show in 1907, and soon production was up to five per day with dealerships as far away as Hawaii and Montana.

However, Moreland's desire to build a four-cylinder car was vetoed by the Durocar board of directors, and he resigned in 1908 to form his own successful Moreland Motor Truck Company in Burbank, California. Meanwhile, the Durocar was built in smaller numbers, and a four-cylinder engine of earlier contention was introduced for the 1910 model year after all.

By 1912, Varney reorganized as the Amalgamated Motors Company moving the factory to Alhambra. A few Durocars were built there from leftover parts, but Varney decided to try and compete with Moreland. Durocars were built from then on as 1/2-ton truck chassis with essentially the same four-cylinder engines as used in the 124-inch wheelbase passenger cars. However, Varney's business acumen was not up to going head-to-head with Moreland, and the Durocar truck builder faded out by 1916.

1903 DURYEA 3-WHEEL DELIVERY   **RD**

DURYEA 1899-1917 — Charles and Frank Duryea have been acknowledged as the first gasoline-powered motor vehicle builders in the United States when they tested their carriage-like highwheeler powered by a 4 hp one-cylinder engine in 1893. However, it was not until 1899 that a commercial vehicle was produced under the name Duryea, representing seven different companies over the years.

The first commercial van was built in 1899 based on the Duryea three-wheeler that was built in Reading, Pennsylvania. It had a single front wheel and was powered by an 8 hp overhead-valve three-cylinder engine mounted transversely at the rear. The engine drove the rear wheels by chain and a two-speed with reverse epicyclic transmission was used. The steering tiller operated throttle, gears and brakes. Pneumatic tires were standard equipment.

One of these three-wheelers was tested a year earlier as a gun carrier by Major R.P. Davidson, commandant of the Northwestern Military and Naval Academy at Lake Geneva, Wisconsin. The Duryea vehicle had an M1895 Colt "Potato-Digger" machine gun and shield over the front wheel and carried a crew of three. It never went into production due to repeated breakdown of the mechanical components. Davidson had the vehicle rebuilt as a four-wheeler, which may have influenced the Duryea vehicles also to be switched back to four-wheel design. However, by 1899 the brothers had parted company on bad terms, and Charles Duryea had established the Duryea Power Company in Reading, Pennsylvania.

By 1904, the Duryea vehicles were once again four-wheelers, and in 1905 a 15 hp engine was used to power a 750-pound capacity delivery van, which could also be set up as a light stage. Charles Duryea resisted the idea of a steering wheel and made all attempts to prove how easily his vehicle could be controlled by the tiller, which also controlled gear selection and acceleration. These vehicles sold for approximately $1,500 at this time, depending on how they were equipped.

Duryea vehicles were also built under license in Coventry, England, as well as by the Waterloo Motor Works in Waterloo, Iowa. In 1903, New York City capitalists Francis D. Carley and Henry Van Arsdale organized the United States Rapid Vehicle Company in Manhattan, but this venture seemed to stall rather quickly. At the same time, various conflicts between Charles Duryea and colleagues in Peoria led to the company's receivership in 1907 after 300 vehicles were built.

After Charles Duryea learned of the takeover by telegram while at the Chicago Automobile Show, he returned to Reading and started another company simply using his own name. He called his new vehicles Buggyaut, and these were powered by 12 hp and 15 hp two-cylinder-opposed air-cooled two-cycle engines with single-lever control once again. Two grooved rollers contacted the rear wheel rims as a form of friction drive, and these vehicles sold for $750.

1910 DURYEA COMMERCIAL CAR   **RD**

Commercial and passenger versions of the Buggyaut were built until 1913. The vehicles had a short hood in front and a turtle deck in the rear giving them the appearance of a buggy. In 1911, Charles Duryea started a coexisting business by the name of the Duryea Automobile Company in Saginaw, Michigan. Buggyauts were built as well as the new Duryea Electa. After taking over the Brooks Manufacturing Company there, which built delivery wagons, Duryea's new company went bankrupt, and the one in Reading was also in financial trouble.

Duryea left town to build a cyclecar with Cresson-Morris in Philadelphia, Pennsylvania. The side-by-side Duryea cyclecar, which was powered by a four-stroke two-cylinder engine, featured the same roller drive as the Buggyaut. In 1916, a 1/2-ton highwheeler van was built with a steering wheel. By this time the Duryea cyclecar became the Crowther-Duryea, which ceased to exist in 1917. Duryea built two more models of light vehicles, known as the GEM, with three- and four-wheel versions being built in Reading, but these were never produced as commercial vehicles. By 1918, the GEM vehicles ceased production, and Charles Duryea at age 55 turned to writing about motor vehicles. He died in 1939 having never produced another vehicle.

Otho C. Duryea, Charles' youngest brother (although he often would not admit to it) started the Western Duryea Manufacturing Company in Los Angeles, California, purportedly building 10 auto-delivery wagons in 1901. Little is known about his company, except that a prototype was assembled by the Maine Machine Shop in Alameda, California. Otho C. Duryea went on to build rock drilling equipment, abandoning the automobile business entirely after 1901.

DUSSEAU 1913 — An early four-wheel-drive system was patented by Dr. Dusseau, although it is not known which of four Dusseaus involved in the company was the patentee. The first Dusseau five-passenger car was shown in Toledo, Ohio, in 1910, but there were no buyers. Subsequently, the Dusseaus tried to sell their patented design on a royalty basis, but also with no success. A four-wheel-drive truck using essentially the same chassis was built in 1913 with the same dismal results. However, after moving to the West Coast, Maurice G. Dusseau was able to sell his patents for U-joints to the Positive Traction Motors Company. Little else is known about the prototype Dusseau truck.

DUTCHER PTV 1984 — The Dutcher PTV was built by Dutcher Industries in San Diego, California. It had a rear-mounted gasoline engine, automatic transmission and a corrosion-resistant chassis. The body was largely made of fiberglass. The van could accommodate seven passengers and 20 cubic feet of luggage, or it could carry two wheelchairs and four seated passengers.

1921 DUTY 2-TON   **RD**

DUTY 1920-1922 — The Duty Motor Truck Company of Greenville, Illinois, built one model of truck during its three years of existence. It was a 2-ton model powered by a 34.6 hp four-cylinder Gray-Bell engine with force-fed lubrication and used a three-speed Covert transmission and Russel internal gear drive. The chassis weight was 3,350 pounds, and the truck's wheelbase was 134 inches. The unusual feature of the design was that the six-inch frame flanges were turned outward not inward. Chassis price was $1,950 in 1920, and the cab cost $85 extra. The following year the company reduced the price to $1,490. Both solid and pneumatic tires were available, the latter being optional at extra cost. The company bragged that "Duty Motor Trucks offer an uncommon selling opportunity -- their future is certain." Approximately 350 Duty trucks were produced in all before the company shut down

in 1922, after a move to Elgin, Illinois, and a controversial attempt to sell out to the American Steam Truck Company of Chicago did not result in further production.

1934 DYMAXION   **GEORGE RISLEY**

DYMAXION 1933-1934 — The vehicle by this name was built by R. Buckminster Fuller, who also used the name Dymaxion for houses, a bathroom design and a boat. The Dymaxion car was in part designed by naval architect W. Starling Burgess. Only three actual Dymaxions were built. Planned manufacture never ensued. The Dymaxion was a three-wheeler, and one of its applications was to be a taxi, hence it could be considered a commercial vehicle.

The Dymaxion was powered by a Ford V-8 engine that provided the vehicle with a top speed of 120 mph while consuming gasoline at 40 mpg at a cruising speed of 50 mph. Wheelbase was 125 inches.

In 1933, Fuller tried to display the car at the New York Automobile Show but was prevented by the organizers, ostensibly due to the fact that Chrysler wanted all the attention on its streamlined Airflow cars. Fuller parked one of the Dymaxions in front of the show building where it drew much attention, nevertheless. However, after the show one of the Dymaxions was in a serious accident outside of Chicago, and its occupants were killed.

The press made much to do about the vehicle's "freak" design, and buyers backed out of the venture. The second Dymaxion was bought by Leopold Stokowski. Fuller went on to gain worldwide fame for his architectural geodesic dome design. He died in 1983 at the age of 87.

DYNAMIC 1911-1912 — The Cleveland Motor Truck Manufacturing Company of Cleveland, Ohio, briefly produced a complex truck with four-wheel-drive and four-wheel-steering. Engines were four-cylinder or six-cylinder gasoline-powered and were spring-mounted, or the vehicle could be ordered as an electric-powered version. A herringbone gear transmission and drive shafts were used to power each wheel. In addition, the customer had a choice of air or mechanical brakes, making this one of the earliest trucks to have pneumatic technology for stopping power.

E

E

1920 EAGLE   RD

EAGLE 1920-1930 — The Eagle Motor Truck Corporation got its
start in 1919 at a St. Louis, Missouri, factory built on land believed
to be in the ownership of J.P. Reis, who was vice-president of
engineering and production at Eagle. Eagle originally built a roadster
in 1909 in St. Louis called the Model N, sometimes referred to as
the American Eagle, which cost $650 but did not sell well. Pro-
duction was discontinued and Eagle started building trucks from
1/2-ton to 5-ton in limited numbers in 1920, all powered by various
Buda engines except for the last year of production.

The first truck sold in May of 1920. It was rated at 2-ton and
used a Buda MU engine with a three-speed Covert transmission
and shaft drive to a Russel rear axle. Price for this truck was $1,925
with pneumatic tires costing $250 extra.

Eagle never produced more than 100 trucks per year. By 1923,
there were a total of 84 Eagle trucks registered in all of St. Louis
County. The 2-ton model was built during all the years of production, whereas the 3-ton was introduced in 1925 and the 5-ton in
1928.

The Eagle 2-ton of 1925 was available as the Model 100 or the
Model 104. The Model 100 was powered by a Buda GTU engine
while the Model 104 was powered by a Buda KTU engine, both
using a Zenith carburetor and Eisemann ignition. Both trucks had
a 130-inch wheelbase and used Russel rear axles and Covert front
axles. The former had Lavine Gear steering and wheels by Standard,
whereas the latter had Ross steering and St. Mary's wheels. Pneumatics were at extra cost, although it appears the Model 104 was
only available with solid rubber rear tires. Although both were rated
at 2-ton, the Model 104 was clearly the more heavy-duty with a
chassis weight of 4,300 pounds and a price tag of $2,395, while
the Model 100 chassis was 200 pounds lighter, had pneumatic
tires on the rear as optional and cost $2,275.

The Eagle trucks had a distinctive radiator guard and eagle ornament, but they were otherwise unexceptional as conventional
assembled vehicles of the era. When the Depression hit, Eagle
offered models from 1-1/2-ton to 5-ton capacity powered by a
choice of Buda, Continental, Hercules or Lycoming engines, but
only a few were sold in 1930, the last year of production.

EAGLE see SILVER EAGLE

EARL 1922-1923 — Earl Motors, Incorporated, of Jackson, Michigan, began when Benjamin Briscoe appointed Clarence A. Earl,
who had been recently fired as vice-president from Willys-Overland,
as president of Briscoe Motor Corporation. By October of 1921,
Briscoe abandoned the automotive field and left the Jackson factory
to Earl. After a variety of financial and philosophical obstacles, Earl

resigned in 1922 leaving the company in the hands of various
bankers and capitalists who could not continue the venture even
with $1 million in capitalization.

1921 EARL SCREENSIDE DELIVERY   RD

For 1922 and 1923, Earl built a Screen Delivery and Panel
Delivery both powered by a 37.5 hp four-cylinder engine. Wheelbase was 112-1/2 inches. The price tags were set at $1,085 and
$1,160, respectively. Both of these commercial versions of the
passenger Earl cars were painted green with black fenders, wheels
and hood. Part of the company logo depicted Buddha. Early in
1924 after about 2,000 Earl vehicles were built in all, the company's assets and remaining stock were sold to the Standard Motor
Parts Company.

1912 ECKHARD 5-TON   RD

ECKHARD 1912 — The Eckhard truck was built in Boston, Massachusetts, and displayed in Madison Square Garden in January
of that year. It was powered by a 54 hp six-cylinder engine, used
two clutches and was rated at five tons. Solid rubber tires of 40x5
front and 40x4 dual rear were used. At the time, its design was
considered radical, according to the motoring press, but it does
not appear to have gone into production.

ECKLAND 1931 — The Eckland Brothers of Minneapolis, Minnesota, had built truck and bus bodies for a number of years for
such companies as Twin City and Will. Will was sold by Greyhound,
the parent company, to Yellow Coach, and this sudden drop in
business prompted the Eckland Brothers to build their own complete bus in an attempt to expand their market.

The body design was based on the Twin City coach, but the
chassis was entirely their own and employed four-wheel-drive.
Amidships on the Eckland frame were two six-cylinder engines
each with its own transmission and drive shaft facing the opposite
way. Two radiators were mounted at the front of the bus for each
engine. The highly unusual design did not attract buyers, and only
a prototype was built. The company survived building bus bodies
until 1935.

ECLIPSE 1911-1913 — By the time this company came into
existence, there had been a half-dozen motor vehicle manufacturers
with this name in various cities of the United States. However, the
Eclipse Motor Truck Company of Franklin, Pennsylvania, was the
only company with this name to produce trucks. Models ranged
from 1-ton to 4-ton capacity, and all used 30 hp four-cylinder

engines, sliding gear transmission, Sheldon axles and double chain drive. Wheelbase was 102-inch for the 1-ton truck. Semi-elliptic springs were used in front while the rear had platform spring suspension. Steering gear was provided by Ross. Top speed was 18 mph for the early trucks.

1911 ECLIPSE 1-TON   RD

The most unusual aspect of the later Eclipse design was the use of compressed air starters for the engine, one of the earliest such applications at a time when the electric starter had just been invented by Charles Kettering. Eclipse trucks were briefly popular in the oil fields of Pennsylvania before the company's sudden demise. Although the company was listed as early as in 1911, the first time any of the Eclipse trucks were publicly shown was at Madison Square Garden in January of 1912.

ECONOMY 1909-1912 — During the era of highwheelers, the Economy Motor Car Company of Joliet, Illinois, was one of many contenders in the business of building light commercial vehicles, if only for a brief period of time. The Economy vehicles were all powered by two-cylinder engines, and used planetary transmissions and chain drive. Vans with 1/2-ton and 1-ton capacity were available, and after using solid tires on wagon-type wheels in the first two years of production, pneumatic tires were introduced. The slightly modernized Economy van still could not find enough buyers to keep the company in business.

1911 ECOMONY   KP

EDISON 1913 — The Edison Electric Vehicle Company of America was located in Lawrence, Massachusetts. The company briefly built 1/2-, 1- and 1-1/2-ton electric trucks using side chain or shaft and worm-gear drive. Edison nickel-iron alkaline batteries were used exclusively. The 1/2-ton had a battery consisting of 60 A-4 Edison cells and the 1-1/2-ton carried 60 A-8 Edison cells. The electric motors were supplied by General Electric and Westinghouse. The lightest truck had a top speed of 12 mph with a range of 55 miles.

The 1-ton truck's range was 60 miles with the same top speed as the previous model. The largest of these had a 50-mile range also with the same top speed. Axles were by Standard or Timken, and in the shaft-driven trucks a David Brown worm-gear drive was used. It is not clear if Edison electric trucks continued to be built past 1913, although there were a few experimental electric passenger cars built, including a 200-pound roadster that was developed in conjunction with Henry Ford in 1927.

1947 EISENHAUER   BHS

EISENHAUER 1946-1947, 1954, 1957 — The Eisenhauer truck design was one of the most unusual of all time. The few trucks built were fabricated by the Eisenhauer Manufacturing Company of Van Wert, Ohio. The first model was a 10x4 powered by two 93 hp 235.5-cubic inch six-cylinder Chevrolet engines that were mounted inline but apparently at different levels, the first under the hood and the second under the cab. They used two manual transmissions synchronized for shifting. Driveshafts extended to the first and third rear axle. Both of the front axles' wheels turned for steering.

The truck was rated at 20 tons, which was the highest capacity for a rigid chassis at that time. It was intended for use instead of a tractor-trailer combination. The roof of the cab was approximately nine feet above the ground, and overall length was 35 feet.

A second version built in the early 1950s (exact date has not been available) had two 302-cubic inch 145 hp GMC gas engines mounted side-by-side. At least three of the latter were built, one of them an Allied moving van, another a stake body and the third a chassis/cab.

Designated as the X-2, the Eisenhauer was tested by the Army in 1957. This version was 10 feet high and 35 feet long. As with the earlier version, the truck had 16 tires: 10.00x20 in front and 9.00x20 duals in the back. The military test vehicle had a 6,176-gallon fuel tank. The suspension system consisted of semi-elliptic springs combined with front and rear chains and sprockets with torque tubes for load equalization. The rear suspension had leading arms and gimbal mounts on the first and third driven axles to allow them to track the arc being run when turning. Air-operated valves permitted those two axles to be locked in the turning position so that the truck could be backed up in the same arc. Chassis lubrication at 102 points was accomplished by automatic air-actuation.

The engines and transmissions were not synchronized but worked smoothly, according to the test. Each engine had a separate electrical system so that the truck could be run on one engine at a time. At about 50 mph, 100 gallons of gasoline was enough for a 300 mile range. After much testing the military determined that there were reliability and maneuverability problems, and the truck was not suited for off-road applications.

E & L 1942-1944 — The E & L Transport Company was formed before World War II by Lloyd Lawson and Robert Ellenstein. Lloyd Lawson was an automobile transporter for Ford. A transportation system was planned by Ford manager Charles Sorenson and Edsel Ford with the cooperation of Consolidated Manufacturing in San

Diego and E & L to haul large bulky parts of the B-24 bombers to other assembly plants in distant locations including the Consolidated plant in Fort Worth, Texas.

The tractor trucks were designed and built by E & L, and a total of 100 such vehicle were manufactured, with E & L operating 96 of them. Four were sold to private companies. The early style of the truck was based on Ford sheet metal while later trucks used simplified squared-off styling.

The complete twin-V-8 power pack with front bumper slid out forward for maintenance and repair work. A parallelogram mechanism was used to shift two transmissions with one lever, and clutch and accelerator pedal also controlled both engines. Twin driveshafts were used. Wing sections of the B-24 were hauled by a tractor-trailer of this type. The B-24's wingspan was 110 feet. Toward the end of the war the same tractor trucks were used to pull trailers that carried B-32 wing sections. Trucks were utilized for this transport because the trip by road from California to Texas took 48 hours instead of seven days by rail. The E & L trucks were also used to haul Waco/Ford military transport gliders from the Ford factory to Iron Mountain, Michigan, which was about 500 miles away.

1915 ELBERT DELIVERY WAGON   RD

ELBERT 1914-1915 — F.W. Topkin, a mechanical engineer for the Chicago Pneumatic Tube Company, designed the Elbert motor vehicles, which began production in Seattle, Washington. A silent partner loaned his name to the venture, which quickly moved to Sunnyvale, California, the center of what is now Silicon Valley. A light tandem runabout was built, but a 1/4-ton delivery wagon was also available for $305. The delivery version featured a C-cab that extended into a box body that had 37-cubic feet of cargo space.

The Elbert was essentially a cyclecar, but it was considered a sturdy one. It had a 102-inch wheelbase and was powered by an 18 hp four-cylinder water-cooled engine and used a sliding gear transmission and shaft drive. Top speed was advertised at 40 mph. A windshield for the delivery wagon was listed at $9 extra. By June of 1915 the company advertised a factory in Sunnyvale and executive offices at the Phelan Building in San Francisco.

Nicholas Wilson was the company president who persuaded nine Seattle families to relocate to Sunnyvale. Instead of finding six large buildings that had allegedly been bought from the Goudy Machine Company, the workers found only "one wayside blacksmith shop," and submitted an official complaint against Nicholas Wilson. The venture was quickly over, although a few vehicles were actually built, all probably in Seattle.

ELCAR 1922-1932 — Having been in the automotive business building the Pratt car, William B. and George B. Pratt began building the Elcar in 1916 in Elkhart, Indiana. The first Elcars were powered by a 35 hp four-cylinder Lycoming engine. The Elkhart Carriage and Motor Car Company built a few ambulances for the military during World War I, but it was not until 1922 that Elcar entered the commercial vehicle field by obtaining a contract for 1,000 taxis with the Diamond Taxicab Company of New York. Both four-cylinder and six-cylinder engines were used in the taxis rated at 40 hp and 55 hp, respectively. They were later also built as the Elfay, Martel and Royal Martel.

In 1925 Elcar started using a 65 hp Lycoming straight-eight engine in its 127-inch wheelbase cars. Later, another version of this engine would develop 140 hp. Prototypes of the Lever and Mercer cars were built on Elcar chassis, but Elcar could not avert the financial disaster of the stock market crash. The company remained open for a while longer into 1932 to build a few Allied and El-Fay (another variation of Elfay) taxis.

EL DORADO 1925-1930 — The El Dorado was a series of buses and coaches built by the Motor Transit Company of Los Angeles, California. Having been dissatisfied with the four-cylinder powered White buses the Motor Transit Company was buying for its El Dorado System passenger transit lines, the Southern California company began building its own six-cylinder Buda-powered buses a year before White offered such an engine in its coaches. Actually, the company first modified a few of its existing fleet before manufacturing entire vehicles of its own.

Over 5-1/2 years the company built 70 buses, almost all for its own use, though a few were sold to other transit lines. Some of the El Dorado vehicles were bus-truck incarnations called "combos" using compound transmissions. Coaches were built up to 33-passenger in size. When Pacific Electric Railway took control of El Dorado Motor Company, bus manufacturing was discontinued.

1927 EL DORADO COACH   MBS

1996 EL DORADO AEROTECH   THOR

ELDORADO 1977 to date — Originally, the ElDorado Motor Corporation (EMC) was organized by William Feldhorn in Minneapolis, Kansas. There the company developed a model line of coaches during the 1980s. Thor Corporation purchased ElDorado in 1991 and has continued production under the ElDorado National name with facilities located in Chino, California; Salina, Kansas; and Brown City, Michigan.

By the mid-1980s EMC offered the ElDorado Falcon T/A, MST and Paratransit buses. The conventional front-engine Falcon was offered with a 460-cubic inch Ford V-8 or Chevrolet 350-cubic inch V-8 engine. Wheelbase was up to 176 inches and capacity was up to 25 passengers. The forward-control MST was offered with up to 31-passenger capacity, and new for 1984 was the Paratransit bus with wheelchair ramp. It was listed for $65,000 that year. The MST also had a 165 hp 8.2L Detroit Diesel engine option.

After Thor Industries acquired ElDorado the model line was expanded to include the Escort FE, Aerotech, AeroXT, Elf Low Floor, MST, Escort RE, Escort RE-A, Escort RE Electric and Transmark RE. All of these have been available in several configurations, each with a variety of optional equipment.

The Escort FE has been offered with a 137-inch or 158.5-inch wheelbase with capacity from 11 passengers to 27 passengers with the FE-25 model. This vehicle has been built on a Chevrolet P-30 chassis powered by a 230 hp 7.4L gasoline engine or optional 190 hp 6.5L turbo diesel engine with CNG and LPG alternative fuel also optional and a four-speed Chevrolet 4L80-E automatic transmission as standard.

1996 EL DORADO MST   **THOR**

The conventional front-engine Aerotech and AeroXT have been offered in a total of 25 different configurations in series 200, 220, 240, 280 and XT. The Aerotech series has used the E-350 Cutaway chassis powered by a 351-cubic inch, 460-cubic inch gasoline V-8 or 7.3L diesel engine using a four-speed E-40D automatic overdrive transmission. The AeroXT has used the Chevrolet GP cutaway chassis with a 7.4L diesel EFI V-8 engine and four-speed automatic transmission.

The Elf 100 Series Low Floor has been offered as a small community bus or as a feeder bus for larger systems. The MST line has been available in series 2400, 2600 and 2800 with at least 11 configurations for up to 31 passengers or 24 passengers and restroom and also depending on wheelchair positions and luggage area. The MST chassis was designed and built by Oshkosh using a 160 hp Cummins 6BT turbo diesel engine and Allison AT-545 transmission. Wheelbases were listed as 158.5, 178 and 190 inches depending on model.

The Escort RE has been offered with up to 41-passenger capacity in series RE-29, RE-A-29, RE-32, RE-A-32, RE-A-35 and RE-A-37. The RE-A chassis was designed and built by ElDorado National available with 160, 190 or 230 hp Cummins 6BT turbo diesel or compressed natural gas and Allison AT-545 standard transmission or MT-643 and MTB-643 optional transmissions. The RE Electric has been available using two Hughes high-speed AC induction motors with integral 4:1 reduction, 60-kilowatt continuous Hughes Power Control System and 80-kilowatt-hour lead-acid battery pack with automatic watering system and thermal insulation, as well as a 20-kilowatt propane-powered generator hybrid range extender with power for air conditioning.

ELDRIDGE 1913-1914 — A four-wheel gasoline-electric hybrid tractor was built by the Eldridge Manufacturing Company of Boston, Massachusetts. These were modified Couple-Gear powerplants having the same front-wheel-drive but with two small wheels added to the back for balance. Such tractors were used to pull wagons. The company did not survive the year 1914.

ELECTRIC VEHICLE 1904-1906 — The Electric Vehicle Company was located in Hartford, Connecticut. H.P. Maxim was the designer of a sightseeing bus that was built for the Blanke Tea Company of St. Louis, which used it to carry passengers during the St. Louis Exposition that year. The open-air bus was eight feet wide and could accommodate 50 people. Wheelbase was 123 inches and top speed was 9-1/2 mph. A battery of 44 cells provided the two 30-volt electric motors with enough power for a range of 30 miles. Reduction gears and chain were used for each rear wheel. The battery was located on a tray below the floor for fast replacement. In 1906 the company built an electric street sprinkler. It is not certain whether this company built other commercial vehicles after 1906. The Electric Vehicle Company was also the name of the taxi operation and vehicle sales and maintenance in New York City.

1904 ELECTRIC VEHICLE SIGHTSEEING BUS   **MROZ**

The Electric Vehicle's Columbia Electrics were the product of the Pope Manufacturing Company, which later branched out as the Pope-Hartford, Pope-Robinson and Pope-Toledo. The companies were the work of Colonel Albert Pope, who began as a bicycle maker. The Columbia and Electric Vehicle Company bought the Selden Patent at the turn of the century, and, under the auspices of the Lead Trust and the Association of Licensed Automobile Manufacturers, aggressively pursued to enforce it. Hiram Maxim, having built his own three-cylinder four-cycle gasoline car in 1895, was apparently upset with the turn of events. By 1907 he severed his ties with Albert Pope and those who were trying to monopolize American automobile manufacturing.

1975 ELECTROBUS MODEL 20   **MBS**

ELECTROBUS 1974-1975 — Electrobus, Incorporated was started circa 1973 in Van Nuys, California, to build battery-powered shuttle buses when vehicle emissions began to be stringently legislated in Southern California. These were low-platform 20-passenger buses, and in 1974 three such vehicles were built for the city of Long Beach. A specially adapted 72-volt battery was used to power a DC traction motor rated at a continuous 50 hp. The battery was mounted in the rear so that it could be easily changed out using a forklift.

The large DC motor also ran the ventilation system, air conditioner and air compressor. Air-assisted hydraulic brakes were incorporated into the design, and the entire bus with batteries weighed 7-1/2 tons. It appears that less than 10 such buses were built by this company before Otis Elevator Company, the parent organization, pulled the plug on manufacturing due to lack of sales.

ELECTROCAR 1922 — Joseph Anglada, designer of the better-known Liberty cyclecar, was also the designer and builder of the Electrocar taxicab in New Brunswick, New Jersey. A General Electric DC motor was mounted under a hood and mock radiator in an attempt to make the Electrocar resemble a gasoline-powered vehicle. Exide batteries could be removed from the car with the use of a built-in jack operated with a crank. The taxi rode on a 112-inch wheelbase. Prices started at $2,975. The Electrocar Corporation settled into new sales offices on Fifth Avenue in New York, and the first car was shown at the New York Edison Company exhibit hall and during the Annual Electric Automobile Show in

1922, following two years of development and experimentation. By this time electric cars had fallen further out of favor, and without any orders, the company folded.

1922 ELECTROCAR TAXI   WLB

ELECTRO-COACH 1913-1914 — The Electro-Coach Corporation was located in New York City and built an electric bus for the People's Five Cent Bus Corporation of New York, which planned to operate electric buses in that city. Each wheel of the bus had a 60-volt 32-amp General Electric motor, eliminating the transmission, chains, shafts and clutch. Sixty cells of Edison alkaline A-12 storage batteries were used. The bus carried from 26 to 32 seated passengers. There was a smaller version "for use in narrower cross streets." Push buttons were installed on all pillars of the interior to contact the driver and conductor. Top speed was 14 mph and a 40-mile range was expected with a single charge.

The New York press evaluated the proposed plans by the People's Five Cent Bus Corporation rather negatively, pointing out "that in order to make a trip from Battery to Harlem under the proposed system it would be necessary to pay a fare of 20 cents, as compared with 10 cents charged by the existing company. However ... no one will want to ride all the way from Battery to Harlem unless time is hanging heavily on his hands." Apparently, the operating company's franchise was hampered by such discussion, and Electro-Coach built few of the 1,040 buses proposed to be delivered within four months.

ELECTROMOBILE 1906 — Little is known about the Electromobile van built by the American Electromobile Company of Detroit, Michigan. What is known is that the battery-powered van was rated at three tons and was offered for only one year. It is quite probable that only one prototype was ever built.

ELK 1912-1914 — Three models of trucks were offered for a brief time by the Elk Motor Truck Company of Charleston, West Virginia, beginning in 1912. The company listed 2-, 3- and 5-ton capacity trucks, starting with a 120-inch wheelbase for the lightest model, each powered by a four-cylinder engine.

These early solid-rubber tire trucks had a maximum speed of 15 mph and were provided for the local Charleston market. The company did not survive 1914.

ELKHART see HUFFMAN

ELLSWORTH 1916-1920 — The Mills-Ellsworth Company offered only a 1/2-ton delivery van over nearly five years of its existence. The manufacturer was located in Keokuk, Iowa, and was not related to the earlier Ellsworth & Fay Company of New York City, manufacturers of an expensive passenger car and chrome nickel steel auto components.

The Ellsworth truck was available as a sheet metal panel delivery van or as an open express body. All Ellsworth vehicles were powered by a 30 hp four-cylinder Lycoming engine with Carter carburetor and Connecticut ignition. It used a three-speed selective sliding gear transmission, cone clutch and shaft drive. Pneumatic tires of 30x3-1/2 dimension on artillery wheels were standard. Rear and front axles were from Gemco, and wheelbase was 108 inches. Front springs were semi-elliptic Sheldon, rear cantilever. Base

price for a chassis in 1916 was $635, and custom bodies were built for different applications. "Completely Equipped," the light commercial car sold for $695.

1916 ELLSWORTH LIGHT COMMERCIAL CAR   RD

ELMIRA 1916-1921 — The Elmira Commercial Motor Car Company, located in Elmira, New York, until 1920, was an obscure manufacturer that listed a lone 1/2-ton light truck for several years, but details are completely lacking regarding its specifications or the company's business dealings. It is known that the enterprise moved to Oswego, New York, in 1920 before fading out completely from the commercial vehicle scene.

ELWELL-PARKER 1905-1908 — The Elwell-Parker Electric Company of Cleveland, Ohio, built a number of components for both the electric and the automobile industries at the beginning of this century. These included: motors, controllers, front and rear axles, chassis, batteries, tires and complete power packages. Large trucks were the company's main product line in terms of commercial vehicles. Models included 5-ton and 7-1/2-ton capacity flatbed trucks. A few passenger cars were also built as demonstrators of the Elwell-Parker components. The largest truck used a 30 hp DC motor. Anderson Carriage Company bought the components business from Elwell-Parker in 1909, and vehicle production ceased. However, the company continued to build industrial electric forklifts.

ELYSEE 1926-1934 — The M.P. Moller Car Company, also a well-known pipe organ manufacturer, was best known for building taxicabs under numerous names such as Astor, Blue-Light, Luxor, Paramount and Puritan (among others), in addition to passenger cars under the names of Crawford, Dagmar and Standish. M.P. Moller was located in Hagerstown, Maryland, although it had subsidiaries such as Luxor Cab Manufacturing in Framingham, Massachusetts, as well as a branch on Long Island in New York. Mathias P. Moller, who owned the Crawford Automobile Company, purchased a new factory in Hagerstown and renamed his company the M.P. Moller Car Company in 1924. Moller vehicles were known for their stylish brass and nickel trim as well as for their 70 hp six-cylinder Continental engines.

The Elysee panel delivery trucks were built for the well-to-do, specifically in the commercial vehicle field for goods distribution to wealthy homes, according to the market strategy. The Elysee was built in five separate models: Band Box, Courier, Fifth Avenue, Mercury and Patrician, at first powered by four-cylinder and six-cylinder Buda engines, but later powered by the six-cylinder Red Seal Continental engine used in other Moller vehicles. Although the bodies were stylishly custom in appearance, the components were standard off-the-shelf, such as Columbia and Timken axles and Fuller transmissions. Moller taxi chassis were undoubtedly utilized, although this was not advertised.

The first two models were rated at 3/4-ton capacity and the others at 1-1/2-ton capacity, although the "cwt" standard was actually used for rating in some advertising. The pointed radiator of the Elysee was borrowed directly from the Standish passenger car.

New York City department stores such as Bonwit Teller & Company, Arnold Constable & Company and Stewart & Company had small fleets of Elysee delivery vans. Most of them were built in the Long Island Moller facilities, although some were assembled in Framingham as well. Specially trained chauffeurs were part of the scheme to sell Elysee trucks out of the New York City sales office.

Moller no longer produced passenger cars after 1926 when his company built a huge seven-passenger limousine for Moller himself to take back to his native Denmark on an extended visit. Upon his return the company concentrated exclusively on taxicabs and delivery trucks until the end of production, which quickly faded out at the beginning of the Depression, even though the company offered vehicles until 1934.

A good deal of confusion had developed early on when Wilhelm and Holgar Moller, also natives of Denmark and builders of motor vehicles, moved to Hagerstown in 1922 and introduced a car named the Falcon at the same time the Halladay auto had a model by the name of Falcon. However, the Moller brothers went out of business 12 years before M.P. Moller followed suit.

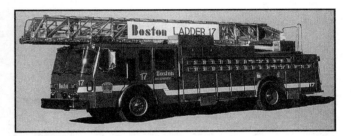

1993 EMERGENCY ONE 110-FOOT HURRICANE LADDER   EO

EMERGENCY ONE 1974 to date — Emergency One, Incorporated has been a relative newcomer to the field of fire apparatus manufacturing, having been established in Ocala, Florida, as a subsidiary of Federal Signal Corporation. The company's Commercial Pumper has been built on commercial chassis supplied by Freightliner, Peterbilt, Navistar, Ford, GMC/White and Volvo. The E-One Hush Pumper has been built with Cummins and Detroit Diesel engine options, while the Protector has been offered with a 250 hp or 300 hp Cummins diesel engine.

Another series of fire engines has been the E-One Tanker trucks built in five distinct configurations with chassis options being designated as Cyclone, Hurricane, Protector, Cyclone TC and Hush -- each of them registered trademarks of Emergency One. The chassis manufacturers have been GMC, Ford, Freightliner and Navistar. The 50-foot Boom truck has been built in five two-axle configurations with the same chassis suppliers but with engines available both as rear-mounted and mid-engine configurations.

E-One has also built ladder trucks in 70-, 80-, 100-, 110- and 135-foot lengths. Tilt-cabs have been available for the 80-, 100- and 110-foot and maximum wheelbase of 249 inches on the tandem axle version of the ladder truck with pump. Transmission options have been HT 740 and HD 4060. E-One has also offered a 95-foot Platform, Industrial Platform and Industrial Pumper. Other industrial trucks have been built on White-Volvo and Kenworth chassis with Caterpillar, Cummins and Detroit Diesel engines and Allison MD, HD and HT transmission choices.

1994 EMERGENCY ONE HEAVY RESCUE   EO

Heavy rescue trucks have been offered as non-walk-in and walk-in conventional and forward-control trucks on a wheelbase up to 232 inches. Both custom chassis and commercial chassis have been offered for this series. E-One has also built glider kits for fire departments that wish to recycle their engine, transmission, rear axle and pump and have it mounted on a new chassis with a new body. E-One advertised a 60-day service time for this type of work and compliance with NFPA 1901 standards.

EMPIRE 1912-1923 — The Empire Automobile Company was organized in Glen Falls, New York, during 1912. It appears the company began as a repair garage and went into truck manufacturing and was reorganized as the Empire Motor Truck Corporation in 1915 with capitalization of $10,000.

In 1922, the *Motor World* advertised a 3/4-ton Empire Light Delivery Truck with a chassis price of $1,000, or $1,200 with an express body and $1,250 with a panel body. The 1-1/2-ton Empire Fast Express was priced at $1,500. Also, a 3-ton and 5-ton chassis was offered for $3,500 and $5,000, respectively. On all models electric lighting and starting was standard equipment, but pneumatic tires were at extra cost.

It is uncertain whether there was an interruption in manufacturing between 1915 and 1922 and it is not known how many trucks this small company actually built. The *Motor World's* ad campaign of 1922 listed the Johnson Motor Truck Company as the distributor, but it is not known if this ad campaign actually represented real production.

EPPERSON see NEUSTADT

ERICKSON 1915-1916 — C.A. Erickson, who had been chief engineer with the Scripps-Booth Company, built a front-drive 3/4-ton delivery truck in Warren, Pennsylvania. The truck's fabrication took place at the Jacobson Machine Manufacturing Company, and the press stated that Erickson had been working on the design for eight years. No further development has been substantiated.

ERIE 1914-1922 — Erie Motor Truck Manufacturing was located in Erie, Pennsylvania. Even though the company built at least four models of trucks, most of the details and specifications are lacking. It is known that the four models comprise 1-1/2-, 2-, 2-1/2- and 3-1/2-ton capacity trucks, all powered by four-cylinder Continental engines. Several chassis were available starting at 144 inches and extending up to 168 inches. By 1919, Erie trucks used Timken worm-drive rear axles. By 1921, when a recession took place in the United States and used military trucks flooded the market, Erie reduced its production to a single 2-1/2-ton model before going out of business altogether.

ERIE & STURGIS see STURGIS

1928 ERSKINE MODEL 50 CLOSED PANEL   A&A

ERSKINE 1928-1930 — Erskine vehicles were named after the president of the Studebaker Corporation, Albert Russel Erskine. Erskine began in 1927 as a low-priced passenger car with the slogan "The Little Aristocrat." By the following year, a 1/2-ton van was also available, along with the sedan and convertible models. All Erskine models, produced along with Studebakers in South

Bend, Indiana, were built on a 108-inch wheelbase chassis at first, then growing to 109 inches in 1929 and 114 inches in 1930. The van was listed only for the years 1928 and 1929. A 40 hp six-cylinder L-head Continental engine powered all Erskines, and prices started at $795 in 1928. The light van was discontinued in 1929, and Studebaker abandoned the Erskine line entirely in 1930.

1928 ERSKINE MODEL 51 BUSINESS COACH SEDAN DELIVERY A&A

1911 ERVING RELIABLE 1-1/2-TON RD

ERVING RELIABLE 1910-1911 — The Erving Reliable commercial car was built for only about one year in the form of a 1-1/2-ton truck. It was powered by a four-cylinder engine and used a three-speed progressive transmission with single disc clutch. Solid rubber tires were employed. The truck's most salient feature was the ease with which its radiator and engine, mounted on a sub-frame, could be removed for service or repair. Bosch ignition was used and suspension was with semi-elliptic springs in front and platform springs in the rear.

1933 ESCO 2-TON VAN ESCO

ESCO 1933-1937, 1945 — The Exhibitors Service Company used its acronym to create a subsidiary in order to manufacture two models of trucks starting in 1933. Esco Motor Company was located in Pittsburgh, Pennsylvania, offering 2-, 2-1/2- and 3-ton capacity trucks powered by six-cylinder Continental engines.

Exhibitors Service Company was organized by G. Callahan in 1911 in order to transport motion picture film to various theaters, originally without necessarily using trucks. However, laws were

passed restricting the transport of nitrate film in passenger-carrying vehicles for safety reasons and this was the impetus for building Esco trucks.

In 1934, the 2-ton model van sold for $2,500, as the company attempted to find outside customers. All Esco trucks were based on a Sterling truck design (after Callahan and his son visited the Sterling factory and decided to build their own trucks) but used five-speed transmissions that had direct drive in high gear. Chassis were bought from Parrish Pressed Steel Company, but most castings and sheet metal were produced at the Esco factory.

The company experimented with fuel oil as a substitute for gasoline, though not successfully. All in all, Esco built nearly 60 trucks, which included a few vehicles built as a result of national transportation restrictions and shortages toward the end of World War II.

ESHELMAN 1957-1959 — Cheston L. Eshelman was described as a "self-made mechanical designer." He began in Baltimore, Maryland, during 1953 building midget cars. He had also built a miniature plane that did not go into production, despite the designer's claims of advance orders for 250 units to be shipped to South America.

By 1955, his shop was reorganized as the Eshelman Motors Corporation. The first vehicle was the Child Sport Car, followed by the Adult Sport Car, both of which went into limited production. By 1957, Eshelman had won a government contract to build 3,400 three-wheel delivery trucks for the Post Office Department. These were powered by a 9 hp engine and were assembled by the Charles B. Briddell Company of Crisfield, Maryland. After 1959, the Eshelman enterprise continued to build a few tractors and golf carts before fading out of existence.

1922 ESSEX PICKUP KP

1933 ESSEX DELUXE PANEL DELIVERY KP

ESSEX see HUDSON

EUCLID 1931 to date — The Euclid Crane and Hoist Company started out in Cleveland, Ohio, in 1926. A subsidiary called Euclid Road Machinery followed nearly a decade later and both companies were the proprietorship of five brothers by the name of Armington after they purchased the businesses in 1931. This was the first year that Euclid pioneered aluminum van trailers and built its first large capacity hauler.

1934 EUCLID   **EUCLID**

An 11-ton Trac-Truk was one of the first models that Euclid built circa 1933. It was intended for the heavy construction and quarrying businesses and included a steel cab, tractor-pattern double rear tires and scow end steel tipping body. Trailerized bottom-dump wagons of 1933 were nicknamed "belly dumps." These trucks had the exclusive Euclid feature of locking one of the rear wheels for a better turning radius and to increase traction in mud by alternately locking the opposite wheels.

A rear dump model was built in 1934 featuring a set back front axle, rear tire cleats, crows nest for backing and separate pedals to operate independent rear brakes. The 1FB Model rated at 15 tons was introduced in 1936. That same year, the well-known diesel-powered FD model began production, which continued through 1954.

Euclid quickly became well known for crawler tractors, dump trucks, loaders and scrapers. A 20-ton coal hauler was built for Truax Coal Company. In 1949, a twin-powered tractor-scraper and tractor-wagon were developed. These had one engine in front and one in rear, and later side-by-side engines for large 6x4 off-highway trucks. By 1951, the Model 1LLD was introduced as a three-axle dump truck rated at 45-ton capacity powered by twin 300 hp Cummins diesel engines.

1964 EUCLID GMC 27-TON   **KP**

In 1953, the company was acquired by General Motors Corporation. Under new ownership Euclid built large crawler tractors in 1954 with twin side-by-side engines and in 1956 a 60-ton log hauler was built as one of many special purpose vehicles. In 1958, the company built one of the world's largest trucks. This was a three-axle truck tractor with a two-axle dump trailer both rated together at 120-ton capacity. It was sold to Western Mining at a cost of $170,000 for its large scale operations. The truck was powered by two 375 hp Cummins diesel engines.

Due to Anti-Trust Monopolies Commission litigation, General Motors was forced to sell Euclid in 1968 and was prohibited from selling off-highway trucks in the United States. GM continued with off-highway truck sales in Canada and Scotland under the name Terex. White Motor Corporation bought Euclid and R.G. Armington, former president of Euclid, became a member of the board of directors of White Motor Corporation. Under White's leadership, Euclid manufacturing was established in Australia, Belgium and Canada.

At that time the U.S. Army's Mobility Equipment Research and Development Command (MERADCOM) at Ft. Belvoir, Virginia, tested a 15-ton Model 99FD Euclid quarry truck. It was powered by a 218 hp 425-cubic inch six-cylinder Detroit Diesel 6-71 engine and used a Euclid 60RA planetary rear axle and Fuller 5F1220 transmission. The stock truck passed all requirements with ease.

In 1969, Euclid built Model R-X, which was a huge 110-ton rear-dump truck. By 1974, Euclid off-highway tractors hauling 85-cubic yard bottom dump trailers were powered by 608 hp Detroit Diesel engines.

The year 1976 marked Euclid's 50th anniversary and a major reorganization took place. A multi-million dollar modernization program was started, a number of prospective buyers were poised to acquire the company once again. The contenders included Clark, Fiat-Allis, Harsco, Paccar and Rockwell International, but in the end Daimler-Benz bought the company in 1977, including the foreign factories.

Euclid continued to build large dump trucks such as the R series two-axle from 22-ton to 170-ton capacity, as well as the B series bottom dump up to 110 tons and the SC series articulated coal haulers for loads up to 150 tons. Cummins and Detroit Diesel engines from 228 hp to 1600 hp were available. One of the largest single orders in Euclid's history was placed in 1979 by Peter Kiewitt Sons. Ten 105-ton bottom-dump haulers and 31 rear dumpers ranging in size from 85 ton to 170 ton were purchased for $17 million.

In 1984, ownership changed once again when the Clark subsidiary acquired Euclid. The R-210 model, which had been developed in 1971 and was temporarily discontinued, went into production with single tires and 4x4 configuration. It was rated at 210-ton capacity and was powered by an 1850 hp Avco-Lycoming turbine, which ran an alternator that provided electricity for DC motors in the wheels. The DC traction motors had dynamic braking along with the air-over hydraulic brakes.

1977 EUCLID R-35   **EUCLID**

The R-170 model of the late 1980s was similar in design to the R-210 in that an alternator was driven by a 1600 hp Cummins V-16 that in turn powered the General Electric traction motors in each rear wheel. An 800 hp Cummins V-12 turbocharged diesel was also available. Euclid made its own double reduction rear axles for the lighter trucks such as the Model R-25 that used a standard drivetrain with an Allison CLBT-750 5F 1R automatic transmission.

The CH series, which was built up to 150-ton capacity, used a 1050 hp turbocharged Detroit Diesel 12V-149-T V-12 engine or the larger displacement 1050 hp Cummins KTA-2300-C V-12 engine. Allison automatic transmissions were used with these engines and the trucks had four braking systems: air/hydraulic service brakes, two independent emergency circuits, parking brake operating on the transmission and a retarder integral with the transmission housing providing constant speed on downhill grades.

Effective August 1986, Clark Michigan Company became VME Americas Incorporated headquartered in Cleveland, Ohio. Equipment continued to be sold under Volvo BM, Michigan Euclid and Ranger names. One of the most common Euclid trucks at that time was the R 190, which had a capacity of 190 ton. Its GVW was 316 ton and it was powered by a Cummins KTTA50C diesel engine or a Detroit Diesel 16V 149TIB engine with 1800 hp. The diesel engine in turn powered a GE electric motor in each wheel. Tire diameter was 11-1/2 feet.

By 1993, VME Industries was building Euclid, and by that year VME (Euclid) had captured 25 percent of the rigid hauler truck market share. Although headquarters continued to be located in Cleveland, Euclid haulers were built in Guelph, Ontario, Canada, by 1994 and the latest development in the complex company history was a joint venture with Hitachi and VME called Euclid-Hitachi Heavy Equipment Incorporated -- still in Cleveland, Ohio, by 1995. With its 70th anniversary in 1996, over all the years of production Euclid has built more than 43,000 units.

1922 EUGOL 1-TON SPEED TRUCK   RD

EUGOL 1921-1923 — The Eugol Motor Truck Company neither lasted for long nor produced many trucks. It was organized by Eugene Goldman in 1921. The small manufacturer was located in Kenosha, Wisconsin, and produced a single model called the 752. This was a 1-ton capacity truck powered by a four-cylinder Buda engine using a three-speed transmission. Rear axle was by Timken, steering was by Ross and pneumatic tires were standard equipment. The company stayed in business only for about one year.

1906 EUREKA 1-1/2-TON   RD

EUREKA 1906 — The C.H. Nadig & Brothers of Allentown, Pennsylvania, built the first Eureka truck, which subsequently was to be manufactured by the Eureka Motor Car Company of Allentown.

Henry Nadig, listed as having built a car in 1891, which has remained extant to date, experimented with gasoline engines with his sons, Charles and Lawrence, through 1896. At about that time, there had been 10 different motor vehicle companies by the name of Eureka in the United States, and the truck that the Nadigs built appears to be the 11th separate effort of this kind.

At least one Eureka truck was built with an 18 hp engine using a Holley carburetor and dual coil ignition. The engine featured pressurized oil lubrication and a water pump for cooling. The truck was rated as a 1-1/2-ton and used solid rubber tires. Whether it went into production is not known.

EVANS LIMITED 1912-1913 — Builder of the Evans Limited, the Automobile Manufacturing and Engineering Company was located in Detroit, Michigan. The Evans Limited was built as a single model for just one year. This was the 3/4-ton Model 1 with 112-inch wheelbase powered by a four-cylinder water-cooled engine. It had a three-speed transmission, shaft drive and pneumatic tires as standard equipment. It was offered in 1913 for $1,200, but the company did not survive the year.

EVO 1968 to date — Evo commercial vehicles were introduced in 1968 by the Lodal Corporation of Kingsford, Michigan. Origins of the trucks, which have been used primarily for refuse collection, date back to 1948 when company president, Ray Brisson, built rearend bucket loaders for trucks in the Brisson Brothers Machine Shop located in Norway, Michigan. A new company by the name of Lodal Incorporated was formed in 1953 for the purpose of building low front-end loaders on truck chassis. Demand for specialized refuse trucks led to the EVO line of trucks. The name was derived from the EVOlution of the loading equipment design.

1976 EVO 1650   LODAL

The EVO system has used two vehicles: a small building-to-building collection truck called the EVO 1650 and a large 34-cubic yard capacity transfer truck called the Load-A-Matic (LAM). This system separates collection from major hauling and has been likened to the Pagefield system from the 1930s.

The low cab-forward EVO 1650 was designed with a loading hopper amidships and steering on both sides. One or two workers could drive and load the vehicle, and each eight-cubic yard refuse container would then be carried to a transfer yard. There the LAM truck would be loaded with the refuse from each container in order to haul it to the dump site. Several EVO vehicles would service one LAM truck saving fuel, equipment and operation costs.

A self-dumping 12-cubic yard EVO has also been available. These vehicles were powered by Chrysler V-8 engines using Allison automatic transmissions and Rockwell-Standard front-drive axles. The Lodal LAM trucks that have been manufactured to date have been constructed on Mack cab and chassis. The company has built a series of ECO and EVO refuse trucks to date, which have been designated the following numbers: ECO-35-R, ECO-35-SR, ECO-SA39-R, EVO-17-XL, EVO-MAG-20 and EVO-T25 Route Builder.

1995 EVO LODAL LOADMATIC   **LODAL**

The ECO truck series is specifically built for recyclables with body configurations for curb separation of up to 10 different materials. Engine, transmission and radiator have been mounted as a single module for fast replacement when necessary. An optional Lodal plastics compactor with 25:1 compaction ratio was designed to hold 4,000 one-gallon plastic milk containers or approximately 30 cubic yards of uncompacted material. Lodal has built various other refuse removal and hauling vehicles to date.

EWBANK 1912 — The Ewbank Power-Transmission and Motor Company began in late 1911 in Portland, Oregon, with a capitalization of $250,000. The company built a gasoline-electric hybrid motor wagon as a fire engine. A separate electric motor was used to drive the water pumper. S.M. Mears was company president, George W. Stapleton vice-president, R.S. Howard treasurer and H.E. Ewbank, secretary. As with many obscure organizations, more is known about who started the company than what they actually produced.

E-Z-GO 1973 to date — Bill and Beverly Dolan founded the E-Z-Go Company in Augusta, Georgia, during 1954. The company built golf carts exclusively. In 1961 Textron Corporation bought E-Z-Go, and in 1973 the company developed light industrial and commercial vehicles both gasoline- and electric-powered.

E-Z-Go has offered a model line consisting of the XI-300 Electric, XI-500 Electric, XI-775 Electric, XI-875P Electric, XI-875 Electric, XI-881 Electric, GXI-804 Gas, GXI-1500 Gas, PC4 Electric/PC4

Gas, PC-952, PC-954, PC-955, PC-956 and PC-957. All of these vehicles have featured direct drive transmissions and 24-volt or 36-volt electric motors rated up to 6.5 hp. The lightest vehicles have used 1.5 hp and 2.5 hp electric motors.

1996 E-Z-GO   **E-Z-G**

Two gasoline engines have been used by E-Z-Go. For the GXI-804 an 8.5 hp four-cycle 295-cubic centimeter displacement engine has been used and for the GXI-1500 and PC-4 a 20 hp horizontally-opposed two-cylinder four-cycle Onan engine has been used. The PC personnel carriers have been listed with either a 6.5 hp electric motor, or in the case of the PC-952, PC-954 and PC-956, the 8.5 hp four-cycle two-cylinder 295-cubic centimeter engine has also been available. The heftiest of the vehicles has been the XI-881 listed with a 3,000-pound payload capacity. The personnel carriers have been listed with four- to 11-passenger capacity. Optional equipment has included van boxes, cabs, galvanized steel cargo deck, light bar, 1,000-pound capacity trailers and steel dropside bodies.

F

F

FABCO 1938-1939, 1955-1977 — The first Fabco trucks built by F.A.B. in Oakland, California, were fire engines manufactured for California Fire Departments before World War II. Although Fabco has stayed in business to date as a manufacturer of steerable axles and transfer cases, it has ceased building complete trucks. Fabco has been a subsidiary of Kelsey-Hayes Company in Oakland, California, which in turn has been a subsidiary of Fruehauf Corporation.

1977 FIELD HARVESTER   **FABCO**

Fabco trucks were produced for highly specialized applications such as agricultural harvesting, crane carrying and power pole erection. The smallest Fabco truck, the early Fab 151, was a one-man-cab yard trailer-spotter. Several flatbed trucks were built with a 10,000-pound Remy hydraulic crane. These FT series were powered by a Ford gasoline V-8 located below the bed using an automatic transmission and were available in 4x2 and 6x4 configurations. They were used primarily to haul pipes and power poles up to 45 feet in length.

The WT series was a "flat-top" with engine above the deck and beside the cab built specifically for harvesting agricultural produce in the field with a minimum of plant damage and without the need of transferring the produce to another on-road vehicle for delivery to stores and warehouses. This was a 6x6 truck with single tires and an 82-inch wide track. They were powered by a Detroit Diesel or Ford gasoline engine. The specially-designed wide track enabled the truck to drive through lettuce fields without damaging the crop. This Field Harvester was designated as the Model WT6630D and used a five-speed Clark 285V 5F 1R transmission in combination with a three-speed Dana 7231D auxiliary transmission and two-speed Fabco TC-33 transfer case providing 30 forward speeds and six in reverse allowing speeds from 1 mph up to 50 mph. Front axle was a Fabco WT-9 while the rear axle was a Fabco DA-20 single reduction tandem spiral bevel type. Brakes were full air-operated.

In addition, Fabco built the UV tandem axle cab-over series starting in 1972. This used a conventional full-width cab. Engine options were Caterpillar or Detroit Diesel and Ford gasoline powerplants were also available. Gross vehicle weight ranged from 27,000 pounds to 56,000 pounds and 4x2, 4x4, 6x4 and 6x6 versions were available. Fabco also offered 4x4 conversions for Ford, GMC and other manufacturers, and these were used primarily for power line installation. The last complete Fabco truck was the Field Harvester sold circa 1976, according to company sources. Fabco is still listed as a truck manufacturer but on a custom basis only.

1921 FACTO   **FACTO**

FACTO 1921-1922 — One of the briefest manufacturers of trucks was the Facto Motor Trucks enterprise of Springfield, Massachusetts. Adolph A. Geisel, who had been a salesman for Federal trucks, was behind this venture. Geisel bought 55,000 square feet of land for the erection of a factory, which appears to have been completed, and the company's offering was a single model truck rated at 2-1/2-ton capacity. It was powered by a 28.9 hp (40 brake hp) four-cylinder Buda ETU engine and a Pierce governor limited the top speed to 18 mph. Wheelbase was 156 inches and the truck used worm-drive. Solid rubber tires were 36x4 front and 36x8 rear. Chassis weight was 5,800 pounds. Standard equipment included weatherproof cab, two dash oil lamps, two gas headlamps, Prest-O-Lite gas tank, rear oil light, mechanical hand horn, jack and full set of tools. The company did not survive the postwar recession from all indicators and it is uncertain how many Facto trucks were built besides two prototypes.

FAGEOL 1916-1939 — The Fageol brothers, Frank R. and William B., started out in 1900 by building an experimental gasoline-powered automobile in their hometown of Des Moines, Iowa. The brothers became dealers of cars rather than manufacturers in Iowa. However, when they moved to California they decided to go into the motor vehicle manufacturing business on a serious level. The first factory was constructed in 1916 in Oakland, California.

The first undertaking was the design and fabrication of an exclusive passenger car using 135-inch to 145-inch wheelbases and a 125 hp six-cylinder engine. Almost from the beginning the Fageol vehicles had a patented hood design that consisted of several rear-facing fin louvers on top in order to assist with cooling by improving air flow. Mostly, however, the large louvers were for appearance sake. Some later tractors even had "blind" louvers. The passenger cars were promoted until 1918, but only three units were actually built and these had an astounding price tag of $12,000 each. It appears that the third auto was built in 1921.

With leadership provided by Louis H. Bill, who was president, and Colonel Elbert J. Hall, the Fageol company became preoccupied with military contracts during World War I and the idea of passenger car production was essentially abandoned. Directly after the war, Fageol began making orchard tractors but these were so overpriced, according to many sources, that the company was forced to take a different tack altogether. Since the Fageol brothers had built a few truck prototypes, it was decided that this would be the main product line.

Fageol trucks were conventional assembled vehicles that started out from 2-1/2-ton to 6-ton in capacity after World War I using four-cylinder Waukesha engines with some cylinders cast in pairs, some as monobloc. Fageol built its own transmissions and used Timken worm rear axles and solid rubber tires on artillery wheels, with dual rear wheels being optional. In the early 1920s, the model line was changed to include 1-1/2-ton to 5-ton capacity trucks with prices ranging from $3,000 to $5,700, substantially higher than many other makes of that time. However, Fageol trucks were designed to be able to climb the amazingly steep streets of San Francisco, among other areas of Northern California where they were primarily sold, and their durability and reputation commanded a higher price range.

1930 FAGEOL 3-1/2-TON   **HAYS**

Fageol also began building buses in the early 1920s. The first model was the Safety Coach of 1921. The low wide-track design allowed for comfortable 22-passenger seating with ease of entry and exit provided by rows of doors on each side of the bus body. These were powered by four-cylinder Hall-Scott engines and a 29-passenger model was added with a six-cylinder engine. Almost immediately, these coaches became successful and many were sold in the Midwest.

Business was so brisk in fact, that by 1924 a sales agency was opened in Cleveland, Ohio, and the former factory of Thomart Motor Company in Kent, Ohio, was acquired solely for building Fageol buses. Hundreds of coaches were built before the American Car and Foundry Company of Detroit, which had acquired the J.G. Brill Company of Philadelphia (builders of streetcars and trolleys), purchased the entire Fageol business in Ohio. The Fageol plant in Oakland remained in the hands of the Fageol brothers, however, even though they were American Car and Foundry vice-presidents.

For 1925, Fageol listed 2-, 3-, 4- and 6-ton capacity trucks. These were designated as models 235, 340, 445 and 645 and were priced at $3,300, $4,000, $5,100 and $5,800, respectively. All were powered by Waukesha engines from 25.6 hp to 32.4 hp except for the 3-ton model 360 Special, which had a 152-inch wheelbase, used a Brown-Lipe transmission, had pneumatic tires in front as standard equipment, duals in rear, and was priced at $5,250. As before, Fageol used its own transmissions as well as Timken axles and Ross steering.

The Fageol Oakland factory continued to build both trucks and buses, while ACF-Brill built buses in Detroit using the Fageol name until 1929. However, the Fageol brothers left ACF-Brill in 1927 when it became apparent that their radical new design for a twin-engine 40-passenger city bus was being shunned by their bosses. They reacquired the Thomart facilities that year to produce the Twin Coach model line.

Fageol trucks adopted industry innovations such as complete electric lighting and starting, full-pressure lubrication and in 1929, four-wheel hydraulic brakes. The model range included a 10-ton six-wheel truck with an optional six-cylinder Hall-Scott engine. By 1930, Safety Coaches had seating for up to 58 passengers, and there were 13 factory branches and many sales agencies in the Pacific West and several foreign countries.

Due to the onset of the Great Depression, a merger with Moreland of Southern California was proposed. It fell through due partly to Fageol's great operating losses and by 1932, this led to bank receivership and reorganization under the name Fageol Truck and Coach Company. That year, Cummins and Waukesha diesel engines were offered and a new innovation of using aluminum frames to save weight was introduced.

Fageol kept up with industry changes and by the mid-1930s adopted an aerodynamic cab design with a V-windshield. A cab-over model was introduced in 1937 when the model line ranged from 2 ton to 10 ton and prices were from $1,340 to $10,800. In 1938, a tandem tractor was built to haul two-section Fruehauf lowbed trailers measuring 74 feet in total length and a Fageol articulated truck pulled a transporter weighing a then-record 104 tons.

But financial trouble continued to plague the company. Fageol's assets were sold to Sterling of Milwaukee in November of 1938. As the year 1939 began, Fageol production ceased entirely and Sterling sold off the remaining vehicles in the inventory. The rest of the assets were sold to T.A. Peterman, who founded the Peterbilt truck line and has continued production to date. The Fageol name was revived by Twin Coach in 1950.

1938 FAGEOL LOGGER   **HAYS**

FAGEOL 1950-1954 — In an attempt to boost sales, Twin Coach introduced a line of moving vans using the name Fageol. These used many International components but integral construction was much the same as the Twin Coach vehicles. Fruehauf sheet metal stampings were used for the van bodies. Eight wheelbase lengths were available from 108 inch to 222 inch. The vans were built by Twin Coach, International dealers sold them, they resembled Fruehauf trailers, but they were known as the Fageol Super Freighters. In 1953, when Twin Coach sold its bus manufacturing to Flxible, a multi-stop delivery van with the name Fageol was introduced briefly, but the new parent company discontinued the Fageol line entirely by 1954.

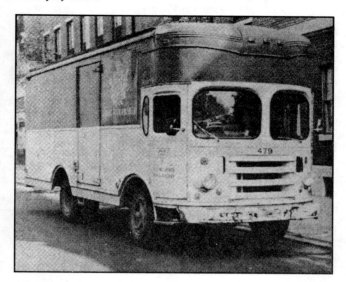

1954 FAGEOL FV24 VAN GNG

FAIRBANKS-MORSE 1908 — Fairbanks-Morse had built a railway inspection car in 1905, a single automobile by the name of Charter prior to 1908 and a single touring car in 1908. This was also the year the company decided to experiment with truck production as well. Delivery wagons of 1,000-, 1,200- and 3,500-pound capacity were built, as was a 3-ton forward-control truck. The latter was powered by a 25 hp Sheffield engine and used a constant-mesh four-speed transmission with double chain drive. A governor limited the top speed to 10 mph. Fairbanks-Morse was better known for its line of tractors, which were built up to 1922. Truck and delivery wagon production lasted for the one year only.

FAIRFIELD 1896 — C.S. Fairfield of Portland, Maine, built a surrey-type buckboard using a 10 hp kerosene engine. It was used to "convey summer excursion parties to resorts in the neighborhood of Portland." However, the Fairfield was not a successful mechanical design, and after its breakdown, its builder refrained from ever building another such commercial vehicle.

FAIRFIELD 1928-1929 — The Fairfield Four truck was designed and built by Victor W. Page in Stamford, Connecticut. Incorporators were Stephen J. Miller, John C. Norton and Joseph Fuger. Victor Page was a proponent of air-cooled engines and his design for a 35 hp powerplant was exactly that, using several of his patents, which also covered the multiple disc transmission brake. Production of only two prototypes of a 1-ton truck have been substantiated. A published prospectus gave a price of $800 for the running chassis and $985 for the complete truck with closed cab and stake body. The stock market crash precluded further development and no other activity appears to have taken place at the small Fairfield factory, which became an independent machine shop that was in business as recently as 1991.

FAIRVIEW 1909 — Announcements in the press divulged that a company by the name of the Fairview Motor Company was to begin manufacturing commercial vehicles exclusively. Backers were affiliated with the Chalmers-Detroit Motor Company but no further activity has been substantiated.

FALCON 1915-1916 — There were several early vehicles with the name of Falcon but it appears that a light delivery 1/2-ton model was the only commercial vehicle with such a name. It was built by the Falcon Motor Truck Company of Detroit, Michigan, and at a time when driving position had not been universally established, the company offered optional left- or right-hand drive. Little else is known about this obscure and short-lived manufacturer.

FAMOUS 1917-1923 — Not directly affiliated with the earlier Famous Manufacturing Company of East Chicago, Indiana, Famous Trucks, Incorporated was located in St. Joseph, Michigan, after having originated in Chicago. It is not clear if this was a reorganization of the earlier automobile builder, but it appears that the company built a prototype called the Model A and then marketed a bare 1-ton chassis as the Model B 10. It was powered by a four-cylinder Continental engine using a three-speed transmission and shaft drive. The chassis wheelbase was 120 inches and it was priced at $1,690. R.H. Grotfeld was president and C.E. Frederickson was vice-president.

FARGO 1913-1921 — The original Fargo Motor Car Company was not affiliated with the later Chrysler vehicles. This earlier manufacturer was located in Chicago, Illinois. The first Model E was a 3/4-ton forward-control panel van with 98-inch wheelbase powered by a two-cylinder engine using a friction transmission. After World War I, the company offered 2-ton trucks using 144-inch wheelbase and four-cylinder engines by Continental. Before the company succumbed to the economic times of the postwar recession, a Fargo 2-ton chassis was priced at $2,200.

1929 FARGO CLIPPER PANEL KP

FARGO 1928-1972 — Chrysler Corporation introduced Fargo in 1928 as a new model line of commercial vehicles, although there actually were some passenger Fargos built at first in the form of a sedan and station wagon on the Clipper and Packet chassis. In fact, the six-cylinder 3/4-ton Clipper and four-cylinder 1/2-ton Packet were advertised with an emphasis on passenger auto design, when the following corporate statement was issued: "Passenger car lines of the most modern accepted standards are characteristic throughout the Fargo line."

1930 FARGO FREIGHTER WITH SPECIAL BODY KP

In the beginning, the Fargo Motor Corporation was Chrysler's fleet sales division. This is associated with Fargo emblems on Plymouth sedans in the 1930s, which were sold to the U.S. Army. The Fargo name continued to be used for Canadian export while proving to be more of an insignia than a separate make and design of commercial vehicles in the United States. Chrysler used the Fargo name for various reasons to penetrate some small foreign markets. Dodge and Fargo trucks were identical but for the emblems and some minor trim over the years, with the exception of a few rare early models based on the Clipper and Packet.

For 1931, Fargo introduced a new line of 21-passenger buses. These were built in "street car coach" and "parlor car coach," with overall length of 20-1/2 feet. The construction of the buses involved wood sections that were "thoroughly treated with lead and oil." The front-engine bus had a two-piece split windshield and a completely circular radiator grille. The vehicle was powered by an inline eight-cylinder engine and used a four-speed transmission. The "street car coach" differed from the "parlor coach" in interior appointments and in that the former used 8.25x20 balloon tires with duals on the rear while the latter had 7.50x20 tires front and rear.

1939 FARGO 1/2-TON PANEL RPZ

For simply a badge-engineered truck, the Fargo sold far and wide. Chrysler sold Australian Dodges produced at Keswick, Adelaide. The Commer sometimes wore the Fargo badge after Chrysler took over Rootes Motors. The Canadian Fargo was discontinued in 1972 but the Fargo name was used elsewhere such as in Africa, the Middle East and Scandinavia.

1972 FARGO B-300 VAN CHRYS

One of the most common Fargo trucks of the 1940s was the Model FL2-33. It had a 128-inch wheelbase and was powered by a 105 hp 228-cubic inch Dodge six-cylinder L-head engine with a Ball and Ball carburetor. Transmission was a New Process four-speed and the rear axle was a Clark spiral bevel type. Suspension was semi-elliptic spring front and rear and tires were 6.50x16 six-ply front and 7.50x16 eight-ply rear. Price for this 1-ton pickup was $1,015 for that year.

The original Clipper and Packet Fargo vehicles borrowed many components from the K and CK series DeSoto six-cylinder models and the four-cylinder Plymouth passenger car, respectively. The Fargo Freighter was really a Dodge 1-ton truck. In 1931 and 1932

the Fargo emblem found its way onto Dodge buses. There were about 75 such buses sold, and these were powered both by six-cylinder engines and Chrysler straight-eight engines. The Fargo PSV line continued for school bus application.

FARMERS 1905-1906 — The Farmers Automobile Company (also known as the Farmer's Auto-Motor Car Company) was affiliated with the Caps Brothers of Kansas City, Missouri. The Caps Brothers had built a small passenger car in 1902 and subsequently produced a few more for the local citizens of Kansas City. Incorporation with a capital of $250,000 took place when the local bank got involved and F. Burleigh became president and J.K. Hudson was chairman of the board. By 1906, production of a truck was announced, which would be powered by a 75 hp engine and would cost $5,000. However, the bankers lost faith in the Caps brothers almost immediately and their factory was taken over by the Kansas City Motor Car Company, which built the Kansas City passenger car. What happened to the Caps brothers is not known but Rhine Caps was listed as secretary of the Kansas City Motor Car Company, which stayed in business until 1909.

FAUBER-BI-CAR 1914 — Of the many cyclecars built at the beginning of the century, the Fauber had one distinction in that it was offered with a delivery van body. W.H. Fauber was the designer, perhaps whose only distinction was that he failed with two different automobiles in one year: the Fauber-Bi-Car and the Auto-Cyclecar. The Fauber-Bi-Car had a motorcycle-type frame, two-cylinder air-cooled engine and tandem seating. Wheelbase was 66 inches and the light delivery van sold for $285, although Fauber advised that "any man can save $100 by assembling the Bi-Car himself." Fauber's offices were located in New York City but the vehicles were actually built in Indianapolis, Indiana, by the Cyclecar Engineering Company. After Fauber's quick exit from the automotive field, he went on to pursue the development of the Fauber Hydroplane, which he had designed.

FAWCETT 1910 — The Fawcett Wagon Works of Tacoma, Washington, built a gasoline stagecoach for transporting passengers between Valdez and Fairbanks, Alaska. It was powered by a 65 hp gasoline engine. No other information has been available to date.

FAWICK 1913-1916 — Thomas L. Fawick was only in his mid-teens when he began designing his first automobile in 1906. By the time he was 18 years old in 1908, he had finished it in his home town of Sioux Falls, South Dakota. He named the car the Silent Sioux. It was powered by a two-cylinder engine and was quite mechanically sound, attracting the attention of local investors. Silent Sioux Auto Manufacturing Company was organized and some cars with this name were produced using four-cylinder Waukesha engines. The Charles Abresch Company of Milwaukee built the aluminum bodies.

In 1910, the Silent Sioux Company became the Fawick Motor Car Company, still located in Sioux Falls. John F.D. Mundt remained as one of the original investors and Fawick's brother also joined the company. What is not clear is exactly if the company built 1/2-, 3/4-, 1-ton and 2-ton trucks, which are listed for the years 1913-1916. It is possible that before Thomas Fawick left the company during World War I to pursue the development of some of his inventions, such as the twin-disc clutch, the Fawick Motor Company had stayed in business long enough to have actually built a few light trucks. Fawick later designed an overdrive mechanism for transmissions, which he sold to Borg-Warner, as well as an engine rubber mount that Chrysler bought from him. After World War II, Fawick merged with the Federal Motor Truck Company.

F.C.S. 1909-1911 — The Schmidt Brothers Company of South Chicago, Illinois, built a 1-ton truck under the name F.C.S. It was powered by an 18 hp two-cylinder engine that was located under a closed delivery body. The air-cooled engine had a planetary transmission attached and power was transmitted to the rear wheels with dual chains. Tires were solid rubber, and the Schmidt Brothers claimed the 1-ton capacity truck could attain 20 mph. Wheelbase was 90 inches.

1911 F.C.S. MODEL C DELIVERY VAN   RD

FEDERAL 1910-1959 — Organizer of the Oakland Motor Car Company in 1907 in Pontiac, Michigan, M.L. Pulcher founded the Bailey Motor Truck Company in Detroit in 1910. By the end of that same year the name was changed to Federal Motor Truck Company.

Capitalization of Bailey Motor Truck Company took $50,000 and with Pulcher's no-nonsense, if somewhat conservative, leadership, the Federal Motor Truck Company prospered as few such independent businesses did. Federal trucks were assembled vehicles and "never an experiment," as the company proclaimed. All Federal trucks were of conventional design until cab-over models were introduced in 1937.

The first Federal was a 1-ton truck powered by a four-cylinder Continental engine using a three-speed transmission and dual chain final drive. The bare chassis sold for $1,800 in 1910. Its weight was listed as 3,000 pounds and its top speed was governed to 15 mph. Federal built bodies, also. These included a stake model with cab roof, plain stake bed and open express.

1911 FEDERAL 1-TON MODEL D   NAHC

The Model C of 1911 featured a 28.9 hp four-cylinder engine, leather-faced cone clutch, sliding selective three-speed transmission, two sets of brakes expanding on the rear wheels and on the transmission jackshaft, 36-inch solid rubber tires, 21-gallon gasoline tank under the seat, semi-elliptic spring suspension and 110-inch wheelbase. The open delivery Model C sold for $2,200 and the Model C full panel C-cab sold for $2,350 at that time. A roofed and screened package delivery body was also available. The Model D had the same specifications as the Model C but used a 144-inch wheelbase.

Wheel winches were introduced in 1912 by L.C. Freeman, chief engineer, at a time when roads were so bad that being stuck in the mud was a regular occurrence. The wheel winches allowed a driver the luxury of "pulling yourself up with your own boot straps," as the press plainly stated.

Federal trucks sold well and by 1913 1,000 had been produced. The U.S. Postal Service had bought 25 Federal trucks, opening a market that the company would continue to pursue. As early as 1911, Federal had established the good business practice of having many sales representatives across the country including: Boston, Camden, Des Moines, Detroit, Los Angeles, New York City, Philadelphia, St. Louis, San Francisco, Portland, and Lynn, Massachusetts, as well as in Ontario, Canada.

For model year 1915, Federal introduced two 1-1/2-ton trucks with worm-drive built by Timken-David Brown. These were the Model J with 120-inch wheelbase and the Model K with 144-inch wheelbase. Both chassis sold for $1,900 and both were powered by the same four-cylinder Continental engine. Ignition was by Eisemann Magneto and a Stromberg carburetor was used with the governor limiting engine rpm to 1190 and again a top speed of 15 mph.

By 1916, Federal listed Model M and Model J at 1-1/2-ton capacity, Model O and Model P at 2-ton capacity, and the Model L had a capacity of 3-1/2 ton. The factory was enlarged to keep up with demand. By this time, chain drive was no longer used and the heaviest truck utilized a disc clutch instead of the cone design. The heftiest Model L had a 146-inch wheelbase and the chassis sold for $2,800. All trucks used the same Continental engine except that the 3-1/2-ton model had a larger displacement with slightly more power.

In 1917, Federal added the 1-ton Model S and the 5-ton Model X, by this time offering a total of five capacities. The larger trucks used steel spoke wheels instead of artillery wheels and C-cabs were common but not universal for Federal trucks. New engine design was described as utilizing five main bearings and a gear pump to circulate oil. Three engines were offered with 25, 30 and 40 hp. Driveshafts were tubular for strength as well as weight savings and Timken-Detroit worm-drive was used.

1923 FEDERAL OIL TANKER   OCW

In 1918, Federal introduced short-wheelbase truck tractors for hauling four-wheel or semi-trailers. The Heavy-Duty truck tractor had a 7-ton capacity with a semi-trailer while the Light-Duty had a 3-ton capacity with a two-wheel semi-trailer. The 2-ton Model U chassis cost $2,600 in 1918 and the 5-ton Model X cost $4,450. Federal advertised that its first truck of 1910, which had been sold to the National Popcorn Works of Lynn, Massachusetts, was still running perfectly "as to seem almost incredible." In some instances the company still referred to its vehicles as "commercial cars."

The 1-ton Model S continued to be quite popular featuring left side driver position, tubular radiator and water pump, full-floating rear axle, 132-inch wheelbase, selective sliding three-speed transmission, 34-inch wooden wheels and a 19.6 hp four-cylinder cast enbloc engine. For 1919, the model line was the same but the designations changed. They now were SD, TD, UD, WC, and XC and a Light-Duty and Heavy-Duty Truck Tractor completed the line of seven trucks. Prices were $1,900, $2,350, $2,600, $3,350, $4,400, $2,500 and $3,475, respectively.

In 1920, Federal offered pneumatic tires on its 1-ton Model SD and in 1921, WE and XE model designations replaced WD and XC. The following year, a Light Delivery truck was available carrying any load "up to the limit of the five-inch cord tires" at a speed up to 35 mph. This was the Model R-2, also known as the Federal Fast Express. By 1923, Federal had built over 27,000 trucks and bus chassis for 18 or 25 passengers became available.

1924 FEDERAL-KNIGHT　　　　　　　　　　**RD**

In 1924, Federal introduced the Knight engine in its new light commercial chassis that sold for $1,095. The Willys-Knight engine was used by Federal until 1928 when Willys-Knight introduced them in its own light trucks. This engine was unique in that it used sleeve valves. In 1925, it was rated at 21 hp on the Model FK 1-ton truck. The Federal-Knight was not a separate make of truck as it has been sometimes listed.

For 1924, model designations changed once again. The 1-ton was offered as the R-2 and the 1-1/2-ton as the S-23. Both of these were powered by a Continental J-4 engine. The 2-1/2-ton Model U-2 with 157-inch wheelbase was powered by a Continental K-4 engine. The 4-ton Model WL had the same wheelbase and engine as the previous model, and the 5-ton Model X-2 with 163-inch wheelbase was powered by a Continental B-5 engine. The light and heavy truck tractors had wheelbases of 125-inch and 121-inch, respectively. The Light-Duty tractor had a Continental K-4 engine, while the Heavy-Duty tractor had a Continental L-4 engine.

1925 FEDERAL C-CAB　　　　　　　　　　**KP**

In 1926, Federal brought out its first six-cylinder powered truck, which was rated at 3-ton and was called the UB-6. The lightest Federal truck was now the 1-1/4-ton Model R-3, while the heaviest was the 5-1/2-ton Model X-5. Federal offered both four-cylinder Waukesha engines, as well as four-cylinder and six-cylinder Continental engines through the end of the 1920s when capacity reached 7-1/2 tons. The six-cylinder engine featured seven main bearings.

Pneumatic tires were available on almost all models, and some of the first sleeper cabs were built by Federal. Styling changes kept up with the industry norm but Federal was not known for extravagance or avant-garde aesthetic design. Front brakes were universal on Federal trucks by 1929 and were of the vacuum-operated hydraulic-type with handbrake acting on the driveshaft.

For 1930, Federal introduced a Walk-in Panel van as well as six-wheel models. The latter had designations U6SW, rated at 6 tons, U6SWAB also rated at 6 tons but with air brakes, and 4C6SW, which was rated at 8 tons. The tandem rear axles were made by Timken and consisted of a SW-200H unit for the U6 series, while the SW-300W was used for the heavier model. Federal offered factory-built dump trucks, and since the Depression had taken its toll, the new six-wheel four-cylinder model was priced competitively at $1,050.

As the 1930s unfolded, Federal trucks continued to resemble those built by GMC. The six-cylinder engine was rated at 72 hp and an 8-ton model was now available. A new bevel-gear tandem axle was announced by Federal's chief engineer George B. Ingersoll. It had been developed in association with the Clark Equipment Company and it differed from other tandem-axle designs in that it did not use a worm or double-reduction, but instead the second bevel ring gear was driven by a pinion shaft from the bevel ring gear of the first axle. Federal built a number of articulated tanker trucks at this time, one of the largest being a two-trailer rig called the "ghost train," which transported 6,500 gallons of gasoline between Muskegon and Grand Rapids four times per day.

1928 FEDERAL BAKERY VAN　　　　　　　　　　**KP**

1930 FEDERAL DUMP　　　　　　　　　　**NAHC**

As the Depression continued, Federal reduced its prices to stay in business. The 1-1/2-ton four-cylinder model was priced at $795 by 1931, while the 1-1/2-ton six-cylinder model was priced at $895. Wheelbases were lengthened to 168 inches to accommodate 12-foot bodies. By 1932, Federal offered a four-cylinder chassis with 130-inch wheelbase and hydraulic brakes for $670, while the six-cylinder 1-1/2-ton was $695. Three wheelbases of the rigid three-axle 10-wheel model were offered: 188-, 206- and 224-inch. These had the dead axle ahead of the driven axle for better traction. The three versions were priced at $3,895, $3,945 and $4,045, respectively. A House-to-House Delivery van was advertised with 108-inch and 120-inch wheelbase, and these featured a 13-1/2-inch low driver step, streamlined utility body and heavy-duty generator for idling and slow speed operation.

For 1934, Federal adopted styling changes that consisted of a slightly slanted visorless windshield and V-type radiator grille. Engine choices were expanded to include Continental, Hercules and Waukesha engines up to 114 hp, and four-cylinder engines were used only on the 3/4-ton and 1-1/2-ton models that were priced at $645 and $845, respectively. Both of these lightest trucks featured full-floating rear axles. Federal continued to supply trucks to the military, such as the Q9 which was powered by an 85 hp six-cylinder Waukesha 6MK engine and used a four-speed Spicer transmission.

By 1935, streamlining was even more pronounced than the previous year. The styling now featured a V-type windshield on most models, as well as horizontal louvers on the hood and fender skirts for the rear. Federal celebrated its 25th anniversary. It advertised a panel truck with a highly streamlined roof line and base price was still $645.

For 1936, the windshields were back to single-piece for some models and hood louvers were now vertical. Model designations consisted of the following: DM, 10, 15, 18, 20, 25, 28, 30, 40, 40DR, T-10B, T-10W, 50, C7, C7W, C8, C8W, X-8, X-8DR, X8R and X8RDR. The Model 10 was offered for $545 with Federal-built standard panel bodies for an additional $270. Federal moved the cab, cowl, engine and radiator forward on its heavy models to improve weight distribution. The company continued to receive contracts from the U.S. military. In 1936, this consisted of an order for 278 units at a price tag of $350,000. By this time Federal had a plant in Windsor, Ontario.

Federal joined in the late 1930s revival of COE design, which was sometimes called "camel-back." Late in 1936, four cab-over-engine models were introduced: Models 75, 80, 85 and 89, which were priced from $1,045 to $1,995. By this time, some of the models up to 2-1/2-ton had drop frames. Models of 4 ton to 6 ton had double reduction drives. The split grille and shape of the cabs were compared to the International D-300, which actually came out a year later.

By 1937, Federal advertised 18 models from 3/4 ton to 7-1/2 ton. There were 100 wheelbases and prices across four lines of models ranged from $645 to $5,345. In the light-duty field, Federal built pickups called Model 7 and Model 8. The H series was unveiled in 10 models featuring heavier axles, springs, brakes and tires primarily for dump application. The 1938 styling, which was spearheaded by Henry Dreyfuss, reached an aesthetic pinnacle with high-crown fenders and slanted radiator grilles with horizontal chrome bars somewhat like those of the acclaimed Diamond T trucks. This design, minus the heavy dose of chrome, was continued through 1950. As R.W. Ruddon became president, by 1939, total Federal truck production over the years had reached 100,000.

1938 FEDERAL 1-1/2-TON   **NAHC**

By this time, the heavy-duty truck line also got a sheet metal face lift with ample chrome and V-type horizontal-bar grille. Waukesha engines with up to 115 hp and Continental engines with up to 138 hp were the choices for the heavier trucks with Hercules powering the lighter models. The engines by this time were all six-cylinder, and all featured seven main bearings. Clark provided the heavy-duty five-speed transmissions, and air brakes were featured throughout much of the Federal truck model line. The U.S. War

Department ordered another 178 2-1/2-ton trucks at a $385,000 cost. All of these were cab-over six-wheel trucks with five-man cabs and 14-foot cargo bodies. The Federal Package Delivery van now sold for $1,095.

The year before the United States entered World War II, Federal's president Ruddon resigned and Thomas R. Lippard was elected company president. At this point, Federal advertised 39 models. The civilian model line continued basically unchanged for almost a decade from this point. When Stewart truck production ended in 1941, Federal adopted Stewart's slogan, "Federals have won by costing less to run." It should be noted that Thomas R. Lippard had been president of Stewart for 25 years.

1939 FEDERAL MODEL B METRO VAN   **NAHC**

Although Federal continued to build trucks for the civilian market, and in 1941 adopted the slogan "Ton for ton in '41 -- Federal leads the way," as soon as World War II started, Federal built 6x6 7-1/2-ton wreckers using a common design with Reo. These had 180 hp six-cylinder Hercules HXD engines with five-speed transmissions multiplied by two ranges. Unusual Cleveland air springs were used in front. A heavy 6x4 transporter truck tractor was also built with a 20-ton capacity. It was powered by a 130 hp six-cylinder Cummins two-stroke diesel and the truck weighed 10 tons. During World War II, Federal continued to advertise its trucks to the general public anticipating further civilian sales once the war would come to an end. By 1944, the U.S. government approved 2,034 Federal trucks to be built for civilian use. By that time, the average civilian truck was 7-1/2 years old.

At the beginning of 1945, the U.S. military ordered another $15 million worth of various Federal trucks. Federal was in excellent financial condition at this time and by keeping tooling costs down with prewar styling, the company prospered after the war. Diesel engines continued to be offered at this time but it was not until 1951 that the company introduced something really new. This took place in the form of the new Styleliner 1800 model line conventional trucks, which were powered by a new 145 hp overhead-valve six-cylinder engine that had been engineered by Federal. The company offered hypoid gear axles and radius-rod drive as standard equipment with double reduction axles being optional. By this time GCW (including a semi-trailer) had reached 45,000 pounds.

Ten other smaller Styleliner trucks were offered, along with the conventional line of heavy-duty trucks and six-wheel gasoline- and diesel-powered vehicles. But with financial stability uncertain, in a reorganization the Federal Motor Truck Company merged with Fawick Airflex and became the Federal Motor Truck Division of the Federal-Fawick Corporation in 1952. At about the same time, U.S. military contracts for Federal amounted to $30 million. The following year, another merger with Orange Roller Bearing of Newark was abandoned. The Federal-Fawick merger was only a year old when a net loss of $1.17 million was announced.

Although 6,020 Federal trucks were registered in 1947, by 1954 that number had dropped to 874. Perhaps that is why Federal embarked on a few specialized ventures at this time. The company built a tall truck tractor for the U.S. Air Force with the cab set high over the wheels and the engine and hood in front. The cab was designed for at least six persons by removing the rear walls of two GMC cabs and welding them together back-to-back. These were used for towing airplanes, a design shared by Coleman.

Another specialized truck from 1954 was the Octo-Quad. This single unit was built as a showpiece for the Timken-Detroit Axle Company. The Octo-Quad had tandem axles front and rear and the cab was built up from a large bus body. The Air Force ordered 100 Federal 4x4 trucks with Hercules RXC and Continental engines with Allison Torqmatic transmissions. These trucks were fitted with five-yard Galion dump beds. Ford cabs of 1956 with wrap-around windshields were utilized. The same trucks were also fitted with Gledhill three-way V-blades for snowplowing.

At the end of 1954, Federal-Fawick had been sold to Mast-Foos Manufacturing Company. Mast-Foos announced it would eventually end Federal truck production and concentrate on servicing. Not long after that, Napco Industries bought Federal. In 1955 the company became known as the Federal Motor Truck Company, Division of Napco Industries, Incorporated, which had its headquarters in Minneapolis, Minnesota. There were to be three ownership shifts within a year.

During this period, the company went through some financial and ownership changes that were quite complex. After a merger of five concerns including Napco, Federal, Berghoff Brewing, Northwestern Auto Parts and R.W.M. Investment Company, the new firm introduced the Golden Eagle line of trucks in the 30,000 to 60,000 GVW class. The Golden Eagles were modern in appearance and were powered by Continental, Cummins or Hercules engines with transmissions by Clark, Fuller or Spicer. Federal did get a $10 million contract from Curtiss-Wright to build axle assemblies for the 2-1/2-ton M series military truck.

A new plant was constructed in Minneapolis and 6x6 Federal crane carriers with 8-ton and 10-ton capacities were one of the first models off the assembly line, but in limited numbers. These were powered by a Chrysler engine with a four-speed transmission and dual range transfer case. A Chilean truck cooperative ordered 200 Federal trucks and Napco reported a good year for 1956.

During this time, the company developed an unusual jet airplane tug called the "Turbo-Tug." It was powered by a Boeing gas turbine with a second turbine used for starting jet engines using compressed air. The Turbo-Tug had four-wheel-drive and was capable of towing aircraft up to a half million pounds in weight.

Despite mergers and modernization, Federal could not resolve its problems with the bottom line. Once the military and Chilean orders were complete and a final shipment of bus chassis was sent to Pennsylvania in March of 1959, Federal ceased production. For a short while, component bus kits called "Mexican Bus" were sent to Argentina for complete assembly and the Masa Motor Coach was built overseas using Federal parts. Including foreign markets, it is estimated that Federal built a total of 160,000 vehicles during all of its years of production.

FEDERAL-KNIGHT 1924-1928 — Federal-Knight was not an independent make but actually built by Federal using Knight sleeve-valve engines. However, because this name has been used independently of Federal, Federal-Knight has often been listed separately. See FEDERAL.

FIFTH AVENUE COACH 1916-1925 — The Fifth Avenue Coach Company was a horsedrawn bus service in New York beginning in 1885. As electric vehicles became popular Fifth Avenue Coach became part of the New York Electric Vehicle Transportation Company in 1899. An effort was made to develop an electric bus but when this failed the company began running gasoline-powered buses in 1906. New York Transportation Company became the holding company. By 1912 double-decker buses were standardized using DeDion-Bouton chassis, Daimler sleeve-valve engines, and open-top bodies were supplied by J.G. Brill.

Fifth Avenue Coach production began as a result of the French Army's confiscation of 25 DeDion chassis for military application during World War I. Fifth Avenue already had bodies for these "commandeered" chassis and so were forced to build their own. Demand for more buses continued with the rapid growth of New York City. A total of 275 "Type A" double-decker buses were built, most of which were put in service in New York. The European design was gradually changed with more up-to-date components. Acetylene tanks were supplanted by storage batteries, for example.

Other modernizations included copper-tube radiators, enclosed driver's cabs, exhaust-pipe heating and illuminated destination signs.

In 1919, the company's former general manager decided to start a similar company in Detroit. However, the Fifth Avenue Coaches built in New York turned out to be too tall for Detroit's bridges and overpasses. Fifth Avenue began building the "Type L" (for Low) buses in 1921 specifically for service in Detroit. These were 55-passenger buses that featured an underslung driveshaft. The "Type 2L" was also built as a 64-passenger bus and these were successful enough to see production of 300 units. The "Type J" single deck model bus was also built between 1923 and 1925 mainly for service in Detroit.

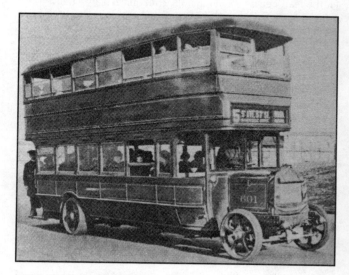

1924 FIFTH AVENUE COACH MODEL 2L BUS   MBS

Yellow, Fifth Avenue and Chicago Motor Coach were under one parent company when Fifth Avenue sold its manufacturing rights to Yellow, which used Fifth Avenue "Type L" design in combination with Chicago Motor Coach "Type K" design to build its own "Type Z." Although Fifth Avenue no longer manufactured complete buses, the company did rebuild its own coaches and built bus bodies in its New York facilities.

FIREBAUGH 1946-1947 — Toolcraft Manufacturing Company of Huntington Beach, California, built three-wheel commercial delivery vehicles. Payload was claimed to be a half ton with 23 cubic feet of cargo area. The three-wheeler had one wheel in front and had a top speed of 35 mph. It was powered by a 8-1/2 hp two-cylinder four-cycle overhead-valve engine, "fluid drive principal with final chain drive," (no transmission or differential) and a foot throttle was used. Wheelbase was 66 inches and chassis weight was 600 pounds. The engine was fully enclosed with an air blower and it had an electric starter. Tires were 12x4 four-ply. Efficiency was claimed to be 55 mpg. Tubular frame construction and rear leaf springs were employed. It is unknown whether the company existed after 1947.

FIRESTONE-COLUMBUS 1912-1913 — The Columbus Buggy Company started building cars in 1903 when it introduced the Columbus Electric. The Columbus highwheeler began production in 1907 but was discontinued when the Firestone-Columbus was introduced in 1909. The car was named after Clinton DeWitt Firestone, Columbus Buggy president. By 1912, a light delivery van was offered using the passenger car chassis and running gear. "The Car Complete" was the company's slogan. The vehicles were built on several wheelbases and were powered by four-cylinder engines from 26 hp up to 33 hp and used three-speed transmissions with shaft drive. The Model 71-C had the shortest of the numerous wheelbases for 1912 (with 106 inches) and was used as a delivery van that was convertible to a five-passenger touring car.

Though success seemed imminent at first, Columbus Buggy was bankrupt in 1913. Early the following year Clinton Firestone died of a stroke at the Vendome Hotel in Columbus. Investors from Buffalo, New York, reorganized the company as the New Columbus Buggy Company, but this failed by 1915 as well. It appears the Model 71-C commercial vehicle was offered only prior to the reorganization of 1913.

1902 FISCHER GASOLINE-ELECTRIC BUS   NMM

FISCHER 1901-1905 — The Fisher Motor Vehicle Company was located in Hoboken, New Jersey, and built hybrid-powered trucks and buses. A 20 hp four-cylinder engine was used to power a 16 kilowatt five-pole generator that produced the power to drive two 10 hp electric motors in each rear wheel. The hybrid trucks were used by breweries and sightseeing coaches as small as 12-passenger buses were built using this technology. However, when the London General Omnibus Company bought a double-decker bus in 1903, the vehicle's inefficient consumption of gasoline and tires forced the return of the coach back to Fischer in Hoboken. Apparently, the hybrid technology had not been thoroughly optimized at that time and the company ceased production by 1905.

1926 FISHER 1-1/2-TON   MROZ

FISHER see STANDARD

FITZJOHN 1938-1958 — Harry A. FitzJohn began building bus and truck bodies in Muskegon, Michigan, during 1919. The company name was Erwin Manufacturing at that time. By 1924, a new plant provided five times more space, but only bus body production continued. Nearly all of the FitzJohn bus bodies of the 1920s were specifically designed for use on Reo chassis.

By the mid-1930s, when body-on-chassis bus manufacturing became outdated, FitzJohn turned to building integral city transit buses after several reorganizations of the evolving company. By 1938, the FitzJohn Body Company offered a complete 27-seat Model 300 bus powered by a six-cylinder Chevrolet truck engine. By the time World War II began, the FitzJohn Coach Company (as it was called from 1940) was also building the Model 500 Duraliner and Model 600 Falcon, both of which were powered by six-cylinder Hercules engines. All three first models were front-engine design.

Business was interrupted in 1943, but after some war production industry restructuring, FitzJohn was allowed to continue bus manufacturing in 1944. The models remained the same except that the front door was placed ahead of the vehicle's axle. In 1946, the Model 500 was superseded by the larger Model 510.

1948 FITZJOHN MODEL 310 CITYLINER   MBS

1954 FITZJOHN ROADRUNNER COACH   MBS

In 1949, a Canadian factory in Brantford, Ontario, began building Cityliner buses for FitzJohn. Competing with large consolidated bus manufacturers became increasingly more demanding during the 1950s and much of FitzJohn's production was aimed at export to Cuba and Mexico. FitzJohn also modernized its design and by 1954 offered the Roadrunner bus, which featured a longitudinally-mounted Cummins diesel engine at the rear of the chassis. Air conditioning, silversiding and picture windows were also part of the new design. About 200 Cityliners were built in Canada. After building approximately 2,600 buses in all, FitzJohn finally succumbed to its competitors in 1958.

1913 FLANDERS PANEL DELIVERY   OCW

FLANDERS 1912-1913 — The Flanders Motor Company was located in Detroit, Michigan. It later became a part of Studebaker. A few light trucks were built on Flanders chassis, but otherwise the company did not build commercial vehicles per se.

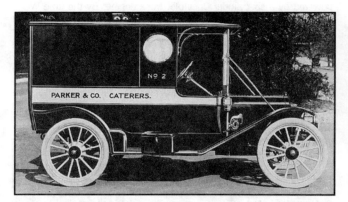

1912 FLANDERS PANEL DELIVERY   OCW

FLEXI-TRUC see IBEX

FLINT 1912-1915 — The Flint was built by the Durant-Dort Carriage Company in Flint, Michigan. Its pedigree has been noted to be the companion marque to the Best auto, although records do not prove this. Capacity was 1,600 pounds and the vehicle was powered by a four-cylinder engine using a three-speed transmission with shaft drive. Chassis prices ranged from $1,285 to $1,375.

FLXIBLE 1922 to date — Hugo H. Young and Carl F. Dudte founded the Flxible Side Car Company in 1913 to build motorcycle sidecars that had a patented design allowing the wheel to stay in contact with the road even during hard cornering. The name Flxible was spelled without the "e" in order to serve as a trade name. With the availability of inexpensive automobiles the sidecar business foundered. By 1922, Young and Dudte were building ambulances and hearses using various passenger car chassis. By 1924, the Flxible Company was building small parlor style buses using either Buick or Studebaker chassis and power trains.

Flxible built numerous 12-passenger coaches during the 1920s on the Buick and Studebaker platform, but it was not until 1936 that a Chevrolet truck chassis was utilized to build a streamlined bus called the "Airway." In 1939, the company built the "Clipper" using Buick and Chevrolet engines mounted longitudinally at the rear of the chassis with seating for 25 and 29 passengers, respectively. The company continued to build small buses on a custom basis and the Clipper was built as a standard assembly line model with minor adaptations for various customers.

1932 FLXIBLE 12-PASSENGER   MBS

Flxible set the styling tone for future buses when the company unveiled its forward-slant parallelogram-shaped windows in 1941. For 1946, the basic buses of 1939 had a two-and-one seat arrangement called the Airporter, and these were common at airports into the 1950s. The 1941-design windows were lengthened into picture windows when the company introduced the Visicoach in 1950.

Flxible did not convert to diesel power during the 1950s as its competitors did. Since diesel power was more economical, Flxible began losing its market share. Twin Coach and Flxible cooperated

on a joint venture to produce "convertible" buses for the U.S. Army. These could be used as trucks or ambulances. At the same time Flxible received a contract for intercity buses from Brazil.

1956 FLXIBLE VISICOACH   JO

When Twin Coach ceased production, Flxible took over the former bus builder's underfloor-engine design to build city transit buses as well as other coaches in its versatile assembly line. During this period propane-powered buses were built for the city of Chicago at a time when fuel cost advantages made this alternative fuel cost effective. Chicago continued to use propane-powered buses after other cities turned back to gasoline and diesel as the fuels of choice.

In 1961, Flxible came out with its "new look" buses, which were patterned after General Motor's design. They were also powered by GM Detroit Diesel engines mounted longitudinally using Spicer torque converters. For Chicago, the "new-look" buses were still propane powered. In 1963, Flxible bought Southern Coach Company of Evergreen, Alabama. The company expanded its business using the Flxible Southern name, building front-engine buses as well as truck bodies. The 19-passenger standard models called Flxettes were powered by Ford V-8 truck engines. These were continued in production without interruption. Meanwhile, the Flxible sold its new motorhome plant to Clark Equipment Company.

At the time, Flxible adopted certain features from GM in the early 1960s, GM also settled a lawsuit and allowed other manufacturers to use a few of its patents, most notably the "angle drive." Flxible buses soon became entirely equal in contemporary technology, comfort and appearance with GM and through federal subsidies, the company tripled its sales of buses after 1966 once the litigation was settled. Intercity bus manufacturing, specifically, was discontinued in 1969.

In 1970, Rohr Corporation acquired Flxible. Rohr has been described as an aerospace company that also built rapid transit cars. In 1977, Rohr sold Flxible to Grumman Corporation. Under the new parent company Flxible built approximately 1,400 buses per year.

By the mid-1990s, Flxible had established offices in Delaware, Ohio and offered three Metro buses in 30-, 35- and 40-foot lengths. Engine options (all transverse rear mounted) have been listed as DDA 6V92TA DDEC 253-277 hp or 6L71TA DDEC 240-270 hp or Cummins LTA10 240-280 hp or LTA10 240 hp CNG, each turbocharged, after-cooled six-cylinder units. The transverse-mounted angle-drive transmission options were listed as ATC V731-VR731 ATEC three-speed automatic, Voith D863ADR three-speed automatic, ZF HP590 or HP-500 four-speed automatic. As with all buses built in the 1990s, wheelchair lifts have been provided.

1996 FLXIBLE METRO   FLXIBLE

The buses' structure has been built using aluminum/composite roof, vertical steel mullions with heavy-wall interlocking aluminum extrusions, stainless steel wheelhousings, HSLA and stainless steel understructure elements and semi-monocoque construction. All Flxible buses during the 1990s have used Rockwell heavy-duty beam-type steering axles and Rockwell banjo-type drive axles with four available ratios rated at 25,000 pounds, having replaceable load tubes.

FMC 1962, 1969 to date — Food Machinery Corporation, as it was once known, was started out as a builder of agricultural machinery and during the 1960s branched out into many new technologies. Its headquarters has been located in Santa Clara, California, where the company developed and tested the Bradley armored personnel carrier and other sophisticated tracked tactical vehicles.

In 1962, and again in 1969, FMC built the M10 and M15 mobile dynamometer. The large three-axle truck featured an adjustable coupling on the front to measure a towing vehicle's drawbar pull while retarding the towing vehicle. The M15 was powered by a 750 hp Continental air-cooled V-12 Model 1790 diesel tank engine. The retardant effect was made possible with the use of three electric motors that could develop 30,000 pounds pull at 4 mph. A large cab housed the driver and measuring and recording equipment.

1970 FMC XR 311   **MROZ**

FMC was the third company to bid on the High Mobility Multipurpose Wheeled Vehicle. The name became an altered acronym dubbed Humvee and later "Hummer". FMC already had similar vehicles by 1970 in the form of the XR 311, a "dune-buggy"-type powered by a Dodge 360 V-8 engine. Top speed was 80 mph and cruising range was 300 miles. Combat loaded it weighed 5,600 pounds. A second version was powered by a 318-cubic inch V-8 engine. A second version had a flatter rear deck with air intakes on the sides, and a third version of the XR 311 was also built with minor changes and advertised commercially in 1974. Nevertheless, AM General received the contract to built the HMMWV.

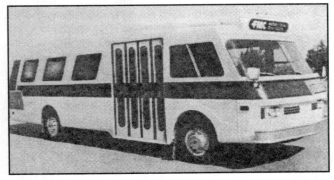

1975 FMC TRANSIT COACH   **MBS**

After World War II, the John Bean Division of FMC began offering high pressure fog fire trucks whose technology was first developed during the war for fighting shipboard fires. The fog could itself knock down a fire or was used to create a curtain to protect fire fighters as they approached a large fire or burning building. Another major advantage of the fog system was the small quantity of water used in order to minimize water damage and flooding. A typical fog system used 60 gallons per minute at 850 psi. FMC built such high-pressure fire apparatus on commercial chassis, but the company also built combination pumpers featuring high-pressure fog guns built on GMC commercial chassis.

In 1980, FMC expanded its product line and began building fire apparatus on custom chassis. The company's marketing focus turned to rural areas. During its expansion the firm moved from its old facility in Orlando, Florida, to Tipton, Indiana, in 1985 where the Sentinel and Starfire lines have been produced to date. The Starfire pumper was built on Ford, GMC and International 4x4 chassis. FMC's Telesqurt combination ladder truck was built on a Ford chassis. The company has continued to build a variety of fire apparatus on custom chassis since 1980.

Before 1974, the Motor Coach Division of FMC was the Recreational Vehicle Division. FMC's transit coach was a highly-modified version of its motorhome recreational vehicle. The first city to obtain the transit coach was Denver, but the buses needed reworking and debugging before they were placed in service in 1975. The specially-designed transit coach featured wheelchair lifts and interlocking devices for connecting several wheelchairs in line.

1905 FORD MODEL C DELIVERY   **KP**

FORD 1905 to date — Henry Ford built one delivery wagon in 1900 but this, his second venture, was not successful. It was not until after he started his third venture at the age of 40 in 1903 (after incorporation) that the Ford Motor Company really began to build trucks and commercial vehicles.

The first commercial vehicles built on the Ford chassis appeared in 1905. Records state a taxicab based on the Model B was built and sold in London in 1905. The same year a Model A was fitted with a cargo box for L.W. Clarke Garage also in London. But neither of these were commercial vehicles produced by the Ford company.

The Model C "Ford Delivery Car" was the first factory-produced commercial vehicle, also called the Model E. The Model E was actually a Model C passenger car sharing the chassis, drivetrain (with two-cylinder engine under the seat) as well as body parts, but it was fitted with a Delivery Top.

All Ford vehicles were considered renegade from the start due to the fact that Henry Ford had not obtained a license from the Association of Licensed Automobile Manufacturers to build automobiles and he chose to fight it out in court. This was to have a profound effect later in 1911, when Ford won the lawsuit based on his four-stroke engine.

In 1906, the first branch assembly plant was opened in St. Louis, Missouri. That year Henry Ford already had controlling interest in the company and in 1907 obtained an even bigger share of ownership when the Ford Motor Company absorbed the Ford Manufacturing Company, a subsidiary. In 1907, Ford announced his interest in building a taxi and he independently developed the "Automobile Plow," which was to become the forerunner of the Fordson tractor. The Model N Runabout was the basis for light delivery vans that were converted by a variety of companies.

After numerous passenger car models were built through 1907, Ford introduced his most famous product in late 1908. It was the ubiquitous Model T. Among several variants from the beginning, it was offered as a Taximeter Cab. Even though the Ford company did not produce a truck per se, numerous aftermarket conversions with chassis extensions were available to build a light, though rugged, 1-ton Model T truck using the passenger car as a basis. The Model T chassis, with semi-elliptic, transverse cantilever springs, powered by a four-cylinder engine with torque tube drive, was ideally suited for such conversions. By 1909, Ford's output was 100 per day in the United States. A Canadian assembly plant also produced another 486 for the year.

By 1910, the taxicab was no longer available from Ford but independent companies custom built them for taxi operators. Ford moved the factory to a new location in the Detroit's suburb of Highland Park, where the plant soon employed 16,000 workers. The same plant would be used for a decade. Ford's court victory in 1911 contributed significantly to the free entrepreneurial spirit of America's automotive industry. William Knudsen joined Ford in 1911 and Ford output in the United States surpassed 32,000 units for that year after a new plant was opened in Kansas City.

1912 FORD MODEL T C-CAB DELIVERY　　　　　　　　NAHC

Ford observed the lucrative commercial market and decided to enter it in 1912 with the Delivery Car that was priced at $700. But this vehicle was not entirely new. Bell Telephone and other companies had tested a fleet of 250 Delivery Car prototypes in 1910 and 1911 before this model was made available to the general public. Also for 1912, Ford offered the Commercial Roadster with a removable rumbleseat to facilitate hauling.

The Delivery Car was discontinued at the end of 1912 due to poor sales. But aftermarket bodies and conversion kits continued to be popular and up to 1916 these were the companies responsible for the plethora of commercial adaptations of the Model T, including taxis, delivery vans, fire trucks, ambulances, buses, farm tractors and jitneys. Extension kits were offered by many companies including Redden Motor Truck, Union Truck Manufacturing, Simplex Truckform, Rayford, Detroit Truck, Commercial Truckmobile, Maxfer Ton Truckmaster, Hudford (later Truxton), F.A. Ames, Jewett Car, Partlow-Jenkins, Motor-Accessory Distributing, Xtend-Ford, Guaranty Motors and Dearborn Motortruck. In 1913, with the cooperation of the Detroit City Gas Company, Ford experimented with a carburetor that mixed natural gas with air.

In 1917, Ford returned to the manufacture of trucks on a permanent basis. In appearance, the Model T changed from a brass radiator to steel painted black that year, perhaps due to styling changes as much as wartime brass shortages. For 1917, Ford also

built its own Fordson farm tractor, 7,000 of which were supplied to Great Britain during the last two years of World War I. The Ford 1-ton Model TT truck resembled many of the prior aftermarket conversions. It had a wheelbase that was 24 inches longer than the passenger chassis, a stronger frame, stiffer suspension, artillery-type wheels with solid rubber tires and a more rugged worm-drive rear axle. The two millionth Model T was built in that significant year of 1917 when Henry Ford's first grandson was born, Henry Ford II.

The two-speed pedal-controlled planetary transmission continued to be utilized, giving accessory makers the opportunity to build both two-speed overdrives, as well as underdrives such as the Supaphord for hilly areas. Ford provided 39,000 vehicles for the war effort in 1918, along with a variety of other military equipment including a submarine chaser boat. Just after receiving a contract to build two-man and three-man tanks, the war ended and the contract was canceled. Well over 34,000 Fordson tractors were assembled in 1918.

The Ford company reorganized and expanded in 1919 with the development of the enormous Rouge River plant in Detroit. This was the year total overall Model T production reached three million and total Model TT truck production reached 100,000. A new plant in Cork, Ireland, began building Fordson tractors and another foreign subsidiary was opened in Copenhagen, Denmark. An optional starter motor with battery and generator was finally offered in 1919, seven years after it was invented. Almost 60,000 Fordson tractors were produced that year.

For 1920, Ford switched its fiscal year to a calendar year, as a result affecting the production figures that would be analyzed decades later. Trucks received demountable rims as an option that year. Under the Fordson name, the first Ford Motor Company heavy truck was designed. It was a 3-ton cab-over-engine truck, but never went into any production. Fordson dealers assembled a few of their own similar trucks using tractor engines. Deluge and American LaFrance, among others, continued to build fire trucks on Ford chassis and a steel dump bed was offered by Galion Allsteel Body Company of Galion, Ohio.

During the economic downturn Ford cut its prices, shut down some plants and enacted austerity programs to stem the company's fiscal emergency, which was compounded by Ford having bought out the minority interest stockholders. Along with drastic price cuts to stimulate sales, Ford forced dealers to accept large inventories to bail out the Ford Motor Company. The half-year interruption of Fordson production as it was moved from Dearborn, Michigan, to the Rouge did not help matters, nor did Ford's acquisition of the Detroit, Toledo and Ironton Railroad for $5 million. But these were temporary setbacks and such investments would pay off as Fordson production neared its new full potential of 250,000 tractors per year. Through reorganization the railway moved Ford's raw production materials at a profit. This was also the year William Knudsen left Ford, prompting him to be hired by minor rival Chevrolet, which quickly became an even competitor after trailing Ford by a ratio of 13:1 in truck sales in 1920.

After the recession of 1920-1921, Ford rebounded dramatically for 1922, selling over 1.1 million Model T cars. A new record in truck production was also achieved. Expansion continued. Ford was now assembling under license in Japan. Ford began building its own batteries and bought out an entire town -- Pequaming, Michigan -- for its lumber mill. The company also acquired Lincoln Motor Company. By this time, the Fordson tractor was $395. A 2-ton truck prototype was built using the Fordson engine but production did not ensue. Both the 2-ton and 3-ton designs would emerge later.

For 1923, Ford produced just over 193,000 truck chassis along with 1.8 million Model T passenger cars, the highest yearly production ever in the United States for a single marque and model. Yet another parts factory began production, this time at Green Island near Troy, New York.

The year 1924 was the first time Ford began building truck bodies. On the otherwise generally unchanged Model TT truck, a canopy top was added to the Express Body in open, curtained or screenside iterations. By March of 1924, Ford offered eight combinations of complete cabs and bodies built in-house on Ford truck

1917 FORD FACTORY PICKUP KP

1918 FORD MODEL T 1-TON KP

1920 FORD MODEL T RM

1925 FORD SCREENSIDE PADDY WAGON RD

1928 FORD MODEL A PANEL A&A

1929 FORD MODEL AA VAN OCW

1929 FORD MODEL AA TANDEM AXLE A&A

1941 FORD DUMP & GRADER A&A

chassis for the first time in company history. Another company first was sending 900 Fordson tractors to the Soviet Union to boost agricultural production.

An important manufacturer of precision machinist's tool gauges, C.E. Johansson, was acquired that year and two huge diesel-powered freighters were launched on the Great Lakes to haul raw materials to the Rouge Plant. Extended Model TT chassis were used to build some 30-passenger buses that year. In October, Ford announced a 2-1/2-ton capacity truck, which was in the development stage but would not, in fact, go into production for the following year as *The Commercial Car Journal* stated.

In 1925, Ford expanded its truck body options. One of the first was an eight-foot platform-stake bed announced on Christmas Eve of 1924. Ford's first closed cab truck appeared in early 1925 and most importantly for that year, the first factory-assembled domestic pickup was produced. It was officially called "Ford Model T Runabout with Pick-up Body" and it was priced at $281 in Detroit. The successful pickup consisted of a cargo box in back of the roadster tonneau instead of the usual rear deck.

Ford's Lincoln division in 1925 offered for the first time a 150-inch wheelbase Lincoln Commercial Chassis for the use of building a professional car body such as a limousine, or it was available as a complete funeral car for $6,800. The Model T and Model TT had engine design improvements with the use of lighter pistons and better lubrication. Ford built its one-millionth truck chassis in 1925, and at that time 75 percent of all trucks in the United States were Fords. In mid-1925, the Ford truck chassis was slightly revised and wheelbase shortened by an inch to 123 inches. The company built 28,266 Express Bodies and 38,722 Stake Bodies for that year. Truck wheels were made by Hayes, Kelsey and Motor Wheel at that time.

For 1926, Ford introduced a new look for its passenger cars, including the Runabout with Pick-up Body light commercial vehicle, as well as some general innovations to keep up with the keen competition. Trucks were available with nickel-plated radiators, but the older design as a carry-over inventory sold briskly. It was not until the end of the year that Model TT trucks were fitted with the new sheet metal.

The long awaited Fordson truck prototype was finally unveiled in 1926. It was a custom-built 2-ton cab-over-engine design with a rack stake body. Ford continued with developments in aviation, and the company opened new plants in Chester, Pennsylvania, and Ploetzensee, Germany, adding to the 86 plants already producing Ford components and/or assembling vehicles.

The year 1927 was the last of Model T mass production. Even though Ford geared up for a new model line of its passenger cars, truck sales had not deteriorated and the Model TT continued to be built late into 1927, while factories retooled for the Model A. However, because of the large degree of interchangeability between the passenger cars and trucks, it was inevitable that a new truck model line would be forthcoming.

For the last calendar year of Model TT, production was broken down into the following numbers: 1,151 Canopies, 3,587 Express bodies, 4,344 Platforms and 7,855 Stakes. Also, 23,888 closed cabs and 91 open cabs were built that year. In place of the standard commercial finish (green), black, blue and brown were offered in an attempt to spruce up the image of the aging Model T design. Beginning in February 1927, steel valves replaced the cast iron ones in Model TT truck engines, and later 32x6 rear tires became available. The departure of the venerable Model T was by some called "The End of the Ford Era."

The Model A debuted in November of 1927 and the Model AA truck followed. Both vehicles were powered by the same new engine at first. The new engine featured pump-assisted splash lubrication and pump-circulated thermo-syphon cooling and it displaced 200.5 cubic inches. A 10-gallon cowl-mounted gasoline tank fed a Zenith updraft carburetor and a forged steel three-main bearing crankshaft was used along with aluminum pistons. With a 4.22:1 compression ratio it developed 40 hp at 2200 rpm. A three-speed selective sliding transmission accompanied the new engine.

Crowned fenders, acorn-shaped headlights and nickel-plated radiator shell were the distinctive styling features of the Model A and Model AA trucks. Light Delivery Cars were expanded in terms of options, although the pickup body was no longer listed. The two cabs were shared between the Model A car and the Model AA truck.

The Model AA truck had a 131-1/2-inch wheelbase and a capacity of 1-1/2 tons with substantial frame improvements, heavier front transverse spring, 13- or 15-leaf longitudinal cantilevered rear springs, 20-inch welded spoke wheels, brake improvements and high pressure truck tires. The powertrain was also improved with larger radius rods, two-piece driveshaft and larger worm-gear rear axle. A planetary two-speed transmission called Dual-High could be ordered coupled to the three-speed, giving six forward and two reverse speeds. The basic Model AA chassis was priced at $460 with an increase to $540 in the spring of 1928 -- Ford Motor Company's 25th anniversary.

For 1929, few changes occurred in the styling and engineering of the successful Model A and Model AA. However, the Model AA trucks did receive six-hole ventilated disc wheels in place of the welded spoke type at the beginning of the year. In October more significant changes took place in the Model AA truck improving its overall ruggedness and performance. First, the Dual-High transmission was discontinued and a four-speed transmission became standard equipment. Also, a heavier spiral bevel rear axle was used, the front axle, radius rods, king pins and spring were strengthened, brakes were enlarged to 14-inch and positive offset five-hole disc wheels were adopted. These were specially designed to be used as duals, which became available in January of 1930.

The Model A was still produced with a variety of commercial bodies including delivery van, roadster pickup, station wagon and taxicab. The station wagon sold for $600 in 1929. A town car delivery was a short-lived model debuting in the year the Depression began. For 1930, the Model AA had an optional 157-inch wheelbase, new cabs had the front end restyled after the 1929 components were finally exhausted and a variety of buses were available through dealerships and coachbuilders.

Ford now had three chassis to use for its commercial vehicles. The new designation was Model AA-131 and Model AA-157. All the trucks adopted the cowl, fender, hood and radiator of the 1930 passenger cars. The Model AA-131 with Type 82-B Closed Cab sold for $510 in Detroit. Stainless steel headlamps and radiator shell were optional, otherwise they were painted black on the trucks. Ford made available all types of bodies to fit the new long wheelbase chassis, as well as a new taxicab that was fitted with the 131-inch wheelbase chassis.

Ford built prototypes of several commercial vehicles in 1930 on an extended 118-inch wheelbase Model A chassis, but these did not go into production. The Briggs Company continued to build the Type 78-A pickup body, as it had since 1925. Ford supplied hydraulically-operated dump models on the AA model truck.

The year 1930 also marked the last year Ford outsold General Motors in passenger cars, GM surpassing Ford the following year and remaining ahead of Ford in overall sales to date. However, for 1930, Ford was still comfortably ahead in truck sales. That year a new plant was completed in Long Beach, California, and a new assembly plant was opened in Richmond, California, replacing the aging factory located in San Francisco. Also, the first Model AA trucks began production under license in the Soviet AMO Plant in Moscow.

The Great Depression really took its toll by 1931 and car and truck sales plummeted for all makes. Nevertheless, this was the year General Motors permanently became the world's largest motor vehicle producer. In spite of slipping sales for the company, Ford introduced 20 new commercial models in 1931, which were all assembled in Ford plants and did not include custom bodies by Briggs, Budd and Murray, among others. The complexity of engineering, building and marketing such a variety of bodies, including ambulances and hearses, did not turn out to be good business for Ford and this was the last time the company would be involved in such manufacturing.

1931 FORD EXPORT MODEL AA   MROZ

For 1931, Ford also announced a new series of Industrial Engines, based on its Model A and Model AA engines. Prices ranged from $120 to $180. A new Ford factory opened in Cologne, Germany, as an assembly plant for the affiliate Ford-Werke A.G.

Ford cars and trucks were redesigned as the Model B and Model BB for 1932, and this was the year a new 65 hp V-8 engine was introduced for commercial application later in the year. The Ford V-8 caused a sensation, and became a successful factor in competition with the popular six-cylinder Chevrolet. It was a design incorporating 90 degrees, as opposed to the 60-degree Lincoln V-8, and had a 221-cubic inch displacement.

With the V-8 engine came a new 106-inch wheelbase chassis for the Model B, featuring double-drop frame, synchromesh transmission and rear-mounted fuel tank. For the Model BB the new frame was seven-inches deep and replacing the Model AA's longitudinal rear cantilever springs were 50-inch free-shackled semi-elliptic springs. On the Model BB, a 17-gallon gasoline tank was now mounted under the seat instead of the previous 11-gallon tank mounted under the cowl. Removal of the new grille's vertical bars in an alternate pattern was common due to the new V-8 engine's tendency to overheat.

Ford's 30th year brought a new passenger car chassis that was six inches longer in wheelbase and featured an X-type double-channel frame. Commercial bodies and components were carried over from 1932 without changes. From 1933 on, truck and passenger car sheet metal rarely coincided as the company focused more on the competitive edge in automobile styling, which was not as significant with commercial vehicles. Also, the increasingly lower passenger car body sheet metal was correspondingly more difficult to adapt to the progressively larger trucks, hence their interchangeability became less of a consequential factor. The raked grilles of the passenger cars were not adapted for trucks until 1935.

Commercial model designations for 1933 included both the Model 40 (station wagon and sedan delivery) and the Model 46, which used the 112-inch wheelbase chassis. Further improvements were made on the V-8 engine with aluminum cylinder heads and higher compression ratio resulting in higher hp. Ford's share of the market slipped, and Dodge's all-new model line and Chevrolet's new car did not make things any easier for Ford. Starting in 1933, Siebert of Toledo, Ohio, began building a line of professional cars, including service cars, ambulances and hearses, using the Model 40 chassis, which was lengthened either 24 or 36 inches using W.G. Reeves extension kits.

Several coach body builders were retained to build various styles and applications of buses, which were the last to use the four-cylinder engine along with trucks as they were gradually phased out in favor of the new V-8 powerplant. The year 1933 was also the first time Marmon-Herrington offered a 4x4 conversion for Ford trucks. The Repeal of the Volstead Act that year stimulated truck sales as companies again began transporting alcoholic beverages in large and legal quantities. Third axle conversions were available from Acme Sixwheeler, Thornton Tandem and Warford Sextette.

For 1934, the V-8 engine underwent another improvement with a double-deck two-runner intake manifold and Stromberg two-barrel downdraft carburetor. Its new fully counterbalanced cast alloy steel crankshaft was a first in the industry. In addition, new open skirt pistons and a new fuel pump all contributed to the V-8's output of 90 hp by that time. The Model BB V-8 80 hp engine differed in that it used cast iron cylinder heads with a lower compression ratio for better octane tolerance and a flatter torque curve. Ford's last Model C four-cylinder engines were installed in cars only for export, as well as in a few Model BB trucks.

The open cabs were phased out in 1934 and only 347 were built that year. Several different special truck and bus bodies were also phased out that year as Ford concentrated less on the specialty markets. The Model BB had a full-floating truck-type rear axle by this time. The Lincoln division adopted the use of a common V-12 powerplant, introduced the previous year, for all of its models, a few of which were built as professional cars. Ford built its one millionth V-8 in 1934.

For 1935, Ford trucks outsold Chevrolet for the first time in two years and sales overall finally surpassed the pre-Depression year of 1929. The new Model 48 had a redesigned chassis with a number of powertrain and component improvements that were also incorporated in the Model 50 commercial cars and, along with the Model 51 trucks, new sheet metal and grilles were utilized to update these vehicles, though not quite to the level of the Model 48. The municipal transit system of Detroit had bought 300 Model 51 buses, and planned to buy 1,000 more for 1936. The open cab, four-cylinder engine, factory-cataloged Fire Engine and Deluxe Panel bodies were all discontinued for 1935. A 160-inch wheelbase was offered by Lincoln for adaptation to professional cars.

In addition to previous aftermarket converters, Truxmore and Twin-Flex offered six-wheel and tandem drives and along with these firms Transportation Engineers of Highland Park, Michigan, produced COE adaptations of the Model 51 truck. The All-Wheel-Drive Ford was built by Marmon-Herrington, perhaps the most important conversion of Ford trucks for 1935. The Ford pickup was now designated Model 50-830 and was priced at $480 and the new panel delivery Model 50-820 sold for $565.

Ford began experimenting with soybean plastics at the Rouge plant, eventually creating body panels for prototype vehicles that never went into production with the revolutionary new material. Ford was also interested in using alcohol as fuel, which would have been easily available in rural areas, but the infrastructure of petroleum-based fuels was already well established and political entities were in place for that to remain the status quo.

For 1936, Ford made few changes in its model lines in terms of styling and engineering, except for the new unitized body (integral with frame) Lincoln-Zephyr, which was powered by a new more economical V-12 engine. However, the Lincoln Twelve continued to be utilized for professional car building, whereas the Lincoln-Zephyr was not.

Ford made a considerable effort to rectify the overheating problem with the V-8 by enlarging the radiator on some vehicles and revising radiator fans and engine compartment louvering on all models. The Model 51 truck was almost identical to the previous year's offering. The commercial car received some chassis updates and was redesignated as Model 67 for 1936. Ford decided to market its own bus, the Model 70, and the first ones rolled off the assembly line in October 1936. They were powered by an 85 hp V-8 and featured a 25-passenger body by Union City on a forward-control 141-inch wheelbase chassis. The company produced its three-millionth truck that year.

Major changes affected the appearance of the model lines in 1937. The Ford trucks and commercial cars still lagged in styling with the passenger cars, but the vehicles did receive a new full-height radiator grille, revised louvers and trim, lowered headlights, V-type windshield and cowl and modified instrument panel. The V-8 got added improvements and the 60 hp 136-cubic inch "European" V-8 was available in all commercial cars except the station wagon, as well as in all 131-1/2-inch wheelbase trucks except for those with dump bodies.

In truck sales, Ford pulled ahead of Chevrolet, Dodge, GMC and International once again, partly as a result of not being crippled by the labor strikes that affected the other manufacturers dependent on auto unions. As a predecessor of sorts to the Jeep, Marmon-Herrington built a Ford-based 4x4 COE truck with convertible top for the U.S. military in 1937, along with 4x4 ambulance chassis for 1938. Ford continued to build numerous specialized vehicles such as propane gas tankers and dump trucks but companies such as Bender Body, Crown Body, Dearborn Line, Gillig Brothers, Charles Olson and Sons, Superior Body and Transportation Engineers provided countless conversions, buses and coaches.

Styling changes on all passenger and truck models were clearly apparent for 1938. Trucks received an oval grille and the first conventional front opening hoods in the industry. Fenders and headlights were redesigned correspondingly. Most importantly, the 1-1/2-ton chassis underwent some of the most comprehensive revisions since the advent of the Model BB. Also, an Eaton two-speed rear axle was available from Ford.

The 1-1/2-ton truck was scaled down to create a 1-ton chassis in addition to the commercial car in order to compete with other truck manufacturers who had been marketing 1-ton models with great success. The year 1938 also marked the first Ford factory-built COE truck and a second version of the Detroit Bus, now two feet longer, was built as the Model 70B. Along with Model 70A, they were built through 1939 with a total production reaching nearly 11,000 units. The year 1938 brought economic recession -- and secondly brought Henry Ford's insistence on continuing with mechanical brakes after an earlier prototype mishap during a test with his son Edsel. Both spelled a downturn in sales for the company's cars and trucks.

1936 FORD 1-1/2-TON TYPE   A&A

1938 FORD UTILITY   A&A

Finally, in 1939, all Ford vehicles got hydraulic brakes. The Mercury model line was introduced to bridge the marketing slot between the Deluxe Ford V-8 and the Lincoln-Zephyr. It was powered by a bored-out Ford V-8 developing 95 hp and known as the Model 99. It was available in Regular and COE truck models and in the Transit Bus, as well as in police cars and light trucks on a special order basis. The basic V-8, as well as the new Mercury V-8 engine now used Ford two-barrel downdraft carburetors.

Mid-year, the Three Quarter Tonner was added to the model lineup and two more aftermarket converters, Grico and Maxim, joined in specialty Ford vehicle fabrications development. Grico

built a Twin-Motor Tractor while Maxim concentrated on heavy fire apparatus up to 22,000 pounds GVW. Marmon-Herrington continued to build 4x4 Ford conversions, including vehicles based on Ford station wagons and passenger cars. The commercial car chassis with 112-inch wheelbase with Type 81 cab sold for $555 that year and included the 85 hp Ford V-8.

As Canada declared war on Germany in 1939, truck production there immediately shifted for military applications, employing a policy of interchangeable parts with General Motors and British Ford. In short order Ford military trucks were being produced in large quantities by GAZ in the Soviet Union and at the same time by Ford-Werke A.G. In the United States, Chevrolet trucks outsold Ford's by 40,000 units that year.

For 1940, driveline modifications modernized Ford vehicles and the truck cabs were extensively reworked. A new hood and grille on all trucks, except the COE series, blended well with the previous year's fenders and headlights, which were now the sealed beam type. Vacuum-boosted power brakes were available on all Regular and COE trucks. The Transit Bus underwent dramatic changes. It was redesigned as a rear-engine vehicle now on a 148-1/2-inch wheelbase and could carry 27 seats. The buses were powered by the 95 hp V-8 engine positioned transversely and they used a three-speed transmission. Due to its new rear-engine design, the buses front end sheet metal was greatly simplified.

1939 FORD COE TRACTOR-TRAILER   MROZ

The year the United States entered the war, Ford restyled its passenger car and repeated its commercial car model line once again. The ambiguous station wagon officially became a passenger car that year and the sedan delivery was entirely the previous year's design. While labor strikes slowed the assembly line, Ford entered the six-cylinder competition with its own in 1941, copied from Continental, but featuring a cast iron crankshaft, direct-drive distributor at the front of the engine and valve seat inserts for durability and replaceability.

Meanwhile the Ford V-8 gained another 5 hp through engineering improvements and the small V-8 was discontinued, being effectively replaced by the six-cylinder engine and in some cases among the commercial car, Three-Quarter and One-Tonner models by the miserly tractor four-cylinder engine. The COE models were updated to resemble Ford's styling that was introduced a year earlier. Ford produced over one million trucks in that one year alone, topping its own record of 1937.

Ford's foreign factories in Europe, the Soviet Union and elsewhere continued to build thousands of vehicles, mostly trucks, as World War II was well underway before the bombing of Pearl Harbor. Ford had designed a series of 3-ton trucks in 1940, designated as the 018T and 098T series. Fueling additional speculation that Henry Ford was a Nazi sympathizer, the Ford company decided to share this new design with the German military and the entire engineering package was shipped to Koln where the Wehrmacht dubbed the new truck series the V 3000 S and over 15,000 were built in 1940 alone. Given these numbers and in view of the historical consequences, the Allied Forces were fighting against technology Ford had developed and handed over to the other side.

Domestically, Ford obtained a contract from the U.S. Army to build 1,500 1/4-ton reconnaissance and command cars and soon after these were called jeep, stemming from the General Purpose (GP) name. The jeep was originally called the Blitz Buggy with an 80-inch wheelbase and 45 hp Ford tractor engine, which was inadequate for the job. The original jeep design had actually come from American Bantam.

Ford also built bomb service trucks and Van Ette field kitchens based on the civilian 1-ton truck chassis. Staff cars were also built using the Type 73 Fordor sedans. COE styling caught up with the vertical-grille style of other trucks in 1941.

1941 FORD GP   **STEVE GREENBERG**

1942 FORD 1-TON PANEL   **MROZ**

By February of 1942, civilian car and truck production was terminated as the motor vehicle industry converted entirely over to military production. Since the tonnage rating system was dubbed "meaningless," the first significant event was the universal adaptation of the Gross Vehicle Weight (GVW) and Gross Combination Weight (GCW) concept, which was also adopted by the Office of Defense Transportation.

Ford truck and commercial car model lines were expanded to include 126 different chassis and body combinations. The light-duty 1/2-ton models were completely revamped starting with a ladder-type four-crossmember chassis and I-beam front axle suspended on longitudinal semi-elliptic leaf springs. The same arrangement carried the heavier 3/4-floating rear axle with Hotchkiss drive and tubular driveshaft.

Although the commercial car's 114-inch wheelbase was the same as with passenger cars, the former vehicles were 3.3 inches higher due to the chassis changes and otherwise departed from the latter in design more so than ever before. For the first time since 1939, the light trucks shared the same grille as the heavier conventional trucks. The rugged utilitarian design was now virtually

flat with vertical bars and contained the headlights, which had been moved off the fenders. Most of the Ford engines had higher compression ratios and higher hp, including the 239-cubic inch Mercury V-8 engine. By the time civilian production stopped in February of 1942, the Ford Motor Company had built 30 million cars and trucks and one million farm tractors.

For the next three years, Ford concentrated on the production of heavy bombers at the new Willow Run factory, and the B-24 Liberator was rolling out at a rate of one per hour by 1945, totalling 8,685 from the beginning of production in July of 1942. Also, Ford was contracted to build the jeep, which had been the culmination of design by American Bantam, Marmon-Herrington and Willys-Overland by that time. Ford built 277,896 jeeps during the next three years. The company also built Model GTB cargo trucks, M-8 and T-17 armored cars, the M-10 Tank Destroyer, M-20 Utility Commando Cars, Universal Carriers, Sherman tanks, Amphibian jeeps and specialized cargo trucks, besides a plethora of war materiel and instrumentation. In 1944, the automotive industry was authorized to build 80,000 trucks of 9,000-pound or larger GVW rating in order to prevent the total fatigue of the nation's civilian transportation industry.

The year 1943 chronicled the untimely death of Edsel Ford, who was 49 years old. Henry Ford again became president of the company, although he had never really left the "top boss" position. Since public transportation was essential for mass production during the war years, Ford continued to build the Ford Transit Bus Model 29B and Model 49B with "blackout" trim for the duration of World War II. Ford also introduced two new trucks in 1944: Model 498T and Model 494T, both powered by the 100 hp V-8 engine.

By the end of 1945, vehicle rationing was abolished and the motor vehicle industry once again retooled for the civilian market. Ford offered 42 different truck chassis models, which were powered by the new Model 59 V-8 engine at first and six-cylinder engines were offered later that year. However, several models were not manufactured and these included the COE trucks, 3/4-Tonners and sedan delivery vehicles. Also, the 221-cubic inch V-8 was discontinued as was the four-cylinder tractor engine for truck application. Henry Ford II took over the reigns as Henry Ford retired toward war's end. For 1945, Ford built a total of 122,473 civilian and military trucks including the jeep.

Although Ford trucks for 1946 were the same in appearance as the 1945 models, Ford brought back its COE, Platform and sedan delivery trucks, which now carried GVW designation for the first time in civilian application. The Mercury line now included trucks, but only in Canada. In the United States, Ford built 2,513 Model 69B Rear-Engine Transit Buses, which were called "The Universal Bus." The year was marked with new labor strikes, including one that affected Ford adversely when steel workers walked off their jobs. The 113-day strike at General Motors benefitted Ford by giving it a larger market share as GM was completely out of the running for nearly four months, but Ford lost over $8 million that year anyway.

Henry Ford died on April 7, 1947, and his grandson continued on, bringing in a new generation of engineering and management talent. Trucks and commercial vehicles continued basically unchanged from the previous year and it was also the last year for Ford's regular production Dump Truck Chassis. Ford introduced a new 95 hp six-cylinder Model 7HA engine later in the year, which at first was used only in passenger cars. Ford's Heavy-Duty line was made up of both 1-1/2-ton and 2-ton models mounted on two wheelbases. That year total Ford truck production over the years had reached five million. In 1947, Marmon-Herrington built the 4x4 Coleman Swamp Buggy that featured 18.00x26 floatation tires and a two-speed transfer case and custom front and rear axles.

Ford's trucks and commercial vehicles were dramatically changed for 1948 with 115 body-chassis combinations. Ford introduced 2-1/2-ton and 3-ton Extra Heavy Duty truck models and the designations for Ford trucks now ranged from the 1/2-ton F-1 to the 3-ton F-8 (standard) using sequential code. All new sheet metal including new cab design gave Ford trucks and commercial vehicles an entirely new look utilizing a horizontal-bar radiator grille. The Extra-Heady Duty F-7 and F-8 trucks also featured a new chassis, new 145 hp 337-cubic inch V-8 Model 8EQ engine and five-speed transmission, heavier axles, better brakes, heftier springs and eight-stud wheels. The COE chassis was also changed to universalize the cab-to-axle dimension and this model line also offered the six-cylinder engine option for the first time. Ford continued to offer the Ford Motor Coach Model 8MB, but transit bus production fell dramatically in light of the fact that Ford offered neither diesel engines nor automatic transmissions, as its competition did.

Trucks and commercial vehicles comprised 164 different combinations in 1949 with the arrival of two factory-cataloged forward-control parcel delivery chassis complete with front sheet metal, instrument panel and seat. These were powered exclusively by the six-cylinder engine and were designated F-3 Parcel Delivery as the Model 9HJ and Model 9H2J. The F-7 and F-8 chassis was now available with up to 178-inch wheelbase, and the two-speed rear axles were supplanted by the single speed type.

1949 FORD F-3 UTILITY   **OCW**

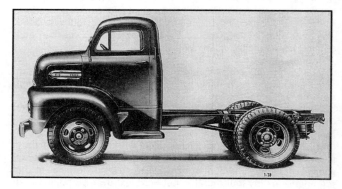

1951 FORD F-6 COE   **FORD**

For 1950, Ford introduced a truck version of the Model 8MB Motor Coach engine called the Model 8MTH, which was available on the F-6 series. The onset of the Korean War brought new demand for both trucks and cars as the American public anticipated the same shortages and rationing as during the previous war. The Ford Motor Company split into six separate divisions concentrating manufacturing toward each of the raw material and major component producing sections in order to be more efficient. Almost at the same time in the year 1950, the public transit bus building business was completely abandoned due to a dive in sales in view of the strength of the competition. The Motor Coach operation was purchased by Marmon-Herrington. A total of 345,801 trucks were built for 1950, the biggest production in 21 years.

A full-width radiator grille distinguished the 1951 Ford trucks from the previous design. The upgraded cab called Five Star had a 50 percent larger window area, dual windshield wipers and a new instrument panel. A waterproof ignition system was introduced, as well as some engine improvements on all truck models. "Scare-buying" due to the Korean War contributed to setting new records for truck sales. Ford received a contract to develop the

jeep's successor, which was to be a parachutable 1/4-ton 4x4 initially called the XM-151. Ford also built M-48 Patton tanks, Model GAA tank engines rated at 525 hp, industrial engines and other war materiel.

For 1952, Ford outspent all other U.S. motor vehicle manufacturers in the development of its products. Two new powerplants constituted Ford's first domestically produced overhead valve engine design. The 215-cubic inch six-cylinder engine was used in passenger cars as well as F-1 through F-5 trucks, F-5 and F-6 School Bus Chassis and in all Parcel Delivery models. The F-8 was powered by the 155 hp 317-cubic inch Lincoln V-8 engine, while the F-7 used a smaller bore version of the same engine. The two displacement sizes of the V-8 engines and the six-cylinder engine had many interchangeable parts, being of the same basic design.

Three new station wagon models also shared much of the sheet metal with a reintroduced sedan delivery. Ford continued to offer the Model 8MTH Big Six engine, and the 239-cubic inch V-8 got some small modifications. With more hp the Big Job F-8 was upgraded to a 41,000 GVW and an F-6 Parcel Delivery was offered with 16,000 pounds GVW. Truck sales fell in 1952, partly due to federal restrictions, partly due to a nationwide labor strike of steel workers.

Ford's 50th anniversary also marked the debut of a significantly updated line of trucks. The new line was marketed as Ford Economy Trucks and designations were changed to be from F-100 to F-900, while prefixes also changed to designate school bus series with the letter "B," Parcel Delivery with the letter "P" and cab-forward trucks with the letter "C." The new designations allowed Ford to offer a larger variety of models with subtle distinctions between them. The previous F-2 and F-3 Series were combined to create the F-250 and the F-4 was down-rated in capacity but expanded in body type selection and called the F-350. The F-7 was replaced by the F-700 powered by the Big Six, while the F-750 was essentially the same truck powered by the V-8 engine. Also, the F-700 used a standard four-speed transmission, while the F-750 used a five-speed overdrive transmission.

The newest series was the F-900 rated at up to 27,000 pounds GVW and 55,000 pounds GCW. It was basically an uprated F-8 Series, except that new Eaton 8,000 pound front and 21,000 pound rear axles were adapted. The springs, steering, tires and brakes were all upgraded as well. School bus Safety Chassis were available as the B-500, B-600, B-700 and B-750, the latter of which was powered by the V-8 engine and was rated at 20,000 pounds GVW. Cab-over models were expanded to include the previous C-500 and C-600 along with the new C-750 and C-800. Also, by reducing the cab-to-axle distance by moving the new wide-track front axle back, Ford trucks had improved weight distribution and created a tighter turning radius. Also, fuel tanks were now mounted on the parallel frame rail chassis rather than on the cab.

An all new "Driverized" cab featured a 55 percent larger curved windshield, armrest height side windows and a four-foot wide rear window. New air vents, handles, wrap-around instrument panel, wider seat and other details completed the improvements of the overall redesign. Front end sheet metal and grille were all new as well. The cab-over and New Pickup/Express and Panel bodies were entirely new. Engines were carried over from the previous year, but transmissions now had synchronizers and the five-speed units were also available in the F, B and C-600 Series.

1954 FORD BIG JOB RESCUE TRUCK   **ERP**

In 1954, Ford completed its transition to all overhead-valve engine design, the first major automaker to do so in the United States despite entering the field later than others. The midsize V-8 engines were similar to the Lincoln and heavy truck units introduced two years earlier and they were almost exactly the same displacement as the earlier Ford and Mercury V-8 engines: 238.6 and 256 cubic inches, respectively, versus 239.4 and 255.4 previously.

Not only did Ford introduce two new overhead-valve V-8 engines but the company also brought out two series with factory installed tandem axles: the T-700 and the T-800. These were based on the F Series using Eaton-Hendrickson dual-axle drive, suspension and power divider. Also new were the C-700 and C-900 cab-over models and the B-600 school bus chassis now had a 210-inch wheelbase. The Fordomatic transmission developed earlier became available on F-100, F-250, F-350, P-350 and Courier panel delivery. The company also continued its experimentation with turbine engines.

The year 1955 was another prosperous one of the motor vehicle industry, primarily because of excellent economic conditions and the industry's efforts to modernize its product lines. Ford was able to obtain 30 percent of the truck market. Total model combinations amounted to 193 with minor changes in regards to all the truck model lines.

For 1956, Ford concentrated on safety in order to try and regain some of the market back from Chevrolet's successful new offerings in 1955. Based on crash tests that Ford had undertaken in the previous two years, Ford cars and trucks received new interlocking door latches and deep dish steering wheels, and safety belts were available. Despite getting the *Motor Trend* Car of the Year Award, marketing safety backfired on Ford as customers were suspicious of "safety problems" and this strategy was abandoned midyear.

This was the year Ford joined other industry procrastinators with a 12-volt electrical system. Wraparound windshields were grafted on to previous year's cabs, yet the incongruous combination turned out to be rather successful. Tubeless tires, four-barrel carburetors and increased engine displacement were offered on Ford trucks for 1956. T-750 Series were added to the model line, which now numbered 289 different combinations. Also for 1956, Ford sold over 10 million shares of company stock to the public and joined the Automobile Manufacturers Association (which had rejected Henry Ford after he had founded the company). This was also the year Highway Act legislation authorized construction of 41,000 miles of the Interstate Highway System, and it was the year that Lee Iacocca was named Ford truck marketing manager.

1957 FORD F-500 STAKE TRUCK   OCW

The Ranchero joined the 300 model 1957 line of Ford trucks and without any competition, briskly sold 18,000 units for the year. Cab-over models were completely changed with flat-faced tilt cabs and set back front axles, as well as new chassis. This COE, although not entirely original, was successful and imitated to the point that Mack and FWD utilized the Ford cabs for their own trucks. Cabs and bodies of F, B and T Series conventional trucks also underwent changes, which mainly consisted of flush fenders and doors, hidden runningboards and wraparound windshield. All-metal slab side cargo beds were featured on pickups as a response to Chevrolet's Cameo truck. The P-400 with 10,000 pound GVW

made its debut in 1957. All heavy-duty trucks received a six-speed Allison automatic transmission called Ford Transmatic as optional equipment.

A new line of heavy-duty trucks characterized the Ford Motor Company for 1958, not just Edsel's famous failure in passenger car sales. With 10 series of trucks now offered, GVW and GCW ratings went up to 36,000 and 65,000 pounds, respectively, and 51,000 and 75,000 pounds with tandem rear axles. An all new trio of V-8 engines specifically designed for trucks were introduced, as opposed to the previous practice of employing modified passenger car engines. Also, eight-speed Fuller R-46 and five-speed Spicer 6000 series transmissions became available along with a heavier 13-inch clutch. Tandem axle tilt cab trucks were offered on special order by the end of the year. Quad headlights were the only basic distinguishing feature setting apart Ford trucks from the previous year's appearance. A national recession brought truck sales down to their lowest level since 1945.

1960 FORD FALCON RANCHERO   OCW

Among the 370 models of commercial vehicles for 1959, Ford truck factory catalogs offered four-wheel-drive for the first time. These were in the form of F-100 and F-250 trucks and would effectively eliminate the Marmon-Herrington conversions. Truck tractor packages on the F-750 through F-1100, C-750 through C-1100 and T-850 and T-950 were made available and automatic transmissions were offered on a larger proportion of the full truck model line.

Ford trucks continued much as the previous year's model line for 1960. The V-8 engine option included two-barrel carburetor-equipped 401- and 477-cubic inch displacement powerplants, but Ford engines by and large were de-rated for durability and economy, the latter being a universal theme in the U.S. motor vehicle industry in general. At the same time, GVW ratings were expanded and overlapped among the medium, heavy and extra-heavy series. The top of the line F-1100 and C-1100 were converted over to strictly off-highway vehicles with heavier axles, while the truck tractor versions in these series were discontinued. Lee Iacocca became vice-president of Ford in 1960.

For 1961, Ford outdid itself with an all new lineup of 619 distinct models of trucks. The F, B and T series were updated completely and Ford entered the market with a compact light van on one end of the spectrum, and a diesel-powered cab-forward linehaul truck tractor at the other end. The Econoline vans, as well as the light bus and pickup iterations, competed directly with Volkswagen "buses" and Corvair-based van commercial vehicles. The Econoline van was a derivative of the Falcon, using most of its drivetrain and various components. The van was rated at 3,600 pounds GVW shortly after its introductory 3,300 pounds that year.

At the same time, the COE linehaul truck tractor was introduced, with diesel engine option a first in company production history. A wide choice of transmissions including 8- and 10-speed Fuller Roadrangers and 12-speed Spicer with three- and four-speed auxiliary gearboxes were also available, while the Allison Transmatic was discontinued. New cab and front end sheet metal gave the 1961 Ford trucks a contemporary if not distinctive appearance. Wheelbases were extended on almost all models, mostly by moving the forward axles further forward and also creating less overhang. The 262-cubic inch displacement 152 hp six-cylinder engine was a new offering after extensive development effort. Most of Ford's engines were further de-rated this year for reasons previously mentioned. Ford Motor Company led the way in the auto industry with the first standard 12-month/12,000-mile warranty for most cars and trucks. In appearance, single headlights returned to the conventional trucks as well as the C-series, which now included a six-cylinder tilt-cab version. The Courier sedan delivery was replaced by the Ranchero sedan delivery for 1961.

For 1962, Ford trucks remained basically the same after the previous year's revamping. The F-700 and F-800 now overlapped in rating and the Styleside slab design pickup beds were reintroduced by popular demand. Ford bought Philco and Autolite that year and adopted a new logo based on the script-in-oval design of 1928-1948.

The N-Series short conventional linehaul truck tractor was a new model line introduced for 1963. These were built from N-500 to N-1100 in size and the single rear axle versions were powered by gasoline engines, while Super-Duty and diesel-powered tandem-axle trucks where also in the factory catalog. Along with the Chassis-Cab bare trucks, 9-foot and 12-foot Platform and Stake bodies were available on the N-500 and N-600 Series trucks.

Besides the diesel heavy linehaulers, Ford also introduced medium/heavy "city-size" diesel trucks in the C- and N-Series that were efficient and maneuverable. Only the heavy trucks received the -D suffix as a designation since Ford wanted only those dealers handling extra heavy trucks who could handle the servicing on those units to sell diesels without changing franchise contracts. Hence, the lighter Ford diesel trucks had a zero added for identification.

For the first time, Ford offered diesel-powered conventional trucks, such as the F-950-D, F-1000-D and F-1100-D, which were single rear axle and the T-850-D and T-950-D tandem axles, which were all powered by the V-6 Cummins 200 diesel engine. By adding the N-Series and the diesel-powered units Ford now had 1,000 truck models, even after excising some of the less popular trucks from its catalog. Cummins diesel engines offered in the COE models included the NH 250, V-6 200 and V-8 265. On F-500 and heavier trucks the GVW ratings were increased.

Also new for the year were the long wheelbase B-600 school bus and Econoline Display and Window Vans. Compression ratios were again decreased on the gasoline-powered models and a new three-speed manual fully-synchronized transmission was available on several lighter trucks, along with Ford passenger cars. As 1963-1/2 models, Ford introduced the V-8-powered Ranchero and sedan delivery along with other passenger cars. This was also the year Ford's Special Military Vehicle Operations began development of the M-656, an eight-wheel 5-ton truck.

For 1964, Ford once again "truckized" three passenger car V-8 engines: known as the 330, 361 and 391 and hp ranged from 186 to 235, while torque was rated between 300 and 372 pound-feet. All models in the series 600 to 800 had these engine options later in the year along with the earlier 330 engine. Development in the F-100 and F-250 4x2 included separately mounted cargo beds on the Styleside models and the industry's first single-latch tailgate. The two pickups were also available with a 128-inch wheelbase "long" chassis to fit campers. GVW ratings were again increased on many models starting with the F-250 going up to the various 850 Series.

The 1/2- and 3/4-ton truck chassis were improved for 1965 and a new line of seven-main-bearing six-cylinder engines were introduced for passenger cars and trucks, the 300-cubic inch displacement version available all the way up to the 600 Series, the latter of which used a heavy-duty iteration. At the same time the 260- and 292-cubic inch V-8 engines were discontinued on passenger cars and trucks.

A prewar French Unic independent front suspension design was adopted for all the F-100 and F-250 4x2 trucks. Also, the F-100 through F-350 Series trucks were available with the 352-cubic inch V-8, which was derived from a passenger car version. Other commercial vehicle news included the availability of the N-600 and N-750 with a 199-inch wheelbase, a crew cab for the F-250 and F-350 and a C-8000 truck tractor with 90-inch wheelbase,

as well as a T-8000 with 158-inch wheelbase, the latter offered with three Cummins diesel engines. This was the year Ford also marketed Camper Special packages on the F-100 and F-250, while the Econoline model series was further expanded. Sedan delivery and 1100 series trucks were discontinued after 1965.

For 1966, Ford introduced some newcomers to its model line such as the Bronco (August 1965 but 1966 model), which had a 92-inch wheelbase and was initially powered by a six-cylinder engine until March of that year when the 289-cubic inch V-8 became available. This was also the year the H-Series high tilt cab was superseded by the W-Series linehaulers. The single rear axle version of this was called the W-1000-D and the tandem was called the WT-1000-D, with GCW rated from 65,000 to 80,000 pounds.

The Bronco's Monobeam type suspension was incorporated in the F-100 4x4 resulting in a much lower silhouette. The Econoline-based vehicles continued to include more body styles including the SuperVan. The F-8000 now had a Cummins 464-cubic inch diesel V-8 in addition to the other engine choices. For the first time, the P-400 parcel delivery was available as a motorhome chassis for aftermarket converters. Also for the year, a heftier transmission was introduced as the C-6. The most important contributing element affecting the U.S. auto industry was the enactment of the Motor Vehicle Safety Act of 1966, which would have a profound influence for years to come.

For 1967, Ford light trucks had all-new cabs and fresh front end sheet metal. Some of chassis changes extended to medium-duty F- and B-Series models but aside from the common cab shell, the heavier models contrasted effectively in appearance with the lighter models. The F-350 chassis was extensively changed with Twin-I-Beam front suspension and F-350 Camper Specials were added to the factory catalog. Both the F-100 and F-250 were offered with a 131-inch wheelbase, and the F-500 was now available with a 174-inch wheelbase. Low-profile tubeless truck tires were adopted for all models up to the 400 series. Medium-duty trucks got integral power steering and light trucks were available with auxiliary fuel tanks. The Ranchero became based on the Fairlane in 1967.

The heavy-duty Ford trucks were now offered with two sizes of the British-built Dorset diesel engine, which superseded the Dagenham models and Detroit Diesel engines included the 6V-53N for the 8000 Series. This was the year the Sports Utility Bronco was introduced, as well as diesel-powered CT-8000 tandem trucks. The former T-700 and T-750 were superseded by the down-rated T-800 and Ford obtained a contract from the U.S. military to build M-151 trucks. Ford trucks sold well, especially in the 16,000 to 26,000-pound GVW class, but a month-long labor strike was a setback for total production.

When General Motors Executive Vice-President "Bunkie" Knudsen joined the Ford Motor Company in 1968, the significant changes in Ford truck production was the discontinuation of the P-100 parcel delivery chassis, CT-750, T-950 tandem bogies, 121-inch wheelbase N-Series diesel engine and the F-100 Camper Special package. Ford continued to be the nation's largest truck seller and by 1969, added special vocational packages as well as P-350 and P-500 motorhome chassis. While the 302-cubic inch V-8 was used in lighter trucks along with a new 250-cubic inch six-cylinder, the Cummins NH 230 was the standard engine for the heavy trucks. The 289-cubic inch V-8 and 743-cubic inch Cummins diesel engines were no longer in the factory catalog.

The Louisville Line of new trucks was introduced for the beginning of the 1970s. These were named after their place of manufacture in Louisville, Kentucky, at the Kentucky Truck Plant and now included the L-Line of trucks. It was the world's largest factory at the time dedicated to production of trucks with 2.3 million square feet and capable of a 336-unit output per day. The L-Series single axle conventional trucks superseded the F-800 through F-1000, the LT-Series superseded the T-Series, the LN-Series superseded the N-Series and the LNT-Series superseded the NT-Series. Ford advertised "600 models, medium through extra-heavy-duty...30 gas and diesel engines to 335 hp."

1965 FORD ECONOLINE VAN   FORD

1966 FORD F-750   WOODARD

1978 FORD CL-9000 TANDEM TRUCK TRACTOR   FORD

1979 FORD ECONOLINE 100 CUSTOM VAN   FORD

1987 FORD RANGER STX   FORD

1993 FORD 9000 AEROMAX CUSTOM TRACTOR   MROZ

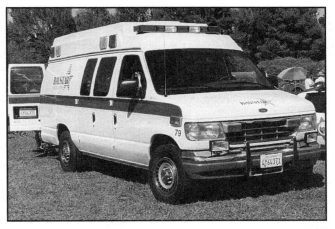

1994 FORD LEADER AMBULANCE   MROZ

1995 FORD LTLS 9000   FORD

147

1972 FORD WT-9000   OCP

The L-9000 and LT-9000 were considered Ford's first bona fide long conventional diesel linehaulers. Other new technologies included higher yield strength steel on frames, dual circuit brakes, electro-coating for corrosion resistance and the industry's largest windshield on the L-Line trucks. Three sets of diesel engines by Cummins and Detroit Diesel were available and transmissions were now offered with 6, 10, 13 or 16 speeds.

At this point the 428-cubic inch V-8 engines and the 390-4V were superseded by three distinct 429-cubic inch V-8 engines and the 351C V-8 (built in Cleveland) was added to the list of choices, complementing the 351W V-8 (built in Windsor), the latter which had been offered in 1969. Although both Cleveland and Windsor engines had the same bore and stroke and displacement, they were actually completely different. The Cleveland engine had a new, stronger block, canted valves and combustion chambers, with ports to match and a higher compression ratio on the 4V version. Ford truck sales surpassed all other makes at this time.

In July of 1970, *The Commercial Car Journal* announced that Ford would build a gas turbine engine the following year, mostly for industrial applications, but some would be fitted into trucks and buses. Two hundred 450 hp Model 707 engines were planned to be built. Continental Trailways, which had been testing the gas turbine Silver Eagle, ordered more turbine engines. Lower output turbine engines from 200 hp to 335 hp were also planned. A year later, the 525 hp Series 4200 turbine engine was announced and the 707 unit was redesignated as the Series 3600. *Fleet Owner* later announced that 20 pilot units were installed into trucks, but the turbine gas engine was never proven successful for vehicle application. In 1970, Lee Iacocca became president of Ford Motor Company.

As the 1970s progressed, Ford's position in truck sales slipped from first in 1974 (having sold 892,736 units), but in the heavy-duty truck range Ford was still third behind International and Mack. The mid-1970s were tough economically for Ford and the nation as a whole with fuel shortages, inflation and a deep recession. Ford brought out its new Econoline Vans and Club Wagons in 1975 despite hard times. On light trucks, the first cosmetic changes in three years included grille and ornament revisions and the 4x4 trucks received disc brakes that the 4x2 trucks had gotten previously. The company offered a number of special editions for the nation's Bicentennial: a Bicentennial Option Group, XLT Luxury Group, Flareside Accent Package, F-150 Special and the Cruising Van.

For 1976, Ford announced its ultimate linehaul truck in the form of the LTL-9000 conventional with tandem axle, powered by a Cummins NTC-350 diesel using a 10-speed Fuller RT-910 Roadranger transmission, Rockwell SQHD rear bogie and a

12,000-pound rated front axle. Owner-operator packages were part of the base price and GVW ratings were from 44,800 to 60,000 pounds, while the GCW was 82,000 pounds. Other heavy trucks were offered with three "economy" diesel engines: Caterpillar Economy 3406, Cummins Formula 290 and Detroit Diesel 8V-71TT, while the 401-cubic inch Super Duty V-8 gasoline engine was discontinued. That year, Ford also offered the W-Series, C-Series, LN-Series, F-Series and L-Series. BBC dimensions ranged from 52-inch for the W-Series to 118 inches for the L-Series and LTL-Series.

1973 FORD UPS TRUCK   MROZ

Celebrating 70 years of commercial vehicle production with the introduction of the Model TT One Ton Truck in 1917, Ford also returned to the number one spot in domestic truck sales. Ford sold 759,660 pickups alone for that year. The FE-Series Y-block V-8 engines were superseded by "truckized" 351- and 400-cubic inch passenger car engines, which provided more horsepower and better fuel economy. Ford also continued to offer light trucks aimed at the youth market in the form of various style accents. Ford announced extensive mid-season changes in its F-250 Regular Cab 4x4 chassis with lower overall height yet better ground clearance. The P-350, P-400 and M-Series motorhome chassis were all dropped from the model line.

For the year 1978, Ford's 75th anniversary, the company brought out new products to offer an enormous range of trucks and commercial vehicles. The model lines included the Bronco, Courier, Econoline, Ranchero and Ranger in the light truck field, with a new Bronco design now based on the F-Series trucks as had been proposed in the first place. Henry Ford II fired Lee Iacocca as president in 1978.

In the heavy truck field, Ford brought out its third-generation COE diesel linehauler, designating it as the CL-9000. It was offered in five single rear axle wheelbases as the CL-9000 and in nine tandem axle wheelbases as the CLT-9000. GVW rating remained the same at 80,000 and 82,000 pounds, respectively. Special 127,000- and 138,000-pound GCW rated trucks were also available in the tandem configuration with certain powertrains. Instrument panels and aerodynamic cabs were state-of-the-art for these new heavy-duty Class 8 trucks, but the air-suspended cab option was the ultimate. Cummins KT and KTA diesel engines were offered with up to 600 hp and Caterpillar, Cummins and Detroit Diesel economy engines were also available. Also, nine Fuller transmissions with up to 13 speeds were also in the factory catalog.

The Ford Ranger made its debut in 1982 and for 1983, a 4x4 version was also available. In March of 1983 Ford introduced the Bronco and for 1984, the smaller Bronco II was added to the model line.

As the 1980s progressed, Ford continued with its largest CL-9000 Series, which as a 6x4 truck tractor had a GCW rating of 80,000 pounds with special versions up to 138,000 pounds. Ford introduced its LTL-9000 conventional in 1981 in order to compete with International, Kenworth and Peterbilt. Nine engine choices were offered with the 435 hp Detroit Diesel the most powerful at that time. Fuller transmissions from 9 to 15 speeds were available and a wide range of options allowed the buyer to select the truck specifications for particular applications.

In the mid-range F-Series trucks, Ford continued to compete one-on-one with Chevrolet throughout the 1980s. The F-600 Series was one of the best selling model lines with three gasoline and two diesel engines, nine wheelbases, 14 transmissions including two automatic and 11 axles giving GVW up to 30,000 pounds. For 1988, Ford advertised its Aeromax LA-9000 single-axle rated at 80,000-pound GCW and the LTA-9000 tandem-axle rated at 82,000-pound GCW. The AeroForce models for that year were the CLT-9000 and LTL-9000. In March of 1990 the Ford Explorer replaced the Bronco II.

By 1994, Ford offered 22 models of Class 7 and Class 8 trucks in 4x2, 6x2 and 6x4 configuration. GVW ratings were from 24,500 pounds up to 66,000 pounds. Maximum GCW ratings were 82,000 pounds, which included seven of the 22 models. Engine options were: D 210-250, D 210-275, D 260-370, D 260-425, D 260-460, D 275-430, D 275-460 and D 280-430. Wheelbases ranged from 117 inches up to 258 inches and BBC dimensions ranged from 79.7 inches on the CF-8000 model up to 178 inches on the LTL-9000 and LL-9000 models.

For 1996, Ford introduced its new AeroMax 9500, the first Class 8 Ford tractor designed exclusively for over-the-road use and the first all-new Ford Class 8 linehaul tractor in more than 25 years. Introduced as a 113-inch BBC conventional linehaul tractor, it featured "solar glass to increase window area while decreasing sunload." Engine options included Caterpillar, Cummins and Detroit Diesel. Sleepers included Able Body Flat-Top Plus and AeroBullet Plus. The second version of the AeroMax 9500 was announced as a 122-inch BBC long-conventional model with "true integrated sleepers" in 57-inch and 77-inch lengths with stand-up/walk-through design and no visible exterior seals.

During the mid-1990s, Ford has offered a wide selection of light and medium duty commercial vehicles. The basic model line has included 23 trucks and vans. The Aerostar Cargo Van has been available with a 3L standard engine and five-speed manual base transmission with a GVW rating of up to 5,180 pounds. The Econoline Vans have been offered in series E-150, E-250, E-250HD, E-250 Super Van, E-250HD Super Van, E-350 and E-350 Super Van. The standard engine for all of these has been the 4.9L and base transmission the three-speed automatic. Heaviest GVW rating was for the E-350 and E-350 Super Van with 9,400 pounds and 9,300 pounds, respectively.

The Econoline Cutaway Chassis Commercial 350 has been available with a 7.3L diesel V-8 engine and four-speed automatic overdrive base transmission. Wheelbase for this vehicle has been listed at 138 inches with a 9,600-pound GVW rating and a payload capacity of up to 4,815 pounds. The Econoline Stripped Chassis Commercial E-350 has been offered with the 4.9L standard engine and three-speed automatic transmission. GVW rating has been listed at 10,000 pounds with a payload capacity of up to 6,065 pounds.

Ranger pickups have been available as the Regular Cab Short-Wheelbase and Long-Wheelbase and as the SuperCab. Standard engine on these three versions has been the 2.3L four-cylinder and the five-speed manual transmission. The F-Series Full Size Pickup has been listed with a 4.9L engine and five-speed transmission as standard equipment in series F-150 Regular Cab, F-150 Super Cab, F-250 Regular Cab and F-250 HD. The latter with 133-inch wheelbase has been available with a GVW rating of up to 8,600 pounds and payload capacity up to 4,115 pounds.

The F-250 SuperCab has been offered with a 5.8L V-8 engine and five-speed manual overdrive transmission as standard equipment and this applied also for the F-350 Regular Cab with dual rear wheels and F-350 SuperCab with dual rear wheels, the latter having a GVW rating of 10,000 pounds with a maximum load capacity of 4,600 pounds. The F-350 Crew Cab truck has been listed with a 7.3L V-8 engine and five-speed manual heavy-duty overdrive transmission as standard equipment.

The F-350 Crew Cab with dual rear wheels has been powered by a 5.8L V-8 standard engine with five-speed manual heavy-duty overdrive transmission and a GVW rating of up to 10,000 pounds. Last of the 23 models has been the F-350 Chassis Cab 4x2 with

a 5.8L V-8 and five-speed manual heavy-duty overdrive transmission and a GVW rating of 8,800 pounds and maximum payload capacity of 4,680 pounds. For a complete history of Ford light commercial vehicles see Krause Publications' *Standard Catalog of American Light-Duty Trucks*.

FORD 1913 — In order to avoid confusion, the Ford Taxicab Corporation of 1913, organized by Newton Dexter, Joseph Reed and Emery Wilson in Portland, Maine, is listed in this compendium to bring attention to the fact that it was not affiliated with Henry Ford and the Ford Company of Detroit, Michigan. Both companies existed simultaneously, albeit this one for only a year. Ford of Portland was capitalized with $10,000. It does not appear production had gone beyond the prototype stage.

FORSCHLER 1914-1924 — The Phillip Forschler Wagon Company was located in New Orleans, Louisiana. The first trucks Forschler built were 1-1/2-ton and 3-ton trucks using water-cooled four-cylinder engines that were spring-mounted on separate frames. These had a 124-inch wheelbase, three-speed transmission and double-chain drive. Chain drive was abandoned in favor of worm-gear drive by 1917. By 1919, the company was reorganized as the Forschler Motor Truck Manufacturing Company, Incorporated still in New Orleans. A variety of trucks including 3/4-, 1- and 2-ton were available. Forschler listed a 2-ton Model D as late as 1924, although manufacturing probably ceased earlier. The Model D with 144-inch wheelbase was powered by a 27.2 hp four-cylinder Continental C-4 engine with Zenith carburetor and optional ignition. Ross steering was used and Smith wheels carried 34x4 front and 36x7 rear solid rubber tires. The chassis alone weighed 4,735 pounds.

1911 FORT WAYNE MODEL AD DELIVERY   **RD**

FORT WAYNE 1911-1913 — The Fort Wayne Automobile Manufacturing Company located in Fort Wayne, Indiana, built a Model A and a Model B truck during its brief engagement in commercial vehicle manufacturing. The company was incorporated by G.C. Dudenhofer, G.T. Fox, W.H. Rohan and L.J. Wilrath with $20,000 in 1910. The Model A (later called AD) was rated at 3/4-ton with a chassis weight of 2,200 pounds and it was powered by an 18 hp four-cylinder thermo-syphon water-cooled engine with force-feed lubrication and used a three-speed transmission with double chain drive. A two-speed planetary transmission was used. It was offered as a panel van "power wagon" for $1,500 in 1911. Wheels were artillery-type "of second growth hickory" and frame was of "second growth ash with steel reinforcements." A governor was used to limit its speed to 18 mph.

The Model B Fort Wayne was rated at 3 tons and was also powered by a four-cylinder engine, though larger than the Model A's. Its top speed was also governed, in this case to 15 miles per hour, and the bare chassis price was $3,000 with a choice of various bodies at extra cost. The company did not survive the year 1913. It should not be confused with the Fort Wayne Automobile Company organized in 1903, which did not produce commercial vehicles. However, one of the investors in the earlier venture was G.C. Dudenhofer who was also involved with the truck builders of

1911. Yet another company with a similar name, the Fort Wayne Motor Sales Company of 1911, did not manufacture any vehicles, it appears.

1916 FOSTORIA CANOPY DELIVERY TRUCK　　　　　　DW

FOSTORIA 1916 — The Fostoria Light Car Company built a gasoline-powered 3/4-ton light truck. The chassis price was $485. The company was briefly located in Fostoria, Ohio.

FOUR WHEEL DRIVE 1904-1907 — Charles Cotta of Rockford, Illinois, sold the patent rights of his four-wheel-drive system to a group of investors in Milwaukee, Wisconsin. Cotta had built his first steam car at the turn of the century using a two-cylinder engine mounted midway between front and rear axles, which were both driven by chain. The Cottamobile also featured four-wheel-steering and after a few were built, Cotta turned his efforts toward the Cotta Gear Company in 1903, which became well known for its transmissions.

H. Theodore Hanson, Charles B. Perry and Lyman G. Wheeler were the principals behind the Four Wheel Drive Wagon Company, which was capitalized with $1 million for the purpose of building "motor vehicles with business purposes." The first delivery wagons, which utilized the Cotta four-wheel-drive and four-wheel-steering design, were powered by a 30 hp four-cylinder Rutenber engine also using chain drive and "wooden tires." However, by 1906, the vehicles were powered by a 40 hp Rutenber engine using shaft drive to differentials on the front and rear axles and had solid rubber tires.

A few Four Wheel Drive vehicles were built in the form of a touring passenger car model using a 132-inch wheelbase. In 1906, the company announced it would expand its manufacturing facilities, but by early 1907, the firm was in bankruptcy. There was no connection between this Four Wheel Drive company and the later Four Wheel Drive Auto Company of Clintonville, Wisconsin, which was organized in 1912.

FOUR TRACTION see KATO

FRANKLIN 1905-1920 — John Wilkinson had built two air-cooled prototype cars for the New York Automobile Company in 1901 but due to a lack of remuneration, he turned to Herbert H. Franklin, who was a manufacturer of die castings in Syracuse, New York. With the additional help of Alexander T. Brown, the Franklin auto was born in 1902 after the New York Automobile Company was absorbed through some litigation. The first runabouts were sold in 1902 and featured a four-cylinder two-cycle overhead-valve engine mounted transversely, which had a throttle control float-feed carburetor, two-speed planetary transmission, full-elliptic springs, shaft drive and wooden frame. A front-mounted gear-driven cooling fan was used, which by 1910 was incorporated into the flywheel as an air-pulling fan.

By 1905, Franklin built a standard control truck using the air-cooled Franklin engine positioned longitudinally. The 3/4-ton vehicle was distinguished by a barrel-shaped hood as were the passenger cars. The following year a 1-ton truck was built using the same essential design and components. The trucks' wooden artillery-type wheels were fitted with solid rubber tires and on passenger cars and later vans, non-dismountable pneumatic tires were good for 20,000 miles due to the full-elliptic suspension that also provided a comfortable ride.

The company sponsored a newsworthy cross-country New York to San Francisco run in 1904 that took 33 days, beating the Winton record by nearly half. In 1908, a 1/2-ton and a 2-ton truck were added to the model line, and a police patrol wagon was sold to the city of Syracuse. The 1-ton truck had semi-elliptic springs. By 1912, the heavy trucks, which had three-speed transmissions and pneumatic tires, were discontinued, while the 1/2-ton Renault-type taxi continued to be available.

1910 FRANKLIN 1-TON VAN　　　　　　NAHC

1911 FRANKLIN COMMERCIAL CAR　　　　　　OCW

Wilkinson was a Cornell engineering graduate and the company reflected his predilection. Franklin spent proportionally more on engineering than most other motor vehicle companies. Six-cylinder engines were used exclusively after 1914 and aluminum pistons were utilized as early as 1915. By 1917, Franklin had won several well-known races and on an economy run by a fleet of Franklins averaged 40.3 mpg. However, by this time commercial vehicle production, except for limousines, had almost entirely faded out at the Franklin factory. By 1920, Franklin was experimenting with its last commercial vehicle prototype, which was a 1-ton truck with full electrics still using the same Franklin air-cooled engine. The U.S. military also experimented with a six-cylinder Franklin air-cooled engine in its trucks as late as 1931.

Wilkinson resigned from the company in protest in 1923, when distributors forced the company to introduce a new car, notably using a false radiator, which went against the grain of Wilkinson's principles. He went on to design and build another car with his own name in 1925. The Franklin Manufacturing Company stayed in business until 1934, having produced V-12 powered passenger car prototypes, but the Great Depression had taken its toll and production had fallen so drastically that the banks had taken over by 1932.

FRAYER-MILLER 1907-1909 — Two years after the turn of the century Oscar S. Lear designed an air-cooled engine, while the same was being accomplished by two other men working together named Lee A. Frayer and William J. Miller. By 1904, the three of them combined their efforts as the Oscar Lear Auto Company, which also absorbed the Buckeye Motor Company that Lear had organized earlier. The Frayer-Miller vehicle's engines were air-cooled using a rotary blower forcing air between aluminum jackets around the cylinders. In 1905, the Frayer-

Miller was distinguished as the first six-cylinder auto sold in the United States, although both four-cylinder and six-cylinder engines were available at that time.

1907 FRAYER-MILLER 1-1/2-TON PLATFORM STAKE   JAW

By 1907, Frayer-Miller introduced a 1-1/2-ton truck using a four-speed transmission and double chain drive. After Frayer-Miller cars won a few races, company policy shifted toward the manufacture of commercial vehicles only. A 1-1/2-ton Frayer-Miller with a stake body was priced at $3,000. Tiller-steered from the rear top, cabs were also built by 1907 under the name Nichols Frayer-Miller. In 1908, the company offered the agricultural Farmobile and Seagrave fire trucks were built on Frayer-Miller chassis. E.S. Kelly, who had helped organize the Kelly-Springfield tire company, bought the Oscar Lear Auto Company and the Buckeye factory and by 1910, the company became the Kelly Motor-Truck Company.

1911 KELLY-FRAYER-MILLER   RD

1923 FREEMAN SECURITY TWIN DRIVE   RD

FREEMAN 1920-1923 — Announcements for the formation of the company and building of the factory in Omaha, Nebraska, appeared in the April 24, 1920, issue of *Automobile Topics*. H.O. Stonebreaker was president, Paul Reiff vice-president and F.L. Freeman general manager. Plans were laid out for the assembly of 500 trucks and 50 passenger cars per year. It would appear only a prototype was built. Frank L. Freeman was awarded patent number 1,416,010 in 1922, having been filed in April of 1920. This patent was for a front-wheel-drive system that Freeman would later use in the subsequent venture of 1928. Although the Nebraska venture was listed only for 1920, *Motor Transport Magazine* wrote about the four-wheel-drive Freeman truck, called Security Twin Drive, in its March 15, 1923, issue, along with photos of the prototype powered by a Buda HTU engine using a Cotta four-speed transmission. The transfer case was located amidships. Other components included Parish & Bingham pressed steel frame, Alemite chassis lubrication, Pierce governor, Zenith carburetor, Detlaff dry-disc clutch, Disteel disc wheels, Westinghouse starting and electrical system, Exide batteries and Wohlrab steering gear.

1928 FREEMAN 4X4   RD

FREEMAN 1928-1931 — The Freeman Motor Car Company of Detroit, Michigan, built a four-wheel-drive truck that was powered by a four-cylinder Buda engine. The company was incorporated as Freeman Quadrive also in Detroit. *The Commercial Car Journal* first covered the six-cylinder-powered four-wheel-drive Freeman truck on October 15, 1928, although the company was already in operation. Articles of incorporation were filed with the Michigan Secretary of State in 1924 but it would appear production did not commence until four years later. Frank Freeman was vice-president of the company. His bevel-gear four-wheel-drive design had already been patented and a prototype of the Buda-powered truck was already built in 1923.

Three engine sizes were offered: 65, 80 and 110 hp. Most common was the 80 hp six-cylinder Buda DA-6 engine. By 1930, Freeman offered 12 different models from 3-1/2-ton to 10-ton capacity ranging in price from $4,900 up to $7,400. All engines were six-cylinder and taxable hp ranged from 33.75 up to 48.60.

In the last year of manufacture the largest Freeman truck could haul 20 tons at 25 miles per hour using two four-wheel trailers. The special design of the drive system involved an eight-speed transmission internal gear drive for the rear wheels while at the front a live axle above the fixed axle used a system of bevel gears instead of a differential. The company began just before the economic downturn of the 1929 stock market crash lasting until 1931 with only a few trucks actually manufactured over approximately three years.

FREIGHTLINER 1940-1942, 1947 to date — Leland James had been a trucker since the age of 19. By the time he was president of Consolidated Freightways he was looking for lightweight, durable trucks with a better ride, but the industry could not provide them to his satisfaction. As early as 1936, the shops at his Salt Lake City, Utah, firm were building aluminum truck and trailer bodies. The first successful experimental cab was added to a Fageol chassis using a six-cylinder Cummins diesel engine in 1937 and 20 of these in various forms were built by 1939. Because the cabs were basic square boxes they were nicknamed "Monkey Ward" Freight-liners, insinuating they could have been built with mail order parts.

James hired engineers who began designing a truck following his ideas, which included the wide use of aluminum and magnesium. The first two prototypes under the supervision of Tom Taylor, shortly to become executive vice-president, were built in 1940. They were aluminum cab-over-engine design weighing 2,000 pounds less than any comparable truck on the road and allowed the maximum legal payload capacity.

A separate company called Consolidated Freightways was formed at this time along with five other freight carriers to serve 10 Western states. Two sets of 10 pilot models were started in August 1940. However, the CF-100 (or Model 100, which was later changed to Model 400) "shovel-nose" truck production was short-lived when material shortages due to the war began by March of 1942. The Model 600 of this period differed in that the aluminum nose was riveted for strength to a flat steel sheet under the windshield and the rest of the cab was also mostly steel. The Salt Lake City plant was converted over to war production where airplane parts and ship hatch covers were manufactured.

1949 FREIGHTLINER MODEL WF 800 (LEFT)   FREIGHTLINER AND 1992 COE TILT CAB (RIGHT)

During the war, the U.S. Justice Department charged that Freightways held a monopoly in 48 states and the cooperative was forced to break up by 1944. The Salt Lake City plant was closed and all equipment and material was sent to Portland, Oregon, where the new Freightliner Corporation was organized after World War II with L.E. Kassenbaum as president and Tom Taylor as general manager. By the end of 1947, Freightliner got back into the business of building trucks.

With the metallurgical advances that World War II had provided, aluminum and magnesium were used extensively throughout the postwar Freightliner trucks. The shop in Portland produced 30 Freightliners in 1947, all for Consolidated Freightways. The cab was redesigned with the bubble of the nose starting just below the windshield in order to make room for a larger radiator and these were referred to as the "bubblenose" Model 800 Freightliner. Forty more were built in 1948 and the first Freightliner sold outside the Consolidated Freightways company was powered by a 275 hp supercharged Cummins diesel.

For 1949, the 5-ton truck tractor Model WF800 4x2 COE with 188-inch wheelbase was powered by a 262 hp Hercules DFXH six-cylinder diesel (743-cubic inch displacement) using a Fuller 4B86 four-speed transmission and Fuller 8016 three-speed auxiliary transmission with Timken front and rear axles. Bendix-Westinghouse brakes were used and tires were 10.00x22 12-ply front and rear. The frame was by Parrish and suspension was semi-elliptic leaf spring front and rear. Steering was the Gemmer 500 type.

By 1950, the company was also building the Model 900, which was essentially the same as a Model 800 but had an integral sleeper. Production was 116 units for that year.

In 1951, Freightliner signed an exclusive agreement with White Motor Corporation of Cleveland, Ohio, to allow the company to market, sell and service Freightliner trucks while letting Freightliner concentrate on the manufacturing. The new trucks were introduced as the White-Freightliner in both the United States

and Canada and the emblem had both names at that time. Production went up to 189 trucks in 1951 as White advertised Freightliners as "Lightweight - More Freight."

1952 WHITE FREIGHTLINER   **FREIGHTLINER**
MODEL WF-8164 6X6

The White-Freightliner COE trucks were available in two basic models. The first was the WF-42, which was a four-wheel single-drive truck tractor that could pull two 24-foot trailers and still fall within the 60-foot overall limit in effect among most of the Western states. The WF-64 was a three-axle dual-drive truck also powered by a diesel engine, but it was usually configured with a 22-foot body and one 28-foot trailer. Because of the great weight savings in the construction of the truck, operators could haul 2,880 more pounds of cargo than standard trucks and for 1952, sales grew to 251 total production.

For 1953, Freightliner introduced its 48-inch cab four-wheel-drive truck tractor known as the WF-4864 Spacemaker. The new cab design was flat in front and the truck was powered by a Cummins "pancake" type engine. Subsequently, the company came out with a 4x4 known as the WF-5844 that featured "on-the-fly" shifting into four-wheel-drive. A tilt-cab design was abandoned because of current litigation involving other companies and the new Freightliner ended up with three-piece removable panels. A large part of the design derived from the company's philosophy of using ODM design (owner-driver-mechanic) and meetings among the three groups led to some of the design parameters and innovations. One of these was the roof-mounted sleeper cab, which White Freightliner introduced by 1953.

For 1954, the company offered a sleeper model with a BBC dimension of 75 inches and this design was known as the WF-7564. It set a new standard for the truck manufacturing industry and sales grew to a total of 430 by 1955, with a grand total of 517 by the following year. A successful tilt-cab was introduced in July of 1958, known as the 8164T. It tilted forward 90 degrees with the use of a hand-operated high-precision tilt pump built by Freightliner. The cab's reinforced monocoque construction using flat glass and sheet metal remained the basic design until some of the aerodynamic cabs of the 1990s.

A new 47,000-foot factory was started in Pomona, California, in 1960, where the largest single truck market in the United States would bring greater sales for the new decade. The first model produced at the Pomona plant was a WFT-7242 single-drive COE truck tractor with a deluxe 72-inch sleeper. The year also marked the company's acquisition of an early IBM computer to deal with its expanding parts business. For 1961, total production reached 1,242 trucks and the company started manufacturing in Canada that year. The 10,000th Freightliner was built in 1963.

For the construction industry, and cement mixing in particular, Freightliner built a half-cab with forward slanting grille, which was also offset. This COE was introduced in 1964 as a 6x4, 6x6 or 8x6. By that time, the Portland plant had reached full production capacity of five trucks per day, which were being built within three acres under roof. The year 1964 was the year that the company began building "Sugar Liners" for the Hawaiian sugar cane fields. These COE trucks had specially low gears for moving one-third-mile per hour while being loaded with 50 tons of sugar cane. They had a top speed of 38 mph.

In 1965, Freightliner introduced its first "Turboliner," which was powered by a gasoline turbine engine developed by Boeing Corporation. It weighed 2,400 pounds less than a similar piston-driven engine powered truck. The Boeing Model 553 turbine produced 300 hp and operated at 7000 rpm, but it consumed gasoline at a great rate. An Allison automatic transmission was used to test it over long distance hauling. Over the next seven years, Freightliner built 10 Turboliners using Boeing, Caterpillar, Ford and Detroit Diesel gas turbine engines. Various problems including high maintenance needs and unresolved application engineering led to the project being discontinued by the gasoline shortage of 1973.

White Freightliner continued to grow at a rapid pace and by 1965, 4,786 trucks were built -- 30 percent more than the previous year. A new 74,000-square foot plant had been opened in Indianapolis, Indiana, and the company now employed 1,541 people. That year also marked production of the 20,000th Freightliner truck and the company continued to grow and prosper. By 1968, the company built 8,313 trucks in North America. By 1970, the Portland Truck Plant was converted to a parts factory and warehouse and COE production was moved to Indianapolis.

**1969 WHITE FREIGHTLINER   FREIGHTLINER
MODEL WF-8164 6X4**

The Powerliner model was introduced in 1973 and the Pomona plant was moved to a larger facility in Chino, California, that year. The Powerliner COE featured a larger grille in order to nearly double the surface area of the radiator up to 2000 square inches in order to accommodate engines over 500 hp.

A new lightweight conventional model also introduced in 1973 and produced for 1974 featured 80 percent parts interchangeability with the full-width COE model, and both models were powered by a Cummins NTC290 with a Fuller clutch and Roadranger 10-speed transmission. Rockwell rear axles were configured as 4x2 or 6x4 drives. Tires were 11x22-1/2 12-ply tubeless nylon with duals on the rear. The semi-elliptic suspension was built by Freightliner, with the weight of the conventional truck tractor chassis being 10,315 pounds, while the 6x4 version weighed 12,465 pounds.

The year 1975 was a disastrous one for the Class 8 truck industry as fuel shortages and rationing raised fuel prices dramatically. Also, federal regulators mandated a new anti-skid brake system be installed in all trucks. Freightliner sales plummeted by 67 percent to 4,673 for that year. Federal Motor Vehicle Standard 121 regarding the early anti-slid brakes was later rescinded by the courts. During this period, Freightliner manage-

ment, with CEO Kenneth Self spearheading the decision, terminated the sales agreement with White Motor Corporation when it expired in December of 1977. The original "Freightliner" emblem reappeared in 1976. Engine options increased to include Caterpillar, Cummins and Allis-Chalmers diesel units. By 1979, Freightliner had over eight percent of the overall Class 8 truck market and about 25 percent of the COE market in the United States. Freightliner also signed an agreement with Volvo AB of Sweden to distribute Class 6, 7 and 8 Volvo trucks.

1975 WHITE FREIGHTLINER MODEL WTF-8164 FREIGHTLINER CONVENTIONAL TANDEM TRACTOR

In 1979, a new plant was opened in Mt. Holly, North Carolina. For 1980, Freightliner added a 60-inch sleeper as optional equipment. However, due to a sag in the market and deregulation in 1980, Daimler-Benz purchased Freightliner in 1981 for $260 million and in consequence, the relationship with Volvo was terminated. Although Class 8 truck sales fell in 1982, Freightliner commanded 10.1 percent of the market with 7,483 units sold that year. The U.S. Surface Transportation Assistance Act of 1983 helped the industry rebound from the earlier recession. The legislation allowed 80,000 pound GVW on interstate highways and disallowed states from setting limits on many tractor-trailer combinations.

For 1984, Freightliner introduced a major model changeover, with upgrades for the COE and conventional trucks, as well as an all new 60-inch Raised Roof Conventional sleeper option. The parent company's Mercedes trucks continued to be assembled in Hampton, Virginia, and later that year Freightliner offered a set-back front axle option for its conventional truck.

In April of 1985, Freightliner introduced its first medium length 112 Conventional, which was the first all-new model since the company's acquisition by Daimler-Benz. As the market shifted toward conventional trucks due to deregulation, Freightliner focused on marketing its design of such trucks. In 1986 the company introduced its new line of construction trucks; the Hard Hat series.

For 1987, a Freightliner/Wabco anti-lock brake system was offered after two years of testing. Freightliner became the first to offer ABS as a production option. This was the year production of the Raised Roof COE commenced. In 1988, the "new generation" of Freightliner vehicles featured aerodynamics and ergonomics and accounted for 27,000 trucks sold. This was also the year the U.S. Army awarded Freightliner a $108 million contract for 775 Long Conventional trucks, with about half being all-wheel-drive off-road design having 133,000 pound GVW rating. In 1989, Freightliner acquired a 280,000-square foot truck plant in Cleveland, North Carolina, from the M.A.N. Truck and Bus Corporation.

As the 1990s unfolded Freightliner brought out numerous new products, including set forward front-axle Conventionals for high-density commodity haulers, Conventionals and Medium Conventionals for construction, logging and cement mix hauling, aluminum cab Medium Conventionals for regional and urban work and the new Business Class line of Class 6, 7 and 8 trucks, replacing the Mercedes-Benz product line in North America. For 1991, the company brought out the FLD120 Classic Conventional and the FLD112SD dump truck for on/off construction applications.

1994 FREIGHTLINER MODEL 911 SCBA FIRE ENGINE **FREIGHTLINER**

1992 FREIGHTLINER 70 SERIES VACUUM TRUCK **FREIGHTLINER**

1993 FREIGHTLINER FLD CONVENTIONAL W/SLEEPER **FREIGHTLINER**

For its 50th anniversary, Freightliner introduced the new 70-inch Raised Roof SleeperCab and 58-inch SleeperCab models. The company also built 1,700 camouflaged Long Conventional military trucks and truck tractors for the U.S. Army Tank Automotive Command and supplied SEE tractors to Egypt, Saudi Arabia and Israel.

For 1995, Freightliner offered 10 basic models: FLD 120 conventional 4x2 and 6x4, FLS 120 SD 6x4 (severe duty), FLD 112 aluminum cab, FLD 112 SD 6x4, FLC 112 4x2 and 6x4 steel cab conventional, FLC 112 SD 6x4, FLB COE 4x2 and 6x4, FL 106 4x2 and 6x4, FL/MB 70 4x2 and FL/MB 80 4x2 and 6x4. Seven engines were used in these trucks depending on model: Caterpillar 3176B-275, Cummins B Series-175, Cummins B Series-210, Detroit Diesel DDC Series 50-300, DDC Series 60-300, Mercedes-Benz OM 366 LA-170 and Mercedes-Benz OM 366 LA-210. GVW ratings were up to 60,600 for the FLB COE and GCW ratings were up to 200,000 pounds for FLD 120 and FLC 112 SD. The COE BBC was 87 inches, the shortest of all Freightliners at this time. Company president James Hebe announced that Freightliner agreed to purchase all assets and rights of fire truck manufacturer American LaFrance for 1996.

1996 FREIGHTLINER CENTURY CLASS **FREIGHTLINER**

Freightliner's 1996 Century Class 8 trucks were designed with circular headlights, the latter distinguishing them in appearance from other recent Freightliner models. But outer appearances were not the only fresh development for the new year. Freightliner developed a 12-liter engine with cooperation from Detroit Diesel and Mercedes-Benz. The new Century Class was intended to be sold side-by-side with the standard line of Freightliner trucks, according to Hebe. The Century Class has been offered as a medium conventional with 112-inch BBC and long conventional with 120-inch BBC dimension. Front axle was specified as a Rockwell FF-961, rear axle as a Rockwell RT-40-145 and transmission as Rockwell RM10-145A.

FREMONT-MAIS 1914-1915 — This obscure truck was produced by the Lauth-Juergens Motor Car Company of Fremont, Ohio. Only a single model rated at 3,000-pound capacity was produced by this manufacturer. It was powered by a four-cylinder Buda engine and had a Warner transmission with shaft drive to the rear axle. A 136-inch or 144-inch wheelbase was available. Burford trucks were successors to the Fremont-Mais when the latter name was changed to Burford after its designer, H.G. Burford, which later in 1917 became the Taylor Truck Company.

FRISBEE 1922-1923 — The Frisbee truck was named after its manufacturer, which was the Frisbee Truck Company of Webberville, Michigan. The only model was a 2-1/2-ton model powered by a 27.2 hp Continental C-4 engine with shaft drive. An altogether different Frisbie passenger car was built at the turn of the century in Connecticut.

1914 FRITCHLE PANEL BODY DELIVERY   OCW

FRITCHLE ELECTRIC 1911-1916 — The Fritchle Electric was named after its designer Oliver P. Fritchle who was a chemical engineer in Denver, Colorado, and began experimenting with storage batteries in 1897, which he patented in 1903. After organizing the Fritchle Electric Storage Battery Company, he proceeded with manufacturing and by 1905, began building electric passenger cars. In 1908, Fritchle challenged other electric auto builders to a range contest and since there were no takers, he made the 2,140-mile trip from Lincoln, Nebraska, to New York City by himself, gaining much publicity along the way.

What his journey proved was that his vehicle could travel up to 100 miles on a single charge. He called his vehicle the "100 Mile Electric" and changed the name of his company to the Fritchle Automobile and Electric Storage Battery Company. By 1909, he planned to go into manufacturing and leased an enormous roller skating rink in Denver to produce electric cars in the price range of $2,000 to $3,000.

By 1911, Fritchle introduced a commercial vehicle with a 1/2-ton capacity and an 80-mile advertised range. The wheelbase was 90 inches and it was fitted with a panel van body. The vehicle's top speed was 15 mph, and it was priced at $2,000. As electric vehicles faded from general popularity, Fritchle built a gasoline-electric hybrid in 1916, the year his commercial vehicles were discontinued. Passenger vehicles were built until 1919, when the company finally faded away.

FROME 1915-1916 — The *Commercial Vehicle* periodical announced in its January 1, 1916, issue that the R.L. Frome Manufacturing Company of Sheboygan, Wisconsin, was making extensive additions to its factory for the production of light delivery trucks with worm-drive after a year's worth of experimentation. Further development has not been recorded.

FRONTENAC 1906-1912 — Starting in 1866, the Abendroth and Root Manufacturing Company of Newburgh, New York, had produced a variety of high grade ironware products including spiral riveted pipe and tube boilers. With a factory consisting of forge, foundry, machine, pattern and sheet metal shops, the company began building large motor cars by 1906. These were powered by a 45 hp four-cylinder engine and used a 123-inch wheelbase.

The first Frontenac truck was rated at 5 tons and used double chain drive. In 1910, the company also offered a 3-ton and 4-ton model, and the following year a 2-ton model was also available. By 1911, the 3-ton was priced at $3,500 and the 4-ton at $3,650. A cone clutch and three-speed transmission was used with final drive by double chain. Both the 3-ton and 4-ton had a wheelbase of 122-1/2 inches.

1911 FRONTENAC 3-TON   RD

In the last year of commercial vehicle manufacture, the 5-ton model, which had a governor limiting its top speed to 12 miles per hour, was available with a flareboard body for $3,800. A limousine was available for $4,500 through 1913, when the company returned to ironware manufacturing exclusively. Motor vehicle manufacturing became the Abendroth & Root Manufacturing Company, builders of A & R trucks in 1913. This Frontenac make should not be confused with the Frontenac of Indianapolis, Indiana, which was in business building passenger cars during the early 1920s.

FRONTMOBILE 1918-1919 — The Safety Motor Company of Greenloch, New Jersey, was the origin of the Frontmobile, whose slogan was "The Car Built on Correct Principles." This vehicle was designed by C.H. Blomstrom and the vehicle's complexity was matched only by the company's unique history. Several patents were applied for regarding the vehicle's front-wheel-drive and LeRoi engine, which embodied the clutch, transmission, differential, worm-drive, radiator, gearshift and control levers. The patented design also involved the transmission gears, which were mounted on the differential housing and revolved at axle speed, as well as other innovations that made the vehicle hopelessly complicated, according to later sources. The Safety Motor Company was a subsidiary of the Bateman Manufacturing Company, manufacturers of farm, garden and orchard equipment.

The Blomstrom design did not sell and it was abandoned just as had been his Queen auto of 1904, Blomstrom of 1907, Gyroscope of 1908 and Rex of 1914. However, Blomstrom moved to Camden, New Jersey, where he organized the Camden Motors Corporation to build the Frontmobile. A 3/4-ton commercial version was developed using a Golden, Belknap and Swartz four-cylinder engine, 139-inch wheelbase and half-elliptic spring suspension. This vehicle incorporated many of the essential elements of the earlier passenger car design with the same end result. Camden Motors Corporation was liquidated in 1922 after producing up to as many as five vehicles.

1912 F-S 800-POUND PARCEL CAR   RD

F-S 1911-1912 — F-S Motors Company was named after Filer and Stowell, builders of the Corliss steam engine in Milwaukee, Wisconsin. F-S management decided to go into gasoline-powered vehicle manu-

155

facturing and acquired two companies for this purpose: Petrel Motor Car Company and Beaver Manufacturing Company, the latter being a builder of gasoline engines. At a large new factory F-S began building engines and cars, as well as trucks by 1912.

Three models of commercial vehicles were offered. The Parcel Car was a small closed van rated at 800-pound capacity and powered by a one-cylinder 12 hp engine. It had a 90-inch wheelbase and was priced at $600. Advertising stated "Any $10 a week boy, who can be trusted with a horse, can run this simple car." The 3/4-ton and 3-1/2-ton trucks were powered by two different four-cylinder engines. The latter was a forward-control design and used a 120-inch wheelbase. This company was short-lived.

1918 FULTON 1-1/2-TON   MROZ

FULTON 1917-1925 — The Clyde Motor Truck Company of Farmingdale, Long Island, New York, began building Fulton trucks in 1917. There had been several other vehicles up to that time named Fulton, but not concurrently with those of Clyde manufacture. William F. Melhuish, president of Clyde, organized the company with the intention of building a medium-size truck with the latest engineering advances of the time and plans were set to build 1,000 units in the first year.

At first, the Fulton truck was rated at 1-1/2 tons and featured a 30 hp four-cylinder L-head engine cast enbloc. Russel internal gear drive was used and the truck rode on 34x3-1/2 front and 34x2-1/2 dual rear tires. Price was $1,090 in 1917. The most notable element of the Fulton was its circular radiator with a prominent top flange and its correspondingly cylindrical hood giving it a distinctive appearance. Also, the radiator had a seven-gallon capacity, one of the largest of any truck built at that time.

By 1919, prices had increased to $1,850 for the 1-1/2-ton model. A 2-ton model had also been introduced for $2,350. Fulton built a right-hand drive passenger car in 1920 powered by a four-cylinder engine, but this vehicle never made it past the prototype stage and it was the only passenger car Fulton assembled. The company decided against going into passenger car production despite positive press coverage. Manufacturing faded out after 1923, although the company continued to offer trucks for sale until 1925. By 1924, the prices were reduced to $1,495 and $2,135, respectively. The 1-1/2-ton weighed 3,450 pounds while the 2-ton weighed 4,950 pounds making this a rather heavy design considering the two trucks' load capacities.

By the end of all production in 1925, Fulton trucks were available as a 1-ton Model A with 130-inch wheelbase or a 2-ton Model C with 137-inch wheelbase, both powered by a 22.5 hp four-cylinder Buda WTU engine. Both engines used a Zenith carburetor and Simms ignition. The Model A had 35x5 front and rear pneumatic tires while the Model C had 34x4 front and 34x7 rear solid rubber tires. Both trucks used a Coventry transmission, Columbia front axle and Sheldon rear axle, the 2-ton fitted with heavier-duty units. Steering was by Lavine Gear and wheels were made by Hoopes Brothers and Darlington. No heavier trucks were built by Fulton Motor Truck Company (the Clyde name used only in the first year of manufacture), which ceased production before the 1926 model year.

FWD 1910 to date — Ottow Zachow and his brother-in-law William Besserdich were machinists in Clintonville, Wisconsin, just after the turn of the century. Ottow Zachow patented a double-Y universal joint in a ball and socket allowing the wheels of a car to rotate and be steered

simultaneously. The two of them built an experimental steam-powered car of their own design, which they called the Z&B and which utilized the new U-joints on the axles.

The steam engine was not a success. They built a second car using a 45 hp gasoline engine, later calling their 3,800-pound vehicle the Battleship. It was used to prove out the worth of their patented U-joints without going into the aspects of sales and marketing.

With the financial backing of Dr. W.H. Finney and investors, they started the Badger Four Wheel Drive Automobile Company in 1909. Seven cars and a 2-ton truck were produced, but Dr. Finney bowed out of the venture and Zachow and Besserdich returned his $1,800 investment. That did not slow them down, and by 1911 the company became known as the Four Wheel Drive Automobile Company and was referred to simply as FWD. Zachow and Besserdich got their patent rights back and Walter A. Olen became president of the company.

One of the first FWD cars was tested by the U.S. Army when it was converted to a scout truck and set out on a grueling 1,500-mile cross-country test run. By 1913, a factory was built near to the Zachow-Besserdich machine shop and as a result of the outbreak of World War I, demand for FWD trucks grew rapidly. The U.S. military ordered so many FWD trucks that Kissel, Mitchell and Premier were licensed to build them in addition to the output from an even larger plant in Clintonville. By the time the war was over, 15,000 Model B FWD trucks had been built for the U.S. military, making FWD the largest producer of four-wheel-drive trucks in the world.

The well-known Model B was powered by a four-cylinder Wisconsin engine using a three-speed constant-mesh transmission. Front and rear axles were built by FWD with torque arms taking the propulsion force. Sixteen mph was achieved by the 6,400-pound vehicle, which used an 8.9:1 high-gear ratio. External-contracting brakes were used on all four wheels. The open cabs had right-hand steering at that time.

After the war, the U.S. military had about 30,000 surplus trucks. Since half of them were FWD that had been allocated to state highway departments, the company stayed in business supplying spare parts at first, until demand for new trucks once again began to grow. A new factory was opened in Kitchener, Ontario, Canada, in 1919. FWD also purchased the Menominee Motor Truck Company in 1921. The standard Model B FWD continued to be built until the early 1930s. Along the way, a number of improvements were made and pneumatic tires became first optional and later, standard equipment.

1918 FWD MODEL B   FWD

1921 FWD MODEL B FIRE TRUCK   FWD

For 1924, the 3-ton Model B with 124-inch wheelbase chassis was listed for $4,200. It was powered by a Wisconsin A engine, with Stromberg carburetor and Eisemann ignition, rated at 36.1 hp. Schwartz wheels still carried 36x6 front and rear solid rubber tires, although pneumatic tires were available at extra cost. The Model B used a Cotta DAE transmission and steering was by Ross. Starter and generator were listed at extra cost.

A conventional FWD was developed in the late 1920s with closed cabs for civilian use and a C-cab for some military applications. Because of the wide range of uses of FWD trucks by state highway departments and various industrial institutions, the company began to build specialized vehicles and equipment as the demand developed. These applications included construction, fire apparatus, logging and oil field work.

1926 FWD 3-TON MODEL B SNOWPLOW TRUCK   KP

Once FWD acquired rights to manufacture Cotta transmissions, the early Model B units with ratios of 48:1 were redesigned for ratios up to 140:1, due primarily to advances in metallurgy such as steel-hardening processes. Five-speed transmissions were available and later, using auxiliary gearboxes along with 10- and 12-speed transmissions, ratios of 600:1. They were made durable for extraordinary pulling power. The four-wheel-brake design was improved continuously through the 1920s and 1930s.

1930 FWD   DW

FWD entered car racing in 1932 and developed a four-wheel-drive Indianapolis car that placed fourth in the Indianapolis 500 that year. It was powered by a Miller air-cooled V-8 engine. The car was raced at Indianapolis without further luck. A similar car was raced at Pike's Peak during the late 1940s and early 1950s with more success. The FWD racing program was terminated in 1953.

FWD expanded its model range in 1934 to include a lighter 2-ton series. In appearance, this series had a more modern cab with a one-piece slanted windshield and a V-type radiator grille. Keeping up with the latest styling in the industry, FWD brought out a more streamlined COE cab with a two-piece V-type windshield in 1937. By that year, FWD listed 23 different models from the 1-1/2-ton Model HS to the 15-ton Model MX6, with chassis prices ranging from $2,440 for the lightest to $12,225 for the latter model. All of these were powered by Waukesha engines except the Model B, which listed FWD's own engine. Horsepower ranged from 56 for the Model B to 198 for the Model M10 (SAE ratings were 33.75 hp to 79.4 hp). Other than FWD's own transmissions, the company also used Brown-Lipe, Cotta and Fuller units on certain models. Also, besides its own front and

rear axles, both Timken and Wisconsin units were used to supply these major components, sometimes in combination such as on the Model HS and 7-ton Model T26 on which the front axles were Timken while the rear axles were Wisconsin.

A four-door COE crew cab was also introduced for the public utility market and, according to some sources, this was the first in the commercial truck field in 1937. By then, double reduction axles were available and multiple speed axles were also offered. The following year Cummins diesel engines were made available in FWD trucks.

During the 1930s, when motor vehicle styling was emphasized year to year as a competitive edge over other manufacturers, FWD concentrated on engineering and ruggedness. COE truck tractors were available in 6x4 configuration. When the industry adopted aerodynamic art deco-type styling, FWD remained more conservative, although the T-40 and T-60 models of the late 1930s did receive pontoon fenders. These two models were rated at 40,000- and 60,000-pound GVW, respectively.

1936 FWD 6X4 TANKER   NAHC

For 1940, FWD announced a new cab for its T-32 model, which was rated by that time at 40,000-pound GVW. It was powered by a 98 hp six-cylinder engine using a five-speed transmission or optional overdrive unit, and both front and rear axles were the full-floating type with single-reduction spiral-bevel design and manually locking differentials for use in severe conditions. A conventional T-32 version was also offered with round grille and V-type two-piece windshield. Other conventional trucks included Models SU, SUA, CUA and MJ5 and these were all in the 4-ton to 6-ton range.

As in World War I, FWD provided the military with trucks during the Second World War. These were heavy-duty civilian styled trucks including a COE SU-based model with open cab and two individual windshields for the Marine Corps.

1957 FWD TERACRUZER XM401   FWD

After World War II, FWD continued to supply 4x4 conventional trucks in all sizes. The heavy-duty were the U series with GVW rating of 44,000 pounds. In the early 1950s, FWD adopted the "Chicago" cab built by International and used by other independent manufacturers. COE trucks used Chicago cabs stretched widthwise. In 1958, a second type was built using Ford C-series cabs with a wire-mesh radiator grille and unique fenders. Some specialty trucks were developed at this time, such as the extra-short wheelbase off-highway Model BXU truck used to drill holes for utility poles. It was distinguished by a windshield canted forward at the top and was dubbed "The Blue Ox," referring to one of its earliest trucks with that nickname.

In 1958, FWD also introduced its Tractioneer line, which was built over a quarter century primarily for concrete mixer and construction work. A flat-faced COE was built in addition to conventional trucks, some with front axle setback under the cab. All were four-wheel-drive, but in addition to the standard model line, FWD built 6x4, 10x8 with tandem front axle, and even a 12x10 version also with tandem front axle. The standard cab at that time was adopted from Dodge with a wrap-around windshield. In 1963, FWD acquired the fire apparatus division of the Seagrave Corporation of Columbus, Ohio, which had already acquired the Maxim Motor Company in 1956.

1966 FWD MODEL C4-4394   **WS**

FWD built a series of huge trucks called the Teracruzer. These were 8x8 off-highway trucks originally prototyped in 1956. They were powered by a 250 hp 628-cubic inch horizontally-opposed eight-cylinder air-cooled Continental engine and the early ones used a non-synchronized four-speed transmission; later had the Allison TX-340 semi-automatic four-speed transmission. FWD designated the Teracruzer as the MM-1, and it was later used for the Pak-Stanvac Pakistan project to haul entire oil well drilling equipment outfits in monsoon climate conditions where no other vehicles were able to maneuver.

The Teracruzer's chassis and cab weight was 22,000 pounds alone, yet due to the huge pontoon tires, the ground pressure was low and allowed the truck access to remote areas in adverse conditions. One military version towed the Martin TM-61 Matador missile on non-driving terra-wheeled trailers. These were known as the FWD Model 8-320 B. The "air-bag" tires were 40x42 made by Goodyear and the vehicle could cruise as 40 mph. The last version, called the XM-401, used 50-inch-wide Goodyear tires, yet the vehicle could still achieve 35 mph.

1979 FWD 8X8 CEMENT MIXER CHASSIS   **KP**

Another similar type of development, which was created by FWD in the late 1960s, was the 8x8 Crash and Fire Rescue (CFR) truck used for emergency work at airports. The P-2 model trucks weighed 65,000 and were powered by two 340 hp engines joined through an FWD-developed collector-box to dual transmissions. Either engine could be used to propel the truck or drive its pumps. When both engines were used to power the vehicle, acceleration was 0 to 55 mph in 55 seconds. The truck had single tires on each of its wheels with double tandem axles and carried 200 gallons of liquid foam concentrate as well as 2,300 gallons of water.

At about the same time, FWD developed the Forward Mover series for highway duty. This series comprised heavy-duty trucks with a 6x4 drive configuration in which the front axle was not driven. The B5-2178 conventional FWD trucks resembled the Tractioneer line with the Dodge cab, although some had an optional forward-slanting windshield. FWD also built numerous crane carriers with drivelines up to 10x8 configuration. As early as 1939, FWD built half-cabs for its crane carriers to make room for the shovel boom during transit.

By 1970, FWD had 93 models using five different drive configurations with conventional, axle-under-cab (set back) conventional and COE versions. Diesel engines were four-, six- and eight-cylinder built by Cummins, Detroit Diesel and International from 145 hp to 238 hp. FWD single reduction rear axles and five-speed Fuller transmissions were most commonly used. Vacuum, air and hydraulic brake combinations were used. For 1970, FWD truck production was 1,097, below 1,645 units, which was the highest output year since 1956.

1983 FWD COE CHASSIS   **FWD**

By 1978, FWD offered three series: the RB 4x4 conventional, the CB conventional 6x6, 8x6, 8x8 and 10x8 and the DF series 4x4 COE model. Diesel engines were up to 350 hp by this time. FWD continued to build custom-designed trucks for specialized application, including four-wheel-steer and front-drive low-bed trucks.

1995 FWD RB-44 PLOW   **FWD**

The FWD factory in Clintonville, Wisconsin, has employed 450 people to date. However, most of the production has been concentrated on Seagrave fire apparatus. About 250 Seagrave fire trucks have been built during the 1990s annually to date. These have included some four-wheel-drive fire engines. Only about 5 to 10 FWD trucks have been built per year as of 1995.

G

GABRIEL 1913-1920 — The Gabriel Motor Truck Company started building 1-ton trucks in 1913 in Cleveland, Ohio. It appears that this company was an outgrowth of the Gabriel Auto Company of Cleveland, which started manufacturing motor vehicles in 1910. The two Gabriels were one and the same.

The company's origin stemmed from the W.H. Gabriel Carriage and Wagon Company, which had been established in 1851. By 1910, Gabriel had built its first passenger car and displayed it at the Cleveland Automobile Show. It was powered by a 30 hp engine and performed well, but the company announced it would add the Grabowsky truck to its model line.

By 1913, the company dropped its passenger car production and built a 1-ton truck model line, which was joined in 1914 by a 2-ton model. Through World War I, Gabriel also built 1-1/2-, 3-1/2- and 4-ton trucks as well. By 1917, the 1-1/2-ton was powered by a four-cylinder engine and used a four-speed transmission with worm-drive. However, the Gabriel company did not survive the postwar recession.

1914 GABRIEL MODEL J   OCW

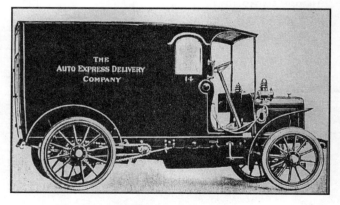

1907 GAETH TYPE K DELIVERY   MROZ

GAETH 1905-1910 — Paul Gaeth built bicycles, stationary engines and an experimental steam car in 1898, and subsequently a gasoline-powered vehicle. After working for People's Automobile Company in Cleveland, Ohio, which went bankrupt, he organized the Gaeth Automobile Company in 1902. His first one-cylinder car was called the Gaethmobile. He built and sold cars with three-cylinder engines, planetary transmission and shaft drive by 1904. The next year he developed a four-cylinder engine and sliding gear transmission, calling the new Gaeth the Triplex.

It was not until 1905 that the first commercial vehicle version of the Gaeth was offered. The early Gaeth 3/4-ton Type K light truck powered by a 12 hp engine using a two-speed transmission and double chain drive. The following year a light truck and van

was built on the Type XII chassis and in 1907 it was built using the Type XV chassis with a 15 hp four-cylinder Gaeth engine. Load capacity was one ton by this time. Swinehart solid rubber tires 34-inch diameter in front and 38-inch in rear were used for the 1907 Type K Delivery Wagon. List price was $1,200 including van body, two side oil lamps and set of tools.

1908 GAETH 1-TON VAN   OCW

Meanwhile, the Gaeth passenger cars were successfully driven on the Glidden Tours of 1907 and 1908 scoring 997 and 1,000 points, respectively. Factory price for a Gaeth was $3,500 from 1907 through 1910. However, as well-engineered as the Gaeth vehicles were, poor management of the company led to its necessary acquisition by Stuyvesant Motor Car Company of Cleveland. Paul Gaeth remained an inventor and antique auto restoration pioneer until his death at age 79 in 1952.

GALE 1905-1907 — When the Sears Roebuck and Company was looking for a car to offer in its all-inclusive catalog, the company's agents finally settled on the Western Tool Works in Galesburg, Ohio. The first one-cylinder Gale Model A cars were sold in 1905 and a van with a 73-inch wheelbase was also available. The one-cylinder engine developed 10 hp, and the vehicles had a planetary transmission with single chain drive to the rear axle. Pneumatic tires were standard equipment. The body was hinged at the rear to create easy access to the driveline. The Model H had a false hood since the engine was located under the seat. The small van's capacity was only 200 pounds and it was priced at $750.

In addition to autos and light vans, the Western Tool Works also produced screw machines, wall safes and emery wheel dressers. The company had an international dealership established and a number of its motor vehicles were sold in Australia, Borneo, Europe and New Zealand. Total production was 140 two-cylinder vehicles and 600 one-cylinder vehicles before financial trouble led to the company's sale to Percy Robson, who reintroduced the vehicles on the market under his own name.

GALLOWAY 1908-1911 — The William Galloway Company of Waterloo, Iowa, sold highwheelers powered by a 14 hp two-cylinder horizontally-opposed engine located under the seat with a planetary transmission and had chain drive to the rear wheels. Suspension was with full-elliptic leaf springs front and rear, and steering was right-hand. The light open cab truck had an 85-inch wheelbase and had 32x1-1/2 front and 33x3 rear carriage-type wood spoke wheels with solid tires suitable for rural areas where the vehicles were marketed. In fact William Galloway scoffed at feeding horses and used the subject of comparison between animal and machine as his sales pitch. Price in 1908 was $570. Although Galloway designed these vehicles, the Dart Manufacturing Company, also of Waterloo, Iowa, manufactured them for Galloway. By 1911, the marque's name was changed to Maytag, and William Galloway was involved in auto manufacturing again in 1915 with a car called the Arabian.

1908 GALLOWAY HAYS

GARDNER 1927-1932 — The Gardner Motor Company was Russell E. Gardner's story of quick financial success and ultimate failure as an automobile manufacturer. Gardner began by building Banner buggies in St. Louis, Missouri. By 1915, his company was producing bodies for Chevrolet alongside his Gardner wagons. Gardner's shop assembled complete Chevrolet cars by 1915, though he subsequently sold his dealership to General Motors.

With his two sons Gardner continued as the Gardner Motor Company, which built assembled cars using Lycoming engines. The first Gardners were powered by a 35 hp four-cylinder engine and had a wheelbase of 112 inches. At the outset the company was successful, but by the late 1920s sales lagged and Gardner entered the field of commercial vehicle fabrication with ambulances and hearses.

The hearses were built in cooperation with the St. Louis Coffin Company. Lycoming straight-eight engines were used with four-speed transmissions available and hydraulic four-wheel brakes as standard equipment. By 1930, sales continued to lag and Gardner built ambulances and hearses using Chevrolet chassis. The Gardner passenger car line was discontinued in 1931 but the company still built a few professional cars using Pontiac chassis through 1932 before the Gardner Motor Company was entirely liquidated.

GARFORD 1908-1933 — The Federal Manufacturing Company of Elyria, Ohio, began building automobile components in 1903, eventually becoming the Garford Company in 1909 at that location. Arthur L. Garford had been treasurer of the American Bicycle Company prior to starting the Federal company. For the first few years of its existence, Federal had a contract with Studebaker to build cars and was legally barred from using the Garford name on its vehicles. However, in 1907 Garford did show two cars under its own name, prompting Studebaker to make legal threats, and subsequently all Garford cars were called Studebaker-Garford or simply Studebaker. The Garford Motor Car Company was listed in New York City by 1908 as a builder of "taximeter cabs," which used their own chassis and featured easily removable engine and transmission.

Once the contract with Studebaker expired in 1910, Garford did build all its cars and trucks under the Garford name. Garford built a few limousines between 1911 and 1913; however, by 1912, the passenger car division of Garford was acquired by Willys-Overland. The truck-building venture continued as a separate marque using the Garford name and emblem.

The first Garford trucks were COE 5-ton models. They were powered by four-cylinder L-head engines with four-speed transmissions amidships with dual chain drive to the rear axle. Garford trucks were easily recognizable with a so-called "Roman Chariot" cowl a the top of which protruded a curved filler pipe.

In 1915, Garford moved to Lima, Ohio, and became the Garford Motor Truck Company. A 3-1/2-ton model was added to the line, and it was also a cab-over design but used worm-drive. By 1916, Garford offered 1-, 1-1/2- and 2-ton conventional models also. Drawbars were standard on the largest Garford trucks for towing two-wheel and four-wheel trailers.

1916 GARFORD 2-TON TANKER MROZ

For 1917, Garford offered three truck tractors. With semi-trailers these had a capacity rating of 4-1/2-, 7- and 10-ton. During World War I Garford trucks were used by the military. Some conventional Garford trucks used Holt-Caterpillar tracks in place of rear wheels as an early version of "halftracks." About 1,000 of the Liberty trucks of World War I were built by Garford, among other companies.

The cab-over-engine design was abandoned in 1920, and these were superseded by conventional models from 1-1/4-ton to 5-ton capacity. All were powered by four-cylinder Buda engines with four-speed transmissions and either Timken worm-drive or Garford chain drive. By 1924, Garford offered a 1-ton Model 15 with 132-inch wheelbase and 34x5 front and rear pneumatic tires as standard equipment. The 1-1/2-ton Model 30 had a 144-inch wheelbase and used 32x6 front and rear pneumatic tires. The 4-ton Model 80 with 162-inch wheelbase used 36x5 front and 36x10 rear solid rubber tires. The 5-ton Model 68D also with 162-inch wheelbase was powered by a 40.0 hp four-cylinder Buda BTU engine with Garford's own 68D transmission. The model had 36x6 front and 40x12 rear solid tires with pneumatic tires being optional on the front along with Timken axles. The 7-ton Model 151 differed from the previous model in that it had the Garford 151 transmission and Garford 151 rear axle, as well as 36x6 front and 40x12 rear solid rubber tires.

By the mid-1920s, seven-speed and eight-speed transmissions were used with two or four speeds in reverse. A bus chassis for up to 29-passengers was available for $4,350. It featured a low frame that was built up and over the rear axle. In addition, for 1925 and 1926 a 17-passenger parlor car and passenger coach chassis was offered with six-cylinder engines.

Relay Motors of Wabash, Indiana, purchased Garford in August of 1927. With this acquisition the conglomerate's headquarters were moved to Lima, Ohio, where Garford was already located, and four trucks were offered: Commerce, Garford, Relay and Service. At this point in time, the Garford designs resembled Relay models in the 1-ton to 4-ton range. Both were powered by six-cylinder Buda engines, but Garford still used worm-drive and steel disc wheels instead of Relay's artillery-style wheels.

After its acquisition, Garford truck sales plummeted from 700 units in 1926 to a little more than 100 by 1929. After the Great Depression started, production faded out until Relay went into receivership and was purchased by Consolidated Motors in 1933. Attempts at revitalizing the Garford truck marque met with no success and after 1933 Garfords were no longer produced by the new parent company.

GAR WOOD 1936-1938 — The Gar Wood Industries, a truck body and boat builder, was located in Detroit, Michigan, and was the result of cooperation with William B. Stout, who was the designer of the Ford Trimotor aircraft and a streamlined streetcar for Pullman in 1934.

1938 GAR WOOD WISCONSIN ROAD CRUISER   KP

The Gar Wood Model C of 1936 used Stout's design that consisted of a framework of welded tubes covered by a thin layer of aluminum alloy. This bus was powered by a Ford V-8 engine and was located behind the rear axle. Gar Wood began building such buses also using Chevrolet and Dodge engines along with the standard Ford engines and 175 of these were built by 1939, when the operation was sold to the General American Transportation Company of Chicago, which built the Aerocoach.

GARY 1909 — The Gary landaulet taxi was built in Chicago, Illinois. The company advertised its vehicle by stating "We Built Nothing But..." The 18 hp engine was easily interchangeable in 20 minutes, it was claimed. Although the passenger compartment was enclosed with stylish coachwork, the driver sat completely in the open without roof or doors for any protection from the Chicago weather. The Gary Taxicab Company had the vehicles built for them, but it is unknown precisely where or how many were actually produced.

1921 GARY   MROZ

GARY 1916-1927 — The Gary Motor Truck Company started in Gary, Indiana, in 1916, just two years after the Gary Automobile Manufacturing Company, also of Gary, Indiana, built a few six-cylinder passenger cars. The earlier Gary lasted only for one year and from all indications was not affiliated with the Gary Motor Truck Company.

The first Gary truck models were 3/4-, 1-, 1-1/2- and 2-ton capacity. By 1922, when the company incorporated as the Gary Motor Corporation, only the 1-ton model was available at first. This was the year when Gary switched to Buda engines and the model

line was again expanded from 1-1/2-ton to 5-ton capacity trucks. The company's reorganization was headed by Frank Dawson, who had presided over the company previously. A recapitalization of $1 million took place in 1922.

Price changes were announced in the following schedule; the 1-1/2-ton Model F was $2,600 dropped to $1,675, the 2-1/2-ton Model I was $2,900 dropped to $2,150, the 2-1/2-ton Model J was $3,800 dropped to $2,550, the 3-1/2-ton was $4,900 dropped to $3,550 and the 5-ton Model M was $5,900 dropped to $4,000. The price slashing apparently had a positive effect on sales and Gary remained in business, although not for long.

By 1925, the 1-ton Model WLD with 132-inch wheelbase was powered by a 22.5 hp four-cylinder Buda engine coupled to a Fuller TU 3/4 transmission. Front and rear axles were Timken and both front and rear Prudden wheels carried 36x5 solid rubber tires. Chassis price was $1,590. The 1-1/2-ton Model G15 with 144-inch wheelbase was powered by a 25.6 hp Buda KBUI engine. Chassis price was $2,590. The 2-1/2-ton Model E25 with 148-inch wheelbase was powered by a 28.9 hp Buda EBUI engine and was priced at $3,250. The 3-ton Model Y30 with 150-inch wheelbase was powered by a 32.4 hp Buda YBUI engine and was priced at $3,550. The 3-1/2-ton Model Y35 with 162-inch wheelbase was powered by the same engine as the previous model and was priced at $4,250. The heftiest Gary truck was the 5-ton Model B50 with 182-inch wheelbase and was powered by a 40.0 hp Buda BTU engine. Chassis price was $4,850. On all models Timken front and rear axles were used, Stromberg carburetors and Eisemann ignition were utilized exclusively, solid rubber tires were universal and steering was by Ross in each case. The three heaviest models used Brown-Lipe transmissions instead of Fuller. The company did not survive the year 1927.

GAS-ELECTRIC 1928 — The Philadelphia Rapid Transit Company commissioned engineers at Mitten Management to design and build an experimental hybrid-powered taxi. The chassis is actually a Willys-Knight Model 70-A. Two General Electric Motors, similar to the ones used in the P.R.T. gas-electric bus, were connected to the Knight sleeve valve engine. The body's special design featured one door on the right side and two doors on the left side. It was claimed that this design provided better acceleration and less maintenance, but the real purpose was to keep passengers from jumping out into traffic. *The Commercial Car Journal* reported on a successful test but only the single prototype was built.

GASMOBILE 1901 — The Automobile Company of America in New York City built a delivery van in 1901 powered by a 10 hp three-cylinder engine and two-speed planetary transmission. Tires were 32-inch solid rubber and advertising stated a front boot gave room for tools "and a bank of radiating coils below cools the jacket water." Four semi-elliptic springs made up the suspension. The carburetor at that time was called a "vaporizer." Passenger cars were also built.

GAY 1913-1915 — The S.G. Gay Company of Ottowa, Illinois, was briefly engaged in the fabrication of 3/4-ton and 1-ton trucks. Both models were powered by four-cylinder Buda engines, located in front under a hood, and they were coupled to a three-speed transmission with double chain final drive. Solid tires were used exclusively, and the suspension consisted of semi-elliptic springs for each wheel.

GAYLORD 1910-1913 — Located in Gaylord, Michigan, the Gaylord Motor Car Company's slogan was "All Roads Are Easy to the Gaylord." Only one model was offered, which was a four-passenger touring car that could easily be converted over to a utility-type vehicle for hauling packages or to a depot wagon that could carry up to eight people. Thermo-syphon cooling, Schiebler carburetor and multiple disc clutch were featured. With Guy Hamilton as chief promoter, the company also claimed to be "Pioneer Utility Car Builders."

The Gaylord was powered by a variety of four-cylinder engines ranging from 20 hp to 40 hp and prices ranged between $1,000 and $1,500. Two slots at the rear of the body allowed for rails that held a short truck bed. The design also featured semi-elliptic springs in front and inverted transverse platform springs attached at the center of the rear frame crossmember on some of the models. By 1912, approximately 350 cars were sold, but Gaylord's decision to expand its line and use different overhead-valve engines led to serious financial woes. The company was no more before the end of 1913.

1917 GEM 1/2-TON PANEL DELIVERY   HAC

GEM 1917-1919 — The Gem Motor Car Company was incorporated in Grand Rapids, Michigan, in December 1917. Chassis for the two models of Gem, a Touring model and a Light Delivery, were purchased from Pontiac. Both models used Golden, Belknap and Swartz engines. The 1/2-ton Light Delivery used a three-speed transmission and shaft drive and the wheelbase was 108 inches. It is believed the bodies for both models were supplied by the Hayes company. All assembly was performed in Grand Rapids, and the plan was to manufacture parts there as well, but this never materialized as the company folded in 1919.

GENERAL 1903 — The General Automobile and Manufacturing Company of Cleveland, Ohio, was the successor to the Hansen Automobile Company when Rasmus Hansen reorganized his earlier business enterprise in 1902. Hansen had built a light runabout, and under the new name also offered a light van with a 1/2-ton capacity. It is unclear whether the van was powered by the earlier 8 hp one-cylinder engine or the later 14 hp two-cylinder engine or if both were available in 1903. Production was up to one vehicle per day, but additional capital was not forthcoming as stockholders anticipated legal action by the Association of Licensed Automobile Manufacturers, which had not given Hansen a license to build motor vehicles per the Selden Patent. No lawsuit followed as General went bankrupt at the end of 1903. The 25 remaining General vehicles along with the company's assets were bought by Studebaker, which began building its own electric vehicles at that time.

1936 GENERAL CAB   A&A

GENERAL CAB 1930-1938 — The Yellow Truck and Coach Manufacturing Company built General Cab taxis, formerly Yellow Cab and also called General Motors Cab. As carried over from previous design when it was renamed in 1930, the vehicle used a six-cylinder Buick engine, which was superseded by a GMC six-cylinder powerplant in 1931. This ended when production was suspended entirely for the year 1935. In 1936, the design changed entirely

by using 124-1/2-inch wheelbase Chevrolets with Chevrolet truck rear axles. The new model was designated as the O-16, and in 1937, the O-17 model used a 127-inch wheelbase Chevrolet chassis, as did the O-18 model in 1938. Divider windows were optional, but jump seats were standard on all General Cab taxis.

GENERAL-DETROIT; GENERAL-PACIFIC 1937-1955 — The General Fire Truck Corporation was located in Detroit, Michigan, and began building fire trucks using a chassis of its own design and construction with a Packard Eight engine and a Ford cab. By the following year, a Packard V-12 chassis was utilized but fire apparatus was mounted on chassis from Federal, Ford and GMC.

By 1939, General expanded its model line to include ladder trucks and quadruple combinations. After World War II, a subsidiary in Los Angeles, California, called General-Pacific also began building pumper fire trucks. The Detroit factory continued to build fire trucks using Available, Duplex and other purchased truck chassis. The 1955 Federal quadruple combination truck was one of the last fire engines built by General-Detroit. General-Pacific production ceased at the same time as that of General-Detroit.

GENERAL ELECTRIC See HOWARD

GENERAL VEHICLE see G.V.

GENERAL MONARCH 1932-1935 — The General Fire Truck Corporation of St. Louis, Missouri, built assembled fire engines for a brief period. The fire trucks were powered by 200 hp engines and were recognizable by their large single spotlight located in the center of the headlights. By 1934, General Monarch trucks had flared fenders, a V-grille and windshield, and were ahead of their time in terms of styling. However, the company did not survive the year 1935.

GENEVA 1910-1921 — The Geneva Wagon Company began in 1894. The factory was located in Geneva, New York, at the former sight of the Pierce, Butler and Pierce Company. The first gasoline-powered motor vehicle was built in 1899 by Geneva, yet the company continued building horsedrawn wagons exclusively until 1910. At that time Geneva went into the commercial motor vehicle manufacturing business with what was described as "auto wagons, light and medium express wagons, panel top delivery wagons, ambulances and wagonettes." President of the company was M.F. Blaine and vice-president was C.G. Blaine.

The light commercial vehicles, which had a 96-inch wheelbase, were rated at 1/2-ton and 3/4-ton capacity. They were powered by a Beaver two-cylinder engine with a planetary transmission and double chain drive. As late as 1919, this tried-and-true design had become obsolete and the company tried to rebound with a passenger car for the first time. With a wheelbase of 139 inches and a six-cylinder Herschell-Spillman engine with a four-speed transmission and floating rear axle, it was an extravagant last-ditch effort to save the company, which it did not.

GENEVA STEAM 1901-1902 — The Geneva Cycle Company, which was started in 1894, became the Geneva Automobile and Manufacturing Company by 1901. With J.A. Carter as president and A. Thompson as chief engineer, the company announced it was ready "to demonstrate to any unbiased mind" that the Geneva steam car was the best that "inventive genius and mechanical skill can produce." The two-cylinder marine steam engine powered the rear axle directly through a differential. A combination water tube and tube boiler was incorporated in the design.

The first Geneva Steam Model A Runabout was finished in 1901. Among the three runabout models, touring and Dos-a-Dos models, Geneva also offered a Steam Light Delivery for 1901 and 1902. The first Geneva car took part in the New York to Buffalo run that was canceled midway due to the assassination of President McKinley.

In 1902, a Geneva steamer was raced at Grosse Point, Michigan, and it defeated its opponent White Steam car as well as a Winton but was bettered by Ford's 999 race car driven by Barney Oldfield. This contributed to media exposure and about 30 Geneva vehicles were sold. However, the small town of Geneva, Ohio, could not adequately support a large manufacturing facility. Despite financial assurances from investors in Cleveland, Ohio, the marque disappeared after one last show at the Macy's Exhibition Hall in 1904, which was the year the Colonial Brass Company bought all of Geneva's assets.

1922 GERSIX 3-1/2-TON FLATBED   **KEN**

GERSIX 1915-1922 — Louis Gerlinger, Sr., along with sons George and Louis, Jr., organized the Gerlinger Motor Car Company in Portland, Oregon, after the collapse of the Stoddard-Dayton Auto Company in 1913, for whom they had been a dealership under that name. Another son, Edward, joined the company, and at that point it became the Gerlinger Motor Car Company, selling Federal, Menominee and Standard trucks in Seattle, Washington, as well.

The first Gersix truck's fabrication started in 1914 in the Portland dealership when demand for a more powerful truck for mountainous conditions prompted the Gerlingers to build their own vehicle. The marque's name derived from a combination of the Gerlinger last name and the fact that the truck was powered by a six-cylinder engine built by Continental.

It is believed that the Gersix was America's first production truck to be powered by a six-cylinder engine. It was designed by shop foreman George Peters, and it was finished in 1915. Without easy access to pressed steel material, the Gersix truck employed structural steel, which was featured on later Gersix trucks. The company moved into another shop in Tacoma, Washington, in 1916. The company tried to market a kit for the conversion of automobiles to tractors.

The second Gersix truck was built using a Buda engine and it is believed that the third Gersix had a six-cylinder Wisconsin engine. However, in 1917, due partly to mismanagement and to parts shortages, the Gerlinger company went bankrupt and was sold to Edgar K. Worthington, the building landlord, and Captain Frederick W. Keen, an ex-Coast Guard Captain and investor.

Having closed the Portland operation, the new owners incorporated as the Gersix Manufacturing Company in Seattle. At first, the company was small employing five people. Parts shortages forced them to seek new vendors without much success. The Gersix company began manufacturing its own castings and various metal components including steel frames and axles, while a few suppliers ensured the delivery of essential components such as engines, constant mesh transmissions and worm-drives. Production was only one per month, and total output amounted to 100 Gersix trucks over all years of manufacturing. The *Automobile Trade Journal* announced that Gersix would build six-cylinder trucks in Tacoma. They were rated at 2-1/2-ton capacity with a wheelbase of 150 inches or 170 inches at prices of $2,500 and $2,550, respectively. However, during World War I production was interrupted and the shop repaired short-wheelbase Japanese trucks.

In 1919, Captain Keen sold his interest to Harry W. Kent, who was a partner of Worthington's in other ventures. In 1922, Gersix acquired the assets of HRM and Vulcan, which were custom builders of trucks in the same area, although it is uncertain if these Vulcan trucks were merely assembled units originally manufactured in Pennsylvania by the Driggs-Seabury Ordnance Company. Details about HRM are unknown. Buda and Wisconsin engines were adopted and the model line was expanded from the single Model G to several others ranging from 1-1/2-ton up to 3-1/2-ton capacity. The year 1922 became the highest production period for Gersix

trucks with a total of 53 units produced. At the end of 1922, Kent and Worthington reorganized as the Kenworth Truck Corporation, which is in production to date.

GIANT 1911-1922 — Giant trucks were first built by the Chicago Pneumatic Tool Company in Chicago, Illinois, in 1911, according to some sources. Apparently, the first was a 3/4-ton delivery wagon powered by a two-cylinder engine and priced at $1,000. In 1912, a 1-ton model was added priced at $1,100. Model designations reached the letter H by 1917. Trucks from 1-1/2-ton to 5-ton were available.

The Giant Truck Corporation was formed later in 1918. Four capacities of trucks were offered by Giant: 1-, 1-1/2-, 2- and 3-ton models. During the first year of production four-cylinder Continental engines were used along with bevel-gear drive and solid rubber tires. However, the following year four-cylinder Buda engines powered the Giant 1-1/2-ton model. Worm-drive was adopted for all models in 1919. By the last year of production, the lightest trucks were discontinued, and the company shut down during the postwar recession.

GIFFORD-PETTIT 1907-1908 — In 1907, the Gifford-Pettit Manufacturing Company was organized in Chicago, Illinois, with $10,000 in capital for the purpose of building automobiles. A.F. Feldt was the designer, but instead of a passenger car the company decided to build a 3-ton capacity forward-control truck. The 5,000-pound chassis had a 120-inch wheelbase and with a 35 hp four-cylinder engine, three-speed transmission and double chain drive with solid rubber tires it had a price tag of $3,500. It was designated as the Model A, but no other models followed and the company was out of business by the end of 1908.

1942 GILLIG 29-PASSENGER BUS   **GILLIG**

GILLIG 1912, 1932 to date — The Gillig Brothers began in San Francisco, California, during the Depression, and the origin of their company goes back to Jacob Gillig, who was their father and had started building carriages in The City back in 1890. The original factory burned down and in 1906 the father and sons reopened as the Leo Gillig Automobile Works building auto bodies, hearses, bus bodies and hearses. In 1912, Leo Gillig built an experimental truck of which little is known. In 1914, a three-story factory was built. The company began building the "California Top," which was a conversion kit to change touring cars to closed models.

By 1932, the Gillig company built its first school bus, which became the mainstay of its business. The company introduced its first transit bus in 1937, and due to growing production, manufacturing was moved across the San Francisco Bay to Hayward near Oakland, where it has remained to date. For 1941, Gillig brought out its first under-floor-engine design bus powered by a Hall-Scot engine. The chassis was made nearby by Fabco.

After World War II, Gillig began building rear-engine buses in 1945. Five years later the plant capacity was able to produce 75 complete buses and another 100 school bus bodies. By that time, Gillig buses adopted diesel engines, which comprised the majority of their powerplants. Caterpillar, Cummins and Detroit Diesel units were available.

By 1970, another front-engine bus called the Microcoach was developed. Seventy-five of these buses were built before the rights to manufacture them were sold to Sportscoach in 1974. In 1976, Gillig Brothers became the Gillig Corporation.

1968 GILLIG MODEL 855-15   MBS

Gillig also built Neoplan buses under license from Germany beginning in 1977. Many American components were adapted and wheelchair access lifts and ramps were added for use in the United States. The first set of these buses were used in Santa Clara County, and these were powered by propane Ford truck engines. Many of these were utilized by the county bus service through the 1980s.

1994 GILLIG 45-PASSENGER BUS   GILLIG

For the 1990s, Gillig has offered three motorhome chassis along with three Phantom Buses. The buses were listed as 30-, 35- and 40-foot in length with maximum seating capacity of 29, 37 and 45 passengers, respectively, including two wheelchair positions. Engine options were DDC 6V92 and S-50, Cummins L-10 and 6CTA diesel and Cummins L-10 NG, along with transmissions from Allison, Voith or ZF. Axles were from Rockwell and steering from TRW. Airport Shuttle or Suburban Commuter configurations have been available, and fuel choices have included Clean Diesel, LNG and CNG to date.

G.J.G. 1912-1913 — George John Grossman, designer of the G.J.G. vehicles, was the president of G.J.G. Motor Car Company in White Plains, New York. The company evolved out of the Mammoth Garage in 1909 after Grossman built the shop and business in 1907, when he was still a dealer of Cadillac automobiles. The company was incorporated with Grossman's wife, Matilda, and his two sons.

As with many vehicles of this era, commercial iterations, in this case as a light van or stake side, were built using the same chassis and drivetrain as the passenger versions. By 1912, the G.J.G. cars were called Pirate Roadster, Scout Touring, Comfort Touring and Carryall Touring. All were powered by a 26 hp four-cylinder engine with a cone clutch and three-speed selective transmission and had a 104-inch wheelbase. Both van and stake side were rated at 1/2-ton capacity. The van has been described as "rakish" due to the fact that its windshield was attached to the front of the frame.

The G.J.G. company never made any money for Grossman and his family, and in 1913 Grossman pronounced and was quoted in *The Motor World*, "there are better places than White Plains for the manufacture of motor cars." Despite plans to move the factory to the Midwest, financial troubles put an end to G.J.G. in 1914, when a few remaining speedster models were assembled from parts on-hand.

1909 GLEASON 1-TON   MROZ

GLEASON 1909-1913 — The same Missouri factory that built the Caps and Kansas City autos also produced the Gleason. These were highwheelers powered by 20 hp two-cylinder engines with three-speed sliding gear transmission and shaft drive. Both 2-ton and 3-ton trucks were available with pneumatic tires from $1,050 to $1,400. The K.C. Vehicle Company was located in Kansas City, Missouri.

1911 GLIDE 3/4-TON DELIVERY   RD

GLIDE 1911-1912 — The Glide was designed and developed by J.B. Bartholomew in Peoria, Illinois, by 1903. Apparently the marque's name derived from the company's address at 210 Glide Street in Peoria. Bartholomew's business was peanut and coffee roasting, but being an inventor and tinkerer, he built his first gasoline-powered car in 1901 using his own name for its marque. Two years later the car went into production as the Glidemobile, which was shortened to Glide by 1904.

Introduced in rapid succession were 6 hp one-cylinder engines, 14 hp two-cylinder engines, 36 hp four-cylinder engines and by 1908, when 200 Glides were sold, 60 hp six-cylinder engines were introduced. It was not until 1911 that Glide introduced 3/4-ton commercial vehicles with either open or closed bodies based on the 45 hp four-cylinder Model 45, which had a 120-inch wheelbase. A three-speed transmission was used with shaft drive. The Bartholomew Company built exactly the same light commercial vehicle for 1912, but dropped the model line later that year. In 1911, the commercial delivery wagon was priced at $2,000, about the same as for three-passenger car models.

"Ride in a Glide and Then Decide" was one of Bartholomew's many slogans. Production of passenger cars continued through 1920, but the company's foray into commercial vehicles appeared to have ended with the 1912 model year.

1917 GLOBE 1-TON MODEL A   RD

GLOBE 1916-1919 — The Globe Furniture Company of Northville, Michigan, began building trucks for its own hauling purposes. The moving vans were powered by an L-head six-cylinder engine. This was one of the first commercial vehicles to use a six-cylinder engine, although a year later the company switched to four-cylinder Continental engines. Also at this time, the Globe company reorganized as Globe Motor Truck Company, also in Northville.

In 1917, Globe trucks consisted of the 1-ton Model A for $1,375, 1-1/2-ton Model B for $1,690, 2-ton Model C for $1,985 and another 2-ton Model EC for $2,085. These were all powered by Continental engines and featured Perfex copper radiator, Raybestos-faced dry clutch, Covert transmission, Celfor internal gear rear axle, Prudden wheels and Vulcan springs. Left-hand drive had been adopted by that time. A Stewart vacuum system supplied a Master carburetor and ignition was by Eisemann. Both foot accelerator and hand throttle was provided. The firm shut down directly after World War I. It was not affiliated with the Globe Motors Company of Cleveland, Ohio, which started in 1920 building passenger cars.

GLOVER 1911-1912 — George T.S. Glover started out in Chicago, Illinois, in 1902 with steam automobile production. His innovation was the utilization of "winter use" equipment, which consisted of a traction wheel mounted amidships, which was hollow and filled with hot water from the steam engine's boiler. It was intended to melt snow and ice. Glover realized its best application would be on his Glover Steam Tractor, which he also built, one of which was sold in 1903 to a logging camp in North Michigan.

By 1911, Glover built a 5-ton capacity truck extrapolating from his "fifth wheel flexible traction" design, which was earlier used to convert horsedrawn wagons to motorized vehicles. This time Glover built a three-wheel commercial vehicle using a 590-cubic inch displacement six-cylinder engine mounted midship with a three-speed transmission and double chain drive. By the following year, a 3/4-ton "trike" using a four-cylinder engine was also built by Glover. In 1911 and 1912, Glover trucks were built ranging from 2-ton to 5-ton capacity. Aside from passenger cars, the trucks were powered by 40 hp four-cylinder engines with a choice of air or water cooling depending on the buyer's preference. Full-elliptic springs were used and the drive wheel, centered between the rear wheels, was 34 inches in diameter and used a 12-inch wood block face that was easily removable for replacement at a cost of $7 in 1912. Large expansion springs pulled the traction wheel against the road surface, and it was claimed its replacement was only needed twice a year. For the 5-ton capacity truck the driving wheel was 35 inches in diameter and had a 24-inch face. The heavy truck's engine was listed as having 60 hp.

1912 GLOVER 2-TON   **RD**

In 1913, George Glover was one of the incorporators of the C.A. Martin Manufacturing Company in Chicago and did not build any other known vehicles under his own name. The later Glover Motor Company of New York City was not affiliated with George Glover.

GMC 1911 to date — With his acquisition of several companies beginning in 1908, which would include truck builders Rapid and Reliance (and later Cartercar and Strenuous Randolph), William Crapo Durant secured established companies that would collectively become the largest truck manufacturing venture in America. At first, the General Motors Truck Company was formed to handle sales of the individual truck and passenger vehicle makes remotely under its control. By the end of July 1911, the General Motors Truck Company was formed and all truck manufacturing was consolidated and soon moved to Pontiac, Michigan. The first GMC truck was shown at the New York Auto Show in 1912, and by that time GMC was already a registered trademark.

Rapid's horizontally-opposed two-cylinder engine design, as well as the

two-cycle two-, three- and four-cylinder engine design of the Reliance trucks continued to be used by General Motors for over a year. Within approximately that much time the decision was made to switch to a conventional four-cylinder L-head Continental engine. By that time, Durant had already lost control of General Motors, as financiers stepped in to prevent bankruptcy only two years after the company's formation.

The investment group of Lee Higginson and Company from Boston and W. Seligman and Company of New York entered the picture. James J. Storrow of Higginson became the president of GMC in November of 1910 but lasted only until the end of January 1911. The bankers' trust appointed Thomas Neal as fourth president of GMC in January of 1911, who remained until Nash took over in November of 1912. George E. Daniels had been the first company president, but lasted only one month. William M. Eaton was second president and lasted two years.

1912 GMC 3-1/2-TON MODEL H   **MROZ**

All along Durant still continued as vice-president, stockholder and a member of the board of directors. He was only forced to step aside "in matters of management." The new conservative group righted the company financially under the philosophy of efficiency and long-term planning.

Badge engineered as General Motors trucks, Rapid trucks were of conventional design with four-speed transmissions and were rated up to 2-ton capacity, while Reliance continued as a forward-control truck up to 5-ton capacity using three-speed transmissions. Both used double chain drive to the rear axle. Aside from the engine change, they retained their original form for at least two years before major design changes were made.

The 1912 GMC Reliance Model H was rated at 3-1/2-ton capacity and received a 40 hp four-cylinder engine with pair-cast cylinders. The 5-ton Model K differed only in that it had larger wheels. Both were known as GMC-Reliance or GMC Model H and Model K after 1912. The GMC-Rapid Model S was rated at 2-ton capacity.

General Motors Company (GMC) also built a range of electric trucks at this time. These used short Renault-type hoods as a finishing touch since the electric motors powered and were located at the rear wheels. The batteries were placed on top of the frame under the driver's seat, unlike other makes whose batteries hung below the chassis. Electric trucks were built in eight models from 1/2-ton to 6-ton capacity until the end of 1915. Chassis prices ranged from $1,200 for the 1/2-ton Model 1-1B to $2,500 for the 6-ton Model 12-12B. These prices did not include batteries.

GMC electric trucks were advertised side-by-side with gasoline-powered vehicles. Ads of the period stated: "In congested traffic and frequent stop work electric trucks excel, while gasoline trucks make the best showing when hauls are long and the stops relatively few." The GMC trucks were designed by John M. Lansden, who had built trucks under his own name that continued to be built after he joined General Motors.

Maximum range for the large GMC electric trucks was about 40 miles on a single charge. The controller, safety switch, ampere-hour meter and lamp circuit were all located under the hood for easy accessibility. Express, brewery, rack, box, stake and platform bodies were available. The Boston Edison Company's "Electric Farm" bought a 2-ton electric GMC in 1912. However, General Motors management decided to concentrate on gasoline-powered engine vehicles, and electric trucks were discontinued.

1914 GMC 2-TON MODEL SC TANKER   **A&A**

Late in 1914, gasoline-powered GMC trucks adopted shaft drive and the forward control Reliance-based trucks were discontinued. The light 3/4-ton trucks used bevel gear rear axles, while all the heavier trucks Model 31. It was powered by a 22.5 hp four-cylinder engine and used a four-speed transmission.

William Crapo Durant had established the Chevrolet Company with Louis Chevrolet during Durant's lesser role at GM, and by increasing the amount of stock of the Chevrolet Company and exchanging for General Motors stock, he effectively took control of GM in 1916. By this time GMC also produced the 3-1/2-ton Model 71 and the 2-ton articulated Model 41 using a wagon-type semi-trailer with steel-shod wooden wheels.

President Nash resigned and with the help of the Boston bankers started the Nash Company, buying out Jeffery. Pierre du Pont, who had been elected as chairman of the board at GM remained and became a major one-third stockholder. It was a little over one year after the June 1, 1916, resignation of Nash that the entire enterprise was reorganized as the General Motors Corporation with Durant as president. The emblem "GMC" had already been used by that time as relating to General Motors Company. The General Motors Corporation became an operating company, not just a holding company as before.

In 1916, General Motors staged a cross-country trek as a promotion gimmick. Driver William Warwick and his wife took a load of Carnation milk from Seattle to New York in 31 days using a 1-1/2-ton GMC truck. They also made a return trip that took much longer, but it got GMC trucks the kind of mention in the press that the company could exploit for its own benefit.

Within a year, GMC trucks were built for the war effort, and the company produced approximately 21,000 vehicles of which 5,000 were 3/4-ton Model 15. Of these 8,500 were built for the U.S. Army, the rest being 1-1/2-ton trucks. Light and medium GMC trucks were widely used as ambulances, fire engines and for ammunition and infantry transport. The 1-1/2-ton Model 31 used solid rubber tires while the 3/4-ton ambulances usually had pneumatic tires and acetylene lights.

At the end of the war, GMC's newly acquired Chevrolet division owned the Scripps-Booth automobile company and built a light delivery van version of its Rocket. Scripps-Booth turned into a Chevrolet spin-off under Durant until Pierre du Pont took over as president of General Motors early in 1921. GMC's venture into farm tractor building under Durant in the form of the Sampson Tractor

Division, originally bought in Stockton, California, as the Sampson Sieve Grip Tractor, was less than profitable and lived up to its name in an unexpected way. However, Durant's acquisition of Guardian Frigerator Company, which became the Frigidaire Division, proved to be an overall boon with later applications to trucking.

1921 GMC FLATBED WITH MODEL BO JOHN DEERE   **EF**

General Motors Acceptance Corporation and United Motors were acquired, and General Motors of Canada was started during the period before du Pont took over. United Motors, also referred to as United Products, consisted of Dayton Engineering Laboratories (where the electric starter motor had been developed by Charles Kettering), Harrison Radiator, Hyatt Roller Bearing, Jaxon Steel Products, Klaxon and New Departure.

Durant's quest for expansion turned into tangible assets under du Pont's presidency, and later Alfred Sloan's management. However, Durant's personal dealings in the stock market led to his resignation, and the du Ponts were deemed generous for taking over his financial obligations, for which he was compensated with 230,000 shares of General Motors stock worth $2,990,000 at that time.

Postwar production of the K series began with a GMC 1-ton truck similar to the 1-1/2-ton Chevrolet Model K based on the 490 and FB series passenger cars using overhead-valve 26 hp or 37 hp four-cylinder engines and pneumatic tires. There were also the larger 5-ton Model K101 and 15-ton K102 truck tractor with solid tires, the latter which was called the Big Brute known for its oversize front bumper and a GVW rating of 22,000 pounds. Starter motors on the heavy trucks did not become standard until 1925. Bus chassis were available based on the 1-1/2-ton K-16 and also the 3-ton K-41, which had an eight-speed dual range transmission.

Overall sales for General Motors in 1918 were $270 million, in 1919 $510 million and for 1920 $567 million, yet financial trouble was still brewing regarding stock sales, inventories and working capital. By 1925, GMC purchased from rental car pioneer John Hertz a controlling interest in Yellow Cab, which was to build Yellow Trucks and Yellow Coaches for GMC. It would not be until 1943 that GMC would buy out the minority interests in Yellow Truck and Coach, which became the GMC Truck and Coach Division. For purposes of clarity, Yellow Coach and GM Coach (General Coach) are treated as one separate entry in this compendium, which deals with the company's buses and coaches built by Yellow.

The importance and interwoven character of GMC's Yellow division underscores the fact that most vehicles escutcheoned as GMC were borrowed at least in significant portion from one of the parent company's subsidiaries. General Motors Corporation has always been comprised of several makes and numerous supporting parts manufacturers. Most significant, however, is the fact that from July 1, 1925, through September of 1943, GMC truck production is not included with corporation sales numbers because that production was listed under the Yellow Truck & Coach Manufacturing Company.

After emerging from the overall national economic slump in the early 1920s under new leadership, GMC gradually caught up with Ford, which was still the top selling automobile and light truck in America. In 1920, for example, General Motors sold 393,075 cars and trucks in the United States and Canada, while Ford produced

1,074,336 cars and trucks for the year. It was also at this time that Charles Kettering, inventor of the electric starter motor, became heavily involved in the development of the "copper-cooled" engine for General Motors. The 2-1/2 years of research and development spent on the air-cooled engine design came to a dead end in 1923, and though as many as 759 such experimental Chevrolets were fitted with these engines, none were considered production vehicles. It is believed that a few light trucks were fitted with these engines, but apparently all air-cooled Chevrolets were eventually recalled by the factory.

1923 GMC 10-TON TRACTOR-TRAILER   OCW

GMC truck sales started at 372 units for 1909 and hit three peaks before interest in Yellow was purchased. These production numbers were 656 units in 1910 with a drop to 293 vehicles for the following year. In 1918, another peak was reached at 8,999 units during war production. And after a slump in 1921 with 2,760 GMC trucks sold for the year, 1923 was again a prolific year with 6,969 units.

For 1925, GMC offered the 1-ton capacity K-16, 2-1/2-ton K-41A, K-41B and K-41C, 3-1/2-ton K-71A and K-71B, 5-ton K-101A and K-101B, and highway tractors K-41T, K-71T and K-101T. The longest wheelbase was 187 inches available on the K-71B and K101B. The K101 engine was rated at 32.4 hp and used Simms ignition. Front and rear axles were from Timken on all but the lightest model, which had GM axles and was the only model with pneumatic tires as standard equipment. On the heaviest truck Dayton wheels carried 36x6 front and 40x12 rear solid rubber tires. This was the year that GM merged with Yellow forming the Yellow Truck and Coach Company, which produced the trucks, buses and taxicabs under the name Yellow.

In 1927, the T series GMC trucks began production, superseding all previous models except the Big Brute, which lasted until 1929. The T series ranged from a 1/2-ton panel delivery up to 6-ton capacity. All had overhead-valve six-cylinder engines, pneumatic tires and complete electrical systems. The lighter trucks of 1927 still had rear brakes only, but by the following year four-wheel-brakes were standardized across the entire line. Worm-drive was used only in the heavier range of vehicles. The exception to the overhead-valve engines was in car-based delivery vehicles and 1-ton trucks, which had been introduced in 1927 as Pontiacs, but evolved into GMC light trucks in 1928 and were powered by 58 hp side-valve six-cylinder engines essentially based on the Pontiac engine. For 1928, the 1-ton Model T-19 exemplified the new styling at GM with headlights relocated next to the chrome-plated radiator along with deeply crowned fenders.

1928 GMC SCREENSIDE DELIVERY   KP

By 1929, the heavier GMC trucks began using the larger four-main-bearing Buick-based six-cylinder engines with up to 89 hp, uprated the following year to 100 hp. In 1931, GMC took over development of the Buick-based six-cylinder engines, which within a year would be fitted with seven main bearings and hydraulic valve lifters. This engine eventually grew to 707 cubic inch displacement and was used until 1960. The original purpose was to supplant the 1920s Knight sleeve-valve engines used in Yellow trucks and coaches, and those engines were designed to be retrofitted to Yellow transmissions.

For 1931, GMC offered trucks with up to 15-ton capacity. By this time GMC concentrated on the heavier trucks and advanced technical development, while Chevrolet built the lighter trucks in large numbers. Tandem rear axles were available on GMC models such as the 10-ton T-95C. Production for the year surpassed 10,000 trucks, achieving a new record for the company. The drastic downturn of the nation's economy influenced GMC to introduce the 2-ton T-18, which used the Pontiac side-valve engine and sold for $600. It shared only its sheet metal with the equivalent Chevrolet truck.

1931 GMC 1-TON   GMC

The first integral GMC bus arrived in the form of the Model 700 in 1932. It seated 40 passengers and had a 616-cubic inch six-cylinder engine mounted lengthwise. In 1933, GMC introduced a sleeper cab for its heavy-duty truck line. Also that year, downdraft carburetors were adopted and overhead-valve engines were used in the 2-ton series. The 707-cubic inch six-cylinder was specifically used in heavy trucks and was rated at 173 hp. These engines used twin-plate clutches and five-speed transmissions with both over-drive and underdrive available from the factory. Worm-drive was used on tandem axles, and Westinghouse air brakes were adopted for the heaviest trucks.

1934 GMC T-74HC 12-TON TRACTOR-TRAILER   GMC

For 1934, GMC used a 70 hp side-valve six-cylinder engine, as well as a larger 120 hp overhead-valve six-cylinder engine for trucks larger than the 1-1/2-ton model. Vacuum servo brakes were introduced for the medium-size trucks and five-speed transmissions were standard on the heavy-duty trucks. Also, a slide-out engine forward-control design was adopted that year. Sleeper cabs were available on the larger trucks, such as the 12-ton articulated T-74HC model.

1935 GMC PADDY WAGON   JERRY SPRINGER

1942 GMC 1-1/2-TON MILITARY FIRE TRUCK   MROZ

1938 GMC 1-TON PICKUP   A&A

1945 GMC STAKE TRUCK   A&A

1940 GMC CCKW 353 A2 6X6   KP

1946 GMC HORSE HAULER   GMC

1941 GMC COE TANDEM-AXLE TANKER   A&A

1948 GMC COE DUMP TRUCK   A&A

In 1935, GMC was restyled along with Chevrolet, following an industry-wide trend. The streamlined cabs were introduced on the larger trucks before they were adopted for the light models. Hydraulic brakes made their debut at GMC that year, with hydrovac for the medium range and full air actuation for the top of the line. The lighter trucks also received streamlined cabs for 1936 in a somewhat gradual switch, not unlike other truck manufacturers.

In 1937, GMC offered 12 conventional models and 11 COE models. The lightest was the 1/2-ton T-14 and the heaviest conventional was the 10-ton T-61H. The F-16 was the lightest COE while the heftiest was the 12-ton F-61H. Prices ranged from $395 to $3,985, respectively, for the two conventional trucks mentioned, and $635 to $4,355, respectively, for the COE trucks mentioned. Engines were rated from 86 hp to 110 hp. The largest displacement listed for that year was the 400-cubic inch six-cylinder engine. Sales surpassed 50,000 units over the year for the first time.

For 1938, seven-bearing engines were used on many models. Some trucks for export were badged Oldsmobile and used side-valve six-cylinder Oldsmobile engines. Total GMC truck production for 1938 was 20,640. Two major developments took place in 1939. Synchromesh was adopted for the transmissions, and diesel engines were used in the 2-ton to 6-ton range of trucks. This distinguished GMC trucks from Chevrolet for many years. The diesel engines were developed by General Motors, called Detroit Diesel, and were two-cycle three-cylinder or four-cylinder powerplants.

General Motors built three-wheel vehicles similar to Harley-Davidson's Servi-Car in 1939. These three-passenger trikes were built by the Delco Division and competed with three-wheelers built by Indian in tests by the Infantry Board at Ft. Benning. Only 20 such vehicles were purchased by the U.S. military. For trucks side-valve engines were not used after 1939 by GMC, when total truck production rose to 44,000. In 1940, production again leaped up to 59,313, and again nearly doubled to 111,382 for 1941.

As World War II began in Europe, General Motors Opel Division was nationalized in Germany and became one of the largest truck builders for the Axis powers. In the United States, GMC quickly converted over to military production. In 1940, there were five 6x6 versions including models CCKW 352, CCKW 353 and AFKWX 353 with and without winches and the latter with a 15-foot body. For the year 1942, GMC produced 148,111 units, which was 16.9 percent of the total U.S. production output.

By 1943, General Motors listed 16 different trucks built for the military: 1) 1-1/2- to 3-ton Small Arms Repair Truck, 2) 1-1/2-ton Radio Sending and Receiving Truck, 3) 1-1/2- to 3-ton Air Compressor Truck, 4) 2-1/2-ton 6x6 Artillery Prime Mover, 5) 2-1/2-ton 750-gallon Tanker, 6) 1-1/2- to 3-ton Traveling Machine Shop, 7) 2-1/2-ton Cargo and Troop Transporter, 8) 2-1/2-ton Cavalry Hauler, 9) 1-1/2- to 3-ton Earth Borer Truck, 10) 1-1/2-ton Recruiting Trailer Tow Truck, 11) 2-1/2-ton Searchlight Carrier, 12) 8-ton Tractor Trailer for Arsenals, 13) 1-1/2- to 3-ton 4x4 Transport, 14) COE Navy Refueler, 15) 4-ton Anti-Aircraft Defense Truck, and 16) 1-1/2-ton 4x4 Troop Transporter.

GMC produced some 560,000 2-1/2-ton 6x6 "army workhorse" trucks powered by 104 hp engines and using five-speed transmissions and hydrovac brakes. The company also built about 20,000 DUKW "Duck" amphibious craft. In 1943, Yellow was acquired in its entirety.

After World War II, GMC again built a full range of trucks starting with the light-duty 1/2-ton Model CC-102 pickup, all the way up to heavy-duty trucks that featured five-speed transmissions, worm-drive, air-operated two-speed rear axles and diesel engines up to 165 hp with the 6-71 six-cylinder powerplant. The West Coast Special had no front brakes and used aluminum extensively for weight savings.

1947 GMC ADVANCE-DESIGN COCA-COLA DELIVERY   **A&A**

For 1948, GMC introduced three medium-duty COE trucks: the FF-350, FF-450 and the FF-351. Wheelbases ranged from 122-inch up to 197-inch and GVW was rated at 16,000 pounds for the FF-350. Rear axles were either hypoid or spiral bevel as standard equipment, as well as two-speed, two-speed double reduction, heavy-service spiral bevel and heavy-service two-speed and double reduction. The largest engine for these COE trucks was the over-head-valve GMC 270 with 104 hp, although governors limited the output about 10 percent. The FF-351 was a special short model with 110-inch wheelbase. Deluxe cabs with rear-quarter window and stainless steel windshield trim were available. The new line also featured solenoid starter motors and a spare tire carrier as standard equipment. Also, a four-speed synchromesh transmission replaced the sliding gear type.

By 1950, GMC listed 20 improved models including pickups, with seven new models for the year and capacity ratings from 1/2-ton to 20-ton. All of the models included conventional chassis, suburban, COE, school bus chassis, truck tractors, six-wheel dual drive and diesel-powered chassis. The new models consisted of two six-wheel trucks, the HCW-400 and HCW-620, two diesel tractors, the HDCR-640 and HDCR-650 (in addition to the earlier 750) and two medium-duty units assigned as the HC-470 and the HF-470, which were similar to the HC-450 conventional unit but with heavier-duty rear axles and increased ratings.

Midyear GMC introduced its new "110" six-cylinder diesel engine with 275 hp. Each cylinder had 110-cubic inch displacement, unlike the earlier 71-cubic inch Detroit Diesel. The new heavy-duty engine featured an efficient gear-driven centrifugal blower with an aluminum impeller. With standard equipment the engine was rated at 229 bhp. The first three-axle truck tractors with this diesel engine were supplied to Pacific Inter-Mountain Express (P.I.E.).

By the end of 1950, GMC announced two series of new highway tractors designated as 640 and 650, the latter GCW rated at up to 55,000 pounds. Wheelbase and cab-to-axle dimensions permitted installation of auxiliary transmissions, sleeper cabs and other equipment for inter-state or intra-state hauling. The GM 4-71 diesel, which had a displacement of 283 cubic inches, was rated at 133 hp at 2000 rpm with 400 pound-feet of torque at 1300 rpm. Push rod/rocker arm operated injectors allowed for engine braking without concern for engine-racing lubrication. All civilian production records were broken when GMC built its 100,000th truck for the year (a 650 Diesel) in December of 1950, surpassing the previous record of 92,677 units for 1948.

In 1951, at the Chicago Auto Show GMC showed its 953 Diesel highway tractor with a 200 hp engine and a GCW rating of 70,000 pounds. There were also two lighter highway tractors: the 650 diesel and the 620 gasoline model, the latter with 50,000 pounds GCW. Also new for 1951 was the M-135 military truck. It was powered by a 302-cubic inch six-cylinder engine rated at 145 hp and used an eight-speed hydramatic transmission that allowed for a top speed of 58 mph carrying a 10,000-pound load. The truck also featured automatic front drive engagement for extra traction. Otherwise only the rear axles were driven. Standard leaf springs were combined with torque rod suspension for the front axle as well. The rear axle springs were assisted by fixed secondary springs for higher load capacity and control of ride clearance. The 24-volt electrical system was dustproof, waterproof, fungus proof and suppressed against radio interference.

At the end of 1952, GMC boosted its hp ratings of both the 4-71 and the 6-71 diesel engine from 133 to 150 bhp and from 200 to 225 bhp, respectively. The governed rpm was increased to 2100 to help performance. The ground surfaces of the block and head eliminated the need for a head gasket. Thus the 4-71 diesel engine that was rated at 110 hp in 1945 had a power output increase of 36 percent and the 6-71, which had 165 hp in 1945, with an increase of 33 percent. Both the 4-71 and the 6-71 engines were dubbed "Million Milers."

In 1952, GMC announced a new 2-1/2-ton diesel, the Model D450-37. The medium-duty conventional truck had a 110 hp three-cylinder diesel engine and featured an electrically-controlled two-speed rear axle. It was rated at 19,500 pounds GVW and 35,000 pounds GCW. This engine was the smaller version of the 4-71 and 6-71 used in the larger trucks up to the 980 model series truck tractors. Later in the year, GMC announced four more similar models as the D450-37, the D470-37, DW450-37 and DW620-47 with up to 21,000 pounds GVW and 45,000 pounds GCW.

All the "71" series engines had interchangeable cylinder liners, pistons, piston rings, connecting rods, main and connecting rod bearings, valves and fuel injectors. Also in 1952, GMC adopted dual-range hydramatic transmissions for its parcel delivery vans, such as the Model P152-22. The latter also featured a wide-track I-beam front axle, hypoid rear axle, 124-1/4-inch wheelbase and GVW of 7,000 pounds. At the end of the year the parcel delivery vans were dubbed Model PM-152 and were advertised as "America's Most Beautiful Delivery Truck." The front sheet metal had a wrap-around design, which was extended up with the two-piece curved windshield. Wide whitewall tires were also featured.

The Korean War spurred GMC under Roger M. Kyes' direction (GM vice-president and general manager of GMC Truck and Coach) to build economical fuel efficient trucks with reduced maintenance requirements. The Korean "conflict" created material shortages, which translated into production cutbacks. The diesel engines of the early 1950s were fitted with a new "fuel modulator" and parts interchangeability with older models were key to the company's success during those hard times.

1953 GMC 2-1/2-TON XM-211 6X6   MROZ

By 1953, GMC engine designations were the following for each engine model: 22 for the 228, 24 for the 248, 30 for the 302, 36 for the 360, 42 for the 426 and 50 for the 503, while for diesel engines these were 37 for the 3-71, 47 for the 4-71 and 67 for the 6-71. Numerous new model designations and ratings were listed for GMC by May of 1952. The heaviest was the HDCW-980, which was formerly known as the DW980-67. Letter designations were F for COE model, D for diesel, M for automatic transmission, P for forward-control model and W for six-wheel model.

The light GMC trucks were nearly identical to those of Chevrolet, distinguished by heavier front grilles and slightly more trim. Hydramatic transmissions were available in pickups by 1953. For 1954, the GMC light trucks got a one-piece curved windshield. In June of 1954, GMC announced the development of its Twin Hydramatic Multiple-Speed automatic transmission for trucks up to 45,000 pounds GCW. By August, GMC also offered Saginaw Power Steering on Models 100 through 450. That month was also when the "Stripaway" COE system was unveiled. It allowed better and quicker access to the engine, transmission and other components by the use of counterbalanced seats that slid up to the ceiling permitting fold-back floorboards as well as side doors that swung open on each side of the large hood.

Major styling changes and introduction of two V-8 engines were in effect for 1955. Light trucks were changed midyear and were distinguished as first and second series, the latter having new sheet metal and 12-volt electrical systems. For the 550 and 650 models up to 55,000-pound GCW a new 96-inch BBC design combined the cab accessibility of conventional trucks with the payload and maneuverability of COE models. The two new V-8 engines were the 155 bhp 288 unit and the 175 bhp 324 powerplant. Forty-four standard models were powered by V-8 engines, and all six-

cylinder engines had power increase up to 225 hp (for the 503). The 288 engine differed from the 324 in that the former had ball-pivot type rocker arms while the latter used a single rocker arm shaft. Both had hydraulic valve lifters.

Sixty-five models used automatic transmissions, up from 13 in 1954. Diesel engine compression ratios were increased to 18:1, resulting in 5 hp increase in the largest unit up to 230 hp. Overall, the second series front sheet metal and grille were heavier and more elaborate than in the previous year. Also, optional plastic panels replaced the former pickup body fenders and short steps.

In 1956, GMC widened its engine options for its medium- and heavy-duty range trucks, which ranged from four-wheel gasoline models with 22,000-pound GVW up to tandem-axle trucks with 90,000-pound GCW. New models were the FW550 dual-purpose tandem-axle tractor and the tandem-axle W670. The former used the V-8 engine introduced the previous year, which was now rated at 210 bhp, while the W670, with a 59,000-pound GVW, used a 225 bhp V-8 engine and a five-speed main and three-speed auxiliary transmission. An inter-axle differential was introduced for locking out the rear tandem axle for off-road operation while connecting it for highway use. Tubeless tires became standard equipment that year. The year 1956 was also the first year for optional 4x4 pickups in the 100, 150 and 250 series.

Starting in 1957, air-suspension was introduced in the heavier trucks, but this innovation lasted only a few years before it was discontinued for over a decade. GM began developing light forward-control vans in the late 1950s, but the protoypes did not lead to production for several more years. In 1959, GMC brought out a new set of engines that were in the form of three V-6 engines and one V-12. These were used for the 1960 model year, although they were already in existence during the previous year. Their displacements were 305, 351 and 401 cubic inches, respectively, while the V-12 had a 702-cubic inch displacement being composed of two 351 V-6 engines.

By August of 1959, these engines were announced in *The Commercial Car Journal*, which stated "Horsepower and torque ratings have not yet been definitely pinned-down." By October of the same year, however, GMC was selling a 48-inch BBC truck tractor Model DFR-8000 along with the DLR-8000 model, available with the new V-6 diesel engine. Both were rated at 76,000-pound GCW, which included "double train" trailer combinations allowed in many states. The two models differed in that the former had a 28-inch bumper-to-front-axle set-back, while the latter had a 50-inch front axle set-back.

Air-suspension allowed height to remain the same regardless of load, permitting fifth wheel and trailer floor to be three inches lower, adding 70 cubic feet in a 35-foot trailer. The diesel engines continued to be two-cycle design, which was not the norm throughout the rest of the diesel industry. For that year, the truck tractor design featured a new 696-pound aluminum tilt-cab, lighter frame by 300 pounds and independent front suspension. The V-6 was rated at 189 hp at 1800 rpm. The tilt-cab used a torsion spring as a counterbalance.

The following year, the company announced a "Completely new line of GMC trucks for 1960." By this time GMC's variety of models combined with the production output was unsurpassed anywhere in the world. For 1960, there were 15 light-duty and pickup conventional gasoline models, 20 "B" conventional models, 16 tilt cab gasoline models, 2 forwar-control models, 7 school bus chassis, 10 "B" conventional diesel models, 5 tilt cab diesel models and 8 short BBC tilt cab diesel models. Also at that time, nine different engines were available, which included an inline gasoline six-cylinder engine, five V-6 gasoline units, a V-12, an inline six-cylinder diesel and a V-6 diesel, the latter of which had two iterations.

Also that year, GMC offered torsion bar independent front suspension, coil spring rear suspension and "vari-rate" spring rear suspension. Light-duty trucks had a combination of independent front suspension with rear coil springs. There were a total of 61 basic new GMC models and the series were numbered as follows: 1000, 1500, 2500, 3000, 3500, 4000, 5000, 5500, 6000, 7000, 860, 8000 and 9000. Newly engineered 4x4s were available as well as the usual package delivery models and school bus chassis. The V-6 engine temporarily superseded the V-8 in GMC trucks for 1960.

1958 GMC TURBOPOWER T1546 TRACTOR-TANKER   A&A

1960 GMC 1-TON MODEL P2503   KP

1965 GMC 1/2-TON PICKUP   A&A

1980 GMC CONVENTIONAL GENERAL TRACTOR-TRAILER   GMC

1969 GMC K SERIES   GMC

1976 GMC ASTRO 95 TRACTOR-TRAILER W/DRAGFOILER   GMC

1982 GMC BEER DELIVERY TRACTOR-TRAILER   MROZ

1983 GMC MILITARY BLAZER   GMC

The model lineup stayed essentially the same at GMC the following year, although such a large company was always able to introduce some new features or options on an annual basis. In 1963, GMC refined its V-6 engines, which had not been entirely debugged when introduced earlier. A 90 hp four-cylinder engine was offered in light trucks, although this was essentially a passenger car engine introduced earlier. Also, General Motors went to a vari-rate I-beam front axle design for medium-duty trucks, while the light trucks had a coil-spring independent front suspension.

The company advertised its "Mylar-sealed printed circuits and Delco-tron diode-rectified AC generator" for 1963. Transmissions for heavy trucks continued to be available in 8-, 10- and 12-speed iterations. The Handi-Van was a new multi-purpose design that became successful over the years, eventually evolving into the mini-van. But GMC continued to build the larger Value Vans for commercial delivery service. Dual headlights were continued into 1964 on the light- and medium-duty trucks, but heavy trucks had a simpler front grille and sheet metal design with single headlights.

For 1964, GMC made necessary refinements in its diesel engines and offered them in V-6, straight-six and V-8 versions. The light-duty was called the "I" series and featured a 140 hp 230-cubic inch straight-six gasoline engine. Models in this series included Suburban "station wagons" and pickups, as well as 1-ton stake and panel trucks.

Also in 1964, GMC caught the imagination of many New York World's Fair visitors with its experimental cargo vehicle called the Bison, a name later used on heavy Chevrolet trucks. It used two turbines that were enclosed in a pod behind the driver who sat in front of the wheels under an aerodynamic forward-tilting canopy. The interior was a study in futuristic obsolescence, which included green, amber and red lights as a warning system for states of disrepair. The combination of turbine power, intended utility and intentional aerodynamics was called a "dream" design, and aside from the latter aspect turned out to be just that.

For 1965, GMC offered diesel engines, called Toro-Flow, in light-duty, medium-duty and school bus chassis. GMC trucks ranged from 1/2-ton pickups to truck tractors with GCW of 150,000 pounds -- a wide variety as usual. Designations changed again two years later as power ratings were increased. Diesel engines were now called Toro-Flow II, and V-6 diesel engines continued to be produced starting with the 305C engine rated at 170 hp gross, which was distinguished from net by a drop to 157 hp. The gasoline V-8 for medium and heavy trucks was rated at 275 hp gross and 250 net. For 1966, new V-8 diesel engines were designated D-637, DH-637 with up to 220 hp, but V-6 engines called Magnum were also available in three sizes.

Production continued to climb during the 1960s and another record number of trucks was built in 1969 with 150,180 units for the year. There were 136,705 commercial vehicles, including pickups, built by GMC in 1965 alone. But 1969 was the last season that GMC was manufactured as an individual make, and from then on GMC vehicles became badge-engineered Chevrolets. GMC introduced the "Jimmy," long a nickname for GMC trucks, in 1970. It was almost identical to the Chevrolet Blazer. The Astro 95 was introduced in 1969.

In the early 1970s, GM experimented with gas turbine engines. Detroit Diesel Allison's engineering test fleet included White Freightliner trucks with 40-foot trailers and loads of 76,800 pounds. But just as Ford's gas turbine engines were 50 percent lighter and 30 percent smaller than diesel engines of the same hp output, tests eventually showed that the gas turbine engines were fuel inefficient, and their limited rpm flexibility made them less than optimum powerplants for motor vehicles.

The largest GMC truck was the Astro 95 COE, which was nearly identical to the Chevrolet Titan. The conventional General was essentially the same truck as the Chevrolet Bison, which was rated for GCW in the category of 80,000 pounds. The Brigadier was one of the largest conventional GMC trucks at that time produced in the 8000 Series and 9500 Series. The 8000 was often powered by a Caterpillar 3208 or Detroit Diesel 6V-53T, while the 9500 usually had a more powerful Caterpillar 3406 or Detroit Diesel 6V-92TTA. Other engine options included six-cylinder Cummins as well as 6-, 8- and 12-cylinder Detroit Diesel up to 412 hp by 1978. By 1980, the Astro 95 was updated with engine options also from Caterpillar, Cummins and Detroit Diesel up to 450 hp. In 1979, GM was the last of three companies to withdraw from the "Transbus" project.

Volvo's acquisition of White in 1981 would be of major consequence for GMC seven years later. White had acquired Autocar in 1954, but the Autocar marque was never abandoned as Diamond T and Reo (later combined as Diamond-Reo) in fact were. In 1982, the large COE Astro 95 tractor trucks all had turbocharged after-cooled engines. That year, GMC adopted more aerodynamic designs for additional efficiency of operation of its medium- and heavy-duty trucks. The Aero Astro was fitted with a patented adjustable roof-mounted air deflector, called the Dragfoiler, to match cab to various trailer heights. Large fiberglass foiler panels closed the gap between cab and trailer to create smoother airflow along the sides. A urethane cab skirt for additional air flow control was also added. The Brigadier was available with sloped hood as well as the tilt hood. Dragfoiler cab-mounted air deflectors were offered on all heavy-duty models.

GMC introduced the S-15 for 1983. The small pickups were nearly identical to the Chevrolet S-10. By this time, GMC offered 95 different color combinations for its heavy-duty line targeting owner-operators to expand into that niche market often exploited by smaller companies. Royal Classic interiors were only available on the 87-inch BBC sleeper cab. The Astro was available as a glider kit.

1983 GMC SCHOOL BUS   MROZ

For the 1984 model year, GMC offered better driver comfort with the use of air-cushion spring and shock absorber cab mounting, which was standard on the Five Star General model. Heavy-duty tandem axle models had Rockwell SQ-200 38,000-pound rear axle with taper-leaf springs as standard and optional air-suspension, which cut weight by 400 pounds. The standard engine was the Detroit Diesel Silver 6V-92TA, both turbocharged and after-cooled. Optional engines included the Cummins L10 Formula and NTC diesel engines with up to 307 hp. The Caterpillar 3208 engine was available with 11 different horsepower ratings. The Detroit Diesel Fuel Pincher V-8 was available for the Series 6000 and Series 7000 trucks. Three gasoline V-8 engines were offered for medium-duty trucks. For dump truck applications the Top Kick used a Caterpillar 3208 V-8 engine. Allison and Fuller automatic and Spicer manual transmissions were available.

1988 GMC VALUE VAN   GMC

In the medium-duty series alone there were 33 different wheelbases offered. Similar to the medium-duty except for the badges, the 5000, 6000 and 7000 Series were built in the same factory. The Top Kick was built as the equivalent of the Kodiak, riding about seven inches higher for better visibility but with a shorter BBC dimension. Engine, transmission and axle options were the same as for Chevrolet, as were cab trims, air conditioning and other interior extras. The 7000 Series was also built as a 6x2 and 6x4 truck.

1984 GMC LCF DIESEL IMPORT   **GMC**

In 1985, GMC brought out its new Safari commercial gasoline-powered minivan with 1,700-pounds carrying capacity and 151 square feet of cargo space. The heavy truck line had a component standardization program in effect but there were few visible changes. The range of engine options was expanded. In the 9500 Series GCW ratings were at 130,000 pounds. The 8000 Series was offered in single-axle form only with GVW up to 36,300 pounds. Caterpillar and Cummins engines were increasingly in demand as fewer buyers chose Detroit Diesel. However, as the Detroit Diesel Engine Division was sold to Indianapolis race car owner Roger Penske, fully-electronic four-cycle diesel engines were being developed, which were successful and were quickly adopted by GMC and other manufacturers.

In December of 1986, the GM-Volvo White merger was announced to be approved by the Justice Department and the Federal Trade Commission. That year, the GMC range of models was covered by the Conventional Medium, W7 Forward, Top Kick, Astro, Brigadier and General models. GMAC financing was offered at 7.9 percent for new trucks.

In 1987, the Detroit Diesel Series 60, which was the relatively new inline four-cycle engine, was adopted in Brigadier and General models in a range from 250 hp to 400 hp. Optional were the Detroit Diesel 6V-92 and 8V-92 and the Caterpillar 3406 and Cummins L-10. GVW ratings were up to 79,000 pounds. A new Jake Brake was available in all GMC heavy-duty models.

The merger between Volvo White and GM officially took place in January 1988, and the trucks became known as WhiteGMCVolvo with Autocar still badged separately, but essentially symbolically because it was the same design and had the same components as other trucks built by the conglomerate. The merger created a dealer selection controversy, as well as other logistical problems that were to be ironed out over the years.

The merger did put the new company in third position in terms of sales of medium and heavy trucks. Before the merger GM had fallen to eighth place for 1987 behind Navistar, Freightliner, Mack, Kenworth, Ford, Peterbilt and Volvo White. The White and Freightliner collaboration that had unraveled 10 years earlier had its impact on the market as well. GM began to penetrate the medium-duty truck line, and the C7 Hot Shot truck tractors and other C-model low-profile units were

successful. A new 530 series was announced for 1990. The Hot Shot models were intended for hauling bulky light freight without having to move to more costly Class 8 equipment. Also for 1990, the all-wheel-drive Safari van was unveiled.

1989 GMC BONUS/CREW CAB   **GMC**

1990 GMC VANDURA EXTENDED CARGO VAN   **GMC**

During 1990, GMC replaced its S-15 line with the Sonoma and Syclone pickups. The name and trim were new, but underneath things had not changed much in the Sonoma truck. However, the latter Syclone was powered by a turbocharged 4.3-liter 280 hp V-6 Vortex engine that allowed 0 to 60 mph acceleration in slightly under five seconds and a standing-start quarter-mile in 13.4 seconds. It also had the first full-time all-wheel-drive system standard with four-wheel antilock brakes. Standard transmission was the sport-calibrated Hydra-Matic 4L60 four-speed automatic.

1993 GMC 1500 SLE CUSTOM   **BILL POWK**

By 1992, GMC introduced a new name for its full-size utility pickup, Yukon. It had a 7,000-pound towing capability, which was 1,000 pounds more than its predecessor. Also that year, a new compact sport utility truck called the Typhoon was unveiled. For heavy trucks in the early 1990s WhiteGMC offered electronic 410 hp Volvo engines, which found their way into six percent of WhiteGMC trucks. This was the same percentage as the mechanical 410 hp Cummins and Detroit Diesel Series 60, which was offered in three different hp ratings. The most common engine by 1993 was the Detroit Diesel 60 425 hp electronic engine, which was in 63 percent of WhiteGMC trucks. Overall, only one percent of Class 8 trucks had Volvo engines that year.

The earlier adjustable air deflectors had given way to the Tall Integral Sleeper on WhiteGMC conventional trucks. Because the aerodynamic rise over and behind the cab was designed into the overall package, this allowed the sleeping compartment to have an eight-foot six-inch ceiling, which was popular with long distance truckers.

For 1995, WhiteGMC offered 22 series of heavy trucks with GVW ratings of 35,000-pounds up to 60,000-pounds in 4x2 and 6x4 configurations. GCW ratings were from 55,000 pounds up to 110,000 pounds. Only one of these series, the WAH42/64 with 215-inch wheelbase, had a Detroit Diesel engine, which was the Series 60-330. All other WhiteGMC trucks used either the Cummins L10-260, Cummins N14-310E, Volvo VE D7-230 or the Volvo VE D12-310. BBC dimensions ranged from 55 inches up to 167 inches and wheelbases ranged from 76 inches to 156 inches.

1995 WHITEGMC WCA 64T PLUS 6 CAB TRACTOR   **GMC**

1996 GMC SAFARI SLT   **GMC**

For 1996, the company planned to drop the Autocar and White names entirely. The change actually took place during 1995. All former Autocar and WhiteGMC models became Volvo as of July 1995. GMC TopKick trucks were enhanced with subtle engine improvements such as cast aluminum front covers and automatic transmission cooling systems good for 100,000 miles. The medium conventional GMC trucks also offered the Caterpillar 3116 diesel, which featured a hydraulic electronic unit injection (HEUI) fuel system with up to 275 hp. Also, the W4 Forward trucks received a five-inch wider chassis resulting in a five-inch wider rear track for better stability with high center-of-gravity loads.

Four TopKick models for 1996 have been listed as the LOPRO with 23,900-pound GVW and 45,000-pound GCW ratings, the C6H042 with 25,950-pound GVW and 45,000-pound GCW rating, the C7H042 with 42,440-pound GVW and 74,000-pound GCW rating and the tandem axle C7H064 with 61,000-pound GVW and 74,000-pound GCW rating. Engine choices have been 225 hp 6.0L gasoline V-8, 255 hp 7.0L gasoline V-8 and the 6.6L turbocharged air-to-air after-cooled Caterpillar diesel engine in hp ratings from 170 to 275. Transmission offerings have been Eaton

and Fuller five-, six-, seven-, eight- and nine-, 10- and 13-speed as well as four-, five- and six-speed Allison automatic. Synthetic lubricant in the manual transmissions have been offered for five-year or 250,000-mile use wear before the first change.

Both the Sonoma and Chevy S Series compact pickups were redesigned for 1994. Standard specifications for the Sonoma Cab Regular Short Box, Regular Cab Long Box and Club Cab Short Box were identical to those of the Chevrolet S Series. The Sierra Full-Size Pickups also had the same specifications as the Chevrolet C Series but on only three wheelbases: 117.5, 141.5 and 155.5 inches. Sierra trucks have been available in the 1500, 2500 and 3500 series with GVW up to 10,000 pounds and payload capacity up to 5,180 pounds for the Club Coupe Longbed 3500 series.

GMC vans' specifications have been somewhat different from those of Chevrolet. The Safari Cargo Van Regular body and extended body both had the 4.3L V-6 standard engine with four-speed automatic overdrive engine. GVW rating for the latter has been listed up to 5,600 pounds with a 1,922-pound payload capacity.

The Vandura Van has been available in the 1500, 2500 and 3500 series. The 2500 series has had the 4.3L V-6 or the 6.5L diesel both with four-speed automatic overdrive transmissions as standard equipment. The 3500 series has been built on a 125-inch or 146-inch wheelbase both with a GVW rating of 8,600 pounds. Payload capacity has been listed up to 3,457 pounds for the shorter wheelbase van, as opposed to 3,536 pounds for the larger van with 306-cubic feet of cargo space. The Rally Vans have also been offered in the 1500, 2500 and 3500 series, each with the 4.3L engine and four-speed automatic overdrive transmission as standard equipment and up to 8,600 pounds GVW rating for the largest vehicle. For the complete history of GMC light vehicles see Krause Publications' *Standard Catalog of American Light-Duty Trucks.*

GOLDEN EAGLE See SILVER EAGLE

1914 GOLDEN WEST 4X4 FOUR-WHEEL-STEER   **MROZ**

GOLDEN WEST 1913-1922 — The Golden West Motors Company was organized in Sacramento, California, at a time when the development of agriculture in the Central Valley attracted light industry to the state's capitol where the Southern Pacific Railroad had earlier established maintenance and repair facilities. In 1914, Edward S. Robinson of Oroville obtained four patents for his designs of a motor vehicle that featured four-wheel-drive and four-wheel-steering. He and three other men founded Golden West Motors the previous year. Mark L. Burns was president, Ferd A. Sloss was secretary and E.C. Binet was treasurer, while Robinson was named as the patentee and director.

The 2-ton Golden West truck used a four-cylinder Continental engine and worm-drive. The transmission included a patented internal brake mechanism and silent Whitney chains. Sheldon worm-drive was used for the front and rear axles, and the universal joints allowed for a maximum deflection of 35 degrees. A 30 x 100 foot factory was hastily built just south of Sacramento, and a few prototype trucks built. The underslung leaf springs gave the truck a rakish appearance. Although light industry had already been established in Sacramento, a city of 60,000 by 1912, attracting working capital became the undoing of the company.

The company was started with much local fanfare and the press duly noted the firm's commencement. Early in 1915, Golden West organized a game of truck polo in downtown Sacramento, attracting a large crowd and notices by the press but apparently few investors. The few trucks built were put through a 7,500 mile test quite successfully, and Golden West showed its vehicle at the first San Francisco truck show held at the Palace Hotel early in 1916. But the truck show apparently did not result in contracts or purchases and production was stopped.

Apparently at this time, Edward Robinson opted out of the company with part of the recompense being that it change its name to Robinson, which it did, but not officially, since company correspondence still carried the Golden West masthead and the press still referred to the firm as Golden West. A few periodicals referred specifically to the truck as the "Robinson tractor." Another reorganization took place in 1917, but the Commissioner of Corporations halted the sale of stock. The company's attorney, Lee Gebhard, left for Washington in June of 1918 to secure a government contract, but he was too late.

In 1919, various listings still noted the Golden West truck with a Buda engine as the Model G. In 1920, the Model H and Model HT were also listed with a Buda engine. For 1921, the truck was called the Model K, and each of these were offered for an even $5,000. No shipping weights or identification numbers were provided, and the trucks were rated as 3-ton and 5-ton models. It is doubtful that any were actually built.

By 1922, another reorganization took place and the company's official name changed to Big Four. It is possible, though highly unlikely, that one or two Big Four trucks, rated at 4-ton capacity, were built. The Model H was listed with a Buda YTU engine, and the Model K with a Buda BTU engine. Parts listings noted the name "Big Four - formerly Golden West," implying that "Robinson" had never really been the company's name after all. After 1922, the Big Four name was associated with a sales dealership, and within a few years it faded out altogether.

GOODWIN See GUILDER

GOODYEAR 1920-1926 — The Goodyear Tire and Rubber Company of Akron, Ohio, built a small number of trucks and buses to illustrate the importance of its pneumatic tire design advances. Before building its own trucks for this purpose, Goodyear had used the 1917 E-Series Packard to begin its road tests. By 1920, many if not most trucks, buses and various commercial vehicles still used solid rubber tires, which limited their speed, hastened road deterioration and did not contribute to the comfort of the driver and passengers. At this time, Goodyear and other tire companies were already developing pneumatic tires for heavier capacity vehicles up to the 6-ton range. But the newly developed "balloon" tires caused trucks to be mismatched with the cargo floor heights of loading docks.

Goodyear hired Ellis W. Templin, who was an automotive engineer, to design and develop six-wheel 5-ton and 6-ton trucks whose tires could be reduced in size by equalizing the load among three axles and six wheels. Templin designed a bogie that was chain-driven from a Timken worm axle and used longitudinal oscillating beams, one on each side with one wheel at both ends. Later, a dual drive Templin designed used two Timken worm axles at the ends of inverted semi-elliptic springs that were in conjunction with slightly telescoping torque arms.

Other than the tandem drives, Goodyear trucks were conventional assembled vehicles that were built with van bodies. A bright aluminum radiator and well-designed front sheet metal gave the trucks

an aesthetic appearance. Artillery wheels carried the Goodyear showcase pneumatic tires, which supported the 8,500 pounds plus cargo that these trucks weighed.

Similarly designed Goodyear buses were also produced. In fact, the first buses used the above mentioned truck chassis and suspensions. A second design used a trolley car body with forward-control and tandem rear axles. A third design used a trolley car body but had tandem axles both front and rear. All trucks and buses used single wheels on each end of the axles.

1921 GOODYEAR 5-TON 6-WHEEL TRUCK   GOODYEAR

In Akron, Ohio, the Goodyear Heights bus line became the first to operate commercial service tandems. For promotional purposes, one of the Goodyear trucks was driven 3,500 miles from New York to Los Angeles in 6-1/2 days setting a new record. With a maximum speed of 45 mph, the 5-ton Goodyear truck was considerably faster than almost any other trucks of that era.

Goodyear used its own 6x4 showcase trucks and 4x2 White and Packard cargo trucks and tractor-semi-trailer combinations as part of its Wingfoot Express between its Akron, Ohio, and Boston, Massachusetts, factories. As Goodyear's point was proven, by 1926, when pneumatic tire sales surpassed that of solid rubber tires, the Goodyear trucks were gradually fazed out of service.

GOPHER see ROBINSON-LOOMIS

1926 GOTFREDSON 6-WHEEL BUS   KLP

GOTFREDSON 1920-1951 — Gotfredson was always an American-owned truck builder in Detroit, and it was almost simultaneously organized in Walkerville, Ontario, Canada. By 1923, it was being produced in the United States and although the Detroit, Michigan, operations were smaller than the Canadian ones, the U.S. factory outlived the Canadian one by about one-and-a-half decades.

This truck was originally called the G & J, which stood for Gotfredson and Joyce Corporation Limited. By 1923, it was incorporated simply as Gotfredson both in Walkerville and Detroit. Gotfredson trucks were conventional assembled trucks using standard components. For example, the 3-ton of 1923 used a four-cylinder Buda engine, four-speed Brown-Lipe transmission and Timken worm-drive.

For 1925, Gotfredson offered five models that were 1-, 2-, 3-, 4- and 5-ton capacity. The 1-ton Model 20 B with 131-inch wheelbase was powered by a 22.5 hp four-cylinder Buda WTU engine with Zenith carburetor and Remy ignition coupled through a Borg and Beck clutch to a Brown-Lipe transmission. The rear axle was made by Clark and the front axle by Salisbury while Van wheels carried 33x5 front and rear pneumatic tires with Gemmer steering.

The 2-ton Model 41 with 146-1/2-inch wheelbase differed considerably in that it was powered by a 25.6 hp four-cylinder Buda KBUI engine and used Timken axles both front and rear. Mechanics Machine wheels carried 36x6 front and 40x8 rear pneumatic tires as standard equipment. Otherwise the component manufacturers were the same as on the 1-ton model.

On the 3-ton Model 60 with 152-1/2-inch wheelbase the powerplant was a 28.9 hp four-cylinder Buda EBUI engine. On this model, Day wheels carried 36x4 front and 36x10 tires with pneumatics at extra cost. On the 4-ton Model 80 with 160-inch wheelbase the engine was a 32.4 hp four-cylinder Buda YBUI. Solid rubber tires were 34x5 front with 36x12 rear. On the 5-ton Model 100 with 169-inch wheelbase a 40.0 hp four-cylinder Buda BTU engine was used. Again, solid rubber tires were used with front being 36x6 and rear 40x14.

Two years later the model line included a 3/4-ton and a 7-ton truck, as well as four-wheel and six-wheel buses and coaches, fire engines and taxicabs. Gotfredson also built car bodies, but this was a small fraction of the business. By 1929, total annual production had risen to 2,000. The company marketed its vehicles throughout Canada and some were sold in Great Britain, including 14-passenger coaches, which were especially popular there.

Most Gotfredson vehicles were easily identifiable due to their bright cast aluminum radiator. Otherwise they were not unusual in appearance. The American division went into bankruptcy in 1929. It was reorganized as the Robert Gotfredson Truck Company in Detroit. Production continued on a much smaller scale. The Canadian factory was shut down in 1932, and soon thereafter, it was purchased by the Ford Motor Company.

Custom-built Gotfredson vehicles continued to be produced in Detroit using Cummins diesel engines and Buda gasoline engines. GMC cabs and fenders were utilized. Gotfredson also became the dealer for Cummins throughout Michigan. After World War II, Gotfredson used 150 hp Cummins diesel engines. According to some records, a handful of these trucks were built up to 1951.

GRABOWSKY 1900-1902; 1908-1913 — Max Grabowsky was best known for building the first heavy truck in the United States. It had a 5-ton capacity and was completed in 1900. Two years later, the Grabowsky brothers established the Rapid Motor Vehicle Company, which was to become the basis for GMC trucks a decade later. In the meantime, Max Grabowsky broke away from the Rapid Motor Vehicle Company in 1908 to form his own Grabowsky Power Wagon Company in Detroit, Michigan.

Max Grabowsky's design was somewhat different from the previous 5-ton creation. His new company built 1-ton and 1-1/2-ton truck chassis, and these were at first powered by a 22 hp horizontally-opposed two-cylinder engine mounted at the front of the truck, and the engine used a cone clutch, planetary transmission with double chain drive. The engines were specially mounted so that they could be easily slid out of the frame for maintenance and repairs. Bodies were also designed to be easily interchangeable. But by 1911, the Grabowsky Power Wagon Company also built another 5-ton capacity truck powered by a four-cylinder engine, and the same special easily-removable mounting was employed as well.

By 1920, a larger four-cylinder engine was also available and, according to scant records, Grabowsky vehicles were all built for commercial purposes. These included trucks with a variety of factory-built bodies, as well as sightseeing buses.

GRAHAM BROTHERS 1919-1928 — The Graham Brothers started producing the Truck-Builder in 1919 in Evansville, Indiana. Joseph, Ray and Robert Grahams' product consisted of the following components: frame, cab, body and Torbensen internal gear drive, which allowed customers to build their own trucks, most often utilizing passenger car engines and transmissions as well as many other components. The product's design was sound, and the Graham Brothers soon began assembling their own complete trucks. For 1920, Graham Brothers introduced a new 18-passenger Speed Bus priced at $3,445, which was based on a 1-1/2-ton Graham Speed Truck chassis.

Graham provided fifth wheel turntables for creating light articulated truck tractors. Conventional models were available in 1-, 1-1/2- and 2-ton capacity, while the articulated truck tractors were available in 3-ton and 5-ton capacity.

After John and Horace Dodge died in 1920 from a widely-known alcohol habit, the subsequent president of Dodge, Frederick J. Haynes, decided to buy majority interest in Graham Brothers and to build Graham trucks in Detroit using Dodge four-cylinder engines and transmissions along with other Dodge components. Marketing was also handled by Dodge. This effectively made Graham trucks a Dodge product, although not specifically by marque, until the Dodge widows sold their deceased husbands' company for a well-publicized $130 million, as well as the subsequent purchase of Dodge Brothers by Chrysler in 1927 (although the name did not change to simply "Dodge" for a couple of years).

1908 GRABOWSKY POWER WAGON   RD

1909 GRABOWSKY 2-TON   RD

1920 GRAHAM BROS. 18-PASSENGER BUS   RD

177

1925 GRAHAM BROS. FIRE ENGINE   S.RAY MILLER

Graham trucks were of conventional design and good reputation. Their chronological appearance was identifiable by the progressive design of the wheels: from disc to artillery to cast steel spoke. The latter carried pneumatic tires by 1924, and spiral bevel rear axles were adopted. That year Graham offered five models. These included the 1-ton Model BB with 130-inch wheelbase for $1,175, and four 1-1/2-ton models: Model CB with 140-inch wheelbase priced at $1,375, Model FB with 158-inch wheelbase priced at $1,425, Model MB with 140-inch wheelbase priced at $1,440 and the Model LB with 158-inch wheelbase priced at $1,490. Front axles, engines, clutches and transmissions were built by Dodge with Graham's rear axles and steering. The electrical systems were built by North East and carburetors were Detroit Lubricator.

1927 GRAHAM BROS. SD-770 PANEL DELIVERY   LAMANO

In 1927, Dodge bought out Graham Brothers outright, and 1/4-, 1/2-, 2- and 2-1/2-ton models were added to the line, some with 60 hp six-cylinder engines, which were designed by Dodge but manufactured by Continental. Graham Brothers produced approximately 60,000 vehicles per year as Dodge reached the number seven spot in overall sales under Chrysler ownership and management. Graham trucks became Dodge Brothers in 1929.

1928 GRAHAM BROS. 2-TON BOTTLER'S BODY   MROZ

1928 GRAHAM BROS. 1-1/2-TON HAND DUMP TRUCK MROZ

As part of the acquisition agreement, the Graham brothers were barred from building trucks and so they purchased the Paige-Detroit Motor Car Company and continued to build the Graham-Paige until 1931 when the marque became known simply as the Graham. The last Graham cars, some of them known for avant-garde styling, were built in 1941. However, the second Graham company as a business became the Madison Square Garden Corporation and has continued to stay viable to date as a sports and circus events sponsor.

1913 GRAMM WILLYS-UTILITY 3/4-TON   OCW

GRAMM 1910-1913 — Although alphabetically this company precedes the Gramm-Logan, Gramm was actually the continuation of the Gramm-Logan, which was organized by Benjamin A. Gramm. Gramm had started out as the general manager of the Motor Storage and Repair Company of Chillicothe, Ohio. He began building steam carriages in 1902, but by the following year he switched to gasoline power. The Gramm-Logan Motor Car Company was organized in 1908 in Bowling Green, Ohio, but as Gramm the firm was moved to Lima, Ohio.

Gramm expanded its model line over the previous company's offerings. The 3-ton cab-over-engine Model X was upgraded to 5-ton capacity, and 1-, 2- and 3-ton capacity trucks were also produced. By 1911, conventional trucks superseded the COE, although forward-control models were still advertised as late as November 1912 when Gramm used the system of analyzing delivery costs as a sales pitch. The Gramm company built some conventional trucks until John Willys purchased the firm in 1913. Benjamin Gramm formed the Gramm-Bernstein Company in 1912 when he joined up with Max Bernstein.

GRAMM 1926-1942 — Once R.M. Kinkaid left Gramm in 1926, Benjamin Gramm continued with his son, Willard J. Gramm. At this point the senior Gramm became the chief financial officer also in charge of marketing, while his son took over the helm as engineer and designer. For 1926, Gramm introduced the "Fast Freighter."

A complete model line of trucks and buses was available from Gramm Motors Incorporated, which was located in Delphos, Ohio. The lightest truck was a 1-ton model, and the heaviest truck was

5-ton capacity at that time. Both four-cylinder and six-cylinder engines built by Continental, Hercules and Lycoming were used. By 1929, the four-cylinder engines were discontinued.

1931 GRAMM 8-TON ARTICULATED TRUCK   **NAHC**

1914 GRAMM-BERNSTEIN   **KP**

Probably because John Willys bought the Gramm factory in Lima, Ohio, and a relationship had been established, Gramm and Willys cooperated throughout the 1920s. Using the Willys-Knight passenger car engine Gramm built 1-, 1-1/2-, 2- and 2-1/2-ton capacity trucks for Willys-Overland. These were exported beginning in 1927 and were sold in the United States and Canada starting in 1928 through 1930.

By 1932, Gramm built its own commercial vehicles for export under the Condor truck name. At first, these were identical to the Gramm trucks but by 1934 different engines were utilized, among other components. The Condor trucks received Waukesha-Hesselman engines instead of the Cummins and Hercules engines that the Gramm trucks had. The Waukesha-Hesselman engine had a specially-designed ignition system in order to burn light oil in areas where fuel grade was poor.

The U.S. government bought Condor trucks for use in penitentiaries, and African explorer Martin Johnson used Condor trucks. In 1934, the design changed when V-shaped radiators were adopted along with new cabs and fenders that resembled Stewart trucks. These trucks were still rated from 1-ton to 5-ton capacity, but in 1936 Cummins and Hercules engines were available and capacity was extended to 7-1/2-ton. That year, Gramm trucks were distinguished by twin trumpet horns. Bickle, the fire engine builders of Woodstock, Ontario, Canada, got involved in assembling Gramm trucks, offering Perkins diesel engines, but only one such truck was known to have been actually constructed. At the same time, Gramm trucks were sold in Western Canada as Condor trucks.

In 1937, Gramm listed the following models from 1-ton to 7 1/2-ton: 15A, 25A, 30A, 40A, 45A, 50A, 55A, 70A, 75A, 85A, DJX40A, DJX55A, DJX70A, DJX75A, DJX85A, GF, EY190, GY, GW, HY, and GWD. Models including EY190 through HY were powered by Continental engines. The last model on the list was the only Cummins powered truck that Gramm offered that year. Gramm used several axle builders at that time including Brown-Lipe, Clark, Timken and Wisconsin, and transmissions suppliers were even more numerous: Brown-Lipe, Clark, Covert, Fuller and Wagner. Prices started at $565 for the Model 15A and went all the way to $6,595 for the Model HY. GVW started at 9,500 pounds and went to 30,000 pounds for the Model GWD.

By 1939, Gramm began building a new series of trucks using cabs of the Willys 1/2-ton pickup. These were not particularly successful due to a shortage of interior space. In 1942, Gramm discontinued truck building but continued to build trailers and specialty bodies before Fruehauf Trailers acquired the factory. Export markets had dried up during World War II and this also contributed to the company's demise.

GRAMM-BERNSTEIN 1912-1930 — After selling the Gramm company to John Willys, Benjamin Gramm joined with Max Bernstein in Lima, Ohio. By 1912, the Gramm-Bernstein trucks were either 2-ton or 3-1/2-ton capacity, and in 1915 a 6-ton model was added. During World War I, Gramm-Bernstein, along with Selden, developed the U.S. Army Class B Liberty truck and built approximately 1,000 of them. At the same time, Gramm-Bernstein continued to build trucks from 1-1/2-ton to 6-ton for civilian use. All of these models had worm-drive.

By 1924, Gramm-Bernstein offered the 1-ton Model 10-Special with 129-inch wheelbase, which was powered by a 22.5 hp Lycoming CT engine with a Muncie clutch and transmission. Both front and rear axles were made by Salisbury and Van wheels carried 33x5 pneumatic tires as standard equipment. The Model 10 was rated at 1-1/4-ton capacity and was equipped the same as the previous model. Two 1-1/2-ton models were available: the Model 115 was powered by a 25.6 hp Lycoming engine while the Model 65 was powered by a 22.5 hp Continental J-4 engine. Both had a 138-inch wheelbase, used Gramm-Bernstein rear axles and Columbia front axles. However, the Model 115 used a Fuller transmission, while the Model 65 used its own. Steering was by Ross and Bimel wheels carried pneumatic tires on the Model 115, while the Model 65 had solid rubber tires. The latter was priced at $2,550.

Gramm-Bernstein also built the 2-1/2-ton Model 125 with 144-inch wheelbase powered by a 27.2 hp Continental K-4 engine. On this model the rear axle was by Sheldon and the truck had its own transmission. The 3-ton Model 30 was powered by a 28.9 hp Hinkley engine and both front and rear axles were by Sheldon. There was also a 3-1/2-ton Model 75P with a 32.4 hp Hinkley engine and its own transmission. The 4-ton Model 40 had the same engine but the 5-ton Model 50 was powered by a 36.1 hp Continental engine. For these two heaviest models Gramm-Bernstein built its own transmissions. There was also a 6-ton Model 56 that used the same engine as above.

By 1926, six-cylinder engines were introduced. Meanwhile, Benjamin Gramm formed a new company with his son, W.J. Gramm and R.M. Kincaid. While the Gramm-Bernstein company continued to build a few trucks until 1930, Gramm-Kincaid built trucks simultaneously in 1925 and 1926.

1925 GRAMM-KINCAID   **EF**

GRAMM-KINCAID 1925-1926 — Gramm-Kincaid Motors Incorporated was formed by Benjamin Gramm and R.M. Kincaid, who had been vice-president of Garford trucks, also located in Lima, Ohio. The Gramm-Kincaids were aesthetically designed trucks from 1-ton to 4-ton capacity. Both four-cylinder and six-cylinder engines were available built by Continental, Hercules and Lycoming.

For 1926, Gramm-Kincaid introduced a bus chassis that had an unusually low double-drop cruciform-stiffened frame and four-wheel-brakes. Two versions were produced: a 21-passenger city bus and a 20-passenger intercity coach. Kincaid left the company in 1926 and the company name once again became simply Gramm, as listed above.

1909 GRAMM-LOGAN   NAHC

GRAMM-LOGAN 1908-1910 — The Gramm-Logan Motor Car Company of Bowling Green, Ohio, built three models of trucks. This was the first company Benjamin Gramm started after producing a few steam cars in 1902, then switching to gasoline-powered surreys in 1903.

The Model Y Gramm-Logan was powered by a 24 hp engine and was built as a delivery van. The Model V was a 1-1/2-ton truck powered by a 25 hp engine and the Model X was a 3-ton truck with a 45 hp engine and chain drive. In 1910, Gramm moved his company to Lima, Ohio, where it became the Gramm Motor Car Company at the end of that year. Gramm went on to become a truck manufacturing pioneer with a variety of partners and collaborators, including his own son Willard, John Willys, Max Bernstein and R.M. Kincaid, among others.

New Grant Speed Truck, Known as Model 17, One and a Half Ton Capacity, Which is Equipped With Pneumatic Tires.

1920 GRANT MODEL 17   MROZ

GRANT 1918-1923 — The Grant Motor Company of Detroit, Michigan, was founded in 1913 by George D. Grant and brother Charles A. Grant, president and vice-president, respectively. They had operated a car dealership and machine foundry right after the turn of the century. By the time the Grant Motor Company was formed the Grant brothers had surrounded themselves with auto-

motive experts. Secretary-treasurer was David A. Shaw, who had been treasurer at the Simplex Motor Car Company. James Howe, the chief engineer, was a Cornell graduate. Factory manager George S. Salzman had built his first car in 1897 and had been production manager for Simplex and Thomas and the sales manager, George S. Waite, had worked for those two companies as well. Despite all the talent, the post-World War I recession spelled doom for the Grant company as it tried to continue large-scale production even after sales had dwindled.

The first Grant roadster was powered by a 12 hp four-cylinder engine and it was built on a 90-inch wheelbase. By 1915, the Model S had a 20 hp six-cylinder engine and along with the four-cylinder Model M, Grant produced 12,000 cars in 1917. During the war, a second factory in Findlay, Ohio, which also had been opened in 1913, produced munitions for the allied military while the Detroit plant built ordnance trailers. Out of this experience, Grant began building trucks in 1918 using four-cylinder Continental engines and Grant-Lees three-speed transmissions with Torbensen rear axles. The model line consisted of 3/4-, 1-1/2- and 2-ton trucks with wheelbases up to 160 inches.

The lightest truck was discontinued in 1920 and overall car production had dropped to 5,400 for that year. But Grant introduced its Model 17-1/2-ton Speed Truck that year, which was equipped with pneumatic tires and had a top speed of 30 mph. It had a 35 hp 220-cubic inch four-cylinder Continental Red Seal engine and used a four-speed transmission with direct drive in fourth gear. Standard equipment included electric starting and lighting, spotlight, bumper, windshield, Moto-meter, speedometer and power-driven tire pump.

With sales plummeting and $500,000 in inventory sitting stranded, Grant sold off its Walker engine division by 1921, but receivership arrived the following year nevertheless. Although passenger car production ceased at that point, some trucks continued to be assembled until June 1923, when the entire company was sold to the Lincoln Electric Company for $425,000.

GRANT-FERRIS 1901 — The Grant-Ferris Company of Troy, New York, briefly built a light van using a horizontally-opposed two-cylinder engine. Load capacity was 1/4-ton and top speed was 12 mph. The van's design included a fairly primitive pulley-type transmission. Other than this information, little else is known about this obscure company. It was not affiliated with the later Ferris company of Cleveland, Ohio.

1936 GRASS-PREMIER DUMP TRUCK   RJ

GRASS-PREMIER 1923-1937 — As a low volume production truck manufacturer, Grass-Premier stayed in business for almost 15 years during a period that saw many such companies go bankrupt or be absorbed by larger firms. Grass-Premier was located in Sauk City, Wisconsin, just outside Madison. Henry Grass, who had built tractors and hoists in Sauk City, was the organizer of Grass-Premier. The first truck model line consisted of three capacities: two 1-1/2-ton vehicles and also a 4-ton model. They were powered by either Continental or Lycoming engines and used Clark or Timken axles.

For 1923, the company produced less than 10 trucks. Two years later, for 1925, Grass-Premier offered the 1-ton Model 40 chassis with 126-inch wheelbase (others optional) for $1,360. It was powered by a 22.6 hp Lycoming CT engine, had a Brown-Lipe transmission with Clark rear axle and Salisbury front axle. Pneumatic tires were standard equipment. The 2-ton Model 70 with 140-inch wheelbase chassis sold for $2,750. This model was powered by a 27.2 hp Waukesha engine and used Timken axles front and rear. Grass-Premier also built the 2-1/2-ton Model 80 for $3,050, which had a 30.6 hp Waukesha engine. The heftiest but similar truck was the 3-1/2-ton Model 90 using a 160-inch wheelbase chassis that sold for $3,700 with a 32.4 hp Waukesha DU engine.

After six-cylinder engines were introduced at this time, Lycoming straight-eight engines were adopted for some models, which prompted the Lycoming company to further improve its eight-cylinder engines, which included the large AEC model. The range included trucks from 3-ton to 10-ton capacity and Waukesha engines and Wisconsin axles were adopted. For 1927, Grass-Premier listed trucks from the 2-ton Model 50 to the 4-ton Model 90-6. Of the eight Grass-Premier trucks available that year, the lightest four were powered by Lycoming engines, while the heavier four used Waukesha, the largest engine being the 6D.

The widest range was offered in 1932, when Grass-Premier trucks were available from 1-ton capacity to a 12-ton truck tractor. Sleeper cabs were offered as early as 1932 and the trucks featured many aluminum weight-saving components.

Grass-Premier developed a heavy-duty 5-ton COE truck using a Ford V-8 engine, but only built a few of these units for a Chicago customer in 1936. (Records conflict showing numbers between 4 and 12). The COE prototype was actually an inline six-cylinder but that design proved too difficult to drive and to service. The final design employed Timken axles and either Fuller or Warner transmissions were available. The cab seemed to be styled after the current Available truck COE design. These were built using an 88-inch wheelbase and were designed so that the engine and transmission could be easily slid out for service and repair. Seeing this innovation, United Parcel Service representatives offered to set up a factory in the east but the Grass-Premier employees refused to move.

The last year of manufacture Grass-Premier listed the 4-ton Model 545 for $2,400, 5-ton Model 555 for $3,600, 7-ton Model 565 for $4,400 and the 10-ton Model 575 for $5,400. Each was powered by a six-cylinder Waukesha engine using Fuller transmissions and Eaton, Timken or Wisconsin rear axles. Engine hp ranged from 85 to 125, and all front axles were built by Timken. Grass-Premier's low production volume slowed to a trickle and dried up entirely in 1937. Production over the years has been estimated at 350 units.

GRAY 1916 — Gilbert M. Anderson and Robert T. Matches teamed up in Sunnyvale, California, to build taxicabs for their Gray Taxicab Company, which operated in the San Francisco and Los Angeles areas. After receiving exclusive rights along the Southern Pacific system, which was no small accomplishment, the two partners started by purchasing the Goldy Machine Company in Sunnyvale, where it lay along the Southern Pacific tracks. It had been the brief home of the Elbert cyclecar and was equipped for manufacturing seven taxis per day.

Soon after the operation started under the combined name of Andermat Machine Company, however, it appears the two partners had a series of major disagreements rather than a series of taxicabs. Anderson stated to the press that he had fired Matches for diverting company funds to outside business, namely the development of the Hydromotor amphibian project.

Matches answered from New York City that he had "resigned voluntarily to give my entire attention to aeroplane interests." He denied wrongdoing and drew attention to the fact that Anderson had been preoccupied with his own outside interests. Anderson was, in fact, "Broncho Billy" of silent film fame and collaborated on a studio venture in Niles, California, where he produced some of Charlie Chaplin's first movies.

That a few taxicabs were built is certain, but any actual specifications have been lacking. Matches was later indicted after the collapse of the Emerson Motor Company.

1925 GRAY 1-TON OCW

GRAY 1923-1926 — The Gray Motor Corporation was formed with $4 million in capital when the Gray Motor Company's factory and assets were sold in 1923. The Gray Company had built engines in Detroit, Michigan, and the new enterprise was formed to build medium-priced four-cylinder passenger cars using much of the existing tooling.

One of the chief organizers was Frank F. Beall, former vice-president of Packard Motor Car Company and William H. Blackburn, former Cadillac superintendent. A year later the vice-president and treasurer of the Ford Motor Company, Frank L. Klingensmith joined Gray as president.

Two commercial iterations were built by 1923 using the same engine and chassis, which were 20 hp and 104-inch wheelbase, respectively. This wheelbase length, which was fabricated as a van, was also used on the 1925 passenger cars. A 1-ton model used an extended chassis with 120-inch wheelbase.

The Gray passenger cars were actually intended to compete with the Ford Model T, using the same original wheelbase and same power four-cylinder engine. The roadster was priced at $490 in 1922 and a record breaking 33.8 miles per gallon was achieved on a promotional run from San Francisco to New York with official observers all along the way speaking with the press. The car was advertised as the "Aristocrat of Small Cars" and production was projected into the hundreds of thousands. It became apparent that beating Henry Ford at his own game was impossible for Gray. A total of 14,772 of them were built. Frank Klingensmith resigned and left for Australia, while plans were announced to build the British Tilling-Stevens Gas-Electric bus, which did not happen as the company was auctioned off in 1926.

GRAY'S 1911 — This short-lived obscure fabricator of a few trucks built a 1-ton vehicle in 1911 only. The Gray's Motor Company was located in Newark, New Jersey. The truck was powered by a 24 hp two-cylinder engine and used a planetary transmission. Wheelbase was 103 inches and early for standard equipment pneumatic tires were sold with the few trucks that were actually produced.

GREAT EAGLE 1910-1915 — The United States Carriage Company announced in 1909 that it would build touring cars, runabouts, motor hearses, cabs and ambulances. Great Eagle vehicles were also built as police patrol wagons and limousines. In 1910, they were powered by a 40 hp engine and had a 126-inch wheelbase. In 1912, a 41 hp six-cylinder engine was introduced on a 138-inch wheelbase. For the final two years, the six-cylinder engine developed 60 hp and the vehicles were on a 142-inch wheelbase. Factory prices started at $3,500 in 1910 but by the last year of production they approached $6,000 for a 10-passenger limousine on a 147-inch wheelbase.

The six-cylinder engine 6-60 superseded the Model C of 1913 but was essentially the same design and had the same components. The Model B of 1913, which had a 50 hp four-cylinder engine, was discontinued after 1913. The company went into receivership in 1915, when the wife of Fred C. Myers, the company president, came to collect a $6,000 note she had against the company, fearing she would lose it all if all the other creditors showed up at the same time. The Great Eagle was going to be resurrected in 1918 but that plan never materialized.

GREAT SOUTHERN 1915-1917 — The Great Southern Automobile Company was formed in 1909 with capitalization of $100,000. President of the company was E.F. Enslen, vice-president was Ike Adler, secretary treasurer was John J. Kyser and general manager was E.F.

Enslen, Jr. Nothing progressed in the field of motor vehicle manufacture but in 1911, the company increased its capital to $500,000. A cotton mill was procured for production and repair but it was not until 1912 that a Great Southern vehicle was produced. There were two passenger car models. The Model 30 had a 30 hp engine and 113-inch wheelbase and the Model 40 had a 55 hp engine and used a 128-inch wheelbase. They sold for $1,400 and $1,750, respectively.

By 1915, however, passenger car production ceased entirely and the company switched to bus manufacturing. That year, a 25-passenger bus was built as a Great Southern. This type of chassis had only a seven-inch minimum clearance. The company built 2-ton and 4-ton versions using underslung worm-drive to achieve the low frame height. These were some of the few commercial vehicles to have been built in the deep south.

GREAT WESTERN 1911-1912 — A degree of controversy surrounds the background information regarding Great Western. It is not certain that Great Western Transportation Company was affiliated with Great Western Automobile Company, both of which existed at the same time, the former in Chicago, Illinois, and the latter in Peru, Indiana. The only thing certain is that a Great Western 10-ton gasoline-electric hybrid-powered truck was built using a 172-inch wheelbase. The solid rubber tires on it were 48x12 front and rear. Two other manufacturers by the name of Great Western existed a few years earlier, one in La Porte, Indiana, and the other in San Diego, California.

GREENE 1908, 1916 — The Greene Motor Car Company was a dealership for Locomobile in Newark and Patterson, New Jersey, while importing Panhard, Mercedes and Renault to the United States from Europe. Records mention that the company displayed an electric truck in 1908. It was not until 1916 that Raymond A. Greene got involved in building what could best be described as a vehicle intended for commercial application.

The Greene vehicle was designed by M.A. Mackay. It had three axles and used a 200-inch wheelbase. Its turning radius was 32 feet, even though both front and rear axles were controlled by the steering wheel. Only the center axle's wheels were non-steering. Businessman were intrigued with the idea and wanted to build a delivery van version of the vehicle. It is not known what type of motor was employed, but the six-wheel goliath went only as far as the prototype stage.

GREYHOUND 1914-1915 — The Greyhound Cyclecar Company began in Toledo, Ohio. Its slogan was the "Aristocrat of Cyclecars" and these vehicles were also fitted with a van body. It was powered by an 18 hp air-cooled four-cylinder engine, although some records show that an earlier 10 hp engine was also used. The narrow track vehicle had a wheelbase of 104 inches, while the track was 30 inches. Shaft drive and a planetary transmission were utilized. The vehicles weighed only 600 pounds and were priced at $385.

Although the company advertised that it was ready to deliver 2,400 vehicles for 1914, no such orders reflected the alleged manufacturing capabilities and the company moved to Kalamazoo, Michigan. There it was reorganized, but no commercial vehicles followed. While it appears the company restarted under various names, a few more Greyhound passenger cars were built up to 1916. This company was not affiliated with the Greyhound Motors Corporation of East Warren, Rhode Island, which began in 1919.

1939 GRICO TWIN-MOTOR TRUCK TRACTOR   RD

GRICO 1938-1939 — The Gear Grinding Machine Company of Detroit, Michigan, built the Grico Twin-Motor Tractor. It would appear the tractor truck was essentially based on a Ford truck with two engines, but the second six-cylinder engine was mounted directly behind the first and drove a second rear axle separately from the forward engine. Combined hp was given as 190. A large box-type hood allowed access to the rear engine. The engines had separate controls or could be operated simultaneously as was intended. Whether more then one prototype was built has not been documented.

1903 GROUT 2-1/2-TON STEAM TRUCK   RD

GROUT 1899-1905 — Although the Grout Brothers Automobile Company started earlier, the first steam vehicle was built in 1899 and this was the basis for the Grout steam trucks of which there were a number of different capacities. The three sons of William L. Grout, Carl, Fred and C.B., who were not interested in their father's New Home Sewing Machine Company in Orange, Massachusetts, were set up by their father in the automotive business. After their experiments in the late 1890s using both steam and gasoline power, the brothers started producing both steam cars and trucks. Some of the early vehicles were extremely tall, others had perfectly round hoods and a single headlight in the center.

Grout "New Home" cars were exported to England under the Weston name. The early trucks were COE design using a one-man pilot-house-type cab centered on a platform ahead of the front axle. The long centered steering column was vertical and the cab was twice as tall, with a roof overhang "visor" and rectangular windows on three sides. One of the vehicle models came with a cowcatcher. The 1903 Grout 2-1/2-ton introduced for the following year had a 12 hp slide valve steam engine amidships with a 15 hp 16-inch diameter boiler mounted directly under the driver's seat, which may have had unforseen consequences. Claims were made of 8 mph top speed and an ability to climb a 15 percent grade. Wooden wheels were 32-inch diameter with solid rubber tires.

By 1904, Grout was producing 18 vehicles per week. Twenty-six gallons of kerosene with enough water gave the truck a 20 mile range at top speed. The high torque of the steam engine allowed for climbing capability as was touted by the Grout brothers. Drive was with countershaft and then to each rear wheel by chain.

In 1905, the brothers added a gasoline vehicle to their model line and by the following year they ceased building steam vehicles. At the same time, it appears they stopped producing trucks and commercial vehicles. Their gasoline-powered model line was not as successful. By 1907, their father objected to the manner in which they were doing their business and served them with a $200,000 lien on their factory. Despite their efforts to have William Grout diagnosed as incompetent due to his 74 years of age, the senior Grout took over the company and the three Grout brothers vanished from the vicinity. However, William Grout died in 1908 and the company was reorganized by Walter J. Gould and his two business associates, who also died suddenly. Production stopped in 1912 and the company was auctioned off the following year. The factory was taken over by the Red Arrow Automobile Company.

1970 GRUMAN MODEL B-100 19-PASSENGER BUS   MBS

GRUMMAN/GRUMMAN-OLSON 1963 to date — The Grumman Allied Industries Incorporated, located in Garden City, New York, was the aerospace company that purchased the J.B. Olson Corporation. Olson was a builder of aluminum truck bodies and in 1963, Grumman launched the Kurbmaster line of commercial vans. Olson's aluminum bodies were supplied on other chassis but the Kurbmaster was built on Chevrolet, Ford and GMC units. These were sold only by Grumman dealers.

For 1970, Grumman built the Model B-100 19-passenger bus. By 1978, Grumman offered a variety of vans from 102-inch to 178-inch wheelbase. These were continued in production through the 1980s. In 1985, Grumman, along with two other companies (POVECO and American Motors), submitted designs for the Long Life Vehicle. Three prototypes were put on a 24,000-mile road test by Uniroyal Tire Company. The postal vans were specified as to be able to last 24 years with maintenance and overhauls. Their design also included automatic transmission and right-hand drive.

1993 GRUMMAN LONG LIFE VEHICLE   MROZ

According to Postal Service transportation director Robert St. Stevens, the postal service placed an order for 143,000 LLV vans from Grumman, which were delivered to the U.S. Post Office by 1995. One of the design criteria was that the gasoline engines were to be easily converted to propane. Two other companies, Mesa Environmental of Fort Worth, Texas, and Beacon Power Systems of Troy, Michigan, received a total of $3.3 million worth of contracts to transform approximately 1,500 Grumman LLV vans to propane power in the mid-1990s. Grumman merged with Northrop Corporation in 1993 and became a division of that giant corporation. All Grumman bodies have been built on Chevrolet and GMC chassis to date.

GUARANTY 1917-1918—Samuel W. Prussian, known as a "furniture man," organized the Guaranty Motors Corporation in Cambridge, Massachusetts. He first started to build truck attachments for Ford Model T cars. It appears that a complete Guaranty truck was built using Motel T components. For that unit, Samuel Prussian fabricated the truck frame, gear drive and attachments, which were also available in kit form. There are no records showing complete vehicle fabrication after 1918, although the company remained viable in Cambridge until 1922.

GUILDER, GOODWIN, GOODWIN-GUILDER, 1922-1936 — The Guilder Engineering Company was located in Poughkeepsie, New York. The Guilder was a truck that evolved from the Goodwin truck built by the Goodwin Car Manufacturing Company also of Poughkeepsie. Goodwin had built railway rolling stock up to 1922 when the company turned its manufacturing efforts to the production of heavy trucks. These were distinctive vehicles with large cast aluminum radiators, and Guilder himself was the design engineer at Goodwin.

The first Goodwin-Guilder vehicle was introduced at the end of 1922. It was a bus chassis using a drop-frame design with complex and expensive one-piece siderail pressings. The bus was powered by a four-cylinder Buda engine.

Guilder became a marque in itself in 1924, when the company built truck chassis from 1-ton to 6-ton capacity. These included the following models: the 1-ton Model B with 132-inch wheelbase was powered by a 22.5 hp Buda WTU engine coupled to a Brown-Lipe transmission. Front axle was by Shuler, rear axle was by Clark and Indestructible Wheels carried 33x5 front and rear pneumatic tires as standard equipment. Chassis price was $1,650 and chassis weight was 3,250 pounds.

The 1-1/2-ton Model D also with 132-inch wheelbase had the same make components as above, except Van Wheels carried solid rubber tires. Chassis price was $2,250 but weight was slightly lower at 3,200 pounds. The 2-ton Model E with 152-inch wheelbase used a 25.6 hp Buda GTU engine. On this model Van Wheels carried 36x4 front and 36x8 rear solid rubber tires. Chassis price was $2,775 and chassis weight was 5,100 pounds.

The 3-ton Model H with 152-inch wheelbase was powered by a 28.9 hp Buda ETU engine. Chassis price was $3,500 and chassis weight was 5,600 pounds. In this case, the rear axle was made by Wisconsin and Van Wheels carried 35x5 front and 36x10 rear solid rubber tires. There was also a 4-ton Model J powered by a 32.4 hp Buda YTU engine with same make components as the previous model. The 5-ton Model K5-6 used a 40.0 hp Buda BTU engine. The largest Guilder was the 7-1/2-ton Model K, which was also powered by a Buda BTU engine. Chassis prices for the three heaviest Guilder trucks were $3,500, $4,500 and $5,250, respectively. In the same chronology, chassis weights for the truck models were 5,600, 7,500 and 8,500 pounds. Zenith carburetors and Ross steering were used throughout the entire model line.

By 1931, Guilder began offering 10-ton and 16-ton six-wheel trucks along with a model line of buses that included 21-, 25- and 30-passenger chassis. Guilder began to concentrate on a trailing third axle design adaptable to all makes of trucks, but especially for Autocar, Ford and International heavy vehicles. After the Depression, truck production waned both because of economic hard times as well as a change in product marketing. Nevertheless, the Guilder Engineering Company was out of business by 1936.

GUMPRICE 1912-1913 — The Gumprice Motor Truck Company was formed at the end of 1912 by H.E. Rice, Jr., W.C. Haight and Paul Corkell in Chicago, Illinois. Manufacturing has not been substantiated.

1914 G.V. FLARE BOARD EXPRESS   OCW

G.V. 1906-1920 — The General Vehicle Company was an out-growth of the Vehicle Equipment Company, both located in New York, New York. The Vehicle Equipment Company, also known as V.E.C., was founded in late 1900 by Robert Lloyd Havemeyer and his two sons Hector and Arthur Havemeyer. The senior Havemeyer had made a fortune in sugar and was known as the "sugar king." The company began producing shaft-driven electric cars but much of the business was concentrated on commercial vehicles, including sightseeing buses and special crane trucks for hoisting safes to upper floors in the city's office buildings.

Reorganized as the General Vehicle Company, the trucks and cars were known as G.V. A full line of commercial vehicles, along with a Ladies Phaeton, was offered. By 1907, nine different models were available, including flatbed trucks and a Chatsworth bus. G.V. trucks were from 750-pound capacity to 5-ton capacity, including heavy commercial vehicles for the brewing industry. The company built its own storage batteries and used General Electric motors. Some of the models had the General Electric motors mounted midway on the chassis and power was transferred to the rear wheels by chain.

1920 G.V. 5-TON   **OCW**

By 1913, G.V. began building gasoline powered trucks under license from Daimler in Germany. In 1915, the truck division of Peerless in Cleveland, Ohio, merged with G.V. Despite financial cooperation, the two companies continued as independent marques. In 1916, G.V. built hybrid-powered gasoline-electric tractors for the New York Sanitation Department. By the end of 1920, G.V. had built its last vehicle.

G.V. MERCEDES 1913-1918 — The General Vehicle Company of Long Island, mentioned above, undertook the assembly of American Daimler trucks under license in the United States. These were 6-ton capacity trucks with large cast steel wheels and were powered by a four-cylinder water-cooled engine using a four-speed transmission and shaft drive. They were virtual copies of the German design. Despite building numerous electric trucks with some technical advancements over the years, the American Daimler G.V. built remained an outdated commercial vehicle with kerosene lamps and hand-crank starting all the way until its demise in the United States in 1918.

G.W.W. 1920-1925 — The Wilson Truck Manufacturing Company of Henderson, Iowa, built G.W.W. trucks. At first the 1-1/2-ton models were powered by Weidley engines. By 1924, a 2-ton model was added to the 1-1/2-ton Super Model. The 1-1/2-ton Super with 142-inch wheelbase was powered by a 25.6 hp Wisconsin SU engine with Zenith carburetor and Bosch ignition coupled through a Fuller clutch to a Fuller transmission. A Clark rear axle was used, front axle was by Shuler and Bimmel wheels carried 35x5 front and rear pneumatic tires as standard equipment. This lighter model was listed as a bus chassis.

The 2-ton model of 1924 and 1925 featured a 147-inch wheelbase and used a heavier Fuller transmission, with Bimel wheels carrying 36x6 front and 38x7 pneumatic tires as standard equipment. The engine was the same as the Super model's and components were of the same make as with the lighter truck. Lavine steering was utilized on both models. Chassis price for the 1-1/2-ton was $1,650 and chassis weight was 3,200 pounds. The 2-ton had a chassis price of $2,250 and a chassis weight of 4,100 pounds.

H

H

HAFER see IBEX

HAHN 1907-1990 — Not affiliated with the earlier Hahn Automobile of Pueblo, Colorado, the W.G. Hahn and Brothers Company of Hamburg, Pennsylvania, began in 1907, when Hahn added trucks to his line of horsedrawn wagons. Only a few trucks were fabricated in the first five years of production and these were powered by Continental four-cylinder engines. By 1914, the 1-1/2-ton chassis was priced at $2,400. The name of the company was changed to Hahn Motor Truck and Wagon Company in 1913.

By 1915, Hahn offered five models ranging from 3/4-ton to 3-1/2-ton capacity and at the same time, the company began building fire trucks. The following year, worm-drive was adopted for all Hahn models. In 1918, a 5-ton model was added to the line, but this higher capacity truck still used chain drive. By 1920, the 5-ton truck's price tag was up to $10,000, a result of the postwar recession and inflation. That year, the company's name was simplified to the Hahn Motor Truck Company as wagons were no longer built.

By 1922, the company listed eight models from 1-ton to 6-ton ranging in price from $1,750 to $4,650. Production averaged five trucks per week during the 1920s. Starting in 1923, some of the models were powered by Hercules engines.

1917 HAHN   **JAW**

Two years later, the model line started with the 1-1/2-ton Model O and went up to the 5-ton Model M and Model M2. The Model O with 138-inch wheelbase was powered by 25.6 hp Hercules OX engine and used Wisconsin front and rear axles. Price was $2,400. Chassis weight was listed at 3,800 pounds. The 2-ton Model K differed considerably in that it was powered by a 27.2 hp Continental K4 engine and used Timken front and rear axles. Optional wheelbases were available on this model, which was listed at $2,850. The Model K Special was rated at 2-1/2-ton and was priced at $3300 but used the same engine as the previous model.

Next up was the 3-ton Model L, which was powered by a 32.4 hp Continental L4 engine and was priced at $3,750. The Model M used the same engine as Model L, but with heavier construction and larger capacity it was priced at $4,250. The most expensive Hahn of that time was the Model M2, which was powered by a 36.1 hp Continental B5 engine and was priced at $4,750. It was not until 1926 that Hahn offered a six-cylinder engine. Both Continental and Hercules powerplants continued to be available. Hahn also built 27- and 35-passenger bus chassis powered by the Continental engine, while a smaller 20-passenger bus chassis used a four-cylinder Hercules engine.

For 1927, Hahn acquired the former Bethlehem plant in Allentown, Pennsylvania, where it moved its office, but the Hamburg facility continued to operate. In August of 1929, Hahn introduced a new model line of trucks which were powered by six-cylinder Continental engines. The model line ranged from 3/4-ton to 5-ton and prices started at $1,098 and went to $4,950. By this time,

all Hahn vehicles had four-wheel hydraulic brakes. They were distinctive with cast aluminum radiator shells. As the Depression took its toll, Hahn and Selden merged but this cooperation lasted only 16 months. At that time, Hahn trucks were sold under both nameplates.

As the Selden deal unraveled, Hahn moved out of Allentown in 1931 and all offices and production returned to Hamburg, leaving Selden in Allentown until 1932, when that company shut down its manufacturing. A few Hahn trucks at that time were powered by a six-cylinder Franklin engine. Although Hahn began to specialize in building fire apparatus after moving back to Hamburg, a full line of trucks powered by a six-cylinder Waukesha engine was available up to World War II.

During the Second World War, Hahn built mobile machine shops and special recovery trucks for the Engineer Corps. After the war, the company received a large order from the United Parcel Service to build delivery trucks using Ford chassis. Once that production was complete in 1948, Hahn again returned to its specialty of building fire trucks.

By the early 1950s, COE fire trucks were built to allow maximum space for the vehicles' fire apparatus. Hahn fabricated its own chassis and bodies but used Waukesha gasoline engines or Detroit Diesel engines. Through 1980, production averaged 100 fire trucks per year. The company went out of business in 1990.

HAL-FUR 1919-1931 — The Hal-Fur Motor Truck Company was located in Cleveland, Ohio. During its 12-year existence, it was always a low-volume producer of trucks with 50 units being the largest output in any one year. The first Hal-Fur trucks were lightweight and medium-duty vehicles from 1-ton to 3-1/2-ton capacity powered by four-cylinder Hinkley engines. Among the conventional models, there was also a 3-ton truck tractor for semi-trailer application.

In 1928, the company introduced the Model 6YB. This was a six-wheel truck and was powered by a six-cylinder Hinkley engine. Hal-Fur developed its own bogie suspension and used air brakes as well as single balloon tires on all six wheels. At that time, the company claimed this was the largest moving van in the world rated at 6-ton capacity.

By 1930, Hal-Fur trucks were made distinctive with four-piece, bolted cast aluminum radiators patterned after those of Rolls-Royce. In the last two years of production, Hal-Fur built less than a dozen vehicles before the Depression forced the company out of business entirely in 1931.

HALL 1915-1922 — The Lewis-Hall Iron Works of Detroit, Michigan, built a few heavy-duty trucks before fading away in 1922. From 1915 through 1916, a 3-1/2-ton and a 5-ton model was available. The company offered both worm-drive as well as double chain drive but in 1918, after a 7-ton model was introduced, both lighter trucks used worm-drive and only the heaviest truck still used chain drive. Each model of truck was powered by a four-cylinder Continental engine coupled to a three-speed transmission and the essential design of Hall trucks did not change over all the years of manufacturing.

The company did not survive the postwar recession. By 1921, it was already on the brink of going bankrupt, which actually took place the following year. There were at least a half-dozen other motor vehicle manufacturers by the name of Hall that were not affiliated with this one located in Detroit.

HALSEY 1901-1907 — James T. Halsey was an engineer from New York who settled in Philadelphia, Pennsylvania, to build heavy steam vehicles under the name of Halsey Motor Vehicle Company. This he accomplished beginning in 1901, when he completed a front-wheel-drive front-wheel-steer truck powered by two single acting four-cylinder steam engines that transferred power via spur gears. In the press he was quoted as stating that he "endeavored to construct a steam wagon that would be free from odors, have no ashes...no dangerous gasoline lamp, require no stoking, so as to require no skilled operator, and to decrease the possibility of repair..."

The first Halsey water-tube boiler 12 hp truck consumed 125 gallons of water every 12 miles. The second one caught fire and was destroyed in 1902. Starting in 1904, Halsey built 30 hp eight-cylinder steam trucks in limited numbers. Using steel rim wagon wheels these trucks were rated at 8-ton and had a top speed of 6 mph when loaded to capacity. Halsey built steam-powered omnibuses and a few touring cars before going out of business in 1907.

HAMPDEN 1921-1922 — Late in 1921, the Hampden Motor Truck Corporation was organized in Holyoke, Massachusetts, for the purpose of manufacturing 2-ton trucks. Plans were made to build a factory on the purchased property in Williamsette. Richard D. Bloom was president, John F. Lynch was vice-president, Ernest S. Steele was treasurer and there was also a board of directors. The Hampden truck was to be a light vehicle selling for $2,000. No production has been confirmed to date.

HANDY WAGON 1911-1916 — The Handy Wagon series of commercial vehicles was built by Auburn Motor Chassis Company in Auburn, Indiana. Although this business enterprise existed simultaneously with the other better-known Auburn Automobile Company, they were not affiliated. Most of the vehicles that were built by the Auburn Motor Chassis Company were for commercial applications. All of these vehicles were highwheelers. Two-cylinder air-cooled engines powered the Handy Wagon. These used chain drive and were available as a Junior or Senior model with 500- and 600-pound capacity, respectively.

Auburn Motor Chassis was best known for the Handy Wagon, which sold for exactly $487.50. But there were also two-cylinder air-cooled Delivery models with 800-pound and 1,500-pound capacity that sold for $365.62 and $562.00, respectively. According to some records, the to-the-penny price tags were specially calculated to show a fair profit. A water-cooled 1,000-pound capacity Delivery was offered for $650 and according to records, this model was powered by a four-cylinder engine. It is possible that two companies with the same name in the same city at the same time building the same products could not coexist after all.

HANDLEY-KNIGHT see CHECKER

HANGER 1915-1916 — The C.F. Hanger Company was located in Cleveland, Ohio, and for a brief period built a 1/2-ton delivery truck. The business started out as the C.F. Hanger Carriage Company and began building auto bodies in 1905. The light truck was distinguished by the fact that it had bevel drive, electric starting and electric lights. It is not clear whether Hanger continued to build vehicle bodies after 1916. The 1916 Hanger truck sold for $785. Wheelbase was 106 inches and the four-cylinder Lycoming engine was rated at 16.92 hp. Top speed was 30 mph. Pneumatic tires were standard and no governor was used as with many of the commercial vehicles of that day, hence the high top speed available. A Carter or Marvel carburetor option was given and the engine used thermo-syphon cooling. Ignition was by Atwater-Kent and a 12-volt electrical system was used.

HANLEY 1940-1941 — Keenan Handley started his own company in 1934 after being chief engineer for the Prospect Fire Engine Company in Prospect, Ohio. At first he used commercial chassis to build pumper trucks. However, in 1940, Hanley built a quadruple pumper combination powered by a V-16 engine designed by Marmon and built by Hanley. From that experience the company was no longer considered just a fire apparatus assembler, although Hanley did use GMC sheet metal and other off-the-shelf components.

In 1941, Hanley built two more V-16 powered fire trucks. One was a triple combination and the other was a long ladder truck. This time Hanley also built the cabs, which have been likened to postwar Ahrens-Fox design. According to records, these three Hanley trucks were the only V-16 fire engines built in the United States.

HANNIBAL 1916 — Hannibal, Missouri, Mark Twain's hometown, was also home to the Hannibal Motor Car Company for one year. Records show only that a 1-ton truck was built there, but all other details are lacking.

HARDER 1910-1913 — The Harder Fire Proof Storage & Van Company, located in Chicago, Illinois, built its own trucks as fire engines and to perform its moving and storage business. In 1911, the company

offered several different models using four sizes of engines ranging from 24 hp to 60 hp. In 1912, the capacities ranged from 1-1/2-ton to 5-ton at prices from $2,250 up to $4,400 for the 5-ton model.

1911 HARDER 1-1/2-TON   NAHC

The company eventually changed its name in 1912 to Harder Auto Truck Company, only to go out of business the next year. Before doing so, the Harder trucks were built as forward-control vans and open body design from 1-1/2-ton up to 7- and 10-ton capacity. Engines were all four-cylinder with three-speed transmissions and final chain drive to the rear wheels. Maximum speed of 10 miles per hour was accomplished with an engine governor.

1913 HARLEY-DAVIDSON BOX BODY TRICAR   H-D

HARLEY-DAVIDSON 1913-1974 — Harley-Davidson of Milwaukee, Wisconsin, announced in 1913 the production of a three-wheel delivery vehicle with 600-pound capacity. The company was started by Arthur Davidson and William S. Harley in 1903. Later, Arthur's brother Walter would become president, and the Davidson brothers' father, William Davidson, was also involved with running the company. The latter man died in 1937.

The company's first commercial vehicle was a three-wheeler with two wheels in front, and the single powered wheel in back. It used the Harley-Davidson two-cylinder "Model J V-twin" motorcycle engine with the new multi-plate clutch. Motorcycle production at Harley-Davidson was up to 10,000 units per year by this time.

187

This type of three-wheeler was superseded by a sidecar-type of commercial delivery car for the 1920s. With a chassis extension to the right of the basic motorcycle frame, this type of vehicle was used throughout the United States for light delivery work. The running gear was the same as H-D's standard motorcycle. The "side-van" was often used for rural postal and package delivery.

Late in 1931, Harley-Davidson introduced the three-wheel Servi-Car. It was powered by a 45-cubic inch V-2 engine and an optional three-speed transmission with reverse was offered for commercial application. The vehicle had an automotive rear differential. An 80-cubic inch V-2 engine was developed by 1934 and it was also intended for heavier commercial applications. Advertising in 1934 announced "Servi-Car - The New Deal Delivery Unit" and claimed a carrying capacity of 500 pounds plus rider.

The Servi-Car was originally intended as a vehicle that car dealerships would use for servicing their customer's vehicles at a time when it was customary (and good for business) that someone from the dealer would pick up the car at the home or business of the auto's owner. The light three-wheeler would then be towed back to the garage and when the car was returned the dealership's agent would return on it. However, numerous other uses were soon found for the Servi-car, including parking patrol, verge-spraying and delivery work as far away as Japan, where the three-wheelers were popular.

1931 HARLEY-DAVIDSON 3-WHEEL COMMERCIAL   **H-D**

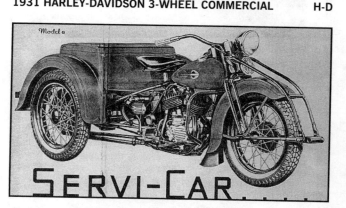

1937 HARLEY-DAVIDSON SERVI-CAR   **H-D**

During World War II, Harley-Davidson three-wheelers were used for such things as emergency fire fighting vehicles. The Servi-Car was offered as the Model GDT with a large capacity body, as the Model G with accessory hardware in the cargo box and as the Model GE, which had its cargo box fitted with an air tank. The U.S. military bought thousands of Harley-Davidsons during the war, many with sidecars, which were called Model XS.

After the war, the company built an experimental Servi-Car with a 50-cubic inch horizontally-opposed two-cylinder engine and another with overhead-valve 74 dual engines but neither went into production. During the late 1960s, the company built the Utilicar, which was similar to a Cushman three-wheeler. The last

year of production for the Servi-Car was 1974. During the 1960s, Harley-Davidson briefly built the three-wheel "Cushman-styled" Utilicar.

1967 HARLEY-DAVIDSON UTILICAR   **H-D**

To date, Harley-Davidson has been the parent company of Utilimaster since 1986, manufacturers of the Utilimaster, Utilivan and Aeromaster bodies in Wakarusa, Indiana. These all have been built on Ford E250, E350 or GMC/Chevrolet cutaway chassis, as well as the bare chassis for the Aeromaster walk-in van. Utilimaster began building commercial bodies in 1973.

HARMON see TULSA

HARRELL 1908 — The Harrell Buggy Company of South Boston, Virginia, built a 1,200-pound capacity commercial vehicle in 1908. The Model 7 was powered by a 18 hp two-cylinder horizontally-opposed water-cooled engine and used a planetary transmission. Final drive was by chain. Suspension was accomplished with four semi-elliptic springs. Solid rubber tires were 39x3-1/2 front and 43x3-3/4 rear. The carburetor was made by Standard and a 10-gallon gasoline tank was provided.

HARRIS 1892 — William T. Harris and William Hollingsworth, who owned the Hollingsworth Machine Company in Baltimore, Maryland, teamed together to build a sightseeing bus for the World Columbia Exposition in Chicago. In February of 1892, the chassis was started by Hollingsworth and he has been credited with most of this early commercial vehicle. It was powered by a 25 hp gasoline engine and had a 48-inch diameter friction clutch transmission amidship.

1892 HARRIS GASOLINE BUS   **RD**

The body was built by Leonhardt Wagon Manufacturing in Baltimore. A patent was applied for in April 1892 and a test run of the finished vehicle was attempted in June 1892. On April 18, 1893, Patent No. 495,733 was granted for the friction discs to propel the vehicle, but during the test run it quickly became apparent that the 6,000-pound vehicle was too heavy for the friction clutch transmission. The vehicle was transported by train to Washington and two years later, it was destroyed by fire.

HARRISON 1911-1917 — The Robert Harrison Company of South Boston, Massachusetts, built heavy trucks using the forward-control design. The first models were 3-1/2 ton and 5 ton. What is notable is that Harrison built the largest truck in the United States of that period. It had a capacity of 12 tons and the chassis weight was 13,000 pounds. However, the market for heavy, expensive trucks was yet to be developed and by 1917, only the 3-1/2-ton model with 142-inch wheelbase was available. All Harrison trucks used four-cylinder engines, three-speed transmissions and double chain drive to the rear wheels. The company did not survive the year 1917.

HART-KRAFT 1907-1913 — The Hart-Kraft Motor Company was located in York, Pennsylvania. The initial organizers were L.M. Hartman, Granville Hartman and Donald H. Yost. The company was incorporated in 1907 with an initial capitalization of $5,000 and later that year another $500,000 was put together for the formation of this manufacturer. Edward L. "Buzzy" Kraft supplied the "Kraft" of the company's name and was appointed superintendent.

Production of automobiles and a few light delivery cars began in July of 1908, but the company's model line was almost immediately switched over entirely to commercial vehicles. By 1909, the company offered four light commercial delivery "power wagons." These were the Model A-0 priced at $1,200, an open delivery Model A-1 for $1,100, Model A-3 for $1,200, and Model A-2, which was the same as the A-3 but had a wheelbase 15 inches shorter and was two inches narrower.

1910 HART-KRAFT STATION BUS   MROZ

1911 HART-KRAFT MODEL C   KP

One of the most significant features of the Hart-Kraft commercial vehicles was the "inter-changeable self contained power plant unit." The engine, magneto, transmission, clutch, differential, jackshaft,

intake, carburetor, exhausts, low-speed reverse levers and direct drive lever were self-contained and suspended from the body frame by five bolts at three locations. The Hart-Kraft engine was a double-opposed four-cylinder type. Standard tires were 36x2-1/2 made by Goodrich or Firestone but smaller 35x2-1/2 Swinehart Clincher Tires were also available.

By 1910, Hart-Kraft offered eight models of Model B "commercial motor wagons" and a station bus. All were built on the same chassis. These were the only vehicles built by the company at that time and all were powered by a 16 hp two-cylinder engine instead of the earlier four-cylinder unit. As the market expanded, sales offices were opened in Philadelphia and the company built a few hearses on special order.

1911 HART-KRAFT LIGHT BUS   JBY/DJS

For 1911, the 1-1/2-ton Model C and 2-1/2-ton Model D made their debut at the Grand Central Palace Show in New York. In 1912, more models appeared from Hart-Kraft in the form of a 28 hp 1-ton Model E, 45 hp 3-ton Model F, 24 hp 3/4-ton Model G and a 35 hp 2-ton Model H. For this line the company adopted four-cylinder Continental engines. The earlier Model C received a 32 hp engine and the Model D a 40 hp engine made by Continental. The first 2-1/2-ton Model D with 140-inch wheelbase and 58-inch tread was sold to the Frings Brothers of Philadelphia.

Standard equipment on all of the Hart-Kraft trucks by that time included four-cylinder engine, tubular radiator, Schebler carburetor, magneto ignition and storage battery, force-fed and splash lubrication, cone clutch, chain drive, three-speed selective sliding gear transmission, armored wood frame, two sets of brakes on rear wheels and jackshaft lined with Raybestos, lamps, horn, jack and tools.

But by this time, the company was sued and a bankruptcy receivership was announced. Apparently, the cost of manufacturing these vehicles was too high and working capital had been depleted. Hart-Kraft was forced to cease operations in 1913. The factory was purchased for the production of the Sphinx vehicles in 1915.

HARVEY 1911-1932 — The Harvey Motor Truck Works was located in Harvey, Illinois. The earliest Harvey vehicles were 1-1/2-ton to 3-ton capacity. By 1916, the company also offered a 5-ton model. By 1920, a full line of trucks from 1-1/2-ton to 5-ton was available from Harvey. Each model was powered by a four-cylinder Buda engine.

By 1925, Harvey listed only two models. These were the 2-1/2-ton Model WFB with 160-inch wheelbase, and the 3-1/2-ton Model WHB with the same wheelbase. The lighter Harvey was powered by a 28.9 hp Buda engine coupled through a Fuller clutch to a Brown-Lipe transmission. Sheldon axles were used front and rear with Smith wheels carrying 36x4 front and 36x8 rear solid rubber tires. Chassis price was $2,950. The heavier Harvey used a 32.4 hp Buda YBUI engine with the same make components as the

189

lighter model. This truck was priced at $3,950 and had front pneumatic tires available at extra cost. Chassis weights were 6,800 pounds and 8,950 pounds, respectively.

In 1927, Harvey attempted to compete with Hug and Super Trucks with a new model called Road Builders' Special. It was a heavy dump truck with seven speeds forward and two in reverse. By 1929, Harvey introduced six-cylinder engines and both 6-ton and 10-ton truck tractors for semi-trailer use were built in limited numbers. Smaller trucks continued to be offered also until 1932, when the company fell victim to the Great Depression.

HASBROUCK 1900-1902 — Almost nothing is known about Hasbrouck vehicle specifications, but the names of all those involved with this arcane manufacturer have been preserved. The principals were Stephen A. Hasbrouck, Joseph Hasbrouck, William H. Hasset, Carl F. Hermann, Lemuel F. Dickerson, F.O. Matthiessen and E.J. Collins. It is known that the company briefly built omnibuses and trucks as well as passenger cars in Piermont, New York, before moving to Yonkers and then to New London, Connecticut, where the business enterprise continued but only as a maintenance and repair facility.

HATFIELD 1907-1908 — Charles B. Hatfield and his son Charles Jr. incorporated their Hatfield Motor Vehicle Company in Cortland, New York, in 1906 before moving to Miamisburg, Ohio, in 1907. They manufactured highwheelers, which they called Buggyabout and Unique. A light open delivery van was built on the same chassis and all versions of this highwheeler were powered by an air-cooled two-cylinder four-cycle engine mounted under the body and coupled to a friction transmission with final double chain drive.

Solid rubber tires were 38-inch diameter in front and 40-inch on the rear. The Model B had a 74-inch wheelbase in 1907, going up to 78 inches in 1908. The Model C was built only in 1907 and had a 101-inch wheelbase. Prices ranged from $600 for the Model B to $750 for the Model C. Capacity was given as 800 pounds with total vehicle weight for the delivery at 1,100 pounds. The running gear and bodies were fabricated by Kauffman Buggy Company, also in Miamisburg. The two companies merged as receivership became inevitable and Charles Hatfield moved back to Cortland to begin manufacturing Hatfield trucks. Charles Hatfield Jr. went on to build the O-We-Go cyclecar.

HATFIELD 1910-1914 — Once back in Cortland, New York, after building Hatfield highwheelers, Charles Hatfield established the Hatfield Motor Vehicle Company and proceeded to build small 1/2-ton and 1-ton trucks. These were powered by air-cooled three-cylinder engines using friction transmissions and double chain drive. At least one model was a forward-control design. Among the various bodies built on Hatfield trucks, there was also a 10-passenger bus. The company moved to Cornwall-on-Hudson, New York, in 1911 and subsequently it was relocated to Elmira, New York.

1910 HATFIELD   **K.H. STAUFFER**

1911 HATFIELD 1/2-TON SUBURBAN   **HAC**

HATHAWAY-PURINTON 1924-1925 — The Hathaway-Purinton Company built 3-ton trucks in Peabody, Massachusetts. This obscure company was listed as a manufacturer in 1925 before it was discontinued. The engine used was a 28.90 hp four-cylinder. It is possible a prototype or only a few of these trucks were ever manufactured.

1957 HAULPAK 32-TON   **HAULPAK**

1988 HAULPAK 240-TON ELECTRIC DRIVE   **HAULPAK**

HAULPAK see WABCO and/or KOMATSU DRESSER

HAWKEYE 1916-1933 — Sioux City, Iowa, was home to the Hawkeye Truck Company. The first Hawkeye truck was a 1-1/2-ton model. It was a conventional assembled truck and in 1919, a

2-ton was also added to the model line. In 1921, a 3-1/2-ton model was introduced. All of the Hawkeye trucks up to 1926 were powered by Buda engines. The company's first advertising slogan was "Manufacturers of Good Trucks Sold at a Fair Price."

The 1-1/2-ton Model K with 149-inch wheelbase used a 22.5 hp Buda WTU engine and Fuller transmission. The rear axle was made by Clark while the front was by Shuler with Dayton wheels carrying 34x5 front and 38x7 rear pneumatic tires as standard equipment. The 2-1/2-ton Hawkeye with 160-inch wheelbase was powered by a 28.9 hp Buda EBU engine with a four-speed Fuller transmission. Both front and rear axles were built by Clark on this model. Pneumatic tires were standard and sized 34x6 front and 36x8 rear. The 3-1/2-ton Model N with 180-inch wheelbase used a 32.4 hp Buda YTU engine. Components were the same make as on the Model K. Chassis price for the 1-1/2-ton was $1,900 and for the 2-1/2-ton $2,800. Chassis weights were 3,750 and 5,000 pounds, respectively, for those two models.

1919 HAWKEYE   **MROZ**

1919 HAWKEYE BEKINS VAN AND STORAGE   **I.H. JENSEN**

In 1927, Hawkeye introduced six-cylinder Buda engines. By 1931, Hercules and Wisconsin engines were also available. The Depression took its toll on the company, and by 1933, production had ceased altogether.

HENDERSON 1916 — The Henderson Brothers of North Cambridge, Massachusetts, built two light truck models in 1916. The 1,200-pound capacity model sold in chassis form for $1,100 and the 1-ton model sold in chassis form for $1,500. Although the Henderson Brothers remained listed in directories for a decade after their limited production, it does not appear they manufactured after 1916.

HENDRICKSON 1913 to date — The Hendrickson Motor Truck Company was established in Chicago, Illinois, by Magnus Hendrickson in 1913, the year he left the Lauth-Juergens Motor Company where he was chief engineer. Henrickson had immigrated from Sweden in 1887 at the age of 23 and by 1900 had built his first truck. Hendrickson's three sons, Carl, George and Robert, were also partners with their father in the company, as were David Nyman and Al Ostby. Robert Hendrickson also had been chief engineer at Lauth-Juergens. Edward, the youngest son, joined the company in 1927.

The first Hendrickson trucks built in the Chicago factory were a cab-over design using chain drive. Artillery wheels carried solid rubber tires and Hendrickson reverted to his previously-developed Lauth-Juergens wooden cab design, which was likened to a three-section bay window. From the beginning, Hendrickson trucks were available with specialized bodies for a great variety of applications. These were usually built at the Hendrickson factory, not by independent builders.

Magnus Hendrickson's imaginative engineering along with his sons' active support created a successful venture that built trucks for many applications including a patented stone hoist for roofers, as well as winch equipment for contractors and dump beds for refuse hauling. There were many vehicle assemblers at that time, especially in the Chicago area, who supplied only the powered chassis and a narrow range of truck bodies. In the highly competitive truck market of that era, Hendrickson was not only willing but capable of providing major finished pieces of equipment to the end user.

By 1919, the company built truck tractors capable of pulling three two-axle trailers with wagon-type steering for the City of Chicago refuse industry. Hendrickson offered a full model line of truck chassis starting with 2-1/2-ton capacity up to 5 tons. The trucks still used solid rubber tires, although gas lamps had given way to electric lights, and chain drive was abandoned in favor of heavy-duty worm-drive. Prices at that time ranged from $3,200 to $5,250.

In 1922, Hendrickson added a lighter model of 1-1/2-ton capacity with chassis price set at $2,200. This truck not only featured worm-drive but also had pneumatic tires as standard equipment. This was the year the company began to offer pneumatic tires as an option on all models except the heaviest 5-ton model. Goodyear was just in the process of proving out its pneumatic tires for such heavy vehicles with trucks of its own manufacture.

The Hendrickson trucks at this time also featured multiple disc clutches and four-speed transmissions with Timken worm-drives. The 5-ton model was superseded by a 6-ton unit in 1924 and special chassis sizes were also available. It was at this time that Hendrickson and his sons Robert and George designed a tandem suspension that featured an equalizing beam with center pivot to distribute weight evenly between the two rear axles while diminishing the effects of uneven road surface. That design, along with a few refinements, has been adopted by numerous heavy-duty truck builders to date.

1928 HENDRICKSON 10-TON 6X4 REFUSE TRUCK   **LIAM**

The first six-wheel truck with "quadridrive" suspension was built in 1926. This used Hendrickson's well-known equalizer suspension, which coupled the two rear axles by means of an underslung beam that was centrally pivoted and combined with conventional leaf springs mounted on the pivot saddle. The company also produced its first crane carrier in 1927. It featured a steel structure riveted to a standard Model SW chrome-nickel frame. A heavy-duty dump truck was also built for brick manufacturing. These featured a new radiator guard and were designated 6-6-4, which stood for six wheels, four-wheel-drive and four-wheel brakes (on the rear axles). Sales continued to increase so that by 1927, an assembly plant was constructed.

At this time, Hendrickson employed about three dozen people. The Model U in 1928 was one of the last heavy-duty Hendrickson trucks with two axles. In 1929, the first specifically-designed crane carrier was built using a channel steel frame with integral outrigger boxes for rollers to facilitate beam extension. Most of the company's trucks were powered by six-cylinder Waukesha gasoline engines starting in 1932. Most of the cabs still used wood frames for the cabs with metal skin and fabric-covered roof, but that year Hendrickson built a cattle hauler using an all-steel cab-over-engine design dubbed "The Midnight Flyer" by the owner to promote overnight service to Chicago.

1933 HENDRICKSON 10-TON 6X4 VAN W/TRAILER   HAC

The company entered a much larger market in 1933, when International Harvester signed an exclusive agreement for the rights to use Hendrickson's patented tandem suspension. This business kept Hendrickson afloat during the Depression, but International also gained business from sales of its heavy three-axle trucks. Hendrickson built fire engines on International chassis and adapted diesel engines for International trucks. By mid-decade the company's model line extended from 2-1/2-ton to 12-ton capacity with prices ranging from $1,760 to $9,000. The Waukesha engines were rated from 33.8 hp to 60 hp.

By 1937, Hendrickson trucks featured radiator shells and massive guards. Cabs were all made from stamped steel panels and the company built streamlined tankers by that time. Cummins diesel engines were available by 1938, and that year the Hendrickson Model A275-F featured narrow doors that could be fastened in the open position flush with the cowl for easy entry and exit for certain applications. This model also had bullet-shaped headlights and the turn signals were mounted on the fenders. A snub nose truck tractor was available by 1939 with set-back front axle to reduce tare weight on the rear axle for added load capacity.

For 1940, Hendrickson adopted the International Model D cab (later K and KB models) and a distinctive radiator ornament was well-recognized. The company developed a four-wheel prime mover for a Heil bowl-type scraper, which featured the company's first planetary reduction axle. The range in 1940 and 1941 began with a 2-ton model and the heaviest was a 10-ton capacity truck. Engines were SAE rated from 35.8 hp to 79.4 hp.

By the end of the 1930s, besides International, Hendrickson had also converted Chevrolet, Ford, Mack and White trucks to the tandem axle design the company had developed. During World War II, Hendrickson supplied 600 suspensions per week to International for the war effort.

After World War II, the company continued to be innovative with designs such as the snub-nose conventional cab and hood that tilted back exposing the engine and transmission for servicing. International K and L cabs were used, which were heavily reinforced in the back for hinge attachment. These were supplanted by COE design that tilted forward. Models such as the AD-42-0-F1 were powered by Caterpillar engines.

In 1948, Hendrickson petitioned for the right to sell its tandem suspension to any manufacturer and to this day a number of truck builders buy the tandem axles directly from Hendrickson. The company was also well-known for its set-back front axle design and this idea continued in 1950 with the B series using International

cabs with curved windshield. The Model B was built in three versions: long hood, standard size and snub-nose with higher cab -- the latter with simple, flat, screen-mesh grille. A taller line-haul COE called the CO-405 was also used from International. Cab-over and cab-forward designs were also adopted from other manufacturers in limited quantities.

1940 HENDRICKSON DUMP TRUCK   KP

A short bumper-to-back-of-cab (BBC) truck tractor was developed, although its first iteration had the engine protruding into the driver's compartment. Hendrickson offset the hood and International cab to provide more foot room. The company also used the Diamond T cab, for which that company won the National Design Award in 1951. This cab was also utilized by International until the early 1970s with different grilles.

1958 HENDRICKSON 8X4 COE   LA

By 1958, Hendrickson built an 8x4 with tandem steering front axles. Its load capacity was 22,000 pounds in front and 34,000 pounds rear. This truck also used the Diamond T tilt cab. The tooling for this cab was purchased by International and used on several truck marques and models. Throughout the 1950s, Hendrickson truck production averaged 80 units per year. Cabs were aluminum, steel and reinforced fiberglass. Along with gasoline and diesel engines, Hendrickson built a few propane-powered trucks in the 1950s.

Throughout the 1960s, Hendrickson continued to build crane and heavy equipment carriers, including a 12x6 narrow cab truck with 200-ton capacity. Refuse trucks continued to be produced and the B series "Pinocchio Nose" was built in various forms including heavy-duty wreckers. A tilt cab truck tractor was developed to pull twin 40-foot trailers with 127,000 GCW powered by a Detroit Diesel 12V-71 engine.

In 1966, Hendrickson built a large truck for operations in Vietnam. This was known as the Liquid Distributor for Dust Control (LDDC). The three-axle truck was built from the ground up to operate in primitive conditions. It had low pressure tires for traveling on sand and mud and was powered by a Detroit Diesel V-6 engine. Nozzles from the tank dispersed liquid at 300 gallons per minute.

This rubber-like dust palliative or bituminous substance hardened into a tacky base that could support light aircraft. The truck was tested in 1967 at Ft. Belvoir, Virginia.

One of the largest truck rigs ever built was constructed at this time to carry a GCW of 1,250,000 pounds to transport 44 transformers, each weighing 500,000 pounds, from railhead to the Churchill Falls hydro-electric plant in Labrador. For this project two 6x6 Hendrickson truck tractors with 360,000 pounds of GVW were built using 700 hp Cummins V-12 diesel engines and Clark power-shift transmissions.

Hendrickson built airport vehicles including fuel tankers, snowplows, plane towers and special cargo and passenger carriers. The company also built entire trucks for Ryder, as well as Manitoc crane carriers. Mid-America Truck Lines has been the largest Hendrickson fleet with approximately 150 trucks used in a seven-state area between Kansas and Illinois. Through the 1970s, Hendrickson production averaged 300 trucks per year. A heavy-duty 6x6 featured an International Fleetstar cab and was used for cement mixer hauling. By 1980, Hendrickson had built about 5,500 trucks over all of its years of production. However, it built many thousands of components and tandem axles for other truck manufacturers to date. A typical Hendrickson truck of the mid-1980s was the Model H powered by a 325 hp Caterpillar 3406 six-cylinder diesel engine and used a Fuller 13F 1R transmission with Rockwell SQHD single-reduction tandem rear axles. Cummins and Detroit Diesel as well as Spicer transmissions were also available. Overall Hendrickson production at that time was about 300 units per year.

1972 HENDRICKSON 6X4 TRACTOR-GINDY TRAILER   OCW

To date, Hendrickson Manufacturing Company is a Boler Industries division and is actually two independent facilities. The Mobile Equipment Division located at Lyons, Illinois, has built crane and heavy equipment carriers, fire trucks and bus chassis. The Tandem Division at Burr Ridge, Illinois, has built truck axles and suspensions in a variety of configurations. It has been headed by Magnus Hendrickson's grandson, Wayne Hendrickson.

1908 HENNEGIN PHYSICIAN'S CAR   NAHC

HENNEGIN 1908 — The Commercial Automobile Company of Chicago, Illinois, built light delivery vans using a highwheeler chassis that had a wheelbase of 87 inches. The Model A, which was priced at $650, was built for only one year in limited numbers. This light commercial vehicle was powered by a two-cylinder engine mounted under the chassis. A friction transmission was employed as was double chain drive to the large diameter rear wheels.

HENNEY 1921-1932 — The Henney family of Freeport, Illinois, started in the buggy and wagon business in the 1870s. John Henney's son, John Jr. started in the business in 1912 and by 1921, under his direction the company produced ambulance and funeral cars, along with a few sports cars. These were assembled vehicles first using six-cylinder Continental engines. By 1924, a 70 hp powerplant was standard. The vehicles had cycle-type front fenders and radiators likened to those of Kissel vehicles of that period, which were also built as professional cars by the early 1920s. At that point, Henney switched to a body design that resembled contemporary Lincoln automobiles.

Besides ambulances and funeral cars, Henney built approximately 30 limousines and sedans per custom order. In 1927, Henney adopted the Eureka three-way loading system for hearses. In 1929, the professional cars were powered by Lycoming straight-eight engines. This was the year Henney built 100 taxis on stretched Model A chassis and the company also got involved in building ambulance aircraft.

For 1931, Henney made an attempt to compete with Cord and built four examples of a luxurious convertible sedan on a 137-1/2-inch wheelbase, just like the L-29 Cord. In 1932, Henney began building bodywork only and exclusively using Packard chassis from 1938 until the company's last year of 1954. Henney also built a special series of Lincolns for the U.S. Government before World War II.

HERCULES 1913-1915 — Not affiliated with the Hercules trucks of Great Britain and Germany, nor with its contemporary (the Hercules Motor Car Company of New Albany, Indiana), the Hercules Motor Truck Company of South Boston, Massachusetts, briefly built a 1-ton truck in express or stake body form. These were priced at $1,775 in 1913.

HERRESHOFF 1911-1912 — The Herreshoff family was known for boat building before they embarked on motorized vehicle production in 1880, when the Herreshoff Company in Bristol, Rhode Island, built a steam-powered road buggy. Charles Frederick Herreshoff reentered the family in the motor vehicle business in 1908, when he founded the Herreshoff Motor Company, occupying at first the former Thomas-Detroit factory in Detroit, Michigan. The Herreshoff vehicles were passenger cars powered by four-cylinder engines that were brought out in 1909.

In 1911 and 1912, the company built the Model 25, which was a light delivery van that used the passenger car chassis and drivetrain, which consisted also of a three-speed transmission and shaft drive. Wheelbase was 98 inches and pneumatic tires were standard. The closed body van was rated at 750-pound capacity and sold for $950. Herreshoff's slogan was "As on blue water so on dry land pin your faith on Herreshoff."

However, a variety of trouble plagued the company by 1911, including strong objections by the local residents when Herreshoff planned to build a new factory on suburban Woodward Avenue in Detroit. Mechanical engine problems beset the Herreshoff vehicles, and this as well as financial problems were blamed on Lycoming in the press. In 1914, the company was sold to Ernst and Otto Kern. Other motor vehicle ventures by Herreshoff family members were attempted later, all the while the original family company continued to build boats in Bristol.

HERSCHMANN 1901-1903 — Arthur J. Herschmann, a mechanical engineer in Brooklyn, New York, designed a 3-ton steam-powered truck at the turn of the century. The first example of this truck was built by the American Ordnance Company of Detroit, Michigan. Thereafter, it was built by the Columbia Engineering Works in Brooklyn. It appears a passenger car of similar design was also built.

The Herschmann steam truck used a fire-tube boiler that was located behind the driver. A compound type engine powered the vehicles. All-gear drive was used, including final drive by internal gear rings on the rims of the rear wheels. The Herschmann trucks were not only likened to the British Thornycroft vehicles, but Herschmann patents were used on British steam wagons from 1903 to 1907.

HEWITT/HEWITT-INTERNATIONAL 1905-1914 — The Hewitt Motor Company was organized in 1905 by Edward Ringwood Hewitt. The company began in New York City when a Selden Patent manufacturing license was purchased from Standard Motor Construction Company. The first vehicles built were town cars and limousines, but Hewitt also introduced a light van in 1906. This was powered by a one-cylinder Adams engine built by the Adams Manufacturing Company of London, England. The vehicles sold in that country were known as the Adams-Hewitt.

Later in 1906, a 4-ton truck powered by a four-cylinder engine was introduced by Hewitt and this vehicle was upgraded to 6-ton as it went into production. It was powered by a 36 hp four-cylinder engine mounted between the seats using a two-speed planetary transmission and chain drive. By the following year, Hewitt also began production of similarly-designed 2-ton and 3-ton model trucks powered by opposing twin cylinder engines. It appears that by this time the Hewitt-International name was also used.

1908 HEWITT 6-TON COAL HAULER   **RD**

In 1909, Hewitt built the heaviest truck in the United States. It was rated at 10-ton and was powered by the same 36 hp engine as on the earlier 5-ton and 6-ton models. Heavier construction of frame, wheels and suspension distinguished it from the lighter Hewitt trucks, as did its lower gearing and 8 mph top speed. Breweries and coal delivery companies bought the 10-ton Hewitt trucks, which were actually manufactured by Machine Sales Company of Peabody, Massachusetts, in 1909 and by Philip H. Gill & Sons of Brooklyn in 1910 and 1911. Meanwhile, the Hewitt Motor Company in New York City built the lighter model trucks.

1910 HEWITT 10-TON MILK VAN   **MACK**

Also, a merger between the Metzger Motor Car Company, builders of Everitt cars, led to the production of a light 1-ton van, which superseded the light one-cylinder vans. The Metzger-type van was powered by a 17 hp four-cylinder Everitt engine using a three-speed transmission. This engine was used also in other Hewitt trucks in 1910 and 1911.

In 1912, Hewitt became a subsidiary of the International Motor Company of Philadelphia, Pennsylvania, which was not affiliated with International Harvester, its contemporary. The International Motor Company was a consortium that included at that time Mack and the American Saurer Company, the latter being an assembler of imported Swiss Suarer trucks. All three, Hewitt, Mack and Saurer, were advertised together, although the lighter Hewitt trucks were replaced by models of the two other makes. The 10-ton Hewitt continued to be built until 1914, when it was discontinued due to

obsolete design and lack of marketing. Edward Ringwood Hewitt went on to become a consulting engineer with Mack trucks until World War II.

1900 HEWITT-LINDSTROM COACH   **GR**

HEWITT-LINDSTROM 1900-1902 — The Hewitt-Lindstrom Company was started by John Hewitt and Charles A. Lindstrom and this firm was not affiliated with the later Hewitt Motor Company. John Hewitt, president and treasurer of Hewitt-Lindstrom, was also owner of the Miehle Company, one of Chicago's largest printing companies. Charles A. Lindstrom was an immigrant from Sweden and the designer of the vehicles the company built.

Hewitt-Lindstrom vehicles were electric-powered. The first commercial versions were coaches and buses. They had an average range of 40 miles per charge and were capable of 22 percent grades. The company promoted simplicity of operation of its vehicles by advertising that Lindstrom's 13-year-old daughter could safely drive a Hewitt-Lindstrom around town at a maximum 16 mph.

By 1901, a 14-passenger omnibus and later a 22-passenger model, used two 4-1/2 hp DC motors, apparently developed earlier by Charles Lindstrom who was described as the "mechanical genius of the institution." A light delivery wagon of similar design was also produced. The company displayed its vehicles at the Chicago Automobile Show in 1902 but seems to have quickly faded out after that. Charles Lindstrom also built another electric vehicle called the Niagara in Buffalo, New York.

1916 HEWITT-LUDLOW   **RD**

HEWITT-LUDLOW 1912-1926 — The Hewitt-Ludlow Auto Company was located in San Francisco, California. It was organized by Edward T. Hewitt, William A. Hewitt and James Ludlow during 1912, but production most likely started the following year. At first the company built trucks from 3/4-ton to 3-1/2-ton capacity. The documented model of 1916 had a wheelbase of 120 inches, was powered by a four-cylinder Buda engine and used worm-drive. Price was $1,650.

By 1917, Hewitt-Ludlow was building trucks from 1-1/2-ton to 5-1/2-ton capacity continuing to use worm-drive. During World War I, the company built 6-ton truck tractors for pulling army artillery. The Hewitt company also built tractor-trailer units under the name of Hewitt-Talbot. The innovative use of the "fifth wheel" concept made the Hewitt-Talbot a standard in the industry. The company's slogan was "The Hewitt trailer doubles the hauling capacity of your truck." The "fifth wheel" ensured "absolute tracking" of the trailer to the truck.

The Hewitt truck line was sold to the Ralston Iron Works in 1926. The Hewitts continued to build trailers until 1930 when that business was phased out and Edward Hewitt developed a line of mobile air compressors for mounting on Ford trucks. Edward Hewitt passed away in 1933 and after a few more years his brother retired from the business.

HEWITT-METZGER 1913-1914 — The name of Hewitt-Metzger was used by Hewitt-International when the two companies merged. The 1-ton model was listed for $1,800 and models up to 10-ton capacity were offered using this name, although they appear to be the same trucks as listed under Hewitt.

1921 HEWITT-TALBOT ARTICULATED LUMBER TRUCK   BE

HEWITT-TALBOT see HEWITT-LUDLOW

HIGHWAY 1918-1919 — The Highway Tractor Company built a three-wheel 3-ton truck tractor that was powered by a Weidely engine. The company was located in Indianapolis, Indiana. The engine and driver's compartment turned 180 degrees so that the single front-wheel-drive vehicle could push its trailer or pull it. The engine was mounted transversely on the frame with radiator and fan on the side. A Martin fifth wheel was mounted for hook-up to trailers and most components were purchased from outside manufacturers. There is apparently no affiliation between this company and its contemporary Highway Knight.

HIGHWAY 1920 — The Highway Motors Company was capitalized with $1.5 million during 1920 in Defiance, Ohio. Among persons involved in the organization were Charles F. Kettering, E.H. Belknap and J.W. Schwartz. This corporation absorbed the businesses of Golden, Belknap and Schwartz, as well as that of the Trucking Machine Company in Detroit, Michigan. It is not clear whether a truck prototype was built but it is known that the company produced engines for a variety of vehicles. This company was not affiliated with the Highway Motors Company that produced the Highway-Knight trucks in Chicago.

HIGHWAY 1960-1975 — Highway Products, Incorporated, of Kent, Ohio, was an outgrowth of the Twin Coach Company as well as Fageol-Twin Coach gasoline engine manufacturing along with the sales network for Fageol-Leyland diesel engines during the 1950s. When these engines became obsolete, Twin Coach focused solely on building truck bodies in 1959.

In 1960, Highway Products received a contract from the U.S. Postal Service to build mobile post offices. J.T. Myers, the company director who had formed Highway Products, first organized manufacturing with leased space at the Twin Coach factory and in 1962, acquired part of the plant for production. The Highway mo-

bile post office was essentially a 6x4 bus powered by either a Cummins diesel or a Fageol-Leyland diesel engine located under the floor. A smaller version was built as a postal van and this was sold for general commercial use as the Compac-Van.

1962 HIGHWAY 6X4 MOBILE POST OFFICE   MBS

The Compac-Van was a forward-control design rated from 13,000-pound to 26,000-pound GVW. These were powered by a choice of engines from Chrysler, Cummins, Ford or Perkins and some of the vans had single cabs with rear- and forward-loading capability. The vans were originally built for White up to 1965 and after that year they were sold by Highway Products, Inc.

For 1968, the company unveiled a 25-passenger bus that had a Chrysler V-8 engine mounted in the rear using an automatic transmission. Federal grant funds helped the development of this project. The new bus was called a Twin Coach, although its real connection was more geographic than by pedigree. In 1969, a 29-passenger model was also introduced. The first production series used a Perkins diesel engine. Subsequent to 1970, the buses used Detroit Diesel 4-53 engines and were built using these engines from then on. The first series also used hydraulic brakes, whereas after 1970 they were replaced by air brakes. In 1971, full air suspension was incorporated.

1968 HIGHWAY 5-TON COMPAC-VAN   LA

The year 1974 was a poor one for Highway Products due to the continuation of production at guaranteed prices during a period when materials and labor became much more costly in a short time. When creditors refused additional financing, production stopped in 1975 for about three months. To fulfil existing obligations, Highway Products resumed production in October of 1975 and at that time delivered the last Twin Coach buses. Altogether 900 buses were built over eight years of manufacturing.

HIGHWAY-KNIGHT 1919-1921 — The Highway Motors Company of Chicago was not affiliated with Highway Tractor of Indianapolis, nor with Highway Motors Company of Defiance, Ohio, although all three companies existed at about the same time. The Knight engine used in these trucks was built by Root and Vandervoort Engine Company under license from Knight, which had developed and patented the sleeve-valve engine design. A 4-ton and 5-ton model of the Highway-Knight was built on the same chassis, which had a 159-inch wheelbase. All Highway-Knight trucks used four-speed Brown-Lipe transmissions and final drive was with worm gear. The company ceased operations in 1921.

1920 HIGHWAY-KNIGHT 4-TON   RNE

HIGRADE 1917-1921 — The Higrade Motors Company began manufacturing in Grand Rapids, Michigan, in 1917. The first model was a 3/4-ton model powered by a "Wisconsin-built" four-cylinder engine using a three-speed Cotta transmission. The wheelbase on this versatile truck was 115 inches. Later the following year a 1-ton model was also introduced. The later truck was basically an upgraded version of the first Higrade model and shared the same specifications. In 1918, the company moved to Harbor Springs, Michigan. Both 3/4-ton and 1-ton models were available up to 1920, but in the last year of production only a 1-ton and 1-1/2-ton model was offered. The company did not survive the post-World War I recession, especially when truck builders were hit hardest in the transportation industry.

HINDE & DAUCH 1907-1908 — The Hinde & Dauch firm was located in Sandusky, Ohio. The company built a single model delivery van that was rated at 1/2-ton. It was powered by an 8 hp one-cylinder water-cooled engine and used a two-speed sliding gear transmission with a single chain drive. The van was a forward-control design and had a wheelbase of 80 inches, although a 90-inch wheelbase has also been listed. In 1907, the Hinde & Dauch van was priced at $800. The fact that Hinde & Dauch might have taken over the production of the 1/2-ton Climax, also built earlier in Sandusky apparently by Dunbar Manufacturing, has not been substantiated. See also CLIMAX.

HOADLEY 1915-1916 — The only information about the Hoadley Brothers' company is that it was located in Gosport, Indiana, briefly, and that the company offered a 2-ton four-wheel-steer four-wheel-drive truck for one year. Each wheel was driven by chain. The press stated in April 1915 that "At both front and rear are fifth wheels beneath which are steel subframes which carry the springs and axles…a four-wheel-driven-and-steered truck of novel design…not actively on the market."

HOFFMAN 1913-1914 — Not affiliated with the Hoffman Automobile and Manufacturing Company of Cleveland, Ohio, or the Hoffman car of Detroit, Michigan, the Hoffman Motor Truck Company was located in Minneapolis, Minnesota. The company briefly built one model of a 3-ton truck that used solid rubber tires. The relatively heavy vehicle of that time was of standard design and conventional assembly. It was powered by a four-cylinder Wauke-

sha engine. The only thing out of the ordinary regarding its design was that it used a single chain drive, which did not contribute much to its reputation.

HOLABIRD — Holabird was not a make but a military installation, Ft. Holabird, where numerous trucks and specialized vehicles were developed and fabricated. Arthur W. Herrington had been involved with the Army's Quartermaster Corps for several years at Ft. Holabird. This was a center for truck development for decades and many military trucks received the "Holabird" name without ever being manufactured by a company of that name. In order to document all these vehicles a separate compendium would be necessary.

1908 HOLSMAN TELEPHONE UTILITY WAGON   DFW/WEPS

HOLSMAN 1908-1910 — Henry K. Holsman organized the Holsman Automobile Company in Chicago, Illinois, in 1903. The company became successful quickly, building simple highwheelers powered by an air-cooled two-cylinder engine using 7/8-inch manila rope for final pulley-type drive. This did not work well in wet weather and the next design involved a chain braided over with manila rope and wire.

1917 HOOVER 1-TON TYPE D-10292   MROZ

It was not until 1908 that the Holsman highwheelers were available as light delivery vans. At first these were powered by the same two-cylinder engine as the early passenger models using a friction transmission and double chain drive. In 1909, a four-cylinder engine was introduced. The two vans had wheelbases of 75 inches and 96 inches, respectively. Brakes were hand operated directly against the steel-tire wheels because "in emergencies and under excitement the foot cannot be relied upon to act sub-consciously or automatically, and to do the right thing instantly."

Holsman refused to add pneumatic tire versions to his model line or to modernize the design in other ways and his vehicles, which were priced from $500 to $1,000, became increasingly obsolete. By 1910, the company went into receivership. However, Holsman moved 50 miles west to Plano, Illinois, and began producing vehicles called Independent Harvester, which was exceedingly similar to the manufacturing company already in existence there. A few of these were even built under the name of I.H.C. The second venture lasted only through 1911.

1920 HOOVER 1-1/2-TON CHASSIS   **RD**

HOOVER 1911, 1917-1920 — The Hoover Wagon Company of York, Pennsylvania, was not affiliated with the Hoover cyclecar built in St. Louis, Missouri, at about the same time. The Hoover wagon company was founded by George Hoover in 1880 who, along with his three sons, built horsedrawn wagons of various types. In 1899, his business was reorganized as the Hoover Wagon Works with George W. Bacon as president, Israel K. Ziegler secretary and Charles C. Frick treasurer. Another reorganization took place in 1902 and Charles H. Dempwolf became president, with Edwin S. Ziegler secretary-treasurer. A fire destroyed the second factory but it was rebuilt. The Hoover Wagon Works began to specialize in building commercial bodies for motor vehicles.

Under contract the company built several 3/4-ton electric trucks in 1911. The firm continued to build auto and truck bodies until 1917, when a 1-ton gasoline-powered truck was unveiled. It was powered by a four-cylinder Continental engine and used bevel drive. Many of the Hoover trucks were built as postal vans. The price tag for a Hoover truck in 1919 was $1,435, but by the end of the following year the company had ceased production. In January of 1920, Hoover still offered a 1-1/2-ton truck powered by a 35 hp four-cylinder Continental engine and three-speed sliding gear transmission.

HORNER 1913-1918 — Horner trucks were built by the Detroit-Wyandotte Motor Company in Wyandotte, Michigan. In 1913, Horner built a 5-ton truck model. The following year the company introduced 1-, 1-1/2-, 2- and 3-ton truck models, all using the same chassis and all had a 145-inch wheelbase. The 5-ton model had a different chassis from the smaller trucks and had a 156-inch wheelbase. All of the trucks were powered by four-cylinder Continental engines with radiators behind the engine block. This allowed for the use of a sloping Renault-type hood and all of the trucks were fitted with three-speed transmissions and double chain drive. By 1918, Horner was out of business.

HOUGHTON 1915-1917 — The Houghton Motor Company built assembled hearses in Marion, Ohio. Only a few were sold without the hearse bodywork. All Houghton vehicles were powered by 22 hp four-cylinder engines and had pneumatic tires as standard equipment. By 1917, vehicle production had ceased all together.

HOWARD 1895-1903 — There were two William Howards at about the same time building motor vehicles. This one was William L. Howard of Trenton, New Jersey, who experimented with a gasoline-powered automobile in 1893 (at about the same time the Duryea brothers were developing what is considered the first gasoline-powered vehicle in the United States). William L. Howard's vehicle was not fully finished and documented until 1895, when he established the Howard Cycle Company and built a gasoline-powered carryall with three bench seats, which was used commer-

cially for public transport around the Trenton Fair Grounds. It was powered by two 3 hp Wing engines and William L. Howard stated "either gasoline, kerosene or city gas can be used as fuel."

1903 HOWARD GASOLINE-ELECTRIC   **RD**

By 1900, Howard organized the Howard Automobile Company and continued to build both gasoline-powered and steam vehicles. The president was George B. Yard, secretary was Frank W. Williams and treasurer was Frank W. Muschert. Another Carryall that Howard built was used for public transportation between Philadelphia and Atlantic City. William L. Howard's brother also built motor vehicles but his were race cars that were run on Brighton Beach at that time. William L. Howard invented a demountable tire for bicycles and cars.

HOWARD 1901-1904 — William S. Howard built his first gasoline-powered car in Troy, New York, at the same time as William L. Howard was building his in Trenton, New Jersey. Undoubtedly, some confusion must have existed regarding the similar and contemporary accomplishments of both men. William S. Howard was first affiliated with the Gas Engine and Power Company and then the Grant-Ferris Company and his first car was built by that firm in 1901. He also founded his own company called the Trojan Launch and Automobile Works. This company began building the Howard automobile in 1901 and both a passenger and goods delivery version were produced, the latter powered by a three-cylinder engine and having a 1/2-ton capacity.

Other engine options included two-cylinder and four-cylinder engines. The company also built a 4-ton gas-electric hybrid-powered truck with a 30 hp four-cylinder engine, which was mounted vertically driving a dynamo that ran two General Electric DC motors, one on each rear wheel. The dynamo weighed 350 pounds, which was as much as the gasoline engine. Its speed was listed as 5 mph loaded and 9 mph empty. The hybrid truck's design also involved two coil radiators, one in front and one in back.

The company was sold to Charles L. Seabury in 1904, who continued passenger car production under the name of Seabury. William S. Howard continued with several other automotive ventures including the development of a rotary sleeve-valve engine in 1912.

HOWARD 1915-1916 — Robert G. Howard established the Robert G. Howard Motor Truck Company in Boston, Massachusetts. By 1915, the firm was producing a light open delivery wagon of 3/4-ton capacity, which was powered by a four-cylinder Continental engine coupled to a three-speed Covert transmission. The design was unusual in that the engine was mounted together with the Salisbury rear axle. The brief venture did not survive beyond 1916.

HOWE 1932-1983 — The Howe Fire Apparatus Company of Anderson, Indiana, was founded in 1872 by J.C. Howe. Using a purchased chassis the company built its first pumper in 1906. The company moved to Anderson, Indiana, in 1917. By that time, Howe was using a Ford Model T chassis for its fire apparatus and the U.S. Army ordered 100 such pumpers. In the early 1920s, the Howe Defender was built on a Defiance truck chassis. Howe also used chassis built by Reo and Mason during the 1920s.

In 1930, when Defiance went out of business, Howe began fabricating its own chassis called the Defender. In 1932, the company began building fire trucks from the ground up using Defender chassis, as well as by utilizing Chevrolet, Diamond, Ford, F.W.D. and International truck chassis throughout the 1930s. In 1936, the Howe Fire Apparatus Company was ironically destroyed by a fire and it moved once again to another plant in Anderson. During the 1940s Howe also used Dodge and Oshkosh chassis for its fire engines.

1960 HOWE FIRE TRUCKS KP

In 1953, Howe introduced the New Defender that used a Duplex chassis and was powered by a Waukesha engine. These were 750-, 1000- and 1250-gpm pumpers and were available with either open or closed cabs. Commercial chassis were used throughout the 1950s and 1960s. In 1961, Howe bought one of its competitors, the Oren-Roanoke Corporation. In 1965, Howe acquired another competitor by the name of Coast Fire Apparatus.

By 1967, a new cab-forward chassis was developed using a Detroit Diesel engine and Cincinnati open or closed cabs. These were still called the Defender. By 1976, the Howe company had been in family hands for 104 years. However, this was the year Grumman Corporation bought Howe and the new parent company continued to build Howe fire apparatus (also using the Oren name that Howe had continued) until 1983, when both marque's names were discontinued.

1913 H.R.L. RD

H.R.L. 1913 — The H.R.L. Motor Company built the 1-ton Model L3/4, 2-ton Model R1 and 3-ton Model H2 in 1920. H.J. Hendricks was president, H.N. Rothweiler was vice-president and J.A. Logue treasurer. The H.R.L. trucks were powered by a four-cylinder Hinkley engine and used a four-speed Brown-Lipe transmission. A semi-floating worm-drive rear axle was also adopted. Marketing was focussed on the Northwest and Orient. How many H.R.L. trucks were sold or how long the company lasted is not certain.

HRM see GERSIX

HUBER 1903-1905 — Emil Huber, Edmund Sprung and Henry G. Ide built an experimental vehicle at the turn of the century in Oxford, Michigan, as the Ide-Sprung-Huber Automobile Company. In 1903, they were joined by Mersden Burch and formed the Huber Automobile Company, which was capitalized with $100,000 in Detroit, Michigan. Sprung was president and Ide secretary treasurer.

Although originally organized to build passenger cars, the Huber company first built a 2-ton delivery wagon, and subsequently built 30-passenger and 40-passenger buses, many of them for sightseeing use. By 1905, the manufacturing portion of the business was faded out as Huber turned to vehicle leasing operations.

In 1907, Ide and Burch tried to secure a chattel mortgage on all company property for the purpose of "protecting the interests held by them and their wives." Sprung alleged the company's books had been altered. Meanwhile, Emil Huber stayed out of the conflict and moved to Iowa where in 1909, he built a runabout that did not go into production. Huber went on to become a successful engineer at Hudson.

1917 HUDSON W.W. I AMBULANCE KP

HUDSON 1917, 1922, 1933-1947 — In the first two decades of the century, there were some 10 motor vehicle companies by the name of Hudson. None were as successful as the Hudson Motor Car Company of Detroit, Michigan. Although the company produced some 4,000 cars by 1910 -- the most sales in the first year of auto production up to that time -- Hudson did not produce commercial vehicles until 1917, when ambulance and light trucks based on the Hudson Super Six were built for the U.S. Army. A few pickups were also built in 1922 for use in the Hudson factory.

The organizers of the Hudson Motor Car Company were Roy D. Chapin, Howard E. Coffin, George W. Dunham and Roscoe B. Jackson, who had all left the Olds Motor Works. Joseph L. Hudson was a wealthy department store owner in Detroit and it was he who put up the $90,000 capital at the urging of his niece, who was Jackson's wife. By 1909, the partners had $100,000 and had obtained the Selden license from the bankrupt Northern company and had started operating in the factory where Aerocar had been produced.

By 1917, when Hudson was part of the war effort the Super Six military vehicles were powered by a Hudson 76 hp 289-cubic inch displacement six-cylinder engine using a Hudson-built sidedraft carburetor. Coupled through a cork-insert wet clutch was a three-speed sliding gear transmission. The vehicles had shaft drive and a semi-floating rear axle. This engine and transmission were also used in 1922 when Hudson built a few experimental pickups.

In 1933, Hudson began building 1/2-ton pickups using the Terraplane 6 chassis and the light commercial vehicles were marketed as Essex Terraplane that year. In 1934, they were known as Terraplane and kept the name until 1937. After that until 1947 they were called Hudson.

1939 HUDSON PACEMAKER DELIVERY RD

All of the pickups were closely based on the company's passenger cars. In 1933, a six-cylinder engine powered the pickups. This engine differed from the earlier Hudson Six primarily in that it had three main bearings instead of four, had a 193-cubic inch displacement and used a updraft Marvel carburetor. By 1938, the chassis had a 112-inch wheelbase. The company built a forward-control short-stop delivery van for 1941 rated at 1/2-ton. At this point, the Hudson pickup was rated at 3/4-ton and had a 132-inch wheelbase, which was the longest in its class. When Hudson introduced its stepdown series in 1947, pickups were no longer produced, although one prototype of a stepdown version was fabricated.

1941 HUDSON MODEL C-10 DELIVERY VAN   OCW

1947 HUDSON 3/4-TON   MROZ

HUEBNER 1914 — O.E. Huebner built the first three-wheel electric cyclecar in America. Its wheelbase was 96 inches and tread was 54 inches. The single driving wheel was at the rear of the prototype, which was fitted with a box in front for light delivery work. A local Brooklyn laundry in New York used the Huebner three-wheeler for eight months carrying loads up to 200 pounds. The light delivery vehicle was driven 2,500 miles averaging 23 miles per charge. Including operating costs and depreciation, Huebner calculated the vehicle's efficiency at four cents per mile. Other similar vehicles were designed by Huebner but did not go into production either.

HUFFMAN 1919-1927 — The Huffman Brothers Motor Company of Elkhart, Indiana, began when William L. Huffman bought the former Sun Motor Company and incorporated with capital investment of $1 million. He took over the company's president while Fred C. Huffman became vice-president, LeRoy Huffman treasurer, R.S. Wiltrout general manager and V.C. Cawley secretary. The press announced that these officers did not receive a salary.

The Huffman trucks were 1-1/2-ton trucks in the first year of operation. These were powered by 22.46 hp Continental Red Seal engines and used worm or bevel gear rear axles with Fuller three-speed transmissions. Wheelbase was 140 inches. In the first year of production, Huffman offered trucks from 1-ton to 5,500 pound capacity starting at $1,495 with internal bevel drive and $1,695 for worm-drive.

1919 HUFFMAN 1-TON   MROZ

In 1920, the company also engaged in passenger car production and truck prices went up by $200. Receivership was requested that year because of a conflict between the stockholders and the Huffman officers. After reorganization, P.J. Schultus of Milwaukee became president. Another lawsuit followed in 1921, when Huffman's creditors by the name of Goshen Buggy Top Company, Ligonier Automobile Body Company, Marion Malleable Iron Works and Woonsocket Manufacturing Company sued the company for payment on debts. Another suit followed in 1923, when Huffman switched to Buda engines and bevel drive. For 1925, Huffman built 1-1/2-ton trucks priced at $1,790 and 2-ton trucks at $1,990. According to some records, there were also a few 3-1/2-ton trucks built.

By the end of 1926, due to delinquency in paying on a bond issue of $165,000, the Valley Motor Truck Company succeeded the Huffman Brothers Motor Company. Trucks continued to be built under the Huffman name, however, and these were rated from 1-1/2-ton to 4-ton capacity, powered by Buda, Continental, Hercules and Wisconsin engines. At the end of that year, the truck's name was changed to Valley Dispatch and Valley Truck. At this point, Hercules engines were used. A fire devastated the factory at this time. In 1929, the name was again changed to Elkhart, and a few trucks under that name were produced until 1931, when all manufacturing ceased.

HUG 1921-1942 — C.J. Hug was in the road construction business and decided to build his own trucks to suit his own specifications. The first Hug was built in 1921 using a 34 hp four-cylinder Buda MU engine. This model went into production in 1922 as the Model T, which was rated at 2-ton. It used a Warner three-speed transmission and Clark spiral bevel rear axle. Along with pneumatic tires, the combination of these components and the selected gear ratio gave this model Hug truck a top speed of 45 mph, which was nearly double that of other equivalent trucks. The Model T Hug had an open cab and was fitted with either a dry goods delivery body or with an inverted trapezoidal body for hauling wet concrete.

Late in 1924, Hug also offered the 1-1/2-ton Model TA with 118-inch wheelbase, the 2-ton Model HA with the same wheelbase and the 2-1/2-ton Model H4 with 121-inch wheelbase. Each of these were powered by a 22.5 hp four-cylinder Buda WTU engine with Zenith carburetor and Bosch ignition. Each of these used a Fuller transmission and Wisconsin axles, except for the lightest model that had a Columbia front and Clark rear axle and the 2-ton used a Hug-built rear axle. The 2-1/2-ton still had solid rubber tires, while the 2-ton was offered with pneumatic tires as standard equipment. In 1925, the company added the 3-1/2-ton Model CH. By 1927, the 6-ton Model 88 was powered by a 43 hp Buda KUBI engine and had a seven-speed Brown-Lipe transmission with a Wisconsin rear axle. By 1930, the 3-1/2-ton was called the Model 43 and was powered by a six-cylinder Buda engine using a Timken rear axle. This model dump truck cost $3,380 in 1930.

1930 HUG DUMP TRUCK   MROZ

1936 HUG MILK TANKER   KP

Hug introduced its heftier Roadbuilder series by 1932. By 1937, these included 6-1/2- 18- and 20-ton models, which were either powered by four-cylinder Caterpillar diesel engines or six-cylinder Buda gasoline engines. They were configured as 4x2 or 6x4 shaft driven trucks or 6x2 and 6x4 chain driven models built by the Six Wheel Company of Los Angeles, California, which built larger trucks under the name Maxi. The front of the dump beds had a large overhang to protect the cab and driver.

The largest Hug built was the Model C99MA, which was rated at 120,000 pounds GVW. In 1938, this vehicle sold for $18,320. The six-wheel version was offered with a Christie detachable halftrack that could be fitted onto the tandem rear wheels for work in soft terrain. Hug trucks proved themselves in heavy construction work but the company also sold many trucks in the Xpress series, which included models rated at 2-, 3- and 3-1/3-ton capacity. These were powered almost exclusively by six-cylinder Buda engines.

At this early stage, Hug built truck tractors with sleeper compartments, as well as cab-over models powered by Buda gasoline and Cummins diesel engines. In 1938, the 10-ton Model 16 cab-over truck tractor was powered by a 468-cubic inch displacement Caterpillar diesel engine. This was also the year Hug began producing rear-engine bus chassis and converting its truck chassis. Fully assembled buses were available at that time and these were of sectional design, which was later adopted by the Mate series of buses built by Wayne, which is where Hug shared its factory in Richmond, Indiana, with the latter manufacturer.

Hug switched from Buda engines to Waukesha engines in 1939, while still offering diesel powerplants made by Caterpillar. The rugged Hug trucks were used in road development and large construction projects including dam building. The Tennessee Valley Authority alone bought 29 of the large six-wheel Hug trucks between 1929 and 1940.

1941 HUG REAR-ENGINE BUS   MBS

Hug built four of the 6x6 51-6 in 1940 and eight of the 6x6 Model 50-6 cargo trucks rated at 7-1/2 ton in 1941. These were powered by Hercules HXC engines with four-speed Fuller 4-A860 transmissions using a Timken-Wisconsin T-77-3 transfer case and Timken axles. They resembled the contemporary Marmon-Herrington trucks, which were shipped overseas under Lend-Lease. Also in 1941, Hug built a series of highway trucks with sheet metal bought from Reo. Many of these latter trucks were bought by the Pet Milk Company, which had purchased 177 Hug trucks over the years.

The last year for Hug was 1942, when the company marked its 20th anniversary. Sold throughout 41 states and 7 foreign countries, total Hug production over the years was 4,014 units, which included about 50 trailers. Four of the Model 50-6 arrived at Ft. Holabird and were crated and sent overseas.

HUNT 1939 — A steam car experimenter since 1908, J. Roy Hunt built what could be considered the first recreational vehicle, which would later be a pattern for building an array of commercial vehicles and buses. The Hunt "House Car" was built in Los Angeles. For 1939, it was unusual in that it was steam engine powered. The vehicle used two high-pressure cylinders coupled to a flash boiler of Hunt's design. Wheelbase was 121 inches while the body measured 222 inches in length. The House Car had seats for five passengers and sleeping accommodations for two. It also had an electric refrigerator, hot water, shower and bathroom facilities.

HUNTER ELECTRIC 1903 — Rudolph M. Hunter was a Philadelphia attorney and electric car experimenter who obtained two patents in 1899 for an electric vehicle and an electric controller and subsequently another patent for an electric tractor. The latter was built as a postal delivery vehicle by the Electric Vehicle Company of Philadelphia, Pennsylvania.

HUNTINGBURG 1901-1903 — The Huntingburg Wagon Works of Huntingburg, Indiana, began motorizing buggies and various horsedrawn wagons, including depot hacks, using a one-cylinder gasoline engine located under the seat. These early motor vehicles were sold with a leather whip and an iron anchor. Ostensibly, the whip was to chase away dogs, while the anchor was intended to stop the vehicle when the brakes failed, which was not uncommon at the time.

HUPMOBILE 1912-1925 — Robert Craig Hupp was an experienced car designer, having already been involved with Ford, Olds and Regal by 1908. He organized the Hupp Motor Car Company in 1909, introducing his Model 20 Hupmobile at the Detroit Automobile Show. In 1912, the first commercial vehicle was produced in the form of the Model H-32, which was a closed delivery van rated at 800-pound capacity. It was powered by a water-cooled four-cylinder engine located under a hood in front and it used a three-speed transmission with shaft drive. The chassis was identical to the 1913 passenger model H-32. Wheelbase was 106 inches and semi-elliptic springs were fitted in front while transverse springs were used in the rear. This commercial version of the Hupmobile was priced at $950. A total of 11,649 Model 32 vehicles were sold but these included the passenger iterations as well as the light delivery van.

The men behind the Hupmobile organization were J. Walter Drake as president, Edward Denby, who was later to become Secretary of the Navy, Charles Hastings, Otto von Bachelle and Emil Nelson. The latter was largely responsible for the engineering of the Hupmobile, while Hastings saw to it that sales were a success. After a promotional tour in 1911-1912, when the Model D Hupmobile was taken on a successful 48,600-mile promotional tour of 26 different countries, Robert Hupp left the company after a dispute with Drake and Hastings. He went on to ventures with R.C.H., Hupp-Yeats, Monarch and Emerson, none of them ultimately successful. In 1918, Hupmobile announced a 1/2-ton commercial vehicle but it never went into production.

1914 HUPMOBILE MODEL 32 PANEL DELIVERY   OCW

Hupmobile passenger cars continued to be produced until 1941. A variety of station wagon type vehicles were built up to 1925 and some of these have been listed as commercial vehicles.

HUPP-YEATS 1911-1912 — After departing from the Hupp Motor Car Company as a result of conflict with the principals there, Robert Craig Hupp was not allowed to use the Hupmobile name as decided by the courts and so using his own initials, the Hupp-Yeats electric vehicles were built by the R.C.H. Corporation. R.C.H. would later stand for something else entirely, but in effect Robert Hupp would never enjoy the success that his first venture, the Hupmobile, did.

The Hupp-Yeats was a 1/2-ton electric truck using lead-acid battery power and was built with several different bodies, including closed and open versions. Out of the 2,700 pounds of total vehicle weight, the 27 battery cells weighed 920 pounds. A screen-side express body truck, which used cushion-type solid rubber tires was priced at $1,600. Hupp-Yeats passenger cars were produced until 1919, when they were discontinued. Robert Craig Hupp died in 1931.

1927 HURLBURT   RD

HURLBURT 1912-1927 — The Hurlburt Motor Truck Company started out in New York City. The factory was moved to the Bronx in 1915. The first models were 1-, 2- and 3-1/2-ton capacity. The model line was expanded in 1918 with 5-ton and 7-ton models. This was also the year Hurlburt switched to a V-shape radiator, which was quite distinctive for that time. The two heavy trucks were powered by six-cylinder Buda engines and used Brown-Lipe transmissions with worm-drive rear axles.

The first five years' production was sold throughout the New York metropolitan area to such companies as Tiffany Studios, Schulz Bread and John Wanamkers. Marketing was expanded to other areas of the East Coast in 1917 and in 1919, the Harrisburg Manufacturing and Boiler Company of Harrisburg, Pennsylvania, continued production of Hurlburt trucks.

In 1920, the 7-ton model was dropped from the line of Hurlburt trucks, only to be reintroduced in 1924. Essentially, all Hurlburt trucks were powered by Buda engines. In the last year of production, the model line consisted of a range starting with 1-ton capacity up to 10-ton capacity. The last Hurlburt, a 10-ton capacity model, was a six-wheel articulated truck. Even with the progressive design, the company did not survive the year 1927.

HYDROCAR 1917 — The Hydrocar was intended as a multi-purpose vehicle, including that of a light truck, with amphibious capabilities. Per the *Automobie Trade Journal* of February 1917 the Hydrocar "is designed to run backward on water by means of special propellers... When land is reached the land wheels take a firm grip." George Monnot, who had been a bicycle builder and auto dealer in Canton, Ohio, was the designer of the Hydrocar. Capitalized with $100,000, the president of the company was Oliver Light, vice-president Harry O. Myers and treasurer was Roy W. Oats.

Monnot wanted to build both commercial and military versions of the Hydrocar, which was powered by a four-cylinder Hercules engine and used two steering wheels on each end, depending whether it was used on land or water. Boattail speedsters were probably an inspiration for the Hydrocar. The propeller was mounted essentially in place of a crank starter under the radiator. Tests showed the vehicle capable of 9 mph in water and 25 mph on land. The military was interested after tests in the Potomac River, but once the Armistice was signed in November 1918 and capital ran out, the Hyrdocar became only a one-off exercise in creative vehicle design.

I

I

IBEX 1964-1978 — The Hafer-Ibex Corporation of Salt Lake City, Utah, started in 1964, with trucks named after an Asiatic mountain goat. The company was renamed simply as the Ibex Motor Truck Corporation of Salt Lake City. The first Ibex trucks were conventional custom-built 4x4, 6x4 and 6x6 models. These were built both as rigid trucks or truck tractors and they were powered by 270 hp six-cylinder, 340 hp V-8 Caterpillar or 194 hp Detroit Diesel engines. Dana or Spicer transmissions were used and transfer cases were made by American Coleman or Rockwell. Axles were built by Eaton or Rockwell and suspensions were from Hendrickson. Ibex trucks were primarily designed for off-highway use in construction, exploration and oil well drilling.

1974 IBEX I   **IBEX**

In 1970, Ibex built the Flexi-Truc, which was a short-wheelbase trailer spotter and these were marketed by Flexi-Truc Incorporated of Secaucus, New Jersey. One version had a low cab and the other a high cab. Ibex also built the 900 series 6x4 construction truck in low cab-forward version and a high COE. The Flexi-Truc and 900 series have been powered by Caterpillar, Cummins and Detroit Diesel engines or Ford gasoline powerplants. Hafers discontinued manufacturing trucks in 1978 but has stayed in business as a truck parts distributor to date.

IDEAL 1910-1916 — Among the more than dozen motor vehicle manufacturers that used the Ideal name, the Ideal Auto Company of Fort Wayne, Indiana, built a 1/4-ton model truck and a 1-ton model truck beginning in 1910. The lighter trucks used a water-cooled two-cylinder engine, while the heavier was powered by a four-cylinder engine. All of the models used two-speed planetary transmission, solid rubber tires and double chain drive.

In 1911, the Ideal truck was listed as having a 1,600-pound load capacity. Wheelbase was 100 inches and chassis weight was 2,000 pounds. Driver's seat was "above motor," which was a 20 hp two-cylinder, four-cycle unit with Schebler or Marvel carburetor and Bosch ignition. A multiple disc clutch was used with the two-speed planetary transmission. Wood wheels carried 36x2-1/2 front and 36x3 rear solid rubber tires. Springs were 3/4-elliptic and steering gear was built by Ideal. Factory price with standard body was $1,200.

For 1912, all Ideal trucks used a forward-control design and the two-cylinder engines were no longer used. All chassis could be fitted with stake bodies or express type beds and for 1915, the company adopted selective gear transmissions. In the last year of manufacture, Ideal offered 1-, 1-1/2- and 2-1/2-ton models.

I.H.C. see INTERNATIONAL

ILLINOIS ELECTRIC 1897-1901 — The Illinois Electric Vehicle and Transportation Company built different models of electric vehicles, including hansom cabs. Actually, the vehicles were pro-

duced by the Siemens-Halske Electric Company in Cicero, Illinois. The hansom cabs were steered by the rear wheels with the driver sitting out in the open above and behind the passengers, much as the earlier Morris and Salom Electrobat cabs. An electric motor in each front wheel provided motive power. Other electric cars made by Illinois were steered by the front wheels and powered with electric motors in each rear wheel. Approximately 30 commercial cabs were built before the company ceased production in 1901.

IMP 1913-1914 — The Imp Cyclecar Company of Auburn, Indiana, was a subsidiary of the W.H. McIntyre Company, which successfully produced highwheelers. The Imp was designed by William B. Stout, who had tried to market a cyclecar under his own name in Chicago but without success. The Imp was a cyclecar that had a 100-inch wheelbase. A light 1/4-ton delivery version was built along with a two-seat passenger model. Both versions were powered by a 15 hp air-cooled V-2 engine and used a friction transmission with V-belt drive. In 1914, a four-cylinder engine was adapted, which the company claimed to achieve 50 mpg and 50 mph. With the two-cylinder engine the whole vehicle weighed 600 pounds and was priced at $375.

1914 IMP LIGHT DELIVERY CAR   **OCW**

One feature of the Imp not shared with most other vehicles of its era was that its wheels were held on the ends of transverse springs, which eliminated the axles altogether. Also, by inserting a crank into the center of the steering wheel, the Imp could be manually started by engaging a ratchet on the crankshaft using a bevel gear. A hardwood block that acted against the pulley groove of the rear wheels was the extent of the braking system. The Imp was first tested on a muddy trip from Auburn to Fort Wayne, Indiana. It proved itself adequately.

Production was approximately 10 vehicles per month in 1913 and this jumped to 50 per month the following, albeit last, year of manufacture. One of the company's advertising lines was "Everyone has Speed Protoplasms in his Blood and Motor Car Driving is the Universal...Manifestation." When William Stout left for the Scripps-Booth company in Detroit, the W.H. McIntyre Company went out of business and the Imp's abundant production was suddenly halted.

IMPERIAL 1903-1904 — The Rogers and Company of Columbus, Ohio, built the Imperial line of automobiles, which included a Model C Light Delivery for both years of manufacture. It was powered by an 8 hp V-2 air-cooled engine and used a 78-inch wheelbase. For both years the Light Delivery was priced at $1,150 as compared to the Model D Physician's Coupe (passenger car). The engine was mounted under a coffin-shaped hood and the vehicles were appointed with 12-spoke wheels and pneumatic tires. Semi-elliptic springs were utilized both front and rear and final drive was by chain. The Imperial was not produced after 1904.

INDEPENDENT 1915-1918 — Independent Motors Company marketed a 1-ton Model F, which was gasoline powered and priced from $1,285 to $1,385. It does not appear that this company was affiliated with the other builders using the Independent name.

INDEPENDENT 1917-1921 — The Independent Truck Company of Davenport, Iowa, built 1-ton and 2-ton model trucks for four years. Both models were conventional assembled trucks powered by four-cylinder Continental engines. The 1-ton model had a wheelbase of 135-inches while the heftier Independent truck had a 146-inch wheelbase. Both were fitted with three-speed Fuller transmissions and Russel bevel-gear rear axles. The company did not survive the post-World War I recession.

INDEPENDENT 1918-1923 — Overlapping in time with the other company producing Independent trucks in Iowa, the Independent Motors Company was manufacturing trucks by the same name in Youngstown, Ohio. For the first two years of existence, the company built trucks rated at the same capacity as well, which must have led to some confusion. In 1919, Independent Motors added a 1-1/2-ton model and a 3-1/2-ton model. To add more to the mix-up, these trucks were also powered by four-cylinder Continental engines and also used three-speed Fuller transmissions. The one distinguishing feature was that the rear axles of the Independent trucks were worm-drive.

INDEPENDENT HARVESTER 1910-1911 — The light Independent Harvester van built commercial vehicles for only about one year between 1910 and 1911 and the design was by Henry K. Holsman. This venture was a continuation of the Holsman vehicle company, which folded in 1910. The vehicles were essentially the same as the previous built in Chicago. They were powered by a water-cooled four-cylinder engine using a friction transmission and final chain drive. Only a few were sold at a price of $750.

Independent Harvester vehicles were built by the Independent Harvester Company of Plano, Illinois, but it was the decision of Holsman to name them as such, which resulted in references to the vehicles as I.H.C. The International Harvester Company of Chicago (also known as I.H.C.) produced highwheelers at the same time until 1911, coincidentally when Independent Harvester, producer of agricultural implements and equipment, stopped building the Holsman-designed vehicles.

INDIAN 1908-1948 — When Oscar Hendee, a bicycle manufacturer, and engineer Oscar Hedstrom joined forces and built their first "Indian" motorcycle in 1904, they had no intentions to go into commercial vehicle manufacturing. By 1908, the company collaborated with the U.S. Postal Service and developed a three-wheel mail delivery van. It was powered by a 2-3/4 hp air-cooled engine and had a 250-pound cargo capacity. A number of these were used for mail and parcel delivery. The two-front-wheel configuration was superseded by the adaptation of cargo sidecars during the 1920s, much as what Harley-Davidson did with its design.

1908 INDIAN MOTORCYCLE POSTAL VAN   RD

The Army Air Corps used an Indian Powerplus to build a "Firecycle," which was used as a rapid deployment fire and rescue vehicle. A sidecar carried a tetrachloride tank built by the Phister Manufacturing Company of Cincinnati, Ohio. The sidecar also held a reel of hose and a stretcher for fast evacuation of injured personnel.

In the late 1920s, Indian introduced its Dispatch-tow three-wheeler. This motorcycle engine-powered vehicle actually preempted Harley-Davidson's Servi-Car of 1931. The Dispatch-tow vehicle was intended for use in auto dealerships to pick up customer's cars and then be towed back to the dealer's garage, thereby using only one person for the job. The three-wheelers found other light commercial uses, but were made in smaller numbers than the Harley-Davidson Servi-Car and were phased out before World War II.

1925 INDIAN 3-WHEEL FIRECYCLE   RD

In 1938, Indian built an elaborate three-wheel vehicle to carry three passengers or cargo and this vehicle was tested by the Infantry Board at Ft. Benning. The three-wheeler shared components with the Model 340 motorcycle. It had dual chain drive to the two-wheel rear axle. Another version was built in 1940 based on the Chief model, but only 16 were bought by the U.S. Army. One type powered by a 24 hp V-2 engine was used for fire fighting by the U.S. Navy. Few three-wheelers were built after World War II, and the company faded out in the early 1950s after becoming an importer of other makes.

1914 INDIANA MODEL B-30   OCW

INDIANA 1911-1939 — Indiana trucks were first built by the Harwood-Barley Manufacturing Company in Marion, Indiana, until 1920, when the firm was incorporated as the Indiana Truck Corporation in that city. Indiana trucks were conventional assembled trucks at first, powered by four-cylinder Rutenber engines. The trucks had a four-speed transmission and double chain drive. Solid tires were standard on this early 1-1/2-ton model but pneumatic tires were also available.

Indiana production rose rapidly and during World War I, the company built 600 trucks for the military. By 1920, the factory assembled 4,000 trucks in that year alone. The full line ranged up to 5-ton capacity and Indiana trucks were powered by either four-cylinder Rutenber or four-cylinder Waukesha engines. By 1923, a 7-ton model was added to the line. The following year, Indiana utilized Hercules engines for all its trucks up to 3-ton capacity.

By 1924, Indiana listed 10 models from 1-ton to 5-ton capacity. The Model 11 was powered by a 25.6 hp Hercules OX engine using a Muncie T-23 transmission. The truck had a Clark rear axle and Salisbury front axle using Bimel wheels and 34x5 pneumatic tires as standard equipment. The Model 11A was generally the same but was rated at 1-1/2-ton capacity and was powered by the same engine using a Brown-Lipe transmission and Sheldon rear axle. The 1-1/2-ton Model 15 differed from the Model 11A in that it had solid rubber tires and used both front and rear Sheldon axles.

In the mid-1920s, the company also offered the 2-ton Model 20, which was powered by an 27.2 hp four-cylinder Indiana engine with Brown-Lipe transmission. The same 38 series engine and component manufacturers were used for Indiana's 2-1/2-ton Model 25. All of these models used Ross steering. The 3-1/2-ton Model 35 with a fixed 172-inch wheelbase (the previous had optional wheelbases) was powered by a still-larger series 40 engine rated at 30.6 hp and used Wohlrab steering. However, the 4-ton Model 40 was powered by a 32.4 hp four-cylinder Waukesha DU engine. The heaviest Indiana trucks at that time were rated at 5-ton, and these were the Model 51 and Model 52. Both were powered by 40.0 hp Waukesha EU engines and essentially differed only in wheelbase and chassis weight, which was 9,160 pounds and 9,310 pounds, respectively.

The 1925 Indiana 5-ton model featured a seven-speed transmission. This truck was styled differently in that it had a sloping detachable radiator grille and both the Waukesha engine and rear axle were made easily detachable for servicing. For 1926, Indiana also built the similarly-designed 3-ton Model 126 but it was powered by a Hercules engine.

1927 INDIANA 1-1/2-TON MODEL 111   HAYS

In 1927, Indiana trucks became a subsidiary of Brockway, although they were still manufactured under the Indiana name. This relationship continued until 1932 when Brockway was forced to sell the company. During this time, Brockway adopted four-cylinder Continental engines as well as six-cylinder Wisconsin powerplants. But for 1927, the 2-ton Model 111 with 152-inch wheelbase had a Hercules OX engine, three-speed Brown-Lipe transmission, shaft drive with Clark rear axle, Shuler front axle and was available with a two-speed auxiliary transmission. The six-cylinder Wisconsin engine model was the firm's first 3-ton Speed truck and it featured a full electrical system, pneumatic tires and spiral bevel drive, which was adopted for all lighter Indiana trucks while the heavier models still used worm-drive.

1930 INDIANA DUMP TRUCK   JOE EGLE

For 1928, Indiana introduced another 1-ton truck powered by a six-cylinder Wisconsin engine. It was called the Ranger and featured four-wheel-brakes. In 1930, Indiana trucks were built with five-speed transmissions, and the heaviest Indiana truck for that year was a 5-1/2-ton capacity six-wheel model. These were powered by six-cylinder Continental engines. Smaller trucks were still powered by four-cylinder Hercules powerplants. In 1931, an Indiana truck was fitted with a Cummins diesel engine for a cross-continent test run.

As Brockway was forced to sell Indiana in 1932, White purchased the firm and moved the operations to Cleveland, Ohio. Under new management, Indiana then received six-cylinder Hercules engines and shared other components such as four-speed and five-speed transmissions and hydraulic brakes. Except for the three-axle trucks, Indiana also adopted spiral bevel drive. The heaviest models were powered by 95 hp six-cylinder engines and featured brakes on all wheels in both 6x2 and 6x4 configurations.

1934 INDIANA STAKE TRUCK   A&A

Indiana/White became the first series-built truck in the United States to use Cummins diesel engines (among many similar types of claims by other truck builders of that time) after Clessie Cummins used the Indiana truck for long distance testing. It was conventional 5-ton model, and it was powered by a 125 hp six-cylinder Cummins diesel powerplant. White management decided to cut Indiana light truck production almost at the same time as the diesel truck was introduced, so that in effect the first diesel trucks were Indiana during testing but were actually fitted into a White chassis for production.

By 1936, the largest Indiana available was a 2-1/2-ton model. Yet the following year, a full range of models were listed from 1-ton to 6-1/2-ton. Indiana was commissioned to build a 7-1/2-ton 6x6 truck for the military at this time. It was powered by a 161 hp six-cylinder Hercules engine, which was more than double the output of the heaviest civilian Indiana truck. The White M3A1 scout car was listed as an Indiana vehicle, in part because it was powered by a Hercules engine, whereas the White M3 halftrack was powered by a six-cylinder engine built by White. A total of 1,706 Indiana trucks were sold in 1936.

1937 INDIANA MODEL 80 STEP VAN   MROZ

By 1937, Indiana continued to feature six-cylinder engines and the civilian range included trucks from 1-ton to 5-ton. The heaviest 5-ton model at that time was available with a six-cylinder Hercules diesel engine and used a five-speed transmission as well as hydro-vac brakes. The lightest Indiana truck, which was rated as a 1-ton, was powered by a 50 hp four-cylinder Hercules engine. This was at a time when the company considered manufacturing in England but by 1938, production was so low that all such plans were abandoned. By 1939, the Indiana marque was all but defunct. Indiana was listed into 1940 but it appears production actually ceased the previous year.

INLAND 1919-1921 — There is scant reference to the Inland Motor Company located in Evansville, Indiana. Two earlier Inland companies associated with motor vehicles were not related. The Evansville firm offered 1-ton and 2-ton trucks for almost two years; however, specifications of the vehicles have not been found to date.

INTERBORO 1913-1914

This early and obscure truck was available as a 1-ton model, which was built by the Interboro Motor Truck Company of Philadelphia, Pennsylvania. It was powered by a 23 hp four-cylinder engine and was listed at $1,850 in 1913. The company did not survive the following year.

INTERNATIONAL 1907 to date — The International Harvester company has traced its origins back to 1831 when Cyrus H. McCormick developed grain reapers. In that century, the company's specialty was farm equipment mechanization. International Harvester Company or IHC as it was called, began doing business as such in 1902, but its first "Auto Buggies" did not appear until 1907.

The first IHC motor vehicles were developed by E.A. Johnson who started with International in 1894, which was five years after the company produced its first tractor. Johnson's first automotive experiments began in 1898 at McCormick and his design work of the Auto Buggy began in 1905. Its actual production started in February of 1907. In October of that year the manufacturing facilities for this vehicle were moved from Chicago, Illinois, to Akron, Ohio. Passenger cars were built in 1910 and 1911. Auto Buggies were built through 1911 and Auto Wagons were built from 1909 until 1912. The IHC highwheelers used wagon-type wheels up to 44 inches in diameter.

1912 INTERNATIONAL MODEL MW 1-TON   **TT**

The 1912 models were the first IHC to carry designations such as Model A and Model M, the latter with a water-cooled engine. An "A" suffix indicated an air-cooled engine and a "W" suffix indicated a water-cooled engine. Many of the two-cylinder horizontally-opposed Auto Buggy and Auto Wagon engines were air-cooled and rated at 15 bhp. In 1914, the IHC logo was superseded with the name International.

Truck production began in 1915 with five models from 3/4-ton up to 3-1/2-ton capacity. The five designations were H, F, K, G and L, with the latter 3-1/2-ton the only model not available with pneumatic tires. Each of the models used a sloping Renault-type hood. The radiator was mounted behind the engine near the firewall for easy access to the engine for maintenance purposes. The vulnerable radiator was also more protected in that position.

On the earlier models a two-speed planetary transmission was used, which had a transverse driveshaft transferring power with a single chain to a double chain final drive. The steel frame had full-

elliptic springs. Tread was 56-inch with an exception for Model B, which used 60-inch tread and was marketed for southern and western regions.

The whole truck line that was started in 1915 was usually shod with artillery-type wheels that had pressed-on solid rubber tires. International used L-head four-cylinder engines for this series, which had different ignitions available including Bosch and Dixie. Also, internal gear drive was used as were enclosed self-adjusting brakes. Transmissions were three-speed selective gear type and springs were semi-elliptic on all models.

1916 INTERNATIONAL SCREENSIDE DELIVERY   **GOODYEAR**

1916 INTERNATIONAL SCREENSIDE DELIVERY   **GOODYEAR**

The smallest truck of the 1915-1923 era was the Model H. Production of this series ended in 1923, as it did with the Model L, which had a 3-1/2-ton capacity. The 2-ton model was the only one to have forward-control. International was able to capture four percent of the truck market by the end of World War I.

Late in 1921, International introduced its speed model truck, which was rated at 3/4-ton capacity and had a 115-inch wheelbase. Standard design was used with radiator in front of a four-cylinder Lycoming engine -- two unexpected choices for a company that also built its own engines. A multiple disc clutch coupled the engine to a three-speed transmission. Top speed was approximately 30 mph. Having opened a new plant in Springfield, Ohio, approximately 7,000 trucks were built in 1921 ranging from 1-ton to 5-ton capacity. The company used a fleet of red "speed" trucks, and with a pickup body this model was nicknamed "Red Baby." The Model G truck had its capacity uprated from 2-ton to 3-ton in 1921. Also that year, the Model 21 replaced the Model H.

For 1923, International began building the "S" series trucks, which lasted until 1929. The following year, a major styling change took place. International trucks were designed with butterfly hoods and prominent front-mounted radiators. Solid tires used steel spoke wheels, and final drive was double reduction bevel type, although a few chain-driven models were built on special order. International had developed a network of 102 factory branches and 1,500 deal-

1924 INTERNATIONAL (LEFT TO RIGHT) TRACTOR TRAILER, 5-TON AND 1-TON   OCW

1926 INTERNATIONAL TANKER   KP

1928 INTERNATIONAL DEPOT WAGON   A&A

1929 INTERNATIONAL TRACTOR-TRAILER   TT

1932 INTERNATIONAL 1/2-TON MODEL AW-1   OCW

1933 INTERNATIONAL ARMORED CAR   KP

1934 INTERNATIONAL MAIL TRUCK   A&A

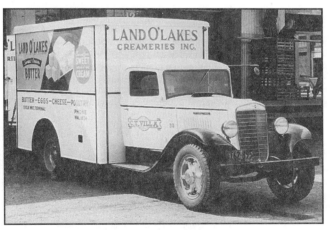

1935 INTERNATIONAL C-30 REFRIGERATED VAN   A&A

1937 INTERNATIONAL D-SERIES PANEL DELIVERY   JH

erships by then. In 1924, International introduced a new model line consisting of Models 33, 43, 63, 94 and 103. Also that year, the Special Delivery trucks were unveiled.

In addition to a bus chassis for 1925, International offered a range of trucks that included the 1-ton Model S, 1-1/2-ton Model 33, 2-ton Model 43, 3-ton Model 63, 4-1/2-ton Model 94 and 5-ton Model 103. The company produced its own engines and transmissions. Between 1924 and 1927, 4,700 Model 43 trucks alone were built by International. At that time the 40.0 hp four-cylinder was the largest standard engine in the company's trucks. However, the bus chassis had a six-cylinder engine, spiral-bevel drive, full-floating rear axle and four-wheel brakes. The six-cylinder engine was adapted for trucks in 1926 when solid rubber tires were phased out.

By the following year, production had risen to 25,000 units for the year. About 3,800 Model SL-36 trucks were built between 1926 and 1929, many with bus bodies. Also in 1926, the company began building the Model S-24 trucks in addition to the SD-34, SF-34, SL-34, SD-36, SF-36, SL-36, SD-44, SF-44, SD-46 and SF-46 type. Between 1927 and 1929, International built several chain-drive trucks that ranged from the 2-1/2-ton Model 54C to the 10-ton Model 104C. The mid-range Model 74C featured a two-speed live axle. The Model 74C had a five-cubic yard capacity as a dump truck. This series used International engines with ball-type main bearings, but a total of only a few hundred were built.

In 1928, International developed the 1-ton Six Speed Special, combining a three-speed transmission and a two-speed auxiliary unit at the rear axle. This truck also had four-wheel brakes and a 1-1/2-ton and 2-1/2-ton version were also produced, as well as a milk-delivery stand-and-drive van chassis. By the time of the stock market crash the company had 170 branches and was producing 50,000 trucks a year. The A series, which had Lycoming or Waukesha engines, was produced between 1929 and 1934. The A-4, A-5 and A-6 were soon followed in 1930 by the A-1, A-2 and A-3. The A-7 and A-8 models did not begin until 1932.

For 1930, however, the economic downturn had a notable effect in that only 29,000 International trucks were produced. Nevertheless, a whole new line of trucks was offered that year plus larger A series and the special W series. These included overhead-valve engines with removable cylinders, a so-called "first." Five-speed transmissions were common with two reverse speeds. The 3-ton Model A and 63 continued to be successful in the more limited market of the Great Depression. Because of lagging sales the earlier models were gradually phased out. The 3/4-ton AW-1 pickup was introduced in mid-1930.

In 1932, International and Willys struck a deal. International would sell the new Willys C-1 pickup and panel truck under the International emblem. This helped sales during times of severe economic hardship. Most importantly, however, in 1933 International began building its own diesel engines. The smaller A series became the B series but along with the W series, production was limited. Also that year, the D-1 pickup went on the market for a chassis price of $360. It was powered by a 70 hp six-cylinder engine.

In 1934, the C series was unveiled. The 1/2-ton pickups were powered by a Willys engine. The trucks in this series featured a V-type aluminum grille and a slightly slanted windshield without the usual visor. That year International began building its own axles exclusively. The range was expanded with 18 models from 1/2-ton to 7-ton capacity. The C series was in production until 1937. Beginning in 1934 up to 1939, International made station wagons that were designed by Alexis De Sakhnoffsky, a well-known designer of that era. Two of the station wagons were brought to Africa by explorer Attilio Gatti on his 10th trip, along with two special International tractor and semi-trailers.

For 1935, International widened its range from 1/2-ton to 10-ton six-wheel design, the latter using a Hendrickson tandem axle. Despite lagging sales, that year the factory network was expanded to 217 branches. The following year, an innovative C-300 COE was introduced and this cab-over was the first in 20 years for International.

1937 INTERNATIONAL D-60 BREWER'S TRUCK   MROZ

A new 1-1/2-ton C-300 COE was offered in 1936 along with conventional models from 1/2-ton to 5-ton. Two A series (A7 and A8) were updated and rated up to 7-1/2-ton capacity for 1937. The sheet metal was redesigned for the D series including new cabs, pontoon fenders, split windshields and passenger car styling. Four-cylinder Waukesha engines were used in the C-5, M3 and C-20 models, the smallest being a 33 hp engine used in the 1/2-ton C-5 truck. All the rest used six-cylinder International engines up to 140 hp in the A8 model. That year, the entire lineup consisted of many overlapping models as the C series was replaced by the D series. This included the C-1, C-5, C-12, C-15, M3, C-20. C-30, CS-30, C-35, CS-35, C-40, CS-40, C-50, CS-50, C-55, C-60, C-300, D-2, D-5, D15, DCO-25, D-30, D-2-M, A7 and A8. The latter two "flat-faced" models lasted until 1942. For the year 1937, overall production reached 100,000 for the first time at International. Production of the D-2 model alone totaled 80,000 units between 1937 and 1940.

1938 INTERNATIONAL COE   A&A

1939 INTERNATIONAL D-30 STREAMNLINER TANKER   A&A

In 1938, International developed a sleeper cab. Metro delivery vans joined the range, with bodies fabricated by Metropolitan Body Company of Bridgeport, Connecticut. This was also the period when many distinctive D series trucks appeared, only to be superseded by the K series introduced in 1940. With the year's production reaching 86,000 units, International had built one million trucks over the years by 1941. The company ranked third in U.S. truck production and sold more trucks over 2-ton capacity than any other manufacturer.

During World War II, International built both civilian and military 2-1/2-ton and 5-ton trucks in 4x2, 4x4 and 6x6 configuration, as well as a great number of halftracks, scout cars and full-tracked personnel carriers. Total combat vehicle production surpassed the 100,000 mark. Kenworth and Marmon-Herrington both built International's H-542-11 military COE, which was distinguished by its slanted hood and bullnose.

1941 INTERNATIONAL MILITARY 6X6   INT

Near the end of World War II, International switched to its more modern logo, the red I over the black H. The K series was continued in 1946 as the KB, which had a wider grille extended out on the front fenders. Models K-6 through K-12 featured a butterfly hood starting just behind the radiator. Model K-1 through K-5 used side-valve engines, but heavier models had overhead-valve engines.

The K series was continued in production until 1950. The KB series was built from 1947 to 1949 and the smaller models featured panel bodies. The largest KB-8 featured an International 360-cubic inch 126 bhp Red Diamond engine that had seven main bearings. The latter cab and 161-inch chassis were priced at $3,765 in 1949. Some 64,000 KB-5 trucks alone were built during this time.

In 1947, International began manufacturing at a new plant in Emeryville, California. The factory produced large western-type truck models with GVW up to 90,000 pounds. The new W series had wider cabs, a flat radiator, flatter V-type windshield and fenders with no skirts. Two gasoline engines along with three diesel engines were available with a large choice of transmissions and wheelbases.

After World War II, both China and the U.S.S.R. copied International KB series trucks almost exactly, without any concern over patent infringements. The 4-ton Jay Fong and ZIS-150 clones remained the same for decades. In the United States, the 1950 L series replaced the KB series. The L range, which debuted late in 1949, was comprised of 87 basic light- and medium-duty models. All had headlights in the fenders and a new conventional cab was designed with a concave dashboard and convex windshield.

1948 INTERNATIONAL ARMORED CAR   BAC

1948 INTERNATIONAL KB-5   INT

1949 INTERNATIONAL DELUXE DELIVERY   INT

1950 INTERNATIONAL L-160 COE   A&A

In addition to gasoline and diesel engines, LP-gas engines were available starting in 1952. These included the BD-240, 264, 282, 308, RD-501, V-8-401, 461 and 549 engines. By 1953, the cab, which was built by Chicago Manufacturing Company, was shared with Diamond T. On the International R series, which debuted that year, the shared cab was distinguished by three thick grille bars. The COE trucks such as the LCFD and 405 were built in 1953 and these used the Diamond T design cab until 1972. This CO model had rear quarter side windows and like the VCO used a V-8 engine, while the DCO was powered by a diesel engine.

1952 INTERNATIONAL L-100 TRAVELALL   **A&A**

1953 INTERNATIONAL COE TRACTOR-TRAILER   **KP**

The Series L (L, LB, LM) became the R series in 1953, but the basic sheet metal remained the same. Then in 1955 the S series was introduced, with the light trucks getting a new sheet metal treatment. The S range superseded the R-100 through R-180 models that year. Total production surpassed 100,000 units once again in 1956. The SM series Metro vans were also redesigned and the 1-ton SM-130 was used as a jitney bus. The 3/4-ton Travelall became a popular light International model during the 1950s.

In 1957, International brought out the A series. The 9,000-pound GVW Metro was available as a school bus for up to 16 passengers. A crew cab was available in the new Utility pickup that year. Once again a 4x4 option was available. The crew cab was offered as the Travelette Utility Pickup in 1959 when the Series A became the Series B (BC replaced AC). The Black Diamond six-cylinder engine continued to be available along with the V-266 V-8. Total yearly production increased to 143,199 units and International held 12.7 percent of the U.S. truck market.

The V-266 and V-304 V-8 engines were announced in March of 1959 and by November of 1959 the V-8 engine was made standard on all Series B. Vertically-arranged dual headlights were another new detail for 1959. F.W. Jenks continued as president of the company.

The 1960 models were similar to the previous ones, and the V-8 model became widely adopted on most light models of International trucks. The C-100 pickup of that year was regularly equipped with the V-266 engine. In 1961, International pioneered the development of the recreational vehicle market with the introduction of the Scout, which had a five-foot bed integral with the cab, whose top was removable. A four-cylinder Comanche engine powered the

Scout, which was available as a 4x2 (GVW 3,200 pounds) and 4x4 (GVW 3,900 pounds). In 1961, the B series was followed by the Series C. The Metro line continued as the AB and AM series.

1961 INTERNATIONAL CREW CAB   **KP**

In 1962, International offered the conventional M series and F-230 with GVW up to 78,000 pounds for the construction industry. Some of these 15-ton 6x6 trucks were up to the legal limit of 35 feet in length for straight trucks. The heavy trucks used angular tread-plate fenders. This was also the time International began building huge 4x2 and 4x4 quarry dump trucks with up to 154,000-pound GVW, some of the largest four-wheel-drive trucks in the world of that period. LP-gas engines continued to be available from International. The first full year of production for the Loadstar 1600 trucks was 1962. The standard equipment for this truck was the 193 bhp V-304 V-8 engine and the T-17 four-speed transmission.

In 1963, the first conventional DC-400 Transtar was unveiled, as was the Fleetstar, introduced in March, which replaced the R series in 1967. The B series was entirely superseded by the Loadstar range also that year. The COE Loadstar would eventually become the Cargostar. The Metro-Mite, Metro and Metroette continued to be manufactured as the Series CM, AB and AM, respectively. The C-900 through C-1500 International trucks were available during 1963 and 1964. These were usually fitted with the BG-241, but other engine options included the BG-265, V-266, V-304 and V-345.

The Payhauler was introduced in 1964 and was unique in that it was the only dump truck to have four-wheel-drive and twin tires both front and rear. The eight smaller tires cost less than six larger ones normally used on a similar 4x2 dump truck and weight distribution was 50/50. Engine options were Cummins VT1710C V-12 or Detroit Diesel 16V-71N-65. During its later financial troubles International sold its Payline Group in 1982 to three former employees who continued to operate as Payhauler Corporation.

1965 INTERNATIONAL TANDEM W/TRAILER   **INT**

In 1965, International once again added a new series designation. It was called the Series D, but generally the same vehicles with essentially the same specifications continued to be produced through the 1960s. There were overlapping series such as the CO-4000 highway tractor, which was powered by a 240 hp diesel IH DVT-573 engine.

The heaviest International trucks in the early 1970s were comprised of seven models from 80,000-pound GVW to 168,000-pound GVW. These were powered by 12-cylinder and 16-cylinder diesel engines with up to 560 hp. Allison or Twin Disc 9-speed and 12-speed transmissions were used along with International axles. The Paystar 5000 appeared in 1973, succeeding the F-230 and M series heavy trucks.

1973 INTERNATIONAL LOADSTAR 1800 6X4 TIPPER   INT

By 1975, International continued to offer a full range of vehicles, many with diesel engines, starting with the Scout 4x2 and 4x4, Travelall, Series 150 and Series 200 pickups and light-duty trucks, conventional Loadstar 4x2, 4x4 and 6x4, conventional Fleetstar 4x2 and 4x4, COE Cargostar 4x2 and 6x4, conventional Transtar 4x2 and 6x4, COE Transtar 4x2 and 6x4, Paystar construction 4x4, 6x4 and 6x6 trucks, school buses and the CO-8190 fire engine chassis. A total of 75 models were available from 5,200-pound GVW to 180,000-pound GVW. Gasoline inline six-cylinder engines up to 215 hp were available, as well as the 200 hp International V-8 diesel and diesel engines from Caterpillar, Cummins and Detroit up to 450 hp. Transmissions were made by International, Fuller, New Process and Warner. Axles were built by International or Spicer.

1978 INTERNATIONAL LOADSTAR 1800 UTILITY   MROZ

1979 INTERNATIONAL TRANSTAR 4300   INT

After 1980, International began concentrating only on medium- and heavy-duty trucks. The Scout business, along with the Ft. Wayne factory where they were built, did not sell and was closed down by November of that year. One of the large construction trucks International built for 1980 was the F-2674 concrete mixer.

International continued having major financial difficulties in 1981. Glider kits were offered by International. These medium-duty trucks consisted of complete trucks less engine, transmission and rear axle. International was not the only company to offer glider kits for such trucks and they were not particularly successful. Iveco began building the new I series for International in 1982. Production was interrupted in the United States, but in 1983 the company was reorganized with the help of the federal government. "We're not giving in -- we're going on," was the slogan for that year.

For 1983, International continued to build the S series (named after the Springfield, Ohio, factory). These were available in a wide range from the smallest two-axle trucks available from International up to four-axle heavy construction trucks and highway tractors with diesel or gasoline engines, transmissions from four-speed to 13-speed manual and four-speed or five-speed automatic. The four-axle was basically a three-axle truck with a tag axle ahead of the tandem unit added as an aftermarket option, creating an 8x4 heavy-duty truck. The latter was typically powered by a six-cylinder PT-270 diesel engine and had a load capacity of 20 tons.

By 1983, the COE Cargostar CO-1750B, which was originally introduced in 1975, was available with six diesel and six gasoline engines, and transmission choices were the same as in the S series. The largest engine was built by Caterpillar, but the 165 hp diesel V-8 was a common engine for this type of truck, which was designed for maximum maneuverability especially suited for local delivery and refuse collection. The Cargostar COF-1950B was also available as a four-wheel or six-wheel truck and used essentially the same cab as the CO-1750B. One of the most common engines for this truck was the Caterpillar 3208 V-8 diesel. After December 1984 only diesel engines were available in International trucks.

At the same time, International built the Paystar, which was the company's premium truck for heavy on/off highway applications. Especially designed for wet concrete delivery work in western United States, the Paystar Weightwatcher weighed about 2,000 pounds less than the regular Paystar due to wide use of aluminum in the frame and cab. A 270 hp Detroit Diesel engine was standard on this model with seven-speed or eight-speed Fuller manual transmission. Paystars were built in Fort Wayne, Indiana, and Wagoner, Oklahoma.

In 1986, International's Truck Group adopted the Navistar International name, and trucks under both names have been built since then. A decade after a brush with financial ruin, the heaviest multi-purpose trucks from International were the Paystar 5000 series. These were available as 4x4, 6x4, 6x6 and 8x4 iterations with tag axles set back or forward, according to state regulations, or with twin-steering tandems. Twenty engines were available with one from International, the 210 hp DT-466, and the rest from Caterpillar, Cummins and Detroit Diesel and transmissions from five-speed to 15-speed. A typical drivetrain for the Paystar 5000 was the Cummins NTCC-4000 six-cylinder diesel coupled to a Fuller RTO 1157DL 9F 2R constant mesh transmission.

The Transtar 4300 series was the heavy-duty truck of the early 1980s for International with GVW up to 120,000 pounds, although state regulations usually limited GVW to 80,000 pounds due to road and bridge conditions. Fourteen diesel engine options were available built by Caterpillar, Cummins and Detroit Diesel. Transmissions from 9-speed to 15-speed were also available. Along with the standard cab, International offered two luxury cabs: the Eagle and the Eagle Brougham, which included upper and lower bunks, fold-down desk, countertop wash basin, clothes closet, refrigerator and fresh water tank. These were primarily aimed at private owner-operators and were available with a personalized dashboard plaque bearing the driver's name.

1994 INTERNATIONAL PAYSTAR 5000 MIXER   INT

International also built the CO Transtar series of forward-control trucks. The most notable was the XL cab, which was originally introduced in 1980 and was continually updated afterwards. The typical Transtar 11 CO-9670 used a Detroit Diesel 8V-92TTAC V-8 turbocharged engine with 12 liters displacement and 365 hp. The long-nosed 9370 conventional replaced the Transtar 4200 and 4300 in 1985 and was continued into the next decade.

1995 INTERNATIONAL EAGLE SERIES 9400, 9300 & 9200 INT (LEFT TO RIGHT)

By 1995, Navistar International offered 30 different iterations starting with the Series 2554 4x2 powered by an International DT-466-230 engine and having a maximum GVW of 44,880 pounds. The 2000 range also included the 2574, 2654 and 2674 series, each available as a 4x2 or 6x4. The 4800 and 4900 series were powered by an International DT-466-195 engine, and the 5000 series used the International 530-275 powerplant. There was also the 8100 and 8200 models, most of which used the Cummins M11-280E engine. The 9000 series was comprised of models 9100, 9200, 9300, 9400, 9600 and 9700. All were built in 4x2 or 6x4 configuration. The heaviest GCW ratings up to 140,000 pounds were offered in the 9000 series range with Cummins M11-280E and Cummins N14-310E diesel engines.

For 1996, Navistar International announced the availability of Cummins 14-liter and DDC Series 60 diesel engines for its new International Pro Sleeper 9800 highway tractors. The larger engines necessitated raising the floor five inches above these trucks' normally level floor. The electronically-controlled DDC Series 60 engine provided hp ratings from 330 to 430. The Cummins N14 CELECT engine was available with 330 to 435 hp.

INTERNATIONAL 1908 — The International Motor Company of Philadelphia, Pennsylvania, was not related to the well-known manufacturer from Chicago, nor related to two other earlier auto companies by the same name located in New York City and Toledo, Ohio, respectively. This small and obscure firm built 3-ton and 5-ton trucks for one year only. The general manager and designer was a man by the name of Lea, hence, the trucks were also announced as the Lea in the press. They differed from other vehicles of that era in that both were front-wheel-drive. The two models were powered by a 40 hp water-cooled four-cylinder engines and used friction drive transmissions. The entire engine and transmis-

sion assembly was mounted on a pivoting front axle with chain drive to each of the two front wheels. The heavier model had a chassis weight of 9,500 pounds and had a wheelbase of 146 inches.

1908 INTERNATIONAL LEA 5-TON FRONT DRIVE   RD

INTERNATIONAL MOTOR CAR see TOLEDO

INTERNATIONAL WHEEL 1900 — The International Wheel Company of New York City built an experimental three-wheel van that used wheel steering for the single front wheel on which a small motor was attached. The rest of the vehicle was essentially a horse-drawn wagon and the front wheel attachment was a mechanical substitute for the horse. Other details have not been available.

1916 INTER-STATE DE LUXE DELIVERY   RD

INTER-STATE 1916-1918 — The Inter-State Automobile Company was announced in 1909 by Thomas F. Hart, who had sponsored a contest to name his new marque in Muncie, Indiana. By the following year, the company began building four-cylinder passenger cars. It was not until late 1916 that Inter-State built an 850-pound capacity commercial vehicle in the form of a Deluxe Delivery model, which was priced at $850. Unlike some of the earlier Inter-State passenger cars, the Deluxe Delivery of 1916/1917 and Delivery Wagon of 1918 were powered by 19.6 hp four-cylinder Beaver engines and had a wheelbase of 110 inches.

The Inter-State company suffered financial troubles early on and was sold to F.C. Ball, who was a manufacturer of glass jars and had invested in the automotive venture from the beginning. The factory was converted over to military production but six months later the war was finished and so was Inter-State.

IROQUOIS 1905-1906 — It appears this company, by the name of Iroquois Iron Works and located in Buffalo, New York, was not affiliated with the Iroquois Motor Car Company that existed at the same time in Seneca Falls, New York. Both were in the motor vehicle manufacturing business, but the Iroquois Iron Works was where 1/2-ton and 4-ton gasoline-powered trucks were built along with steam-powered and gasoline-powered road rollers. "Built Like a Locomotive" was the company slogan in 1906.

1906 IROQUOIS 15-PASSENGER BUS RD

The 1/2-ton truck was powered by a 25 hp four-cylinder engine and used shaft drive. The 4-ton truck had a 60 hp engine with water pump cooling and was mounted under the driver's seat. A three-speed sliding gear transmission was used as well as standard chain drive. A 15-passenger bus was built in 1905 using a 3-1/2-ton chassis powered by a 25 hp engine. The Iroquois Iron Works did not manufacture automobiles at all, nor did it produce vehicles after 1906, even as so listed in various publications. It appears that the confusion lies with the fact that W. Grant King, who was the manager of the Iroquois Iron Works, had built a steam runabout in 1902. After using it for four years, he sold it to a local farmer and it became known as the King Steamer. In 1909, *Motor Magazine* listed the Iroquois Iron Works in its "Historical Table of the American Motor Car Industry" as a builder of steam automobiles from 1906 to 1908. The only auto built was by King himself years earlier and all other vehicles were for commercial purposes built only during 1905 and 1906.

ISCO 1972-1990 — The Isco Manufacturing Company started out in the communications, finance and insurance business. In 1972, Isco organized the merger of four separate companies for the purpose of manufacturing a variety of commercial vehicles. The list of merging companies consisted of the Cline Truck Manufacturing Company, Hardwick Manufacturing Company, which built Eject-All rock haulers, W.T. Cox Ryd-A-Rail and the Shuttle Wagon Corporation.

Once the companies were merged on paper, they were also merged by location in one factory. Large trucks for mining above and below ground were introduced, as well as rock hauler semi-trailers and large haulers for quarrying, construction as well as various road/rail vehicles.

The first truck models included seven two-axle versions from 13-ton to 50-ton capacity, a 15-ton cab-over model, a 22-ton front-wheel-drive articulated rock hauler, a 75-ton steel and copper mill single-axle slag hauler, a 70-ton coal hauler and 90-ton logging tractor. The semi-trailers were built in three versions. Each was a horizontally unloading type designed to be pulled by any prime mover. Other vehicles also included underground personnel carriers for mining applications, the Shuttle Wagon rail car mover and trailer spotter, locomotive re-railers and a Ryd-A-Rail conversions of 80,000-pound GVW. One 22-ton side dump low-bed semi-trailer hauler was custom made for gypsum mining and later joined other Isco trucks as a production model.

In many cases the Cline badge was used because many of the truck designs originated with the acquired company. Over the years, however, the Cline badge virtually disappeared as the Isco name became more well known. No matter what the name, the trucks were powered by a variety of engines. Some had six-cylinder Cummins engines from 250 hp up to 420 hp. Others were powered by four-cylinder, straight-six, V-6, V-8 and V-12 turbocharged Detroit Diesel engines from 140 hp up to 434 hp. Also, Ford V-8 engines were used in the Shuttle Wagons. Allison six-speed transmissions were used almost exclusively, including one such automatic transmission. As a business entity, Isco prospered but was no longer directly affiliated with truck production including Cline, which got into crawler tractor production by the mid-1990s.

J

J

JACKSON 1907-1923 — The Jackson Motor Car Company began as an outgrowth of a printing business that used steam power. It had been started by Byron J. Carter and his father, Squire B. Carter, in 1896 as the U.S. Tag Company. By 1899, Byron Carter built a gasoline-powered car, and basically the same car was produced as the Michigan by the Michigan Automobile Company in 1901. Subsequently, Carter patented a 6 hp three-cylinder steam engine and persuaded both George A. Mathews, director of the Jackson City Bank and owner of the Fuller Buggy Company, as well as Charles Lewis, president of the Lewis Spring and Axle Company and director of the Union Bank in Jackson, to go into manufacturing with him as the Jackson Automobile Company, which became the Jackson Motor Company.

The first vehicles were built under the name Jaxon in 1903. Carter soon left to build his own Cartercar when his partners, who controlled finances, refused to develop a not unusual friction drive idea Carter had in mind. The Jackson was a conventional car using four-cylinder engines by 1906. The following year, the company introduced light commercial vehicles including vans based on the passenger car chassis.

1908 JACKSON PANEL DELIVERY NAHC

Jackson introduced six-cylinder Northway engines in 1913 and V-8 Ferro engines in 1916, but it is unclear if any of those were used in the commercial versions. The company's slogan was "No Hill Too Steep - No Sand Too Deep." The company also built a car called the Duck, which was steered from the back seat. Later Jackson cars were likened to Rolls-Royce in appearance but not necessarily in quality.

1921 JACKSON 4X4 EF

Mathews bought out Lewis and installed his three sons as president, secretary and treasurer. For 1917 and 1918, the Jackson line was marketed as the Wolverine. The following year, the factory was converted to produce trucks only. At this time the Jackson company unveiled a 3-1/2-ton capacity truck that was four-wheel-drive and was powered by a four-cylinder Continental engine. It also featured a four-speed transmission and self-starter. There is some evidence that the only Jackson 4x4 remaining extant is the only unit ever built by the company.

In regards to the engineering of the Jackson vehicles, which resumed production in 1920, one of the assembly line workers opined in a quote to the press that he "should have raised chickens instead." In 1923, which was the last year of any commercial vehicle production by Jackson, the company merged with the Dixie Flyer of Louisville, Kentucky, and the National firm of Indianapolis under the new name of Associated Motor Industries. It took one more year before that company met its demise and along with it went all three vehicle's marques.

JACTO 1912-1913 — This little-known company by the name of Jacto was listed in the January 1913 issue of *The Commercial Vehicle* as a builder of a 1/2-ton Model C and D, which were similar. Each had the same wheelbase and was powered by electric motors using batteries. Final drive was by chain. No other details are known.

JAQUET 1906 — F.G. Jaquet of Toledo, Ohio, designed and built an unusual commercial vehicle for 1906. It was a huge vacuum cleaning machine mounted on a chassis of 110 inches. A 24 hp two-cylinder engine powered both the vehicle and an air compressor that allowed the vacuum cleaning of houses and offices with 900 feet of flexible hose. A two-speed transmission was used. Since the vehicle was stationary for its vacuum cleaning purposes, a 60-gallon tank of water located behind the driver's seat was provided for cooling the engine. The first truck was built in Wauseon, Ohio. Tires were Firestone 32-1/2x3-1/2 solid rubber front and rear. Timken axles and platform springs were used for the suspension both front and rear.

1906 JAQUET VACUUM CLEANER TRUCK RD

The engine was placed at the front of the "platform" and an 18-inch compressor tank along with a 42-inch high "dirt tank" was positioned behind it. The machine could run for 10 hours on less than 10 gallons of gasoline. The vehicle weighed 4,700 pounds and the cab was eight feet, two inches tall. Whether more than one such vacuum cleaner truck was built is not known.

J & J 1920-1921 — Originally organized in Lorain, Ohio, in 1905, the Lorain company appears listed as having produced a 2-ton truck called the J&J during 1920 or 1921. It is possible that it was confused with the Lorraine Car Company of Richmond, Indiana, which also existed only during 1920 and 1921 building professional vehicles such as hearses and limousines, or possibly the Lorraine Motors Corporation of Grand Rapids, Michigan, which was in business from 1920 to 1922. No other details have been available to date.

JAMIESON 1902 — Mark W. Jamieson started the Jamieson Automobile Works in Warren, Pennsylvania, purely as a hobby. He built one or two small delivery trucks among the eight vehicles total, using a 7 hp two-cylinder engine, high wire wheels with pneumatic tires, tiller steering and double chain drive. The vehicles never went into production and were intended for family use around the farm.

Fifty years later, one of these 1902 vehicles was found in a barn on the Jamieson property. The surviving Jamieson vehicle can truly be considered a crossover between early established family-business "home-built" mechanized transportation and the mass-produced commercial vehicles that have been built by the industry since that time.

JANNEY STEINMETZ 1901 — Although Janney, Steinmetz and Company advertised coal-burning steam wagons that had "no odors, no stoking, no visible exhaust, no ashes, no vibration," it appears that the firm's vehicle production was a wishful thought and not a verifiable reality, as with several others of that post-positivism era. The company did manufacture gasoline storage tanks, boiler shells, malleable iron castings, tire iron and tubing, but there is no direct proof supporting production of vehicles, especially ones as described above. However, because Janney Steinmetz has been listed as a builder of commercial vehicles in the past, available information is included here for reference purposes.

1925 JARRETT 1-1/2-TON MODEL J   **HAYS**

JARRETT 1917-1934, 1937 — James C. Jarrett, Jr. started out in Colorado Springs, Colorado, in 1916 when he formed the Jarrett Motor and Finance Company selling Scripps-Booth autos and a few trucks. Upon demonstrating an All-American truck in Cripple Creek, he and his potential customer discovered that the truck could not climb the 4th Street hill at that elevation, which was and is 9,000 feet. Jarrett promised his customer he would return in one year and bring him a truck that could make the grade.

Jarrett assembled a truck by the following year using a six-cylinder Waukesha engine and a seven-speed Fuller transmission along with a double reduction rear axle and Ross steering. Production was minimal in the first few years and, according to some records, Jarrett truck output did not begin until 1921, which is erroneous. One of the first Jarrett trucks was the 2-1/2-ton Model J. The early trucks sported a distinctive JCJJ script logo.

In the 1920s, Jarrett built 2-1/2-ton and 5-ton model trucks using Shuler and Wisconsin axles. Nearly all the Jarrett trucks used pneumatic tires on wood spoke wheels up until 1925. By 1927, headlights were moved from the cab front to the front fenders and a new arrowhead emblem was adopted. Dual rear wheels were available by 1927. By 1930, side-dump trucks capable of pulling road graders were sold to the Colorado State Highway Department. Jarrett also built four-wheel-drive trucks by 1934.

By the late 1920s, all Jarrett trucks had six-cylinder engines and were used by highway and street departments in Colorado and Texas. Over all the years total production was approximately 200 units. The company was not bankrupt as previously indicated in literature; it simply closed its doors for 1935 and 1936 during James Jarrett's illness. It appears that seven trucks were built in 1937 for $4,900 each. After that, the company closed down its production due to the owner's failing health.

1912 JARVIS-HUNTINGTON 5-TON   **MROZ**

JARVIS-HUNTINGTON 1911-1914 — Out of the Jarvis Machinery and Supply Company in Huntington, West Virginia, evolved the Jarvis-Huntington Automobile Company, which was incorporated with $100,000 in 1911. The first vehicles were passenger cars with a 142-inch wheelbase and these were powered by a 70 hp six-cylinder engine.

In the final analysis Jarvis-Huntington trucks were all powered by four-cylinder engines with overhead-valves and overhead cams. The models ranged from 2-ton up to 5-ton capacity. A Hele Shaw clutch was used and all trucks had double chain drive. Three-speed transmissions were used in the lighter trucks. The largest truck had a 144-inch wheelbase.

The 2-ton was $2,750, 3-1/2-ton $3,500 and the 5-ton model was priced at $4,400. Standard equipment included electric lights, electric horn, "reliable self-starter" (which must have been one of the earliest as standard equipment on a truck) and a "liberal supply of spare parts." Its top speed was mechanical-governor limited to 10 mph. The company also built passenger cars in 1912 only. Truck production ceased by 1914, or possibly earlier. It appears that the Jarvis-Huntington repair garage lasted longer than the manufacturing side of the business.

1963 JEEP POSTAL CARRIER DISPATCHER 100   **KAISER**

JEEP 1963 to date — The Kaiser-Jeep Corporation of Toledo, Ohio, was the new name of Willys-Overland beginning in 1963. Kaiser had bought Willys-Overland in 1953 but kept the name Willys Jeep for 10 years. Willys-Overland had built the jeep since World War II and this versatile vehicle continued to be built as before, although the Wagoneer was actually a new model for 1963.

The Wagoneer was similar to previous Jeep station wagons but wheelbase was now 110 inches, six inches longer than any previously. Both two-wheel-drive and four-wheel-drive versions were available. For the first time, the company offered independent optional front suspension and automatic transmission. A new 140 hp (155 gross hp) hemi-head six-cylinder Tornado engine powered the Wagoneer, the only engine being built in the United States with an overhead-cam.

The basic 4x2 Wagoneer of 1963 was priced at $2,546, which was up by $451 from 1962. The Custom 4x4 version cost $3,526 plus options. There was also a panel delivery version of the Wagoneer. Due to problems with detonation an economy version of the SOHC straight-six with a lower compression ratio was offered in 1964. It was rated at 133 hp.

In 1965, Jeep introduced the Dauntless V-6 engine for its CJ series and the 250 hp Vigilante V-8 for its Gladiator and Wagoneer vehicles. The earlier Borg-Warner transmission was superseded by a GM Turbo-Hydramatic unit. During the year the J-200 and J-300 Gladiator were joined by new J-2000 and J-3000 Gladiator models, which included pickups and panel delivery versions and were sometimes used as tow trucks. The Gladiator trucks were built on 120-inch and 126-inch wheelbase chassis in 4x2 and 4x4 configuration with 1/2-ton and 1-ton capacity.

The Jeep FC-170 forward control light truck was built as a pickup, but did not sell well. Military versions as ambulance and cargo pickup were quite successful. Kaiser offered 76 Jeep models for 1965, which included 46 different Gladiator models, 16 conventional trucks, 8 forward-control models, 3 Dispatchers and 3 Utility Jeeps. In addition there were also the Wagoneers, Utility Wagons and Wagoneer-based sedan delivery. The year 1965 was also the last time the CJ-3B was produced, and the following year was the last for the forward-control.

1966 JEEP PANEL AMBULANCE 4X4 KAISER

By 1966, the SOHC was no longer produced and a less expensive overhead-valve straight-six was offered in its place. The Super Wagoneer was built from 1966 to 1968. It cost $2,163 more than the Custom model and included every option possible. The independent front suspension was also discontinued due to durability problems with off-road use. A Perkins Four 192 diesel engine was optional in the CJ series. Also for 1966, a 270 hp Vigilante V-8 engine was optional, as was the Buick V-6 engine for the CJ series.

1967 JEEP KAISER M-715 HE

In 1967, Kaiser reintroduced the Jeepster, albeit a new and improved version over the 1940s original. It was available as a pickup, convertible, station wagon and roadster. Initially it was powered by the venerable F-head Go-Devil four-cylinder engine or the Buick-

designed V-6. Tooling for the engine had been purchased by Kaiser from Buick by that time. Automatic transmission was optional with the Jeepster, as was a V-8 engine in later years.

Kaiser wanted to use the original tooling for the Jeepster, but unable to locate it, the company had to fabricate it anew. The Jeepster Commando, as it was called, used the CJ-6 101-inch wheelbase chassis and Jeep Universal front sheet metal. Styling closely resembled the original Jeepster but was more subdued. Many buyers paid the extra $194 for the 160 hp Dauntless V-6, which had more than double the power of the four-cylinder engine. A paramedic truck and a dump body were offered from the factory in 1967, and Jeep built ambulances for UNICEF that year. Fire truck conversions were also common.

In 1968, the Vigilante engine was discontinued. In its place, the 350-cubic inch Buick V-8 was offered. Sales were up and the company was making a profit by this time. In 1969, the Gladiator series wheelbase was stretched to 132 inches. Only 20 models were offered by Kaiser that year and few changes were made from the previous year's models. An experimental XJ-001 model with fiberglass body did not go into production and the prototype was destroyed in a highway accident.

In 1970, Kaiser sold its Jeep division to AMC in an unusual merger between the two companies in which Kaiser obtained both cash and AMC stock. The value of the sale was listed as $75 million, but it included 5.5 million AMC shares, $9.5 million in five-year AMC notes and other assets besides $10 million in cash. Edgar Kaiser decided to concentrate on other areas of his empire, which included Kaiser Aluminum, Kaiser Steel, National Steel and Shipbuilding, Kaiser Broadcasting, Kaiser Aerospace and several other companies. Kaiser ended up with 22 percent of AMC stock, which was a controlling interest, although eventually the holdings were sold.

In 1970, AMC created AM General to build the vehicles that had been produced by Kaiser's Defense and Government Products Division. AMC engineers jumped on the opportunity to improve and modernize the Jeep model line. First, the Jeepster Commando and Wagoneer received new trim. The Renegade II was one of the first attempts at trend packaging of the Jeep by the new parent company. At the same time, the Jeepster name was dropped from the Commando title, the convertible was discontinued and the F-head four-cylinder and V-6 engines were no longer produced. The Gladiator received new front sheet metal styling and there were two new six-cylinder engines and a V-8 unit. The trucks were called Thriftside and Townside and were available with automatic transmissions and independent front suspension.

In 1972, the Renegade package was offered on the CJ-5 Jeep, which included styled wheels, roll bar, extra gauges, rear-mounted spare, special trim and a 304-cubic inch V-8 engine. The following year was the last for the Commando of which 9,538 were built for 1973. The previous year the Commando, as it was now called, was mounted on a 104-inch chassis to make room for the three new aforementioned engines. This was also the first time the CJ had a factory-installed V-8 engine. The V-8 was standard with the Renegade package.

AMC introduced the Quadra-Trac full-time four-wheel-drive system in 1973. It was manufactured by Borg-Warner, and it differed essentially from previous four-wheel-drive in that it allowed each of the four driven wheels to turn at its own speed, something that had not been accomplished before in a production four-wheel-drive vehicle. Full lock-up was still available with the turn of a knob located inside the glove compartment. Quadra-Trac was standard on the Wagoneer with automatic transmission and 360-cubic inch 175 hp V-8 and optional with the top-of-the-line 195 hp V-8. The heftiest Jeep by that time was the 3/4-ton J-4800 with a GVW rating of 8,000 pounds.

The first Jeep Cherokee appeared in 1974, designed to compete with the GMC Jimmy and Chevy Blazer. The Wagoneer's base engine was the 360 hp V-8 with four-barrel carburetor or the 401-cubic inch optional V-8, while the Cherokee was powered by the 258-cubic inch six-cylinder as standard and V-8 engine optional. Earlier brake fade problems were overcome in 1974 with the use of power-assisted disc/drum brakes. And the Dana 44 front axle cut the turning radius by three feet while only reducing the wheelbase by an inch. The turning circle had been criticized previously for contributing to poor off-road maneuverability.

The Cherokee and CJ series was the main focal point for improvements in 1975. Both had an electronic ignition system and were mandated to use catalytic converters for use with unleaded fuel only. The CJ's frame was strengthened and a Levi's interior package was available. The Cherokee Chief debuted in January of 1975 at an extra cost of $349 over the S model. Wider axles and larger wheels were featured on this upgraded version. The Pioneer package was available on pickup trucks that year. It consisted of a number of amenities such as dual horns, special interior, chrome bumpers and additional trim. Overall Jeep production rose from 93,316 vehicles in 1974 to 108,612 vehicles for 1975.

In 1976, the CJ-7 replaced the CJ-6, although the CJ-6A continued as an export model until 1981. The wide-axle Honcho pickup was also introduced that year for the American Bicentennial. The CJ-7 wheelbase was 93.4 inches, which was 10 inches longer than the CJ-5. The CJ-7 had an optional automatic transmission that could be coupled to the Quadra-Trac full-time four-wheel-drive. Also, a new removable polycarbonate hardtop was available, as were optional roll-down windows and lockable steel doors. The Renegade package was available in the CJ-5 and CJ-7. The truck line had several packages available for 1976, which included a Snow Boss plow, winches, locking hubs and auxiliary fuel tank for the long-wheelbase J-20.

In 1977, Jeep offered a four-door Cherokee that was standard with the six-cylinder engine and standard part-time four-wheel-drive. Quadra-Trac was optional. Anti-sway bars were introduced in order to make the Jeeps handle better on-road, but this did not help with off-road performance. The CJ series was again upgraded with a fully boxed frame and optional power disc brakes and air conditioning. For an extra $200 the Golden Eagle option was offered, which included a Levi's soft top, larger tires and better instrumentation. Only 2,200 Golden Eagles were produced.

For 1978, the Golden Eagle package was made available with the short wheelbase pickup trucks. The package cost an extra $999 and included off-road driving lights mounted on a roll bar, as well as fancy wheels and flashy trim and interior details. The Wagoneer Limited appeared midyear and sold out almost immediately. Its standard engine was the 360-cubic inch V-8 and it came with the Quadra-Trac, automatic transmission, power steering, disc brakes and full instrumentation. The Limited had such things as air conditioning, AM/FM/CB radio, roof rack, power back window and other accoutrements.

With all of these comforts Jeep was penetrating the upper end of the market, moving upscale from Chevrolet and Ford. AMC Jeep vehicles were offered with a multitude of smooth-ride suspension and quiet-interior packages, but the most obvious outer change was the new vertical bar grille and rectangular headlights for 1979.

AMC recorded a profit of nearly $84 million for 1979, which was quite a contrast to the sudden plummeting with a loss of $155 million for 1980 (calendar year loss was nearly $200 million). A new standard engine was introduced for 1980 called the Hurricane. It was in reality Pontiac's Iron Duke four-cylinder engine with 82 hp. The fuel crises of the 1970s prompted AMC to offer more economical powerplants by this time. Both part- and full-time four-wheel-drive was offered in the J and SJ series using a four-speed Tremec model transmission and New Process 208 transfer case. The Quadra-Trac unit was improved with viscous drive supplanting the previous cone clutch. The Tremec transmission could also be fitted to the Chrysler TorquFlite transmission.

By this time, AMC was selling Renault cars in the United States in order to diversify its product line, but instead AMC was forced to sell 20 million in shares of stock for $122.5 million, which gave Renault 46 percent control of AMC. For 1982, Jeep introduced the CJ-8, or Scrambler as it was also called. The Cherokee and the J series trucks were fitted with a Warner Gear T5 five-speed transmission. The year 1982 was also the 30th anniversary of the Jeepers Jamboree and 2,500 Commemorative Edition Jeeps were built. W. Paul Tipper Jr. was elected chairman of AMC and Renault effectively took control of the company. The AM General division was sold to LTV Corporation for $170 million.

AMC lost $146 million for 1982, although sales were slightly higher than the previous year with 266,000 vehicles produced. For 1983, Jeep sold 4,705 Gladiator/J series pickups, 20,019 Wagoneers, 6,186 Cherokees, 37,673 Universal/CJ-7 jeeps and 5,405 CJ-8/Scramblers.

For 1984, AMC redesigned the Jeep entirely. The Jeep family of vehicles was now called the XJ series and used unibody construction for the first time ever. The Wagoneer was renamed the Grand Wagoneer, but J series trucks continued to be built on the same platform as before. As the Wagoneer and Cherokee, the XJ Jeeps were all-new with a 101.4-inch wheelbase and were powered by a new 150-cubic inch four-cylinder engine or by the General Motors V-6. Similar to the Selec-Trac four-wheel-drive system of the Wagoneer, the Command-Trac was a part-time four-wheel-drive system available "on-the-fly."

Introduced as 1984 models, the entry-level XJ was named the Cherokee and the larger version was dubbed the Wagoneer, names that had already been well-established much earlier with a completely different design. The four-door body style was particularly successful in light of the fact that it would take the competitors until 1990 to introduce their four-door equivalents. A manual four-speed transmission was standard with both the 105 hp four-cylinder engine and with the 115 hp V-6. A manual five-speed transmission or a Chrysler automatic were optional. The new Cherokee's handling was considered superior to its competition by much of the automotive press at that time. The CJ-5 was finally dropped after 603,000 were built beginning in 1954.

For 1984 and 1985, Jeep sales grew rapidly and the company showed a profit with its new sport utility vehicle lineup. A Renault 2.1-liter turbocharged engine was optional. The older design Grand Wagoneer was still selling briskly, and 17,200 of these were sold for 1985. The J-10 and J-20 pickups shared a 131-inch wheelbase chassis with a 115 hp six-cylinder engine powering the former and a 150 hp V-8 powering the latter. The pickups did not sell as well, but sales of other Jeep models still put the company in the black.

The Scrambler pickup was discontinued for 1986 after a five-year production of nearly 28,000 units. The Wagoneer's appearance changed with new grille styling. It was announced that the CJ-7 would be discontinued for 1987. Renault continued to sell about 10,000 Jeeps a year in France, most of them being the diesel-powered Cherokee.

This was also the period during which the CJ was attacked in the press and the courts for its propensity to roll over in certain conditions; conditions that were artificially created by insurance industry lobby analysts for their dramatic effect to scare the public. However, the National Highway Traffic Safety Administration concluded there was no safety defect that would cause the Jeep to roll over.

The Jeep Comanche was introduced for 1986. It was powered by a 117 hp four-cylinder engine and transmission choices were four-speed or five-speed standard or three-speed automatic. In May of 1986, AMC unveiled the successor to the CJ series -- the Wrangler, codenamed the YJ. It was powered by the existing four-cylinder engine or the optional 112 hp straight-six engine. The XJ Dana front and rear axles were carried over, and a five-speed transmission with shift-on-the-fly capability was accomplished by the New Process Gear transfer case. An optional five-speed transmission was built by Aisin in Japan.

By then Jeeps had disclaimer stickers warning the driver of possible injury if the vehicle was mishandled, which in some cases it was, apparently by a new category of buyers who were not familiar with off-road conditions. The Laredo was a dressed up Wrangler that sold for about $2,000 more than the base model.

By the end of 1986, Chrysler was poised to buy out AMC. AMC had lost $91 million in 1986. In March of 1987, Chrysler announced the purchase of AMC for $1.5 billion acquiring Renault's 46 percent and buying out 110,000 private shareholders. With AMC seriously in debt and Chrysler inheriting all liabilities, the actual cost of acquisition was $2 billion. AMC had only one percent of the auto market in the United States at the time of the buyout.

Chrysler quickly discontinued the most unprofitable AMC models including the 4x4 Eagle wagon. However, the name was not entirely lost when the new division was named Jeep-Eagle whose sales force consisted of 1,400 AMC/Jeep/Renault dealers.

The J-10 and J-20 pickup production was terminated in September of 1987, only one month after the deal was finalized. The Comanche pickup would continue with a shorter 113-inch wheelbase so as not to compete with Chrysler's own line of pickups. A new AMC-designed 242-cubic inch fuel-injected straight-six engine, called the Power Tech, replaced the flaccid GM V-6. It was rated at 173 hp up from 115 hp for the GM V-6. The Renault-built 85 hp four-cylinder engine continued to be available outside California, where apparently it could not be made to pass emission regulations. A joint-venture result of Aisin and Warner Gear was the four-speed automatic transmission available in 1987. The Jeep Wrangler made its debut for 1987 and was available with a four-cylinder or six-cylinder engine.

1988 JEEP WRANGLER SAHARA   AMC

For 1988, Chrysler dropped the Renault four-cylinder engine, which did not sell well in the United States for a number of reasons. Cherokee and Wrangler sales were up under the new parent company's management, but Wagoneer sales fell. Chrysler was able to market all Jeep models except the Wagoneer, but sales were up overall. Except for the Comanche, in 1989 Jeep-Eagle vehicles could be ordered with ABS for the first time.

1989 JEEP WRANGLER   CHRYS

In order to compete with the likes of Suzuki, which was selling its mini 4x4 Samurai for about $8,500, a new entry level S model priced at $8,995 was added to the Wrangler line. In 1990, the Cherokee and Wagoneer were joined by competition from Ford and Japanese companies that built a five-door 4x4 sport utility vehicle for that year.

Without many changes in two years, the most notable improvement for 1991 was the upgrade of the 242-cubic inch (4.0 liter) straight-six engine to 190 hp. The four-cylinder engine's hp was raised to 130, up by 9 hp over the previous version. The Wrangler's four- and six-cylinder engines were also upgraded to 180 hp and 123 hp, respectively. Sales fell again by 10 percent due to stiff competition, especially taking into account Ford's new Explorer, which was very successful.

The ZJ program was delayed, and the engineering team that came from AMC developed the concept to include a V-8 engine option. The ZJ was named Grand Cherokee by Lee Iaccoca, chairman of Chrysler, and the new vehicle continued alongside the older

design Grand Wagoneer for 1991. The Grand Cherokee had a new suspension and was powered by a 190 hp Power Tech six-cylinder engine. The top-of-the-line Grand Wagoneer received the 318-cubic inch 220 hp (5.2 liter) V-8 engine. A four-speed automatic fit both engines, and the six-cylinder engine could also be mated to a five-speed transmission. For 1993, the Grand Cherokee was also available with the V-8 engine, and it was the only entry in its market segment with an airbag that year. The Wrangler for 1993 was the only mini 4x4 to offer antilock brakes.

1995 JEEP WRANGLER SAHARA   CHRYS

Few changes were made to the Jeep line in 1994, although trim and interior details were updated as usual. The Grand Cherokee's average price for that year was $36,000, but it was also the fastest accelerating vehicle in a field of half a dozen comparison rivals from Japan and Great Britain. For 1996, Chrysler was working on the Wrangler, and the company planned to use the Grand Cherokee's Quadra Coil suspension.

JEFFERY 1914-1917 — Thomas B. Jeffery was the man who built the Rambler automobile in Kenosha, Wisconsin, at the turn of the century and organized the manufacturing of passenger automobiles there. Thomas Jeffery's son, Charles Jeffery, renamed the company after his father suddenly passed away. In 1914, the company continued to build passenger cars but also got into manufacturing trucks and commercial vehicles.

1914 JEFFERY QUAD   KP

The first Jeffery truck was a 3/4-ton capacity delivery vehicle based on the passenger car chassis. Soon thereafter, the company produced other 3/4-, 1- and 1-1/2-ton capacity trucks. The company's reputation became well known based on the introduction of the Jeffery Quad 4x4 army truck in 1913, which was rated up to 2-ton capacity and used by the Army Quartermaster Corps. It was first built as a 1-ton capacity truck per U.S. Army specifications. For the year 1914, the company built 3,096 Quads. Some records show that production for 1913 and 1914 totaled 5,500.

The Jeffery Quad was powered by a 36 hp four-cylinder Buda engine using a four-speed transmission with a central transfer case and shaft drive to both front and rear axles. The Jeffery Quad also had four-wheel-steering. Turning circle for the Quad was 45 feet and top speed was approximately 20 mph.

In 1915, Jeffery built a 2-ton four-wheel-drive Quad chassis that was "reversible." It had a seat, steering wheel and controls at both ends of the vehicle. Aside from being double-ended, the "reversible" Jeffery had a more compact grouping of components at the front end. The driver's seat was placed "very low" and the radiator dropped between the frame members. The engine was covered with a light steel guard and had a Bijur electric starter. The transmission's reverse gear was replaced by a fourth gear, while the driveshafts were fitted with a separate reverse gear so that the vehicle had four speeds in either direction.

The double-ended Jeffery's steering wheels and brake and clutch pedal were interconnected, but the engine and transmission controls were not, being operated by the driver in front only. "An electric buzzer signal serving to establish communication by the two operators," was what the *Commercial Vehicle Magazine* stated in March 1915. With the addition of the fourth gear the truck was capable of 35 mph in either direction and at least three such chassis were known to have been built. Two of them were fitted with an armored body, while the third was shipped to Europe for evaluation.

A few of the first Jeffery four-wheel-drive trucks (prior to being called Quad) were sent to San Diego, California, where they were "put to use along the southern border hauling supplies over the rough roads and mountainous country." Although most Jeffery Quad trucks were bought by the army, a number of them were sold to the private sector and demand was so great that three other factories were hired to produce these vehicles: Hudson, National and Paige.

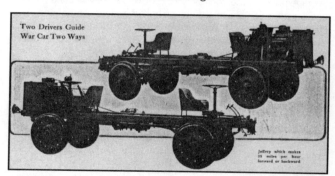

1915 JEFFERY 4X4 REVERSIBLE   RD

1915 JEFFERY QUAD   RD

The Jeffery company's history as well as that of the rest of the world changed dramatically during Thomas Jeffery's voyage to Europe in 1915. The ship on which he set sail was the *Lusitania*. It was torpedoed by a German submarine and it quickly sank on May 7th. Jeffery spent four hours in the icy water before being saved by a passing trawler. He was one of 761 survivors the day 1,198

passengers lost their lives. Upon his return he decided to pursue personal interests and at the age of 40 retired when Charles W. Nash bought the Jeffery company in July of 1916.

1916 JEFFERY W.W. I QUAD   KP

Prior to the sale of the company, two Jeffery Quad trucks set an altitude record in the Andes Mountains hauling ore from 15,000 feet down to the Pacific Ocean on a 75-mile run that included 20-degree road grades and temperatures of zero degrees Fahrenheit. After 1917, the Jeffery Quad became the Nash Quad, which remained essentially the same truck for a number of years. Production for 1918 was 11,940 Quads, the largest production number for any one make up to that time.

1901 JENKINS STEAM COACH   RD

JENKINS 1900-1902 — C. Francis Jenkins organized the Jenkins Automobile Company at the turn of the century in Washington D.C. Jenkins built steam-powered vehicles and electric cars. His first commercial vehicle was a "16-foot-long steam truck."

The Jenkins Observation coach was claimed to be the largest self-propelled bus in America at that time. It was powered by a 30 hp horizontal four-cylinder compound steam engine using a marine-type water-tube boiler with power transmitted through a differential shaft to ring gears on the inboard sides of each rear wheel. The bus was built for sightseeing around Washington D.C. and featured revolving seats for the passengers with steam heat for comfort in winter.

Jenkins became better known for the 24-inch wheelbase 24-inch tread electric car that he built for a Cuban midget named Chiquita who was 26 inches tall. The car was dubbed the "littlest automobile ever built" and Chiquita used it for personal transportation as well as in his carnival act, which was also part of the Pan American Exposition in 1901. There was another Jenkins motor vehicle manufacturer in New York that was unrelated to this one.

JOHNSON 1901-1912 — Warren S. Johnson invented the mercury thermometer electric thermostat circa 1885, which made him wealthy and somewhat well-known. His Johnson Service Company of Milwaukee, Wisconsin, built a 1-ton steam truck in 1901. It was a forward-control design, had an underfloor boiler and used single chain drive. It was used at his company until overloaded with sheet iron one day and Johnson quickly built a heavier version using stronger axles. A 2-ton and a 3-ton steam truck was built as a moving van and for the Pfister-Vogel tannery.

Johnson built eight steam-powered vans for the Milwaukee U.S. Postal Service, one of the first such collaborations in America involving motor vehicles. Pabst Brewing bought Johnson's truck and other commercial vehicle sales prompted the expansion of the company in 1905. Ten steam limousines were produced for "touring in civilized countries by civilized tourists." The vehicles featured boilers on which meals could be cooked during touring.

The company also built ambulances, hearses, a fire truck, a trolley-wire maintenance vehicle, a sightseeing bus, portable stone crushers, police patrol wagons and street-cleaning equipment. Many of the later vehicles were gasoline-powered using Renault engines of 30, 40 and 50 hp built under license at the Johnson factory. There were also COE design trucks from 1-ton up to 4-ton capacity. Smaller trucks and passenger cars used shaft drive, while the larger trucks and buses used double chain drive.

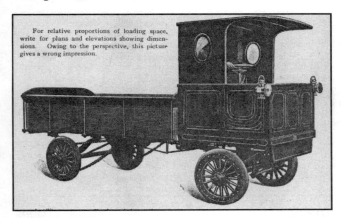

1907 JOHNSON POWER WAGON   **MROZ**

Professor Johnson died in 1912 and vehicle manufacturing was suspended. Afterwards and to date the company has been specializing in electronic temperature control systems.

JOHNSON see EMPIRE

1912 JOLIET LIGHT DELIVERY   **MROZ**

JOLIET 1912 — During the brief existence of the Joliet Auto Truck Company in Joliet, Illinois, light electric trucks were built up to 1/4-ton capacity. Several models were offered but most likely only the lightest was actually built. It had a 70-inch wheelbase, used tiller steering and vehicle weight with batteries was 1,400 pounds. Top speed was 10 mph and a range of 30 miles between charges was claimed. It appears this company had no connection with the earlier Joilet Automobile and Garage Company, which was also located in Joliet, Illinois.

JOLY & LAMBERT 1916 — The Joly and Lambert Electric Auto Company built a 1/2-ton and 1-ton model truck chassis. Prices were $925 and $1,590, respectively. Manufacture period was brief for this ephemeral venture.

1918 JONES 1-TON   **MROZ**

JONES 1918-1920 — John J. Jones started out as an oil field laborer in Oklahoma. He eventually settled down in Wichita, Kansas, and became a successful car dealer, selling many Ford Model T cars, among others. In 1914, he decided to build a car under his own name and his Jones Motor Car Company began building passenger cars that sold so successfully, that investors from the East recapitalized the company with $2.5 million in 1917.

Along with passenger cars, the Jones factory built light trucks by 1918. Specifications on the first trucks included a 1-ton capacity rating and power from a four-cylinder Continental engine. The loading space was nine feet long. Wheels were solid rubber 34x3-1/2 front and 34x4 rear. Chassis weight was 2,750 pounds and chassis price was $1,100. Plans were made to build 2,000 such trucks in the first year of production, but this has not been substantiated and would seem rather inflated. A 2-ton truck was planned, but it does not appear to have been put into production.

By 1919, Jones began building roadster-pickups with a drill bit rack on the rear deck. Called the Oil Field Special, these had a 126-inch wheelbase and were powered by a 29.6 hp six-cylinder engine. They sold for $2,000 in 1919 and 1920. It should be noted that in one corner of Jones' plant, a man named Clyde Cessna built his first airplane. Fire destroyed the factory in 1920 and the following recession prevented the Jones Motor Car Company's revival.

JONZ 1911-1912 — Chester Charles Jones was an automobile dealer in Nebraska. Among details of notoriety regarding his career, he was arrested in the town of Beatrice in 1906 for exceeding the speed limit of 6 mph. Jones patented a two-cycle engine in 1908, which had only five moving parts and was internally air-cooled. Later that year, he organized the Jonz Automobile Company with his brother Ellsworth, who was a local druggist. They ran out of money before even showing their car at the Chicago Automobile Show in 1909, despite an alliance with a local lawnmower company.

In 1910, Berton B. Bales arrived from Kentucky and financed the Jones brothers business enterprise, whose name at that point was changed to the American Automobile Manufacturing Company. It was moved to New Albany, Indiana. An elaborate effort was made to find stock buyers and the company succeeded in finding some 8,000 such investors. The main advertising point of the Jonz vehicles was that its "vapor-cooled engine...has no valves, no cams, no gears, no push-rods, no rollers, no rocker arms, no pumps, no radiator and no water." The cars were named "The Tranquil Jonz."

The company offered a 1/2-ton version of its three-cylinder two-cycle passenger car and a 1-ton and 3-ton capacity truck was available, although the latter was most likely never actually manufactured. A light delivery van was built using shaft drive, pneumatic tires and selective gear transmission. The two-cycle engine that Jones patented apparently was far from perfected and it was abandoned at some point in 1912, when Continental engines were bought. However, at that point, the company went into receivership. In 1913, Fred Kahler bought the factory where he would produce the Pilgrim automobile.

1918 JUMBO 2-TON MODEL 20   **MROZ**

1919 JUMBO 2-1/2-TON   **HAYS**

JUMBO 1918-1924 — Jumbo trucks were built by the Nelson Motor Truck Company, which was located in Saginaw, Michigan. It was unrelated to the various other motor vehicle manufacturers by the name of Nelson. The truck's name referred to a large elephant and an image of the pachyderm was used as the vehicle's emblem.

Jumbo trucks were first built as a 2-1/2-ton capacity model for 1918 and 1919. Late in 1920, the model line was expanded to include 1-1/2-, 2-, 2-1/2-, 3-, 3-1/2- and 4-ton models. Each and every one of them was powered by a four-cylinder Buda engine and used a four-speed Fuller transmission with a Clark bevel gear rear axle, although these components varied in size for the truck's capacity. The company did not manufacture vehicles after 1924.

1912 JUNO FLATBED   **CHAD ELMORE**

JUNO 1912-1914 — When Brodessor trucks were renamed Juno, they were still being built by Brodesser Motor Truck Company in Milwaukee, Wisconsin. When the Juno Motor Truck Company was formed in 1912, Brodesser was bought out and the operations were moved to Juneau, Wisconsin, also in 1912. The incorporators of the Juno Motor Truck Company were Theodore P. Hemmey, Henry Henning, F. Lindeman, Martin Lueck, Peter Peters and L.C. Pautsch.

1913 JUNO   **CHAD ELMORE**

Juno trucks were assembled cab-over design and were powered by four-cylinder Wisconsin T-head engines with cylinders cast in pairs. These were built in either 30 hp or 40 hp versions to power either 2-ton or 3-ton capacity Juno trucks. Multiple disc clutches coupled the engines to three-speed selective gear transmissions, which were mounted amidships. Chain drive was used as well as solid rubber tires which were 36x3 and 36x4. The service brakes were external, while the emergency brake was internal. Suspension was by semi-elliptic front springs and platform type on the rear axle. The 2-ton Juno chassis sold for $2,659, while the 3-ton Juno chassis sold for $3,250. The company's brief venture into truck manufacturing ended suddenly in 1914.

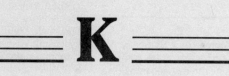

K

K

KADIX 1912-1913 — The Kadix-Newark Motor Truck Company was located in East Grange, New Jersey. Kadix trucks were conventional powered by four-cylinder engines using three-speed transmissions with jackshafts and double chain drive. The entire model line included 3-,4-,5-,6- and 7-ton capacity trucks. Chassis lengths were from 144-inch up to 186-inch and could be specified by the customer. The company only lasted for just over one year.

KAISER 1943, 1946, 1949-1950 — During World War II, the Office of the Chief of Ordnance established the Extra Light Weight truck program, which included testing of light off-road trucks that included the Crosley Pup and small jeep-type vehicles from Chevrolet, Ford, Kaiser and Willys. The program did not go past 1943 but it did inspire a few manufacturers to build vehicles they would most likely not have experimented with otherwise.

Henry J. Kaiser had already established his empire in the American industry when he got the opportunity to build vehicles in the defense of the nation. All of the entered vehicles were prepared for a 10,650-mile test run and only the Willys made it that far. The rest never made it close to the halfway point.

The Kaiser vehicles submitted to the program all had front-mounted Continental engines. Continental was a subsidiary of Kaiser by this time. The heaviest Kaiser to arrive at Aberdeen was a 1,525-pound "jeep" with a 42 hp 142-cubic inch horizontally-opposed four-cylinder engine. It had a 72-inch wheelbase. It made it through about one-third of the test but was generally deemed adequate.

1946 KAISER ARTICULATED BUS   MBS

The second version designated by the factory as the Model 1160 was similar but weighed less and two of three delivered had a wet sump 52 hp Continental four-cylinder engine. These vehicles had a top speed of 60 mph, a 160-mile cruising range with a nine-gallon gasoline tank and could ford 14 inches of water. Tires size was 6.00x14. A few more even smaller versions were built but none were accepted by the military for purchase. However, Kaiser had whet his appetite for building motor vehicles and when he teamed up with Joseph Frazer after the war, he was not entirely a newcomer to the business.

As part of the Kaiser empire, but independent of the previous venture, Kaiser Industries in Permanente, California, was hired to build a 60-foot articulated coach for National Trailways. It was actually fabricated by the Permanente Metals Corporation, which was a subsidiary of Kaiser, for Santa Fe Trail Transportation Company, which was a subsidiary of National Trailways.

The three-axle bus had a body made of a magnesium-aluminum alloy. In the front section a Cummins diesel engine was fitted under the floor while the rear section had an air conditioner mounted in similar fashion. Baggage space under the floor was given as 378 cubic feet. The coach used "Torsilastic" suspension, which consisted of concentric tubes with layers of rubber bonded between the walls.

The Torsilastic suspension design was developed by Twin Coach and was used on Bus & Car's Silver Eagle and on Flxible buses. The single example of Kaiser Industries coach was made distinctive by its split V-type windshield as well as oval and porthole windows, elaborate paint scheme and wide whitewall tires. It was used on a regular schedule over-the-road between Los Angeles and San Francisco until 1951, when it was removed from service.

Henry J. Kaiser and Joseph Frazer were already in the automotive manufacturing business when sales of their Kaiser and companion Frazer automobiles began to slip after two successful years of post-war market demand. Their answer was to get directly involved in the building of taxis for 1949 and 1950.

The Model K491, taxi Body Style 4916, of 1949 and Model K501, taxi Body Style K5016, of 1950 were identical to the four-door Special Series sedans. They were powered by a 100 bhp 226.2-cubic inch L-head six-cylinder engine with Carter carburetor. The front grille had been redesigned from 1948 and featured three full-width chrome moldings. A large wing-shaped molding on the nose of the car just above the grille carried the company logo consisting of the letter 'K' and the outline of a Buffalo. The taxi version also featured a reinforced suspension and heavier upholstery. For 1949, the Kaiser taxi was priced at $2,216. Production numbers for the taxi in 1950 was 2,641, which was about five percent of overall sales that year. The taxi idea was abandoned after 1950 and Kaiser ceased production after the 1955 model line.

KALAMAZOO 1913-1920 — The Kalamazoo Motor Vehicle Company was located in Kalamazoo, Michigan, and for the first three years, manufactured one model of truck that was rated at 1-1/2 tons. It was powered by a four-cylinder Buda engine and used a three-speed transmission with double chain final drive. For one price of $1,590 it was available as either a stake body or express body. For the year 1915, the Kalamazoo truck was sold in Great Britain as the Shakespeare. In 1916, similarly designed 2-1/2-ton and 3-1/2-ton models were built and the company reorganized in 1920 as the Kalamazoo Motors Corporation.

KALAMAZOO 1920-1924 — Essentially a continuation of the previous Kalamazoo company in the same city, the Kalamazoo Motors Corporation built 1-1/2-, 2-1/2- and 3-1/2-ton model trucks. These differed from the previous design in that they used four-speed transmissions and worm-drive, as well as Wisconsin engines in the larger two models. The 1-1/2-ton model with a wheelbase of 144 inches was powered by a Continental engine.

Kalamazoo expanded its model line for 1923 with capacities from 1-ton up to 5-ton. Except for the smallest 1-ton model, all the rest used four-speed transmissions and worm-drive. The company offered a variety of four-cylinder engines built by Continental, Hercules and Wisconsin, but 1924 became the last year of manufacture for Kalamazoo Motors Corporation.

KALAMAZOO CRUISER see PONY CRUISER

KANAWHA 1911-1912 — The Kanawha Auto Truck Company was located in Charleston, West Virginia. The only model built by this company was a 2-ton capacity model with 130-inch wheelbase, which had a four-cylinder engine with a three-speed transmission. Power was supplied to the rear wheels using jackshafts and double chain drive. For 1912, the 2-ton Kanawha truck was priced at $2,850. It appears that the company built firefighting equipment up to 1916.

KANKAKEE 1924-1925 — The Kankakee Automobile Company was started in 1916 in Kankakee, Illinois, when it was capitalized with $500,000. The Chiniquy brothers and R.E. Parker were the organizers. Two six-cylinder touring prototypes were completed in 1916. Then the company was idled for some time before any vehicles were offered for sale and it appears that it was this same Kankakee company that listed a single model of truck for 1924 and 1925. This was the 2-1/2-ton Model H, which was powered by a 27.2 hp four-cylinder Continental K-4 engine with a Fuller clutch and transmission. Rear axle was made by Wisconsin while the front axle was a Shuler. Steering was by Ross and Bimel wheels carried 36x5 front and 36x8 solid rubber tires.

KANSAS CITY 1905-1909 — The Kansas City Motor Car Company was organized in 1905 and was located in Kansas City, Missouri, at the factory where the Caps brothers had tried to build their own car without success. J.C. Caps remained to design the Kansas City Car, which was built in light delivery form at first. Later, the company also built buses and trucks up to 2-ton capacity. The early commercial vehicles were powered by a 35 hp two-cylinder engine. One of the trucks had a track of 69 inches with a wheelbase of 91 inches.

Caps only stayed with the company for a year, when the president of Kansas City announced that the new chief engineer was L.M. De Dieterich, who had worked for Aerocar, Cadillac and Waltham as Dieterich, and whose name was now changed to appear as if he was associated with the successful French company by the name of Dieterich. The press was duly confused.

De Dieterich designed a 60 hp four-cylinder engine and two new passenger car models, as well as a truck, which was called Dieterich. Nevertheless, the Kansas City company was in receivership by December of 1907. Reorganization followed. By 1909, the name changed to the Wonder Motor Car Company, which attempted to market the Kansas City Wonder automobiles. The entire venture folded and the new business enterprise that took over the factory was the Kansas City Vehicle Company, which would briefly produce passenger car highwheelers by the name of Gleason.

KARAVAN 1920-1921 — There is only scant information that the Caravan Motor Corporation built a few 1-1/2-ton Karavan trucks in Portland, Oregon, for just over one year.

1906 KARBACH MOTOR BUS RD

1907 KARBACH 1-1/2-TON RD

KARBACH 1905-1908 — Erroneously spelled Karback in some previous literature, it was P.J. Karbach and Sons, a large carriage building business, which also got into building motor vehicles in Omaha, Nebraska. The carriage builder's first vehicle was a passenger-carrying wagon put together in 1901 using a 10 hp engine purchased from the St. Louis Motor Carriage Company. No other motor vehicles were built by Karbach until 1905, when the company was capitalized with $75,000.

Although the original intent was to build passenger cars, the Karbach Automobile and Vehicle Company started by building a 1-1/2-ton truck, which was not a success and was converted to a 22-passenger sightseeing bus. Subsequent trucks and buses were improved and marketed in Omaha. Both the 1-1/2-ton truck and the bus based on its chassis were powered by a 20 hp two-cylinder engine using a three-speed transmission and double chain drive.

KARIVAN 1955 — Tri-Car Incorporated of Wheatland, Pennsylvania, built a forward-control three-wheel van powered by a 30 hp V-2 Lycoming engine. A Westinghouse-Schneider torque converter was used with drive to the single rear wheel. The Karivan had torsilastic suspension on all three wheels and it was priced at $1,045. Load capacity was 700 pounds. It appears that this vehicle was only made for one year.

1909 KATO 1-1/2-TON 4X4 MHS

KATO 1908-1913 — The Four Traction Auto Company of Mankato, Minnesota, was organized by candymaker Ernest Rosenberger. He designed four-wheel-drive trucks and passenger cars to climb the Minnesota hills. By the end of 1908, 25 such vehicles had been completed with the help of A.G. Wasson and J.W. Schmitt. These were powered by two-cycle Brennan engines. The vehicles were referred to as Four Traction, Mankato or Kato, the latter being used for the company's delivery wagon. This was a 1-1/2-ton model with power transmitted by a driveshaft to a transfer case amidship and then to front and rear axles via two more shafts.

In 1911, a 3-ton model was offered priced at $3,500 using a four-cylinder engine with a Schebler transmission and Remy ignition. A cone clutch was used with a three-speed selective sliding gear transmission. Wheelbase was 120 inches. During 1913, the entire company was sold to the Nevada Manufacturing Company of Nevada, Iowa. At this point, the new company received a government contract for 500 trucks and promptly folded. Total production was approximately 12 cars and 30 trucks by the sudden end in 1913.

KAYSER see UTILITY TRAILER

1914 KEARNS MODEL A PANEL DELIVERY   **OCW**

KEARNS 1909-1928 — The Kearns Motor Buggy Company started out in Beavertown, Pennsylvania, and occupied the former Eureka shop to build highwheelers for both passenger and commercial applications. Becoming the Kearns Motor Car Company in 1909, the first commercial vehicle built was a brewery truck. Engines were two-cylinder and three-cylinder two-cycle Speedwell air-cooled units, although the commercial versions used three-cylinder engines almost exclusively at this point. Friction transmissions were used as well as dual chain drive and wheel steering. By 1912, a 3/4-ton Kearns truck sold for $900. Water-cooling was optional. This was the year the company became the Kearns Motor Truck Company of Beavertown.

In 1913, Kearns introduced a 20 hp four-cylinder engine and a standard truck was built using this powerplant along with a three-speed transmission, cone clutch and Hotchkiss drive. The chassis price was $1,175. The chassis was shared with a few touring cars, while the company also built the Lulu cyclecar in 1914. For 1916, Kearns built a Light Delivery using a 12 hp four-cylinder engine and 90-inch wheelbase, which was priced at $750.

After World War I, Kearns built a 1/2-ton model using a Lycoming engine and a 1-1/2-ton model with a Herschell-Spillman powerplant, which was superseded by a Continental engine. The trucks used dry plate clutches and internal gear drive. They were priced at $850 and $1,800, respectively.

The company moved to Danville, Pennsylvania, in 1920 becoming the Kearns-Dughie Corporation specializing in fire engines chassis. It built equipment for the Foamite-Childs Corporation of Utica, New York. These fire engines were sold as the Childs Thoroughbred and conventional trucks from 1-ton up to 5-ton were also built until 1928, when the factory was closed down permanently.

KELDON 1919 — The Keldon has been listed in previous literature as a 2-ton truck built by the House Cold Tire Setter Company of St. Louis, Missouri. Other information has not been available.

1920 KELLAND ELECTRIC DELIVERY VAN   **DFW/HAC**

KELLAND 1922-1925 — The Kelland Motor Car Company built electric trucks only and only for two-and-a-half years. The Kelland trucks were 1/2-, 3/4- and 1-ton capacity designed as Model A, B and C, respectively. All had the same chassis with 102-inch wheelbase. The company was located in Newark, New Jersey. The vehicles were powered by General Electric DC motors and used solid rubber tires on all models. The Model A was priced at $2,200. Kelland did not survive the year 1925.

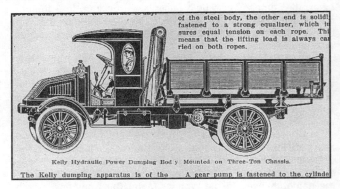

1913 KELLY-SPRINGFIELD DUMP TRUCK   **RD**

1913 KELLY-SPRINGFIELD OPEN EXPRESS   **RD**

1914 KELLY-SPRINGFIELD CHASSIS   **HAYS**

KELLY; KELLY-SPRINGFIELD 1910-1929 — The Kelly Motor Truck Company of Springfield, Ohio, was the successor of the Frayer-Miller automobile built by Oscar Lear Auto Company in Columbus, Ohio. The same air-cooled engines were powered the Kelly vehicles until 1912. That year, Kelly introduced its own four-cylinder water-cooled engine and became the Kelly-Springfield Motor Truck Company. These trucks had the radiator behind the engine and featured Renault-type hoods. They also used three-speed transmissions and double chain drive. Three models including 1-, 2- and 3-ton capacity were built with open express bodies available from the factory on the two heavier chassis. The 3-ton Model 50 for 1914 was available with a 150-inch wheelbase, had solid rubber tires and cost $3,400.

In 1917, one of the largest civilian contracts up to that time was made between Kelly-Springfield and the United States Circus Corporation. The circus placed an order for 100 3-1/2-ton trucks to use for transporting its show around the country instead of using railcars.

By 1918, the model range had been expanded to eight, which included a 1-1/2-ton truck and went to 6-ton capacity. The 1-1/2-ton of 1918 featured worm-drive, while the heavier trucks continued to use double chain drive, with the 6-ton model having this type of drive through 1926. Starting in 1920, most of the Kelly-Springfield trucks adopted internal gear drive. By 1925, Kelly-Springfield listed five models from 1-1/2-ton to 6-ton. These included the 1-1/2-ton Model K70 with 150-inch wheelbase powered by a 27.2 hp Continental K-4 engine. Chassis price was $2,900. The two 2-1/2-ton trucks were Model K75 and K76, both with 154-inch wheelbase and powered by the 28.9 hp Continental L5 engine and priced at $3,600. The primary difference between them was that the K75 used a Clark rear axle and the chassis was slightly lighter than that of the K76.

The 3-1/2-ton Model K41 was powered by Continental's own engine and used a Kelly-Springfield K41 rear axle. The heaviest model used Clark wheels that carried 36x5 front and 36x12 rear solid rubber tires. The K41 chassis was priced at $4,400 and chassis weight was 7,900 pounds. The 6-ton Model K61 featured another Kelly-Springfield proprietary engine rated at 32.4 hp and used a factory-built K-61 transmission.

The lighter models differed in that wheels were by St. Marys carrying optional pneumatic tires and steering gear was by Ross instead of Gemmer. Towards the end, Kelly-Springfield offered Hercules engines. By 1927, production was fading out and it appears that by the following year the company had ceased production, although it was listed until 1929 in some literature.

KELSEY see MOTORETTE

KENAN 1915 — The Kenan Manufacturing Company was located in Long Beach, California. The company built a 3/4-ton light truck chassis priced at $1,600. It appears that the people involved in this company were affiliated also with Van Winkle a decade earlier.

1923 KENWORTH TANKERS   OCW

KENWORTH 1923 to date — Having evolved from the Gersix Manufacturing Company, which had started in Portland and Seattle, two partners by the name of Harry Kent and Edgar K. Worthington formed the Kenworth Motor Truck Company in Seattle, Washington. Two other companies in the area, Vulcan and H.R.L., had failed and this left Kenworth with no competition in the Northwest at that time. Although the Kenworth company was organized in 1923, the first Kenworth trucks were not built until 1924, when 80 vehicles were sold, according to the firm's archives. All the first Kenworth trucks were customized to buyers specifications but the basic models were 1-1/2-, 2-1/2- and 4-ton capacity powered by four-cylinder Buda engines.

For 1925, Kenworth offered a variety of models. The 1-ton Model OS and Model OL were both powered by the 22.5 hp Buda WTU engine and used a Brown-Lipe transmission with Sheldon axles. The Model OS differed from the Model OL in that the former had a 131-inch wheelbase as opposed to a 140-inch wheelbase for the latter, which was priced at $2,250, $100 more than its companion 1-ton model. Both models used 30x5 front and rear solid rubber tires. The

2-ton Model M with 153-inch wheelbase was powered by a 25.6 hp Buda KBU engine and was priced at $3,100. Pneumatic tires were optional with the 3-ton Model K-S, which was powered by a 28.9 hp Buda EBU engine. It was priced at $3,750, had a 160-inch wheelbase and a chassis weight of 6,300 pounds.

Both 4-ton and 5-ton were offered in the mid-1920s by Kenworth. The 4-ton Model L with 170-inch wheelbase was powered by a 32.4 hp Buda YBU engine and used a Cotta transmission. The chassis was priced at $4,500. The 5-ton Model RS with 178-inch wheelbase was powered by a 40.0 hp Buda BTU engine. It was fitted with a Brown-Lipe transmission and base chassis price was $5,500.

By 1926, production was 99 trucks for the year continuing the custom-built focus of the company. In 1927, when production reached three trucks per week, a 78 hp six-cylinder engine was adopted along with a seven-speed transmission. The company expanded its assembly facilities to Vancouver in 1927, effectively doubling its West Coast market.

1929 KENWORTH 25-PASSENGER BUS   KEN

1930 KENWORTH 10-TON ARTICULATED VAN   OCW

1932 KENWORTH MOVING VAN   KEN

1933 KENWORTH TANKER W/TRAILER   KEN

227

By 1930, when the Depression hit the company struggled but continued to introduce new technology such as torsion-bar suspension and vacuum boosters for hydraulic brakes. Along with buses in the 1920s, by 1930 Kenworth introduced six-wheel trucks, available with either a tandem drive axle or trailing third axle. In 1932, the company began building fire engines, expanding on its custom-built marketing scheme as well as its sales.

In 1933, Kenworth was the first American manufacturer to offer diesel engines as standard equipment. This was the 100 hp Cummins HA4 engine. At that time, diesel fuel cost one-third that of gasoline. Kenworth also sold its first sleeper cab that year. The company continued to build a few buses, most of which were intercity coaches, some with one-and-a-half deck bodies and either forward-control or conventional layout and a few of which had under-floor pancake engines.

1937 KENWORTH 346C 10-TON TRACTOR-TRAILER   OCW

The year 1935, when the Motor Carrier Act was passed, was the year Kenworth began using aluminum components in order to reduce weight, which was restricted by the new regulations. This was the year Kenworth began building its own cabs and sheet metal and from this era Kenworth was recognizable by its aesthetic chrome grille. In 1936, the first Kenworth "bubblenose" cab-over-engine model was unveiled. Harry Kent died suddenly of a heart attack in 1937 and Phil Johnson became president. That year Kenworth built 10 models of trucks from the 2-ton Model 88 powered by an 83 hp Hercules JXC engine, which sold for $1,582, up to the 7-ton Model 241C powered by a 125 hp six-cylinder Cummins diesel engine, which sold for $8,333. Buda and Herschell-Spillman gasoline engines were also used on models such as the 4-ton Model 146B and the 7-ton Model 241A. All gasoline powerplants by 1937 were six-cylinder, but the 505, 506 and 507 models were powered by four-cylinder Cummins diesel engines. One of the custom-built vehicles Kenworth produced at this time was the 18-passenger Tri-Coach. Five of these canvas-top vehicles were delivered in 1938 to the Rainier National Park Company. Small buses were also produced and at least 17 six-wheel truck models were available with nine of them diesel-powered.

1938 KENWORTH TRUCK TRACTOR   KP

By 1940, Kenworth truck production had risen to 226 units. Special low-bed models, sleeper cabs and milk delivery trucks continued to be offered. A new upright radiator shell was introduced and this look continued for four decades. In 1941, Cummins built the world's first aluminum diesel engine, instigated by Kenworth and installed in one of its trucks.

In 1941, after Pearl Harbor was bombed by the Japanese, Kenworth received a contract to build 430 4-ton M1A1 heavy-duty "wrecker" trucks. Another 1,500 were ordered before the end of the year. These were six-wheel-drive and were equipped with cranes, winches fore and aft, cutting and welding equipment and special floodlights. In 1943, Kenworth began building components for the Boeing B-17 and B-29 "Fortress" aircraft and was induced by the government to move some of its facilities further inland to the Yakima fairgrounds for national security. The company also developed a pilot model of an 8-ton 6x6 truck. Production of civilian commercial vehicles was down to 87 for 1943.

In 1944, Phil Johnson died and the widows of Johnson, Kent and former company director Frederick Fisher, decided to sell their shares of the company to the employees. However, since financing did not materialize, Kenworth was purchased by PACCAR (Pacific Car and Foundry) and became a wholly owned subsidiary of that company. This was also the year the company developed an extruded aluminum frame. In 1945, Kenworth built 484 military vehicles and 427 commercial vehicles.

Once the war was over, Kenworth's first large customers were Hawaiian sugar cane plantations. A new factory was acquired and for 1946, a total of 705 trucks were manufactured. This was also the year the company moved back to Seattle, occupying the former Fisher body factory where it has remained to date, although with additional facilities opening elsewhere as well. Kenworth continued to build heavy experimental trucks for the military, such as the T30 in 1946. It was powered by a 290 hp water-cooled overhead-valve six-cylinder Continental X6748 gasoline engine. This truck was also built as a tractor with a 30,000-pound GCW rating. Fording depth was 72 inches.

By 1950, 40 percent of total Kenworth sales was accounted by foreign business. The flat-faced K series was begun in 1950. The year 1950 was when Kenworth began experimenting with a Boeing gas turbine engine for scheduled freight service. This was a joint venture between Boeing, Kenworth, the U.S. Navy Bureau of Ships and West Coast Fast Freight. The first 175 hp Boeing 502-8A turbine weighed 230 pounds, which was 2,500 pounds lighter than the comparable diesel engine. A seven-speed hydraulic-shift transmission was mated to the turbine. Tests were undertaken for 12 years; however, due to high fuel consumption and initial costs, as well as other problems with maintenance and application compatibility the turbine adaptation ultimately proved to be unsuccessful.

In 1951, Kenworth's Model 853 was developed for the Arabian Oil Company (ARAMCO) and eventually 1,700 of these were ordered. At the same time, the Model 801 was developed as an 11-cubic yard capacity hauler for large construction projects. In 1952, Kenworth's yearly production surpassed the 1,000 unit mark. Cab-over-engine models continued to be in high demand, especially articulated truck tractors. One special project that Kenworth was involved with at this time was the development of the T-10 Heavy Equipment Transporter for the U.S. Army. The rig was double-ended with a truck tractor at each end moving a 250mm gun with a total weight of 85 tons.

1954 KENWORTH CBE   MROZ

For 1953, Kenworth unveiled a new cab-beside-engine model for maximum visibility. A few were built as 6x4 trucks and almost all were produced as truck tractors. The cab was essentially a single-seat design with a small canvas seat for a passenger behind the driver. Some were built as sleepers, with quarters behind the engine. Another production facility was opened in Burnaby, British Columbia, for 1955. Canadian Kenworth Limited was formed as a wholly owned subsidiary of PACCAR.

For 1956, Kenworth developed the four-axle "Dromedary" with twin steering axles in conjunction with Pacific Intermountain Express. It included a short cargo van between the cab and the fifth wheel coupling for the semi-trailer. This was also the year that PACCAR dissolved the independent charter Kenworth had up until then and the Kenworth Motor Truck Company became a division of Pacific Car and Foundry. At this time, the Model 900 made its debut. It was a conventional cab design and featured a new frame with dropped front section, which shortened and lightened the chassis.

At the same time, oil exploration brought Kenworth trucks to the ice and tundra of the Yukon. A fleet of Model 923 Kenworth trucks powered by Cummins NH 200 diesel engines with compression brakes worked 24 hours a day without switching off the engines in cold that reached minus 60. In 1957, the company built a full-tilt cab-over-engine truck for ease of serviceability. The following year, the Model 953 powered by a Cummins NTC 350 diesel engine was the culmination of truck development for the oil exploration industry.

Expansion arrived once again in 1959, when Mexican regulations induced Kenworth to build production facilities south of the border in Mexicali, Baja California. The W900 conventional (W stood for Worthington) and the K100 (K stood for Kent) cab-over-engine were both introduced in 1961. With Kenworth selling well in the eastern states, where the cab-over-engine K100 met new regulations, a new factory was opened in Kansas City, Missouri, for 1964. The large factory produced 2,037 trucks in the first year of operation, which was a new production output record for Kenworth. Another record was set in 1966, when a total of 3,900 trucks were sold in one year.

Again, due to tariff restrictions, Kenworth opened a plant in Melbourne, Australia, in 1968, where right-hand drive conventional and cab-over-engine trucks were built by 1970. The following year, the PD series was introduced. Its straight cab forward design was utilized in the urban delivery vehicle market sharing the sheet metal with the Peterbilt 200 series.

1977 KENWORTH BRUTE MIXER   **KP**

In 1972, vehicle production reached 10,000 units for the year. Kenworth celebrated its 50th anniversary in 1973. To commemorate the occasion, Kenworth fitted gold-background hood emblems called the Kenworth Bug replacing the polished aluminum ornament. That same year, the company brought out the Brute series, which was a conventional 6x4 marketed in the heavy construction industry. For 1974, Kenworth expanded once again by building a factory in Chillicothe, Ohio. This brought annual production output capability up to 16,000. Top speed records were set by Kenworth in 1975, with 154 mph for a truck tractor and 92.083 mph with a tractor and trailer combination.

The W-series conventional linehaul truck tractors and the K-series cab-over-engine line-haul trucks continued into the 1970s, with gross-vehicle-weight from 50,000 pounds up to 89,000 pounds for the construction models and with gross-train-weight with semi-trailers for these series from 76,800 pounds up to 130,000 pounds.

For the Bicentennial Kenworth celebrated again by issuing a Very Important Trucker (VIT) series that featured standing room, luxurious double beds, refrigerators and hot plates. And each truck bore the name of a different state effectively making them limited edition series for that year. At the same time, Kenworth brought out the Arctic Transporter (ATX), which featured six-axle steering using torsion bar suspension.

Another special project arrived in 1979 for Kenworth. This time a W900 model transported a "High Resolution Spectrometer Magnet," stronger than the Earth's magnetic field by a factor of 36,000, and the 140-foot-long load weighing 107 tons was moved from Illinois to Palo Alto, California. The custom Kenworth was powered by a 450 hp Caterpillar 3408 PCTA diesel engine and a Spicer 24-speed transmission.

By this time, the W-900, like the K-100, still looked like the Kenworth of 1940, with its vertical nearly square grille. It was available in 4x2 and 6x4 version and it was commonly powered by diesel engines from 230 hp up to 525 hp. A common engine for the standard conventional W-900 was the 300 hp turbocharged six-cylinder Cummins NTC-300 engine along with a Fuller RT-910 10F 1R transmission and Rockwell single reduction hypoid tandem rear axle.

Also offered by Kenworth at this time was the C500, intended for the construction industry. It was available in 6x4 and 6x6 versions and was powered by a choice of engines that included Caterpillar, Cummins and Detroit Diesel in straight-six, V-6 and V-8 forms. Maximum gross vehicle weight was rated at 40,000 pounds. The three-axle version of this truck continued to be called the Brute, which differed also in that it had a set-back front axle and steel and fiberglass cab instead of the standard C500 aluminum cab. For the C500, the typical configuration was comprised of a 270 hp turbocharged six-cylinder Cummins NTC270 diesel engine with a Fuller RTO1157DL 8F 1R constant mesh transmission and Eaton single reduction spiral bevel tandem rear axle.

The K-184 was a truck that offered twin steering axles, much as some European trucks were configured. The truck featured a short bumper-to-back-of-cab (BBC) dimension, along with a sleeper cab. Cummins diesel from 350 hp to 450 hp were available along with Detroit Diesel engines from 270 hp to 435 hp. Fuller and Spicer transmission from five-speed to 15-speed were offered with the K-184. Rear axles were Eaton or Rockwell single or double reduction tandem.

1984 KENWORTH K100E   **KEN**

Another notable Kenworth of this period was the L700, which had essentially been introduced in 1961. At first, it was known as the Hustler. These were built in the Quebec plant along with the nearly identical Peterbilt 310 model trucks, except for the badge and trim. Engine offerings were Caterpillar, Cummins and two-cycle Detroit Diesel.

The modified W900B arrived in 1982 and the K100E cab-over-engine was introduced in 1984. The latter was especially designed for aerodynamics, which generally hampered fuel efficiency in previous years. A more refined aerodynamic design arrived in 1985 in the form of the T600A, which was a slope-nosed conventional with set-back front axle. Wind tunnel tests showed that the T600A was a 40 percent improvement in aerodynamics over the company's conventional W900 with a 22 percent savings in fuel consumption.

Kenworth launched the T800 in 1986. The design featured set-back front axle geared for heavy-duty operations and for on/off highway use. For 1988, Kenworth introduced the C500B construction truck, which was a design combination of its preceding C510 model and the T800 cab comforts. The same year, the company also unveiled its new T400A designed especially for the regional-haul market. And in 1989, the T450 construction truck with 112-inch bumper-to-back-of-cab dimension went into production, as well as the second generation T600A.

Fuel economy was the marketing strategy behind the new T600A and a "Tour America" fuel economy run took place in 1990. Three different T600 trucks were used, each equipped with a different size Cummins engine. Using real-life driving conditions including poor weather, road construction, steep grades and traffic jams, the 330 hp L10 engine averaged 8.21 miles per gallon, the 370 hp N14 engine averaged 7.99 mpg and another N14 Cummins rated at 460 hp gave 7.68 mpg. Also for 1990, Kenworth introduced its W900L long-nose conventional model with 130-inch bumper-to-back-of-cab dimension.

For the end of 1991, Kenworth brought out the T884 offering customers dual steering again as in the K-184 model. The design utilized two steering axles, front and rear, which allowed for sharper turns as well as all-wheel-drive for off-road use where the truck's turning circle can be even more critical than on the highway. The T884 found customers in the mining and heavy construction industry. It was at this same time that Kenworth embarked on another special project, when the company was contracted to move the SR71 Blackbird spy plane from the Mojave Desert to the Seattle Museum of Flight.

For 1992, Kenworth initiated a new driver involvement program called Board Members, which included 500 truck drivers nationwide. The company also introduced K300 Class 7 cab-over-engine model. Kenworth's Class 7 production facility was moved from Brazil to Ste. Therese, Quebec, Canada. And in July of the same year, the B-Series trucks were unveiled, which featured the "Quiet Cab" package.

1994 KENWORTH T600 KEN

1995 KENWORTH T300 KEN

It was not until 1993 that Kenworth celebrated its 70th year anniversary. A new production plant was opened in Renton, Washington, where the T600 AeroCab began production. Aerodynamic drag was further decreased by three percent over the T600B. The same year, Kenworth also introduced the Studio Sleeper, one of the roomiest in the industry to date. For 1994, the company introduced its T300 conventional, which utilized the T600 cab and listed a gross vehicle weight of 30,000 pounds. Also for 1994, the AeroCab line was expanded to include a 62-inch model along with the 72-inch version as well as the FlatTop Aerocab, which still allows a person of six-foot, one-inch height to fully stand inside the sleeper.

1993 KENWORTH C500B KEN

1919 KEYSTONE 2-TON MROZ

KEYSTONE 1919-1923 — In the beginning, the Commercial Car Unit Company of Philadelphia, Pennsylvania, built the truck named Keystone. Founded by H.W. Sofield, the company was not affiliated with the earlier Keystone from Pittsburgh, Pennsylvania. The first two trucks were the 1-ton Model 20 and 2-ton Model 40. The latter was powered by a 26 hp four-cylinder engine manufactured by Commercial Car itself. The Commercial Car Unit had specialized in Truxton Ford conversions before going into the truck manufacturing business as Keystone Motor Truck Corporation in Oaks, Pennsylvania, at the end of 1919.

H.W. Sofield left the company in 1921. By this time, the Model 20 was discontinued. Starting with that year, Keystone trucks were fitted with four-cylinder Buda engines. The Model 40 was priced at $2,200 in 1921 and featured an optional power-driven tire pump and whistle. The price was reduced to $2,175 in 1922 and even further to $1,975 in 1923, but the company was in financial straights. Sofield founded Penn Motors Corporation, which purchased Keystone in its entirety in 1923.

KIDDER 1900-1903 — Wellington P. Kidder was the inventor of the Kidder press and the Wellington and Franklin typewriters. He built two steam carriages in 1899 before forming the Kidder Motor Vehicle Company. Funding for this venture came from T. Attwater Barnes who became the company president. The former New Haven Chair Company became the sight of the Kidder business in Connecticut.

Kidder had also built a gasoline-powered vehicle called the Petromobile, but he chose instead to concentrate on steam power. The Kidder was built in two forms: the Model 2 runabout, which sold for $1,000, and the Model B delivery wagon, which sold for $1,600. Twin cylinders of the engine were configured on each side of the boiler with direct drive to the rear axle on the runabout, but the commercial version had a train of gears for a lower ratio. Thirty-five Kidder vehicles were reported being built in 1900 but upon the death of Barnes, the company dissolved. On his own, Kidder went on to experiment with electric and gasoline vehicles until 1907.

KIMBALL 1917-1926 — Kimball trucks were built in Los Angeles, California, by the Kimball Motor Truck Company. Kimball offered 1-1/2-, 2-, 2-1/2-, 4- and 5-ton models. These were powered by four-cylinder Wisconsin engines and used worm-drive rear axles. In 1922, the model line was pared down to 2-, 3-1/2- and 5-ton trucks. In 1924, there were two additional trucks available and these were 1-1/2-ton and 4-ton trucks with a wheelbase up to 168 inches.

For 1924, Kimball offered the 2-ton Model AB with optional wheelbase as before and powered by a 25.6 hp four-cylinder Wisconsin TAU engine using a Brown-Lipe transmission and Timken axles. Chassis price was $3,435 and pneumatic tires were optional at extra cost. The 2-1/2-ton Model AC was similar, except it was powered by a 28.9 hp Wisconsin UAU engine. Chassis price was $3,960.

For the last two years, Kimball also offered two 4-ton and one 5-ton truck. The 4-ton Model AM differed from the Model AE in that the former was powered by a 32.4 hp Wisconsin VAU engine while the latter was powered by a 36.1 hp Wisconsin RAU engine. The Model AE sold for $4,960 while the Model AM was cheaper by $125. The 5-ton Model AF was powered by a 40.0 hp Wisconsin RBU engine and was priced at $5,160. Its chassis weight was 8,800 pounds. Each model used a Brown-Lipe clutch and transmission, Timken front and rear axles, Ross steering and Smith wheels. These were continued until 1926, when the company ceased production.

KING 1912-1918 — The A.R. King Manufacturing Company of Kingston, Ohio, built the Model 3-1/2, which was also the truck's load capacity. The King was a forward-control design with a wheelbase of 120 inches. It was powered by a four-cylinder engine using a three-speed transmission and final drive was by double chain. The chassis price was $3,350 in 1913. The Model 3-1/2 chassis weight was 6,000 pounds. It appears material shortages put King out of business by the time World War I ended.

1913 KING 3-1/2-TON   MROZ

KING STEAMER see IROQUOIS

1924 KING-ZEITLER   RM

KING-ZEITLER 1919-1929 — Starting out as the Zeitler and Lamson in 1914, the marque was revived as the King-Zeitler in 1919. The company offered a full range of trucks from 3/4-ton up to 5-ton, and a bus chassis was manufactured by 1923. The typical 1-ton of 1919 had a 150-inch wheelbase and was powered by a 19.6 hp Continental engine with a four-speed selective sliding gear Brown-Lipe transmission and Timken worm-drive. By 1924, King-Zeitler built trucks from 1-ton up to 5-ton capacity.

The 1-ton was powered by a 22.5 hp Continental J4 engine using a Brown-Lipe transmission and Timken front and rear axles. Bimel wheels carried 34x4 front and 34x5 rear tires, which were available as pneumatic at extra cost. The more heavily constructed 1-1/2-ton was powered by the same engine. Price difference was $2,050 for the former and $2,375 for the latter.

The 2-1/2-ton model was powered by a 27.2 hp Continental K4 engine and chassis price was $2,875, and the 3-1/2-ton was powered by a 32.4 hp Continental L4 engine. It sold for $3,625. All of these models were available with pneumatic tires at extra cost. The 5-ton used a 36.1 hp Continental B5 engine and chassis price was $4,525. This was the heaviest King-Zeitler, also known as the Model 90, and its chassis weight was 8,000 pounds. All models used Bimel wheels and Brown-Lipe clutches. The 5-ton was available only with solid rubber tires measuring 36x7 front and 40x14 rear. By 1929, production had come to a standstill.

KISSEL 1907-1931 — The Kissel started out as the Kissel Kar, but the ethnic-appearing "Kar" was dropped during the war with Germany. The elder Kissel family members behind the firm were indeed immigrants from that country who had settled in Hartford, Wisconsin. Under the parent company L. Kissel and Sons, the

Kissel Car Company came into existence. George and Will Kissel, the two sons, had built an experimental car in 1905 and by 1906, they were in production for the model year 1907.

1912 KISSEL 3/4-TON RACK BODY   KM/HW

The first Kissel commercial vehicles were based on the passenger car models, which were powered by Beaver engines. The bodies were made by the sleigh manufacturer Zimmerman Brothers. A Chicago auto distributor named W.A. McDuffee ordered 100 vehicles and at the same time, the Kissel company hired Herman Palmer, a university-educated engineer passing through town giving cello performances, and J. Friedrich Werner, who had been a coachbuilder for Opel in Russelsheim, Germany. The whole combination was fortuitous and by 1909, reliable Kissel cars were available in a number of sizes along with several truck models.

By 1910, Kissel offered trucks up to 5-ton capacity. They were powered by either Wisconsin or Waukesha engines and the heftier models used chain drive. Models at this time were called Dreadnought, Goliath and Heavy Duty. Kissel patented a differential lock for use in soft or slippery terrain. At about the same time as its "All Year Car" was introduced, Kissel also offered similar amenities on its trucks including removable winter cab and enclosed plate glass windows.

1915 KISSEL 3/4-TON DELIVERY   OCW

In 1915, Kissel received its sixth order from European governments and one set of the company's trucks was sent to the Serbian government. Kissel briefly adopted the Weidley V-12 engine in 1917, but it was not continued as the company was converted over for the war effort.

During World War I, Kissel manufactured Liberty trucks and its well-informed staff contributed to a number of improvements on Class A and Class B military trucks. In 1918, the Kissel factory was switched over to the production of FWD trucks under license from that company, but under government contract. By 1919, the prewar models returned, including standardized units such as the "General Utility" model.

1921 KISSEL MODEL "HEAVY-DUTY" TANKER   MROZ

1922 KISSEL 18-PASSENGER COACH   EEH

1923 KISSEL PIRSCH FIRE TRUCK   HARTFORD

After the war, Kissel continued with its L-head long-stroke six-cylinder engine in both cars and trucks. By 1920, Buda and Waukesha engines were also used in the commercial vehicles, which included fire engine chassis and buses, such as the 18-passenger "Coach Limited" of 1923. These were well known for their drop-frame design with 202-inch wheelbase and featured 20-inch disc wheels. Well-known celebrities such as Fatty Arbuckle, Amelia Earhart and Al Jolson bought Kissel automobiles in the early 1920s.

Kissel production peaked in the mid-1920s. At that time, Kissel offered the 1-ton capacity truck powered by its own 24.1 hp engine with a Warner transmission and Timken axles for $1,585. Pneumatic tires were standard. The 1-1/2-ton model had a 152-inch wheelbase and sold for $1,975. It, too, was powered by Kissel's own Model 40000 engine. The 2-1/2-ton model was powered by Kissel's 50000 engine and chassis price was $2,875. Next up in size was the 4-ton Kissel Heavy Duty powered by the Kissel 14000 engine and selling for $3,675. This model used Sheldon front and rear axles and pneumatic tires were available at extra cost. The year 1925 was when Kissel developed its own straight-eight engine based on the Lycoming block, as well as its Heavy Duty Safety Speed Truck.

Production began to slip dramatically starting in 1926. Kissel entered the field of ambulance and funeral car production, which became a greater overall portion of its business as other sales tumbled. A lengthened Model 75 stock car chassis with Kissel's 61 hp Model 6-55 engine were used for the professional cars. After 1928, Lycoming WS engines were used. The funeral cars were distributed by the National Casket Company and were called National-Kissel. The company also built 285 taxis during 1929. This was accomplished through an agreement with Bradfield Motors of Chicago, Illinois, and the Bradfield taxis, also built as the New Yorker taxis, were briefly assembled with Continental engines by Bradfield even after Kissel's demise in 1930.

1929 KISSEL-BRADFIELD TAXIS   **A&A**

1929 KISSEL-BRADFIELD TAXIS   **A&A**

In 1930, with bank credit shut off and with the company already heavily mortgaged, entrepreneur Archie Andrews agreed to finance the company in order to continue Kissel production alongside his front-wheel-drive Ruxton automobile. One funeral car and one taxi were slated for daily production but Andrews came up with only $100,000 of the $250,000 he promised. Almost one year after the Stock Market Crash, Kissel bankruptcy was declared in September 1930. Production for 1930 was 93 Kissel cars (including 16 1931 models), 77 funeral cars, 2 trucks and 49 taxis. Compared with 1925 production output of 2,122 units, it was the only move

George Kissel could do but to ask for receivership. A few vehicles were assembled for 1931, including the Bradfield taxis, and Kissel would never again manufacture motor vehicles. The company was reorganized and built marine engines until 1942, when it once again went into war production. That year, George Kissel passed away and his widow sold the company two years later.

1914 KLEIBER BEER TRUCK   **KP**

KLEIBER 1914-1937 — One of the first West Coast truck assemblers was Kleiber and Company, which was located in San Francisco, California. Paul Kleiber was not a native of the city, as has been erroneously written, but immigrated from the Alsace Lorraine area of Europe in 1894 at the age of 25. He began experimenting with horseless carriages in the late 1890s. After acquiring the Gramm truck distributorship around the turn of the century, he organized the Kleiber Motor Truck Company in 1913.

1918 KLEIBER 3-1/2-TON   **MROZ**

Starting in 1914, Kleiber built trucks from 1-1/2-ton to 5-ton capacity. Production output was three for the first year and the company occupied 140,000 square feet, which was the largest truck plant west of Chicago at that time. At first, four-cylinder Continental engines were used along with purchased components such as Brown-Lipe transmission, Bosch ignition, Timken worm-drive and Ross steering. Between 1918 and 1923, Kleiber built the 1-ton Model AA, 1-1/2-ton Model A, 2-ton Model BB, 2-1/2-ton Model B, 3-1/2-ton Model C and 5-ton Model D. Prices at that time ranged from $2,600 to $5,600. In 1924, the 2-ton model was discontinued and did not reappear until 1928. The Model D, which had been powered by a four-cylinder Buda engine since 1921, was reduced in price to $5,300. This truck was often assembled as a dump truck.

By the mid-1920s, Kleiber added a line of passenger cars powered by the 60 hp six-cylinder Continental Red Seal engine. At that time, the 1-1/2-ton model with 147-inch wheelbase was powered by a 27.2 hp Continental K-4 engine and the chassis price was $2,600. The 2-1/2-ton model with 163-inch wheelbase was powered by a 32.4 hp Continental L4 engine and chassis price was $3,850. There was also a 3-1/2-ton model selling for $4,850 and a 5-ton model selling for $5,300, the latter powered by a 36.1 hp

Continental B5 engine. Major component manufacturers were the same as on the first model and pneumatic tires were optional on every model by 1925.

A few Buda six-cylinder engines were used by 1926. At that time, Kleiber offered two Speed Truck models. They were 1-ton and 1-1/2-ton capacity, powered by a 19.8 hp six-cylinder Continental engine and a 27.34 hp six-cylinder Continental engine, respectively. Component suppliers were the same as on previous models. In 1928, Kleiber introduced four-wheel hydraulic brakes made by Lockheed. That year Kleiber offered 10 different trucks with capacities from 3/4-ton to 5-ton and wheelbases from 136-inch to 185-inch. The uprated 2-ton "Speed Truck" for that year was powered by a six-cylinder engine, but the 3-ton "Special" bus chassis had a six-cylinder Buda "bus" engine.

1930 KLEIBER 2-TON   NAHC

By 1929, the passenger car line was eliminated (although two straight-eight powered prototypes were built) and the truck model line ranged from a 1/2-ton pickup up to a 5-ton model. In 1930, Kleiber built its first six-wheel truck, and only six-cylinder engines were used throughout the model line. The six-wheel trucks featured Timken bogie axles and large air springs and the six-wheel models found buyers, with Cummins diesel engines being custom-installed as early as 1932. Total yearly production at that time was approximately 200 units. By 1934, diesel engines were introduced and in the mid-1930s Continental-powered Kleiber trucks were up to 9-ton capacity. Continental and Hercules engines continued to be employed, but the KD-4 and KD-6 were powered by Cummins four-cylinder and six-cylinder diesel engines, respectively.

After acquiring the lucrative Studebaker franchise, Kleiber production was reduced even further, although by 1937, the last year of manufacturing, Kleiber still offered the 2-1/2-ton Model 80, 3-1/2-ton Model 100, 4-1/2-ton Model 120, 5-1/2-ton Model 140, 6-ton Model 210, 4-ton Model KDB-6 diesel and 6-ton Model KD-6 diesel, along with three six-wheel trucks from 5-ton to 9-ton capacity. Continental, Cummins and Hercules engines were available. Few of these trucks were built and Kleiber essentially produced some vehicles on custom order only. One such example was a diesel-powered tandem truck tractor with a Cummins KD-4 engine and a 100-gallon tank providing a 1,000-mile range. Paul Kleiber passed away in 1938.

KLINE/KLINE-KAR 1909-1914 — James Allen Kline organized the B.C.K. Motor Car Company in 1909 along with investors Samuel E. Baily and Joseph C. Carrell, whose last name initials also formed the company name. Kline was a talented inventor and self taught engineer. Both Kline and Baily had been involved with the York and Pullman Motor Car Companies, also in York, Pennsylvania, which was a hotbed of motor vehicle development in the first two decades of the century.

Kline experimented with a steam auto in 1899 and brought the first motor vehicle to Harrisburg, where he had set up a bicycle manufacturing business. He was an Oldsmobile dealer from 1903 to 1905. A prototype of the first Kline truck had been built by the York Carriage Works where Kline had teamed up with Baily in 1905 to design the York car, which later became the Pullman.

Kline vehicles were on the market by October 1909. Aside from six-cylinder passenger cars, the model line included a light truck. The first large order for commercial vehicles (delivery trucks) was

placed by the James B. Claffing Company and the James M. McCreary Company, both of New York. Passenger car and commercial vehicle production was about even by 1910 and the company's slogan was "Sell a Winner and Win a Seller." Kline cars were successful in races and endurance tests at a time when such events had major marketing and sales impact, as national auto production reached 200,000 units in 1911.

1912 KLINE-KAR MODEL 2-16   RD

In 1912, the B.C.K. firm was sold to a consortium in Richmond, Virginia, and became the Kline Motor Car Corporation. The Kline Kar continued to be built, along with a few light trucks powered by a 12 hp two-cylinder engine and chain drive. The passenger cars were popular partly as a result of Kline's success in dirt track racing. Motors and transmissions continued to be manufactured by Kirkham Motor and Parts Company of Bath, New York.

1913 KLINE-KAR   OCW

Once the move to Richmond took place, a few delivery trucks were built on the standard Kline chassis, which was available from 115-inch wheelbase to 132-inch wheelbase. Under new management and reorganized by this time, Kline was using 30 hp and 40 hp four-cylinder engines and 50 hp and 60 hp six-cylinder engines. It is unclear which, if any, of these, were used in the commercial vehicle versions, which were discontinued in 1914. Passenger car production continued until 1923. The postwar recession took its toll on the company, and Kline was quoted as saying "I would rather see my children dead than prostituted to cheapness and inferior workmanship."

K & M 1905 — Enos H. Kreider organized the Kreider Machine Company in Lancaster, Pennsylvania. His idea of making a high-wheeler vehicle easily convertible from passenger to commercial use went considerably further than other efforts. Not only did his K & M vehicle serve both functions, it was also a "stationary powerplant for driving such farm essentials as wood saw, water pump, corn grinder, churn, root cutter or washing machine."

The 102-inch wheelbase vehicle was powered by an 18 hp two-cylinder engine located amidship. Large diameter solid rubber tires were fitted, as was a back bench seat, a canopy and side curtains, all removable for light delivery work, although the canopy could be left in place to protect a cargo of produce. The power takeoff was from a shaft under the step for the rear seat and by pulley and belt, the various tools could be run off the engine while the vehicle sat in neutral gear.

Kreider built a few of these vehicles before starting the Lancaster Automobile Company, which was a garage and dealership for various well-known automobiles. By 1913, Kreider closed down the car business and the Kreider Machine Company to become an instructor at the Stevens Industrial School.

KNICKERBOCKER 1911-1916 — It appears that the Knickerbocker Motor Truck Company could have been related to the earlier Knickerbocker vehicles built by the Ward Leonard Electric Company. Both companies existed in New York, although the Ward Leonard Electric Company ceased passenger car production in 1903. However, Ward Leonard stayed in New York City developing an electric lighting system for motor vehicles among a hundred other patents in commercial use at that time. The Knickerbocker Motor Truck Company listed its address in Bronxville and its move to Mount Vernon, New York, along with the cessation of vehicle manufacturing also coincided with the death of Ward Leonard in 1915.

The Knickerbocker trucks were electric vehicles at first in 3-1/2-, 4- and 5-ton versions including a coal dump truck. By 1915, a 2-ton model was added to the line and four-cylinder gasoline engines were adopted. These were forward-control and used double chain drive. For the last year of manufacture, only the 2-ton and 3-1/2-ton were available. By then, each used worm-drive and had its engine under a front hood. It appears that the Knickerbocker company was reorganized and has continued to manufacture various electronic components.

1902 KNOX LIGHT DUTY JAW

KNOX; KNOX MARTIN 1901-1924 — Harry A. Knox got some encouragement from his next door neighbor, J. Frank Duryea. Knox was a graduate of the Springfield Technical Institute and worked for the Elektron Company, which built elevators in Springfield, Massachusetts.

The Knox Automobile Company was organized by its namesake with former Elektron boss E.H. Cutler in 1900 and the company began by building 15 three-wheel runabouts that year and 100 the following year. Another 250 of the "Old Porcupine" air-cooled one-cylinder 4 hp runabouts were built in 1902. Starting in 1901, a delivery version of this vehicle was produced. All the three-wheel Knox vehicles had pins on the cylinder barrel instead of fins for cooling, hence the nickname. A 3-ton model was built in 1905. "The Car That Never Drinks," was the early company slogan until 1908, when water-cooled engines were adopted. The three-wheel vehicle's two forward speeds were provided by the epicyclic transmission, which had no reverse. Steering was by tiller.

The first four-wheel commercial vehicle was produced in 1902. Its one-cylinder "porcupine" engine faced forward (mounted lengthwise) and the transmission had two forward speeds with one reverse. Up until then, all commercial vehicles were passenger vehicle conversions. These had tiller steering and wood spoke wheels with clincher rims that held 30x3-1/2 front and rear pneumatic tires. One such version sold for $1,600 in 1903. In 1904, the first purpose-built commercial chassis was offered by Knox. It had a 96-inch wheelbase and was rated at 1-1/4 tons or it could carry 14 passengers, according to sales literature. Many different bodies were fitted on this Knox chassis. What the company called the Knox Davis Delivery of 1904 had a 10 hp one-cylinder engine and a 72-inch wheelbase. It sold for $1,500. The Adams Delivery used a two-cylinder 18 hp engine and sold for $2,500.

1904 KNOX CANOPIED EXPRESS DELIVERY JAW

1905 KNOX JAPANESE HOTEL BUS RD

The year 1904 was also when Knox himself resigned from the company to go on to build the Atlas and Atlas-Knight automobiles. Although the parting was a sudden and unexpected one, the Knox company continued on successfully and in 1906, a Knox car completed the Glidden Tour with a perfect score. This was also the year that Knox unveiled a 1-1/2-ton model truck similar to its previous commercial vehicle and the company also built its first fire engine, which was delivered to the Springfield Fire Department in

235

September 1906. It was powered by a four-cylinder engine and was designated as the Knox Model G. Its successful design and application provided much business in the following years.

By 1907, the company was controlled by its creditors and went into receivership to finance a much needed expansion. In 1908, water-cooled engines began to supersede the air-cooled engines and the last air-cooled model was a light delivery wagon offered towards the end of that year. In 1909, Charles Hay Martin, a former employee, returned to Knox and patented a system for attaching two-wheel trailers to a tractor, known as the Martin Rocking Fifth Wheel. The "fifth-wheel" turntable was carried by semi-elliptic springs attached directly to the tractor's rear axle. The weight of the two-wheel trailer was supported by the tractor's rear wheels, while the lesser weight of the tractor itself was supported by lighter springs.

1905 KNOX STAKE TRUCK   **RD**

1906 KNOX 15-PASSENGER SIGHTSEEING COACH   **RD**

1910 KNOX MODEL 64 AMBULANCE   **KP**

The first such Knox tractors were three-wheel vehicles and were powered by a 40 hp four-cylinder overhead-valve engine. They were primarily used for pulling horsedrawn fire apparatus and attracted many buyers who did not want to spend capital on a new complete fire engine. The road tractors were also employed for general hauling work, such as in the brewery business.

By 1911, Knox was building 2-, 3-, 4- and 5-ton capacity trucks using forward-control design. The Knox fire engine was a conventional design truck powered by the same 40 hp engine that the 5-ton model had. Late in 1912, the Knox company began operating under a trusteeship after the death of company treasurer A.N. Mayo.

The Martin Tractor Company was formed in 1913 by Charles Martin just 200 yards away from the Knox plant. There were two versions of the three-wheel tractor, one a 5-ton capacity model and the other a 10-ton model. Both had the same engine and the primary difference was the wheelbase. For general hauling top speed was 10 miles per hour, but the sprocket ratio could be changed for fire apparatus so that the vehicle could attain 33 mph. The steering allowed for a 90 degree lock so that the entire rig could turn in its own length. Martin's tractors were called Knox-Martin and were some of the first truck tractors purposely-built for semi-trailer hauling.

1912 KNOX 6-TON CHASSIS   **MROZ**

1914 KNOX-MARTIN 3-WHEEL TRACTOR   **JAW**

In 1914, the Knox company was bought by Edward O. Sutton for $631,090 and was reorganized as the Knox Motors Company. By 1915, the three-wheel tractors were replaced by four-wheel units that had better stability and maneuverability in soft or uneven terrain. The same four-cylinder engine design was used, with the exception that the cylinders were cast in pairs. Martin formed the Martin Rocking Fifth Wheel Company in Chicopee Falls, Massachusetts, during the year 1916. The four-wheel tractors were used during World War I. In France, these were used as one of the world's first tank transporters.

In 1919, Knox merged with Militor Corporation in Springfield and plans were made to build the Militor motorcycle as well as a passenger car. The latter was never marketed. As the need for retrofitting horsedrawn trailers diminished so, too, did sales for Knox-Martin. Knox offered the innovation of fan-vanes for cooling its brake drums as early as 1916. The postwar recession was yet another factor in the final demise of the company, which took place in 1924.

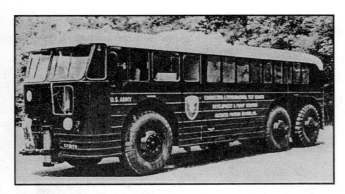

1955 KNUCKEY M9   **RD**

KNUCKEY 1943-1956 — The Knuckey Truck Company of San Francisco was formed during World War II, when ample production numbers of a custom-built hefty hauler could not be met by other manufacturers along the Pacific Coast at that time. The Knuckey was built in two-axle and three-axle versions with a capacity of up to 125,000 pounds. Both versions were powered by Cummins diesel engines using Fuller transmissions and Timken axles, although butane- and gasoline-powered engines were also available.

The company patented a center pivot double chain drive system on its 6x4 model and these were used on the West Coast for tank transporting. Worm-drive or double reduction drive were also optional and these were used in dam construction and mining. The Knuckey M26 tank retriever tractor was well known during World War II. It used the Knuckey chain-drive rear bogie. Its design stemmed from the utilization of one of Knuckey's large quarry truck chassis and mounting the required armored cab, a pair of 60,000-pound capacity winches in the back, one 35,000-pound capacity winch in front and using a 1,090-cubic inch Hall-Scott engine with a 12-speed transmission. Pacific Car and Foundry Company produced these vehicles due to Knuckey's small manufacturing facilities.

The company ceased truck production in 1955 but in 1956, Knuckey built an Aberdeen Proving Ground M9 tandem-axle dynamometer bus, which could develop 20,000 pounds of absorption capacity using an electric generator and retarder. It was originally fitted with a 500 hp Ford V-8 tank engine and while still in use during the 1970s, refitted with a 430 hp Cummins Turbo Diesel VTS-430-CR. Original cost was $185,000.

1910 KOEHLER VAN   **RD**

KOEHLER 1910-1923 — The H.J. Koehler Sporting Goods Company started out in New York City selling available automobiles in 1898. In 1910, the company ventured into motor vehicle manufacturing and began producing both passenger cars and trucks. The first chassis in 1910 was a 112-inch unit used both for the Koehler touring car and a light truck. The first truck had 1,600-pound capacity and was powered by a two-cylinder four-cycle water-cooled engine. The planetary transmission was mounted at

the jackshaft, instead of at the engine. The forward-control type truck had only a radiator in front of the vertical steering column. With canvas sides it was priced at $800. L.E. Schlotterback manufactured trucks for Koehler until 1916, when the two companies merged.

1914 KOEHLER 1-TON   **OCW**

1916 KOEHLER 1-TON FLATBED   **RM**

By 1913, the company began to concentrate solely on truck manufacturing, and used a 24 hp four-cylinder engine for 1-ton truck, which was priced at $750 with flareboard body. A 12-passenger stage was priced at $1,000. Other bodies available were: Express, Canvas-side, Stake-side, Panel, Plumbers and Contractors Job, Bakers and Confectioners Body and Furniture Body.

The Koehler was known as the Model K by 1916 and later had a Herschell-Spillman engine, Torbensen internal gear drive, 34x4 solid rubber tires and cost $895. In 1918, a 1-1/4-ton model was also offered. By that time, Hercules and Herschell-Spillman engines powered a range of truck from 1-1/2-ton to 5-ton capacity. The Koehler company production facilities were located in Bloomfield and Newark, New Jersey. Motor vehicle manufacturing faded out after World War I but the company was listed as a viable business until 1923.

KOEHRING 1939-1941 — Koehring Excavators, Incorporated were located in Milwaukee, Wisconsin. Before World War II, the company built a short-wheelbase truck that was designed to carry a 7-1/2-ton load of iron ore for open pit mine application. It was powered by a four-cylinder diesel engine set over small driving wheels. The driver sat backward facing the dump box. There was no lift mechanism -- the driver simply slammed on the brakes to dump the load. Koehring's production of these trucks was small, but the company continued to build mining equipment for several decades after World War II and apparently faded out during the 1980s.

KOENIG & LUHRS 1916 — The Koenig & Luhrs Wagon Company was started in 1901 in Quincy, Illinois. For the first 15 years the company built horsedrawn wagons. In 1916, it was announced in the press that Koenig & Luhrs was building a light motor truck chassis. In *The Automobile*, a press release stated "Before undertaking its new line the company installed the necessary machinery and employed a number of experienced mechanics to look after the new department." No further activity in the truck manufacturing business appears to have followed.

KOMATSU DRESSER 1988 to date — Komatsu Dresser went into partnership with the Dresser Construction and Mining Equipment Company in September of 1988. Dresser had acquired the Haulpak mining truck division from Wabco three years earlier, which was a continuation of LeTourneau Westinghouse truck manufacturing. During that period, the trucks were called Dresser Wabco Haulpak

By 1995, Komatsu Dresser had acquired a 100 percent interest in KDC (Komatsu Dresser Corporation). Komatsu Ltd. has continued to build large mining trucks using both the Haulpak and Dresser names. The model line has consisted of the 210M, 330M, 445E, 510E, 630E, 730E, 830E and 930E. Only the first two lighter (60-ton and 100-ton capacity) trucks have used mechanical drive consisting of a 675 hp Cummins KTTA-19C six-cylinder diesel engine with an Allison CLT-6063 transmission and a 1050 hp Cummins KTA38-C 12-cylinder diesel with a Torqueflow transmission.

Both the 445E and 510E trucks have used the Detroit Diesel 12V-149TIB 12-cylinder engine rated up to 1350 hp for the latter vehicle. GE 776 HS and GE 791 electric motors are used, respectively, to drive the rear wheels of the two models. The next two sizes of truck have been powered by a 1600 hp Cummins K 1800 E 16-cylinder diesel and a 2000 hp Cummins K 2000 E diesel 16-cylinder engine. These trucks have used the GE 776 and GE 788 electric motors.

1996 KOMATSU 930E 310-TON HAULPAK　　　**KOMATSU**

The 830E truck with 240-ton load capacity has used a 2,500 hp 20-cylinder Detroit Diesel 20V149TIB engine and GE 787 electric motor drive. The largest truck built by Komatsu, called the Komatsu Haulpak 930E, has been powered by a 2686 hp MTU 16V396 TB44L 16-cylinder diesel engine using AC Induction Traction Motors giving the 310-ton capacity goliath a 40 mph top speed. Tire size was listed as 48/95 R 57.

KOPP 1911-1916 — The Kopp Motor Truck Company was a commercial vehicle business enterprise located in Buffalo, New York, for less than five years. During that time the company built trucks of 1-, 1-1/2-, 2-, 3- and 5-ton capacity. Specifications are known only for the largest model, which was powered by a 605-cubic inch displacement four-cylinder engine. Its wheelbase was 129 inches, chassis weight was 6,900 pounds and it was priced at $4,500.

KOSMATH 1914-1917 — The Kosmath Company of Detroit, Michigan, built 1/2-ton trucks starting in 1914. This was a continuation of essentially the same truck built by Miller Car Company. The chassis price was $850 but in an apparent attempt to be more competitive, Kosmath utilized a smaller gasoline engine and shorter chassis by 1916 in order to bring the truck's price down to $675.

This did not meet with success and the Pennsy Motors Company of Pittsburgh, Pennsylvania, took over Kosmath late in 1916. The remaining trucks were assembled by Pennsy as Kosmath vehicles in January of 1917 before being discontinued as Pennsy went into passenger car production for one additional year.

1914 KOSMATH PANEL　　　**KP**

1915 KREBS 3/4-TON EXPRESS　　　**JAW**

KREBS 1912-1917 — J.C.L. Krebs organized the Krebs Commercial Car Company in Clyde, Ohio, early in 1912. The first Krebs trucks had Renault-type sloping hoods with the radiator behind the engine. These were powered by two-cylinder two-cycle engines. The Krebs trucks of Clyde, Ohio, ranged from 3/4-ton to 3-ton capacity. The Krebs factory was located in the Elmore Manufacturing Company plant after Elmore was acquired by General Motors.

1923 KREBS 2-1/2-TON TANKER　　　**MROZ**

KREBS 1922-1925 — Just as it is unclear that it was the same Krebs of Ottowa, Ohio, who built an automobile in 1901, it is also unclear to what extent, if any, the Krebs Motor Truck Company of Bellevue, Ohio, was an affiliation of the Krebs Commercial Car Company of Clyde, Ohio. The Krebs in Bellevue built conventional trucks ranging from 3/4-ton to 6-ton capacity.

All trucks of the later Krebs company were powered by four-cylinder Continental engines. In 1923, the 2-1/2-ton Model 75 had a 163-inch wheelbase, four-speed transmission, Timken worm-drive, steel wheels with solid rubber tires and cost $2,850. Two years later, the company listed the 2-1/2 ton as the Model K45 with 140-inch wheelbase and powered by a 27.2 hp Continental K-4 engine and Brown-Lipe transmission. Pneumatic tires were at extra cost. There was also a 3-1/2-ton Model L110 with 170-inch wheelbase that year. It was powered by a 32.4 hp Continental L-4 engine and used solid rubber tires. Some Krebs trucks were used as oil and gas tankers. The Krebs name was changed to Buck in 1925. That marque survived essentially in the same form until 1927.

1914 K.R.I.T. 1/2-TON PANEL DELIVERY   **OCW**

K-R-I-T 1911-1915 — The Krit Motor Car Company was organized in 1909 by Kenneth Crittenden. S. Briggs and W.S. Piggins were his partners, and the Blomstrom plant was secured for manufacturing. The first models were built for 1910 and these were passenger cars powered by a 22.5 hp four-cylinder engine on a 96-inch wheelbase chassis. In 1911, the company was purchased by a syndicate under the leadership of Walter S. Russel. Crittenden remained as vice-president and head of engineering. It was not until 1912 that the Model K with 106-inch wheelbase was assembled as the Model KD closed delivery van. It was also powered by the same engine as previous K-R-I-T cars. By 1914, when wheelbase was lengthened to 108 inches, the Model L Delivery Car sold for $1,000. Bankruptcy arrived early in 1915.

KUNKEL 1915-1916 — The Kunkel-Lebman Company, organized in 1909 in Brooklyn, New York, could have been the progenitor of the Kunkel Carriage Works, which was listed in Galion, Ohio. J. Kunkel, C.F. Lebman and K.K. Kunkel were the incorporators of the former company but it is not certain if they were also the organizers of the latter business enterprise. The Kunkel company specialized in hearse coachwork on numerous chassis, including a few of its own, hence it has been listed as a commercial vehicle manufacturer between 1915 and 1916. Funeral cars on Cadillac and Ford chassis were listed as late as 1925.

L

L

LAFRANCE-REPUBLIC 1929-1942 — LaFrance-Republic became a business entity on its own when two separate commercial vehicle manufacturers merged in 1929. Those two companies were American LaFrance and Republic Motor Truck Company, the latter being the largest American truck manufacturer just one decade earlier. By the late 1920s, both companies were in financial straits and the merger postponed Republic's inevitable demise. Although the merger took place in 1929 and trucks by the name of LaFrance-Republic were sold that year, the two truck manufacturers were listed separately until 1930.

American LaFrance was a well-established fire apparatus manufacturer since 1910, when the LaFrance-Republic subsidiary was established in Alma, Michigan, which was the former Republic plant. Republic trucks of 1929 comprised a new range from 1-ton to 6-1/2-ton capacity. Republic chassis were being utilized for the premier fire engines and in 1929, 815 LaFrance-Republic trucks were sold. The onset of the Great Depression quickly took its toll when sales plummeted to 598 units in 1930 and 461 in 1931. Efforts to penetrate Republic's Canadian market failed as well.

1930 LA FRANCE-REPUBLIC MODEL A-1   **MROZ**

In 1931, LaFrance-Republic introduced its large "Mogul" Q6 six-wheel truck powered by the American LaFrance 240 hp V-12 engine. The bogie was built by Timken and oversize tires were used in place of rear springs. It was designed for speeds up to 60 mph with a gross vehicle weight of 20 tons. The large truck did not generate any sales for reasons most closely associated with the economic times of the period. There were 14 LaFrance-Republic models listed for 1931.

The following year, LaFrance-Republic was bought by the Sterling Motor Truck Company. The Alma factory was shut down, although parts and service continued at that location. Sterling attached the LaFrance-Republic emblem to some of its lighter trucks. In 1933, eight models were listed; in 1935, seven models; in 1937, seven models; in 1939, 10 models. By 1940, chassis prices ranged from $3,035 to $5,715. The badge-engineered marque was continued until 1942, when the United States entered World War II.

LAMBERT 1891, 1906-1918 — The Buckeye Manufacturing Company of Anderson, Indiana, was not affiliated with its contemporary Ohio Buckeye company. The Indiana Buckeye venture was organized by John William Lambert, whose first vehicle was not truly a commercial one as Morrison's was in 1891, but both are the earliest references in this compendium. It appears John Lambert's gasoline buggy of 1891 predates the Duryea effort of the early 1890s, although Duryea is "credited" as the first to build a gasoline-powered motor vehicle in the United States. The date of 1891 is referenced here as a historical footnote; the real date of Lambert's first vehicle has not been substantiated, although the vehicle's successful testing and $550 price tag actually dates back to this time period.

John Lambert built several gasoline-powered vehicles during the 1890s, some of them under the auspices of his Buckeye company, which manufactured stationary engines, and also under the name "Union," whose fabrication began in Union City, Indiana, eventually moving back to the Anderson Buckeye plant in 1905. By 1906, Lambert was in the business of manufacturing vehicles on a regular basis.

1907 LAMBERT   **MROZ**

1914 LAMBERT MODEL V-3   **DFW/MVMA**

Lambert trucks were light delivery highwheelers with engines built in-house until about 1911, when the company began buying powerplants from various sources including Buda, Continental, Davis, Rutenber and Trebert. Friction transmissions were used throughout and nearly all Lambert vehicles used chain drive. The Buckeye Manufacturing Company stopped passenger car production in 1917 but continued building commercial vehicles for one more year.

LAMSON 1911-1919 — The Lamson Truck and Tractor Company of Chicago, Illinois, built trucks ranging from 1-ton up to 5-ton in capacity. Wheelbases were from 144 inches to 180 inches and trucks were powered by four-cylinder engines with three-speed transmissions and final worm-drive. It appears that the United Four Wheel Drive Company acquired Lamson in 1919 but this has not been substantiated.

1914 LANDSHAFT MODEL C FLAREBOARD EXPRESS   **OCW**

LANDSHAFT 1911-1920 — William Landshaft and Sons organized their company on Milwaukee Avenue in Chicago, Illinois, in 1909. By 1911, the company produced a few commercial vehicles powered by two-cylinder engines. The vehicles used planetary transmissions and chain drive. The first models were 1/2 ton and 1 ton, but in 1913, the company also manufactured a 1-1/2-ton truck. From 1916 until the end, 1 ton and 2 ton were the only Landshaft trucks produced. These later vehicles had three-speed transmissions and shaft drive. It appears the postwar recession knocked Landshaft out of business.

LANE 1916-1920 — The Lane Motor Truck Company of Kalamazoo, Michigan, first built 3/4-ton capacity trucks in 1916. These were powered by a four-cylinder engine and used a worm-drive rear axle. The same model was offered for 1917 but in 1918, the model line changed considerably. Lane offered 1-1/2-, 2-1/2- and 3-1/2-ton capacity trucks all powered by Continental engines, the largest two having six-cylinder powerplants. Up to 1920, which was the last year of production, Lane trucks had wooden spoke wheels and solid rubber tires. Timken worm-drive rear axles were used in all Lane vehicles. The company did not survive the postwar recession.

1914 LANGE MODEL C   OCW

1920 LANGE 2-TON   GOODYEAR

LANGE 1911-1931 — The H. Lange Wagon Works started out in Pittsburgh, Pennsylvania, in 1911. Announcements for the production of a motor truck and light delivery car appeared in the *Motor World* as early as September 1909, but apparently Lange used Gramm-Logan chassis until 1911. Starting that year, 1-ton and 2-ton models were offered on Lange chassis. In 1912, the wagon works became the Lange Motor Truck Company. All Lange vehicles were conventional assembled trucks powered by Continental engines. By the mid-1920s, the company offered a 1-1/2-ton model powered by a 22.5 hp Continental J4 engine with a Brown-Lipe clutch and transmission and Timken front and rear axles. Hoopes wheels carried 34x4 front and 34x6 rear tires with pneumatics at extra cost. The chassis price was $2,950. The 2-1/2-ton Model E of that period was powered by a 27.2 hp Continental K-4 engine and sold for $3,650. Chassis weight for the latter was 5,650 pounds. Lange also built the 3-1/2-ton Model F, which was powered by a 32.4 hp Continental L-4 engine. Chassis

price was $4,650. Component manufacturers were the same for all models and wheelbases were optional. The company faded out when the Great Depression ensued.

LANPHER 1910 — Carthage, Missouri, was the home of the Lanpher Motor Buggy Company, which began in 1906 and lasted until 1916. Earl and Norman Lanpher were the organizers of the company, which evolved from their Lanpher Brothers Carriage Works. Both horsedrawn wagons and motor vehicles were built side-by-side.

The Lanpher auto was a typical highwheeler with a 14 hp two-cylinder air-cooled engine, planetary transmission, double chain drive and solid rubber tires. For 1910, a delivery van version of the passenger car was built. The engine was beneath the body and suspension was by transverse springs front and rear on a chassis of 76-inch wheelbase. The Lanpher family left Carthage in 1916.

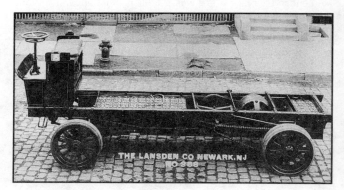

1920 LANSDEN 8-TON CHASSIS   NAHC

LANSDEN 1904-1928 — The Lansden Company began in Birmingham, Alabama, as the Birmingham Electric Manufacturing Company. John M. Lansden and William M. Little began experimenting with electric cars in 1901 before moving to Newark, New Jersey, in 1904.

The first Lansden Electric to go into production was a commercial vehicle called Type 36, Style A, which was powered by a 3/4 hp DC motor. The vehicle was built on a wooden frame and had a wheelbase of 87 inches. Final drive was by double chain. By 1906, three models were available of similar design. For 1907, a 1/2-ton and a 1-1/2-ton model was offered. Many Lansden vehicles had long hoods where the batteries were located, but forward-control vans were also built from 1-ton to 5-ton capacity. An electric taxicab was built in 1910, which was also the year that the company stopped building passenger cars, although a few were built after that on a custom order basis.

John Lansden left the company in 1911 to manage electric truck production at General Motors. The Lansden Company continued without him in Allentown, Pennsylvania. For 1912, the new plant under the auspices of Mac-Carr also produced a 5-ton capacity model with a wheelbase of 136 inches. A 50-mile range was guaranteed between charges on batteries developed by Thomas Edison. These were alkaline storage batteries instead of the commonly used lead acid type. In 1914, the Lansden Company moved to Brooklyn, New York, and in 1921, the company was incorporated in Danbury, Connecticut. Edison batteries were used exclusively. Production dwindled in the late 1920s, until the company faded out completely.

LANSING 1917-1920 — The Lansing Company of Lansing, Michigan, briefly built battery-powered electric trucks. Two models were available during the three-and-a-half years of manufacture. Lansing offered a 2-1/2-ton model and a 6-ton model.

LAPEER 1916-1920 — The Lapeer Tractor Truck Company was located in Lapeer, Michigan. As the company name denotes, the Lapeer truck was an articulated truck tractor of 5-ton capacity. It was powered by a four-cylinder Wisconsin engine with a three-speed transmission and Torbensen internal gear drive. Lapeer was one of the first truck builders to offer a cab that was completely enclosed as early as 1917. Truck production ceased by 1920, although the company continued to build trailers for a number of years.

LARRABEE 1916-1932 — The Larrabee-Deyo Motor Truck Company of Birmingham, New York, was named after H. Chester Larrabee and R.H. Deyo. This company evolved from the earlier Sturtevant-Larrabee Company, which built carriages, sleighs and wagons. Larrabee trucks were conventional assembled vehicles starting with 1-ton capacity and going up to 5-ton capacity by the end of World War I. Most Larrabee trucks were powered by four-cylinder Continental engines and had solid rubber tires until the early 1920s. Clutches and transmissions were provided by Brown-Lipe and worm-drive rear axles were from Sheldon. A Speed-Six Larrabee-Deyo was introduced in 1921. It featured a six-cylinder engine and two radiators for slow-running capability.

In 1922, Larrabee unveiled a 1-ton speed truck, which was powered by a six-cylinder Continental engine. Rear axle was a Salisbury spiral bevel type and pneumatic tires were standard. In 1923, the 1-1/4-ton Model L5 with 138-inch wheelbase was powered by a six-cylinder Continental engine and used a three-speed Brown-Lipe transmission and 36x6 pneumatic tires. It was priced at $1,835.

By the mid-1920s, Larrabee listed models from 1-1/2-ton to 3-1/2-ton. The 1-1/2-ton Model XH with 168-inch wheelbase was powered by a six-cylinder Continental 6B-6 engine and used a Brown-Lipe clutch and transmission. Both front and rear axles were Sheldon. Smith wheels carried 34x7 front and rear solid rubber tires. Chassis price was $3,200. The 2-1/2-ton Model K-5 with 176-inch wheelbase was powered by a Continental L-4 engine. Chassis price was $3,550. The 3-1/2-ton Model L-4 was powered by the same engine but had a 186-inch wheelbase and the major components were heavier-duty, although the suppliers were the same.

1927 LARRABEE STAKE   NAHC

By the late 1920s, Larrabee used four-speed transmissions, spiral bevel rear axles, steel spoke wheels, four-wheel hydraulic brakes, handbrake expanding on the rear drums, electric lights and starter, instruments on the dash and two-bar front bumper. Single pneumatic tires were on all four wheels. The one arcane feature on Larrabee trucks was the gravity-fed fuel system. The company provided fenders for all four wheels as well as full-length running-boards on all models as standard equipment. Prices went as high as $4,750 for the earlier 5-ton model.

A bus chassis of the late 1920s was offered for $3,900. Larrabee also assembled several hundred taxicabs under the name "Majestic" for use in New York City. Before the Depression began, Larrabee truck production reached 400 per year. After 1929, sales rapidly plummeted and the company was out of business by 1932.

LA SALLE-NIAGARA 1906 — The La Salle-Niagara Automobile Company was located in Niagara Falls, New York, at a former button factory. It was the continuation of the Wilson Automobile Manufacturing Company and E.A. Kinsey and George E. Whiteside were behind this brief venture, the latter being the patentee of the La Salle-Niagara passenger car, which was in production from 1905 into 1906.

The company also produced a 1-ton capacity flatbed delivery truck that was powered by an 18 hp horizontal two-cylinder engine mounted under the seat. Final drive was by double chain and wheel-

base was 90 inches. It appears that this was the same engine and chassis used on the Model B La Salle-Niagara Touring auto. Chassis price for the commercial vehicle was $1,500.

LASALLE see CADILLAC

1914 LAUTH-JUERGENS MODEL K   OCW

LAUTH; LAUTH-JUERGENS 1907-1915 — Jacob Lauth and Company was a tanning plant in Chicago, Illinois. The first Lauth truck was fabricated by Magnus Hendrickson, hence the date of 1907 is referenced as the first year of the marque. It was not until 1908 that Theodore Juergens joined Lauth and they built a few cars and light trucks.

As an employee of Lauth's, Hendrickson developed a number of important components including the hollow-spoke wheel in 1906, a three-speed transmission in 1909, a two-speed bevel gear transmission for chain driven vehicles, a jaw clutch transmission and the first worm-drive axle. The Lauth-Juergens passenger car was displayed at the Chicago Automobile Show in 1907, but this market did not develop and in 1910 the Lauth-Juergens Motor Company moved to Fremont, Ohio, to build trucks exclusively. Hendrickson joined them and was appointed chief engineer and designer. His sons, George and Carl, also joined in at the Fremont plant.

The Lauth-Juergens were conventional assembled trucks with cab-over-engine design, double chain drive, artillery wheels, solid tires and right-hand drive. The fully enclosed cabs had flat vertical windshields. In 1911, the company built a tilt-cab model truck. A bus was also available and it featured a three-piece windshield in the form of a bay window, which would later be adopted by Hendrickson when he and his sons returned to Chicago in 1913 to build Hendrickson trucks and components. The Lauth-Juergens trucks were available in 1-, 2-, 3- and 5-ton capacity. The most remarkable feature was that the engine was guaranteed for life. A third son of Hendrickson's, Robert, took charge of the Lauth-Juergens plant while his father and two brothers were organizing their own manufacturing sight. The Lauth-Juergens was renamed the Fremont-Mais in 1914 and in 1915, the company was bought by H.G. Burford.

LA VIGNE 1913-1915 — J.P. La Vigne had failed with his La Petite and Griswold cars and after obtaining some 224 sundry patents, he returned to automobile manufacturing in 1913 with the La Vigne cyclecar. It had a 96-inch wheelbase and was powered by a 15 hp four-cylinder air-cooled engine. A van version was available with planetary transmission and shaft drive. The vehicle's weight was 650 pounds and the price was $600. At the same time, La Vigne also built a car named the Traveler. Company brochures were presented under two names: La Vigne and JPL but by the end of 1914, the business enterprise was entirely defunct.

L.A.W. 1912-1913 — The L.A.W. Motor Truck Company, located in Finlay, Ohio, recorded a brief foray into the motor vehicle manufacturing business. The company offered 1-, 1-1/2- and 2-ton model trucks that were powered by four-cylinder engines. The trucks featured a sloping Renault-type hood. The light model used shaft drive and double reduction gears in the drive axle. Another early standard feature was left-hand drive. Chassis price was $2,200. The company stopped manufacturing at the end of 1913.

LAWSON 1917-1918 — The Lawson Manufacturing Company was located in Pittsburgh, Pennsylvania, and lasted for about one year. The only truck offered was the Model 35. It was powered by a four-cylinder Golden, Belknap & Schwartz engine and had a three-speed transmission. It also featured shaft drive. Wheelbase was 102 inches. Other details are not available.

L & E 1934-1942 — Lundelius and Eccleston formed a business partnership in 1922 and built a motor car prototype in Los Angeles by 1924. The L & E auto was promoted as "the car without axles." Four transverse springs were used front and rear to hold the wheels, presumably with stub axles. Each rear wheel was driven by a short shaft having two universal joints. The shaft connected with a bevel gear and differential hung from crossmembers. Despite heavy promotion in Long Beach, the Franklin-powered L & E did not go into production and Lundelius and Eccleston tried the same approach with other make vehicles. Ultimately, their product was a commercial vehicle chassis produced during the Great Depression until World War II. Further details are lacking.

LEA see INTERNATIONAL (1908)

LEACH 1899-1900 — The Leach Motor Vehicle Company was a builder of steam vehicles, mostly passenger cars, although a delivery wagon was also produced using a common chassis. John M. Leach, owner of the Everett Cycle Company, was the mastermind behind this venture located in Everett, Massachusetts. The steam vehicles he built used a tubular steel frame, much as his bicycles had. The suspension was comprised of three elliptical springs. The water boiler was fed automatically. Remarkably, the fuel used to heat it was gasoline. The vehicle itself was powered by a 6 hp slide valve steam engine. The delivery wagon was rated at 750 pounds. In 1900, Leach told the press that "a New York capitalist who undertook to raise funds failed to connect, and the works have been closed until the necessary capital can be secured."

LEAR see BROBECK

LE BLOND-SCHACHT see SCHACHT

LECTRA HAUL 1963 to date — Unit Rig & Equipment Company of Tulsa, Oklahoma, was best known for its oilfield equipment dating back to 1935. The company also built various off-road military vehicles for U.S. and foreign governments, as well as trailer-mounted oilfield machinery and truck-mounted ditch digging machines. The first truck prototype was built in 1960 but production did not start until three years later. In 1963, Lectra Haul unveiled its giant 4x2 dump truck, which started as the M-85 rated at 85-ton capacity. At the time, this was the largest dump truck in the world. Lectra Haul has built the M-200, which was rated at 200 tons, again the largest two-axle truck in the world at the time of its introduction.

All Lectra Haul trucks have had one thing in common: final drive was by large DC electric motors powered by generators driven by internal combustion engines, mostly diesel units. In the M-85, M-100 and M-120, the most common engine was the 700 hp Cummins VTA-1710. The M-200 was powered by a 2475 hp Electro-Motive Division (EMD) of General Motors. General Electric generators and General Electric wheel motors provide the motive power through planetary gears. Rubber-cushion Dynaflow columns were used as suspension. Unit Rig sold many of the M-200 trucks to Russia for hauling coal and phosphates in Siberia.

Lectra Haul introduced its articulated bottom-dump coal hauler in 1973. This was designated as the BD-180 and was powered by a 1100 hp Detroit Diesel V-12 engine. Capacity was 180 tons.

Large airport tow tractors and 60-ton forklift trucks have also been made by Unit Rig. By the end of 1975, total production of dump trucks and mining haulers was 2,000.

The Mark 36 Lectra Haul was added to the line as a companion model to the M-200. The Mark 36 was powered by a 1600 hp EMD engine and the truck was rated at 170-ton capacity. Without a clutch or transmission, the GE776 series-wound DC motors were driven by a rectified alternator. Rear axle was a fully-floating type. In addition to the dual circuit air-hydraulic brakes, electric braking was also available at the rear wheels. Wheelbase was 208 inches and overall height to top of cab was 19 feet. Top speed was 35 mph.

The BD-180 was superseded by the BD-270, which has been available to date with its smaller companion the 240-ton capacity BD-240. Along with these two articulated diesel-electric drive bottom dump trucks, through 1990 Lectra Haul has offered the Mark 24, Mark 30 and Mark 33 with payload capacity from 100-ton to 150-ton. In addition, the company has also built the MT-3600, MT-3700 and MT-4000, which were also diesel-electric two-axle back dump trucks from 190-ton to 240-ton capacity.

1993 LECTRA HAUL BD 270　　　　　　　　**UNIT RIG**

1994 LECTRA HAUL MT-3700　　　　　　　　**UNIT RIG**

1995 LECTRA HAUL MT-4400　　　　　　　　**UNIT RIG**

For 1993, the Mark 33 was discontinued while the Mark 30 was upgraded from 120-ton to 130-ton capacity. Load capacities for the three MT series did not change. However, for 1994, the Mark 24 was replaced by the Mark 27 with a 100-ton capacity while the Mark 30 was again rated at 120 tons. In addition to the three MT series, the MT-4400 with 260-ton capacity was added to the model line for 1995. The latter featured an 2467 hp MTU 16V396TE44 (1840 KW) engine, General Electric GTA 26 Alternator and G.E. 787 Series Wheel Motor with Statex III solid state logic control. Gear ratios from 26.625:1 to 31.875:1 have been available and suspension used nitrogen with oil struts.

LEHIGH 1925-1927 — The Lehigh Company was located in Allentown, Pennsylvania. Three models were built, each rated at 2-ton capacity. Two different Hercules engines were used for two of the models and the third was powered by a Buda HS-6 engine. In 1927, Lehigh merged with Bethlehem Motors Corporation.

1925 LEHIGH 2-TON CHASSIS　　　　　　　　　**RD**

1914 LEMOON MODEL D-1　　　　　　　　　　　**KP**

LEMOON; NELSON-LEMOON 1910-1939 — Nelson & LeMoon was located in Chicago, Illinois. Records show that the first truck produced by this company appeared in 1910. It was powered by a four-cylinder engine and used double chain drive. Its capacity was 1 ton. A.R. LeMoon won the Chicago-Detroit-Chicago commercial vehicle trial with one such truck in 1911. By 1912, a 1-1/2-ton truck was built using the same essential design. In 1913, a 2-ton and 3-ton model were added to the line. Chain drive was superseded by Timken worm-drive in 1915 on all but the heaviest truck but right-hand drive continued on all models until 1920. The 1915 3-ton Model E3 had a four-speed transmission and chain drive. Wheelbase was 156 inches. Wooden wheels carried 36x5 front and 36x5 rear dual solid rubber tires. Price was $2,950 for this model. Engines were provided by Continental and this was the case with few exceptions until 1930.

The trucks were called Nelson-LeMoon from 1913 until 1927 but after 1927, the single name of LeMoon was resumed. The company introduced a 5-ton capacity model in 1918, which was powered by a Buda engine. The rest of the model line consisted of 1-ton to 3-1/2-ton trucks all powered by Continental engines. By the mid-1920s, Nelson-LeMoon offered 1-, 1-1/2-, 2-, 2-1/2-, 3-, 3-1/2- and 5-ton models. All of them featured Continental engines, Brown-Lipe clutches and transmissions, Timken front and rear axles, St. Marys wheels and Ross steering.

In 1928, six-cylinder engines were adopted. Eight different models were offered by that time. By 1930, there were 11 models to chose from starting at $1,500 and going to $7,300. In 1931, LeMoon unveiled a six-wheel truck with a 12-ton capacity, which featured finned hood ventilators somewhat after the Fageol design, as well as cycle-type fenders. Waukesha six-cylinder engines were adopted for the larger trucks at that time.

1938 LEMOON 6X4 TRACTOR W/LOWBED TRAILER　　**CAT**

LeMoon introduced Lycoming straight-eight engines in the early 1930s and Cummins diesel engines were also offered by 1932. In 1936, the models ranged from 2-ton to 12-ton capacity. Cab-over-engine design was adopted for some models and articulated truck tractors were also introduced. By the following year, LeMoon listed the following models: 207, 307, 407, 507, 508, 510, 607 and 1100. These were all powered by six-cylinder Waukesha engines from 73 hp to 127 hp. The 1100 model was a cab-over-engine truck tractor priced at $6,500. The rest of the model line ranged in price from $1,275 to $3,250. The two lightest models used Warner transmissions, the rest used Brown-Lipe. All front and rear axles were Timken. In 1938, LeMoon introduced a more streamlined cab for its truck tractor likened to that made by Available. Engine options included powerplants built by Caterpillar, Continental, Cummins and Waukesha.

In the last few years of manufacture LeMoon built a motorhome designed and marketed by Brooks Stevens, which was sold also as a portable office or showroom. LeMoon built taxicabs at this time as well. LeMoon bought the Chicago branch of the Federal truck company and production ceased in April 1939. The company became known as the Federal-LeMoon Truck Company, which was a dealership and no longer a manufacturer. Over all years of production, it has been estimated LeMoon and Nelson-LeMoon trucks totaled 3,000.

LEONI 1925 — A.M. Leoni of Philadelphia, Pennsylvania, built an electric truck that had a motor forming the rear axle. Drive was through double planetary gear reduction for a top speed of 16.5 mph. Wheels were 33-inch in diameter. The battery was composed of 42 cells with 11 plates each providing a capacity of 150 amp-hours. Range was listed at 70 miles per charge after a test of the prototype but it does not appear many more Leoni electric trucks were built.

LESCINA 1916 — The Lescina Automobile Company began in Newark, New Jersey, and displayed several of its vehicles at the New York Automobile Show in 1916. Among the 11 different body styles on three different chassis Lescina offered a Model H Delivery Deluxe for $990. Standard purchased components and mass production was the intent to keep Lescina vehicles affordable. The Delivery Deluxe was powered by a 30 hp four-cylinder engine and had a 112-inch wheelbase. While a nationwide dealership organization was being established during 1916, the company's plans failed altogether. By January 1917, only the prototypes had been completed.

1996 LETOURNEAU T-2200   **LETOURNEAU**

LETOURNEAU 1985 to date — After Wabco sold its truck division to Marathon, the company's name was changed to Marathon-LeTourneau. The name LeTourneau derives from R.G. LeTourneau who began building earth-moving equipment in 1922 at Birk's Hollow, Illinois. He built the first self-propelled scraper in 1923, a rubber-tired scraper in 1932, a two-wheel prime mover called "Tournapull" in 1937 and an electrically-controlled self-propelled rubber-tired scraper in 1946. The first mechanical trucks called Haulpak were built in 1957, when the LeTourneau company co-operated with Westinghouse. In 1968, LeTourneau became a division of the Westinghouse Air Brake Company (Wabco).

Marathon-LeTourneau continued to build essentially the same trucks that Wabco had designed in the early 1980s. In 1993, the Rowan Corporation bought Marathon-Letourneau and the company name was returned to LeTourneau.

For the 1990s, LeTourneau has built two truck models designed for large scale mining operations: the T-2190 and the T-2200. Both of these were designed with diesel-electric drive systems and have been rated at 190-ton and 200-ton capacity, respectively. The lighter truck has been listed with a 1800 hp Cummins K1800-E 16-cylinder, 1800 hp Detroit Diesel 16V-149TI 16-cylinder or 1850 hp MTU 12V396TE44 12-cylinder engine. All of these have been built with turbocharger and intercooler. A 12B A.C. Generator has been used to power the two G-2 traction motors.

For the T-2200 model engine options have been listed as 2000 hp Cummins K2000E 16-cylinder diesel, 2000 hp Detroit Diesel 16V-149TI 16-cylinder and 1850 hp MTU 12V396TE44 12-cylinder diesel engine. Generator and traction motors have been the same as for the T-2190 model LeTourneau.

LEWIS 1912-1914 — The Lewis Motor Truck Company was located in San Francisco, California. Three models were available: 2-1/2-, 3- and 5-ton capacity. Each was powered by a four-cylinder side-valve engine whose location was listed as optional. All Lewis trucks used three-speed transmissions and double chain final drive from jackshafts. The wheelbase was 144 inches and only one chassis was used for all three models. Suspension was by semi-elliptic springs in front and platform springs in the rear. Lewis built bodies for brewery application as well as back and side dump beds and flatbeds. Production was limited over about two years of manufacture.

LEWIS 1939-1941 — The Lewis Construction Company of Los Angeles built at least one large dump truck for the San Gabriel Canyon project near Azusa, California. The truck was powered by twin V-8 190 Caterpillar diesel engines and GVW was 100 tons. Triple tires were used on both rear axles. It would appear that the company built more than one such truck before the beginning of World War II, but additional information has not been available.

1918 LIBERTY PICKUP   **DFW/OHS**

LIBERTY 1916-1923 — Light trucks by the name of Liberty were built by the Liberty Motor Car Company. These appear to have had six-cylinder engines and were not affiliated with the Liberty trucks of World War I. The Liberty Motor Car Company was located in Detroit, Michigan.

1917 LIBERTY   **OCW**

LIBERTY 1917-1918 — Fifteen different truck manufacturers actually built the Liberty Class B truck of World War I. There were also two other classes of Liberty trucks, but these were not produced in quantity as was the Class B model. The impetus for building the Liberty Class B truck (also called the USA, which was derived from lettering on the radiator header tank) was a general lack of standardization for truck design and specifications, resulting in maintenance and repair chaos for the Allies during the early part of the war.

By July of 1917, the military submitted the desired specifications for a general utility 4x2 truck that could be used in different branches of the armed forces. The Society of Automotive Engineers met in August of 1917 and organized 50 engineers in eight groups to design the truck's components. The engine was to be a 424-cubic inch displacement four-cylinder powerplant of which Continental manufactured the block, Waukesha the cylinder heads and Hercules the pistons. Wheelbase was 144 inches. Assembly of two prototype trucks was begun in Lima, Ohio, and Rochester, New York. The goal was to have a standardized truck built in large quantities having all parts interchangeable, with units built by different companies in various locations. A total of 150 companies were involved in producing components for the Liberty trucks.

By October of 1917, the two prototypes were driven to Washington D.C. without any mechanical problems and were delivered to the Secretary of War. By January of 1918, production began. The first five Liberty trucks were completed by the middle of the month. By May of 1918, production was geared up to 1,000 per month by the 15 different companies contracted for the job. Before the Armistice was signed in November of 1918, records show a total of 9,364 Liberty Class B trucks were completed. Once the war ended, the order for 43,000 more Liberty trucks was canceled. This resulted in financial doom for many small companies.

The total production of 9,364 units for 1917 and 1918 has been assigned to 15 companies that assembled the Liberty trucks in the following breakdown: Bethlehem 675, Brockway 589, Diamond T 638, Garford 978, Gramm-Bernstein 1,000, Indiana 475, Kelly-Springfield 301, Packard 5, Pierce-Arrow 975, Republic 967, Selden 1,000, Service 337, Sterling 479, U.S. Motor Truck 490 and Velie 455.

The Liberty was the basis for truck designs used by the U.S. military for many years after the war, including 6x4 variations, halftracks and fire engines. Liberty trucks continued to be assembled at various U.S. Army depots after 1918. They were used throughout Europe for civilian work during the 1920s and also became the basis for the design of the Willeme trucks in France.

LIEBHERR 1995 to date — Liebherr Mining Truck, Incorporated, a Swiss-based company, purchased Wiseda in 1995 and has continued to build the Wiseda KL-2420 and KL-2450 mining trucks with up to 240-ton capacity. See WISEDA.

1914 LIGHT TRICAR BOX BODY   OCW

LIGHT 1913-1914 — The Light Commercial Car built a three-wheel parcel delivery van in Marietta, Pennsylvania, in 1913. The following year, the company became the Wayne Light Commercial Car Company of New York City. The light van had a 750-pound capacity and the early vehicles were powered by a 6 hp one-cylinder air-cooled engine superseded by a 14 hp two-cylinder engine at the time of the company's move. Single chain drive to the single rear wheel was used and the later version of the three-wheel van was priced at $475 in 1914. This company was not affiliated with the Light Motor Car Company of New York City that existed at the same time.

LIMA 1915-1916 — The Lima Light Car Company was organized by C.E. Miller and F.E. McGraw in Lima, Ohio, during the year 1915. By midyear, the company was capitalized with $50,000 and plans were for the production of 10 vehicles per day.

Three versions of the Lima were available; roadster, speedster and light delivery. All were powered by an 18 hp four-cylinder engine and the common wheelbase was 100 inches. Price was $500 for each of the versions, but it appears only pilot models were ever built and the company faded out by 1916. This company was not affiliated with the nearly contemporary Lima Roadster, also of Lima, Ohio. It appears William Townsend Marsh built one prototype of the latter in 1912.

LINCOLN 1912-1913 — The Lincoln Motor Works of Chicago, Illinois, obtained machinery and rights from Sears when the large catalog and department store sold off its unprofitable automobile manufacturing division. The company continued to build vehicles that were essentially the same as the Sears design. Light vans were available with up to 800-pound capacity powered by a 14 hp two-cylinder air-cooled engine using two-speed friction transmissions and single chain drive. Prices ranged from $585 to $650.

1912 LINCOLN LIGHT DELIVERY VAN   MROZ

1912 LINCOLN FLAREBOARD   MROZ

LINCOLN 1916-1917 — The Lincoln Motor Truck Company of Detroit, Michigan, built a single model 3/4-ton capacity truck during one year encompassing 1916 and 1917. It was powered by a four-cylinder overhead-valve engine using a three-speed transmission. Wheelbase of this vehicle was 122 inches. During 1916, the Lincoln Motor Truck Company acquired the O.K. Motor Truck Company. The reasons for Lincoln's demise in 1917 is not known, although material shortages during the war contributed to problems of manufacturing.

LINDSLEY 1908-1909 — Sometimes listed as located in Seymour, Indiana, J. Victor Lindsley & Company actually did business from a small plant in Dowagiac, Michigan. Having built a high-wheeler prototype in Chicago, Lindsley returned to get his father's financial assistance for the manufacture of the vehicle. The younger Lindsley proceeded to purchase the Dowagiac Automobile Company, which had been started by machinists Frank Lake and Doras Neff, who had as yet to go into actual manufacturing. Lindsley began by selling complete chassis for the do-it-yourself coachbuilder at a price of $250.

The J.V. Lindsley Auto Chassis Company did only modest business this way and Lindsley decided to build complete vehicles for $475. As a 3/4-ton delivery truck with a 96-inch wheelbase the cost was $600. The vehicle was powered by a two-cylinder air-cooled engine featuring force-fed lubrication, a multiple-disc clutch, two-speed planetary transmission and double chain drive. Later, a 1-1/4-ton capacity truck was also available, although it is not certain if any were actually built as the Lindsley or were actually the later Dowagiac. The Lindsley business was not profitable, J. Victor temporarily disappeared and Lindsley's lumber industry millionaire father paid off the debts. Frank Lake bought back the assets including machinery to restart the Dowagiac company in order to build light delivery trucks. He was killed in an accident in 1909

247

and the enterprise, cut short, was acquired by the Tulsa Auto Manufacturing Company, which moved operations to Oklahoma by 1912.

1928 LINN HALF-TRACK LOGGER   KP

LINN 1916-1952 — The Linn Manufacturing Corporation of Morris, New York, specialized in building halftracks intended for load carrying or as towing tractors. Applications included construction, logging, mining, snowplowing and military use. Holman H. Linn was the organizer behind the venture, which began during World War I.

The design of the Linn halftracks was conventional apart from the tracks themselves. The first series was powered by a four-cylinder Continental engine. This was superseded by four-cylinder and six-cylinder Waukesha engines and subsequently six-cylinder Cummins and Hercules diesel engines were used. The tracks were mounted between the framerails and the auxiliary extensions with the rear axle being gear-driven.

In 1922, Linn halftracks had snowplows built by Carl Frink as a regular option. Holman Linn left the company in 1927 to start the Linn Trailer Company, which became Lyncoach (listed as Linn Coach and Truck Company of Oneonta, New York, builders of buses and large ambulances for the military during World War II and mobile television vans for the Signal Corps in 1950-1951). After 1927, the Linn company continued without its founder and built a special military version called the T3 rated at eight tons in 1933, which was powered by a 246 hp American LaFrance V-12 engine.

1930 LINN CAB/CHASSIS   HAYS

The Linn company developed special four-speed and eight-speed transmissions in the late 1930s in conjunction with a heavy two-plate clutch. This allowed high-speed reversing, providing the halftrack with equal speed in both directions. The lowest gear for towing and rough terrain had a ratio of 116:1. The shuttle shift-equipped Linn was called the "Contractor's Special" and the six-cylinder Linn was called the "County and Township Special." Top speed of the latter was 7.5 miles per hour, which was about double of a regular crawler tractor.

Fenders were a special order option and the early open cabs were supplanted by closed wooden cabs in the 1920s. A fully enclosed steel cab with visor was adopted just before World War II. A conventional truck tractor with twin wheels in back was developed in 1930 for delivering Linn halftracks to customers. The single example built had a sleeper cab and two 50-gallon gasoline tanks. Fully loaded it could cruise at 40 mph.

Holman Linn returned to the Linn company in 1937. Linn models included the A, B, C and T series. The founder died in a plane crash the year he returned to the company that he had started over 20 years earlier.

The C series was developed by Philip W. Sloan, a consulting engineer, after Linn's death. The C-5 was a 5-ton hybrid halftrack with front wheel drive and a non-driven axle behind the tracks, which could be lowered hydraulically for road use giving the Linn a top speed of 35 mph. The C-5 was a cab-over-engine design with 170-inch wheelbase and used a six-cylinder Hercules gasoline or diesel engine. The transmission provided five forward speeds and two reverse. The C-5 was the first Linn to be available in a color other than the standard forest green. It was available in highway equipment orange.

For a variety of reasons, production of the C-5 in Buffalo was abandoned after just a few months. The C-5 was redesigned, patented and the trademark of "Catruk" was issued to the company. Twenty were built for the Navy. In 1946, the C-5 was redesigned again. The rear axle was made entirely removable with the use of two hydraulic bottle jacks that were permanently attached to the end of the rockerbeam axle, the main load-bearing crossmember that distributed the load to the bogie wheels. The jacks were swung down and manually operated. Using four link pins and two air hose couplings, the whole rear axle and toggle frame could be removed or attached.

The C-6 Halftrak was developed during World War II, when problems with the C-5 prompted the company to produce a conventional halftrack. Twenty-five were completed to be sent to Russia before the Berlin Blockade stopped all exports to that country.

After World War II, Linn halftracks carried price tags of up to $15,000 each. The 25-ton D-25 model was built, which was the largest Linn, but by 1949, demand faded to the point that the board of directors decided to liquidate the company. It was sold to two local businessmen, Harold Mills and Maurice Bridges, who built a few more Linns before closing down the company in 1952.

LION 1920-1921 — The only information known about this obscure make was that the company resided in New York City for a year and built a single model 3/4-ton truck. The Lion Motor Truck Company was succeeded by the Pitt Motor Car Company, but no other details have been available.

1911 LIPPARD-STEWART LIGHT EXPRESS   NAHC

1912 LIPPARD-STEWART PANEL DELIVERY   RD

LIPPARD-STEWART 1911-1919 — The Lippard-Stewart Motor Car Company was located in Buffalo, New York. The Lippard-Stewart trucks were distinguished by their Renault-type sloping hoods. The first model was rated at 3/4-ton. The radiator was located behind the four-cylinder engine in each case.

Lippard-Stewart also built at least three 1-1/2-ton trucks for the U.S. military to serve on the Mexican border. These featured David Brown worm-drive rear axles and 35 hp Continental four-cylinder engines. The Renault-type hoods continued to be used. Later Lippard-Stewart offered trucks from 1/2-ton to 2-ton capacity also powered by four-cylinder Continental engines with three-speed transmissions and worm-drive. Following World War I, the company ceased production.

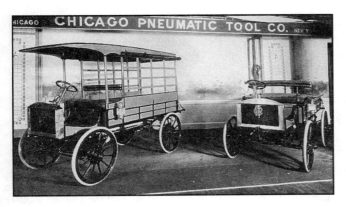

1912 LITTLE GIANT   NAHC

1912 LITTLE GIANT MODEL H   OCW

1916 LITTLE GIANT WORM-DRIVE DELIVERY   OCW

LITTLE GIANT 1912-1918 — The Chicago Pneumatic Tool Company of Chicago, Illinois, built light trucks powered by two-cylinder engines with planetary transmissions and double chain drive. These forward-control trucks were rated at 3/4-ton and 1-ton up to 1915. The company switched to four-cylinder Continental engines that year and adopted three-speed transmissions as well as worm-drive. The later trucks were rated up to 3-1/2-ton capacity. Trucks under the abbreviation C.P.T. were also built by this company and a few carried the name Chicago.

1932 LITTLE MAC PANEL TRUCKETTE   JEFF GILLIS

LITTLEMAC 1929-1934 — Herbert and Ralph Thompson organized the Thompson Motor Corporation in Muscatine, Iowa, in 1929. The Littlemac car was the idea of Clayton E. Frederickson, who had built cyclecars in Chicago. The Littlemac was powered by a four-cylinder Star engine on a chassis with an 80-inch wheelbase and 40-inch tread. Both a coupe and a light delivery were offered for $350 and $500, respectively. William Durant cooperated by providing the Star parts when he phased out that marque to start the Durant 4-40 in 1928.

It was not until 1931 that the first Littlemac "Truckette" was built. The Littlemac vehicles were advertised as "The Fastest Small Automobile in the World." Cruising speed was 55 mph and top speed was 75 mph, with average fuel consumption at 35 miles per gallon. According to records, the coupe was discontinued and a new "Truckette" was sold as late as February 1934, although its production was probably earlier. The company closed down entirely by 1935.

L.M.C. 1919-1920 — The Louisiana Motor Car Company of Shreveport, Louisiana, built one model of truck that was rated at 2-1/2-ton capacity. The Model 2-20 used a four-cylinder Continental engine and a four-speed transmission with final drive by bevel gear. Wheelbase was 164 inches and chassis price was $2,950.

1974 LOCKHEED TWISTER DRAGON WAGON   RD

LOCKHEED see TWISTER DRAGON WAGON

LOCOMOBILE 1901-1916 — The Locomobile Company of America was incorporated in 1899 in Watertown, Massachusetts, by John Brisben Walker, editor and publisher of *Cosmopolitan Magazine*, and Amzi Lorenzo Barber, who had made a fortune in asphalt. The Stanley Brothers sold their business to Walker and Barber that year for $250,000 and the new owners continued to assemble 100 steam cars under the new name of Locomobile. After Walker and Barber broke off their partnership at the turn of the century, Barber became the sole owner of Locomobile and eventually moved all manufacturing to Bridgeport, Connecticut.

In 1901, a 1/2-ton "Locodelivery" steam vehicle was built. It had a 21-1/2-gallon fuel tank and a 50-gallon water tank with a 16-inch boiler. It was priced at $2,000. By 1902, about 4,000 of the primitive Locomobile steam cars were built.

249

Upon improvements made to the Locomobile cars by the Overman Wheel Company, builders of the Victor steam autos in Chicopee Falls, the two companies merged. Locomobile had Andrew Lawrence Riker on its team by 1902. It was he who designed the first gasoline-powered vehicle that was the prototype for Locomobile cars and trucks when steam power was discontinued by that company in 1904. The gasoline-powered Locomobile gained an excellent reputation. The company slogan was "Easily the Best Built Car in America" and a number of racing victories helped sales considerably.

1913 LOCOMOBILE MODEL A 5-TON NAHC

By 1912, Locomobile introduced a 5-ton model truck powered by a 431-cubic inch displacement four-cylinder engine. Wheelbase was 140 inches. The truck had a three-speed transmission and double chain drive. In 1913, the company introduced a demountable dump body. By 1914, Locomobile had acquired such a high reputation that a custom department built special cars for people such as William Carnegie, Reggie Vanderbilt and William Wrigley. General Pershing took his Locomobile overseas. Lamps and metal work on some of the Locomobile autos were crafted by Tiffany at this time.

In 1915, the company introduced a line of trucks that included 3-, 4-, 5- and 6-ton models, although the following year only the two latter were available. Great Britain, France and Russia ordered hundreds of Locomobile trucks for the war effort in Europe. Both the 5-ton and 6-ton trucks were powered by a 45 hp four-cylinder engine built by Locomobile. Clutch was a dry disc type coupling the engine with a four-speed selective gear transmission. Both trucks had a wheelbase of 140 inches (with 170 inches optional on the 6-ton model) and tires were 40x6 front and rear with duals on the back. The 5-ton chassis price was $4,500.

1914 LOCOMOBILE CHASSIS HAYS

250

In 1916, the Locomobile trucks were renamed Riker in honor of the vehicles' designer. Locomobile supplied 3-ton trucks to the American Expeditionary Force chasing Pancho Villa after he raided Columbus, New Mexico. The Riker trucks had special wheels to convert over for use on railroad tracks and after a successful demonstration the military bought 30 such vehicles.

Locomobile became part of William Durant's business venture in 1922 and truck production under the name Riker also ceased. Locomobile car production was shut down when Durant's firm was hit by the stock market crash of 1929.

LODAL see EVO

1905 LOGAN MODEL E EXPRESS JAW

LOGAN 1904-1908 — The Motor Storage and Manufacturing Company was the original producer of Logan vehicles, both commercial and passenger types. Benjamin A. Gramm was the man behind this company, which was renamed the Logan Construction Company and produced cars and light trucks for four years. Under Gramm's leadership, this company became the predecessor of the Gramm-Logan when Gramm moved the manufacturing facilities from Chillicothe to Bowling Green, Ohio. For commercial vehicle specifications refer to Gramm-Logan.

LOMBARD 1901-1919 — The Lombard Auto Tractor-Truck Corporation was located in Waterville, Maine. It was organized by Alvin O. Lombard, whose first halftrack was based on locomotive design, but with tracks in the rear and skids in front in place of wheels. The tracks were mounted inside the chassis frame.

By 1916, the Lomabard tractor-trucks were powered by a 75 hp four-cylinder Model engine. One hundred-four were sold to the Russian army just before the Bolshevik Revolution to haul artillery and supply trains. Lombard sold such tractor-trucks in the United States for use in the logging industry. The vehicles were capable of pulling 60-ton trailers.

1920 LONE STAR 1-1/2-TON RD

LONE STAR 1920-1921 — The manufacture of a 1-1/2-ton truck by the name of Lone Star has been traced to the brief existence of a company by the name of the Lone Star Truck and Tractor Association of San Antonio, Texas.

1902 LONG DISTANCE   RD

LONG DISTANCE 1902 — Also known as the U.S. Long Distance Automobile Company, this venture was organized in 1900 by Lewis Nixon, Lt. John C. Fremont and D.J. Newland. Marine engines were the first product of the company until 1901, when passenger cars designed by C.C. Riotte were built using two-cylinder and three-cylinder water-cooled engines.

In 1902, the company built a 1-1/2-ton truck for the U.S. Army per military specifications. It was equipped with two engines, one for motive power (24 hp four-cylinder) and the other to power a generator, lathe and grindstone. Its 110-inch wheelbase chassis with all machinery and box body weighed 10,500 pounds. It carried tools for shoeing horses, carpentry, blacksmithing and saddlery. It was tested at Ft. Leavenworth, Kansas, and proved a top speed of 10 mph with a range of 390 miles on one tank of gasoline. It appears only one such truck was built and the Long Distance Automobile Company of New Jersey (also listed in New York) continued production of passenger cars until 1904, when the name was changed to Standard.

1911 LONGEST   RD

LONGEST 1907-1912 — The Longest Brothers, W.B., T.F., and C.F. started in Louisville, Kentucky, in 1906. At first they were dealers for Stoddard automobiles but it appears that by 1907, they began manufacturing 4-ton and 6-ton trucks powered by a 40 hp four-cylinder engine located under a front hood and using a four-speed transmission with double chain drive. Both models had solid rubber tires and sold for $4,250 and $4,750, respectively. H.J. Edwards and C.G. Stoddard (formerly of Stoddard-Dayton) took over the company in 1912. Edwards announced that the company would continue producing trucks but this has not been substantiated.

LOOMIS 1900-1901 — Frank P. Loomis was a mechanical engineer in Akron, Ohio. He has been credited with building the first motorized police patrol wagon ever used in the United States. It was powered by two 4 hp electric motors in each rear wheel. A battery of 40 cells provided electric power and these were carried under the seats of the vehicle in four sets of 10 each. By switching from one to all four sets, four speeds were available up to 20 mph. Braking was accomplished with two sets of friction rollers that were engaged against the solid rubber tires of the rear wheels by means of a "foot-lever." A handbrake was also provided, which was connected to the gearing of the rear wheels. Wheel steering was used. The vehicle weighed 5,500 pounds. It cost the city of Akron about $3,000. It is not certain if Frank P. Loomis was related to Gilbert J. Loomis, who built a number of cars in Westfield, Massachusetts, at about the same time.

1900 LOOMIS   RD

LOOMIS 1900-1902 — Gilbert J. Loomis was an engineer who experimented with steam vehicles as early as 1896. He holds the distinction of being the first to buy automobile liability insurance in the United States. This took place in 1897 for a $1,000 policy for an annual premium of $7.50. The Loomis Automobile Company went into production in 1900, with three models of gasoline vehicles. Model 1, 2 and 3 were each powered by a 5 hp two-cylinder air-cooled engine. The Model 3 was a light delivery vehicle that was priced at $1,200 and was produced for three years. Loomis obtained an important contract from Bloomingdale's department store for 500 light delivery vans, which he accepted. When he could not produce this number of vehicles in two months Bloomingdale's canceled the order. Loomis continued building passenger cars until 1904, when he sold his company to Samuel Squires. He continued to work as an engineer for Pope-Tribune, Payne Modern and Speedwell.

1912 LORD BALTIMORE COVERED EXPRESS   RD

LORD BALTIMORE 1911-1915 — The Lord Baltimore Motor Car Company was organized in 1910 to build trucks designed by John Luntz Jr. By 1911, the company built a 3-ton Model A truck in

Baltimore, Maryland. It used a four-cylinder engine and was built with a stake side body. The transmission was a three-speed unit and final drive was by chain.

By 1913, the company offered five models of trucks from 1-ton to 5-ton capacity. Luntz attempted to go into the passenger car manufacturing business at that time but without any success. Each of the trucks his company built used a different chassis. For 1914 and 1915, only the 1-ton and 2-ton models were built. By 1916, Luntz was no longer in the manufacturing business but was listed as the proprietor of The Service Company, which sold tires and accessories.

LORRAINE 1920-1924 — The Lorraine began as an independent company started by D.H. Cummings. It was soon taken over by the Pilot Motor Car Company, which was an outgrowth of the Seidel Buggy Company also located in Richmond, Indiana. "The Car Ahead" was the company's slogan. The company's success was in building reliable passenger cars. After World War I, the economic recession proved insurmountable for the Pilot and Lorraine companies and the Lorraine became a sideline activity for the former and larger Pilot firm.

As part of the Pilot company, the Lorraine vehicles were mostly funeral cars, although a few were built as limousines. These gray and silver professional cars rode on a 122-inch wheelbase and were powered by a 55 hp six-cylinder 7R Continental engine and later by six-cylinder engines from Herschell-Spillman and Teetor-Harley. When the postwar recession hit, Cummings stated to a press reporter that "It has been calculated that the number of funerals, the country over, have (sic) been only two-fifths of normal, since last October." The Pilot company went into receivership and was sold to a local junk dealer named Sam Jaffe for $28,500.

LOS ANGELES 1913-1914 — The Los Angeles Motor Truck Manufacturing Company was formed in Los Angeles, California, in 1913 for the purpose of building trucks with up to 20-ton capacity. Its authorized capital was $1,000,000. W.B. Joslyn was general manager and M.S. Walton was chief engineer. The first Los Angeles truck was announced in *Motor World* in March 1913 as having "double worm-drive to each rear wheel." Underslung construction allowed the loading platform to be only 21 inches off the ground. Two driveshafts were employed, each following closely and protected by the channel steel frame of the bed. It is uncertain whether this truck ever went past the prototype stage.

LOYAL 1918-1920 — The Loyal Motor Truck Company of Lancaster, Ohio, built 1/2-ton and 3/4-ton trucks for the first two years of its short existence. For the last year of manufacture, a 1-ton truck was offered. A four-cylinder LeRoi engine was offered in the 1/2-ton model, but the company went out of business that year.

1912 LOZIER PATROL WAGON   MROZ

LOZIER 1910-1912 — Henry Abram Lozier started out building steam vehicles in 1898. After selling his bicycle factories that made up the Lozier Manufacturing Company for four million dollars, Lozier senior died leaving the business to his son, who, after undertaking some industrial espionage, went into auto production by 1905. With a substantial capitalization, the company began producing

top quality cars, which also won a number of races. In 1911, when Lozier won second place in the Indianapolis 500, the price range of the factory cars was from $4,600 to $7,750. At that time, Lozier introduced water-cooled brake drums, a feature used on racing cars half a century later. What many people thought was bronze striping on the cars was actually 24-karat gold. About 600 cars per year were built at the Plattsburgh plant in New York.

Meanwhile, Lozier had a large new factory started in 1910 in Detroit. Because of the financial stress this project had caused, he was ousted from the company in 1912. The year 1910 was the year financial difficulties induced Lozier into building trucks. The first Lozier truck that year was the Model 25, which had a forward-control design and was powered by a four-cylinder water-cooled engine. A four-speed transmission transmitted power to the rear wheels through jackshafts and double chain drive. The Model 25 was rated at 5-ton capacity and was governed to a maximum speed of 13 mph. Its wheelbase was 134 inches and its chassis price was $4,500. The truck was discontinued by 1912 but the company continued in an effort to stay in business.

After several managerial shakeups and changing of leadership, the Lozier firm was taken over by a bankers' group named the Associated Lozier purchasers. The Plattsburgh plant and the Detroit facility were both sold in 1915. The new reorganizers leased the former plant of the Standard Auto Truck Company but by the end of 1918, production had faded out completely.

LUCK UTILITY 1911-1914 — Harry Eugene Luck, a Texas preacher, organized the Cleburne Motor Car Manufacturing Company in Cleburne, Texas. F.L. Deal was vice-president and R.H. Crank was secretary. The Luck Utility was intended as a roadster that could easily be converted into a light delivery truck. One of the company slogans was "Never runs away or kicks the wagon to pieces." The Luck Utility was powered by a 30 hp four-cylinder engine and had a 115-inch wheelbase. The engine was mounted under a hood between the two front seats and the vehicle used a three-speed transmission and shaft drive. The hard rubber tires were on wheels suspended by semi-elliptic springs in front and two-thirds elliptic at the rear. The company also built a single "Luck Truck," which was heftier than the light delivery, although specifications are unknown. After production of about 20 vehicles, the company was shut down in 1914.

1924 LUEDINGHAUS   RD

LUEDINGHAUS 1920-1933 — The Luedinghaus-Espenschied Wagon Company built trucks by the name of Luedinghaus in St. Louis, Missouri. After building horsedrawn wagons for many years, the company began building trucks when demand forced the company to change to more modern technology. The first Luedinghaus trucks were 1 ton and 2-1/2 ton powered by four-cylinder Waukesha engines. By the mid-1920s, Luedinghaus offered 1-1/2-, 2-1/2-, 3-1/2- and 5-ton models. The 1-1/2-ton truck was powered by a 25.6 hp Waukesha engine and used a Borg and Beck clutch and Detlaff transmission. The front axle was a Shuler, rear axle was made by Wisconsin and steering was Lavine Gear. Chassis weight was 4,500 pounds. Pneumatic tires were optional at extra cost. The 2-1/2-ton model differed from the previous one in that it was powered by a 28.9 hp Waukesha RU4R engine, the transmission was supplied by Detroit Gear and rear axle was made by Timken. The 3-1/2-ton Luedinghaus truck model used a 32.4 hp Waukesha DU engine and Brown-Lipe transmission. Rear axle was made by Wisconsin and steering gear was Ross. Bimel wheels carried 36x6 front and dual rear optional pneumatic tires. The 5-ton model had the same make components as the previous model but was powered by a 40 hp Waukesha EU engine, and pneumatic tires were once again optional.

Luedinghaus built a custom six-wheel truck in 1928. It featured set-back front axle, enormous balloon tires and Hendrickson tandem axles. By 1933, only a few trucks were being produced, and only 1-1/2-ton and 2-1/2-ton capacity were available before the company went out of business.

LUMB 1918 — The Lumb Motor Truck and Tractor Company was located in Aurora, Illinois. The company built a single model truck rated at 4,500-pound capacity. It was powered by a four-cylinder Buda engine and used a three-speed transmission. The truck's wheelbase was 148 inches. Chassis price was $1,900. It appears that production was limited over less than one year. The company was bought out by Pan-American Motors, builder of passenger cars.

1926 LUVERNE MOVING VAN   NAHC

LUVERNE 1912-1923 — Ed and Fenton Leicher began by building horsedrawn buggies and gradually switched over to automobile manufacturing by 1905 in Luverne, Minnesota. By 1910, the Luverne automobiles were mostly large touring cars, but it was not until 1912 that the company entered the commercial vehicle business by building a hearse and a fire engine, both powered by six-cylinder Rutenber engines. Truck production began the following year. That was the same year that Luverne built the Montana Special six-cylinder motor car, which was soon eclipsed by the "Big Brown Luverne" touring and roadster of 1914, distinguished by a 130-inch wheelbase, "Old Spanish brown leather with all hair filling" and a solid German silver radiator.

Late in 1916, passenger car production ceased as the company dedicated itself to building farm trucks for the war effort. In the early 1920s, the Luverne Motor Truck Company evolved into the Luverne Fire Apparatus Company. The last Luverne truck was a 3-ton capacity model powered by a four-cylinder Continental 7N engine. After 1923, the company produced fire apparatus using chassis built by other companies. After passing out of the Leicher family's hands in 1970, the firm has survived to date as the Luverne Fire Equipment Company.

LUXOR 1924-1927 — The M.P. Moller Company built the Luxor taxicabs, although the first pilot models were built by the Luxor Cab Manufacturing Company in Framingham, Massachusetts. Allie S. Freed and Mickey Heidt were the organizers of the company having named the cab after the city next to King Tut's tomb, which was discovered in Egypt at that time. The two of them approached M.P. Moller who was in Hagerstown, Maryland, producing the Dagmar automobile.

Moller bought a substantial interest in the Luxor business. In 1925, the decision was made to move the cab building enterprise to Framingham, where they would be assembled alongside Bay State cars at the factory of the R.H. Long Motor Car Company. The cabs were built on a 114-inch wheelbase and were powered by four-cylinder Buda engines. Their leather-upholstered interior was described as commodious and the cream, yellow and black with red striping color scheme distinctive. The New York Supreme Court awarded Luxor the exclusive rights to the color scheme after another cab company adopted the same design, prompting a lawsuit. Luxor ended up buying the Bay State factory machinery after R.H. Long's business failed and the company proceeded to follow suit in 1927.

LYNCOACH 1938-1970 — Lyncoach was founded by H.H. Linn, designer of the Linn halftrack. The Lyncoach & Truck Manufacturing Company was founded in 1929 and by 1938, was located in Oneonta, New York, where the first complete assembled vehicle was built by the company. Up to that time, only bus, trailer and truck bodies were manufactured. The first Lyncoach was a radio operations truck for station WOR in New York City. It was powered by a Waukesha engine and became the pilot model for other similar traveling showrooms and motorhomes.

During World War II, Lyncoach built complete ambulances powered by either V-8 Ford engines or six-cylinder Dodge units. The company also built various bodies assembled on chassis by a variety of manufacturers. After the war, Lyncoach built a series of front-wheel-drive vans powered by Waukesha engines.

In 1960, a new factory was started in Troy, Alabama, for the production of aluminum truck bodies and trailers. The Lyn Airvan was built at the new plant using Ford chassis primarily. These were built in various capacities from 1/2 ton to 3 ton. Before the end of van production, the name was changed to Lyn Arrow; however, after 1970, the company produced bodies and trailers only. The Oneonta factory was closed at about the same time.

M

MACCAR 1912-1935 — Jack Mack, one of the Mack brothers of Mack truck fame, teamed up with Roland Carr in 1912 to form the Mac-Carr Company in Allentown, Pennsylvania, builders of Maccar trucks. The first trucks built by this company were conventional 3/4-ton and 1-1/2-ton capacity vehicles. During 1912 and 1913, Maccar vehicles were built in the factory that was also occupied by the Webb Motor Fire Apparatus Company and the Lansden Company that built electric trucks. By 1915, the company was reorganized in Scranton, Pennsylvania, as the Maccar Truck Company without the presence of Mack or Carr, the company's founders.

At the new location, the company began building trucks from 3/4-ton to 2-ton capacity using Wisconsin engines. By 1917, the model range included 3-1/2-ton and 5-1/2-ton trucks. The 1919 3-1/2-ton Model M had a four-cylinder Continental engine, three-speed Brown-Lipe transmission and Timken worm-drive. Wheelbase was 174 inches and price was $4,300. Maccar became well known throughout New England and New York in the 1920s.

By the mid-1920s, Maccar produced the 1-1/4-ton Model EX with 132-inch wheelbase powered by a 25.6 hp Wisconsin SU engine using a Brown-Lipe clutch and transmission. Front and rear axles were by Salisbury and Van wheels carried 34x5 front and rear pneumatic tires as standard. The 2-ton Model V-3 was powered by a 28.9 hp Wisconsin UAU engine and both front and rear axles were Timken while Dayton wheels carried solid rubber tires with pneumatic as optional.

1914 MACCAR MODEL A   **KP**

Two 3-ton models were available: the H1 and the H-3. The H1 was powered by the same engine as the previous model, while the H-3 had a 32.4 hp Wisconsin VAU engine. Chassis weight was 6,300 pounds for both and wheelbase for the H1 was 163 inches, while for the H-3 it was optional. There was also a 4-ton Model M2 with the same engine as the H-3, which had a wheelbase of 173 inches. The heftiest Maccar at that time was the 5-ton Model G1, which was powered by a 40.0 hp Wisconsin RBU engine and had a seven-speed transmission available. Component suppliers for the H1, H-3, M2 and G1 were the same as on the V-3 model.

For 1926, Maccar offered six-cylinder engines made by Buda and Wisconsin. Front axles were by Shuler and the heavier models had heat-treated frames. Cast-iron radiators and sheet metal were quite distinctive for Maccar during this period. By 1929, Maccar offered the 1-1/2-ton Model 36 for $1,950, the 2-ton Model 46 for $3,100, the 3-ton four-cylinder Model 64 for $3,800, the 3-ton six-cylinder Model 66 for $4,100, the 4-ton four-cylinder Model 84 for $4,100, the 4-ton six-cylinder Model 86 for $4,400 and the 6-ton Model G for $5,100. This was the first year that tandem axle six-wheel trucks were available, and that year Maccar joined Hahn and Selden as a conglomerate to ride out the Depression.

1926 MACCAR   **BOSTON MUSEUM**

1931 MACCAR MODEL S6 3-TON TANKER   **NAHC**

By 1930, Maccar introduced six-wheel trucks, which primarily used Hendrickson tandem axles. From that year on, no four-cylinder engines were used. For 1931, Maccar introduced two heavy-duty high-speed models rated at 4 ton and 5 ton distinctive with four-piece radiators. They had air brakes and were powered by six-cylinder engines. An experimental 15-ton six-wheel truck was built using a six-cylinder Sterling Petrel engine and Maccar built its own tandem bogie for this single example.

By 1933, the model lineup consisted of the 2-ton Model 100 with a Buda H-260 engine, the 4-ton Model 40A with a Buda H-298 engine, the 5-ton Model 180 with a Buda K-393 engine, the 6-ton Model 60A with a Buda BA-6 engine, the 6-ton Model 66A with a Hercules YXC3 engine, the 6-ton Model 220W with a Waukesha 6SRK engine and the 8-ton Model 86A with the same engine as the previous truck. Chassis prices ranged from $1,330 to $5,950. Horizontal side hood louvers spaced diagonally were the distinctive look of the later Maccar trucks.

The Depression finally sunk the joint venture of Hahn, Maccar and Selden in 1935. Hahn continued on its own after reorganization.

MCCREA see CHAMPION

MACDONALD 1920-1952 — MacDonald trucks were built by the MacDonald Truck and Tractor Company in San Francisco, California. There were essentially two models: the front-wheel-drive Model O, which was rated at 5 tons, and the Model AB, which was rated at 7-1/2 tons. Both used four-cylinder Buda engines. The Brown-Lipe transmission was coupled directly to the differential through a single rubber-bonded fiber coupling. Whitney roller chains transferred power to planetary drives in the front wheels.

The massive front axle had two transverse, centrally-pivoted springs. Hydraulic band brakes applied stopping power to the front wheels, while secondary brake bands were applied to the differential. There were no brakes or springs at the rear axle. A large hydraulic pump mounted on the right side of the engine provided power steering. There was no direct link between the front wheels and the steering column. The frame was made of structural steel and dropped to a 16-1/2-inch floor height behind the cab for dock use on the San Francisco waterfront. The low flat beds with usually with stake sides were eight feet square. The Model O had 40x12 front and 40x14 rear solid rubber tires. The rear axles were of a crank-type design to provide the low platform height. A vertical windlass (capstan) was mounted on the front left corner of the truck bed. It was chain driven from a power takeoff on the transmission and was used for loading large heavy objects.

The low beds were essential at a time when most products were unloaded by manual labor. Such things as cement, flour and paper as well as plate glass were hauled from dockside to warehouse by MacDonald trucks into the 1950s. However, production of MacDonald, which was taken over by Peterbilt after World War II, was sporadic. A combination Diamond T and MacDonald lowbed stake was built in 1942. The powerplant and cab front section were built by Diamond T and the rear bed, frame and crank axle were built by MacDonald. For 1948, production output was a total of four trucks. For 1949, it was two trucks. The company was listed as being open for business until 1952, but production for the last three years has not been substantiated.

1923 MACDONALD   **RNE**

1907 MACK 7-TON DUMP TRUCK   **MACK**

MACK 1901 to date — Five Mack brothers were the founders of the Mack Brothers Company in Brooklyn, New York. They had a successful wagon-building enterprise by the turn of the century and in 1901 they built their first motor vehicle -- a 1-ton 15-passenger sightseeing bus (20 passenger seating possible) powered by a 24 hp four-cylinder horizontally-opposed engine, which was replaced by a 36 hp vertical four-cylinder engine built by the Mack brothers. The successful operation of the bus in New York led to another order in 1903.

1909 MACK 5-TON   **OCW**

In 1905, the bus-building business was moved from New York to Allentown, Pennsylvania. After the move, production had reached 51 vehicles for the year, most of them being the "Manhattan" bus, but trucks were also being built. Two delivery style trucks were built using bus chassis, and these were rated at 1-1/2-ton and 2-ton capacity, respectively. In a short time, a 5-ton truck was also built. These were powered by a 50 hp Mack engine and used a constant-mesh selective gear transmission designed by Gus Mack. The engines remained in production until 1915. For 1905, Mack advertised an automatic starter consisting of a spring "which imparts a number of revolutions to the engine without relieving the compression. The engine re-energizes the spring and disconnects it, ready for use."

1910 MACK 4-TON TANKER   **TEX**

The company built 1-, 1-1/2- and 2-ton trucks powered by a 32 hp engine, and these became the Mack Junior series along with Mack Senior trucks, differing not only in that they were light- and heavy-duty (from 1-1/2-ton to 5-ton), but also in that Mack Juniors were left-hand drive and Mack Seniors were right-hand drive. The Mack Senior trucks were soon uprated to 7-1/2-ton capacity. In 1910, the company adopted the bulldog crest trademark, which has been used to date.

By 1911, the Mack Brothers Company was employing 700 people and a newly acquired engine plant in New Jersey employed an additional 75 people. By that time, the youngest brother, Joseph, who had a silk mill in Allentown, had joined the company and become treasurer. The "Manhattan" bus was not only sold in New York but as far away as New Orleans and Havana, Cuba. After 1911, factory output reached approximately 600 units per year.

As production increased, expansion became necessary. In 1911, Mack joined with the Saurer Motor Company, which held a license to build Swiss Saurer trucks in the United States. Under the financial holding company called International Motor Company (IMC) both Saurer and Mack continued separate manufacturing. The heavy Mack trucks from 3 ton to 5 ton were forward-control design only until 1908, when the company introduced conventional design trucks up to 5-ton capacity. The holding company was backed by J.P. Morgan and Company, and sales of the two truck builders were combined. By March of 1912, Hewitt trucks also joined the International Motor Company and although manufacturing continued separately, sales and marketing were all under "one roof," with all three makes carried in the same advertisements.

Mack built buses and trucks, and also introduced fire engines. However, after the involvement with IMC the Mack brothers all left with the exception of Willie, who retired from Mack in the 1920s but not before starting his own company in 1916 by the name of Metropolitan Motors Incorporated, which built light trucks called Mackbilt. Gus and Joseph left the motor vehicle business while Jack Mack formed Mac-Carr, which later became Maccar, building trucks until 1935. Jack Mack was killed in 1924 when his car was hit by a trolley.

1917 MACK BULLDOG TANK CARRIER   GTC

By acquiring the Hewitt Motor Company, IMC also acquired the engineering talents of Edward R. Hewitt and Alfred F. Masury. Edward Hewitt designed the Mack AB, which was built from 1914 until 1936. Alfred Masury designed the Mack AC "Bulldog." It was he who created the Bulldog hood ornament that would be mounted on every Mack truck after 1932.

IMC began having serious competition in 1913 from Packard and General Motors and it was during this time of financial uncertainty that Joseph and Jack Mack left the company. The International Motor Truck Corporation was formed, which absorbed the earlier IMC and dropped the Hewitt truck line. A total of 98 Model S Mack trucks were built at that time, and a prototype of the Model T Mack, before production was concentrated on the AB and AC models.

The AB replaced the Junior line of Mack trucks, although Junior models were built until 1916 in 1-, 1-1/2- and 2-ton versions. The AB model was powered by a 30 hp four-cylinder engine. The AB also had a worm-drive rear axle, new for Mack trucks, which were exclusively chain driven until then. In the beginning, the AB model used a Brown-Lipe transmission, Timken axles and Gemmer steering but after 1915, these components were all built by Mack.

1920 MACK BOTTLER'S TRUCK   A&A

1924 MACK MODEL AC BULLDOG   OCW

In 1919, International Motor Corporation dropped Saurer as well. The following year, the AB trucks' worm-drive axles were succeeded by Hotchkiss-type double reduction axles, with chain-drive remaining as an option. Because of some confusion between International Motor and International Harvester, the company directors voted to change the name to Mack Trucks Incorporated in March of 1922. That year, R.D. Hatch of San Francisco, California, built a refrigeration unit on a Mack truck, achieved by evaporating anhydrous ammonia. Coiled pipe, which was insulated with ground cork and paper, lined the body of the truck.

The AB Mack was used as the basis for fire engines and in 1921, an AB bus chassis was introduced. The AB engine's cylinders were cast enbloc and side-valve design was used. The crankcase had large inspection ports to view the condition of the connecting rod bearings. This utilitarian feature was also used on the AC Mack. The 30 hp engine would later be rated at twice that, although early Mack trucks with solid rubber tires were governed to a top speed of 16 mph. Electric starting and lights were available in 1921 on the AB model.

1926 MACK SCHOOL BUS   OCW

A larger radiator was adopted in 1923, changing the appearance of the AB model slightly as the fin-and-tube radiator stood taller than the hood. The AB bus chassis was changed to a drop-frame design in 1924 and for it specifically, pneumatic tires were adopted.

The AC Mack was introduced in 1916 in 3-1/2-, 5- and 7-1/2-ton versions. This model was powered by a 75 hp engine that was actually smaller than the Mack Senior engine but was more powerful. The AC models used a pressed steel frame as did the lighter Macks after 1909. The AC was most recognizable for its sloping hood due to the radiator being mounted behind the engine against the firewall/dashboard. All AC Macks had chain drive as standard equipment until the end of their production in 1938. The similar-looking AK model used shaft drive and was built from 1927 until 1936.

The sloping hood was also used on the AC six-wheel trucks, as well as on the six-cylinder AP models, the latter which were built as four-wheel and six-wheel versions. The four-wheel had a capacity of 7-1/2 tons as a four-wheeler, 10 tons as a six-wheeler and 15 tons as a six-wheel articulated truck.

In 1928, Mack began production of the 1-1/2-ton BB model, which survived only until 1932. In 1930, the "Baby Mack" name of the AB was transferred to the 1-ton BL model, which was the first light-duty chassis since 1918 for the company. The six-cylinder AB became known as the BG and was continued six more years until 1936. The AB Mack surpassed the AC in sales with a total of 51,613 units plus 3,813 AB buses and six AB railcars.

1930 MACK TANDEM AXLE BULLDOG　　　　　　　　　　**TEX**

The sloping hood of the AC Macks with the radiator being behind the engine was explained as a precaution to radiator damage, which could occur by accident or by the "carelessness" of teamsters who considered motorized transportation as the death knell to their horsedrawn business. There were other advantages such as motor accessibility and steering gear configuration improvement. The British ordered 150 5-ton AC Macks, and after being put through rigorous testing in the field, they nicknamed them "Bulldog" Macks as an endearing term, which to the English has represented toughness.

The AC "Bulldog" used pressed chrome-nickel steel frame channels that were heat treated for durability. Aluminum was used for the radiator tank, transfer case, timing cover and engine crankcase. The pair-cast cylinders were also heat-treated, and the compacting of the metal resulted in longer life for the engine. Gray cast iron used for pistons was also heat-treated and crankshafts were case-hardened. Drop-forged alloy steel was used for the front axle, which was also specially designed to withstand rough terrain. A squirrel cage blower was used to cool the two-section radiator straddling the rear of the engine, another Mack specialty. All in all, the AC Mack had 18 patents covering its various innovations.

The AK Model, similar in appearance, was produced beginning in late 1927. Almost all AK Macks had shaft drive and a dual reduction differential. Most AK trucks wore pneumatic tires after 1929 and had four-wheel brakes. The AK engine was a mono-bloc, unlike the cast-in-pairs unit in the AC. The AK engine was rated at 70 hp, which was four less hp than the AC engine of the mid-1920s. The early AK engine also featured an aluminum cylinder head. However, due to problems with this engine, another was developed for the AC model and the mono-bloc AC/AK engine was offered in 1929 with thick aluminum cylinder heads that led to the nickname "high hat."

The AK, fitted with a four-speed transmission, was intended as a medium-duty highway truck with load capacity up to 5 tons. In 1931, that capacity was raised to 8 tons. To offset increased speeds, Mack added vacuum-boosted mechanical brakes. The AK Mack was used more often in urban areas where its tighter turning radius was an advantage, along with other features such as rubber shock absorber cab supports and spring brackets, and a covered cab fitted with a one- or two-piece windshield.

Mack introduced a six-cylinder engine in its AC models and soon thereafter, offered it in the AK, which became known as the AK-6. Unveiled in 1931, the Depression reduced sales of this truck

drastically. A total of 2,819 AK trucks were built by Mack. Mack's first six-cylinder engine, called the AH and built under chief engineer A.F. Masury, was developed in 1923. It was rated at 120 hp but was too expensive to produce in number. Another smaller six-cylinder engine called the AJ was built in 1924. It was rated at 100 hp and was mounted in the Greatcoach, an experimental six-wheel bus. It was also unsatisfactory for trucks because of its long stroke and low speed. In 1926, yet another smaller 97 hp six-cylinder engine called the AL was developed and found application in buses and fire engines. The six-cylinder vehicles looked similar to the AC model but had 13 side louvers instead of the usual 10.

With the requirements for higher speeds and heavier loads, Mack continued development of six-cylinder engines and late in 1926, the AP engine was completed. It was rated at 150 hp, which was nearly twice the power of the four-cylinder AC engine. The first AP model was rated at 7-1/2-ton capacity and could carry such a load at 30 mph. Mack also introduced a six-wheel version capable of carrying 10 tons. These were similar to the AC in that they used the sloping hood and chain drive.

A thicker radiator and longer hood distinguished the AP from the AC, but this difference was further complicated by the introduction of a six-cylinder AC in 1931, which used the BK six-cylinder engine until 1932, when it was adopted to both the AC and AP. The AC-6 used the longer AP-6 hood while the AP-4 used the shorter AC hood. The first six-wheel AP trucks used a nonpowered bogie rear axle. By 1931, Mack developed the Power Divider differential that drove both axles.

The Power Divider was located between the front and rear jackshafts and allowed one set of drive wheels to turn faster or slower than the other. The distance-compensating feature also supplied power to the wheels that had the most traction rather than the least. The result was a truck with driving power to all rear wheels, while providing maximum traction over difficult terrain. Six-wheel AC and AP Mack trucks were used extensively in the construction of the Hoover Dam, one of the largest construction projects in the world.

Mack developed the B series in 1928 to answer the demand for long distance high-speed trucking. The first B model was the BJ, which had a maximum load capacity of 4 tons, which would later be uprated to twice that in 1931. Also in 1928, the light-duty fast delivery BB model was introduced. It was powered by the same 57 hp four-cylinder engine used in the AB model Mack. The BB has been credited as the first truck model to be fitted with a hypoid rear differential in contrast to most light-duty trucks then, which usually used worm-drive.

Styling of the BB was at first boxy, with the cab sitting high and using a two-piece windshield. As the next decade progressed, the enclosed BB cab became lower and more modern in appearance, resembling the International A line. The spartan enclosed cabs were an improvement over open cabs, although only the deluxe cab offered any insulation. The BB was nicknamed "Baby Brother."

A heavier version of the BB was built and dubbed the BC. It had a larger engine modestly rated at 60 hp, which had a higher 85 hp output at 2000 rpm. The BC trucks had a dual reduction rear axle and were fitted with either a C-cab or the enclosed cab of the BB model. They could be ordered with a 154-inch or 172-inch wheelbase and like the BB model, used a four-speed transmission.

In 1932, the BF series began to be produced and these also had a maximum load capacity of 4 tons. The six-cylinder BF was advertised for fast, economical highway service. The same engine was used in the BG Mack, but the BF had the same hypoid rear end as the BB model. The BF was available with a 156-inch or 174-inch wheelbase, with 192-inch and 210-inch wheelbase on special order. This series could also be fitted with a five-speed transmission.

The BB model was replaced by the BG Mack. It had a more powerful 70 hp six-cylinder engine and was rated at 1-1/2-ton capacity. It was intended for fast delivery work and could be fitted with platform, panel or other special bodies. Wheelbase of the BG was either 156-inch or 168-inch. A BG truck tractor was also produced.

For 1932, Mack introduced three more models: the BM, BQ and BX. The BQ and BX were the heavy-duty versions of the B series. The largest was the BQ with up to 8-ton capacity and was powered

1932 MACK MODEL AP 15-TON NAHC

1933 MACK MODEL BJ OCW

1934 MACK MODEL BC TANKERS TEX

1936 MACK 20MB MACK JR. KP

1938 MACK MODEL AB A&A

1936 MACK 20MB MACK JR. KP

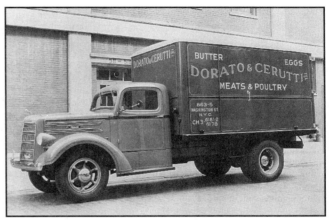

1939 MACK MODEL EF VAN A&A

1939 MACK MODEL EF VAN A&A

1949 MACK MODEL EH TRACTOR-TRAILER OCW

by a 128 hp six-cylinder engine and dual reduction rear axle. Wheelbase was either 157-inch or 181-inch. The four-speed transmission was placed amidships. Advertising called it the "heavy-duty highway freighter and long distance high-safe-speed-schedule-clipper." The BQ was capable of 40 mph with a full load, or it could be fitted with chain drive for construction and mining applications.

The BX had shaft or chain drive and a GVW rating of 36,000 pounds and 40,000 pounds, respectively. The BX was powered by a 105 hp six-cylinder engine and had vacuum-boosted brakes. It was used for long distance hauling and also as a dump truck. The BX Mack was distinguished by door ventilators in the hood, and the front axle was set back, which helped with weight distribution. This model could be bought with a C-cab for off-road work or with the Mack enclosed "coupe" cab. For heavier work, the 117 hp six-cylinder CF engine was also available, as was the Power Divider (which replaced the Krohn Compensator) for the six-wheel version of the BX Mack.

Truck tractors with semi-trailers were built shortly after World War I, but this type of design was slow in its development as heavy loads over long distances were still handled by railroads and so-called speed trucks were generally light-duty. As paved roads became more widespread, the use of pneumatic tires and six-cylinder engines provided trucks with the ability to haul heavier loads over longer distances, effectively creating some competition between rail and truck transportation. The early Mack truck tractors were modified AB and AC chassis, but these were quite slow. Beginning in the 1930s, Mack built semi-trailer tractors in the BG, BF, BC, BM, BX and BQ series.

Cab-over-engine design was adopted by Mack as early as 1933, with the "Traffic Type" trucks first designated as the CH and CJ models. The CH had a 5-ton maximum load capacity, while the CJ had a maximum 6-ton capacity. The CH engine was rated at 107 hp while the CJ truck had an engine rated at 117 hp. Both used updraft carburetors to limit the height of the engine. The early C line was described as being "pug-nosed" while beginning in 1936, a flat-nosed Traffic Type was introduced with doors hinged at the rear. These had engines removable on a sliding platform.

Mack suffered from dismal sales figures in the early 1930s, just as other companies did. In order to broaden its appeal, Mack struck a deal with Reo in October of 1934 to rebadge and slightly restyle Reo's light- and medium-duty trucks and sell them as Mack Juniors. The Mack Junior appeared in 1936. These trucks' grilles were slightly different from the Reos' as a distinguishing feature. There were basically four models of the Mack Junior: the 1/2 ton was designated as the 1M, the 1-1/2 ton 10M, the 2 ton 20M and a 3 ton 30M. A COE version of the latter was also available and was called the 30MT, the "T" designating "Traffic," which was a reference to the short length of the more maneuverable forward-control truck.

For 1937, Mack added the 2M Mack Junior, which was a rebadged Reo Speed Delivery truck. It was available with a four-cylinder or six-cylinder engine, just as the Reo version would be, and could have a wheelbase of 114 inches or 120 inches. The two engine and two wheelbase options created four versions of this truck: 2M4A, 2M4B, 2M6A and 2M6B, respectively. Each of these could be ordered as a 1/2-ton or 3/4-ton truck, the latter having a heavier-duty rear axle, larger tires and the suffix "S" in its designation. Overall, few Mack Junior pickups were sold but across the full line, sales improved to just over 4,000 in 1936, which was the first time that number had been reached since 1930.

Mack began building its ED Series trucks, and this line overlapped with the Reo-built Juniors. The ED trucks were powered by a 67 hp L-head six-cylinder engine, which was also built by Continental. These light-duty Mack trucks were engineered and styled after the heavier-duty E series. They were available with a 120-1/2-inch wheelbase or with a 136-1/2-inch wheelbase with the Special model.

The standard ED Model did not have chrome, and the stripped chassis was priced at $675. From there, several different commercial vehicles could be built, including a cab-over "retailer" that resembled International's Metro, a standard delivery truck, a pickup and a variety of utility body iterations along with the pickup cab.

The ED was built through 1944, although during World War II these were in the form of fire engine pumpers. Production of the ED never exceeded 750 in one year. For its first year of production

in 1936, only a few were built and even two years later, a total of 152 were produced. The largest production was in 1941, with 707 units built. A Traffic Type "cabover" E model was also built with dual rear tires and these were designated as EC and EB. They were similar to the Mack C Series Traffic Type but were lighter-duty.

Starting in 1936, a heavier EH model was also introduced. This model was powered by the six-cylinder EN310 engine formerly used in the BG model. Its GVW rating was 18,000 pounds or 19,500 pounds, depending on equipment. The E line also included the EE model with GVW rating of 12,000 pounds and the EF model with GVW rating of 14,000 pounds.

All conventional E type Mack trucks shared the same cab, which had a one-piece windshield distinguished from the two-piece Mack Junior line. The fenders were high-crowned cycle style in design and looked similar to those on the heavier E series trucks. More importantly, the E line Macks had hydraulic brakes, used the "Archemoid" steering mechanism and were fitted with five-speed or 10-speed monoshift transmissions.

In 1937, the E line was expanded with the EG, EJ, EH and EM series, the latter being the heftiest of the group with a GVW rating of 23,000 pounds. Also that year, the superduty F series was started, which was the replacement for the heavy AC and AP models. The F series trucks used the BG radiator, C-cabs and chain drive. By 1938, the F series consisted of the FG with GVW of 35,000 pounds, FJ with 45,000-pound GVW and FK with 50,000-pound GVW. There were also two special permit trucks: the FC 6, which could pull trailers with 50-ton load capacity and the FCSW (SW meaning six-wheel) for 30-ton trailer hauling. The F series used chain drive and in 1941, the FP model replaced the ER and ES model. Mack offered its own diesel engine as well as Buda and Cummins diesel powerplants. Some Mack engines shared blocks for both gasoline and diesel use, with "EN" as an engine number prefix for the former and "END" as a prefix for diesel.

Also, a new cab-over E Series was introduced with the engine slightly ahead of the seats to reduce the size of the "doghouse." The cab-over E trucks were also distinguishable with the E style grille and bulldog ornament. The stub-nosed cab-over-engine E line was available in six models: the EEU and EHU with a GVW rating of 12,000 pounds, and EFU and EMU, rated at 14,000-pound GVW, and the EGU and EQU, both rated at 16,000-pound GVW. Engine sizes distinguished these models besides load rating and prices ranged from $3,600 to $5,150 for the heaviest. Midyear, Mack also added the EQ cab-over truck with a GVW rating of 23,400 pounds and the AB truck, built since 1914, was replaced by the ER Model.

In 1938, the EM and ES were added to the range of Macks, the latter having the same specifications as the EQ but using chain drive. Also that year, the agreement with Reo was ended and Mack Junior trucks were no longer produced. Mack also built truck tractors in the E Series and these were designated with the letter "T." Depending on the load rating they were called EFT, EHT and EMT, each fitted with a five-speed transmission and different size engines. Mack began building its heavy L series in 1940.

Meanwhile, Mack was building buses. In 1926, the AL model was powered by a six-cylinder engine. This line was replaced by the BK buses that had a more powerful six-cylinder engine and used air brakes. Front engine buses were replaced in 1934 with a new series of streamlined rear-engine buses. These had their engines mounted transversely and were small enough to use a right-angle drive design. About 7,000 were sold over 10 years, the largest fleets being in Buffalo, Philadelphia, Portland and St. Louis. Between 1935 and 1943, two sizes of trolley buses were also built. Starting in 1938, Mack began building diesel engines using the Lanova precombustion chamber design. Also beginning in 1938, school bus chassis based on the E Series were available.

As World War II started in Europe, the U.S. military ordered 368 trucks, most of which were the EEU "cabover" type, and the contract also included 80 EE models fitted with dump beds. French and British forces ordered several hundred EXBX tank transporters and NR4 trucks in 1939 and 1940. The British also ordered hundreds of EH, EHT, EHU and EHUT trucks. In 1944, the U.S. Army ordered an additional 700 COE 4x4 Model NJU 6-ton trucks, which were essentially the same as the earlier Traffic Type discontinued in 1941.

1944 MACK FIRE ENGINE   **MACK**

Mack also produced 26,000 NO and NR trucks between 1940 and 1945, the former 6x6 primarily being used to haul the 155mm Long Tom field guns. Mack factories in Allentown built the Vultee naval torpedo bombers and in Brunswick, New Jersey, tank power trains were produced. Fire engines were built on Brockway and Kenworth chassis and an experimental double-ended tank transporter was built, but only as a prototype.

1950 MACK MODEL LJ   **HAROLD DAY**

After World War II, the light E Series Mack trucks were no longer produced and the CH and CJ cab-over were reintroduced. The lightest Mack truck in 1947 was the EE with a GVW rating of 12,000 pounds. The E series were discontinued in 1950, along with COE Macks. The A series superseded the E series and in 1951, bowing to demand for cab-over-engine-type trucks, Mack reissued its EFU snub-nose as the A20U, which remained in production for just two years. Mack also built E series chassis for use as fire apparatus as well as for buses. A total of 53 EH and 38 EJ buses

were built. The small number reflected the higher price of Mack quality construction, which was not a priority among cost-conscious community-based buyers.

Just before the series was discontinued Mack used the E model to reintroduce diesel engines. To publicize its medium-duty diesel power, Mack set up a specially-painted EH tractor to lead a diesel caravan that carried a 672 diesel engine on display. Within a year, Mack eliminated all trucks under 17,000-pound GVW. The EF was continued into 1951, but at that point the E series was finally finished. The heavier L series trucks were continued into the 1950s, and some special models into the 1960s.

1953 MACK MODEL LN TANDEM AXLE TRACTOR   **OCW**

Mack did not build any L series trucks during World War II, but between 1940 and 1953 a total of 12,453 LF, LFT and LFSW Macks were built. These were usually powered by overhead-valve six-cylinder Thermodyne engines and the most common choice was the EN 510 engine rated at 160 hp. Both five-speed and 10-speed duplex transmissions were available.

Mack also built heavier versions in the L line, notably the LJ and LM, and the truck tractor versions called LJT and LMT. END405, 519 and 605 diesel engines were offered with the heavier L line. The LM included a heavy off-road dump truck called the LMSW-M. The tractor version had a GVW rating of 100,000 pounds.

Another even heftier model was the six-wheel LRSW with 115,000-pound GVW or 180,000-pound GCW. It featured Mack's Planidrive system, which superseded chain drive. In 1947, the LTSW was introduced to haul full and semi-trailers. For the West Coast, this truck, called the LTLSW (L for light), was modified with weight saving materials cutting out over a ton of bulk for additional payload capability. The heaviest L series trucks were the LV and LY, which were continued into the 1960s. A special LRVSW off-highway version built in the 1950s had a load capacity of 34 tons. Mack continued to build complete fire trucks, such as the Type 75 powered by Mack's own ENF510A gasoline engine.

In 1950, Mack unveiled its A series while celebrating its 50th anniversary. Three years later, the B series appeared. These were Mack's medium-duty trucks at first, consisting of four models: the A-20 rated at 17,000-pound GVW (replacing the EF), A-30 rated at 21,000-pound GVW (replacing the EG), A-40 rated at 24,000-pound GVW (replacing the EH) and A-50 rated at up to 45,000-pound GVW (replacing the EQ). During the advent of the B series, the A line was also expanded. By 1952, Mack offered the A-54T and A-51T diesel as well as the A-54S six-wheeler. Initially three six-cylinder Mack Magnadyne L-head engines were offered. The 158 hp overhead-valve Thermodyne gasoline engine was also available, as was the END 510 diesel engine with its Lanova-licensed combustion chamber.

To fill the market demand for lighter COE trucks, the A-20U and the A-52U were introduced in 1951, but neither sold well. The L series was often used to build aesthetically acclaimed fire trucks in the early 1950s. In the spring of 1953, the B series was introduced and this line was completely restyled and re-engineered. The B series was an outgrowth of an engineering study made in 1948 called the M8. The tall vertical grille, wide fenders and "frenched" headlights were all derived from this earlier study. The B line consisted of a wide range of models starting with the B-20, rated at 17,000-pound GVW and powered by the 290 Magnadyne engine and the B-30 with a 21,000-pound GVW, which was also available as the B-30T truck tractor. The most common of this series was the B-42, which was also built as the B-42SW six-wheel semi-trailer tractor. This truck's standard engine was the EN 401 Magnadyne and several five-speed and 10-speed duplex transmissions were available.

The year 1956 was marked by the introduction of the B-53 Model, which was powered by the END 673 engine. Also that year, Mack acquired Beck, the fire apparatus manufacturer and continued building pumpers, ladder trucks and articulated fire engines with either open or closed cabs and with optional automatic transmissions. The B line of trucks was expanded that year and included the B-72, B-73 and B-75 models, which replaced the LTL and LTLSW models.

Within three years the market for Mack trucks not only increased but changed its preference in fuels by opting for diesel engines in a ratio of 3:1. Mack also developed the 15-speed Triplex and 20-speed Quadraplex transmissions during the late 1950s. In 1956, Mack debuted its B-70 and B-80 series of Super-Duty trucks, which were intended as replacements for the LJ and LM models. These trucks exceeded 60,000-pound GVW.

1957 MACK MODEL H-63 TRUCK TRACTOR   OCW

1957 MACK MV-620-D BUS   RD

The B series was built for 13 years and amounted to a total of 127,000 trucks in that series. During production of the B series, Mack built many specialized trucks that can be grouped in the order in which they were built under the letter designations H, D, N, G, MB, F and C. Most of these were the cab-over-engine design, including the first H series that came out in 1953, which was nicknamed "cherry picker" because of its high cab. This cab was redesigned for 1954.

The D series was built in five sizes: D-20, D-30, D-42 P, D-40 and D-42. GVW ratings were from 20,000 pounds for the smaller delivery style trucks to 53,000 pounds GVW for the large tractor-trailer combinations. In 1958, the D line was replaced by the N

line, which used Budd built cabs that were nearly identical to the Ford C class cabs. The elevating mechanism of the D cabs was abandoned and the N cabs tilted forward instead. The N series of trucks, from N-42 to N-61, had a GVW rating from 28,000 pounds to 65,000 pounds.

In 1962, Mack discontinued the N series, replacing it with the MB line of trucks. Mack also began production of its END 864 V-8 diesel engine. This powerplant was used often in the largest vehicles. Most MB trucks used the 140 hp six-cylinder END 475 engine, which was built by Scania-Vabis. Mack also offered gasoline Chrysler hemi-head V-8 engines rated up to 189 hp.

1960 MACK P2 DIESEL TANDEM   OCW

The G series was a line of trucks composed of short tractors that were introduced in 1959. These had BBC dimensions of 51 inches and with a sleeper cab this dimension was 80 inches. The G truck tractors were available with Cummins or Mack diesel engines, both turbocharged and normally aspirated. Despite a modern appearance and engineering, less than 2,000 G series Macks were sold in three years of production. They were replaced in 1962 with the successful F series, which had a 50-inch BBC dimension and with a standard sleeper cab that dimension was only 70 inches. The F series featured a modern look, upgraded cab interior and a wide range of diesel engines. The C series Mack used existing parts and cab sheet metal from the B series to create a truck tractor with a BBC dimension of 89 inches. The C series was built for only two years, being replaced by the U series.

1965 MACK MODEL R TRACTOR-TRAILER   OCW

In 1966, Mack opened its West Coast plant in Hayward, California, where RL conventional and FL cab-over trucks were built for western operators. The R line had entered production a year earlier and the B line was phased out in 1966. The R line has consisted of the R-400, R-600 and R-700. The early R models had engines from 140 hp to 255 hp. Mack developed its Maxidyne engine in 1966. This was a "constant horsepower" engine that provided from 206 hp to 237 hp between 1200 rpm to its maximum governed 2100 rpm.

In 1970, Mack began building a larger version of the Maxidyne diesel with 325 hp. Another set of trucks that was built by Mack was the U series, which were easily identifiable by the 11-inch right-hand-offset cab. This design was intended for better visibility. With a BBC dimension of 90 inches, the U series replaced the C series. By combining the features of the R and U trucks, Mack created the DM model, which stood for Dumper/Mixer. The R, U and DM series trucks have been continued in production to date.

1979 MACK CRUISELINER TRACTOR-TRAILER   OCW

By 1975, Mack began building the COE highway tractor Cruiseliner whose cabs measured 54-inch to 90-inch BBC. There were 31 engine options for the Cruiseliner from a 235 hp Mack six-cylinder to a 430 hp Detroit Diesel V-8. Engines for the late 1970s R and U models consisted of Cummins, Detroit Diesel, Mack and Mack-Scania units. For the western conventional RL and RS models Caterpillar engines were also available. Mack also built the HMM 8x6 front-discharge concrete mixer truck with a Mack Maxidyne six-cylinder engine, and the M series off-highway dump trucks with load capacity up to 120 tons using an articulated bottom dump trailer. These had engines up to 800 hp as with the Detroit Diesel 16V71TI V-16.

By the mid-1980s, Mack continued to build the heavy-duty DM Series at its Macungie, Pennsylvania, factory. The DM was built as a 6x4 and also as a 6x6 known as the DMM. The DM800 was powered by a 400 hp Mack EM9-400 V-8 diesel engine and used a Mack Maxitorque 6F 1R transmission. In Canada, production also continued for the 8x6 DMM 6006EX. Additional tag axles produced DM Series trucks with up to five axles. The latter was sometimes used with a six-axle trailer known as the Michigan centipede where restrictions have existed on maximum weight per axle. Cummins Formula 350 and Caterpillar 3208 and 3406 were also available.

At the same time, the Mack Midliner series was also built for the United States, but these were essentially rebadged Renault G models. They were powered by the turbocharged 175 hp Renault 175200P or the 210 hp 175300P six-cylinder diesel engine. Transmission was a Spicer 5052A 5F 1R all-synchromesh for the MS200P or a Renault transmission with the MS300 engines. Rear axle was a Renault single reduction hypoid type. The truck was available in four wheelbases plus a tractor version.

Another set of trucks for the 1980s was the DM Series. The largest was the DM800 offered with many engine options including six Caterpillar units from 300 hp to 380 hp, five Cummins units from 350 hp to 450 hp and six Mack diesel units from 237 hp to 400 hp. The most common heavy-duty transmission was the Fuller

RTO-14613 14F 1R and rear axle was the Mack SW80 double reduction. The DM was built in several versions including as straight truck, dump truck, concrete mixer, refuse hauler or as a tractor for hauling low-bed trailers with up to 10 axles and 40 wheels.

1983 MACK MODEL MH ULTRALINER COE   KP

In 1984, Mack ceased production of all fire apparatus, although the company has continued to offer chassis to other fire apparatus builders. Mack was the only company in recent years to build fire engines using its own engines and major chassis components, but this was not a profitable business by the 1980s. The last Mack fire engine was a CF custom pumper delivered to the city of Westbury, New York, in August of 1984. It was powered by a Mack diesel, had a 600-gallon tank and was fitted with a 1,500 gpm pump.

1986 MACK MS250P MIDLINER   OCW

Mack became a division of Renault (Renault had acquired 20 percent of Mack stock in 1979) and also continued production with the CH and CL series trucks to date. These trucks have been aerodynamic in appearance and have been offered with various diesel engines both in six-cylinder and V-8 form with the most powerful engine being the 500 hp Mack E9 engine. Transmissions have featured triple countershaft overdrive. The Renault SA company of France and AB Volvo of Sweden merged in 1993.

1992 MACK DM600 SERIES CONCRETE MIXER MACK

1993 MACK FDM SERIES W/BULLDOG 500 BARREL MACK

By 1995, many of the models had vehicle management and control (VMAC) electronics and the complete model lines consisted of the CH 602, CH 603, CL 602, CL 603, CL 703, DM600X, DM600S, DM600SX, DMM6006S, DM6006EX, MR600P, MR600S, RB600S, RB600SX, RD600P, RD600S, RD600SX, RD600S Western Contractor, RD800SX, CS200P, CS250P, CS300P, CS300T, MS200P, MS250P, MS300P and MS300T. The shortest BBC dimension is 63 inches for the MR600P and MR600S. Available engines were designated as EM7-300 V-MAC, EM7-300, E3-190 and E3-220. GVW ratings ranged from 26,000 pounds for the CS200P to a maximum of 103,000 pounds for the RD800SX.

1995 MACK CH613 SERIES (LEFT) MACK
AND CL613 SERIES (RIGHT)

For 1996, Mack introduced its V-MAC II second generation electronic engine control system. This was described as a network of sensors and actuators in conjunction with a PC-compatible hardware and software system that was adopted to the Mack E7 12-liter displacement engine. The second generation electronics included a sophisticated data log and trip recorder, field programmable flash memory, an on-off fan control, variable end regulation, accessory bus relay control, engine brake/cruise interfacing, fuel control, minimum/maximum governor control, low idle adjust, timing control, engine protection shutdown, course control, engine speed control, speed limiting, torque limiting, limp home capability, self diagnosis, fault logging, diagnostic clamp, serial data link and an enhanced tamper resistant program.

MACKBILT 1917 — William C. Mack, one of the Mack brothers of Mack truck fame, founded Metropolitan Motors Incorporated, which was located in New York City. A 3/4-ton model was designed and one single chassis with a wheelbase of 115 inches was fabricated. It was powered by a four-cylinder Buda engine and had pneumatic tires. Only one prototype was built in the Bronx shop before Willie Mack gave up the idea.

MADSEN 1948-1973 — Madsen built numerous chassis on a custom order basis. Vehicles included buses, fire engines and refuse haulers. Buses were two-axle and three-axle and the buyer had the full choice of engine locations: front, amidship or rear-mounted. Engine choices were Ford, Hall-Scott, International or White for gasoline-powered and Cummins, Detroit or Waukesha diesel units. Dual cabs were featured on the last Madsen trucks built after the Jay Madsen Equipment Company moved from Bath, New York, to Allentown, New York, in 1971, becoming the Jay Madsen Division of Air Springs Incorporated. This truck was designed for refuse hauling and its two cabs were seven feet ahead of the front axle with a Ford V-8 engine mounted between them. Production stopped entirely at the end of 1973.

1901 MAHONING CLOSED TOP DELIVERY VAN JAW

MAHONING 1904-1905 — The Mahoning Motor Car Company built a delivery car model priced at $950. It was powered by a 9 hp one-cylinder engine and had a wheelbase of 82 inches. The company's delivery car was one of four models of motor vehicle available. The company was located in Youngstown, Ohio. The company was a cooperation between W.P. Williamson, owner of the Youngstown Carriage & Wagon Company, and Charles T. Gaither, a mechanical engineer of the Fredonia. A man named Mahoning provided the capital, but the company soon closed after building only a few vehicles. Apparently, mechanical design problems plagued the vehicles from the beginning.

1914 MAIS COVERED FLAREBOARD   **OCW**

MAIS 1911-1916 — Albert F. Mais was vice-president and Charles A. Bookwalter was president of the Mais Motor Truck Company, which got its start in Peru, Indiana, and shortly thereafter moved to Indianapolis. The first Mais truck was powered by a 24 hp four-cylinder Model engine that was mounted under a short hood. It used a three-speed transmission and internal gear drive. Claims were made that this was the first American truck to use this type of drive. In 1912, the model range also included 1-1/2-, 2-1/2- and 5-ton capacity trucks. That year Mais built a high-speed ladder fire truck that featured what was claimed as the largest pneumatic tires at that time, 38x8 inches.

In 1913, a 1/2-ton and a 3-ton model were also added to the line. In 1916, the company was acquired by the Premier Motor Manufacturing Company of Indianapolis. Premier had been reorganized in 1915 under the leadership of F.W. Woodruff, an Illinois banker who kept the Premier Motor Car Company going until 1920 when other investors took over.

MAJESTIC CAB see LARRABEE

MANHATTAN see MACK

MANKATO see KATO

MANLY 1917-1920 — Beginning as the Manly Motor Corporation of Waukegan, Illinois, the company offered three models: the 1-1/2-ton Model 30, the 2-ton Model 40 and the 2-1/2-ton Model 50. In 1918, the company's name became O'Connell Manly Motor Corporation and the following year, it was reorganized as the O'Connell Manly Motor Truck Corporation. The three models were offered each year of production, which ended in 1920. The trucks were powered by four-cylinder Waukesha engines and used worm-drive rear axles. The heaviest of the trucks had a four-speed transmission. It appears that the Manly hydraulic transmission built in 1909 by Manly Drive, considered the first fluid transmission built in the United States, was designed by Manly Motor's founder.

MANSUR see SALVADOR

MARATHON 1912-1913 — The Marathon Motor Works began in Jackson and moved to Nashville, Tennessee, in 1910. By 1912, the company offered commercial vehicles along with the passenger car model line. A Light Delivery shared its chassis with the Runner Series of passenger cars, which had a wheelbase of 104 inches and were powered by a 25 hp four-cylinder engine. The company also briefly produced 1-1/2-, 3- and 5-ton trucks, which had larger four-cylinder engines and all used worm-drive rear axles. The Light Delivery model sold for $850 in 1913. Sales literature attempted to bring together the image of Nashville's recreation of the Greek Parthenon and the historic reference of the word Marathon in Olympiad history. Sales were dismal, nevertheless, and by the summer of 1914, the company declared bankruptcy. Herff-Brooks bought Marathon and built automobiles by that name in Indianapolis for two years.

MARATHON-LETOURNEAU see LETOURNEAU

MARKEY 1912 — The Markey Manufacturing Company of Mt. Clemens, Michigan, built a four-wheel-drive commercial car in 1912 that had a 3-ton capacity. Apart from the announcement made in 1912 in *Automobile Topics*, no other information has been available.

MARMON 1913-1915 — The Nordyke & Marmon Manufacturing Company, famous for its high quality passenger cars, went into the commercial vehicle market in 1913, although announcements to the press were made in 1912. The company was started by Howard C. Marmon about 10 years after he graduated from the University of California at Berkeley in mechanical engineering along with his brother Walter Marmon, who was also an engineer. The Nordyke & Marmon Manufacturing Company was a family business that produced flour milling machinery. Howard Marmon was highly interested in automobiles and built a few experimental ones starting in 1902. By 1905, automobile production output for the year was 25.

The Marmon Truck of 1913 was rated at 3/4-ton capacity and was powered by the same engine as the passenger car with a reduced stroke that also reduced the displacement from 318 to 251 cubic inches and horsepower from 32 to 25.6. The engines vertical drive from the camshaft to the oil pump was extended for the addition of a speed governor, which limited the truck to 20 mph. It appears that the Model 48 passenger car transaxle assembly was utilized. The passenger car chassis was reinforced with gussets and heavier gauge crossmembers, stiffer springs and stronger wheels and tires. Dual pneumatic tires were used in the rear mounted on wooden artillery wheels. A van body and an open delivery body were offered by the company. The stamped steel banjo rear axle housing with full-floating axle shafts and four-inch wide brake drums over internal brakes with S-cam actuation of roller-ended rigid brake shoes has been considered well ahead of its time in 1913. However, the company withdrew from the commercial vehicle market after 1915.

1914 MARMON PANEL   **OCW**

MARMON 1912-1916 — Howard C. Marmon, a graduate mechanical engineer from the University of California-Berkeley, worked for the Nordyke & Marmon Company of Indianapolis, Indiana. The firm manufactured flour milling machinery and Howard Marmon's father appointed him chief engineer. In 1902, Howard Marmon built his first experimental car using an overhead-valve V-2 engine and three-speed selective sliding gear transmission, both of his own design.

Having built a number of high quality passenger cars, Marmon introduced a 3/4-ton delivery car in 1912. It was based almost entirely on the Model 32 car, which had a 32 hp four-cylinder engine and 120-inch wheelbase. One difference was that the gasoline tank was removed from under the right seat to outside of the seat panel. The vehicle featured a transaxle, as did the passenger cars. The delivery car was built only for a few years, but Marmon passenger cars continued to be manufactured until 1933.

MARMON 1963 to date — Although listed alphabetically before Marmon-Herrington, Marmon has been the continuation of Marmon-Herrington when the truck division was sold to Adrian Roop and was set up as the Marmon Motor Company in Denton, Texas.

The following year a Marmon highway tractor was built in Denton. However, in order to secure further capital for manufacturing, the Marmon Motor Company was acquired by the Space Corporation, a military contractor with subsidiaries in the mobile home and forging industry. Marmon truck fabrication was moved to Garland, Texas (a suburb of Dallas), where Space had room for such facilities.

1975 MARMON HDT-BC-86 6X4 TRACTOR   MARMON

Compared to the first truck tractors built by Marmon-Herrington, the Marmon had a more conventional roof line and dual headlights. Steel and aluminum cabs were offered. The 220 hp Cummins NH-220 was available as was the Caterpillar 673 engine. The two-axle model was rated at 34,000-pound GVW and 66,000-pound GCW and the three-axle model was rated at 45,000-pound GVW and 76,800-pound GCW. Minimum BBC dimension was 51 inches without sleeper and 86 inches with sleeper.

By 1969, Marmon brought out a conventional diesel highway tractor in addition to the COE HDT truck. By that time, Caterpillar, Cummins and Detroit Diesel engines were available and transmissions were from Fuller or Spicer. Rear axles were built by Eaton and Rockwell for both single or tandem units. A tilting hood and fender piece was made by "hand layup of sheets of woven fiberglass cloth." A butterfly type hood was offered for construction and other heavy-duty applications.

In 1973, Marmon and Space Corporation were purchased by Interstate Corporation, a Chattanooga, Tennessee, insurance business. Robert A Thornell became president of the Marmon Motor Company division.

For 1974, Marmon introduced a second generation pair of COE and conventional highway tractors. The cab received some luxury appointments as standard equipment. The standard engine was the Cummins NTC 350 coupled to a Fuller RTD 9513 transmission and driving Rockwell FF 921 or SQHD axles fitted on the Reyco 101 suspension. The much larger frontal area could hold a 1,200-square inch radiator for the larger engines anticipated to be up to 600 hp by the end of the decade.

However, the OPEC oil embargo of 1973 ended the growth of engine horsepower, but large radiators were still needed to expel heat of less efficient, lower-emitting engines. The larger diameter, slower-speed fans also added to this problem in order to meet air and noise regulations. The new COE cab and conventional hood unit could tilt a full 90 degrees without any disconnections. During the second half of 1973, 300 Marmon trucks were assembled in Garland, Texas. Two assembly lines were used, one for the chassis and one for the cab. The cabs had many features as standard that were only optional on other trucks, such as tinted windshields and acoustical insulation.

In 1976, Marmon began building sleeper cabs on the tandem conventional highway tractors. These were designated as Model CHDT-BC-110. The 110 stood for a 110-inch BBC dimension and the B for a 6x4 configuration. These were called "Cadillac of the Industry" by the press.

More changes to the truck tractor took place in 1983. These were in styling and aerodynamics. The cab roof was raised, the corner radii increased and the visor deepened and rounded. A metal tilt hood was optional for those who were not convinced of the advantages of the fiberglass type. New fenders held twin rectangular headlights.

During the mid-1980s, Marmon built the F (fleet) and P (premium) series in both conventional and COE configuration. The COE was available only as a 6x4 with a BBC dimension of 60 inches for the day cab, 86 inches with the single sleeper cab and 110 inches for the double sleeper cab, hence the model numbers 60-F, 60-P, 86-F, 86-P, 110-F and 110-P. The Marmon 86-P, standard COE representative of this series, was powered by a turbocharged 400 hp Cummins NTC-400 using a Spicer twin dry plate clutch and Fuller RTO-14613 13F 1R constant mesh transmission. Rear axle was an Eaton DS401P single reduction spiral bevel tandem unit. The Cummins Formula 300 was used for the F Series.

At the same time, Marmon also built the F Series and P Series conventional highway tractors. Square headlights were becoming popular and Marmon made the transition during this time while utilizing a butterfly type aluminum front bumper. The conventional Marmon tractor trucks were available in the F and P series with sleepers or without and were built in 4x2, 6x2 and 6x4 formats. The typical 54-F truck was powered by a 300 hp Cummins Formula 300 engine with a Spicer 1372-A 7F 1R constant mesh manual transmission. These models were available through the 1980s. In 1991, Marmon discontinued building COE highway tractors.

1996 MARMON SB 57 S   MARMON

1996 MARMON SB 125 SHR   MARMON

To date, Marmon trucks have been assembled in a new plant in Garland, Texas, at a rate of about three per day. The frame is a completely huck-bolted assembly with 10-inch steel heat treated alloy steel channels and steel crossmember and gussets. The trucks are essentially hand-built with cabs being of all aluminum construction. Using highly modular extrusion tooling allows Marmon to build five different cabs using the same essential "building blocks." Aluminum skins, which are not part of the cab's structure, are bond-sealed to the frame without riveting.

Marmon has offered D, L, P, R and S series conventional trucks for 1996. The standard powerplant has been the 305 hp Caterpillar 3306C Air-to-Air after-cooled engine, with optional Cummins and Detroit Diesel with up to 500 hp. Standard front axle has been the Eaton E-1200I and rear axle the Eaton DS404. Standard transmission has been the Eaton RT116906A, but other options have also been available. For 1996, Marmon has employed 175 people and has had 40 dealers across the United States.

1932 MARMON-HERRINGTON DSD-800   **MARMON**
6X6 TRACTOR W/DESERT BUS TRAILER

MARMON-HERRINGTON 1931-1963, 1973 — Walter C. Marmon and Arthur W. Herrington organized Marmon-Herrington Incorporated in 1931 in Indianapolis, Indiana. Walter Marmon's brother, Howard Marmon, had earlier founded the Marmon Motor Car Company, and the British-born Herrington had served in the U.S. military and had worked at Harley-Davidson. By terms of the Moskovics-Herrington contract the company was formed in March of 1931 with G.M. Williams, president; F.E. Moskovics, chairman of the board; Arthur W. Herrington, vice-president; Walter C. Marmon, director and other officers of the Marmon Motor Car Company had corresponding capacities.

Marmon-Herrington was essentially a subsidiary of the Marmon Motor Car Company. The purpose of the new business enterprise was described in the following terms: "To build a new truck of a type...which the government uses for mobilization purposes."

First, one of the plants of the Marmon Motor Car Company was taken over for production of 33 trucks that had been ordered by the U.S. military. Almost immediately the new company went into a financial crisis and was bailed out by Walter Marmon. F.E. Moskovics dropped out quickly and the new officers were Walter C. Marmon, chairman; A.W. Herrington, president and chief engineer; Bert Dingley, executive vice-president and D.I. Glossbrenner, secretary-treasurer. Dingley became president a few years later.

In 1931, production began for the 33 T-1 four-wheel-drive aircraft refueling trucks and seven more were built to establish other markets. These first trucks were powered by six-cylinder Hercules engines. The company's focus was on building multiple-axle-driven trucks primarily for the military. In 1932, the DSD-800 6x6 truck tractor was built for desert applications, as were many subsequent 4x4 and 6x6 Marmon-Herrington trucks outfitted as mobile machine shops, balloon winch trucks, reconnaissance trucks, armored cars, load carriers and wreckers. Some of the armored and scout cars had four-wheel steering.

In 1932, an all-wheel-drive truck was built for oil pipeline construction in Iraq. In 1931, Herrington had personally dropped in at a meeting in London where the construction engineers were discussing the problems of hauling heavy pipe across the desert sand. The truck pioneer promised he could deliver a truck capable of carrying 40 tons at 20 mph. In August of 1932, the finished prototype made a test run with 40 tons of cargo at 26 mph. Three more were ordered by the Iraq Petroleum Company at $35,000 each. This truck was designated as the TH-300-6 Series Six Wheel Drive and was powered by a 185 hp 707-cubic inch six-cylinder Hercules diesel engine. A truck tractor was built using the same type of engine and designated as the TH-320-6.

The following year, a 31-passenger articulated coach was bought by Norman and Jerry Nairn for the Damascus-to-Baghdad desert route. The Syrian desert entrepreneurs also bought a 20-ton semi-trailer freight unit to be used with the M-H TH-315-4 four-wheel-drive truck tractor, which was powered by the same six-cylinder Hercules diesel engine as used in the pipe hauler. The coach used a 4x4 configuration with a tandem trailing axle unlike the 6x6 configuration of the pipeline trucks.

For 1934, Marmon-Herrington offered a complete line of all-wheel-drive vehicles in five series. The 4x4 A Series was comprised of five different capacity trucks from 1-1/2 ton to 4-1/2 ton. The 4x4 TH Series designated TH-300-4 to TH-340-4 included seven different capacity trucks from 4-1/2 ton to 20 ton. There was also a TH 6x6 series from 10-ton to 35-ton capacity and the similar THD Series, which was powered by diesel engines. The fifth series was also designated with a THD prefix and was powered by diesel but was built in a 4x4 configuration. Once Marmon-Herrington established a reputation, the company's growth was rapid.

The year 1934 was also when A.W. Herrington obtained U.S. Patent 1,981,173 for his 4x4 steering mechanism that avoided irregular rotation of the axle, which was the weakness of the usual Cardan-type design. His design was innovative and made a tremendous impact on the company's business future.

By 1935, Marmon-Herrington built armored cars, scout cars and trucks for Shah Reza Pahlavi's Persian military, which quickly became one of the best outfitted mechanized armies in the world. Another project was the fabrication of a large mobile home for the King of Saudi Arabia. But the company's success was also based on the domestic market, especially regarding the well-known Marmon-Herrington Ford conversions.

While Arthur Herrington negotiated business deals in the Middle East in 1935, Walter Marmon and Robert C. Wallace, one of the company directors and later chief engineer, began designing the Ford all-wheel-drive conversion to which Herrington was strongly opposed at first. However, once the prototype was built, using a 1-1/2-ton Ford V-8 truck, Herrington embraced the idea. The conversion created a 2-1/2-ton 6x6 out of the Ford 4x2 and the model line also included a 4x4.

By using the existing Ford sheet metal, engine and other components, the cost of the final product was greatly reduced, which was the original intent of the concept. Nevertheless, the conversion involved major chassis modifications requiring complete disassembly of the Ford truck and removal of the forward frame and transverse suspension assembly. New frame extensions were added and parallel semi-elliptic springs were used. The central frame cross-members were also changed to mount the Marmon-Herrington transfer case. Also, hydraulic brakes were retrofitted on the Ford trucks. Within a few years, other Ford vehicles, such as the 1-ton truck, panel delivery and the suburban station wagon, were converted to M-H four-wheel-drive. A number of the heavier conversions were supplied to the U.S. and the Belgian armies.

Another development in 1935 for Marmon-Herrington was the fabrication of the CTL-1 tank for the U.S. military. It was also a Ford derivative, as was the trailer designed to carry it. The tank prototypes were tested at the Indianapolis Motor Speedway with military personnel on hand. The Combat Train, as the complete set of equipment and crew were called, performed well and this demonstration quickly led to the procurement of the T-2 Scout Car by the Ordnance Department in 1935.

It was in 1936 that the Ford pickup was first converted to four-wheel-drive. This involved the addition of a secondary quarter elliptic spring paralleling the rear half of the usual M-H half elliptics, which were changed over from the factory springs. Also, the four-speed T-9 transmission was used instead of the standard three-speed. One hundred such conversions were sent to Belgium and this became the pilot run of the first light 4x4 trucks that were considered the "Granddaddy of the jeep."

Another breakthrough in military truck development took place in 1937 when Marmon-Herrington developed the T9 Half Track Truck. This was also a Ford conversion and used a driving front axle. A variety of such Herrington-designed vehicles were produced through World War II. The year 1937 epitomized Marmon-Herrington's success at building military vehicles for various branches of the armed forces. In addition to the aforementioned vehicles, M-H also built a series of T-13 armored cars based on the B 4x4 Ford conversion. The U.S. Army and Marine Corps bought 2-1/2-

ton C-5 6x6 truck conversions. The U.S. Navy ordered a series of crash fire trucks, and the U.S. Coast Guard bought 1/2-ton 4x4 Ford conversions.

In 1938, Marmon-Herrington developed the Marsh Buggy, predecessor of the so-called "Big Foot" trucks by several decades. It was available as the Model F5MB-4 in 1939. It was offered in several different versions and used 13.50x24 oversize tires, with dual front and triple rear tires as optional. Also that year, M-H sold a large shipment of 1/2-ton 4x4s to Belgium and similar vehicles to the U.S. Marine Corps. A prototype of the C30-6 6x6 8-ton dump truck was shipped to Moscow, U.S.S.R. Combat tanks were sold to Mexico, a TA-30 track-laying tractor was sold to the Netherlands and a TA-40 to Egypt.

The Merz Engineering Company was acquired by Marmon-Herrington in 1939, and a new plant was built just south of the Marmon-Herrington plant in New York. That year, the U.S. Coast Guard bought 1/2-ton International 4x4 conversions from M-H. The U.S. Quartermaster Corps, the U.S. Public Health Service and the U.S. Army Air Corps each bought numerous M-H Ford 4x4 trucks. More sales took place to Canada and the U.S. military in 1939 and 1940. The DSD400-6 truck was introduced in 1940. It was rated to 9-ton capacity and was powered by a WXC3 Hercules engine.

Other versions of the DSD series included the DSD-200-4, DSD-200-6, DSD-300-6, DSD-500-4, DSD-800-6, DSD-900-6, DDSD-900-4 and DSD-1000-6. All used Hercules engines including a six-cylinder diesel in the DDSD-900-4. The suffix referred to the number of driven wheels and most of the DSD series was available in both 4x4 and 6x6 format. The DSD-1000-6 was rated at 20-ton capacity.

As America entered World War II, Marmon-Herrington production of combat tanks and trucks increased dramatically without any need for retooling, which hampered production at other civilian-based manufacturers. M-H built a prototype amphibious jeep for Ford Motor Company production and a 1-1/2-ton airfield utility and bomb carrier was designed by M-H but handed over for production by the latter company as well. Marmon-Herrington's tanks were shipped in large numbers to the Netherlands, besides delivery to the U.S. Ordnance Department.

1941 MARMON-HERRINGTON 7-1/2-TON 6X6   MARMON

New light tanks were developed in 1942. Although Marmon-Herrington production concentrated on tank production during the war, a large number of All-Wheel-Drive Barrage Balloon Winch trucks and TD-600-6 wrecker trucks were also built. Large numbers of M-H CO 1 Q axles were used for conversions, which were also produced at Ford of Canada in the hundreds of thousands for the British Empire countries using M-H components built under license agreement with the Canadian Traction Company.

An unusual venture by Marmon-Herrington took place in 1943 when the company began experimenting with the Rhino, a vehicle designed by Elie P. Aghnides. It used two large hemispherical drive wheels and a single spherical wheel for maneuverability "by swiveling as easily as an office chair." The large wheels were also flotation devices and acted as paddlewheels.

In 1944, the Ordnance Department ordered such a large quantity of truck tractors that Marmon-Herrington and Kenworth were given the job to build the H-542/G 671 4x2 truck that International had

been building. These truck tractors were powered by a 451-cubic inch 124 hp Model RED-450-D International six-cylinder engine and were designed to haul 20-ton trailers over long distances. They provided the European truck industry with transportation in the immediate postwar era.

Marmon-Herrington manufactured a similar truck 4x4 tractor, which was originally built by Autocar. It was rated to 50-ton capacity and was powered by a 529-cubic inch 112 hp Hercules RXC-6 engine. Tank production was phased out in 1944 and truck production of 20 per day took its place at M-H. Tire shortage was the main constraint.

Near the end of the war, the company's management decided to diversify in the motor vehicle market and began building multistop delivery vehicles as well as buses and trolleys. Marmon-Herrington's Delivr-All was a short-wheelbase maneuverable van that could be driven from a standing or sitting position and whose entire front axle, engine and steering assembly was removable as a unit. Delivr-All production began late in 1945 and ended in 1952.

In 1946, the company went into the business of building electric trolleys and motor coaches. About 1,500 were built until 1955 and the largest fleet was in Chicago, with a single order for 349 units having been placed in 1950.

The first postwar truck models built by Marmon-Herrington were the MH 440-4 and MH 555-4. These were powered by the Hercules WXC3 and the Hercules RXC engines, respectively. W.C. Lipe clutches and five-speed Fuller transmissions were also used on both models.

In April of 1948, six models of the Q Series Marmon-Herrington trucks were introduced. These were all based on the largest F-7 Ford trucks, which had a new 145 hp V-8 engine. Three of these models were 4x4 and three were 6x6. The GVW rating for the former was up to 21,000 pounds and for the latter 35,000 pounds. Wheelbases ranged from 136-1/2 inches to 220 inches. That year, M-H also built 12 other lighter Ford conversions and four heavy-duty models of its own manufacture and design. The total of 22 models covered a GVW rating of 4,700 to 42,000 pounds.

Ford's light bus manufacturing was continued by M-H in 1950 also, with the 27- and 31-passenger transit buses formerly offered by Ford being built by Marmon-Herrington until both these and the trolleys became unprofitable in the mid-1950s.

In 1951, the U.S. Air Force placed a $10 million order for airport crash trucks. These new 6x6 trucks were designated as Model O-10. The trucks were designed to operate in temperatures from minus 65 degrees to plus 130 degrees on the Fahrenheit scale. A separate engine placed amidships in the vehicle powered a pump that delivered air-foam and water under high pressure from a remote-control turret on top of the truck. Seven hundred-twenty-six such trucks were built along with 134 similar MB-1 crash trucks for the U.S. Navy. M-H also built 2,246 MA1 and NC5 All-Wheel-Drive chassis for ground servicing jet aircraft of the U.S. Navy and Air Force.

The following year, Marmon-Herrington announced a new series of trucks with new cabs, styling and sheet metal. The all-new cabs, built from 14-gauge sheet steel throughout, sported a V-windshield that was 62 inches wide, and wrap-around corner windows for optimum visibility as well as a vertically-opening center rear window were standard equipment. The new series was designated Models 610, 615, 620, 625 and 630. The three pairs had engines of 139, 145 and 180 hp, and GVW ratings were from 24,000 to 33,000 pounds. The all-new heavy riveted frames did not have the traditional Marmon-Herrington kick-up over the front suspension, but the 12-1/4-inch flat-top channels tapered to six inches in that area of the chassis. The 600 Series lasted until the end of Marmon-Herrington production and continued to be built by UNIC division Marmon-Bocquet (Marmon-Simca) in France as late as 1982.

For 1952, Marmon-Herrington introduced its "21st Anniversary Models" and in 1956 another 21st Anniversary was announced - this one commemorating the first Ford 4x4 conversions of 1935. During those 21 years, 100,000 such conversions were built. The Ford designations had a 4 added to the number referring to four-wheel-drive. For example the Ford F-750 became the M-754. Ford had changed its numerical designations to three digits for its own 50th anniversary in 1953. Ten conventional and six COE conversions were available. All-wheel-drive was available as a conversion for all Ford bus and parcel delivery models. Also for 1956, M-H developed a new series of air force crash trucks and these were designated as the O-12.

Two years earlier, Marmon-Herrington built a pusher-type school bus chassis called the Model R225-D-V-8, which used a Cummins V-8-185 diesel engine. However, bus production was not lucrative until the company received a $10 million contract in 1958 to refurbish 1,000 Greyhound buses over 11 months with new diesel V-8 engines.

In 1960, Marmon-Herrington acquired the Oneida Bus Division of the Henney Corporation in Canastoga, New York, in an attempt to stay in the bus manufacturing business. The rear-engined Safeway chassis were particularly well suited for school bus and transit application. The Oneida plant was expanded to 263,000 square feet with 16 acres of additional outside space. The two Oneida models were called the "Starline" and the "Guardian," but Oneida chief engineer William De Capua's redesign using the monocoque principle delayed production while the previous line had already been discontinued. However, De Capua died suddenly of heart failure at age 47 and Slim Swinford took over the job.

Also for 1960, Marmon-Herrington began building Class 7 and Class 8 truck tractors at the Oneida plant, with Swinford also in charge of the engineering. The first prototype emerged in June 1961 and was rated to 40,000-pound GVW and 72,000-pound GCW. A 6x4 three-axle tandem V-belt drive truck tractor was also designed. The shorter tractor had a BBC of 52 inches. In 1962, production of the truck tractor began with optional Caterpillar diesel power and the original 90-degree wrap-around windshield had to be abandoned. A far less costly flat two-piece windshield was adopted instead.

1962 MARMON-HERRINGTON HIGHWAY TRACTOR   WOOD

About 50 of the HTD-1 truck tractors with Caterpillar engines were built in a finalized version that was rated at 70,000-pound GVW. The Mayflower moving company performed a field test of the new trucks, but a surprise announcement in July 1963 stated that the Marmon-Herrington Truck Division had been acquired by Adrian H. Roop, a Marmon-Herrington distributor. As the Oneida bus operation was closed down, the truck manufacturing was moved to Denton, Texas.

Other business moves in 1960 included the purchase of the Long Company, whose president John B. Long later became president of Marmon-Herrington. The acquisition of Flash Perforating Company that year also foreshadowed the diversification and change in business plan for Marmon-Herrington. Another earlier acquisition of Airdox combined with Long resulted in new product lines for the coal-mining industry. M-H purchased Cardair in 1963, which built four-stage air compressors.

The heavy investment in bus manufacturing turned into a losing proposition and the Oneida division was closed down without any interested buyers to be found. Herrington sold his 25 percent ownership to the Fritzker family of Chicago, who later bought out the rest of the business and converted it over as a holding company for a number of smaller enterprises.

With the formation of the new Marmon Motor Company in Texas, the U.S. Marmon-Herrington firm ceased to be involved in commercial vehicle manufacturing. According to some records, in 1973 Marmon-Herrington's Knoxville, Tennessee, plant built a single prototype of a Ford-powered 4x4 construction truck. In July of 1963, Herrington announced to the press that the plant was closing and thereafter only the operation in France was set up for motor vehicle and parts manufacturing.

MARQUETTE 1911-1912 — A good deal of confusion surrounds the name Marquette as a motor vehicle manufacturer. In 1904, there was an electric car referred to as the Marquette, built by the Berwick Auto Car Company of Grand Rapids, Michigan. Subsequently there were listings for the Marquette Motor Vehicle Company and the Marquette Motor Company, both of which either existed simultaneously in 1912, or more likely were erroneously mentioned as separate business entities in Chicago, Illinois, and Saginaw, Michigan, respectively. It is quite possible that the two companies existed separately at the same time and not far apart geographically. The Chicago company advertised its vehicles as powered by two-cylinder engines using planetary transmissions and double chain drive, while the Saginaw company offered a four-cylinder engine in 1912. In any case, a few open stake body trucks and a 12-seat bus were built under the name Marquette, which should also not be confused with the Buick Marquette built in 1930.

1927 MARSH FRONT-DRIVE DELIVERY WAGON   RD

MARSH 1927 — C.M. Marsh of Hudson, New York, experimented with front-wheel-drive. In 1927, *Automotive Industries* announced a delivery wagon with this type of design, which had the four-cylinder engine mounted under the seat with flywheel facing forward. The press release further stated "At the center of the frame in front there is a fifth wheel, by means of which the car is steered and through which the power is transmitted to the front driving wheel." After a lengthy explanation of the complex mechanism the press also stated "It is to be expected that automobile engineers will not look favorably on the fifth wheel method of steering, owing to the heavy shocks which collisions with road obstacles must impose on the steering mechanism." Apparently this evaluation reflected the fact that the Marsh did not go into production.

MARTEL see ELCAR

1911 MARTIN FIRE TRUCK   **MROZ**

MARTIN 1908-1916 — The Martin Carriage Works of York, Pennsylvania, started out as a builder of horsedrawn wagons, most of which were used commercially. Milton D. Martin was president and P.A. Elesser was secretary-treasurer.

The company went into the motor vehicle manufacturing business in 1908 with a highwheeler of 800-pound capacity called the Model J, which was priced at $1,400. Early in 1909, for the Grand Central Palace Show in New York, Martin also displayed its 18 hp 1/2-ton Model E and similar Model G priced at $1,650. A planetary transmission and chain drive were used. The company had reached a production level of 20,000 horsedrawn wagons by 1908 before going into the "motor wagon" business. Many of the first motor vehicles were "Undertaker's Cars."

In 1910, Martin showed well at the "Reliability Run" from Philadelphia to Atlantic City and that year began building buses. The West York Council Reliance Fire Company ordered the first 3,000-pound capacity Martin fire engine. Soon, 2-ton and 3-ton trucks were also added to the model line.

In 1911, four models were produced. These were from 1-1/2-ton to 6-ton capacity. A passenger car model (Suburban Car Model J-3) was built by removing the bed and adding seats and an optional convertible top on the 88-inch wheelbase light truck chassis with a 16 hp engine.

1915 MARTIN COMMERCIAL WAGON   **OCW**

The lighter models were powered by a 29 hp Wisconsin engine, while the heavier trucks used a 36 hp four-cylinder engine of the same make. All of the trucks used disc clutches and three-speed transmissions. Price of the 2-1/2-ton Martin in 1913 was $2,750. The 3-1/2-ton model sold for $3,500 that year. The company continued to build the two-cylinder model until 1913. In 1916, M.D. Martin passed away and the company was bought by John J. Watson, president of Lee Rubber Company. The Martin marque was superseded by the Martin-Parry Corporation and Atlas trucks.

MARYLAND 1900-1901 — The Maryland Automobile & Manufacturing Company was incorporated in Luke, Maryland, at the turn of the century. The company took over the machine shops of the Twin Towns Manufacturing Company and directly thereafter, the buildings were knocked down by gale force winds. However, being insured against such a calamity, the plant was put back together and production resumed.

Maryland vehicles were all steam-powered using a 12 hp two-cylinder vertical double slide engine. The 1/2-ton Delivery Wagon had a top speed of 30 mph and sold for $1,500. The company also produced a Tourist Carriage for $1,400 and two Omnibus vehicles for $1,800 and $2,500, respectively. Receivership came midyear in 1901.

1910 MAYTAG MODEL A FARMER'S CAR   **DFW/ACTHR**

1911 MAYTAG MODEL 11 LIGHT DELIVERY   **DFW/ACTHR**

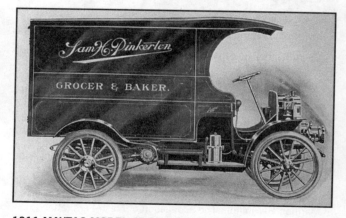

1911 MAYTAG MODEL 10 PANEL DELIVERY   **OCW**

MASON; MAYTAG-MASON; MAYTAG 1906-1912 — Edward R. Mason was an attorney in Des Moines, Iowa, who funded the incorporation of the Mason Motor Car Company in that city during 1906.

Fred Duesenberg supplied the two-cylinder automobile that he and his brother August had designed at their garage in Des Moines two years earlier. The company began producing commercial vehicles based on its passenger car models.

Three models were built using a 14 hp flat two-cylinder air-cooled engine and two-speed planetary transmission with final chain drive. The Model 10 was a delivery van, the Model 11 was a delivery wagon and Model 12 was a hybrid car that could be fitted with a touring body and light delivery body. The bodies were interchangeable within 20 minutes. Prices were $1,150, $1,175 and $1,250, respectively.

In 1909, F.L. Maytag and his son Elmer Maytag, manufacturers of washing machines and agricultural machinery, bought controlling interest in Mason and moved the plant to Waterloo, Iowa, at the former factory of the Waterloo Motor Works. In 1910, the company was reorganized as the Maytag-Mason. The company's slogan had been "The Fastest and Strongest Two-Cylinder Car in America" and Senator Maytag had enough faith that he invested heavily in the company. The Duesenberg brothers went off to race cars and took the Mason name with them, effectively leaving the Maytag name as the marque emblem but only for the year 1911. At that time, a four-cylinder car was added to the model line. But as quickly as the Maytags got into the automobile manufacturing business, they got out just as fast. By 1912, under pressure from creditors, the Maytags sold the company back to Edward R. Mason. It appears that by 1912, commercial vehicles were no longer produced. The company folded late in 1914.

MASON ROADKING 1922-1925 — The Mason Motor Truck Company was located in Flint, Michigan, and was part of William Crapo Durant's conglomerate. The company was established to build 1-1/2-ton trucks to supplement Durant's smaller trucks built by Star. The Mason Roadking was originally a 1-ton capacity truck that was uprated to 1-1/2-ton in 1923. It was powered by a 25.6 hp Herschell-Spillman Model O engine with Zenith carburetor and Autolite ignition. The truck used a three-speed Warner Gear transmission with double reduction final drive. Both front and rear axles were made by Flint, steering was made by Lavine Gear and Hayes wheels carried 34x5 front and rear pneumatic tires. Wheelbase was either 130 inches or 150 inches and chassis price was $1,495. Chassis weight was 3,320 pounds.

1919 MASTER JUNIOR   **KP**

MASTER 1917-1929 — Master Truck Incorporated was located in Chicago, Illinois. Master produced trucks from 1-1/4-ton up to 6-ton capacity. The Model 11 was the lightest truck and was powered by a 22.5 hp Buda WTU engine. Clutch and transmission were built by Fuller and front and rear axles were by Timken. The electrical system was provided by Westinghouse. St. Marys wheels carried 33x5 front and rear pneumatic tires and the wheelbase was 132 inches. The Model 21 with 142-inch wheelbase was rated at 1-1/2-ton capacity and was powered by a 25.6 hp Buda GBU engine. Chassis price was $2,290. Next up was the 2-1/2-ton Model 41 with 154-inch wheelbase and powered by a 28.9 hp Buda EBU engine. The Model 51 was rated at 3-1/2-ton capacity and was

powered by a 32.4 hp Buda YBU engine. Wheelbase was 158 inches. The Buda YBU engine also powered the Model 61, which was rated at 5-ton capacity. The largest Master truck was the Model 64 rated at 6-ton capacity. It had a 170-inch wheelbase and was powered by a 36.1 hp Buda ATU engine. A few of the later Master trucks were powered by Jackson engines. Between 1921 and 1924, the company offered a 21-passenger and a 29-passenger bus chassis.

1920 MASTER JUNIOR 1-1/2-TON FARM TRUCK   **RD**

1975 MASTER REFUSE TRUCK CAB/CHASSIS   **MASTER**

MASTER TRUCK 1972-1985 — The Master Truck was a low cab-forward truck built for the refuse collection market. The axles were configured 4x2, 6x2 and 6x4 and four diesel engines were offered: Caterpillar 1150, Cummins V-210, Detroit 6V-52N and Perkins 180. Master Trucks were specially designed for quiet operation in residential neighborhoods. The Engineered Fiberglass Company designed a special engine shroud for sound dampening, keeping the engine noise level below 78 decibels. The Model 6000 with tilting cab appears to have been the only model produced by this company, which was located in Fountain Valley, California.

MATHESON 1906 — The Matheson Motor Car Company was established by Frank and Charles Matheson in Grand Rapids, Michigan. After purchasing the Holyoke Motor Works and hiring its engine designer, Charles G. Greuter, the Matheson company began producing passenger cars with the 24 hp four-cylinder overhead valve Greuter engine in 1903. In 1906, the company moved to Wilkes-Barre, Pennsylvania, and that year produced a large 5-ton capacity truck powered by a 45 hp four-cylinder engine, which was mounted between the seats. It appears that this engine was the same as the one used on the Matheson Touring car of 1906. This was the only year that the company built trucks and those were on a limited production basis. Passenger cars were built until 1912, when receivership forced the company's closure. The factory later became a munitions plant during World War I. After the Armistice, Frank Matheson was involved in the unsuccessful Owen-Magnetic car. After that company failed, he bought back his old plant in Wilkes-Barre to use as a distributorship for GMC trucks.

MAXFER 1917-1919 — The Maxfer Truck & Tractor Company of Chicago, Illinois, began by building rear axle kits for transforming Ford Model T passenger cars into 1-ton capacity trucks. In

1917, Maxfer assembled an entire 1-ton truck using a 31 hp four-cylinder engine and a semi-floating worm-drive with a Bailey non-stalling differential. Electric lights and an electric starter were standard components. Pneumatic tires were used only in the front with solid rubber on the rear wheels. The complete Maxfer truck was made for a little over two years.

MAXI 1940-1942 — Six Wheels Incorporated built Maxi truck tractors, which were marketed for heavy-duty off-highway construction work. This 6x4 truck was powered by a 225 hp Waukesha-Hesselman engine and had a Fuller clutch and transmission. The company built its own rear axle and drive, which was by means of a walking beam housing reduction gears. Final drive was by chain to the rear tandem axles. Drawbar pull capacity was 32,000 pounds and load capacity was 110 tons. The cabs were open and dual wheels were not used on this giant truck. The Six Wheel Company also assembled Hug trucks with their own tandem axles.

1914 MAXIM BOX BODY TRICAR   **KP**

MAXIM 1911-1914 — Maxim Tricar Manufacturing started out in Thompsonville, Connecticut. The three-wheeler was designed by Maxim Karminski, who was from France, and George Peters, who was from Germany. The design borrowed heavily from Gustav Hiller's Phanomen (or Phanomobil) that had been built in Zittau, Germany.

The first Maxim Tri-Car was built in 1911 for the 1912 model year. It was tiller-steered and had a one-cylinder engine mounted on the forks of the front wheel, which was driven by a single chain. Later vehicles used an 8 hp two-cylinder engine but the drive remained the same. It was rated at 3/4-ton capacity. Wheelbase was 96 inches and the price was $395. The delivery box was easily removable for the mounting of two more seats. After the purchase of the Jefferson, Long Island, factory where the Only car had been built, the Maxim Tri-Car Company, as it was called by then, went bankrupt in 1914.

1927 MAXIM MODEL BA 1 FIRE ENGINE   **MAXIM**

1937 MAXIM MODEL M-3   **MAXIM**

1976 MAXIM MODEL S   **MAXIM**

MAXIM 1914-1985 — The Maxim Motor Company of Middleboro, Massachusetts, began as a manufacturer of fire apparatus and in 1914, began assembling complete light trucks. By the following year, the company decided to specialize in fire engines. The first Maxim trucks were built on Thomas chassis but by 1916, Maxim began fabricating its own chassis. These were powered by Maxim's own six-cylinder engine that featured triple ignition. The trucks all had worm-drive and by 1918, the company offered a full range of fire engines including combination vehicles, motor pumpers and hook and ladder trucks.

Maxim continued to build a variety of fire engines through the 1920s. A special 6x4 pumper-tanker was built for the city of Fallmouth, Massachusetts, where poor road conditions prevailed. The same year, Maxim built a prototype of an upgraded 2-ton Ford truck. Improvements were made by reinforcing the chassis, using oversize tires and adapting heavy-duty Timken axles. The truck was rated at up to 5-ton capacity but never went into production.

After World War II, Maxim resumed fire engine manufacturing and produced pumpers capable of 750 and 1,500 gallons per minute. Quad combinations were built using open cabs. A new V-grille was introduced, which was kept until 1961. In 1952, Maxim began building the German Magirus rear-mounted aerial ladder under license on the company's own chassis. Both rigid and articulated aerial ladders were sold to Ward LaFrance and Mack, who were competitors.

In 1956, Seagrave acquired Maxim, although the Massachusetts plant continued to build fire engines including bodies and aerial ladders. In 1959, Maxim introduced the F Series truck, which was company's first cab-forward design. Conventional Maxim trucks continued to be built and in 1960, the S Series was introduced. This was a short-wheelbase conventional truck that remained unchanged for 20 years. When FWD acquired Seagrave in 1963, Maxim also became a subsidiary of the new parent company but continued to produce fire apparatus under its own name.

By 1980, Maxim offered gasoline engines built by Waukesha, as well as diesel engines from Cummins and Detroit. Spicer synchromesh manual transmissions were available, as were Allison automatic transmissions. Manufacturing ceased by 1985.

MAXWELL-BRISCOE, MAXWELL 1905-1913, 1917-1925 — Benjamin Briscoe and Jonathan Maxwell were the founders of the Maxwell-Briscoe Motor Company, which started in Tarrytown, New York.

Briscoe owned a prosperous sheet metal manufacturing company and had already invested in the Buick automobile. Right from the start, the company built delivery vans on the 85-inch wheelbase chassis also used for the "Dr. Maxwell" car, which was marketed especially for physicians. The delivery vans were powered by the same 20 hp two-cylinder water-cooled engine, which Maxwell had designed.

In 1908, Maxwell offered taxicabs when total production had risen to 4,455 for the year. Cadwallader Washburn Kelsey was the sales manager for Maxwell-Briscoe and staged many unusual events to promote the company. These included chases with police, driving up steps of venerable buildings, races and a 1909 cross-country trek by four women in a Maxwell. Most of these events were captured on film to be shown in nickelodeons for additional public exposure.

1917 MAXWELL 1-TON BOX/STAKE BODY   CP

By 1910, some 20,500 Maxwells were sold. That year, Briscoe formed the United States Motor Corporation in an attempt to compete with the only two motor vehicle companies in America larger than Maxwell: Buick and Ford. Kelsey abruptly left the company and Jonathan Maxwell became the president of Maxwell-Briscoe. Briscoe could not compete with General Motors and Ford and his new venture collapsed in 1912. Maxwell factories in Pawtucket, Rhode Island; Auburn, New York; Cranston, Rhode Island; and the main plant in Tarrytown (where Durant would produce Chevrolet) were sold and Maxwell moved production to Detroit, Michigan.

1922 MAXWELL 1-1/2-TON   KP

1925 MAXWELL PANEL MERCHANT'S CAR   OCW

Between 1913 and 1917, only passenger car production continued. In 1917, a 1-ton truck was introduced. It was powered by a 21.03 hp four-cylinder engine used in passenger cars but it had a 124-inch wheelbase, which was not one of the passenger car chassis. That year, total production of Maxwells since 1905 reached 100,000. In 1918, Maxwell used the 108-inch wheelbase passenger car chassis to build a delivery van. In 1920, the truck was uprated to 1-1/2-ton capacity. This was also the year that the postwar recession hit the Maxwell hard. At one point, dealers had 17,000 unsold Maxwells. A merge with Chalmers would bring Walter Percy Chrysler in as president in 1924, and the last Maxwell was built in 1925. The following year, Chrysler began building cars after his own name. Jonathan Maxwell died two years later.

MAYFLOWER 1906 — The Mayflower "station wagon" was built by Peter and Michael Burgard in York, Pennsylvania, in 1906. It was powered by a 10-hp air-cooled engine and used a two-speed planetary transmission with a disc clutch. The vehicle could carry six passengers and had a drop tailgate for use as a delivery vehicle. Its first owner was the Sultner's Meat Market in York. It had 35x2 solid rubber tires and a top speed of 18 mph. The vehicle has remained extant and it is believed no others were built.

MAYTAG see MASON

MCBRIGHT 1953-1955 — McBright Incorporated of Lehighton, Pennsylvania, built a truck that was powered by a White engine. The engine, transmission and radiator were all mounted behind the rear axle under the floor. McBright built two-, three- and four-axle versions of this design for about two years. Other details are unknown.

MCFARLAND 1918 — The McFarland Carriage Company of Connersville, Indiana, began building passenger cars in 1910. In April of 1918, *Motor World* announced that McFarland would be producing a 3-1/2-ton truck that would be manufactured by the Teeter-Hardly Motor Company of Hagerstown, Indiana. The estimated price of the truck was $4,000. It does not appear that this vehicle made it past the prototype stage. McFarland continued building passenger cars until 1928.

1929 MCGEE TRACKLESS TRAIN   MROZ

MCGEE 1917-1930 — Although the H.O. McGee Company of Indianapolis, Indiana, never built its own chassis, the commercial/advertising vehicles the company built deserve to be acknowledged in this compendium. The McGee Company began in 1917 by building a trackless train that was a type of truck fabricated in the form of a steam locomotive but powered by an auto engine. It used truck wheels and tires as it was not intended for the tracks. The truck/locomotive was used for recruiting military personnel during World War I and it was an effective attention grabber. After the war, it was purchased by a large carnival company and used in parades and as a show vehicle.

In order to advertise a new paint system for automobiles, McGee built another trackless train in 1925 in order to advertise the new venture with which he was involved. It consisted of a "locomotive" and a luxurious club car complete with observation platform. The club car was large enough to accommodate 15 passengers and had a baggage and dining compartment. The vehicle toured the state of Indiana promoting Lykglas auto paint before it was sold to Metro-Goldwyn-Mayer. The new owner made use of the "International Beauty Train" not only across the United States but also in several other countries in Europe, Central and South America and Australia.

The "trackless train" was so successful that McGee and his company built at least 16 additional such vehicles. They were constructed on Cord, Dagmar or Graham-Paige chassis as locomotives and a few "tractor-trailer" units built for broadcasting were among these. They were powered by twin 150 hp engines with synchronized transmissions permitting a 40 mph cruising speed. Price was $52,000. Crude oil could be dripped into the exhaust manifold at the control of the driver to create the locomotive smokestack effect. Revolving blades in the smokestack emitted puffs instead of a constant stream of smoke.

Companies such as Kelly-Springfield tires, Majestic Radio, cigarette companies and Paramount Pictures were some of the buyers of the McGee trackless trains. They were used for advertising and broadcasting. Several of the vehicles were fitted with a "wireless receiving set and amplification system." Most of the vehicles were built just before the Great Depression began, after which the McGee Company quickly faded out.

MCI 1963 to date — Motor Coach Industries started as the Fort Garry Motor Body Company in Winnipeg, Manitoba, Canada. Fort Garry was already an established bus and truck body manufacturer when it built its first complete buses in 1937. The first buses were powered by front-mounted International engines. In 1938, five more buses were built using the Yellow Coach styling. When Greyhound opened new routes in Canada in 1940, Fort Garry built 22 buses for its new American customer. The company has always been primarily a Canadian company.

Fort Garry was renamed Motor Coach Industries in 1942. After World War II, production immediately increased to 50 buses per year for Canadian Greyhound. In 1946, MCI introduced its rear-engine Courier model. By 1950, MCI became part of Greyhound, continuing to build buses under the MCI name. In 1957, Greyhound Lines of Canada was the company formed to hold subsidiaries such as MCI. In 1959, MCI began a new series numbering system beginning with the MC-1 Challenger. This MCI designed bus was the first to use the distinctive slanted-and-straight window dividers.

It was in 1963 that MCI buses began to be built in the United States; hence the starting date of 1963 is given as American commercial vehicle production was launched that year in Pembina, North Dakota. Up to that time, about 750 MCI buses had been built in Canada. The MC-5 bus was already in production when Greyhound started building buses in North Dakota. This vehicle was powered by a Detroit Diesel 8V-71 engine with a Spicer mechanical transmission. Greyhound specified belt-driven accessories instead of gear drive on this 39-passenger 35-foot single-level bus.

By 1978, 2,300 MC-5 buses were produced but the demand for the 47-passenger MC-7 with tandem axles, which was introduced in 1968, overtook the MC-5 production with 2,550 built by that year. The MC-6 was an experimental model 102 inches wide and was powered by a 12-cylinder Detroit Diesel engine. One hundred MC-6 buses were built before that series was discontinued. Efforts to change regulations allowing the six-inch wider buses were not successful and the MC-6 buses ended up in California, where they were legal. Many of them had their 12-cylinder engines changed over to the Detroit Diesel 8V-71 units.

Even greater demand for the MC-8 series, which was produced between 1973 and 1978, resulted in a total production of 3,000 buses within five years by MCI. Another factory was established in Rosewell, New Mexico, in 1975, partly as a result of labor strikes in Canada. The New Mexico plant has assembled Greyhound buses

from stampings made in Winnipeg, but all Canadian buses are built entirely in Winnipeg. In the late 1970s, MCI introduced the 47-passenger MC-9 series, which was built through the 1980s. These were essentially the same as the previous series, except for window and trim styling. MCI has been producing approximately 40 percent of all intercity buses in the United States and Canada to date.

1911 MCINTYRE MODEL 251 RD

MCINTYRE 1909-1915 — The W.H. McIntyre Company was located in Auburn, Indiana, and was an outgrowth of the Kiblinger highwheeler. W.H. McIntyre had been the factory manager of Kiblinger and bought out the company in 1909. Passenger cars were produced primarily, some with light cargo bodies. Two-cylinder and four-cylinder engines were used and in 1910, McIntyre introduced a power wagon that was powered by a 24 hp engine with front axle set back under the dashboard of the open cab. This vehicle used two-speed transmission, solid rubber tires and chain drive. Price was $1,350.

A new model line of commercial vehicles was introduced in 1913, when styling was also updated to include C-cabs, front fenders (absent on many previous models) and the front axle location was moved under the engine. This model line included 3/4-, 1-1/2-, 3- and 5-ton capacity trucks priced from $1,500 up to $4,200. The lighter trucks had pneumatic tires by 1914, but this was the year that the company's Imp cyclecar was discontinued due to a lack of sales and commercial vehicle production followed suit. The following year, the company went into receivership and folded. It was succeeded by the DeKalb Manufacturing Company of Fort Wayne, Indiana.

1915 MCKEEN HIGHWAY COACH RD

MCKEEN 1915 — The McKeen Motor Car Company of Omaha, Nebraska, was a manufacturer of gasoline-powered railway coaches. In 1915, the company built two coaches for Minneapolis. The McKeen coach was powered by a four-cylinder Continental engine with Stromberg carburetor and Eisemann magneto and used a three-speed Brown-Lipe transmission with shaft drive. Springs were supplied by Perfection Company and front axle was from Sheldon while the rear axle was from Timken. Six-inch structural steel was employed for the chassis. Tires were solid rubber of the dimension 36x5 front and rear with duals in the back. Chassis weight was given as 6,700 pounds and the weight of the body was an additional 3,800 pounds. Pneumatic mechanisms were used in the seat cushions and two-foot circular windows were hinged to the ceiling. The interior was finished in Cuban mahogany and ventilator motors also provided fresh air for the passengers. The chassis was supplied by the United Motor Truck Company. It is not certain whether more than two of these buses were built.

MCQUAY-NORRIS 1933-1934 — The McQuay-Norris Manufacturing Company of St. Louis built six teardrop-shaped cars as rolling laboratories to promote its company. The company had been in business building engine and chassis components since 1910. The promotional cars were built on Ford chassis and carried a complete arsenal of instrumentation, including gauges to measure exhaust temperature, compression pressure, oil level, oil pressure, oil viscosity, oil temperature, water temperature, a Moto Vita combustion indicator and other more common instruments such as ammeter, clock, speedometer, et cetera. The Hill Auto Body Metal Company of Cincinnati, which had built the similar-looking Arrow Plane car in 1932, was contracted to build the McQuay-Norris vehicles. They toured the country visiting auto repair shops and wholesale distributors and other McQuay-Norris customers for several years following their fabrication.

M & E 1913-1915 — The M & E, which stood for Merchant & Evans, was a short-lived company in Philadelphia, Pennsylvania, which built a 4-ton capacity truck with a 114-inch wheelbase in 1913. The company listed a 3-1/2-ton and a 5-ton capacity truck for 1915, but specifications and production numbers are not available to date.

1908 MEISELBACH RD

MEISELBACH 1904-1909 — August D. Meiselbach was the organizer of the Meiselbach Motor Wagon Company in North Milwaukee, Wisconsin. The company originally began in Washington D.C. in 1903 with E.T. McKaig, who owned a number of patents. Meiselbach owned a bicycle manufacturing company in Chicago as well as the Meiselbach Typewriter Company. Meiselbach and McKaig parted company before any vehicles could be built. The following year, Meiselbach managed to acquire some of McKaig's patents and production began of a 1-ton highwheeler truck.

The Meiselbach highwheeler was powered by an opposing twin-cylinder water-cooled engine and used a friction transmission and chain drive. The company introduced double disc friction drive in 1906. Discs were mounted on each end of the transverse crankshaft. By 1908, Meiselbach offered 1-, 2- and 3-ton capacity highwheeler trucks with wheelbases of 84, 96 and 108 inches, respectively. Friction drive was continued with only one speed forward and one in reverse, giving the vehicles a top speed of 10 mph.

MENOMINEE 1911-1937 — The Menominee Motor Truck Company was named after a northern Indian tribe that had at one time occupied territory not far from the factory's location in Clintonville, Wisconsin. The first Menominee trucks were 3/4-ton and 1-ton capacity models and only these were built until 1917, when the model range was extended up to 3-1/2-ton. As an example, the 1-ton Model HT Express Delivery for 1917 had a four-cylinder Continental engine with Stromberg carburetor and Eisemann ignition and used a three-speed transmission with Timken worm-drive. Wheelbase was 130 inches and 34x4-1/2 tires were pneumatic

front and rear. Price was $2,080. By 1923, the truck models ranged from 1-ton to 6-ton capacity along with 20-passenger and 25-passenger bus chassis.

1914 MENOMINEE MODEL A-3 RD

By the mid-1920s, the Menominee 1-ton, known as the Hurry-ton, with 132-inch wheelbase was powered by a 25.6 hp Wisconsin SU engine and used a Borg & Beck clutch and Detlaff transmission. Both front and rear axles were made by Columbia and steering gear was built by Lavine. The chassis price was $1,650. Next up was the 1-1/4-ton Model HT with 130-inch wheelbase powered by the same engine as the previous model. However, the front axle was made by Shuler, rear axle was Wisconsin, transmission was provided by Cotta and Ross steering was used. Chassis weight was 3,525 pounds compared to 2,925 for the 1-ton model. The Model HT chassis price was $2,000. The 1-1/2-ton Model H with 144-inch wheelbase had the same components as the previous model but sold for $2,475.

At that time, Menominee also built the 2-1/2-ton Model D with 144-inch wheelbase, which had the same make components as the previous model but was powered by a Wisconsin TAU engine. Chassis price was $2,875. The company also offered the 3-1/2-ton Model G with 160-inch wheelbase for $3,800. Up to this model, pneumatic tires were available at extra cost but the 5-ton Model J3 had hard rubber tires and was powered by a 36.1 hp Wisconsin RAU engine. Chassis weight was 8,250 and chassis price was $4,850.

1917 MENOMINEE HAYS

Menominee had an extensive sales department and sold trucks as far away as New York despite small scale production. In 1928, the Four Wheel Drive Auto Company acquired Menominee as a subsidiary, continuing to build trucks under that name. The Menominee plant was used as a source for utility bodies and pole trailers and other equipment. In 1932, the Menominee model range included trucks from 1-1/2-ton up to 8-ton capacity and three bus chassis up to 35-passenger. The following year, a new model line was introduced powered by Waukesha engines.

For 1937, Menominee still listed seven models: A-15, DX-6, DN-6, A-30, N-6, JX-6 and 6W-8. All were powered by the six-cylinder Waukesha engines adopted in 1933. The models still ranged from 1-1/2-ton to 8-ton capacity, but few trucks were built. Axles were provided by Shuler, Timken and Wisconsin and transmissions were exclusively provided by Brown-Lipe, except for the lightest model which used a Fuller unit. Plant production was devoted almost entirely to truck bodies. By the following year, Menominee as a marque was entirely discontinued. The Menominee truck company was not affiliated with the Menominee Electric Company that built an electric car in Menominee, Michigan, during 1915.

1914 MERCURY HIGHWHEELER   OCW

MERCURY 1910-1917 — Of the more than half-dozen motor vehicle manufacturers by the name of Mercury, the Mercury Manufacturing Company appears to be the only one that resided in Chicago, Illinois. The company built 1/2-ton capacity highwheelers from 1910 to 1916. These were all forward-control design and were powered by two-cylinder two-cycle air-cooled engines using a planetary transmission up to 1912. Wheelbase was 85 inches. The Mercury used a progressive transmission in 1912. The company also built the Bulley tractor, named after the company president. Most of the Bulley tractors were three-wheel vehicles with a single chain-driven wheel in back, although a few had single wheels in front. The company stopped all vehicle production in 1917.

MERIT 1911 — The Waterville Tractor Company of Waterville, Ohio, built a 1/2-ton Model B truck during 1911 only. The truck had an 88-inch wheelbase and was powered by a two-cylinder air-cooled engine that was mounted under the body. The truck used a friction transmission and final drive was by chain. The price was $1,000, which included an open delivery body.

MERZ 1913-1915 — The Merz Cyclecar Company, located in Indianapolis, Indiana, built a cyclecar designed by Charles Merz, who had been a well-known race car driver. It was powered by a 9 hp two-cylinder De Luxe engine and used a friction disc transmission with final drive by V-belt. The tread dimension was 40 inches. Full-elliptic springs were used all around and a single headlight was integrated into the top of the radiator and hood.

A Light Delivery version was listed for $485 in 1914. It is known that Merz built a prototype for the 1914 Chicago Automobile Show, which took place in January, but he arrived too late to secure exhibit space. Road tests showed that the Merz vehicle would cost less than one cent per mile for gasoline, oil and tires. Receivership arrived in the summer of 1914. It is uncertain how many vehicles were built, if in fact there were any more than the prototype itself.

MESERVE 1901-1904 — William Forest Meserve built a steam truck in Canobie Lake, New Hampshire, during 1901. This truck was used by Pemberton Mills in Lawrence for the next 20 years. The truck was powered by a two-cylinder steam engine built by Edward of Dorchester, Massachusetts. The Meserve Auto Truck Company was organized at Canobie in 1902 and William Meserve offered 2-ton capacity steam trucks using wooden chassis and double chain drive. It appears he built a second truck for Pemberton Mills.

In 1902, Meserve built a similar gasoline-powered truck using an 11 hp two-cylinder horizontally-opposed Upton engine. It used a two-speed transmission and final drive was by chain from a jackshaft. Top speed was 8 mph. In October 1902, an announcement was made that 10 more trucks of this type would be built, but it is not certain if in fact they were.

1902 MESERVE   RD

Meserve was also known for having built a touring car in 1904. It was on a 108-inch wheelbase using a four-cylinder two-cycle engine that had a compressed air self-starter. Meserve got out of motor vehicle construction and was later known for the assembly of jail cells in Derry.

MESSENGER 1913-1914 — The Messenger Manufacturing Company of Tatamy, Pennsylvania, built railroad cars. During one year, the company an experimental 2-ton truck powered by a 30 hp four-cylinder engine. It was priced at $2,400. Apparently this vehicle was not affiliated with the Messenger cars built by Brasie in Minnesota during the same time. Other specifications of the Messenger truck have not been available to date.

MESSERER 1897-1901 — Stephen Messerer started out as a jeweler and watchmaker in Newark, New Jersey. He transformed the back of his store into an inventor's studio, where he and others could develop their ideas -- one of them being motor vehicles. He built his first automobile in 1897 and established the S. Messerer Motor Wagon Company. The Messerer delivery wagon had a 1/2-ton capacity and used a four-cylinder engine with four-inch bore and six-inch stroke developing 6 hp at 350 rpm.

Messerer secured $300,000 worth of capital stock to incorporate his firm in 1899. He continued to build the delivery wagons, which also had a combination gear and belt drive using a six-inch pulley. Maximum speed was 12 mph. Messerer also built a 4 hp one-cylinder engine that powered his stanhope in 1901. He closed his vehicle building operation by the end of that year.

METEOR 1914-1932, 1941 — Maurice Wolfe started out in Minneapolis, Minnesota, where he was involved with the H.E. Wilcox Company, which built the four-cylinder Wolfe passenger car. In 1912, he ventured to Shelbyville, Indiana, where he bought the failing Motor Car Company for $37,219 and established the Meteor Motor Car Company. Within only a few months he moved his plant to Piqua, Ohio, where the factory could produce 15 cars per day, which was five times as many as in the previous location. By 1914, he began producing vehicles, most of which were hearses.

The first Meteor used a factory-built chassis and a body by A.J. Miller. Engines were six-cylinder Continental or Model. Besides funeral cars, the company also added a model line of ambulances also powered by the six-cylinder Continental engine. Price for such a vehicle was $1,750 in 1915. The following year, for $2,050, a Meteor could be bought with an overhead valve V-12 Weidely engine, which was discontinued in 1917. In addition to Miller, Bellefontaine also produced professional car bodies for Wolfe, who was also in the phonograph business. The company's slogan for the early 1920s was "Kills 'em with Music, and Hauls 'em Away."

By 1920, limousine bodies were available and all Meteor vehicles used Warner transmissions and Columbia axles. A companion model to the Meteor hearse was built and named "Mort," which means dead in French. By 1924, Meteors used four-wheel hydraulic brakes and balloon tires. Continentals' straight-eight engine was available by 1927 and standard the following year. By 1932, Meteor changed over to Buick components and also adopted Cadillac chassis for its professional cars. The company stopped producing complete vehicles in 1932 but stayed in business specializing in coachwork.

In 1941, Meteor built the Model 101 29-passenger transit bus, but only one prototype was completed. After World War II, the company manufactured bodies for the Reo 96-HT between 1945 and 1947. A merger took place with Miller in 1957 and the Miller-Meteor continued to build bodies on Cadillac, Chevrolet and Dodge chassis. This company evolved into the Miller-Meteor Division of Divco-Wayne Corporation, surviving as such until 1979.

METROPOLITAN 1917 — Metropolitan Motors produced 3/4-ton trucks in 1917. The chassis was priced at $895. There was also a Model AA 3/4-ton priced at $995 and Model AB priced at $1,035. The latter was a panel truck. It does not appear that this company was affiliated with the later Metropolitan Motors of Kansas City, Missouri.

1916 METZ COMMERCIAL DELIVERY CAR   DFW/HAC

METZ 1916-1917 — Charles Herman Metz started his Waltham Manufacturing Company in Waltham, Massachusetts, during the year 1893 for the purpose of building bicycles. In 1898, he motorized one of his bicycles and this was acknowledged at the time as America's first motorcycle. After having a falling out with investors, he left the company and became an editor of *Cycle and Automobile Trade Journal*. He also continued to build motorcycles. In 1908, he got his old company back, which was in financial ruin. In order to pay off debts, he created a 14 package kit for customers who wanted to assemble their own cars and pay incrementally. The idea was a success and Metz paid off the company's debts, then reorganized in 1909 as the Metz Company.

After winning the Glidden Tour in 1913 with a perfect score, Metz continued to sell kits as well as completely assembled cars. By 1915, the company built 7,200 cars that year. It was the following year that Metz entered the commercial vehicle market with a 1-ton truck priced at $695. Unlike the Metz passenger cars that had chain drive, the truck used shaft drive. It was powered by a 25 hp four-cylinder engine mounted under the front hood and had a wheelbase of 130 inches. Tires were pneumatic. The truck was not produced after 1917, although the company continued to build passenger cars until bankruptcy arrived in 1921, when the company's name had been changed again to Waltham.

1914 MICHAELSON BOX BODY TRI-CAR   OCW

MICHAELSON 1914 — Joseph M. Michaelson built a three-wheel box-body delivery vehicle in 1914, which was shown at the Minneapolis Auto Show in Minnesota. The company was started during 1909 in Minneapolis and used the name Minneapolis Motorcycle Company. Joseph Michaelson and his brother Walter left the company in 1912. Thereafter, the company was first reorganized as the Michaelson Motor Company, then as the Shapiro-Michaelson Company. How many of the tri-cars were built is uncertain. The company was also involved in the development of a cyclecar.

MICHIGAN 1915-1921 — Not related to the Michigan Steam cars also built earlier in Grand Rapids, Michigan, the Michigan Hearse and Carriage Company specialized in funeral cars. These had assembled chassis and were powered by six-cylinder Continental engines using worm-drive. The last year of production included a notable model called the "Gothic," which had stained glass windows.

MIDLAND 1919 — The Midland Motor Car and Truck Company was incorporated in Oklahoma City with a million dollars in stock by James M. Aydelotte, George L. Cooke, Robert P. Inglis and Floyd Thompson. The company planned to build "battleplanes" and cars, but no evidence of such manufacture has been uncovered. However, the company did build a 2-1/2-ton capacity truck in 1919. The only known specifications are that the truck had cast steel spoke wheels that carried solid rubber tires. It appears the company ceased existing by 1920.

MILBURN 1914-1916 — The Milburn Wagon Company began as a horsedrawn carriage builder in 1848 in Toledo, Ohio. The company decided to go into building electric vehicles in 1914. The Light Delivery had a 100-inch wheelbase and used a General Electric motor along with Philadelphia storage batteries. Price for the Light Delivery was $985, $300 less than the Roadster. Range was 60 to 75 miles between charges. The Light Delivery model was discontinued in 1917 but in 1920, a taxicab on a 111-inch wheelbase was produced. By that time the batteries were mounted on rollers for quick exchange. The factory suffered a disastrous fire in 1919, with damage totaling $900,000. By 1921, after the company was recapitalized with a million dollars, the 800-man workforce was only partly involved in building electric cars. Six hundred people were building bodies for Oldsmobile. The Milburn factory was bought for $2 million in 1923 by General Motors.

MILITOR 1917-1918 — Two companies built the Militor truck: Militor Corporation of Jersey City and Sinclair Corporation of New York City. The Militor was a standardized truck ordered by the U.S. military intended to replace the F.W.D. and the Nash Quad. It had four-wheel-drive and could be built as a load carrier or tractor. It was powered by a 36 hp four-cylinder Wisconsin engine and to protect the radiator it was mounted behind the engine. The truck used a four-speed transmission and used internal gear drive. Between the two companies, 150 Militor trucks were built before the Armistice prompted the military to cancel further orders.

1918 MILITOR 3-TON 4X4   B.H. VANDERVEEN

1906 MILLER BRIDGEPORT SIGHTEEING BUS　　RD

MILLER 1906-1908 — The Miller Garage Company organized in Bridgeport, Connecticut, planned to build trucks and buses. A few sightseeing buses were built using a 45 hp four-cylinder Continental Type O engine and a three-speed transmission with final chain drive. Top speed was 20 mph. By that time, the company's name was changed to the Miller Motor Company and it also produced a surrey powered by a 30 hp engine. This vehicle featured a mahogany dashboard and aluminum hood. By 1908, this business was no longer in existence.

1914 MILLER MODEL A PANEL BODY　　OCW

MILLER 1913-1914 — The Miller Car Company of Detroit, Michigan, was established in 1911 with a capital stock of $50,000. Theodore Miller was president and his organization also consisted of E.L. McMillan, proprietor of the Continental Can Company, and J.C. Hallock who owned the Excelsior Works and where the Miller vehicles were produced. Guy Sintz, who had built gasoline engines, joined as the factory manager and the Miller car went into production.

By 1913, the Miller Model A was a 1/2-ton delivery wagon powered by a four-cylinder side valve engine mounted under a hood. The light truck used a three-speed transmission and shaft drive. Wheelbase was 112 inches and pneumatic tires were standard with the delivery van body. In 1914, the company went into receivership. By early 1915, Miller was bought out by the Kosmath Company, which produced the delivery van for one more year.

MILLER 1917-1924 — The A.J. Miller Company of Bellefontaine, Ohio, was established in 1870 as a coachbuilding enterprise. By 1912, the company began building hearse bodies for Meteor, using the latter make chassis. Beginning in 1917, Miller also built its own chassis on which were mounted its own professional car bodies powered by six-cylinder Continental engines. These were continued until 1924, although Miller stayed in business for many years after that specializing in coachwork on Cadillac, Chevrolet, Chrysler, Ford, Hudson, Nash and Packard chassis. Miller merged with Meteor in 1957.

MILLER-QUINCY 1922-1924 — The E.M. Miller Company was located in Quincy, Illinois, and to distinguish the company from its contemporary, the Miller Car Company of Detroit, these ambulances and hearses were called Miller-Quincy. They were also powered

by six-cylinder Continental engines. The company did not survive the year 1924, as did the aforementioned Miller professional car builder.

1902 MILWAUKEE STEAM DELIVERY WAGON　　GNG

MILWAUKEE 1901-1902 — The Milwaukee Automobile and Brass Specialty Company was located in Milwaukee, Wisconsin, at the turn of the century. It was capitalized with $15,000 but employed 40 people. The company built a phaeton and runabout along with a light delivery truck based on the common engine to all models, which was a 5 hp two-cylinder engine with a load capacity of 800 pounds and sold for $1,000. The organizers of the company were Frederick D. Bergman, George A. Rosenbauer and William Spence, the latter being president. It was Rosenbauer who had designed the car and had sold it briefly under his own name. The Milwaukee delivery wagon was marketed in Great Britain under the Shippey Brothers name.

In 1902, Milwaukee also built a 2-ton capacity truck. This was also powered by steam using a paraffin-fueled fire-tube boiler and a three-cylinder single acting engine. The truck used a seasoned oak frame. Two speeds were available: 4 and 10 mph. This later heavy truck was designed by W.L. Bodman, who had been with the British Simpson and Bodman Company. The undercapitalized venture closed in 1902.

1966 MINIBUS MB-711　　MBS

MINIBUS 1963-1980 — The Passenger Truck Equipment Company was started in 1963 in Huntington Park, California, and built sightseeing buses for zoos and parks. The company built a shoppers' shuttle called the MB-711, which first appeared in Washington. These were powered by Dodge or Chrysler V-8 engines and in the mid-1970s, were available with propane or natural gas conversions. The company specialized in custom body configurations for specific shopping mall and city themes. It appears production faded out by 1980.

MINNEAPOLIS 1910 — The Minneapolis Motor and Truck Company was formed to build 1-, 3- and 6-ton capacity trucks in Minneapolis, Minnesota. The company showed a prototype truck at the Minneapolis Auto Show in 1910. It was powered by a three-cylinder two-cycle engine. The venture was not heard from after the show.

MINNEAPOLIS 1912-1913 — The Minneapolis Motor Cycle Company of Minneapolis, Minnesota, built a three-wheel delivery tri-car, with a box over the front wheels. It was rated at 300-pound capacity and the rear wheel was driven by chain. Wheelbase was 82 inches and the vehicle was sold during 1912 and 1913 for $375. The company also built a motorcycle by the same name. R.M. Page was superintendent of the company, which stopped production in 1914.

1913 MINNEAPOLIS BOX BODY TRI-CAR   OCW

MINO 1914 — The New Orleans Cyclecar Company, Limited was organized in New Orleans, Louisiana, by W.S. Campbell, I.T. Rhea and Julius C. Weiner. It was powered by a two-cylinder air-cooled engine, although sources also indicate a four-cylinder air-cooled engine, which is doubtful. A two-speed planetary transmission was used with V-belt drive, although here again shaft drive has also been listed. The discrepancy in mechanical component specifications may answer why the cyclecar went from $375 as the initial price to $465 by the time it was produced. A small closed delivery body was available. Wheelbase was 100 inches and track was 36 inches. Although originally intended to be called the New Orleans Cyclecar, its name was changed to Mino once production ensued, which was minimal.

1908 MITCHELL 1-1/2-TON   NAHC

MITCHELL 1905-1923 — Henry Mitchell built wagons in Racine, Wisconsin, and when William Turnor Lewis joined the company and married his daughter, Lewis gained control of the business, which became the Mitchell and Lewis Wagon Company in the 1880s. It also produced bicycles in the 1890s with its subsidiary,

the Wisconsin Wheel Works. By 1901, the company produced a motorcycle and by 1903, one-cylinder runabouts were also built by the Mitchell Motor Car Company, as it was called by then.

By 1905, Mitchell built a 1-ton capacity truck using a 7 hp two-cylinder horizontally-opposed engine mounted under the driver's seat. A three-speed transmission was used as was shaft drive to a spiral bevel axle. In 1908, this truck was also built in a 1-1/2-ton capacity version. The company also built some hotel buses that were electric powered.

It appears that Mitchell built light panel delivery vans based on its six-cylinder passenger cars until 1923, when the factory was sold to Nash.

MITCHELL 1906 — The J. Henry Mitchell Manufacturing Company of Philadelphia, Pennsylvania, was an obscure and short-lived motor vehicle manufacturer in comparison to the previous Mitchell company. J. Henry Mitchell built a 1-ton truck, with solid rubber tires on a wheelbase of 100 inches, using a 14 hp two-cylinder engine that was mounted under a hood in front and used a three-speed transmission. Other details are not available.

MOBILE 1900-1903 — John Brisben Walker established the Mobile Company of America, which built the Mobile Steam vehicles. He persuaded the Stanley brothers to sell their steam vehicle manufacturing company and with the help of Amzi Lorenzo Barber, who had made a fortune in asphalt, the two created the Automobile Company of America, whose name had to be changed because of previous incorporation under such name. Their new company was the Locomobile Company of America. Due to unknown disagreements, the partners split up almost immediately, with Walker establishing the Mobile company in Tarrytown, New York, where he had yet to build a factory. Both Locomobile and Mobile vehicles were closely based on the early Stanley designs.

While Barber was already producing the Locomobile, Walker built his factory and started manufacturing steam vehicles in a variety of body styles by March of 1900. There were several commercial Mobile vehicles built between the turn of the century and 1903. These included the Model 22 Steam Wagonette for $2,000, Model 16 Light Delivery for $1,350, Model 42 Merchant's Delivery for $2,000, Model 36 Rapid Transit Omnibus for $3,000, Model 40 Light Delivery for $1,085, Model 46 Heavy Truck for $3,000 and Model 41 Heavy Delivery for $1,800. All were based on essentially the same chassis except the Heavy Truck, which had a capacity of 3 tons and used double chain drive. The rest had single chain drive and used a 10 hp two-cylinder steam engine.

The former partners got into serious competition, except for the fact that Barber had gotten a major head start and by 1903, 5,000 Locomobiles were sold compared to 600 Mobiles. This was not alleviated by an inadvertent promotion when Virginia Earle sang "My Mobile Gal" on Broadway in *The Belle of Bohemia*. Walker sold the Mobile factory to Maxwell-Briscoe and no further production ensued in 1904.

MOBILETTE see Woods

MODERN 1911-1912 — The Modern Motor Truck Company was located in St. Louis, Missouri, during its ephemeral existence. The Modern shop built a 2-ton stake body truck with 118-inch wheelbase, which was powered by a four-cylinder engine and used a three-speed transmission with double chain drive to the rear wheels. An engine governor was used to limit speed to 15 mph. Price was $2,850 in 1912, the last year of manufacture for this Modern company.

MODERN 1911-1919 — At the same time as the Modern Motor Truck Company was building Modern trucks in St. Louis, Missouri, the Bowling Green Motor Car Company of Bowling Green, Ohio, built 1/2-ton and 3/4-ton light trucks. Both had solid rubber tires and were powered by a four-cylinder engine using a three-speed transmission. The 1/2-ton vehicle used double chain drive, while the 3/4-ton Modern had optional shaft drive or chain drive and forward-control was also on the option list. A variety of closed and open bodies were available from the company.

1914 MODERN MODEL F FLAREBOARD EXPRESS   OCW

In 1914, Bowling Green adopted four-cylinder Continental engines exclusively, and the company upgraded its model line with a 1-ton and 1-1/2-ton model truck. The former used shaft drive while the latter was chain-driven. For 1916, the company added a 2-ton and 3-1/2-ton truck. Wartime material shortages could have contributed to the fact that by 1917, only the 1-1/2-ton model was available. Modern trucks were not produced after 1919.

MOELLER 1911-1916 — Also known as the New Haven, H.L. Moeller & Company built two models of trucks both rated at 5-ton capacity. The Model A was a forward-control design and the Model B was a conventional design and was specifically marketed for the widespread ice delivery business of that time. A governor limited both trucks to 10 mph. The company built a 3-ton model for 1912 and the following year, demand induced Moeller to build a 1-1/2-ton truck. Production stopped during World War I.

MOGUL 1911-1916 — The Mogul Motor Truck Company began in Chicago, Illinois, with three truck models that were all forward-control design. These were 2-, 4- and 6-ton capacity and all were powered by four-cylinder engines using three-speed transmissions. Double chain drive was used on each model as well. In 1913, the Model U, which was primarily built for the lumber industry, had a 188-inch wheelbase and a chassis weight of 11,000 pounds. In 1914, the company set up a plant in St. Louis, Missouri. Mogul trucks were listed as late as 1920 but it appears manufacturing stopped at the end of 1916.

MOLINE 1920-1923 — The Moline Plow Company, located in Moline, Illinois, also got into the truck building business when the company produced the Model 10 starting in 1920. It was rated at 1-1/2-ton capacity and was powered by a four-cylinder engine using a three-speed transmission. The truck was built on a 130-inch wheelbase. In mid-production, it carried a price tag of $1,695.

MOLLER 1927-1931 — Often confused with the Moller brothers of Lewiston, Pennsylvania, the M.P. Moller Motor Company of Hagerstown, Maryland, was not affiliated with the Falcon and Halladay cars of the early 1920s. Mathias Moller was the organizer of the Dagmar automobile, which faded out in 1926. He was a manufacturer of pipe organs and when Moller's passenger cars could no longer find customers, the company received a lucrative contract to build taxicabs. The four-cylinder Moller taxis were known as the Astor, Blue Light, Moller and Twentieth Century. The six-cylinder versions were known as the Aristocrat, Five Boro, Paramount and Super Paramount. The Paramount featured a small rear window for passenger privacy in New York.

The taxicabs' names usually reflected the names of the operators, such as Blue Light (Baltimore), Five Boro (New York City) and Twentieth Century (Philadelphia) or were simply chosen as names of prestige. Each one was customized for its application. For example, the Astor cab, which was built on a 118-inch wheelbase and was powered by four-cylinder Buda engine, had a V-radiator and a two-tone paint scheme consisting of a black top with beige lower section set off by a bright orange belt line. Also, disc wheels were used. With standard equipment, prices ranged from $2,295 to $2,345, depending on body styles, which included landaulet and limousine.

Moller ceased production in 1931 but continued to fit factory built bodies onto Model T chassis as late as 1933. Also, Ford V-8 chassis and engines were used up to 1936. Production crested about 1927, when the plant was building 125 cabs per week.

1910 MONITOR   RD

1914 MONITOR MODEL E   OCW

MONITOR 1910-1916 — "Cars That Run, Stand Up and Make Good" was the Monitor Automobile Works' slogan. Sometimes listed as two businesses, the company was first located in Chicago, Illinois, and later moved to Janesville, Wisconsin. J. Frank Waters was the designer and manager of the company. The principals were J.E. Norling and William Westerlund. Aside from passenger cars built on an 86-inch wheelbase and powered by a 20 hp two-cylinder engine, the company also built 1/2-ton and 1-ton capacity commercial vehicles with a variety of bodies, including a wicker panel van.

One of the early Waters' designs was a four-passenger surrey dual purpose car dubbed the "Milk Wagon/Pleasure Car." It won an endurance race in Kansas City in 1910 and the company began to concentrate on trucks exclusively after 1911. "Designed Right, Priced Right and Built Right" became the company slogan. The 1/2-ton model used the two-cylinder engine that the Monitor passenger car had, while the 1-ton truck used a four-cylinder engine and a selective sliding gear transmission. Double chain drive was utilized at first before shaft drive was adopted. The 1-ton was usually a forward-control design.

MOON 1912-1918 — Joseph W. Moon began building automobiles in St. Louis, Missouri, during 1905. The first Moon car was an expensive five-passenger touring car powered by a 35 hp Rutenber engine. It was priced at $3,000 in 1906 and called "The Ideal

American Car." Its designer, Louis P. Mooers, formerly of Peerless, quickly moved back to Ohio to design the Ewing. Moon continued with less expensive cars and got into the truck building business.

1914 MOON MODEL A   OCW

The Moon trucks were built on separate chassis from the passenger cars. The Model A was a 1/2-ton capacity light truck capable of 35 mph. It was powered by a four-cylinder engine, used a three-speed transmission and had shaft drive. Wheelbase was 102 inches. The Model A was also the designation for the first Moon passenger car in 1905 but by 1912, Moon was using designations of 30, 40 and 45 for the automobiles that also had longer wheelbases.

The Model B Moon was a 1-1/2-ton capacity truck that used a four-cylinder Continental engine and chain drive. It was priced at $1,900 with an enclosed van body and other bodies were available including a bus. In 1915 and 1916, the Model A was no longer offered. In 1916, when Moon cars became powered by six-cylinder engines, truck production ceased. Joseph Moon died in 1919 but his son-in-law Stewart MacDonald took over. The company faded out in 1929 amid much controversy.

MOORE 1911-1916 — The F.L. Moore Motor Truck Company started out in Los Angeles, California. Moore trucks were offered in 2-, 3-, 5- and 6-1/2-ton capacity. The heavier trucks were powered by a 605-cubic inch displacement four-cylinder engine mounted under a front hood and they used a four-speed transmission with jackshafts for double chain drive. Towards the end of production, during World War I, when the Pacific Metal Products Company of Torrance, California, produced the Moore vehicles, a 1-1/2-ton model was also available.

MOORE 1912-1914 — The Moore Motor Truck Company of Philadelphia, Pennsylvania, offered six models of trucks during its brief existence. Moore began with the Model C, which was a 3/4-ton capacity truck for 1912 and 1913. In 1914, the company greatly expanded its model line to include 1-1/2-, 2-, 3-, 4- and 5-ton capacity vehicles. Each was powered by a four-cylinder engine mounted under a front hood and used double chain drive. All the trucks had three-speed transmissions except for the heftiest, which used a four-speed transmission and was built on a 193-inch wheelbase. The 5-ton model cost $4,500 in 1914, which was the last year of production.

1913 MOORE (PALMER-MOORE) OPEN DELIVERY   RD

1914 MOORE (PALMER-MOORE) MODEL C PANEL   OCW

MOORE; PALMER-MOORE 1913-1914 — The Palmer Moore Company of Syracuse, New York, built the Model C 3/4-ton capacity truck that used a three-cylinder two-cycle air-cooled engine under a sloping Renault-type hood. The vehicle had a planetary transmission and final drive was by double chain. Fitted with a panel body the truck cost $1,300 in 1913. It was listed under both Palmer and Palmer-Moore names.

MORA 1911-1914 — Not affiliated with the earlier Mora Motor Car Company of Newark, except that they were both organized by Sam H. Mora, The Mora Power Wagon Company was located in Cleveland, Ohio. The company built a 3/4-ton capacity truck that was powered by a two-cylinder engine mounted under a front hood. Wheelbase was 94 inches and only an open express body was available from Mora. The Power Wagon Company was formed after Mora's New Jersey passenger car manufacturing venture failed in 1910.

1911 MORA 3/4-TON DELIVERY   RD

1914 MORA MODEL 24 STANDARD OPEN EXPRESS   OCW

1914 MORA MODEL 25   OCW

MORELAND 1911-1941 — The Moreland Motor Truck Company started out in Burbank, California, having been established by Watt Moreland, an engineer who had begun his career with Winton automobiles in 1903 and Durocar in 1908. Having designed passenger cars, Moreland turned successfully to commercial vehicles with his own company in Southern California.

1912 MORELAND 5-TON DISTILLATE TRUCK   RD

By 1912, Moreland had produced 203 trucks and six touring cars, the latter for factory use. The first models were 1-1/2-, 3-, 3-1/2- and 5-ton capacity trucks with driver situated over the engine and chain drive. Continental and Hercules engines were utilized with Brown-Lipe transmissions. Moreland trucks were available with a gasifier so that by 1916, low-gravity distillate fuel could be used.

1924 MORELAND 6-WHEEL BUS   MBS

By 1924, a 6 ton was available and Moreland built its first six-wheel chassis for use as a double decker bus. Both rear axles were driven by a six-cylinder Continental engine and the chassis had both Lockheed hydraulic and Westinghouse air brakes. Watt Moreland would later be a spokesman for the truck industry urging

weight allowances that would allow such six-wheel vehicles on the roads of the United States, although the six-wheel bus itself did not go into production due to the high price of the vehicle.

By the mid-1920s, Moreland offered trucks from 1 ton to 5 ton. The 1-ton Model RR and Model RC differed in wheelbase with 130 inches and 180 inches, respectively. Price of the RR chassis was $1,875 and for the RC chassis it was $2,280. Both were powered by 25.6 hp Hercules OBX engines with Zenith carburetor and Auto-Lite ignition. Brown-Lipe clutch and transmission were standard, as were pneumatic tires. Moreland built the 1-1/2-ton Model BX with the same components including Timken front and rear axles, but the 2-ton Model EX and EC with 150-inch and 178-inch wheelbase, respectively, were both powered by a 27.3 hp Continental K-4 engine. The EX truck, which sold for $2,950, used a transmission built by Moreland in-house. The EC truck had a Brown-Lipe transmission and sold for $3,780.

At that time, Moreland built two 3-ton chassis. These were the Model AX and Model AC, the latter intended for bus coachwork with 187-inch wheelbase and dual Van wheels in the rear. It cost $4,700, as compared to the Model AX, which cost $3,900. The 5-ton Model RX with 192-inch wheelbase was powered by a 36.1 hp Continental B-5 engine, had solid rubber tires and used a transmission built by Moreland. The Moreland Roadrunner light delivery truck was also popular during the 1920s and early 1930s.

The company also developed the TX6 truck at this time, which had a Moreland-designed bogie, wherein the dual rear axles were located by equalizing rockers pivoting from the center of semi-elliptic springs attached to the frame. Both Fageol and Moreland developed the first six-wheel trucks at about the same time. A Continental 14H engine powered the TX6 truck, which was rated at 10-ton capacity. It sold for $7,000 and a slightly less expensive 6-ton version became available the same year. The six-wheel Moreland trucks pioneered the new concept in 4x6 drive, which led to orders across the country as well as from the Philippines, Australia and South and Central America.

During the late 1920s, Moreland not only built its own transmissions but also began manufacturing its own axles. Before the Great Depression hit, Moreland's plant occupied 25 acres in Burbank and for the year 1929, the company built approximately 900 trucks and buses. The company also produced trailers and the trucks were fitted with a variety of equipment including cranes and refrigeration units.

Moreland continued to build four-wheel trucks, namely the 1 3/4-ton Ace and the 7-ton capacity Californian, which was built of aluminum alloys and other weight saving materials to give it an unladen weight of 8,000 pounds. The Ace was powered by a Continental engine, while the Californian had a Hercules engine.

When the stock market crash occurred, Moreland sales quickly slipped from four vehicles per day to 35 per year. The company continued to struggle, although innovation was not shunned. Diesel engines by Cummins and Hercules were adopted, a few trucks were fitted with Waukesha engines and streamlined cabs were designed. A merger between Fageol and Moreland was negotiated starting in 1931 but years went by with no agreement reached. Moreland continued to build trailers and special equipment. Because of poor truck sales, this became an increasingly more important part of the company's business.

By 1937, Moreland listed six standard truck models: the 4-ton Model R-170, 5-ton R-190, 5-1/2-ton R-200, 6-ton Model E-220, 7-ton E-260 and 9-ton H-300. All of these were powered by six-cylinder Hercules engines from 85 hp to 110 hp. Transmissions were all provided by Spicer and axles were all by Timken. Prices ranged from $2,135 to $4,685. Moreland also built the TA-420CD for 1938, which was powered by a 125 hp Cummins diesel engine and was rated as a 42,000 pound GVW weight straight truck or it was rated at 68,000 pounds as a tractor-trailer combination. Few Moreland trucks were actually manufactured after 1938, though the company listed vehicles until 1941. After World War II, the Cook brothers bought the company in 1949 for $35,000 and it became strictly a parts and service enterprise.

1902 MORGAN STEAM WAGON   NMM

1910 MORGAN MODEL A 5-TON   NAHC

1912 MORGAN 5-TON COAL TRUCK   RD

MORGAN 1902-1903; 1908-1913 — The Morgan Motor Company of Worcester, Massachusetts, built steam trucks starting in 1902. These were powered by a two-cylinder compound engine fed by a vertical water tube boiler reaching 600 psi, which used crude oil for fuel. After a break in production during the 1904 to 1907 period, Morgan returned to manufacturing with a gasoline-powered truck using forward-control. This truck was powered by a 40 hp four-cylinder engine, used a planetary transmission, double chain drive and artillery wheels.

As the R.L. Morgan Company since its reopening, in 1910 the company switched to disc wheels with the rest of the design remaining essentially the same. For 1912, when the business changed to the Morgan Motor Truck Company still located in

Worcester, 2-, 3-, and 5-ton trucks were introduced with the latter using a 144-inch chassis. These same models were continued until 1920 under the name Steele.

1896 MORRIS & SALOM HANSOM CAB   RD

MORRIS & SALOM 1894-1897 — Henry G. Morris and Pedro G. Salom organized the Electric Carriage and Wagon Company in 1894. Morris was a mechanical engineer, while Salom was an electrician. The first vehicle they built in Philadelphia, Pennsylvania, was called the Electrobat. It was a converted delivery wagon. The name was derived from "electro" along with the Greek word "bainein" meaning "to go." It was powered by a 3 hp General Electric motor and 60 chloride batteries of 100 ampere-hours. Out of the 4,250 pounds of vehicle weight, the "accumulators" contributed 1,600 pounds.

Morris and Salom built a series of electric vehicles and several types were used commercially as taxis. By 1895, their Electrobat was powered by two 1-1/2 hp Lundell motors and four sets of 12 cells each, giving 200 amperes total. Using battery switching, the vehicle had four speeds forward and one in reverse. Hansom-type cabs were used in New York City commercially by November 1896. The first type used wooden spoke wheels, while later vehicles had wire spokes. The front wheels were larger than the rear, the former driven and the latter used for steering. Turning radius was 20 feet. The vehicles used 44 chloride lead acid cells yielding 88 volts.

Morris and Salom also built two delivery wagons for silk merchants Charles A. Stevens and Brothers. The American Electric Vehicle Company was the next business venture for the two entrepreneurs and four more similar delivery wagons were ordered. Electric vehicles were in their infancy but even in the technology's primitive stages, there were many useful and efficient applications.

A fleet of 13 Morris and Salom taxis were in operation by 1897 in Manhattan. They were the first electro-mechanically powered taxis ever introduced in America. Advantages over horsedrawn cabs were quickly proven. They were both cheaper and more reliable, even if their range was about 25 miles between charges. Salom promoted his electric vehicles in an article for the *Journal of The Franklin Institute* by stating "All the gasoline motors we have seen belch forth from their exhaust pipe a continuous stream of partially unconsumed hydrocarbons in the form of thick smoke with a highly noxious odor. Imagine thousands of such vehicles on the streets, each offering up its column of smell."

Since the first commercial vehicles were electric, it is pertinent to explain the demise of electric road vehicles in America by taking a glimpse at the investors in this industry at that time. One of the trends of capitalism toward the end of the 19th century was the formation of various Trusts, including the Beef Trust, Cement Trust,

Sugar Trust, Rockefeller's Oil Trust and finally Widener and Whitney's Lead Trust, considered by many to be an attempt at monopoly, as were the other trusts. President Theodore Roosevelt would take on the problem of monopolies and "anti-trust" a few years later.

Since the Morris and Salom taxi business was doing well, it caught the attention of entrepreneur Isaac Rice, who bought the company in 1897. The Widener and Whitney Trust in turn bought Rice's taxi company and placed an order for 200 more vehicles with Colonel Albert A. Pope's Pope Manufacturing Company, which had started out as a bicycle manufacturer located in Hartford, Connecticut. Pope, in turn, contracted with the Studebaker brothers for vehicle fabrication and the Studebaker company would later produce its own electric cars.

Meanwhile, Pope merged his company into the Lead Trust and this conglomerate, which owned car and battery manufacturers and electric street car franchises, purchased the Selden patent in 1902. George B. Selden had obtained the sweeping patent on all internal combustion engine automobiles in 1895. All those wishing to manufacture such vehicles would have to do it under license from the new patent owners.

It was not until Henry Ford refused to buy such a license that the Lead Trust sued Ford, who won eight years later on the principle that he was using an Otto-type four-cycle engine, not a two-cycle engine as the Selden patent specified. Shares of the Lead Trust immediately collapsed with that legal decision and Henry Ford avoided paying millions of dollars in licensing fees for the years 1903 to 1911. This freed the other emerging automobile manufacturers, while ruining many of those who had invested in electric vehicles. With the invention of the electric starter by Kettering in 1912, electric vehicles, which were expensive and short-ranged due to underdeveloped battery technology, faded out during the next two decades.

1891 MORRISON RD

MORRISON 1891 — This is the earliest reference to commercial vehicles in this compendium. Although there were numerous steam tractors built prior to 1891, their application was usually limited to agricultural activity and they were generally not road vehicles; hence they deserve a separate tome. However, William Morrison's electric surrey, built in 1891 (also the year of the first concrete street in the United States built in Bellefontaine, Ohio), is considered to have been the first four-wheel electric vehicle built in the United States. It was used to carry visitors at the Chicago Columbia Exhibition in 1893.

Morrison's vehicle was powered by a 4 hp DC motor with a Siemen armature. Electricity was supplied by 24 storage batteries yielding 48 volts and 112 amperes. Each cell weighed 32 pounds for a total of 768 pounds in batteries alone. The electric motor was geared to the rear axle. Forward steering was accomplished by a

gear coupling to the pivoting front axle. The vehicle's speed was controlled by voltage switching between batteries with top speed being 14 mph.

J.B. MacDonald, president of the American Battery Company, bought the vehicle in 1892 and the firm of Harold Sturges and John A. Qualey showed the vehicle at the Chicago Columbia Exhibition. The Morrison surrey was the first to be used to carry passengers in a public exhibit and it was the first electric vehicle to be seen on the streets of Chicago, although it was technically not used commercially after that. Another one was built by the Sturges Electric Motorcycle Company in 1895. It differed in that it used solid rubber tires, as opposed to the iron rims of the earlier surrey, and had 36 cells providing 72 volts and 250 ampere-hour batteries.

MORSE 1914-1916 — The Morse Cyclecar was located in Pittsburgh, Pennsylvania. It was organized by Frank H. Morse, who had built a steam car in Milwaukee in 1902 and also worked for the Four Wheel Drive Wagon Company, Wisconsin Motor Manufacturing and Kissel. He was also chief engineer for Duquesne in Pittsburgh. The Morse Cyclecar differed from all others in that it was front-wheel-drive. It was powered by a two-cylinder Spacke engine and used a two-speed planetary transmission. The wheelbase was 105 inches. A Light Delivery version was built and was priced the same as the Tandem Roadster at $350. Manufacturing lasted less than one year.

MORT 1917-1924 — The Meteor Motor Car Company in Piqua, Ohio, began producing a companion model to the larger Meteor series of professional cars. Maurice Wolfe, the company's founder, thought that "mort," which means "dead" in French, was a good name for his funeral cars. They were powered by a 40 hp Continental engine and had hydraulic four-wheel brakes in their last year of production, although it appears the Mort was listed until 1926. This is probably due to the fact that Mort bodies were fitted on four-cylinder Dodge chassis for about two years.

MORTON 1912-1916 — The Morton Truck and Tractor Company of Harrisburg, Pennsylvania, offered trucks from 1-1/2-ton up to 5-ton capacity. The company also listed a four-wheel-drive tractor. Every Morton truck was powered by a 30 hp four-cylinder engine using a four-speed transmission and chain drive. For 1915, Morton filled in its model line with 3-ton and 6-ton four-wheel-drive and four-wheel-steering versions, also adding a standard 3-ton capacity model. Russia was one of Morton's best customers with many trucks shipped there starting in 1914. Morton was a predecessor to the Hurlburt trucks in that both were manufactured at the factory of the Harrisburg Manufacturing and Boiler Company.

1914 MOTOKART BOX BODY DELIVERY OCW

MOTOKART 1913-1914 — The MotoKart was a cyclecar-based delivery van briefly built by the Tarrytown Motor Car Company in Tarrytown, New York. Wheelbase was 69 inches and track was 44 inches. The vehicle was powered by a two-cylinder four-stroke water-cooled engine using a friction transmission and single chain drive to one of the rear axles. The small engine was located under the driver's seat. Wire spoke wheels carried pneumatic tires giving the small van a 400 pound carrying capacity. Price was $400 in 1914.

1911 MOTORETTE KELSEY 3-WHEEL MOTOR VAN   **RD**

MOTORETTE 1911-1914 — The Motorette was a registered trademark of the C.W. Kelsey Manufacturing Company. "Carl" Kelsey was the man responsible for promotion stunts at Maxwell-Briscoe that helped sell many Maxwell cars. After a falling out with Benjamin Briscoe, who had automotive empire building in mind, Kelsey designed a small four-wheel car called the Spartan that he thought would be able to compete with the Ford Model T. When Henry Ford cut the Model T's price by another $100 at that time, Kelsey turned to the idea of a three-wheeler.

The Motorette was powered by a 10 hp two-cylinder two-cycle air-cooled engine and used chain drive to the single rear wheel. Later versions had two-cylinder four-cycle water-cooled engines. Tiller-type steering was utilized and two iterations were developed. The 200-pound capacity Model L 1 Motorette had its seat in front of the rear wheel, while the 500-pound capacity Model N 1 had the seat above the rear wheel.

Kelsey augmented his three-wheel vehicle design by adding a crossbar and a system of links and levers attaching the front axle with the frame so that both of the full-elliptic springs acted together and in conjunction with a truss over the rear wheel, the resulting anti-sway bar configuration, which Kelsey called a stabilizer, prevented the trike from tipping over to some degree. The vehicle was unveiled at the 1910 Grand Central Palace New Year's Eve celebration in New York City. The Motorette featured a pressed steel frame and I-beam front axle, vanadium springs and tubular radiator, all components associated with larger and more expensive motor vehicles of that era.

Commercial versions were offered after the Motorette was put through various tests and races, including a cross-continent trek and a climb up Mt. Washington. Another market idea was explored with a rickshaw design for the Orient. However, the switch to four-cycle water-cooled engines was to become an unanticipated turning point for the entire company when machinists at the contracted firm of Lycoming went on strike. Upon the employees' return to work, the Lycoming engines were quickly installed in the waiting Motorettes, only to be returned by scores of buyers when it turned out most of the engines were sabotaged with sand in their crankcases. Motorette was effectively put out of business, although Kelsey assembled a few more units and tried to power his three-wheelers with Edison electric motors. A total of 210 Motorettes were produced over the years. He later built the Kelsey automobile in New Jersey. Cadwallader Washburn Kelsey died in 1970 after a career in banking during which time he developed a crop-dusting helicopter.

MOTOR TRANSIT see El Dorado

MOTOR WAGON 1912-1913 — The Motor Wagon Company of Detroit, Michigan, built light trucks also known as Detroit Motor Wagons. These vehicles were built as 800-pound or 1/2-ton capacity open express trucks with a wheelbase of 100 inches. The early Motor Wagon was powered by a 101-cubic inch displace-

ment 16 hp two-cylinder, horizontally-opposed water-cooled two-cycle engine. Later trucks were listed with four-cylinder engines. All had a two-speed planetary transmission and chain drive. Front springs were transverse semi-elliptic leaf and rear springs were full-elliptic. Wood spoke wheels 30x3-1/2 carried pneumatic tires. Prices ranged from $610 to $900.

1912 MOTOR WAGON MODEL A   **NAHC**

1904 MOYEA   **RD**

MOYEA 1903-1904 — Henry Cryder founded the Moyea Automobile Company in Middletown, Ohio, where the cars were built prior to the completion of the Rye, New York, factory, which was also the company's headquarters. The name Moyea was derived from an Indian word meaning "swift running." At the beginning of 1904, the company's name was changed to Consolidated Motor Company. Due to the fact that the Rye factory was not ready, the Alden Sampson Machine Company of Pittsfield, Massachusetts, was contracted to finish the European-designed passenger car.

At the same time, a forward-control chain-drive truck was also built and shown at Madison Square Garden. The 1-1/2-ton rated truck was powered by a 7 hp one-cylinder engine and used friction drive. The press announced yet another factory site in Gloversville, New York, and both solid rubber tires and pneumatics were illustrated. Alden Sampson bought out Consolidated Motor by the end of 1904 and continued to build Alden Sampson cars and Sampson trucks.

1912 M & P 1-TON OPEN FLAREBOARD EXPRESS RD

M & P 1911-1913 — The M & P Electric Vehicle Company of Detroit, Michigan, built light commercial vehicles of 1/2-ton and 3/4-ton capacity. Both had a wheelbase of 100 inches and held 40 cells of Gould accumulators that amounted to 900 pounds in weight. Westinghouse DC motors powered the electric trucks and delivery and express bodies were available from the factory. In 1913, the marque's name was changed to Victor.

1912 M & P 1-TON EXPRESS RD

1904 MUNSON GASOLINE-ELECTRIC RD

MUNSON 1904 — The Munson gasoline-electric tractor-truck was built by the Oil Well Supply Company of Pittsburg, Kansas. It was intended for switching freight cars in the company's yard and for hauling steel and other oil well supplies from the factory and depots. The truck was powered by a 25 hp two-cylinder horizontally-opposed engine that, in turn, drove a dynamo that could start the gasoline engine with current from a storage battery. The engine and dynamo were hung from the platform frame and the truck was

capable of carrying five tons or, on level ground, capable of moving six 100-pound rail cars in either direction. It is uncertain whether more than one such truck was built.

1911 MURRAY 3-TON RD

MURRAY 1911 — Murray trucks were built briefly in Norwalk, Connecticut. These were conventional assembled trucks in 3-ton and 5-ton capacity. Both models were powered by a 40 hp four-cylinder engine with a multiple-disc wet clutch and a three-speed sliding gear transmission.

MURTY 1952-1965 — Established in 1949, the Murty Brothers began in Portland, Oregon, building off-highway trucks for logging. The company pioneered eight-wheel crane carriers. In 1952, Murty built its only on-highway truck, which was called the Flat-Top. These were produced in two-axle and three-axle form and both versions were powered by a 150 hp 486-cubic inch displacement six-cylinder White engine. The four-wheel truck used a five-speed 270V transmission and a two-speed rear axle, while the six-wheel truck used the same five-speed transmission along with a three-speed Brown-Lipe auxiliary unit giving 15 speeds forward. The two-axle Flat-Top had a capacity of 10 tons and a deck length of 25 feet. The three-axle version had a capacity of 15 tons and a deck length of 30 feet.

The Murty trucks were designed primarily for carrying long or bulky loads including pipes and girders. Both versions had one-man cabs and were built between 1952 and 1956 for West Coast customers. In total, about 25 were built over the five years of production. Murty Brothers has been in business to date supplying industrial equipment and, according to a company spokesman, a few of the steel carrier trucks were built as late as 1965.

MUSKEGON 1917-1920 — The Muskegon Engine Company, named after Muskegon, Michigan, where it was located, built one model of truck starting in 1917. The only truck built by this company was called the Model 20, which was rated at 2-ton capacity. It was powered by a four-cylinder Continental engine and used a three-speed transmission with shaft drive. The truck's wheelbase was 144 inches and its price tag was $2,325. The Muskegon Engine Company appears to have been the victim of the postwar recession.

MUTUAL 1919-1921 — The Mutual Truck Company was located in Sullivan, Indiana. The company first offered 2-1/2-, 3-1/2- and 5-ton capacity models. All of the trucks were powered by four-cylinder Wisconsin engines and had four-speed transmissions and Sheldon worm-drive rear axles. In the last year of production, the company built a 2-ton and 2-1/2-ton model truck before shutting down entirely.

MYERS 1918-1919 — The only available information about the E.A. Myers Company was that it was located in Pittsburgh, Pennsylvania, and built a 1-ton and a 1-1/2-ton model truck for approximately one year. It is not known what relationship this builder had to the Myers of Sheboygan, Wisconsin, if any.

N

O

N

NAPOLEON 1919-1923 — The Napoleon Motors Company was located in Traverse City, Michigan. A.O. George, F.N. McGrew and G.W. Russell were the organizers of the firm, which started out in 1916 in Napoleon, Ohio, as the Napoleon Motor Car Company. When Traverse City offered $75,000 in working capital and free rent for three years at the former Williams flooring factory, the operation was quickly moved there in 1917. W.J. Chase was president, C.E. Culver vice-president, Frank Trude secretary-treasurer and Leon Gauntlett, resident of Traverse City who initiated the business deal with Napoleon, was general manager. The company built four-cylinder and six-cylinder passenger cars.

Early in 1919, the company built a 1-ton and a 1-1/2-ton model truck, both of which were powered by a four-cylinder overhead valve Gray engine and used a three-speed transmission and bevel-gear rear axle. In 1921, the firm became Napoleon Motor Cars and Trucks still in Traverse City. The postwar recession slowed production to a minimum and by 1923, production was discontinued all together.

1917 NASH MODEL 2017 CANOPY EXPRESS   OCW

NASH 1917-1930; 1947-1955 — Abandoned by his parents, Charles W. Nash began working as a child. By age 31 in 1895, he was manager of the Durant-Dort Carriage Company. In 1910, he became manager of the Buick Motor Car Company and by 1912, he was president of General Motors. After a dispute with William Durant, accompanied by GM man James Storrow, he bought the Thomas B. Jeffery Company of Kenosha, Wisconsin, makers of the Jeffery Quad 4x4 four-wheel-steering truck. By 1918, the 2-ton Jeffery Quad became the Nash Quad. It was powered by a four-cylinder Buda engine and a standard 1-1/2-ton and a 2-ton 2x4 Nash truck was also built. For the first full year of production Nash built 11,490 trucks, immediately becoming the largest truck manufacturer in the world.

1918 NASH QUAD   MROZ

1919 NASH QUAD   RD

After 1919, the 2-ton Model 4017F Nash used a four-cylinder Buda engine rated at 28.9 hp with Stromberg carburetor and Eisemann ignition. The truck also used a Borg & Beck clutch and a Nash four-speed constant mesh transmission. Lavine steering was optional on all four wheels. Wheelbase was 124 inches and suspension was semi-elliptic front and rear. Cast steel wheels carried 36x5 front and rear solid rubber tires. Top speed was 18 mph and the truck weighed 6,250 pounds with a standard open cab. Price was $3,250.

1921 NASH 1-TON   WOM

Along with passenger car production, Nash continued to build the Quad and standard truck models, the latter being powered by large four-cylinder side valve monobloc engines that had coil ignition. The trucks had three-speed transmissions with shaft drive and electrical lighting was a standard feature. Starter motors were not introduced until 1921. During the 1920s, sales of Nash trucks quickly faded so that by 1924, only 203 were built. By that time, the company offered two models: the 3018 and the 4017.

1949 NASH WRECKER   MROZ

The 3018 model had a 144-inch wheelbase and was powered by a 22.5 hp Nash engine and used a Detroit Gear transmission. The rear axle was built by Clark. Auto Wheel Company rims carried solid rubber tires with pneumatics at extra cost. Chassis price was $2,150. The 4017 model was powered by a 28.9 hp Buda HU engine. Transmission and axles were built by Nash. Steering gear was provided by Lavine on both models. The chassis price for the 4017 model truck was $2,750.

Nash discontinued the Quad in 1928, largely due to the fact that it had not been modernized as its competitors moved ahead with new designs. By 1930, truck production had faded out, with a few sedan delivery vehicles built until 1931.

After World War II, Nash built a few 3-ton trucks using the six-cylinder Ambassador car engine and also some of the sheet metal with fenders enlarged by spacers. The chassis and cab were listed for export only, but Nash built wreckers and sold a few hundred to American dealerships. A total of 5,000 such trucks were built between 1947 and 1955. Also, in 1951 and 1952 Nash built a delivery van based on its Rambler passenger car.

1914 NATCO TYPE 15 COVERED EXPRESS   **OCW**

NATCO 1912-1916 — The National Motor Truck Company of Bay City, Michigan, built a 2-ton truck powered by a four-cylinder engine mounted under a front hood. Wheelbase was 104 inches and the company offered four types of open and closed bodies on the single chassis.

NATIONAL-KISSEL see KISSEL

NAVISTAR see INTERNATIONAL

NELSON LE MOON See Le Moon

NETCO 1914-1938 — The New England Truck Company of Fitchburg, Massachusetts, first built a 1-1/2-ton model truck powered by a four-cylinder Continental engine. The Netco truck had worm-drive, as did a 2-ton model that appeared in 1916. In the 1920s, the company continued production with a 2-ton and a 2-1/2-ton model also powered by Continental engines and using Brown-Lipe transmissions and Timken axles.

Netco trucks were conventional assembled vehicles and few were actually manufactured. The 2-ton Model DK with 156-inch wheelbase used a 27.2 hp Continental K-4 engine. Chassis weight was 5,200 pounds. It sold for $3,300. The 2-1/2-ton Model DH was powered by a 32.4 hp Continental L-4 engine. Model DK used Ross steering, while the Model DH used Lavine steering gear. The Model DH chassis with 168-inch wheelbase was priced at $3,500. There was also a 3-ton Model DHX with 170-inch wheelbase powered by a 32.5 hp Continental L-4 engine. That model differed in component sourcing by the fact that it had Gemer steering. Chassis price was $3,700. A 4-ton model was listed with a 32.4 hp Hinkley engine. The heaviest Netco used a Wisconsin rear axle and a Shuler front axle. It was priced at $4,500. All four models had pneumatic tires as optional equipment.

By 1934, Netco listed several models from 2-ton to 10-ton capacity with engines from Lycoming and Waukesha. Straight-eight Lycoming engines were available, but it has not been substantiated that there were any Netco trucks ever built with such engines given the fact that the company's facilities were the size of a large garage, just across the street from the Wachusett company. Netco's main business was building snowplows and hoists and occasionally a truck, mostly on special order. By 1938, truck assembling had stopped, although the company lasted building municipal equipment until the mid-1950s.

1906 NEUSTADT DELIVERY   **RD**

NEUSTADT 1905, 1911-1914 — J.H. Neustadt began at the turn of the century in a partnership called the Neustadt-Perry Company in St. Louis, Missouri. He became well known for motor vehicle kits, both for steam- and gasoline-powered vehicles. This company was also known as Neustadt Supply and a gasoline hose wagon was built in 1905. At about this time, he bought out Perry and organized the Neustadt Motor Car Company.

In 1907, Neustadt stopped selling passenger car kits and only commercial vehicles were available in unassembled form. By 1911, he assembled a few trucks, which he called Model A for the 1-ton capacity and Model B for the 2-ton capacity. Both were powered by four-cylinder engines mounted under a front hood. Solid rubber or pneumatic tires were available. In 1912, these trucks were listed under the E L Epperson Commercial Truck Company, most likely the marketing firm for the vehicles. In 1916, Neustadt assembled three special four-wheel-drive cars for a customer. After World War I, he retired to California as an auto dealer.

NEVADA 1913-1916 — The Nevada Manufacturing Company built four-wheel-drive trucks under license from the Four Traction Auto Company of Mankato, Minnesota, where these vehicles were originally designed. Nevada trucks were built in Nevada, Iowa. They were 3-ton capacity trucks using forward-control and shaft drive to the front and rear axle.

NEVADA see KATO

NEVADA FLYER see DESERT FLYER

NEW ERA 1911-1912 — Apparently not affiliated with at least three other companies by the same name, the New Era Auto Cycle Company, located in Dayton, Ohio, built the Tricar, which was a three-wheel vehicle driven by a one-cylinder, air-cooled engine turning the single rear wheel by chain. The front axle could be fitted with a parcel box and capacity was 400 pounds. Steering was by handlebars as on a standard motorcycle.

NEW HAVEN see MOELLER

NEW YORK 1900-1901 — The New York Motor Vehicle Company was short-lived venture of New York City at the turn of the century, which built a 20-passenger steam bus. The bus had a two-cylinder horizontal compound engine fed by a vertical Morrin Climax boiler, most often used on stationary steam engines. Paraffin was used as the main fuel, while wood alcohol was the fuel for priming the burner. F.R. Wood and Sons built the chassis and one such bus is known to have been driven from New York to Buffalo for the Pan American Exposition of 1900.

NEW YORK 1912 — The New York Motor Works of Nutley, New Jersey, built 3/4-, 1-1/2-, 3- and 5-ton capacity trucks. The first two lighter trucks were powered by four-cylinder engines, while the heavier two were powered by six-cylinder engines, making this possibly the first sixes used in trucks in America. All four models had solid rubber tires and double chain final drive. The company existed for less than one year.

1913 NEW YORK 1-1/2-TON   **RD**

NEW YORK 1913-1921 — Tegetmeier & Riepe Company of New York City were the producers of this New York truck, which was not affiliated with the earlier New York truck built in Nutley, New Jersey. Model L was the first vehicle introduced. It was rated at 1-1/2-ton and was powered by a four-cylinder side valve engine located under a hood in front. It also had a three-speed transmission with chain drive. Wheelbase was 129 inches. In 1915, the Tegetmeier company introduced its first worm-drive and by 1917, this was standard on a second model New York, which was rated at 2-ton capacity. This model was also powered by a four-cylinder engine and its wheelbase was 144 inches. Both models were discontinued in 1921, when the company shut down entirely.

NEW YORKER TAXI see KISSEL

NEWARK 1911-1912 — Light, open delivery vans were built by the Newark Automobile Manufacturing Company. They were powered by four-cylinder water-cooled engines and used three-speed transmissions with shaft drive. Wheelbase was 105 inches for the smaller vehicle and 115 inches for the 3/4-ton capacity van. The 1/2-ton van, which was called the Commercial Car, had a capacity of a 1/2 ton and vehicle weight was only 1,700 pounds. It was priced at $1,250 in 1912. The company was located in Newark, New Jersey.

NILES 1915-1920 — A 1-ton and a 2-ton truck were built by the Niles Car and Manufacturing Company of Niles, Ohio. The company was incorporated by H.A. Wilson and R.G. Adams in 1913. For the first year, it appears the venture stayed in the business of auto repair. According to some records, Niles announced production of trucks in 1915. By 1918, only the 2-ton model was available. Other details have not been found to date.

NOBLE 1917-1931 — The Noble Motor Truck Company of Kendallville, Indiana, built a total of eight models of conventional assembled trucks. These included 1-, 1-1/2-, 2-, 2-1/2-, 3-, 3-1/2, 4- and 5-ton capacity trucks, although not all were available every year of manufacture.

The 1-ton Model A-76 with 130-inch wheelbase was powered by a 22.5 hp Buda WTU engine and used a Fuller transmission, Clark rear axle and Sheldon front axle. Chassis weight was 3,400 pounds and pneumatic tires on Bimel wheels were standard. The 1-1/2-ton Model A-21 differed from the previous model in that it had a 144-inch wheelbase and used a Clark rear axle. The 2-ton Model B-31 was powered by a 25.6 hp Buda GTU engine, had a 162-inch wheelbase and pneumatic tires were optional. The 2-1/2-ton Model D-51 had the same wheelbase as the previous truck but was powered by a Buda ETU engine, which were also the specifications for the 3-ton Model D-52. The 3-1/2-ton Model E-71 was powered by a 32.4 hp

Buda YTU engine. The 4-ton Model E-72 was powered by the same engine as the E-71 but used a Warner transmission. Its chassis weight was 7,300 pounds. All models except the lightest used Sheldon axles front and rear and Ross or Lavine steering. Chassis prices were $1,875, $2,200, $2,900, $3,350, $3,500, $3,995 and $4,150, respectively, as listed. Beginning in 1921, all Noble trucks were powered by six-cylinder Buda engines. The company failed at the start of the Great Depression.

NOLAND 1985 — Noland commercial vehicles were built in Edgewater, Florida. The two models built were a three-wheel and four-wheel utility vehicle. The former was similar to a Cushman, the latter similar to a golf cart. Detailed specifications are lacking.

1993 NORDSKOG ELECTRIC SHUTTLE BUS   **NORDSKOG**

NORDSKOG 1946-1994 — Nordskog Industries' sister company, Nordskog Electric, started out in Redlands, California, building industrial electric vehicles for government, factory, hotel and recreational uses. Both three-wheel and four-wheel light-duty vehicles were built during the 1950s and 1960s in direct competition with Cushman and Taylor-Dunn, with many of the specifications being nearly identical. Nordskog Industries has produced aircraft composites and a variety of components.

In the early 1990s, Nordskog entered into shuttle bus manufacturing largely as a result of California's emission regulations. The first multi-passenger electric shuttle was developed for transporting the company's employees at the Van Nuys corporate headquarters. The 14-passenger shuttle had four-wheel-drive using electric motors that permitted a top speed of 40 mph and a 55-mile range between charges, which could be accomplished between four and eight hours with 110 or 220 voltage. The shuttle featured aircraft honeycomb construction and a switch-out battery pack with solar cell roof panels. Additional units began to be built in 1993 and then U.S. Electricar bought Nordskog in 1994. See U.S. ELECTRICAR.

NORTHERN 1906-1908 — Charles B. King and Jonathan D. Maxwell, both formerly of Oldsmobile, organized the Northern Manufacturing Company. They began by building passenger cars called Silent Northern, which were powered by a 5 hp one-cylinder engine of King's design. About 300 of these were sold in 1903. A two-cylinder engine followed in 1904 and in 1906, when Maxwell left the company, a four-cylinder engine was introduced.

"Utility if the Basis for Beauty" and "Built for Business" were the company slogans when its name changed to Northern Motor Car Company, still located in Detroit, and the firm began producing commercial vehicles. Another plant was opened in Port Huron, Michigan, for the manufacture of the two-cylinder vehicles including a Model C 1,200-pound capacity delivery van powered by the 20 hp Northern engine. Its wheelbase was 106 inches and it sold for $1,600. The Model C had a planetary transmission and used shaft drive. Northern merged with the Wayne Automobile Company in 1908 and E-M-F took over all the factories. Charles King left to produce a car under his own name and Northern vehicles were only produced until the end of that year.

NORTHLAND see WILCOX

NORTHWAY 1918-1922 — The Northway Motors Corporation was organized by Ralph E. Northway in Natick, Massachusetts, after General Motors acquired his engine factory earlier in Detroit and his Ohio Motor Car Company failed in Carthage. Boston capitalists were behind Northway and the company's first vehicles were trucks. These were 2-ton and 3-1/2-ton models that were powered by four-cylinder overhead valve engines built in-house. Northway trucks were one of the first to have fully enclosed heated cabs. Passenger car production ensued in 1921, but the following year Northway himself left the company to build Maxim fire engines. Car designer A.J. Romer also left to produce a car under his own name.

1922 NORTHWAY 3-1/2-TON   NORTHWAY

1923 NORTHWAY 2-TON   NORTHWAY

Receivership followed in 1923 and production stopped. A reorganization took place the following year, which united the American, Bessemer, Krebs, Northway and Winther truck companies under the umbrella company named Amalgamated Motors Corporation with executive offices in Plainfield, New Jersey. The company announced its new truck called the Rocket in 1924, but all production ceased soon thereafter, with the various marques under Amalgamated fading out within the following three years.

1919 NORTHWESTERN 1-1/2-TON CANOPY EXPRESS   MROZ

NORTHWESTERN 1913-1933 — The Star Carriage Company began in Seattle, Washington. By 1913, the company embarked on building commercial motor vehicles. Up to 1916, only a 1-1/2-ton model was built. It was a conventional assembled truck using a Continental engine and Sheldon axles. The company advertised it as "Built for Seattle for Seattle's Hills" and it sold for $2,150. In 1919, a 2-ton was added to the line, built in the same way as the lighter truck. For the last years of its existence, Northwestern offered a 2-1/2-ton and a 5-ton capacity truck, which were designated as Model WS and Model LB. These were powered by a 32.4 hp Continental engine and were priced at $3,500 and $5,000, respectively.

1920 NORTHWESTERN C-CAB VAN   MROZ

NORWALK 1918-1919 — Arthur E. Skadden founded the Norwalk Motor Car Company in 1910. It evolved out of the Auto Bug Company that produced the eventually obsolete highwheelers by that name. The Norwalk company began in Norwalk, Ohio, but within the first year was in such deep financial trouble that its assets and machinery were taken over by its biggest creditor, the Model Gas Engine Company of Peru, Indiana. Skadden moved to Martinsburg, West Virginia, where he found willing investors: Gilbert W. McKown as president, James M. Rothwell as vice-president, Charles F. Glaser as secretary and Thomas W. Martin as treasurer.

Norwalk cars featured a 251-cubic inch displacement four-cylinder engine and an underslung frame with a 144-inch wheelbase and a four-speed Vulcan electric transmission. Again, financial troubles closed the factory in 1915 and it was sold again with Skadden taking over along with A.E. Clohan and T.G. Coppersmith. When production resumed the new Norwalk cars were standard assembled vehicles with a 35 hp four-cylinder Lycoming engine. The underslung chassis was no longer used and wheelbase was 154 inches. It was on this chassis and with the Lycoming engine that the company also assembled its 1-ton and 1-1/2-ton trucks using a three-speed transmission and worm-drive. Neither of the two models were provided with electric lights.

The company badge-engineered such cars as the Marshall in Chicago and the Stork-Kar in New York City. Skadden died in 1919 and his wife took over as president. Since the Norwalk company had been making parts for two other motor vehicle manufacturers, Bush and Piedmont, they tried to take over Norwalk. Because Mrs. Skadden was a republican, she refused to sell to the company's owners, who were registered socialists. She simply dissolved the Norwalk firm in 1922.

NOTT 1911-1914 — The Nott Fire Engine Company existed in Minneapolis, Minnesota, built steam fire engines and by 1911, began building complete four-cylinder and six-cylinder gasoline fire trucks, as well as gasoline-powered tractor attachments for earlier steam pumpers. In 1912, the company introduced a modern fire engine with worm-drive. It was called the Nott Universal and was distinguished by a V-type radiator likened to the Mercedes. It was produced until 1914.

NOVA see TMC

NYBERG 1912-1913 — Henry Nyberg bought the former Rider-Lewis plant in Anderson, Indiana, and began production of an automobile in 1911 named after himself. He also built a 1-1/2-ton model truck with a stake body. It appears he used the same engine in the truck as in his passenger cars. This was a 40 hp four-cylinder engine mounted under a front hood. The truck's wheelbase was 124 inches. Double chain drive was used from the transmission jackshafts. Financial trouble and major flooding at the end of 1913 brought receivership by 1914. A.C. Barley bought the factories, the main one in Anderson and another that had been opened earlier in Chattanooga, Tennessee. Despite promises to continue building the Nyberg vehicles, the factory reopened to build the Madison car in 1915.

NYE 1920-1921 — The Hood Manufacturing Company was located in Seattle, Washington, for a brief period. The company offered 5-ton and 7-ton truck tractors specifically marketed for the logging industry. Other details are not known.

1921 O.B. ELECTRIC   **RD**

O.B. 1921-1933 — O.B. Electric Vehicles Incorporated of Long Island, New York, built 1-, 2-, 3-1/2- and 5-ton capacity electric trucks with double chain drive. The company offered a variety of commercial bodies. In 1925, O.B. also listed a 10-ton capacity truck. By the time the stock market crashed, the company was already fading out, but it still listed the following models: 1-ton Model A, 2-ton Model B, 3-1/2-ton Model C, 5-ton Model D, 6-ton Model DH and 10-ton Model GL. Prices started at $2,175 and went to $6,000. For the last year, the 6-ton truck was superseded by the 7-1/2-ton Model DHL. Manufacture was officially discontinued in 1933, although few were built after 1929.

O'CONNELL see SUPERTRUCK

OFELDT 1901-1902 — F.W. Ofeldt & Sons was a well-known company in Brooklyn, New York, that built steam launches. In 1899, one of Ofeldt marine steam engines was fitted in a carriage. It was a compound engine with cylinders set at 90 degrees, one of the earliest V-type steam engines in the United States. This delivery wagon was rated at 3/4-ton capacity and was announced in *The Horseless Age* in August 1901.

After securing another plant in Newark, New Jersey, Ofeldt built a 2-ton steam delivery wagon that had a water-tube boiler and double chain drive. It also used the Ofeldt compound engine. After a few various vehicles were built, F.W. Ofeldt stated to the press that "We wanted to have the car look as much like a horsedrawn vehicle so it wouldn't scare horses." Another delivery wagon was fitted with a four-cylinder engine but no details are available. The company remained in the steam launch business but other vehicles were not built after 1902.

OGDEN 1919-1929 — Ogden Motor and Supply was not affiliated with the earlier company by the same name in Ogden, Utah. This Ogden was located in Chicago, Illinois, and became the Ogden Truck Company. The company offered several models including the 1-ton Model A2, 1-1/2-ton Model D2, 2-1/2-ton Model E2, 3-1/2-ton Model F and the 5-ton Model G. All of the models were powered by Continental engines from 22.5 hp N engine up to the 36.1 hp B-5 engine. Each used a Brown-Lipe clutch and transmission and Timken front and rear axles. Only the 1-ton had pneumatic tires as standard equipment. Ross steering was used on all models.

OHIO 1912 — The Ohio Motor Car Company's headquarters was located in Cincinnati, Ohio, with the factory in Carthage. The company started out in 1909 as part of the Jewell Carriage Company. When that firm went into receivership in 1912, the company's president, C.F. Pratt, reorganized as the Ohio Motor Car Company, occasionally written OhiO. Among the various four-cylinder passenger cars, Ohio built two light delivery vans known as the Model 40-P and Ohio Service Car Delivery. They used a 40 hp four-cylinder engine, three-speed transmission and shaft drive and were built on the 115-inch wheelbase chassis that the passenger cars also used. Price was $2,150. The commercial vehicles were built for one year only.

OHIO ELECTRIC 1911-1913 — The Ohio Electric Car Company of Toledo, Ohio, marketed its cars with the female driver in mind. Tiller steering was provided both from the front and rear seat for a woman's privacy, so that it would not appear she was a chauffeur. Using the 80-inch wheelbase standard chassis, the company also offered a closed delivery van for $2,000. Magnetic control and double steering were patented by the Ohio company. Brakes were applied with the touch of a button. The incorporators in 1909 were Henry P. Dodge, Rathbun Fuller, Henry E. Marvin, James Brown Bell and Robert E. Lee. After sharing space with the Milburn Wagon Company, Ohio moved to its own quarters. The principal leaders of the company changed a few times and by 1918, the company was dissolved with machinery and equipment sold at public auction.

OILFLYER see TOLEDO

1914 O.K. 1200-POUND DELIVERY VAN   **OCW**

O.K. 1913-1916 — The O.K. Motor Truck Company of Detroit, Michigan, built a 1,200-pound and a 1-ton model truck during 1913 and 1914. The lighter vehicle had an open delivery body. Both were powered by four-cylinder side valve engines. In 1914, the company moved to Flint, Michigan, and became the O.K. Light Delivery Car Company. A 1-1/4-ton model was then built until the end in 1916. It appears that the Star-Tribune Motor Sales Company of Detroit became the parent company of O.K.

O.K. 1917-1929 — The second O.K. company that built trucks, unaffiliated with the first, was the Oklahoma Auto Manufacturing Company of Muskogee, Oklahoma. The first two models produced were the 1-1/2-ton and 3-ton capacity trucks with a wheelbase of 150 inches. The 3-ton model used a four-speed transmission. Both had worm-drive.

In 1921, the company moved to Okay, Oklahoma, and became the Nolan Truck Company, introducing its line that year, which included 1-1/2-, 2-1/2- and 3-1/2-ton capacity trucks. In 1923, a 1-ton model was also available. The Oil Field Special was designed and built for the local petroleum industry and for the last two years of manufacturing, only a 3-ton model was built.

All of the O.K. trucks were powered by Buda engines. The 1-ton truck was powered by a 22.5 Buda WTU engine. The lightest truck had a 131-inch wheelbase, a chassis weight of 3,250 pounds and sold for $1,575 in the mid-1920s. It used a Fuller transmission, Timken axles and Motor wheels carried 33x5 front and rear pneumatic tires. The 1-1/2-ton used a Shuler front axle, Wisconsin rear axle and Bimel wheels. Chassis price was $1,750. With the same make components as the previous model, the 2-ton O.K. truck had a 149-inch wheelbase and cost $2,250. The 2-1/2-ton truck had a Timken rear axle and was powered by a Buda ETU engine. Wheelbase was 150 inches and this Model A sold for $3,250. There was also a 3-1/2-ton model with 164-inch wheelbase, which sold for $3,975 by 1925. This was the heaviest O.K. truck and it was powered by a 32.4 Buda YTU engine and used a Fuller clutch and transmission. Front axle was provided by Shuler while the rear axle was by Timken. Solid tires were 36x5 in front and 36x10 rear. In 1928, six-cylinder engines were introduced. By 1929, trucks named Mogul superseded the O.K. marque. These were not affiliated with the earlier Mogul trucks of Chicago and St. Louis and once the stock market crashed, so did this company's manufacturing.

OLD HICKORY 1915-1923 — The Kentucky Wagon Works of Louisville, Kentucky, began by building a 1-1/2-ton capacity truck model in 1915. It featured worm-drive. The Kentucky Wagon Works became the Kentucky Wagon Manufacturing Company, still located in the same city. The following year, only a 3/4-ton model was available. It was powered by a four-cylinder engine located under a front hood and used bevel-gear drive. It also featured pneumatic tires and had a wheelbase of 112 inches. By 1918, this model truck was fitted with a four-cylinder Lycoming engine and the following year, a new 1-ton Old Hickory model used a four-cylinder Continental engine. Old Hickory also manufactured electric commercial vehicles under the name Urban. Production of the gasoline-powered trucks ended in 1923. The Urban electric vehicles were discontinued by 1918.

1915 OLD HICKORY COVERED FLAREBOARD   **RD**

1921 OLD RELIABLE 2-1/2-TON   **MROZ**

OLD RELIABLE 1911-1927 — The Henry Lee Power Company of Chicago, Illinois, began building a 3-1/2-ton truck in 1911 and 1912. It featured forward-control, a four-cylinder engine with twin spark plugs and double chain drive. Wheelbase was 126 inches, wheels were wooden spoke and tires were hard rubber. Before the company had reorganized as the Old Reliable Motor Truck Company, 2-, 4- and 5-ton capacity trucks were available. Each one also had forward-control, double chain drive and wooden spoke wheels with solid rubber tires.

By 1915, the model line had been expanded to include trucks from 1-1/2-ton capacity up to 7-ton. The lighter trucks continued to use worm-drive, while the heavier trucks continued to use double chain final drive. Except for the lightest model, Old Reliable trucks continued to be forward-control. The 1-1/2-ton model was discontinued by 1924, but the 2-1/2-, 3-1/2-, 5- and 7-ton models were available until 1927.

The 2-1/2-ton Model B was powered by a 28.9 hp Wisconsin engine and used a Fuller clutch and transmission. Both front and rear axles were Sheldon. Chassis price was $3,500. The 3-1/2-ton Model C had

the same make components and chassis price was $4,250. The 5-ton Model D differed in that it used a Brown-Lipe transmission. Its chassis price was $4,500. The heaviest 7-1/2-ton Model L (which superseded the 7-ton Model KM) was powered by a 36.1 hp Waukesha engine and clutch, transmission and rear axle were all manufactured by Old Reliable in-house. The front axle was made by Continental and chassis weight was 10,250 pounds. The truck sold for $6,000. In all cases, wheelbase was optional and Ross steering was used. By 1928, the Old Reliable Motor Truck Company was out of business.

OLDSMOBILE 1904-1908; 1919-1924; 1936-1939; 1949 to date — Olds Motor Works of Lansing, Michigan, began in the commercial field by building a delivery van version of the Curved Dash Runabout in 1904. It had a 7 hp one-cylinder (1600cc) horizontal engine located under the floor, two-speed planetary transmission and central chain drive. The chassis was essentially that of a horsedrawn buggy, though it was fitted with pneumatic tires. A year later, the tiller steering gave way to wheel steering, solid rubber tires returned and a non-functional hood was attached in front.

1904 OLDSMOBILE BOX BODY RUNABOUT   **OCW**

The Olds Motor Vehicle Company was organized in Lansing during the year 1897, making it the oldest American motor vehicle manufacturer in the United States that is still in business to date. Ransom Eli Olds actually built his first vehicle in 1887. This was a three-wheel steam vehicle followed by another in 1891. He built his first gasoline-powered vehicle in 1896, while the family business of P.F. Olds and Son, which was renamed Olds Gasoline Engine Works in 1897, prospered by building gasoline engines. The Olds Motor Works was organized in 1899, with a half million dollars in capital stock, and absorbed the other Olds businesses into one. Olds himself invested $400 while lumber millionaire Samuel L. Smith put in $199,600. A new plant was built in Detroit and several different cars were built by 1900, among them electric-powered vehicles. After a devastating fire at the factory, only one car survived and it was the Curved Dash Runabout, which became the company's only product. By the time a commercial version was built in 1904, production was up to 5,508 for the year.

Ransom Olds had major disagreements with Samuel Smith and his two sons about the future of the company. Since it was Smith's money behind the venture, Olds went off in 1904 to start the Reo company, named from his own three initials. Between 1905 and 1907, a few 1-1/2-ton commercial vehicles were built at Olds, some of these as 18-seat buses. These were powered by two-cylinder engines and used double side chain drive. When Olds left the company, the Smiths turned to building large expensive cars and their sales plummeted. William Crapo Durant bought the Olds company in 1908 for $17,279 in cash and $3 million in General Motors stock. It was not until 1918 that Olds got back into producing commercial vehicles again.

1905 OLDSMOBILE 10-PASSENGER WAGONETTE RD

1906 OLDSMOBILE PLATFORM TRUCK RD

1919 OLDSMOBILE ECONOMY TRUCK OCW

In 1919, after Durant had regained control of General Motors, Olds built a 3/4-ton (also rated at 1-ton) commercial chassis called the Model T, which was used both as a light truck or as a 16-seat bus. It was powered by an overhead valve 40 hp four-cylinder Northway engine -- the same as was used in Chevrolets at that time. The carburetor was built by Zenith and ignition was Delco-Remy. It had a three-speed selective-sliding Muncie transmission, cone clutch, Jacox steering gear and a full electrical system. Wheelbase was 128 inches and the truck used wooden spoke wheels that carried 35x5 tires front and rear. Top speed was 22 mph. With a Matthews body the Oldsmobile Economy Truck sold for $1,245 in 1919. After 1924, the Oldsmobile truck was discontinued.

In 1936, Olds began producing trucks for export only. These were identical to Chevrolet and GMC trucks but were badged as Oldsmobiles for Australia, Holland and Great Britain. The only real Oldsmobile component was the side valve six-cylinder engine used in Oldsmobile passenger cars. A 6-ton capacity forward-control

truck of this type appeared in 1937 with hydrovac brakes and two-speed rear axle. Once World War II began in Europe, no other Oldsmobile trucks were produced.

1922 OLDSMOBILE FIRE TRUCK KP

More recently, Oldsmobile professional chassis were used to build ambulances and hearses since 1949. In the 1970s, Cotner-Bevington used Olds chassis for such work. Between 1968 and 1970, the American Quality Coach Company built an eight-door 15-seat airport limousine called the AQC Jetway 707. It featured twin rear axles and Toronado front-wheel-drive. By 1990, Oldsmobile introduced a V-6 powered van, which has been essentially the same as the Chevrolet and Pontiac, except with a more luxurious interior and trim. The vans have been used for light delivery work. The streamlined Oldsmobile Silhouette van featured a 3.4-liter or a 3.8-liter V-6 with four-speed automatic transmission and front-wheel-drive for 1996.

OLIVER 1910-1913 — The Oliver Motor Car Company of Detroit, Michigan, which became the Oliver Motor Truck Company in 1913, was not affiliated with the earlier Oliver "fifth-wheel" car of 1905. Oliver trucks were available as 3/4-ton and 1-1/2-ton capacity highwheelers powered by a two-cylinder horizontally-opposed engine using a planetary transmission. The lighter truck had shaft drive, the heavier used double chain drive. The Oliver "panel top express" was priced at $1,400.

1983 OLSON KURBMASTER 1-TON PANEL DELIVERY EK

OLSON see GRUMMAN

OLYMPIC 1923-1928 — The Olympic Motor Truck Company was located in Tacoma, Washington. The only vehicle built was a 2-1/2-ton capacity model truck powered by a 28.9 hp Buda ETU engine. The truck was priced at $3,200 from 1923 to 1925. In 1926, it increased to $3,250. It appears that only about 30 trucks were built over all the years of manufacture.

OMASKA 1911 — The Omaska was built by George H. Downs, a railway traction expert. The Omaska truck built by Downs in 1911 weighed eight tons and had a capacity of 20 tons.

1911 OMASKA GASOLINE-ELECTRIC RD

The Omaska was described in the June 1911 issue of *The Commercial Vehicle* as "practically an electric locomotive carrying its own powerplant." A six-cylinder Wisconsin gasoline engine turned a 20-kilowatt generator that produced 250 volts powering two large DC electric motors. However, storage batteries were also used as auxiliary power for starting and hill climbing.

Controls were likened to those of a street car. At 1025 rpm, the dynamo output provided 27-1/2 hp. Downs claimed his truck to run at 80 percent efficiency. Batteries also increased the power of the generator by 50 percent giving a maximum of 41-1/4 hp. Final drive was by double chain. Whether Downs ever built additional units of his Omaska truck is not known.

1925 OMORT DUMP TRUCK AMERICAN AGGREGATES

OMORT 1923-1934 — Omort Trucks was a division of the American Aggregates Corporation in Greenville, Ohio. Omort stood for One Man Operated Road Truck. The truck was specially designed to handle sand and gravel for the construction industry. It was based on the Model T chassis at first, using chain drive, and was fitted with a bottom dump bed. For the first three years, a 22.5 hp Hercules engine was used. Between 1926 and 1929, a more powerful Hercules engine was adopted. Prices started at $1,750 in 1923 and went to $3,750 by 1929. That year, Hercules engines were standardized as were double reduction axles, both of which had been optional on earlier Omort trucks. During the early 1930s, 2-, 3-, 4- and 5-ton capacity trucks were built. American Aggregates continued in the gravel and rock crushing machinery business but stopped assembling trucks in 1934.

1929 OMORT 3-TON TYPE D RD

1918 ONEIDA OCW

ONEIDA 1917-1930 — The Oneida Motor Truck Company of Green Bay, Wisconsin, began building four truck models in 1917. These were built as the 1-ton Model A, 1-1/2-ton Model B, 2-ton Model C and 3-1/2-ton Model C. All were powered by four-cylinder Continental engines and used three-speed Cotta transmissions and Timken worm-drive. In 1919, the company added a 5-ton model and engines were also available from Hinkley, as were Wisconsin axles. Each model had at least two wheelbases and overall, they ranged from 130 inches to 190 inches.

Oneida ventured into the agricultural tractor business and also built electric trucks between 1920 and 1922. The electric trucks were forward-control-type with storage batteries suspended under both sides of the chassis. Once the company was reorganized in 1924 due to financial trouble, the model line consisted of the following: the 2-ton Model B9 with 144-inch wheelbase was powered by a 25.6 Hinkley 400 engine and used a Fuller clutch and transmission with Shuler front axle and a Wisconsin rear axle. Prudden wheels carried pneumatic tires up front but rear pneumatics were optional. Chassis price was $2,825. There was also a 2-1/2-ton Model C9 with 160-inch wheelbase with the same engine and components as the previous model. Only the frame and axles were heftier. Price was $3,200. Next up was the 3-1/2-ton Oneida Model D9 with 170-inch wheelbase powered by a 32.4 hp Hinkley 200 engine. Rear axle was from Timken and front axle was from Continental for this model. Its chassis price was $4,050. The heaviest Oneida at that time was the 5-ton Model E9 with 180-inch wheelbase and powered by a 33.5 hp Hinkley 1600 engine. Chassis weight was 9,400 pounds and chassis price was $4,725. Steering gear was from Ross on all Oneida trucks during this period.

Oneida also produced bus chassis in 25-, 30- and 42-seat sizes. After 1926, a few Continental engines were used along with Hinkley powerplants but after 1927, Hercules engines were adopted exclusively. Due to financial trouble once again, the firm was reorganized in 1928 as the Oneida Truck Company, still residing in Green Bay. Production diminished to only a few trucks a year so that by the time the stock market crashed, the company was ready to close, which it did in 1930. The Oneida name came from an Indian tribe that had migrated to Wisconsin.

1955 OREN TRIPLE PUMPER COMBINATION OMM

OREN 1949-1974 — The Oren-Roanoke Corporation of Roanoke and Vinton, Virginia, built fire trucks and equipment on various commercial chassis. The company's advertising boasted "the South's only fire truck manufacturer." In 1949, the company built its own chassis and these fire trucks were powered, respectively, by 190 hp and 240 hp engines. Corbitt was one of the component suppliers. A custom chassis from Duplex was used from 1963 and these fire engines used a Cincinnati cab. In 1974, the company was purchased by the Howe Fire Apparatus Company located in Anderson, Indiana.

295

ORLEANS 1920-1921 — The New Orleans Motor Truck Manufacturing Company was located in New Orleans, Louisiana. In 1920, the firm introduced its first trucks, which were 1-1/2-, 2-1/2- and 3-1/2-ton capacity. The 1-1/2-ton used a three-speed Cotta transmission, while the two heavier models used four-speed units. All were powered by four-cylinder Hercules engines with 25.6, 29.0 and 32.4 hp, respectively. Each model used worm-drive, Continental front axle and Wisconsin rear axle. Springs were half-elliptic and the four-speed transmissions were mounted amidships. Force fed lubrication was used in the Hercules engines and a centrifugal water pump was also incorporated. Wheelbases were 144, 156 and 164 inches and prices were $2,700, $3,150 and $3,800, respectively. The company only lasted for a little over one year.

OSHKOSH 1917 to date — After gradually giving up on the FWD company of Clintonville, Wisconsin, which he founded with Otto Zachow, William R. Besserdich set out with Bernard A. Mosling to form a competing business building four-wheel-drive vehicles. The company was first organized in Clintonville, but the first truck (since then named "Old Betsy" and still in running condition) was actually built in a Milwaukee machine shop.

Besserdich had been awarded one of the patents on the FWD vehicle in 1908, along with his brother-in-law Zachow who held the rest of the patents. However, during the early formation of the FWD company, both Besserdich and Zachow had sold their share of stock, which had been given to them in exchange for the earlier patent rights. Besserdich sued FWD unsuccessfully and subsequently teamed up with Mosling to form their own company by the name of the Wisconsin Duplex Auto Company.

Mosling and Besserdich were awarded patents in 1914 and 1915 for a locking differential and a steering mechanism, respectively. While Besserdich supervised the design and fabrication of the first truck, Mosling hit the road to sell stock in the new company. The capital raised through stock sales, a quarter million dollars, was put together in 1917 when the company was incorporated.

The first truck, which was rated at 1-ton capacity, was powered by a four-cylinder LeRoi engine and used a three-speed transmission. The truck used 32x4 Firestone gum-dipped pneumatic tires. From the start, pneumatic tires became standard equipment on Oshkosh trucks. Late in 1917, the name was changed to Oshkosh Motor Truck Manufacturing Company and a factory was leased in Oshkosh, located about 50 miles south of Clintonville. The name originated from American Indian Chief Oshkosh of the Menominee tribe, who lived from 1795 to 1858.

In 1918, Oshkosh built its first truck with an automatic positive-locking center differential along with four-wheel-drive. The first production Oshkosh truck was designated as the Model A. It was powered by a 72 hp Herschell-Spillman four-cylinder engine that used a system of heating the gasoline at three points prior to combustion in order to gain as much power as possible out of the low octane gasoline of that era. A four-speed Brown-Lipe Model 35 transmission was used and the frame was built by the A.O. Smith Company. Tires were Goodyear 36x6 diamond-pattern pneumatic. Standard features also included thermo-syphon cooling, demountable artillery-type rims, Allis-Chalmers electric starting, two headlights and a taillamp, a speedometer and an electric horn. The truck sold for $3,500.

1920 OSHKOSH MODEL A FIRE TRUCK   **OSHKOSH**

In January of 1921, Oshkosh moved its facilities to a new factory site and has occupied it continuously since that time. The previous facilities later became the location of the University of Wisconsin-Oshkosh. At the new plant, the Model B began production. It was rated at 2-ton capacity, then increased to 3-1/2-ton. Sales increased from seven trucks in 1918 to 54 in 1919 to 142 in 1920. However, due to the postwar recession and to the fact that the U.S. government was giving away thousands of FWD trucks as war surplus, profits for Oshkosh lagged. Besserdich, who was only directly involved with the startup of the business venture, was succeeded by Mosling as the company president in April of 1921.

Advertising of that period stated the "Oshkosh Truck Goes Anywhere The Wheels Can Touch the Ground." Publicity stunts included a female driver by the name of Blanche Rahr driving up the steps of the local high school and library.

1920 OSHKOSH MODEL A FIRE TRUCK   **OSHKOSH**

The 5-ton Model F quickly followed the Model B. The Model H was announced in late 1924. It was first built with a four-cylinder engine, but it was soon offered with a six-cylinder engine and double reduction axles. This truck model kept the business alive for about five years. The Model H was used often as a snowplow and for road construction. In 1930, the Great Depression forced the reorganization of the company, which became the Oshkosh Motor Truck Company, Incorporated. R.W. Mackie was installed as president while Mosling again became the chief salesman for the company.

In 1932, Oshkosh built the Model FC and FB with capacity up to 44,000 pounds GVW. These models were powered by six-cylinder Hercules engines from 102 hp to 200 hp. Transmissions from four-speed to 12-speed were offered. These heftier trucks were matched with larger V-plows and wing plows or with rotary plows, which were beginning to see wider use at that time.

The Model TR truck was introduced in 1933 and marked diversification for the Oshkosh company. The Model TR was intended for earth moving and used rubber tires and bottom-dump semi-trailers. Goodyear made the tires, which were the largest pneumatic tires up to that time. The Oshkosh TR had four-wheel-steering, could travel at 35 mph and was able to turn 180 degrees in 31-1/2 feet. The set-back front axle achieved an even load distribution. Large construction contractors bought the Oshkosh TR and more than 100 were sold in England. The U.S. Army evaluated these trucks for pulling 105mm guns but declined to buy any because of the vehicles' tall profile and the vulnerability of the large pneumatic tires. Some of the TR trucks were fitted with bulldozer blades, which was a first for a rubber tire vehicle.

The first diesel engine appeared in an Oshkosh G series truck in 1935. The engine was a Cummins powerplant. This was the year that the J series trucks were introduced. The J series had new cabs with one-piece windshields, large wing-type fenders and rounded V-type grilles. Capacity was from 2-ton to 3-1/2-ton.

Oshkosh built a few 4x2 Express models during this time in an attempt to compete with larger manufacturers, but these were soon discontinued in order for the company to concentrate on building what it was known for, four-wheel-drive. The FB series continued with a square cab and front grille, but were later fitted with the J cab. Oshkosh trucks were used often for snow removal in many states where roads had to be kept open in order for dairy farmers to stay in business. By 1938, Oshkosh trucks were priced from $2,885 to $13,500 depending on size and equipment.

Production of the W series began in 1940 and lasted for 20 years. This series had a new cab with a V-windshield and an Indian-head grille. The first type of this series to be used for the military was the W-700. It was placed in service with the U.S. Army Corps of Engineers who used them with snowblowers to keep runways clear. A 175 hp Climax R61 six-cylinder engine mounted on the back of the truck powered the rotary snowblowers, often a Klauer TU-3. The trucks were powered by a 112 hp six-cylinder Hercules RXC truck engine, and both were gasoline powered.

Oshkosh continued to produce trucks for the war effort without retooling or borrowing and B.A. Mosling again became president of the company in 1944. He remained in the capacity until 1956 when his son John Mosling took over. During the war, truck design was steadily improved. As the war ended, the W-1600 model began production. The W-1600 was a large 6x6 intended for off-road use to pull trailers with heavy machinery and oil field equipment.

In 1947, the Model W-2200 was unveiled. It was powered by Buda or Hall-Scott gasoline or diesel engines and was larger, heftier and faster than the competition. It was usually fitted with large plows and wings with hydraulic actuation so that only one person was required to operate the truck and its equipment. The W-2200 was also purchased by sugar companies and mining operations for large scale hauling. The W-2200 was soon followed by the W-2800, which was a 35-ton capacity mining truck featuring planetary axles and a torque proportioning transfer case differential.

In 1955, Oshkosh produced the 50-50 series 4x4, which had a deep set-back front axle under the cab doors with the engine and hood protruding far forward. Its first application was for concrete mixer use and the set-back front axle gave the vehicle an even load distribution with the rear axle, hence the name 50-50. Producers could haul more material and go off road where concrete was specifically needed on large construction jobs.

1955 OSHKOSH 4X4 CONCRETE MIXER　　　　**OCW**

The 50-50 was so successful that later in the year Oshkosh built the diesel-powered 45-55. The rear axle was rated at 23,000-pound capacity, compared to 18,000-pound capacity for the 50-50 truck. GVW rating for the 50-50 was 36,000 pounds, and for the 45-55 it was 41,000 pounds.

In 1956, Oshkosh built the Model 1832, which was a 6x6 tandem axle truck with a load rating of 32,000 pounds for the rear axle and 18,000 pounds for the front axle. During this period, concrete mixer barrels grew in size and the chassis and supporting axles grew with them. Oshkosh built ever larger capacity trucks later as the C-, F- and D-Series including 8x6, 8x8 and 10x6 drives, with the largest being

the 16-cubic yard D-Series, which had two tandem steering front axles and four rear axles creating a 12x10 drive. The last axle in the rear was hydraulically retracted after the barrel was emptied.

A complete restyling took place in 1960, with a new all-steel cab that had a one-piece forward-slanting windshield, rearward-slanting roof, flat-top fenders and squared-off chrome grille. That year, the 3000 series truck was also introduced. It was a COE tractor-trailer dump truck combination for off-road use that had a 60-ton capacity.

At the same time, Oshkosh was building the WT-2206 for the U.S. Air Force. This truck was designed to operate with a large roll-over plow or rotary snowblower to clear runways no matter how much snow fell. They were indispensable for the Strategic Air Command during the Cold War. The trucks were powered by 325 hp Hall-Scott engines with Allison TG 602-RM automatic transmissions and operated at 55 mph. The company eventually built 1,000 of these trucks and many were used at commercial airports.

Many of the trucks Oshkosh built for the military were remanufactured at less than two-thirds the cost of a new unit. Upgrades included change-over to diesel engines from gasoline power. A new truck warranty was included and by 1987, remanufacturing was calculated to have saved $83 million of taxpayers' dollars.

In 1962, Oshkosh built a new all-wheel-drive utility truck tractor designed to be used with earth-boring machines. The truck used the well-known set-back front axle long-nose design and was designated as the U-44-L, nicknamed "Pogo Stick."

Aircraft Rescue and Firefighting (ARFF) trucks, designated as MB-5, were built for the U.S. Navy beginning in 1968. These trucks carried 400 gallons of water, which was mixed with a foam concentrate expanding the extinguishing foam material to 5,000 gallons. Three hundred such trucks were ordered in 1968 and 73 more were ordered as 1,000-gallon versions called MB-1 in 1971. Seventy-two MB-2 trucks were built. Also in 1968, Oshkosh built the U-30, which was a large tow tractor used with the C5A cargo aircraft. The MB-2 was a smaller tow tractor built from 1968 to 1977 and 72 of these trucks were built for the U.S. Air Force.

The M-1000 and M-1500 were a similar series, with the former 4x4 having a 1,050-gallon water tank and a 135-gallon tank of foam concentrate and the latter 6x6 using a 510 hp diesel pumping engine with a roof turret and two frontal sweep nozzles. Another crash truck called the P-4, which was a 6x6, carried 1,500 gallons and 542 such vehicles were sold to the U.S. Air Force in the early 1970s.

Also in 1971, Oshkosh built the E series tilt COE, which was 103 inches tall and available as a 4x2 or 6x4 highway tractor. After initial production in Wisconsin, these were later produced in South Africa. Subsequently, the R-Series were produced, which like the E-Series, was powered by Caterpillar diesel engines. As well as being assembled in kit form in Australia, it was manufactured in South Africa into the 1980s. Oshkosh standardized its trucks in 1973 with diesel engines from Caterpillar, Cummins and Detroit Diesel.

1974 OSHKOSH E SERIES 6X4 W/TRAILER　　　　**OSHKOSH**

In 1974, the J-Series Desert Prince and Desert Knight were introduced for oil field work. These were 6x6 conventional trucks based on the F-Series but were powered by 325 hp to 485 hp diesel engines and used 2,000-square inch radiators as well as enormous balloon tires. This J-Series bore no relationship to the J-Series of the 1930s. On some models, the tubular front bumpers held fresh drinking water.

In 1975, the B-Series concrete carrier was introduced. It had a one-person cab placed over the front axle with the engine in the back. The chute was placed in front for ease of delivery and control from inside the cab. The B-Series was built also in 6x6 and 8x6 configuration. Also that year, the L-Series 6x4 COE chassis was developed with a low profile 72-inch dimension to the top of the cab roof. It was powered by a 350 hp 8V-71 diesel engine and used an Allison automatic transmission. For 1976, the company won a contract from the U.S. Army for 744 tractors to pull tanks or heavy equipment. These were designated as M-911 Heavy Equipment Transporter (HET) by the U.S. Army. The truck was based on a truck tractor then currently in production. This was one of the bidding criteria. The HET was derived from the F-Series.

The P-4 was superseded by the P-15 in 1977. This was an 8x8 66-ton vehicle powered by a pair of 492 hp Detroit Diesel V-8 engines. The truck carried 6,000 gallons of water, which turned into 60,000 gallons of foam. This was the largest fire engine built in the world at that time. The smaller P-19 was a derivative of the P-15 and 715 were built for the U.S. Air Force beginning in 1984.

In 1981, Oshkosh won one of the largest contracts ever to have been awarded by the U.S. military. Oshkosh was the successful bidder for the Heavy Expanded Mobility Tactical Trucks (HEMTT), which provided crucial ground support during the Operation Desert Storm. General H. Norman Schwarzkopf told the House Armed Services Committee that without trucks, "We never would have had the supplies far enough forward to go ahead and launch the war..." Over 13,000 HEMTT vehicles were built over the next dozen years. The HEMTT was built in five 8x8 models: two cargo trucks, a tanker, a tractor and a recovery vehicle. Each was powered by a 445 hp Detroit Diesel V-8 engine and used a four-speed Allison automatic transmission.

By 1983, Oshkosh built three J models of six-wheel-drive trucks. The J-2065 was in the middle of the range and was powered by a 325 hp Caterpillar 3406-DIT six-cylinder engine and used a Fuller RTO-12509 9F 2R constant mesh manual transmission or an Allison HT-740D 4F 1R automatic transmission. The transfer box was a two-speed type built by Oshkosh, as was the front single-reduction axle. Rear axle was a single-reduction hypoid type from Rockwell. The largest J-3080 model was powered by a Caterpillar V-8 diesel engine and was unusual in that it did not have brakes on the front wheels. All J series Oshkosh trucks were available as load carriers or as tractors with straight- or low-loading trailers, the latter having GVW ratings up to 300,000 pounds. Large section tires allowed for travel on sand so that even with a 100,000 GVW single wheels were used on the rear. These trucks had a top speed of about 50 mph.

At the same time, Oshkosh built the twin-steer K-2444, which was the only truck of this type built then by the company, and one of the few forward-control twin-steer trucks built in the United States. This vehicle was primarily used for oil field work, although it could also be used as a bulk tanker. It was powered by a Cummins NTC-400 or KT-450 and the Allison CLBT-750 5F 1R automatic transmission was standard. Rear axle was an Eaton DT-440-P.

1980 OSHKOSH 6X6 TRACTOR W/SEMI TRAILER   OCW

During this period, Oshkosh began building the Dragon Wagon, which had been developed by the Lockheed Missile and Space Corporation in 1974 and built by that company until 1980. At that time, Oshkosh acquired the patents to the vehicle (called Twister Dragon Wagon by Lockheed) and introduced its own Dragon Wagon in 1981. It had a lower profile cab and a different engine, a turbocharged 445 hp Detroit Diesel 8V-92A with an Allison HT704D 4F 1R transmission. The Dragon Wagon had a center-articulated frame with 32 degree yaw capability and six degree roll capability. The vehicle consisted of two modules that drove each of its four wheels. The rear module could be fitted with a fifth wheel for semitrailer highway application for loads up to 65 tons. For off-road work the capacity was 12.5 tons. The Dragon Wagon was the precursor to the LVS.

Starting in 1985, Oshkosh began building 1,400 articulated Logistics Vehicle Systems (LVS) trucks. These were four-wheel diesel-powered tractor trucks used to pull a variety of pieces of equipment, essentially based on the Dragon Wagon design.

In 1988, the company began producing the 6x4 R-11 truck, which has had a 6,000-gallon capacity as a refueler of U.S. Air Force planes. It was powered by a 250 hp diesel engine and used a five-speed automatic transmission. Oshkosh built 1,267 R-11 trucks in the following years.

To date, Oshkosh has continued to build heavy snow removal trucks, the latest having either blower or plows that can remove 3,000 tons of snow per hour. These latest trucks were designed as four-wheel-drive four-wheel-steer for maximum maneuverability. The U.S. Army also ordered Heavy Equipment Transporter (HET) M-1070 trucks in 1990. The contract specified a total of 1,044 such vehicles to be built through the 1990s. The M-1070 8x8 was powered by a 500 hp engine, featured a five-person cab and was intended to haul the 70-ton M1A1 main battle tank.

1978 OSHKOSH R SERIES TANDEM TRUCK   OSHKOSH TRACTOR

1989 OSHKOSH LVS   MROZ

Yet another U.S. Army contract in 1990 called for 2,626 Palletized Load Systems (PLS) vehicles. These use a hydraulic load-handling system that places a flat-rack cargo bed weighing up to 33,000 pounds onto its bed in a single motion. This truck was designed as a 10x10 vehicle powered by a 500 hp diesel V-8 and featured an automatic transmission, central tire inflation and rear-steer axle in addition to the front-steering axle. Oshkosh has continued to diversify its model line as of 1996 and has expanded its operations with the acquisition of trailer manufacturing facilities and the development of its new recycler/refuse hauler.

The lightest commercial chassis built by Oshkosh during the mid-1990s has been the MT10FD powered by a 3.9L diesel as the standard engine with a four-speed manual transmission. Wheelbase was listed at 158.5 inches and GVW rating at 9,998 pounds. But vehicles produced by Oshkosh have mostly been large aircraft and rescue fire fighting vehicles, snow removal trucks, waste disposal vehicles, concrete mixers, and military trucks composed of the Heavy Expanded Mobility Tactical Truck (HEMTT) and the HET and PLS series.

The HEMTT series trucks have been built as the M977, M978, M983, M984A1 and M985. The M977 has been built as a cargo truck, the M978 as a fuel servicing truck, the M983 as a truck tractor, the M984A1 as a recovery truck and the M985 as a cargo truck with material handling crane or drum winch. All of these have been powered by a 445 hp 8V92TA Detroit Diesel engine. Transfer case has been a two-speed Oshkosh 55000 and transmission an Allison HT740D. This has been the same engine used for the ARFF T-1500 and T-3000.

1994 OSHKOSH P-SERIES 4X4   **OSHKOSH**

1995 OSHKOSH T-3000 FIRE & RESCUE TRUCK   **OSHKOSH**

The F-Series 6x6 load carriers have used the 260 hp Cummins L10-260 with a Fuller RT-11609A transmission. The Oshkosh snowblower has used a Series 60 inline six-cylinder Detroit Diesel engine with a four-speed Allison HT-740 automatic transmission. The J-Series 6x6 conventional load carrier has used a 450 hp CAT 3408-DI-TA engine with an eight-speed Clark 8820 Power Shift transmission.

Yet another line of conventional special-application trucks has been the 4x4 P-Series powered by a choice of engines: the Detroit Diesel Series 60 with hp ratings from 325 to 470, Cummins N14E diesel engine with hp ratings from 330 to 435 and Caterpillar 3176B diesel engines with hp from 275 to 350. A 13-speed Fuller RTO-14613 manual transmission or a four-speed Allison HT-740 transmission has been offered with the aforementioned engines in the P-Series. In addition to the S-Series concrete mixers, Oshkosh has also built the Waste Disposal series of trucks powered by a 250 hp to 315 hp Detroit Diesel Series 50 engine with an Allison HT740RS automatic transmission.

OTIS see WESTCOASTER

1930 OVERLAND 2-TON   **OMM**

OVERLAND see WILLYS

1911 OWOSSO 2-TON   **NAHC**

OWOSSO 1910-1914 — The Owosso Motor Company of Owosso, Michigan, built a 1-ton model truck during the few years of production. It used a 22 hp two-cylinder engine mounted under the floor and had a planetary transmission with double chain drive. Semi-elliptic springs and solid rubber tires were used throughout. Wheelbase was 106 inches. It appears that Owosso may have built another model in 1914 but specifications have not been available to date.

P

Q

PACIFIC 1942-1945 — The Pacific Car and Foundry Company was organized in 1905 for the manufacture of metal components. It was not until 1942 that the company was contracted to design and build a large cab-over 6x6 truck tractor that was rated at 12 tons. These were used for towing M15 and M15A1 semi-trailers for the transport of tanks, being one of the most powerful trucks built during World War II. These three-axle vehicles designated M26 were powered by a 240 hp Hall-Scott engine and used a four-speed transmission with a three-speed central transfer case connected to the rear eight-wheel tandem drive as well as by shaft to the front two-wheel steering axle. The M26 used divided rim wheels with bead locks, which carried 14.00x24 20-ply non-directional military tread tires and spread duals were also used on the semi-trailers.

The M26 had a front-mounted winch controlled from the cab and it had a 35,000 pound capacity for recovery of tractor and trailer in rough terrain. In the rear of the cab, two winches were mounted, which could be controlled together or separately and these were rated at 60,000-pound capacity for loading the semi-trailer and for tank recovery. Both the M26 and the M26A1 had a seven-man cab, but the earlier version had a roof as the later one did not. Plate armor of 3/4-inch thickness was used on the front and 1/4-inch thickness on the sides. As in many military vehicles of that era, no doors were provided, only openings to the rear of the cab behind the wheels. A ring mount on the roof was used to carry a .50 caliber machine gun. The windows slanted toward the center of the cab and had plate openings.

The later M26A1 cab had a different appearance besides being of the open top design. It also had the .50 caliber machine gun mount. Armor was up to the windows sills only, with only the frame rails and windshield above the plates. This later version used double chain drive for the rear tandem axle. The M26A1, weighing up to 24 tons, was rated to pull trailers up to 44,000 pounds with capacities of up to 45 tons for a gross combat load of a maximum 91 tons. Total production of the M26 and M26A1 was 1,272 trucks. Many were converted for civilian use after the war.

PACKARD 1905-1923 — James Ward Packard began his company in 1899, after having purchased a Winton automobile and found it wanting for a number of reasons. When Winton refused to improve his vehicle, Packard set out to build his own car with the help of Winton defectors William A. Hatcher and George Weiss. Packard introduced the automatic spark advance and the "H" gear slot in 1900. Both later became industry standards.

1908 PACKARD 3-TON   **RD**

The first Packard commercial vehicle was a 1-1/2-ton forward-control truck powered by a 15 hp horizontally-opposed two-cylinder engine that had been used previously with slight differences in some of the passenger cars. This model was built for three years before a larger model was introduced for 1908, powered by a 24 hp four-cylinder engine also using a three-speed transmission and double chain drive. The second model (known also as the TD with 144-inch wheelbase) was rated at 3 tons and was powered by a 350-cubic inch four-cylinder Packard engine and used a three-

speed sliding gear transmission with chain drive. It was priced at $2,800 in 1910. One such truck crossed the Continent in 1911 from New York to San Francisco in 46 days; the first truck to make such a journey, which was copied by a loaded 3-ton capacity Alco the following year in nearly twice that amount of time.

1911 PACKARD FORWARD-CONTROL 3-TON   **OCW**

1911 PACKARD MOVING VAN   **RHINEBECK**

Up to 1911, passenger car chassis were fitted with police patrol bodies and fire fighting equipment, but it was not until 1912 that Packard added a 2-ton and 5-ton truck in addition to the 3-ton model already in production. The lighter truck had worm-drive by 1914, although chain drive was kept on the heavier trucks until 1920. During World War I, the U.S. Army bought 4,856 Packard trucks and more were sent overseas to other Allied countries engaged in the war effort. Some of these Packard trucks were fitted with Holt tractor tracks instead of rear wheels.

1912 PACKARD MAIL DELIVERY   **GOODYEAR**

Beginning in 1917, Goodyear used E-Series Packard trucks for an extensive development program to improve its pneumatic tires. Seven Packard trucks were used for these road tests, and highly durable pneumatic tires for commercial vehicles were only part of the outcome. Building the Wingfoot Express also resulted in the construction of one of the first sleeper cabs and a tractor semi-trailer as early as 1918. One Packard truck made a round trip of 4,288 miles from Detroit into Mexico and back using knobby-tread pneumatic tires. That year was also the first time these Packard trucks, which were fitted with pneumatic tires, were driven across the Continent from Boston to San Francisco. In the last of four such treks, the Packard caravan made the coast-to-coast journey in 14 days, a new record at that time. Firestone also initiated this type of promotion with its own fleet in 1919. Goodyear built its own trucks in 1920 for further tests and development.

1916 PACKARD 1-TON CHASSIS   KP

1918 PACKARD STAKE BED   OCW

1920 PACKARD MOVING VAN   LIAM

In 1920, Packard offered five truck models from 1-1/2-ton to 7-ton capacity. The 2-ton Model X of that year featured a four-speed transmission and pneumatic tires, the only such equipped Packard truck ever, since the entire model line was discontinued in 1923 as Packard concentrated on high quality passenger car manufacturing. A few truck chassis were used to fabricate buses and the first trolley bus in Toronto in 1922 used a Packard truck chassis. Some ambulances and hearses were built on Packard chassis through the early 1950s. These were manufactured by body fabricators such as Henney. Packard merged with Studebaker and faded out entirely after 1958.

PACKERS 1910-1913 — The Packers Motor Truck Company of Pittsburgh, Pennsylvania, built 1-, 2-, 3- and 4-ton capacity trucks each powered by a four-cylinder engine. The trucks used a three-speed transmission and double chain drive. The two lighter truck models were built on a custom order basis, if in fact any were built. The 4-ton model had a chassis weight of 6,700 pounds and a wheelbase of 150 inches.

PACKET see BRASIE or FARGO or SCRIPPS-BOOTH

PACO 1908-1909 — The Paco Automobile Company was incorporated during 1906 in Chicago by Laurence J. Pietsch, Edward A. Becker and Carlos J. Ward. By 1908, when delivery wagons were built, the company's name was the Pietsch Auto & Marine Company of Chicago. A closed delivery van was the only commercial version built and it was powered by a 12 hp two-cylinder engine mounted under the seats, although a hood was fitted on the front of the Paco vehicles, which used wheel steering. Final drive was by double chain and the Light Delivery sold for $500, $100 more than the Paco Runabout. Plans to increase capitalization and to move to Kalamazoo failed in 1910 and the company folded.

1923 PAGE, BECK & WHITE STEAM BUS   MBS

PAGE, BECK AND WHITE 1923 — Page, Beck and White was an engineering firm located in Chicago. The company built a 29-passenger steam-powered bus that used a Winslow boiler located under the front hood and a compound steam engine placed alongside the driver. The bus was tested for several months and was retired.

PAIGE 1918-1923, 1931 — It was Harry M. Jewett who brought financing and in 1909, installed former Reliance designer Fred O. Paige as president of the Paige-Detroit Motor Car Company. After getting rid of Fred Paige in 1910, Jewett became president, although he continued with the Paige marque for his automobiles, having dropped the word "Detroit" from the name. Manufacturing prospered as production rose from 4,631 cars in 1914 to 12,456 by 1916. It was in 1918 that Paige got into the commercial vehicle market.

The first Paige truck was a 2-ton capacity model with 150-inch wheelbase. It was powered by a four-cylinder Continental engine. It used a three-speed transmission with shaft drive and worm gear rear axle. Wheels were wood spoke and tires were solid rubber. The truck was upgraded for 1919 as a 2-1/2-ton capacity model and a 3-1/2-ton was added to the Paige line. The latter had a four-speed Brown-Lipe transmission and Timken worm-drive. Wheelbase was 160 inches. It sold for $4,150 in 1920.

Paige cars were selling well in the meantime, with races won and speed records set. Although the postwar recession had its effects on the company, Paige survived intact through 1921, when it introduced a 1-1/2-ton model and switched to Hinkley engines for all of its trucks.

The year 1923 was the year Paige introduced its Jewett passenger cars and it was also the year truck manufacturing was discontinued. After 1926, automobile sales dropped dramatically. Harry Jewett sold out to the Graham Brothers, who began producing the Graham-Paige passenger cars, having agreed not to build any trucks when they sold their Graham Brothers company to Dodge. However, they did build a screen-side express pickup in 1931 called the "Paige" utilizing the Graham-Paige 612 Series chassis, albeit briefly.

1927 PAK-AGE-KAR   NAHC

PAK-AGE-CAR 1926-1941 — The Pak-Age-Car Corporation began building the Pac-Kar, as it was first called, in Chicago, Illinois. The boxy multi-stop van, whose body was a unitized wood and steel design, was introduced in 1926 and featured a steering wheel at each side and a low walk-through-floor for easy exit and entry. The driver stood while driving. The first version of this vehicle was powered by a 7 hp two-cylinder horizontally-opposed engine that was located at the rear along with the transmission. It was claimed that as a unit the engine and transmission were removable in 15 minutes. The suspension was composed of transverse springs above and below the worm-drive differential. With a long structural spacer between the springs, which acted as the axle housing and were held similarly in the front, the vehicle had a type of independent suspension. Only a single lever was used to control the vehicle.

1936 PAK-AGE-KAR   S. RAY MILLER

By 1932, the Pak-Age-Car Corporation was in deep financial trouble due to the hard economic times of the day, and the Stutz Motor Car Corporation acquired the company. The Pak-Age-Car, as it was called by then, was redesigned with a longer wheelbase, a four-cylinder engine and a more rounded, aesthetically oriented body. In 1936, sliding doors and a two-piece V-windshield were also incorporated. By 1938, the company was sold again.

In 1938, Auburn (Auburn-Cord-Duesenberg) was already bankrupt, but the Auburn Central Company continued to operate. It was an offshoot of the Auburn Automobile Company, begun by the Eckhart Brothers in 1900 and later acquired by Errett Loban Cord who bought the Central Manufacturing Company of Connersville, Indiana, in 1929. There, the Pak-Age-Car continued to be built with a four-cylinder Lycoming engine. However, since Auburn was without a sales, marketing or service network, these operations were handled by Diamond T in Chicago, Illinois, and the Pak-Age-Car vans were badged as Diamond Ts until production ended in 1941. Total production over 16 years was 3,500 units.

1912 PALMER-MEYER 3/4-TON DELIVERY WAGON   RD

1914 PALMER-MEYER FLAREBOARD   OCW

PALMER; PALMER-MEYER 1912-1918 — There were other early makes of motor vehicles under the name Palmer, but this company was the only one that existed in St. Louis, Missouri. The trucks were listed under both Palmer and Palmer-Meyer, the latter being the full name of the company. The company's first truck was the 3/4-ton Model B, which had a four-cylinder engine mounted under a front hood. It was built with a stake body and sold for $1,550. In 1914, Palmer trucks were also available in 1-ton and 1-1/2-ton capacity and these were also powered by four-cylinder side valve engines. All of the company's trucks were assembled with three-speed transmissions and double chain final drive. Although shaft drive was used by 1915, solid rubber tires were standard on Palmer trucks throughout the years of production. For 1917 and 1918, only 1-ton and 2-ton capacity trucks were offered by the Palmer-Meyer company.

1914 PALMER-MOORE OPEN FLAREBOARD EXPRESS   OCW

PALMER-MOORE 1913-1916 — The Palmer-Moore Company was located in Syracuse, New York. The company built 3/4-ton and 1-ton trucks for a brief period. The 3/4-ton Model K was priced at $1,150. It used a Renault-style hood and was powered by a four-cylinder Buda engine.

PANHARD 1918-1919 — Although this name was associated with a famous motor vehicle manufacturer, Panhard Motors of Grand Haven, Michigan, was not evidently affiliated with the French company by the same name. The American company's Model A was a

1-ton truck and the Model B was rated at 1-1/2 tons. Both trucks used the same chassis, which had a wheelbase of 130 inches. As standard assembled vehicles, both were powered by four-cylinder Gray engines, Fuller transmissions and Torbensen rear axles.

1919 PARKER 3-1/2-TON CHASSIS   MROZ

PARKER 1918-1933 — The Parker Motor Truck Company of Milwaukee, Wisconsin, assembled conventional trucks from 1-ton to 5-ton capacity. Parker trucks were powered by Continental, Waukesha and Wisconsin engines. In the early 1920s, Parker's 3-1/2-ton capacity truck was powered by a 43 hp side valve Continental engine and used a four-speed Warner transmission with front and rear axles built by Parker. The truck was advertised for its passenger car track dimension, which allowed it to follow the ruts of a country road. Wheelbase was 160 inches standard, with 180 inches optional. Pneumatic tires were also optional, which gave the truck a top speed of 20 mph instead of 16 with solid rubber tires. Price for the 3-1/2-ton model was $4,400.

1920 PARKER 3-1/2-TON   KP

The company survived the postwar recession but in 1924, new ownership initiated a change of name to the Parker Truck Company, Incorporated. The firm continued to build trucks in Milwaukee, adding a 1-ton model powered by a Buda WTU engine. After the new owners took over, the 5-ton model was discontinued and only 1-ton to 3-1/2-ton trucks were built as the company gradually faded from manufacturing. It appears that by 1933, Parker was no longer in operation.

PARR 1909-1910 — The Parr Wagon Company of Huff Station, Pennsylvania, built one truck model during its brief entry into the commercial vehicle manufacturing field. This was a 3-ton capacity forward-control vehicle that used a 36 hp four-cylinder Waukesha engine and a friction transmission with double chain final drive.

1916 PATHFINDER   S. RAY MILLER

PATHFINDER 1912-1914 — The Pathfinder evolved from the Parry Auto Company, which went into receivership in 1910. Former executives of Parry, Dayton, Standard Oil and American Ball Bearing organized the Motor Car Manufacturing Company, which built Pathfinder passenger cars with names such as Armored Roadster, Martha Washington Coach and Leather Stocking Touring. The company also built a 3/4-ton Delivery Wagon based on the 118-inch wheelbase chassis used in its Series XIII passenger cars of 1913. These were powered by a 40 hp four-cylinder engine and used a three-speed transmission with shaft drive. A 1-ton delivery was also built on the same chassis, selling for $2,000 in 1913.

The company's slogan was "Known for Reliability" but it seemed to be highly preoccupied with styling. This included a boattail speedster, covered spare wheels, bright color combinations and a Conestoga wagon top on one of its Delivery Wagon models. Commercial vehicles were no longer built after 1914, although the company continued into 1916 with passenger cars, including a 12-cylinder Weidely Pathfinder car called "Pathfinder the Great, King of Twelves." Once World War I began, however, material shortages put the company under. Its assets were bought out for $59,000 and its factory was taken over to make shoe polish.

PATRIOT 1918-1926 — The Patriot Motor Car Company evolved from the A.G. Hebb Quality Bodies factories in Lincoln, Nebraska. Hebb Motors Company was listed in late 1917, when Patriot trucks were assembled for the 1918 model year. Two models were built: the 1-1/2-ton Lincoln and the 2-1/2-ton Washington. Both were powered by four-cylinder Buda engines with four-speed transmissions. The Lincoln truck had internal gear final drive while the Washington used worm-drive. One year later, the company switched to Continental engines. Hebb built its own chassis and bodies, as well as supplying bodies to other truck builders such as Douglas in Omaha, Nebraska.

1918 PATRIOT BUS   RD

The Patriot Motors Company was the result of a reorganization of Hebb in 1920. "Made in the West; Built for the World," was the company slogan. A year later, the Revere 3/4-ton "speed model" was unveiled. It featured pneumatic tires and full electrical system as standard equipment that was only optional on the other two models, which continued to be assembled. At that time, the company used a Continental engine for the Revere while switching to Hinkley engines for the other trucks. Patriot trucks were built for agricultural use as well as for bus and fire engine applications.

1920 PATRIOT 1-1/2-TON   **MROZ**

By 1922, the company's business had unraveled and the Woods brothers bought out Patriot. Under new management as the Patriot Manufacturing Company, the plant was moved to Havelock, Nebraska, and continued production with 1-, 2- and 3-ton capacity trucks powered by either Buda or Hinkley engines with Covert transmissions and Empire or Wisconsin worm-drive. By 1926, the Woods brothers placed their own name on the company emblem. Woods trucks were built until 1931 back in the city of Lincoln.

PATTON 1899 — The Patton Motor Vehicle Company of Chicago, Illinois, designed an 8-ton capacity truck that was actually built by the Fischer Equipment Company, also located in Chicago. This was a hybrid electric design that used a vertical three-cylinder two-cycle engine supplied by the American Petroleum Motor Company that drove an kilowatt Crocker-Wheeler dynamo, which, in turn, provided the electricity for two 7-1/2 hp motors driving each rear wheel. Maximum speed was 8 mph. It appears only one such vehicle was built.

PAULDING 1913-1916 — Paulding trucks were built by the St. Louis Motor Truck Company in St. Louis, Missouri. The company built commercial vehicles ranging from 800-pound to 3-ton capacity. Chain drive was used on the first series but for the last year of manufacture, the company switched to shaft drive. Engines were mounted under a front hood. Other details have not been available.

PAYHAULER see INTERNATIONAL

1980 PAYMASTER REFUSE TRUCK   **PAYMASTER**

PAYMASTER see RYDER

1911 PEERLESS   **RD**

PEERLESS 1911-1918 — Having started as a bicycle manufacturer and maker of clothes wringers, the Peerless Manufacturing Company had built its first car in 1897, before hiring Louis P. Mooers as chief engineer. Peerless Motor Car Company had been formed in 1902. The firm's cars were quite modern in design, including such things as tilt steering and limousine coachwork by 1904. Mooers believed that racing was the best way to advertise as well as improve the breed and at this time, he designed a huge 60 hp car that would be driven by the well-known Barney Oldfield to set new records. However, in 1905, Mooers left to build the Moon car. Peerless hired Charles B. Schmidt away from Packard to design a series of luxury cars. "All That the Name Implies," was the company slogan.

It was not until 1911 that Peerless got into the commercial vehicle market with a model line of trucks ranging from 3-ton to 6-ton capacity. Under the leadership of Lewis H. Kittredge, Peerless built high-quality passenger cars and some conventional conservatively-designed trucks. All used four-speed transmissions and double chain final drive. Peerless built its own engines for the trucks. These were 412-cubic inch displacement four-cylinder water-cooled engines, which were used in all the models.

1914 PEERLESS 5-TON   **LIAM**

In 1916, the company introduced a 2-ton truck that featured worm-drive. In 1918, Peerless built a 3-ton truck for the U.S. military. It was known as the Model TC3 and was powered by a 32.4 hp 412-cubic inch four-cylinder Peerless engine and used a four-speed transmission. Truck tractors were also built with capacities of 3 tons and 6 tons, respectively. All Peerless trucks were painted a gray color called "Lead." By 1918, trucks were discontinued, although passenger car production continued successfully into the mid-1920s. In 1921, the company was bought by Richard H. Collins, former president of Cadillac. After various management upheavals, the company succumbed to the Great Depression in 1931.

PENN 1911-1912 — The Penn Motor Car Company was organized in Pittsburgh, Pennsylvania, in 1910 and began producing both the Penn Thirty Roadster and a 3/4-ton delivery truck, the latter being powered by a 22 hp four-cylinder engine and using shaft drive. By 1912, the delivery truck sold for $1,250 while the Comet Roadster was priced at $1,000 for that year. It appears that both used the same 105-inch wheelbase chassis. That year, a $90,000 factory was built in New Castle, Pennsylvania, but the backers petitioned for bankruptcy before any vehicles were produced there. The Penn Motor Car Company was dismantled by early 1913.

1910 PENN-UNIT   **RD**

PENN-UNIT 1910-1912 — The Penn-Unit Car Company of Allentown, Pennsylvania, built the Penn-Unit truck in 1910. It was a 3/4-ton capacity vehicle powered by a 20 hp two-cylinder water-cooled engine. The truck's name alluded to the fact that the engine and clutch, as well as the transmission, differential and jackshaft, were all easily removable as a "unit." In 1911, the truck was priced at $1,800. In 1912, the company was reorganized as the Penn-Unit Manufacturing Company but it appears production did not continue.

PENTON 1927-1928 — The Penton Motor Car Company was incorporated by E.W. Penton, who was president, H.S. Sherman as vice-president and J.F. Potts as secretary-treasurer. The company was founded with $50,000 in capital in Cleveland, Ohio, and announced the production of "electric goods." It is known that the company did build the Penton Cantilever, which was a "walk-thru" van powered by a four-cylinder engine using front-wheel-drive.

PERFEX 1913-1916 — James R. Fouch was the designer of the Perfex car, which made a debut in its hometown of Los Angeles, California, in 1912. Fouch was also the factory manager. Capital was provided by various early Los Angeles entrepreneurs, who had tried earlier with a car called the Moro. Former Moro secretary Ora Hutchings stayed with Perfex and the company offered a roadster for $1,050 in 1912, when 12 such cars were built.

The roadster model was joined by the Model 19 1/2-ton truck by the following year. The truck had a 116-inch wheelbase, 10 inches longer than the roadster. Both were powered by the T-head four-cylinder Golden, Belknap and Swartz engine and used a three-speed selective sliding gear transmission and shaft drive. Pneumatic tires were standard equipment and the truck sold for $875. In 1913, the company's president, Paul Brown Jr., unveiled that the Perfex company would continue building commercial vehicles only, at which time Fouch quickly departed. The light Perfex trucks were built until about 1916.

PETERBILT 1939 to date — Having been in the logging business and having modified many old trucks for hauling purposes, Theodore Alfred (Al) Peterman bought the Fageol Truck and Coach Company of Oakland, California, in 1939 on 13-1/2 acres of land for approximately $200,000. His goal was to build trucks per his specifications based on Fageol design. Fageol had been acquired by Sterling on November 1, 1938, but the company did not have adequate working capital to continue operations on the West Coast. Peterman had invented the Flex Axle, which was used on a number of early Peterbilt trucks.

The first Peterbilt trucks were nearly identical in appearance to the Fageol trucks except that the trademark hood fins of the former make were no longer used. One of the first Peterbilt trucks was the Model 260 chain drive logger built the year of the company and factory purchase. W.H. Bill was the first company president and, according to some sources, mechanics first referred to the trucks as Bill-Bilt, which prompted Peterman to name the trucks Peterbilt.

1939 PETERBILT 6X4   **RNE**

Fortuitous access to some arcane company records show who purchased the first seven Peterbilt trucks in 1939. In June, the first truck was serial number S-100, which was delivered as a bare chassis to O.M. Hirst Company in Sacramento where it was built up as a fire engine. The second truck sold was number L-100, a three-axle truck, to Beckley Brothers in Stockton, and M-101 went to P. Bordenave in August, also of that city. Kent Lines of San Francisco bought the fourth truck, which was M-102, and Winkler bought the fifth truck, which was serial number M-103. A.W. Hays who founded the Hays Antique Truck Museum bought the sixth truck, which was L-101. Serial number S-101 was bought in December by the Centerville (now Fremont) fire department after it was displayed at the 1939 World's Fair in San Francisco.

1942 PETERBILT TANDEM AXLE DUMP TRUCK   **RNE**

Production rose to 82 (or 111 depending on source) trucks in 1940. This included 10 supercharged HBS-600 Cummins-powered "Freightliner" COE trucks for Freightways Manufacturing Company of Salt Lake City. Peterbilt built a dump truck for the U.S. Army in 1942 and the Model 270 also made its debut that year. Engine options included Cummins, Waukesha and Hall-Scott engines -- both gas and butane -- Brown-Lipe, Spicer and Fuller transmissions, dual reduction worm-drive Timken-Detroit axles, Ross cam-and-lever steering and Westinghouse air brakes. Most of the early Peterbilt trucks were 6x4 load carriers and truck tractors used in logging, sugarcane transport, quarrying, mining and oil field applications. All used conventional layout design.

Peterbilt used aluminum extensively in its frame (which had extruded channels), cabs, wheels, bumpers and other components in order to reduce weight by as much as 1,500 pounds per truck compared with steel construction, which was available as an option. In 1944, the Oakland plant built 225 trucks for the U.S. government. T.A. Peterman passed away from cancer in the fall of 1944 and his widow took over the company's ownership. Five employees got together and bought the company from Ida Peterman in 1946 for the sum of $450,000. L.A. Lundstrum became president, F.E. Mathews vice-president and W.M. Fanning secretary-treasurer. By 1947, the company's sales surpassed $4.5 million.

For 1948, Peterbilt offered Models 270DD, 344DT, 345DT, 354DT and 355DT, and the Model 350 also made its debut. Peterbilt trucks were available as two- and three-axle versions from 27,000 pounds to 77,000 pounds GVW. Product line revision did not take place until 1949. The cabs were enlarged and made more ergonomic. The bumpers were lowered exposing more of the radiator and resulting in a taller stance. The headlights were moved up on brackets that were mounted to each side of the radiator, which was mounted on Lord rubber bushings.

1949 PETERBILT OFF-ROAD TRUCK   **RNE**

Although *The Commercial Car Journal* had earlier stated that Peterbilt trucks had a maximum GVW rating of 77,000 pounds, in November of 1948 that figure was published as 56,000 pounds. Cummins diesel engines continued to be used and Waukesha gasoline engines or Hall-Scott 400 gasoline or butane engines were optional. Peterbilt acquired the MacDonald Truck and Manufacturing Company of San Francisco in 1949. MacDonald continued to build a few low-bed trucks as a division of Peterbilt before MacDonald faded out entirely three years later. Peterbilt model number series for 1949 were listed as 280, 350, 360, 370, 380 and 390. Prices ranged from $14,800 to $20,500.

Peterbilt introduced its first cab-over in 1950, when company sales grew to $7 million. A COE prototype called the Model 280/350 was built and after road testing, production began two years later. Peterbilt also pioneered the design of the Dromedary truck design. This consisted of a long truck tractor with additional cargo space, which was also capable of pulling a trailer. The vehicle could therefore be used as a straight truck or in combination with a semi-trailer as a highway tractor. The first of such trucks was delivered to the Pacific Inter-mountain Express (P.I.E.). For Ringsby Company Peterbilt also manufactured the Model 451 Dromedary, which had twin-steer tandem axles in front. There was also the off-highway Model 381 with a deeply set-back front axle.

Another Peterbilt COE of that period was the tilt-cab Model 352 that was built between 1952 and 1956. The year 1952 was also when Peterbilt switched from a rectangular cast aluminum nameplate to a chrome cloisonne oval with the Peterbilt name in script. Models 281 and 351 were successful and were built for 11 years after being introduced late in 1954. COE versions of the Model 281 and 351 were introduced late in 1955 and these had wide cabs and two-piece curved windshields. The trademark tapered bumper and skirted fenders of previous models gave way to circular fenders and a straight bumper flush with the new grille shell.

In June of 1958, Peterbilt Motors was bought by the Pacific Car and Foundry Company (PACCAR) of Renton, Washington. Two years later, Peterbilt Motors Company, as a division of PACCAR, relocated to a new $2 million plant in Newark, California, located just south of its Oakland factory. By this time, the Model 310 COE had been placed into production. In 1962, the company introduced the lightweight dumper/mixer chassis Model 341. A face lift was

adapted for the Model 282 and 352 COE in 1963 and this consisted of quad headlights and a four-piece windshield with curved corner sections. The "H" versions of these models were fabricated with higher cabs and larger radiators.

The tilt-hood Model 288 and 358 arrived in 1965 and the Model 289 and 359 were unveiled in 1967. Models 281 and 351 were still being offered in 1965 but there is no evidence any were actually built that late. For 1968, conventional highway tractors were available with aluminum or fiberglass tilt hoods and wide grilles. Another huge factory was started in Madison, Tennessee, in 1969. Engine choices during the 1960s included Caterpillar, Continental, Cummins and Detroit Diesel, which were available in the form of the V-6, V-8, straight-six, straight-eight and V-12. J.M. Bodden was general manager of the company. Peterbilt production for the decade was 21,000 trucks, four times that of the previous decade.

During the 1960s, the most common engine used by Peterbilt was the Cummins NH 220 diesel coupled to a Spicer 12-speed transmission. Axles were usually Timken full-floating hypoid or double-reduction. GVW ratings were up to 84,000 pounds and GCW was up to 250,000 pounds.

1977 PETERBILT MODEL 353 6X4   **PETERBILT**

Peterbilt began production of its Model 346 6x6 and 8x6 mixer/dump in 1973. Front driving axle was a Rockwell Standard FDS-1800 and the rear axle was most often a Rockwell Standard SQHD. Standard engine was the 255 hp Cummins V-555 and optional engines were Caterpillar 1673 and 1674, Cummins VT-555 and Detroit Diesel 6V53 and 6171. Models 200 and 300 LCF were built in the 1970s for refuse service and the Model 353 was introduced for the logging and heavy construction industries. Model 387 was designed for off-highway mining and oilfield work. Peterbilt used Kenworth cabs on its conventional cabs except for its off-highway trucks.

The 1970s were a time when fuel economy became of utmost importance. One of the trends that Peterbilt followed was the "gear fast/run slow" drivetrain design application. Also fan clutches and radial tires were adopted. Fuller 15-speed transmissions were standardized equipment. By 1978, GVW was from 34,000 to 62,000 pounds and GCW was from 55,000 to 125,000 pounds for highway work. Caterpillar, Cummins and Detroit Diesel engines continued to be offered from 210 to 450 hp. By 1980, Peterbilt was building 9,000 trucks per year. For the entire decade the company had built 72,000 units. Experiments with turbine engines in 1972 were short-lived.

The COE Model 362 was introduced in 1980. During the 1980s, Peterbilt concentrated on niche marketing. In 1980, another large facility was opened in Denton, Texas, while manufacturing was discontinued at the smaller Newark factory in California during 1986, although engineering and management offices remained.

1985 PETERBILT MODEL 359 W/LOWBED TRAILER   MROZ

For 1986, Peterbilt's conventional line was redesigned and it consisted of the Model 375, aerodynamic Model 377 and traditional Model 377. Peterbilt developed aerodynamic elements for its product line, although the company's trucks were distinguished by large, flat, square radiator grilles. Detroit Diesel engines were used much less often with only about three percent of the trucks powered by those units compared to Caterpillar and Cummins.

In 1988, it was announced that Peterbilt's Class 8 market share was 11 percent, which was double that of a decade before. That number translated to mean 18,000 Class 8 trucks produced for one year. Peterbilt's market share in the refuse and construction industry also grew to eight percent. The aerodynamic COE Model 372 made its debut in 1988 and it featured a sloping windshield, curved front and integral roof fairing.

In 1989, Peterbilt celebrated its 50th anniversary and gave away a Model 379 in a sweepstakes contest. At that time, Peterbilt trucks could be ordered with commemorative Caterpillar 3406 or Cummins 444 engines, 48- or 63-inch high roof sleepers, any Fuller transmission and any Peterbilt air suspension. A restored 1939 Model 334DT toured the United States. The Model 375 was advertised with a 300 hp engine and Peterbilt continued to refine its trucks with aerodynamic elements and more luxurious cabs and sleeper compartments.

1991 PETERBILT REFUSE TRUCK   PETERBILT

During the 1990s, Peterbilt struggled to maintain its share of the Class 7 and Class 8 markets. By 1995, the company offered seven basic models: 320 LCF, 362 COE, 357 CONV, 379 CONV, 377 CONV, 378 CONV and 375 CONV. The 320 LCF was available in 4x2, 6x4 and 6x6 and dual steer versions with a 58-inch BBC dimension. Standard engine was the Caterpillar 3306B-300. The rest of the models listed were all available in 4x2 or 6x4 configu-

ration except for the Model 357, which was also available as a 6x6 truck. All of these models' standard engine was the Caterpillar 3176B-350.

1994 PETERBILT MODEL 357   PETERBILT

1995 PETERBILT MODEL 378   PETERBILT

For 1996, Peterbilt enhanced its Model 362E COE with a lighter and five-inch lower cab. A 90-inch and a 110-inch BBC dimension was available. Also, the front axle was moved back for better maneuverability and aerodynamics were improved giving these cab-over trucks a more modern appearance.

PETER PIRSCH 1926-1988 — Peter Pirsch & Sons had started as fire apparatus and wagon builders in the late 1800s. Peter Pirsch's father had patented a compound-truss extension ladder in 1899 and soon thereafter, the company began building motorized fire equipment using various chassis including Rambler (the first) as well as Couple Gear, Dodge, Duplex, Nash and White.

1940 PIRSCH MODEL 38   **PIRSCH**

1945 PIRSCH   **MROZ**

The first complete Peter Pirsch fire engines were unveiled in 1926. These were 150 to 750 gallon per minute pumpers, chemical and hose trucks. All were powered by six-cylinder Waukesha engines. The first fully enclosed cab from Peter Pirsch arrived in 1928 on a pumper fire engine. This was the first of its type in America; the previous fire engines' cabs, including all other manufacturers', never used a fully enclosed design. In 1931, Pirsch introduced another innovation in the form of a one-man-operational hydro-mechanical aerial ladder hoist mounted on an 85-foot articulated ladder truck.

1950 PIRSCH COMBINATION FIRE TRUCK   **KP**

1977 PIRSCH SENIOR AERIAL LADDER TRUCK   **PIRSCH**

Pirsch used its own chassis but also built on Sterling in 1933, International in 1936 and Diamond T in 1937. General Motors provided cabs from the 1930s for the following decades. In the 1930s and 1940s, the numerous Pirsch articulated ladder trucks were powered by Hercules or Waukesha engines, which were located under a hood in conventional layout. The first cab-forward design did not appear until 1961 and this design was kept for the next three decades. Ford and Mack CF chassis were also used by Pirsch since the 1960s. By 1970, most of the Pirsch trucks were of cab-forward design powered by diesel engines. Production continued until 1988, when the company went out of business.

PHILADELPHIA 1911-1912 — The Philadelphia Truck Company in Pennsylvania built a 3/4-ton delivery van with forward-control. It used a four-cylinder engine and featured a brass shell radiator, which set it off from other vehicles of that time. The van was priced at $2,200 and weighed 2,065 pounds. Its wheelbase was 102 inches.

PHIPPS-GRINNELL 1910-1911 — The Phipps-Grinnell Auto Company was located in Detroit, Michigan. Ira and C.A. Grinnell were music dealers and Joel Phipps was an electric car designer in Detroit. The partners built a battery-powered electric delivery van rated at 800-pound capacity. The batteries were located in front under a hood, which made it appear as if it were a gasoline engine-powered vehicle, at a time when the internal combustion engine was rapidly becoming the dominant powerplant in the motor vehicle industry.

In 1912, the partnership disbanded and the Grinnell Brothers went on to build their own electric car. Phipps formed a new partnership with C.W. Whitson and built the Phipps in 1912. The company was out of business by year's end. The Grinnell Electric was built until 1916 but not as a commercial vehicle.

1908 PHOENIX 3-TON   **RD**

PHOENIX 1908-1910 — The Phoenix Auto Works occupied a small plant in Phoenixville, Pennsylvania. The Phoenix commercial vehicle this company built was a 1/2-ton capacity highwheeler that was powered by a 12 hp two-cylinder DeTamble air-cooled engine mounted under a front hood. The light truck used a friction transmission and chain drive. For the first year of manufacture, the vehicle was priced at $800 and for 1909 and 1910, its price went up to $900. The company also built small eight-passenger buses based on the same design. This company was not affiliated with the Phoenix Motor Car and Truck Company of Brooklyn, New York, which was formed in 1911, and appears not have gone into manufacturing.

PHOENIX CENTIPED 1909-1918 — The Phoenix Manufacturing Company was located in Eau Claire, Wisconsin. The first vehicle was called the Centiped and was a tractor using a locomotive boiler and a 100 hp four-cylinder vertical steam engine, which turned Lombard Patent tracks using a bevel and spur-gear transmission. Steerable sled tracks were mounted in front for use in winter logging.

In 1916, the company announced a new Centiped, which was powered by a high torque 50 hp four-cylinder gasoline engine that could also run on paraffin. The same type of tractor tracks were mounted at the rear but in front steel-shod wheels were used. A sliding gear transmission allowed three speeds, which were 1-1/2, 3 and 5-1/2 mph.

P.H.P. 1911-1912 — The P.H.P. Motor Truck Company was located in Westfield, Massachusetts. The company built the 3/4-ton Model 25 and 1-ton Model 28 truck during its brief foray into manufacturing. The lighter truck was listed with a 24 hp four-cylinder engine and used a three-speed transmission with shaft drive, while the later and heavier truck had a 30 hp engine. The Model 25 had a wheelbase of 100 inches while the Model 28 had a wheelbase of 115 inches. Semi-elliptic springs were used in front, while full-elliptic springs were used in the rear. The lighter truck was priced at $1,050, while the heavier truck was an additional $450.

1929 PICKWICK NITE COACH   MBS

PICKWICK 1927-1933 — The Pickwick Stages began in 1912 as a Los Angeles interurban and long distance coach operator, part of a diversified holding company by the name of the Pickwick Corporation. Pickwick used a variety of chassis to build its early buses. The early ones were based on Pierce-Arrow passenger cars. These chassis were stretched and custom bodies were built in Southern California. After 1924, the work was done on the Pierce-Arrow Model Z chassis in Pickwick's own shops. Fageol, Packard and White chassis were also utilized for bus construction. Pickwick pioneered such features as reclining seats and on-board kitchens and restrooms.

In 1927, Pickwick began building its own bus, which was unveiled to the public in 1928. This was the Alsacia Nite Coach that featured an all-metal chassisless construction built with longitudinal beams from which the axles were suspended and on which the body was attached. Two levels were divided by a center aisle creating 13 interlocking compartments, each intended for two passengers. Each compartment had its own running water, folding berths, storage space and dressing room. The bus also provided two restrooms and a kitchen and contained a crew of three including driver. The overnight coach was intended to shorten long trips by eliminating hotel stay-overs and would be leased to other carriers. Pickwick built only four such buses before the Great Depression stymied the continued manufacturing of such luxurious mass transit vehicles. Another 40-day coach version called Duplex was built, based on designer Dwight Austin's work.

Because of the poor economic times, the Pickwick Corporation went into receivership in 1931, and much of the bus operation was sold to Greyhound. By 1932, all of Pickwick's bus lines had been acquired by Greyhound. The manufacturing plant was bought by Dwight Austin, who proceeded to build 18 more Nite Coaches with some similarities to the original design. However, instead of using front-mounted Sterling engines as in the original version, the latter Nite Coaches had a transverse rear-mounted Waukesha engine with Austin's patented angle drive. The buses were too expensive for the market at that time and none were built after 1933.

Austin designed and built the rear-engine Austin Utility Coach for 1933 and 1934, before being hired by Yellow Truck and Coach. His patented angle drive system was used in Yellow and General Motors buses for the next three decades. The name "Pickwick Sleeper" was used by the Columbia Coach Works in 1936 for its prototype bus, which was powered by two rear-mounted Ford V-8 engines and which featured a mechanical air-conditioning system -- one of the first ever to be used in a bus. The single experimental bus was bought by All American Bus Lines in 1937.

1919 PIEDMONT 1-TON MODEL O   RD

PIEDMONT 1919-1920 — The Piedmont Motor Truck Company was located in Lynchburg, Virginia. The 1-ton Model O and 1-1/2-ton Model P trucks were built briefly using a four-cylinder Lycoming engine with Borg & Beck clutch and three-speed selective gear transmission. Artillery type wheels were made of "second growth hickory" and were 33x4 pneumatic on the front and 33x4 solid or 34x6 pneumatic on the rear. It does not appear that the company survived the postwar recession.

PIERCE 1983 to date — The Pierce Manufacturing Company, based in Appleton, Wisconsin, built fire apparatus for other manufacturers until 1968 when the company began fabricating its own fire trucks using commercial chassis. The original Pierce Auto Body Works was incorporated in 1913 in Appleton, Wisconsin, by Dudley H. Pierce and his father Humphrey Pierce, who were not related to anyone of the Pierce-Arrow company.

During the 1920s, Pierce expanded its range, building bodies for a number of truck manufacturers. Dudley Pierce's son, Eugene, entered the business in 1927. The two men managed the company for many years and in 1958, Douglas A. Ogilvie became president when the name of the company was changed to Pierce Manufacturing Incorporated.

Once the company began building its own fire trucks, the name Power Chief was adopted in 1970. In 1971, Pierce moved to larger facilities still located in Appleton. Rights to use the Pierce-Arrow name were obtained in 1979, which was the year Pierce began building its new line of complete trucks, although bare chassis were built by Oshkosh and later by Duplex. One well-known model was called the Arrow, which has been built to date.

In 1983, Pierce began building its own chassis, establishing itself as a builder of complete trucks from the ground up. The utility trucks were named Fleet Arrow, which was a name first used by Pierce-Arrow in 1928. The following year, Pierce offered tilt-cab COE models called Dash and the name Lance was used for its variety of fire trucks. These could be ordered with a raised roof to serve as a mobile command station. The canopy cab could seat six fire fighters. Aerial ladders were available in 55-, 75- and 105-foot lengths. A Pierce trademark has been the black vinyl pump controls panel.

In the late 1980s, Pierce introduced the Javelin line of rear-engine front-wheel-drive fire trucks. The engine was located just forward of the rear axle, allowing the cab to be spacious enough for 10 people. The Pierce Dash trucks used a hydraulic tilt cab.

By 1989, Pierce developed its own Fleet Arrow chassis, which used a heat treated 110,000 psi frame that was available in two-, four- and six-wheel-drive. The company has continued to build fire apparatus to date. Advertising used the Pierce-Arrow name and product line.

During the 1990s, Pierce has built a number of fire truck models, including the Saber Pumper, Dash Pumper, Lance Pumper, Suburban, Responder Pumper, Pumper Tanker, Heavy Duty Rescue, the articulated Tiller tractor semi-trailer fire truck and Aerial trucks with up to 105-foot ladders.

For 1995, Pierce offered an All-Wheel-Steer chassis for fire apparatus application. Advertising compared a chassis with a 45 degree turning angle of front wheels as having a 71-1/2-foot turning diameter. With the Pierce All-Wheel-Steer system, which also had a 45 degree turning angle of the front wheels but in addition, also had a 17 degree turning angle of the rear wheels, the truck's turning diameter was reduced to 54 feet or about one-third less. Also for 1995, Pierce introduced its Quantum fire truck, which used a new chassis, new cab aerodynamic styling and featured the latest in technical improvements such as Wabco ABS with front disc brakes, Micro Controller II self-diagnostic vehicle monitoring system and a DDC Series 60 diesel engine from 350 hp to 470 hp.

1908 PIERCE RD

PIERCE-ARROW 1907, 1909-1935 — The first truck that was built by Pierce (later Pierce-Arrow) had its design initiated in 1905, four years after the motor vehicle manufacturer was formed from a company that had built birdcages as well as ice boxes and other household items. That company was Heintz, Pierce and Munschauer, which had started in Buffalo, New York, in 1865. In 1872, George N. Pierce bought controlling interest in the company. By 1896, the reorganized firm was building bicycles.

In 1901, Pierce entered the motor vehicle market by building 150 Motorette one-cylinder cars that had been designed by David Fergusson, the former engineer for Stearns who became chief engineer at Pierce-Arrow for the next two decades. At first Pierce-Arrow used DeDion engines, but then all engines were built by the company until financial trouble forced the use of Hercules engines after the stock market crash of 1929.

It was not until 1907 that the first truck was completed after the company moved to its Elmwood plant late in 1906. After a thorough testing at the Goodrich Rubber Company, the Pierce directors decided to build 100 such 5-ton trucks in 1909; hence, by the time of actual completion most sources refer to Pierce production as having started in 1910, when the name had been changed to Pierce-Arrow. H. Kerr Thomas, formerly with Saurer, joined the company at that time and it was he who implemented some design changes in order to optimize the trucks' ruggedness and performance. David Fergusson, once employed at Leyland, also helped shape the design of the company's high-quality trucks.

However, before the chain-drive 5-ton truck was completed another switch to worm-drive was chosen by the directors as a result of user information from the field. The company also bought an English 5-ton Dennis truck to further acquaint themselves with this

type of vehicle before completing their design. Pierce-Arrow's engineer John Younger had worked for Dennis and director H. Kerr Thomas had worked at Hallford.

The finalized Pierce-Arrow design was completed late in 1910 and the "second" truck was shown at the New York Auto Show in January of 1911. This first production truck, designated as X-1, was sold in June to the International Brewing Company that year. The truck was of conventional layout and was powered by a 38.0 hp T-head four-cylinder Pierce-Arrow engine and used a three-speed transmission. Tires were 36x6 front and 40x6 rear and wheelbase was 156 inches. Chassis price was $4,500. Only a few of these trucks were built and they were characterized by not having louvers in the hood, instead having horizontal louvers in the radiator for temperature control. In 1912, Pierce-Arrow built a truck with an all-steel, one-piece brewery body supplied by the Fale and Kilburr Body Company.

In October of 1913, the 2-ton Model X-2 was completed. It was similar to the X-1 but had a smaller engine with 25.6 hp. It was available in two wheelbases, unlike the X-1. Also, it was distinguishable from the earlier model in that it had four louvers on each side of the hood, four openings in the side of the radiator shell and vertical elements in the radiator front. For 1915, a 5-ton truck was developed and designated as the Model R-5.

As with several other companies, passenger car demand became secondary to the demand for trucks as World War I developed. The earlier truck production has not been established precisely but by 1917, annual truck production was over 7,000 compared to 2,500 for passenger cars. By the end of the following year, Pierce-Arrow had built 14,000 trucks, but passenger car design stagnated somewhat because of the disproportionate sales success of commercial vehicles at that time. Pierce-Arrow was also contracted to build approximately 1,000 Class B Liberty trucks for the war effort. Its 2-ton and 5-ton trucks were used by the United States, Great Britain and France during World War I. It has been noted that Britain, France and Russia preferred the R model trucks, while the U.S. Army preferred the 2-ton Model X. In England, the Wolseley company built 48 armored cars on Pierce-Arrow chassis in 1915.

1918 PIERCE-ARROW MROZ

In 1918, the 2-ton truck was called the X-4 and sold for $3,750. The Model R received two optional windshield wipers in 1918, but otherwise remained unchanged for the next decade. The 5-ton capacity model became the R-9 and sold for $5,500. The postwar recession adversely affected sales at Pierce-Arrow and for 1921, only 709 trucks found new customers. However, the company continued to develop new products and the 3-1/2-ton W-2 model was added to the line and the R-9 became the R-10 as the X-4 became the X-5. The W-2 was powered by a 32 hp engine and was priced at $4,950. All three (R-9, X-5 and W-2) were discontinued in 1922.

Major changes in the truck model line took place in 1923. A four-cylinder dual-valve dual-ignition engine was introduced (which had been developed two years earlier by Pierce-Arrow) and the model line included the 2-1/2-ton Model X-A, the 3-ton Model X-B, the 4-ton Model W-C, the 5-ton Model W-D, the 6-ton Model R-E and the 7-1/2-ton Model R-F. One hundred heavy-duty Pierce-Arrow trucks were ordered that year for the New York City Department of Street Cleaning.

Also for 1923, the two lightest models were powered by a 25 hp engine while the other four were powered by a 32 hp engine. Truck tractor versions and dump trucks were available in this model line, but sales continued to fall both in the passenger car line as well as in the truck line. Less than 2,000 trucks were being built per year in the early 1920s. In 1924, capital was invested in the lagging passenger car model line with the introduction of the Series 80 for the following year.

In 1924, the Z truck chassis was introduced and fitted with the 38 hp six-cylinder Model 33 passenger car engine. The two available wheelbases were 196-inch and 220-inch, some of the longest standard in the industry. This truck's four-speed transmission and gearing allowed a top speed of 60 mph, far higher than most other trucks of that time. Prices were between $3,300 and $5,500 and most of these chassis were used for buses, although a few fire engines and the Caravan "deluxe traveling home" were also built. However, between 1924 and 1928, fewer than 1,000 Z chassis were built by Pierce-Arrow.

For 1925, Pierce-Arrow listed the 2-ton Model XA for $3,300 chassis price, 3-ton Model XB for $3,500, 4-ton Model WC for $4,600, 5-ton Model RD for $5,000 and 6-ton Model RF for $5,200. The XB, RD and RF were available in truck tractor form. All used Pierce-Arrow engines, transmissions, steering and axles. The largest engine was rated at 32.4 hp and Stromberg carburetors with Dayton ignition were used throughout this lineup.

1928 PIERCE-ARROW MODEL Z BUS KP

As financial troubles continued to burden the company, a new truck model was developed for 1928 in the hope of stimulating new sales. This was the Fleet Arrow announced in 1927 for the following model year. It used a 70 hp six-cylinder engine that was derived from the Model 80 passenger car unit. Available wheelbases were 140-inch, 160-inch and 180-inch. The year 1928 was a milestone for the Pierce-Arrow company, as Studebaker acquired most of its stock. After building 500 of the Fleet Arrow trucks, truck production was suspended in 1929 in order to redesign the truck line.

Up to the suspension of production, Pierce-Arrow built three models in the Fleet Arrow line and also offered six in the larger truck range. But the latter vehicles remained mostly unchanged from the World War I era with solid rubber tires and open C-cabs. All in all, they were outdated. But overall, Pierce-Arrow had made a $2 million profit for 1929 and much of this money was put back into new design work.

In December of 1930, a whole new truck line was introduced. It consisted of the 2-ton Model PT with a 70 hp engine, the 3-ton Model PW with a 77 hp engine, the 4-ton Model PX with a 103 hp engine, the 5-ton Model PY with a 103 hp engine and the 8-ton Model PZ with a 130 hp engine. The six-cylinder engines were new and straight-eight engines were adopted for the passenger car line.

The new line found increased sales, but those numbers were still quite small. It is only estimated that for 1931 and 1932 about 200 trucks were built. Studebaker-sponsored Pierce-Arrow trucks were offered in 28 chassis versions and eight engine sizes, which included Hercules units, as well as Clark and Covert transmissions, Timken axles and Westinghouse air brakes. Production figures were 22 for 1930, 126 for 1931 and 70 for 1932.

Over the years, many commercial body fabricators used Pierce-Arrow for building ambulances, fire trucks, funeral cars and some early police cars. These included funeral bus-type coaches. A.J. Miller and Henney built funeral cars until Pierce-Arrow could no longer supply chassis.

1931 PIERCE-ARROW 5-TON DUMP TRUCK OCW

By November of 1932, all truck production was stopped at Pierce-Arrow. A new 2-ton model with a straight-eight engine and dual ignition capable of 55 mph was announced but it appears that only a few were actually fabricated.

The controlling interests at Studebaker who had decided to acquire White (which had bought the Indiana truck company in 1932) transferred production of Pierce-Arrow trucks over to Cleveland where the trucks carrying the Pierce-Arrow name continued to be built into 1933. The White-built Pierce-Arrow trucks were listed under 22 four-wheel chassis, six six-wheel chassis and eight truck tractor chassis. Seven six-cylinder engines from 298-cubic inch to 779-cubic inch were offered and one 385-cubic inch straight-eight was also available. Studebaker's acquisition of Pierce-Arrow resulted in a separate company called SPA Truck Corporation (Studebaker Pierce-Arrow), which was the financial vehicle for the acquisition of White.

Pierce-Arrow trucks were "available," according to some literature, until 1935 but only a handful were actually built in 1934. These were the SPA 3/4-ton Panther trucks, which were only for export to Great Britain. Studebaker/White sold the Pierce-Arrow passenger car operations for approximately $1 million. The truck operation was sold separately.

Reorganized, Pierce-Arrow built a few nine-passenger and 15-passenger "buses" with 140 hp eight-cylinder engines in 1935 on a stretched 204-inch wheelbase chassis. These were stretched passenger car "airport limousines." Luxurious passenger cars were built into 1938. The Pierce-Arrow V-12 engine continued to be produced by Seagrave for three decades with only minor modifications.

PIERCY 1915-1916 — The Piercy truck was built by the Hub Motor Truck Company in Columbus, Ohio. This was a hybrid design using a four-cylinder gasoline engine mounted in front under the hood. The engine powered a generator that, in turn, drove two electric motors mounted on each rear wheel. The truck was rated at 2-1/2-ton capacity. It was no longer manufactured after 1916.

1912 PIGGINS 1-TON CHASSIS RD

PIGGINS 1912-1916 — Charles R. Piggins and his brother Frederick H. Piggins started out as machinists in Racine, Wisconsin. They had built a steam car in 1883, an electric vehicle in 1897 and their first gasoline auto in 1902. Concluding from their experiments that the gasoline engine was the best powerplant, they began manufacturing two-, four- and six-cylinder cars and two-cycle marine engines. Their company was reorganized as the Racine Manufacturing Company and in 1912, the brothers founded the Piggins Motor Truck Company.

The Piggins trucks were 1-, 2- and 3-ton capacity vehicles powered by a four-cylinder engine. The two smaller trucks were conventional layout with a three-speed transmission and shaft drive while the 3-ton model was a forward-control design. The company's slogan was "The Practical Piggins." Their manufacturing business evolved into the Reliance Motor Truck Company in 1917, when operations were moved to Appleton, Wisconsin. This later Reliance was not related to the earlier company that was purchased by General Motors.

PIONEER 1920-1924 — Not related to the earlier Pioneer cyclecar in Chicago, Illinois, the Pioneer Truck Company was also located in that city and built a 2-ton capacity truck in 1920 and 1921 using a four-cylinder Continental engine. For 1921, a 1-ton truck was introduced but for 1922 and 1923, only the 2-ton model was built. In 1924, the 1-ton model was again offered powered by a four-cylinder Golden, Belknap and Swartz engine.

1929 PIONEER STAGE   MBS

PIONEER STAGE 1923-1930 — The California Body Building Company started out in San Francisco, California. The firm evolved from a taxi garage started by W.W. Travis in 1914. Travis was the operator of a taxi service in San Francisco, whose taxicabs were built on heavy White chassis. As expensive as these vehicles were, Travis stretched the chassis and began building buses, which he called "stages," and these were sold to a number of operators throughout California.

Having gone into the bus building business, Travis also formed the California Transit Company in 1921. He had built the first all-metal bus body in 1919. The first completely assembled bus, including in-house built chassis, arrived in 1923. The company immediately set out building six-wheel buses for 1923 and 1924, and after 50 such vehicles were built, it became apparent that traction problems would necessitate retrofitting dual wheels in the rear. It was at this point that the "Pioneer Stage" name was adopted both for the manufacturing company and for the California Transit Company, which had become the largest long distance bus system in northern California, much as Pickwick was in southern California.

The California Body Building moved to larger facilities in Oakland, California, just across the San Francisco Bay. In 1929, California Transit became part of the Greyhound Pacific Lines, as did Pickwick soon thereafter. At that time, the manufacturing part of Pioneer became the Pioneer Motor Coach Manufacturing Company and remained in Oakland. One bus series totaling 60 parlor coaches was fabricated before that company was absorbed into Greyhound's subsidiary by the name of C.H. Will Motors Corporation located in Minneapolis, Minnesota. Bus production over the years from 1923 to 1930 was approximately 400.

PITTSBURG 1908 — The Pittsburg Machine Tool Company in Allegheny, Pennsylvania, built a heavy steam truck in 1908. It was powered by a three-cylinder single-acting steam engine using a fire-tube boiler with double chain drive and two speeds. The truck featured two brake systems. One was a handbrake acting on the rear wheels and the other was a foot-operated air brake acting on the differential. The truck also featured a winch (winding drum) powered by the engine for lifting and carrying loads up to 10 tons.

PITTSBURG 1905-1910 — The Pittsburg Motor Vehicle Company of Pittsburg, Pennsylvania (the spelling change to "Pittsburgh" took place almost two decades later) was started by Charles A. Ward. The vehicles built by this company were all for commercial applications and were all electric powered using storage batteries. The first Pittsburg trucks were light vehicles powered by 2 hp electric motors. Type L had a wheelbase of 75 inches and Type 2 had a wheelbase of 100 inches. In 1910, the company offered a range of six models from 1/2-ton to 3-ton capacity. The three largest had two electric motors, one for each rear wheel, and all used double chain drive. Charles Ward went on to organize the Ward Motor Car Company in New York in 1910, after closing down the Pittsburg company.

PITTSBURGER 1919-1923 — The Pittsburger was a truck built by the Pittsburgh Truck Manufacturing Company located in Pittsburgh, Pennsylvania. The first iteration of this truck was a 2-1/2-ton capacity model powered by a four-cylinder Continental C4 engine. By 1921, a 5-ton model was added and the heavier truck was powered by a Midwest engine. In 1922, a 1-1/2-ton and a 3-ton model were available, both also powered by a Midwest engine. Each model of the Pittsburger used a four-speed transmission in conjunction with worm final drive.

PITTSBURGH see AUTOCAR

PITTSBURGH MACHINE see CURTIS

1907 PLYMOUTH STAKE BED   RD

1914 PLYMOUTH MODEL D-3 COVERED FLARE   KP

PLYMOUTH 1906-1914 — The Commercial Motor Truck Company of Toledo, Ohio, built Plymouth trucks before unaffiliated Chrysler Corporation brought out its Plymouth cars in 1928. After its organization in Toledo, the firm moved to Plymouth, Ohio, later the same year. In the first two years of production, the company built trucks from 1/2-ton to 3-ton capacity using four-cylinder Continental engines, friction transmissions and double chain drive. In 1908, Plymouths were offered with engines up to 50 hp and some of these were built as buses for up to 20 passengers. One version was a combination bus and truck. In 1909, the company was reorganized as the Plymouth Motor Truck Company. By 1912, only

313

a 1-ton model powered by a 25.6 hp four-cylinder engine was offered along with a 2-ton model truck, which was powered by a 40 hp four-cylinder engine. These had a single "cyclops" headlight mounted on top of the dash with two small lights at the sides. Manufacture was discontinued after 1914.

1914 PLYMOUTH MODEL D-3 COVERED FLARE   KP

1937 PLYMOUTH SEDAN DELIVERY   RD

PLYMOUTH 1935-1942; 1974; 1984 to date — Chrysler Corporation unveiled its first Plymouth cars in 1928. They were intended to compete with Chevrolets and Fords and kept the company afloat after the stock market crash. In 1935, Plymouth introduced a two-door commercial sedan and in 1936, offered a panel delivery. By 1937, a separate commercial range was unveiled. Also starting that year, Plymouth listed its own seven-passenger taxi of which 500 were built in 1937, 35 for 1938 and only 12 for 1939.

Plymouth commercial cars resulted from a demand by Chrysler-Plymouth and Plymouth-DeSoto dealers for additional sales opportunities that up to that time were assigned to Dodge dealers for Chrysler Corporation. The Plymouth commercial vehicles' styling was based on that of passenger cars but in actuality, few sheet metal parts were interchangeable. The "woodie" Westchester station wagon debuted in 1936, along with a sedan delivery and these were at first built on the light Dodge truck chassis. Within two years, a longer passenger car chassis was used. These Plymouths were really Dodges, aside from the Plymouth engine and trim.

For 1938, the Plymouth commercial line sold only half as many vehicles as the previous year, partly due to the recession of that year. This year was the last year for any Plymouth sedan delivery to be built on a truck chassis as before. It would also be the last year that the pickup styling would be based on the passenger cars, notably with spare tire mounted on the front fenders.

For 1939, the Plymouth commercial line had a new "truck" look to it but actually borrowed the chassis from its companion passenger cars. The new three-man cab pickup was advertised as the largest in its class. The spare tire was now mounted under the bed and the cab and chassis were standard with front and rear fenders as well as full length running-boards. The engine was a 201-cubic inch displacement side valve six-cylinder unit rated at 70 hp, but it was essentially the same cast iron six with 6.7:1 compression ratio that was rated at 82 hp at 3600 rpm in the standard passenger car.

For 1940, the commercial series was the last Plymouth entry into commercial vehicles until 1974 with the Dodge-based Trail Duster. Starting with 1936, the commercial vehicle designations were PT50, PT57, PT81, PT105 and PT125, respectively. By 1940, the sealed beam headlights introduced the year before were moved outward and

the grille and trim were changed for a new look that has since met with mixed acceptance. From the introduction of the 1939 body style, Plymouth truck production was limited to the Detroit and Los Angeles plants exclusively. The PT105 of 1938 was priced at $585 as a pickup and $555 for cab and chassis, while the PT125 of 1939 was priced at $625 as a pickup and $590 for cab and chassis. A few Plymouth vans in 1938 and 1939 were marketed as Chryslers in Great Britain.

1941 PLYMOUTH 1/2-TON PICKUP   OCW

1975 PLYMOUTH VOYAGER PB300   KP

In 1984, Plymouth introduced its first Voyager minivan and these have been used for light delivery by small stores, florists and other businesses. The Voyager became a successful model line almost immediately for Plymouth and in 1987, the company introduced its Grand Voyager with more cargo capacity. By 1988, Plymouth had sold one million Voyager minivans. In 1991, a second generation of the Voyager was introduced featuring the first airbag for a minivan. By the following year, total Voyager sales had reached the two million mark.

1996 PLYMOUTH VOYAGER   CHRYS

For 1996, the third generation of Voyager has been introduced with the following powertrain options: 2.4L DOHC engine with three-speed automatic, 2.4L DOHC engine with four-speed automatic, 3.0L Mitsubishi V-6 with three-speed automatic, 3.3L V-6 engine with four-speed automatic and a planned 3.8L V-6 with four-speed automatic transmission for Grand Voyager All-Wheel-Drive. Four-wheel antilock brakes were made standard on all Plymouth minivans. The two rear seat benches were made easily removable for convenient cargo carrying capability or they could both be folded down for the same purpose with less vertical room. Model line has been listed as Voyager, Voyager SE, Grand Voyager, Grand Voyager SE and Grand Voyager AWD for late 1996.

PNEUMATIC 1896-1899 — The Pneumatic Carriage Company was founded in New York City with half a million dollars in capital stock in 1895. The first experimental vehicle was a carriage prototype intended for urban transit. The Pneumatic carried a tank of air under pressure, which fed a reciprocating motor that weighed 400 pounds. With the use of a pressure reducing valve the motor turned at 350 rpm when the carriage was traveling 15 mph. The air was "surcharged" with hot water carried in a separate tank and used five pounds of water for each mile of travel. Range was about 20 miles per tank. The experimental carriage with seating for six was built at the American Wheelock Engine Company in Worcester, Massachusetts. It had 32-inch front and 40-inch rear wooden wheels that carried pneumatic tires. The first successful public test ride took place on Flag Day, October 31, 1896, in Worcester. No further development was undertaken and the company faded out in 1899.

PONTIAC 1905-1908 — The Pontiac Spring and Wagon Works began in 1899, when Albert G. North organized the company in Pontiac, Michigan. In 1905, North's venture took over Max Grabowsky's Rapid truck company, which had been started in 1902. In 1907, this Pontiac company also built about 35 highwheelers powered by a 12 hp two-cylinder engine and used a friction transmission with double chain drive. In 1908, the Motorcar Company of Detroit acquired Pontiac and moved to the city by that name to build the Cartercar.

PONTIAC 1906 — The Pontiac Motor Company was organized by Martin Halfpenny in Pontiac, Michigan, during 1904. Nothing took place until 1906, when Halfpenny changed the company's name to the Pontiac Motor Car Company and built a prototype delivery wagon featuring patented Halfpenny auxiliary springs. The press announced the performance of road tests, but there is no evidence that the planned production of trucks from 1 ton to 3 ton ever took place.

PONTIAC 1926-1928; 1949 to date — General Motors embarked on a low-priced six-cylinder automobile in the early 1920s. The first Pontiacs were built by the Oakland Motor Car Company in order to boost Oakland sales, which were fading at the time. When the new marque debuted, it set a new all-time record for first year auto sales -- 76,696 Pontiacs sold in 1926. By 1927, there were 3,611 Pontiac trucks registered in the United States.

1936 PONTIAC DELIVERY PROTOTYPE   **KP**

The commercial vehicle was based on the passenger car in the form of a light van and designated as the 6-27 Deluxe Delivery. The Pontiac of that first year was powered by a side valve 186.5-cubic inch 40 hp six-cylinder engine and used a three-speed transmission. Wheelbase was 110 inches. The same 1/2-ton van was built for 1927 and continued into 1928 as the 6-28. In 1928, five styles were listed: delivery van, screenside delivery, canopy delivery, sedan delivery and pickup. No evidence exists that the 1928 pickup was ever built as a Pontiac. Later that year, the GMC T-11 made its debut. Pontiac was the supplier of its 26.3 hp Pontiac 200 L-head six-cylinder engine to 16 different GMC trucks up to 2-ton capacity.

For 1935 and 1939, a prototype of a Pontiac sedan delivery was built but neither one went into production. Flxible built a few hearses and ambulances on Pontiac chassis during the 1930s. It was not until 1949 that Pontiac (now officially Pontiac Division of General Motors Corporation) built sedan delivery versions of its passenger cars. The Pontiac sedan delivery was called Steamliner and by 1950, it used the passenger car deluxe trim package. Both the six-cylinder and straight-eight engines were available. Production plummeted from about 2,488 in 1949 to 2,158 in 1950, 1,822 in 1951, 984 in 1952 and 1,324 in 1953.

1951 PONTIAC SEDAN DELIVERY   **RD**

During the 1950s and 1960s, the Superior Body Company built ambulances and hearses on Pontiac professional chassis once again. A prototype Pontiac light truck was built in 1959, when the company built its own version of the Chevrolet El Camino, dubbed the "El Catalina." Dealers also transformed stock passenger Pontiacs into light pickups. Another factory prototype pickup was built in 1980.

1990 PONTIAC TRANS SPORT SE   **PONTIAC**

1996 PONTIAC TRANS SPORT VAN   **PONTIAC**

By 1990, Pontiac introduced its streamlined Trans Sport van, which has been almost identical to the Oldsmobile Silhouette. The Trans Sport featured a 3.4-liter or a 3.8-liter V-6, four-speed automatic transmission and front-wheel-drive for 1996.

PONY 1919-1920 — The Minnesota Machine & Foundry Company, located in Minneapolis, Minnesota, attempted to revitalize interest in the cyclecar concept by building the 1/4-ton Pony delivery van. It used a small four-cylinder water-cooled engine, friction transmission and chain drive to the rear wheels. The narrow chassis had a 90-inch wheelbase and the Pony was priced at $350. The popularity of cyclecars had passed almost a decade before and few Pony vans were sold before being discontinued in 1920.

1941 PONY CRUISER 19-SEAT BUS   MBS

PONY CRUISER 1938-1951 — People's Rapid Transit Company was an urban passenger carrier based in Kalamazoo, Michigan, serving about 200 miles of routes in the vicinity. The company built a 16-passenger intercity bus in 1938. It was based on a Ford commercial chassis with engine mounted in front. For 1940, the bus was restyled and resembled the contemporary FitzJohn buses. That year, bus operations were separated from the manufacturing part of the company and the latter became Kalamazoo Coaches, Incorporated. A 19-passenger version of the Pony was introduced. Many small bus operators bought the Pony Cruiser, which was inexpensive, economical and easy to service. The British Yukon Navigational Company along the Alcan Highway made notable use of these buses between 1946 and 1951. By 1947, Chevrolet and International K-7 chassis were offered in addition to the Ford chassis. The company built a larger bus called the Kalamazoo Cruiser with up to 29 seats and along with the Pony, about 625 were produced over the years.

1913 POPE-HARTFORD 3-TON STAKE   MROZ

POPE-HARTFORD 1906-1914 — Colonel Albert A. Pope had already built a bicycle and sewing machine manufacturing empire by the time he entered the motor vehicle industry. The Pope-Hartford was only one of several Pope-backed manufacturers but it was the longest-lived and the only one to be produced in Hartford, which was the Pope Manufacturing headquarters. The company began by building a one-cylinder Model A and Model B passenger car in 1904. By 1906, the first Pope truck was built using a 20 hp two-cylinder water-cooled engine with a four-speed transmission and double chain drive. There were several ambulances and fire trucks as well. Pope-Hartford built 3-ton and 5-ton trucks, which had double chain drive throughout their production into 1914. The largest had a 170-inch wheelbase. The factory furnished stake bodies only.

Colonel Pope died in 1909 at the age of 66. His brother George took over but in 1913, after a third receivership, the company faded out selling off its assets until the factory itself in Hartford was purchased by Pratt & Whitney in 1915 for $300,000.

POPE-WAVERLY 1904-1908 — Starting out as the Waverly in 1898, the company became a subsidiary of the Pope Manufacturing Company in 1904. All of the Waverly vehicles were battery-powered electric, the commercial ones ranging from light delivery wagons up to 5-ton capacity trucks. The 1904 Model 23 Delivery Wagon with 80-inch wheelbase sold for $1,400. There was also a Model 24 Service Wagon with the same wheelbase and price. A 1-ton truck was available on a 96-inch wheelbase with a track of 82 inches. By 1906, there were six commercial vehicle models, which were comprised of one delivery van, two closed delivery vans and trucks of 1-, 3- and 5-ton capacity.

Originally produced in Indianapolis, Indiana, by 1907, the Pope-Waverly and Pope-Tribune went into receivership. Both makes were briefly built in Hagerstown, Maryland, before the company was sold to local businessmen. Manufacturing continued under the Waverly name back in Indianapolis until 1916.

1911 POSS MODEL A 1/2-TON EXPRESS   NAHC

POSS 1912-1914 — The Poss Motor Car Company began in Detroit, Michigan, during 1911 with a capital stock of $250,000, incorporated by Frank P. Poss, George W. Bailey, Robert R. McKinley and Joseph M. Ness. The company built one model of a 1/2-ton delivery on a chassis with a 98-inch wheelbase. The truck weighed only 1,350 pounds but was powered by a four-cylinder water-cooled engine and was available with either solid rubber or pneumatic tires for $850.

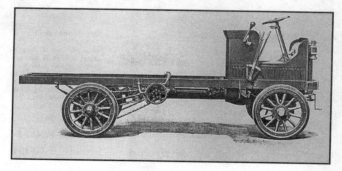

1910 POWELL 1-1/2-TON CHASSIS   MROZ

POWELL 1910-1911 — The Powell Engine Corporation was organized in 1910 by L.P. Powell, R.W. Powell and C.I. McLaughlin. The company was capitalized with $50,000 in Brooklyn, New York. It is believed the company built at least a few Powell Motor Trucks, but actual proof has not been found to date.

A well-designed brochure provided illustrations and specifications. The engine was a 30 hp four-cylinder vertical overhead valve-type with a Schebler carburetor. Dual Remy ignition was provided. Cooling was by centrifugal pump.

Powell trucks were also specified with a three-speed selective sliding gear transmission and multiple disc clutch. Suspension springs were semi-elliptic. Wheelbase was 112 inches with weight of chassis being 3,500 pounds. The Powell truck was rated 1-1/2-ton capacity. Front and rear axles were Timken. Chassis price was given as $2,250.

1955 POWELL PICKUP   **HAYS**

POWELL 1955-1956 — Powell pickups and station wagons were built by Hayward and Channing Powell in Compton, California. The two brothers started out building motor scooters, then motorhomes. A prototype "Sport Wagon" was built on a Chevrolet chassis in 1952. Ultimately, they chose the Plymouth to build a light pickup that would ride like a passenger car. The 1941 Plymouth was chosen partly due to availability of used or dilapidated cars. Operations began in 1954.

The 117-inch wheelbase chassis was completely rebuilt. Bodies were made of heavy-gauge sheet metal, except for the fiberglass nose section that required compound curves. All Powells were powered by six-cylinder side valve Mopar engines, which had been rebuilt from used vehicles. A three-speed synchromesh transmission was used and front suspension was independent with coil springs. Steering was Gemmer worm and roller. Rear suspension was with longitudinal leaf springs.

The slab-side styling preceded Chevrolet's Cameo Carrier by a full half year. A two-door station wagon was added in 1956. The price for the Powell Sport Wagon pickup was $998.87 in 1955 and went to $1,095 for 1956. The deluxe version with turn signals, two-tone upholstery and chrome hubcaps was priced at $1,195; still $250 less than any of the competitors' offerings and enough to pay for the pop-up camper option. The light trucks had a 1/4-ton capacity. It has been approximated that 1,000 pickups and 300 station wagons were built over two-and-a-half years of production, with some vehicles being built in 1956 and registered for 1957.

POWER 1917-1923 — The Power Truck and Tractor Company started out in Detroit, Michigan. The first truck this company built was a 2-ton model. By 1918, 1-, 3-1/2- and 5-ton trucks were also offered. All were powered by four-cylinder Continental engines and used worm-drive. The largest truck had a wheelbase of 180 inches. It appears the company moved to St. Louis, Missouri, in 1922. At that time, only 2-ton and 3-1/2-ton trucks were available. The later Power trucks used Hinkley engines, four-speed transmissions and worm-drive rear axles.

POYER 1915 — This company has been listed as a manufacturer of 3/4-ton and 1-ton trucks in Menominee, Michigan. No other details have been available.

PRECEDENT 1984 — The Precedent was a luxury minivan built by Alain Clenet and shown at the National Automobile Dealers Association convention in 1984. The platform was a Chevrolet S-10 pickup, but the body and styling was entirely original, having been completed with the help of Mark P. Stehrenberger, Fred L. Lands and Dick Gulstrand.

PROGRESS 1911-1914 — The Universal Machinery Company of Milwaukee, Wisconsin, offered 3/4-, 1-1/2- and 3-ton trucks powered by four-cylinder engines. All three were forward-control design and had a three-speed transmission with double chain final drive. The company's primary market was Milwaukee's brewery business. In 1913, there were six models of Progress trucks. The company stopped manufacturing vehicles in 1914.

PROSPECT 1924-1934 — Not affiliated with the earlier Prospect car also built in Prospect, Ohio, the Prospect Fire Engine Company built rotary pumper fire trucks under the name Deluge. Keenan Hanley was

the chief designer who started his own company in 1940. These were built of Ford and Reo chassis. Beginning in 1924, the company built the Prospect-Biederman Deluge Master Fire Fighter. It was constructed on a special Biederman chassis. In 1930, the company adopted a Mars chassis, which was powered by a Lycoming eight-cylinder engine. The Prospect company was forced into bankruptcy during the Great Depression.

1916 PULLMAN LIGHT DELIVERY   **RD**

PULLMAN 1911-1917 — The Pullman Motor Car Company started in 1905 in York, Pennsylvania. Albert P. Broomwell designed the first Pullman in 1903, which was a six-wheel vehicle that did not find any ready acceptance. Broomwell was the president of Broomwell, Schmidt and Steacy Company, a heating equipment manufacturer that had been in business since the mid-1800s. He chose the Pullman name so that potential buyers would associate his product with the luxury of the well-known railroad cars.

Along with Samuel E. Baily, owner of the York Carriage Company, which had just been rebuilt after a devastating fire, they formed the York Automobile Company. Twenty cars were built in 1905 using the standard four-wheel configuration after the six-wheel experimental car turned out to be impractical.

1916 PULLMAN EXPRESS DELIVERY   **MROZ**

By 1906, the company was reorganized as the York Motor Car Company with J. Calvin Schutte as vice-president. The general manager was James A. Kline, who would later build the Kline-Kar in York. Starting with Model C and Model D, Pullman cars were high quality and rather expensive. The enterprise grew quickly and by 1911, Pullman was building taxis. All of the vehicles were powered by a four-cylinder engine of the company's own manufacture. A year later, Pullman cars were switched to left-hand drive. In 1914, after business had taken a downturn, Pullman entered the economy car market and began building some light trucks a year later when Hans Hayden joined the company.

The 1/2-ton Pullman Light Delivery was priced at $750 for an Express body with roll-down canvas. With panel body, featuring 103-cubic feet of cargo space, the price was $775. The bodies were built by York Hoover Body Corporation since by that time, York and Hoover had merged. A Pullman touring car chassis was used and these featured a magnetic push-button clutch, which eliminated the pedal. Rejecting the advice of sound engineering practice, management ran the company with a "sell regardless" philosophy, which has been documented in earlier writing. Pullman closed its doors in 1917 for the last time.

317

1945 PULLMAN TROLLEY BUS   **MBS**

PULLMAN 1932-1952 — Although the Pullman-Standard Company of Chicago has been listed as a commercial vehicle manufacturer, its sole production was of trolleybuses. Hence, it really deserves to be in a compendium of trolleys and light rail, a separate category in itself.

PULL-MORE 1914-1917 — The Pull-More Truck Company of Detroit, Michigan, was incorporated by Frank C. Krueger, Henry M. Marker, Ralph S. Moore and Marvin A. Smith with a capitalization of $250,000. E.M. Leavitt was president and treasurer.

It appears the company built 1-, 2- and 3-ton capacity truck prototypes. The entire front-wheel-drive unit (including engine and cab) were detachable, with easy access to mechanical components. The 3-ton truck pictured had power steering, with the entire driving unit pivoting on a king ball located midway between the front wheels -- somewhat akin to the MacDonald. Illustrations showed small wheels that swung down from the back bottom of the cab so that the entire drive unit could sit upright and be moved without the bed and rear axle -- essentially a primitive version of a truck tractor.

A factory was secured in New Castle, Pennsylvania, but by 1917, the company had been reorganized with E.M.S. Young as president and general manager and H.P. Pope as vice-president. Plans were made to build 100 trucks per month and the company was by then capitalized with $1 million, it was announced. A 3-ton Pull-More chassis was priced at $3,400. In 1918, the company went into receivership and was shut down permanently.

1914 PURITY ELECTRIC   **MROZ**

PURITY 1914-1915 — The Purity electric delivery van was first built for the Purity Bread Company's own use in distribution. Two models were built: a 1,200-pound and a 1-ton capacity van, both battery-powered and both using a chassis with a wheelbase of 102 inches. The vans wore pneumatic tires and were available for sale to other companies in 1915.

Q

QUADRAY 1904-1905 — The Commercial Motor Vehicle Company of Detroit, Michigan, built large electric vehicles up to 6-1/4-ton capacity called Quadray. The company also produced buses for up to 50 passengers. In 1905, Quadray built four-wheel-drive four-wheel-steering trucks that used a 3-1/2 hp DC motor mounted in each wheel. These were assembled as vans and open delivery trucks using wooden tires with 8 mph as the maximum speed. Also produced was a hybrid gasoline-electric bus, with a 25 hp engine running a generator that drove four 2-1/2 hp electric motors. The latter was designed for interurban and sightseeing applications where the vehicle's range with storage batteries alone was inadequate. A 10-ton truck was offered in 1904, with a top speed of 6 mph. The company advertised itself in the *Automobile Review* as "manufacturers of heavy trucks, buses and interurban cars."

QUADRU 1911 — The Quadru was a prototype of a gasoline-electric hybrid truck with a 15-ton capacity. A 32 hp gasoline engine drove a generator that, in turn, powered motors in all four wheels. A crane and jack were carried on the truck for loading and unloading cargo and a trailer was also attached at the rear. R. Fuller showed the Quadru at the 1911 Detroit Auto Show.

1911 QUADRU 4X4　　　　　　　　　　　　　　**RD**

QUAKERTOWN 1916 — The Quakertown Auto Manufacturing Company of Quakertown, Pennsylvania, offered a 1/2-ton truck powered by a 35 hp four-cylinder engine for $500. It is believed that this is the same company that began in Quakertown in 1902 and was organized by J.S. Nicholas originally as the Quakertown Buggy Works. The name was changed to Quakertown Auto Manufacturing in 1903.

R

RAINIER 1903-1911; 1916-1927 — The Rainier Motor Corporation began in Flushing, New York, where John T. Rainier began in 1905 with his Rainier Motor Car Company. The earlier Rainier firm built passenger cars on chassis from Garford. In 1908, the company moved to Saginaw, Michigan, and produced 300 passenger cars using chassis built by Rainier. Following bankruptcy in 1909, the company was acquired by General Motors but John Rainier returned to New York City to begin over again, this time for the production of commercial vehicles.

1903 RAINEIR BUS RD

Rainier's first truck was a 1/2-ton model powered by a four-cylinder engine built in-house. The truck used worm-drive and was available with a closed or open express body. In 1917, the company moved to Flushing where Rainier had originally set up his first venture. By 1918, a 3/4-ton and a 1-1/2-ton model was added to the line. Each of the Rainier trucks used three-speed Brown-Lipe transmissions, pneumatic tires and worm-drive. In each case, the engine was mounted in front under a hood and closed delivery bodies were available from the factory. The 1-1/2-ton model was powered by a four-cylinder Continental engine. Rainier expanded its model line in 1921 with 2-, 2-1/2-, 3- and 5-ton trucks.

1903 RAINIER 4-TON RD

In 1924, the company was reorganized as Rainier Trucks Incorporated. At that time, Rainier offered seven models. The lightest was the 3/4-ton Model R-31 with 125-inch wheelbase. Chassis price was $1,970. The 1-ton Model R-29 had a 133-inch wheelbase and was priced at $2,150. Both of these were powered by the four-cylinder Continental N engine, had Lavine steering gear and pneumatic tires were standard. The 1-1/2-ton Model R-36 had a Continental J-4 engine and was priced at $2,590. Pneumatic tires were optional and steering gear was from Ross.

All three models up to this size used Timken front and rear axles. The 2-ton Model R-28 was powered by a Continental K-4 engine and Sheldon front and rear axles were used. Chassis price was $3,190. The 2-1/2-ton Model R-20 with 165-inch wheelbase used

the same engine as the previous model but had Timken front and rear axles. Chassis price was $3,550. The 3-1/2-ton Model R-25 had a 170-inch wheelbase and chassis price was $4,400. The heftiest Rainier truck was the 6-ton Model R-27 with 170-inch wheelbase and a chassis price of $5,300. Its chassis weight was 9,000 pounds and it was powered by a 36.1 hp Continental B-5 engine. It was the only truck in this model line to use Smith wheels. The rest used Jones-Phineas wheels with solid rubber on the R-25 or heavier models. Each and every model had a Brown-Lipe clutch and transmission. The Rainier company did not survive the year 1927.

RALSTON 1913 — The Ralston Motor Car Company of Omaha, Nebraska, offered a 1/2-ton truck called the Model 1/2. It was powered by a four-cylinder air-cooled engine and had an open van body. A friction transmission was used with double chain drive to the rear wheels. The truck used 36x2 solid rubber tires and had a wheelbase 110 inches. A wooden frame was used for the Ralston, which was priced at $750. This company was not affiliated with the Ralston Iron Works of San Francisco, California, which built four-wheel trailers a few years later.

1904 RAMBLER TYPE 1 DELIVERY VAN OCW

1905 RAMBLER PANEL DELIVERY VAN OCW

RAMBLER 1897-1913 — Organized by Thomas B. Jeffery, this company built delivery vans based on the Rambler passenger cars. Prices ranged from $850 to $1,000. The company advertised that the Rambler Type 1 Light Delivery could carry "one-quarter cubic yards of merchandise, accessible front and rear of wagon." Thomas

B. Jeffery became well known for the Jeffery 4x4 trucks. Before building the famous Quad, the company also built a Jeffery 3/4-ton express truck in 1914.

1911 RAMBLER MODEL 63 PICKUP   OCW

1910 RANDOLPH 1-TON MODEL 14   NAHC

RANDOLPH 1908-1912 — The Randolph Motor Car Company began in Flint, Michigan. The first light delivery vans were powered by two-cylinder engines. The 1-ton Model 14 used a 206-cubic inch displacement 22.1 hp four-cylinder engine. Randolph also built flatbed trucks up to 4-ton capacity and called its trucks the Strenuous Randolph. It featured two radiators in side panels under the driver's seat and water was circulated by a large centrifugal pump. Semi-elliptic springs were used in front and full-elliptic in the rear.

1911 RANDOLPH   HAYS

The 1-ton had 34x4 front and 36x6 rear solid rubber tires and had a top speed of 14 mph. It sold for $1,850 in 1911. In 1912, the firm moved to Chicago and became the Randolph Motor Truck Company. All models used three-speed sliding gear transmissions and had solid rubber tires.

RANGER 1920-1923 — The Southern Motors Manufacturing Association was organized during 1920 in Houston Texas by Jacques E. Blevins, E.F. Reid and C.E. Shively. The first vehicles built by the company were passenger cars with Southern-built four-cylinder and six-cylinder engines, but it appears that the 2-ton Ranger truck had a four-cylinder Continental engine. It also used Timken worm-drive and had a wheelbase of 136 inches. In 1922, it was derated to 1-1/2-ton capacity. About that time, the company went into receivership. Southern Motors merged with National Motors and it appears manufacturing continued, but it is not clear if any commercial vehicles under the name Ranger were built in 1923. In 1924, 14 people affiliated with Southern and National Motors were indicted for fraud.

1905 RAPID EXPRESS WAGON   RD

1909 RAPID 1-TON   NAHC

RAPID 1904-1912 — The Rapid Motor Vehicle Company of Detroit, Michigan, built a light delivery van in 1904. Rapid and Reliance were two of the first companies in the United States whose production was dedicated to commercial vehicles, not as a sideline or as a secondary product based on passenger vehicle chassis. The first Rapid van was powered by a two-cylinder engine mounted under the seat and used a planetary transmission with single chain drive to the rear axle. It had a wheelbase of 80 inches, weighed 1,900 pounds and was priced at $1,250. Rapid moved to Pontiac, Michigan, in 1905.

In 1906, Rapid launched a full line of trucks and vans starting with a 1-ton commercial vehicle and it included several buses with up to 20 seats. The following year a 1-ton delivery van was built, as were two 1-1/2-ton capacity trucks and five buses from 12 to 24 passengers, now powered by four-cylinder engines. In 1909, 24 hp and 36 hp four-cylinder engines were used throughout the model line of 17 different commercial vehicles. These included an ambulance, police patrol wagon, a fire engine and buses from nine-passenger to 22-passenger. The 1-ton and 1-1/2-ton trucks were also built at that time.

1911 RAPID 1-TON   MROZ

In 1910, Rapid offered two models of the 1-ton vehicles and one model of the 1-1/2-ton. The following year, 1-, 2- and 3-ton commercial vehicles were produced. Rapid and Reliance were both purchased by General Motors in 1912. For a brief time, both makes of trucks were continued with the GMC emblem.

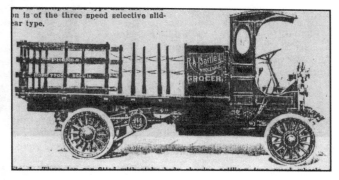

1912 RASSEL 3-TON   MROZ

RASSEL 1910-1912 — The E.C. Rassel Manufacturing Company of Toledo, Ohio, produced a 1-ton and a 2-ton open delivery truck over approximately two years of operation. Both models were powered by four-cylinder engines and used three-speed selective sliding gear transmissions with double chain drive. The 1-ton was priced at $1,700 and the 2-ton at $2,400. In 1912, the company was reorganized as the Rassel Motor Car Company in Toledo. A 3-ton and a 5-ton model truck were added to the line but the company did not survive the year.

RAUCH & LANG; RAULANG 1922-1929 — Started by wagon builder Jacob Rauch and real estate magnate Charles E.J. Lang in 1884, the Rauch & Lang Carriage Company began building its own electric cars during 1905 in Cleveland, Ohio. After buying out the Hertner Electric Company, production rose quickly before Baker Motor Vehicle Company merged with Rauch & Lang, becoming the Baker R & L Company, usually called Baker Raulang. Coachbuilding began in 1919 as a separate division named Raulang. Ray S. Deering, president of Stevens-Duryea, bought out Baker R & L and reorganized it as Rauch and Lang Incorporated in Chicopee Falls, Massachusetts. By 1920, the least expensive Rauch & Lang electric was selling for $3,700.

1924 RAULANG ELECTRIC TAXICAB   FLP

Rauch & Lang entered the taxicab business having moved into the Stevens-Duryea factory in 1922. Three hundred gasoline taxis were built in 1923, powered by 22.5 hp four-cylinder engines. The company also built a few electric taxis and the Model C-505 passenger car, which sold for $4,250. The gasoline taxi sold for $2,350 and the electric taxi sold for $2,750. By 1928, which was the end of production, the taxis' price tag remained the same, while the Model S-68 sedan was priced at $5,000. A hybrid gas-electric was developed for 1929. It was powered by a 35 hp sleeve valve six-cylinder engine. It does not appear that any production followed.

RAYNER see STANDARD

READING STEAMER 1902-1902 — Irving D. Lengel founded the Steam Vehicles Company of America in Reading, Pennsylvania. Reading Steamers were powered by a four-cylinder steam engine with a top speed of 14 mph. "Runs indefinitely without attention" was the company slogan. A 14-hour test ride to New York seemed to prove that. The Reading Steamer was built in various forms, including a Steam Delivery that sold for $1,000. By the end of 1902, the company was bankrupt and Lengel incorporated the Meteor Engineering Company, which bought out the Reading assets and continued some production for a year with the same vehicles under the Meteor name.

REAL 1914-1915 — The H. Paul Prigg Company of Anderson, Indiana, built a cyclecar that had a two-cylinder air-cooled engine mounted in the rear with a friction transmission and belt drive. The vehicle had a 100-inch wheelbase with a spruce frame overslung to create a 15-inch ground clearance. Tread option was 36 inch or 56 inch. The steel body was removable with two bolts and a delivery van was available for two years priced at $375. The Tandem Roadster was priced at $290. Late in 1914, the company's name was changed from the Real Cyclecar Company to the Real Light Car Company.

RED BALL 1924-1927 — The Red Ball Motor Truck Corporation was located in Frankfort, Indiana, and was part of the Red Ball Transit Company of Indianapolis. The first Red Ball trucks were standard conventional assembled. In 1926, a six-wheel truck with drop-frame design was produced. Red Ball built its own bogie using an eight-leaf spring suspension. The tandem was single drive. A four-cylinder Wisconsin engine was used and the low chassis was designed for bus application or as a low-loading van. Some of these trucks were sold to Red Ball Transit affiliates. The company continued to build light-alloy van bodies after 1927.

RED SHIELD HUSTLER 1911-1912 — The Red Shield Hustler Power Company of Detroit, Michigan, built three models of high-wheelers. All of them were powered by a 20 hp two-cylinder engine mounted under the body and used a planetary transmission with double chain drive. The 1/4-ton light trucks had a wheelbase of 75 inches and the 1,200-pound capacity Red Shield trucks had a wheelbase of 86 inches. All had solid rubber tires.

1912 RED SHIELD MODEL A NAHC

REEVES 1897-1898 — Milton O. Reeves was the owner of the Reeves Pulley Company in Columbus, Indiana. He began building a few vehicles under the name Motocycle. Two of these were buses powered by two-cylinder Sintz engines that used a variable speed geared transmission of Reeves' design and double chain drive. One of Reeves passenger cars had a muffler and a papier-mache horse's head to prevent equine panic. The "Big Seven" bus had three rows of seats in ascending elevation for seven passengers. The Reeves bus was built in 1898. It had room for 20 passengers seated on a single level and its wheels were six feet in diameter with axles seven feet long. This larger bus was not suited for the roads of South Dakota, where it was intended to provide service and it was fitted with flanged wheels for use by the Big Four Railroad between Columbus and Hope, Indiana.

The Reeves variable speed transmission was not practical for automotive application, but Reeves had also designed a four-cylinder engine that found customers such as Alexander Y. Malcomson, who ordered 500 units for his Malcomson Aerocar. When Malcomson's company went under, Reeves large inventory of powerplants induced him to go into automobile manufacturing once again in 1905. Among the cars he built between 1905 and 1912 was the Sextoauto and the Octoauto, the latter having a wheelbase of 180 inches and an overall length of 20 feet. It used four axles, two in front and two in the rear.

REGAL 1911-1912 — Charles R. Lambert, J.E. Lambert, Bert Lambert and Fred W. Haines were the three brothers and their partner who started the Regal Motor Car Company in Detroit, Michigan. Paul Arthur was hired to design the four-cylinder car, which was driven across the continent several times in 1909 to demonstrate its durability. Production rose rapidly from 175 units of 1907 to 5,800 by 1912, which was the only model year a commercial version was built. The Model LB was rated at 1/2-ton capacity and was powered by a 30 hp four-cylinder engine. It had a wheelbase of 107 inches and used a different chassis from the one on which the passenger cars were built. Some Regal motor vehicles were sold in England. Material shortages during World War I put an end to the company in 1918.

1926 REHBERGER 5-TON RJ

REHBERGER 1923-1938 — Arthur Rehberger & Sons of Newark, New Jersey, assembled conventional trucks from 1-1/2-ton to 7-ton capacity. They used four-cylinder Buda engines and Brown-Lipe or Fuller transmissions and Timken axles. In 1925, Rehberger offered a 3-ton chassis with bus coachwork. The chassis differed from the other Rehberger trucks in that the frame was lower, engine was set back, air springs were used in front and pneumatic tires were standard on disc wheels. The 5-ton model used a two-speed rear axle giving eight forward speeds.

1934 REHBERGER 30-SEAT BUS RJ

Once the Depression set in, Rehberger specialized in buses from 1933 until the end. Most of its trucks were sold in the Newark area and buses were bought by small transit companies. By 1938, production shifted to the manufacture of industrial trailers, which continued through World War II. Despite plans to resume truck building the company did not manufacture vehicles after the war.

RELAY 1927-1933 — The Relay Motors Corporation was started in Wabash, Indiana, by eastern bankers when they acquired three truck companies: Commerce of Ypsilanti, Michigan; Garford of Lima, Ohio; and Service in Wabash. With $10 million in capital, the new company advertised it was able to build 25,000 trucks per year. Records show production, which took place mostly in Lima and Wabash, to have been nowhere close to that number.

Eight different models ranged from 1-ton to 4-ton capacity and all used Buda six-cylinder engines with four-speed transmissions. Although Commerce, Garford and Service trucks used worm-drive, some Relay trucks used the "Relay Drive," which was a variation on the commonly used internal gear drive design. This design resembled a standard planetary concept, except that the live axle carried all the weight and was attached firmly to the chassis with leaf springs and torque arms. The dead axle, which supported the wheels, was able to float both vertically and horizontally using a patented D-shaped forging that held a bushing. The live axle would climb up the internal ring gears of the two rear wheels and the vehicle would move up as much as 3-1/2 inches and back and forth as much as 6-1/4 inches, with the advertised advantage being that the weight of the truck helped get it started especially when stuck in sand, mud or a pothole. A man climbing the spokes of a wagon wheel was used to illustrate the principle. Also, in the conventional planetary drive the pinions on the live axle were near the bottom, leaving little ground clearance for the differential, which would rise only when an obstacle or uneven terrain was encountered. It was claimed that the Relay Drive smoothed out the ride so that speeds of 45 mph were possible with solid rubber tires.

Steel spoke wheels also distinguished the Relay trucks from the three other "sister" makes, which used steel disc wheels. Production numbers were best in 1928 with 639 units built, of which 205 had the Relay badge, and also in 1929, with 679 units built of which 511 were Relay trucks.

Despite the Great Depression, Relay expanded its model line in 1931. A light 3/4-ton model was added, which used a Continental engine, as well as a 5-ton and 7-ton model. The 7-ton was a six-wheel truck and each of the new trucks was built only with the Relay badge.

This was also the year Relay completed the Duo-Drive, claiming to have developed the most powerful truck in the world. The 6x4 design used two 420-cubic inch Lycoming straight-eight engines placed side-by-side, each driving one of the rear axles with separate five-speed transmissions that also had two reverse gears. These Fuller transmissions were pneumatically operated while the Vickers steering and Jones twin-disc clutch were hydraulically controlled. The two heavy engines required 12-leaf springs as well as air springs for the front axle. Each rear axle had semi-elliptic springs, two radius rods and a torque rod.

1929 RELAY 3-TON MODEL 40A   **HAYS**

1930 RELAY   **OCW**

Extensive use was made of aluminum in the frame of the Duo-Drive 300A. The engines could be used together or separately with a combined output of 275 hp and top speed of 60 mph. (Each Lycoming engine was rated at 130 hp.) Westinghouse air brakes were used and the truck had three fuel tanks that could hold a total of 150 gallons of gasoline. Along with a sleeper berth, the design was well ahead of its time, except that maximum weight limits per axle were enacted in most states at that time and the design shifted to the more flexible tractor-trailer combination for large trucks.

The Duo-Drive was a last gasp effort. In 1932, Relay Motors went into liquidation. Consolidated Motors, the new owner, built Garford and Relay trucks for one more year before it closed for business permanently.

RELIABLE-DAYTON 1906-1909 — The Reliable-Dayton Motor Car Company was started in Chicago, Illinois, in 1906 by William O. Dayton. The Reliable-Dayton vehicles were highwheelers. The first ones used rope drive, solid rubber tires and a fine-tube radiator over the front axle. With Renault-type hoods, the second series of Reliable-Dayton looked similar to the early International trucks also made in Chicago at that time. However, the engine was actually mounted under the seat. The early two-cycle engines were supplanted by four-cycle engines at the request of the company's customers. The open box bed was the only factory cargo body for the early long wheelbase vehicles.

The second series model line used two-cylinder horizontally-opposed 15 hp and 20 hp four-cycle engines that were water-cooled. The trucks were right-hand tiller drive with a shifter for the two-speed forward and two-speed reverse transmission. The frames were of wagon design made from ash. The Reliable-Dayton had front fenders and a panel body with roof, which extended forward up above the dashboard. Chain drive was used on all Reliable-Dayton trucks and top speed was claimed to be 25 mph. The vehicle's price started at $1,100.

One of the unusual aspects of the engine design for that time was that the connecting rods had lubrication through passages drilled in the crankshaft as in later engines. Also, the engines used an external contracting clutch lined with camel's hair belting.

The large Reliable-Dayton factory in Chicago produced passenger highwheelers but light truck production was also a portion of the overall business. In 1909, the F.A.L. Motor Company of Chicago acquired Reliable-Dayton but no records show production after that year.

RELIANCE 1906-1911 — The Reliance Motor Car Company was founded in Owosso, Michigan, and was to become part of a much larger, far-reaching enterprise called GMC when it was purchased along with the Rapid Motor Vehicle Company in 1909. The company first began in 1904 with a two-cylinder passenger car that used a selective transmission and shaft drive. The company's slogan was "The Car Too Good for the Price." In 1906, the company built its first commercial vehicle and production was shifted entirely away from passenger cars.

The Reliance company produced a varied model line listed by letters of the alphabet going up to 5-ton capacity, including passenger stages and buses. This company was not affiliated with later Reliance Truck Company of Appleton, Wisconsin. From the start, Reliance built forward-control trucks with double chain drive. Fred Paige was the chief executive officer until going off to build the Paige-Detroit cars in 1909.

Reliance trucks were powered by two-cycle water-cooled engines, some using water pumps, others using the "Thermo-Siphon system." The company offered two-, three- and four-cylinder versions in a modular-type design of 30, 45 and 60 hp, respectively. These two-cycle engines were advertised as "two-cycle with the power of four." The three-cylinder engine had a displacement of 309 cubic inches. Literature of that period stated "There are fewer parts and hence less liability to disorder..." Drive was with jackshafts by side chains to the rear wheels. Transmissions were three-speed sliding gear type. Only the Model K chassis was wider at the rear than in front with a 77-inch tread. Otherwise a 58-inch tread was standard. Top speed for the Model G-3 was 18 mph.

1908 RELIANCE RACK BODY   **OCW**

Although models were listed alphabetically, the earliest Model F used a finned radiator up to 1909. The later Models A through N varied largely in body design. Model G had a 108-inch wheelbase, Model H 132-inch and Model K 136-inch. The company advertised capacity from 1/2 ton to 5 ton. Prices ranged from $2,700 for the

Model G, $3,100 for the Model G-3, $3,500 for the Model H, $3,750 for the Model H-4, up to $4,400 for the Model K. Most of the bodies were express type up to Model G. Model H and Model L were available with a 26-passenger sightseeing bus body. Model M was offered as a depot wagon with drop windows. The Model N was an omnibus with side curtains built to customer specifications.

1908 RELIANCE STAKE OCW

All Reliance trucks were fitted with artillery wheels and solid rubber tires at the factory. Suspension was semi-elliptic in front and platform spring in rear. Standard equipment was listed as two side oil lamps, oil taillamps, horn and full set of tools.

1910 RELIANCE FLATBED HAYS

When William Crapo Durant chartered the General Motors Company in New Jersey, one of the many acquisitions he was to make was the Reliance Motor Truck Company. Already part of GMC, in June of 1910 Reliance announced plans to build a new plant in Owosso, which was to employ 1,400 men, up from 200. As the newspaper headlines proclaimed, for the town of Owosso this meant an additional payroll of $80,000 each month, at a time when houses rented for $15 there. A building and loan association was formed there to construct 600 new homes, but production was moved to Detroit as truck manufacturing was consolidated by General Motors. Under GM ownership since 1908, Reliance trucks were built until 1911 but when production was consolidated, the Reliance badge was soon dropped as were the two-cycle engines. For a brief period, the GMC trucks were known as GMC-Reliance or GMC Model H and Model K, rated at 3-1/2-ton and 5-ton capacity, respectively.

RELIANCE 1917-1927 — The Racine Motor Truck Company was located in Appleton, Wisconsin. In 1918, it became the Reliance Motor Truck Company. The company built a 1-1/2-ton and a 2-

1/2-ton model truck powered by a four-cylinder engine. There was a choice of three-speed or four-speed transmissions and Badger external gear drive was used. In 1922, the company became the Appleton Motor Truck Company and it faded out over the following few years.

1911 REMINGTON 5-TON RD

REMINGTON 1911-1913 — The Remington Standard Motor Company was organized by Philo E. Remington who was the grandson of the man who founded the well-known Remington Arms Company, where experiments with a kerosene engine mounted on a three-wheel vehicle took place as early as 1895. The original Remington Automobile & Motor Company built a four-cylinder car that ran on acetylene gas. It was designed by William A. Schmidt who had previously built Remington typewriters. By 1904, the company went into receivership and Philo Remington was forced to start over in Charleston, West Virginia, in 1910.

In Charleston, the company occupied the former factory of the Baldwin Steel works and announced that cars and aeroplanes would be built there. Trucks from 5-ton to 10-ton capacity were to be built there, but it appears only the prototype was completed. It was a forward-control design with a four-cylinder engine that had dual spark plugs. A patented Manly hydraulic transmission was used "with any number of speeds forward and reverse." A 7-1/2-ton truck chassis with these components was priced at $5,500 but it appears no orders followed. Charles M. Manly sued the Remington Standard Motor Company for payment, effectively bringing it into involuntary receivership.

1918 RENNOC-LESLIE 8-TON TRUCK TRACTOR RD

RENNOC-LESLIE 1918-1919 — Rennoc-Leslie, also known as Renno-Leslie, was organized in Philadelphia, Pennsylvania, in 1917 with a capitalization of $750,000. Records show that at least one 2-1/2-ton truck and at least one 2-1/2-ton truck tractor was built in 1918 and 1919. The truck had a 144-inch wheelbase and the truck tractor had a wheelbase of 116 inches. Both were powered by four-cylinder Buda engines and used four-speed Warner transmissions with worm-drive rear axle.

RENO FLYER see DESERT FLYER

RENVILLE 1912 — This company was listed both as the Motor Buggy Manufacturing Company and as the Renville Buggy Manufacturing Company. Both a passenger car and a light truck were offered, most likely using an interchangeable design. However, the 3/4-ton and 1-ton truck, priced at $800 and $1,150, respectively, were powered by a two-cylinder engine. The Renville touring car had a 45 hp four-cylinder engine. The latter was advertised as "The car for the farmer."

REO 1906-1967 — Having left Olds, the company he established, Ransom Eli said his farewells to his business associates and bankers whose philosophy he did not share and who forbid him to use his own name on other cars. Within a year, he started a new company and finished building a new car by October of 1904. The official press release explanation for his sudden departure was given as "for certain reasons."

The first Reo Gasoline Commercial Cars were illustrated in the March 1906 *Cycle and Automobile Trade Journal*. A photo of the Wagonette Bus showed 10 passengers on board and it was priced at $1,600. A drawing of a delivery wagon was also shown and priced at $1,700. The latter was powered by a 16 hp two-cylinder four-cycle horizontally-opposed engine, used a planetary transmission and had a 90-inch wheelbase.

1909 REO FLAREBOARD EXPRESS   **BWA**

By then Ransom Eli Olds had become known for the curved dash Oldsmobile, which his partners, the Smiths, wanted to phase out in order to build large luxury cars. Since they had controlling interest, Olds made his departure and began the Reo Motor Car Company in Lansing, Michigan. The 16 hp engine was also used in the first five-passenger detachable tonneau car priced at $1,250. He also built a car with a 24 hp four-cylinder engine by 1906, although this car was not promoted. One of his first Reo cars was sent on a double transcontinental journey, something that had never been done up to that time. By 1907, the Reo Motor Car Company was third in the industry behind Ford and Buick. The company built a Light Flare Board Express in 1909.

In October of 1910, a sister business venture, the Reo Motor Truck Company, was announced in Lansing with Ransom Olds holding a 51 percent controlling interest. The first two advertised vehicles from this company were the 3/4-ton Model H and the 1/4-ton Model J light delivery truck priced at $600. Both used a maximum-rated 12 hp engine, planetary transmission and multiple-disc clutch. The heavier had double chain drive and 36-inch wheels with hard rubber, while the lighter used single chain drive and had pneumatic tires. Wheelbase was 86 inches and 78 inches, respectively. In 1912, a stake body or express body Model H was priced at $750.

1911 REO   **SMOKEY MTN CAR MUSEUM**

In 1913, the Model H continued to be offered with a 9.03 hp one-cylinder engine, planetary transmission and 90-inch wheelbase. The Model J was now a 2-ton capacity truck priced at $1,800 with factory stake body or $1,650 for chassis and cab. It had a 25.6 hp four-cylinder engine and a three-speed transmission with direct drive in third gear. Between 1911 and 1913, some 2,300 Model H Reo trucks were sold.

1915 REO SPEED WAGON   **WALTER MILLER**

By 1915, Reo advertised a 3/4-ton "Speed Wagon," also called a "Hurry Up Wagon." The latter name did not catch on. Top speed with load was claimed to be 40 mph, although 22 mph was the speed stated in the specifications. Electric starting was standard and a 45 hp four-cylinder engine was used with a 13-plate clutch and three-speed selective sliding gear transmission and bevel drive. With the standard express body the price was $1,075. The 2-ton Model J continued to be priced at $1,650 without body and the engine was uprated to 27.23 hp. By 1917, the "Hurry Up Wagon," as it was still advertised, was priced at $1,000 complete with covered express body, but later in the year the same 3/4-ton truck was shown as a "Speed Wagon" for $1,125.

The "Hurry Up Wagon" name was not abandoned just yet. By 1918, it was used interchangeably with "Speed Wagon." No matter what it was called, it sold well. Different bodies began to appear on the Speed Wagon chassis, including hearses and ambulances. By the following year, 19,900 Speed Wagons had been sold since production began. The Reo factory provided several bodies by 1920, including the Carryall, Low Open Express, Grain Box, Stock Rack, Canopy Top Express and Double Deck Canopy Express at prices ranging from $1,435 to $1,485. The chassis price, which did not include a cab or seats but did include four fenders, lights and hood, was selling for $1,245 by 1921.

1920 REO 3-TON SPEED WAGON TANKER   TEX

1920 REO STAKE BED   KP

Late in 1920, Reo began production of the Power Wagon. Twelve different standard bodies were available from the factory. Most of the components were built by Reo itself, unlike many of the other assembled vehicles of the day. Also that year the Hotchkiss drive was available on the Reo trucks and the 2-ton model continued to be built but did not sell as well as the lighter trucks. The Speed Wagon was even built as a light bus.

In 1923, Reo introduced a new Parcel Delivery model rated at 1/2-ton capacity. It was based on Reo's taxicab chassis and was priced at $1,485. The taxicab had been introduced for 1922 using a 113-inch wheelbase, according to literature of that period. The Parcel Delivery based on this chassis was available as a solid panel or screen side body. Even with a solid panel body, the driver still sat inside a C-cab, with side curtains available for inclement weather. The Speed Wagon was in fact available with a fully enclosed cab.

1924 REO CROSS-COUNTRY BUS   RD

All advertisements and listings of that time referred to the "Speed Wagon" not "Speedwagon," as was used in later literature. Gradually the two words were hyphenated, then became one word, although much factory literature still used the two words separately until the early 1930s. In later literature, the T-6 taxicab, which was powered by a 50 hp six-cylinder engine, was listed as having a 120-inch wheelbase. By 1920, that was the standard wheelbase of Reo passenger cars, which were being built alongside Reo trucks from the beginning.

For 1925, the "Speed Wagon" concept was expanded to include a 1-1/4-ton version, which was powered by a 27.2 hp four-cylinder Reo engine and used 33x5 front and rear pneumatic tires. It was

also known as the Model F and had a wheelbase of 128 inches. The closed cab version without body was priced at $1,185 but many variations were available directly from Reo. The chassis alone was priced at $1,035, but with a panel delivery body and closed cab the price went up to $1,385.

1925 REO 1/2-TON CANOPY EXPRESS   OCW

Also in 1925, Reo introduced the 2-ton Heavy Duty Speed Wagon. It was powered by a six-cylinder engine and featured spiral bevel gear drive, double frame chassis, pneumatic tires, all with a chassis price tag of $1,985. After some success with jitney operators, the new six-cylinder Model W chassis was also intended for bus application. Streetcar-type bodies were built by FitzJohn and parlor car bodies were fabricated by Fremont, among other body makers. By 1927, Reo had sold nearly 2,400 Model W chassis. Lockheed four-wheel hydraulic brakes were fitted on the lighter trucks at this time.

1928 REO FIRE TRUCK   OCW

The "Junior Speedwagon" appeared in 1928. It was rated at 1/2-ton and the chassis was priced at $895. Ads proclaimed "The Lowest Priced Six-Cylinder Truck of its Size in America." It was offered in addition to the 1-ton Tonner for $995, the 1-1/2-ton Standard for $1,345, the 2-ton Master for $1,645 and the 3-ton Heavy Duty for $2,185. Starting with the 1-1/2-ton trucks and up the six-cylinder "Gold Crown" engine was used, which featured a chrome-nickel block. Expanding-type hydraulic brakes were fitted on all models by this time.

By 1929, the Junior, DA and DC model trucks used a 16-E six-cylinder Continental engine. The Standard Speed Wagon was the FA model usually built with a 137-inch wheelbase and 32x6 tires. The 3-ton Heavy Duty GA model was usually built with a 163-inch wheelbase, but altogether, Reo's trucks were offered in 14 wheelbases from 115 inches to 179 inches. The Flying Cloud engine, used for passenger cars, was adapted to the "New Speedwagon" truck using a heavier flywheel, larger fan and water pump and integrally-cast cooling fins on the oil pan.

1930 REO SPEED WAGON   OCW

The 60 hp Continental 6-E engine continued to be used in the 1/2-ton Junior 15 Speedwagon. The DF Tonner used a more powerful six-cylinder Reo engine, as did the 1-1/2-ton FA, FE and FF trucks. Next up were the 2-ton FC, FD and FH models and the 3-ton was offered as GA, GC, GD and GCS. The FH and GD were tractor-trucks. Also, about 1,300 FB and GB kick-up frames, used primarily for buses, were sold by 1933.

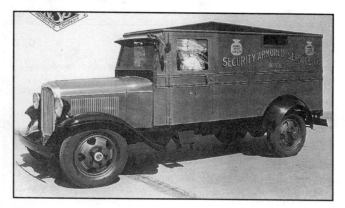

1932 REO 1-TON ARMORED CAR   KP

1933 REO 1-1/2-TON SPEEDWAGON   MROZ

A new, well-designed horizontal-bar V-grille made its debut in 1931. Reacting to the sudden economic downturn, Reo advertised its 1-1/2-ton Speed Wagon chassis with a four-cylinder engine for only $625. The following year, Reo introduced a 4-ton truck, designated as 4H, 4J and 4K, with a 110 hp straight-eight, one of the few truck builders to do so. In 1933, wheelbases ranged from 136 inches to 205 inches. Some Reos still had flat radiators and nearly all had 20-inch wheels.

In 1934, Reo slashed its base price to $595 for a 1-1/2-ton and 2-1/2-ton chassis. The 1/2-ton Speed Wagon pickup was offered for $660 and the 1/2-ton Speed Wagon panel truck for $695. Reo trucks were assembled in Great Britain and sold well there. The following year, the first Reo cab-over-engine model was introduced. The heaviest Reo by then was a 6-ton capacity truck, but Speedwagon chassis started at an even lower price, $445. The 1/2-ton used 6.25x16 tires, while the rest had 20-inch wheels. A new Silver Crown 209-cubic inch 70 hp engine was also introduced for 1935. For both 1935 and 1936, Reo did not build any trucks with four-cylinder engines.

1936 REO 3-TON SPEED WAGON   NMM

In order to stay competitive in the marketplace, under an agreement with Mack, Reo began building Mack Junior trucks and buses late in 1935. The Mack Junior series consisted of the 1/2-ton 1M, 1-1/2-ton 10M, 2-ton 20M, 3-ton 30M and a Traffic type 3-ton model called 30MT with the engine between the seats. For 1937, the last year of the Mack Juniors, designations were 2M for the 1/2-ton to 3/4-ton, which was available with a four-cylinder or six-cylinder engine, MF for the 1-1/2-ton route delivery, 11M for the standard 1-1/2-ton, 21M for the 2-ton, 31M for the 3-ton, 31MT and MT for COE trucks and a transit bus designated as 91MT.

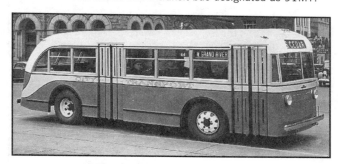

1937 REO 3P7 REAR-ENGINE CITY BUS   FLP

At the same time, Reo also offered the "Brilliant New" Speed Delivery chassis for $555. The front sheet metal, grille, fenders and windshield were restyled for 1937. The Speed Delivery was available on a 114-inch or 120-inch wheelbase with four-cylinder or six-cylinder Silver Crown engines. Bus chassis continued to be built and in 1937, Reo used six-cylinder Buda engines in its 3L6H model line in addition to the metropolitan 2LM and 3P7. The latter was a pusher chassis with Bender or FitzJohn bodies but Reo also embarked on building integral buses and a team of engineers was "hired away" from Yellow Coach. The result was a series of buses called Flying Cloud that were produced from 1939 until 1942. However, from a business point of view, this project was a failure when only 170 of these buses sold over three years.

In the truck line for 1938, more restyling took place and the advertising slogan used often was "Out in Front with Reo!" referring to its COE trucks. That year, Reo announced capacity ratings from 12,000 pounds to 15,000 pounds GVW for its heavy-duty models, which were powered by 228-cubic inch or 268-cubic inch six-cylinder Gold Crown engines and had wheelbases from 105 inches to 166 inches. The heftiest Reo truck that year was the six-wheel COE Truxmore Model 1B7M, which was powered by a 228-cubic inch 73 hp six-cylinder engine and used a four-speed or optional five-speed transmission.

Between 1937 and 1939, Reo built 1/2-ton Speed Delivery light trucks in two series, the 450 45 hp four-cylinder and the 650 70 hp six-cylinder. Both had a standard 114-inch wheelbase or could be ordered on a 120-inch wheelbase, the latter having an L suffix. With a heavier axle, larger rear springs and 16-inch tires, the two models were also available as 3/4-ton capacity trucks. Both used L-head Continental engines, which were called Silver Crown. The 450 and 650 series trucks had two-piece windshields that opened individually, doors with armrests and ashtrays and the front bumpers were chrome. Despite such luxurious appointments, these light trucks did not sell well. Over three years of production, only 2,000 found buyers of which only 77 were four-cylinder models.

In 1939, the Speedwagon name was phased out and a new heavy-duty range developed the previous year continued with rounded hood and set-back front axle. The Silver Crown engine was originally designed for Reo passenger cars and had four main bearings and full-pressure oiling. Reo discontinued building passenger cars for 1937 and Ransom Eli Olds, who was 70 years old at the time, resigned from the board of directors. He much preferred building passenger cars and this corporate decision did not please him in the least.

1940 REO 20 BS TANKER OCW

1940 REO SCHOOL BUS KP

During World War II, Reo built 300 front-engine buses with Wayne sectional bodies for the U.S. Navy. Most of the production was concentrated on the 29 Series 6x6 trucks and truck tractors, which Federal also built for the military. "Steady Pace for Victory" was Reo's slogan during the war. Reo built a 2-1/2-ton prototype called the Model 23 BHRS, which used a Waukesha 6 MZR six-cylinder engine in 1941, but it was not selected for production. Reo later built the Studebaker US-6 U3 model instead.

The postwar "Victory" bus, whose design had been started as early as 1943, was built with the body furnished by the Meteor Motor Car Company of Piqua, Ohio, an ambulance and funeral car builder. Between 1945 and 1947, nearly 1,000 of these buses

were sold in comparison to 3,000 school buses during the same period. A new assembly line was set up in Lansing to produce a line of Flying Cloud buses using under-floor Continental six-cylinder engines and Spicer torque converters. Only about 100 of these buses were sold and Reo quickly discontinued bus production entirely.

1945 REO 6X6 WRECKER OCW

For 1948, Reo had a new perforated sheet metal front grille on its heavy-duty trucks, which were up to 76,000 pounds GVW for the Models 30 and 31. The rest of the line was comprised of Models C19 to C25. Models 30 and 31 were available with a 200 hp six-cylinder engine. The following year, the tandem axle Models 30A and 31A had 513-cubic inch and 602-cubic inch six-cylinder engines, respectively. Reo did not adopt diesel engines and all seven six-cylinder engines were gasoline powered.

Ransom Eli Olds died in 1950. He had had little to do with the Reo company since his resignation in 1937. For 1950, Reo's E-19, E-21, E-22 and E-23 trucks had a heavier grille with a single row of horizontal slots on each side and the letters REO placed vertically on the nose of the front sheet metal. The company introduced round-nosed vans called Step-and-Serve and forward-control vans called Merchandiser. The name Speedwagon reappeared, albeit briefly, on smaller round-nose pickups and stake trucks.

The Reo 2-1/2-ton 6x6 M34 was the replacement for the GMC CCKW of World War II and it was first shown in 1951. The U.S. Army specified that its trucks could run submerged and the M34 could operate in water up to 11 feet deep with snorkel devices and the driver wearing scuba gear. Reo called these trucks the "Eager Beaver." GMC and Studebaker also built this truck and its production eventually outlived the Reo company itself.

In 1953, Reo introduced liquid propane gas (LPG) engines and the following year, a heavy-duty V-8 truck of its own design was offered by the company. In 1954, plans to sell the company to Henney Motor Company, hearse and special body fabricator for Packard, was agreed to by Reo directors but did not get stockholder approval. This was the year Reo introduced a sleeper cab. The Henney deal fell through and Bohn Aluminum and Brass Corporation of Detroit bought Reo.

In 1955, with John C. Tooker as president and John L. Adams as Reo sales manager, the company offered a 100,000-mile warranty on all new Gold Comet engines. Gold Comet engines included gasoline and LPG six-cylinder units and the heavy duty V-8. The warranty covered engines 255 OA, 292 OA, 331 OA, OH 160, OV 195, OV 220, OH 160 LPG, 255 OA LPG and 331 OA LPG. The heaviest Reo trucks had a new flat trapezoidal grille with a second rectangular section underneath just above a massive front bumper.

Also for 1955, Reo introduced a COE truck tractor and a conventional tractor with a 96-inch BBC. Reo advertised its LPG-powered trucks as costing 2-1/4 cents per mile to operate, largely due to the low maintenance for LPG engines. Diesel engines were finally adopted in 1956 and these were turbocharged Cummins units.

Sales increased dramatically under the new ownership, although John Adams was the only new member of the management team. Bohn began negotiating to buy Diamond T, but in 1957 White bought Reo from Bohn.

The following year, White bought Diamond T and consolidated both operations at the Reo plant as a separate division. By this time, the Reo D-600 and D-700 series were offered in six models. Conventional trucks had a GVW rating up to 52,000 pounds with tandem axles and up to 78,000 pounds for the tandem axle highway tractors. The new E series featured diesel engines, which were from Cummins and ranged from 180 hp to 262 hp. LPG engines continued to be sold and the Reo AC 63-inch COE was quite successful. The company's slogan was now "Reo - Gold Standard of Values."

In 1961, Reo offered a tilt-cab highway tractor that used simple flat sheet metal on the cab in order to minimize tooling costs. By the following year, Reo advertised eight truck models, eight highway tractors and four tandem axle trucks. Both COE tilt-cabs and conventional trucks were offered. There were 43 basic Reo models at that time, with 14 diesel engines from Cummins, Detroit Diesel and Perkins. Reo was also building a 7-1/2-ton 6x6 military truck called the Type F1, which was identical to the one built by Federal. Reo's designation for this truck was as Model 29XS.

In 1964, a tri-drive-axle truck was built, along with numerous models in the D, E, DF and DCL series. A new swing-open hood was available in 1966. LPG engines were available, and Reo built a wide range of 6x4, 6x6 and 8x6 chassis. However, Diamond T and Reo models overlapped in specifications to such an extent that White consolidated both makes under the name Diamond-Reo in May of 1967.

1914 REPUBLIC STAKE PLATFORM   **OCW**

1915 REPUBLIC CANOPY EXPRESS   **VINCENT KOVLAK**

REPUBLIC 1912-1929 — Republic trucks were first made by the Alma Motor Truck Company of Alma, Michigan. According to some records, the first unit was built in 1912. For 1913, the Republic trucks were conventional 3/4-ton and 1-ton capacity and they continued to be built when the Alma company changed its name to the Republic Motor Truck Company in 1914. For 1915, there were three shaft drive models and two chain drive models available. By the end of that year, chain drive was discontinued and Torbensen Internal Gear Drive was advertised.

1916 REPUBLIC BUS W/PASSENGER TRAILER   **LIAM**

1917 REPUBLIC ARMY TRUCK W/TRAILER   **OCW**

By 1917, the Republic company had been incorporated and the model line consisted of five capacity trucks from 3/4 ton to 3-1/2 ton. With production up to 10,000 trucks per year, Republic was the nation's largest truck manufacturer by 1918. By that year, there had been a total of 30,000 Republic trucks sold by 1,300 dealers. Republic trucks were distinguishable by their yellow chassis and other eye-catching colors for bodies and cabs.

By 1920, a total of 70,000 Republic trucks had been sold. However, production fell to 500 trucks a month in 1922. During the next several years, Republic built a range of trucks from 1-1/2-ton to 4-ton capacity and also introduced a bus chassis. Continental, Lycoming and Waukesha engines were used. Republic's bus chassis had a 185-inch wheelbase and was powered by a 25.6 hp Lycoming four-cylinder engine. The bus had seating for 15 passengers. By this time, there were 71 different bus chassis available from 43 different manufacturers.

By the mid-1920s, the company offered several models starting with the 1-1/4-ton capacity Model 75. It was powered by a 22.5 hp Lycoming C engine and used a Fuller clutch and transmission. The Model 75 had Eaton front and rear axles, Saginaw steering and Northern wheels carried 33x5 pneumatic tires front and rear. The next heavier Republic truck was the 1-1/2-ton Model 10F with 140-inch wheelbase and powered by a Lycoming CT engine. This truck had solid rubber tires, whereas the 2-ton Model 11X had optional pneumatic tires on Van wheels and was powered by a Continental J4 engine.

Republic also offered two 3-ton model at that time with the same component manufacturers as previously stated. However, the 3-ton Model 19 used a 27.2 hp Continental K-4 engine, whereas the 3-ton Model 19W used a 25.6 hp Waukesha engine. The heaviest Republic truck listed by 1925 was the 4-ton Model 20 with a 165-inch wheelbase and a chassis weight of 6,700 pounds. It was powered by a 32.4 hp Continental L-4 engine and had the same components as the lighter model except Smith wheels carried 36x5 front and 36x10 rear solid rubber tires with pneumatics being listed as optional.

Early Republic trucks used Torbensen internal gear drive, later replaced by Eaton and Timken worm-drive. In the second half of this decade, the company built trucks up to 5-ton capacity, which included drop frame bus chassis for 16, 20, 26 and 32 passengers.

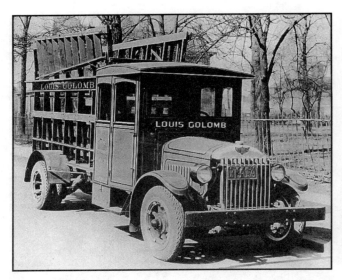

1927 REPUBLIC 2-TON   **OCW**

In 1927, there were eight models available and six-cylinder engines were introduced. Half of the models still used solid rubber tires. Republic bought Linn Manufacturing Corporation in 1928 (Linn halftracks continued to be built under their own name) and Republic merged with the commercial division of American LaFrance in 1929, forming the LaFrance-Republic Corporation. There were 28 distinct models of Republic trucks for that year and Republic and American LaFrance were listed separately until the end of the year. Although Republic trucks were no longer made under the single original name, some trucks with the Republic badge were sold in England into 1931.

Due to the economic downturn, only 12 models of LaFrance-Republic were listed for 1930. See LaFrance-Republic.

REX 1921-1923 — The Royal Rex Motors Company of Chicago, Illinois, built Rex trucks of which there were six sizes consisting of five capacities from 1 ton to 5 ton. These trucks were exported under the marque C.K.D. and used a swastika as a trademark. It does not appear that Royal Rex built Rex or C.K.D. trucks after the postwar recession of the early 1920s.

REX VIAPLANE 1932 — The Rex Finance Corporation of Chicago, Illinois, was founded by five Fitzgerald brothers, who were brokers of intercity bus lines throughout Minnesota starting in 1920. In 1932, the oldest of the Fitzgeralds, Roy, built a 13-passenger parlor bus powered by an International engine. The Rex Finance Corporation was set up to market this bus, which was named the Rex Viaplane. However, no customers were found and only the prototype was completed.

REYA 1917-1919 — Although the Reya Company has been listed as a commercial vehicle manufacturer in Napoleon, Ohio, no details or specifications have been available to date.

REYNOLDS 1920-1923 — The Reynolds Motor Truck Company was located in Mount Clemens, Michigan. The company began by offering trucks from 1-1/2-ton to 5-ton capacity. The heaviest truck was available only with solid rubber tires, while the rest had optional balloon pneumatics. All Reynolds trucks were powered by four-cylinder Hinkley engines and used four-speed transmissions that were mounted amidships with power takeoffs on either side. Sheldon worm axles were used as the final drive. An engine driven compressor was available for trucks with pneumatic tires. For the last two years of its existence, the Reynolds Motor Truck Company only built 1-1/2-ton and 2-ton capacity trucks.

RIKER 1897-1903 — The Riker Electric Motor Company was started by Andrew Lawrence Riker in Brooklyn, New York. Riker was the first president of the Society of Automotive Engineers. His first vehicles were built in the mid-1890s and by the turn of the

century, he was building electric cars and winning races. His first commercial sales came in 1897 with orders for electric vans and hansom cabs.

1900 RIKER ELECTRIC DELIVERY WAGON   **LIAM**

In 1899, Riker incorporated as the Riker Electric Vehicle Company and moved to the former Lewis & Fowler factory in Elizabethtown, New Jersey. The following year, he sold his company to the Electric Vehicle Company, makers of the Columbia electric and Riker became a vice-president of that company. The E.V.C. enterprise briefly continued to build cabs, vans, hotel buses and trucks up to 2-1/2-ton capacity under the name Riker in Elizabethtown before moving production to the Hartford, Connecticut, plant. One of the first ambulances built in the United States was produced by Riker in 1901. According to records, this type of electric tiller-steered ambulance transported President William McKinley when he was shot at the Pan American Exposition in 1901.

Riker commercial vehicles were produced until 1903 when the name was dropped in favor of Columbia. This was the parent company's name, which had built Columbia electric vehicles in parallel with Riker from 1900.

1916 RIKER STAKE BED   **GOODYEAR**

RIKER 1916-1921 — Andrew Lawrence Riker was the designer of the Locomobile located in Bridgeport, Connecticut. Having previously designed electric cars and trucks, he was hired by that company in 1902 to build internal combustion-powered vehicles and his engineering efforts were quite successful. By 1916, the Locomobile trucks were renamed Riker in honor of their chief designer. Riker had resolved an engineering problem for the Army Quartermaster Corps in 1916, when he added railroad wheel flanges on Locomobile trucks for rapid deployment over train tracks against Pancho Villa who had raided Columbus, New Mexico.

1916 RIKER 4-TON HIGH-LIFT COAL TRUCK　　　**LIAM**

Riker trucks were built in 3-ton and 4-ton forms using a common 150-inch wheelbase chassis. A four-cylinder Locomobile T-head engine powered the two truck models that used four-speed transmissions and worm-drive. Riker trucks had the same wooden spoke wheels that Locomobile used. Priced at $4,600 for the 3-ton model, Riker trucks were considered high quality and were distinguished by notable bronze castings of the transmission casing and engine parts.

After suffering receivership in 1919, Locomobile cars and Riker trucks were briefly built by the Hares Motors Company in Bridgeport, Connecticut, which also owned Mercer and Simplex. Emlen S. Hare was the former vice-president of Packard, but his company was soon undone by financial trouble and Locomobile (along with its Riker truck division) was sold again, this time to William Crapo Durant, who was building up General Motors. Riker truck production was immediately dropped, although Locomobile passenger cars were continued until 1929. Andrew Lawrence Riker died in 1930.

RIMPULL 1975 to date — The Rimpull Corporation started out in Olathe, Kansas, during 1972 building replacement components such as axles and powertrains for mining trucks. By 1975, the company went into the production of off-highway dump trucks for mining and large construction projects. The Rimpull trucks used proprietary engines and incorporated the company's own Quad-Reduction axle made up of a double reduction differential and double reduction planetary transmission. Coal haulers have been built as end dump and bottom dump trucks.

Rimpull also built water-sprayer trucks for off-road dust control with optional fire fighting apparatus. The dump trucks were powered by engines with 600 hp to 1200 hp. The water/fire trucks were powered by a 600 hp engine. The two-axle dump trucks had a 65-ton capacity, while the three-axle articulated bottom dump trucks had a 170-ton capacity, which was uprated to 200-ton capacity.

By the mid-1990s, Rimpull has offered nine models of trucks. The lightest model has been designated the RD-85B rear dump truck with up to 100-ton capacity powered by either a 1050 hp 12-cylinder Detroit Diesel or 1050 hp Cummins diesel engine. The truck has used the Allison DP 8963 transmission and both steering axle and drive axle have been built by Rimpull.

The Model R3051 rear dump truck has been rated at 115-ton capacity powered by 1200 hp 12-cylinder Cummins or Detroit Diesel engines with a CLBT 9681 Allison transmission. Next up was the R3351 model Rimpull with 150-ton capacity and 1350

hp diesel engine options. Rimpull has also offered the WT-20B water truck with 20,000-gallon capacity powered by the same engine as the RD-85B model.

1995 RIMPULL WT-20B　　　**RIMPULL**

1996 RIMPULL CW-280　　　**RIMPULL**

Rimpull has also built a series of articulated bottom dump coal haulers starting with the CW-150 powered by the same engine as the WT-20B and RD-85B as well as the CW-160S bottom dump coal hauler. The next size up Rimpull bottom dump hauler has been offered as the Model CW-180 powered by 1350 hp Cummins or Detroit Diesel with the same transmission as the R3051 truck. The two largest coal haulers built by Rimpull have been designated as the CWT-270 bottom dump coal trailer-train and the CW-280, the latter powered by a 1600 hp Detroit Diesel or Cummins engine using a Twin Disc Model 8500 transmission. Rimpull has built all of its steer, drive and trailer axles and the company has continued manufacturing in Olathe, Kansas, to date.

1971 RITEWAY 8X6 CONCRETE MIXER　　　**EK**

RITEWAY 1961-1979 — The American Rite-Way Corporation began in Dallas, Texas. The original Riteway was a purpose-built concrete mixer with up to 10-cubic yard capacity. This truck had either three or four axles, with one or two in the form of tag axles, the fourth also being retractable. Smaller eight-cubic yard versions were also built. The Riteway trucks were powered by Cummins or Detroit Diesel engines.

Riteway was reorganized and moved to Fort Wayne, Indiana. The company built larger concrete mixer trucks with three, four or five axles, each with a single front axle. Six-wheel-drive using the front axle was common. Engines were mounted in the rear with concrete discharge at the front over the cab.

By 1976, Riteway was built by the Arlan Manufacturing Company of Arlington, Texas, and marketed by the Rexnord Company of Milwaukee, Wisconsin. Some of these were rebadged as Rex and most were built on Diamond-Reo, Hahn or Hendrickson chassis. In 1978, Rexnord bought out Arlan and the Riteway (Rite-Way) name was phased out, although the company has continued to build purpose-built concrete mixer trucks on commercial chassis.

1913 ROBINSON MODEL D   **MHS**

ROBINSON 1909-1920 — Thomas F. Robinson began building trucks in Minneapolis, Minnesota, with a forward-control 1-ton model named the Gopher. Robinson formed a partnership with Freeman M. Loomis and the company built 57 of these trucks, which sold for $1,800 each. By 1910, the business was called the Robinson-Loomis Truck Company but in 1912, Thomas Robinson went on his own again with the Robinson Motor Truck Company, which was not affiliated with the Robinson trucks built at the same time in Sacramento, California.

The second Robinson truck model line began in October of 1912. A 1-1/2-ton and a 2-ton truck were offered that year and in 1913, a 5-ton truck was also built. The latter was powered by a 50 hp engine. Subsequent production included a kit to transform passenger cars into light trucks. The company faded out by 1920.

1915 ROBINSON/GOLDEN WEST 4X4 POLO TRUCKS   **MROZ**

ROBINSON see GOLDEN WEST

334

ROBINSON-LOOMIS 1909-1920 — Thomas F. Robinson built the Gopher truck in Minneapolis, Minnesota. This was a 1-ton capacity unit priced at $1,800. A total of 57 Gopher trucks were documented to have been built. During this time, Robinson was in partnership with L. Loomis and their company was known as the Robinson-Loomis Truck Company from 1910 to 1912. This company was not related to the Robinson Brothers of St. Louis who built a fire engine pumper on a Chadwick chassis in 1910, which was delivered to the city of Wichita Falls, Texas.

In 1912, Robinson went off on his own again as the Robinson Motor Truck Company, still in Minneapolis. The truck model line was expanded with 1-1/2-ton and 2-ton capacity trucks available and in 1913, a 5-ton truck with a 50 hp four-cylinder engine was built. Truck production faded out during World War I, most likely as a result of material shortages. In 1920, Robinson advertised a conversion kit for passenger cars which could be turned into light trucks, but truck manufacturing was terminated.

ROCKET see NORTHWAY

ROCK FALLS 1909-1925 — The Rock Falls Manufacturing Company began by building hearses in Sterling, Illinois, during 1909. Ambulances were also built starting in 1912 and these were standard assembled vehicles using Buda four-cylinder engines. One of the unusual features of the Rock Falls hearses was that the gasoline tank was mounted on the left side of the chassis with the filler cap and gas gauge on the floor under the driver's legs.

By 1920, the company was producing one vehicle a week. Few of the 136-inch wheelbase vehicles were limousines -- most were professional cars in the $5,000 range. In the early 1920s, 73 hp six-cylinder Continental 9A engines were used and prior to the company's demise, the wheelbase changed to 132 inches and 70 hp six-cylinder Continental 6T engines were used. Also, between 1920 and 1923, a 1-1/2-ton truck was available from Rock Falls.

ROCKFORD 1914 — The Rockford Motor Truck Company was located in Rockford, Illinois. The firm listed a 3/4-ton and 1-ton chassis with bodies available on a custom order basis. It is uncertain whether or not this company stayed in business for more than a year.

1906 ROCKLIFF 3-TON   **RD**

ROCKLIFF 1902-1906 — Charles Rockliff of Brooklyn, New York, was the builder of the 3-ton Rockliff Express Wagon, which was announced midyear during 1906. After two years of experimenting, Rockliff had built a gasoline-powered surrey by 1901 and demonstrated it to members of the Long Island Automobile Club that year. According to *The Motor Vehicle Review*, his intent was to show a vehicle that could be used in the operation of a stage line. Instead, he began building trucks the following year, which were sold to New York department stores and to the Brooklyn Rapid Transit Company.

The Rockliff Express Wagon was powered by a water-cooled 18 hp vertical two-cylinder engine and used a two-speed planetary transmission. From a jackshaft, final drive was by chain. Chain was also used from the transmission to the jackshaft. Wheelbase was 126 inches and tread was 64 inches. Tires were 36x3 front and rear solid rubber on wooden artillery type wheels. The frame was built from white oak shod with half-inch steel plates. A 2-ton capacity truck was upgraded to 3-ton capacity by 1906, the last year of the Rockliff's manufacture.

ROCKNE 1932-1933 — Knute Rockne was a well-known football coach at Notre Dame, who also happened to be friends with Albert Russel Erskine, president of Studebaker. Knute Rockne was appointed sales promotion manager in March of 1931. On the last day of that month he died in a plane crash. The car that was to be marketed by Rockne Motors Corporation of Detroit ended up being a memorial to Knute Rockne.

1932 ROCKNE PANEL DELIVERY   A&A

1933 ROCKNE POSTAL DELIVERY   A&A

1933 ROCKNE DELUXE PANEL DELIVERY   A&A

The Rockne was intended to compete in the economy range and its total production of 23,201 vehicles was due in part to the $600 to $800 price. One version was a light commercial delivery van based on the Model 65, which had a 110-inch wheelbase and was powered by an 66 hp six-cylinder L-head Studebaker powerplant. It also featured a three-speed transmission with freewheeling. Production ended midway through 1933 when the Rockne plant was shut down, engine production was moved to South Bend, Indiana, Studebaker went into receivership and Albert Erskine committed suicide.

ROCKWELL 1910-1911 — The New Departure Manufacturing Company was the builder of the Rockwell Light Delivery Wagon and Rockwell taxis. The vehicle was named after Albert F. Rockwell, who was associated with Ernest R. Burwell, Charles Treadway, Ira Newcomb and T.H. Holdsworth at the Bristol Engineering Company in Bristol, Connecticut, where this commercial vehicle was designed. The New Departure Company was considered one of the

best manufacturers of automobiles in the country at that time and Rockwell was at the head of the enterprise. The company also built the Houpt-Rockwell and Allen-Kingston cars.

1910 ROCKWELL LIGHT DELIVERY   MROZ

The Rockwell taxi was a laundelet-type with a 20 hp four-cylinder water-cooled engine with a selective speed transmission and shaft drive. It was priced at $3,000. About 200 of these taxis plied their trade in New York City in 1910. The Light Delivery apparently used the same engine and had a three-plate clutch coupling, the same three-speed selective type transmission. The driving axles were fitted with hub driving clutches.

RODEFELD 1915-1917 — Rodefeld vehicles were built in Richmond, Indiana, and included both cars and trucks. Between 1915 and 1917, the company built a 1-ton model truck. Chassis price was $1,100 in 1915. A.H. Rodefeld was the organizer, who also employed his two sons Gus and Bill Rodefeld. The Rodefeld vehicles used four-cylinder air-cooled engines and chain drive. The company built its own engines, transmissions and all other mechanical parts but purchased bodies, wheels and electrical equipment from other companies. One Rodefeld truck was built with seating for 12 and was bought by the Wayne County Highway Department for transporting prisoners to and from work as a chain gang.

ROGERS 1911-1914 — The Rogers Motor Car Company was located in Omaha, Nebraska. It was founded by Ralph F. Rogers, who began in 1909 with his own car designs in Chicago. Manufacturing was organized for the 1911 model year in Ralston, Nebraska, which was near the main offices in Omaha. The Roger highwheelers were built as runabouts, roadsters and surreys, but only one model 1/2-ton truck was available, which was powered by the same 18 hp two-cylinder engine that the other models used. Wheelbase was listed at 100 inches (10 inches longer than the passenger cars) and the Rogers commercial version sold for $800.

ROGERS UNA-DRIVE 1919-1922 — The Rogers Una-Drive Motor Truck Corporation was located in Sunnyvale, California. The company built a four-wheel-drive truck with 3-ton capacity. A central transfer case transmitted power to front and rear axles using shaft drive. The truck was powered by a four-cylinder Buda engine. It is not certain when the Rogers company faded out of business in the early part of the decade.

ROLAND 1914-19151 — The Roland Gas-Electric Vehicle Company was located in New York City. The company built commercial vehicles using a gasoline engine that turned a generator that powered the electric motors for final drive. Trucks of 1-, 3-and 3-1/2-ton capacity were built, as were city buses rated up to 7 tons. The 3-1/2-ton truck chassis was priced at $3,750 in 1914.

ROUSTABOUT see TRIVAN

ROTARY 1917-1918 — The Rotary Motor Company was a short-lived business located in New York City. Arthur S. Alexander was president and the company built a 1/4-ton capacity three-wheel delivery car late in 1917. The engine was a rotary type with three cylinders enclosed within the spokes of the driving wheel, which was located at the center rear of the chassis. The body was mounted forward on the axle that carried two wheels in front. The driver sat above the engine as on a motorcycle.

The motor weighed 34 pounds and it was claimed could develop 10 hp while providing an efficient 50 miles per gallon in fuel consumption. Top speed was 25 mph. Tires were 30x3 front and rear pneumatic and the entire vehicle weighed 300 pounds. It was priced at $295. *The Commercial Vehicle* announced in January that one Rotary had been built and orders were being taken for further production, but there is no evidence that the vehicles were manufactured in any quantity. The earlier Rotary invented in 1906 by Edward C. Warren in New York City was not related. There was also a Rotary car built later in Hoboken, New Jersey, which was not related either.

1911 ROVAN FLAREBOARD EXPRESS   **JAW**

ROVAN 1911-1914 — Kinnear Manufacturing of Columbus, Ohio, built the Rovan commercial vehicles that featured front-wheel-drive. A horizontally-opposed two-cylinder engine was mounted under a short hood and drove the light trucks through a three-speed transmission, which was bolted to the front axle with worm gear final drive. The vehicles were available with a 104-inch wheelbase or a 124-inch wheelbase and both were rated at 3/4-ton capacity. Solid tires were used exclusively and the vehicles' top speed was 22 mph. The shorter standard model sold for $1,600.

1911 ROWE MODEL A 3/4-TON COVERED EXPRESS   **DJS**

ROWE 1911-1925 — Samuel D. Rowe designed an air-cooled five-cylinder engine in 1908, which he marketed without success after organizing the Rowe Motor Company in Waynesboro, Penn-

sylvania. The company built an experimental car in 1910 but it was not until 1911, when he moved his firm to Coatesville, Pennsylvania, that successful manufacturing of trucks ensued.

The first Rowe truck was a 3/4-ton capacity model powered by a 25 hp five-cylinder water-cooled engine. The Model A and Model B had four-cylinder engines and prices were in the $2,000 range. By the following year, when the company moved to Downington, Pennsylvania, a complete line of trucks was offered from 3/4-ton to 5-ton capacity designated by letters of the alphabet. All Rowe trucks had four-speed transmissions and chain drive was standard until 1915, when worm-drive was adopted. That year, the company also built a 5-ton cab-over-engine truck rated at 5-ton capacity, which was powered by a six-cylinder engine. Beginning in 1915, Rowe offered Models CW, DW, EW and GW from 1-1/2-ton to 5-ton capacity. Prices ranged from $2,450 to $4,500 and Wisconsin engines were used.

1914 ROWE COVERED FLAREBOARD EXPRESS   **OCW**

1914 ROWE OPEN FLAREBOARD EXPRESS   **OCW**

1921 ROWE MODEL HSW 3/4-TON   **DJS**

Rowe used early "air bag" suspension and built a few fire engines. Designations changed again in 1917, when the Model CW and Model EW were discontinued. For 1918, when the company moved to Lancaster, Pennsylvania, the largest Rowe truck was the 5-ton Model FW with 171-inch wheelbase selling for $4,500. Late the following year, Rowe introduced the 3-ton Model GW speed truck, which had pneumatic tires and was powered by a Herschell-Spillman V-8 engine. It was priced at $4,500 while the 5-ton Model FW went up to $4,900. The V-8 chassis was fitted with bus bodies and a few Continental and Hercules engines were used. Total production of the V-8 speed trucks was about 25 up to 1921. In 1922, overall production peaked at 900 units for that year. The following year, a fire destroyed most of the factory and the company quickly faded out after that. For 1925, the last year of production, the company offered the 2-1/2-ton Model CDW for $3,575, the 3-ton Model GSW for $4,150, the 4-ton Model HW for $4,500 and the 5-ton Model FW for $4,850. Total production over the years amounted to approximately 4,500 vehicles.

ROYAL 1914-1919 — The Royal Motor Truck Company of New York City built large trucks starting in 1914 with a 3-1/2-ton and a 5-ton capacity model line. By 1916, worm-drive was optional in place of the standard double chain drive. For 1916, the company offered eight different capacity trucks: 1-, 1-1/2-, 2-, 2-1/2-, 3-1/2-, 5-, 6- and 7-ton. All of them were powered by four-cylinder Wisconsin engines with Timken worm-drive rear axles.

ROYAL 1923-1927 — The Royal Coach Company was started in Rahway, New Jersey, in order to manufacture buses under stringent specifications that the state of New Jersey enacted in the early 1920s. The Ace bus chassis was adopted, which was built in Newark, Ohio, by the American Motor Truck Company. Royal Coach also hired some of American Motor Truck's employees who helped develop and oversee the assembly of chassis and bodies in Rahway. The Royal buses were powered by Waukesha engines and were designated as Model A and Moded D. Model B and Model C were not used as designations for Royal because Ace trucks had already built buses using those letters. Model A was a 29-passenger model and Model D was slightly smaller. A Model E announced in 1927 does not appear to have seen production. Total output for the Model A and Model D was about 50 buses up to 1927.

ROYAL REX see Rex

R-S 1915-1916 — R-S stood for Reading-Standard Company, which was located in Reading, Pennsylvania. This was a three-wheel vehicle with a one-cylinder motorcycle engine mounted under the seat driving the single rear wheel through a three-speed transmission. The engine was built by Reading-Standard and the cargo box over the front wheels had a capacity of one-third ton. It does not appear that this company was affiliated with the earlier Reading car also built in that city.

1928 RUGBY 1-TON   **HAYS**

1929 RUGBY CANOPY EXPRESS   **OCW**

1931 RUGBY 1-TON PANEL DELIVERY   **NAHC**

RUGBY see STAR

RUGGLES 1905, 1921-1928 — Frank W. Ruggles first built a light delivery wagon with friction drive in Ware, Massachusetts, in 1905. Manufacture did not follow and Ruggles became president of Republic Motor Truck Company from 1917 until 1920, when he left abruptly.

When Ruggles moved to Saginaw, Michigan, in 1921, he established the Ruggles Motor Truck Company with $3 million in capital. The former Saginaw Ship Building Company plant was acquired. William J. Wickes and Julius B. Kirby became vice-presidents, Ezra L. Smith secretary and Walter C. Hill treasurer.

Production began in August 1921. The first two models were the 1-ton Model 20 and 2-ton Model 40. The Model 20 was called the "business truck" and with a chassis price of $1,195 78 were sold the first year. Ten of the Model 40 were sold the first year with a chassis price of $1,795.

1922 RUGGLES SIGHTSEEING BUS   **WJP**

For 1922, the same models were continued with the addition of the Model 20R and Ruggles built its first dump bed that year. About 100 men were employed at the factory by this time. A 24-passenger 168-inch wheelbase "Char-a-Banc" bus was built in 1922.

For 1923, the Ruggles 3/4-ton Model 15 "Go Getter" was introduced. It had a 32 hp engine and chassis price was $795. There was also the 1-1/4-ton Model 20R for $1,375, 1-1/4-ton Model 20AR for $2,095, 2-ton Model 40 also for $2,095 and 2-1/2-ton Model 40H "Road Builder" for $2,195. At first, Ruggles produced its own four-cylinder engines. After 1923, Ruggles switched to Herschell-Spillman powerplants on some trucks for the first time.

At that time, the 3/4-ton Model 15 was powered by a 19.6 hp four-cylinder Herschell-Spillman engine and used a Fuller transmission and Columbia front and rear axles.

Also for 1923, the company built the 16-passenger "Chanticleer Highway Parlor Car" bus and priced it at $3,190. Ruggles had a second plant in London, Ontario, Canada, which also assembled trucks.

1924 RUGGLES 1-1/4-TON MODEL 20R   MROZ

1924 RUGGLES CARTAGE TRUCKS   MROZ

In 1924, Ruggles offered the 1-1/2-ton Model 21 for $2,095, the 2-1/4-ton Model 41 for $2,395 and the 3-ton Model 40HRB for $2,395, which had been added the previous year. The "Highway Parlor Car" was discontinued.

In 1925, Ruggles entered the fire engine, ambulance and police patrol market. It was the first time a six-cylinder engine was used. Models included the ones carried over from 1924 plus the 1-ton Model 16 for $1,165, 1-1/2-ton Model 22 for $1,595, 1-1/2-ton Model 60 for $2,750, 2-1/4-ton Model 65 (with 75 hp six-cylinder engine and called "Super-Express Six) and 3-ton Model 70 for $4,500. By this time, Hercules OX engines were adopted for some models.

Frank Ruggles stepped down as president and left the board of directors in 1926 and was replaced by Joseph Warren Fordney, an ex-congressman. That year, only Models 15, 20R, 22, 40H and 70 were continued. Buses were built on the Model 60, 65 and 70 chassis, but no trucks were assembled on the larger frames. The company was losing money rapidly and by this time, the cumulative deficit had reached $633,593.

Ruggles tried to revamp its model line for 1927 and only the Model 22 was carried over. The line now consisted of Models 18 (four-cylinder or six-cylinder engine), 22G, 22H, 25, 42, 45, 45A, 45B, 45D and 45RB plus the bus models 60, 65 and 70. Lycoming engines were used for Models 18 and 25. The last new model introduced by Ruggles was the 2-ton Model 30 of 1927.

For 1928, Ruggles continued its model line but financial woes were so severe the company finally shut down amid disputes and accusations. Dalles E. Winslow bought the remaining assets and 100 leftover Ruggles trucks in 1928 and disbanded the company. Frank Ruggles headed a new company called the "Double Duty Company," which manufactured assemblies to convert Chevrolet and Ford trucks into six-wheel vehicles. He left the company in 1930 and passed away in 1933.

RUMELY 1919-1928 — The Advance Rumely Thresher Company of LaPorte, Indiana, built a 1-1/2-ton truck between 1919 and 1923. It was powered by a four-cylinder Buda engine and used a Fuller transmission and Sheldon worm-drive rear axle. Wheelbase was 144 inches and chassis weight was 4,050 pounds. Steering gear was provided by Gemer. The 1-1/2-ton Model A Rumely chassis price was $2,150 by 1925. The company also built agricultural tractors.

1916 RUSH LIGHT 1/2-TON DELIVERY VAN   WOM

RUSH 1915-1918 — The Rush Delivery Car Company of Philadelphia, Pennsylvania, was in the business of building light trucks for four years. The truck was powered by a four-cylinder Lycoming engine that featured a counterbalanced crankshaft. Its original chassis price was $625 and a canopy express body was $95 more. By 1917, the price for the Rush chassis had gone up to $750, partly due to the wartime inflation. With a closed van body the Rush 1/2-ton truck was advertised for $845.

1917 RUSH 1/2-TON LAUNDRY TRUCKS   OCW

The light trucks used 31x4 pneumatic tires front and rear, cone clutch and bevel gear drive. These were standard conventional assembled vehicles with Carter carburetor, Splitdorf ignition and Lavine steering. In 1916, the company's name changed to the Rush Motor Truck Company. Higher prices put Rush out of the running with its competition by the end of 1918.

RYDER 1973-1974 — Ryder System of Miami, Florida, developed the original Ryder Paymaster truck tractor with Dean Hobgenseifken as chief designer. This line-haul tractor was built using an aerodynamic cab with air foil spoiler to reduce air turbulence on the semi-trailer. After acquiring patent rights, Ryder hired Hendrickson to build 10 such trucks. Engine choices were Detroit Diesel 6-71, 6-71T and 8V-71T or Cummins VT 903. Transmission was a Fuller RT910. The engine was mounted under the fifth wheel. The complete powertrain including transmission, two radiators, engine and rear end were mounted on a separate removable aluminum frame for easy maintanance. Ryder System Truck Rentals evaluated these trucks, which did not go into further production.

S

S

S & S 1907-1935 — Sayers & Scovill Company, known as S & S, was organized by William A. Sayers whose partner was A.K. Scovill. Sayers had opened his carriage company in 1876 and as part of the model line, he built horsedrawn hearses. In 1907, he branched out into gasoline engine vehicles and his first commercial effort was a 1-1/2-ton truck with 90-inch wheelbase. The 1-1/2-ton Sayers & Scovill truck continued to be produced until 1912, while the company also built ambulances and hearses. The truck was a forward-control design with a 27 hp four-cylinder Carrico air-cooled engine mounted under the seat and using chain drive. The truck also had semi-elliptic springs and Timken axles.

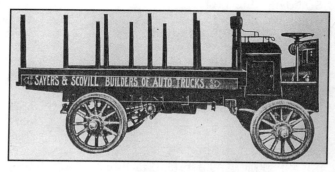

1907 S & S 1-1/2-TON FORWARD CONTROL　　　MROZ

Ambulances and hearses were known under the name S & S and became the main product line over the years for Sayers & Scovill. By 1913, these were powered by either Continental or Lycoming engines. In 1915, Continental engines were adopted both for S & S professional cars as well as for Sayers passenger cars, which were essentially similar. The professional and passenger cars shared the same 55 hp (33.75 hp) six-cylinder Continental engine, but the passenger cars' 118-inch wheelbase was extended to 132 inches (and later to 136, 140 and 143 inches) for ambulances and hearses. In 1924, the company announced it would discontinue building passenger cars, although a funeral limousine was reintroduced by 1926. Between 1924 and 1928, prices ranged from $4,000 to $6,000.

Four-wheel-brakes began to be fitted by 1927 and were standardized in 1928, when S & S vehicles were fitted with 85 hp eight-cylinder Continental engines. For 1929, the company unveiled its extraordinary Signed Sculpture hearse, which had a price tag of $8,500. Bronze side panels showed the Angel of Mercy. For 1929, the horsepower was increased to 114 using the eight-cylinder Continental 15K engine. By 1930, ambulances resembled town cars and featured louvered hoods, twin trumpet horns and dual sidemounts in cellulose covers. Engine output was again increased to 118 hp in 1931, when syncromesh transmissions and ride control dampers appeared.

1930 S & S FUNERAL COACH　　　CP

In 1933, a Buick overhead valve engine was adopted and by 1935, the company began using lengthened Oldsmobiles for a cheaper line of professional cars. In 1936, the S & S vehicles were entirely Buick except for badge and hubcaps. In 1938, another switch was made to Cadillac chassis and in 1942, the company was reorganized as Hess and Eisenhardt, which continued to build ambulances and hearses on Cadillac chassis.

SAFEWAY see SIX WHEEL

SAF-T-CAB see CHECKER

ST. CLOUD 1920 — The St. Cloud Truck Company of St. Cloud, Minnesota, was organized by J.R. Brown, who had been manager of Pan Automobile Company in St. Cloud in 1919. The company assembled a few 2-1/2-ton trucks primarily for local rock quarries. After announcing a 1-ton model, St. Cloud shut down soon thereafter.

1901 ST. LOUIS GASOLINE DELIVERY　　　RD

ST. LOUIS 1900-1901 — The St. Louis Motor Carriage Company of St. Louis, Missouri, began in 1899, when George Dorris and John L. French became partners and incorporated with Callie French, H.E. French and Jesse French, Jr. Their business venture became the first successful automobile manufacturing facility west of the Mississippi. In 1900, the firm built 130 cars, some of which were light delivery vehicles and buses.

For 1901, specifications are known for two models of the St. Louis Delivery. The first was powered by a 10 hp one-cylinder engine and sold for $1,250. The second Delivery was powered by a 15 hp two-cylinder engine. A small bus was powered by a 25 hp two-cylinder engine. Some of the early St. Louis vehicles were tiller steered and used wire spoke wheels, pneumatic tires and a wood block braking system. By 1901, the Gasoline Delivery Truck had wheel steering, wooden wheels and a capacity of 2,500 pounds. In April 1901, *The Horseless Age* stated that the St. Louis Heavy Delivery Wagon powered by a 15 hp horizontally-opposed engine had been driven 624 miles by that time, "according to cyclometer reading."

The company's slogan at that time was "Rigs That Run." John French expanded the company when he moved to Peoria, Illinois, leaving chief engineer and designer George Dorris behind. The company was "financially embarrassed" by 1907.

ST. LOUIS 1921-1922, 1930-1951 — The St. Louis Car Company of St. Louis, Missouri, which was not affiliated with the earlier company by the same name, was a builder of streetcars, railroad passenger cars and, by 1914, assembler of buses, the latter having open-top double-decker bodies fitted on Kelly-Springfield and Mack chassis. These were built specifically for a fleet that was placed in operation in San Francisco during the Panama-Pacific Exposition. The Chicago Motor Bus Company also built similar buses in 1917 using bodies fabricated by the St. Louis Car Company.

In 1921, St. Louis began development of two trolley-coaches, four of which were completed for Windsor, but the company concentrated its production on streetcars and train cars during the 1920s. Trolley coach production continued for fleets in Atlanta, Cleveland and New Orleans. In 1929, St. Louis built a six-wheel gas-electric hybrid bus and during the 1930s, continued to build a few bus prototypes, which never went into production. Production of trolley-coaches totaled about 1,100 over the years of manufacturing, which ended in 1951.

SALVADOR 1915-1916 — The Mansur Motor Truck Company of Haverhill, Massachusetts, built a 2-ton truck that had the engine covered by a short hood and was mounted between the seats. The Salvador truck model used worm-drive and was available in three lengths of wheelbase. This company was not affiliated with the Salvador cars built at the same time in Boston.

SAMPSON 1905-1912 — Sometimes listed as two separate businesses, the Alden Sampson Manufacturing Company began in Pittsfield, Massachusetts (before moving to Detroit), and got into the motor vehicle manufacturing business in a rather circuitous way. When the Moyea Automobile Company of Middletown, Ohio, did not have time to complete the prototype of its 1904 passenger car (still waiting for the completion of its Rye, New York, factory), the Alden Sampson company was contracted to build the vehicle. By the time that company president Henry Cryder saw the car's completion, he bought out Moyea at the end of 1904 and by the end of the year, the company's name became Consolidated Motor, although the vehicles' name continued to be Sampson. In 1905, passenger car production was discontinued and Alden Sampson built trucks.

The company eventually built a full range of trucks, but its main model was a 5-ton capacity vehicle powered by a 40 hp four-cylinder engine using chain drive. It was not until 1909 that the company offered 1-, 2-, 3- and 4-ton capacity trucks, which all had chain drive. The following year, a 1/2-ton model was available with an 18 hp horizontally-opposed two-cylinder engine and shaft drive. An enclosed oil-tight steel case was used for the chain drive and a differential interlock allowed both wheels to lock together.

1910 SAMPSON ROAD TRAIN   **CP**

1911 SAMPSON 4-TON BREWERY TRUCK   **MROZ**

Alden Sampson built the "road train" between 1908 and 1910. This was made up of a truck tractor powered by a 40 hp Sampson engine and a generator that provided DC current to each of the trailer's electric motors. Maximum speed for the "road train" was

8 mph and only a few were built. All Sampsons used engines built in-house until the company's sale late in 1910. Its manufacturing was moved to Detroit, Michigan, at that time.

1911 SAMPSON 5-TON STAKE BED   **MROZ**

1912 SAMPSON DELIVERY VAN   **NAHC**

Production amounted to 50 trucks per year until 1911, when the company once again embarked on passenger car manufacturing. Alden Sampson was sold to the United States Motor Company, which was Benjamin Briscoe's attempt to create a large conglomerate to compete with General Motors and Ford. The Alden Sampson factory was moved to Detroit, Michigan, and both the Sampson trucks and passenger cars were built there briefly until the collapse of the United States Motor Company in 1912. The later Sampson truck was powered by a 30 hp four-cylinder Continental engine and was priced at $1,775. It was also known as the Hercules truck but was not powered by an engine of that manufacture.

1919 SAMSON 3/4-TON   **OCW**

1920 SAMSON 3/4-TON MODEL 15   EEH

SAMSON 1920-1923 — The Samson Tractor Company was part of William Crapo Durant's General Motors effort to compete in the farm vehicle market. Samson built farm tractors and also produced two truck models. The first was a 3/4-ton vehicle with a Chevrolet 490 engine. The second was a 1-1/4-ton truck with a Chevrolet FB engine. Samson trucks were designed for farm applications and were fitted with extension rims, which had plain cleats in front and shallow cleats in the rear for driving over plowed fields. The Janesville, Wisconsin, factory was converted over to Chevrolet assembly when GM executives realized Samson tractors could not compete with Fordson. The successful Samson trucks were discontinued at the same time in 1923.

1911 SANBERT 1-TON   MROZ

SANBERT see SANFORD

1914 SANDOW MODEL I PANEL DELIVERY   OCW

SANDOW 1914-1928 — The Sandow Motor Truck Company was located in Chicago, Illinois. The first trucks produced by this company were rated at 1-1/2-, 2- and 3-ton capacity. The lightest used a worm-drive rear axle while the two heftier models had double chain drive. Electric lighting and starting was optional through

1925, according to listings. By the mid-1920s, the 1-ton Model GA with 120-inch wheelbase had pneumatic tires. A Fuller clutch and transmission was used and front axles were provided by Sheldon while the rear axle was from Timken. The 1-1/2-ton model was powered by a 16.9 hp Buda WTU engine and used a Sheldon rear axle. Tires were solid rubber and chassis price was $1,895. The 2-ton Model JS was powered by a 25.6 hp Hercules O engine, while the 2-1/2-ton used a 28.9 hp Buda ETU engine, Brown-Lipe clutch and transmission and Timken front and rear axle. There was also a 3-1/2-ton Model M with 170-inch wheelbase that sold for $3,895. The heaviest Sandow was the 5-ton Model L with a 32.4 hp Buda BTU engine and a 175-inch wheelbase. Ross steering was used on all models. The company did not survive the year 1928.

1915 SANDOW   HAYS

1914 SANDUSKY MODEL B PANEL DELIVERY   OCW

1914 SANDUSKY MODEL B FLAREBOARD   OCW

SANDUSKY 1911-1914 — This later Sandusky was not affiliated with the earlier Sandusky of 1904, both of which did business in Sandusky, Ohio. The Sandusky Auto Parts and Truck Company first built a 1-ton model with an enclosed express body. The following year the truck was upgraded to 1-1/2-ton capacity. Sandusky attempted to enter the passenger car field without success and by 1914, closed down entirely. It should be noted that the company was listed as Sandusky Truck, Sandusky Motor and Sandusky Motor Truck.

SANFORD 1911-1937; 1969-1989 — The Sanford-Herbert Company of Syracuse, New York, began building trucks by the name of Sanbert in 1911. The first model was a 1-ton capacity truck called the Model J priced at $1,500. It was powered by a 25 hp three-cylinder two-cycle engine that was mounted under the seat. A two-speed transmission was used and final drive was by double chain.

1913 SANFORD 1-TON MODEL K   RD

For 1913, the Sanbert was powered by a four-cylinder engine and a 1-1/2-ton model was added to the line. A three-speed transmission was also introduced and in 1913, the company's name was changed to the Sanford Motor Truck Company, still located in Syracuse. By 1916, the company offered five models from 3/4-ton to 2-ton capacity. The engine was mounted ahead of the driver under a hood and worm-drive was adopted.

1920 SANFORD MODEL W-50 5-TON TIPPER   FLP

In the early 1920s, Continental engines were utilized and in 1923, a 1-1/2-ton Greyhound "speed truck" was introduced as well as a bus chassis, the latter being discontinued almost immediately. For 1924, Sanford introduced six-cylinder engines.

By 1925, Sanford offered seven models with five different capacities. The 1-ton Model W-10 with 140-inch wheelbase was powered by a Continental 8-R-6 engine and used a Fuller clutch with Brown-Lipe transmission and front and rear axles were from Salisbury. Front and rear tires were 33x5 pneumatic. The 1-1/2-ton Model W-15 was powered by the same engine but had a Fuller transmission and Sheldon front and rear axles. Instead of Hoopes wheels, Van wheels carried 36x6 front and rear solid rubber tires. Wheelbase was the same and chassis price was $2,150.

There were two 2-1/2-ton models at that time: the W-25A and W-25B. They differed in wheelbase in that the first was 156 inches and the second was 174 inches but chassis price was the same, $3,350. Both had Continental L-4 engines, Fuller transmissions and Sheldon front and rear axles. The same essential components were used on the 3-1/2-ton Model W-35B and Model W-35SC, which were priced at $4,200 and varied only in wheelbase. The

heaviest Sanford was the 5-ton Model W-50, which used a Continental B-7 engine and was priced at $5,100. For each model a Stromberg carburetor and Owen Dyneto ignition were used.

1931 SANFORD FIRE TRUCK   OCW

Spiral bevel drive did not appear until 1926. Sanford's business increasingly concentrated on fire trucks throughout the late 1920s and into the 1930s. Beginning in 1929, Sanford offered a variety of fire trucks including four pumpers from 350 to 750 gallons per minute. Production faded out entirely by 1937.

The Sanford Fire Apparatus Corporation, which was located in East Syracuse, New York, was revived in 1969 and built fire trucks and apparatus on custom chassis, including those supplied by Duplex, using Cincinnati cabs and diesel engines. The company faded out once again in the 1980s.

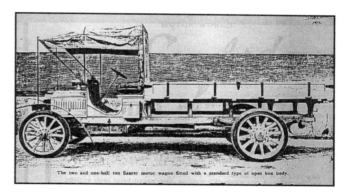

The two and one-half ton Saurer motor wagon fitted with a standard type of open box body.

1912 SAURER 2-1/2-TON OPEN BOX BODY   MROZ

SAURER 1911-1918 — Originally designed and built in Arbon, Switzerland, in 1903, Saurer trucks were imported into the United States beginning in 1908. Subsequently in 1909, components were imported and the trucks were assembled by the Quincy, Manchester and Sergent Company. Saurer was best known in Europe for the further development and application of the diesel engine during 1908, under the supervision of Rudolf Diesel at the Safir Company in Zurich. During a voyage to England, Rudolf Diesel disappeared overboard and his body was never found.

In 1911, the 4-ton Saurer was manufactured in Plainfield, New Jersey. Late that year, the International Motor Company was formed. This was a holding company that sold Hewitt, Mack and Saurer trucks in the United States. The Hewitt truck, which was sold by International Motor in 1912, included the heaviest of all three makes, which were advertised together. Hewitt production stopped in 1914. After the Mack AC engine began to be manufactured in Plainfield in 1916, American Saurer was discontinued in 1918. Saurer trucks were also produced in France until 1956.

SAVIANO SCAT 1955-1960 — Arnold P. Saviano built a jeep-type vehicle in Warren, Michigan, during this period. Saviano was the owner of a machine shop but no other details have been available.

1914 SAXON DELIVERY CAR   RD

SAXON 1914-1916 — The Saxon Motor Company began in 1913 in Detroit, Michigan, with the production of passenger cars. Hugh Chalmers was the company president. The Saxon was an inexpensive vehicle sold as a cyclecar but featured a 21.1 hp four-cylinder Ferro water-cooled engine and shaft drive. An open express body was offered between 1914 and 1916, although the company survived until 1922. In 1915, total production was almost 12,000 vehicles. The following year, that figure would nearly double but commercial bodies were discontinued. Saxon motor vehicles have been listed with Continental engines, but this did not take place until late 1916. In the final analysis, the company succumbed to bankruptcy.

SAYERS & SCOVILL See S & S

SCHACHT 1909-1938 — The Schacht Manufacturing Company of Cincinnati, Ohio, was a horse buggy manufacturer that got into building motor vehicles in 1904. Gustav A. Schacht was the president and his brother William was also one of the principals. The company's slogans were the "Invincible Schacht" and the "Three Purpose Car," which referred to a runabout, family car and delivery wagon that were convertible from a single vehicle. This type was available when the company was renamed the Schacht Motor Car Company in 1909. Approximately 8,000 cars were built by that time, when a decision was made to concentrate on commercial vehicles.

The company was reorganized as the G.A. Schacht Motor Truck Company in 1913. The first line of trucks ranged from 1/2 ton to 4 ton and all of these were conventional vehicles using four-cylinder engines and solid rubber tires. Both Continental and Wisconsin engines were used in various models. In 1922, the entire range of models was shifted to heavier capacities starting with 2-ton trucks.

1925 SCHACHT DUMP TRUCK   NAHC

During this time, Schacht built its own transmissions, front and rear axles and many of the small components. However, the 1-ton Schacht of 1925 used a Fuller clutch and transmission, Shuler front axle, Wisconsin rear axle and Ross steering. This model was powered by a 25.6 hp four-cylinder Wisconsin SU engine and had pneumatic tires as standard equipment. The next size up was the

1-1/2-ton Model H, which was priced at $2,500. It had the same engine and major components as the 1-ton model. There were two 2-ton models. The Model G was powered by a 28.9 hp four-cylinder Wisconsin UAU engine and used a Schacht transmission and axles. Chassis price was $3,200. The 2-ton Model J was powered by the smaller Continental SU engine and used a Fuller transmission, Shuler front axle and Wisconsin rear axle. Chassis price was $2,600. The 2-1/2-, 3-, 4- and 5-ton models each had Schacht transmissions, axles and steering gear. Chassis prices were $3,400, $3,800, $4,400 and $4,600, respectively. In many cases, the same model designation referred to different truck sizes such as the 1926 Model M-MP, which was available as 4-, 5- and 7-1/2-ton capacities.

1926 SCHACHT BUSES   OCW

For 1926, Schacht added the Super Safety Coach to its model line of commercial vehicles. This was a low chassis powered by a 48.6 hp six-cylinder engine using an eight-speed transmission. For the first year, the chassis was priced at $5,900. In 1927, it was dropped to $4,900. That year, the company merged with LeBlond and became the LeBlond-Schacht Truck Company. In 1927, the 3-1/2-ton Model L and Model LN used a Wisconsin engine and in the dump model a 10-speed Fuller or 10-speed Schacht transmission was available with Wisconsin double reduction rear axle at a vehicle price of $4,000. Wheelbase was 156 inches and Gruss air springs were optional. At this time, Schacht offered the "Dreadnaught" Model MP dump truck, which was rated at 7-1/2-ton capacity and had an eight-speed or optional 10-speed transmission, the latter giving the vehicle a top speed of 20 mph. The dump hoist was built by St. Paul, which measured 11x6x20 feet. A worm-drive rear axle was used and solid rubber tires were 36x7 front and 40x16 rear.

1928 SCHACHT DUMP TRUCK   BUD STENDER

In 1928, Schacht purchased the Armleder Truck Company and the two makes overlapped while being merged over the following eight years. By 1929, Schacht had set up 10 sales offices in the Northeast with sales of 280 vehicles there that year and 359 the following year.

Between all of the Armleder trucks and the models of Schacht, there was a full range of vehicles in the 1930s from 1-1/2-ton to 11-ton capacity. Truck tractors were introduced in 1932. Continental engines continued to be used in the lighter trucks, while the heavier ones had either Hercules or Wisconsin engines. After 1929, all were six-cylinder powerplants. Schacht trucks were distinguished by wide radiators and fenders and large headlights. In 1932, Schacht offered 19 models from 1-ton to 3-ton capacity, including two truck tractors. Prices ranged from $1,495 to $8,020 for the 3-1/2-ton Model 66HA.

1930 SCHACHT 3-TON FLAREBOARD EXPRESS   NAHC

1937 SCHACHT 3-TON STAKE TRUCK   OCW

Schacht merged with Ahrens-Fox in 1936, although the marques remained separate. A general redesign of Schacht cabs and grilles took place in 1937. The A series were conventional trucks from 1-1/2-ton to 3-1/2-ton capacity. The CU series were cab-over-engine design from 2-1/2-ton to 5-ton capacity. One year before withdrawing from the truck manufacturing business, Schacht still offered 19 models. They were the 8A, 10A, 12A, 15A, 18A, 20A, 25A, 28A, 35A, 40A, 66A, 75A, 110CU, 115CU, 120CU, 125CU, 128CU, TRA and TRCU. Capacity ranged from 1-1/2-ton to 15-ton and chassis prices were listed from $1,085 to $5,495. Ahrens-Fox-based design fire engines were built until 1942 and the Schacht name disappeared all together. Ahrens-Fox continued as a marque until 1956.

SCHLEICHER 1911-1919 — The Schleicher Motor Vehicle Company was located in Ossining, New York. Schleicher trucks were from 3-ton to 10-ton capacity. The 3-ton and 5-ton trucks had 45 hp Continental engines. All Schleicher trucks were essentially built to order. The large 10-ton chassis with a wheelbase up to 156 inches was priced as high as $10,000. Few were actually constructed. All had four-speed transmissions and double chain drive.

SCHLOTTERBACK 1912-1916 — The L.E. Schlotterback Manufacturing Company of East Orange, New Jersey, built delivery wagons for the Koehler Sporting Goods Company when the latter decided to go into commercial vehicle manufacturing after a brief venture into passenger car production from 1910 to 1912. The delivery wagon this company built was powered by a horizontally-opposed two-cylinder four-cycle engine and used a two-speed planetary transmission. The countershaft was located near the trans-

mission and chain was used for the final drive to the rear wheels. As a complete vehicle, it was priced at $750. In 1916, the H.J. Koehler merged with Schlotterback and trucks continued to be built under the Koehler name until 1923.

SCHMIDT see F.C.S.

SCHNABEL 1914-1916 — The G.A. Schnabel and Son company was located in Pittsburgh, Pennsylvania. The company specialized in professional cars, especially hearses, and it is listed because it manufactured a few of its own chassis. The company built both conventional-looking vehicles and some with Renault-type hoods and the radiator in back of the engine.

SCHNEER 1916 — The J.J. Schneer Company built fire engines and some commercial chassis in San Francisco. Other details are lacking.

SCHURMEIER 1910-1911 — The Schurmeier Wagons Company began as a horsedrawn buggy manufacturer that built some experimental trucks. By 1910, a new factory was opened specifically for the production of commercial motor vehicles. The company built 1-, 2- and 3-ton trucks. The lightest vehicle was powered by a two-cylinder vertical two-cycle engine, while the heftier two had a three-cylinder vertical two-cycle engine. All were forward-control design and used chain drive. Production over nearly two years amounted to 100 vehicles before the Schurmeier trucks were discontinued.

1920 SCHWARTZ 2-TON   MROZ

SCHWARTZ 1918-1923 — The Schwartz Motor Truck Corporation was founded by H.B. Schwartz, who was an automobile dealer in Reading, Pennsylvania. In 1918, Schwartz began manufacturing light trucks powered by a four-cylinder engine using worm-drive. Two years later, the model line included 1-1/2-, 2-1/2- and 5-ton trucks. The two lighter trucks were powered by Continental engines while the largest used a four-cylinder Buda engine. For 1922, Schwartz introduced a "speed truck" powered by a Lycoming engine and bevel drive. That year, Schwartz offered Models A, K, L, LS, LL and MS ranging from 1-ton to 6-ton capacity. Prices were from $1,685 to $4,900 at this time. Clinton Motors acquired Schwartz and its factory in Reading during 1923 and the Schwartz name was dropped as Clinton continued production of worm-drive trucks under its own name until 1934.

SCRIPPS-BOOTH 1914-1915 — James Scripps-Booth, a wealthy publisher, began in 1912 with his Bi-Autogo, a car whose two side auxiliary wheels folded up above 20 mph turning the three-seat vehicle into a motorcycle powered by Detroit's first V-8 engine and capable of 75 mph. It used a compressed air starter, four-speed transmission and 450 feet of copper tubing alongside and over the hood.

This prototype evolved into a simpler cyclecar called the Rocket, which had a rocket-like bulge on the hood that was actually the fuel tank. The tandem seat vehicle was powered by a 10 hp V-twin-cylinder Spacke engine and used a two-speed planetary transmission with belt drive. Wheelbase was 100 inches and the vehicle featured tilt steering. The Rocket and Packet names were used later by Northway and Brasie, respectively, but these companies were not related.

1914 SCRIPPS-BOOTH PACKET LIGHT DELIVERY MROZ

The commercial version of the Rocket was called the Packet and sold for $395 in 1914, $10 more than the Tandem Roadster Rocket. Total vehicle weight was 750 pounds with van body. A combined total of about 400 Rockets and Packets were built up to 1915. One advertising slogan was "Climbs All Grades - Will Not Skid."

In 1916, James Scripps-Booth resigned from the company and a year later the company was absorbed by Chevrolet. Scripps-Booth continued production with passenger cars until 1922 and after that, built several high-performance prototypes until 1935. The founder died in 1955 at age 66.

1914 SEAGRAVE LADDER TRUCK LA

SEAGRAVE 1907 to date — The Seagrave Company began in 1907 in Columbus, Ohio. The first three motorized vehicles, which were powered by a four-cylinder two-cycle engine, were built for Vancouver, British Columbia, Canada. In 1909, Seagrave built a truck tractor for articulated ladder use and this vehicle was also powered by the four-cylinder air-cooled engine as before. The Model AC apparatus appeared in 1910, also featuring the driver's seat ahead of the engine. Then in 1911, the company built its first centrifugal pumper using a six-cylinder engine, although the air-cooled "buckboards" continued to be built up to 1915. In 1912, Seagrave offered pumpers up to 1,000 gpm. For 1914, Seagrave built a passenger-type fire vehicle. It was called the Chief's Auto and featured seats for two and a chemical tank or seating for five.

1920 SEAGRAVE PUMPER OCW

Seagrave built front-wheel-drive conversions for ladder trucks up to 85 feet long. This was called the Model K and as with the Chief's car, it was available with a 30 hp four-cylinder or 45 hp six-cylinder

engine. Ladder trucks were also built on Couple Gear electric vehicle chassis. The first Seagrave motor water tower was introduced in 1917, which was also the year Seagrave offered a Herschell-Spillman V-8 engine. All Seagrave trucks were chain driven until 1922, the Chief's Auto being an exception with shaft drive.

1925 SEAGRAVE OCW

In 1922, Seagrave began building pumpers with shaft drive. These were described as having a "gabled" hood and were likened to the contemporary Mercedes. Seagrave built a large variety of fire engines during the 1920s, including pumpers from 750 gpm to 1,300 gpm. Starting in 1923, a 350 gpm pumper called the Suburbanite was produced. It was powered by a six-cylinder Continental engine and continued to be built for a dozen years. The largest Seagrave pumper at the time was the Metropolite with a 1,300 gpm capacity. A 600 gpm pumper called the Special was introduced in 1926.

The Sentry began production in 1931. This pumper featured a windshield and a siren mounted between the headlights. In 1932, Seagrave introduced its 240 hp V-12 engine one year after American LaFrance had unveiled its 12. Because of the Depression, however, some Seagrave fire trucks were assembled on commercial truck chassis supplied by Ford and Reo, although these amounted to only a small number of total production, which was itself limited due to difficult economic times.

Another V-12 engine based on the Pierce-Arrow passenger engine block arrived in 1935. This was the same year that new styling was introduced at Seagrave, reflecting an industry-wide trend for the mid-1930s. The new V-radiator grille that appeared in 1935 was kept until 1951. In 1936, the Safety Sedan Pumper was designed in the form of a limousine. Open and closed cabs continued to be built through the 1930s for rigid and articulated fire trucks, but 1937 marked the first enclosed canopy cab.

1942 SEAGRAVE PUMPER OCW

Because Seagrave had built horsedrawn fire apparatus in the 1800s, the 70th Anniversary Series arrived in 1951. These were restyled with a horizontal grille and a distinctive round chrome siren at the upper center of the radiator, which was kept for 20 years. During this period, the V-12 engine was used in many of the pumpers, articulated ladder and rigid trucks and in 1955, a new model with 300 hp was produced. Seagrave wholly acquired

Maxim Motor Company, although the two companies continued to operate as separate entities. During the 1950s and 1960s, commercial truck chassis were supplied by Ford and International for many of Seagrave's vehicles.

1958 SEAGRAVE   **KP**

In addition to the conventional fire trucks, the first Seagrave cab-forward design trucks arrived in 1959. In 1961, Seagrave pioneered the first aerial platform "snorkel," which was available in 65-foot and 85-foot lengths. By 1962, Seagrave offered Hall-Scott and Waukesha engines and the V-12 was gradually phased out of production.

Seagrave was bought by FWD in 1963 and manufacturing was gradually transferred to Clintonville, Wisconsin. By 1965, the Rear Admiral began production. This was a rear-mounted turntable design first announced in 1963, but due to the acquisition by FWD it did not see production until the Clintonville factory was placed in full operation, where the FWD Tractioneer cab-forward pumper was also built. Another company was formed in 1969 by the name of Seagrave Commercial-by-Timpco located in Columbus, Ohio.

In 1972, Seagrave built a new cab-forward design using Detroit Diesel engines. A FWD chassis was used for one model of Seagrave fire engine. Seagrave fire engines were built exclusively in the old Clintonville FWD factory through the 1980s and 1990s. By 1995, Seagrave production was approximately 250 trucks per year. The company offered the Patriot Rear Mount Aerial with Rockwell single or tandem rear axles and Cummins or Detroit Diesel engines up to 470 hp.

1993 SEAGRAVE PATRIOT LADDER TRUCK   **SEAGRAVE**

1994 SEAGRAVE CUSTOM PUMPER   **SEAGRAVE**

1995 SEAGRAVE PATRIOT TRACTOR AERIAL   **SEAGRAVE**

The Patriot Tractor Drawn Aerial had the same engine options with Allison automatic transmission. A 100-foot four-section aerial ladder has been available along with full-length pre-piped telescopic waterway, pinnable feature and automatic nozzles. Travel height was advertised as 10 feet, 8 inches and turning radius as low as 24 feet, 7 inches.

Seagrave has also offered the Apollo 105 Aerial Platform, which could be elevated from minus 5 degrees to 80 degrees and rotated 360 degrees. The Marauder has been totally engineered and built by Seagrave with Hale and Waterous fire pumps. The Marauder featured a six-man tilt, six-man split tilt or 10-man split tilt raised roof cab with optional medical compartment and optional top mount controls. The company has been a single source manufacturer of the entire unit including chassis and serial device "eliminating divided responsibility."

1909 SEARS   **HAYS**

SEARS 1908-1912 — The Sears & Roebuck Company of Chicago, Illinois, began offering a highwheeler in its catalog in 1908. Even though it was built as a runabout, a small "cargo" box was mounted on the back, hence the Sears cars are included as commercial vehicles. For 1911 and 1912, there was a Model P Business/Pleasure model that had an 87-inch wheelbase -- 15 inches longer than the runabout and coupe models. Wood spoke wheels carried 38x1-3/4 front and rear solid rubber tires. For the first two years, Sears motor cars were built by Colonel William W. McCurdy in Evansville, Indiana.

Designed by Alvaro S. Krotz, all Sears vehicles of this period were powered by a two-cylinder horizontally-opposed air-cooled four-cycle engine mounted under the seat. The engine was rated at 10 hp for the first two years and upgraded to 14 hp in 1910. The Sears featured friction drive transmission, tiller steering, full-elliptic springs and front and rear fenders as standard equipment. The Model P was priced at $445. Sears used catalog number 21R333 for its vehicles. Total production was approximately 3,500, along with the manufacturing that took place in Chicago, Illinois, from 1910 to 1912. The Sears & Roebuck Company discovered it was losing money on its motor vehicle venture and sold its production machinery and rights to the Lincoln Motor Car Works after the 1912 model year was abruptly finished. Lincoln Motor Works built a few more cars by the name of Lincoln, which were essentially Sears vehicles, until 1913.

1909 SEARS   HAYS

1911 SEITZ 3-TON STAKE   NAHC

SEITZ 1908-1913 — Seitz built 3/4-, 2-, 3- and 5-ton trucks. The Seitz Automobile and Transmission Company was located in Detroit, Michigan. All models used the Seitz double friction transmission. The 3/4-ton truck was a delivery van and all Seitz vehicles were forward-control using chain drive and solid rubber tires. The larger trucks were powered by a 45 hp four-cylinder engine. The company advertised that its transmission could be used as a brake by throwing the vehicle into reverse.

SELDEN 1913-1932 — George Baldwin Selden was best known for his patent on all internal combustion engine vehicles, which he obtained in 1895. This was one of the most influential of all patents at that time in that it forced all manufacturers to pay a royalty in order to build automobiles and trucks that were not steam or electric driven. The patent was acquired at the turn of the century by the (Columbia) Electric Vehicle Company, which was absorbed by the Lead Trust in 1902, which had its own agenda in limiting the development and expansion of petroleum power.

George Selden continued to receive a percentage of the royalties, which were administered by the Licensed Automobile Manufacturers Association. When Henry Ford turned down a license in 1903, the Lead Trust sued, effectively allowing Ford to challenge the famous patent in court. Ford eventually won on appeal in 1911, using the technicality of differentiating between two-cycle and four-cycle engines, which Selden had not cleared up in his patent. In the meantime, the Lead Trust, which had become a virtual monopoly in the electric vehicle industry, lost millions of dollars and after a short reorganization went bankrupt in 1913. Meanwhile Rockefeller's Oil Trust and Henry Ford went ahead with their plans.

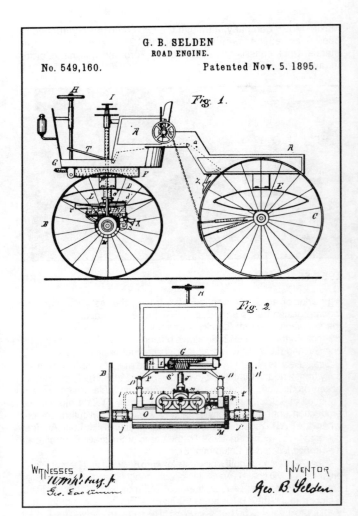

1895 SELDEN PATENT ON ALL GASOLINE VEHICLES   OCW

1914 SELDEN MODEL J COVERED FLARE   OCW

As good a patent attorney as he was, George Selden went into gasoline engine vehicle manufacturing by 1907 himself but with the help of a hired car designer by the name of E.T. Birdsall. For the first six years, the company built only passenger cars with four-cylinder engines on wheelbases between 109 inches and 125 inches, selling for $2,500 to $3,750. In 1913, the Selden Motor Vehicle Company of Rochester, New York, began building light trucks powered by either 20 hp or 40 hp four-cylinder Continental engines and using either three-speed or four-speed Brown-Lipe Transmissions. Rear axles were by Russel or Timken. From the beginning, Selden offered his trucks on a deferred pay plan to attract customers, which the company did.

By World War I, Selden had a large contract to build the Class B Liberty truck and eventually built 3,700 of them. Civilian production included 1-, 2- and 3-1/2-ton trucks, many of which were exported overseas. The company was incorporated as the Selden

348

Truck Corporation in 1919. By 1920, the 2-1/2-ton Model A11 had a wheelbase of up to 170 inches and used Timken worm-drive. George Selden died in 1923 but the company he started lived on, having suffered through the postwar recession. It continued to build trucks from 1-1/2-ton to 3-1/2-ton capacity.

1920 SELDEN HAYS

1924 SELDEN 1-1/4 TON PACEMAKER RD

The 1-1/2-ton Model 30 was powered by a 22.5 hp Continental J-4 engine with Stromberg carburetor and Eisemann ignition and used a Brown-Lipe clutch and transmission. Wheelbase was 137 inches, front and rear axles supplied by Timken and Archibald wheels carried 34x3-1/2 front and 34x5 rear solid rubber tires with pneumatics at extra cost. The 2-ton Model 33 was powered by a 27.2 hp Continental K-4 engine, which was also used in the 2-1/2-ton Model 50. The 3-ton Model 53 had a 32.4 hp Continental L-4 engine, which also powered the 3-1/2-ton Model 70. There was also a 4-ton Model 73 with a Continental B-5 engine and a 5-ton Model 90 with a Continental B-7 engine. Ross steering was used on the lighter trucks, while Gemer was used on the heavier models. Model 90 had a wheelbase of 164 inches and a chassis weight of 9,650 pounds. Pneumatic tires were listed as optional up to Model 73.

For 1928, Selden introduced a six-cylinder LeRoi engine and a new light series consisted of the 3/4-ton Roadmaster and 1-1/2-ton and 2-1/2-ton Pacemaker. By that time, the 7-ton Model 77 was the heftiest Selden truck available. However, in 1929, for financial reasons, Selden merged with the Hahn Motor Truck Corporation of Allentown, Pennsylvania. A few trucks were built there under both names before Selden faded out as Hahn went into fire apparatus vehicle manufacturing.

SENECA 1917-1921 — After the Fostoria cars did not do well in the marketplace, the company was renamed the Seneca Motor Car Company under Ira Cadwallader, who took over as president. Seneca of Fostoria, Ohio, built mostly passenger cars but also offered a 1/2-ton light truck with a 27 hp four-cylinder LeRoi engine and three-speed transmission. The wheelbase was 108 inches and price was $1,020 compared to $990 for a Roadster in 1919. The company later switched to a 40 hp Lycoming engine for its cars

and wheelbase was increased to 112 inches. In 1924, the production of vehicles was ceased, although the company continued to build replacement and spare parts for its vehicles.

1914 SERVICE MODEL J FLAREBOARD EXPRESS OCW

SERVICE 1911-1932 — The Service Motor Car Company was located in Wabash, Indiana. The first Service truck was the Model A. This was a delivery vehicle that used a 22.5 hp four-cylinder engine and had a friction transmission and final chain drive. In 1914, the company was renamed the Service Motor Truck Company, reflecting the specific product line the company produced. By 1917, the company offered trucks from 1-ton to 5-ton capacity powered by four-cylinder Buda engines using three-speed or four-speed transmissions with Timken worm-drive.

1914 SERVICE MODEL K COVERED FLAREBOARD OCW

1921 SERVICE 5-TON MODEL 101 CHASSIS HAYS

In 1923, the company was reorganized as Service Motors Incorporated. In the following year, the lightest Service truck was the 1-1/4-ton Model 25 with 132-inch wheelbase and was powered by a 22.5 hp Buda WTU engine with Brown-Lipe clutch and transmission. Front axle was from Shuler and rear axle was made by Eaton. Bimel wheels carried 34x5 pneumatic tires front and rear. The 1-1/2-ton Model 33 differed in that it was powered by a 25.6 hp Buda GBU-1 engine and had a Timken rear axle. There was also a 1-1/2-ton Model 25C with components essentially the same

349

as the Model 25. Next size up was the 2-ton Model 42, which had a 28.9 hp Buda EBU-1 engine and Timken axles front and rear. Pneumatic tires were optional on Interstate wheels. The same essential components including engine and Brown-Lipe transmission were used on the 3-ton Model 61, which had a 163-inch wheelbase. Next size up Service truck was the 4-ton Model 81 with 173-inch wheelbase powered by a Buda YBU engine. The heaviest Service truck at that time was the Model 103.

1924 SERVICE ADVERTISING TOUR TRUCK   RD

In 1927, Service was bought by Relay, which had just been organized as a conglomerate by East Coast financiers. The factory equipment was moved to Lima, Ohio, where both Relay and Service trucks were built side-by-side. They were essentially the same except that Service trucks used worm-drive instead of internal gear drive and had steel disc wheels instead of Relay's artillery wheels. Relay drive was also exclusive to that make. Commerce and Garford trucks had also been acquired by Relay and all of these makes were quite similar, although each carried its own emblem. However, Service trucks were not successfully marketed and in 1928, the company sold a total of 80 vehicles. For 1929, only half of that number found buyers. Relay went into receivership in 1932 and the Service marque was suspended permanently.

SHAKESPEARE see KALAMAZOO

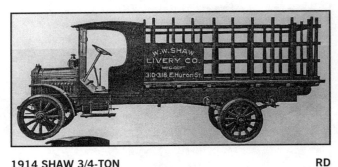

1914 SHAW 3/4-TON   RD

SHAW 1913-1914; 1918-1920 — The Walden W. Shaw Livery Company of Chicago, Illinois, got into the automobile business in 1908 selling passenger cars. Walden Shaw hired John Hertz, who organized the running of the company and by 1913, the Shaw company was building taxi chassis. In 1915, the Yellow Cab Manufacturing Company was set up also in Chicago, Illinois, for the manufacturing of the cabs with the Walden W. Shaw Livery Corporation as the holding company. In 1918, Shaw offered a 2-ton truck but production did not ensue. It appears that a prototype was probably the only vehicle built. Passenger car production was attempted in 1920 but this also met without success.

SHELBY 1917-1918 — The Shelby Tractor and Truck Company of Shelby, Ohio, has been listed as a manufacturer of a tractor and a 3/4-ton truck, both priced at $900. It is not certain if the same 9 hp engine that was used in the tractor also powered the truck.

SHERIDAN 1916-1917 — The Sheridan Commercial Car Company built a Model A in 1916. This was a gasoline-powered open delivery truck rated at 650-pound capacity and was priced at $465. In 1917, the company introduced a 1/2-ton stake bed truck, which was priced as chassis for $490 and as a canopy express or stake body for $540.

SHUTTLECRAFT see AMERICAN CARRIER EQUIPMENT

1914 SIEBERT MODEL H COVERED FLAREBOARD   OCW

SIEBERT 1911-1916 — Siebert was located in Toledo, Ohio, and built a 1,200-pound and 1-ton capacity truck. The lighter vehicle was powered by a two-cylinder engine, while the 1-ton model had a four-cylinder engine and a wheelbase of 120 inches. Two years later, a 3/4-ton truck was introduced. It featured a four-cylinder engine, three-speed transmission and double chain drive. Another 1-ton model similar to the earlier 3/4-ton truck was available by 1915. Production stopped in 1916 as material shortages during World War I took their toll on small manufacturers such as the Siebert company.

1914 SIGNAL 3/4-TON CHASSIS   OCW

1914 SIGNAL SCREENSIDE FLAREBOARD   OCW

1922 SIGNAL STAKE SIDE   **RD**

SIGNAL 1913-1923 — The Signal Motor Truck Company was located in Detroit, Michigan, and the first truck built there was a 1-1/2-ton capacity model that used a four-cylinder side-valve engine, a three-speed transmission and double chain drive. The company built both open and closed bodies on this chassis through 1914. In 1915, 1-, 2- and 3-ton capacity trucks were added, each with double chain drive. By the following year, however, worm-drive was adopted on all four models. Both left-hand and right-hand drive was available, the former largely for export to Europe. A 5-ton capacity truck was added to the line in 1917 but the company rapidly faded. Only the 1-3/4-ton Model F was built in 1923.

1967 SILVER EAGLE 6X2 COACH (BUILT IN   **MBS**
AND IMPORTED FROM GERMANY AND BELGIUM)

SILVER EAGLE 1975 to date — Eagle buses were originally built in Belgium but in 1975, a factory was started in Brownsville, Texas. The buses built in Belgium and Germany originally had MAN and Detroit Diesel 8V-71 engines. The first units were called Silver Eagle, although that name was dropped later. Approximately 3,500 Silver Eagle and Golden Eagle buses were imported by Trailways between 1961 and 1974. By 1976, importing was discontinued due to the decline of the dollar against other currencies and Eagle buses have been built for domestic use in Brownsville.

1995 EAGLE COACH   **EAGLE**

For 1995, Eagle has continued to build the 45-foot coach, which is also manufactured in the form of the 45-foot Seated Coach and 45-foot Conversion Coach. All three use the Detroit Diesel Series 60 engine. This engine was designed with a turbocharger and charge air cooling. Output has been listed as 400, 430 and 470 hp. Transmission has been the five-speed or six-speed Automatic Allison World unit. Front axle has been the Rockwell Model FF942 and rear axle the Rockwell Series S-163QX. The Intermediate axle has been a Independent Torsilastic. Steering system has been the Ross Model TAS 65 Series. Wheelbase has been listed as 343

inches and turning radius as 53 feet, 9 inches. Seating capacity was listed as 57 passengers without bathroom and 55 passengers with bathroom for the Coach and Seated Coach.

SIMPLO 1908-1909 — The Cook Motor Vehicle Company of St. Louis, Missouri, built the Simplo highwheeler, which was available in several versions including a conventional delivery wagon. The Simplo was powered by 16 hp two-cylinder engines; one was air-cooled and the other water-cooled. A friction transmission was used with double chain drive and the vehicles all had right-hand steering. Brakes were double internal expanding and wheelbase was 86 inches. The delivery version was rated at 1/2-ton capacity and cost $700. Tires were 36x1-1/2 solid rubber, or for an extra $50 28x3 pneumatic tires were available. The Simplo did not sell well and the Cook company became a dealership for other motor vehicle manufacturers.

1926 SIX-WHEEL SAFEWAY COACH   **MBS**

SIX-WHEEL 1924-1928 — Six-Wheel buses, sometimes known as "Safeway" buses, were manufactured briefly by the Six-Wheel Company of Philadelphia, Pennsylvania. The Six-Wheel Company was an outgrowth of the American Motor Body Corporation, which was formed in 1920 and reorganized in 1923 by well-known investor Charles M. Schwab of Bethlehem Steel and other financiers. The American Motor Body Corporation was a successor to the Wadsworth Manufacturing Company of Detroit, whose plant was sold to Chrysler in 1925. At the same time, American Body acquired the Hall and Killburn Company, which built railroad car and street car components. The new venture began building Six-Wheel buses.

Six-Wheel also built a few trucks with up to 5-ton capacity and these were sold to India, South Africa, Sudan and Turkey. The heavy-duty Six-Wheel buses found buyers in the form of Cleveland, Detroit, Kansas City and New York transit companies. Bodies were built by American Car Company, Auto Body Company, Fitzgibbon and Crisp Company, Kuhlman, Lang and Hoover and most often by Wolfington of Philadelphia. Over the short period of manufacture, a total of approximately 400 Six-Wheel buses were built.

SLEEPER COACH 1937 — After the Pickwick Nite-Coach was used for long distance passenger service, Sleeper Coaches Incorporated of Detroit, Michigan, built a prototype of a similar type of coach based on a rear-engine Reo chassis. The venture was initiated by Paul W. Seiler, former president of the General Motors Truck Company. The bus had 16 overnight berths. However, the high cost of such luxurious transportation precluded further production.

SMITH FORM-A-TRUCK see FORD

1912 SMITH-MILWAUKEE 3-1/2-TON MODEL A   **AOS**

351

SMITH-MILWAUKEE 1912-1915 — The A.O. Smith Company of Milwaukee, Wisconsin, began building trucks in 1912. The first was the 3-ton Model A, which featured a four-cylinder engine with twin-ignition. The Model A also used a three-speed transmission and had a wheelbase of 168 inches. The Model A was upgraded to 3-1/2-ton capacity for 1913 and the company also introduced the 6-ton Model B. The latter was priced at $4,750 with a platform body. These were the only trucks built until the company ceased operation in 1915.

SNYDER 1914 — The Snyder Motor and Manufacturing Company of Cleveland, Ohio, built cyclecars for one year only. The Snyder vehicle had a 100-inch wheelbase and was powered by a 9 hp two-cylinder engine or an optional 12 hp four-cylinder engine. G.J. Snyder and R.E. Blackwell, who also built the Snyder motorcycle, were the organizers of the company. Among standard passenger models, there was a delivery van priced at $425.

1907 SOULES LIGHT DELIVERY   JAW

SOULES 1905-1915 — The Soules Motor Car Company was located in Grand Rapids, Michigan. The company built a 1-ton truck powered by a 22 hp two-cylinder horizontally-opposed engine with shaft drive. According to some records, the company moved to Detroit in 1911 and continued to offer 3-, 4- and 6-ton trucks.

1915 SOUTH BEND 2-TON   RD

SOUTH BEND 1913-1916 — The South Bend Motor Works was started in 1912 and a small factory went into production early in 1913. The company built 2-ton and 4-ton trucks and fire apparatus in South Bend, Indiana. South Bend trucks used chain drive until 1916, when worm gear drive was adopted and the model line was expanded to include 1-1/2-, 2- and 3- and 4-ton trucks. Wisconsin engine power output was listed at 30, 40, 80 and 95 hp, respectively. Prices were $1,750, $2,000, $3,000 and $3,850, respectively. Timken or Sheldon axles were available and Warner transmissions and Ross steering were used. Internal gear drive was also optional in the last year of manufacture. The company built Double-Duty Fire Apparatus as well. Until 1914, South Bend also manufactured long-wheelbase passenger cars powered by a six-cylinder engine.

SOUTHERN 1919-1921 — The Southern Truck & Car Corporation was located in Greensboro, North Carolina. The only records available to date show that this company built 1-ton and 1-1/2-ton trucks for a brief period. This Southern company was not affiliated with one by the same name and same year of manufacture in Memphis, Tennessee, which built passenger cars.

1954 SOUTHERN   MBS

SOUTHERN 1945-1961 — The Southern Coach Manufacturing Company was founded by Stanley Green in Evergreen, Alabama, during 1941. As World War II began, however, bus overhaul and rebuilding operations were the primary business at Southern. Southeastern Greyhound Line's front-engine conventional White buses were entirely rebuilt with new forward-control Wayne bodies.

In 1945, Southern began building its own buses with underfloor engine design and forward-control. The first such transit buses were 32-passenger but 35-, 41-, 45- and 50-passenger buses were built during the 1950s. Waukesha engines with Spicer transmissions were used during the 1940s. A switch was made to Fageol Twin Coach engines until that company folded in 1953. Leyland and Cummins engines were used after that with hydraulic transmissions.

By the mid-1950s, Southern obtained a lucrative government contract to build buses and some were exported, although most units remained in the southeastern part of the United States. A total of approximately 1,400 buses were built by Southern. The company's production plummeted after 1956 and the plant was closed before most of it was sold off to Flxible. The factory was used to build buses and truck bodies until the building burned down in 1968.

1913 SOWERS 1-1/2-TON STAKE   MROZ

SOWERS 1913-1914 — The Sowers Motor Truck Company was located in Boston, Massachusetts. For a brief time, the company built a 1-1/2-ton model truck but other information has not been available.

1947 SPANGLER DUAL-ENGINE 8X4   **NAHC**

SPANGLER 1947-1949 — The D.H. Spangler Engineering and Sales Company of Hamburg, Pennsylvania, briefly got into the business of manufacturing trucks after World War II, when demand for specialized commercial vehicles was high. The Spangler trucks were heavy-duty four axle units with each rear axle driven by a 100 hp Ford V-8 engine. Separate chain drives were used on the engines, which were mounted side-by-side.

D.H. Spangler was president of Hahn Motors and the Spangler trucks were built at the Hahn plant, better known for its fire apparatus. There was a Spangler fire truck and a truck tractor. The Spangler "Dual" had three axles. After 1949, Spangler concentrated on heavy-duty conversions of Ford, GMC and White trucks. Spangler's production trucks, of which there were small numbers, were based on Ford components and were serviced at Ford dealers.

SPARTAN 1946-1949 — The Spartan Coach & Manufacturing Company was located in Sturgis, Michigan. A demand for more economical buses after World War II led Howard Munshaw to design a 21-passenger bus with a 170-inch wheelbase. The chassis and frame of the body were built with welded steel tubing and the first model was powered by an International engine using a five-speed Fuller transmission. A few Spartan buses were used by operators between cities in the Midwest and at least five were sold to Nairn Transport in Syria. In the last year of manufacture, 25- and 29-passenger models were built but soon thereafter the company shut down and Munshaw went on to form Cub Industries.

1995 SPARTAN GLADIATOR FIRE ENGINE   **SPARTAN**

SPARTAN 1975 to date — Spartan Motors Incorporated was an outgrowth of the failed Diamond-Reo factory in Charlotte, Michigan. Former Diamond-Reo employees formed this company and began building the earlier-designed 2000 series chassis primarily for fire

engine application. Also, the HH-1000 6x4 off-road truck was built for coal hauling with a 40-ton capacity. Cummins and Detroit Diesel were available, although other engines could be ordered as well.

Spartan has continued to offer the EC-2000 chassis for motorhomes, fire trucks and buses. It has been powered by the Cummins 6B5.9 engine with up to 230 hp and has used an Allison automatic transmission. For specific fire fighting applications, Spartan has built the GT-One chassis powered by a 300 hp Caterpillar 3116 engine mounted in the rear as standard equipment and Allison MD 3060 electronic five-speed transmission. The cab could seat seven people with raised crew area roof. GVW has been rated at 30,000 pounds for this fire engine.

Spartan has also offered the Mountain Master chassis. This chassis has been powered by a 250 hp or 300 hp Cummins diesel engine with a six-speed electronic Allison automatic transmission. An M-11 engine was also offered as optional with 350, 370 or 400 hp and up to 1,350 pound-feet of torque. Other features included engine roll-out for fast maintenance, chassis rust protection, stainless steel exhaust system and air suspension.

The largest selection of Spartan fire apparatus trucks has been offered to date as the Series 95. This includes the GT One, Diamond, Gladiator, Charger, Baron and Silent Knight fire engines. The GT One design included engine location behind the rear axle, aluminum cab with seating up to seven and 300 hp Caterpillar 3116 engine as standard equipment.

The Diamond's design has featured engine mounting ahead of the front axle with horsepower of 250, 300 and 320 available. The Gladiator has had the same engine position as the Diamond but horsepower has been offered at 330 and 470. The Charger's engine was located behind the front axle with up to 430 hp. The Baron fire truck's engine was located amidships with up to 470 hp and the Silent Knight engine was located behind the rear axle. All of the above fire trucks have been offered through 1995.

1913 SPAULDING MODEL T   **ISHS**

SPAULDING 1913 — Henry W. Spaulding was a blacksmith who arrived in Grinnell, Iowa, in 1876. Henry's two sons, Frederick and Ernest, joined him at the turn of the century when their father's business was one of the largest manufacturers of horsedrawn carriages west of the Mississippi. In 1910, the Spaulding Manufacturing Company began building passenger automobiles that were powered by a 30 hp four-cylinder engine and used a three-speed sliding gear transmission. Three years later, the company also produced a 1-ton truck called the Model T. It used the same engine and transmission as the passenger car but had dual chain drive and solid rubber tires. With an express body it sold for $1,100.

SPECIALTY VEHICLE 1983 to date — Specialty Vehicle started out in 1983 and has built manufacturing facilities in Downey, California. The company's model line has consisted of buses, shuttles, trams, trolleys and vans.

The Model 4146 has been designated as the name of the Specialty Vehicle 46-passenger tram that uses a forward-control open-sided battery-powered electric bus with a single open-sided trailer with applications for resorts, sightseeing tours and other similar uses. An enclosed version of the bus has been built as Model 4122 18-passenger shuttle.

The Model 5122 has been built as a 22-passenger electric bus or shuttle. This vehicle has been powered by a 35 hp three-phase AC induction motor with 4.28:1 gear ratio, eliminating the need for a transmission. Input voltage has been listed as 240 to 336 DC provided by traction batteries. Listed features were air ride suspension, power steering and power brakes. The air suspension allows the bus to be lowered to eight inches off the ground for wheelchair accessibility.

1994 SPECIALTY AVS 22-PASSENGER ELECTRIC BUS　　SV

Model 3122 has been built as a retro-styled trolley-type electric bus with 21-passenger capacity. Maximum speed was listed as 35 mph. At a constant 25 mph range has been listed at 60 miles depending on type of batteries used.

1995 SPECIALTY VEHICLE ELECTRIC SHUTTLE　　SV

1996 SPECIALTY VEHICLE ELECTRIC STEPVAN　　SV

Model 5129 has been built as a 28-passenger electric bus and a more aerodynamic version of this tandem-axle bus has been designated Model 5131.

Model 8118 has been built as a purpose built lightweight step van. Its wheelbase has been listed at 125 inches with 465-cubic feet of cargo room. This front-wheel-drive vehicle has been rated at 55 mph with a 60-mile range using GNB, Trojan or Chloride batteries. A 60-kilowatt or 75-kilowatt motor has been available.

SPEEDWELL 1907-1915 — The Speedwell Motor Car Company was located in Dayton, Ohio. Pierce D. Schenck was the founder and his first vehicles were passenger cars powered by four-cylinder and six-cylinder Rutenber engines. The first commercial vehicles the company built were light vans based on the passenger car chassis but by 1912, with the help of design engineer Gilbert Loomis, Speedwell began producing 2-ton and 3-ton trucks. These heavier trucks used forward-control and were powered by four-cylinder engines with dual chain drive and solid rubber tires. A power winch was an option beginning in 1912 and it added $200 to the price of the truck, which could be as high as $4,400 for a 6-ton model that appeared in 1913.

1916 SPEEDWELL SPECIAL STAKE BODY　　RD

Although the company built vans and trucks, it was better known for its passenger cars. Part of Speedwell's factory was leased to Wilbur and Orville Wright in 1907. When Schenck left Dayton in 1912, Cyrus Mead entered the picture as the company's financier who quickly attempted to change over to a rotary valve engine but before the revamped venture could succeed, Mead died in an auto accident and the Dayton factory was flooded during the winter. Bankruptcy was filed at the start of 1915 but by that time, production had already ceased.

1902 SPENCER STEAM DELIVERY VAN　　RD

SPENCER 1902 — The Spencer Auto-Vehicle Company began building steam delivery vehicles in 1902 but despite some refinements, the business venture did not survive the year. The Spencer delivery wagon had a 72-inch wheelbase, hard rubber tires and tiller steering. The vehicle's patented boiler used an automatic water feed regulator and a Jenkins kerosene burner. The steam engine was a single-acting four-cylinder-type capable of providing 6 hp at 150 psi of steam pressure. Splash lubrication was used. The engine drove a countershaft using a Brown-Lipe equalizing gear. The Spencer made only a brief appearance on the market before both gasoline and electric trucks became widely accepted throughout the United States.

SPHINX 1914-1916 — In 1914, with the help of Theodore F. Freed, H.R. Averill founded the Sphinx Motor Car Company in York, Pennsylvania. Theodore C. Auman was president, Samuel K. McCall secretary and Howard Rohrer treasurer. The company's slogan was "Quiet as a Sphinx." In December of 1914, the Hart-Kraft Motor Car Company factory, a defunct truck builder, was acquired for the purpose of building passenger cars. E.T. Gilliard designed the Sphinx vehicles, which included a 1/2-ton truck, powered by the same 17 hp Lycoming four-cylinder engine that was used in the touring car. The chassis was built by Parrish Manufacturing.

A cone clutch and bevel gear drive were also used and the panel-body truck was priced at $675. A three-speed sliding gear transmission, starter and electric lights were standard equipment. Few Sphinx trucks were built out of a total of about 1,000 Sphinx vehicles assembled in 1915 and 1916.

1915 SPHINX COMMERCIAL VAN   OCW

A company announcement of 1915 stated that the name of Du-Pont was also going to be used, although another company in Delaware already used that name. Apparently, truck production stopped but a few more Sphinx cars were sold. A few cars were built for the Bush Auto Mechanics School of Chicago and they were badged as "Bush Cars." Gilliard went back to Pullman, where he had been a designer for many years and the factory was sold to Pullman, which continued to use the facility to build auto bodies after 1916. Apparently, only a few cars under the DuPont name were built by Sphinx.

1912 SPOERER MODEL 40 C DELIVERY WAGON   WJP

SPOERER 1912-1914 — Charles and Jacob Spoerer, sons of carriage builder Carl Spoerer, built a car in 1907, which finished seventh in a 1,282-mile reliability run from Boston to Washington D.C. Carl Spoerer's Sons Company of Baltimore, Maryland, built 10 cars by the time of the race in 1908, and subsequently went into production. Commercial vehicles based on the Model 40C were mechanically the same as the 40 hp passenger car and the Model 25A used a 27 hp four-cylinder engine, both of them water-cooled engines. The universal 120-inch wheelbase was the same as that of the passenger Spoerer and both used shaft drive as did the lighter model. Basic design was compared to Mercedes of that time period and a considerable amount of effort went into detail. The heavier model was priced at $3,000 while the lighter one was $2,000. Production ended after 1914 due to financial trouble.

SPRINGFIELD 1901 — The Springfield Motor Vehicle Company of Springfield, Massachusetts, was the builder of large steam vans using two compound engines, one on each side and driving each rear wheel. The vehicles were designed by S.H. Barrett and R. Hale Smith. The prototype Springfield Steam used a 4 hp steam engine

and was bought by one of 10 company backers who owned the Royce Laundry Company. This was the first commercial vehicle in Springfield. As heavy as the production vehicles were, capacity was 1/2-ton and range was about 50 miles with a full supply of fuel and water. A condenser allowed 200 miles between fill-ups of water but fuel supply still limited the range. This company was not affiliated with Springfield of Ohio, which existed at the same time and was intertwined with the Springfield Automobile Company, which would later build the Bramwell passenger cars.

STANDARD 1907-1908 — The Standard Gas-Electric Power Company of Pennsylvania built a hybrid-powered truck using a two-cylinder horizontally-opposed engine under the seat, which drove a shunt-wound generator. However, it did not drive the vehicle but instead, was used as a motor when engine speed fell below 1,000 rpm. The transmission had three forward speeds and final drive was by dual chain. Batteries also provided a few miles of range.

1920 STANDARD 3-1/2-TON GROCER'S VAN   LIAM

STANDARD; FISHER-STANDARD 1912-1933 — The Standard Motor Truck Company of Detroit, Michigan, began building trucks using Continental engines, Brown-Lipe transmissions and Timken worm-drive. Continental engines would be used throughout the dozen years that the company was in existence. Chain drive was used on all Standard trucks up to 1920. The largest capacity truck at that time was a 5-ton model.

1929 FISHER-STANDARD MOVING VAN   NAHC

In 1925, Standard expanded its line to include a 7-1/2-ton capacity truck powered by a 36.1 hp Continental B-5 engine. A choice of four-speed and nine-speed transmissions was offered. The largest truck had a wheelbase of 165 inches and used 36x6 front and 40x14 rear solid rubber tires. There were also two lighter trucks models, the 3-1/2 5 K and 3-1/2 5 KS, both with a 160-inch wheelbase and powered by 32.4 hp Continental L-4 engines. The company also built Models 2-1/2 and 3-1/2 K and KS, which were powered by Continental K-4 engines. Both of these had a 147-inch wheelbase. The 1-1/2 K truck had a 144-inch wheelbase and used a Continental J-4 engine. The lightest Standard model was the 1-1/4-ton Model 75 powered by a Continental N engine. All the models used Timken front and rear axles and Ross steering.

A speed model called the Fisher Fast Freight was introduced in the mid-1920s. By 1928, the smaller trucks used the Fisher name. The 1-ton was called the Fisher Junior Express, the Fisher Fast Freight was rated at 1-1/2-ton, the Fisher Mercantile Express was a 2-ton truck and the Fisher Heavy Duty Six was rated up to 3-1/2-ton. Heavier trucks, vans and light models with solid rubber tires continued to be available, as was a 28-passenger bus called the Standard AK. After 1930, the Fisher-Standard name was used for all models of vehicles the company produced, which were marketed primarily in the Detroit area and to Canada. By 1933, the Depression took its toll on the firm and production was discontinued.

STANDARD 1913-1914 — The Standard Motor Truck Company of Cleveland, Ohio, is known to have built a 1-ton and 1-1/2-ton truck. No other details have been available.

STANDARD 1913-1915 — The Standard Motor Truck Company of Warren, Ohio, built a model line of trucks consisting of 3/4-, 1-, 1-1/2-, 2- and 3-1/2-ton capacity. For 1916, the name of the company was changed to Warren Motor Truck Company. No other information regarding this company has been available. There is no apparent connection with the Standard Motor Truck Company that existed in Cleveland, Ohio, at about the same time.

STANDARD TRACTOR 1915-1916 — The Standard Tractor Company was located in Brooklyn, New York. The company's vehicles were designed as some of the earliest truck tractors for pulling independent four-wheel trailers. These were forward-control and had a worm-drive jackshaft to the rear of the back axle and then chain drive to the rear wheels giving an overall axle wheel ratio of 18:1. Air brakes were used and compressed air hoses ran to the back for attaching to the trailer.

STANDARD 1917-1918 — Standard trucks of World War I were not a make but were built by 15 different companies with shared mechanical components. These were called Liberty trucks. See Liberty.

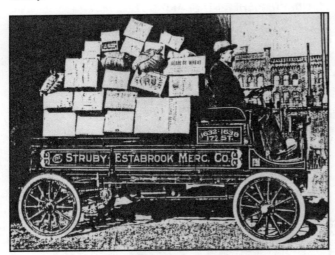

1908 STANLEY STEAMER DELIVERY WAGON   **RD**

STANLEY STEAM 1909-1916 — The Stanley Brothers, Francis and Freeland, began in Watertown, Massachusetts, in 1897. Their first successful efforts resulted in a steam passenger vehicle, which was built near their Newton, Massachusetts, photographic laboratory. After demonstrating their steam carriage near Boston, orders quickly followed and the brothers were building steam cars by the hundreds.

John Brisben Walker soon made an offer the brothers could not refuse -- $250,000 for the company in which they had $20,000 invested. The new owner teamed with asphalt producer Amzi Lorenzo Barber but the two had a falling out early on and went separate

ways to build the Locomobile and Mobile steam cars, respectively. The Stanley brothers were soon back in business. After settling a patent infringement lawsuit with George Whitney and taking care of contracts with Walker and Barber, they began production of steam vehicles under the name Stanley Motor Carriage Company in Newton, Massachusetts, with manufacturing restarting in 1902.

It was not until 1909 that Stanley built commercial vehicles and these were in the form of 12-passenger open-side hotel buses called the Mountain Wagon. Several were specifically built for use at the Stanley Hotel at Estes Park in Colorado. Powered by a 30 hp two-cylinder steam engine, they could climb the rugged dirt roads in and out of the park with ease. Several other hotels used Mountain Wagons, some being used 80 years later at the Magic Age of Steam Museum in Yorklyn, Delaware. The Mountain Wagon was built from 1909 until 1916, with 1-ton and 1-1/2-ton truck versions also being available in small numbers.

1914 STANLEY EXPRESS WAGON   **WOM**

1914 STANLEY EXPRESS WAGON   **WOM**

Although the Stanley brothers remained in business until 1927, commercial vehicle production was suspended after 1916. Announcements were made in 1924, 1935 and 1936 regarding the production of steam trucks and buses but none of these vehicles ever materialized. Steam vehicles were entirely discontinued by the time World War II began.

STAR 1913-1914 — Among several manufacturers by this name, the Star Motor Car Company of Ann Arbor, Michigan, built two models of trucks. Both were powered by a four-cylinder side-valve engine mounted under a front hood and used a three-speed transmission and dual chain drive. The 1-ton model was similar to the 1-1/2-ton that had a wheelbase of 132 inches, used solid rubber tires and was priced at $1,800.

STARBUCK 1912-1913 — The Starbuck Automobile Company of Philadelphia, Pennsylvania, offered a 1-1/2-ton truck with express body for $1,800. The truck was powered by a 28.9 hp four-cylinder engine and had an advertised top speed of 20 mph. A Schebler carburetor was used along with Michigan ignition system. A disc clutch and chain drive were featured and the rear suspension consisted of a transverse leaf spring arrangement. Wheelbase was 110 inches. This company was not affiliated with the later Starbuck venture that William P. Deppe was involved with around 1919.

1913 STARBUCK MODEL G   RD

1923 STAR PANEL DELIVERY   OCW

1924 STAR CANOPY STATION WAGON   OCW

STAR RUGBY 1922-1932 — William Durant organized his company under his own name after leaving General Motors, which he had helped found earlier. The Star Four was intended to compete with Chevrolet and was priced at $400. The vehicle was available as a delivery van and as a depot wagon with roll-up side curtains. The Mason was a 1-ton commercial vehicle, which was upgraded as a 1-1/2-ton light truck for export.

In 1926, a six-cylinder engine was introduced and used in the 1-1/2-ton Star Six Compound Fleettruck, which was renamed Rugby in 1927, although this name had been used for exported vehicles to England from the beginning. A 1/2-ton van once again used the 36 hp Durant Four four-cylinder engine. The van had four-wheel-brakes, which were not yet available on the heavier chassis. The 1-ton van was available with the four-cylinder or the six-cylinder engine and featured a four-speed transmission and four-wheel handbrake. An auxiliary two-speed transmission in conjunction

with a standard three-speed unit provided six forward speeds in 1929 but this was too expensive to produced, especially by the end of the year after the stock market crash.

1926 STAR CLOSED BOX ROADSTER PICKUP   OCW

1927 STAR CANOPY FLAREBOARD   OCW

The heavier Rubgy 1-ton and 1-1/2-ton trucks used a four-speed transmission for 1931 and 1932. A 58 hp six-cylinder engine was used in the latter vehicles, which was also available in the 1/2-ton van. It was the same engine as the Durant 6-14 passenger car. Durant went out of business in 1932 and the company was liquidated in 1933. Durant filed personal bankruptcy in 1936 and he died in 1947 at the age of 85.

STAR TRIBUNE see O.K.

STEAMLINE see BAKER

STEAM-O-TRUCK 1918-1920 — The Steam Automotive Works of Denver, Colorado, built the Steam-O-Truck, which was at first called Stokesbary. In 1918, the single model was a 5-ton capacity truck powered by a four-cylinder single expansion steam engine geared directly to the rear wheel with a 3:1 reduction ratio. A two-cylinder compound engine was used starting in 1919. The water tank held 40 gallons of water and the boiler was fitted under the hood giving the truck a more modern appearance. Wheelbase was 137 inches and operating pressure was 600 psi. The truck was priced at $5,000. Few were actually built.

STEAMOBILE 1919 — The Winslow Boiler and Engineering Company of Chicago, Illinois, built a 5-ton capacity truck that used a Uniflow V-4 steam engine and a Winslow high-pressure boiler. Although the design was an advanced one, using shaft drive as well, by 1919, the market for steam powered trucks had vanished nearly entirely and the Steamobile ended up being an anachronistic experiment. This company was apparently not related to the earlier Steamobile of Keene, New Hampshire.

STEAMOTOR 1917-1920 — Another company late in the business of using steam power was the Steamotor Truck Company, which became the Amalgamated Machinery Corporation in 1919.

The truck used a Doble-built steam engine with a 600 psi 45 hp boiler, which was located under a hood, while the engine was located under the seat. Shaft drive and worm gear were used on the Steamotor 2-ton truck, which had a 144-inch wheelbase and was priced at $3,000 for chassis.

1917 STEAMOTOR DOBLE-ENGINE TRUCK   RD

STEAM POWER SYSTEMS see BROBECK

1901 STEARNS UTILITY WAGON   JAW

STEARNS-KNIGHT 1901-1913, 1915-1916 — Frank Ballou Stearns built his first car in 1896 in the basement of his family home, where his father had set up a high quality machine shop. F.B. Stearns & Company was organized in 1898 and Stearns soon became known for building excellent cars with wheel steering in 1901, a sliding gear transmission in 1902, magneto in 1904 and a four-speed transmission in 1905. "Runs Like a Deer" was the company slogan. By 1911, Stearns bought the Knight engine factory and set up production at the Royal Tourist facilities where sleeve-valve Knight engines were to be produced. All of the Stearns cars were powered by Knight engines after 1911.

It was not until 1911 that the Stearns company built its first commercial vehicle, which was 3-ton truck powered by a standard 44 hp four-cylinder engine and used double chain drive. From 1912 on, Stearns built only a 5-ton model truck with platform body, three-speed transmission and double chain drive. Wheelbase was optional from 180 inches to 236 inches. Production of commercial vehicles was interrupted in 1913 for almost two years when the 5-ton truck was redesigned using the sleeve-valve Knight engine, which was spring mounted on a subframe using inverted semi-elliptic springs. Optional wheelbase was extended to 230 inches and double chain drive was still used.

1912 STEARNS STAKE BED   NAHC

In 1917, Stearns left the company and commercial vehicle manufacture also ceased at that time. John North Willys later bought the company in 1925. It was shut down when the stock market crashed.

1908 STEEL SWALLOW POSTAL DELIVERY   WLB

STEEL SWALLOW 1908 — David Dearing's patents were the basis for the Steel Swallow, which was built by the Steel Swallow Automobile Company in Jackson, Michigan. Dearing was joined by several investors who capitalized the company in 1906 with $100,000 of which $60,000 was actually paid commencing production in 1907. The first vehicle was a runabout but for 1908, a light delivery van was built using an 8 hp two-cylinder engine and friction transmission. The U.S. Post Office used some Steel Swallow vehicles called "Special R.F.D." that were also built in 1908.

STEELE 1914-1919 — W.M. Steele of Worcester, Massachusetts, built Morgan trucks before that company ceased operations in 1913. Steele built its own four-cylinder engines, which powered 2-, 3-, 4- and 5-ton capacity trucks also manufactured in Worcester in small numbers. Steele used three-speed Cotta transmissions and double chain drive. The front seats were mounted on either side of the hood creating a type of forward-control layout. Steele also built its own jackshafts and for a brief time, experimented with cyclecars.

STEGEMAN 1911-1918 — The Stegeman Motor Car Company built six models of trucks ranging in capacity from 3/4 ton to 5 ton. All but the lightest shared the design of having solid rubber tires and double chain drive, which was available in a fully enclosed oil bath for an extra $150. The 3/4-ton Stegeman had shaft drive and pneumatic tires. Four-cylinder engines were used exclusively until 1917, when a six-cylinder engine with electric start was introduced for the heavier models. In 1917, a 7-ton model was brought out that featured a fully floating worm-drive rear axle fabricated by Stegeman. This was the year the company ceased operations. The company was located in Milwaukee, Wisconsin.

1911 STEGEMAN 2-TON   MROZ

1914 STEGEMAN PANEL BODY DELIVERY   OCW

STEINKONIG see WORLD

1925 STEINMETZ DELIVERY VAN   WJP

STEINMETZ ELECTRIC 1922-1926 — Charles Steinmetz was well known as an electrical engineer and inventor when he chose to enter the electric auto manufacturing field at the late date of 1922. Prototypes of his electric cars were built by the Thorne Machine Tool Company in Syracuse, New York. A factory was established in Baltimore, Maryland. Steinmetz himself tested one of his electric closed sedans at 40 mph with a claimed range of 200 miles. Almost immediately, the decision was made to go into commercial vehicle production instead.

The company built a 1/2-ton and 3/4-ton truck using Diehl DC motors and bevel gear rear axle drive. The 1/2-ton had a wheelbase of 108 inches while the 3/4-ton had a 114-inch wheelbase. For 1925, the lighter truck was discontinued and the heavier model continued to be built only through 1926.

1920 STEPHENSON UTILITY DELIVERY WAGON   RD

STEPHENSON 1910-1913 — The Stephenson Motor Truck Company specialized in building 1-ton and 3-ton trucks in Milwaukee, Wisconsin. A water-cooled four-cylinder engine was used coupled to a friction transmission and double chain drive. The 1-ton truck had a wheelbase of 112 inches, while the heavier model had a wheelbase of 132 inches. Both trucks had solid rubber tires. The Stephenson trucks were priced at $2,000 and $3,500, respectively.

STERLING 1909-1910 — Of the half dozen companies that manufactured motor vehicles under that name, the Sterling Vehicle Company was the only one to be located in Harvey, Illinois. The company built a Model C truck that used a water-cooled two-cylinder engine, three-speed transmission and shaft drive. Wheelbase was 88 inches.

STERLING 1916-1953 — Sterling began as the Sternberg Motor Truck Company. Because of anti-German sentiments at the beginning of World War I, William Sternberg changed the name to Sterling in 1916 and the company continued to build conventional trucks from 3/4-ton to 7-ton capacity. All used four-cylinder engines and worm gear drive except for the 7-ton truck, which used chain drive. The 3/4-ton truck had a three-speed transmission while the 1-1/2-, 3-1/2- 5- and 7-ton trucks used a four-speed transmission.

There were four engine sizes at that time. The lightest truck had a 138-cubic inch 30 hp engine. Next up was a 289-cubic inch 35 hp engine and a 326-cubic inch 45 hp unit. The two largest Sterling trucks were powered by a 478-cubic inch 52 hp four-cylinder engine. Windshields, electric headlights and oil side lamps were standard equipment and all but the 3/4-ton truck had standard half doors. On the lightest truck they were optional. Widely spaced hood louvers were also featured on Sterling trucks of this period.

During World War I, Sterling built 489 Class B "Liberty" trucks. Production of the earlier models also continued. In January of 1919, the Hayssen family took over the corporation. Robert G. Hayssen became president with Ernst M. Sternberg as vice-president and Frank Luick as secretary-treasurer. The name "Sterling" was cast into the smooth triangular radiator shell crown on almost all Sterling trucks up to 1920.

A patent was obtained on February 7, 1922, in regard to the exclusive wood inlay of the truck frames developed by Sternberg. By 1923, worm gear drive trucks were available in 1-1/2-, 2-, 2-1/2-, 3-1/2- and 5-ton capacity while chain drive was offered on 5-ton and 7-ton trucks. Also, there were two 5-ton chain drive models, the ELD and the EHD, which were powered by two different engines depending on whether light-duty service or heavy-duty service was the application. The lightest three trucks had four-speed sliding gear transmissions, while the rest were equipped with constant mesh three-speed transmissions. The chain drive models also had a two-speed jackshaft unit that gave six speeds forward and two in reverse.

1923 STERLING 1-1/2-TON CHASSIS HAYS

From 1921 to 1924, Sterling's engines were built in four displacements: 289, 346, 398 and 491 cubic inch. Electric headlights and taillamps were standard equipment. Solid rubber tires were standard but the lightest three capacity trucks had single pneumatic tires for each wheel as optional equipment.

By 1925, Sterling was building a wide range of trucks starting with the 1-1/2-ton model carried over from previous years up to 7-1/2-ton capacity. Worm-drive trucks at that time were rated up to 27,000 pounds GVW and chain drive trucks were rated up to 35,000 pounds GVW. Cycle-type fenders were used on Sterling trucks through the Teens and 1920s. The 1-1/2-ton model for 1925 was priced at $3,345. The 2-ton Model 2 chassis was priced at $3,545 and the 2-1/2-ton chassis was priced at $3,805. Next up was the 3-1/2-ton chassis for $4,750. In the 5-ton range, Sterling offered the Model W for $5,400, the Model EHD for $5,750 and the Model ELD for $6,000. The 7-1/2-ton Model 7-1/2 was priced at $6,500. There were also six truck tractors from $3,905 to $6,600.

During this period, Sterling built the D series and the E series of trucks. The aforementioned E series was a continuation of previous design, while the D series was available in two basic configurations: the first was a "speed" chassis with up to 12,000 pounds GVW and the DW series was rated up to 18,000 pounds GVW. The lighter D series trucks were powered by a 251-cubic inch engine with 43 hp, while the heavier were powered by a 346-cubic inch 46 hp engine. The D series had solid rubber tires as standard equipment while pneumatic tires were optional.

From 1927, the D series was expanded to include higher GVW ratings. Horizontal hood louvers replaced the vertical louvers and a new enclosed cab was substituted for the open cabs and half doors. Buses for 21 or 25 passengers continued to be built in small numbers. These were priced at $6,800 and $7,575, respectively, in 1926. They remained virtually unchanged in appearance until the end of the decade.

Additional chain drive models were offered by 1928. The "speed" trucks were superseded by the Model DB8, which was powered by a 260-cubic inch six-cylinder engine and used a three-speed transmission with a spiral bevel rear axle. Pneumatic tires were standard. GVW ratings were 11,000 pounds for Model DW11, 14,000 pounds for Model DW14 and 18,000 pounds for DW18, 20,000 pounds for Model EW20, 21,000 pounds for Model DC21, 25,000 pounds for Model DC25, 27,000 pounds for Model EW27, 29,000 pounds for Model EC29 and 35,000 pounds for Model EC35. Models DC19, DC23, DC26 and DC 27 were available by 1929.

In January of 1929, Sterling issued $1.8 million in preferred stock, which was sold by brokers. It was intended to pay off bank loans and mortgages on the factory and liquidate accounts payable. Henry C. Keenan became a second vice-president and Carl G. Hayssen became secretary.

1928 STERLING DUMP TRUCK OCW

1929 STERLING TANKER ZIERDEN

For 1931, the F series was introduced by Sterling. The new trucks had a more modern appearance with new cabs and sheet metal as well as a separate radiator shell. Spiral bevel, double reduction, worm and chain drive were used in Sterling trucks at this time.

In 1931, Sterling bought the LaFrance-Republic Corporation of Alma, Michigan. Production was continued by Sterling in Milwaukee. According to some records, once inventory of the LaFrance-Republic truck parts was exhausted, the Sterling F series was badged as LaFrance-Republic until 1942.

The day before Christmas of 1931, due to a failure to meet dividend requirements of the preferred stock, control was taken away from the Hayssen family and Ernst M. Sternberg took over as president of the company. In 1932, banks gave the company a 20-month extension on $700,000 outstanding and William G. Sternberg, Jr. became vice-president. At the end of 1933, a reorganization took place and the company was incorporated in Wisconsin. Old common stock was retired and exchanged for new common stock at a ratio of six to one. The new corporation received an authorized capital of $1,060,000 represented by 100,000 shares of cumulative preferred stock and 60,000 shares of common stock.

The first diesel engine that Sterling installed was a Cummins H series. It was fitted in a model FD195H in 1932 and became standard equipment. Sterling was one of the first to use diesel engines as a standard powerplant but due to other such claims it cannot be said with absolute certainty that Sterling was *the* first. In 1935, Sterling developed its first supercharged diesel engine for use at high altitudes to haul lead and zinc ore in Argentina. The truck was a HCS210H 6x4 dual chain drive. For low altitude, the engine used an automatic bypass to regulate air volume. A second such truck with a Rootes blower was built as a tractor-trailer with a GCW rating of 93,600 pounds. Production of other similar trucks followed.

Sterling developed its first COE truck in 1934. The Model GD97 was a 4x2 truck comparable to the F series conventional design and was rated at 22,000 pounds GVW. The cab tilted backwards splitting at the top of the windshield.

The Shell Petroleum Corporation ordered COE trucks that had weight specifications of a maximum 8,300 pounds with 35 gallons of fuel. This was due to the fact that a 4x2 highway tractor with single axle semi-trailer had a permissible gross weight of only 38,000 pounds. With elaborate use of aluminum in the framerails, crossmembers, brackets, cab, bumper, fuel tank, battery box and other smaller parts, the final weight of the truck tractor was only 8,070 pounds with 35 gallons of diesel. The revolutionary highway tractor with forward tilting cab was powered by a 100 hp Waukesha 6D100 diesel engine. One variation of this COE had a sleeper over the driver's compartment to keep a short BBC dimension. Another variation was a short BBC COE cab with room for four persons. The two who sat above the engine in the center had extra headroom with a higher cab roof and auxiliary windshields.

1937 STERLING DIESEL DUMP TRUCK OCW

In 1937, 4x2 worm gear trucks were not selling and the line was discontinued except for one model with GVW rating of 22,000 pounds. Five Sterling models were spiral bevel drive up to 37,000 pounds GVW rating, three were chain drive up to 34,000 pounds GVW and eight were double reduction up to 40,000 pounds GVW. The largest engine was the 462-cubic inch unit, which was used in the 6x4 trucks with double reduction drive, and the 517-cubic inch engine used in the 4x2 truck with double reduction drive. The entire F series, of which there were 17 basic models, used six-cylinder Waukesha engines. There were no four-cylinder engines available in the F series, which were built as standard trucks or truck tractors.

In addition to the gasoline engines Cummins H series diesel units were often used, with 40 percent of Sterling trucks between 1938 and 1940 being so equipped. The largest of these was the FWS180H, which had dual worm gear drive rear axles and was set up to pull a full trailer with a GCW rating of 68,000 pounds. Also in 1937, the H Series with an F Series cab was produced for dump, mixer and other severe service. The Model HC140 was rated at 36,000 pounds GVW, the HC170 at 44,000 pounds and HCS210 at 55,000 pounds. These were all chain drive and the two larger trucks were powered by a 677-cubic inch six-cylinder engine.

In 1938, Sterling unveiled a smaller, less expensive M series truck and tractor. The cab was similar to the J and H series, which were to debut in 1939. The radiator and fender combination resembled that of the H series. The conventional M series 4x2 was offered with chain drive, spiral bevel drive or double reduction gear rear axle. GVW rating was from 18,000 to 24,000 pounds. Two gasoline six-cylinder engines were available along with a Cummins AA6 diesel engine. A typical M series chain drive was the MC96 with 24,000 pounds GVW.

Sterling acquired the assets of Fageol in 1938 through the Waukesha Motor Company, who was Fageol's chief creditor and at the same time, owned a large amount of preferred stock in Sterling. Fageol truck production ceased in January 1939. Because Sterling lacked the capital to purchase the Fageol factory and all equipment, a Sterling factory branch in San Francisco was set up to handle the sale of Sterling trucks and to handle the sales and service of Fageol. Similar branches were set up in Portland, Oregon, and Seattle, Washington. The sales outlets were kept by Sterling. The rest of the Fageol business was sold to T.A. Peterman, who established Peterbilt Motors Company in Oakland, California.

1939 STERLING MODEL J NMM

Also in 1939, Sterling brought out the J series trucks. The J series was designed with style in mind and a distinctive radiator shell with aluminum bars was the first eye-catcher of the new look. The streamlined fenders were easily removable for access to the engine and components. Horizontal chrome bars along the sides of the hood followed ventilation apertures. Both gasoline and diesel engines were available and trucks with tandem rear axles and dual wheels were built in this series.

During World War II, Sterling built a variety of huge trucks for specialized services. The Navy Department ordered DDS150, DDS225 and DDS235 6x6 trucks as well as HCS330 6x4 trucks. Most of these were used for aircraft crash recovery operations. The DDS150 was used as a torpedo crane carrier. Sterling also built the 12-ton T26 8x8 standard truck and truck tractor for the Ordnance Department. The T26 had dual steerable axles and dual tires could be installed all around, the latter being designated the T26E1. The T26 trucks were powered by a 275 hp American LaFrance V-12 and had a GVW rating of 85,000 pounds.

Sterling also built the T28, T29 and T35 series truck tractors. The T29 was a 20-ton 6x6 powered by a 500 hp Ford V-8 tank engine, while the T35 was powered by a 750 hp Ford V-12 tank engine. These T series were built toward the end of the war and only a few were completed. The company also built the model HC145 4x2 for construction of U.S. Air Force bases in the North Atlantic and models HWS160H and HC297 6x4 trucks for the Army Corps of Engineers.

After the war, Sterling built the H and R series trucks. The H series consisted of 4x2 enclosed cab with up to 36,000 pounds GVW, 4x2 chain drive with up to 60,000 pounds GVW and the 6x4 enclosed with up to 52,000 pounds GVW. The R series consisted of a 4x2 enclosed with up to 36,000 pounds GVW and a 6x4 enclosed with up to 52,000 pounds GVW. All of these were available with either gasoline or diesel engines.

The company issued debentures paying 3.5 percent interest in the amount of $400,000 in 1945. A three for one stock split was made in 1946 and Donner Estates of Philadelphia, Pennsylvania, purchased the debentures, converting them during 1947 and 1948 and effectively taking control of Sterling until the sale of the company to White. William G. Sternberg and Ernst M. Sternberg continued as president and vice-president, respectively. However, Ernst M. Sternberg passed away in 1947 and William F. Sternberg and Ernest R. Sternberg were elected vice-presidents.

In 1948, Sterling began production of the TE and TG series trucks. The TE series was a cab forward design with a short stout hood with the engine partially extending into the cab area. The TG series was a COE design, although it actually had a short hood. Both had an insulated engine housing that was relatively easy to remove. At that time, Sterling also built the CC235 crane carrier for Bucyrus-Erie Company of Milwaukee. These were either 20-ton capacity with single rear axle or 25-ton capacity with tandem rear axles. Later in Cleveland, Sterling built 10- and 15-ton crane carriers for the same customer.

1949 STERLING TRACTOR-TRAILER   **OCW**

Also for 1948, Sterling built the model DD115 4x4 trucks with 32,000 pounds GVW and the DD145 with 36,000 pounds GVW. They were superseded late in the year by Models HB1604 and HB1904. The latter differed from the former in that the axle set-back dimension was increased. Late in 1948 and early 1949, the SB series was also introduced. The SB3001D 4x2 truck was fitted with a 10-cubic yard dump body and used a Sterling-designed planetary axle with a torque proportioning differential.

Sterling continued chain drive longer than most other U.S. truck manufacturers. The last chain drive model was built in 1951. Sterling cited five advantages to chain drive: 1) the driveline is straight and rotating shafts are parallel, 2) application of power is direct, 3) application of drive torque is equal to the torque at the wheels divided by the sprocket ratio creating less strain on the jackshaft, 4) final drive ratios are easily changed, and 5) there is better road clearance with chain drive.

Sterling's model line between 1948 and 1951 remained essentially unchanged, except that the 126 series cab superseded the previous standard cab. The new cab had a larger windshield and did not open for ventilation. A pivot panel was installed on the dashboard so that access was made easier for installation and servicing of the instruments. On June 1, 1951, Sterling was bought by White Motor Company.

STERLING-WHITE 1951-1957 — When White Motor Company purchased Sterling in June of 1951 the transaction was handled by exchanging the Sterling stock for the White stock with a ratio of four to one being the numerical formula. Sterling became a division of White. Vice-president in charge of the Sterling-White Division was William G. Sternberg while Ernest R. Sternberg became general manager of the division. Sterling-White trucks remained essentially unchanged except for the new Sterling-White emblem plate.

On July 1, 1953, all operations were moved to the White factory in Cleveland, Ohio. William G. Sternberg retired and Ernest R. Sternberg was transferred to Cleveland as assistant to the vice-president of production.

The Sterling-White trucks built in Cleveland were similar to the previous trucks built in Milwaukee, with the exception that on the Model HB2755D 6x4 the composite steel and wood cabs were fabricated in all-steel form. Fifty of the HB2755D trucks were built in Cleveland. Cardox Corporation, one of Sterling's earlier customers, ordered 78 Model TG1207 fire crash chassis, which were built up for the U.S. Air Force. As mentioned earlier, crane carriers were built for Bucyrus-Erie for about four years after the move to Cleveland. Subsequently, the Sterling-White trucks were discontinued. The Sterling name was revived in 1973 by Sterling Custom Built Trucks in Kansas City, Kansas.

STERLING 1973-1982 — Sterling Custom Built Trucks Incorporated revived the name of Sterling but the Kansas City company located in Kansas had nothing to do in terms of business association with the earlier Sterling company of Milwaukee and Cleveland. This later Sterling built a few custom crane carriers, prime movers, railroad service trucks and trailers before fading out around 1982.

STERNBERG 1907-1915 — William Sternberg organized the Sternberg Motor Truck Company in Milwaukee, Wisconsin. The first Sternberg trucks were COE-type in 1-, 1-1/2-, 3-1/2- and 5-ton capacities. The smallest engine used by Sternberg was a 29 hp four-cylinder unit, while the heavier trucks used a 44 hp four-cylinder engine. All of the engines were T-head-type with cylinders cast in pairs. A multiple disc clutch and three-speed selective sliding gear transmission mounted amidship were used on these models with the exception of the 1-ton truck, which used friction drive. Semi-elliptic springs were used throughout with the exception of the 1-1/2-ton, which had platform springs at the rear.

1913 STERNBERG 2-TON MODEL 2   **OCW**

1914 STERNBERG OPEN BOX BODY   **OCW**

Bow-shaped radiators gave Sternberg trucks a distinctive look. Artillery wheels carried solid rubber tires. The frames had oak planks bolted into the channels and bolts, instead of rivets, were used throughout the chassis.

In 1914, Sternberg introduced conventional design trucks with worm-drive, although the 7-1/2-ton used COE design. Sternberg changed its name to Sterling during World War I under pressure from anti-German reaction. For 1916, the company became the Sterling Motor Truck Company.

STEWART 1912-1916 — The Stewart Iron Works of Covington, Kentucky, built a single model 1-ton called the Model 1 throughout its five years of production. The truck was forward-control and was powered by a four-stroke two-cylinder engine and had double chain drive. Wheelbase was 96 inches. The Stewart Iron Works produced cast iron fences, yet the truck's chassis crossmembers were made out of hickory wood. This company was not affiliated with the Stewart Motor Corporation of Buffalo, New York, which was organized the same year. The Stewart Iron Works was also listed in Cincinnati, Ohio.

1912 STEWART 1/2-TON COVERED FLAREBOARD EXPRESS   RD

STEWART 1912-1941 — Thomas R. Lippard and R.G. Stewart both left the Lippard-Stewart company and organized the Stewart Motor Corporation in July 1912. Stewart and Lippard-Stewart produced trucks concurrently until 1919 when Lippard-Stewart went out of business.

The Stewart Motor Corporation was incorporated in Buffalo, New York, with $250,000 in capitalization. The first Stewart trucks resembled those of Lippard-Stewart in that both used a Renault-type hood. It was a 3/4-ton capacity vehicle priced at $1,650. A 221-cubic inch 27 hp four-cylinder Continental engine was used along with a three-speed transmission and Timken bevel drive.

1914 STEWART MODEL A PANEL   OCW

No major changes took place in the design of the Stewart truck until 1916. In the meantime, the Navy bought some ambulances in 1914 and used them in the Washington D.C. area. Also that year, a light bus was built on the Stewart chassis. Pneumatic tire size was increased from 34x4 to 34x4-1/2 that year and electric starting, invented two years earlier, was adopted in Stewart trucks. A number of body styles were available from the factory and from

the National Body and Top Corporation of Buffalo. In 1915, Stewart built passenger cars but this sideline only lasted through the following year.

In 1916, the 3/4-ton Series No. 2 was replaced by the Series No. 3 and 4. The Model No. 3 was rated at 1-ton and the Model No. 4 was rated at 1-1/2-ton. Stewart switched to solid rubber tires. Stewart also advertised a 1/2-ton truck for $750 complete with covered express body. In 1918, Stewart offered the 3/4-ton Model No. 6, 2-ton Model No. 7, 1-ton Model No. 8 and 1-1/2-ton Model No. 9. Contrary to some reports, Stewart did not switch to chain drive, although a few custom trucks might have been built using this type of drive. Four bodies were offered in 1918 designated Model A through Model D. The Model A was a steel-panel totally enclosed type. Model B was a covered express type, Model C was an open express with cab and the Model D was a stake platform body. Stewart's ads claimed "One Stewart truck supplants 10 horses."

In 1919, Stewart began producing a 3-1/2-ton truck. Most Stewart trucks were Continental powered but Buda, Milwaukee and LeRoi engines were used in some trucks. Also in 1919, the company announced an expansion program that would allow production of 10,000 trucks per year. The company had 345 distributors in the United States by then and was represented in 27 countries. Edward K. Roberts became general sales manager in 1920. Despite a coal strike and a railroad strike in 1920, production more than doubled.

Late in 1921 a 3/4-ton "speed" model truck was introduced. Chassis was priced at $1,395. Stewart claimed to have trucks in 41 foreign countries by this time. The factory covered a half million square feet of floor space and employed about 400 people.

For 1922, Stewart offered seven models. The lightest was the Utility Wagon with a capacity of 500 to 2,500 pounds priced at $1,245. The Model 15 was a 1-1/2-ton truck priced at $1,445. The Model 9 was a 2-ton capacity truck with a chassis price of $1,790. The 2-1/2-ton Model 7 had a chassis price of $2,190 and the 3-ton Model 7X was priced at $2,390. There was also the Model 10 and Model 10X both rated up to 4-ton capacity and priced at $3,190.

In 1925, Stewart built 18- to 25-passenger buses using six-cylinder engines. The 1-ton Model 16 of that year was powered by a 22.5 hp Lycoming CT engine and used a Fuller transmission, Clark rear axle, Columbia front axle and Gemmer steering gear. The 1-1/2-ton Model No. 17 had the same make of components but used a more powerful 25.6 hp Lycoming C engine. Chassis price was $1,595 for the latter. The 2-ton Model No. 9 was still powered by a Continental engine and was offered with a Durston transmission. The 2-1/2-ton Model No. 7X used a 29.0 hp Buda HTU engine and a Fuller transmission. Tires were 34x4 front and 34x8 rear solid rubber with pneumatic as optional. The 3-1/2-ton Stewart Model No. 10X was powered by a Buda YTU engine. This model also had optional pneumatic tires with standard being solid rubber 36x5 front and rear. Steering gear was by Ross.

1927 STEWART 1-TON PANEL DELIVERY   OCW

For 1926, six-cylinder engines were adopted as standard and the new "Buddy" Stewart model was introduced. The "Buddy" was a 3/4-ton speed truck with bevel gear rear axle and a 40 hp six-cylinder Continental engine. The transmission was a three-speed unit. For 1927, a new 1-ton "Buddy" truck was offered for a chassis price of $985. Sales continued to grow, with the company claiming an increase of 41 percent over 1925. In 1928, sales were 50 percent higher than in 1927. Stewart built trucks up to 4-ton capacity in 1928 and both four-cylinder and six-cylinder engines were available in the 1-1/2-ton model.

1929 STEWART DELUXE PANEL BODY   MORALES

1930 STEWART BUS   LIAM

1930 STEWART SPECIAL SEDAN DELIVERY   NAHC

For 1929, Stewart built its first aluminum panel delivery truck, believed to be the first in the industry. The company slogan continued to be "Stewart Trucks have won - By costing less to run." For 1930, Stewart produced trucks up to 7-ton capacity. The 1-ton chassis was priced at $695 and was the only model with a four-cylinder engine. Trucks up to 2-1/2-ton capacity used bevel drive while the heavier trucks used worm-drive.

In 1931, Lycoming straight-eight engines were adopted, although the heaviest truck still had a Waukesha engine. Transmission options included 12-speeds forward and three in reverse, created by a three-speed auxiliary unit. The lightest Stewart was the 1-ton model, which had a chassis price of $695. The 3-1/2-ton eight-cylinder Stewart chassis was priced at $3,990 and advertised to be capable of 60 mph with load. Wheelbases were from 150 inches to 241 inches for this model. The "Buddy" truck was discontinued on 1930 but reintroduced in 1935. The year 1930 was the best year for Stewart in terms of overall sales, which amounted to 2,315 units.

Stewart built a three-axle 10-wheeler in 1930 to carry a 4,000-gallon 22-foot long gasoline tank. The GVW of the truck was 43,500 pounds. School bus chassis were also built in 10 different versions, from the 130-inch wheelbase 30X to the 190-inch wheelbase 32X. Chassis prices ranged from $913 to $1,611. As the Depression set in, prices dropped to boost sales. For 1932, the Stewart 1-1/2-ton truck chassis cost $795 and the 2-ton truck chassis was $995.

That year, Stewart advertised its fire engines, which included combination ladder, hose and chemical trucks. Also that year, a sleeping cab was offered for $380 available painted green or red. The Lycoming eight-cylinder trucks were favored by long distance carriers and with a tandem axle, the truck's capacity was eight tons. Specialized van bodies were available, as well as ice cream truck bodies.

1935 STEWART DUMP TRUCK   OCW

1936 STEWART 2-TON STAKE BODY   MROZ

In 1935, Stewart restyled its light truck cabs with streamlining and V windshields and grilles. A 1/2-ton chassis appeared priced at only $495. For 1937, further restyling included pontoon fenders and teardrop headlights. Waukesha engines were used exclusively along with Waukesha-Hesselman semi diesel engines. Only a few cab-over trucks were built by Stewart. Raymond Stewart and company superintendent William F. Stuhlmiller both died suddenly in 1937.

"Stewart acknowledges no peer in truckdom" was the company's motto at that time, although by 1938, total sales had dropped to 390 and fell again to 90 units for 1939. Stockholders approved the liquidation of Stewart Motor Corporation in 1939 and a Chinese business group purchased the plant. The factory that had at one time employed 650 people was down to 32 employees in 1940. A few more trucks were built before Stewart ended all production in 1941. Peak sales of $6,651,000 was attained in 1929 before the Great Depression began.

STOCKTON see VAN WINKLE

1911 STODDARD-30 2-1/2-TON   CP

STODDARD-DAYTON 1911-1912 — John W. Stoddard, along with his brother Charles G. Stoddard, were members of a family whose business of building farm implements had formally started when the Stoddard Manufacturing Company was incorporated in 1884. The first auto appeared in 1904, largely a result of design engineer H.J. Edwards' efforts. Soon the Stoddard farm equipment business was abandoned and the two brothers dedicated themselves to building automobiles. "As Good As It Looks" was the company slogan.

Commercial vehicles appeared in 1911 in the form of 1-ton and 2-1/2-ton trucks, which were forward-control. Chain drive and solid rubber tires were used. The two truck models were built only for 1911. In 1912, a light delivery van was built based on the 28 hp four-cylinder Savoy model passenger cars, which had a wheelbase of 112 inches. The company was out of business by 1913.

STOKESBARY see STEAM-O-TRUCK

STORMS 1915 — William E. Storms, formerly with the Colonial Electric Car Company and the Anderson Electric Car Company, got into the business of building cyclecars, except that his was the only American electric cyclecar. The Storms electric had a wheelbase of 90 inches and a tread of 44 inches. The pressed steel frame used semi-elliptic springs in front and three-quarter elliptics in the rear. A top speed of 18 mph was advertised and range was up to 50 miles on a single charge. Besides the coupe and the roadster, a light delivery was offered for $650.

1926 STOUGHTON DUMP TRUCK   **HAYS**

STOUGHTON 1920-1928 — The Stoughton Wagon Company was located in Stoughton, Wisconsin. The first models of trucks that the company built were 1-, 1-1/2- and 2-ton capacity. The two lighter models used Waukesha engines while the 2-ton model was powered by a Hercules engine. Each model used a Brown-Lipe transmission and worm-drive. In 1922, the company added a 3-ton model with a wheelbase of 158 inches.

For 1925, Stoughton listed the 1-1/4-ton Model C with 138-inch wheelbase as its lightest truck. It was powered by a 27.3 hp four-cylinder engine unlike most other models, which used engines from Continental, Midwest and Waukesha. Front and rear axles were made by Columbia and steering gear was from Ross. Next up was the 1-1/2-ton Model B and Model BJ with 140-inch wheelbase. The Model BJ used Stoughton's own 31.5 hp engine, while the B model had a Waukesha engine. A combination of Columbia and Sheldon axles were used front and rear on these two models. There was also the 2-ton Model D and 3-ton Model F.

In 1926, Stoughton built three models of fire trucks with 250, 350 and 500 gpm ratings. In the last year, Stoughton's heaviest truck had a maximum capacity of 4 tons. Also for 1926, it appears Stoughton used Hercules engines and Brown-Lipe transmissions for some of its trucks. The company ceased production for 1929.

STRICK 1978-1980 — The Strick Corporation of Fairless Hills, Pennsylvania, built what they named the Strick Cab Under. The cab and chassis could be slotted under a semi-trailer allowing for a maximum amount of payload within a limited overall length. The twin-steer chassis was powered by a turbocharged Cummins 903 V-8 diesel located behind the cab, which was only four feet high. A 13-speed Roadranger transmission was used. The Strick design

has been likened to the 1965 Bussing Decklaster cab. Apparently, this type of truck was built only for a brief period. The Strick Corporation has continued to build bodies and various fire apparatus to date.

STUDEBAKER 1902-1964 — The Studebaker brothers began building horsedrawn wagons in 1852 and continued such production until 1920. The company supplied wagons for the Union Army during the Civil War. In 1868, the company was incorporated as the Studebaker Brothers Manufacturing Company. Fred Fish, John M. Studebaker's son-in-law, experimented with horseless vehicles as early as 1897. In 1902, the company began building electric vehicles, which were largely designed by Thomas A. Edison, and the original sales brochure included a brake body.

Twenty-nine electric Studebakers were sold the first year and according to records, 1,841 were built in the 10 years before the company ceased production of electric vehicles. The first models with a folding rear seat allowed the operator to carry a few hundred pounds of cargo, although they could not be considered trucks by any stretch of the definition. Late in 1902, the company announced the production of 1/2-ton to 4-ton capacity trucks.

Within three years, Studebaker was offering electric truck chassis up to 5-ton capacity. The first vehicles used a single Westinghouse D.C. motor while the heavy vehicles had one electric motor for each rear wheel using chain drive. A number of heavy-duty vans and stake trucks were produced, which used forward-control design with the steering column placed vertically. Battery boxes were built integral with the chassis.

By 1906, of the 12 electric models that Studebaker offered seven were commercial vehicles. The 5-ton capacity model was priced at $4,250 and all models carried a one-year guarantee. The heavier models used 4 hp electric motors with power fed from a 44-cell No. 17 M.V. Exide battery underslung amidships giving a range of 30 miles at the speed of 9 mph. The 3-1/2-ton model was equipped with Firestone hard rubber tires and sold for $3,500. Among the early Studebaker electric commercial vehicles was the "automobile transfer" truck that could carry a disabled car on its bed with ramp and winch behind an open cab, which was positioned over the front wheels. Studebaker displayed a 16-passenger opera bus in 1907 at the November Madison Square Garden show. In 1909, the H.C. Piercy Company of New York bought 25 Studebaker electric delivery trucks to replace 300 horses and 200 wagons.

1909 STUDEBAKER 2-1/2-TON ELECTRIC VAN   **NAHC**

The first Studebakers with gasoline engines were built in 1904, with Garford Company of Elyria, Ohio, supplying the chassis. By 1911, 2,481 Studebaker-Garfords were built. There were a few

Suburban vehicles built in 1908 and 1909, but otherwise the Studebaker-Garfords were not trucks. However, outside firms built custom delivery bodies.

1914 STUDEBAKER PANEL BODY GASOLINE TRUCK   OCW

In 1911, the Everitt-Metzger-Flanders Company was combined with the Studebaker Brothers Manufacturing Company to form the Studebaker Corporation. Studebaker marketed a Flanders Delivery Car and Suburban Utility Car for a brief period. Also in 1911, Studebaker took over the former Ford plant on Piquette Avenue in Detroit, where all Studebakers were assembled from 1913 to 1919.

Late in 1913, Studebaker announced a 3/4-ton capacity light delivery vehicle that had a new straight commercial chassis and used the four-cylinder passenger car engine with a governor that the press stated "will insure the owner against the evils of high speeds." The light truck featured a complete Studebaker-Wagner electrical system including an electric starter, which had been developed at General Motors for Cadillac only the previous year. The 3/4-ton Delivery Car was based on the 108.5-inch wheelbase of the Model SC passenger car, which had a 30 hp 192.4-cubic inch four-cylinder engine.

A 3-ton chassis with a four-cylinder T-head Studebaker truck engine and four-speed transmission was shown in 1913. It was designed by Albert Mais of Fremont-Mais fame but it was not marketed. The word "pickup" was first used by Studebaker in 1913.

In 1915, Studebaker announced a C-cab 1/2-ton capacity Commercial Car. It was powered by a 48 hp four-cylinder engine with Schebler carburetor and was available as chassis only for $785 or with Panel Body for $885, Express for $850 and Combination Passenger and Express Body for $875. The C-cab was elegantly incorporated into the panel body and spare tires were mounted above the runningboards on each side. A cone clutch was used and the three-speed transmission used Timken bearings and chrome-nickel gears. A generator-supplied Willard six-volt battery provided the power for starting and ignition. As with many commercial vehicles of that period, the gasoline tank was mounted ahead of the dashboard. A heater in conjunction with the exhaust manifold was available and standard equipment included a speedometer, gasoline gauge, battery indicator, oil pressure gauge, horn and windshield.

1916 STUDEBAKER MODEL SF PANEL DELIVERY   OCW

Early in 1916, Studebaker introduced a 1-ton model, which was to be produced at 10,000 units per year. The open express version was priced at $1,200, stake body at $1,250 and a 16-passenger bus at $1,400. The 1/2-ton truck continued to be built also. Both were designed for commercial use and were not warmed-over passenger car conversions. In 1917 and 1918, Studebaker offered finished 1/2-ton C-cab trucks with open express body for $960, panel delivery for $985 and station wagon for $985. The 1-ton truck was also offered with open express body and either stake body or as a 16-passenger enclosed bus, the latter for $1,600 by then. These models continued into the 1920s without major changes. The 40 hp 235.8-cubic inch engine was adopted for the commercial line.

In March of 1917, John Mohler Studebaker passed away. He had been a strong proponent of commercial vehicle production. Albert Erskine, company president, was the first to offer the company's services to President Woodrow Wilson, the first such offer made in the United States as our country entered World War I. The company soon received many orders for horsedrawn vehicles and such things as artillery wheels but not for motor trucks. Commercial vehicle production ceased by midyear and by the end of the war, car production was nearly at a standstill as Studebaker dedicated manufacturing for the war effort. After November of 1918, production was shifted to South Bend, Indiana.

In the early 1920s, Studebaker expanded its commercial vehicle models by teaming up with Superior Body Company and others that built ambulances and hearses on lengthened chassis -- which were not available from the factory -- as well as pickups, panel and delivery bodies. Some 1,000 Big Six buses were built by outside vendors up to 1925.

1925 STUDEBAKER AMBULANCE   OCW

In 1925, Studebaker unveiled its own new bus chassis, which was powered by a 75 hp six-cylinder engine that year. A few six-cylinder buses had already been road tested by that time but the A-158 and M-184 model chassis were announced in the press by midyear. Springs were semi-elliptic and the rear axle was semi-floating. The buses' wheelbases were defined by the model numbers: 158 inches and 184 inches, respectively. Pneumatic balloon tires were 34x7.50 six-ply and dual wheels were optional on the M-184 model. Hydraulic brakes were fitted to all four wheels at that time, which was earlier than many other companies' buses.

The anti-lock patented hydraulic brakes were actuated by a two-cylinder hydraulic pump mounted at the back of the transmission, which imparted a 60-40 proportioned force of 200 psi on the rear and front brakes, respectively. Since stopping the driveshaft also shut down the hydraulic pump, locking the brakes was "impossible," although certain aspects of this method were not entirely worked out and mechanically-actuated brakes were used soon afterwards. The A.J. Miller Company of Bellefontaine, Ohio, also built 12-, 15- and 19-passenger bus bodies on Studebaker Big Six Chassis. Model 75 was also built to accommodate 21 passengers.

The Bender Company of Cleveland, Ohio, became a bus body vendor for Studebaker in 1927. That year, Studebaker also introduced a 3/4-ton Delivery truck, which was available as a screenside express or with a full panel body. The L-head engine was rated at 27.3 hp and wheelbase was 113 inches. Spiral bevel gears and Hotchkiss drive were used. The trucks also featured pressurized lubrication, centrifugal water pump, four-wheel-brakes and 33x6 balloon tires front and rear.

1927 STUDEBAKER BIG SIX DEPOT WAGON   A&A

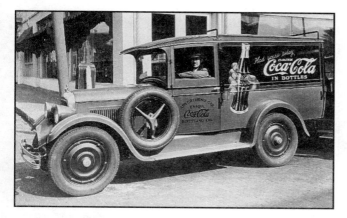

1928 STUDEBAKER PANEL EXPRESS   A&A

In 1928, Studebaker had purchased controlling interest in Pierce-Arrow. The result was a short-lived collaboration called the S.P.A. (Studebaker Pierce-Arrow) Truck Corporation, which announced its new 1-1/2- and 2-ton capacity trucks in 1930. The 1-1/2-ton model was built with 130-inch and 160-inch wheelbases with chassis prices of $695 and $775. The 2-ton model was available with 148-inch and 160-inch wheelbases with chassis prices of $895 and $945, respectively. A 205-cubic inch 70 hp six-cylinder engine powered both models.

1929 STUDEBAKER FIRE ENGINE   OCW

The Studebaker factory built a 22-passenger Seminole Parlor Car bus in 1928 and in 1929, the company announced a new line of delivery wagons with three different chassis and 13 body combinations. Later that year, a 25-passenger parlor bus was built on Studebaker's 220-inch wheelbase chassis. *The Commercial Car Journal* listed seven basic truck models from 3/4-ton to 3-1/2-ton capacity.

The S.P.A. venture quickly unraveled when the market crash of 1929 forced Studebaker to sell its Pierce-Arrow stock. An attempt to purchase the White Motor Company at that time also ended in financial disaster. At the same time, the new Studebaker Rockne division was abandoned after Knute Rockne, a famous football player and coach, died in an airplane crash. Studebaker's low-priced Erskine auto was also discontinued due to poor sales. In March of 1933, Studebaker went into receivership and in July, company president Albert Erskine committed suicide.

1930 STUDEBAKER 3/4-TON OPEN EXPRESS   A&A

Harold Vance and Paul Hoffman took over the helm and with $1 million from the Pierce-Arrow stock sale, Studebaker went on. In fact, $100,000 was spent on an ambitious advertising campaign using the slogan "Studebaker Carries On." The company introduced its new line of four trucks for 1933, which were designated as the Model S-2 with up to 2-ton capacity, Model S-4 with up to 2-1/2-ton capacity, Model S-6 and Model S-8 with 3-ton and 4-ton capacity, respectively. Chassis prices ranged from $670 to $1,425. These trucks were powered by the 75 hp six-cylinder engine that had been brought out a decade earlier.

1934 STUDEBAKER T 241 BREAD TRUCK   A&A

1935 STUDEBAKER 3-TON LUMBER AND COAL TRUCK   A&A

Studebaker sought out new distributors across the country including Kleiber on the West Coast, Ward LaFrance in New York, Nelson-LeMoon in Chicago and Autocar in over two dozen cities. Studebaker vehicles were also marketed in Mexico and South America and color ads in Spanish were printed. Chassis prices were revised and ranged from $625 to $1,795 at that time. The company sold a total of 1,872 trucks in 1933 and 1,697 for 1934. Capacity was up to 4 tons and ads for 1933 Studebaker trucks had "The White Motor Company, Cleveland, Ohio" as the parent organization, which was brief. "Handsome Brutes the new Studebaker trucks," ads proclaimed.

In September of 1936, Studebaker showed its new COE truck line, which was available as the 1-1/2-ton Metro Ace and the 2-ton Metro Boss. The Metro Ace was offered with wheelbases of 101 inches or 125 inches, while the Boss was built with these wheelbases and also with a 157-inch wheelbase. The Ace used Studebaker's 75 hp six-cylinder engine but the Boss was powered by an 80 hp Waukesha six-cylinder powerplant. Timken axles were used throughout on both models. Access to the cylinder head was from inside the cab.

1936 STUDEBAKER 2M657 FURNITURE VAN   A&A

1937 STUDEBAKER EDWARDS BODY SPECIAL   OCW

By the time Studebaker displayed its vehicles at the Second Annual Show of the New Jersey Motor Truck Association in October of that year, the Boss was rated at 2- to 3-ton capacity. The "Metro" name had already been registered as a trademark by the Metropolitan Body Company of Bridgeport, Connecticut, so Studebaker adopted "Cab-Forward" and the conventionals were called "Standard." Studebaker's exclusive Hill Holder was gradually introduced in all trucks. Total truck sales for 1936 amounted to 3,300 units. For 1937, sales shot up to 5,100, then again dipped to 2,000 for the recession year of 1938.

Studebaker's Coupe Express was built between 1937 and 1939. This was a light truck first based on the Dictator passenger car series. When the Dictator name was dropped for 1938, partly due to the political climate in Europe, the Coupe Express for 1938 and 1939 was based on the Commander series. The entire front of the vehicle shared its sheet metal and mechanical components with its related passenger car, much as the Chevrolet El Camino and Ford Ranchero did two decades later.

An 86 hp version of the Studebaker Big Six powered the Coupe Express in 1937. It was uprated to 90 hp for 1938 but wheelbase remained the same at 116 inches. The Coupe Express sold for $647 in 1937, which was about $175 more than a Ford pickup. About 3,000 Coupe Express light trucks were sold for that year, with sales dropping to one-third that for each of the two following years. Hercules engines were adopted for the heavier trucks in 1937 and a 68 hp Hercules diesel engine was used by 1938 in the 3-ton Studebaker trucks. Special refrigerated cab-forward Model K15M-01 vans were available by 1938, as were K series truck tractors with integral sleepers.

1937 STUDEBAKER COUPE EXPRESS   A&A

1937 STUDEBAKER J2SMB SUPERIOR BUS   A&A

Aside from the Coupe Express, from 1935 to 1941 truck styling was independent of the passenger car line. After dropping the Cab-Forward series in 1940, for 1941 Studebaker began building its M series trucks and the M3 was another attempt at entering the pickup market. The Waukesha engine was rated up to 106 hp but with the advent of the M series, Studebaker went back to using only its own engines, which were based on the Champion and Commander six-cylinder units, the latter being rated at 94 hp. Hydrovac brakes and two-speed rear axles were available in most of the heavier Studebaker trucks before World War II. Wheelbases were up to 195 inches for use with 18-foot bodies. The company also produced cab-forward-type buses when the COE trucks were introduced.

1938 STUDEBAKER K-15 VAN   OCW

For Lend Lease and World War II production, Studebaker built nearly 200,000 6x4 and 6x6 2-1/2-ton trucks. However, nearly all of these were again powered by Hercules engines. A light, full tracked vehicle called the Weasel was powered by the Champion six-cylinder engine and was produced as an amphibious version. The Champion engine was used in the pickup and 1-1/2-ton light truck. Thousands of Studebaker 6x4 and 6x6 trucks were shipped to the U.S.S.R., and most of the Russian Army during World War II was mobilized by Studebaker and GMC. Having major design problems with the ZIL trucks after World War II, the U.S.S.R. brought back thousands of 1940s vintage Studebaker trucks and rebuilt them for military use during the 1950s.

1939 STUDEBAKER K-5 PICKUP   **A&A**

1939 STUDEBAKER K-10 1-TON CUSTOM PANEL   **MROZ**

1941 STUDEBAKER M15 VAN   **A&A**

1941 STUDEBAKER 6X6 ARMY TRUCK   **OCW**

1946 STUDEBAKER M16-52 HEAVY-DUTY STAKE BED   **OCW**

1947 STUDEBAKER MAIL TRUCK VAN   **A&A**

In the United States, the M series was continued exclusively after World War II until 1948. In 1946, Studebaker trucks were available in 1/2-, 1- and 1-1/2-ton sizes with four-speed transmissions and overdrive optional with the 1/2-ton Coupe Express. Highway tractors had a 24,000-pound GVW rating and the M16 was used often as a tanker. The 1945 civilian M series was really a warmed-over 1941 design. Production reached 67,000 trucks per year in the first three postwar years. By 1948, 3/4-ton and 2-ton trucks were also available from Studebaker in addition to the range from 1946.

1950 STUDEBAKER R15 STAKE BED   **A&A**

Studebaker introduced its modernized and restyled R2 series in 1949 but these were still powered by a side-valve six-cylinder engine. Pickups were available in 1/2-, 3/4- and 1-ton capacities with up to eight-foot beds for the latter vehicle type. Studebaker produced 1-1/2-ton and 2-ton trucks and showed a variety of bodies that included the grain-stock rack, closed van, three-cubic yard dump bed, 12-foot platform, refrigeration van, tanker and bottler's body. As a single rear axle tanker, Model 2R16 was rated up to 14,000 pounds GVW. Overdrive and automatic transmissions were available in light trucks beginning in 1950.

1954 STUDEBAKER 2-1/2-TON 4X4 ARMY TRUCK   OCW

By 1954, Studebaker introduced a short-stroke V-8 engine for its trucks, having brought its V-8 for the Commander series in 1952. The essential design remained unchanged, although fender and grille styling changes were an attempt to keep up with the times. Studebaker's merger with Packard in 1955 placed the combined output in fourth place among U.S. auto and truck producers. The Scotsman pickup sold well during the 1950s. Studebaker used the name Transtar for its heavier trucks starting in 1956.

1957 STUDEBAKER 2-TON TRANSTAR   NAHC

1957 STUDEBAKER 3E11 BREAD VAN   OCW

For 1958, the Studebaker truck V-8 was rated at 182 hp. Hydrovac brakes were standard on the heaviest models and a five-speed transmission was optional. Studebaker offered a 1/2-ton 4x4 and the Scotsman was advertised as "America's Lowest-Priced Pick-

up! Only $1,595." There was a car-based light panel truck with independent front suspension. The following year, the Scotsman was available with a V-8 engine and automatic transmission.

1961 STUDEBAKER DETROIT DIESEL TRUCK TRACTOR   KP

1963 STUDEBAKER MODEL 8E40 TRANSTAR MILITARY   KP

In 1959, Studebaker introduced its Lark Series, which was used also to create the new Champ pickup by June of 1960. Studebaker still offered 1-ton and 2-ton trucks that year. Packard disappeared altogether after 1958. Studebaker manufactured vehicles in the United States only through 1964. From 1957 through 1963, new Studebaker yearly truck registrations were between 5,000 and 6,000. In the last year of U.S. production, that number dipped to 1,539. Studebaker continued building motor vehicles for only two more years at its Canadian plant. One of the last development projects finished by Studebaker was a "squareish" COE pickup truck, which never had a chance to go into production.

STURGIS 1900-1905 — John Philip Erie and Samuel D. Sturgis formed a partnership in Los Angeles, California, and experimented with electric- and gasoline-powered cars beginning in 1897. At the turn of the century, Erie returned to the East Coast and John Sturgis, with his brother William Sturgis, switched to building mostly gasoline-powered trucks. Their first vehicle was one of the heaviest built in the world at that time. The Sturgis truck had a 5-ton capacity and could pull a trailer with an additional five tons of cargo.

The vehicle was powered by a large 40 hp four-cylinder horizontally-opposed engine mounted amidships under the bed, which had friction clutches in conjunction with a type of transaxle. The forward-control design involved having the driver directly over the front axle and using a vertical steering column. Maximum speed was 6 mph. It is not certain whether the Sturgis truck was built in more than a few examples. One truck was known to have been bought by W.H. Manchester and used between Los Angeles and Pomona and, according to the *Standard Catalog of American Cars* by Beverly Rae Kimes, a photo depicts one of the Sturgis trucks in 1905. The time of manufacture has not been established beyond this evidence.

1924 STUTZ PUMPER/LADDER FIRE TRUCK   RNE

STUTZ 1919-1940 — The Stutz Fire Engine Company of Indianapolis, Indiana, operated from 1919 until 1928. This company was "only related through Harry Stutz" to the Stutz Motor Car Company, which existed from 1911 until 1935. The Stutz cars were well known for collecting racing trophies.

The Stutz fire engines were better known for their four-cylinder and six-cylinder Wisconsin engines and that they were built in various configurations including ladder, pumper and combination trucks. Stutz specialized in fire apparatus and even during the peak years of sales success the company did not list its trucks in chassis form on the market.

Stutz fire engines were successful and gained prestige to the point that fire companies as far as Tokyo, Japan, purchased its vehicles by 1926. That year, Stutz also began using its own 175 hp six-cylinder engine.

By 1931, the Stutz Fire Engine Company had been reorganized due to the Great Depression and Harry Stutz lost control of the company. In 1934, the Stutz Motor Car Company also went into financial crisis. The last attempt to salvage it was the company's entering into the production of the Pak-Age-Car, the sister company's only apparent commercial vehicle venture. Through Harry Stutz, the two companies became more intertwined nearer their demise. But the New Stutz Fire Engine Company, as it was incorporated, which moved to Hartford, Indiana, in 1932, would continue to stay in business and build one of the first American diesel-powered fire engines using a Cummins engine in 1939. The last Stutz fire engine was built in 1940.

SUBURBAN 1912-1913 — The Suburban Truck Company of Philadelphia, Pennsylvania, built a 1-1/2-ton truck powered by a 29 hp four-cylinder engine with disc clutch and worm-drive for 1912. Advertisements quoted a chassis price of $2,500 but how many were actually built is in doubt. For 1913, a 2-ton model was listed for $3,000. It was also powered by a four-cylinder engine using a cone clutch and shaft drive.

SULLIVAN 1910-1923 — The Sullivan Motor Car Company of Rochester, New York (not related to the Sullivan Manufacturing Company of St. Louis, Missouri), built light delivery wagons using a 16 hp two-cylinder horizontally-opposed engine with a two-speed planetary transmission and double chain drive. The vehicle had solid rubber tires and an 800-pound capacity.

1914 SULLIVAN MODEL 51 PLATFORM STAKE   OCW

In 1912, the Sullivan company introduced 1/2-ton and 3/4-ton models, also using solid rubber tires and chain drive. By 1914, there was also a 1-ton truck and in 1916, a 2-ton model was added to the line powered by four-cylinder Buda engines. Brown-Lipe transmissions and Timken worm-drive were also used. Sullivan's trucks used this design until 1923, when the company went out of business.

1918 SULLIVAN 2-TON TANKER   RD

SULTAN 1904-1912 — The Sultan Motor and Car Company was located in New York City. The company was formed in 1904 by Henri de Buren whose chief engineer was Nelson Bliss. The first vehicles were taxicabs, which were manufactured for Sultan by the Elektron Manufacturing Company of Springfield, Massachusetts. By 1908, Sultan went into private car production but it was the Otis Elevator Company that manufactured the vehicles. The vehicles were powered by a four-cylinder gasoline engine, not electric motors as might be surmised. Sultan also produced a 2-ton truck powered by a 32 hp four-cylinder engine and used a three-speed transmission. It had a 116-inch wheelbase and was priced at $3,000.

There was also a lighter Series 800 commercial vehicle with a 15 hp four-cylinder engine using a cone leather-faced clutch, three-speed transmission and shaft drive. Wheelbase was 98 inches and the price was $2,000. The latter appeared to have the same exact mechanical specifications as the Sultan passenger cars of 1910-1912.

SUPER-TRACTION see WISCONSIN

SUPER TRUCK 1919-1936 — The O'Connell Motor Truck Company of Waukegan, Illinois, built the Super Truck, whose primary difference from other trucks was in that the driver's seat pivoted around the steering column providing travel in either direction. The Super Two Way Drive chassis were available from 2-1/2-ton to 7-1/2-ton capacity.

By 1925, the 2-1/2-ton Model 50 was powered by a 25.6 hp four-cylinder Wisconsin TAU engine and used a Fuller transmission and Sheldon front and rear axles. Wheelbase was 156 inches and chassis price was $3,300. Pneumatic tires were optional at extra cost. The 3-ton Model 60-D had a shorter 126-inch wheelbase but was powered by the larger 28.9 hp four-cylinder Wisconsin VAU engine. Front axle was from Sheldon and rear axle was made by Wisconsin. Next up was the 3-1/2-ton Model 70 with 164-inch wheelbase with a chassis price tag of $4,100. It was powered by a Wisconsin UAU engine. The heaviest Super Truck listed that year was the 5-ton Model 100, which had a Wisconsin RAU engine.

The later models had a transmission built by O'Connell and used a large cast iron radiator. The only sheet metal on the vehicle consisted of a short hood. Other conventional trucks up to 7-ton capacity were built powered by four-cylinder Wisconsin engines. After 1928, six-cylinder Wisconsin engines were used along with Fuller transmissions and Timken and Sheldon axles.

SUPERIOR 1911-1913 — The Superior Motor Car Company of Detroit, Michigan, built an enclosed delivery van powered by a 25 hp water-cooled four-cylinder engine. A three-speed transmission was used with double chain drive. The vehicle had a wheelbase of 110-inches, solid rubber tires and a 1,200-pound capacity. With factory body, the Superior van was priced at $1,700.

SUPERIOR 1912-1914 — The F.G. Clark Company of Lansing, Michigan, built the Superior Model A, which was a 1-ton express truck that had a four-cylinder engine, three-speed transmission, double chain drive and a wheelbase of 110 inches. Chassis weight was given as 2,500 pounds. With solid rubber tires the truck cost $1,700.

1939 SUPERIOR MODEL 411   **MBS**

SUPERIOR 1938-1948 — The Superior Coach Corporation of Lima, Ohio, began by building bus bodies in 1923 for Garford of Lima. The company became known as Superior in 1930. In 1931, Superior pioneered one of the first all-steel school bus bodies with safety glass in all windows. The first complete bus, which had a V-8 engine mounted in the rear, was dubbed the Avenue and appeared in 1938. The long distance version of the Avenue was named the Rocket. With an interruption of production during World War II, after the war a slightly redesigned version of the transit bus was put into production. The largest fleet of Superior buses numbering 14 was in Lima, Ohio.

1974 SUTPHEN AERIAL TOWER FIRE ENGINE   **EK**

SUTPHEN 1967 to date — Sutphen originally started building fire apparatus in 1890. The Sutphen Fire Equipment Company has been located in Amlin, Ohio, since its relatively recent entry into complete vehicle production in 1967. The Sutphen aerial tower fire engine was originally built on commercial chassis in 1963 but by 1967, the company began building its own chassis. The first complete aerial tower fire engines used a custom three-axle chassis and a Cincinnati cab. Cummins and Detroit Diesel engines were available, although most of the engines were the latter from 265 hp to 525 hp. An experimental turbine-powered 2,000 gpm pumper was built in 1972 but it did not go into production. The engine was a Ford 3600 gas turbine. Sutphen continued to build custom fire apparatus throughout the 1980s using the same basic design.

Newly designed custom chassis and fire engines have been produced to date by Sutphen. The company expanded its offices to Monticello, New York, and by the 1990s, offered a 105-foot tractor-trailer whose ladder telescoped from a 55-foot collapsed section, one of the shortest in the industry. A 104-foot rigid truck was also available with Cummins or Detroit Diesel engine and Allison automatic transmission. This fire truck has featured a 94-inch wide aluminum four-door cab and a stainless steel apparatus body. A Hale pump has been optional along with a 300/500 gallon composite laminate booster tank. Aircraft huck bolts have been

used instead of welds. Another two-axle fire truck used a platform and patented box ladder with up to 75-foot reach. Sutphen fire trucks have been offered with wheelbases from 166 inches to 210 inches with fixed or tilt enclosed cabs through 1995. The company's slogan has been "Custom Built With Family Pride."

1995 SUTPHEN FIRE ENGINE   **SUTPHEN**

1986 SWEEPLITE UTILITY DUMPSTER   **EK**

SWEEPLITE 1986 — The American Sweeping Service marketed this commercial vehicle in Clearwater, Florida. It was powered by a John Deere four-cylinder diesel engine and used a half-cab design. The vehicle was used for street cleaning and also had a hydraulically-operated dump box.

1903 SYNNESTVEDT ELECTRIC DELIVERY WAGON   **MROZ**

1903 SYNNESTVEDT PASSENGER BUS   RD

SYNNESTVEDT 1903-1907 — The Synnestvedt Machine Company was located in Pittsburgh, Pennsylvania. Paul Synnestvedt was a patent attorney there and his business consisted of patent law application. His first vehicle was an electric stanhope that appeared in 1903 -- 10 years after Synnestvedt began experimenting with the idea of an electric car. The first commercial vehicles were battery-powered electric vans with wheel steering and double chain drive. The same chassis was used to build light buses. The Synnestvedt bus weighed 3,500 pounds with batteries and had a top speed of 15 mph. The vans were 200 pounds lighter and featured a glass windshield. Final drive was by chain.

Passenger car production ended in 1905 but commercial vehicles continued to be built for another two years. This included the double chain drive 3-ton capacity Type F and the 5-ton capacity Type D, the latter whose chassis weight was also five tons. The Type D, which was priced at $4,500, had a wheelbase of 124 inches and a track of 68 inches. The Type F had a wheelbase of 87 inches and a track of 56 inches.

T

T

TARRYTOWN 1914 — The Tarrytown Motor Company built a box body delivery van based on a cyclecar with a 1/4-ton capacity. It was priced at $400.

TAYLOR 1917-1918 — The Taylor Motor Truck Company of Fremont, Ohio, was the successor to the H.G. Burford Company, also located in Fremont. Like the Burford vehicles, Taylor assembled its trucks from purchased parts including four-cylinder Continental engines, Covert transmissions and Timken worm-drive rear axles. The Taylor trucks were available in 1-, 1-1/2-, 2-1/2-, 3-1/2- and 5-ton capacity. The lightest truck had a wheelbase of 130 inches and the heaviest had a 160-inch wheelbase. All models used the same make components.

TAYLOR-DUNN 1949 to date — Taylor-Dunn started out building light electric off-highway commercial vehicles primarily intended for government, warehouse and factory yard use. For nearly four decades, Taylor-Dunn's three-wheel and four-wheel electric-powered vehicles competed with those of Cushman and Nordskog and were similar. The company began in Anaheim, California. The early vehicles consisted of the Model B three-wheel and four-wheel 1-ton capacity burden carriers, which complied with MIL Spec 3997-A. The Model C was a three-wheel vehicle capable of towing five tons.

The three-wheel Model E tractors had a 1,000-pound drawbar pull and there was also a four-wheel Model P with a 2,000-pound drawbar pull. The Model R was a three-wheel or four-wheel pickup and the Model M was a personnel and luggage carrier. Automotive differentials were used in Taylor-Dunn vehicles and the company advertised its electric vehicles for their "silent operation…elimination of fatigue-causing noise…clean and odorless…no need to ventilate buildings or tunnels." Diamond plate was used almost entirely throughout the vehicle bodies.

1991 TAYLOR-DUNN AIRCRAFT TENDER   **T-D**

The manufacturer remained located in Anaheim, California, after its acquisition by Arthur J. Goodwin and Milton L. Sneller in 1990. Under the new ownership, none of the 200 employees were laid off during the economic recession that took place in the early 1990s.

By 1991, when Cushman entered the market for a zero-emission three-wheel on-road electric commercial vehicle, Taylor-Dunn focused on the off-highway market with its ElecTruk. Taylor-Dunn advertised this electric vehicle as a "full-sized" new truck with a 3/4-ton capacity. At a speed of 32 mph, it had a range of 30 miles. The truck used 12 six-volt deep-cycle lead-acid batteries giving a 72-volt operating system. A 20 hp GE motor was used with a solid

state controller and hydraulic brakes. The ElecTruk's base price was $15,000. General applications included airports, transport and processing facilities, resorts, schools and universities, military bases and other government institutions. By 1995, Mexico City bought approximately 500 ElecTruks in an effort to curb air pollution.

1993 TAYLOR-DUNN ELECTRUK   **T-D**

In addition to the ElecTruk, Taylor-Dunn has produced the electric Loadmaster, electric and gasoline Truckmaster, electric Model B Series with up to 5,000-pound capacity, gasoline Cargomaster with up to 6,400-pound capacity, electric Mule, electric and gasoline Roadmaster, electric Stepsaver, electric Towmaster with a 20,000-pound tow capacity, Pullmaster with up to 30,000-pound tow capacity as well as the Stockchaser, Aristocrat fiberglass truck and Model E electric Tractor with 15,000-pound capacity.

For 1996, Taylor-Dunn has the factory narrow-aisle C4-15 cargo vehicle priced at $6,985. Another vehicle introduced for the mid-1990s has been the Taylortruck electric burden carrier with a load capacity of 3,000 pounds. Operating costs have been claimed to be 10 cents per mile, about half that of similar gasoline-powered vehicles. Options include hydraulic dump bed, metal boxes and tool cabinets. Another vehicle with similar applications has been introduced as the MX600 mobile repair shop that includes a workbench and a five-drawer toolbox for fast repairs in a wide variety of industrial and military environments.

1962 TECHNO CONTAINER TRUCK   **TECHNO**

TECHNO 1962 — The Techno Truck Company of Cleveland, Ohio, was a short-lived effort to create a refuse container vehicle using a novel concept that involved converting an International B170 short conventional truck to front-wheel drive. The Techno truck did not have a standard body to the rear of the cab. Rather, the entire back section was a framework for loading and unloading a large container that could be lowered to the ground by means of a hydraulic-operated mechanism.

The Techno design also incorporated two or three smaller containers. Open lumber or pipe carriers were also available. Planned production included 4-, 5-, 6- and 8-ton versions, but only a 6-ton truck was built, and after some initial testing, the concept was dropped. However, this experiment served as a test bed for other more simplified container trucks that are used to date.

T.E.C.O. 1948 — The Tibbets Engineering Company of Highland, Illinois, built only three trucks for a local quarry. Keith Tibbets was the son-in-law of C.J. Hug and had been vice-president and general manager of the Hug company, which built trucks from 1922 to 1942. The three T.E.C.O. trucks were built from leftover Hug parts and therefore have the same basic specifications as the last 7-1/2-ton Hug truck model built in the early 1940s.

TEC-TRUK 1920-1921 — This vehicle was built by the Terminal Engineering Company of New York City. It was a battery-powered truck tractor used in conjunction with trailers with up to 2-1/2-ton capacity.

1912 TEEL-WOODWORTH 3-TON   **MROZ**

TEEL-WOODWORTH 1912-1913 — The Teel Manufacturing Company was located in Medford, Massachusetts, hence its vehicles have also been listed as Teel-Medford. The Teel company had been in business for nearly a century building horsedrawn vehicles prior to fabricating trucks, which were exhibited in March 1912 at the Boston Commercial Motor Vehicle Association Show, where some 60 manufacturers showed their trucks.

The first Teel-Woodworth vehicles shown were two 3-ton trucks and one 3-ton chassis. Specifications included a 30 hp four-cylinder Continental engine, Cotta transmission, Hele-Shaw 28-disc clutch, Timken front and rear axles and jackshaft as well as Ross steering. Cooling was by centrifugal pump using a Mayo radiator. Solid rubber tires were 36x5 front and 36x4 duals in the rear. Dash and taillamps were lighted by battery. Wheelbase was 125 inches and suspension was by half-elliptic springs.

A review of the Teel-Woodworth trucks in the April 1912 issue of *The Motor Truck* mentioned the fact that Teel Manufacturing was already in the business of building "high grade automobile equipment... All the parts are jigged to ensure perfect interchangeability, these being produced by one of the best known of the fine machine builders." However, despite such high praise, Teel-Woodworth trucks did not continue production for more than a year. Announcements for the manufacture of passenger cars ended with similarly curtailed results.

TELEDYNE 1970-1977 — Teledyne Continental entered its own prototype of the HUMMV. It was powered by a 140 hp inline six-cylinder engine with a three-speed automatic transmission and featured independent torsion bar suspension. Cross-country it had a payload of 2,500 pounds and its height could be reduced to 50 inches, although with some sacrifice in ground clearance. Out of several prototypes submitted, AM General got the contract to build the Hummer, which has been in production to date.

In 1977, Teledyne introduced Cheetah, a full-time 4x4 powered by a 360-cubic inch Chrysler V-8 with a three-speed automatic. It had a top speed of 90 mph and a cruising range of 340 miles. These were originally designed and marketed by Lamborghini. The vehicle used 34.5x14 tires and had a self-contained winch.

TEMPLETON-DUBRIE 1910 — The Templeton-DuBrie Car Company was a Detroit, Michigan, builder of cars and light trucks for only one year. The company's reported production of up to 20 vehicles has been a total mystery, since no dealerships carried the line at that time. Beside limited passenger car production, a truck was also listed with a two-cycle two-cylinder engine for 1910.

1975 TEREX TITAN 350-TON DUMP TRUCK   **GMC**

1975 TEREX R-17 17-TON DUMP TRUCK   **GMC**

TEREX 1973 to date — After selling Euclid to White, the General Motors Scotland division continued to build trucks overseas. It was in 1973 that Terex (Latin for Earth King) began building large dump trucks in Hudson, Ohio. These ranged from 17-ton to 150-ton capacity and were powered by Cummins and Detroit Diesel engines. In 1974, the Terex Titan was introduced, which had a capacity of 350 tons. It was powered by a 3300 hp GM diesel locomotive engine and electric drive at the rear wheels. Three years later, the largest capacity Terex truck was a 550-ton. Terex has built trucks and equipment in Australia, Brazil, Canada, India, Luxemburg, Scotland and South Africa.

Until 1980, Terex was a division of General Motors. The division was formed after GM sold its Euclid truck manufacturing to White. Although the home offices remained in Hudson, Ohio, three years later Terex was a part of the German IBH group. By 1984, the Terex 33-09 was powered by a turbocharged 665 hp Detroit Diesel 16V-71T V-16. Transmission was an Allison CLBT-6061 6F 1R. The 22-ton Model 33-03B was powered by the smaller 228 hp 6V-71N but larger engines, such as the 1200 hp 12V-149TI, were used in the 130-ton Model 33-14. The bottom-dump articulated coal hauler was designated as the Model 33-14.

In 1988, Terex purchased the assets of Unit Rig, which included Dart and Lectra Haul trucks. Unit Rig became a Division of Terex, whose truck line by this name includes five models of rigid trucks, three articulated dump trucks and four variants. The lightest rigid dump truck was designated as the 3305B with a 34-ton capacity. Next up was the Model 3307 with 49.5-ton capacity. The 55-ton Model 3308E, 66-ton Model 3310E and 94-ton Model 3311E have all been two-axle trucks. The lightest truck has been powered by a 329 hp (net) engine and the Model 3311E has been powered by a 975 hp (net) engine.

1980 TEREX 33-15B   GMC

1981 TEREX 34-11C COAL HAULER   GMC

The three articulated trucks consisted of the 25-ton Model 2566B 6x6 with 240 hp engine, 30-ton Model 3066 6x6 with 258 hp engine and the 40-ton Model 4066B 6x6 with 375 hp (net) engine. Terex has also built a 39-cubic yard Coal Truck, Tipping Frame truck for 20-foot container, Container Transporter for 30-foot refuse containers and a Load Handler with self-loading and unloading systems.

1995 TEREX 3310 RIGID DUMP TRUCK   UNIT RIG

In addition to the aforementioned trucks, for 1996, Terex has built five models of Wheeled Loaders up to 30-ton capacity and five models of Motor Scrapers, the largest being the TS46C Coal Scraper with tractor axle suspension and 740 hp (net) engine.

Many of these trucks have been built in Scotland but main offices have been located in Tulsa, Oklahoma. Trucks built to date have listed capacities in British tonnes -- add 10 percent to obtain U.S. tons.

1995 TEREX 3066 ARTICULATED DUMP TRUCK   UNIRIG

1934 TERRAPLANE PICKUP   RD

1937 TERRAPLANE 8058 FUNERAL COACH   KP

TERRAPLANE 1933-1937 — The Terraplane began in 1932 as a model of the Essex built by Hudson. By 1933, Hudson began using the Terraplane chassis to build pickups and the following year, only the name Terraplane was used. By 1935, Terraplane was available as a 3/4-ton chassis for $430, chassis and cab for $515, pickup for $545, utility coach for $565 and sedan delivery for $675. Wheelbase was 112 inches. For 1936, the same 21.6 hp six-cylinder engine was used but the wheelbase was increased by three inches and prices were up by $15. For 1937, the standard Terraplane chassis was 117 inches but there was also the Big Boy series with 124-inch wheelbase. In addition to the bodies mentioned, Terraplane was also built as a station wagon with wood sides and as a Utility Coupe Pickup with a box that slid out from the trunk. The 3/4-ton Big Boy Custom Sedan Delivery was up to $880. After 1938, the Terraplane name was dropped entirely, including passenger car production, but Hudson continued to build light commercial vehicles until 1947. See HUDSON.

1937 TERRAPLANE SERIES 71 TAXI   KP

1937 TERRAPLANE 3/4-TON CUSTOM PANEL DELIVERY   RD

1919 TEXAN MODEL TK   MROZ

TEXAN 1918-1922 — The Texas Motor Car Association was organized in 1917 by H.J. Wells and F.E. Crotto in Fort Worth, Texas. One aspect of the organization was that no stockholder could own more than $500 worth of shares. The first vehicle listed for this make was the Model A-36 Light Delivery for $1,100 and the Model A-36 Oil Field Special for $1,150. The Model TK had the same 19.6 hp four-cylinder engine but was rated as a 1-ton. Chassis and cab were listed for $1,525.

For 1920, the Texan was listed as a Model D-38 Delivery, with pneumatic tires, for $1,395 and the Model C-38 Light Oil Field Special for $1,440. The Model TK was listed with the same price but noted pneumatic tires as standard equipment.

For 1920, the company also began building passenger cars and all vehicles had large tires "In Texas Oil Fields, Where the goin' is rough." J.C. Vernon became president and William Ginnuth vice-president. Receivership was announced by the end of the year. The company was financially floated to complete the 100 unfinished vehicles and then the factory was sold to the Moco Monkey Grip Rubber Company, boot and patch manufacturers.

TEXTRON see E-Z-GO

THOMAS 1905-1911 — The E.R. Thomas Motor Company was located in Buffalo, New York. Erwin Ross Thomas established this company and the Buffalo Automobile & Auto-Bi Company in 1902, merging them for 1903. Up to that time, the company had been selling Buffalo cars with engines supplied by Thomas. Thomas became well known after winning the New York to Paris race of 1908. The company also built taxicabs, hence it is listed as a commercial vehicle manufacturer. The taxi had its own 100-inch wheelbase chassis and was powered by a 16 hp four-cylinder engine. By 1910, the Model R taxi had a 123-inch wheelbase and was priced at $4,000. Passenger cars had longer wheelbases and cost between $4,100 and $7,500 for 1910. Taxi production ceased after 1911 but the company continued to build luxury cars as late as 1918.

THOMAS 1906-1908 — The Thomas Wagon Company of Vernon, New York, built motorized wagons in the literal sense. What would otherwise be a horsedrawn wagon was fitted with a two-cylinder air-cooled engine. The wagon used a patented steering knuckle on its front axle. Wheel steering, friction transmission and dual chain drive were featured. In 1907, a 3-ton model with 180-inch wheelbase was priced at $1,500. The truck featured an open box body that was easily removable for inspection of the engine and chassis. For 1908, the company moved to Lititz, Pennsylvania. The company appears to have ceased motorized production and continued to build horsedrawn wagons until 1910.

THOMAS 1916-1917 — The Thomas Auto Truck Company was located in New York City. Charles K. Thomas was the organizer who had been vice-president of the Federal Motor Truck Company. Thomas built a 2-ton model truck powered by a four-cylinder Buda engine. For 1917, the company listed the 2-1/2-ton Model 40 for $2,700 and the 3-1/2-ton Model 60 for $3,250.

Thomas trucks featured Covert-Brown-Lipe three-speed transmissions and Timken-David-Brown worm-drive rear axles. Before production ceased, the company was incorporated as Consolidated Motors.

THOMPSON 1901-1907 — The Thompson Auto Company was located in Olneyville, Rhode Island, although Providence has also been listed as the company's location. J.P. Thompson was the organizer of the venture, which was intended for the purpose of building "delivery wagons, trucks and buses." Most of the vehicles were powered by a 10 hp Fitzheney steam engine and a Tonkin dry plate boiler. A single roller chain was used for the drive mechanism. A reach frame was used with solid rubber tires and the wheelbase was 104 inches. The Thompson Steam Wagonette, which seated up to 10 passengers, was successful. This was called the Model B and had a 104-inch wheelbase. It was priced at $2,200. A delivery wagon and three 16-passenger buses were sold to Puerto Rico.

1929 THORNE GAS-ELECTRIC DELIVERY VAN   RD

THORNE 1929-1938 — The Thorne Motor Corporation began in Chicago, Illinois, and by 1929, had established production of multi-stop delivery vans rated at 1-1/2 tons, which competed with Divco and Pak-Age-Car. The first design used an 18 hp four-cylinder Continental engine that drove a generator that powered a 90-volt electric motor located just ahead of the rear axle. Hydraulic four-wheel brakes were used and the driver was in a standing position. By 1932, a 24.02 hp four-cylinder Continental engine was used, which was 2-1/2 hp higher than the earlier engine. However, the hybrid gasoline-electric design was not successful and the company faded out by 1938.

THREE POINT 1917-1924 — The Three Point Truck Corporation was actually a subsidiary of the New York Air Brake Company of Watertown, New York. The Three Point vehicle had a pivot-type front axle and radius-rod design intended to eliminate frame distortion. The radiator was copied from Rolls-Royce and fenders were flat military style.

For 1917, Three Point listed the 6-ton Model A-10 (short) and 6-ton Model A-13 (long), both powered by a 28.9 hp four-cylinder Buda engine. List price was $3,800. The same models were listed through 1921 but the prices had risen to $4,650. After 1922, only the Model A-13 was available. Production appears to have ended in 1924, although some vehicles may have been assembled after that.

1914 TIFFIN COVERED FLAREBOARD OCW

1914 TIFFIN MODEL A PLATFORM STAKE OCW

TIFFIN 1913-1923 — The Tiffin Wagon Works of Tiffin, Ohio, began by building 1,200-pound and 2-ton capacity commercial vehicles. By 1916, the company listed the 3/4-ton Model A, 1-ton Model G, 2-ton Model M, 5-ton Model S and 6-ton Model SW. Prices ranged from $1,600 to $4,650. Buda four-cylinder engines were used with a three-speed transmission and double chain drive. Electric starting and lighting were standard on the light Tiffin trucks. By 1921, the company listed the 1-1/2-ton Model GW with a 27.23 hp engine (35 brake hp), 2-1/2-ton Model MW with the same engine, 3-1/2-ton Model PW with a 32.4 hp engine (42 brake hp), 5-ton Model TW with a 36.1 hp engine (55 brake hp) and the 6-ton Model UW with the same engine as the previous vehicle. By this time, the postwar recession had seriously affected the company's business and production fell. Only the two largest capacity trucks were offered in the last two years.

TIGER 1914-1915 — The Automobile Cyclecar Company of Detroit, Michigan, built a delivery version of its cyclecar. The company was started by William Andrew de Schaum, who had earlier built

the de Schaum and the Suburban cars. The Tiger was powered by a 12 hp four-cylinder water-cooled Farmer engine, three-speed sliding gear transmission and shaft drive. The Model D was the parcel delivery version among two other passenger versions. The delivery vehicle was priced at $300. In February of 1915, William de Schaum died and along with him died his company.

1911 TITAN TAXICAB RD

TITAN 1911 — The Central Motor Company of Detroit, Michigan, was a division of the US Motor Company. The Titan taxi was built on a Brush chassis, which included a wood frame and coil springs on all four corners. It was powered by a one-cylinder water-cooled engine and used a planetary transmission with double chain drive. Wheelbase was 80 inches.

TITAN 1916-1917 — The American Machine Company of Newark, Delaware, built a steam-powered truck. It was rated at 2-1/2-ton capacity. The Model A had a 144-inch wheelbase and the chassis weight was 4,650 pounds. A two-cylinder steam engine with four-inch bore and five-inch stroke was directly attached to a Torbensen rear axle. The complete chassis price was $3,000. The truck was listed until 1920 but due to its lack of success, production appears to have been limited between 1916 and 1917 only.

1920 TITAN HE

TITAN 1917-1932 — The Titan Truck and Tractor Company started out by building 5-ton trucks in Milwaukee, Wisconsin. The Titan truck was powered by a four-cylinder engine and used a Titan four-speed constant-mesh transmission with internal gear final drive. Similar to Walker electric trucks, Titan used solid cast-steel disc wheels and solid rubber tires.

The company reorganized as the Titan Truck Company but remained in Milwaukee. The model range included 1-, 1-1/2-, 2-, 2-1/2- and 3-1/2-ton trucks, the latter with a price tag of $5,400. All of the models were powered by four-cylinder Buda engines. By

1927, the company's small production output dwindled and faded out, although according to some records, it is believed a few Titan trucks were assembled as late as 1932.

1995 TMC RTS TRANSIT BUS   **TMC**

TMC/NOVA 1975 to date — The Transportation Manufacturing Corporation, located in Roswell, New Mexico, was a subsidiary of Greyhound and built about 350 buses per year for its parent company. The buses have been identical to those with MCI escutcheons and TMC built Canadian Orion buses under license for use in the United States. In 1987, TMC acquired GM Coach.

After being purchased by Nova Bus Incorporated in 1994, TMC became a division of its parent company. Nova Bus has continued manufacturing three types of buses to date. The Low Floor model, which has had a floor 14-1/2 inches up from the ground, was designed with seating for up to 39 passengers, including tie-down positions. For 1996, plans have been made to lower the floor to 9-1/2 inches from the ground in order to shorten the ramp by half. The Low Floor bus has been offered with the 8.3 Cummins diesel or the Series 40 Detroit Diesel.

Nova's Classic bus design is the oldest of the three. This bus was designed with seating for up to 49 passengers, including tie-down positions. The 8.3 Cummins diesel and the Series 50 Detroit Diesel engine have been available for this model. Allison B400 five-speed or six-speed transmissions have been used with the Nova Classic and Low Floor buses.

Nova's TMC RTS bus design was an outgrowth of the GM Transbus, which was originally planned to be introduced in the early 1980s. Body structure has been composed of five-foot welded stainless steel modules. Engine choices have been Detroit Diesel Series 50, Cummins L-10, M-11 or C8.3 diesel engines and a natural gas engine. Allison ATEC or ZF Economat transmissions have been used for all of Nova's RTS Transit Buses with up to 45-passenger capacity. RTS buses have been equipped with ramps and wheelchair lifts complying with the Americans with Disabilities Act (ADA) and California Title 13 certification.

TOLEDO 1901 — This company started out as the American Bicycle Company in Toledo, Ohio. At the turn of the century, the company announced it would be going into the production of steam vehicles and Frederick Billings designed the first car, which was shown at the New York Automobile Show. At the show, the car was displayed as the Billings but the designer assigned all rights to the American Bicycle Company, which was immediately reorganized as the International Motor Car Company. The first two models were called the Toledo and the Westchester but the latter name was dropped.

The company built a truck using a paraffin-fueled horizontal cross-compound engine with piston valves and Stephenson link motion. Final drive was by internal gears. The truck's capacity was 2 tons and it was used at the company's factory until passenger car production stopped in 1903. It was not affiliated with at least two other commercial vehicle companies using the name International.

TOLEDO 1912-1913 — The Toledo Motor Truck Company of Toledo, Ohio, acquired the little known Rassel Motor Car Company in 1912 and began production at that factory. The forward-control Toledo truck design was not based on that of Rassel vehicles. The 1-ton Toledo Model A was powered by a water-cooled four-cylinder engine. Also, a three-speed transmission and double chain drive were used. The Model A with stake body was priced at $1,850. The 2-ton Model B, which had a longer 130-inch wheelbase, was priced at $2,600 with the same type of body. The company existed for only slightly over one year. This company was not affiliated with the earlier Toledo, Pope-Toledo and Apperson-Toledo companies.

1918 TONFORD   **RD**

TONFORD 1917-1919 — Tonford trucks were built by the Detroit Truck Company in Detroit, Michigan, for a brief period. The vehicles' specifications are lacking, although it is known that both chain drive and internal gear drive were available. Tonfords were conventional trucks up to 3-ton capacity. At the beginning of 1918, the company advertised "For the first time in months we are now in a position to take on a few more energetic, dependable dealers... We have been too busy filling orders to cover the field." This appears to have been a slight exaggeration. For the following year, Tonford was not listed any longer in most directories. By the time the post-war recession took place, the company had faded out entirely.

1907 TORBENSEN DELIVERY WAGON   **LIAM**

TORBENSEN 1906-1911 — The V.V. Torbensen Company started out in 1901 in Newark, New Jersey. It was established by Viggo V. Torbensen, who had arrived in the United States from Denmark.

After moving to Bloomfield, New Jersey, he changed the name of his business to the Torbensen Motor Car Company and began producing passenger cars.

By 1906, Torbensen began building light commercial vehicles as well. The first was a small forward-control delivery van powered by a 14 hp two-stroke air-cooled three-cylinder engine. It was rated at 3/4-ton capacity. The second version of the van used a similar two-cylinder engine and planetary transmission with double chain drive. The wheelbase was 92 inches. Torbensen also established the Torbensen Gear Company, which went on to manufacture axles for cars and trucks for many years after vehicle manufacturing was suspended.

TOURAINE 1914 — With fresh capital, the Nance automobile was resurrected as the Touraine in Philadelphia, Pennsylvania. The company also produced a light truck called the Vim. Apparently, a Touraine truck was also offered for 1914 only at $550. The company switched to building Vim trucks after phasing out its passenger car production in 1916.

1907 TORBENSEN DELIVERY WAGON   LIAM

TOURIST 1902-1910 — The Auto Vehicle Company of Los Angeles, California, built passenger cars but also was involved in fabricating some fire engines and commercial trucks. The company was organized by William H. Burnham of Orange (County), Carroll S. Hartman of Pasadena and Willis D. Longyear of Ocean Park. The company hired Ralph B. Hain, a local machinist, and he designed a 6 hp one-cylinder prototype. This version did not succeed and Waldemar Hansen was hired to build a two-cylinder version, which went into production. Watt Moreland joined the company. Production reached 500 by 1905, and some of the vehicles included a hose and chemical truck for the City of Hollywood. Partly due to the lack of a Selden manufacturing license, the company had difficulty in obtaining parts and was bought out by the California Automobile Company in 1909. Vehicles under the name California and Tourist were built in 1910.

1915 TOWER 2-TON STAKE SIDE   MROZ

TOWER 1915-1923 — The Tower Motor Truck Company was located in Greenville, Michigan. The first model was a 2-ton capacity truck but in 1920, the model line consisted of 2-1/2-ton and 3-1/2-ton capacity vehicles that were powered by four-cylinder Continental engines. Transmissions were from Fuller and rear axles

were Timken worm-drive. The largest truck had a wheelbase of 165 inches and a price tag of $4,100. The company ceased operations by 1923.

1914 TRABOLD PANEL BODY   OCW

TRABOLD 1911-1932 — The Trabold Truck Manufacturing Company was located in Johnstown, Pennsylvania. Adam G. Trabold had started out experimenting with motorized vehicles in 1898. He built another vehicle in 1905 and established a dealership. By 1911, Trabold built a forward-control truck powered by a four-cylinder Buda engine. By 1913, Trabold trucks were of conventional design using Buda engines. After 1915, bevel gear drive was used in some models.

In 1922, the company was reorganized as the Trabold Motors Company of Johnstown. Worm-drive was adopted in 1923 and the company moved to Ferndale, Pennsylvania, in 1924. By 1925, Trabold was building approximately two trucks per week. These consisted of 1-1/2-ton and 2-1/2-ton models. In 1929, the company went through a financial crisis and production lasted through 1932 on a custom basis only. After 1932, the Trabold Company, back in Johnstown, built truck bodies until 1960.

TRACTOR 1912 — The Denlock Manufacturing Company built a 1-ton truck called the Tractor. It was priced at $1,200. The company was briefly located in Atlanta, Georgia.

TRADER see PEERLESS

1919 TRAFFIC 2-TON EXPRESS BODY   KP

1920 TRAFFIC 2-TON CHASSIS   HAYS

TRAFFIC 1918-1929 — The Traffic Motor Truck Corporation was located in St. Louis, Missouri. From the outset, Traffic trucks used four-cylinder Continental Red Seal engines, three-speed Covert transmissions and Russel internal gear drive. The 1920 2-ton Model C used a 22.5 hp four-cylinder Continental engine with Carter carburetor and Bosch ignition. The truck also featured a three-speed Covert transmission, shaft drive with Russel rear axle and steering gear built by Traffic. The 133-inch wheelbase Traffic truck was priced at $1,395 for 1920.

Up to 1925, the frame was combined into a front (and rear) bumper with semi-circular sections of channel steel. For 1925, Traffic trucks were available in three capacities: 1-1/2-, 2- and 3-ton. The 1-1/2-ton with 128-inch wheelbase used a 22.5 hp four-cylinder Continental N-4 engine with Carter carb and Bosch ignition. A Covert clutch and transmission were used along with a Russel rear axle. The front axle was built by Traffic, as was the steering gear and mechanism. Day wheels held 35x5 front and rear pneumatic tires. Chassis price was $1,750.

The 2-ton Model 4000C used the same engine and make of components but wheelbase was 132 inches and pneumatic tires were optional. Chassis price was listed as $1,695 -- less than the 1-1/2-ton model. The 3-ton Model 6000 had the same engine and make of components but wheelbase was 135 inches and chassis price was $2,145.

From 1925, the curved chassis front and rear pieces were discontinued as were the smaller Continental engines used up to that time. Traffic offered a six-cylinder engine for 1929 but this was the last year of manufacture.

1974 TRANSCOACH   **MBS**

TRANSCOACH 1974-1980 — The Transcoach was built by Sports-coach Corporation in Chatsworth, California. Transcoach, a division of Sportscoach Corporation, built small buses for 17 to 27 passengers. The vehicles had a built-in wheelchair lift as optional equipment. In 1975, Transcoach built an experimental bus with air suspension powered by a 4-53 Detroit Diesel engine. This bus did not go into production. The Dodge RM-400 chassis was used until Dodge went into financial crisis and ceased production of its commercial chassis.

1948 TRANSICOACH   **MBS**

TRANSICOACH 1948-1950 — Transicoach was based in Richmond, Indiana, where about 200 school buses were built using a sectional body design by C.J. Hug. The buses used underfloor-mounted engines built by Hercules and five-speed Fuller transmissions. Crown Coach of Los Angeles was the western distributor.

TRANSIT 1902 — The Steamobile Company of Keene, New Hampshire, built steam-powered passenger cars under the name Steamobile and Keene Steamobile but a truck called the Transit was also built by the company. It was powered by a 6 hp double-acting two-cylinder engine and single chain drive. The driver sat at the rear with cargo area in front.

1914 TRANSIT COVERED FLAREBOARD   **OCW**

TRANSIT 1912-1916 — The Transit Motor Car Company was located in Louisville, Kentucky. The first model the company built was a 3-ton truck powered by a 32 hp four-cylinder engine. It used a three-speed transmission, double chain drive and its wheelbase was 144 inches. For 1913, Transit offered 1-, 2-, 3-1/2- and 5-ton trucks. Each of them was a forward-control-type and used double chain drive. The company built dump bodies for its trucks by 1914. That year, the 1-ton truck was not listed. However, for 1915 and 1916, the model line consisted of the four capacities available in 1913. For the last two years, the 1-ton truck had its engine mounted under the floorboards, while the other trucks were of conventional design with engine under the front hood.

1948 TRANSIT MODEL 81 BUS   **MBS**

TRANSIT 1948-1949 — Transit Buses Incorporated was a short-lived company located in Dearborn, Michigan. The business began as a dealership during 1941 for rear-engine Ford Transit buses. A split from Ford occurred in 1947 and the company's Union City Body Company factory was used to build a newly-designed 31-passenger bus for the 1948 model year.

The Transit bus' chassis was built by Checker Cab Manufacturing Company. Continental engines were mounted crosswise at the rear. The City of Detroit bought 300 Transit buses but only a total of 200 more were sold to other cities. The company quickly got into financial trouble. By January of 1950, it was acquired by the Checker Cab Manufacturing Company.

1918 TRANSPORT   **MROZ**

TRANSPORT 1918-1925 — The Transport Truck Company of Mt. Pleasant, Michigan, began in 1918 with 1-, 1-1/2- and 2-ton capacity trucks. Buda and Continental engines and Fuller transmissions were used. In 1920, Transport also built the 2-1/2-ton Model 50. The truck's 27.2 hp four-cylinder engine used a Stromberg carburetor and Eisemann ignition. Semi-elliptic springs supported a Clark internal-gear rear axle, which was driven by a shaft drive from a Fuller four-speed transmission. It was priced at $2,585.

By 1925, Transport added a 3-1/2-ton and a 5-ton model. The 1-ton Model 15 with 128-inch wheelbase was powered by a 22.5 hp four-cylinder Continental N engine with Zenith carburetor and Remy ignition. The transmission was made by Fuller and both front and rear axles were made by Columbia. Steering gear was from Lavine and Motor Wheels carried pneumatic tires.

The 1-1/2-ton Model 26 with 140-inch wheelbase was powered by a 22.5 hp four-cylinder Buda WTU engine with Zenith carb and Remy ignition. A Fuller transmission was used along with a Columbia front axle and Clark rear axle. Saginaw steering was used and Motor Wheels carried pneumatic tires. Next up was the 2-ton Model 36 with 140-inch wheelbase powered by a 25.6 hp four-cylinder Buda KTU engine. The same make components were used as the previous model but pneumatic tires were optional at extra cost.

The 3-1/2-ton Model 61, which came out only for 1925 along with the 5-ton Model 75, was powered by a 28.9 hp four-cylinder Buda ETU engine and used a Shuler front axle. Otherwise, the component suppliers were the same. Wheelbase was 150 inches. The heaviest Transport was powered by a 32.4 hp four-cylinder Buda YTU engine and its components were made by the same companies as the Model 61. Wheelbase was 170 inches.

TRANSPORT TRACTOR 1915-1917 — The Transport Tractor Company, Incorporated, was located in Long Island City, New York. The company built one model of a truck tractor for pulling a 5-ton trailer. This was a forward-control vehicle powered by a 25 hp four-cylinder engine with three-speed transmission and worm-drive. In order to tow such a heavy trailer the lowest gear was 45.8:1.

1920 TRAYLOR   **RD**

TRAYLOR 1920-1928 — The Traylor Engineering & Manufacturing Company was located in Allentown, Pennsylvania. The first model line included 1-1/4-ton, 2-, 3- and 4-ton trucks built with four-cylinder Buda engines with three-speed and four-speed Brown-Lipe transmissions and Sheldon worm-drive rear axles.

By 1925, the 1-1/2-ton Model B with 140-inch wheelbase was powered by a 22.5 hp four-cylinder Buda WTU engine. The transmission was from Covert and front and rear axles were from Sheldon. Ross steering was used and pneumatic tires were standard. Chassis price was $2,390. The 2-ton Model C was powered by a 25.6 hp four-cylinder Buda ITU engine. Components were from the same manufacturers as on the Model B, except pneumatic tires were optional at extra cost. Chassis price was $2,850. The heaviest Traylor truck by this time was the 3-ton Model D with 150-inch wheelbase, which was powered by a 28.9 hp four-cylinder Buda HTU engine. On this model, the transmission was built by Traylor. Chassis price was $3,300. The three models introduced in 1925 were continued until 1928, when the company ceased production.

TRIANGLE 1917-1925 — The Triangle Motor Truck Company of St. Johns, Michigan, began by building a 1-1/2-ton truck powered by a four-cylinder Waukesha engine and used a three-speed transmission. Wheelbase was 144 inches. In 1924, a 2-1/2-ton model was added. It was powered by a 25.6 hp four-cylinder Waukesha FU engine and used a Fuller clutch and transmission. Front axle was from Eaton and rear axle was from Clark. Gemmer steering was used and Royer wheels carried solid rubber tires, with pneumatic tires at extra cost. Chassis price was $2,785. Some records show that manufacturing was discontinued in 1924 but Triangle trucks were listed for model year 1925, possibly leftover units.

1912 TRI-CAR DELIVERY   **RD**

TRI-CAR 1911-1912 — The Tri-Car was built by Coates-Goshen in Goshen, New York. Joseph Saunders Coates was the owner of Historic Track, birthplace of sulky racing. At his Miller Cart Company, he built sulky carts and in 1905, it was there that he built his first gasoline-powered car. His first production car was shown at the 1909 New York Auto Show and featured a 25 hp four-cylinder engine along with a pressed steel frame that predated modern frames by dozens of years. The 112-inch wheelbase Town Car was priced at $3,250. After building 32 cars, his factory in Goshen burned down along with half the town.

Coates declared bankruptcy and began again with the Coates-Goshen Tri-Car, which was a three-wheel delivery vehicle powered by a 16 hp two-cylinder horizontally-opposed water-cooled engine with a Schebler carburetor. The Tri-Car open van with a box mounted over the two front wheels had a capacity of 800 pounds. The vehicle used a steering wheel and had 28-inch pneumatic tires. Ads for the Tri-Car stated that the vehicle had been tested in Europe "for several years" before being marketed in the United States. After 1912, Coates went back to sulky racing and designing sulky carts.

TRIUMPH 1909-1912 — The Triumph Motor Car Company was located in Chicago, Illinois. It was started by John H. Behrens in 1907 and managed by Eric Christopher and his two brothers. That year, Vincent Bendix and O.M. Delauney bought the company, which was already producing the Model A Triumph passenger car that was marketed as the "Self-Starting Car." A compressed air mechanism devised by C.L. Halladay, company superintendent, was operated by a switch and a foot button to start the engine, instead of hand cranking, as almost all internal combustion-powered vehicles had to be before the advent of the electric starter motor. "A car to direct - not to labor with" was the company slogan.

By 1909, the company introduced a light delivery van powered by an 18 hp horizontally-opposed two-cylinder Monarch engine and planetary transmission located under the seat. In contrast, the passenger cars used four-cylinder engines and four-speed sliding gear transmissions. The Monarch engine was available with either air- or water-cooling. Depending on this option and type of delivery body, prices ranged from $650 to $850, which was considerably less than the $2,250 to $3,500 for the Triumph passenger car models. The first year the electric starter motor was adapted to some cars was also the last year of Triumph production.

1963 TRIVAN 1/2-TON 3-WHEEL UTILITY   DJS

TRIVAN 1962-1964 — The Roustabout Company of Frackville, Pennsylvania, built the Roustabout light commercial vehicle and in 1962, the company began production of the 1/2-ton Trivan. Power to the single rear wheel was supplied by a 32 hp two-cylinder air-cooled Kohler engine using a three-speed transmission. The chassis consisted of a steel-tube frame with air-bag suspension. Production totaled 150 units.

TROJAN 1914-1920 — This vintage of Trojan trucks was built by the Toledo Carriage Woodwork Company of Toledo, Ohio. The first model was 3/4-ton capacity vehicle and in 1916, a 1-ton was added to the line. Both were powered by four-cylinder engines. Prices ranged from $1,400 and $1,600, depending on size and options.

TROJAN 1937-1940 — The Trojan Manufacturing Company was located in Los Angeles, California. The company was organized in 1937 and by 1938, the first Trojan truck was built for off-highway use in mining and large construction projects. Raymond Lewis was president and Stanley G. Mitchell was secretary-treasurer. According to some records, Paul B. Cason was the chief designer who had at one time been production manager for Kimball trucks.

The Trojan was powered by a 1662-cubic inch Caterpillar D-17000 V-8 diesel engine, which was rated for 190 hp at 1100 rpm. The clutch was from Twin Disc and the transmission had three forward speeds and reverse. There was also a three-speed auxiliary transmission that provided a ratio 40 percent of one-to-one and 50 percent under drive. Steering was supplied by Ross.

The Trojan had a dump bed capacity of 55-cubic yards flush and its GVW was up to 210,000 pounds. The empty vehicle weighed 72,000 pounds. The front springs were semi-elliptic with 13 leaves of half-inch steel, each four inches wide. The rear axles were suspended by two longitudinal springs on each side using 14 leaves of 5/8-inch steel, each five inches wide. Rear wheels had triple tires. Final drive was by double chain from a jackshaft.

TRUCKING MACHINE see HIGHWAY 1920

TRUCKSTELL 1937-1942, 1946-1947 — Truckstell Incorporated began in Cleveland, Ohio, late in 1937. Some of the company's first products were parts for other truck companies. There was an interruption in truck manufacturing during World War II. By the end of the war, Truckstell listed 10 models once again, half of them powered by Chevrolet engines and half by Ford powerplants.

Directly after World War II, Truckstell offered the following models of trucks: F2X262F, F2X272F, F2X342F, F4X264R, F4X294R, C2X262F, C2X282F, C2X342F, C4X264R and C4X294R. The first five models were powered by Ford engines and the second five were powered by Chevrolet engines. Rear axles were built by Chevrolet, Clark, Eaton, Ford or Timken depending on the vehicle capacity. Transmissions were also from Chevrolet or Ford, except for Model F2X342F, which also had a Brown-Lipe transmission available. Truckstell quickly faded out after the war, when the demand for new trucks was filled by numerous larger competitors.

1917 TRUCKTOR   RD

TRUCKTOR see CHRISTIE

TRUMBULL 1914-1916 — The Trumbull Motor Car Company was located in Bridgeport, Connecticut. The Trumbull was a cyclecar designed by Harry J. Stoops and engine designer K.L. Hermann, who had his own engineering company. Alexander H. Trumbull and his brother Isaac B. Trumbull were the financiers of the company, hence the name Trumbull.

The first Trumbull vehicles were powered by an 18 hp water-cooled four-cylinder engine and used a three-speed selective sliding gear transmission and shaft drive. Wheelbase was 80 inches and tread was 44 inches. After the Trumbull brothers bought out Stoops, a friction transmission was adopted. A 1/4-ton light delivery model was built but few of this version were produced. Most of them were in the form of the Roadster and Coupe. Of the 2,000 Trumbulls built, 1,500 were exported to Australia and Europe. Isaac Trumbull and 20 of his cars were aboard the *Lusitania* when it was torpedoed on May 7, 1915, and all went to the bottom putting an end to the Trumbull company as well.

TULSA 1912-1916 — The Tulsa Automobile & Manufacturing Company was located in Tulsa, Oklahoma, after buying out the assets of auto builders J.V. Lindsley & Company of Dowagiac, Michigan. The company also bought out the Pioneer Car Company of Oklahoma and established a small factory, which was set up to produce a "light delivery wagon for oil field work." There was also a connection with the Harmon Motor Truck Company of Chicago, about which there is almost no information except that it was most likely an outgrowth of the Harmon Manufacturing and Distributing Company established by Henry Harmon in 1904.

Once production began, it appears that the leftover vehicles of the Pioneer firm were badge engineered as the Oilflyer, another make assembled by Tulsa. The company announced itself in directories as "Manufacturers of good commercial motor trucks, that's all." According to some records, the company built 3/4-, 1- and 1-1/2-ton trucks for a brief period. Constant changes in management contributed to the company's rapid demise. It was not affiliated with the later Tulsa Automobile Corporation of 1917, except that the latter took over the former company's factory in the city of Tulsa.

TURBINE 1904 — The Turbine Electric Truck Company was located in New York City. The truck used a 24 hp Roberts marine water-tube boiler and a steam engine turned a generator, which powered two General Electric motors geared to the rear axle. The hybrid vehicle used 40 pounds of coal per hour. Both front and rear axles were pivoted at the center using steel guide plates to assure wheel alignment under spring deflection. Wheelbase was 115 inches, track was 72 inches and the vehicle weighed 12,000 pounds. Steel wheels were used. The cab was enclosed and the condenser was mounted above it. Although the vehicle was called a truck, it was rather a road locomotive.

TUTTLE 1913-1914 — The Tuttle Motor Car Company was located in Canastota, New York. Daniel M. Tuttle was the organizer who started the D.M. Tuttle Company in 1903 for the purpose of building engines, boats and automobiles. The company was reorganized in 1910 with several financiers. It would appear that no commercial vehicles were built until 1913, when the company produced a 1-1/2-ton truck powered by a four-cylinder Hazard engine. Sheldon axles, worm gear drive and Sheldon wheels were used. The vehicle used solid rubber tires and had a wheelbase of 130 inches.

1918 TWIN CITY 2-TON   **OCW**

TWIN CITY 1917-1922 — Not affiliated with the earlier Twin City Auto-Car Company, the Twin City Four Wheel Drive Company of St. Paul, Minnesota, built 4x4 trucks designed by J.L. Ware, who had built trucks under his own name between 1912 and 1915. Twin City trucks were simultaneously built at the Four Wheel Drive Manufacturing Company in Minneapolis, Minnesota. Two models were produced. Both the 2-ton and 5-ton model were powered by four-cylinder engines and used three-speed transmissions.

By 1917, four-wheel brakes were introduced. In 1920, according to some records, the company developed a four-cylinder engine with four valves per cylinder with cylinder walls being removable. This company was also not affiliated with the earlier Twin City vehicles built by F.R. Brasie and the concurrent vehicles built by the Minneapolis Steel & Machinery Company.

1925 TWIN CITY MODEL DW 25-SEAT COACH   **MHS**

TWIN CITY 1918-1929 — These vehicles were built by the Minneapolis Steel & Machinery Company of Minneapolis, Minnesota. The company's best-known product was agricultural tractors, which later were known under the Minneapolis-Moline name. Twin City trucks were built in 2-ton and 3-1/2-ton capacity. The company began producing buses in the early 1920s. The successful 25-passenger Model DW low parlor coach was introduced in 1925. It was powered by a 60 hp engine and had front-mounted air springs. The company did not survive the stock market crash of 1929.

TWIN COACH 1927-1953 — The Twin Coach Company of Kent, Ohio, was organized by the Fageol brothers two years after the Fageol Motors Company was expanded to Kent, Ohio, primarily for the purpose of building buses. The Fageol company began in Oakland, California. The Twin Coach was a dual-engine 40-passenger heavy-duty transit bus and parlor coach.

The Fageol brothers had merged their Ohio operation with ACF. ACF management did not embrace the dual-engine design, so the Thomart Motor Company factory was acquired by Fageol in 1925 and then absorbed by ACF in 1926. Because of the management conflict it was reacquired by the Fageols in 1927.

Utilizing forward-control design, the 40-passenger Model 40 Twin Coach buses were 30 percent bigger than existing buses at the time and were one of the first designed to enclose the engine(s) within the coach bodywork. They were at first powered by two four-cylinder Waukesha engines but because of specific technical inadequacies for the application, the company switched to Hercules engines in 1928. These powerplants were used until 1943. Trolley coach versions of the Model 40 were also built beginning in 1928 until 1934.

Twin Coach began building smaller buses with single four-cylinder engines and forward-control in 1929. The company experimented with street car development, of which four were fabricated, as well as with rail buses and railroad maintenance vehicles. Twin Coach also built 1-ton delivery vans for postal and food distribution applications. These were produced from 1929 to 1936 in both gasoline-powered and battery-powered iterations. That division was sold to Continental-Divco in 1936 and these vehicle would be incorporated into the Divco model line, which had been acquired by Continental in 1934.

1935 TWIN COACH MILK DELIVERY TRUCK   **CARBONELLA**

The dual-engine Model 40 and the front-engine 20-seat buses were phased out beginning in 1934 and were supplanted by rear-engine-design buses over the next two years. For 1935, Twin Coach built the first production diesel-powered buses in America. About 300 of these were diesel-electric buses and a few gasoline-electric hybrid buses were built up to World War II. In 1936, rear-engine 40-passenger and 44-passenger trolley coaches were introduced and continued in production until 1942. About 2,700 dual-engine and front-engine buses had been built by 1936.

For 1938, Twin Coach introduced the Super Twin, which was a 56-passenger four-axle diesel-electric hybrid bus hinged vertically in the last one-third of the body, but it was not articulated for turns. Only two of these were built along with two three-axle units, but sales did not materialize. Rear-engine bus production from 1934 to 1943 amounted to 6,200 units.

1938 TWIN COACH MODEL 27-R BUS   MBS

1938 TWIN COACH MODEL 58-GDE   MBS
DIESEL-ELECTRIC BUS

During World War II, the Twin Coach factory built control cabins for U.S. Navy blimps and tail assemblies for Curtiss-Wright airplanes in Kent as well as in Buffalo, New York, where there was a government-owned aircraft plant. This factory was bought by Twin Coach in 1946 and converted to bus assembly. Another plant was established in Ontario during 1948.

After the war, Twin Coach introduced a new design of buses styled by Dwight Austin. Austin's enduring design was easily recognizable in the six-piece windshield constructed entirely of inexpensive flat glass. In Kent, a new engine manufacturing facility was set up to build high-compression six-cylinder engines, which were mounted on their sides under the floor for efficient space usage and maximum power transmission using a Spicer torque converter that had been optimized for military vehicle application during the war. Only a few 44-passenger postwar Twin Coach buses were built using the dual-engine design.

Twin Coach moved away from diesel engines and this turned out to be a rather fateful decision, as transit companies opted for efficiency and low cost maintenance. Only two contracts for Super Twin coaches and trolley coaches were completed by 1948. In 1950, the company offered LPG engine options. This helped sell some buses to transit operators, such as the City of Chicago, at a time when propane was inexpensive and easily available but this alternative fuel did not catch on with many operators.

In 1953, Twin Coach sold its manufacturing business to Flxible as well as most of its Kent factory. The engine plant continued to build powerplants for other manufacturers. Twin Coach had sold a total of 5,800 units after World War II. The Buffalo factory went back into aviation technology. Highway Products bought the Kent plant and produced a small bus called the Twin Coach but it really had nothing else associated with the original firm of Twin Coach. Total Twin Coach production was approximately 14,710 units.

TWISTER DRAGON WAGON 1972-1980 — The Lockheed Missile and Space Company, Incorporated, built the Twister Dragon Wagon, which consisted of two center-articulated four-wheel-drive modules. Apparently, the project began in 1972. The two modules were capable of roll and yaw and were powered by a 225 hp Caterpillar 1160 diesel engine and used a six-speed transmission with a two-speed transfer case. Selection between four-wheel-drive of the front module or to all eight wheels was manually controlled. Rockwell-Standard tandem axles and high-traction differentials were used. Suspension was six-rod independent walking beam-type. Air brakes acted on all four axles and a disc brake on the drivetrain was used for parking. The vehicle had a top speed of 55 mph. It was capable of climbing a 60-degree slope and traversing a side slope of 40 degrees. Production began in 1974, and the vehicle was used primarily for oil exploration and military use. In

1980, Lockheed sold the Twister Dragon Wagon patents to Oshkosh. The vehicle was redesigned and continued in production as the Oshkosh Dragon Wagon.

1914 TWOMBLY LIGHT DELIVERY CAR   RD

TWOMBLY 1914-1915 — William Irving Twombly made three attempts at motor vehicle manufacturing, all of them in New York City. The first was in 1904 as the Twombly Motor Carriage Company when he built a large steam car. After building a second gasoline-powered car, he went on to develop his Twombly Power Corporation in Manhattan. In 1910, he tried again with a steam car on which he had spent some $250,000 in development, according to the press.

In 1913, Twombly once again got into the automotive field with a cyclecar. The underslung chassis had a 98-inch wheelbase and at first, it was powered by a 7 hp V-2 engine. It had a friction transmission and double chain drive. By 1914, it had a 10 hp water-cooled piston-valve four-cylinder engine and the wheelbase was lengthened to 100 inches. The Light Delivery car was built for 1914 and sold for $395, which was the same price as for the tandem roadster.

Sensing the lack of enthusiasm for cyclecars, Twombly redesigned his vehicle later in 1914. The engine he adapted was a poppet-valve 16 hp water-cooled four-cylinder. He used worm gear drive and a three-speed sliding gear transmission. The price went to the $600 to $700 range and a taxicab was also in the lineup. The taxicab was built by Twombly in the leased former New York Motor Works plant in Nutley, New Jersey. His financial backer was Presbyterian minister Dr. Dodge, who could not wait for the 3,000 cars Twombly ordered to be built by the Driggs-Seabury Company in Sharon, Pennsylvania. Dr. Dodge petitioned for bankruptcy in February of 1915, and the business venture was over before any more vehicles could be built.

TWYFORD 1901-1907 — Robert E. Twyford applied for a patent on four-wheel-drive in 1898 and it was granted to him in 1900. The original vehicle was designed to use an electric motor but by the turn of the century, Twyford had built a few four-wheel-drive passenger cars using gasoline engines. Twyford's design consisted of a shaft extending from the rear-mounted engine to the front axle, which pivoted as in horsedrawn wagons. Two pairs of friction clutches within the solid shafts combined with a network of gears provided a crude if complicated 4x4 drive.

By 1901, both passenger cars and commercial vehicles were being produced in limited number at the Twyford Motorcar Company's shop in Pittsburgh, Pennsylvania. By 1902, the operation was closed down, largely due to design problems of the four-wheel-drive system. Robert Twyford redesigned some of the vehicle's mechanical components and reorganized in Brookville, Pennsylvania, during 1904 with the support of local investors.

A delivery truck was listed for 1905 using an 8 hp engine. For 1906, a 16 hp engine was also listed. All of the following vehicles were powered by 20 hp two-cycle two-cylinder engines. Twyford listed 6-, 10- and 15-passenger buses in 1906 but it is uncertain how many were ever actually produced. After a management shakeup during which time Robert Twyford resigned as factory superintendent, the company ceased operations by 1907. Twyford made a brief second effort with the Brandon commercial vehicle venture in Houston, Texas.

U

V

U

ULTIMATE 1919-1925 — Ultimate trucks were built by Vreeland Motor Company, Incorporated in Hillside, New Jersey. This conventional truck was assembled from purchased parts, which included four-cylinder Buda engines. The 2-ton Model A used a 25.8 hp unit and the 3-ton Model B used a 28.9 hp unit. Ultimate also built the 25-seat Model AJL bus and the 30-seat Model BU bus. The trucks were hand cranked for starting, whereas the buses used Westinghouse electric starters and lights. In 1924 and 1925, only the Model BU was produced by Ultimate before the company ceased operations altogether.

UNION 1901-1904 — The Union Motor Truck Company was located in Philadelphia, Pennsylvania. The Union truck was powered by a 380-cubic inch two-cylinder engine mounted under the frame. Company literature described the transmission as a "reversible roller ratchet and movable crank pin." The company entered two of its tall trucks in the commercial vehicle contest of 1903 in New York City. According to records, one of the trucks had a mechanical failure while the other lost a wheel and overturned. The company made a special effort for the following year's contest and won first place in its class, but production was discontinued.

1905 UNION   JAW

UNION 1905 — The Union Automobile Manufacturing Company, one of half dozen to use the Union name, was located briefly in St. Louis, Missouri. This was actually a division of the Union Automobile Company of Indiana but it is treated as a separate business venture due to its listing as such.

The first vehicle produced by this company was a friction-drive motor buggy. "You Auto Take This Home With You" was the company slogan. The venture was headed by Benjamin Hulbert and George Martin. The company built a light delivery van version of its 16 hp two-cylinder vehicle with shaft drive. Both solid and pneumatic tires were offered on a wheelbase of 92 inches. The vehicle was priced at $1,275. When the parent company located in Anderson, Indiana began building the Lambert, the St. Louis branch became a dealership and ceased manufacturing. It was not affiliated with the Union Carriage Company of St. Louis, which began production three years later.

UNION 1912-1914 — The Union Motor Truck Company of San Francisco, California, was a small producer of assembled trucks for a brief period. The company first offered a 1-1/2-ton Model U-1 truck in 1912. In 1913, this model was superseded by a 2-ton model, which was built until 1914 before the company ceased manufacturing altogether.

UNION 1917-1925 — Yet another company using the Union name was the Union Motor Truck Company of Bay City, Michigan. The first model was a 2-1/2-ton truck and in 1921, the company introduced a 4-ton and 6-ton capacity truck. A bus was built in 1922, and all vehicles up to that time used Wisconsin engines, bevel gear rear axles and Fuller transmissions.

Toward the end of production, the Union company continued to build the 1-1/2-ton Model E with 150-inch wheelbase powered by a 27.3 hp four-cylinder Continental 6M engine using a Fuller clutch and transmission. The rear axle was provided by Shuler and the front axle by Clark. The Indestructible Wheel Company provided the vehicles with rims for 34x7 front and rear pneumatic tires. A Zenith carburetor and Bosch ignition were used.

At the same time, the company also built the FLW, FV, FWC and FW model trucks. Each of these was rated at 2-1/2-ton capacity and all were powered by a four-cylinder Wisconsin TAU engine. All but the FWC model had a 155-inch wheelbase and used 36x5 front and 36x10 rear solid rubber tires. The FWC model had a 200-inch wheelbase and used 38x7 front and 42x9 rear solid rubber tires. All four models used Fuller GU-7 transmissions. The FLW and FW trucks had a Walker rear axle and a Sheldon front axle, while the FV model used a Vulcan 4-R rear axle. The FWC truck had a Walker rear axle and a Shuler front axle.

Union also made the 4-ton Model H and Model HW powered by the 32.4 hp four-cylinder Wisconsin VAU engine. Both of the 4-ton Union trucks used Shuler front axles, Saginaw steering and Smith wheels, which carried solid rubber tires. Union's last year of manufacture was 1925.

UNIT RIG 1960 to date — Unit Rig & Equipment Company was started in 1935 by a group of businessmen in Tulsa, Oklahoma. The company was involved in equipment production during World War II, while continuing to manufacture draw works. After the war, Unit Rig continued to produce military products that included track-mounted entrenching machines and tank-mounted bridge launchers. The original partnership was dissolved in 1946 and the company was reorganized in 1947.

Unit Rig developed the diesel electric drive for rear-dump trucks in open pit mining. The first truck was introduced in January of 1947. The first production model did not appear until 1963. This type of large dump truck with a diesel engine turning a generator that powered DC motors in each rear wheel has been built to date.

In 1984, Unit Rig purchased Dart truck and loader model line. In 1988, Terex Corporation purchased the U.S. and Canadian assets and the stock of its foreign subsidiaries. Unit Rig has been a Division of Terex to date. See also DART, LECTRA HAUL and TEREX.

UNITED 1914-1915 — The National United Service Company built a cyclecar that was sold as the United. It used a 12 hp four-cylinder water-cooled engine and a friction transmission with final drive by double chain. Tread was 40 inches and wheelbase was 96 inches. In addition to the roadster for $395, there was also a light delivery version that sold for $425. The National United Service Company was also a marketing agency for the Beisel manufactured in Monroe, Michigan, and the Arrow built in Dayton, Ohio. The United cyclecar was built for only about one year.

UNITED 1915-1930 — The United Motor Truck Company was organized in Grand Rapids, Michigan. The first models were 1-1/2-, 3- and 5-ton capacities. These were all conventional trucks powered by four-cylinder Continental engines. The 1-1/2-ton model and one of two 3-ton models used worm-drive. The second 3-ton model and the 5-ton truck used double chain drive. The company was reorganized as the United Motors Company in 1916.

In 1922, the company was once again reorganized as United Motors Products Company in Grand Rapids. A 1-ton truck was also available by this time and the heaviest model was still 5-ton capacity. By mid-decade, the company listed 1-, 1-1/2-, 2-, 2-1/2-, 3- and 5-ton capacity models. The 1-1/2-ton Model 30 and Model 32 were powered by a 25.6 hp four-cylinder Hercules OX engine. Both used a Brown-Lipe clutch and transmission and Shuler front axle. The difference was that the Model 30 used a Columbia rear axle, while the Model 32 had a Wisconsin rear axle.

1924 UNITED CONSTRUCTOR DUMP TRUCK   CCJ

The 2-ton Model 35 and 2-1/2-ton Model 50 had the same engine and make of components as the Model 32. The 5-ton Model 100 was powered by a 32.4 hp Hercules MU3 engine, with components the same make as Model 35 and Model 50.

In 1927, the company was acquired by Acme and the model line was merged with that of the new parent company located in Cadillac, Michigan.

UNITED 1917-1920 — The United Four Wheel Drive Company was an obscure manufacturer located in Chicago, Illinois. The company built a 1-1/2-ton model truck that used four-wheel-drive. Other information has not been available to date.

1911 UNIVERSAL 3-TON MODEL A   NAHC

UNIVERSAL 1910-1920 — The Universal Motor Truck Company was organized in Detroit, Michigan. The first model truck to be built by this company was 3-ton capacity truck that used forward-control design. Wheelbase was 132 inches. It was powered by a 30 hp four-cylinder engine using double chain drive. In 1913, a 1-ton and 2-ton truck was added to the model line. The lightest truck used shaft drive and was of conventional design, whereas the 2-ton model was similar to the 3-ton, which was offered in addition to the two lighter trucks. By 1915, the 1-ton truck was upgraded to a 1-1/2-ton but the other two models remained the same. The postwar recession took its toll on the Universal Motor Truck Company and production ceased in 1920.

UNIVERSAL GAS ELECTRIC 1919-1921 — The Universal Gas and Electric Company was first organized in April 1919 for the purpose of manufacturing "Gas Electric" vehicles under the patents of the Maximum Power Company of Lawrence, Kansas. The Uni-

versal Gas and Electric Company was located in Kansas City, Missouri. Its first trucks were found to be defective in design. By 1921, the company was reorganized with a capitalization of $1 million.

1921 UNIVERSAL GAS ELECTRIC 6X4   MROZ

Details of the electro-mechanical design have not been clear to date. It is known that a gasoline engine was used to turn a generator that powered electric motors in the wheels. The first versions had four-wheel-drive with a trailing rear axle, hence it was a 6x4 configuration, which also used solid rubber tires.

By 1921, in a highly unusual combination photograph-and-airbrush illustration, the company advertised another 6x4 gas-electric truck chassis. This time the front axle was not driven but the two rear axles were. Pneumatic tires were employed. Five tons was the rated capacity. Maximum speed was advertised as 30 mph and it was stated that "two loaded five-ton trailers" could be hauled at a constant 12 mph on level roads.

The company's brochure failed to mention any details regarding the gasoline engine, dynamo or electric motors employed in the design. Advantages were that the truck had "no geared transmission, gearshift, propeller shaft, universal joints or differential gears" and electric braking was available. The fact that the company's earlier trucks had a problem with high gasoline consumption was addressed only superficially. As much as the conceptual design of the Universal Gas Electric Truck was ahead of its time (in that huge earth movers would later use this type of drive configuration), it would appear that the company did not go any further with its own plans for manufacture after 1921.

UPPERCU 1924-1927 — The vehicles built by this company were named after the founder, who was Inglis M. Uppercu. The company was named the Aeromarine Plane and Motor Corporation, which was located in Keport, New Jersey. Inglis Uppercu had been building training airplanes and seaplanes and acquired the coach-building company of Healy in 1921. He first used Cadillac chassis to build ambulances, hearses and custom passenger cars.

In 1924, the company began building single- and double-decker buses, which were powered by Continental engines and had front-wheel-drive. The entire engine, transmission and axle mechanism was removable as a unit. Production was approximately 30 single-decker buses and only two double-decker buses. The Tompkins Bus Corporation was the primary buyer of Uppercu vehicles, although the company resold the buses to the city of Chicago. For 1926, and the last year of vehicle manufacture, Waukesha six-cylinder engines were listed.

UPTON 1902-1903 — Colcord Upton organized the Upton Machine Company in Beverly, Massachusetts, during the year 1900. The company was set up to manufacture planetary transmissions, which Upton had earlier invented. The first vehicle was a passenger car powered by a 3-1/2 hp De Dion engine but this car was built only to demonstrate the planetary transmission.

Upton apparently had disagreements with his associates and left the company in 1903. Meanwhile, some records show that the Upton company went into the manufacture of 2-ton trucks, which were powered by a 10 hp two-cylinder engine. As of Upton's departure, the company was assembling 10 such trucks. However, Upton took his company name with him to Lebanon, Pennsylvania, where he continued to build passenger cars under his name. A contract to build 700 taxicabs for New York City fell through and his second venture was finished by 1907. The company he left behind switched to the name of Beverly but survived only through 1903.

1914 URBAN MODEL 10 PANEL DELIVERY OCW

1914 URBAN MODEL 20 COVERED FLAREBOARD OCW

URBAN 1911-1918 — The Urban was a battery-powered electric truck built by the Kentucky Wagon Manufacturing Company of Louisville, Kentucky. The 1/2-ton capacity vehicle was offered for the first three years before the company expanded the model lineup to 2-ton capacity trucks. Edison alkaline batteries were used in all Urban vehicles as well as double chain drive. A wheelbase of 130 inches was used for vans and enclosed trucks up to 1918, when the company stopped manufacturing commercial vehicles altogether.

1915 U.S. 3-TON FLATBED RNE

U.S. 1909-1930 — The United States Motor Truck Company was located in Cincinnati, Ohio. The first model was powered by a 20 hp horizontally-opposed two-cylinder engine mounted under the seat. Capacity was listed at 1-ton and 1-1/2-ton for the two versions in the first model line. For 1912, a four-cylinder engine was also

available. These included a forward-control 1-1/2-ton truck and a conventional 3-ton unit. Most of the vehicles produced by that time used the four-cylinder engine, although the earlier two-cylinder engine was still available.

By 1916, trucks by the name of U.S. were also available in 3-1/2-, 4- and 5-ton capacities with worm and chain drive. Hinkley and Continental engines were used after World War I. By 1922, the model range expanded to include trucks from 1-1/2-ton to 7-ton capacity. Three years later, the 3-ton Model R U.S. truck used a 25.6 hp four-cylinder Hinkley 400 engine. But the same year, the 2-ton Model NW24 was powered by a 22.5 hp four-cylinder Buda WTU engine and used a Fuller clutch and transmission, Sheldon rear axle and Shuler front axle. The heavier trucks used a Brown-Lipe clutch and transmission and Sheldon rear axle.

The 7-ton Model T was powered by a 36.1 hp four-cylinder Buda ATU engine. Component manufacturers were the same, but steering was from Lavine and Smith wheels carried 36x6 single front and 40x6 dual rear solid rubber tires. Stromberg carburetors were used throughout and Bosch ignition was used on all except the heaviest truck, which had Eisemann Magneto ignition.

U.S.A. see LIBERTY

U.S. CARRIAGE see GREAT EAGLE

1996 U.S. ELECTRICAR 282HD FLATBED USE

U.S. ELECTRICAR 1994 to date — U.S. Electricar bought out the Solar Electric Corporation of Santa Rosa, California. In 1994, the company was reorganized and acquired Nordskog in Redlands, California. Industrial electric vehicles and an electric shuttle bus has been this company's product to date. The electric industrial and commercial vehicles have been a continuation of the vehicles previously manufactured by Nordskog in Redlands, California.

U.S. Electricar has built electric shuttle buses, which were developed by Nordskog before the company's acquisition. The 14-passenger buses were enlarged to 22-passenger capacity and the vehicle model line was expanded to include the Electricar Sedan, Pickup and Electricar Van. These have used the new Dolphin AC Drive System developed by the Hughes Electronic Corporation, a part of GM Hughes Power Control System.

Along with the aforementioned vehicles, U.S. Electricar has continued to build electric commercial and industrial vehicles that have included dump trucks, resort bellhop vehicles, fire rapid-response units, courtesy cars, customer service vehicles, welding light trucks, multi-passenger trams, tunnel vehicles and the U.S. Electricar Pushmaster.

The latest addition to the commercial products group has included the Model 282HD electric flatbed with 76-inch wheelbase. This series of vehicles has been powered by a 4.13 hp 36/48 volt DC series wound electric motor using a solid state transistorized speed controller with reverse switch. Tires are 5.3x10 and 5.3x12 optional pneumatic. Batteries are either six six-volt or eight six-volt. Capacity has been rated at 3,800 pounds with a top speed of 15 mph. U.S. Electricar vehicles have also featured disc brakes, quick change battery systems and unitized diamond plate chassis construction. For 1996, U.S. Electricar's company slogan has been "The Competition is Fuming."

U.S. LONG DISTANCE see LONG DISTANCE

U.S. STEEL 1967 — The United States Steel Corporation built a 2-1/2-ton 6x6 truck as an experimental test bed in 1967. The truck used a Continental LD-465 engine and had a six-speed automatic transmission. It was put through extensive evaluation over 12,000 miles of desert near Carson City, Nevada. Tires were 16.00x20 front and rear and it used advanced steels including two-leaf front springs and independent coil springs in back. Governed speed was 52 mph. It appears this was the only unit built by United States Steel.

UTILITY 1910-1911 — Commercial vehicles by the name of Utility consisted of 1-ton and 3-ton trucks built by the Stephenson Motor Car Company of South Milwaukee, Wisconsin. Utility trucks were forward-control design and both models were powered by four-cylinder engines mounted under the seat, had friction transmissions and used double chain drive. The 1-ton Type B had a wheelbase of 110 inches and was powered by a 35 hp engine. It was listed at $2,000 in 1910.

The heavier Model C had a 136-inch wheelbase and used a 50 hp engine. It was briefly listed for $3,500 with a stake body and 136 wheelbase. Both trucks had a top speed of 25 mph. The company was out of business by the end of 1912.

UTILITY 1912 — The second truck by the name of Utility was built by the Gaylord Motor Company. Refer to GAYLORD.

UTILITY COACH see AUSTIN UTILITY COACH

UTILITY TRAILER 1937 — Cooperating together, designer Allan J. Kayser, Utility Trailer and the Six-Wheel distributor in Denver, Colorado, built what has been claimed as America's first air-conditioned truck. Four such trucks using Cummins diesel engines were built for the Cunningham Oil Transport Company of La Junta, Colorado. At the completion of the first truck, *Western Fleet Owner* announced the business venture in its October issue. A series 700 five-speed Brown-Lipe transmission was used with a two-plate clutch.

A Utility third axle was used for the tanker truck and a corresponding six-wheel trailer was built to complete the full rig. The truck carried 2,700 gallons of fuel and the trailer tank carried 3,550 gallons. The cab was insulated with Master Metal and Rock Wool "without any danger from poisonous gases." The air-conditioning system used a separate gasoline engine that drove a two-cylinder compressor. Sulphur gas was used for the cooling element and the coils were located "between the seats of the driver and rider at the back of the cab." The cost of the air-conditioner was $500.

V

VALLEY see HUFFMAN

VAN 1908-1909 — Van was the name used for highwheelers built by H.F. Van Wambeke & Sons located in Elgin, Illinois. Two versions, both with wheel steering, were available. One was a 1,600-pound capacity truck and the other was a 1-ton capacity vehicle. The two models were powered by an 18 hp air-cooled two-cylinder engine using friction transmission and double chain drive to the rear axle. The 1,200-pound capacity vehicle was fabricated as a light delivery van, while the other one was built as an express delivery truck. Both versions used the horsedrawn wagon design, which did incorporate a frame. Wagon wheels were used with solid rubber tires in dimensions of 36x1-1/4 front and 40x1-1/4 rear. Wheelbase was 92 inches and the vehicle weighed 1,600 pounds.

1913 VAN AUKEN 1-TON ELECTRIC DELIVERY   HHB

1914 VAN AUKEN MODEL A STAKE BODY   OCW

VAN AUKEN 1913-1914 — Howard Van Auken was the designer of the Van Auken vehicles built by the Van Auken Electric Car Company organized in Connersville, Indiana, during 1913. The incorporators were A.K. Babcock, G.C. Babcock, C.L. Millard and H.M. Wylie. An electric van with 1/2-ton capacity was the only model vehicle built and it was assembled at the Connersville Buggy Company. A General Electric motor was used with shaft drive for motive power. Front axle was tubular and chassis weight was 1,240 pounds with a wheelbase of 80 inches. This was a short-lived company.

VAN DYKE 1910-1912 — The Van Dyke Motor Car Company, located in Detroit, Michigan, built a 1/2-ton delivery van that was powered by a 12 hp two-cylinder engine using a friction transmis-

sion and shaft drive. Chassis weight was 1,900 pounds with a wheelbase of 86 inches. Both solid and pneumatic tires were offered and with the former, the vehicle's price was $950.

1913 VAN DYKE DELIVERY VAN   MROZ

VAN-L 1911-1912 — The Van-L Commercial Car Company was located in Grand Rapids, Michigan. The company built 1-, 1-1/2- and 2-ton capacity trucks during its brief existence. All were forward-control and were powered by four-cylinder engines using a three-speed transmission and double chain drive. The heaviest truck was listed as having a 32 hp engine and a chassis weight of 4,000 pounds. With solid rubber tires, it was listed at $1,900. By 1913, this company became the Commercial Service Company, which did not go into manufacturing.

1908 VAN WAMBEKE MOTOR WAGON   RD

VAN WAMBEKE 1907-1909 — With the help of his sons, H.F. Van Wambeke built at least seven highwheelers in Elgin, Illinois. Air-cooled two-cylinder engines of 10 hp to 20 hp were used. Planetary transmissions were used with dual chain drive. The whole operation took place in a barn behind the Van Wambeke's grocery store. Most of the vehicles were delivery trucks, except for one known runabout. According to some records, the Van Wambekes built one delivery vehicle for themselves powered by a four-cylinder engine.

VAN WINKLE 1913-1914 — Charles W. Van Winkle was an inventor in San Joaquin, California, who built a four-wheel-drive passenger car in 1905. His four-wheel-drive mechanism consisted of a single shaft that transmitted power to both front and rear axles. After fabricating a prototype, Van Winkle sold the patent rights to a company called the Stockton Four Drive Auto Company of which he was manager, U.S.G. Mowry of Farmington was president and John Marshal of Stockton was secretary.

The four-wheel-drive concept did not progress any further, although there may have been an indirect connection with Golden West and Robinson whose four-wheel-drive trucks appeared shortly thereafter in nearby Sacramento. Charles W. Van Winkle moved to Atlanta, Georgia, and by 1913, went into the truck manufacturing business himself but not using the four-wheel-drive idea.

1913 VAN WINKLE MODEL B   RD

The Van Winkle truck was a conventional truck built as the 2-1/2-ton Model E and 4-ton Model K, both powered by a four-cylinder L-head engine cooled by a centrifugal pump. A Stromberg carburetor and Bosch ignition were used. The transmission was a three-speed selective sliding gear type and the clutch was a multiple disc type running in an oil bath. A driveshaft transmitted power to the transmission, which was located amidship. The universals were of one-piece construction so that the two universals and the driveshaft were made up of three pieces. This was accomplished "by a round square section on the shaft, working in a round square section on the shaft, working in a round square hole in the universals." From the jackshaft, power was transmitted to the rear wheels by dual chain.

Charles Van Winkle's truck manufacturing enterprise did not last for long and it appears to have faded out within a year or two. His inventiveness also included the design of "imaginative aircraft" in White Plains, New York.

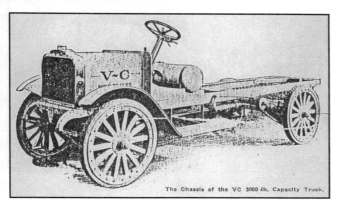

1912 V-C 1-1/2-TON CHASSIS   RD

V-C 1912-1913 — The V-C Motor Truck Company of Lynne, Massachusetts, began late in 1912 with a capitalization of $100,000, organized by company president Frank S. Corlew. Frank E. Vallier was treasurer and general manager. By 1913, the company built a 1-1/2-ton Model B truck that was powered by a 22.5 hp four-cylinder engine with Schebler carburetor and Bosch ignition. A cone clutch was used to couple to a three-speed selective sliding transmission and chain drive. Wheelbase was 130 inches and suspension was semi-elliptic front and rear. Solid rubber tires were used with dimensions of 34x4 front and rear. With lamps and stake body, the price was $2,350. The company was out of business the same year.

V-CON 1971-1980 — The Marion Power Shovel Company, Incorporated, Vehicle Construction Division, was started in Dallas, Texas. The V-Con diesel-electric end-dump trucks that were built by this company were some of the largest in the world. By the late 1970s, the company built four models with capacities from 250 tons to 270 tons. These were powered by 8- and 12-cylinder Alco

diesel engines or 12- and 16-cylinder Detroit Diesel engines. Horsepower was from 1340 to 3000. Engines were mounted amidships and powered a GTH 11 alternator, which drove the General Electric 772 motorized wheels.

1974 V-CON MODEL 3006 270-TON 8X6 DIESEL   MARION
ELECTRIC DUMP TRUCK

Each truck had two sets of wheels on short axles and most of the trucks had six powered wheels. Brakes and front wheel steering were hydraulically actuated and the trucks had a 51-foot turning radius. The truck bodies were 28 feet wide, making them too large for on-highway driving. Each truck was delivered in pieces and assembled at the construction site. The largest Model 3006 was priced at $1,200,000. About one truck per month was built until the company withdrew from the manufacture of trucks.

1903 V.E.C. 5-TON ELECTRIC HOIST TRUCK   OCW

1905 V.E.C. SIGHTSEEING BUS   LIAM

V.E.C. 1901-1906 — The Vehicle Equipment Company of Brooklyn, New York, was organized by Robert Lloyd with Hector H. and Arthus H. Havermeyer late in 1900. The Havermeyer brothers were sons of sugar magnate William F. Havermeyer, so substantial capital allowed the company to go into what would be considered large scale production for that time. The company built both passenger and commercial vehicles and all of them were electric battery-powered.

The first model line of commercial vehicles was a series of sight-seeing buses, which were used in New York, Washington and other cities. The company began to specialize in vehicles for the transport and installation of heavy safes in upper stories of office buildings. V.E.C. also built ambulances, brewery trucks and coal dump trucks.

1905 V.E.C. STAKE CANOPY   **RD**

In 1904, a balloon that landed on the factory roof started a fire that destroyed the plant. It was rebuilt in Long Island City and continued manufacturing until 1906, when bankruptcy forced reorganization. In 1906, the venture became the General Vehicle Company and electric commercial vehicle production was continued in Long Island City until 1920.

VEERAC 1910-1914 — Frank H. Merrill of Plainfield, New Jersey, began experimenting with a two-stroke gasoline engine of his own design in 1892. The name Veerac was derived from the abbreviation for "Valveless, Explosion Every Revolution, Air-Cooled" engine. The first company organized by Merrill began during 1905 in Plainfield, New Jersey. There, however, the needed capital of $300,000 was not procurable and after building only a roadster prototype, the company was closed down. *The Motor World* stated "Frank H. Merrill...is responsible for the inventions that suffered the company to be born."

1912 VEERAC 3/4-TON OPEN FLAREBOARD (LEFT)   **OCW**
AND PLATFORM STAKE BODY TRUCKS

Five years later, the Commercial Club of Anoka, Minnesota, invited Merrill to produce commercial vehicles. A factory was set up to build light vans using the two-stroke two-cylinder engine that Merrill had developed. A 3/4-ton and a 1-ton model were the only two offered. The vehicles used planetary transmissions and double

chain drive. The heavier truck was listed as having a 20 hp engine and a wheelbase of 86 inches. A governor was used to limit top speed to 15 mph.

1914 VEERAC MODEL B PLATFORM STAKE   **OCW**

VELIE 1911-1924, 1927-1929 — The Velie Carriage Company began producing horsedrawn vehicles in 1902. Willard Lamb Velie was the organizer of this company in Moline, Illinois. Within a few years, the citizens of Moline were interested in automobiles and Velie began manufacturing passenger cars for the model year of 1909. Financing arrived from Velie's mother Emma Deere, whose father John Deere had already made a fortune with a plow he had invented, along with other farm implements.

American and British Manufacturing Company provided the first set of engines and 1,000 cars were sold the first year. The first Velies were in the John Deere Plow Company catalog. A switch was made to Lycoming engines and by 1911, the company was building its own four-cylinder engine. This was the year the first commercial vehicles were introduced. It was also the year a Velie came in 17th out of 40 cars in the Inianapolis 500.

1911 VELIE 3-TON STAKE BED   **RD**

1912 VELIE 3-TON MODEL Z MOVING VAN   **NAHC**

Velie began building a 1-1/2-ton and a 3-ton truck in 1911. Both were powered by four-cylinder engines. The 3-ton truck was advertised for its design, which allowed for the easy removal of the engine by unbolting the front crossmember and sliding out the unit. The 1-1/2-ton truck was listed at $2,850 and the 3-ton truck for

$3,350. Both trucks were available with a 148-inch or 172-inch wheelbase. By the following year, the 1-1/2-ton model was discontinued and in its place Velie offered instead a 1-ton truck by 1913. At this time, Velie introduced a six-cylinder engine for its passenger cars, which was actually built by Continental.

According to some records, by 1915 Velie adopted worm-drive. The following year, the company offered 1-1/2-, 2- and 3-1/2-ton "Biltwel" trucks equipped with four-cylinder Continental engines. Models 25 and 26 were governed to a top speed of 18 mph and 14 mph, respectively. A dry disc three-plate clutch was used. At the end of 1916, a 1,200-pound capacity vehicle in the "Velie Commercial Car Line" was announced. The factory moved once again and by 1917, only two models were listed: 2-ton and 4-ton maximum capacity trucks. The company also went briefly into farm tractor manufacturing at that time.

1914 VELIE MODEL X FLAREBOARD EXPRESS   OCW

During World War I, the company prospered on government contracts. It was reorganized as the Velie Motors Corporation with a stock capitalization of $2 million. Among many manufacturers, Velie was a builder of the Liberty Standard B trucks. The 3-1/2-ton Velie Standard B was delivered to the U.S. Army in August 1918. They used a 32.4 hp 349-cubic inch four-cylinder Continental engine and a four-speed Brown-Lipe transmission with Timken worm-drive. Front tires were 36x5 and rear were 40x5 dual solid rubber. The steering wheel was still mounted on the right of the truck.

After the war, the Velie company promoted its vehicles again by racing, and showing well, at the Pike's Peak contest. In May 1919, Velie offered 1/2-, 2- and 3-1/2-ton model trucks. By the following year, perhaps due to the postwar recession, the company only listed a 1-1/2-ton truck for its lineup. Vehicle output was between 5,000 and 6,000 on the average during the early 1920s. In 1921, the Velie truck was upgraded to 2-ton maximum capacity and was offered with 36x3-1/2 front and 36x5 rear balloon tires. A 1-1/2-ton and a 2-1/2-ton Velie truck was listed for 1923.

By 1924, Willard Velie Sr. was taken ill and hired an efficiency expert to take control of production. After three years of Edwin McEwen helping the company go downhill, Willard Velie returned and installed his son Willard Velie Jr. at the helm. It is during Edwin McEwen's tenure that Velie truck production was interrupted. No trucks were listed until 1927, when the company introduced its Velie 40 Speed Truck. Advertising read "Airplane Type Motor in Speed Truck Creates New Standards of Service."

The company slogan was "Ask the Driver." Velie was referring to a six-cylinder engine that the company began building in 1922 for its passenger cars and now it was an overhead-valve design that permitted the 1-1/2-ton truck to reach 50 mph. By May 1928, a 3/4-ton speed truck was listed for $1,165 and the 1-1/2-ton model for $1,395. Willard Velie died suddenly of an embolism in October 1928. Five months later, his son died of heart failure. Without the two men at the top, the stock market crash another five months later put an end to the Velie company.

VERSARE 1925-1931 — The Versare Corporation was located in Albany, New York. Company president was Frederick Pruyn, vice-president was Oliver F. Warhus and treasurer was Randall MacDonald. The United Traction Company provided public transportation for the Capitol District of New York and it was to be Versare's first customer.

1925 VERSARE 8-WHEEL BUS   MBS

The Versare company specialized in building a large bus using hybrid gasoline-electric technology. A four-cylinder Buda engine under the giant front hood powered a generator that, in turn, drove an electric motor located in each of two four-wheel bogies at either end of the chassis. The bus was a hybrid, also, in the sense that it could serve as a streetcar. Clerestory-type roof windows on one of two versions accentuated the resemblance to a streetcar. The other model had a flat roof. Both were constructed of aluminum-alloy welded framing and aluminum-alloy skin.

Production of the first version is known to have been at least four buses and a prototype side-dump truck. Late in 1925, one Versare bus was assigned to a route in Albany, New York, and this was probably the first commercial use of the enormous vehicle.

Then in 1927, a new design was employed in a prototype with the engine mounted at the rear within the body. The more "streetcar-type" bus had its front entrance door ahead of a single front axle. The same basic hybrid drive system was employed. Customers appeared more interested, partly because the new design made it much easier to operate such a large vehicle amid pedestrian and car traffic. Transit companies from Albany, Boston, Cleveland, Lynchburg, Montreal, Salt Lake City and New York would become buyers of the Versare buses.

In 1928, a streetcar manufacturer by the name of the Cincinnati Car Company bought Versare and went into manufacturing both the three-axle hybrid-powered bus and a three-axle trolley-coach, which was later revised to a single rear axle. The trolley-coaches were sold under the Cincinnati name, while the buses stayed with the Versare emblem.

In 1930, a Versare flatbed truck rated at 20-ton capacity was tested by the Ordnance Department. It was powered by the same Buda engine as earlier Versare buses were. One Vesare bus was used at Fort Holabird for several years. Approximately 100 buses and 40 trolley-coaches were built up to 1931 with production continuing in Watervliet near Albany until 1931, when economic hard times put an end to production.

VIALL 1913-1919 — The Viall Motor Car Company was started by Clarence S. Viall and Roswall A. Viall in Chicago, Illnois. Both passenger cars and trucks were built there. The 1-ton Model B1 was priced at $1,400. Other heavier trucks were also built but details are lacking.

1912 VICTOR 2-TON   RD

VICTOR 1910-1914 — The Victor Motor Truck Company was located in Buffalo, New York. Several companies using the name Victor had come and gone by that time. At first, the company offered a 3/4-ton standard express truck for $1,650. Wheelbase was 104 inches. It was powered by a 25 hp (at 900 rpm) four-cylinder engine with Shebler carburetor and used a metal disc clutch coupling to a three-speed selective sliding gear transmission. Wooden wheels carried 34x2-1/2 front and 34x3 rear solid rubber tires. Top speed was 25 mph. Oil lamps, horn and tools were the only standard equipment.

The company began offering four more commercial vehicles that were built as delivery vans, although production numbers are uncertain. By 1912, the model line was expanded even though factory production was not set up for an efficient assembly line with such variety. Ambulances, fire apparatus, police patrol wagons and sightseeing buses were also offered. At one time, the company listed trucks up to 10-ton capacity but by 1913, a 3-ton and 5-ton truck were the only ones available from Victor, which did not survive the year 1914.

VICTOR 1913-1914 — The Victor Automobile Manufacturing Company began in St. Louis, Missouri, in 1905. It started out by building highwheelers, which were advertised as being "Hand Forged." They were powered by a one-cylinder two-stroke water-cooled engine and used a friction transmission. Price was $450. A two-cylinder engine was introduced by 1909 and later a four-cylinder was also added but by 1911, the company was in financial trouble.

It appears that after president and founder Joseph F. Harrington died in 1911, the company was reorganized in 1913 to build battery-powered electric commercial vehicles. The 1/2-ton capacity vehicles used a 32-cell Gould battery pack and a Westinghouse D.C. motor along with bevel gear final drive. Suspension was by elliptical springs on all four wheels. Wheelbase was 92 inches with as chassis weight of 1,800 pounds. The single model chassis was priced at $1,500. It is uncertain how, during this time period, the Victor Motor Car Company of St. Louis fit into the overall picture but in all probability, it was the name of the interim company after Harrington passed away.

VICTOR 1918-1920 — The Victor Motor Truck & Trailer Company was located in Chicago, Illinois. The company used a single chassis to build two models: 1-1/2-ton and 2-ton capacity trucks. Wheelbase was also shared at 140 inches. Both were powered by four-cylinder Continental engines and used three-speed progressive transmissions built by Fuller. Internal gear rear axles were obtained from Clark. As with a number of small truck builders after World War II, economic hard times and a glut of surplus trucks helped drive the companies into oblivion.

1923 VICTOR 2-1/2-TON LIAM

VICTOR 1923-1928 — Victor Motors Incorporated was located in St. Louis, Missouri, just as the Victor Automobile Manufacturing Company was, but there is no evidence that the two were directly connected. This Victor company built conventional trucks for about five years ranging from 1-1/4-ton to 6-ton capacity. The 6-ton truck was only available during 1925 and 1926. The lighter Victor trucks were powered by Hercules four-cylinder engines, while the 3-1/2-

ton and heavier trucks used Continental engines. In the last years of production, a 35-passenger bus was listed and it is believed that at least one such vehicle was actually fabricated. The company did not survive the year 1928.

1916 VIM STAGE LIAM

VIM 1913-1923 — The Touraine Company of Philadelphia, Pennsylvania, began in 1912 by continuing to build a newly-escutcheoned Nance passenger car. Harold B. Larzelere was the president of the company, who began to lose faith when sales of the 40 hp six-cylinder-powered car dipped into dire prognosis. The resulting resurrection of the company was due to the VIM truck of 1913, which was powered by a four-cylinder Northway engine using a cone clutch and bevel drive. Because it was assembled with purchased parts on a modern production line, the finished chassis was priced at $620 in 1915. For the next two years, the company sold about 13,000 trucks per year. Passenger cars were phased out in 1915, with a few leftover units assembled for 1916.

In 1918, the company offered a 1-1/2-ton and a 3-ton truck powered by an engine built by the Vim Motor Truck Company, which was the name adopted during reorganization in 1915. After World War I, the company went back to purchased engines from Continental and Hercules. The Standard Steel Car Company took over Vim in 1921. Within two years, the company assets had been sold off. Vim was listed in some directories until 1926.

VIXEN 1914-1916 — The Davis Manufacturing Company of Milwaukee, Wisconsin, built the Vixen cyclecars. These had a wheelbase up to 106 inches and a 36-inch tread. A Merchants Light Delivery was priced at $395, which was the same as for a three-passenger and a roadster model. Davis stopped building cars early in 1917 and returned to engine manufacturing.

VOLTACAR 1914-1916 — The Cyclo-Lectric Car Company was founded in New York City. The company briefly went into building a battery-powered electric delivery van, which was considered crude even at the time. The van's batteries were mounted underneath the seat: on the Model A the driver sat behind, or in the Model B the driver sat in front of a box that could carry a 500-pound load. Wheelbase was 68 inches with tread at 40 inches -- essentially an electric cyclecar. Tires were 28x2 front and rear solid rubber. Drive was by Timken-David Brown worm gear with the shaft enclosed in a tubular housing.

Steering was "from the left side of the driver's seat, the wheel being mounted upon a vertical post." A General Electric controller was operated by a lever just below the steering wheel. Maximum speed was 15 mph with a range up to 50 miles per charge. The vehicle was priced at $585 in 1914 but it was also available without batteries and instead, a leasing arrangement could be obtained from the company's service station.

Both 14-plate lead-acid or Edison alkaline A-4-type batteries were offered. A single 40-volt GE DC motor was used mounted "just back of the center of the chassis." Full elliptic springs were used on all four wheels, although the lower halves of the rear axle were "clipped under the center," while the front springs were attached above the axle. The rear axle was considered a semi-floating-type with expanding brakes only on the rear wheels. This design did not attract many buyers.

1914 VOLTACAR PARCEL DELIVERY　　　　　　　**RD**

VOLTZ 1915-1918 — Daniel W. and Edward C. Voltz were the organizers of the Voltz Brothers Company, which started in 1912 as a carriage builder at one location and as a garage at a second location in Chicago, Illinois. By 1915, the company began building a 3-ton and a 5-ton truck. Both were conventional layout with engine under the hood and used double chain drive from jackshaft to rear wheels. The company offered electric taillights and headlights as standard equipment. Little else is known about the company, which apparently ceased production in 1918.

1913 VULCAN OPEN EXPRESS　　　　　　　**MROZ**

VULCAN 1912-1916 — Not affiliated with the British Vulcan manufacturer nor the Gersix Vulcan trucks from the West Coast, the Vulcan trucks in the United States were built by the Driggs-Seabury Ordnance Company of Sharon, Pennsylvania. This company also built the Driggs-Seabury, Ritz, Sharon and Twombly motor cars, which included cyclecars. The Vulcan was a successor to the American-built Commer truck line. Five models with capacities from 3-ton to 7-ton were offered by 1913. The company built its own four-cylinder engine, pressed steel frame, cone clutch and double chain drive.

In 1915, the Driggs passenger car went into production briefly. By the beginning of World War I in Europe, Driggs-Seabury listed three models of Vulcan trucks from 2-ton to 5-ton capacity but in 1916, truck manufacturing was discontinued as the company geared up for armament manufacturing. In 1921, the company tried again with passenger car production for two years.

W

W

WABCO 1956-1984 — Wabco was the acronym for Westinghouse Air Brake Company, which first began doing business in 1869. The trucks built by this company were produced by R.G. Le Tourneau Company, which began building road construction machinery in 1919. By 1953, its earth-moving equipment division had become part of Westinghouse. In 1957, the Le Tourneau-Westinghouse Company of Peoria, Illinois, began building trucks under the name Haulpak.

1977 WABCO 3200B WABCO

Le Tourneau also began by building a huge truck-like vehicle for the U.S. Army. The application of the vehicle was to carry large payloads over the frozen tundra. Le Tourneau was already in the process of building a commercial version in 1956 for Alaska Freight Lines Company of Circle, Alaska. That one was a non-articulated tractor with five powered trailers. The military version was somewhat different in that it was articulated and had 120-inch diameter tires. The military version was built in 1957 and was called the Overland Train, Mark I, which had a payload capacity of 45 tons. The tractor had two Cummins diesel engines with two DC generators and two AC alternators. The power tractor alone weighed 29 tons. The army's name for this off-road tractor/trailer combination was "Logistical Cargo Carrier X1." Another version with eight cargo trailers totaling 572 feet in length was built in 1962 by Le Tourneau.

The first two Wabco models were of 27-ton and 30-ton capacity. Within a decade, the company was producing 65-ton capacity trucks. In 1968, Le Tourneau was bought out and Wabco trucks were manufactured by the Construction Equipment Division of Westinghouse. By 1970, the load rating had gone up to 100 tons. The following year, a diesel-electric driven tractor and semi-trailer were up to 200-ton capacity. However, Wabco continued to build what would be considered the smaller trucks, such as the Model 50 50-ton capacity truck into the 1970s. The 200-ton tractor-trailer combination was superseded by the rigid Model 3200B 235-ton diesel-electric rear-dump truck.

By the late 1970s, Wabco built 35-, 50-, 75- and 85-ton diesel-powered dump trucks as well as 120-ton and 170-ton capacity diesel-electric behemoths along with the Model 3200B. The trucks up to 85 ton were powered by six-cylinder and V-12 Cummins diesel engines from 420 hp to 700 hp or V-12 and V-16 Detroit Diesel engines from 475 hp to 700 hp. Allison six-speed automatic powershift transmissions were used with Wabco double reduction rear axle.

In the diesel-electric trucks, Caterpillar, Cummins and Detroit Diesel V-12 engines were available for the 120-ton truck and V-16 engines for the 150-ton and 170-ton trucks. For the 235-ton Model 3200B the engine used was the General Motors EMD V-12 rated up to 2475 hp, which was previously used as a locomotive engine. General Electric motors were used on all except the Model 3200B, which used two EMD electric motors in conjunction with spur and planetary gear reductions.

Wabco also built bottom-dump articulated coal trucks from 120 ton to 150 ton, which were powered by Cummins V-12 and Detroit Diesel V-16 engines that were each rated at 700 hp. Wabco trucks were assembled in Australia, Belgium and Brazil. The Australian Model W22 was the smallest of all Wabco trucks. It was powered by a 230 hp six-cylinder Detroit Diesel engine. Wabco was acquired by Dresser, which became Komatsu Dresser Corporation (KDC). The splintering of Wabco has resulted in the formation of three -- to date -- independent companies: Le Tourneau, Komatsu and Liebherr with U.S. competition from trucks built under the names of Dart, Lectrahaul, Unit Rig, Euclid, Terex and Rimpull.

1922 WACHUSETT MROZ

WACHUSETT 1922-1930 — Watchusett Motors Incorporated was located in Fitchburg, Massachusetts. Fred Suthergreen left the New England Truck Company, builders of Netco trucks, and built a factory across the street. Wachusett trucks were conventional assembled vehicles with capacities of 1-, 1-1/2-, 2- and 2-1/2-ton. The 1-ton Model S with 152-inch wheelbase was powered by a 27.3 hp four-cylinder engine and used a Brown-Lipe clutch and transmission. Front and rear axles were from Timken, steering gear was from Ross and Smith wheels carried 34x5 front and rear solid rubber tires. Chassis price was $2,400.

The 1-1/2-ton Model J with 148-inch wheelbase was powered by a four-cylinder Continental J4 engine. Tires were 36x6 front and rear solid rubber. Chassis price was $2,800. The 2-ton Model K with 154-inch wheelbase used a Continental K4 engine with chassis price at $3,200. The heaviest was the Model L with 170-inch wheelbase powered by a Continental L-4 engine. Chassis price was $3,800. All models used a Brown-Lipe clutch and transmission and Ross steering gear. The stock market crash was the final blow for the company in 1930.

1914 WADE FLAREBOARD EXPRESS OCW

WADE 1913-1914 — The Wade Commercial Car Company was located in Holly, Michigan. This company bought a unexceptional highwheeler with 800-pound capacity. The vehicle was powered by a one-cylinder air-cooled engine mounted under an open express body. A friction transmission and double-chain drive was used. Wheelbase was 72 inches and the open express body vehicle was priced at $400. The company only existed for about one year.

1916 WAGENHALS PARCEL POST DELIVERY   RD

WAGENHALS 1910-1914 — The Wagenhals Manufacturing Company began in St. Louis, Missouri, by building a three-wheel light electric delivery car. By 1912, the company was reorganized as the Wagenhals Motor Car Company and moved to Detroit, Michigan. The company also built an 800-pound capacity three-wheel delivery car powered by a 14 hp two-cylinder engine. A planetary transmission was used with single chain drive to the single rear wheel. By the time of the move to Detroit, an underslung suspension design was adopted to improve stability of the 80-inch wheelbase chassis.

By 1913, a switch was made to a four-cylinder engine. It appears the electric version was short-lived and by this time, no longer in production. All versions had wheel steering to the front axle and the driver sat behind the cargo box. Most of the Wagenhals were used by the parcel post service of the U.S. government.

In 1914, a lighter four-cylinder version was introduced with smaller four-cylinder engine mounted cross-wise on the right side. The radiator was placed on the left side of the chassis and a sliding gear transmission was adopted. The vehicle had a 500-pound capacity and the wheelbase was 67 inches. Otherwise, the design was unchanged. Above the main frame a sub-frame supported by semi-elliptic springs was used to carry the body, which was available both in open or closed form. The latter vehicle was priced at $425. However, the company's announcement of the lighter version vehicle ended with the company's shutdown in 1915.

1891 WALDHAUSER/GRILL STEAM BUS   FLP

WALDHAUSER/GRILL 1891 — John L. Waldhauser was a mechanic and Godfret Grill was a wood carver in Baltimore, Maryland. The two of them built a steam-powered eight-passenger bus in 1891, with the ornate wood body being the work of Grill while the mechanical work was done by Waldhauser. The bus had two large rear wheels and a single front wheel for steering over which the driver sat.

A trial run was made with eight passengers, who later submitted written statements before a notary public that they had ridden in the bus. The problem was that Waldhauser had neglected to include a differential, so going around corners was nearly impossible despite the front steering wheel. The differential had been invented in France in 1827, but its absence in the Waldhauser/Grill vehicle led to the abandonment of one of the earliest commercial vehicles ever built in the United States.

1923 WALKER ELECTRIC PLATFORM TRUCK   SWEET

WALKER 1906-1942 — The Automobile Maintenance & Manufacturing Company of Chicago, Illinois, began building electric vehicles under the name Walker Balance Gear. This design incorporated a separate electric motor for each rear wheel but in 1909, this was replaced by a single large 3-1/2 hp electric motor mounted integrally in the rear axle. A gasoline-electric hybrid power system was used briefly but was not successful.

In 1912, the company was reorganized as the Walker Vehicle Company in Chicago. That year, the model line consisted of five models ranging from 750-pound to 3-1/2-ton capacity. All of the vehicles were built for commercial purposes and used the single rear axle motor, which used internal gear reduction inside each solid cast steel rear wheel. Up to 1/2-ton capacity, Walker vehicles had hoods that were strictly decorative, in line with the appearance of gasoline-powered light trucks. The Walker trucks and vans continued to be built through the 1920s, with the only major change being the availability of pneumatic tires by mid-decade. All of the heavier models were forward-control.

1924 WALKER ELECTRIC VAN   KP

In 1929, the Model 10 Special rated at 3/4-ton capacity was styled close to that of contemporary gasoline-powered light trucks and helped sell Walker electric trucks through the 1930s, when most other electric vehicle manufacturers had faded out of existence. The heaviest Walker for 1929 was a 7-ton capacity truck.

In 1938, Walker returned to the gasoline-electric hybrid design called Walker Dynamotive. These used either four-cylinder Waukesha engines or six-cylinder Chrysler engines, which powered a 15 kilowatt generator mounted on the flywheel bellhousing that drove the electric motor in the rear axle. The four-cylinder truck had a 1-ton capacity and the six-cylinder had a 1-1/2-ton capacity. A number of Walker electric trucks were exported to Great Britain, where sales continued during the 1930s. Along with the two hybrid vehicles, trucks up to 5-ton capacity were built until 1942.

WALKER-JOHNSON 1919-1924 — The Walker-Johnson Truck Company was located in East Woburn, Massachusetts. The first truck built by this company was a 2-1/2-ton capacity vehicle powered by a four-cylinder Buda engine and used a four-speed Brown-Lipe transmission and Timken worm-drive rear axle. Wheelbase was 150 inches. In 1920, the company moved to Boston, Massachusetts. By 1922, the single 2-1/2-ton model was superseded by a 1-ton model powered by a four-cylinder Midwest engine. This vehicle was not particularly successful and the company closed down by 1924.

WALL 1903 — The R.C. Wall Manufacturing Company was organized in Philadelphia, Pennsylvania. It was produced as a working prototype for the Ward Bread Company and was powered by a 21 hp three-cylinder two-stroke "vertical" water-cooled engine, which was located in front under a prominent hood. The C-cab van had a cone clutch and a three-speed "spur-gear" transmission with a countershaft and double chain drive. Engine rpm was advertised in the range from 150 to 800. Artillery wheels were shod with solid rubber tires of dimensions 38x4 front and 42x4 rear. Brakes were on each rear wheel and a separate foot-operated brake acted on the differential gear. Semi-elliptic springs were used on all four wheels.

The company also advertised a foot warmer and dash with glass panels for winter use. Front side opera windows gave a close resemblance to the 1903 White van. An announcement in July 1903 stated, "This wagon has just been finished by the R.C. Wall Mfg. Co., which is in position to duplicate it without further charges, having tested it until satisfied that all parts are right." There is no evidence that any more Wall Business Wagons were built.

1922 WALLACE COACH NMM

WALLACE 1919-1922 — The Wallace truck was assembled in England by Richmond Motor Lorries Limited at Shepherd's Bush, London. The 1-1/2-ton vehicles used American-made components including a four-cylinder Continental Red Seal engine, three-speed transmission and bevel drive rear axle. A char-a-banc model was added to the model line but the company's plans to manufacture the entire vehicle in England did not materialize and it closed down by 1922.

WALTER 1909 to date — William Walter was a Swiss immigrant who owned the first automobile on Staten Island, which is where he had made his new home in 1883. He had imported the car from Europe in 1898 but Walter was not satisfied with it. He had another car built at the American Chocolate Machinery Company in Manhattan, which is where he was involved with building confectionery production equipment. After testing the car for a few years he placed it on the market in 1902 as the Waltmobile. The next car, which appeared in 1903, was called the Walter and in 1904, yet another car with a 30 hp engine and three-speed sliding gear transmission was shown at the New York Automobile Show.

During this time the American Chocolate Machinery Company became the manufacturer of the luxurious Walter cars. It was not until 1905 that the Walter Automobile Company was formed. After several partnerships and a foreclosure, the Walter Automobile Company went out of business in 1909. William Walter moved on to form the Walter Auto Truck Manufacturing Company in New York City.

1914 WALTER 4X4 WALTER

Walter truck production began in New York City in 1909 and the first vehicles were conventional units similar in design to the passenger cars produced up until then. However, in 1911, a four-wheel-drive truck was introduced based on the French Latil design with the radiator behind the engine, which was covered by a so-called Renault hood. This type of truck was to be the essential model line for the company, although rear-wheel and front-wheel-drive trucks were also built. All had internal gear drive. In 1911, the company became the Walter Motor Truck Company. Within a few years, the Walter four-wheel-drive trucks were being built for the war effort.

Up until 1920, Walter built its own four-cylinder engines but after the postwar recession, the company switched to Waukesha engines with only a few exceptions. The company moved to a new factory at Long Island in 1923. Engines were set ahead of the front axles for weight distribution. Walter pioneered this design, which later was adopted by FWD, Oshkosh and other companies.

1925 WALTER SNOW FIGHTER HAYS

401

By the mid-1920s, the company was building highway tractors in 7-, 10- and 15-ton ratings. These were designated as models FL, F and FR, respectively. Each of them was powered by Walter's own four-cylinder engines from 25.6 hp to 32.4 hp. The lighter model used a Stromberg carburetor while the two heavier had Zenith carbs and all had Westinghouse ignition. Transmissions and front and rear axles were all manufactured by Walter. Ross steering was used and Day wheels carried 40-inch diameter solid rubber tires. Model FR had dual wheels on the back. Chassis weights ranged from 7,700 pounds to 9,200 pounds.

1935 WALTER MODEL FMD CHASSIS   MROZ

1935 WALTER SNOW FIGHTER WITH PLOW   MROZ

In 1929, the company introduced its Walter Snow Fighter truck, which would become a successful design also used for construction and concrete mixer use. The company expanded into fire engine production during the 1930s, supplying a number of units to New York City. Two-axle truck tractors were also used for coal hauling and in the logging industry. By the end of the decade, Walter offered six models of four-wheel-drive trucks from 3-ton to 12-ton capacity. Six-cylinder gasoline engines were purchased from Hercules and Waukesha and six-cylinder diesel engines were supplied by Cummins.

Walter built 4x4 artillery tractors during World War II as well as snow removal trucks for the Canadian and U.S. Armies. The artillery tractor was powered by a 672-cubic inch six-cylinder Hercules engine. The snow removal trucks/plows had six-cylinder Waukesha engines.

After the war, Walter returned to building both 4x4 rigid trucks as well as tractor trucks used for heavy construction and mining applications. Rigid trucks were also built as heavy-duty wreckers. In the late 1940s, Walter built specially-designed snowplows for New York International Airport (now JFK). From that experience, the company got the opportunity to focus on fire apparatus once again and in cooperation with the U.S. government, the National Fire Protection Association and the Port of New York Authority, developed a series of airport crash tenders, emergency vehicles and foam-spraying fire engines. This design incorporated both single engine and dual engine 4x4 chassis, which were also used for snowplows.

Walter again began to concentrate on airport fire engines. In the 1950s, controls for water and foam were mechanical and transmissions were all manual on the first airport crash fire trucks, which used Maxim apparatus briefly from 1949. The company received a $9 million contract in 1956 to build fire trucks. Walter moved to upstate New York in 1957. The Class 1500 crash units and "CF" civilian version of 1959 were superseded in 1962 with the CB series, which used dual engines,

both with automatic transmissions, and dual water pumps. The trucks could be operated with either engine, or both, and either pump, or both. About 200 of the CB vehicles were built.

1968 WALTER CB-3000   WALTER

1970 WALTER AIRPORT CRASH TRUCK   OCW

1975 WALTER MODEL CBK   OCW

The CB-3000 was introduced in 1965 and the first units were delivered to Chicago's O'Hare International Airport. The CB-3000 weighed 28 tons when fully loaded but could still reach 60 mph powered by Ford V-8 or Detroit Diesel engines through a pair of torque-converter transmissions. Total pumping capacity was 2,000 gallons per minute using two single-stage centrifugal pumps, each rated at 1,000 gpm. The truck carried 400 gallons of foam. The CB-3000 was produced until 1980 and about 100 were built for U.S. and foreign airports.

In 1980, a group of Canadian businessmen bought the Canadian subsidiary, which had been organized in 1932. When banks foreclosed on the Walter Motor Truck Company in the United States during 1980, Walter Equipment USA was formed as a subsidiary of the Canadian company. This new business venture in turn bought all the assets of the former Walter Motor Truck Company in 1981. The resurrected Walter Equipment Company relocated to the Northeastern Industrial Park in Guilderland, New York.

1988 WALTER B-3000   WALTER

For the mid-1980s, Walter completely redesigned its 4x4 trucks, which included several patented drive features. The new model was called the B-3000, which incorporated an exclusive four-point positive drive and suspended double reduction drive along with automatic torque proportioning differentials. The B-3000 trucks have also featured full compensating differential action, Suspended Drive resulting in minimum unsprung weight, dropped position axles for lowest frame height and center of gravity, as well as more equal weight distribution between axles, higher ground clearance under axles and large diameter tires for minimum rolling resistance and improved traction. Walter has also used constant velocity steering drive universal joints.

1995 WALTER 4X4 UTILITY CHASSIS   WALTER

For the 1990s, Walter has built Snow Fighters, Airport Crash Trucks, Tractor Trucks and Special Purpose Trucks. The Walter "U" Series Snow Fighters have incorporated the above features along with Allison fully automatic or Fuller manual shift transmission. Engine options have been the 270 hp Cummins PT-270, 300 hp Cummins NTC-300, 350 hp Cummins NTC-350, 290 hp Detroit 6-71T or 350 hp Detroit 8V-71. The Walter Snow Fighter has been powered by up to 450 hp providing a maximum speed of 40 mph.

1995 WALTER RAPID INTERVENTION VEHICLE   WALTER

Another Walter vehicle built to date has been the Model BDG 1,500-gallon ARFF. This airport fire truck has used a 540 hp Detroit Diesel 8V92T and an Allison HT750 fully automatic five-speed transmission.

Walter double reduction axles have been used along with a Walter single-speed automatic-locking, torque-proportioning center differential. GVW rating for this vehicle was 40,000 pounds. Top speed was 65 mph with 0 to 50 mph in less than 30 seconds, with typical loaded weight of 38,365 pounds. The BDT-3000 is the largest airport crash truck Walter has built to date. It used the 540 hp Detroit Diesel 8V92T engine with an Allison HT750 five-speed automatic transmission. Acceleration has been rated at 0 to 50 mph in less than 45 seconds with top speed of 65 mph.

1907 WALTHAM MODEL DC DELIVERY WAGON   RD

WALTHAM/WALTHAM-ORIENT 1906-1908 — The Waltham Manufacturing Company began in Waltham, Massachusetts, in 1893 for the production of Orient bicycles. Charles Herman Metz was a founder but soon left after disagreements with the board of directors. The company began to experiment with a light car called the Buckboard, which went into production at the turn of the century. These were soon joined by larger cars called Orient. By 1905, the company became known as Waltham but vehicles under the Waltham-Orient name were also produced.

The commercial vehicles were derivatives of the passenger car chassis and were built as light vans from 600-pound to 800-pound capacity. By 1907, there were eight models, all quite similar to one another. These were powered by 4 hp or 8 hp two-cylinder engines and used friction transmissions. Wheelbase was from 96 inches to 99 inches, the latter including the largest Waltham vehicle called the Democrat Wagon built as a small bus for up to six passengers and selling for $1,850 in 1908, which was the last year of manufacture for commercial vehicles.

Charles Metz got his company back in 1908 and the following year, it was reorganized as the Metz company. The company continued until 1921, when financial trouble arrived once again. The passenger cars built for 1922 were once again called Waltham. That year, the company went bankrupt.

1914 WARD MODEL EB FLAREBOARD EXPRESS   OCW

WARD 1905-1934 — The Ward Electric was first built by the Pittsburgh Motor Vehicle Company in 1905 in Pittsburgh, Pennsylvania. The company was organized by Charles A. Ward, an engineer from Cornell University who designed a light van intended as a delivery vehicle for his family's Ward bread baking business. For the first five years, the vans were used exclusively to distribute Ward's "Tip-Top" bread throughout Pittsburgh until the business expanded to New York City.

1914 WARD MODEL EO ELECTRIC PLATFORM TRUCK   OCW

In 1910, the Ward Motor Vehicle Company was established in the New York City's Bronx section. The company continued to build delivery vans from 800-pound to 2-ton capacity. In 1912, the company introduced a 3-1/2-ton capacity vehicle and the following year, a 4-ton truck was also available. The year 1914 was also the time that the company went into electric passenger car production. For 1915, a 5-ton capacity truck was introduced and the company moved to Mt. Vernon, New York.

1916 WARD ELECTRIC DELIVERY VAN   OCW

1929 WARD 1/2-TON WALK-IN ELECTRIC VAN   OCW

1930 WARD DAIRY DELIVERY TRUCK   OCW

By 1916, passenger car production ended and in 1918, the company's trade name was changed to Ward-Electric. That year, house-to-house delivery trucks featured a hinged dashboard that swung away for easier access and exit with the front bumper acting as a step. Up to 1920, all Ward vehicles were powered by Westinghouse DC motors but in 1921, the company switched to General Electric motors. Production of 1/2-ton to 5-ton capacity trucks and vans continued until 1925, when a 10-ton capacity truck was introduced. The model line stayed essentially unchanged until 1934, when production of complete vehicles ceased. Ward built truck bodies for various companies until 1965.

WARD LAFRANCE 1918-1993 — The Ward LaFrance Truck Corporation of Elmira, New York, was organized by A. Ward LaFrance in 1918. A. Ward LaFrance was from the same family that established the American-LaFrance fire engine company but the Ward LaFrance business was entirely separate from the earlier firm established in 1910.

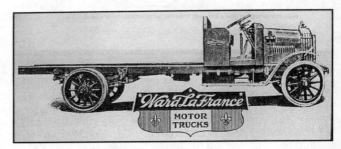

1920 WARD LAFRANCE CHASSIS   RD

Ward LaFrance built assembled trucks for the armed forces during World War I. The first series had a capacity from 2-1/2 ton to 7 ton and was powered by four-cylinder Waukesha engines and used Brown-Lipe transmissions and Timken axles. Almost from the beginning, Ward LaFrance trucks featured an effective though bulky self-lubricating system.

By 1920, Ward LaFance introduced a 2-1/2-ton truck especially designed to use pneumatic tires at a time when vehicles of such capacity all had solid rubber tires. A two-cylinder Kellog pump was made standard as an accessory for the early pneumatic tires, which needed repair quite often. By 1925, the 5-ton Model A with 164-inch wheelbase was priced at $5,490 for chassis, which weighed 9,300 pounds. Component manufacturers included Brown-Lipe, Timken, Ross steering gear, Smith wheels and Stromberg carburetion.

In 1926, Ward LaFrance introduced six-cylinder engines and the model line was extended to include a 7-ton capacity truck. Three years later, two bus chassis were also available. In 1930, the company introduced its "Bustruk," which was a high-speed chassis for use as a bus or truck van that was powered by an inline eight-cylinder Lycoming engine. Sales for the company averaged 100 units per year and most of the vehicles were sold to the city of New York.

In 1930, Ward LaFrance introduced an eight-cylinder engine for its "Bustruk" chassis. During the 1930s, Ward LaFrance specialized in custom-built trucks for crane transportation. Some of these were used as tow vehicles for illegally parked cars in New York City and a number of such trucks were produced in 1934. This was also the year the company adopted the use of diesel engines supplied by Cummins. The engines were first used in Ward LaFrance heavy-duty six-wheel trucks. Highway tractors rated to 20 tons were built by mid-decade. In 1935, the first COE six-wheel truck was introduced. An extraordinary option at that time was a fabricated chassis frame made from steel or Duralumin, which was soon abandoned due to extremely high cost.

Ward LaFrance built heavy-duty wreckers during World War II. These were 6x6 trucks at first designated as M1 vehicles, later M1A1, which were powered by six-cylinder Continental engines also manufactured for the war effort by Kenworth. The company also produced 6x4 and 6x6 load carriers for the U.S. Army.

1945 WARD LAFRANCE MODEL D   FLP

With the additional capitalization of the Elmira factory during the war based on military contracts, the company expanded its range with the addition of the D series in 1945. The new line of trucks were rated at 40,000 to 60,000 GCW and were powered by either Continental gasoline engines or Cummins diesel engines. Flat fender styling was carried over from the military vehicles and the postwar demand for new trucks boosted sales to 509 for 1947 and 271 for 1948. An attempt to market a bus for export did not meet with success, although it appears a few units were sold to Argentina and Mexico.

After the war, once the market for trucks was filled, sales fell drastically. Load carriers were dropped from the model line and the company began to concentrate on fire engines. During the 1950s, the company built conventional open-cab ladder trucks. In 1959, a forward-cab design was introduced, which was built with a variety of pumper and aerial platform bodies powered by Ford, Hall-Scott, International, Roiline or Waukesha engines. Both five-speed and six-speed transmissions were available and air brakes were standard.

In 1962, Ward La France built a long-wheelbase truck tractor that had no compound curves in its sheet metal. About 390 of these were supplied to the U.S. Air Force and these were powered by 336 hp 567-cubic inch Detroit Diesel Model 7087 V-8 engines with five-speed Fuller Model 5-C-72 transmissions.

During the late 1960s and 1970s, Ward LaFrance increasingly used Chevrolet, Ford and International commercial chassis to build fire engines. The largest truck built through the 1970s was the 532 hp twin-V-8 engine 4x4 airport crash tender, which had a maximum speed of 60 mph. In 1971, Ward LaFrance pioneered the change of fire truck color from red to lime yellow, which scientific studies showed to be more clearly visible than the previously accepted fire engine red. With the new paint color analysis accepted by experts, Ward LaFrance shipped trucks to 140 different fire

departments in 1975 alone. These included fire departments in the United States as well as Columbia, El Salvador, Saudi Arabia and Venezuela.

1975 WARD LAFRANCE CUSTOM PUMPER WARD LAFRANCE

By the end of the 1970s, Ward LaFrance was also supplying the U.S. Army with a heavy-duty 8x8 transporter powered by a 600 hp diesel engine. The company continued to build specialized fire apparatus on its own chassis through the 1980s, but the company finally succumbed to financial woes in 1993.

WARE 1912-1915 — The Ware Motor Vehicle Company was established in St. Paul, Minnesota. This company was organized by J.L. Ware, who also designed the Ware truck, which was one of earliest four-wheel-drive trucks built using a driveshaft and power dividers at the rear differential. Two shafts then returned power to each front wheel. Ware trucks were built in three sizes from 3/4-ton up to 3-ton capacity. This company was succeeded by the Twin City Four Wheel Drive Company, which utilized the same Ware design for its own trucks.

WARREN/WARREN-DETROIT 1911-1913 — The Warren Motor Car Company was founded by Homer Warren, who was a successful real estate entrepreneur and also the postmaster of the city of Detroit. The company was formed at the end of 1909 with the participation of W.H. Radford, a former Hudson engineer, and John G. Bayerline, formerly of Olds Motor Works. The passenger cars that first appeared for 1910 were powered by a 30 hp four-cylinder engine. The following year, there were eight different passenger car body styles, all under the Model 11 moniker, and a light van was also introduced.

The Warren cars met with racing success and the company continued to offer the light commercial versions of its car with both open and enclosed van bodies. Shaft drive and three-speed transmissions were standard equipment. Wheelbase was 110 inches for the commercial vehicles, which was also the wheelbase of the Model 11 of 1911 and of the Model 12-30K of 1912. The "Winged Express" Warren commercial car was priced at $1,300. Financial problems led to a reorganization in 1912. The failure of the main sales organization by the name of Taylor Distributing Company in Philadelphia appears to be the reason that Warren ceased production in 1913.

WARREN 1912-1913 — Not affiliated with its contemporary, the Warren Motor Car Company of Detroit, the Warren Motor Truck Company of Warren, Ohio, built one model of a truck that was designated as the Model 30. This was a 1/2-ton open express commercial vehicle with a 110-inch wheelbase powered by a 30 hp four-cylinder engine, just as the other Warren was during the same time period. The company faded out after 1913 but it is uncertain when all production actually ceased.

WASHINGTON 1909-1912 — The Washington Motor Vehicle Company, located in Washington D.C., built four models of electric commercial vehicles. The lightest was a 750-pound capacity van and the heftiest was a 2-ton capacity truck. All four used Edison alkaline batteries, which gave the vehicles an approximate 50-mile range. Final drive was with double chain. In 1911, the company's name was changed to Capitol Car and a passenger vehicle was produced for a brief period.

1910 WASHINGTON OPEN EXPRESS　　　　**WJP**

WASHINGTON 1914-1916 — Although the Washington Motor Car Company listed 5-, 6- and 7-ton trucks, there is no evidence that any were actually manufactured. This company was an outgrowth of the Carter Motor Car Corporation, which went bankrupt in 1912 and was reorganized three times, also using the name Independence Motor Company.

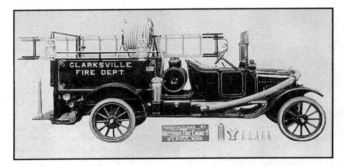

1919 WATEROUS/FORD　　　　**WATEROUS**

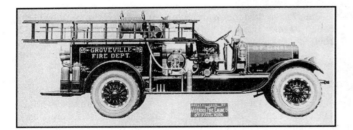

1923 WATEROUS FIRE ENGINE　　　　**WATEROUS**

WATEROUS 1906-1923 — The Waterous Engine Works of St. Paul, Minnesota, was a builder of horsedrawn steam fire engines. According to some sources, Waterous was the first company to build a gasoline-powered fire engine in the United States, which was bought by the city of Radnor, Pennsylvania. It was a forward-control vehicle and used one engine for propelling the vehicle and a second engine to drive the pump. In 1907, a conventional design was adopted using a four-cylinder engine that was mounted under a large hood. This type of fire engine was built in small numbers until 1923, although the company continued to stay in business building pumps. Waterous built fire apparatus on commercial chassis, such as Reo, until the Great Depression. The company has built pumps for fire engines to date.

1928 WATEROUS/REO　　　　**WATEROUS**

1920 WATSON 5-TON ARTICULATED TRUCK　　　　**FLP**

WATSON 1917-1925 — The Watson Wagon Company of Canastota, New York, built what the firm called "Trucktractor." This was an assembled truck using a forward-control design with a crescent cab and a shallow parabolic radiator. A bumper protruded from the extended frame in front of the vehicle. The short wheelbase truck was rated at 5-ton capacity. It was powered by a four-cylinder Continental engine with centrifugal water pump cooling and used a Brown-Lipe clutch and four-speed transmission. Timken worm-drive was used and solid rubber tires were mounted on artillery wheels with duals on back. The truck had right-hand drive and was priced at $4,050 with electric lights at extra cost.

In 1919, the company became known as the Watson Products Corporation. Semi-trailers were also built and these included dump-body trailers for construction with large steel-shod artillery wheels. Solid rubber tires were used on trailers for more conventional road use. In 1920, Watson also built conventional trucks with C-cabs with capacity ratings from 1-ton to 3-1/2-ton. The company switched to four-cylinder Buda engines and adopted left-hand steering location. Electric lights became standard equipment and bumpers were spring loaded. The company was reorganized in 1923 as the Watson Truck Corporation in Canastota but by 1925, it was out of business for good.

WAVERLY 1898-1903, 1908-1916 — The Waverly Electric began in Indianapolis, Indiana, when the Indiana Bicycle Company merged with the American Electric Vehicle Company. The firm also operated as the American Bicycle Company and the International Motor Car Company, but all of the names were simply different incarnations of Colonel Albert Pope's business empire.

By the turn of the century, Waverly offered 18 different models, which included open and closed delivery vans and a station bus in addition to the passenger cars with names such as Piano-Box Runabout. In 1904, the name was changed to Pope-Waverly and production was continued until 1908, when the company was sold to former Waverly executives who reorganized as the Waverly Company without Albert Pope. H.H. Rice, W.B. Cooley and W.C. Johnson were the key organizers who continued manufacturing "The Silent Waverly" until 1916. The largest Waverly was a 5-ton capacity brewery truck.

WAYNE 1914 — The Wayne Light Commercial Car Company was located in New York City and briefly produced a three-wheel delivery vehicle with an 800-pound capacity. The cargo box was over the front two wheels ahead of the driver. The vehicle was powered by an air-cooled two-cylinder engine that had belt drive to the single rear wheel. A two-speed transmission was used and the three-wheeler was steered by handlebars. The price was $475. The Wayne was in production for less than one year.

1945 WAYNE BUS   **MBS**

WAYNE 1931-1994 — Richmond, Indiana, has been the home of The Wayne Works. The company started out as a wagon builder in the 1840s. During the 1920s, Wayne built composite school bus bodies for Chevrolet, Dodge and Ford chassis. During the 1930s, Ford used Wayne bodies to build standard buses and this was repeated for 1949 and 1950. During World War II, Wayne built approximately 300 sectional bus bodies, which were similar to those made by C.J. Hug. The Wayne bodies were mounted on rear-engine Reo chassis. In 1959, Divco purchased Wayne and a forward-control transit bus called the Bantam was built by the division of what had become the Divco-Wayne Corporation. Since that time, Wayne Corporation has built buses on a variety of commercial chassis.

In 1991, Wayne went bankrupt and was purchased by the BMY Corporation of Marysville, Ohio. BMY, a supplier to the U.S. military, changed the name to Wayne Wheeled Vehicles but this venture lasted only about one year. In 1994, Carpenter acquired the tooling, engineering and rights to the Wayne name. Carpenter moved its operations to the large and modern 533,000-square foot facilities that Wayne had built during the 1960s in Richmond, Indiana. The Wayne name was discontinued by Carpenter.

WEBSTER 1910-1911 — The Chicago Coach and Carriage Company was the builder of the Webster truck and bus. The single model chassis was rated at 3/4-ton or 12-passenger. Wheelbase was 93 inches and tread was 56 inches. The vehicle was powered by a 16 hp two-cylinder four-cycle engine with Schebler carburetor and used a two-speed planetary transmission with countershaft and double chain drive. Wooden wheels carried 1-3/4-inch wide solid rubber tires front and rear. Maximum speed was 20 mph. Front springs were semi-elliptic, while the rear springs were full-elliptic. Lamps and horn were standard equipment. Exactly when the Webster ceased to be manufactured has not been determined.

1907 WEEKS LIGHT DELIVERY VAN   **JAW**

WEEKS 1907-1908 — The Weeks Commercial Vehicle Company was located in Chicago, Illinois. One model of commercial vehicle was built by this firm and this was in the form of a closed van rated at 1/2-ton. Mounted under the floorboards, it was powered by a 20 hp two-cylinder Advance engine and used a friction disc transmission with double chain drive to the rear wheels.

WEIER-SMITH/W-S 1915-1919 — Nearly all of the trucks built by the Weier-Smith Truck Company were called W-S. The firm was located in Birmingham, Michigan. For the first year, only a 1-1/2-ton truck was built. For the second year, only a 2-1/2-ton truck was produced. For 1918 and 1919, W-S trucks were up to 3-1/2-ton capacity powered by four-cylinder Continental engines using an eight-speed transmission and worm-drive rear axle with a wheelbase of 158 inches.

WERNER 1925 — Ralph M. Werner was a mechanic from Brooklyn, New York, who had a maintenance and repair service and worked on United Parcel trucks. From his experience in disassembling many Hahn trucks, Werner built his own truck, which could be rapidly disassembled. With the use of cotter pins and snap couplings, the truck's engine could be removed in four minutes, the transmission in one-and-a-half minutes, the clutch in less than one minute and the driveshaft in five seconds, it was claimed. An article in the January issue of *Motor Magazine* described these features, although otherwise the truck was entirely conventional in appearance.

The *Motor Magazine* article stated "...it is no criticism of the industry to remark that present backwardness in quick repair construction is unquestionably due to a real lack of understanding by engineers and draftsmen as to what the serviceman is up against." Right angle slots at the transmission-to-engine mounting permitted removal of the gearbox by loosening the bolts and turning the transmission one inch. Components were not built by Werner but purchased from known manufacturers, such as the Timken-Detroit rear axle. The four-cylinder engine used a Zenith carburetor and Eisemann ignition, both further modified by Werner.

In addition, the truck frame was made of I-beam structural steel eight inches in depth with five-inch flanges and a weight of 17 pounds per foot. Crossmembers were made of heavy steel tubing set in bronze sockets bolted to the frame. The tubes were "filled with waste soaked in oil so that no squeaks will develop..." Werner had several original and not impractical ideas that were incorporated in the few trucks he built and at least one carried the emblem "Werner Brooklyn N.Y." However, several of the quick-disconnect designs would have led to problems with quick disconnection at inopportune times and Werner did not go into manufacture on any scale of more than several individually crafted vehicles.

1975 WESTCOASTER ELECTRIC MAIL VAN   **OTIS**

WESTCOASTER 1927-1975 — The West Coast Machinery Company started out in Stockton, California, during 1927 with the intent of producing farm equipment. Almost from the beginning, the company began building light three-wheel commercial vehicles

407

similar to those built by Cushman. They were powered by gasoline or battery depending on the model. The internal combustion engine was a 50-cubic inch 17.6 hp two-cylinder unit. The electric-powered versions used a 36-volt system. Automotive hypoid-type drive was used to the rear axle and most of the vehicles had wheel steering, although some of the lightest "carts" used tiller steering.

In 1970, Westcoaster was sold to Otis Elevator Company and became a division of the parent firm. Vehicles produced were for police patrol, mail service, refuse haulers, ambulances for factories, hotel transporters, building complex security vehicles and other non-highway applications.

Westcoaster also built two four-wheel vehicles. One was a 1-ton flatbed hauler and the second was a 750-pound capacity delivery van with a top speed of 43 mph. The van/flatbed was called the Otis and it was powered by a 30 hp electric motor using 16 six-volt lead-acid batteries, which raised the van's weight to 3,700 pounds with a double wall fiberglass body. The company advertised that the van could climb a five percent grade at 30 mph and in 1974, it cost 1-1/2 cents per mile to operate. It was priced at $8,000.

Under the ownership of the Otis company, production was forecast at 50 van/flatbed units per year. A 20-passenger Electrobus was designed and a few were built, but the entire Westcoaster division was closed in September of 1975 due to poor sales performance.

WESTERN 1917-1923 — The Western Truck Manufacturing Company was located in Chicago, Illinois. The company initially entered the market with a 7-ton model truck. It was powered by a four-cylinder Wisconsin engine and used a four-speed transmission and double chain drive. Wheelbase was 146 inches.

By 1919, the 7-ton was in its last year of manufacture and the following year, Western built a series of three trucks that were rated at 1-1/2-, 2-1/2- and 3-1/2-ton. All three of these used Timken worm-drive. The lightest could be distinguished from the other two by the fact that it had a three-speed transmission, while the heavier trucks used a four-speed transmission. The company did not survive the year 1923.

WESTERN STAR see WHITE

WESTERN see FLYER

1912 WESTFIELD 3/4-TON MODEL O　　　　**MROZ**

WESTFIELD 1912-1913 — The Westfield Motor Truck Company was located in Westfield, Massachusetts. The company built 3/4-, 1- and 2-ton capacity trucks. The 3/4 ton was called the Model O and was priced at $1,500 with canvas canopy and open express body.

The trucks featured four-cylinder engines, three-speed selective sliding gear transmissions and shaft drive. The engine used splash lubrication exclusively and the clutch was a multi-disc-type running in oil. Thirty-inch artillery-type wheels carried pneumatic tires front and rear. Front suspension was with semi-elliptic springs and rear suspension was with full elliptic springs. It does not appear that the company continued production beyond 1913.

1901 WESTINGHOUSE HUB BUS　　　　**RD**

WESTINGHOUSE 1901, 1977 — In 1901, the Westinghouse Electric & Manufacturing Company of Pittsburgh, Pennsylvania, built an omnibus using the newly-developed Hub Motor Company. The 20-passenger bus used four Hub electric motors, one in each wheel and each rated at 7 hp. The motors could be momentarily overloaded 500 percent. A tray under the body carried an 80-cell battery. The battery was invented and patented by J.K. Pumpelly. Innovations in the battery design included one set of chemically-formed plates and the others were pasted plates. Glass wool was used to protect the battery plates.

Wooden wheels carried solid rubber tires but the company was "experimenting with a pulp or composition hemp tire which is expected to outlast two sets of rubber." The buses were used primarily in Chicago by the Hub Motor Transit Company, which assigned its patent rights to Westinghouse.

1977 WESTINGHOUSE MARKETEER　　　　**SEVA**

Among many vehicle development projects with which Westinghouse was involved, the electric Marketeer of 1977 was a notable one. This was a four-wheel industrial/commercial-type vehicle with a capacity of 3/4-ton. It was capable of running 50 miles on a single charge and was delivered to the military installation at Ft. McNair. It is not known how many Marketeer light electric trucks were built.

WESTMAN 1912-1914 — The Westman Motor Truck Company of Cleveland, Ohio, built a single model of its 1-1/2-ton truck. It used forward-control design and had a three-speed transmission and shaft drive. A dual ignition system was featured with the truck's four-cylinder engine. Although several bodies were available from the factory, a covered express was known as the Model E. With a 104 inch wheelbase, the Model E's chassis weight was 3,800 pounds.

WESTRAM see WARD LAFRANCE

WEYHER 1910 — The Weyher Manufacturing Company went into the production of trucks for a brief period in Whitewater, Wisconsin. The one model the company built was a 1/2-ton capacity vehicle powered by a 16 hp two-cylinder water-cooled engine located under a front hood. A friction transmission was used along with double chain drive to the rear wheels. Solid rubber tires were standard equipment and wheelbase was 94 inches.

1928 WHIPPET CANOPY TOP EXPRESS   **HAC**

WHIPPET see WILLYS

WHITCOMB 1928-1930 — The Whitcomb Wheel Company operated in Kensoha, Wisconsin. The company built a six-wheel bus using integral "uni-body" construction and coil independent front suspension. The Whitcomb bus was powered by a 105 hp six-cylinder Wisconsin Z engine that could attain 60 mph. It was built to accommodate 24 passengers, or as a long distance luxury coach there was room for 18 passengers. The price ranged from $13,000 to $15,000 depending on the appointments. For 1930, the company offered a 3-ton truck using the same essential design but by that time, the stock market had crashed. That turned out to be the last year for Whitcomb's vehicle manufacturing.

WHITE 1900-1903 — The White Engineering Works of Indianapolis, Indiana, built a 2-ton steam wagon in 1900. The vehicle used a marine water-tube boiler and a four-cylinder horizontal double compound engine. Double chain drive was used at the rear axle. The vehicle was capable of 5 mph. In 1901, the company's name was changed to the White Steam Wagon Company but it was not related to the White truck manufacturer of Cleveland, Ohio.

WHITE 1900-1995 — Thomas H. White began building sewing machines in 1859 in Orange, Massachusetts, and moved his business to Cleveland, Ohio, by 1866. The company expanded its product line and new divisions were organized to include the manufacture of roller skates and bicycles. In 1900, his four sons, Thomas II, Rollin, Walter and Windsor, built their first steam vehicle and by 1901, production was up to three vehicles per week.

One of the first commercial vehicles was a steam van sold to the Denver Dry Goods Company in 1901. The vehicle featured a two-cylinder engine, mounted under the floor, with underslung condensers. Chain drive and tiller steering were used.

In 1902, four of five White steam vehicles made a perfect score in the Boston-to-New York endurance run and two of those were delivery wagons. The 1902 White Steam Delivery Wagons had tiller steering but were fitted with radiator condensers "in order to avoid the appearance of steam in crowded traffic, where they are certain to be used." The 1/4-ton C-cab vans had porthole windows on each side and were intended for use "in light retail trade, such as dry goods, laundry and mail delivery." A 5-ton steam truck was also built in 1902.

1902 WHITE STEAM DELIVERY   **MROZ**

By 1903, the White steam trucks had compound engines and semi-flash boilers and radiator condensers allowed 100 miles between fill-ups. Tiller steering was replaced by wheel steering and shaft drive was adopted. Pneumatic tires were used almost from the beginning. A few 1/2-ton commercial steam vehicles built by White appeared in 1904 powered by a 10 hp engine. A heavier chassis was built as White's first bus that year.

White offered numerous types of bodies by 1906, which included buses. It has been documented that one was sold to a company in Japan. A police patrol wagon was sold to the city of Rio de Janiero. Fire apparatus was built on White chassis. For the U.S. government, the company produced mail trucks and military ambulances. The heaviest vehicles built at that time by White were rated to 3-ton capacity. By 1906, production was up to 1,500 units per year, including both passenger and commercial vehicles. The White Company was incorporated that year to handle only motor vehicle manufacturing. Thomas White left that business for his sons to run while he continued with the earlier sewing machine venture he had founded.

The first gasoline-powered vehicles appeared in 1909 using engines manufactured by Delahaye. Steam vehicles were still available but by December of that year, a 1-1/2-ton truck was advertised with a White four-cylinder gasoline engine coupled through a leather-faced cone clutch to a four-speed transmission. The 1-1/2-ton truck had a 144-inch wheelbase and used 36x4 dual pneumatic tires in the rear with single wheels in front. Bevel drive was standard, as were pneumatic tires for the light vehicles, although in the following years, many trucks were fitted with hard rubber tires and sometimes steel tractor wheels. In 1910, White showed a 3-ton platform truck but this heavier truck used dual side chain drive and single hard rubber tires on all four wheels.

White's "Domestic Express" was announced in *The Motor World* early in 1910 where it was described as a "light tray body, built after the approved form of all express wagons, with outside stiffening molding and hinged tail board. As its name implies, it is purposed for the domiciliary uses of the owner in hauling luggage to and from the depot, bringing home the Sunday dinner and transporting discarded furniture to the homes of poor relations."

In 1912, the commercial model line was expanded to include 3/4-ton vehicles up to the 5-ton model T.C., which had a larger four-cylinder engine and dual chain drive. The 3/4-ton Model G.B.E. canopy express was priced at $2,100 while the 1-1/2-ton Model G.T.B. was $3,150. Both featured pneumatic tires and shaft drive. The 3-ton Model G.T.A. was priced at $3,850, while the 5-ton Model T.C. was $4,700. The two heaviest models had hard rubber tires and chain drive as before and there was also a 145-inch wheelbase 5-ton Model T.K.A. In 1912, the profitable Chicago

Motor Transport Company ordered eight more White buses when a ride in a motor bus cost 10 cents, while a ride in a horsedrawn bus cost 50 cents.

1914 WHITE GOOD ROADS MODEL TKA-ATC 5-TON   WTD

In 1913, the U.S. Army Corps of Engineers made an 826-mile crossing of Alaska in a 3/4-ton White truck. The trip took 22 days. By 1914, all White trucks were built with left-hand drive, whereas only the 5-ton model had been designed this way until then. That year, the company built a 5-ton steel-wheel log truck powered by its new 60 hp six-cylinder engine. Thomas White died June 22, 1914.

In 1915, White displayed a bus built on a 1-1/2-ton chassis. It was praised in the press as being luxurious, bearing "no resemblance to a street car, as most bus bodies do, but is constructed more on the order of a limousine. It is of unusual width, with flush sides and drop-sash windows. The interior is upholstered in black leather with cork carpet on the floor." Engineer Rollin White left the company to start the Cleveland Tractor Company (Cletrac).

1916 WHITE 5-TON   OCW

The company was reorganized in 1916 as the White Motor Company with $16 million in capital, which was soon increased to $25 million. That year, the White company advertised that it had 800 trucks owned by dry goods and department stores in the United States, Canada and England. The U.S. Army standardized 1-ton and 3-ton White trucks and 18,000 were built for World War I.

In 1917, White began building open-sided sightseeing buses for Yellowstone National Park. These were based on the 20-45 T.D.B. truck chassis and were designated as the YP-type. The municipal transit system of San Francisco was using White buses as early as 1918. Similar buses appeared in 1919 in Ohio. The Star Auto Stage Association was expanded in California with the use of White taxicabs and the Motor Transit Company of Los Angeles grew quickly with the fleet mostly composed of White vehicles.

By 1919, White heavy chassis of 3-ton and 5-ton rating received double-reduction two-piece shaft drive. Chain drive was discontinued. White had all but ceased production of passenger cars in 1918. Truck brakes were greatly improved and cast vertical-tube-type radiators with removable heads were adopted, as were removable cylinder heads. During World War I, White produced about 18,000 trucks.

1917 WHITE TRANSIT BUS   OCW

1919 WHITE 3/4-TON STAKE TRUCK   OCW

1920 WHITE SIGHTSEEING BUS   OCW

1920 WHITE 5-TON CANOPY EXPRESS   WTD

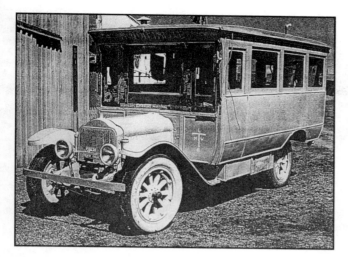

1921 WHITE MOTOR HOME PAT

1921 WHITE ARMORED BANK TRUCK OCW

For 1921, the new company president, Walter White, announced an operating profit of $3,486,000 on sales of $51,998,000 for 1920. But because of the recession of 1921, the company had a loss of $2,346,000 on sales of $30,320,000, a considerable drop from the previous year. Windsor White also became chairman of the board that year. White introduced its new Model 50 late in 1921, which was based on its 20-45. The four-cylinder GN engine used in this chassis later evolved into the GR and GRB engines. White continued to build trucks to 5-ton capacity, such as the Model 45-D Power-Dumping Truck, which was powered by a 28.9 hp four-cylinder engine and was priced at $5,100 for 1922. For that year, the bus chassis was listed at $4,400 using the Model 45 engine. Dual or single rear wheels were available with pneumatic tires at an extra cost of $250.

1923 WHITE 5-TON MODEL 45 TANKER OCW

The Model 50 chassis wheelbase was 198 inches. It was powered by a 50 hp engine. The bus was designed to carry 25 passengers and the frame had built-in "outriggers" to support the custom body, gas tank and battery. The two-piece driveshaft had a double-band brake. The Edgewater Beach Hotel Bus was fitted with luxurious seats in 1922, with the seatbacks on a movable anchorage to absorb road shocks. Doors on the bus opened electrically and were controlled by the driver.

1924 WHITE 3-TON OCW

1925 WHITE C-CAB WITH TRAILER OCW

1925 WHITE MODEL 15 LIAM

By 1925, White offered a variety of commercial vehicles starting with the 3/4-ton Model 15 powered by a 22.5 hp four-cylinder GK engine with a chassis price of $2,400. The 2-ton Model 20 had the same engine and the chassis price was $3,250. The Model 45 had a 50 hp (28.9) engine and the truck chassis price was $4,500. An open Yellowstone sightseeing bus of that year was designated as a Model 15-45. It used the 50 hp four-cylinder engine and the body was by Bender.

1927 WHITE MODEL 15-B MARKEY

The new Model 54 bus, also called the White "Six" and powered by a 100 hp six-cylinder overhead-valve seven-main-bearing engine, was shown in 1926 at the American Electric Railway Association annual convention. Wheelbase was 227 inches and air brakes were standard. A corresponding four-cylinder model was

411

designated as the Model 53. New York City bought 126 Whites that year, increasing its fleet to 1,072. White introduced a new dump truck called the Model 52-D for 1926. It featured an auxiliary transmission and gear-type hoist. The Model 51 was rated at 2-1/2 tons and the Model 40A at 3-1/2 tons. Prices were $3,750 and $4,350, respectively, for 1927. The Model 52 chassis was priced at $5,100 for that year.

In March of 1926, White introduced its new 2-ton Model 56. It was powered by a side-valve mono-bloc four-cylinder engine with a removable cylinder head, which had been developed earlier, and the transmission had four forward speeds. A centrifugal water pump had already been adopted by that time. A year later, White introduced a 1-1/4-ton truck chassis, the Model 57, which was priced at $2,725. One more year later, White introduced the De Luxe Package Car and the Town Car Deluxe, available on two high speed chassis of 1-ton and 1-1/4-ton capacity. Each vehicle had two sidemount spare tires on disc wheels and chrome, two-tone paint and special upholstery were used to create an upscale appearance.

1928 WHITE MOVING VAN WITH TRAILER BEKINS

Also for 1928, White improved its bus design with its Model 54-A of 1928 by moving the dashboard forward over the rear of the engine, which was also relocated over the front axle. By extending the wheelbase only 10 inches to 250 inches without major chassis modifications, the bus' capacity was effectively increased from 29 to 38 passengers. A 180-inch wheelbase iteration was available as the Model 65 and an intermediate chassis was designated as the Model 65-A. This was also the year that White built an experimental gas-electric hybrid bus that used a six-cylinder engine in conjunction with two G.E. electric motors at the rear wheels. The latter bus did not go into production.

In April of 1928, White announced its new Model 58, which had a "gross weight carrying capacity of 22,000 pounds, and was designed to meet conditions created by legal weight restrictions which have been set up in 22 states." The Model 58 was distinguished by a high, narrow aluminum radiator, full crown fenders and was available with dump, stake or van bodies. Altogether, White expanded its chassis model line from 12 for 1927/1928 to 17 for 1929.

White's lightest chassis for 1929 was the 1-ton four-cylinder model, which was priced at $1,545. The 1-ton 54 hp six-cylinder Model 60, new for 1929, was priced at $1,850. Hydrovac brakes became widely used in heavy-duty White trucks and buses, the most expensive being the 54A for up to 41 passengers, which was listed at $8,000 for 1929 and 1930. Company president Walter White died on September 29, 1929, as a result of an auto accident.

1930 WHITE BOTTLER'S BODY OCW

White's new heavy-duty model line consisting of the 620/640 series was rated at 16-ton GVW. Overhead-valve six-cylinder engines were up to 100 hp at that time. The top-of-the-line featured full air brakes on all wheels, auxiliary transmissions, double reduction drive and electric pump feed. By this time, White was building articulated truck tractors with up to 12-ton rating such as the Model 64T. The first factory-built White 6x4 using Timken worm-drive was built for the U.S. Army.

1931 WHITE 64T TRACTOR TRAILER OCW

A.G. Bean was elected president of White in 1931. As the Depression took its toll, White first acquired Indiana trucks, then merged with Studebaker, which had acquired Pierce-Arrow. Pierce-Arrow trucks were assembled at the White factory in Cleveland but the entire association was brief, as Studebaker was forced to liquidate its Pierce-Arrow and White holdings. For 1932, White sold only 2,138 vehicles.

At the same time, White pursued its development of its 505-cubic inch 143 hp horizontally-opposed 12-cylinder engine, which was shown in *Automotive Industries Magazine* on November 5, 1932. This engine was mounted amidship under the floor in buses for up to 100 passengers. The engine featured a dry-sump oil lubrication system and two downdraft carburetors. A second version was built with 811-cubic inch displacement and 225 hp and was introduced for 1933. The "street-car-type bus" as it was called, also featured power steering, power clutch and power brakes, twin starter motors and the four-speed helical-gear transmission was designed with heavy-duty intermediate bearings. A five-speed version was also developed.

A prototype of the bus with the larger engine was ready in October of 1932. The "pancake" engine would have been well-suited for its job if it were not for its high fuel consumption. The engine as well as the wood-and-steel composite bus body were discontinued after 1937. By 1935, a long distance version with raised rear compartment and a second mid-section windshield was developed for carriers such as the Washington Motor Coach System. White sold a large number of buses to transit systems in Boston, Cleveland and Los Angeles, among other cities.

1934 WHITE MOVING VAN OCW

In 1934, the 700 series White trucks were restyled with V-type radiators and all vehicles over 3-ton capacity were powered by overhead-valve six-cylinder engines, not including the 12-cylinder buses. Five-speed transmissions were also standard on the heavier trucks, as were coil ignition systems. Robert F. Black assumed the office of company president when A.G. Bean died on July 13, 1935. The well-known Alexis de Sakhnoffsky designed streamlined cabs for 1936 and the conventional White trucks retained this design for two decades.

1936 WHITE MODEL 731 12-CYL. HEAVY-DUTY   MROZ

White continued to build smaller sightseeing buses. The Model 706 powered by a 94 hp six-cylinder engine was constructed for Yellowstone National Park in 1936. The streamlined van body was available from the factory, such as on the 1-1/2-ton Model 703 powered by an 80 hp side-valve engine. The Model 703 had a price of $1,185. Indiana trucks had become a subsidiary of White but the two makes were quite separate in design. Whereas Indiana was one make that pioneered the use of diesel engines, White continued to use only gasoline engines throughout the 1930s, except for a few export models that were fitted with Cummins diesel units. The cab-over-engine Model 731 appeared in 1935.

1937 WHITE MODEL 802 COE   OCW

By 1937, White listed 48 different standard truck models from the 3/4-ton Model 700P to the 10-ton Models 623X, 722A and COE 731H. In White trucks, engine horsepower ranged from 148 for the Model 700K "250" White engine up to 226 hp for the heavier units. Special dual axle 6x4 trucks were built with a 16-ton rating. The Model 704 was a smaller version of the 706 and was used primarily to build school buses whose bodies were fabricated by Bender in Cleveland.

The earlier conventional buses were replaced by streamlined forward-control types designated 706M, 800M, 805M and 810M. A new factory was set up in East Cleveland for 1937, where the new buses and their chassis could be manufactured by Bender. Despite this effort, Bender went out of business by 1942. Meanwhile, White also built 6x6 trucks for the U.S. Army in 1939 and beginning in 1938, the company also introduced two multi-stop commercial delivery vans. The Merchandor used an underfloor engine design.

For 1939, the White Horse was unveiled for similar application. The latter 2-ton model had uni-body construction, a rear-mounted detachable air-cooled Franklin-designed 40 hp four-cylinder engine, three-speed transmission and coil rear suspension. About 2,000 of these sold the first year alone. White Horse vehicles were built from 1940 to 1942, and then again after World War II for a

brief period. In 1942, White Horse trucks were designated as the Model 99 and Model S-99 (with 99-inch wheelbase) and Model 116, Model S-116 and Model H-116 (with 116-inch wheelbase).

1939 WHITE YELLOWSTONE COACH   KP

1942 WHITE M3A1 SCOUT CAR   STEVE GREENBERG

During World War II, White built 20,000 M3A1 scout cars, which had been designed by engineers at the Indiana subsidiary. White also built 4,000 halftracks using its own side-valve six-cylinder engine, as well as 4x4 truck tractors and 6x4 and 6x6 trucks powered by Cummins diesel engines or Hercules gasoline six-cylinder units.

1948 WHITE DE SAKHNOFFSKY TRACTOR-TRAILER   OCW

Just after World War II, a surge of orders to update aging transit systems resulted in a large production of buses from 1945 to 1948 but once the contracts were fulfilled, White's main business returned to truck manufacturing. Forward-control trucks were built in the form of the Super Power 3000, which had tilt cabs. With two-speed rear axles and five-speed transmissions, White offered a total of 10 speeds along with disc-type handbrakes. Introduced in 1949, by 1950 the White 1100 production model bus was powered by a 743-cubic inch 200 hp six-cylinder four-cycle Cummins engine mounted underfloor amidship just as the earlier buses had been configured.

1949 WHITE SUPER MUSTANG REFRIGERATED TRUCK OCW

1951 WHITE 3000 COE   OCW

1952 WHITE TRUCK TRACTOR   OCW

White bought out Sterling in 1951 and merged with Freightliner. Trucks built by those companies continued in production badged as Sterling White and White Freightliner. White absorbed Autocar in 1953, the year transit buses were discontinued. Up to 1955, some of the light White trucks were powered by Packard side-valve six-cylinder engines but these were rare. That year, a turbocharged diesel Cummins engine was adopted for the 100,000 GCW rated trucks and the White Mustang engine's output was increased to 215 hp. In 1957, the Reo Motors was acquired by White and the following year Diamond T was bought out, although both continued briefly as separate makes.

COE models were redesigned for 1959 with entirely different cabs that had split windshields and dual headlights, such as the Model 5464TD. The use of aluminum throughout White's cabs reduced about a ton from the basic TDL. Cummins engines were available from 180 hp to 262 hp. White had continued to build school bus chassis and in 1960, a new series called 48, 54, 60

and 68 were brought out using the White 2000BA chassis with wheelbases from 187 inches to 256 inches. These were powered by the standard White OA-110 engine or the optional OA-130 unit. A 335 hp Cummins diesel was offered in the 6x4 COE Turnpike Cruiser of 1960.

1959 WHITE 5464 TD DIESEL FREIGHT SYSTEM   OCW

As the new decade began, White offered Clark, Fuller and Spicer transmissions with the 5000 series. Special trucks included 6x2 twin steer trucks in the 3000 series with automatic transmissions for airfield application. The heavy-duty Construktor 6x4 was used for off-road and concrete mixer work. The five-speed transmission in conjunction with a three-speed auxiliary provided 15 speeds total and both gasoline and diesel engines were available from 145 hp to 220 hp.

The Highway Compact van was offered until 1965. It was built for White by Highway Products but after 1965, the two companies ceased their cooperative venture. Gasoline engines from Chrysler and Ford were available, as were diesel engines from Detroit Diesel and Perkins. The White Horse series was resurrected at that time with a conventional engine mounting in the PDQ vehicles, which were powered by several engines including a Chrysler marine V-8, Continental six-cylinder unit, Plymouth Valiant overhead-valve six-cylinder, a Perkins four-cylinder diesel and the Willys F-head four-cylinder engine. However, a fire at the PDQ Montpelier, Ohio, factory destroyed the production facilities and White did not resume PDQ manufacturing.

Both the 1500 and 3000 series were built by White during the early 1960s, the latter being developed into the Utilideck half-cab for carrying pipe and steel girders. The 1500 series had low-tilt cabs over the front axles with the front grille protected with a heavy bumper. The 1500 truck tractor wheelbase was 74 inches, one of the shortest in the industry. Hydrovac brakes and four-speed transmissions were standard. The four-cylinder Perkins diesel engine was available for this series by 1964. Half-cabs were also built in the form of White-Freightliner trucks, many of them for the concrete mixer market.

In 1966, White's Mustang V-8 engine was offered as an optional engine in the 4000 and 9000 conventional trucks and highway tractors. The Mustang engine was actually a modified Cummins diesel unit rated at 250 hp. Few trucks were actually fitted with these engines. For 1967, White produced 4x2, 6x2, 6x4 and 6x6 versions of its conventional and COE trucks. The following year, 8x6 trucks were introduced. Also that year, White engines were discontinued and Caterpillar, Cummins, Detroit Diesel, Diamond Reo and Perkins engines were available. White combined Diamond T and Reo as Diamond Reo in 1967.

White's Western Star division produced trucks for western markets in Ogden, Utah, and Kelowna, Canada. Western Star built only conventional trucks powered by diesel engines. Western Star's headquarters and main plant are located in Canada and have produced conventional 6x4 and 6x6 highway tractors there to date. U.S. production of Western Star was discontinued.

The Road Xpeditor 2 evolved from the Compact into the 1970s. Caterpillar and Cummins six-cylinder diesel engines powered the low-tilt cab Road Xpeditor 2 trucks. COE highway tractors with GVW rating up to 68,000 pounds and GCW rating of 125,000 pounds were built in the form of Road Commander. These were available in 4x2 or 6x4 configuration with engines up to 450 hp and a wide choice of transmissions. Conventional trucks by the name of Road Boss had tilting fiberglass hoods. Available with power steering and Allison automatic transmissions, Construktor trucks were built by White's Autocar Division by this time. The well-known William Knudsen of Ford and GM fame joined White in 1971.

1975 WHITE CONSTRUCTOR 8X4 DUMP TRUCK   OCW

1978 WHITE ROAD BOSS TRACTOR TRAILER   OCW

By 1975, the White Truck Group consisting of Autocar, Diamond Reo, Freightliner as well as trucks built under its own badge amounted to 30,000 units for the year's production, yet the company lost $50 million. The White Freightliner marketing relationship was severed in 1977, although Freightliner continued to be a subsidiary of White. The Diamond Reo division was sold off in 1977. Cruse Moss joined White as the new president and CEO in August 1979.

White still badge engineered Autocar and had a licensing agreement with Western Star. The three makes were advertised together using a new combined logo. The original Road Boss that was introduced in 1973 was superseded by the Road Boss II in 1980, which was restyled and had some relatively minor mechanical and electrical improvements. A factory in New River Valley, Virginia, began production and was aimed at modernizing White's outmoded manufacturing facilities in Cleveland.

Despite optimistic announcements by February of 1981, White was operating under U.S. and Canadian bankruptcy laws and openly seeking a buyer. The first possibility was the sale of its truck manufacturing divisions to Consolidated Freightways Incorporated of San Francisco, California, and Daimler-Benz of West Germany. But the major financial obstacle was the assumption of $70 million in promised pension payments. However, by the end of the year, it was Volvo of Sweden that bought White for $17 million in cash and $34 million in notes. The company's name was changed to Volvo White Truck Corporation. It was two years later that Western Star became an independent corporation based in Canada when

Volvo White terminated their sales and licensing pact. Due to bankruptcy proceedings, total losses by White were estimated at $60 million. Most of White's 9,500 employees found work with their new owner, Volvo, but Northeast Ohio Axle, which was formed during reorganization under Chapter 13, as well as administrative offices, laid off workers.

In December 1986, the GM-Volvo merger was announced and took place the following year. Many of White's truck designs were simply eliminated and the company's name became WhiteGMC Volvo. By 1991, the WhiteGMC Tall Integral Sleeper Aero ES conventional featured a 310 hp Cummins N14-310 engine and nine-speed Fuller RTO-12609A transmission as standard equipment. A 40,000-pound rated Rockwell SQ-100 rear axle with the WhiteG-MC parabolic four-spring suspension and a 12,000-pound rated Rockwell FF961 front axle were also standard equipment. The truck also featured a 50-inch front axle setback, parabolic front springs, air-sprung cab suspension, second generation aerodynamic refinements, air dam integrated with front bumper, medium-length sloped hood and curved windshield.

For 1993, the Tall Integral Sleeper ES was standard with a Caterpillar 3406B engine, Spicer clutch, Fuller RTX-14715 rear axle and Volvo VF series front axle. In September of that year, the parent companies of VolvoGMC and Mack announced a merger. These companies were Renault SA of France and AB Volvo of Sweden. The two companies intended to achieve cost savings and improved component manufacturing by combining purchasing, R&D and engineering.

For 1995, WhiteGMC listed 21 models from 161-inch to 216-inch wheelbase and with BBC dimensions ranging from 55 inches to 167 inches. Of the 21 models listed, 16 were available both in 4x2 and 6x4 configuration. GVW ratings were up to 60,000 pounds on the WX64 and WXLL64 models. GCW ratings were up to 110,000 pounds for several models. Standard engines on specific models were Cummins L10-260, Cummins N14-310E, DDC Series 60-330, Volvo VE D7-230 and Volvo VE D12-310. WhiteGMC Volvo dropped both the Autocar and White names for 1996, hence, as a marque, 1995 was the last year for White.

WHITE FREIGHTLINER   see FREIGHTLINER

WHITE HORSE   see WHITE

WHITE HICKORY 1917-1921 — The White Hickory Wagon Manufacturing Company of Atlanta, Georgia, built the 1-1/2-ton Model H, which was continued in production through 1920. This truck was powered by a four-cylinder Continental engine and used a three-speed progressive gear transmission with a Timken worm-drive rear axle. For 1921, the company expanded its model line to include 2-1/2-ton and 3-1/2-ton capacity trucks, but the expansion was futile in light of the postwar recession and the company's final demise.

WHITESIDES 1911-1912 — The Whitesides Commercial Car Company was located in Franklin, Indiana. This vehicle was built as a 1-ton capacity "flat dray" (flatbed), van and stakeside truck. It was powered by a 30 hp four-cylinder water-cooled engine. Prices started at $1,265.

1914 WHITE STAR MODEL 1 COVERED FLAREBOARD   OCW

WHITE STAR 1912-1914 — The White Star Motor & Engineering Company of Brooklyn, New York, began during 1912. For model year 1913, a 2-ton and a 3-ton capacity model were offered. The 2-ton model was an enclosed van powered by a four-cylinder engine. The truck used a four-speed transmission and had a wheelbase of 168 inches. A similar 5-ton truck was introduced in 1914 before the company forever closed its doors. Just a few years before the start of this company, there was also the White Star Automobile & Truck Manufacturing Company of Pleasanton, Kansas, which does not appear to have gone into production. At the same time, there was a White Star Automobile Company in Atlanta, Georgia, which built passenger cars up to 1911.

1905 WHITING 5-TON CONVERTIBLE GASOLINE TRUCK   RD

WHITING 1904-1905 — This commercial vehicle manufacturer started as the Whiting Foundry Equipment Company in Harvey, Illinois. The Whiting was one of the largest trucks of its time with a vehicle weight of 10,000 pounds. It was powered by a 680-cubic inch four-cylinder engine and used a three-speed transmission and double chain drive to the rear wheels. The truck was built only as a flatbed with a structural steel frame and its top speed was governed to 10 mph.

1914 WICHITA MODEL B   RNE

WICHITA 1911-1932 — The Wichita Falls Motor Company was located in Wichita Falls, Texas. It was not affiliated with the Wichita Falls Motor Company of Wichita Falls, Kansas, which operated during 1914. The truck's designer by the name of McKeirnan went into partnership with two local businessmen to build a factory.

McKeirnan's invention consisted of a single lever located at the steering wheel, which controlled the spark, throttle, clutch and transmission. The device was first tested on a Maxwell car before production began. The Texas firm first built vehicles intended for oil field operations, then expanded into several other markets including vans and buses. In the first few years, the company built a 1-ton and 2-ton truck with right-hand steering and "center control." The model range was expanded to include trucks from 1-1/2-ton up to 5-ton capacity and all were powered by Waukesha engines.

1918 WICHITA BUS   RD

In 1920, the company introduced a utility car referred to as the "oil field tool pusher." It was powered by a 50 hp four-cylinder engine and had a wheelbase of 127 inches. It could carry three persons and a half ton of equipment and sold for $2,150. The company sold many of its trucks to Mexico, China and reportedly 85 other countries where the easy forward-and-backward single lever control found acceptance with people who were mechanically unsophisticated at a time when driving a vehicle needed a lot of skill and attention. The company's slogan was "The Sun Never Sets on the Name of Wichita." The business remained afloat until 1932, when the Depression finally took its toll.

Press coverage in 1912 mentioned that Wichita had become the first motor vehicle company in the United States to be directed by a woman. That person was Mrs. Nettie C. McIntyre of Denver, Colorado. She was not only the principal stockholder of the Wichita Falls Motor Company, but also the chief organizer.

1912 WILCOX 1-1/2-TON MODEL K   OCW

WILCOX 1910-1927 — The H.E. Wilcox Motor Car Company had been established in Minneapolis, Minnesota, by H.E. Wilcox, John F. Wilcox and Maurice Wolfe in 1910. The Wolfe Motor Car firm was formed in November 1906 and first produced the Wolfe passenger car until 1910, when the Wolfe was superseded by the Wilcox as the two parties joined forces. A few car-based delivery vehicles were built under the name Wolfe using a 40 hp four-cylinder engine and a chassis with 115-inch wheelbase. By 1913, the Wilcox passenger cars were discontinued and the company concentrated only on trucks and buses with the name Wilcox Trux.

The first Wilcox truck of 1910 was a 1-ton model, followed soon after by a 3-ton capacity truck. This was also the year of the first bus built by the company, which described it as a combination mail wagon and stagecoach. Within a few years, the Wilcox Motor Truck Company became the largest producer of commercial vehicles in Minneapolis.

By 1918, the company offered six capacities of truck from 3/4 ton to 5 ton, the larger being COE design. Buda and Continental four-cylinder engines were used but Wilcox also began building its own engines as well. In 1921, the company was incorporated as Wilcox Trux of Minneapolis.

Wilcox also built buses at that time, primarily for transporting copper and iron miners. In 1922, the company started to build a chassis specifically intended for bus application. The low drop frame used fabricated arches instead of the more common one-piece siderails. The rear axle was a live Huck-type design with differential-mounted planetary gear for final reduction. Bodies were made by Eckland, which was also located in Minneapolis and worked with the Will company.

1917 WILCOX TANKER   OCW

1919 WILCOX CHASSIS   HAYS

The Wilcox bus was powered by a six-cylinder Continental engine and by mid-decade, the 29-passenger model was advertised as having a top speed of 62 mph. At this time, the Model 1-ton Model AA with 130-inch wheelbase was powered by a 22.5 hp four-cylinder Buda WTU engine with Stromberg carburetor and Westinghouse ignition. Wheels carried 35x5 solid rubber tires with pneumatic tires at extra cost. Transmission and clutch were made by Brown-Lipe, front axle was from Russel, rear axle was from Shuler and steering gear was by Gemmer. Chassis price was $1,900.

The 1-1/2-ton Model BB with 135-inch wheelbase differed in that it was powered by a 28.9 hp four-cylinder Wilcox engine and used a Wilcox clutch, transmission and steering gear. Front axle was from Walker and rear axle was from Shuler. Chassis price was $2,250 and solid rubber tires were used with dual wheels on the rear. There was also the 2-1/2-ton Model CC, which was powered by a 28.9 hp four-cylinder Wilcox CC engine. Otherwise, component suppliers were the same as on the Model BB. The heaviest Wilcox truck was the 5-ton Model F with a 36.1 hp four-cylinder Buda ATU engine. Clutch, transmission and steering were built by Wilcox. Smith wheels carried 36x5 front and 40x12 rear solid rubber tires on a chassis with a 162-inch wheelbase. Chassis weight was 9,000 pounds and it was priced at $4,350.

By 1925, the Northland Transportation Company ordered 39 of the 29-passenger six-cylinder bus, but these were badged as Northland to distinguish them from the Wilcox trucks. Bus production had eclipsed truck manufacturing by this time and H.E. Wilcox sold the whole business to the Motor Transit Corporation, which was formed in 1926 as a holding company for Greyhound bus lines. These became known as Will buses.

WILL 1927-1931 — The holding company for Greyhound bus lines bought Wilcox. Naming the operation after its general manager, Carl H. Will, production turned entirely to buses for Greyhound. Most of these were used in the Midwestern region of the

United States. The buses were also called "W.M.C." as simple an abbreviation for the C.H. Will Motors Corporation, which was located in Minneapolis, Minnesota.

Under Greyhound specifications, Will built a parlor car on wheelbases of 239 inches at first, and then 249 inches. These were all powered by six-cylinder Waukesha engines. Also, drop frames with one-piece siderails were used and air springs at the front held Timken axles, which were also used at the rear. In 1929, Greyhound acquired the California Body Building Company of Oakland, California, and the buses built by this combination of plants were called the Pioneer-Will. By the time the Oakland factory finished 60 of the buses for Pacific Greyhound in 1930, that plant was closed.

The last Will buses built in Minneapolis were completed in January 1931, and subsequently that factory's manufacturing was switched over to overhaul-and-rebuild services for Greyhound. The buses built in Minnesota, of which there were about 500, were used by Northland Greyhound. All of the Minneapolis-built units had bodies by Eckland. Greyhound, in the meantime, signed a contract in November 1929 with Yellow Coach to develop and manufacture buses for its growing transit operations.

1913 WILLET 3/4-TON DELIVERY   RD

WILLET 1911-1915 — The Willet Engine & Carburetor Company built small vans powered by two-cylinder and three-cylinder two-stroke engines until 1913, when it was reorganized as the Willet Engine & Truck Company. By then, the Model L with a Renault-type hood was powered by a four-cylinder two-stroke engine. It had a rated capacity of 2 tons and used a friction transmission and chain drive. Wheelbase was 144 inches.

For 1915, the company discontinued its previous vehicles and introduced a 3/4-ton truck that used shaft drive. Unlike the previous vehicles, which used solid rubber tires, the new truck, which had a wheelbase of 133 inches, had pneumatic tires. It was priced at $2,100. The year 1915, however, was the company's last.

WILLYS, WILLYS-KNIGHT, WILLYS-OVERLAND, OVERLAND 1903-1963 — The first Overland of 1903 was available as a delivery van with tiller steering and solid rubber tires. However, no records actually attest to the fact that any such vans were built until 1908 when, according to some sources, passenger car chassis were used to construct postal vans. These were powered by a four-cylinder engine and used a two-speed planetary transmission. The Overland 37, an 800-pound capacity commercial car, was built in 1910. A year later, the company advertised a forward-control 1-ton truck that used a 40 hp four-cylinder engine. This model was most likely supplied by Federal. All in all, the aforementioned manufacturers listed after Willys were inextricably intertwined in matters of design and production and to address them separately would be ineffectual.

John North Willys took over at the helm of Overland in 1907 and in 1909, the company became Willys-Overland. Willys acquired controlling interest in the Gramm Motor Car Company of Lima, Ohio, and the Garford Automobile Company of Elyria, Ohio, in 1912. Vans continued to be built until 1913 when 3/4-ton Gramm-built Utility trucks were first introduced as Willys-Overland, the first time the Willys name appeared on a vehicle, even before the well-known Willys-Knight was produced. The Utility was powered by a 30 hp 240-cubic inch four-cylinder engine and had solid tires on the rear while the front was fitted with pneumatic tires as standard equipment. Pneumatic tires on the rear were available at extra cost.

A brochure from 1913 showed 15 variations of the basic 120-inch wheelbase chassis, including a Short-Haul Hotel Bus, Hearse, Ambulance, Screened Delivery Body, Fire Engine Hose Wagon, Department Store Delivery, 200-Gallon Tank Wagon, 12-Passenger Sight-Seeing Bus, Express Delivery (windshield $18.50 extra), Quick Delivery Express, Spring Water Delivery, Stake Body, Cab and Flatbed, Express Parcel Delivery C-Cab and Grocery Delivery Special. There were 42 different options listed that year.

The 800-pound capacity Model 69 of 1913 was available with an express body for $950 or closed panel body for $1,000. Both used the same 25.6 hp four-cylinder engine, three-speed transmission, 3/4 floating rear axle and 33x4 front and rear pneumatic tires.

The following year, John Willys bought the Edwards Motor Car Company of Long Island, New York, and installed the firm and H.J. Edwards himself at the Garford plant in Elyria, Ohio, which Willys had bought earlier. Within a year, the company was offering numerous models of passenger cars under the Willys, Willys-Knight and Overland names. Left-hand drive vans were offered with a full electrical system for $850 in 1915. Both Gramm and Garford were sold off that year but both makes continued to be sold by Willys dealers.

By 1919, the Light Four engine was used in vans and this venerable engine remained in production in various forms for several decades. With commercial vehicles only as a side line, including the 27 hp Light Four Overland truck of 1920, John Willys was trying to expand his automotive empire as quickly as possible and acquired the former Duesenberg factory in Elizabeth, New Jersey. There he hired the engineering team of Zeder, Skelton and Breer, formerly of Studebaker, to develop a six-cylinder engine. However, by overextending himself, Willys unintentionally invited Chase National Bank to step in and install its own company manager, Walter Chrysler, formerly president of Buick.

Walter Chrysler only stayed for two years before leaving for Maxwell-Chalmers. John Willys placed the Willys Corporation, a holding company for the motor vehicle manufacturing divisions, into receivership and regained control of the company through shrewd stock transactions. The former Duesenberg plant was sold to William Durant and sales and production of the Willys-Knight and Overland vehicles was multiplied 10-fold by 1925.

From 1924, both four-cylinder and six-cylinder sleeve-valve Knight engines were used in Willys-Knight taxicabs. Overland chassis were used to build 1-ton trucks in England but these were not the same design as the British Overland trucks, which began production in 1926. In 1924, 30 hp four-cylinder engines were used in the Light Four Overland truck chassis, which was priced at $395.

Knight engines were sold to Yellow Cab at that time and both the taxis and Yellowcab Trucks and Yellow Trucks, also called Yellow-Knight, used this sleeve-valve engine through 1927. That was also the first model year of the Whippet truck, which was powered by a side-valve four-cylinder engine. This powerplant was the basis for the engine used in World War II jeeps.

By 1928, the Yellow-Knight trucks were discontinued and the cabs soon received Buick engines. Meanwhile, the Overland Four was superseded by the Overland Whippet, which was called Whippet for 1927 and 1928, and then became the Willys-Whippet. The Willys-Whippet was available as a panel van and had an optional six-cylinder engine. Willys-Knight built trucks starting in 1927, which were powered by a sleeve-valve six-cylinder engine. Capacity for these trucks was from 1-ton to 2-1/2-ton. Gramm became the truck builder for Willys again in 1927, although the company continued to build a few of its own commercial vehicles. In 1928, the company offered a 190-inch wheelbase coach chassis for export, or by special order, also with the six-cylinder sleeve valve engine and a four-speed transmission as well as vacuum servo brakes. The Gramm-built commercial vehicles became available in the United States and Canada in 1928.

By 1929, Willys offered the 1-1/2-ton C101 and T103 trucks, which used Whippet front sheet metal. The C101 used a seven-main-bearing side-valve engine while the T103 was powered by another sleeve valve six-cylinder engine. In 1930, the Gramm-Willys contract ended, largely due to financial problems brought on by the stock market crash. By 1933, the entire truck line was discontinued and the company concentrated all its efforts on the new Willys 77. It was powered by a small four-cylinder engine and a utility version was offered, also in panel delivery form. The Willys 77 kept the company in business during the Depression and in 1936, it was updated with new sheet metal and mechanical improvements. A 1/2-ton pickup was built, including an updated version for 1937.

1922 WILLYS-OVERLAND LIGHT DELIVERY   **BC**

1941 WILLYS MODEL 441 1/2-TON VAN   **RD**

1924 WILLYS-OVERLAND PANEL DELIVERY   **RD**

John North Willys died in 1935 and Ward Canaday took over at the helm. Canaday was the financial head of the company and he watched as four company presidents succeeded Willys in short order. First Dave Wilson took over as president then in 1939, Joseph Frazer took the helm. Canaday took over for a while after 1942, then Charles Sorensen came over from Ford. However,

James Mooney became president in 1946. After financial difficulties appeared on the Willys ledgers, Canaday took over once again in 1949, but he stayed on only until 1953.

1942 WILLYS JEEP   MVPA

The Willys name would become virtually synonymous with the "jeep" after the Quartermaster Corps Ordnance Technical Committee invited 135 manufacturers to bid on a General Purpose reconnaissance car after seeing Bantam's prototypes in 1940. Given only two months to produce some pilot models, Bantam was the only company to meet the deadline with a small vehicle based on its diminutive passenger car. The deadline was extended and both Ford and Willys fabricated General Purpose vehicle prototypes.

The G.P. abbreviation would soon become pronounced "jeep," which was the name of a silent cartoon character who could walk through walls and had magical powers and appeared in Popeye cartoons in 1936. A story in the *Washington Daily News* quoting that name appeared on February 19, 1941, and the American public was introduced to a vehicle that would become legendary in years to come. The name "jeep" would later be capitalized when Willys obtained a registered trademark and called its vehicles Jeeps. What did not stick were the "BRC," "Quad" and "Pigmy" names used in 1940 by the three companies that built the prototypes.

At first, Ford's design, which was slower and heavier, got approval for manufacturing because of production capabilities. Former General Motors President William S. Knudsen, who became a lieutenant general and was appointed by Franklin D. Roosevelt to the National Defense Advisory Committee, intervened and approved a combined design for the jeep that would use the best aspects of all three designs. The Willys 61 hp Go-Devil engine was the most powerful and flexible of the three choices. Its design was incorporated into the final model MA and model MB jeep. A three-speed transmission and two-speed transfer case were standardized, as were all other components for military application.

Bantam produced a total of 2,643 jeeps before production was entirely awarded to Ford and Willys, despite vehement protest from the former company's management and design team. All three companies were awarded a first production run of 1,500 jeeps, which were distributed to Russia and China under the Lend Lease program. A General Purpose Amphibious vehicle, called the "seep," was also built in small numbers by Marmon-Herrington but was not successful.

In October of 1941, Ford was given the contract to build the "General Purpose Willys" and the first order was for 15,000 units at a price of $14,624,000. Willys turned over its blueprints and patents to Ford "without hesitation" in January of 1942. The United States had already been directly drawn into World War II after the Japanese attack on Pearl Harbor. By the end of the war, Willys had built 362,841 jeeps while Ford had produced 281,448 of the nearly identical 1/4-ton vehicles during the same period.

In 1945, before the end of the war, Willys announced the Jeep Universal Model CJ-2A, which was the first civilian version of the well-known military vehicle. These jeeps had a few changes, such as larger headlights and a side-mounted spare tire, but otherwise they were the same "Jeep" as had been built for the military. The

major difference was that there were many options that could be ordered, many of which were intended for farm application, including front and rear power takeoffs and an engine governor. A hydraulic lift option was by far the most expensive at $225.

1946 WILLYS FIRE CHIEF'S JEEP   E.B. COMBS

A station wagon and derivative sedan delivery arrived in 1946. Despite claims to the contrary by Plymouth, Willys had the first all-steel wagon. Late in 1946, the Jeep pickup came out for 1947. A 1-ton 4x4 was also available. That series was available as pickup, platform stake, chassis and cab or base chassis, all on a 118-inch wheelbase.

Based on the Jeep, light fire apparatus vehicles were also developed by Willys at that time. However, it was not until 1948 that a six-cylinder engine was introduced and the wagon was also made available with four-wheel-drive that year. The Jeepster made its debut that year as well. At the time, the CJ-2A had a base price of $1,270. It was in 1949 that Willys brought out its CJ-3A and obtained a trademark on the name Jeep. The Jeep CJ-3A was distinguished by its one-piece windshield and a number of detail changes.

Despite growing sales in the 1940s by 1949, Willys was losing money. Overall production had increased from nearly 79,000 units in 1946 to almost 100,000 units in 1947 and 159,000 for 1948. However, 1949 production was half of that as for 1948 and it barely improved for the following year. For 1951, production jumped up to 119,000, then leveled off at an average of 60,000 for an entire decade.

1950 WILLYS M38   MVPA

One of the notable aspects of the Willys sheet metal during the 1940s and 1950s is that no more than six inches of draw were required to form the shape of any body piece. Compound curves were almost entirely avoided. This not only helped to keep the cost of tooling down, but it also allowed Willys to mass-produce sheet metal that would otherwise have to be fabricated by vendors too busy at the time working for other larger motor vehicle manufacturers.

The MC military Jeep was the replacement for the MB. It was dubbed the M38 by the U.S. military. It used a 24-volt electrical system, heavier body and chassis components, and a snorkel device allowed for complete submergence -- a military specification handed down to manufacturers of trucks at that time. It required scuba gear for the drivers and was basically not a practical requirement other than to ensure that the electrical system and carburetor were truly protected from the elements. About 60,000 M38 Jeeps were eventually built for the military. The M38 became the basis for the CJ-5.

In 1950, the Jeep pickups were restyled and given a five-bar horizontal grille with a slight V-shape. The following year, the 63 hp side-valve four-cylinder engine was superseded by a 72 hp F-head four-cylinder engine called the Hurricane. Trucks constituted about one-fourth of Willys sales. The 4x2 Willys truck cost $73 more than the Chevrolet 3/4-ton pickup. In July of that year, a six-cylinder engine designed by Barney Roos called the Lightning Six became available. Later that year, the engine's displacement was increased to 161-cubic inches and horsepower went from 70 to 75.

The year 1953 marked a major transition for Willys-Overland, which was purchased by Kaiser-Frazer Corporation for approximately $60 million. Just prior to the sale, the CJ-3B was introduced, which used the F-head engine. Then in 1955 came the CJ-5, based on the M-38, although the headlights received a chrome bezel and the 24-volt system was replaced by a more-conventional-for-the-time six-volt system. The front fenders had a distinct curve to them that the CJ-3A and CJ-3B did not have. A lightweight Jeep called the Bobcat, or BC, was built only as a prototype in 1953 and did not go into production -- just as the earlier lightweight MBL met a dead end a decade earlier.

By 1954, a 115 hp six-cylinder engine was available with the four-wheel-drive station wagon and panel delivery. The next important development at Willys took place in 1956. In November of that year, Kaiser-Jeep unveiled a forward-control pickup designated as the FC-150. With only an 81-inch wheelbase, it had a six-foot cargo area. It was over three feet shorter than a 1/2-ton Chevrolet pickup. The FC-150 was powered by the 75 hp Hurricane F-head four-cylinder engine and had a three-speed standard and four-speed optional transmission. Its base price was $2,320.

In 1957, the similar FC-170 was produced on a 103-1/2-inch wheelbase. The FC-170 was built as a pickup with a nine-foot bed or it was used to build fire apparatus and other specialty commercial vehicles.

1958 WILLYS JEEP PANEL DELIVERY   **WILLYS**

During this time, the company built the Mechanical Mule for the military and the CJ-6 was introduced as an extended wheelbase CJ-5. Its sales did not go well. Based on the FC chassis, three van prototypes were built but did not go into production. By this time, Jeeps were being manufactured and/or assembled in 19 countries.

For 1961, the Fleetvan was introduced. It was similar to the postal van the company had built and it was powered by the F-head four-cylinder engine. Wheelbase was 81 inches and there was 170 cubic feet of cargo space. It was listed at $2,380, which was $166 cheaper than a Chevrolet Walk-In Delivery. The M38

was transformed into the M151, also known as the A-1 MUTT. It had more cargo room and used a rear suspension with a trailing arm to help overcome the rollover tendencies of the M38.

1958 WILLYS 4X4 JEEP UTILITY WAGON   **WILLYS**

The extended wheelbase CJ-6 became the M170 built specifically for the military. In 1963, American Motors Corporation (AMC) bought Kaiser-Jeep and the vehicles, identified by the name Jeep, are listed under that name in this compendium, covering the years 1963 to date.

1917 WILSON MILITARY TRUCK   **RD**

1925 WILSON SAFETY SPEED TRUCK MODEL C   **OCW**

WILSON 1914-1925 — The J.C. Wilson Company of Detroit, Michigan, began by building horsedrawn wagons. In 1914, the company entered the truck manufacturing market with a 2-ton model that at first used chain drive and in 1916, was updated with worm-drive. The following year, 1-ton and 3-ton capacity trucks were also built and some were assembled for military use overseas. For 1918, the line was expanded even further with 3-1/2-ton and 5-ton models. The latter used a four-speed transmission. By 1920, the company offered 1-1/2-, 2-1/2-, 3-1/2- and 5-ton models all with four-speed Brown-Lipe transmissions, four-cylinder engines and Timken worm-drive. However, by 1925 the company was in such poor financial condition that it did not list any new trucks for the model year, which turned out to be its last.

WINKLER 1911-1912 — The Winkler Brothers Manufacturing Company was located in South Bend, Indiana. Winkler trucks were offered in two sizes, the lighter 1-ton being powered by a 25 hp engine and the heavier 3-ton capacity had a 45 hp engine. The latter used a three-speed progressive transmission and had a wheelbase of 120 inches. As a stakeside truck it was priced at $4,000.

1975 WINNEBAGO SHUTTLE BUS   EK

WINNEBAGO 1973-1993 — By the same name as the Wisconsin lake and resort, Winnebago Industries has been located in Forest City, Iowa. Originally, the company built house trailers and in 1973, expanded its line of products to include motorhomes. One version of this vehicle was built as a small bus constructed on either of two Dodge chassis: the RM-350 with a 318-cubic inch V-8 and the RM-400 with a 400-cubic inch V-8. Winnebago continued to offer a small shuttle bus based on the company's recreational vehicle until 1993.

1917 WINTHER 6-TON LOGGING TRUCK   HAYS

1918 WINTHER-MARWIN MODEL 430   FLP

1920 WINTHER-MARWIN 4X4   HAYS

WINTHER, WINTHER-MARWIN, WINTHER-KENOSHA 1917-1927 — Martin P. Winther, an engineer who had worked for the Jeffery Company, started his own firm in 1917. The Winther Motor Truck Company began in Winthrop Harbor, Illinois, building conventional trucks up to 6-ton capacity. In 1918, the company moved to Kenosha, Wisconsin, and became the Winthrop Motor Truck Company, producing its first four-wheel-drive truck called the Winther-Marwin, which was similar in design to the Jeffery 4x4 truck. During World War I, Winther claimed to have the dominant truck in the U.S. Navy.

In 1920, the company also tried to enter the passenger car market without success and in 1921, the name of the company became Winther Motors Incorporated, once again producing Winther trucks.

The pre-1920s Winther-Marwin and Winther trucks were built as 4x2 and 4x4 vehicles all powered by four-cylinder Wisconsin engines of various ratings. Borg & Beck clutches and Cotta three-speed and four-speed transmissions were used along with Celfer internal gear axles. In the early 1920s, the model line included 2-, 3-, 4- and 6-ton trucks with prices ranging from $2,750 to $4,700. In the early 1920s, the model line was expanded to include 1-ton and 7-ton trucks, the latter briefly using a four-cylinder Herschell-Spillman engine. Transmission suppliers included Brown-Lipe, Fuller and Warner. Internal gear axles were from Clark, Midway, Torbensen as well as Timken front axles. Electric starters were used throughout the 1920s.

By the mid-1920s, Winther listed the 1-1/2-ton Model 34 and Model 434. The latter was a 4x4 but otherwise, both were powered by a 25.6 hp four-cylinder Wisconsin engine and used a Fuller transmission. The 4x2 used a Timken front axle and steering was from Lavine. Prices were $2,450 and $2,850, respectively. The 2-1/2-ton Model 44 with 161-inch wheelbase was powered by the same engine as the 1-1/2-ton trucks. Steering was from Lavine and chassis price was $3,100.

The 3-ton Model 54 and Model 454 with 152-inch wheelbase were powered by a 28.9 hp four-cylinder Wisconsin engine. These heavier trucks used Ross steering, Borg & Beck clutches and Brown-Lipe transmissions. The 4x2 Model 54 had a Clark rear axle and a Timken front axle. The 4x4 used Winther's own front axle, as did all of the company's four-wheel-drive trucks. Chassis prices were $3,500 and $3,800, respectively. The 5-ton Model 104 was powered by a 36.1 hp four-cylinder Wisconsin RAU engine and used the same make components as a the previous model. The heaviest Winther truck was the 7-ton Model 144 with a 40.0 hp Wisconsin RBU engine, Brown-Lipe transmission, Timken front axle and Clark rear axle. Both the 5-ton and 7-ton trucks had Ross steering. Prices for the last two models were $5,000 and $6,000, respectively. The 7-ton chassis weighed 9,500 pounds.

In a refinancing strategy for the last year of production, the company became Winther-Kenosha. Financial problems led to the sale of the company in 1927 to H.P. Olsen. Truck manufacturing was discontinued for 1928.

1898 WINTON DELIVERY   RD

WINTON 1898-1918 — Alexander Winton immigrated to the United States from Scotland in 1884. He established the Winton Bicycle Company in 1891 and by 1896, was experimenting with a single-cylinder gasoline car. The following year, he established the Winton Motor Carriage Company and built his second car, which was powered by a 10 hp two-cylinder engine. This car was driven at a speed of 33 mph around the Glenville Track known for horse racing in Cleveland, Ohio, which is where Winton's company was established. Winton's vice-president was Thomas W. Henderson, secretary-treasurer George H. Brown and chief engineer Leo Melanowski, who passed up the chance of hiring Henry Ford as a mechanic.

Winton has been credited with building the first truck in the United States. This vehicle was a forward-control light delivery van that was completed in 1898. It was based on the two-cylinder passenger car chassis and used wire spoke wheels with pneumatic tires and tiller steering. One hundred such delivery wagons were ordered by Dr. Pierce Medical Company of Buffalo, New York, but it is not certain how many were actually purchased.

By 1901, Winton car sales reached 700 but few of these were commercial vehicles. In 1903, Winton made headlines by driving across the continent. The car was driven from San Francisco to New York by Dr. H. Nelson Jackson and his chauffeur Sewell H. Croker.

1904 WINTON SIGNAL CORPS WAGONETTE   SMITHSONIAN

In 1905, the Model C featured a four-cylinder engine and shaft drive. Winton vehicles used compressed air starters, wheel steering and planetary transmissions. In 1906, the first 20 hp two-cylinder Winton van was imported to England by the Goodrich Motor Tyre Company.

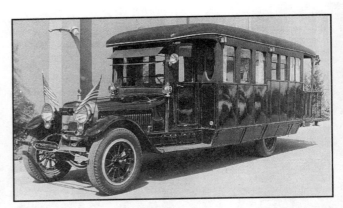

1917 WINTON CUSTOM HOUSE CAR   HAC

In 1907, Winton introduced a six-cylinder engine, which was used in most Winton vehicles after that. The compressed air starter could also be used to inflate tires by 1909. It was not until 1915 that electric starting was adopted by the company. Passenger car chassis were used for the few commercial applications of the Winton during this time. During World War I, Winton built heavy equipment and some load carriers but after the war, the company stayed away from commercial vehicles and faded out of business by 1924.

1918 WISCONSIN TANKER   JAW

WISCONSIN 1912-1926 — The Wisconsin Motor Truck Works was first located in Baraboo, Wisconsin. For the first three years, the company built 3/4-ton light trucks. In 1916, the Wisconsin Motor Truck Works became Myers Machine Company and moved to Sheboygan, Wisconsin, where 2-ton trucks were the first model line. By 1919, the name again changed to Wisconsin Truck Company as the firm moved to Loganville, Wisconsin.

In 1921, a 5-ton truck was added to the model line. Trucks were built in capacities from 1-1/2-ton to 5-ton during the 1920s. Continental, Herschell-Spillman and Waukesha engines were offered, the latter being the most common. In 1923, the company acquired the Six Wheel Truck Company of Fox Lake, Wisconsin, which had built the six-wheel Super-Traction truck. This design was used to develop a six-wheel 28-passenger bus chassis for 1924, which was powered by a six-cylinder Continental 6B engine with two underslung worm-drive axles. A simpler four-wheel bus chassis was listed at the same time but by 1925, the company was fading out. In 1926, it ceased production.

WISEDA 1980-1995 — The company was started by William S. Davis whose family had invested in the off-road industrial truck business prior to 1980. The manufacturing facilities were established in Baxter Springs, Kansas. Wiseda utilized the new 787 General Electric drive motor and alternator system, which was developed in the late 1970s. All of the Wiseda trucks used diesel-electric drive technology. The largest trucks built by this company were 220-ton and 240-ton capacity goliaths used almost exclusively for large-scale open-pit mining operations. Each rear wheel was driven by an electric motor that used planetary gears with a 28.8:1 ratio.

Wiseda used A710 alloy steel composed of nickel-copper for its heavy frames to withstand the severe shock and stress when half a million pounds in the form of about 250-cubic yards was loaded on its rear-dump trucks. By the mid-1990s, the cost of moving a ton of ore was down to about 16 cents due to the efficiency of using huge trucks such as those built by Wiseda. The Wiseda Model 2450 was powered by any of four basic engines: a Detroit Diesel V-16 149 two-stroke with up to 2200 hp, a Cummins KTTA-50C or Cummins K2000 four-stroke diesel engine with up to 2000 hp, or an MTU V-12 396 four-stroke diesel engine with 1850 hp. By 1994, MTU was offering a 3200 hp diesel engine for this type of application. Tire size for the Wiseda 2450 was 40x57 and cost approximately $15,000 each. Wiseda was purchased by the Swiss firm of Liebherr Mining Truck, Incorporated, in 1995, which has continued manufacturing in Baxter Springs under the name Liebherr.

WITTENBERG 1966-1981 — The Wittenberg Motor Company of Midway, Washington, was a used military dealer since the early 1950s. Beginning in 1966, the company began rebuilding military vehicles using new cabs, hoods, fenders and the Wittenberg badge. The trucks were mostly M-series GMC and Reo 6x4 and 6x6 units. Also included were 3/4-ton Dodge 4x4 trucks and 5-ton 6x6 COE with offset "half-cab." Wittenberg offered custom bodies and equipment as well. The company appears to have faded out in the early 1980s.

1913 WITT-WILL   RD

WITT-WILL 1911-1931 — Washington D.C. was the home of the Witt-Will Company, Incorporated. Witt-Will began by building conventional assembled trucks using Continental engines, Brown-Lipe transmissions and Timken worm or Timken bevel axles. Through the 1920s, the company built trucks from 1-1/2-ton to 5-ton capacity. In the mid-1920s, six-cylinder engines were adopted. The 1-1/2-ton Model N with 144-inch wheelbase was powered by a 27.2 hp Continental C-4 engine and used a Brown-Lipe clutch and transmission with Timken supplying the front and rear axles. Ross provided the steering gear and Archibald wheels carried 36x3-1/2 front and 36x6 rear solid rubber tires. The 2-ton Model P had the same engine and component suppliers but chassis weight was 4,600 pounds as opposed to 4,000 pounds and the chassis price was $2,450 and $2,650, respectively.

Witt-Will also built the 2-1/2-ton Model S with 146-inch wheelbase powered by a 27.2 hp Continental K-4 engine. Chassis weight was 5,000 pounds and chassis price was $2,950. The 4-ton Model A with 172-inch wheelbase used a 36.1 hp Continental B5 engine. This was the same engine and wheelbase for the 5-ton truck, the latter having Westinghouse ignition and Smith and Day wheels, respectively. Chassis weight was up to 9,500 pounds and it had a price tag of $4,500.

This company was a small one located near the White House in Washington D.C. and it received a number of federal contracts. Most of the trucks were sold in the company's geographical area but soon after the stock market crash of 1929, production faded out. The company specialized in truck body manufacturing and auxiliary equipment on other commercial chassis.

W.M.C. see WILL

WOLFE see WILCOX

1961 WOLFWAGON 6X4   LA

WOLFWAGON 1956-1964 — Wolfe Engineering Corporation began in Dallas, Texas. L.J. Wolfe of the St. Louis Car Company designed and managed the production of Wolfe half-cab trucks. Wolfe's company developed a system in which a series of its trucks could be tethered together using the controls of one operator. An A-type drawbar was mounted on each truck and stored vertically when the truck was used as a single unit. Connecting cables were used to control the brakes, throttle and transmission when the trucks were hooked together. Both two-axle and three-axle Wolfwagon trucks were built with a 40-ton GVW rating for two three-axle units. Trucks in pairs were the most common arrangement, although up to six trucks could be hooked together. Engine and transmission were mounted above the front axle or amidships. The manufacturing was accomplished by the St. Louis Car Company in St. Louis, Missouri, until the company faded out around 1964.

WOLVERINE 1918-1922 — The American Commercial Car Company of Detroit, Michigan, built a 3/4-ton and a 1-1/2-ton truck for a brief period and in small numbers. The lighter vehicle was a delivery van with pneumatic tires, which was only made during the company's first year of existence. The heavier truck model was built for nearly five years. It was powered by a four-cylinder Continental engine and used a three-speed Fuller transmission and Russel rear axle. Its wheelbase was 140 inches and solid rubber tires were standard equipment. The Jackson Motor Company also built a motor vehicle using the name Wolverine.

1912 WOLVERINE MODEL C FLAREBOARD   RD

WOLVERINE-DETROIT 1912-1913 — The Pratt, Carter, Sigsbee Company of Detroit, Michigan, built two models of commercial vehicles over a span of slightly less than two years. The first was an 800-pound capacity light delivery van that was priced at $850. These used Timken axles and had friction drive, as did the 1/2-ton rated open express delivery truck, also powered by a one-cylinder water-cooled engine using double chain drive. Both solid and pneumatic tires were available. Wheelbase was 89 inches and chassis price was $775.

During the second and final year of manufacturing, the Wolverine-Detroit Model C was a 1/2-ton truck that used worm-drive. Its one-cylinder engine was mounted under the body, which was only available from the factory as a flareboard express. Its wheelbase was 96 inches. There were several other companies during this era that made vehicles by the name of Wolverine but they were not affiliated with Pratt, Carter and Sigsbee.

WONDER 1917 — The Wonder Company was listed in Chicago, Illinois, as having been the manufacturer of two 1-ton truck models. The Model 1 was offered with an open top for $800 and the Model 2 "with top" was priced at $850.

WOOD 1900-1902 — Frederick R. Wood & Son of New York City specialized in building electric ambulances. St. Vincents, Roosevelt and Presbyterian hospitals were among its customers. One of the first electric ambulances built in the United States was constructed by Wood in 1900 for St. Vincents Hospital. It used two 2 hp DC motors that were suspended on the rear axle. A battery of 44 cells provided the electricity and the controller was located under the seat out of view. Forward speeds of 6, 9 and 13 mph were available and speeds of 3 and 6 mph in reverse were also allowed by the controller.

The driver was in communication with the attendants via a speaking tube. Opening windows were made of beveled plate glass and the interior was finished with leather. Interior and exterior lights were provided and the bed slid out, being caught by irons and protruding parallel with the sidewalk for comfort of the patient. The Wood ambulance was tiller steered and had an Elliott type of front axle with full elliptic springs.

Wood ambulances proved superior during extreme weather spells and were more quickly dispatched without the need to hitch horses. Unhygienic horse stable conditions were also avoided at the hospital where the electric ambulances were used. The company also built delivery wagons for B. Altman's department stores but after 1902, Wood only built bodies for other companies. Passenger car bodies were also built until 1926, and bus and truck were built until 1939.

WOOD 1902-1905 — The Wood Vapor Vehicle Company of Brooklyn, New York, experimented with motor fuels and propulsion methods for several years, building test vehicles intended primarily for the commercial market. The company, which carried its owners name, completed a 7-ton truck in 1905. It was a steam-powered vehicle using coal for fuel and had a low cab-over design. Two single-acting steam engines were used, which were mounted below the frame and drove the two rear wheels directly with a chain to each. Maximum horsepower was listed as 100 and the truck could be started from a standstill without the need of a clutch or transmission. The truck's large artillery wheels were steel-shod and the front wheels' diameter was considerably smaller.

The Wood steam truck incorporated wheel steering whose column protruded vertically through a low platform between the front wheels. A step was provided for the driver in front and the driver's seat was mounted on the chassis just ahead of a large rear-dump body. The truck's application was for hauling asphalt. It appears it may have been the only example built by the company.

WOODS 1899-1916 — The Woods Motor Vehicle Company was organized in Chicago, Illinois, with $10 million in capital stock. The principals of the company were Samuel Insull, August Belmont and "Standard Oil magnates and investors from Toronto." The company's goal was to compete with the giant Electric Vehicle Company of New York and this company was not affiliated with the Woods company of New York, which also built electric vehicles as the same time. The Woods Motor Vehicle Company of Chicago was named after Clinton E. Woods, whose patents the company had bought with the purpose of building such vehicles under the management of Clinton E. Woods himself. Making things even more complicated, during 1901 the Chicago-based company formed a marketing firm called the Woods Motor Company of New

York, which sold two types of passenger cars and two delivery cars. The latter firm was closed during the parent company's reorganization in 1901.

The Woods Motor Vehicle Company went into receivership at the end of 1901 and Clinton E. Woods left to become an automobile dealer. Thus far, few Woods electric vehicles had been built, although one electric carriage was known to have been shipped to the manager of the Honolulu Iron Works, making it one of the first, if not the first, motorized vehicles in Hawaii. Also, a number of electric delivery vehicles had been sold to Chicago businesses.

After reorganization, the company began to build large numbers of electric passenger cars. With Louis Burr (who had left Kimball) as president, the company's production output reached 500 units per year. One of the commercial vehicles that the company built at that time was the Style 11 Hansom Cab.

Woods vehicles had electric motors at the rear axle and after 1902, they also had a hood under which the batteries were mounted. Gas-electric hybrid-powered vehicles were built from 1905 to 1907, but the company returned to battery-powered electric vehicles in 1908. Wheelbases varied from 64 inches to 96 inches and prices were in the $2,000 to $3,000 range. After 1912, sales plummeted. By 1916, the company built the Woods Dual Power, another attempt at hybrid gasoline-electric motive power, which did not appear to have been built for commercial vehicle application. In 1918, the company faded out altogether.

WOODS 1927-1931 — The Patriot Manufacturing Company of Havelock, Nebraska, built trucks under the name Woods, having built trucks under the name Patriot from the time the Woods brothers bought Patriot in 1922. The Woods trucks were the same as the Patriot in almost every respect, except for the new badge that appeared in 1927. Truck capacities were 1-, 2- and 3-ton for the years 1927 through 1929. These were mostly Buda-powered, although Hinkley engines had also been listed. Covert transmissions were used and Empire or Wisconsin worm-drive rear axles were offered.

In 1929, the Patriot Manufacturing Company became a division of The Arrow Aircraft & Motors Corporation of Lincoln, Nebraska. Production was transferred to the main factory in Lincoln and the dealership network was enlarged for Woods trucks, which were sold to Arrow's airport fueling facilities, state highway departments and telephone companies. Semi-trailers and truck bodies were added to the product line. By 1930, the range of Woods trucks was from 1-1/2-ton to 4-ton capacity. The largest was a six-wheel truck powered by a six-cylinder Hercules engine with Timken and Shuler axles. Woods attempted to compete with Diamond T and Woods styling was similar. However, the Depression put an end to the latter, while Diamond T survived.

1916 WOODS MOBILETTE MODEL NO. 4 FULL   RD
PANEL DELIVERY CAR

WOODS MOBILETTE see MOBILETTE

WOOLSTON 1913 — The C.T. Woolston Company was located in Riverton, New Jersey. The company built 1-, 2-, 3- and 5-ton capacity trucks, which were all built as express-type vehicles despite the large capacities. The two lighter trucks were forward-control, while the two heavier models were of conventional design.

All were powered by four-cylinder engines and the 1-ton Model A was listed with a three-speed transmission. All used solid rubber tires and were governed to a maximum of 15 mph.

WORLD 1927-1931 — The World Motors Company was located in Cincinnati, Ohio. World trucks were built from 1-1/2-ton to 5-ton capacity and many were powered by straight-eight engines from Continental and Lycoming. The company was an outgrowth of the reorganized Steinkoenig Motors Company, which had built assembled Waukesha-powered trucks in the 1920s. World's market was generally limited to the state of Ohio. Once the Depression arrived, the expensive World trucks did not sell. By 1931, the company was out of business.

WORTH 1906-1910 — Willis Copeland, president of the Single Center Buggy Company, hired a New York engineer by the name of William O. Worth. Copeland had agreed to build a car designed by J.A. Windsor of Chicago, but that venture failed, and Worth persuaded Copeland to build a highwheeler he had designed. These were built as five-, nine- and 16-passenger buses. Most were powered by an air-cooled two-cylinder engine and used a friction transmission that Worth had designed. Final drive was by double chain drive. The largest used a 60 hp four-cylinder engine and had a wheelbase of 140 inches. There was also a Model D delivery van with a wheelbase of 100 inches. In 1907, Copeland and Worth had a disagreement over the vehicles' design and Worth moved the plant from Evansville, Indiana, to Kankakee, Illinois. In 1910, Worth declared bankruptcy.

W.S. see WEIER-SMITH

X

Y

Z

X

XENIA 1914 — The Xenia, named after the town it was built in in Ohio, was a cyclecar designed by Paul Hawkins of Cleveland, Ohio. George Little, a Xenia banker, was president of the small company. The car was powered by 13 hp air-cooled two-cylinder DeLuxe engine and used a planetary transmission and belt-drive. Wheelbase was 102 inches and tread was 36 inches. The Xenia had a single "cyclops" headlight. With a delivery body the vehicle was priced at $395, which was $10 more than with two tandem seats. One of the cars was successfully test driven from Xenia to San Francisco. The company did not survive the year 1914.

Y

YALE 1920-1922 — The Yale Motor Truck Company was located in New Haven, Connecticut. The company built one model of truck, which was rated at 1-1/2-ton capacity. The only known specification is that the truck was powered by a four-cylinder Hershell-Spillman engine.

1924 YELLOW CAB   KP

YELLOW CAB 1915-1929 — John Hertz, known for the car rental company named after him, was the organizer of the Yellow Cab Manufacturing Company in Chicago, Illinois. The company began doing business as a taxi company in 1910, but manufacturing did not begin until 1915. The first Yellow Cab taxis were powered by four-cylinder Continental engines and had bodies made by Racine. Yellow Cabs were built for use by the parent company in Chicago but once the fleet was built up, the taxis began to be sold to other companies in other cities. In 1924, a chassis production run of 120 were sold to W & G du Cros, a taxi operator in London, England. These had English landaulette bodies. In 1923, Hertz expanded into bus manufacturing and in 1924, he started a "self-drive hire company" (car rental agency) using the Ambassador sedan that his firm manufactured.

For 1924 and 1925, the company built a 1-ton capacity truck called the Yellowcab Truck. It was built in two versions: as the Model T1 and Model T-1-5. They were identical except for the respective 130-inch and 150-inch wheelbase. Both were powered by a 22.5 hp four-cylinder Continental V-4 engine with Zenith carburetor and North East Electric ignition and used a Brown-Lipe clutch and transmission, Timken front and rear axles and Gemmer steering. The only other difference was that the T1 truck had 33x5 front and rear pneumatic tires, while the longer wheelbase truck had solid rubber tires. Chassis weight for the shorter truck was 3,130 pounds while the longer truck had a chassis weight of 3,210 pounds. Prices were $1,450 and $1,550, respectively.

Yellow Cabs changed model designations from year to year. In 1915, it was Model H, Model J for 1916, Model K for 1917 and 1918, Model L for 1919, Model M for 1920 and Model O for 1921. Thereafter model designations changed to letter prefixes with single digit numbers such as the Model O-3 for 1922 and 1923. By 1924, NACC horsepower ratings were 19.6 for the four-cylinder Model A2 and 22.5 for the Model O4. In 1925, a 25.3 hp six-cylinder engine was introduced in the Model D taxi. Factory price was $1,795 compared to $2,340 for the four-cylinder Model O-4 and Model O-5. The six-cylinder factory prices remained lower for two more years before the four-cylinder engines were phased out.

By 1925, Yellow's operations were acquired by General Motors with John Hertz remaining as president. The car rental business was renamed Hertz in 1925 and remained a separate operation. The Yellow cab model line was expanded to include the Yellow-

Knight, which was powered by a Knight sleeve valve engine. Cabs were mostly powered by Continental, although some used Lycoming and Northway engines.

1926 YELLOW CAB MODEL T-2 VAN   GMC

In 1927, all cars were manufactured by Yellow Coach & Truck in Chicago, Illinois. A new taxicab was introduced, which had front wheel brakes. In 1928, the Model O-6 received a six-cylinder overhead-valve Buick engine (the Buick Standard Six). Yellow-Knight built trucks by that time from 3/4-ton to 4-ton capacity. The lighter models had Continental engines while the heavier ones used Buick or the Knight sleeve valve engines. Truck production ceased at the end of 1927. In 1929, all Yellow Cabs used Buick engines and the following year, the company's name was changed to General Cab as it was absorbed into General Motors along with bus manufacturing.

1926 YELLOW COACH TYPE X   OCW

YELLOW COACH/GM COACH 1923-1987 — The Yellow Coach Manufacturing Company was organized by John D. Hertz, who had earlier started the Yellow Cab Manufacturing Company, which was also located in Chicago, Illinois. The Yellow Coach venture started when Hertz got control over the Chicago Motor Bus Company and its manufacturing plant, the American Motor Bus Company. By putting these together with the Fifth Avenue Coach Company, he created a new holding business called the Omnibus Corporation.

The new bus manufacturing plant was headed by Col. George A. Green, who worked for Fifth Avenue Coach and had also been involved in the development of buses in London, England. Using the London double-decker and the Fifth Avenue double-decker, both of which he had largely designed, Green combined the best features of each and created the first Yellow Coach called Type Z. Fifth Avenue buses had been already dubbed Type A. The Type Z was a double-deck bus with seating room for 67 passengers. In 1924, the Type Z evolved also into the Type Y, which was a single-deck bus for 29 passengers, or in the deluxe express version for 25 passengers. In 1925, the Type X was also introduced. This was a single-deck feeder bus with seating for up to 21 passengers.

In 1923, Hertz had acquired the Silent-Knight sleeve-valve engine manufactured by the R&V Engineering Company of East Moline, Illinois, and it was renamed the Yellow Sleeve-Valve Engine Works. The Type Z bus used this engine and because it had already been proven in the field, this bus sold successfully. In 1925, the Type Z 200-inch wheelbase was extended to 230 inches and in conjunction with General Electric, a fleet of hybrid gasoline-electric buses was built. In hybrid version, these were named Z-230. A standard gasoline-powered version of these was called Z-33. A second series was called Z-200 and Z-29.

In 1925, General Motors acquired controlling interest in Yellow Coach for $16 million. The GM truck manufacturing operations were combined into the Yellow plant facilities. At that point, the Yellow Sleeve-Valve Engine Works were shut down and engine production was transferred to Pontiac, Michigan. Bus manufacturing was also transferred to Pontiac soon afterwards and the Chicago plant was shut down entirely.

1926 YELLOW KNIGHT 1-TON MODEL T2 CHASSIS   KP

According to some sources, the sleeve valve engine was not durable enough for heavy-duty bus and truck applications and most of the Type X buses were rebuilt by their operators using Buick or Ford engines. By 1928, the Type X was discontinued and superseded by the Type W. This replacement not only had new styling but also used a Cadillac V-8 engine. Many Type X buses had been sold as parlor coaches to small operators, so the Type W was offered with a newly styled parlor car body manufactured by Lang or Yellow.

1929 YELLOW COACH   RD

In 1929, Yellow introduced the Z-240 and Z-39 buses, which were essentially Type Z chassis extended by 10 inches. By also moving the dashboard forward over the rear of the engine, this increased passenger capacity to 40. Also, this was the end of the double-decker production after 100 were sold to Fifth Avenue Coach and 12 to Baltimore in 1930. The Z-200 and Z-230 were replaced by the Z-225. The latter was styled after the Z-240 and had seating capacity for up to 33 passengers. The year 1930 was also the advent of the poppet-valve engine introduced by Yellow. The Type V made its debut and also that year, the Type U was introduced, which was powered by a six-cylinder Buick engine.

By this time, Greyhound sold its C.H. Will Motors Corporation manufacturing subsidiary to Yellow Coach. The 250-inch wheelbase Type Z was produced by Yellow for Greyhound, which had become the dominant U.S. intercity bus company. This Type Z was the last conventional full-size bus before new designs that enclosed the engine within the coach body were introduced. The Z-250 had a 707-cubic inch inline six-cylinder engine, while the smaller Yellow buses used 568- and 616-cubic inch six-cylinder engines. Buick and Cadillac engines were superseded by GM truck engines for the smaller buses.

In 1931, Yellow introduced a few city transit buses with rear-mounted engines with rear axles just ahead of the engine block. These were not successful due to clutch problems, since the design precluded large enough engines for the size of the vehicles. Production of this type of bus was suspended in 1934. Type U and Type W buses were superseded by forward-control front engine buses. Type V and Type Z buses were built until 1936, at which time all Yellow buses had model numbers in the 700 series without letter prefixes. Under sales manager Herbert J. Listman, Yellow worked closely with its customers such as Greyhound, National City Lines, Omnibus Corporation and National City Lines. These dominant bus-line operators kept Yellow in business during the depressed 1930s.

Dwight Austin, formerly with Pickwick, Nite Coach and Utility Coach, was hired in 1934. His design of a rear-engine transverse drive was patented as "angle drive." It used a configuration of gears to turn the driveshaft by more than 90 degrees from the engine crankshaft. The final shaft connected forward to an offset differential. The advantage was more available space within the body and easier access to the engine and transmission for maintenance. However, the extra set of gears reduced fuel economy and the entire mechanism was more expensive.

In 1934, The Omnibus Corporation finally received permission to change over its fleet of streetcars in Manhattan, New York, to bus service. Using the same 616-cubic inch six-cylinder engine and angle drive, a 41-passenger bus was developed. It was dubbed Model 718 and used an air-assisted clutch for easier operation in heavy traffic. About 400 of these were built for Omnibus, as well as a few for other transit operators.

Between 1936 and 1938, Yellow built 300 double-decker rear-engine buses. These were called Model 720 and Model 735 and 160 of them were sold to Fifth Avenue Coach Company. The rest were sold to the city of Chicago. Many of these one-driver-operated buses were converted to diesel power, which was slow to catch on during the 1930s. By this time, almost every bus manufacturer had abandoned the front engine coach design. Yellow first used diesel engines in 27 buses it built for Public Service Coordinated Transport, which specified that diesel engines be used. Hercules four-cycle six-cylinder diesel engines had been used in some Twin Coach buses successfully and these were installed in the Yellow buses in 1936.

During the mid-1930s, Dwight Austin helped develop the long distance Model 719 Super Coach. The bus featured transverse engine and underfloor luggage space. By 1940, these were diesel-powered with 6-71 engines and had air conditioning. They did not have torque converters in order to improve highway fuel consumption. Dubbed "Silversides," their development was financed by Greyhound, which put 2,500 of these buses into service between 1940 and 1948.

General Motors Research began developing diesel engines for bus application. In 1938, the company introduced two-cycle diesel engines, which were two-, three-, four- and six-cylinder units with interchangeable pistons and other components. This was called the "71" series, which referred to the cubic inch displacement for each cylinder. The two-cylinder and three-cylinder units were not used for buses, but the entire series was modified for use in marine applications and for heavy trucks. Transmissions that could handle the increased torque were developed with many problems along the way so that until the design was refined, Yellow shipped diesel engines and transmissions free of charge to operators whose buses broke down in the field.

In 1939, Yellow adopted a new bus model designation system. The first bus to use this code was Model TD-4501. The "T" stood for "transit" (as opposed to parlor or intercity), the "D" stood for "diesel," "45" was the seating capacity, and the final two digits refer to the specific version of that type of vehicle. A third prefix letter was used for many years to denote what type of transmission was used: electric, hydraulic or mechanical.

During World War II, bus production was suspended. However, during this time diesel engine and transmission development made great progress as this technology was applied to tanks and heavy military vehicles. By the end of the war, the diesel-hydraulic drivetrain was entirely debugged with many fine improvements. In 1943, GM bought out the minority interests in Yellow. By 1944, when bus production resumed, the nameplates read "GM Coach."

1940 GM INTERCITY BUS   KP

1955 GM COACH   KP

By 1953, air suspension was adopted for both transit and intercity buses. The compressed-air-type suspension was one more additional comfort feature in an attempt to make bus travel as comfortable as possible in an era when private use of the automobile grew at a tremendous rate. This was also the year that GM in conjunction with Greyhound developed the Scenicruiser. The Scenicruiser had two 4-71 diesel engines with a fluid coupling merging the output of the two engines to a single driveshaft. Despite reliability problems from the outset, about 1,000 of these buses were built between 1954 and 1956.

Bi-level seating, which was popular during the 1920s, was readopted in the mid-1960s, providing even more luggage space and allowing room for rest room facilities. The additional luggage area allowed for the development of an extensive package express business, which replaced some of the railway parcel service.

1959 GM TRANSIT COACH   GMC

In 1959, a new V-type diesel engine was introduced in the form of the 6V-71. Two years later, the 8V-71 was introduced. The latter became a universal engine for almost all buses in the United States and Canada. Detroit Diesel-Allison of Indianapolis, Indiana, sold the engines to GM Truck & Coach at that time.

During the 1960s and 1970s, GM Coach built the following essential types of buses: 35-foot and 40-foot split-level intercity buses powered by 8V-71 engines with Spicer mechanical transmissions; 35-foot city transit buses with 6V-71 engines and Allison torque converter transmissions; and 40-foot city buses, either 96

inches or 102 inches wide with either 6V-71 or 8V-71 engines and Allison transmissions. Production of this series, which was built in the form of several different models, ended in 1977 with a total of 33,500 built starting in 1959.

1972 GM SUBURBAN COACH MOBILE POLICE SUBSTATION   MROZ

1975 GM 47-PASSENGER RTS TRANSIT BUS   GMC

The Rapid Transit Series (RTS) was planned for the 1970s, but the U.S. government delayed this program because of the mandated low-floor design for accessibility to the elderly and handicapped that needed to be incorporated into the new buses. These buses featured a stainless steel superstructure with fiberglass outer panels. This "Transbus" was mandated as the only federally funded 40-foot transit bus that could be built by interested manufacturers after 1981.

In 1977, GM Coach introduced its RTS with many of the features of the Transbus, but without the revised axles, tires and brakes that the 22-inch floor height would necessitate. In 1979, GM was the last of three companies to withdraw from the Transbus project. AM General and Flxible (Division of Grumman) had already refused to bid on buses that had government-mandated bus specifications. The withdrawal prompted the press to announce "Death of Transbus Revitalizes Bus Industry." Eventually, most of the Transbus specifications were adopted for allowing the physically challenged to be able to board a public bus. By 1980, Yellow/GM Coach had built over 112,000 buses since 1923. GM Coach was purchased by TMC in 1987, which, in turn, was acquired by Nova Bus in 1994.

YOUNG 1920-1923 — The Young Motor Truck Company was a small manufacturer based in Geneva, Ohio. The company built 1-1/2-ton and 2-1/2-ton capacity trucks powered by four-cylinder Continental engines. More information has not been available.

YOUNG 1970-1990 — The Young Fire Equipment Corporation began in Lancaster, New York. The company built two types of fire engines. The smaller was called the Bison, which used two axles, and the larger was the Crusader, which was a three-axle vehicle. The latter had an extremely low-profile cab and carried a snorkel with an 85-foot boom. Detroit Diesel or Caterpillar engines were both available.

During the 1980s, Young built fire trucks with engines mounted amidships with pumps located at the front of the vehicles. The company pioneered the use of fiberglass and used large doors on both sides of the engine for easy accessibility. Custom pumpers were built for cities in Florida until 1990, when, according to founder Richard Young, auto unions forced the company into shutting down manufacturing. Richard Young reorganized to form the Performance Advantage Corporation, which builds components for fire apparatus builders to date.

Z

ZACHOW & BESSERDICH see FWD

1915 ZEITLER & LAMSON 2-1/2-TON FIRE TRUCK   **RD**

ZEITLER & LAMSON 1914-1916 — The Zeitler & Lamson Motor Truck was located in Chicago, Illinois. Trucks in one-ton increments from 1-ton to 5-ton capacity were built until 1916. All were powered by four-cylinder Continental engines and chassis prices were from $1,550 to $4,150. Production ceased by 1917 but the company was revived under the name of King-Zeitler in 1919.

ZELIGSON 1946-1989 — The Zeligson Company was started directly after World War II by three ex-servicemen who later also started the Crane Carrier Company. The Zeligson company was located in Tulsa, Oklahoma, and its purpose was to remanufacture military trucks for civilian use, as well as for the conversion of standard 4x2 and 6x2 trucks to all-wheel-drive. Zeligson also fabricated custom chassis for the oil industry and other specialized applications using military and civilian proprietary components, including Detroit Diesel engines and custom equipment assembled at the Tulsa plant. Samuel Zeligson sold his company in 1980. Under new management and ownership, the company continued on a small scale until it faded out in 1989.

ZIMBRICH 1912 — A.M. Zimbrich was the owner of the United States Garage in Rochester, New York. In 1912, his company built two hotel motor buses, which were powered by four-cylinder Con-

tinental engines with Bosch ignition. Half of the engine extended into the driver's compartment to reduce the length of the wheelbase for better maneuverability. Front and rear axles were from Timken.

1912 ZIMBRICH HOTEL BUS   **RD**

The body design used Colonial styling and was totally enclosed. Half of the forward section was arranged for carrying hand baggage. The interior was finished in walnut and leather and opening windows were made from plate glass. The bus was tall enough to stand inside and could seat 14 passengers. It does not appear that Zimbrich built more than the two buses of 1912.

ZIMMERMAN 1912-1915 — The Zimmerman Manufacturing Company of Auburn, Indiana, started out by building horsedrawn buggies. Elias Zimmerman was president and brothers Franklin T. Zimmerman was vice-president while John Zimmerman was secretary-treasurer. The company began building highwheeler passenger cars in 1908. In 1910, the company added a four-cylinder car but the 1/2-ton light truck that appeared in 1912 was powered by 20 hp air-cooled two-cylinder engine and used a planetary transmission with double chain drive. In 1910, Franklin Zimmerman died and in 1914, Elias Zimmerman also passed away at the age of 85. The Zimmerman truck was uprated to 1-1/2-ton in 1915 but that year, the remaining brother, John, closed down the company and went on to help establish the Union Automobile Company, which took over the Zimmerman factory.

LIST OF ILLUSTRATION CREDITS AS ABBREVIATED IN CAPTIONS:

A&A	Applegate & Applegate	JO	Jim O'Malley
ACTHR	American Truck History & Research	KEN	Kenworth
ATHS	American Truck Historical Society	KM/HW	Kissel Museum, Hartford, Wisconsin
A-L	American LaFrance	KP	Krause Publications
AMT	Alaska Museum of Transportation	LA	Larry Auten
AOS	A.O. Smith	LIAM	Long Island Auto Museum
BAC	Bill and Ann Clark	MCA	Motor Coach Age
BB	Bluebird Corp.	MBS	Motor Bus Society
BC	Blackhawk Classic Auto Collection	MC	Micheal Carbonella
BE	Bill Emery	MHS	Minnesota Historical Society
BHS	Berkeley Historical Society	NMM	National Motor Museum
BR	British Rail	MROZ	Albert Mroz
BS	Bob Strand	MVPA	Military Vehicle Preservation Association
BWA	Burkhart Wilson Associates	MVMA	Motor Vehicle Manufacturer's Association
CAT	Caterpillar	NAHC	National Automotive History Collection
CCJ	Commercial Car Journal	NMM	National Motor Museum
CHA	Chance Corporation	OCP	Old Car Publications
CHEV	Chevrolet	OCW	Old Cars Weekly
CHRYS	Chrysler	OHC	Oregon Historical Society
CP	Crestline Publishing	OMM	Old Motor Magazine
DJS	Donald J. Summar	PAT	Pioneer Auto Museum
DT	Diamond T	PJMMOA	Petit Jean Mountain Museum of Automobiles
DW	Donald Wood	RD	Ralph Dunwoodie
EEH	Eugene E. Hustings	RJ	Rolland Jerry
EF	Eric Foley	RJG	Robert J. Gaylord
EK	Elliot Khan	RM	Reynolds Museum
EO	Emergency One	RNE	Railway Negative Exchange
ERP	Edward R. Pomonio	RPZ	R. Perry Zavitz
FLP	Free Library of Philadelphia	RSC	Republic Steel Corporation
FTS	Frank T. Snyder	SAH	Society of Automotive Historians
GMC	General Motors Corporation	SEVA	Sacramento Electric Vehicle Association
GNG	G.N. Georgano	SV	Specialty Vehicle
GTC	General Tire Corporation	T-D	Taylor-Dunn
HAC	Harrah's Automobile Collection	TEX	Texaco
HAYS	Hays Antique Truck Museum	TM	Tania Martinez
HD	Hugh Durnford	TT	Truck Tracks Magazine
H-D	Harley Davidson	TWC	Taylor Woodrow Construction
HE	Hope Emerich	USE	U.S. Electric
HHB	Henry H. Blommel	WEPS	Western Electric Photographic Services
INT	International	WJP	Willard J. Prentice
ISHC	Iowa State Historical Society	WLB	William L. Bailey
JAG	John A. Gunnell	WOM	Walter O. McIlvain
JAW	James A. Wren	WJP	Willard J. Prentice
JH	Jerry Heasley	WREN	James Wren
JBY	John B. Yetter	W&S	Warner & Sweeney
JM	Joe Mazzarella	WTD	White Truck Division